ANTHROPOLOGY

ANTHROPOLOGY

BARBARA D. MILLER
The George Washington University

BERNARD WOOD
The George Washington University

with contributions from

Andrew Balkansky
Southern Illinois University, Carbondale

Julio Mercader
University of Calgary and The George Washington University

Melissa Panger
U.S. Environmental Protection Agency and
The George Washington University

PEARSON

Boston   New York   San Francisco
Mexico City   Montreal   Toronto   London   Madrid   Munich   Paris
Hong Kong   Singapore   Tokyo   Cape Town   Sydney

To our families, friends, teachers, and students with gratitude for their support and inspiration

Series Editor: Jennifer Jacobson
Series Editorial Assistant: Emma Christensen
Marketing Managers: Kris Ellis-Levy and Laura Lee Manley
Production Editor: Susan Brown
Development Editor: Ohlinger Publishing Services
Editorial Production Services: Kathleen Deselle
Composition Buyer: Linda Cox
Manufacturing Buyer: Megan Cochran
Electronic Composition: Publishers' Design and Production Services, Inc.
Interior Design: Anne Flanagan
Photo Researcher: Sarah Evertson, Image Quest
Cover Administrator: Linda Knowles

For related titles and support materials, visit our online catalog at www.ablongman.com.

Photo credit pg. ii: Marc C. Abrahms. Acknowledgments appear on p. 683, which constitutes a continuation of the copyright page.

Library of Congress Cataloging-in-Publication Data
Miller, Barbara D.
  Anthropology / Barbara D. Miller, Bernard Wood ; with contributions from Andrew Balkansky, Julio Mercader, Melissa Panger.
    p. cm.
  Includes bibliographical references and index.
  ISBN 0-205-32024-4 (paper)
  1. Anthropology—Textbooks. 2. Physical anthropology—Textbooks. I. Wood, Bernard A. II. Title
  GN25.M55 2006
  301—dc22
  2004060199

Printed in the United States of America

10 9 8 7 6 5 4 3 2   VHP   09 08 07

BRIEF CONTENTS

CONTENTS

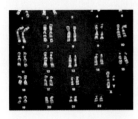

3
Science, Biology, and Evolution 65

4
Research Methods in Anthropology 99

5
The Nonhuman Primates   135

6
The Earliest Human Ancestors   165

7
Emergence and Evolution of Archaic *Homo* 195

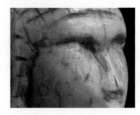

8
Modern Humans: Origins, Migrations, and Transitions 223

11
Economic Systems 319

12
Reproduction and Human Development 353

13
Illness and Healing 383

14
Kinship and Domestic Life 411

15
Social Groups and Social Stratification   439

16
Political and Legal Systems   467

PART IV COMMUNICATION AND THE SEARCH FOR MEANING

17
Communication 499

18
Religion 523

19
Expressive
Culture   553

20
People
on the
Move   581

21
Development Anthropology 607

Anthropology in the Real World profiles highlight five career paths of anthropologists.

ANTHROPOLOGY
in the Real World

Crossing the Fields sections emphasize the connections among the four fields of anthropology: archaeology, linguistic anthropology, biological anthropology, and cultural anthropology.

CROSSING THE FIELDS

Critical Thinking boxes explore an issue and how it has been interpreted from two or more perspectives, others prompt rethinking of existing concepts.

CRITICAL THINKING

LESSONS APPLIED

Lessons Applied boxes provide examples of how research in anthropology is applied to real-world problems.

Methods Close-Up boxes focus on diverse methods including how anthropologists gather data, analyze and present their findings, and pay attention to ethical considerations.

METHODS CLOSE-UP

Welcome to *Anthropology* and its fresh approach to the study of humanity's past and present. In the four-field view, anthropology encompasses human evolution and biology (biological or physical anthropology), our cultural past (archaeology), our ways of communicating (linguistic anthropology), and the rich variety and dynamism of contemporary cultures (cultural anthropology). Mirroring the discipline's wide scope, the methods used are also diverse, ranging from genetics research in a lab to recording and transcribing the songs of village women. Anthropology's findings often make headlines when a new fossil in the human lineage is discovered. Anthropologists are increasingly in the public eye when they figure in policy debates and contribute to the solution of local and global problems.

Early in the twentieth century, Franz Boas was an advocate of using the four-field approach in anthropology to understand the complexities of the human condition. Partly through his influence, the four fields became institutionalized in North American anthropology departments. The authors of this book all taught in a four-field department, at The George Washington University, and share an interest in learning more about each other's fields. We decided that one way to do that would be to collaborate on this book. Since beginning that collaboration in the late 1990s, the three younger contributors (Andrew Balkansky, Julio Mercader, and Melissa Panger) have taken up new positions, but the book project has kept us together, even if only virtually. In addition, writing *Anthropology* has made us more convinced than ever that Boas was right to urge anthropologists to think broadly about humanity through the four-field approach. We feel that writing this book made us better anthropologists by prompting us to think harder, both within our own field and across the four fields. We hope that our enthusiasm for the discipline of anthropology comes through in the pages of this book.

The fact that we have written this book as a team means that *Anthropology* is more current because the authors work at the cutting edge of their fields. Examples of **currency** include:

- coverage of *Homo floresiensis,* a new species discovered in 2004 (Chapter 7)
- up-to-date discussion of the conflict over Kennewick Man (Chapter 9)
- review of the "grandmother hypothesis" and menopause (Chapter 12)

Currency is also reflected in the many photographs that provide images of new research methods, such as computer-based reconstruction of prehistoric buildings, de-mining programs for women in Afghanistan, and nonhuman primate endangerment from deforestation.

Anthropology emphasizes **connections** among the four fields. Our philosophy is that each field should initially be presented as a coherent body of knowledge with its own questions, methods, and findings so that readers will understand what is distinct and valuable about each field. Building on this foundation, we provide connections among the fields throughout the text. In this way, each field gains value from the

explicit linkages around particular issues. These connections are made in several ways. First, each chapter contains a section called *Crossing the Fields*. Here are a few examples:

- Crossing the Fields: What Is Europe? A Four-Field View (Chapter 1)
- Crossing the Fields: Learning about Chimpanzee Tool Use through Archaeology (Chapter 5)
- Crossing the Fields: An Evolutionary Perspective on Baby Talk (Chapter 17)

We also connect the fields through discussion and examples. In Chapter 9, on the Neolithic and urban revolutions, we discuss the contemporary globalization of potatoes. Chapter 17, on communication, covers historical linguistics and Proto-Indo-European language origins and expansion. Another connecting strategy is the inclusion, in each chapter, of photographs that "cross the fields."

Anthropology demonstrates the **relevance** of the discipline to contemporary policy issues and debates and to students' lives and careers, thus addressing the "so what?" challenge. Each chapter contains a *Lessons Applied* box. As the following examples suggest, these features illustrate a variety of ways anthropology can be applied to real-world problems.

- Lessons Applied: Anthropologists Advocate for World Heritage Status for Atapuerca, Spain (Chapter 7)
- Lessons Applied: The Role of Cultural Brokerage in the Newborn Nursery (Chapter 12)
- Lessons Applied: Helping to Resolve Conflicts about Repainting Australian Indigenous Cave Art (Chapter 8)

Five *Anthropology in the Real World* profiles, one at the beginning of each of the five major parts of the text, highlight different career paths of anthropologists, including a forensic anthropologist, an independent business owner, and an international development policy maker.

A successful textbook must also ensure **student engagement.** The authors have taught in a wide variety of contexts, in small colleges and large universities, in large lectures and small seminars. In doing so, we have gained much experience in understanding how to engage students' interest, and we hope

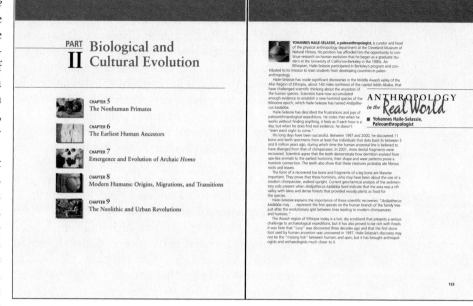

that is reflected in *Anthropology*. Of course, there is a lot of material—concepts, debates, sites, fossils, group names—that students need to learn. This textbook's pedagogy enlivens that learning process through its thought-provoking boxed material and intriguing photographs. The *Thinking Outside the Box* feature prompts students to learn more about an issue by visiting a web site, drawing on their personal experiences that are related to an issue, or formulating a hypothesis about a perplexing phenomenon. For example:

- Listen to some Kiowa songs at *www.uspress.arizona.edu/extras/kiowa/kiowasng. htm*. (Chapter 4)

- How do your consumption patterns compare to those of your parents? To those of your grandparents? What explains the variations? Are differences in age a factor? (Chapter 11)

- In your microculture, what are the prevailing ideas about wedding expenses and who should pay for them? (Chapter 14)

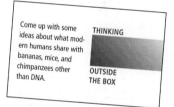

Come up with some ideas about what modern humans share with bananas, mice, and chimpanzees other than DNA.

THINKING OUTSIDE THE BOX

Through our team approach to four-field coverage, carefully chosen examples, and clear writing, *Anthropology* illuminates the key ideas and findings of the discipline, demonstrates how they are connected, and illustrates how anthropology is relevant to today's world. The rationale underlying all the pedagogical features in *Anthropology* is that every person who reads this book can learn to think like an anthropologist and live a life that is better informed about the richness of humanity's past and present.

HOW THIS BOOK IS ORGANIZED

Anthropology pursues its goal of promoting learning about humanity's past and present in two ways. One is familiar—the delivery of information. The second may be less familiar to readers—asking questions about the information at hand and presenting some of the key debates in the discipline. In this way, we combine traditional learning with a critical thinking approach.

Readers will encounter abundant, up-to-date information about humanity's past and present: What is the evidence for human evolution? What do archaeological discoveries tell us about the human past? What are the biological characteristics of the world's living people? How do people in different parts of the world obtain food, conceive of their place in the universe, and deal with rapid cultural change?

Part I, Introducing the Study of Humanity, contains four chapters that establish a solid foundation for the rest of the book. Chapter 1, Anthropology: The Study of

Humanity, discusses what the discipline of anthropology covers, including its theoretical roots. These theories are also presented, in context, throughout the book so that their relevance is clear. Chapter 2, Culture and Diversity, is concerned with what human culture is and with the diversity of contemporary human cultures. Chapter 3, Science, Biology, and Evolution, describes biological approaches in anthropology and discusses the basics of how biological evolution has helped shape humanity. Chapter 4, Research Methods in Anthropology, presents some of the important methods that anthropologists use in studying humanity's past and present.

Part II, Biological and Cultural Evolution, contains five chapters that explore humanity's past. Chapter 5, The Nonhuman Primates, offers an overview of humanity's closest relatives, concluding with a detailed examination of our closest living relatives, the chimpanzees and bonobos. Chapter 6, The Earliest Human Ancestors, explains what fossil evidence reveals about the earliest stages of human evolution, starting around 7 million years ago. Chapter 7, Emergence and Evolution of Archaic *Homo*, takes the narrative of human evolution through stages when stone toolmaking began and early forms of *Homo* moved from Africa to most of the Old World. Chapter 8, Modern Humans: Origins, Migrations, and Transitions, introduces *Homo sapiens* and describes the global migrations and innovations of this stage of human evolution, including the emergence of art. Chapter 9, The Neolithic and Urban Revolutions, covers the origins of plant and animal domestication, cities and civilizations, and states and empires.

Part III, Contemporary Human Social Variation, begins with a discussion of aspects of contemporary human biological variation in Chapter 10, Contemporary Human Biological Diversity. This chapter is a bridge connecting the previous section on humanity's past with the following sections on contemporary cross-cultural variation. It discusses human genetic variation, the nonviability of a biologically based concept of "race," genetic diseases, and urbanization as a new stressor for human biological adaptation. The next six chapters present up-to-date material on cross-cultural patterns in the following areas: economies (Chapter 11), reproduction and the life cycle (Chapter 12), health, illness, and healing (Chapter 13), kinship and domestic organization (Chapter 14), social groups and social stratification (Chapter 15), and politics and law (Chapter 16). Consideration of cross-cultural patterns continues in Part IV, Communication and the Search for Meaning, with chapters on communication (Chapter 17), religion (Chapter 18), and expressive culture (Chapter 19).

Part V, Forces of Change and Humanity's Future, contains two chapters that pull together many earlier topics through a focus on major factors of contemporary change. Chapter 20, People on the Move, discusses migration in a globalizing world, highlighting several "new immigrant" groups in North America. This unique chapter is especially engaging for the many students from immigrant populations. Chapter 21, Development Anthropology, examines international development from the perspective of cultural anthropology. While it highlights the "action" aspect of cultural anthropology and underlines how that perspective can be relevant to urgent issues in the contemporary world, it also shows how each field of anthropology is connected to the study of international development.

DISTINCTIVE FEATURES

In addition to offering currency, connections across the four fields, relevance, and student engagement, *Anthropology* is distinctive in devoting attention to four enduring themes in anthropology that run through the entire textbook. These themes are the environment, culture, social diversity and inequality, and change.

The importance of the **environment:** The subject of the environment in relation to humanity's past and present is examined in terms of interactions that make a difference. These interactions go two ways: the environment to some extent shapes humanity and our culture, and humanity and culture in turn affect the environment. The concept of adaptation is discussed in several places in the book, as is the concept of anthropogenic (human-made) changes to the environment. For example, in Chapter 6, the environment is mentioned as being related to changing patterns of adaptation in early human evolution, including bipedalism. In Chapter 10, the relatively new environment of large, polluted cities is related to new biological stresses. Some of the boxes, such as Lessons Applied: Studying Pastoralists' Movements for Risk Assessment and Service Delivery (Chapter 20), also highlight environment.

Culture is key: The story of humanity—how we became human and why we are the way we are now—is mainly about the increasing importance of culture as our primary means of adapting to the environment and to environmental change. Chapter 2 offers an introduction to the concept of culture and the importance of microcultural worlds based on class, ethnicity, gender, and age. Links between biological and cultural approaches to understanding humanity appear throughout the book. For example, Chapter 3's Crossing the Fields section discusses how British ideas about breeding top race horses mirror a sense of how proper "breeding" is related to human elites. Chapter 10 most directly brings human biology and culture together in its consideration of contemporary human biology. Students will find the material in that chapter on Iceland's Human Genome Project particularly engaging. Later chapters continue to pull in biological questions and material as in the discussion of an evolutionary view of baby talk in Chapter 17 and the health effects of immigration to the United States in Chapter 20.

Social inequality and social diversity: We consistently present substantial material on class, race/ethnicity, gender, and age, linking examples to economies, reproduction, health, kinship systems, politics, religion, and language. The focus on social inequalities is maintained throughout the book, with more in-depth attention in certain places. The major categories of class, race/ethnicity, age, and gender are introduced in Chapter 2 and revisited in greater depth in Chapter 15, Social Groups and Social Stratification. In fact, there is enough material on social diversity and gender for courses using this textbook to fulfill curriculum requirements in these areas. For example, Chapter 1 introduces the perspective of feminist anthropology. Chapter 5, on the nonhuman primates, presents critiques of the now-rejected model of dominant males as typical of the species and describes various male–female interaction patterns. Chapter 9, on the Neolithic and urban revolutions, presents information on burial evidence for gender hierarchies and the role of queens in several early states. Chapter 15 includes discussion of women's craft cooperatives in Panama and the women's movement in China. Chapter 21 includes an entire subsection on the topic of women in development. Several of the boxes and Crossing the Fields sections reinforce gender issues as important in the discipline. See, for example, Crossing the Fields: Linking the Gender Division of Labor to Diet and Growth (Chapter 11).

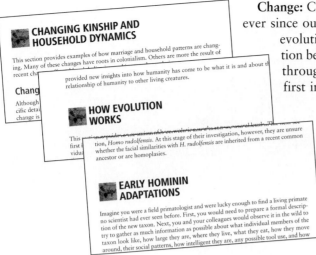

Change: Change has been a key theme in humanity's past and present, ever since our beginnings. This textbook thoroughly reviews biological evolution in Chapters 3, 6, and 7, at which point cultural evolution begins to be a more important factor of change. In Chapters 10 through 21, the forces of globalization and cultural localization, first introduced in Chapter 2, become threads connecting all the ethnographic material, often linked in the text to change in human biology and language. Changing patterns of consumption as a result of globalization, including changing food consumption and shopping practices, are reviewed in Chapter 11. The decline of matrilineal kinship, as noted in Chapter 12, is another result of globalization. In Chapter 20, the effects of migration on cultural change, and sometimes on continuity, are examined in several contexts, including the important role of religion in providing identity for migrants.

BOXED FEATURES

The pedagogical goals of this book are advanced through the use of three distinctive boxes—Lessons Applied, Methods Close-Up, and Critical Thinking—many of which have been previously mentioned. These boxes illustrate the importance of questioning received wisdom, demonstrate how anthropologists do what they do, and underscore the relevance of anthropological research to solving social problems. They also exemplify some of the many careers available to anthropologists. Boxes present one or more questions to the readers. These questions are designed to encourage critical thinking and to enhance engagement with the material.

Lessons Applied boxes provide examples of how research in anthropology can be applied to real-world problems. These boxes show how anthropological knowledge can make a positive difference in policy, projects, or an aspect of human interaction. They highlight different anthropological roles in applied work such as in conducting social impact assessments or in advocacy anthropology working with indigenous peoples. Here are some examples:

- Lessons Applied: Archaeology Findings Increase Food Production in Bolivia (Chapter 1)
- Lessons Applied: Using Primatology Data for Primate Conservation Programs (Chapter 5)
- Lessons Applied: Anthropologists Advocate for World Heritage Status for Atapuerca, Spain (Chapter 7)
- Lessons Applied: Helping to Resolve Conflicts about Repainting Australian Indigenous Cave Art (Chapter 8)

Methods Close-Up boxes focus on diverse methods in anthropology and prompt students to consider how anthropologists gather and analyze data, and the importance of research ethics. The Methods Close-Up boxes bring research methods alive, invite further critical thinking about anthropologists' findings, and inspire students to do their own research. Examples include

- Methods Close-Up: Studying Egyptian Mummy Tissue for Clues about Ancient Disease (Chapter 4)
- Methods Close-Up: Recovering Mammalian DNA from Neanderthal Stone Tools (Chapter 7)

- Methods Close-Up: Taking Gender Into Account When Surveying Sexual Behavior (Chapter 12).

- Methods Close-Up: Studying Birth Rituals in Indonesia (Chapter 18).

Beyond the delivery of information, *Anthropology* promotes engaged learning and critical thinking as its second pedagogical cornerstone. Our commitment to encouraging students to think critically is manifest in each chapter through the third type of boxed feature, **Critical Thinking**. In most of these boxes, students will read about an issue and how it has been interpreted from two different or conflicting perspectives, while in others they are prompted to rethink existing concepts.

- Critical Thinking: Adolescent Stress: Biologically Determined or Culturally Constructed? (Chapter 2) asks students to consider how the researchers approached the issue, what kind of data they used, and how their conclusions are influenced by their approach.

- Critical Thinking: Unfair to Neanderthals? (Chapter 8) asks students to reflect on "received wisdom" from a new angle.

- Critical Thinking: Probing the Categories of Art (Chapter 19) introduces anthropological categories that prompt a reshuffling of the reader's ideas.

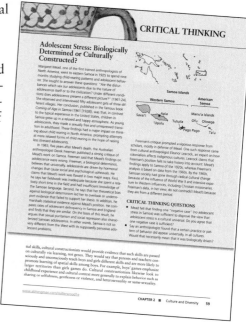

The boxed material enriches the in-text discussion of our four themes: environment, culture, social diversity and inequality, and change. For example,

- Lessons Applied: Archaeological Findings Increase Food Production in Bolivia (Chapter 1) highlights the environment.

- Lessons Applied: The Saami, Snowmobiles, and the Need for Social Impact Analysis (Chapter 21) highlights cultural issues.

- Critical Thinking: Missing Women in the Trobriand Islands (Chapter 4) highlights gender.

- Methods Close-Up: Love Letters and Courtship in Nepal (Chapter 14) highlights change.

IN-TEXT PEDAGOGY

Anthropology's overarching goal is to achieve greater student engagement than other textbooks. We use several approaches and pedagogical devices.

First, as previously noted, we provide carefully selected examples, clear writing, and an exciting program of features.

Second, the book's design includes features that will engage students in the material. Visually stimulating page layouts, with attention-getting photographs, will draw students into the text. Most of the photographs include **thought questions** to pique interest and invite students to get involved with what the photographs show. Each chapter in the book includes many pedagogical tools

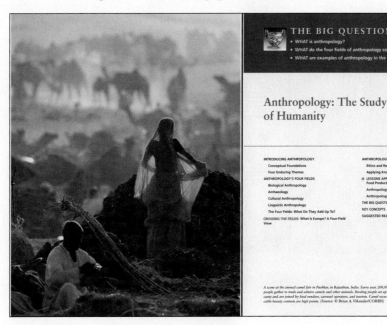

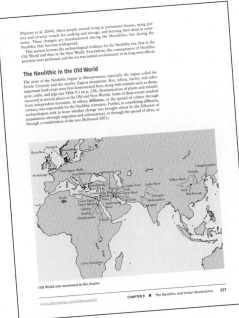

(Piperno et al. 2004). More people started living in permanent houses, using pottery and ceramic vessels for cooking and storage, and burying their dead in cemeteries. These changes are foreshadowed during the Mesolithic, but during the Neolithic they become widespread.

This section reviews the archaeological evidence for the Neolithic era, first in the Old World and then in the New World. Everywhere, the consequences of Neolithic practices were profound, and the era was indeed revolutionary in its long-term effects.

The Neolithic in the Old World
The story of the Neolithic begins in Mesopotamia, especially the region called the Fertile Crescent and the nearby Zagros mountains. Rye, wheat, barley, and other important food crops were first domesticated here, along with animals such as sheep, goat, cattle, and pigs (see Table 9.1 on p. 258). Domestication of plants and animals occurred in several places in the Old and New Worlds. Some of these events resulted from independent invention. In others, diffusion, or the spread of culture through contact, was responsible for the Neolithic transition. Further, in considering diffusion, archaeologists seek to learn whether change was brought about by the diffusion of populations (through migration and colonization), or through the spread of ideas, or through a combination of the two (Bellwood 2001).

Old World sites mentioned in this chapter.

www.ablongman.com/millerwood1e

CHAPTER 9 ■ The Neolithic and Urban Revolutions   257

to help students learn and to help teachers teach. Chapters begin with a chapter outline that lists the main topics covered and the boxed features.

Chapter introductions discuss the broad areas addressed in each chapter so that students can see how topics are connected and can navigate the material more easily. In turn, each of the three major sections in each chapter includes a brief preview of the topics covered in that section, providing further guideposts for the reader.

The Big Questions, a feature located at the beginning of each chapter, identifies the three key themes that students should keep in mind as they read the chapter. Chapters conclude with *The Big Questions Revisited*, a section that reviews concepts and provides answers to The Big Questions in a summary format. This feature offers an accessible way for students to review the major points of the chapter, helping them see how all the "trees" add up to the "forest."

Given the importance of environment and spatial issues in *Anthropology*, this text offers a rich set of maps to guide readers to fossil and archaeological sites, regions of interest, and locations of various cultural groups. Boxes often include a locator map to increase engagement with the material, as in the locator map of the Andaman Islands in the Methods Close-Up box in Chapter 3. Chapters 6, 7, 8, and 9 include up-to-date maps of fossil and archaeological sites mentioned in each chapter. In Chapter 17, a map shows two possible areas of the origin of Proto-Indo-European and offers a link to material on the evolution of human language in Chapter 9. In-text cross-references to maps prompt students to review.

A *Key Concepts* list is provided at the end of each chapter. Each key concept that is boldfaced in the text is listed here, along with the page number on which it is defined. The key concepts are also defined in the Glossary at the end of the book.

Chapters end with a list of *Suggested Readings*. Each reading comes with a brief annotation to guide students who may be looking for books to read for a class project or report.

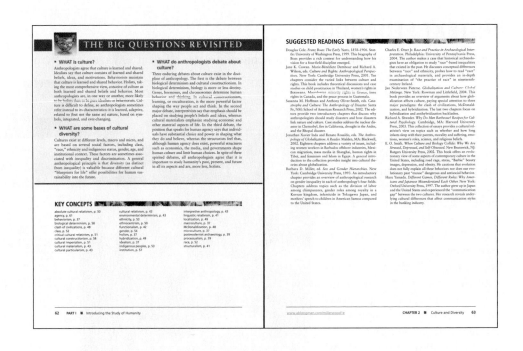

SUPPLEMENTS

Available for use with this textbook are many supplements that will assist instructors in using the book and enriching the students' learning experience.

Anthropology Experience Web Site

The **Anthropology Experience** provides online resources for the four fields of anthropology. Illustrated text is provided, along with introductory content that incorporates photographs and downloadable figures and tables. PowerPoint presentations for each field serve as tutorials for students, who can use the presentations to review key concepts about each field. Instructors may wish to use these presentations in their lectures. A special video section provides opportunities for students to view footage that has been carefully selected to illustrate important anthropological concepts. Many video clips serve as "lecture launchers." In addition, an interactive glossary organized alphabetically within each field provides key terms and definitions, many in written and audio format. Web links, organized within each field, provide students with easy access to helpful anthropology resources—ideal for students interested in taking more anthropology courses or considering a major in anthropology. Visit *www.anthropologyexperience.com*.

Online Study Guide

An online study guide available at *www.ablongman.com/millerwood1e* offers students an opportunity to test their understanding of material in the text.

Instructor's Resource Manual

For each chapter in the text, the Instructor's Resource Manual (IRM) authored by Michelle Croissier, Southern Illinois University, and Nancy Gonlin, Bellevue Community College, with contributions from Jessica Gibson and Barbara D. Miller, The George Washington University, provides At-a-Glance grids that link main concepts to key concepts in the text as well as to other supplements. Each chapter includes chapter summaries based around the text's Big Questions, learning objectives, chapter outlines, key concepts, key people, discussion topics, classroom activities and student projects, service learning suggestions, suggested films, Internet exploration Web links, and suggested readings and additional references. Included in this IRM is *The Blockbuster Approach: A Guide to Teaching Anthropology* with video by Casey Jordan, Western Connecticut State University. Organized by topic, this guide offers many suggestions of popular films to incorporate into the course. The manual is available in print or in electronic form.

Test Bank

The printed version of the test bank, authored by Keith M. Prufer, Wichita State University, and Marjorie Snipes, University of West Georgia, with contributions from Jessica Gibson and Barbara D. Miller, The George Washington University, includes 75–100 questions per chapter in four formats: multiple choice, true/false, fill-in-the-blank, and essay.

Computerized Test Bank

This computerized version of the test bank, with full editing capability for Windows and Macintosh, is available with Tamarack's easy-to-use TestGen software, making it possible for instructors to prepare tests for printing as well as for network and online testing.

Allyn & Bacon Interactive Video and User's Guide

This custom video covers a variety of topics, both national and global. The video segments are useful for opening lectures, sparking classroom discussion, and encouraging critical thinking. The user's guide provides detailed descriptions of each video segment and suggested discussion questions and projects.

Allyn & Bacon Video Library

Qualified adopters may select from a wide variety of high-quality videos from such sources as Films for the Humanities and Sciences and Annenberg/CPB.

PowerPoint Presentation and User's Guide

This PowerPoint presentation for *Anthropology,* by Sally Billings, Community College of Southern Nevada, combines many graphic and text images into teaching modules. Using either Macintosh or DOS/Windows, a professor can easily create customized graphic presentations for lectures. PowerPoint software is not needed to use this program; a PowerPoint viewer is available to access the images. Adopters may visit *www.ablongman.com* on the Internet to register for access to this PowerPoint presentation.

Research Navigator: Anthropology

This guide offers a general introduction to the Internet, a virtual tour of anthropology and its four fields, and hundreds of anthropology Web links, along with practice exercises.

Careers in Anthropology

Written by W. Richard Stephens, this accessible volume contains biographies of professional anthropologists in all four fields and helps students and professors answer the often-asked question "What can I do with a degree in anthropology?" The biographies include discussions of what can be done with a B.A., an M.A., a Ph.D., or a combination of degrees. The booklet also provides information about career options related to anthropology.

Themes of the Times: Cultural Anthropology

This brief supplement includes twenty articles from the *New York Times* that illustrate applications of cultural anthropology from the headlines.

Anthropology, SafariX WebBook

SafariX Textbooks Online is an exciting new *choice* for students looking to save money. As an alternative to purchasing the print textbook, students can *subscribe* to the same content online and save up to 50% off the suggested list price of the print text. With a SafariX WebBook, students can search the text, make notes online, print out reading assignments that incorporate lecture notes, and bookmark important passages for later review. For more information, or to subscribe to the SafariX WebBook, visit *www.safarix.com.*

We authors have worked long and hard to write this book, but we realize with great humility how much our effort depended on the work of many other people. At the risk of sounding slightly ridiculous, it seems important to us first to thank humanity itself for being so diverse, changing, and interesting and for allowing anthropologists access to its past and present, to its bones and artifacts and innermost thoughts. Thanks to humanity for enriching our intellectual and social lives.

A bit closer to home, we wish to thank our teachers and their teachers before them, many of whom will live forever in their writings and in the contributions they have made to the "intellectual DNA" of subsequent researchers and authors. We wish to thank the hundreds of anthropologists and other writers whose work fills the pages of this book. Our research prompted us to keep up on the most recent findings and publications and, at the same time, reminded us of the enduring value of many of the classics.

We are grateful, as well, to our students. Over the years, in both the United States and Canada, they continue to inspire us with their enthusiasm for anthropology and their thoughtful questions, comments, and contributions. Thank you all.

Invaluable contributions to the content of this book have been made by the many anthropologists who reviewed all or parts of it. They include

Abigail E. Adams, Central Connecticut State University

James Adovasio, Mercyhurst College

Alice Baldwin-Jones, The City College of New York

Gina Bessa, Illinois State University

James R. Bindon, University of Alabama

Paul F. Brown, Minnesota State University, Mankato

Susan Love Brown, Florida Atlantic University

Raymond A. Bucko, Creighton University

Elizabeth Cartwright, Idaho State University

Leslie Grace Cecil, Baylor University

Cynthia Clarke, Everett Community College

Phyllis Ann Fast, University of Alaska, Fairbanks

Ilsa Glazer, Kingsborough Community College

Nancy Gonlin, Bellevue Community College

Sharon Gursky, Texas A&M University

Russell R. Hamby, Coker College

S. Homes Hogue, Mississippi State University

Kevin Keating, Broward Community College

Robert W. Keeler, Clackamas Community College

James McClenon, Elizabeth City State University

John Mitani, University of Michigan

Christopher J. Norton, William Paterson University

Deborah Joanne Overdorff, University of Texas, Austin

Keith M. Prufer, Wichita State University

Yorke M. Rowan, Pennsylvania State University, Erie

James J. Sheehy, Pennsylvania State University

Andris Skreija, University of Nebraska, Omaha

Bev Smith, West Virginia University

Marjorie M. Snipes, University of West Georgia

Thomas G. Sparhawk, Central Virginia Community College

Denise To, Arizona State University

Mark Tromans, Broward Community College

Donald A. Whatley, Blinn College

Jennifer Wies, University of Kentucky

Mary S. Willis, University of Nebraska, Lincoln

Steven Ybarrola, Central College

Kathleen Young, Western Washington University

We also thank those who reviewed the three editions of Barbara's *Cultural Anthropology* textbook, at various stages of its development. They include

Jason Antrosio, Albion College

Diane Baxter, University of Oregon

Peter Brown, University of Wisconsin

Howard Campbell, University of Texas, El Paso

Charles R. de Burlo, University of Vermont

Elizabeth de la Portilla, University of Texas at San Antonio

William W. Donner, Kutztown University

Elliot Fratkin, Pennsylvania State University

Ann E. Kingsolver, University of South Carolina

Leslie Lischka, Linfield College

William M. Loker, California State University, Chico

Maxine Margolis, University of Florida

Corey Pressman, Mt. Hood Community College

Russell Reid, University of Louisville

Ed Robbins, University of Wisconsin

G. Richard Scott, University of Nevada, Reno

Wesley Shumar, Drexel University

Robert Trotter II, University of Arizona

Katrina Worley, Sierra College

Special thanks go to our friend Mark Weiss of the National Science Foundation, who reviewed several drafts of Chapters 3 and 6 and made detailed comments that led to much improvement in their clarity and accuracy. On top of that, he reviewed the final versions of Chapters 1–10 before they went to press, again making valuable suggestions that we incorporated to the best of our ability.

Many other anthropologists have provided invaluable material, comments, encouragement, photographs, and other forms of support: Lila Abu-Lughod, Vincanne Adams, Catherine Allen, Joseph Alter, Donald Attwood, Don Brenneis, Alison Brooks, Judith K. Brown, Christina Campbell, D. Glynn Cochrane, Angela E. Close, Jeffery Cohen, Liza Dalby, Loring Danforth, Patricia Delaney, Timothy Earle, Elliot Fratkin, David Gow, Daniel Gross, Marvin Harris, Michael Herzfeld, Barry Hewlett, Danny Hoffman, Michael Horowitz, Robert Humphrey, Cheryl Jamison, Don Johanson, Laurel Kendall, David Kideckel, Stuart Kirsch, Dorinne Kondo, Ruth Krulfeld, Joel Kuipers, Meave Leakey, Lamont Lindstrom, David Lordkipanidze, Steve Lubkemann, Samuel Martínez, Shannon McPherron, Jerry Milanich, Gananath Obeyesekere, Marcia Ponce de León, David Price, Jennifer Robertson, Joel Savishinsky, Nancy Scheper-Hughes, Kathy Schick, Richard Shweder, Chunghee Soh, Fred Spoor, Dietrich Stout, Nick Toth, Barth Wright, Kevin Yelvington, and Christoph Zollikofer.

Other people who are not anthropologists made similar contributions: Elson Boles, Matthew Goodrum, Cornelia Mayer Herzfeld, Edward Keller III, Qaiser Khan, and Roshani Kothari.

Several former or current graduate students and student assistants at The George Washington University helped by obtaining library and Internet materials, scanning photographs, and providing comments on the manuscript: Justin Bedard, Paul Constantino, Jessica Gibson, Matthew Skinner, and Phillip Williams. In the anthropology department at The George Washington University, senior administrator Jonathan Higman and assistant Jamie Grisham kept the UPS packages moving and gently inquired about our mental health from time to time.

We have been fortunate in working with an excellent team in designing and producing this book. The series editor at Allyn & Bacon, Jennifer Jacobson, is a smart and trustworthy manager. Susan Brown was overall coordinator of the production process. Kris Ellis-Levy was our initial marketing manager followed by Laura Lee Manley. Jennifer's editorial assistants, first Amy Holborow and later Emma Christensen, always provided prompt attention to our needs. Throughout the writing process, we worked closely with a dedicated development team at Ohlinger Publishing Services in Columbus, Ohio. Monica Ohlinger managed the long and arduous drafting and revising process with great skill, combining the necessary attention to detail with a strong grip on priorities and time. Thanks, Monica, for making it all work. Joanne Vickers drafted the Anthropologists in the Real World profiles. Erin Denny, development editor, and Cortney White, assistant editor, helped in many ways, including replacing a lot of text that was lost after Barbara's computer crashed in 2003. Kathleen Deselle, in New Hampshire, calmly managed the critical tasks of copy editing, creation of artwork, photograph layouts, and proofreading. Our copy editor, Connie Day, who lives in Vermont, is simply super. In Boston, Sarah Evertson of Image Quest conducted much of the photo research and did some great detective work, tracking down many hard-to-find images. In Washington, Jessica Gibson, former assistant to the Culture in Global Affairs Research and Policy Program, contributed to the supplements package.

Acknowledgments tend to list families last. We follow the convention here though, in fact, they are our first and foremost partners and supporters in the long process of research, writing, and revising. The authors collectively thank their parents. Melissa also thanks her husband, Norm Birchfield, and her son Carter, for their patience and support.

BARBARA D. MILLER

Barbara Miller is Professor of Anthropology and International Affairs, and Director of the Culture in Global Affairs (CIGA) Research and Policy Program, at The George Washington University. She received her Ph.D. in anthropology from Syracuse University in 1978. Before coming to GW in 1994, she taught at the University of Rochester, SUNY Cortland, Ithaca College, Cornell University, and the University of Pittsburgh.

For thirty years, Barbara's research has focused mainly on gender-based inequalities in India, especially the nutritional and medical neglect of daughters in northern regions of the country. In addition, she has conducted research on culture and rural development in Bangladesh, on low-income household dynamics in Jamaica, and on Hindu adolescents in Pittsburgh. Her current interests include continued research on gender inequalities in health in South Asia, the role of cultural anthropology in informing policy issues, and cultural heritage and public policy, especially as related to women, children, and other disenfranchised groups. She teaches courses on introductory cultural anthropology, medical anthropology, development anthropology, culture and population, health and development in South Asia, and migration and mental health. In addition to many journal articles and book chapters, she has published

"Cultural anthropology is exciting because it CONNECTS with everything, from FOOD to ART. And it can help prevent or SOLVE world problems related to *social inequality* and injustice."

several books: *The Endangered Sex: Neglect of Female Children in Rural North India,* 2nd ed. (Oxford University Press, 1997), an edited volume, *Sex and Gender Hierarchies* (Cambridge University Press, 1993), a co-edited volume with Alf Hiltebeitel, *Hair: Its Power and Meaning in Asian Cultures* (SUNY Press, 1998), and *Cultural Anthropology,* 3rd ed. (Allyn & Bacon, 2005).

BERNARD WOOD

Bernard Wood is the Henry R. Luce Professor of Human Origins in the Department of Anthropology at The George Washington University and Adjunct Senior Scientist at the National Museum of Natural History, the Smithsonian Institution. He served as founding Director of the Center for the Advanced Study of Human Paleobiology at The George Washington University. A medically qualified paleoanthropologist, he practiced briefly as a surgeon before moving into full-time academic life in 1972. He earned a Ph.D. and D.Sc. from The University of London. He has taught at The University of London and The University of Liverpool. In 1995 he was appointed Dean of The University of Liverpool Medical School where he served until moving to Washington in 1997. He teaches a problem-based learning seminar for first-year undergraduates, courses on the fossil evidence for human evolution, evolutionary anatomy, and research methods, as well as teaching anatomy in the GW medical school.

In 1968, when a medical student, Bernard joined Richard Leakey's first expedition to what was then called Lake Rudolf, and he has remained associated with that research group and pursued research in paleoanthropology ever since. His research centers on the reconstruction of human evolutionary history by developing and improving the analysis of the hominid fossil record. A "splitter," his interests include distinguishing between intraspecific and interspecific variation in order to devise sound taxonomic hypotheses, refinement of cladistic techniques for the recovery of phylogenetic information, reconstruction of early hominin function such as chewing and locomotion, and exploration of methods for studying the evolution of human growth and development. Bernard's books include the definitive monograph on the cranial remains from the Koobi Fora site. He regularly publishes journal articles, book reviews, and essays.

> "The BEST THING about *science* is being able to COLLABORATE with other *scientists*."

ANDREW BALKANSKY

Andrew Balkansky is Assistant Professor of Anthropology at Southern Illinois University, Carbondale. He earned his Ph.D. in anthropology from the University of Wisconsin, Madison in 1997. From 1998 to 2002, he was Assistant Professor of Anthropology at The George Washington University, where he taught courses on introductory anthropology, Mesoamerican archaeology, and ethics and intellectual property rights. Among other courses that Andrew teaches in his current position at SIU is an introductory course in four-field anthropology. An anthropological archaeologist, Andrew has been conducting fieldwork in Southern Mexico for the past ten years in order to illuminate the evolution of complex societies. His current field project is the excavation of a site called Tayata that dates between 1300 to 300 BCE, the period immediately prior to the urban revolution and a time about which little is known. His publications include journal articles, chapters and book reviews, and the monograph *The Sola Valley and the Monte Albán State: A Study of Zapotec Imperial Expansion,* published by the Museum of Anthropology at the University of Michigan in 2002.

> *"Archaeology means* I get to PLAY in the DIRT for a LIVING. It's the next best thing to being a *professional baseball player."*

JULIO MERCADER

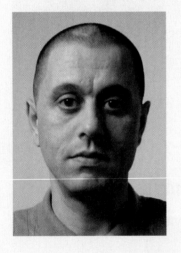

Julio Mercader is a Canada Research Chair and Assistant Professor in the Department of Archaeology at the University of Calgary, Canada. He holds a simultaneous appointment as Research Associate in the Department of Anthropology at The George Washington University and at the Smithsonian Institution. He earned a Ph.D. from Universidad Complutense de Madrid in 1997 and was subsequently awarded a joint postdoctoral research fellowship with The George Washington University and the Smithsonian Institution. His teaching includes courses on African archaeology, hominoid behavior, and European prehistory. He has conducted fieldwork in the Democratic Republic of the Congo, Equatorial Guinea, Cameroon, and Mozambique. Julio's recent publications include the edited book *Under the Canopy: The Archaeology of the Tropical Rain Forests,* published by Rutgers University Press in 2003. In 2003, he received a grant from the Canada Foundation for Innovation and the Canada Research Chairs Program to build the newly created Tropical Archaeology Laboratoy at the University of Calgary, which he directs.

> *"Being an archaeologist* means I get to go to the FIELD, gather NEW DATA, and ANALYZE it."

MELISSA PANGER

Melissa Panger is a wildlife biologist in the U.S. Environmental Protection Agency and holds a simultaneous appointment as Research Associate in the Department of Anthropology at The George Washington University. She earned her Ph.D. in anthropology from the University of California, Berkeley in 1997. From 2000 to 2003, she was an NSF IGERT postdoctoral research fellow with the Hominid Paleobiology Program at The George Washington University. During much of that period, she was also Assistant Professorial Lecturer in the Department of Anthropology and taught courses on primatology and biological anthropology. She has conducted field research on nonhuman primates in Côte d'Ivoire, Panama, Costa Rica, and Florida. Melissa is the recipient of many grants and scholarships, and she has published widely. Most recently, she is one of the editors of a book entitled *Primates in Perspective*, to be published by Oxford University Press.

"*Being a primatologist* gives me opportunities to TRAVEL, do RESEARCH with fascinating animals, get to KNOW people in different cultures, and help preserve *endangered primate species.*"

PART I Introducing the Study of Humanity

FREDY PECCERELLI, a forensic anthropologist, risks his personal security working for victims of political violence in his homeland. Peccerelli is founder and executive director of the Guatemalan Forensic Anthropology Foundation (FAFG), a group that focuses on the recovery and identification of some of the 200,000 people, mostly indigenous Maya living in mountain regions, that Guatemalan military forces killed or "disappeared" during the brutal civil war that occurred between the mid-1960s and the mid-1990s.

Peccerelli was born in Guatemala. His family immigrated to the United States when his father, a lawyer, was threatened by death squads. He grew up in New York and attended Brooklyn College in the 1990s. But he felt a need to re-connect with his heritage and began to study anthropology as a vehicle that would allow him to serve his country.

ANTHROPOLOGY
in the Real World

■ **Fredy Peccerelli, Forensic Anthropologist**

The FAFG scientists excavate clandestine mass graves, exhume the bodies, and identify them through several means, such as matching dental and/or medical records. In studying skeletons, they try to determine the person's age, gender, stature, ancestry, and lifestyle. DNA studies are few because of the expense. The scientists also collect information from relatives of the victims and from eyewitnesses of the massacres. Since 1992, the FAFG team has discovered and exhumed approximately 200 mass grave sites in villages, fields, and churches.

Peccerelli sees the foundation's purpose as applying scientific principles to basic human concerns. Bodies of identified victims are returned to their families to allow them some sense of closure about what happened to their loved ones. Families can honor their dead with appropriate burial ceremonies.

The scientists also give the Guatemalan government clear evidence on the basis of which to prosecute the perpetrators of these atrocities. However, Guatemala was long structured in terms of a ruling military and a largely disenfranchised indigenous population. Many members of the former militia are still in positions of power within the government.

Peccerelli, his family, and his colleagues have been harassed and threatened. Eleven of the FAFG scientists have received written death threats. Bullets have been fired into Peccerelli's home, and it has been burglarized. The United Nations and other human rights organizations have made it clear to the government that they support FARG's investigations, and exhumations continue with heightened security measures.

The American Association for the Advancement of Science, an organization committed to "advance science and serve society," honored Peccerelli and his colleagues in 2004 for their work in promoting human rights at great personal risk. In 1999, *Time* magazine and CNN chose Peccerelli as one of the 50 "Latin American Leaders for the New Millennium." During the same year, the Guatemalan Youth Commission named him an "Icon" for the youth of the country.

Currently, Peccerelli is on sabbatical to work on a master's degree in forensic and biological anthropology at the University of Bournemouth, UK. He intends to return to Guatemala: "There is enough work for another 25 years." ■

THE BIG QUESTIONS

- WHAT is anthropology?
- WHAT do the four fields of anthropology cover?
- WHAT are examples of anthropology in the "real world"?

Anthropology: The Study of Humanity

A scene at the annual camel fair in Pushkar, in Rajasthan, India. Every year, 200,000 people gather to trade and admire camels and other animals. Herding people set up camp and are joined by food vendors, carousel operators, and tourists. Camel races and cattle beauty contests are high points. (Source: © Brian A. Vikander/CORBIS)

Isotopic Data Pinpoint Iceman's Regional Origins
Fifty Percent of Reunions between Long-Lost Siblings Result in Obsessive Emotion
Europeans, Like Neanderthals, Are Dying Out
Sweden May Be First Country to Repatriate Australian Aboriginal Remains
Ancestral Lands in Botswana Parceled Out for Diamond Exploration Concessions

These headlines confirm popular images of what anthropology is about: old bones, buried treasure, *Indiana Jones and the Temple of Doom*, intrigue, and even danger. Popular impressions of anthropology from movies and television depict anthropologists as adventurers, heroes, and heroines. Many anthropologists do have adventures. Some do discover ancient pottery, hidden tombs, medicinal plants, and jade carvings. But for most anthropologists, their research is less glamorous, involving the careful repetition of tedious activities and painstaking analysis.

What do anthropologists do and why do they do it? What knowledge has their work produced? What questions motivate anthropologists to do research? What relevance does anthropology have to "real-world" problems? Should anthropologists be responsible for making their work relevant to the public? This book provides insights into these questions that take us deeper into the study of humanity than magazine articles or television shows but also communicate the excitement of discovering lost treasures, forgotten rituals, and exotic behavior.

THINKING What are your impressions of anthropology? How did you acquire them? Make notes of these impressions and then review them at the end of the course.

OUTSIDE THE BOX

 # INTRODUCING ANTHROPOLOGY

Anthropology is the study of humanity, including our prehistoric origins and contemporary human diversity. Compared to other disciplines that also study humanity (such as history, psychology, and sociology), anthropology is much broader in scope. First, anthropology embraces a much greater span of time than these disciplines. Second, in studying contemporary humans, anthropologists consider a much broader range of topics. Anthropology is a unique discipline because it takes both a deep and a broad view of humanity.

One hundred years ago, cultural anthropologists conducted research in places considered "exotic." Here, a team of anthropologists and student researchers discuss their research project on Silicon Valley culture. ■ If you were given a grant to conduct anthropological research, where would you go and what would you study? (Source: J.A. English-Lueck, Cofounder Silicon Valley Cultures Project)

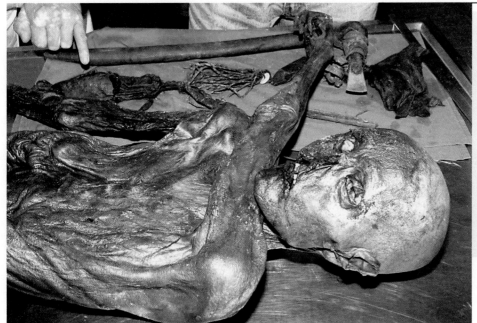

In 1991, a couple hiking along a ridge in the Alps discovered a frozen corpse in a melting glacier. Since then, research on Ötzi, or the "Iceman," has provided information about how he died, where he lived, what he ate, and what he was wearing at the time of his death about 5,000 years ago. ■ On the Internet, review sources on Ötzi and choose one that appears to provide the most scientific information about these findings. (Source: © Bettmann/ CORBIS)

Some anthropologists spend years in difficult physical conditions searching for the most ancient fossils of our ancestors. Others live among, and study firsthand, contemporary residents of Silicon Valley, California, trying to document and understand how people work, organize family life, and adapt to a situation that is permeated by modern technology. Some anthropologists are skilled in conducting laboratory analyses of the contents of tooth enamel to reveal where an individual once lived. Others pore over ancient pottery designs and attempt to understand the meanings of symbols. Others observe chimpanzees in the wild to learn how they find and share food, communicate with each other, care for their offspring, and resolve conflict.

The breadth of anthropology includes methods that range from the more scientific to the more humanistic. Some anthropologists consider anthropology to be a **science**: a form of inquiry that involves first the formulation of a hypothesis, or hunch, about the way things work and then observation or testing to see whether the hypothesis is correct. A scientific approach is more likely to rely on quantitative, or numeric, data. Other anthropologists consider their research to reflect a **humanistic approach**: a more subjective attempt to understand humanity through the study of people's art, music, poetry, language, and other forms of symbolic expression. This approach avoids working from a pre-set hypothesis but instead seeks insight through culturally informed understanding. The humanistic approach is more likely to be qualitative, relying on verbal description or other forms of representation of themes and patterns. Both the scientific approach and the humanistic approach are valued in anthropology, because both provide insights about humanity, emphasizing different aspects of human life and viewing it from different angles. Hence the study of humanity is a vast project that employs a wide range of techniques, from hard science to intuitive interpretation.

No matter whether it is pursued from a more scientific or a more humanistic perspective, anthropology seeks to produce new knowledge, and this is its primary goal as an academic field of inquiry. But its findings are also relevant to significant real-world issues and, therefore, to the public at large. Anthropologists' research findings can influence government policy makers, businesses, technology developers, health care providers, teachers, and the general public. You will learn more about these contributions in this chapter and throughout the book.

The team of five authors who wrote this book has, collectively, spent decades researching, teaching, and writing about anthropology. Despite differences among us in topical interests and expertise, we all share an excitement about anthropology and are involved in contributing to its new discoveries and applications. We also try to bring the thrill of new discoveries and new questions into our teaching. Here, through this book, we invite you to join us in the adventure of anthropology. Be forewarned, however, there is hard work to do along the way: dates to be remembered, concepts to be understood, and categories to be learned. But the effort will pay off, we promise.

We begin the adventure by providing an overview of the discipline of anthropology. After considering the origin of anthropology, we discuss four themes that are important in the discipline's history. These themes serve as organizing principles for much of the material in this book. The second section offers a brief overview of each of anthropology's four fields, followed by an example of how the four fields fit together to create a "whole greater than the sum of its parts."

In the chapter's third section, we consider what anthropologists do and the relevance of anthropology to everyday life. We introduce three issues: ethics, relevance, and responsibility. Next, we talk about the importance of anthropology to the general public. We are convinced that knowledge of anthropology, just like acquaintance with history and philosophy, contributes an urgently needed perspective in everyone's education as a citizen of the world. Finally, we offer advice about the relationship between anthropology and careers.

Anthropologists raise, and seek to answer, serious questions about humanity: What are humans? How do humans differ from other animals? Where did humans come from? Are all humans the same? Why do humans behave the way they do? Why do humans have language? How can we explain conflict among humans? How are humans changing? Anthropologists, though, were not the first people to ask these questions.

Conceptual Foundations

The discipline of anthropology, according to available written records, arose in Europe. If you have studied Western philosophy, you know that thinkers such as Plato (fifth century BCE) and his student, Aristotle (fourth century BCE) pondered many of the same questions about humanity that concern us today: What makes humans different from animals, and how did humans come to be the way they are? (*Note:* BCE stands for "Before the Common Era" which is a secular transformation of BC, or "Before Christ." Similarly, CE stands for "Common Era" and is used in place of AD which stands for the Latin phrase that means "Year of the Lord.") It is highly likely, though, that the classical Greek philosophers were not the first people to wonder about humanity. They were the first, however, to have provided enduring written evidence of their thinking.

A prominent feature of anthropology's classical heritage today is the existence of two basic ways of knowing about humanity. The tradition of Aristotle supports the scientific approach, which says that we can learn about humanity through careful observation. The humanities approach owes more to Plato, who was skeptical about knowledge gained through observation. He said that knowledge is better gained through understanding (see Figure 1.1).

The major animating force of early anthropological thinking was an awareness of "the other"—especially "other" people but also "other" beings, such as apes and

FIGURE 1.1
Classical roots of two ways of knowing in anthropology.

Plato, fifth century BCE	Skeptical of observation-based knowledge	Humanistic approach in anthropology
Aristotle, fourth century BCE	Believed that knowledge can be gained from observation	Scientific approach in anthropology

chimpanzees, or "monsters" as represented by the fossil evidence of extinct creatures. Long-distance wars of conquest were a major way in which Europeans gained exposure to "other" peoples. The Greeks colonized the entire Mediterranean region and thus had interactions with many non-Greek peoples. The ambitious explorer and conqueror Alexander the Great extended the boundaries of his empire from Greece to India during the fourth century BCE and thus expanded Europeans' exposure to distant lands and peoples. Later on, the Romans went even further and encountered Celtic people in Britain.

The Greek writer Herodotus, chronicler of the Persian Wars during the fifth century BCE, is considered by many to have been the first anthropologist, though a self-trained one (historians claim him as the first historian, too). Herodotus recorded astute descriptions of the diverse peoples he met during his travels. In what we now consider good reporting, he is often careful to distinguish between what he witnessed firsthand and what was hearsay.

Other travelers, explorers, and conquerors added to early awareness of peoples and places beyond the known world. But most ordinary people's experience, during the many centuries before the development of ocean-going ships in the fifteenth century, was limited to what they could see in roughly a 25-mile radius from their place of birth (Brace 1997). Roads were poor, there was no public transportation, and little printed material was available outside cities. Human appearance, language, and behavior within that 25-mile radius would have been quite similar. During the Middle Ages (the sixth to fourteenth centuries), Christianity was widespread in Europe, and most people accepted the Bible's explanation of the origin of humanity and why humans appear to differ in culture and language. During this period, the classical Greek heritage of human reasoning and questioning was abandoned in favor of faith-based explanations about the origin and characteristics of humanity.

The European Enlightenment, beginning in the fifteenth century, ushered in dramatic changes to the prevailing views of humanity. It led to controversial questioning of the biblical narrative. Once again, people began asking "Who are we?" and "Where did we come from?" Two important factors underlay the European Enlightenment. The first factor is Islamic science and philosophy. Through the Crusades, many Europeans became aware of Islamic accomplishments in the Middle East. In addition, the Moorish (Arabic) conquerors of Spain in the fourteenth century brought with them a scientific tradition of learning. The second major factor was the increased rate of contact with "other" people through European explorations in Africa, Asia, and the Americas. Both exposure to Islamic learning and contact with non-European peoples and places led to scholars' questioning of biblical explanations about humanity.

The early explorations and colonization also produced the first classifications of "other" people. European descriptions of "others" emphasized their physical characteristics, including skin color and facial features, dress (or lack of dress), and practices that struck European observers as bizarre or even odious, such as worship of non-Christian deities and human sacrifice and cannibalism, as some reports claimed. In the New World, one of the first important distinctions that Europeans made was between "Christians" (the Europeans) and "non-Christians" (the Native Americans).

This fifteenth century European depiction of indigenous peoples of the New World includes views of brutality and cannibalism. ∎ One interpretation of such primitivist depictions is that they justified the conquest of people considered to be little more than animals. Five hundred years later, how has the world's understanding of "the other" changed, and what accounts for such change? (Source: © Leonard de Selva/ CORBIS)

Distinctions based on skin color emerged later. In the New World colonies, the terms *White* and *Black* first corresponded to legal differences between people who had rights, "White" people, and those who did not, the enslaved "Black" people (Orser 2004:7).

In the second half of the nineteenth century, the scientific approach to studying natural and social phenomena began to gain acceptance among Europeans and Euro-Americans (the contributions of Charles Darwin and other scientists of the time are detailed in Chapter 3). Its rise influenced the emerging discipline of anthropology. Anthropology began to take shape as a formal academic subject worthy of being taught in universities, first in Europe, then in North America. In its formative years, anthropology was dominated by the concept of **evolution,** a term that refers to the process of gradual and cumulative change in the characteristics of species, populations, and culture. Early anthropologists wrote about the evolution of the human species, social organization, and languages, and all their models showed an upward path of change from "savagery" or "barbarism" to "civilization." Civilization, defined in terms of European criteria, was the culmination of human evolution.

Anthropology has changed substantially since the late 1800s. Its knowledge base has expanded dramatically, its theories have developed, and modern research methods would astound the founding figures in the discipline. The number of anthropologists has increased, along with the emergence of many specialties. The high degree of specialization found in anthropology today means that anthropologists often cannot understand what other anthropologists are saying. To add to this richness and complexity, anthropology is no longer carried out only by Europeans and North Americans. It is global. Departments of anthropology are now found worldwide, from Argentina to Kenya to Japan. Anthropology in different countries and regions takes on particular characteristics that respond to the cultural context in which it is found. For example, in Latin American countries, social inequality and human rights are prominent topics of study. Anthropology develops a particular character even within individual countries. In Argentina, for example, anthropologists focus on topics as varied as the decline of the welfare state, the "Dirty War" of the 1970s, and the relationship between tango and gender identity (Guber 2002).

Thus anthropology has moved from being a small discipline in which Euro-American people studied non-Euro-American people and phenomena in exotic locations to a global discipline in which anthropologists worldwide participate. Another feature of contemporary anthropology is the growth of *native anthropology,* in which anthropologists study their own cultures.

In spite of these positive changes, power inequalities still exist in anthropology—and other disciplines, too. Global inequalities shape funding opportunities and the sheer ability of students to be able to study anthropology (Kuwayama 2003). European and North American countries have the most money to support anthropological research, data collections, and museums. Far more Euro-Americans can afford to become anthropologists than can people in poorer countries. Globally, the power of the English language places Euro-Americans in a central position; writings published in other languages are less likely to gain worldwide attention. Within the wealthy nations, social inequalities also exist in terms of who becomes an anthropologist. In the United States and Canada, although numbers are rising somewhat, ethnic minorities are severely underrepresented in anthropology. Archaeologist Anna Agbe-Davies points out that in the United States, the disciplines of history and political science attract more African American students than archaeology does (*Archaeology* 2003:22). Her explanation is that African Americans are more likely to choose history or political science because they feel that they will have more social impact in those disciplines. On the bright side, more and more anthropologists are finding ways to make their research relevant to social issues.

Important changes have also occurred in the way anthropologists relate to the communities in which they conduct research. It used to be that anthropologists would arrive at a site or community, proceed to extract objects or information, take the objects or information home where they established data collections, teach about them, and publish their findings. This approach has been modified. Anthropologists now take a more community-based approach that is collaborative and sensitive to local people's interests and rights. For example, an archaeology project not only hires local workers for digging and sifting but also trains them in skills including preservation, conservation, and museum management so that they can take care of their heritage themselves.

Four Enduring Themes

Over the centuries in the history of anthropological thought, four themes recur: the effects of environment and landscape in shaping humanity, culture as key to humanity, the unity and diversity of humanity, and how humanity changes (see Figure 1.2).

Environment and Landscape Shape Humanity

Early thinkers often explained differences found around the world in people's lifestyles and physical appearance as the result of environment and climate. They associated cold, dark regions with light skin and associated hot, bright regions with dark skin. Some anthropologists still seek explanations for variations in human biology by considering environmental factors (discussed in Chapter 10).

FIGURE 1.2
Four enduring themes in anthropology.

Environment and landscape shape humanity	Like all living things, humans have been shaped by a wide range of environments. Humans have also exerted significant effects on the environment.
Culture is key	Learning that is transferred from generation about shared beliefs and behavior.
Unity and diversity	Humanity is one species, yet cultures differ, enhancing adaptation to different environments.
Humanity changes	Throughout human prehistory and history, humanity has changed biologically and culturally.

The Mangshan Irrigation Pumping Station, in Henan province, China, located in the midst of terraced rice fields. ■ For thousands of years, humans have altered the environment in many ways. Think of an example from your experience of a technological development that could be considered an "adaptive compromise." (Source: © Lowell Georgia/CORBIS)

Explanations for aspects of the human evolutionary past, such as the transition to walking on two feet as opposed to swinging in trees, often take the natural environment and landscape into account as explanations. For example, one theory of why early human ancestors began to walk on two feet is that global climate changes reduced the amount of rainforests and increased open grasslands. These changes prompted early human ancestors to abandon the trees for the ground. Such changes that contribute to the survival of the species are called **adaptations.**

Humans act to transform, and sometimes destroy, the environment and landscape in which we have evolved. We refer to human-created changes in nature as **anthropogenic,** or caused by humans. Deforestation is a powerful, anthropogenic source of environmental change. Mass clearing of forests began only a few thousand years ago, with the invention and spread of agriculture. In those few thousand years, a dramatic reduction in forest coverage has been accompanied by a decline in biodiversity, including plants, animals, and the human life that depended on forests. The increased food production from farming has had high costs in terms of the environment. Changes that involve trade-offs between positive and negative effects are called **adaptive compromises.** In other words, some things are gained while others are lost. We shall encounter many examples of adaptive compromises in this book.

Culture Is Key

The story of humanity—how we became human and why we are the way we are now—is mainly about the increasing importance of human culture as our primary means of adapting to our wider environment and to environmental change. The concept of culture is one of the most complicated in the English language (Williams 1990). We propose this basic working definition: **culture** consists of learned and shared ways of living and thinking. By saying that culture is learned, we mean that culture is not biologically transmitted through genes or any kind of "hard wiring." Culture is passed down through the generations by learning, or **enculturation,** the term anthropologists use for the acquisition of culture through learning. By saying that culture is shared, we exclude idiosyncratic and highly individualized ways of living or thinking. One person alone cannot have a culture. Culture is bigger than any one of us.

Anthropologists have long taken culture to be a distinguishing feature separating humans from other animals. Scholars who study human evolution throughout prehistory search for evidence of the beginnings of culture such as tool-making or symbolic behavior such as art or language. Culture relies heavily on the use of symbols. A **symbol** is a thing or a concept that stands for something else. Symbols are "arbitrary"; that is, there is no logical or necessary relationship between a symbol and that for which it stands. Some nonhuman primates can understand symbols, and recent research is showing that a culture-based boundary between humans and nonhuman primates is not clearly defined. As we will see in the chapter on nonhuman primates (Chapter 5), evidence is accumulating that some nonhuman primates exhibit some features of culture.

Unity and Diversity

All living people belong to one species, yet anthropologists also recognize the existence of human diversity. Anthropologists attempt to define and study "difference" and face the challenge of saying what constitutes a real and significant difference as opposed to a superficial difference. From the fifteenth century on, European colonizers referred to the peoples they met in Africa, Asia, and the Americas as "primitive," "non-Christian," and less than human (Jahoda 1999). Their definitions of difference as equivalent to primitive, pagan, and not quite human served the interests of the colonial powers by legitimizing their intrusion into people's lives and lands, the promotion of Europeanization, and the often ruthless enslavement of non-Europeans for labor. Given this history, anthropologists take a cautious position when it comes to defining and describing difference, because such definitions may play into the interests of the more powerful over the less powerful and may stigmatize specific groups.

Sometimes, anthropologists agree that certain differences, which appear to be negative, cannot be dismissed. For example, if a particular genetic pattern is linked to a greater likelihood of having a life-threatening illness, then this difference is important and is something that health researchers and care providers should address. The sickle-cell trait, and associated anemia and other health problems, is a case in point revealing how important the links are between patterns of genetic variation and their social consequences. The sickle-cell trait in hemoglobin, within the red blood cells, is the result of a genetic mutation that occurred thousands of years ago in parts of Africa, the Mediterranean, and India. In those regions, children born with the sickle-cell trait had a survival advantage in the face of malaria.

Where malaria is not a problem, however, the sickle-cell gene provides no survival advantage and can cause seriously impaired health, including anemia, pain, fatigue, and eye problems in some people. In the United States, sickle-cell anemia is the most common inherited blood disorder, affecting mainly people whose ancestors lived in the areas where the gene first emerged. The highest frequency occurs among African Americans, but sickle-cell disease also afflicts people of other ethnic groups, including Latinos and Arab Americans. In addition to health concerns, people with sickle-cell disease have experienced various kinds of discrimination, in the job market for instance. The sickle-cell trait is a clear example of a biological "difference" that has both health effects and social effects.

Anthropologists also use labels and terms for various cultures with care because a seemingly simple term such as *British* can refer to many different groups and characteristics. Consider, for example, what the term *American* might mean. Is there an "American" culture that we can discuss without many qualifications such as North or South, urban or rural, rich or poor, young or old, male or female, and from which

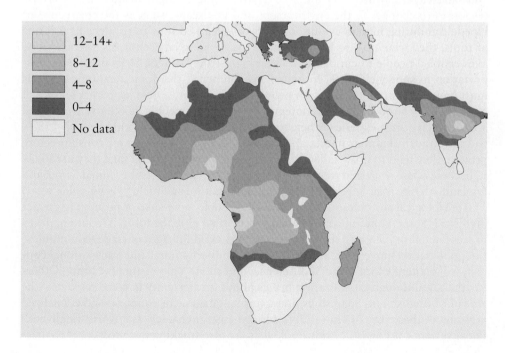

12–14+

8–12

4–8

0–4

No data

Percent of the population with the sickle cell trait in Africa and Eurasia.

The Berber people live in North Africa and the Middle East. Most make their living herding animals, though many are now settled farmers and urbanites. Left: Dressed as a prospective bride, a Berber girl takes part in a group engagement ceremony in Imilchil, Morocco. Right: A young woman of the Kabylie people, a Berber group of Algeria, wears a headband that signifies mourning during a public march to protest the government's denial of human rights to the Kabylie people. ■ Think of two images of people in your culture that illustrate intracultural variation. (Sources: © Nik Wheeler/CORBIS, left; © Tiz/CORBIS SYGMA, right)

ethnic group and which region? Does it ever make sense to speak of "American" culture? Attention to intracultural differences is important everywhere. No matter how homogeneous a culture appears, not all its members are from the same cookie cutter. Thus, while anthropologists focus on describing and explaining variations across cultures around the world, we also pay attention to variation within cultural groups.

Humanity Changes

Changes in humanity are linked to the three themes already discussed: environment and landscape, culture, and unity–diversity. Some changes in humanity may be responses to changes in the environment and landscape, such as the emergence of bipedalism during human evolution. As people learned how to produce new forms of tools, they were able to adapt to more challenging environments. Strong stone axes enabled people to cut down trees and construct shelters. Sleds provided transportation in snowy climates. In desert environments, the domestication of camels must have had dramatic effects on peoples' entire lifestyle, just as, perhaps, the cell phone is having today. Among contemporary humans, people who move from rural areas to a city often experience heightened blood pressure (Hackenberg et al. 1983). Cultural transformations in diet affect human biology. When people consume more protein, they tend to grow taller. When they eat more sugar and fats, they are likely to become obese. Referred to in the media as an "epidemic" in the United States and England, obesity is an important issue that links culture and biology in complex ways.

Are biological and cultural changes making people more alike or promoting greater diversity? Some contemporary thinkers say that **globalization,** a contemporary process of cultural change related to dense and rapid linkages of trade, communication, population movement, and other forms of international and transnational contact, will obliterate local cultural differences and create a global mono-culture. Others say that even though globalization brings about greater unity in some respects—the spread of English and Spanish as dominant languages, for example—new localized versions of these mega-cultural patterns are emerging, such as "World Englishes" (local variants of English). Anthropologists are also tracking the effects of globalization on human biology. For example, the distribution of vaccines against infectious diseases will bring an end to polio. On a less positive note, it is possible that the spread of American-style fast food may bring with it the spread of obesity.

ANTHROPOLOGY'S FOUR FIELDS

In North America, anthropology is divided into four fields (see Figure 1.3) that focus on separate, but connected, subject matter: biological anthropology, archaeology, cultural anthropology and linguistic anthropology. Some anthropologists argue that a fifth field, applied anthropology, should be added. **Applied anthropology,** also called practicing or practical anthropology, is the use of anthropological knowledge to prevent or solve problems or to shape and achieve policy goals. Our position is that the application of knowledge, just like theory, is an integral part of each of the four fields and should not be separated from them. Thus, in this book, applied anthropology is an intrinsic part of all four fields.

Biological Anthropology

Biological anthropology, or physical anthropology, is the study of humans as biological organisms, including their evolution and contemporary variation. It is a large and growing discipline that encompasses three subfields. Although these subfields rely on different kinds of data, they share an interest in the relationship between **morphology** (physical form) and behavior.

Primatology is the study of the nonhuman members of the order of mammals called primates. Primatologists study nonhuman primates in the wild and in captivity. The category of nonhuman primates includes a wide range of animals from very small, nocturnal creatures to gorillas, the largest members. Primatologists record and analyze how the animals spend their time, how they collect and share

FIGURE 1.3
The four fields of anthropology.

(*Source:* Reprinted by permission of Allyn & Bacon.)

food, their social groups and interactions, how they rear offspring, their leadership patterns, conflict and conflict resolution, and how their behavior is affected by captivity. They ask how the environment and access to resources such as food and water shape nonhuman primate behavior. They study the effect of body size on dominance patterns.

A second subfield is *paleoanthropology,* the study of human evolution on the basis of the fossil record. An important activity is the search for fossils to increase the amount and quality of the evidence related to the way human evolution occurred. Genetic evidence suggests that human ancestors diverged from the ancestors of chimpanzees between five and eight million years ago in Africa. Fossil evidence is scarce for this period, and researchers are busy hunting for fossils to fill the gap. Discoveries of new fossils provide "ah hah!" moments and arresting photographs for the covers of popular magazines. A less glamorous but equally important activity in paleoanthropology is dating and classifying new fossils. The excitement of discovery must be followed by careful analysis in order to test and revise theories.

In the third subfield, biological anthropologists study *contemporary human biological variation.* They define, measure, and seek to explain differences in the biological makeup and behavior of modern humans. In the past, biological anthropologists defined what they perceived as significant differences across modern humans as "racial" (we use quotation marks to indicate that the meaning of this term is not universally agreed upon) or regional. Among early anthropologists, the concept of "race" referred to social categories defined on the basis of one or more biological markers, including skin color, hair texture, head shape, and facial features. In this view, people born with particular biological markers were thought to behave and think in predictable ways. The controversial book *The Bell Curve: Intelligence and Class Structure in American Life* (Herrnstein and Murray 1994) is an example of enduring racial thinking in the United States. It asserts that "race" determines intelligence and class position.

Most anthropologists now reject this view, just as they would reject any biological link between gender and intelligence, or height and intelligence, or eye color and intelligence. DNA evidence clearly demonstrates that "races," defined on the basis of external physical features, are not scientifically valid categories. So-called races lack internal consistency in both biological and cultural features, and there are no clear boundaries among so-called races. Anthropologists do, however, recognize the reality of "social race" and racism—that is, the fact that many people still think "race" exists and still treat people differently on the basis of this thinking. At the same time, some groups now consciously adopt a social identity tied to "race" and find positive feature in such group identity. "Race" is a cultural construction rather than a biological given.

Archaeology

Archaeology means, literally, the "study of the old" and is therefore connected with paleoanthropology. Archaeologists focus on human culture and thus are less concerned with the earliest human ancestors (who presumably lacked culture) and with the more purely biological aspects of life. One caricatured difference is that paleoanthropologists concentrate on fossils ("bones") whereas archaeologists concentrate on tools ("stones"). This oversimplification masks the fact that some archaeologists study bones to see, for example, whether our ancestors used them as a food source. Paleoanthropologists, likewise, often examine artifacts to illuminate the contexts in which fossils are found. Both types of anthropologists often collaborate on research projects, the paleoanthropologist examining human fossils found at a site while the archaeologist analyzes the material objects discovered with the fossils.

Archaeology has been a topic of scholarly interest for centuries. The classical Greeks and Romans considered the past a golden age when their heroic ancestors lived. They revered fossilized animal bones, enshrined them in their temples, and created myths about monsters and giants of the past on the basis of their observations of fossilized dinosaurs (Mayor 2000). For many decades in the early history of archaeology, the terms *civilization* and *Europe* were regarded as synonymous. This Eurocentric view led to errors in interpreting the archaeological record. Early writings denied that Africans built the pyramids at Giza in Egypt and that Native Americans built the great mounds of the Mississippi valley. It was assumed that, because the structures were so large and complicated, they must have been built by lost European civilizations. We now know that many aspects of "civilization," such as sophisticated art and architecture, scientific thinking, and urban planning, first emerged outside Europe.

Archaeology encompasses two major areas: *prehistoric archaeology,* which concerns the human past before written records, and *historical archaeology,* which deals with the human past in societies that have written documents. This distinction makes sense because archaeological interpretation in the absence of written records faces the challenge of having only material objects to study. Prehistoric archaeologists often identify themselves with broad geographic regions, studying, for example, Old World archaeology (Africa, Europe, and Asia) or New World archaeology (North, Central, and South America).

Another set of specialties within archaeology is based on the context in which the archaeology takes place. One such specialty is underwater archaeology, the study and preservation of submerged archaeological sites. Sites may be under water because of rising water levels over time or because of an accident such as a shipwreck. Underwater archaeological sites may be from either prehistoric or historic times. Some prehistoric sites include early human settlements in parts of Europe, such as household sites discovered in Switzerland that were once near lakes but are now submerged. Prominent historic contexts include shipwrecks.

Underwater archaeologists record remains of a shipwreck, dated 1306 BCE, at Uluburun, off the southern Turkish coast. They are placing tags on copper ingots that the ship was carrying. ■ Find out more about the Uluburun excavation by visiting the web site of the Institute of Nautical Archaeology. (Source: Courtesy of the Institute of Nautical Archaeology, Texas A&M University/Photo by Don A. Frey)

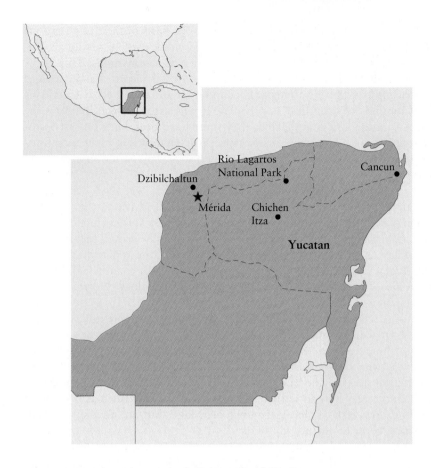

An ongoing, six-year project in underwater archaeology is being carried out on the Yucatan peninsula of Mexico (Pilar 2003, Vesilind 2003). This research provides insight into Maya funerary and religious practices dating from hundreds of years ago. Throughout the region are deep holes filled with water, created by a meteor crash around 65 million years ago. These pools are called *cenotes* (pronounced sen-OH-tays), from the Maya word for "abyss." Most cenotes are so deep and difficult to enter that the archaeologists undergo special diving training. There is no light at the bottom of the cenotes, so the divers have to carry lighting equipment in addition to their excavating equipment. Bringing materials back to the surface intact is difficult. Through this arduous and dangerous work, archaeologists are discovering rich finds of human skeletons and other artifacts. Some skeletons show the marks of sacrificial wounds. According to Maya beliefs, the rain god lived at the bottom of the cenotes. Sacrificing virgin girls, and sometimes other people, by casting them into the cenotes would bring much-needed rain.

The cenotes are an important part of the cultural heritage of Mexico, but they are endangered. Their contents are being disturbed by the activities of sports divers. As many as 10,000 sports divers a year enter the cenotes along the coast alone. Therefore, the team of professional archaeologists is working with some urgency to survey and document as many cenotes as possible.

Another specialty is industrial archaeology, which focuses on changes in material culture and society during and since the Industrial Revolution. Although it is pursued worldwide, industrial archaeology is especially active in Great Britain, home of the industrial revolution. There industrial archaeologists study such topics as the design of iron bridges, the growth and distribution of china potteries, miners' housing, and cotton mills. An important role of industrial archaeology is the conservation of industrial sites, which are more likely to be neglected or destroyed than are sites that have natural beauty or cultural glamour attached to them.

Ironbridge, England, is an important site of industrial archaeology. Considered the "birthplace of industry," the site includes the world's first iron bridge and remains of factories, furnaces, and canals. ∎ Take a virtual tour of the site by going to www.ironbridge.org.uk. (Source: Barbara Miller and Bernard Wood)

Archaeologists seek to understand the entire range of human lifestyles in the past, including everything from people's everyday work and eating patterns to special events and ritual practices. They share with paleoanthropologists an interest in attempting to trace changing patterns of human diet and the implications of diet for changes in human biology and culture. Some theorists claim that meat-eating was a key factor in the increase in size of the human brain and the consequent ability to think symbolically. Others dispute this theory and maintain that early humans relied more on fruits and roots during the early stages of brain enlargement. They say that the practice of cooking food is a more likely explanation for the emergence of culture: the controlled use of fire for cooking food meant that our human ancestors could eat a wider range of foods, which made larger group size possible. The greater social interaction that resulted may have led to the emergence of verbal language, and more.

Archaeological data on the size and floor plan of domestic sites can indicate the number of people who lived together, enabling us to reconstruct the evolution of family life. Stylistic analysis of tools and of other domestic items such as pottery provides insights about individual and group creativity and cultural identity. Treatment of the remains of the dead provides tantalizing clues to the development of a sense of an afterlife or soul.

An important characteristic of archaeology research is that it is **multiscalar**. This term means that archaeological thinking and interpretation move from the microscale of a single tool, potsherd, piece of ceramic from pottery, or site, to wider levels of regional and even global ties and patterns. The detailed study of the contents of a single grave, for example, is not an end in itself. Rather, such research sheds light on the evolution of power, wealth, status, and symbols. Tools, potsherds, and other archaeological findings are always related to a larger cultural and environmental context.

The ultimate goal of archaeologists is to understand human life in the past. Most of their evidence is in the form of objects, places, and other largely silent material remains, and this "silence" poses a serious challenge for interpretation of what the evidence might mean. Archaeologists debate how closely interpretation must stick to the artifacts and how much imagination the archaeologist can apply. For example, some archaeologists contest the conventional view that the makers and users of stone tools were primarily men. They suggest that women may just as well have done so and claim that the prevalent perspective is biased by a male perspective. Such debates are the lifeblood of any academic subject.

Serpent Mound, Ohio, is a pre-historic monument stretching over more than a quarter of a mile. It is uncertain who built the mound, when it was built, and what the serpent shape signified. Today, the mound is situated within a state park and is accessible to the public. ■ Do some research to find out more about this and other serpent-shaped mounds. (Source: © Tony Linck/Superstock, Inc.)

Cultural Anthropology

Cultural anthropology is the study of living peoples and their cultures, including attention to variation and change. Cultural anthropologists learn about culture by spending extended periods of time with the people they are studying (discussed in Chapter 4). Since World War II, cultural anthropology has grown dramatically in North America. This growth has brought about the development of many specialties within the field.

Prominent areas of specialization include economic anthropology, political anthropology, medical anthropology, psychological anthropology, and development anthropology (the study of the effects and patterns of international development policies and plans in cross-cultural perspective). In all these areas, cultural anthropologists explore cross-cultural variation in behavior and beliefs. The prefix *ethno* is often applied to an English term to suggest a cross-cultural view of whatever topic is being considered. For example, *ethnobotany* is the cross-cultural study of people's knowledge about and use of various plants in their environment. This is urgent research because many of the world's plants and their uses are still undocumented, many are being lost through development projects and deforestation, and much of the knowledge about their uses is dying out.

Cultural anthropologists, like archaeologists, look at the entire range of human behavior and thought: how people make a living, their reproduction and family patterns, health and healing, social organization and political systems, religion, language, and other expressive aspects of life such as art and music. In contrast to archaeologists, cultural anthropologists can observe living people working, arguing, and dancing and can ask them about their beliefs and thoughts related to these activities. While a woman is weaving a blanket, the cultural anthropologist can ask her why she chooses a particular motif.

Cultural anthropologists also study and document contemporary cultural change. Cultural anthropologists are studying the effects of globalization on all aspects of cultures worldwide. For example, research on the use of the Internet sheds lights on changing patterns of consumption and trade. It can also reveal how communication via the Internet helps members of migrant groups stay in touch with distant relatives or share information about their cultural identity with people they have never met. In this way, cultural anthropologists see how contemporary people create, maintain, and transform their cultures in a new, virtual world.

Another way in which some cultural anthropologists study change is to look at recent cultural history on the grounds that we cannot fully understand contemporary cultures without reference to their past (Brumfiel 2003). A prominent topic of cultural history is European colonialism. Colonial policies had major effects on local systems of land ownership, social status, gender roles, law, religion, and more. In contemporary Zimbabwe, for example, the current challenges to peace and internal security are due in part to its colonial legacy of a long period of White-minority political and economic domination (United States Institute of Peace 2003). Prospects for internal peace are blocked or slowed by historical traditions that promote the use of violence, rather than peaceful means, to bring about change. The hope here is that such patterns of violence will be reversible, because they are not biologically programmed but, rather, culturally learned.

Since the 1980s, several important developments in cultural anthropology have raised new questions and generated new data that have transformed the field. *Feminist anthropology,* or a perspective in anthropology that emphasizes the need to study female roles and gender-based inequality, is a major area of interest. Feminist anthropology has moved beyond cultural anthropology into the other fields of anthropology where it has also had a transformative effect. Another new area is *gay and lesbian anthropology,* or *queer anthropology,* which focuses on the study of gay and lesbian sexuality and culture.

Linguistic Anthropology

Linguistic anthropology is devoted to the study of communication, mainly (but not exclusively) among humans. In anthropology, the term **communication** refers to the conveying of meaningful messages from one person, animal, or insect to another through language. **Language** is a set of symbols that convey meaning; are shared among a group, and are acquired through learning. The major kinds of language among humans are verbal (speech, writing, singing) and nonverbal (eye movements, body posture and positions, movement of the limbs, dress and hair style, art and performance). Language, thus, may be spoken, signed, written, worn, sung, danced, and

Children playing video games in southern China in 1991. Since 2004, China's Ministry of Culture screens foreign games in terms of how their content relates to Chinese national interests and the possible effects of sexual and violent material on young people. ■ What is your position on the role of governments in censoring video games? (Source: © Michael S. Yamashita/CORBIS)

more. But communication is more than language itself. Among modern humans, it also involves technology and institutions such as mass media and the Internet.

Linguistic anthropology emerged in Europe and North America in the latter half of the nineteenth century. At that time, its major topics of interest were the origins of language, the historical relationships of languages of different regions and continents, and the languages of "primitive" peoples. Two important factors shaped linguistic anthropology in its early days: the discovery that many non-European languages were unwritten and the realization that the languages of many non-European peoples were dying out as a result of the negative consequences of contact with Europeans. Linguistic anthropologists responded by developing methods for recording unwritten and dying languages. In this pursuit, they learned that non-European languages have a wide range of different phonetic systems (pronunciation of various sounds) that do not correspond to the Western alphabet. To address this situation, they invented the *International Phonetic Alphabet,* which contains symbols to represent all known sounds. For example, the symbol "!" represents a click sound found in many languages of southern Africa.

Early linguistic anthropologists, thus, were interested in both the past and the present, and this breadth characterizes the field today. Some linguistic anthropologists work on topics linked to paleoanthropologists in their study of the evolution of verbal language. Others share interests with primatologists in the study of language capabilities in chimpanzees. Yet others who study the development and spread of writing are more associated with archaeology. This range of interests is reflected in linguistic anthropology's three major subfields: *historical linguistics,* the study of language change over time, how languages are related, and the relationship of linguistic change to cultural change; *descriptive* or *structural linguistics,* the study of how contemporary languages differ in terms of their structure, such as in their grammar and sound systems; and *sociolinguistics,* the study of the relationships among social variation, social context, and linguistic variation, including nonverbal communication. Most linguistic anthropologists are closely connected to cultural anthropology through their study of communication among contemporary humans, but other linguistic anthropologists see themselves as more closely connected to biological anthropology or archaeology.

Since the 1980s, several new directions have emerged that connect linguistic anthropology to important real-world issues. First, there is a trend to study language in everyday use, or *discourse,* in relation to power structures at local, regional, and international levels (Duranti 1997). For example, in some contexts, powerful people speak more than less powerful people, whereas, sometimes the more powerful people speak less. Besides sheer quantity of speech, power relations may be expressed through intonation, word choice, and such nonverbal forms of communication as posture and dress. Second, study of the media is a major growth area. Important and exciting work is being done on the relationship between language and nationalism, the role of the mass media in shaping culture more widely, communication and violence, and language rights. Third, increased attention is being paid to the role of information technology in communication. Along with many cultural anthropologists, linguistic anthropologists are studying the effects of the Internet on communicative practices and the formation of identity; the impact of cell phones on social relationships; and mass media as both a homogenizing force and a source of local cultural creativity.

The Four Fields: What Do They Add Up To?

Anthropology's four fields are now highly specialized, and no individual anthropologist has expertise in the entire discipline. The authors of this book continually strive to gain insights from the other fields, through four-field conferences, discussion, and the very process of writing a textbook together. As one illustration of how all four fields contribute important knowledge to a particular issue, consider the question "What is Europe?"

THINKING
OUTSIDE
THE BOX

Think of what you know about your home country in terms of the subject matter of anthropology's four fields. Do you know more in some of the fields than in others? What might account for that difference?

T he creation of the European Union (EU) in 1993 established a new political and economic entity intended to play a more powerful role in global affairs than could any single European country. In 2004, the EU included fifteen member states: Austria, Belgium, Denmark, Finland, France, Germany, Greece, Ireland, Italy, Luxembourg, the Netherlands, Portugal, Spain, Sweden, and the United Kingdom. Several states of Eastern Europe are negotiating for either membership or some other form of association with the EU: Estonia, Poland, the Czech Republic, Slovakia, Hungary, Romania, Bulgaria, and Turkey. Morocco applied for membership but was rejected, and Norway decided not to join. EU policy makers are concerned that excessive enlargement will weaken the organization. They are faced with two challenges: defining boundaries for membership and creating a sense of internal solidarity.

What is Europe? Where does it begin and end? What commonalities join its peoples together? Research in the four fields of anthropology sheds light on why the EU's attempts to define "Europe" and provide internal homogeneity have been elusive (Rathgeb 2002).

CROSSING
THE FIELDS

What Is Europe?
A Four-Field View

A circle of standing stones at Mzoura, Morocco. This circle is similar to many stone circles in Europe, illustrating prehistoric Celtic connections between Europe and Africa. ■ Where else are stone circles found? (Source: Barbara Miller and Bernard Wood)

The population of Europe has been formed through thousands of years of immigration. Most biological anthropologists accept that all modern humans (*Homo sapiens*) originated in Africa and then spread throughout the world (Stringer and Andrews 1988). Research in biological anthropology indicates that the first migrations of *anatomically modern humans* (discussed in Chapter 8) into Europe came from Africa and Asia, through the Middle East, beginning around 40,000 years ago (Cavalli-Sforza 1997, Chickhi et al. 1998). Over time, many waves of immigration have contributed to the genetic variation found among contemporary Europeans (Sokal 1991). There are no genes that are distinctively "European." The European genome is a patchwork quilt made of many genetic bits and pieces originating mainly in Africa and the Middle East (Barbujani and Bertorelle 2001).

Archaeological data mirror the biological evidence in revealing longstanding patterns of internal cultural diversity and movement across political borders. For example, one view says that the Neolithic and Bronze Age circular stone monuments popularly associated with Western Europe actually originated in Eastern Europe, beyond the present boundaries of the EU (Bradley 1997). Also, elements of so-called Celtic civilization, with its heartland currently in western Ireland, Scotland, Wales, and northwest France, extended beyond continental Europe into northern Africa. Thus early European cultures were not restricted to "Europe." For centuries, trade, migration, and circulation of people and ideas through conquest have created shifting borders and internal complexity. EU leaders, however, tend to ignore this fact and instead highlight selected features of the archaeological record as proof of clear boundaries between Europe and not-Europe and to create a myth of internal commonality.

The EU also attempts to form a cultural entity by recalling a shared cultural foundation in ancient Greece and Rome, Christianity, the Enlightenment, and the democratic tradition. But cultural anthropology research also shows that there is no bounded and internally homogeneous "European" culture. One anthropologist uses the wider term *Eurasia* to indicate the fluid cultural terrain between the two continents (Goody 1996).

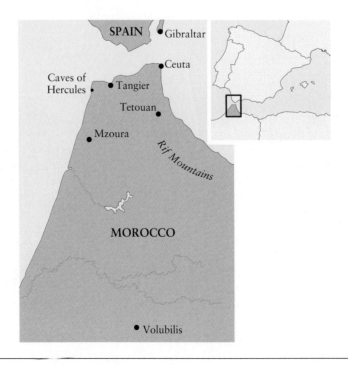

Similar family structures and inheritance patterns indicate that this term is more valid than either *Europe* or *Asia*. Cultural anthropologists question the usefulness of EU attempts to create European symbols such as a flag, currency, anthem, and heritage sites (Shore 1993). Yet even though most such attempts have been unsuccessful to date, many people who live in EU states appreciate the convenience of a single EU passport and currency. Perhaps these two highly functional items will form a more coherent sense of unity than any other symbols.

Linguistic anthropology shows that language is often a key factor providing people with a sense of shared identity. The EU chose English as the language used in policy making and for communication among member nations. This choice overlooks ten other official national languages and at least one hundred other distinct languages spoken in EU member countries. The EU has two different categories for nonofficial languages. It recognizes Irish and Basque, for example, as "regional minority" languages and has drafted legislation to promote their use as important "heritage" languages. Conversely, the EU classifies "immigrant minority" languages (such as Arabic and Turkish) as languages of "foreigners." This differentiation seems to reflect a wish to mute subordinate immigrant groups.

Taken together, findings from anthropology's four fields provide convincing evidence that it is erroneous and probably futile for EU policy makers to attempt to forge a vision of a bounded and homogeneous Europe. Doing so would require the erasing of thousands of years of prehistory, history, and recent patterns of immigration. Rather than ignoring the rich plurality of its peoples and its dynamic international relationships, EU leaders might be wiser to take a boldly pluralistic view of EU identity and build on that rich foundation. ■

FOOD FOR THOUGHT

■ If the concept of a bounded and homogeneous Europe is invalid, are other world regions equally invalid? Is there an Asia? Is there an Africa?

ANTHROPOLOGY IN THE "REAL WORLD"

In this section, we launch the discussion of several topics related to doing anthropology in the "real world" and to the relevance of anthropology beyond academia. We introduce the important topics of ethics and relevance and discuss them in terms of research, teaching, and application. We then review some connections between anthropology and careers.

Ethics and Relevance

Ethics comprises rules of conduct about what is right and wrong in terms of both motives and actual behavior. These issues were not prominent in the early phases of anthropology, but they are extremely important now. When the earliest archaeologists opened an ancient tomb, removed the contents and put them on display in museums in their home countries, they were not thinking about the ethical implications of their actions. The earliest anthropologists who encountered isolated tribal groups were not aware that they might spread diseases among people who had no resistance. Now, however, ethics, relevance, and responsibility are high on the agendas of all anthropologists. Because of this importance, we begin a discussion of ethics, relevance, and responsibility in this chapter, and we will provide examples throughout the book.

THINKING
OUTSIDE
THE BOX

What other courses that you have taken included discussion of ethics? Should ethics be part of every academic discipline, or part of some but not of others? Be prepared to explain your position.

Starting in the 1950s and 1960s, serious, and often heated, discussions about ethics in anthropology arose in the United States, surrounding the possibility that the United States government was using anthropologists as spies conducting secret research in Latin America and then in Southeast Asia during the American–Vietnam war. These cases were never resolved, and claims and counterclaims went largely unproven. Accusations included the possibility that such research had been used by the government to kill suspected enemies and destroy villages where the anthropologists had done research. The possibility that anthropologists might have consciously gathered data that would later be used against the people they studied horrified most anthropologists. Some anthropologists, though, took a different position, saying that when one's country is at war, it is a citizen's duty is to do everything possible to aid that effort, even if it means posing as an anthropologist to gain information about the enemy.

The first formal statement on anthropological ethics was issued in 1971 by the American Anthropological Association (AAA). It was subsequently revised in 1986 and again in 1998. The code of ethics has three major sections: research, teaching, and application (see Figure 1.4). Under research, the anthropologist's first responsibility is to avoid doing anything that would harm the people, animals, and materials they study. Another point made in the 1971 code of ethics was that anthropologists should never do covert (secret, undercover) research. This point has been rephrased to ensure that researchers always inform their human research participants about the research and tell them how the data will be used. Participants must be assured of anonymity unless they explicitly give investigators permission to reveal their identity. Another important point is that researchers should recognize their debt to the study population and that they must reciprocate appropriately. Finally, researchers bear the responsibility of disseminating their findings to the public in such a way as to ensure that those findings are well understood and used responsibly.

The section on research provides guidance for protecting research populations, sites, and materials. Clearly, such protection must be the number-one priority on general ethical grounds. Underlying this important objective, however, is the need to protect the future of anthropology. In doing anthropological research, the reminder that "one cannot step into the same stream twice" is fitting. Excavating an archaeological site alters that site forever—in many cases, excavation actually involves destruction of the site. Conducting interviews with people in a village can be done only once in that particular time and context. The research interaction will affect, often in unknown ways, the people involved. The very presence of a researcher can have major effects on the host population and site. Researchers are usually from a relatively wealthy country, they have expensive equipment and canned food, they have foreign ways of behaving, and they will eventually leave, perhaps never to return. Given the inevitable and often negative "anthropogenic" (and here we intend a double meaning of "human-created" and "anthropology-created") changes, the discipline needs ethical guidelines for conducting research and, just as important, for helping to decide whether it is appropriate to do the research at all.

In terms of teaching, the 1998 code sets down principles that apply to good teaching in any field: treating all students equally and fairly, being responsive to students' needs and interests, and acknowledging student assistance in research and publications. The single point about ethical teaching specifically related to teaching anthropology is that professors should engage students in the discussion of ethical issues and discourage students from participating in ethically questionable projects.

The ethical principles for conducting research also guide anthropologists who undertake applied work. The code suggests that anthropologists should carefully consider the ethical implications of any such involvement before getting involved. Further, the code says that inaction or even noncooperation with certain projects may be ethically justifiable. The AAA sets out ethical guidelines but has no role in enforcing them. If a claim is made that an anthropologist has behaved unethically, the AAA will review the case and write a report, but that is as far as its power and responsibility extend.

FIGURE 1.4
The Code of Ethics of the American Anthropological Association, 1998.

Research

1. Primary ethical obligations are to the people, species, and materials they study and to the people with whom they work. These obligations can supersede the goal of seeking new knowledge:

   - Avoid harm or wrong, understanding that the development of knowledge can lead to change, which may be positive or negative for the people or animals worked with or studied.

   - Respect the well-being of humans and nonhuman primates.

   - Work for the long-term conservation of the archaeological, fossil, and historical records.

   - Consult actively with the affected individuals or group(s), with the goal of establishing a working relationship that can be beneficial to all parties involved.

2. Ensure that anthropological research does not harm the dignity or privacy of the people with whom they conduct research, or harm the safety, well-being, and survival of animals with which they work.

3. Determine in advance whether human research participants wish to remain anonymous or receive recognition. Informed consent of persons being studied must be obtained in advance. Informed consent does not necessarily imply or require a written or signed form, but involves the quality of consent that is provided on the basis of a clear understanding of possible effects of participation in the research.

4. Recognize their obligations to individuals, groups, and host institutions that participated in or otherwise facilitated the research.

Responsibility to Scholarship and Science

1. Anticipate possible ethical dilemmas and raise these issues in their research proposals.

2. Assume responsibility for the integrity and reputation of the discipline and abide by general moral rules of science:

   - Do not deceive.

   - Do not knowingly misrepresent.

   - Do not prevent reporting of misconduct.

   - Do not obstruct the research of others.

3. Preserve opportunities for future fieldworkers.

4. Use findings in an appropriate fashion and, whenever possible, disseminate findings to the scientific and scholarly community.

5. Consider all reasonable requests for access to data and ensure preservation of data for posterity.

Responsibility to the Public

1. Make findings appropriately available to sponsors, students, decision-makers, and other nonanthropologists and ensure that such information is well understood and properly utilized.

2. It is possible to move to a position of advocacy, but this is an individual decision rather than an ethical responsibility.

Teaching

1. Do not discriminate on the basis of sex, marital status, "race," social class, political convictions, disability, religion, ethnic background, national origin, sexual orientation, age, or other criteria irrelevant to academic performance.

2. Strive to improve teaching, availability, counseling, and helping students obtain professional placement.

3. Impress upon students the ethical challenges in every phase of anthropological work.

4. Publicly acknowledge student assistance in research and preparation of work and compensate students justly for their participation in all professional activities.

5. Avoid sexual liaisons with students for whose education they are in any way responsible.

Application

1. Follow the same ethical guidelines in all anthropological work, be open with funders, and make carefully considered decisions about what types of work in which to be involved.

2. Be honest with employers about qualifications, capabilities, and aims and do not accept conditions contrary to professional ethics.

3. Be alert to dangers of compromising anthropological ethics and understand that contributions to public or private sector actions and policies may include both proactive participation and noncooperation, depending on circumstances.

Note: The AAA code does not dictate behavior or include sanctions. It is designed to promote discussion and provide general guidelines for ethically responsible decisions.

(*Source:* Adapted from *www.aanet.org* by permission of the American Anthropological Association from the Code of Ethics of the American Anthropological Association, approved June 1998.)

Besides the AAA code, each of the four fields has developed its own field-specific codes of ethics. For example, ethics within archaeology addresses issues such as stewardship of the archaeological record through preservation and advocacy for public support, accountability to groups affected by research, avoiding activities that add to commercialization of artifacts, and the responsibility to public education. Ethics codes have been developed by anthropology associations in many countries in professional organizations whose interests intersect with anthropology, such as museum associations and scientific associations; and in international organizations such as the United Nations Educational, Scientific, and Cultural Organization (UNESCO) (see Figure 1.5).

FIGURE 1.5
Codes of ethics of professional associations of anthropology and related areas.

American Academy of Forensic Sciences (AAFS)
  Bylaws

American Anthropological Association
  Ethics Homepage
  Sections and Interest Groups with independent bylaws

American Association of Physical Anthropologists (AAPA)
  Code of Ethics

American Cultural Resources Association (ACRA)
  Code of Ethics

American Society of Primatologists (ASP)
  The Long-term Care of Chimpanzees

Archaeological Institute of America (AIA)
  Code of Ethics
  Code of Professional Standards

Association of Social Anthropology (ASA)
  Ethical Guidelines for Good Research Practice

Canadian Archaeological Association (CAA)
  Principals of Ethical Conduct
  Statement of Principles for Ethical Conduct Pertaining to Aboriginal Peoples

European Association of Archaeologists (EAA)
  Code of Conduct
  Code of Practice

International Council of Museums (ICOM)
  Ethics Policy

National Association for the Practice of Anthropology (NAPA)
  Ethical Guidelines for Practitioners

Society for American Archaeology (SAA)
  Principles of Archaeological Ethics

Society for Applied Anthropology (SfAA)
  Ethical and Professional Responsibilities

Society for Historical Archaeology (SHA)
  Bylaws

World Archaeological Congress (WAC)
  Code of Ethics

(*Source:* Adapted from *www.web~miner.com/anthroethics.html.*)

Since the 1960s, some anthropologists have insisted that anthropologists must go beyond simply "doing no harm" in our research and work. They ask, "What is anthropology for? For whom are its activities conducted?" The AAA code does not require service to the public other than through the obligation to make research findings accessible to the public. For many anthropologists, service to the public should be implicit and unquestioned if the discipline is to be more than an "ivory tower" preoccupation of an academic elite. Anthropology can be made relevant to the public through applied work, teaching, and transferring anthropological knowledge to the public via museums, media, and popular writing. We first consider some examples of applied anthropology and then turn to the role of anthropology in public education.

Applying Knowledge

Applied anthropology emerged as a separate branch of cultural anthropology after World War II. Anthropologists had often worked in a professional capacity before that time, but the term "applied anthropology" had not yet been coined. During European colonialism of the late nineteenth and early twentieth centuries, many anthropologists were employed by their governments to study the languages, cultural practices, and people's attitudes in colonized areas. If a colonial power wanted to know about "traditional customs" of the people concerning marriage, for example, an anthropologist would be asked to gather information related to that topic and provide a report. During World War II, several prominent anthropologists in the United States served as consultants to government, offering cultural insights about Japanese culture and mentality in order to help the United States defeat the enemy. More recently, applied anthropology has expanded from its base in cultural anthropology to the other three fields.

Several areas of biological anthropology are amenable to applied work. Applied primatologists help provide data to support primate conservation projects. In designing primate conservation projects, primatologists often work with cultural anthropologists because of the need to complement knowledge about nonhuman primates with knowledge about neighboring people's relationships with the primates and the environment. The cultural anthropology part may include research on local people's need for farm land or on the potential environmental and economic impact of international tourism in the area. Biological anthropologists who study contemporary human variation provide knowledge relevant to social welfare programs based on their research about how health and nutrition change when people migrate to cities or about growth patterns of children in refugee camps. Welfare programs can then more effectively target their resources to those most in need. *Forensic anthropology* is another applied area of biological anthropology. It involves biological anthropologists in criminal investigations using laboratory analysis to identify human remains, to provide information about the context of the death, time of death, and cause of death, and to identify victims' age, sex, and ethnic heritage. In addition to lab work, forensic anthropologists may also provide expert testimony in the courtroom. They often join the efforts of international humanitarian aid organizations in identifying the victims of natural disasters such as earthquakes. In many parts of the world, forensic anthropologists work closely with human rights advocates by providing information on deaths from state terror.

In archaeology, applied work is growing. Since the 1970s, in the United States a major impetus to this involvement has been the national policy of *cultural resource management (CRM)*. This policy requires an archaeological survey of "cultural resources" that may be affected whenever a major new construction project, such as

People watch as forensic anthropologist Francisco de Leon conducts an exhumation of more than 50 bodies in a highland Guatemalan village in 1997. Anthropologists are increasingly involved in applied research related to human rights abuses. ■ Are courses in forensic anthropology offered at your school? (Source: AP/Wide World Photos)

Archaeology Findings Increase Food Production in Bolivia

AN ARCHAEOLOGICAL RESEARCH project near the shores of Lake Titicaca in highland Bolivia uncovered prehistoric remains of raised fields separated by an intricate system of canals (Straughan and Schuler 1991). When the Spanish colonialists arrived, they abandoned the raised-field system and replaced it with their own type of cultivation. In the 1990s, farmers were struggling to produce adequate crops of potatoes from the boggy soil. Frosts also took their toll on the plants before they matured.

Two archaeologists who had been working in the region for years convinced a local farmer to experiment with the indigenous raised-field system, suggesting that what worked a thousand years ago might succeed again. The other villagers were skeptical but watched with interest as the potato plants on the raised field grew taller than they had ever seen. Then, right before the harvest, frost threatened and 90 percent of the village crop was lost. Most of the potatoes in the experimen-

tal field, though, were fine. They had been protected by a thick mist that had formed over the field. The sun's warmth during the day heats up the canal water, which, in turn, warms the fields at night when the temperature drops.

The community eventually adopted the new–old system, and crop yields rose significantly. Moreover, algae and aquatic plants began to grow in the canals along with nitrogen-fixing bacteria. When the canals are cleaned annually, there is now a rich residue of organic material in them that can be used to fertilize the fields. The Bolivian government has started a training program to promote the old technique as a way to increase the nation's food supply. The archaeologists are now welcomed with great enthusiasm when they visit Lake Titicaca—a region that once was the center of a rich civilization, was reduced to poverty by the effects of colonial extractive policies, and now, through study of the past, is a revitalizing agricultural economy.

FOOD FOR THOUGHT

- What are some pros and cons of anthropologists applying their knowledge to contemporary social problems?

Raised beds in Bolivia. This strategy helps prevent erosion, improves the organic content of the soil, captures moisture, and provides protection for crops from frosts. The main feature of the system, termed waru waru *in the Quechua language, is a network of embankments and canals.* ■ To find out more about *waru waru,* go to *http://www/oas.usde/publications/Unit/oca59ec/ch27.html.* (Source: © Bettmann/CORBIS)

a highway, is planned. It also requires plans for preservation of the affected cultural resources. The phrase *cultural resources* includes properties and objects such as buildings and structures, sacred places, historic and modern landscapes, historic documents, museum collections, and individual artifacts (Bergman and Doershuk 2003). The requirement for CRM surveys led to major growth in employment opportunities for archaeologists. About one-third of the professional (nonacademic) archaeologists in the United States are currently involved in CRM work. Internationally, such survey work is not always mandated, and valuable sites and artifacts are destroyed by bulldozers in the name of progress—for example, building an airport or road.

Internationally, archaeologists have become increasingly active in providing knowledge that can help improve the lives of people in poor countries. This effort parallels a wider search throughout anthropology for ways to provide findings relevant to key social issues such as poverty and food scarcity (see the Lessons Applied box). Lessons from archaeology can help alleviate contemporary problems.

Linguistic anthropologists play important roles in applied research and policy advising. For example, they consult for educational policy makers in North America about language teaching in schools and how to meet the needs of multilingual populations. They conduct research on classroom dynamics—student participation and teachers' speech patterns—and ask whether there are practices that could be changed to alter gender or ethnic inequalities. Internationally, linguistic anthropologists are promoting the rights of indigenous peoples to use their own language as an aspect of cultural rights. Their documentation of dying languages of the past has proved useful to indigenous people who wish to revive their ancestral language.

Applied anthropology is a vigorous part of cultural anthropology. Several professional associations in the United States and elsewhere reflect that importance. These include NAPA (National Association of Practicing Anthropologists) and WAPA (Washington Association of Professional Anthropologists) and Internet groups such as Anthropology in Action, based in the United Kingdom. Applied cultural anthropologists provide input to such activities as needs assessment, project design, social impact analysis, social marketing, and project evaluation. Cultural anthropologists have helped design HIV/AIDS prevention programs by making their messages more culturally relevant. They have documented environmental destruction by mining companies and helped the affected villagers protest that destruction and gain redress. They have helped prevent the construction of large dam projects that would have displaced thousands of local people. They have done social surveys of malnutrition in famine areas to help aid agencies provide food most effectively. In health care settings in the United States, they have served to enhance cross-cultural understanding between medical doctors and members of immigrant populations.

Cultural anthropologists also contribute to policy formulation, analysis, and critique. For example, they contribute to framing policy objectives to alleviate rural poverty in Nepal—an effort that will address social inequality. They critique policies related to international trade. A growing set of experiences now points to "best practices" in terms of how culture can and should be taken into account in projects and policies. We now have many decades of experience showing how ideas imposed by uninformed but well-meaning outsiders can have damaging effects or can simply be a waste of effort. It is clear that one of the main problems in international relations and aid is that people in the "first world" lack knowledge about "other" people and their values, needs, and lifestyles. Cultural anthropologists help fill that knowledge gap by sharing their findings with policy makers and program designers.

Anthropology and the Public

Contemporary anthropologists are concerned that anthropology should be relevant to public education. Archaeology has taken the lead in this effort. Archaeologists have provided guidelines and examples of how to incorporate archaeology into middle school and high school education curricula, and into college education at both the undergraduate and graduate levels. The goal of public education is normally to produce knowledgeable citizens, and that of archaeology is normally to preserve the archaeological record and develop awareness of the significance of archaeological resources. These two goals can fit together well. Citizens should know about their country and its history and prehistory, as well as about that of the wider global world. Teaching about archaeology can fill that need, expanding on the range of what is normally taught in history and social studies classes.

An archaeologist working in Florida once examined his daughter's eighth-grade social science textbook and was dismayed to see that the discussion of the history of the United States began with Jamestown and the Pilgrims (Milanich 2001). The 12,000 or more years in which Indians had lived in Florida were not mentioned, nor were the Spanish missions and French settlements. Nearly 15 years later, he received an email from a school in St. Petersburg mentioning that the fourth-grade class was

Did you learn about local archaeology in your grade school, middle school, or high school?

THINKING

OUTSIDE THE BOX

doing a project on famous Floridians, and one girl had selected Cacique María. The teacher was seeking some advice on how to help find information for the student's project. The archaeologist was impressed at the change. The Florida Department of Education now mandates that social studies courses emphasize Florida history in the fourth and eighth grades. Standards require that students learn about "early Spanish settlements" and "loss of Native American homelands." Educators are collaborating with archaeologists to prepare lesson plans. Archaeologists are helping by writing texts for fourth and eighth graders that cover topics such as changing climatic conditions at the end of the last Ice Age, the state's first inhabitants, native chiefs, and Spanish colonialism. Incorporating archaeological knowledge into grade school texts is a good way to share it with a wide public. Such textbooks provide a more accurate and richer story of the past, help build interest in and respect for the past, and thus enhance public stewardship of the past.

Turning to education at the college and university level, we find that most efforts of archaeology devoted to curriculum and course content focus on students who are majoring in archaeology. The main goals in this respect are to ensure that archaeology programs include course work on ethics and relevance and that they help to prepare archaeology students for careers either in or beyond academia. One could, however, push a step further, applying the insights from the Florida grade school initiative. A case could be made that archaeology is just as important for a well-rounded liberal education as history and that archaeology classes could fulfill the same distributional requirements that history classes do. Given the increasing global links and intracountry cultural diversity driven by migration, it seems imperative to the authors of this book that "citizens of the world" benefit from exposure to humanity as a whole—and thus, to anthropology.

Anthropology and Careers

For those who are not interested in majoring in anthropology as undergraduates, anthropology can be an excellent minor or double major. Anthropology complements almost any other area of study by adding greater "time depth" and a cross-cultural perspective. If you are majoring in music, complementary study in the music of the world will greatly enrich your primary interest. The same applies to subjects as different as interior design, psychology, and criminal justice.

For students interested in pursuing a major in anthropology (or in one of its fields, depending on what your college or university has to offer), we recommend that you make this choice with your eyes wide open. A B.A. in anthropology, just like a B.A. in most other liberal arts subjects, is not a professional degree. Like degrees in history, psychology, and sociology, it is a "good liberal arts degree." It provides a solid background relevant to many career directions that are likely to require further study: law, law enforcement, medicine, social services, education, and business, for instance. The emphasis in anthropology on cross-cultural awareness, understanding of connections among aspects of humanity, and awareness of the dynamics of change are all intellectual assets and skills that employers value (see inside front cover).

Not many of you will decide to go on to pursue a master's degree (M.A.) or doctorate degree (Ph.D.) in anthropology, but we have some advice for those who do: Be passionate about your interest, pay attention to the ethical aspects of your involvement, and be aware that full-time jobs as professors are rare and highly competitive, as are full-time jobs as professional anthropologists. It is often wise to combine a "professionalizing" skill with anthropology, such as a law degree, an M.A. degree in project management, a Master's of Public Health (M.P.H.), a certificate in disaster relief, or attendance at a training program in conflict prevention and resolution. Useful skills in a variety of areas can be gained to complement each of anthropology's four fields. In biological anthropology, it may be your knowledge of anatomy that helps you get a job teaching anatomy in a medical school or working in a forensics lab. In archaeology, it may be your experience on a summer dig that helps you find a job with the CRM people in your home state. In cultural anthropology, your interviewing skills may land you a position with a marketing company. In linguistic anthropology, your knowledge of bilingualism means that you can help design a more effective program for teaching English to refugees.

Studying anthropology makes for smart people and people with breadth and flexibility. In the United States, current college graduates are likely to change careers (not just jobs, but careers) several times in their lives. You never know where you are going to end up working or in what endeavor—so it pays to be smart, broadly informed about the world, and flexible. Anthropology will help you to ask original and important questions about humanity and to provide original and important answers.

THE BIG QUESTIONS REVISITED

▪ WHAT is anthropology?

Anthropology is the study of humanity, including the prehistoric origins of humans, our nonhuman primate relatives, contemporary human biological and cultural variation, and human communication past and present. It is the only discipline that provides such a comprehensive view of humanity. Anthropology's roots go back at least to the time of the classical Greek and Roman philosophers, who raised questions about humanity's origins and diversity. During the Middle Ages, the Bible was the source of explanations about humanity in most of Europe, but after the European Enlightenment of the seventeenth and eighteenth centuries, the biblical view began to be displaced by a scientific view. Since the latter half of the nineteenth century, anthropology has emerged as a formal academic discipline and has grown substantially. It is now a global activity, although most anthropologists are still found in Europe and North America. Throughout its history, four enduring themes in anthropology have been how environment and landscape shape humanity, culture as the key to humanity, unity and diversity, and change over time.

▪ WHAT do the four fields of anthropology cover?

North American anthropology is divided into four fields: biological anthropology, archaeology, cultural anthropology, and linguistic anthropology. These fields contain distinct but related subject matter. Most anthropologists specialize in one field. Biological anthropology, or physical anthropology, is the study of humans as biological organisms. It includes the subfields of primatology, paleoanthropology, and contemporary human variation. Archaeological anthropology, or archaeology, is the study of past human cultures through their material remains. It contains two subfields: prehistoric archaeology and historic archaeology, and several other domains (such as underwater archaeology and industrial archaeology) based on characteristics of the sites involved. Cultural anthropology, or social anthropology, is the study of living people and their cultures and of variation and change therein. Cultural anthropology contains many subfields, including economic anthropology, political anthropology, psychological anthropology, medical anthropology, and more. Linguistic anthropology is the study of human communication—its origins, history, and contemporary variation and change. Most linguistic anthropologists study contemporary communication among humans and are thus closely linked to cultural anthropology. Applied anthropology is sometimes put forward as a possible fifth field in the discipline. This book takes the perspective that application of knowledge, just like theory, is an integral part of each of the four fields and should be studied as such, not as a discrete field. As an example of how the four fields fit together, we explored the question "What is Europe?"

■ WHAT are examples of anthropology in the "real world"?

Anthropology is not just an academic discipline populated by professors in universities. One aspect of anthropology's public role is its concern with ethics in all its activities, from research to teaching to applied work. Ethics are rules regarding what is right and what is wrong in motives and behavior. Anthropological ethics about research state that the anthropologist's primary responsibility is to protect the well-being of people, sites, species, and materials involved in his or her research. Ethics about teaching involve principles that apply to teaching in any field, such as treating all students fairly, but also include the specific goal of engaging students in discussion of ethical principles. Anthropologists who undertake applied work should abide by the principles governing research as well as by additional guidelines about honesty in dealing with sponsors and not taking on any work that is ethically questionable. Applied work is an important way in which anthropologists can share their expertise with the public. Examples of applied work in each of the four fields demonstrate the relevance of anthropology to the solution of real-world problems.

Anthropology has relevance to public education, from grade school on up. Anthropologists are increasingly active in helping to provide advice about curriculum to make it more inclusive. Anthropology is relevant to many kinds of careers. As a minor or double major, it complements and strengthens many other disciplines by adding greater time depth and cross-cultural breadth of understanding. As a B.A. major, it is an excellent foundation for future professional study—for example, in legal, business, and health fields. In M.A. programs, a professional degree in anthropology can lead to careers in many areas. At the Ph.D. level, it prepares anthropologists for teaching in colleges and universities and for research and policy roles in organizations such as governments and international organizations.

KEY CONCEPTS

adaptation, p. 10
adaptive compromise, p. 10
anthropogenic, p. 10
anthropology, p. 4
applied anthropology, p. 13
archaeology, p. 14
biological anthropology, p. 13

communication, p. 19
cultural anthropology, p. 18
culture, p. 10
enculturation, p. 10
evolution, p. 8
globalization, p. 12
humanistic approach, p. 5

language, p. 19
linguistic anthropology, p. 19
morphology, p. 13
multiscalar, p. 17
science, p. 5
symbol, p. 10

SUGGESTED READINGS

James Deetz. *In Small Things Forgotten: An Archaeology of Early American Life*. New York: Doubleday, 1996. Deetz argues that understanding past cultures is best accomplished through studying everyday things such as gravestones, doorways, musical instruments, and pottery shards. The updated version of this classic study includes more material on women and African Americans.

Jane Goodall. *Reason for Hope: A Spiritual Journey*. New York: Warner Books, 1999. Primatologist Jane Goodall provides her memoirs (including recollections of her childhood in London during World War II, Louis Leakey's mentorship when she was a young fieldworker, and her long-term fieldwork in Tanzania with chimpanzees) and reflections on the ethical implications of animal research.

Cori Hayden. *When Nature Goes Public: The Making and Unmaking of Bioprospecting in Mexico*. Princeton, NJ: Princeton University Press, 2003. The exchange of plants for corporate promises of royalties or community improvement projects is studied from the perspective of cultural anthropology. Using the results of in-depth research at several sites in Mexico, the author considers who stands to win and lose, how companies should pay, and to whom.

Gustav Jahoda. *Images of Savages: Ancient Roots of Modern Prejudice in Western Culture*. New York: Routledge, 1999. The author examines the historic roots of prejudice in Western thinking, tracing such beliefs as monstrous cannibals, wild men of the woods, and ape-like savages. These beliefs peaked in the nineteenth century, when many of them gained scientific respectability. Some of these themes persist today in descriptions of people perceived as "other," including the poor and the mentally ill.

Richard J. Perry. *Five Concepts in Anthropological Thinking*. Upper Saddle River, NJ: Prentice-Hall, 2003. After a brief introduction on theory in anthropology, the author discusses the following concepts: evolution, culture, structure, function, and relativism. A final chapter provides a summary and a discussion of "unsettled issues."

Adriana Petryna. *Life Exposed: Biological Citizens after Chernobyl*. Princeton, NJ: Princeton University Press, 2002. A cultural anthropologist considers the aftermath of the disaster and how the people affected face their new lives of disability and uncertainty. Attention is also given to how the nation of Ukraine is dealing with the management of risk.

Hugh Raffles. *In Amazonia: A Natural History*. Princeton, NJ: Princeton University Press, 2002. This book provides a wide view of the region and its people.

W. Richard Stephens. *Careers in Anthropology: What an Anthropology Degree Can Do for You*. Boston: Allyn and Bacon, 2002. Sixteen profiles of careers in, and related to, anthropology, provide insights about career options and paths to a career in anthropology. The mini-biographies include people working in cultural resource management, international development, computer engineering, coroner's investigation, the administration of not-for-profit organizations, and more.

THE BIG QUESTIONS

- WHAT is culture?
- WHAT are some bases of cultural diversity?
- WHAT do anthropologists debate about culture?

CHAPTER 2

Culture and Diversity

A circle of standing stones, dated around 3500 BCE, and the world's first full-scale nuclear power station at Sellafield, England, both important monuments of their respective eras. (Source: © Macduff Everton/CORBIS)

I can't pass a rock
like you
without being mystified
or hypnotized

I have heard stories
of rocks
and have known some
rocks personally

They represent the
world by their presence
wisdom has no
relationship to size

One time, perhaps many times
a man became a rock
thinking that a fine way
to gain immortality

This Native American poem of the Wintu people of California refers to a rock formation called the "Bag of Bones" (Theodoratus and LaPena 1994:24–25). It also expresses a more general message about the connectedness between humans and natural sites that has persisted for thousands of years among cultures around the world. Today, however, many people in industrialized cultures have replaced a connectedness to stones, streams, and mountains with a connectedness to technology and to modern monuments such as the Eiffel tower, satellite dishes, and huge shopping malls.

Culture today seems less and less connected to nature, but perhaps that is an overgeneralization. One of anthropology's goals is to study the relationship between nature and culture and the power of each to shape humanity's past, present, and future.

 THE CONCEPT OF CULTURE

As we mentioned in Chapter 1, our working definition of *culture* is that it consists of learned and shared behavior and beliefs. The topic of culture crosses all four fields of anthropology. Paying in-depth attention to it is a necessary step before going further in the exploration of humanity. Many scholars agree that although biology was the major actor in humanity's earliest evolution, culture is now the key shaper of humanity. The fossil and archaeological record of human evolution supports this view. Linguistic anthropology, too, provides evidence of the important cultural role of human communication that goes far beyond the biological ability to speak or the muscular and neurological ability to communicate with hand, eye, or facial movements.

Definitions of Culture

The question of how to define culture has intrigued anthropologists for over a century. Even now, spirited discussions take place between animal scientists and cultural anthropologists about whether nonhuman animals have culture and, if so, how it resembles or differs from human culture. This section reviews some important differences in how anthropologists define culture, then considers some characteristics of culture, and, last, discusses ethnocentrism and cultural relativism.

Because culture is a core concept in anthropology, it seems likely that anthropologists would agree about what it is. This may have been the case in the early days of the discipline in the nineteenth century, when there were far fewer anthropologists. But by the middle of the twentieth century, an effort to collect definitions of culture produced 164 different ones (Kroeber and Kluckhohn 1952). We first look at the history of attempts to define culture and then bring us up to the present, when three perspectives prevail.

The earliest definition of culture was proposed by British anthropologist Edward Tylor in 1871: "Culture, or civilization . . . is that complex whole which includes knowledge, belief, art, law, morals, custom, and any other capabilities and habits acquired by man as a member of society" (Kroeber and Kluckhohn 1952:81). The phrase *that complex whole* has been the most durable feature of Tylor's definition. Three other features have not stood the test of time. First, most anthropologists now avoid using *man* to refer to all humans and instead use generic words such as *humans* and *people*. One might argue that the word *man* can be used generically according to its linguistic roots, but studies indicate that this usage can be confusing. Second, most anthropologists no longer equate culture with civilization. The term *civilization* implies a sense of "highness" versus noncivilized "lowness" and sets up an invidious distinction placing "us" (the so-called civilized nations of Europe and North America) in a position superior to "them"—the other societies. Third, many anthropologists now think that culture is not limited to humanity but that, to an extent, it is also found in some nonhuman animals in which observed variations in behavior are not determined genetically but are learned and shared (McGrew 1998).

We can divide contemporary views about the question "What is culture?" into three perspectives: **idealism**, **behaviorism**, and **holism** (see Figure 2.1). These views differ in terms of whether they conceive of culture as consisting mainly of internalized meanings, or mainly of observable behavior, or both. The idealist view, also called symbolist and interpretivist, is that culture consists of learned and shared beliefs, thoughts, meanings, and symbols. The behaviorist view is that culture consists of learned and shared ways of behaving. The holistic view is that culture consists of learned and shared beliefs, meanings, and symbols *as well as* learned and shared ways of behaving. In reality, most anthropologists would agree that beliefs and behavior are both important and are interrelated aspects of culture.

Culture is found universally among human beings, and thus it exists in a general way as something everyone has, a kind of culture with a capital "C." Culture also exists in a more specific way. The term **microculture**, or local culture, refers to distinct patterns of learned and shared behavior and ideas found in localized regions and among particular groups. Microcultures include ethnic groups, racial groups, genders, and age categories. The term **macroculture** refers to learned and shared ways of behaving and thinking that cross local boundaries, such as the sense of national culture that some governments seek to promote to enhance unity, and the global consumer culture that pervades upper-middle-class and upper-class groups transnationally.

FIGURE 2.1
Three views of culture.

Idealism: emphasis on learned and shared ways of thinking

Behaviorism: emphasis on learned and shared ways of behaving

Holism: emphasis on learned and shared ways of thinking and behaving

A Brief History of Anthropology's Focus on Culture

Three fields of general anthropology are most directly concerned with the study of culture: archaeology, linguistic anthropology, and cultural anthropology. This section provides an abbreviated intellectual history of these three fields (Chapter 3 provides a parallel history of biological anthropology).

Archaeology and Culture of the Past

The study of culture in the human past has been a topic of popular and scholarly interest for centuries (Trigger 1989). As noted in Chapter 1, the Greeks and Romans revered the past, and they collected relics and fossils unearthed from construction sites. The biblical age also envisioned the ancient past as a golden age—the time of Adam and Eve in the Garden of Eden. The biblical description of human prehistory, though, was shaken during the early centuries of European colonialism. Europeans were especially perplexed about the existence of people in the New World, because

A panel of the so-called Elgin marbles, a collection of marble friezes and other sculptures originally located at the Acropolis in Athens, Greece, now housed in the British Museum in London. ■ Learn more about the Elgin marbles as "contested" and take an informed position in the debate as to whether they should remain in London or be returned to Athens. (Source: British Museum, London, UK/ Bridgeman Art Library)

the Bible never mentioned them. When the Spanish arrived in Mexico and saw the advanced cities and massive wealth of the Aztec empire, it became clear there was a flaw in the Eurocentric vision of Europe as the only civilized region and of European people as the only people capable of civilization.

In the 1600s, the Danes established the first museum of antiquities, or "ancient objects" (Bahn 1996). The seventeenth and eighteenth centuries saw increased interest in antiquities in Europe and among Europeans in the American colonies. Collectors at this time were called *antiquarians,* untrained people who collected and studied relics of the ancient past as a hobby. Early antiquarians, however, laid the basis for contemporary archaeological methods. Thomas Jefferson, in 1784, undertook the first recorded excavation to be conducted in North America (Patterson 2001). With the goal of learning about the origins of Native Americans, his project is now recognized as an early example of the scientific method: he had a research goal and a method to achieve that goal. The method involved careful excavation and detailed recordkeeping of several mounds on his Virginia estate at Monticello.

Over the centuries, countless objects were taken from their original sites and displaced into private collections or museums. Many of these objects are the focus of heated debates about whether they should be returned to their place of origin.

During the mid-nineteenth century, antiquarianism began to evolve into archaeology, a formal area of study with science defining its goals and methods. A Danish scholar, Christian Jurgen Thomsen, was an important figure in this transition period. He devised a three-age system of prehistory based on the evolution of tools: the Stone Age, the Bronze Age, and the Iron Age. He introduced the concept of *association* by which non-tool artifacts are dated on the basis of their association in the site with tools made of stone, bronze, or iron. He organized the Danish museum's collections in accordance with this principle and, in 1836, published a major book on his findings called the *Guide to Northern Archaeology.* In 1843 another Dane, Jens Worsaac, published an account of Danish prehistory entitled *Primeval Antiquities of Denmark,* which established his career as a full-time professional archaeologist and his being recognized as the father of modern archaeology (Bahn 1996:90).

Daniel Wilson, active during the mid- and later nineteenth century, coined the term *prehistory* and popularized it in Britain and North America through his several publications. Born poor in Edinburgh, Scotland, he migrated to Canada where he undertook excavations in the Great Lakes region. At a time when the prevailing European sentiment was that Native Americans were "savages," he recognized the existence of civilization among non-Western peoples and claimed that all humans can be civilized. In 1857, he taught an honors course in archaeology at the University of Toronto, probably the first formal course taught on archaeology anywhere.

The information and theories set out in Darwin's 1859 publication, *On the Origin of Species,* were consistent with the emerging evidence of human antiquity. In turn, archaeological findings helped Darwin revise his original timeframe for human evolution. During the latter half of the nineteenth century, collections grew and chronological categories were redefined. For example, the Stone Age was divided into two ages: the Paleolithic (Old Stone Age) and Neolithic (New Stone Age).

The second half of the nineteenth century also saw the beginnings of the search for evidence of modern human origins. The new, nonbiblical model was evolutionary, moving from "savagery" or "barbarism" to "civilization" as exemplified by Europe. The perception that *civilization* and *Europe* were synonymous led to many interpretive errors. For example, it was denied that Africans built the pyramids at Giza in Egypt. The structures were so large and complicated that it was assumed that they must have been built by a lost European civilization.

Important Old World sites excavated during this period include Athens and Troy. Excavations in the Indian subcontinent, led by the British archaeologist Sir Mortimer Wheeler, focused on the major monuments there and produced rich documentation

The site of Great Zimbabwe in southeastern Africa has generated intense speculation among archaeologists since its discovery by European explorers in the nineteenth century. British archaeologist Gertrude Caton-Thompson conducted excavations there in the 1920s and reported that Bantu people built the monuments several centuries earlier. ■ Assume that the Government of Zimbabwe has just hired you to construct a web site about Great Zimbabwe, and you have one week to accomplish this task: what information will you include? (Source: © Robert Holmes/CORBIS)

of early Buddhist and Hindu temples. The first European archaeological expedition to China was led by a Swede, Sven Hedin, in 1895. Japan was the first Asian country to adopt archaeology. Japan pioneered a cultural properties protection law in 1876 and launched its first excavation a year later. Archaeology was first taught in Japan in 1907 at Kyoto University.

In 1871 in Africa, a German geologist discovered the site of Great Zimbabwe, capital of the fourteenth-century Shona kingdom. This discovery prompted a heated debate in Europe about who had built such an impressive and large settlement, with clear distinctions between the elite who lived inside the walls and the commoners who lived outside. The prevailing Eurocentrism denied an indigenous African heritage for the site, whereas archaeologists insisted on its African origins.

In the New World, archaeologists have been drawn to Maya sites in Mexico and Central America since the late 1800s. Temple sites and hieroglyphics provided rich material for collection and interpretation. In 1911, a Yale University historian named Hiram Bingham discovered the remains of an ancient Incan city, Machu Picchu, located high in the Andes mountains in Peru (see the photograph on p. 254). This discovery generated great excitement in New World archaeology and once again prompted questions about what "civilization" consists of and who has it.

A major theoretical change since the 1960s in North America was a move away from the earlier emphasis on simply providing detailed descriptions of particular sites. American archaeologist Lewis Binford was influential in pushing for theory building and generalization across sites. He launched **processualism**—the theory that environment and other material factors determine certain kinds of cultural changes. Processualists ask "why" questions and seek to find general principles to explain changes over time, such as the emergence of cities and states. For example, processualists would ask why the Maya state emerged when and where it did, and they would search for environmental influences such as the availability of critical natural resources (water, for example). This approach still characterizes most archaeological research worldwide.

Since the 1980s, however, **postmodernist archaeology**, or postprocessual archaeology, has gained followers (Hodder 1996). This perspective rejects the search for general theories as ways of understanding the human past and instead emphasizes the rich description of particular cases and the intuitive interpretation of evidence. Postmodernist archaeology says that objective interpretations of sites and artifacts are not possible, because the interpreter is inevitably biased by his or her position and perspectives (as male or female, middle-class, or White). Postmodernist archaeology

THINKING

OUTSIDE
THE BOX

Consider the garbage
you create within a typi-
cal week and make a list
of its contents. What
would a processual
model say about your
garbage? What would a
postmodernist (or post-
processual) perspective
say? Compare your
results with those of
other students.

is closely associated with Ian Hodder, formerly of Cambridge University and now at Stanford University in the United States. Hodder urges archaeologists to study meaning and symbols in archaeological remains and to search for the role of individuals and creativity. Such archaeologists link their attempts to understand, for example, gender-related symbols, cosmology (ideas about the universe), and sacred sites with the work of cultural anthropologists, thereby demonstrating the value of greater integration between these two fields (Robb 1998).

Linguistic Anthropology and the Study of Language as Culture

Linguistic anthropology as a professional area of research and teaching emerged in the United States in the later nineteenth century when researchers began to document disappearing Native American languages. As with the other fields of anthropology, its intellectual roots extend much further back. Within European history, in the early pre-Christian era, Greek philosophers thought that the earliest humans were distinguished from modern humans by their lack of language. Later, biblical writings said that language began when God, through Adam, named the animals (Patterson 2001:10). The Bible also explained why languages differ: in order to punish the people who built the Tower of Babel, God scrambled their language and scattered them around the globe. The Christian view that God alone could have invented words, grammar, and writing retained a prominent position in Western thinking into the nineteenth century (Harris 1968:57).

The European Enlightenment inspired study of non-Western languages. In the United States, George Washington and Thomas Jefferson supported the collection of Native American vocabularies over several decades of the 1700s (Patterson 2001:11). Comparisons of the word lists of many languages convinced some people that all Native American languages must have come from a single language and that they were related to European languages. Both Washington and Jefferson were interested in demonstrating the shared humanity of Native Americans and Europeans.

At about this time, the *comparative method* in language study was established. By comparing features of contemporary languages, one could reconstruct language history. A major advance based on the comparative method occurred in 1786 when Sir William Jones proposed that Greek, Latin, Celtic, and Sanskrit (the classical language of India) had a common origin. This discovery also supported the view of the unity of humankind by showing the close connections between Europeans and the people of India.

The mid-nineteenth century was a major watershed in the emergence of a scientific approach to the cross-cultural study of language. The reasons are similar to those discussed earlier: colonialism's encounters with non-Western peoples, the rise of evolutionary theory in the mid-1800s and the decline of the biblical model. Edward Tylor, a founding figure of cultural anthropology, paid considerable attention to language (Lounsbury 1972). Tylor was interested in origins and in the "progress" toward "civilization"—issues that had been pursued in the preceding century but were given a new impetus and a much longer timeframe by writers such as Darwin. He and others moved the question of origins from the supernatural domain to the natural domain. Language was now seen as part of humanity's natural endowment rather than as God-given.

A key question of Tylor's time was whether the ideas necessary for language are innate within the human mind or are acquired through experience. Prominent theories stated that verbal language started with the natural cries of animals, through imitating the sounds of nature. Another question was why people have language in the first place. Is it primarily for psychological self-expression or to serve social purposes?

Another concern of the late nineteenth and early twentieth centuries was the question of differences among languages and the significance of such differences (Lounsbury 1972). By the early twentieth century, most linguistic anthropologists had abandoned the idea that languages differ because their speakers are at different stages of evolution. This change was largely due to the contributions of Franz Boas (discussed in the following section on cultural anthropology). In contrast to his contemporaries, Boas argued that the structure of a language could not hinder thought and could not (if different from English or French) be a marker of a less psychologically advanced people. He said that languages are adapted to the circumstances of life but are not limiting. Boas invented the concept of **linguistic relativism,** the idea that all languages are equally sophisticated and competent. Further, Boas insisted that one cannot understand another culture without knowing its language (Duranti 1997:53).

Edward Sapir, the founding father of linguistic anthropology, followed the relativist lead of Boas by saying that languages could differ in structure (grammar) but still have equally sophisticated content and competence. Writing in the 1920s and 1930s, he argued that language is a prerequisite for the development of culture. He also believed that languages have the power to train people into certain ways of thinking, and, that thereby languages actually create different "thought worlds" for their speakers.

A later approach called **structuralism,** which originated in France, attracted attention in the United States in the 1960s. Structuralism is a theoretical perspective prominent in both linguistic and cultural anthropology. Its premise is that meaning in language and other aspects of culture emerges from the relationships between and among various elements of a language or culture (Barnard 2000:120). For example, meaning does not come from individual sounds or words but, rather, depends on how sounds or words are placed in relation to each other. The French cultural anthropologist Claude Lévi-Strauss is the leading figure of structuralism. He claimed that all human thinking is based on binary oppositions: two opposed factors such as male and female, culture and nature, or raw food and cooked food. These oppositions, he says, reflect the deep problems that human thought and culture must deal with—major issues such as the difference between people and animals, for example, or between life and death. He found, in his study of 813 myths from North and South American indigenous peoples, that these basic binary oppositions are always mediated by a third, middle-ground element, which then forms a kind of solution to the basic problem of duality. Mediating elements are often categorically ambiguous, or crossovers (such as the Sphinx, which is part human and part animal, and rotten food, which is neither raw nor cooked). French structuralism emphasizes the need to analyze the symbolic meanings and relationships of cultural elements. Currently, French structuralism is not accepted in its pure form by many anthropologists. But certain features are still influential, especially the idea that the true meaning of language lies beneath the surface and can be discovered only through symbolic analysis and the appeal of binary oppositions in interpreting linguistic, textual, and social data.

The latter half of the twentieth century, from the 1980s to the present, brought a new vitality to linguistic anthropology with an emerging emphasis on discourse (language in use) in the context of social roles and power relations. Many contemporary anthropologists use a blended theoretical approach that sees language and other forms of communication, especially mass communication, as shaped by the material realities of life and, in turn, as shaping those realities (Duranti 1997).

Cultural Anthropology and the Study of Human Culture

The history, goals and findings of cultural anthropology are linked with those of the other fields of anthropology. An early landmark is Charles Montesquieu's book, *The Spirit of the Laws,* published in 1748 (Barnard 2000:22ff). Based on library research, this book discusses the temperament and government of people around the world. Montesquieu's explanation for differences among various people was the environment, not biology or mental ability. He stated that nature and climate dominated "savages" more than the Romans, Chinese, or Japanese.

By the mid-nineteenth century, the concept of evolution began to gain ground among Western thinkers. Herbert Spencer published works about cultural evolution a few years before Darwin's publications emerged (Harris 1968). He attempted to

Claude Lévi-Strauss, French cultural anthropologist, is most noted for his contribution to structural anthropology, or the study of underlying patterns in culture especially through the analysis of themes that recur in myths and rituals.
■ Choose a myth that you know and look for themes of female/male. (Source: © Sophie Bassouls/CORBIS SYGMA)

Select a folktale or story **THINKING** such as "Cinderella" or "Star Wars," and apply a structural analysis to it, including the drawing **OUTSIDE** of a formal diagram of **THE BOX** key elements and their relations. See whether a nature/culture, good/evil, or other dichotomy fits, and then see whether you can find a mediator, or third element.

devise an evolutionary scheme for all components of culture, including the family, the economy, and language. Like other thinkers of this period, Spencer relied on reports about non-European cultures from explorers and missionaries, and thus his schemes relied on faulty and often fanciful examples. However, it may be that another thinker of the time, Karl Marx, was more influential than either Spencer or Darwin in shaping ideas about cultural evolution. Marx's contributions to the emerging field of cultural anthropology include a focus on material aspects of culture, such as the *mode of production* as the basic feature of cultures and emphasis on the role of social conflict as the major force driving cultural change. Marx was also a founding father of the study of social inequality, and he may be one of the first policy-oriented social scientists, as demonstrated by his statement that "The philosophers have *interpreted* the world in various ways: the point however is to *change* it" (quoted in Harris 1968:219). The Marxist model of cultural evolution exhibits striking parallels to Darwin's in that both view progress as achieved through competition and struggle. Marxism was the basis of anthropology in the former USSR and China. In the West, Marxist thinking gained prominence in cultural anthropology in the 1970s (Patterson 2001:137–138).

Three men, considered the founding fathers of cultural anthropology and all writing in the late eighteenth and early nineteenth centuries, were Sir Edward Tylor and Sir James Frazer in England and Lewis Henry Morgan in the United States. All three proposed evolutionary models for culture and for particular features of culture, such as kinship systems and religion. Early forms of kinship were said to be centered on women, with inheritance passing through the female line, whereas more evolved (European) forms centered on men, with inheritance passing through the male line. Magic was said to precede religion, which was said to precede science.

The early cultural anthropologists were predominantly "armchair" anthropologists whose research involved reading reports written by others. Tylor, working in this mode, proposed the first definition of culture in 1871. Frazer's multivolume publication *The Golden Bough* (1970 [1890]) is a compilation of myths, rituals, and symbols from around the world organized thematically. It includes sections on sacred trees, deities related to corn, and harvest rituals, for example. Morgan, a lawyer in Rochester, New York, abandoned the armchair to conduct field research over several years with the Iroquois of central New York (Patterson 2001:26). Morgan was interested in the main question of the time: whether living humans are all related to each other or are descended from different roots and therefore unrelated. He compared Native American kinship terms with Asian kinship terms and concluded that they were similar. On these grounds, he argued that Native Americans and Asian people were related, thus supporting the position that humanity is biologically and culturally one.

Polish-born Bronislaw Malinowski is generally considered the father of *participant observation*, the cornerstone research method of cultural anthropology (discussed in Chapter 4). For his first research project, he spent many months living with people of the Trobriand Islands, off the east coast of Papua New Guinea, learning their language, eating their food, and trying to gain a comprehensive picture of all aspects of their culture from sexual behavior to canoe magic to musical instruments (Barnard 2000:66ff). By learning the local language, he was able to dispense with interpreters and thereby gain a much more direct understanding of Trobriand culture. Malinowski's work established a theoretical perspective called **functionalism** wherein a culture is viewed as similar to a biological organism with various parts working to support the operation and maintenance of the whole. Thus a culture's kinship system or religious system contributed to the functioning of the culture of which it was a part. The medical specialty of anatomy inspired this model.

Another landmark figure in cultural anthropology, whose impact extended to the discipline of anthropology as a whole, is Franz Boas. Born in Germany and educated there in physics and geography, Boas came to the United States in 1887 and played a major role in establishing anthropology in the United States during the first half of the twentieth century (Patterson 2001:46ff). He brought with him a skeptical view

Franz Boas is considered the father of North American anthropology. He promoted the concept of cultural relativism, rejected the notion of biological "race," and supported a four-field approach to understanding humanity.
■ Learn more about his ethnographic research projects. (Source: © Bettmann/CORBIS)

about Western science gained from a year's study with the Inuit of Baffin Island, where he learned that a physical substance such as "water" can be perceived very differently in different cultures. Boas recognized the plural validity of different cultures and is considered the father of the key concept **cultural relativism,** or the position that each culture must be understood in terms of the values and ideas of that culture and should not be judged by the standards of another. Accordingly, no culture is any more "advanced" than another. Boas thus launched an enduring critique of evolutionism in cultural anthropology.

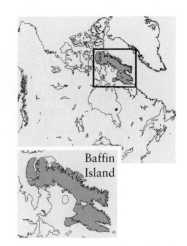

Baffin Island

Boas rejected comparison and theory-building and promoted **cultural particularism,** an emphasis on the uniqueness of each culture and on the need for detailed study and description of individual cultures within their own historical contexts. Boas built the discipline of anthropology in the United States through his role as a professor at Columbia University, where he trained many prominent students. He was an activist anthropologist and was inspired by a politically progressive philosophy to promote social justice, racial equality, and gender equality in the United States. Once he was commissioned by President Theodore Roosevelt to study the effects of the United States environment on immigrants and their children (Patterson 2001:49). He and his research team measured 17,821 people and concluded that head size responds quickly to environmental change and that, therefore, bodily form is not "racially" determined. His report was dismissed by the U.S. Immigration Commission and the Congress, which passed the Immigration Restriction Act in 1924. Boas was outraged and called the act racist and xenophobic (Patterson 2001:49).

In the 1950s, **environmental determinism,** the theory that environment shapes culture, arose in the United States as a prominent challenge to cultural particularism. This movement was led by two American anthropologists, Julian Steward and Leslie White. Although Steward's and White's theories differed in certain details, both gave primacy to material, environmental factors in shaping culture. In comparison to earlier, unilineal views of evolution (which says that all societies have to pass through the same stages), their model allowed for multilineal evolution, with different stages occurring in different environmental contexts. Beginning in the 1960s, a related perspective emerged. **Cultural materialism** emphasizes examining the material aspects of life, such as the environmental context and how people make a living within particular environments. Marvin Harris is the anthropologist most closely associated with this perspective. This approach parallels processual theory in archaeology.

Another theoretical position, which also began gaining prominence in the 1960s, is **interpretive anthropology** or symbolic anthropology. This perspective emphasizes understanding culture by studying people's ideas, their interpretations of their lives, and the meanings that are important to them. Interpretive anthropology is an idealist view as opposed to the more behaviorist view (review Figure 2.1, p. 37). It emphasizes what people think as the most important part of culture. Leading proponents of the interpretivist/symbolic view are Clifford Geertz and Mary Douglas.

Characteristics of Culture

This section outlines some important characteristics of the elusive concept of culture. Culture, we will emphasize, is learned, adaptive, related to nature but not the same as nature, based on symbols, integrated, and changing.

Culture Is Learned

Culture is learned, not innate. Cultural learning begins from the moment of birth, if not before (some people think that an unborn baby takes in and stores information through sounds heard from the outside world). Much of people's cultural learning is unconscious, occurring as a normal part of life through observation and imitation. Schools, in contrast, emphasize formal learning, although much informal learning occurs in schools, too—through peer pressure, for example. Throughout most of humanity's prehistory and history, children learned appropriate cultural patterns by

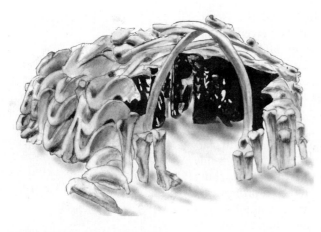

FIGURE 2.2

A reconstruction of an Upper Paleolithic dwelling with mammoth bones as the framework. Remains of such houses are found in Ukraine and central Asia.

receiving guidance from elders, hearing stories, and watching performances. The learning of one's culture through a combination of direct and indirect means is referred to as enculturation, as noted in Chapter 1.

Primatologists' studies of culture in nonhuman primates point to two kinds of learning that differ in some ways from learning among humans (Alvard 2003). First is *imitation,* or learning through behavioral duplication. Young chimpanzees watch their mother using a stick to get termites out of a termite mound, and they repeat the action. The second form of learning is called *local enhancement,* or stimulus enhancement. This term refers to the increased probability that individuals will learn a trait on their own when they are exposed to the conditions that make the acquisition of the behavior likely. In this view, young chimpanzees learn to use sticks to collect termites not because they watch their mother and imitate her. Instead, given the proximity of sticks and termites, they are likely to learn on their own that using the sticks is an effective way to get food. Thus far, primatologists have not witnessed formal attempts by adult nonhuman primates to teach particular behaviors to offspring.

Culture Is Adaptive

As we mentioned in Chapter 1, the story of humanity is one of adaptation and change in both biology (body size, body shape, and physical capabilities such as walking and talking) and culture (learned and shared behaviors and beliefs). It is likely that biological and cultural adaptations during the early evolution of humanity were closely linked to the natural environment and climate at the time.

Human economic systems, or ways of making a living, are basic elements of cultural adaptation that have changed throughout human evolution. The earliest ways of making a living were directly dependent on the environment: if the most preferred fruit is there, eat it; if not, go for second best. Many economic systems are now independent of the environment to a large extent and therefore reflect modern humans' greater adaptive capacities. For example, a computer software specialist can make a living while residing in Dublin, Ireland, or in Bangalore, India. As human evolution proceeded (Chapters 6, 7, and 8), culture became the most important adaptive mechanism mediating between humans and their environment (see Figure 2.2).

Some aspects of contemporary human culture, however, may be nonadaptive in that they are actually dangerous to the survival of humanity. The development and spread of weapons of mass destruction means that humans have the ability to destroy everyone on the planet. Now, as never before, our cultural capacities are changing more rapidly than we can foresee the costs and benefits to humans, other living creatures, and the environment.

Culture Is Related to, But Not the Same as, Nature

The relationship between nature and culture is of great interest to anthropologists in their quest to understand people's behavior and thinking in the past and the present. One way of seeing how culture is related to, but diverges from, nature is to consider that basic "natural" demands of human life are met in different ways in different cultures. Take, for example, the biological functions that everyone must perform to stay alive: eating, drinking, sleeping, and eliminating (requirements for shelter and clothing vary, depending on the climate, and procreation is not necessary for individual survival). We know that living people have to perform these functions. Otherwise, they would not be alive and well. But we have no way of predicting how, when, or where these functions will be fulfilled. That is because culture plays a major role in defining how we eat, drink, sleep, and eliminate. Thus these functions are to some extent arbitrary: they involve culturally shaped meanings. We can determine what cultural rules govern their performance, and what the deeper meanings are, only by spending substantial time in that culture—becoming enculturated. Nature takes us only so far.

Eating. The human body requires certain nutrients for survival, but these nutrients can be provided in many ways. For example, eating meat is not necessary for survival. Culture shapes what one eats, how one eats, and when one eats, and it affects ideas about eating. People living in vegetarian cultures have survived quite well without eating meat of any sort for centuries.

Preferences about what tastes good vary markedly, and many examples exist of foods that are acceptable in one culture and not in another. In China, most people think that cheese is disgusting, but in France, most people love cheese. Another distinction exists between eating animals that are alive and animals that are dead. In a few cultures, consumption of live (or nearly live) creatures is considered a gourmet specialty; for example, one Philippine dish includes ready-to-be-born chicks. In many cultures where hunting and fishing are dominant ways of procuring food, people believe that the freshness of the catch is important. They consider canned meat or fish highly undesirable. Food and how it is consumed convey symbolic meaning about social status, gender, and even age. For example, upper-class people in England eat dinner in a specific set of courses. Middle-class people are more likely to have fewer courses. In the United States, one stereotype is that "real men" do not eat quiche. Older people and younger people in the United States often go to different types of restaurants when they are eating out, not just because of the kind of food served but also because of ambience and social context.

Taste categories, too, are culturally constructed. Although anthropologists and other scientists have attempted to delineate universal taste categories into four basic types (sweet, sour, bitter, and salty), cross-cultural research disproves these four as universals. Among the Weyéwa people of the highlands of Sumba, an island in Eastern Indonesia, the flavors recognized are sour, sweet, salty, bitter, tart, bland, and pungent (Kuipers 1991).

How to eat is another important aspect of food behavior. Rules about eating are one of the first things one confronts when entering another culture. Proper dining manners in India require that a person eat using only the right hand, because the left hand is reserved for cleaning oneself after elimination. A clean right hand is believed to be the purest dining implement, because silverware, plates, and glassware that have been touched by others, even though they have been washed, are never truly clean.

Drinking. The cultural elaboration of drinking is as complex as that of eating. Every culture defines what is appropriate to drink, when to drink, and with whom. In French culture, it is normal to drink wine, not water, with lunch and dinner. In the United States, water typically accompanies lunch and dinner, although children are supposed to drink milk. In India one drinks water only after the meal is finished, not during the meal itself.

Different social categories of people drink different beverages. Particular drinks and the style of serving and drinking them, like food, have different meanings. If you were a guest and the host offered you a glass of water when you arrived, you might think it odd (just as you would if the host offered you a peanut butter and jelly sandwich for dinner). If your host explained that it was "sparkling water from France," you might be more impressed. In cultures where alcoholic beverages are consumed, men tend to consume more than women. Social drinking, whether the beverage is coffee, beer, or vodka, creates and reinforces bonds. Beer-drinking "rituals" of American college fraternities are a dramatic example. In a brief ethnographic film entitled "Salamanders," made at a university in the northeastern United States, during parties

Two Ethiopian women dining at an Ethiopian restaurant. The main meal consists of several meat and vegetable dishes, cooked with special spices and laid out on injera bread, a soft, flat bread that is torn into small pieces and used to wrap bite-sized bits of meat and vegetables. The entire meal can be eaten without utensils. ■ How does this dining scene resemble or differ from a recent meal that you have had in a restaurant? (Source: © Michael Newman/PhotoEdit)

Sumba

A Maya vessel found in Belize, Central America, contains residues of cacao dated around 600 BCE. Documents from the time of the Spanish conquest indicate that liquid chocolate was poured from one pot to another to produce foam. The foam was the most desirable part of the drink. ■ Compare this technology to ways of producing preferred hot drinks in your culture. (Source: © Terry G. Powis/Photo courtesy of Thomas R. Hester)

the brothers run to various "stations" in the fraternity house, downing a beer at each (Hornbein and Hornbein 1992). At one point, the film shows us a brother who chugs a beer, turns with a stagger toward the next station, and then falls flat on his face and passes out. (Most of our students, as they watch the film, laugh when he falls down.) The movie also documents a drinking ritual in which both young men and women at some fraternity parties swallowed live salamanders, sometimes two or three at a time, with large gulps of beer.

Sleeping. Going without sleep for an extended period of time can eventually lead to insanity and even death. Common sense might say that sleep is the one natural function that is not shaped by culture, because people tend to do it every twenty-four hours, everyone shuts their eyes to do it, everyone lies down to do it, and almost everyone sleeps at night. But there are many cultural aspects to sleep, including the question of who sleeps with whom. Cross-cultural research reveals varying rules about where infants and children should sleep: with the mother, with both parents, or by themselves in a separate room.

In indigenous cultures of the Amazon, mothers and babies share the same hammock for many months, and breastfeeding occurs whenever the baby is hungry, not on a schedule.

Culture also shapes the amount of time a person sleeps. In rural India, women sleep fewer hours than men because they have to get up earlier to start the fire for the morning meal. In fast-track, corporate North America, "A-type" males sleep relatively few hours and are proud of it—to sleep too much is to be a wimp.

Elimination. This subject takes the discussion into more private territory. How does culture affect the elimination process? Anyone who has traveled internationally knows that there is much to learn about elimination when you leave familiar territory. The first question is where to eliminate. Differences emerge in the degree to which elimination is a private act or can be done in more or less public areas. Public options often include street urinals for males but not for females, as in Paris.

In most villages in India, houses do not have interior bathrooms. Instead, early in the morning, groups of women and girls leave the house and head for a certain field where they squat and chat. Men go to a different area. Everyone carries, in the left hand, a small brass pot full of water with which they splash themselves clean. This practice has ecological advantages because it adds fertilizer to the fields and leaves no paper litter. Westerners may consider the village practice unclean, but village Indians would think the Western system unsanitary because paper does not clean one as well as water.

In many cultures, urine and feces are considered dirty, polluting, and disgusting. People do not try to keep such things, nor do they in any way revere them. Among some groups in Papua New Guinea, in the South Pacific, people take great care to bury or otherwise hide their fecal matter. They fear that someone will find it and use it to work magic against them. A negative assessment of the products of elimination is not, however, universal. In some cultures, these substances are believed to have positive effects. Among some Native American cultures of the Pacific Northwest region of Canada and the United States, urine, especially women's urine, was believed to have medicinal and cleansing properties and was considered the "water of life" (Furst 1989). In death rituals, it was sprinkled over the corpse in the hope that it might rejuvenate the deceased. People stored urine in special wooden boxes for ritual use, including the first bath that a baby was given, in which the urine was diluted with water.

Culture Is Based on Symbols

Making money, creating art, and practicing religion are all activities based on symbols. As defined in Chapter 1, a symbol is something that stands for something else. Symbols are arbitrary, unpredictable, and diverse. Because symbols are arbitrary, we cannot know in advance how a particular culture will symbolize any particular thing.

In India, a white sari (women's garment) symbolizes widowhood. ■ What might these women think about the Western custom of a bride wearing white? (Source: Barbara Miller)

Although we might predict that people who are hungry would have an expression for hunger involving their stomach, no one could predict that in Hindi, the language of much of northern India, a colloquial expression for being hungry says that "rats are jumping in my stomach." The linguistic history of *Barbara* (the name of one author of this book) reveals that originally, in Greek, it referred to people who were outsiders, "barbarians," and, by extension, uncivilized and savage. On top of that, it implied that such people had beards. The symbolic content of the contemporary American name Barbara no longer conveys a sense of foreignness or beardedness. Symbolic content can and does change.

Cultures Are Integrated

To state that cultures are internally integrated is to assert the principle of holism. Thus, studying only one or two aspects of culture provides limited understanding.

Consider what would happen if a researcher were to study intertribal warfare in Papua New Guinea and focused only on the actual practice of warfare without examining other aspects of culture. A key feature of highland New Guinea culture is the exchange of pigs at political feasts (Rappaport 1968). To become a political leader, a man (most political leaders in this area are men) must acquire many pigs. Pigs eat yams, which men grow, but pigs are cared for by women. This division of labor means that a man with more than one wife will be able to produce more pigs and hence to rise politically by giving more feasts. Such feasting enhances an aspiring leader's status and makes his guests indebted to him. With more followers attracted through feasting, a leader can gather support from his followers and wage war on neighboring villages. Success in war brings territorial gains and influence over even more people as potential supporters. So far, this example reflects mainly economics, politics, and marriage systems. But other aspects of culture are involved, too. Supernatural powers affect the success of warfare. Painting spears and shields with particular designs helps increase their power. At feasts and marriages, body decoration (including paint, shell ornaments, and elaborate feather headdresses) is an important expression of personal identity and status. Looking only at warfare, without considering the wider cultural context in which it occurs, will yield a severely limited view.

Cultural integration is extremely relevant to applied anthropologists who are involved in suggesting certain kinds of cultural change. Attempting to introduce change in one aspect of a culture without considering what its effects will be in other

Aymara women of the Andean highlands in South America wear distinctive clothing including rounded hats made of felt and multi-colored shawls. In the cities, this distinctive clothing is giving way to more cosmopolitan styles and the abandonment of the hat and shawl. ■ What clues do you gather about people's culture from the clothing they wear? (Source: © Wolfgang Kaehler/CORBIS)

areas is irresponsible and may even be detrimental to the survival of the culture. For example, Western missionaries and colonialists banned head-hunting in parts of Southeast Asia such as Borneo and the Philippines. Head-hunting was embedded in many other aspects of culture, including politics, religion, and psychology (a man's sense of identity depended on the taking of a head). Although stopping head-hunting might seem like a good thing, the suddenness of the change had negative consequences for the cultures in which it had been practiced.

Cultures Interact and Change

Cultures interact with each other and change each other through contact. Trade networks, international development projects, telecommunications, education, migration, and tourism are just a few of the factors that affect cultural change through contact. Globalization (defined in Chapter 1) is a major force of contemporary cultural change that moves vertically, from the global level to the local level. It has gained momentum through recent technological change, especially the boom in information and communications technologies, which is closely related to the global movement of capital and finance (Pieterse 2004).

Globalization is not spreading evenly, nor are its effects the same everywhere. Four paradigms capture some of this variation (see Figure 2.3). First, the **clash of civilizations** argument says that the spread of Euro-American capitalism and lifeways throughout the world has created disenchantment, alienation, and resentment among other cultural systems, most notably among people in Islamic countries. This model divides the world into the "West and the rest." It is not generally supported by anthropologists, who see it as excessively binary and therefore misleading because it overlooks the vast amount of cultural interaction around the world and the intermingling of cultural and religious groups through international migration.

The second view is **McDonaldization.** This model says that, under the powerful influence of United States–dominated corporate culture, the world is becoming

FIGURE 2.3

Four models of cultural interaction.

Clash of civilizations	conflict model
McDonaldization	takeover and homogenization model
Hybridization	blending model
Localization	local cultural remaking and transformation of global culture

culturally homogeneous. "Fast-food culture," with its principles of mass production, speed, standardization, and impersonal service, is taken to be at the center of this new global culture.

Hybridization is the third model. Also called syncretism, creolization, and cultural crossover, hybridization occurs when aspects of two or more cultures are mixed to form something new, a blend. In Japan, a grandmother may bow in gratitude to an automated banking machine. In India, languages such as Hindi and Tamil incorporate English phrases. In the Amazon region, indigenous people use satellite imagery to map and protect the boundaries of their ancestral lands.

Anthropologists have observed a fourth pattern of social change called **localization,** which is cultural change that occurs when global changes are received and transformed through interaction with existing cultures (Figure 2.4 provides examples of cultural localization in Japan). There is no doubt that fast-food culture can now be found in many parts of the world, but anthropologists also provide strong evidence of localization. For example, in many countries, people resist the pattern of quick eating, insisting on leisurely family gatherings. The McDonald's managers in these contexts alter the pace of service in their restaurants to allow for this much slower turnover of tables.

FIGURE 2.4

Localization of Western culture in Japan.

Language

On average, Japanese speakers' language includes 10 percent loan words, most of which are from English, such as *hambāgā shoppu,* hamburger joint, and *birru,* beer. Advertising uses many English loan words to generate catchy phrases that cannot be precisely translated: "Do you know me?" for American Express, and "My life my gas" for the Tokyo Gas Company, and "My beautiful human life" for Shiseido cosmetics (Stanlaw 1992).

Public bathing

A Japanese value on daily bathing, preferably in a *sentō,* public bath, involves status, purity, cleanliness, and bonding through *hadaka no tsukiai,* noneroticized "naked bonding." In Tokyo now, about 70 percent of families have a private home bath and use public baths less frequently. The rise of home bathing is not associated with Westernization. Instead,

the home bath is viewed as essentially Japanese, in spite of the Western-imported bathing products used (soap, towels). Along with the rise in home baths there has been a dramatic increase in the popularity of *onsen,* hot springs, as sites for family vacations and business meetings that convey a sense of Japanese identity (Clark 1992).

Shopping

Depāto, Western-style department stores that sell a variety of goods in one building, have played a major role in introducing Western goods into Japanese society by cleverly contextualizing them within Japanese customs. One such item is the diamond engagement ring, which has been promoted not as a sign of emotional love between the two engaged people but as part of *yuinōhin,* a series of gifts from the groom's household to the bride that symbolize a long and happy life together (Creighton 1992).

Throughout human prehistory and history, clashes between cultures, cultural homogenization, cultural hybridization, and cultural localization can all be documented, at different times and in different contexts, and sometimes within the same context. For example, in terms of understanding contemporary cultural change, anthropologists may view the hybridization model as valid in a certain setting but may also point to many examples in which outside cultural forces result in the extinction of local culture rather than in coexistence and blending. This scenario is especially likely to occur when the outside culture is materially and technologically much more powerful than the local culture and can overwhelm it.

Ethnocentrism and Cultural Relativism

Most people grow up thinking that their culture is the only way of life and that other ways of life are strange and inferior—and other people less than human. Anthropologists label this attitude **ethnocentrism:** judging other cultures by the standards of one's own culture rather than by the standards of those other cultures. Ethnocentric views have fueled centuries of efforts to change other people in the world, sometimes in the guise of religious missionary proselytizing, sometimes in the form of colonial domination.

The European colonial expansion that began in the fifteenth century was intended to extract wealth from the colonies. In addition to plundering their colonies, the Europeans ethnocentrically imposed their culture on indigenous groups. The British poet Rudyard Kipling reflected the prevailing view when he said that it was "the white man's burden" to spread British culture throughout the world. Christian missionaries played a major role in transforming non-Christian cultures.

Many contemporary Western powers exhibit similar attitudes, making foreign policy decisions that encourage the adoption of Western economic, political, and social systems. There is much that is good about many Western institutions, including democratic political processes, but the notion that these same institutions can work everywhere and should be transplanted to different contexts without modification is testimony that ethnocentrism is alive and well in the world today.

The opposite of ethnocentrism is cultural relativism, the idea that all cultures must be understood in terms of their own values and beliefs and should not be judged by the standards of another culture. Cultural relativism assumes that no culture is better than any other. How does a person gain a sense of cultural relativism? Besides living with other peoples, the best ways to develop a sense of cultural relativism include traveling (especially extended periods of study abroad), taking a course in cultural anthropology, eating different foods, listening to music from Appalachia or Brazil, reading novels by authors from other cultures, making friends who are "different" from you, and exploring the multicultural world on your campus. In sum, exposure to "other" ways, with a sympathetic eye and ear to understanding and appreciating differences, is the key.

Can a person ever completely avoid being ethnocentric? The answer is probably no, because we start learning about other cultures from the standpoint of the one we know first. Even the most sensitive person who has spent a long time living within another culture still carries an original imprint of her or his native culture. As much as we might say that we think we are viewing Culture B from the inside (as though we were natives of Culture B), that is impossible because everything we learned about Culture B—the language, dress, food preferences, social organization, work habits, leadership patterns, and religion—we learned in relation to or in comparison with what we already knew about Culture A.

One way in which some anthropologists have interpreted cultural relativism can be termed **absolute cultural relativism,** the conviction that whatever goes on in a particular culture must not be questioned or changed because no one has the right to question any behavior or idea anywhere—it would be ethnocentric to do so. But absolute cultural relativism can lead in dangerous directions. Consider the example of the Holocaust during World War II, in which millions of Jews and other minorities in much of Eastern and Western Europe were killed as part of the German Nazis' Aryan supremacy campaign. To be consistent with its own logic, the absolute cultural relativist position must maintain that, because the Holocaust was undertaken in accordance with the values of the culture, outsiders have no business questioning it.

Critical cultural relativism offers an alternative view that poses questions about cultural practices and ideas in terms of who accepts them and why, and who they might be harming or helping. In terms of the Nazi Holocaust, a critical cultural relativist would ask, "Whose culture supported the values that killed millions of people on the grounds of racial purity?" Not the cultures of the Jews, Gypsies, and other victims. It was the culture of Aryan supremacists, who were one subgroup among many. The situation was far more complex than a simple absolute cultural relativist statement takes into account, because there was not just one culture and its values involved. Rather, it was a case of **cultural imperialism,** in which one dominant group claims supremacy over minority cultures and proceeds to impose its will and exploit the situation in its own interests and at the expense of other cultures. Critical cultural relativism avoids the trap of adopting a homogenized view of complexity. It recognizes internal cultural differences and acknowledges the existence of winners and losers, oppressors and victims. It pays attention to different interests of various power groups. Beyond the clear case of the Nazi Holocaust, critical cultural relativism can be applied to illuminate many recent and contemporary conflicts, such as those in the former Yugoslavia, Rwanda, and Iraq.

A growing number of cultural anthropologists seek to critique the behavior and values of groups from the standpoint of some set of generally agreed-upon human rights. (Here *critique* means to probe underlying power interests, not just to make negative comments as in the general usage of the term *criticism.*) But even these anthropologists recognize how difficult it is to generate a universally agreed-upon list of values and principles different cultures view as good and right. Clearly, no single culture has the answer, and none has the right to dictate to others. As French anthropologist Claude Lévi-Strauss commented, "No society is perfect" (1968: 385). While considering the "imperfections" of any and all cultures, anthropologists should examine and discuss their own biases and then try to view all cultures objectively. This means critiquing all cultures—one's own and "other's"—on an equal basis.

This pre-Hispanic Maya calendar in stone was more accurate than European calendars, which required the Gregorian Reform to eliminate 11 days in 1572. It relies on a base-20 mathematics and a celestial cycle of 18,980 days. Western ethnocentrism often led to overlooking scientific achievements embedded in non-Western modes of thinking. ■ In math and science classes you have taken, how much have you learned about non-Western ideas? (Source: © Otis Imboden/ National Geographic Image Collection)

MULTIPLE CULTURAL WORLDS

Culture exists at several levels. Numerous microcultures exist within larger cultural clusters. Much of this internal variation is shaped by the factors of class, race, ethnicity, gender, age, and institutions (see Figure 2.5). An individual is likely to be a member of several microcultures and may identify more strongly or less strongly with a particular microculture.

Microcultures are not necessarily positioned next to each other. They may overlap or they may be related to each other hierarchically. The contrast between difference and hierarchy is important. People and groups might be considered different from each other on a particular dimension, but not unequal. For example, people with blue or brown eyes might be recognized as different, but this difference might

FIGURE 2.5
Some bases of microcultures.

Class
"Race"
Ethnicity and indigeneity
Gender and sexuality
Age
Institution

A view into the yard of a house of a low-income neighborhood of Kingston, Jamaica. ■ Why do you think people in these neighborhoods prefer the term *low-income* to *poor*? (Source: Barbara Miller)

not entail unequal treatment or status. In other instances, differences *do* become the basis for inequality.

Class

Class is a social category based on people's economic position in society, usually measured in terms of income or wealth and exhibited in lifestyle. Class societies may be divided into upper, middle, and lower classes. An earlier definition of class proposed by Karl Marx and Frederick Engels, who wrote during the second half of the nineteenth century, says that class membership is determined by people's relationship to production, or how people make a living. Separate classes include, for example, the working class (people who trade their labor for wages) and the landowning class (people who own land on which they or others labor). Classes are related in a hierarchical system, with certain classes dominating others. Class struggle is inevitable, in the Marxist view, as those at the top seek to maintain their position while those at the bottom seek to improve theirs. People at the bottom of the class structure may attempt to improve their class position by gaining access to more material resources or by adopting aspects of upper-class symbolic behavior, such as speech, dress, and leisure activities.

Class is a recent development in human history. For example, in tribal groups in the Amazonian region before they were affected by outside European cultures, all members had roughly equal wealth. Contemporary global systems of social integration mean that indigenous tribal groups are now part of a global class structure, occupying a position at the bottom.

Race

Race refers to a group of people defined by selected biological traits, usually visible features. In South Africa, race is defined mainly on the basis of skin color, as it is in the United States. In nineteenth- and early twentieth-century China, in contrast, body hair was the main basis of racial classification, although nose shape was also used to distinguish among so-called races (Dikötter 1998). Greater amounts of body hair were associated with "barbarian" races and the lack of "civilization." One early Chinese survey of humankind provided a detailed classification on the basis of types of beards, whiskers, and moustaches (see the Crossing the Fields section in Chapter 6, pp. 176–177).

Scientists now know that such biological traits do not determine a person's behavior or in any way explain or account for culture. Franz Boas proved this point a century ago. Rather than being a biological category, race is a cultural or social construct. "Race" does not exist as a biological fact. Racism and its effects on people *do* exist, of course, and are real. Racist thinking has been the basis for some of the most terrible oppression and cruelty throughout history. Racial apartheid in South Africa denied citizenship, security, a decent life, and sometimes life itself to those labeled Black.

Some scholars argue that racism is the most important factor supporting social difference in the United States (Hacker 1992). In the book, *Two Nations: Black and White, Separate, Hostile, Unequal,* political scientist Andrew Hacker discusses the racial income gap, inequities in schooling, and crime. In all these areas, the Black population of America, in general, participates in a world that is resource-poor compared to the better-off White population, is less well served in terms of the public school system, and is more at risk of violent crime.

Many Tibetans have left their homeland as refugees since China took control of the region. Most live in India and Nepal. This scene is the inside of a Tibetan Buddhist monastery in Nepal. ■ Do some Internet research to learn about current policies in Nepal toward Tibetan refugees. (Source: © Galen Rowell/ CORBIS)

Ethnic Groups and Indigenous Peoples

Ethnicity is a sense of group affiliation based on a distinct heritage or worldview as a "people." Examples of ethnic groups include African Americans and Italian Americans of the United States, the Croats of Eastern Europe, and the Han peoples of China. This sense of identity can be vigorously expressed through political movements or more quietly stated through family gatherings at which familiar foods are eaten. It can also be a basis for social ranking, claimed entitlements to resources such as land or artifacts, and a perceived basis for defending or retrieving those resources.

Social scientists find the term *ethnicity* to be a more positive term than *race*. But ethnicity, too, has often been a basis for discrimination, segregation, and oppression. The "ethnic cleansing" campaigns in the early 1990s by the Serbs against Muslims in the former Yugoslavia are an extreme case of ethnicity-based discrimination. Expression of ethnic identity has been politically suppressed in many cultures. Among many Native American groups in South and North America, shared ethnicity is an important basis of tribal revival movements. Among many recent immigrant groups throughout the world, the resilience of ethnic culture is being tested.

Another important but also hard-to-define category is that of **indigenous peoples.** Following the guidelines laid down by the United Nations, indigenous people are groups who have a long-standing connection with their home territory that predates colonial or outside societies prevailing in the territory (Sanders 1999). They are typically a numerical minority and often have lost the rights to their original territory. The United Nations distinguishes between indigenous peoples and minority ethnic groups such as the Rom of various European countries, the Tamils of Sri Lanka, and African Americans. Although this distinction may be useful in some ways, it should not be taken as a hard-and-fast difference (Maybury-Lewis 1997b). Many indigenous groups are now taking active steps to recover their lost lands, to revive their forgotten languages and rituals, and to build a new and stronger future for themselves through various forms of organization and resistance to negative outside forces. Often, anthropologists have been able to support these efforts through their research (see the Lessons Applied box).

Historical Archaeology and the Story of the Northern Cheyenne Outbreak of 1879

The Northern Cheyenne long resisted the takeover of their native lands in Montana, first by Euro-American settlers in the latter half of the nineteenth century and then, since the mid-twentieth century, by energy companies (McDonald et al. 1991). They have also resisted the dominant culture's telling of their history. The Cheyenne collaborated with historical archaeologists from the University of South Dakota Archaeology Laboratory to document their version of an incident in their resistance to domination, the Cheyenne "Outbreak" from Fort Robinson, Nebraska, in the winter of 1879.

For several generations, some Cheyenne have accepted the White version of the Outbreak. The story begins with the signing by several chiefs in 1867 of a treaty they did not fully understand. The treaty provided for the relocation of Cheyenne people from Montana to "Indian Territory" in present-day Oklahoma. Once this condition was understood, a party of chiefs traveled to Washington, DC, to inform President Grant of their desire to remain in their homelands. Grant allowed them to stay, temporarily. After the Custer Massacre at Little Big Horn, the Cheyenne chiefs feared reprisals, even though the Cheyenne were not involved in the battle. Over the next few years, the U.S. military attacked Cheyenne settlements, destroying their food supply, killing their horses, and driving them from their homes. Under the leadership of Chief Dull Knife, the Cheyenne agreed to move south on what they considered to be a trial basis. Many fell ill and died during the difficult 70-day journey.

Two years later, the U.S. military told Dull Knife that his group would be relocated again. On the way to the new location, some of the Cheyenne tried to escape but were recaptured, locked into barracks, and told they had to move south. Dull Knife refused to return to the "land of sickness." Their food and water supplies were cut off in order to force their submission. With only a few guns, Dull Knife's people broke out from the barracks on an evening in January 1879. Nearly half of them were killed in the ensuing battle, but the survivors fled via an escape route toward home. They were recaptured after eleven days; most of them were killed.

The controversy between White and Cheyenne accounts of the Outbreak concerns the escape route. The White narrative designates Area C, a long, barren ridge. The Cheyenne version, has the route going through Areas A and B. Archaeological fieldwork was conducted to check the accuracy of each version. Representatives of the Northern Cheyenne tribes provided geographic information. They also ensured the spiritual integrity of the project by incorporating prayers and story-telling into the research, a practice that expressed reverence for the land and artifacts. Methods included visual inspection, random shovel testing, and use of metal detectors. Most of the artifacts were spent ammunition. No artifacts of any kind were found in Area C, whereas a number of artifacts likely to have been deposited during the Cheyenne Outbreak were found in Areas A and B. With no firm evidence that they went into Area C it is more likely, then, that they chose a route through terrain that provided natural cover. The deeper significance of this controversy lies in the fact that if Area C was the escape route, then Dull Knife and his people made a serious mistake, taking a route that would expose them as easy targets on what was a brightly moonlit night.

The collaboration between the Northern Cheyenne and the archaeologists helped the Cheyenne validate their version of their history. It demonstrated the use of archaeology to support indigenous people's resistance to dominant cultural narratives. It also showed that the different interests of Native Americans, who seek knowledge of their cultural history and identity, and of archaeologists, who seek data about land and materials controlled by the tribes, are both served through collaboration and mutual respect.

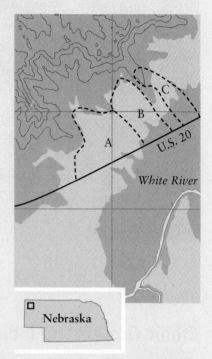

Survey project near Fort Robinson, Nebraska. (*Source:* Adapted from p. 69, "The Northern Cheyenne Outbreak of 1879: Using Oral History and Archaeology as Tools of Resistance" by J. Douglas McDonald et al. In *The Archaeology of Inequality*, ed. by Randall H. McGuire and Robert Paynter. Cambridge, MA: Basil Blackwell, 1991.)

FOOD FOR THOUGHT

- Go to the Web and learn about Dull Knife Memorial College and the current status of the Cheyenne Outbreak Trail.

Gender

Microcultures that reflect **gender** differences exhibit patterns of culturally constructed and learned behaviors and ideas associated with masculinity, femininity, or sometimes a "third," or blended, gender. Gender can be contrasted to sex, which uses biological markers to define categories of male and female such as genitals, chromosomes, and hormones. Anthropology, however, shows that a person's biological makeup does not necessarily correspond to his or her gender. Only a few tasks, such as giving birth and nursing infants, are necessarily tied to biology.

Cross-culturally, gender differences vary from societies in which male and female roles and worlds are similar or overlapping to those in which genders are sharply differentiated. In much of rural Thailand, males and females are about the same size, their clothing is quite similar, and their agricultural tasks are complementary and often interchangeable (Potter 1977).

In contrast, among the Hua people of the New Guinea Highlands, extreme gender segregation exists in nearly all aspects of life (Meigs 1984). The men's house physically and symbolically separates the worlds of men and women. The men live in strict separation from the women, and they engage in rituals seeking to purge themselves of female influences and substances: nose or penis bleeding, vomiting, tongue scraping, sweating, and eye washing. Men possess the sacred flutes, which they parade though the village from time to time. If women dare to look at the flutes, men have the right to kill them for that transgression. Strict rules govern the kinds of food that men and women may eat.

In many cultures, the lives of gay and lesbian people are adversely affected by discrimination based on their gender identity and sexual preferences. Other cultures are more open to varieties of gay, lesbian, and blended gender identities.

Age

The human life cycle, from birth to old age, takes people through biological and cultural stages for which appropriate behavior and thinking must be learned anew. In many African herding societies, elaborate age categories for males define their roles and status as they move from being boys with few responsibilities and little status, to young men who are warriors and live apart from the rest of the group, to adult men who are allowed to marry, father children, and become respected elders. "The Hill," or the collective members of the United States Senate and the House of Representatives, is a highly age-graded microculture (Weatherford 1981). The Hill can be considered a gerontocracy (a group ruled by senior members) in which the older politicians dominate younger politicians in terms of amount of time for speaking and how much attention a person's words receive. It may take a junior member between 10 and 20 years to become as effective and powerful as a senior member, by which time, of course, she or he has become a senior member.

In many cultures, adolescents make up a particularly powerless category because they are neither children, who have certain well-defined rights, nor adults. Given this threshold position, many adolescents behave in ways that the larger society disapproves of and defines as deviance, crime, or even psychopathology (Fabrega and Miller 1995). Females, at most ages in many societies, have lower status than males do. Cross-cultural research shows that in many nonindustrial societies, though, middle-aged women have the highest status in their life cycle, especially if they are married and have children (Brown 1982).

CROSSING THE FIELDS

Elderly Females Take the Lead in Baboon Societies

Beginning in 1971, several decades of observation of baboons in Amboseli National Park, southern Kenya, reveal a pattern in which an elderly female serves as a leader at critical times in group movements (Altmann 1998). Adult males are usually in the forefront during actual fights with predators or other baboon groups. In such instances, each individual seems to decide for itself whether to threaten the intruders, hang back, or flee.

The decisive role of elderly females appears at controversial points in group movements when the question is which route to take. An elderly female typically makes the choice that is followed. The researchers wonder why the "opinions" of these females carry so much weight. It is not necessarily because of social rank: elderly females of high, middle, and low social rank have been observed to take the lead. A more promising explanation lies in the number of female offspring an elderly female has. Among baboons, females are the permanent members of the group, whereas males move to another group at maturity. An elderly female with many female offspring has a large following. This explanation works in most cases, but there are some elderly female leaders who have few offspring and some females with many offspring who do not assume leadership roles.

Another possible explanation is the size of an individual female's social network beyond her offspring. Bearing offspring is a time when social networks are extended and affirmed as relatives and acquaintances cluster around the infant and mother. These ties are reinforced through grooming. For males, social relationships are less enduring— though of broader range—given the fact that they leave their birth group, have to establish themselves in another group, and may change groups several times. ■

FOOD FOR THOUGHT

- Think about what your microculture involves in terms of residence during adulthood. How does staying in or near one's home area, or moving away from it, affect friendship and other ties?

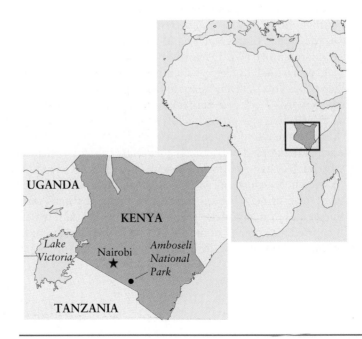

Institutions

Institutions, enduring group settings formed for a particular purpose, have their own characteristic microcultures. Institutions include hospitals, boarding schools and universities, and prisons. Anyone who has entered such an institution has experienced a feeling of strangeness. Until you gain familiarity with the unwritten cultural rules, you are likely to make mistakes that offend or perplex people, that fail to get you what you want, and that make you feel marginal.

Consider the microculture of a large urban hospital in the United States. Melvin Konner, an anthropologist who studied among a hunting–gathering group of southern Africa, later decided to go to medical school. In his book *Becoming a Doctor* (1987), he reports on his experience in medical school, providing an anthropologist's insights into the hospital as a cultural institution. One of his most striking conclusions is that medical students undergo training that functions to dehumanize them, numbing them to the pain and suffering that they will confront each day. Medical training involves, for example, the need to memorize massive amounts of material, sleep deprivation, and the learning of a special form of humor and vocabulary that seems crude and even cruel. Some special vocabulary items: *boogie*—a verb meaning to move patients along quickly in a clinic or emergency room (as in "Let's boogie!"); *dud*—a patient with no interesting findings; and *gomer*—an acronym for Get Out of My Emergency Room, referring to an old, decrepit, hopeless patient whose care is guaranteed to be a thankless task and who is usually admitted from a nursing home.

Relationships of power and inequality exist within institutions and between different institutions. These relationships cut across those of other microcultures, such as gender. In the United States, women prisoners' recent claims of rape and abuse by prison guards are an example of intra-institutional inequality linked with gender inequality. Schools have their own institutional cultures. Within the classroom, studies show that many teachers are not egalitarian in the way they call on and respond to students, depending on their gender, race, or "looks." In the Kilimanjaro region of Tanzania, a lesson about proper sexual behavior directed to secondary school students advised boys to "preserve your bullets" and girls to "lock your boxes" (Stambach 2000:127–130). The surface message is that boys should learn to control their mental processes and girls should look after their possessions, which each girl keeps in a metal trunk beneath her bed. The underlying message is that boys should learn to control their sexual desire and that girls should protect their bodies. The separate metaphors, bullets and boxes, for the boys and the girls, reflect and reinforce gender differences in moral codes and expected behavior.

Valuing and Sustaining Diversity

Most anthropologists value and are committed to cultural diversity just as environmentalists value biological diversity and are committed to sustaining it. Thus cultural anthropologists deeply regret the decline and extinction of different cultures. Anthropologists contribute to the preservation of cultural diversity by describing cultures as they have existed, as they now exist, and as they change. Many cultural anthropologists have become advocates or activists in the area of cultural survival. An organization called Cultural Survival has been helping indigenous peoples and ethnic minorities deal as equals in their interactions with outsiders. Cultural Survival's guiding principle is printed on the inside cover of its publication, *Cultural Survival Quarterly*:

> We insist that cultural differences are inherent in humanity; protecting this human diversity enriches our common earth. Yet in the name of development and progress, native peoples lose their land, their natural resources, and control over their lives. The consequences often are disease, destitution, and despair—and war and environmental damage for us all. The destruction is not inevitable. (1988)

Cultural Survival sponsors programs to help indigenous peoples and ethnic minorities help themselves in protecting and managing natural resources, claiming land rights, and diversifying their means of livelihood.

Native American dancers perform at the annual Gateway Pow Wow in Brooklyn, New York. ■ Are there examples in any of your microcultural experiences of attempts to revitalize aspects of the culture? (Source: © CRDPHOTO/CORBIS)

 # CONTEMPORARY DEBATES ABOUT CULTURE

Within anthropology, enduring theoretical debates both divide the discipline and give it coherence. Three important contemporary debates, discussed here, will resurface throughout the book. Each is concerned with the basic question of how people behave and think and why they behave and think the way they do.

Biological Determinism versus Cultural Constructionism

Biological determinism is an approach in anthropology that emphasizes how genes and hormones shape human behavior and thoughts. Biological determinists search for the gene or hormone that might lead to behavior such as sharing, art, social organization, homicide, alcoholism, or adolescent stress. (See the Critical Thinking box.) They examine cultural practices in terms of how these practices contribute to the *reproductive success* of the species, in other words, how they contribute to the gene pool of subsequent generations by boosting the numbers of surviving offspring produced in a particular population. Behaviors and ideas that confer reproductive advantages are, in this view, more likely than others to be passed on to future generations.

Biological determinists, for example, provide an explanation for why human males apparently have better spatial skills than females. They say that these differences are innate in males, genetically inherited as a result of evolutionary selection. Throughout human evolution, males with better spatial skills would have an advantage over other males in securing food and mates. Males with better spatial skills would thus have both an individual survival advantage (through more effective food procurement) and greater reproductive success (through impregnating more females and thus having more offspring who, in turn, have better spatial skills). Spatial skills would not, however, result in differences in reproductive success among females.

Cultural constructionism, in contrast, maintains that human behavior and ideas are shaped by one's culture through learning. In terms of the example of better male spa-

Adolescent Stress: Biologically Determined or Culturally Constructed?

Margaret Mead, one of the first trained anthropologists of North America, went to eastern Samoa in 1925 to spend nine months studying child-rearing patterns and adolescent behavior. She sought to answer these questions: "Are the disturbances which vex our adolescents due to the nature of adolescence itself or to the civilization? Under different conditions does adolescence present a different picture?" (1961:24). She observed and interviewed fifty adolescent girls of three different villages. Her conclusion, published in the famous book *Coming of Age in Samoa* (1961 [1928]), was that, in contrast to the typical experience in the United States, children in Samoa grew up in a relaxed and happy atmosphere. As young adolescents, they made a sexually free and unrepressed transition to adulthood. These findings had a major impact on thinking about child rearing in North America, prompting attempts at more relaxed forms of child rearing in the hope of raising less stressed adolescents.

In 1983, five years after Mead's death, the Australian anthropologist Derek Freeman published a strong critique of Mead's work on Samoa. Freeman said that Mead's findings on adolescence were wrong. Freeman, a biological determinist, believes that universally, adolescents are driven by hormonal changes that cause social and psychological upheavals. He claims that Mead's work was flawed in two major ways. First, he says her fieldwork was inadequate because she spent a relatively short time in the field and had insufficient knowledge of the Samoan language. Second, he says that her theoretical bias against biological determinism led her to overlook or underreport evidence that failed to support her thesis. In addition, he marshalls statistical evidence against Mead's position. He compares rates of adolescent delinquency in Samoa and England and finds that they are similar. He therefore argues that sexual puritanism and social repression also characterized Samoan adolescence. In other words, Samoa is not so very different from the West with its supposedly pervasive adolescent problems.

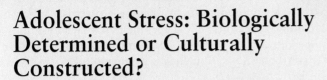

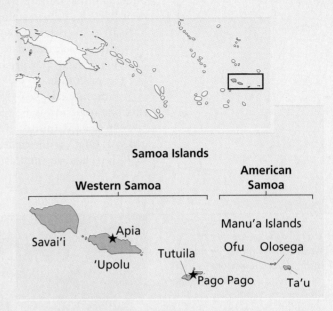

Samoa Islands

Western Samoa　**American Samoa**

Savai'i　Apia　'Upolu　Tutuila　Pago Pago

Manu'a Islands

Ofu　Olosega　Ta'u

Freeman's critique prompted a vigorous response from scholars, mostly in defense of Mead. One such response came from cultural anthropologist Eleanor Leacock, an expert on how colonialism affects indigenous cultures. Leacock claims that Freeman's position fails to take history into account: Mead's findings apply to Samoa of the 1920s, whereas Freeman's analysis is based on data from the 1960s. By the 1960s, Samoan society had gone through radical cultural change because of the influence of World War II and intensive exposure to Western influences, including Christian missionaries. Freeman's data, in her view, do not contradict Mead's because they are from a different period.

CRITICAL THINKING QUESTIONS

■ Mead felt that finding one "negative case" (no adolescent stress in Samoa) was sufficient to disprove the view that adolescent stress is a cross-cultural universal. Do you agree that one negative case is sufficient?

■ Say an anthropologist found that a certain practice or pattern of behavior did appear universally, in all cultures. Would that necessarily mean that it was biologically driven?

tial skills, cultural constructionists would provide evidence that such skills are passed on culturally through learning, not genes. They would say that parents and teachers consciously and unconsciously teach boys and girls different skills and are more likely to promote learning of spatial skills among boys. For example, boys' games emphasize larger territories than girls games do. Cultural constructionists likewise look to childhood experience and cultural context to explain behavior such as sharing or selfishness, gentleness or violence, and heterosexuality or same-sexuality.

Interpretivism versus Cultural Materialism

The two perspectives considered here, interpretivism and cultural materialism, differ in terms of how culture should be studied and understood. Interpretivism focuses on understanding culture by studying what people think about, their explanations of their lives, and the meanings that are important to them. Thus interpretivists largely have an idealist view of what culture is, and this view shapes their approach to studying culture. Cultural materialism, in contrast, seeks to explain beliefs and behavior in terms of how they are related to questions of making a living and other "material" aspects of life.

A famous example of this debate concerns India's many cows. To interpretivists, this phenomenon is best understood by paying attention to Hindu beliefs about cows as sacred animals that must not be killed and that must be protected in their old age. On the other side, cultural materialists maintain that there are many cows in India because they are important economically. Cows, even when scrawny-

Top: Traffic in the city of Varanasi (Banaras), in northern India. Foreign visitors to India have often commented that the presence of wandering cows is a sign of wastefulness and inefficiency. Bottom: SUVs, trucks, and buses share the road in Los Angeles. SUVs are increasingly popular in the United States even as environmentalists criticize them for their poor gas mileage. ■ If you were an energy policy-maker, what lessons would you draw from these two photographs? (Source: © Jack Fields/CORBIS, top; AP/Wide World Photos, bottom)

looking to a Wisconsin farmer, are worth more alive than dead (Harris 1974). They can be used for plowing fields and are less costly than motorized equipment to the farmer and to the environment, because fossil fuel is not needed to run them. As they wander along village lanes and city streets, they consume trash (including wet garbage such as orange peels and dry materials such as paper and cast-off clay drinking cups), which they transform into dung. The dung is collected and used as farm fertilizer or, after being mixed with straw and dried as patties, as cooking fuel. For these reasons, cultural materialists would say that the sacredness of cows among Hindus provides a form of religious protection against the killing of these economically useful animals.

Individual Agency versus Structurism

This debate concerns the question of how much individual will, or agency, affects the way people behave and think, compared with the power of major forces, or "structures," that are beyond individual control. Western philosophical thought gives much emphasis to the role of **agency,** the ability of individuals to make choices and exercise free will. In contrast, structurism holds that free choice is an illusion because choices are structured by forces such as the economy, social and political organizations, and ideological systems.

For example, explaining why people are poor, unemployed, or on welfare in the United States has been approached from both positions by anthropologists and others. Those who emphasize agency in explaining behavior and ideas say that people are poor, unemployed, or on welfare by their own (direct or indirect) choice. If they wished, they could choose to be otherwise. Structurists would say that the poor and unemployed are trapped by structural forces and cannot escape these traps. They would argue that the people at the bottom of the economic ladder have little opportunity to exercise choice about being elsewhere than at the bottom.

Beyond the Debates: Holists at Heart

Some anthropologists emphasize people's ideas as the most important feature of humanity and human culture, whereas others look first to how people make their living and organize themselves in groups. We find useful as a starting point, a model of culture as a "messy cake" with three marbled layers (see Figure 2.6).

Besides having different theoretical positions, some anthropologists apply the findings of their research to solving or preventing real-world problems, whereas others stick more to academic pursuits. In spite of the diversity among anthropologists, we believe that all anthropologists are deeply interested in just about everything having to do with humanity, including its past, its present, and its future. We are all, more or less, holists at heart.

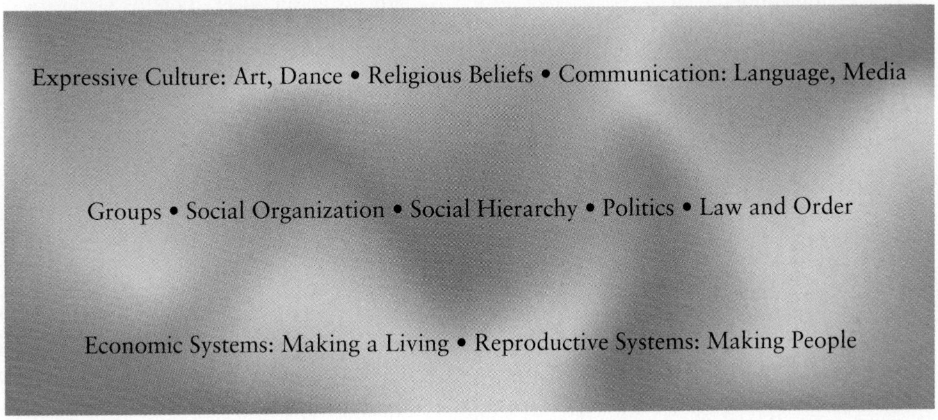

THINKING OUTSIDE THE BOX

Imagine that you are on a debating team. The issue is cars in the United States. Prepare to support both an interpretivist and a cultural materialist position about how to understand why people in the United States have so many cars.

Expressive Culture: Art, Dance • Religious Beliefs • Communication: Language, Media

Groups • Social Organization • Social Hierarchy • Politics • Law and Order

Economic Systems: Making a Living • Reproductive Systems: Making People

FIGURE 2.6
The "messy cake" of culture.

THE BIG QUESTIONS REVISITED

WHAT is culture?

Anthropologists agree that culture is learned and shared. Idealists say that culture consists of learned and shared beliefs, ideas, and motivations. Behaviorists maintain that culture is learned and shared behavior. Holists, taking the most comprehensive view, conceive of culture as both learned and shared beliefs and behavior. Most anthropologists are more likely to be holists than to be pure idealists or behaviorists. Culture is difficult to define, so anthropologists sometimes refer instead to its characteristics: it is learned, adaptive, related to (but not the same as) nature, based on symbols, integrated, and ever-changing.

WHAT are some bases of cultural diversity?

Cultures exist at different levels, macro and micro, and are based on several social factors, including class, "race," ethnicity and indigenous status, gender, age, and institutional context. These factors are sometimes associated with inequality and discrimination. A general anthropological principle is that diversity (as distinct from inequality) is valuable because different cultural "blueprints for life" offer possibilities for human sustainability into the future.

WHAT do anthropologists debate about culture?

Three enduring debates about culture exist in the discipline of anthropology. The first is the debate between biological determinism and cultural constructionism. In biological determinism, biology is more or less destiny. Genes, hormones, and chromosomes determine human behavior and thinking. In cultural constructionism, learning, or enculturation, is the more powerful factor shaping the way people act and think. In the second major debate, interpretivists say that emphasis should be placed on studying people's beliefs and ideas, whereas cultural materialists emphasize studying economic and other material aspects of life. In the third debate, the position that speaks for human agency says that individuals have substantial choice and power in shaping what they do and believe, whereas the structurists feel that, although human agency does exist, powerful structures such as economics, the media, and governments shape human culture and limit human choices. In spite of these spirited debates, anthropologists agree that it is important to study humanity's past, present, and future and are holists at heart.

KEY CONCEPTS

SUGGESTED READINGS

Douglas Cole. *Franz Boas: The Early Years, 1858–1906.* Seattle: University of Washington Press, 1999. This biography of Boas provides a rich context for understanding how his vision for a four-field discipline emerged.

Jane K. Cowan. Marie-Bénédicte Dembour and Richard A. Wilson, eds. *Culture and Rights: Anthropological Perspectives.* New York: Cambridge University Press, 2001. Ten chapters consider the varied links between culture and rights. This book includes theoretical discussions and case studies on child prostitution in Thailand, women's rights in Botswana, Macedonian minority rights in Greece, Innu rights in Canada, and the peace process in Guatemala.

Susanna M. Hoffman and Anthony Oliver-Smith, eds. *Catastrophe and Culture: The Anthropology of Disaster.* Santa Fe, NM: School of American Research Press, 2002. The editors provide two introductory chapters that discuss why anthropologists should study disasters and how disasters link nature and culture. Case studies address the nuclear disaster in Chernobyl, fire in California, drought in the Andes, and the Bhopal disaster.

Jonathan Xavier Inda and Renato Rosaldo, eds. *The Anthropology of Globalization: A Reader.* Malden, MA: Blackwell, 2002. Eighteen chapters address a variety of issues, including women workers in Barbados offshore industries, Mexican migration, mass media in Shanghai, human rights in Tibet, and feminism and Islam in Egypt. A general introduction to the collection provides insight into cultural theories about globalization.

Barbara D. Miller, ed. *Sex and Gender Hierarchies.* New York: Cambridge University Press, 1993. An introductory chapter provides an overview of anthropological research on gender inequality in each of anthropology's four fields. Chapters address topics such as the division of labor among chimpanzees, gender roles among royalty in a Korean kingdom, infanticide in Tokugawa Japan, and mothers' speech to children in American Samoa compared to the United States.

Charles E. Orser Jr. *Race and Practice in Archaeological Interpretation.* Philadelphia: University of Pennsylvania Press, 2004. The author makes a case that historical archaeologists have an obligation to study "race"-based inequalities that existed in the past. He discusses conceptual differences between "race" and ethnicity, probes how to read "race" in archaeological materials, and provides an in-depth examination of "the practice of race" in nineteenth-century Ireland.

Jan Nederveen Pieterse. *Globalization and Culture: Global Mélange.* New York: Rowman and Littlefield, 2004. This book provides an overview of arguments about how globalization affects culture, paying special attention to three major paradigms: the clash of civilizations, McDonaldization, and hybridization. The last two chapters focus on hybridization and antihybridization backlashes.

Richard A. Shweder. *Why Do Men Barbecue? Recipes for Cultural Psychology.* Cambridge, MA: Harvard University Press, 2003. This collection of essays provides a cultural relativist's view on topics such as whether and how long infants sleep with their parents, morality and suffering, emotions, women's roles, science, and religious beliefs.

E. O. Smith. *When Culture and Biology Collide: Why We Are Stressed, Depressed, and Self-Obsessed.* New Brunswick, NJ: Rutgers University Press, 2002. This book offers an evolutionary view of some aspects of contemporary culture in the United States, including road rage, stress, "Barbie" beauty images, depression, and obesity. He cautions that evolution does not fully explain all these behaviors nor does our evolutionary past "excuse" dangerous and antisocial behavior.

Haru Yamada. *Different Games, Different Rules: Why Americans and Japanese Misunderstand Each Other.* New York: Oxford University Press, 1997. The author grew up in Japan and the United States and experienced the "communication gap" between the two cultures. Her research reveals underlying cultural differences that affect communication styles in the banking industry.

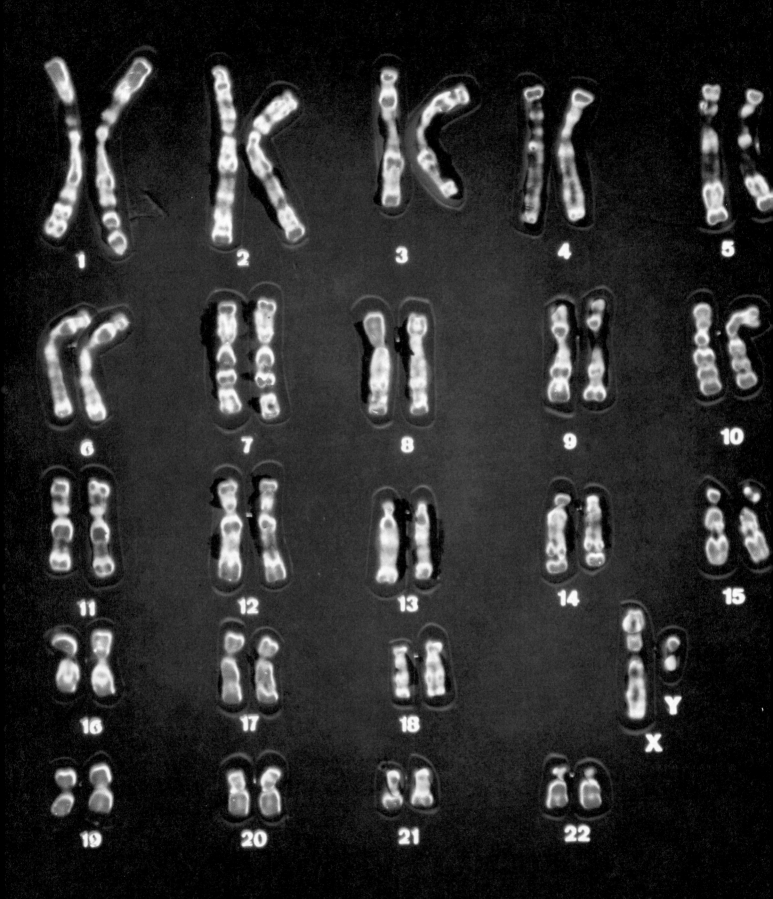

THE BIG QUESTIONS

- WHAT is the scientific view about humanity?
- HOW does the concept of evolution explain humanity?
- HOW does evolution work?

CHAPTER 3

Science, Biology, and Evolution

Human chromosomes. Each nucleated cell in the human body contains a full set of genetic instructions. Most of them are encoded in nuclear DNA distributed among the 22 pairs of autosomes and the two sex chromosomes shown here. What each cell looks like and what each cell does is determined by which of thousands of instructions are switched on. (Source: © CNRI/Photo Researchers, Inc.)

With respect to the horse, I have collected cases in England of the spinal stripe in horses of the most distinct breeds, and of all colours; transverse bars on the legs are not rare in duns, mouse-duns, and in one instance in a chestnut: a faint shoulder-stripe may sometimes be seen in duns, and I have seen a trace in a bay horse . . . .
In the north-west part of India the Kattywar breed of horses is so generally striped, that, as I hear from Colonel Poole, who examined this breed for the Indian Government, a horse without stripes is not considered as purely bred . . . . (Darwin 1859:151)

I n 1842 Charles Darwin moved to a village southeast of London. The village, given its location near London, had a good postal service—a fact that was important to Darwin in his research. Each day he wrote to breeders of domestic animals asking them for information about their breeding practices and outcomes. Such information about artificial selection was crucial to his development of the theory of natural selection as the key process driving evolution.

In this quotation from his groundbreaking book, *On the Origin of Species,* Darwin discusses variations in the color and pattern of horses' coats. By accumulating such information, he subsequently concluded that the coats of the ancestors of domesticated horses were likely to have been striped.

This chapter is about the role of biology and evolution in shaping humanity's past and present. Biology and evolution do not explain everything about humanity's origin and present variation, as discussed in Chapters 1 and 2. Although anthropologists may debate the role of biology and culture in such human behaviors as mate selection, sharing, or aggressiveness, there is no debate about how humans acquired the particular proteins on the surface of our blood cells that determine our blood group or the color of our skin. We inherit these characteristics from our parents in the form of a genetic message. Nor is there any scientific debate about the notion that all forms of life are connected by the process of evolution.

We first provide a historical context for the scientific view of how humanity emerged and changed through evolution. Next we describe the development of the scientific concepts of evolution, natural selection, and heredity. Last, we consider how evolution works in terms of humanity.

SCIENCE AND THE TREE OF LIFE

Anthropologists now take for granted the scientific evidence that connects modern humans with the rest of the living world. Long before such scientific evidence was available and its significance understood, some thinkers had applied the power of reasoning to the problem of human origins and to the relationship between humans and other animals. This section focuses on European thinking, because in it lie the roots of the discipline of anthropology. Philosophies and religions from other parts of the world, such as Hinduism in India and Islam in the Middle East, had their own theories about humanity, but these are not part of the scientific approach that anthropology adopted.

Before Science

Intellectual history tells us that the classical Greeks and Romans were the first to put their thoughts about humanity into writing. Centuries later, the spread of Christianity throughout Europe led to the decline of Greco-Roman ideas and to the rise of

Biblical explanations for the origin of humanity and humanity's place in nature. We briefly discuss these two phases in Western thinking as background to the later emergence of science and its views about humanity.

Greco-Roman Thinking

As noted in Chapter 1, the earliest recorded ideas about the origin of humanity are contained in the writings of Greek thinkers such as Plato and Aristotle in the fifth and sixth centuries BCE (see Figure 3.1). These early philosophers developed the concept that all the components of the natural world are parts of one system. Another aspect of their thinking was the conviction that universal laws govern the natural world,

FIGURE 3.1
Timeline of Western thought about humanity and evolution.

6th–5th century BCE	Greek philosophers consider humans part of the natural world.
1st century BCE	Lucretius suggests human ancestors were brutish cave dwellers.
5th century CE	Biblical narrative predominates in Europe through to the 19th century.
11th–12th century CE	Islamic scholars build on Greco-Roman ideas about the natural world.
13th century CE	Aquinas reconciles Greek ideas with the biblical narrative.
16th century CE	Vesalius writes the first detailed and accurate description of the human body.
17th century CE	Bacon sets out the basic elements of the scientific method. Ussher and Lightfoot calculate the time of the biblical creation using "begats."
18th century CE	Linnaeus assembles the first comprehensive taxonomy of living things. Cuvier establishes the principles of scientific paleontology. The Great Chain of Being metaphor predominates. Malthus publishes work emphasizing competition among individuals for scarce resources.
19th century CE	Lamarck proposes that existing species arise independently and are then transformed through the inheritance of acquired characteristics. Lyell publishes a scientific version of the origin of the earth and establishes geology as a science. Amateur archaeologists discover fossils of extinct animals in association with stone tools. Wallace and Darwin suggest that evolution through natural selection best explains the Tree of Life. Darwin publishes *On the Origin of Species* and provides compelling evidence that natural selection drives evolution. Mendel presents the results of his experiments on heredity.
20th century CE	The words *genetics* (1906) and *gene* (1909) are first used. Avery et al. show that DNA carries genetic messages (1943). Watson and Crick publish findings on DNA (1953). Two international teams of scientists sequence the human genome (2001).

Note: BCE = Before the Common Era, and CE = Common Era. In the text, we use the BCE abbreviation but dispense with CE. Thus any date in this text without the letters BCE refers to the Common Era.

The Judeo-Christian narrative of human origins is set out in the Bible. It says that all living things are unchanged since they were made by God, and it traces all people back to Adam and Eve, who were also created by God. ■ How does this explanation for the origin of modern humans differ from the one set out by the Roman philosopher Lucretius? (Source: © Bettmann/CORBIS)

including humans. Humans, in classical Greek philosophy, were part of, not separate from, the natural world, and scholars wrote that animals and humans shared a common origin in natural processes.

Several hundred years after the time of Plato and Aristotle, a Roman philosopher named Lucretius, writing in the first century BCE, proposed that the earliest humans differed from contemporary Romans. He suggested that they were brutish (animal-like), lived alone in caves, ate berries, and lacked tools and language. Both classical Greek and Roman thinkers viewed the ability to make tools, the use of fire, and verbal language as crucial steps in the ascent of humanity from its bestial state (Cole 1990). Thus the basic elements of a view of humanity as changing from an earlier, primitive form to later, more complex forms was established early in Western thought.

The Early Christian Perspective

The collapse of the Roman Empire in the fifth century brought a radical change in how Western thinkers, nearly all Christian by that time, viewed humanity and its origin. The account given in the Old Testament of the Bible largely replaced Greco-Roman ideas. According to the biblical view, the Judeo-Christian God created humans—first in the form of a man, Adam, and then in that of a woman, Eve. As a result of humanity being the result of God's work, the first people were fully equipped with language, a rational and cultured mind, and the ability to live together in societies. All their mental and moral capacities placed humans apart from and superior to other animals (Goodrum 2002).

Most Western philosophers living in and immediately after the periods described as the Dark Ages (the fifth to twelfth centuries) and the Middle Ages (twelfth to fifteenth centuries) held to a literal biblical explanation of human origins. For them, the Bible provided a true and accurate explanation for human origins and their place in nature. According to the book of Genesis, all creatures had been created at one time, about 6000 years earlier, and they continued to exist in the form in which they had been created. There was no understanding of the earth's great age, of extinct species, or of the transformation of humanity over time.

Insights from Greco-Roman times were mostly abandoned by Western thinkers during the Dark and Middle Ages when faith replaced reason. Greek classical texts, however, were read by Islamic scholars who translated them into Arabic. Before and during the time when Christian armies drove the Muslims from Spain in the twelfth and thirteenth centuries, a few curious Medieval Christian scholars translated into Latin the manuscripts left behind. Some of these translated texts dealt with the natural world, including animal and human origins (Lindberg 1992). In the thirteenth century, the noted Christian philosopher Thomas Aquinas integrated elements of Greek ideas about nature and humanity with Biblical interpretations (Ruse 2003). Despite his writings and those of other philosophers of the time, the prevailing explanations in Europe about the origin of humanity remained biblically based throughout the Middle Ages.

Science Emerges

Science, which we defined in Chapter 1, is a form of knowledge seeking that involves a set of steps now called the **scientific method.** The first step of the scientific method is making observations of a particular phenomenon. These observations then lead

The Mezquita (mosque) in Córdoba, Spain. Córdoba was the capital city of Islamic Spain. Construction of the Mezquita began in the early eighth century, and it soon became a center of Muslim worship and scholarship. The Christians retook Córdoba in the thirteenth century and converted much of the Mezquita into a church. Later additions during the Renaissance brought an even more hybrid appearance. ■ A distinctive Islamic feature that remains is the *mihrab*, the octagonal structure with high arched windows. Research the significance of this feature of Islamic architecture. (Source: © Patrick Ward/CORBIS)

to a hypothesis, or possible explanation, to account for what was observed. Next comes the testing of the hypothesis by performing experiments or making new observations that lead to the confirmation, amendment, or rejection of the hypothesis. The scientific method, overall, involves a repeated pattern of hypothesis—testing—hypothesis. Each round of hypothesis generation and testing should be informed by the previous round. This continuing process is needed because the goal of science transcends simple description, or knowing *that* things happen. Science seeks to know *why* things happen.

The Renaissance and the Scientific Method

The foundation of the scientific method lies in the European Renaissance, which ushered in the revival of art, architecture, and literature in Italy in the fifteenth century. Over time, the influence of the Italian Renaissance spread to other parts of Europe.

Its impact on the development of science as a way of thinking was especially strong in England, where Francis Bacon, in the early seventeenth century, developed the basic ideas of how scientific investigations should be pursued. His contribution can be summed up as follows: Instead of reading about something in a book, go out and observe the phenomenon for yourself. Then investigate its causes by devising your own explanation (hypothesis) and then testing it.

Scientific Bases of Human Evolution Emerge

In addition to prompting development of the scientific method as a general approach to thinking about humanity, advances in the understanding of the earth and its creatures, generated during and after the Renaissance, led to a new way of thinking about human origins and to the foundation of the scientific study of human evolution. These streams of thinking included the study of human anatomy, geology (earth science), and paleontology (the study of **fossils,** which are the preserved remains of a plant or animal from the past).

The foundations of scientific anatomy, the study of the human body, were established in the sixteenth century by Andreas Vesalius, a scholar from the Low Countries, or what is now Belgium. He realized that the textbooks used by his professors were based on a confusing and inaccurate mixture of human and monkey anatomy.

THINKING OUTSIDE THE BOX Do some research to find out why the practice of dissection was abandoned in Europe at the same time that Christianity became the dominant religion.

The illustrations, he knew, were not derived from or checked against careful dissections. Once again, it was the classical Greeks who had, ten centuries before, dissected human bodies for the purpose of studying how the body works. But after that time, and into the Dark Ages, the practice of dissection was abandoned. Vesalius decided to do his own dissections and to write his own, accurate human anatomy book. His efforts ensured that, from then on, scientists would have access to reliable information about the structure of the human body.

Just as the structure and working of the human body were confused and shrouded in mystery by nonscientific thinking, so too was thinking about the age of the earth and the living creatures that inhabit it. In 1650 James Ussher, then Archbishop of Armagh in Ireland, used the number of "begats" in the Book of Genesis to calculate the precise year of the act of Creation. According to his arithmetic, the act of Creation took place in 4004 BCE. A little later, a theologian at Trinity College, John Lightfoot, calculated that the act of Creation took place at 9 a.m. on October 23 in 4004 BCE.

In the eighteenth century, a new science devoted to studying the earth arose: geology. Its development received much impetus in the nineteenth century, with the beginnings of industrialization. The excavations required to build canals and railroads gave people an opportunity to see rock formations that previously had been accessible only by looking at seaside cliffs and riverbanks.

A Scottish scientist named Charles Lyell is considered the father of geology. In 1830, he provided a scientific version of the history of the earth in his book *The Principles of Geology*. This book influenced many scientists of the time, including Charles Darwin. In it, Lyell established two important principles that explain the earth's landscape. The first, *fluvialism*, says that water erosion shaped the earth's surface by reducing the height of mountains and creating valleys. The second, *uniformitarianism*, says that the earth's surface, throughout its history, has been shaped by the same processes, such as fluvial erosion and volcanoes, that still shape it today. Another major and enduring contribution made by Lyell is his emphasis on the importance of **stratigraphy,** the study and description of a vertical series of sediment or rock layers that have accumulated over time. Lyell pointed out that strata (layers) increase in age the further down they are in any geological sequence. This principle also applies to fossils or stone tools contained within the strata. In other words, the lower in a sequence of rocks a fossil is, the older it is likely to be. Lyell recognized, as we do today, that certain factors could disrupt this rule, such as upheavals in the earth's surface due to natural causes or deliberate burial, which places an object beneath the level where it would be found naturally.

The implications of the new science of geology were profound. It provided a scientific alternative to the biblical explanation for the earth's appearance, which is based on the story of the great flood during which Noah built his ark. Second, it raised serious questions about the biblical view of the earth's age by providing evidence that the earth had to be much older than 6000 years.

A third stream of thinking further contributed to the questioning of the biblical narrative about humanity in favor of an evolutionary perspective. This thinking emerged from the scientific study of fossils. Classical Greek and Roman writers had discussed fossils and speculated that they were the remains of ancient monsters, and many of these monsters figured in their myths and legends (Mayer 2000). The existence of fossils caused a serious conceptual problem for biblical scholars, because the story of the flood and Noah's ark makes it impossible for any life forms to have existed from before the flood (a period referred to as antediluvian, "before the flood"). Starting in the eighteenth century and increasing into the nineteenth century, stone tools were discovered in England and France, in association with fossils of extinct animals such as mammoths. Scientists began to accept that fossils were the remains of extinct animals and plants. Their association with evidence of humans further called into question the theory of the Big Flood. Writings in the first half of the nineteenth century by amateur scientists, such as Jacques Boucher de Perthes in France and geologist William Falconer in England, were radical for the time. Their

This skull cap was recovered in 1856 by quarry workers in a cave exposed by erosion from the Neander River, Germany. It took nearly a decade for scientists to appreciate its significance. ■ Consider what happened between the time of its discovery and 1864 that may have influenced this change. (Source: © Giraudon/Bridgeman Art Library)

reports about human fossils found in association with stone tools provided evidence that humans were much older than the biblical story said.

At this time, French scientist Georges Cuvier emerged as a key figure in the study of fossils, and he is recognized as the founder of paleontology. For Cuvier, the study of fossils provided a means to piece together the story of the earth and life on it. Many of his contributions, including how to categorize fossils and how to reconstruct broken fossils, endure to the present day (Rudwick 1997:49).

Science and Classification

Beginning in the fifteenth century, the European exploration of the non-European world produced eyewitness accounts of humans using simple tools and acquiring their food by hunting, fishing, and gathering. Explorers and traders also brought back descriptions—and examples—of many plants and animals that were new to Europeans. These discoveries were not consistent with the existing understanding of the natural and human world. The presence of people in the New World was perplexing to those who accepted a literal reading of the Bible, because nowhere in the Bible are such people mentioned. Scholars were challenged to think of new ways to understand and organize all this variation. Several thinkers proposed methods for making sense of the new information.

The goal of scientific classification schemes is to group similar things together in increasingly broad, or inclusive, categories. The classification system of Swedish scientist Karl von Linné, first proposed in 1758, is still used by scientists today. Called the Linnaean system after its founder, it originally included seven major levels for all living things, from the most inclusive category to least inclusive: kingdom, phylum, class, order, family, genus, and species. As a parallel, consider an example of classification from art with seven levels. It begins with the most inclusive category and ends with an individual work of art. The levels are fine arts, paintings, oil paintings, twentieth-century oil paintings, Picasso's oil paintings, Picasso's anti-war oil paintings, and *Guernica*.

By the middle of the eighteenth century, the European voyages of exploration had produced a bewildering array of new plants and animals. Karl von Linné, a Swedish Botanist, recognized the need for a way to organize and catalog the discoveries. The scheme he introduced in the tenth edition of his book, **Systema Naturae,** *is the one that is still used now.* ■ How do modern humans fit into Linnaeus' scheme? (Source: © 2001 The Natural History Museum, London)

FIGURE 3.2
Modified Linnaean categories.

Linnaean Category	Modern Humans
Kingdom	Animal
Phylum	Chordate
Class	Mammal
Order	Primate
Family	Hominid
Tribe	Hominin
Genus	*Homo*
Species	*Homo sapiens*

The complexity of the living world, scientists realized later on, requires more than seven levels. Thus Linnaeus's original system was expanded by adding the new category tribe, between the genus and family, and by introducing the prefix *super-* above a category and the prefixes *sub-* and *infra-* below it. These additions increase the potential number of categories below the level of order to a total of twelve (eight of these categories that apply to modern humans are displayed in Figure 3.2).

As you will see in later chapters of this book, the principles of Linnaean classification are important in many areas of biological anthropology, especially primatology and paleoanthropology. Given the importance of this system, we should spend some time discussing how it works. First, anthropologists use the term **taxon** (plural, *taxa*) to refer to any group named at any level in the Linnaean hierarchy. A taxonomy, then, is a classification scheme that shows how various taxa are related to each other. The **Linnaean taxonomy**, a hierarchical structure for classifying all organisms, is a binomial system. Two categories, genus and species, make up the Latinized name for all species, extinct or living. For example, *Homo sapiens* is the genus and species of modern humans. According to convention, scientists can abbreviate the name of the genus, but not that of the species. Thus, we can write *H. sapiens* but not *Homo s.* The reason for this rule is that a species name, within its genus, is unique. If the species name were abbreviated, and there were more than one species in the genus with the same first letter, confusion would result.

Biological anthropologists must place any new fossil evidence about human prehistory into the most appropriate species. Members of the same species should be more like each other, in *morphology* (the size, shape, and appearance of an organism) and in behavior, than they are like the members of another species. The prevailing definition of a **species**, according to the biological species concept, is that a species is a group of interbreeding organisms that are reproductively isolated from other such groups (Mayr 1982). Thus members of a species can mate successfully (that is, can produce fertile offspring) only with each other and not with members of any other species. Such interbreeding keeps members of a species looking more like each other than like individuals that belong to other species. This definition, however, is problematic for paleoanthopologists who study human evolution. They have no information about the breeding patterns of extinct taxa. Instead, they identify species in the fossil record on the basis of morphology—what a fossil looks like—as a proxy for information about the individual's breeding pattern. The working assumption is that fossils that look similar are from animals that were capable of interbreeding. Another analytical challenge is deciding what degree of difference to allow within species and when to decide that a fossil is different enough that it almost certainly belongs to a separate species. We will discuss this challenge in Chapters 6, 7, and 8. Yet another challenge is determining which fossil primates belong to the human genus, *Homo* (see the Critical Thinking box).

Classification: Phenotype versus Molecules

Unlike many other classification schemes that have been proposed, the one introduced by Linnaeus has stood the test of time because scientists find it to be a reasonable and effective way of interpreting and organizing the living world. Assigning taxa to its various categories, however, is a somewhat subjective exercise involving judgments about degrees of similarity and difference. This subjectivity is nowhere more obvious than in the heated debates about which taxa should be included in the human genus, *Homo*. For many decades, membership in the genus *Homo* has been defined on the basis of phenotype, or physical features—such as a large brain, a rounded brain case, and straight knees, for example.

Advances in molecular biology provide new information about the structure of the genome. In the case of the higher primates, these new data have prompted a radical proposal concerning the genus *Homo* (Wildman et al. 2003). Derek Wildman and a team of researchers compared a segment of nuclear DNA consisting of 90,000 base pairs (out of a total of 3 billion) that in modern humans codes for 97 genes (out of an estimated total of 30,000). They recorded the sequences of bases in modern humans, chimpanzees, gorillas, and orangutans. The results showed that the similarity between modern human and chimpanzee DNA justifies including modern humans and chimpanzees in the same genus, *Homo*.

Other researchers argue that genetic relatedness is not the only criterion that should be taken into account when making decisions about what taxa to include in a genus. Wood and Collard (2000) agree with the Wildman team that all the taxa in a genus should belong to the same **clade**—that is, they are all descended from a recent common ancestor. They propose, however, that what the animal looks like and how it behaves (its phenotype) should also be taken into account. In other words, Wood and Collard argue that the taxa within a genus, in addition to belonging to the same clade, should belong to the same **grade** (a category based on what an animal does). If the "clade plus grade" criteria were applied to the living higher primates, then, modern humans and chimpanzees would not be in the same genus because they are not in the same grade with respect to behavior, despite the fact that between 98 and 99 percent of their DNA is the same.

CRITICAL THINKING QUESTIONS

- How would you feel, as a member of the genus *Homo,* if chimpanzees were reclassified into *Homo*?
- What behavioral criteria might be used to argue that humans should be in a separate genus from chimpanzees?
- How important are taxonomies in the real world—for example, in terms of classifying cars or music—and does the clade/grade argument have any relevance in these classification systems?

EVOLUTION EXPLAINS THE TREE OF LIFE AND HUMANITY'S PLACE ON IT

In this section, we discuss the scientific approach to understanding humanity that involves evolution and the three processes that evolution requires: variation, heredity, and natural selection. Evolution, as defined in Chapter 1, is a process of cumulative change in the characteristics of organisms or populations, occurring in the course of successive generations related by descent. It usually is a slow process, and it tends to lead to a more complex animal evolving from a less complex predecessor.

THINKING OUTSIDE THE BOX

Consider the category of running shoes. What features do all running shoes have in common that make them running shoes and not some other category of footwear? What are the major subcategories within the category of running shoes?

Evolution and the Tree of Life

Individuals within the same species are more closely related to each other than they are to an individual from another species. Likewise, species within the same genus are more closely related to each other than they are to a species from another genus. And so on, up to the highest levels in the Linnaean hierarchy. Scientists use the same classification system for all living animals because they have concluded that all living animals ultimately share a common ancestor.

FIGURE 3.3

The wing of a bird and a human arm are structurally different, but the signaling genes involved in their development are the same. Birds and modern humans must have inherited these genetic instructions from a distant (millions of years ago) common ancestor.

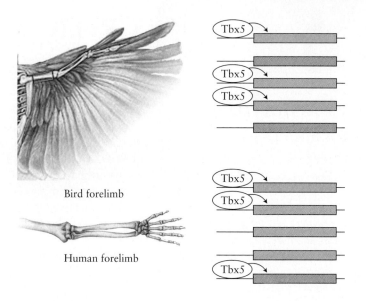

Bird forelimb

Human forelimb

FIGURE 3.4a

The Great Chain of Being, the Judeo-Christian view, depicts all living creatures in a sequence with humans occupying the place closest to God.

At first, scientists determined relationships morphologically—by comparing animals in terms of anatomical features that are visible to the naked eye or with a conventional light microscope. The assumption was that the larger the number of shared structures, the more closely related the animals. Then, beginning with pioneering studies in the early 1900s, scientists became able to compare and classify animals using the morphology of molecules. Now they determine the relationships among taxa by comparing their **DNA** (short for deoxyribonucleic acid), a complex molecule made up of units called **nucleotides** that carries the **genetic code** (the information needed to make proteins), encoded as distinctive sequences of DNA nucleotides. Over time, it became apparent that animal species similar in morphology also had similar molecules and similar genetic codes. Researchers have also shown that even though the wing of an insect and the arm of a primate look very different, the same basic genetic instructions are used during their development (Carroll et al. 2001) (see Figure 3.3).

These structural similarities and shared developmental instructions are compelling evidence that all living things are connected within a single *Tree of Life*, or TOL (see Figure 3.4b). This metaphor of a tree is now the prevailing image that scientists have for all living creatures, including humans. The TOL metaphor is a product of Darwinian thinking. Prior to Darwin, the dominant metaphor for humanity and its relationship to other animals was the *Great Chain of Being* (see Figure 3.4a). According to this image, a single chain links primitive animals with more advanced forms of life. Introduced by Medieval Christian philosophers, it persisted into the nineteenth century. According to the Great Chain of Being metaphor, modern humans are at the top end of the chain, and their superior position means that they are dominant over the creatures below them. In some renditions of the Great Chain of Being model, creatures are placed at different heights corresponding to their order in boarding Noah's ark.

The TOL metaphor gained prominence in the latter part of the nineteenth century. In a scientific TOL, the relative size of the part of the tree occupied by any particular group of living things reflects the number of taxa in that group. The branching pattern of the tree reflects the way scientists think the plants and animals within the TOL are related. Unlike a linear chain, the tree model emphasizes complexity and "bushiness," with lots of branches and sub-branches. In the TOL model, the branches of life have different lengths and run in different directions. Some become dead ends and die out.

In terms of humanity's place on the tree, all current evidence—including evidence from anatomy, molecules, and DNA—says that modern humans and chimpanzees shared the same small branch of the TOL until around 8 to 5 million years ago, after which the branch split into separate twigs. Research into primate **genomes** (a genome is the totality of genetic information encoded in the DNA of an individual) shows substantial overlap between humans and chimpanzees, a finding with important implications for the treatment of chimpanzees in the world outside academia (see the Lessons Applied box on p. 76).

What is the prevailing view of human origins and evolution in your cultural background? Does it reject or accept the Darwinian view, or does it provide some kind of accommodation with it?

THINKING

OUTSIDE THE BOX

FIGURE 3.4b
The scientific model sees all forms of life, living and extinct, as part of a tree-like structure. Modern humans are located on the end of one of the many branches connected to the vertebrate part of the Tree of Life.

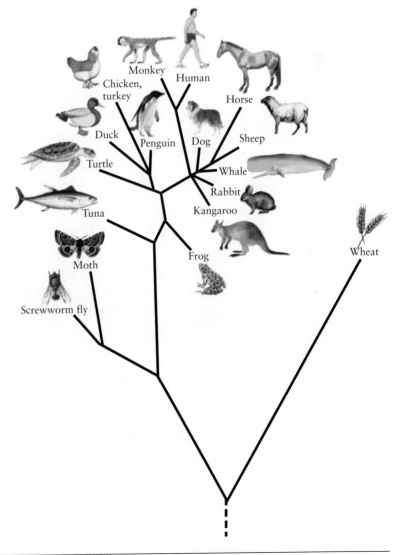

Applying Science to the Ethical Treatment of Nonhuman Primates

DNA evidence reveals that the genomes of humans and chimpanzee genomes overlap substantially. In addition, recent research shows many similarities between their cognitive processes that further blur the distinction between modern humans and chimpanzees (Gallup et al. 1977, Miyamoto et al. 1988). These findings are being used in two different areas: by animal rights activists and by medical researchers.

This research has been used as a rationale by animal rights activists in many parts of the world. One area of vigorous activity is in New Zealand, where an organization called the Great Ape Project New Zealand (GAPENZ) was formed. Members of the group lobby for special protection for the living animals closest to modern humans (Cavalieri and Singer 1993). Supporters of GAPENZ seek three basic rights for the great apes (Taylor 2000):

- not to be deprived of life
- not to be subjected to torture or to cruel, degrading, or disproportionately severe treatment
- not to be subjected to medical or scientific experimentation where it is not in the best interests of the individual

The close biological link between modern humans and chimpanzees strengthens the case for chimpanzee protection, but it also increases pressure from medical researchers to use chimpanzees as surrogates for humans in medical research. The New Zealand Animal Welfare Act of 1999 included no "rights" for nonhuman primates, but it does prohibit research on them unless it is in their own "best interests."

FOOD FOR THOUGHT

- What are the protections in place for nonhuman primates in your home country? Do you think they are adequate? Why or why not?

Scientists ask how the TOL grew and how best to explain the connectedness of various branches and twigs. The process of evolution, with natural selection as the mechanism for evolution, is accepted as the only explanation that has scientific merit. The first scientific explanation for one species changing into another was called transmutation. It was proposed by Jean Baptiste Lamarck, a French scientist, in his book *Philosophie Zoologique*, which was published in 1809. Lamarck's thinking was made available to the English-speaking world in a book by Robert Chambers called *Vestiges of the Natural History of Creation*, which appeared in 1844. According to Lamarck, species arose independently. He did not believe that all life could be traced back to a single ancestral form.

By the mid-1800s, the concept of evolution was gaining acceptance in spite of often strong negative reactions from biblical literalists—and in spite of the fact that no one yet understood how evolution worked. But progress in this direction was soon to come, partly through the inspiration of Chambers's *Vestiges*, which influenced many people, notably Charles Darwin and Alfred Russel Wallace.

Natural Selection

Darwin and Wallace both, independently, came up with a key concept in understanding species change: natural selection. **Natural selection** is the process by which organisms are better adapted to the environment reproduce more effectively and increase in numbers faster than less well-adapted forms. Natural selection accounts for both the diversity and the branching pattern of the TOL. It is the main driving force behind evolution.

Although Charles Darwin is often considered the originator of the concept of evolution, he is more appropriately acknowledged as providing a coherent theory about the way evolution works with his landmark contribution of developing the concept of natural selection. Working in parallel to Darwin was another English scientist, Alfred Russel Wallace. Wallace was a natural historian who spent much time in what is now Malaysia, studying wild plants and animals. In 1858 Wallace submitted a paper about natural selection to The Linnaean Society of London. Other British scientists were aware that Darwin was also writing a book about natural selection. Friends of Darwin urged him to summarize his ideas and send them at once to The Linnaean Society. Thus a paper entitled "On the Tendency of Species to Form Varieties, and on the Perpetuation of Varieties and Species by Natural Means of Selection," co-authored by Darwin and Wallace, was presented at a meeting of The Linnaean Society, in London, in July 1858. The realization that he was not alone in understanding the importance of natural selection stimulated Darwin to finish his book. On November 24, 1859, the first edition of his groundbreaking book, *On the Origin of Species by Means of Natural Selection,* was published. In this work, Darwin explained how the principle used by breeders to select the fastest racing pigeon could work in nature to produce new and diverse species.

Given the importance of Darwin's role in developing the theory of natural selection, it is worthwhile paying attention to the intellectual influences on his thinking. In addition to Chambers's *Vestiges,* three other books were influential. One of these was by William Paley, who supported the idea of a divine designer to explain the fact that animals were so well adapted to their habitat. Such adaptation, according to Paley, could not be due to chance but must be due to design. If there was design, there must, he reasoned, be a designer, and that designer must be the Christian God. Paley's book provoked Darwin to provide an alternative to the creationist view that could account for the highly adapted nature of animals.

Another important influence was Charles Lyell's *Principles of Geology.* Lyell's fluvial explanation for the evolution of the surface of the earth was similar to the gradual morphological change proposed by Lamarck and others as responsible for the modification of existing species into new ones.

Perhaps most influential of all was Thomas Malthus's *Essay on the Principle of Population,* published in 1798. Malthus, the founder of demography, or the study of population, wrote about the relationship between population growth and the material resources needed to support more people. His famous theory is that population grows exponentially, whereas resources increase arithmetically. Thus the world will increasingly undersupply its growing population, and famine, disease, and violence will result. Malthus's overall message is that competition is inevitable when resources are limited. Darwin adopted this competition model, linking resources and demand for them, as a foundation for his notion of how natural selection drives evolution (Ruse 1999).

Natural selection suggests that because resources are finite, and because of random variation, some individuals will be better than others at accessing those resources. That variant will then gain enough of an advantage that it will produce more offspring than the other individuals belonging to the same species. Biologists refer to this advantage as an increase in an animal's **fitness,** or the probability that an animal of a particular **genotype,** which is the genetic basis of a trait, will survive and reproduce. Darwin's notebooks are full of evidence about the effectiveness of the type of artificial selection used by animal and plant breeders. Darwin's genius was to think of a way in which the same process could occur naturally—a natural kind of "breeding" that would lead to improvements in a species over time.

Variation

Darwin also recognized the significance of the observation that no two individual animals are exactly alike: there are no perfect copies, or clones. Differences, even small ones such as leg length or strength, can be crucial in determining whether an individual can escape from a predator. The individuals that do escape survive to reproduce, passing on their genes to the next generation. The ones that do not survive

Left: After his five-year journey around the world on the HMS Beagle, *Charles Darwin became a laboratory scientist, using his house and garden as his lab. He collected evidence for his theory of natural selection from his own observations and through correspondence with people who bred plants and animals. Right: The naturalist Alfred Russel Wallace is less well-known than Darwin, but he also realized, independently, that natural selection was the mechanism driving evolution.* ■ Do some research to find out where Wallace made his observations that led to his ideas about natural selection. (Source: © Bettmann/CORBIS, left; © Hulton Archive/Getty Images, right)

make no genetic contribution to succeeding generations. Before Darwin, philosophers and scientists thought that each species had an optimum size and shape and that any variation was an unproductive deviation from the perfect form. Darwin recognized that the small differences among individuals within a species provide the raw material on which natural selection operates.

Heredity

Artificial selection works only if the offspring of a mating faithfully inherit the feature or features desired by the breeder. In natural selection, it works only if the offspring inherit the feature that confers greater fitness. Darwin understood that heredity existed, but he did not understand the mechanism for it. Nor did he realize that variation and heredity were part of a single genetic system.

While Darwin was finishing his book, a Catholic monk named Gregor Mendel was painstakingly working out the essential rules of inheritance in a monastery garden in Brno, in what is now the Czech Republic. The discipline of **genetics,** the field of biology that deals with heredity, was established on the basis of his deductions based on breeding experiments conducted on collections of artificially bred plants. In 1865 Mendel presented the results of his research to the Natural Science Society in Brno. His findings are summarized in two propositions known as Mendel's laws. We will discuss them in the next section when we consider how evolution works.

Mendel deduced the basic rules governing heredity, but he had no means of investigating what determined the color and texture of the peas, or the color of the flowers produced by the pea plants, in his monastery garden. The word **gene,** meaning the smallest unit of heredity, was not coined until 1909, several years after Mendel's pioneering experiments came to the notice of scientists. Mendel was, however, fortunate that his peas provided several examples of a simple one-to-one link between a gene and a trait, which is called a single-gene, or monogenic, effect. We now know that most traits are controlled by more than one gene; that is, they are *polygenic effects.* In addition, many genes, under different circumstances, can have more than one effect, and these are called *pleiotropic* effects.

These nineteenth-century advances in scientific thought carved out a new direction for thinking about humanity's past and present. The twentieth century heralded the contributions of scientists working at ever smaller levels of evidence—from cells to chromosomes and then to DNA. This new evidence, especially evidence from DNA,

provided new insights into how humanity has come to be what it is and about the relationship of humanity to other living creatures.

HOW EVOLUTION WORKS

This section provides an overview of how evolution works at two general levels. The first is **microevolution,** the evolutionary processes that operate at the level of the individual and over short periods of time. It includes all the short-term genetic changes (over tens and hundreds of years) that have occurred and still occur, generation-by-generation, within local populations. The second level is **macroevolution,** evolutionary processes that operate at large scale and over long periods of time. It includes long-term genetic changes (over hundreds of thousands of years) that have occurred in human evolutionary history.

Microevolution

The section describes the molecular mechanisms that are involved in sexual reproduction and small-scale evolution. Much of this discussion is rooted in Mendelian genetics.

Mendel's Two Laws

We now return to Mendel and his peas in order to understand the scientific view of microevolution. Mendel began his work with the important observation that the pea plants in his garden produced pods containing either yellow or green peas. He set out to understand the "rules" that determined traits such as pea color. First, he selected plants that produced either green or yellow peas. Then he bred within each pea color until all the cross-pollinations, or crosses, were producing plants that produced all yellow peas or all green peas. Next he crossed the plants that faithfully produced yellow peas with plants that faithfully produced green peas. Mendel found

FIGURE 3.5

The results of Gregor Mendel's experiments convinced him that pea color was determined by two sets of instructions, one dominant and one recessive.

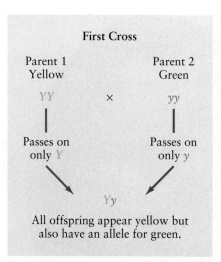

First Cross

All offspring appear yellow but also have an allele for green.

Y = yellow y = green

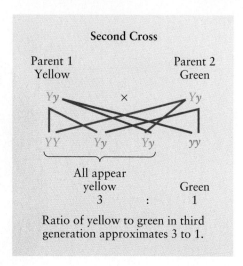

Second Cross

Ratio of yellow to green in third generation approximates 3 to 1.

that all the plants of the first cross produced yellow peas; none of the plants produced green peas, nor did any exhibit a mixture of yellow and green peas. Finally, Mendel took the plants that produced yellow peas and bred them with each other; this is called the second cross. This time, for every three plants with yellow peas, there was one that produced green peas. Mendel was painstaking. His notebooks show that the 3:1 yellow/green ratio was based on 6022 plants with yellow peas and 2001 plants with green peas.

Mendel reached two important conclusions. First, pea color is discrete. Mendel's plants produced peas that were either yellow or green; no plants produced peas that were shades in between. Mendel reasoned that a single mechanism could explain the dominance of yellow over green and the subsequent 3:1 yellow-to-green ratio. He suggested that a trait such as pea color was controlled by two sets of instructions, one inherited from the male parent plant and one from the female parent plant. Mendel proposed that his results could be explained if one of these sets of instructions is dominant and the other recessive. He suggested that for pea color, the instructions for yellow (Y) are dominant and those for green (y) are recessive. Mendel reasoned that if, in an individual plant, at least one of the two sets of instructions is the dominant version (YY or Yy), then that plant will produce yellow peas. The only circumstance under which a plant will produce green peas is when it has inherited recessive versions of the instructions from both parents (yy).

Mendel conducted similar experiments with the flowers of the pea plants. In this case he showed that purple flowers were dominant and white flowers recessive. The combination of two recessive instructions appears in only a quarter of the crosses (see Figure 3.5). The fact that pea and flower colors are discrete, and that they do not blend together, is known as Mendel's First Law or the *Law of Segregation* (see Figure 3.6).

Mendel's experiments showed that there is not always a one-to-one correspondence between an organism's **phenotype** (or **morphology**, meaning its size, shape, appearance, or internal structure)—in this case the color of peas or pea flowers—and its genotype (the genetic basis of a trait). Sometimes, different genotypes can produce the same phenotype. For example, plants that produce only purple flowers, the purple phenotype, can be either PP or Pp. However, the plants that produce white flowers, the white phenotype, can be only the genotype pp. Mendel found that other traits, such as the texture of the surface of the peas (smooth or wrinkled) behaved in the same way.

When Mendel studied pea and flower color, he was dealing with dichotomies of yellow/green or purple/white, which are called discontinuous traits. Most of the characteristics with which biological anthropologists work, however, are not

FIGURE 3.6
Mendel's laws.

Law of Segregation	Consequence
Each parent has a pair of genes (alleles) for traits such as pea color and flower color, but each gamete (egg or sperm) has only one of the two versions.	The appearance of the offspring depends on which of each pair of genes it inherits from its parents.

Law of Independent Assortment	Consequence
During the formation of gametes, chromosomes and the genes they carry are distributed randomly.	Traits on different chromosomes, such as pea color and flower color, vary independently.

dichotomous. For example, paleoanthropologists studying fossils deal with *continuous* traits, such as the size of a tooth or the thickness of a limb bone. These features have smooth, continuous distributions. Likewise, biological anthropologists who study contemporary human variation deal with continuous traits such as body weight and level of hormones in the blood. How do you get continuous curves if traits are discrete? There are two explanations. The first is that, unlike pea and flower color, many genes are involved in determining the size of a tooth or the thickness of a limb bone. What looks like a continuous curve really reflects the combination of the effects of many genes (see Figure 3.12 on p. 88). The second is that nongenetic factors such as nutrition also contribute to making a smooth curve.

From the results of Mendel's experiments, we know that genes may come in several versions called alleles. The genotype of an individual is made up of its own particular combination of alleles. If the versions, or alleles, for any trait inherited from the individual's parents are the same, then the genotype of that individual is described as homozygous. If the alleles are different, the individual is described as heterozygous. Each allele has an effect, but as Mendel discovered, some effects are stronger than others. In homozygous individuals, such as Mendel's *PP* and *pp* plants, there is no trial of strength between the alleles; the instructions they give are the same. However, in heterozygous individuals, one allele, the dominant allele, exerts the decisive influence on the phenotype. The allele whose effect is masked is the recessive allele. Remember Mendel's peas and his demonstration that what look to be similar versions of the same dominant phenotype, a purple flower color, can be produced by either of two combinations of alleles (*PP* and *Pp*), whereas the recessive phenotype, a white flower color, always has the same pair of alleles (*pp*). The form a particular animal or plant takes, which is called its overall phenotype, is the sum of the biological effects of all the genes in that individual, combined with the environmental effects the animal encounters during and after its development.

The next issue to consider is what carries the message. Genes do not exist in cells as individual units. Most genes exist in packages called **chromosomes.** Mammalian cells are composed of a dense nucleus and clear cytoplasm. The nucleus is dense because the chromosomes it contains are made up of a mixture of proteins and nucleic acid. Except for the male and female sex cells that unite at fertilization, the nuclei of modern human cells have 23 pairs of chromosomes. Twenty-two of these pairs, called autosomes, are common to both sexes. The pair of chromosomes that brings the total number of chromosomes up to 46 consists of the two sex chromosomes. Females have a pair of X chromosomes, whereas males have one X chromosome and one Y chromosome.

Every human being starts out as a single cell, the fertilized egg. How does each of us become an organism consisting of literally millions and millions of cells? The answer is the process called **mitosis,** whereby one somatic cell with 46 chromosomes

FIGURE 3.7

A short section of DNA showing how its two strands of nucleic acids are held together by chemical bonds between pairs of complementary bases.

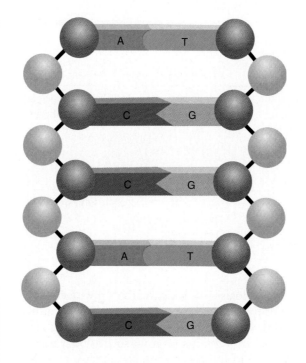

divides into two cells, during which time each strand of the genetic material replicates itself so that each daughter cell also has 46 chromosomes. In this way, mitosis maintains the number of chromosomes in the daughter cells. A different process, called **meiosis** or reduction division, is the process by which sex cells, or gametes, are produced. Meiosis reduces the number of chromosomes in the daughter cells by half. Thus, when two sex cells combine at the time of fertilization to form the zygote, the new individual will have the same number of chromosomes, 46, as the parents. At fertilization each parent provides one of each of the 22 pairs of autosomes, and either an X or a Y chromosome.

At the time of meiosis, the chromosomes that go into the sex cells (a process called sorting) do so independently. Thus, because modern humans have 23 pairs of chromosomes, there are 2^{23} (over 8 million) possible combinations of chromosomes in the sex cells produced by one parent. This finding, known as Mendel's Second Law or the *Law of Independent Assortment,* explains the independence of traits, and it is also the main reason why siblings of the same parents differ genetically.

DNA Enters the Scene

We now turn to the question of where genes are located. Genes in the nucleus must be in either one or the other of the two molecules, proteins and nucleic acids, that make up the chromosomes. Proteins are mostly large molecules with complex shapes that fulfill important functions in cells. Nucleic acids are made up of units called nucleotides. Each nucleotide consists of three components: a sugar, a phosphate group, and a base (see Figure 3.7). There are two types of nucleic acids, DNA and RNA. The sugar in DNA is deoxyribose, and that in RNA is ribose—hence their different names. The type of nucleic acid found in chromosomes is DNA.

In the early years of genetic research, most scientists thought that genes were in the protein component of the chromosomes, for it was clear that the genes had to be in some sort of code, and proteins seemed to be more complex (and thus more likely to carry a code) than nucleic acids. But a series of experiments conducted in the 1940s using bacteria showed conclusively that genetic information was encoded in the nucleic acid component of the chromosomes. Even though scientists had shown that DNA was the site of the genetic code, there was still much to explain. How is the genetic message encoded in the nucleic acids, and how is the code translated into instructions for the machinery that makes proteins? How do the genes make copies of themselves when cells divide?

The puzzle of how DNA copies itself was solved in the 1950s when American scientist James Watson and British scientist Francis Crick worked out the details of the structure of DNA. They reasoned that only the bases were variable enough to carry a coded message. There are two sorts of base: purines and pyrimidines. Each of these comes in two forms. At any one location on your DNA you have one purine (adenine, A, or guanine, G) or one pyrimidine (cytosine, C, or thymine, T) base. Experiments using extracts of DNA had previously shown that the amount of A always matched that of T, and the amount of G always matched that of C.

When X-rays were directed at crystals made from DNA molecules, the images suggested that DNA was made of two ribbons, or strands, lying side by side and arranged in the form of a helix of constant width. Pyrimidines are larger molecules than purines, so pairings made either of two pyrimidines or of two purines did not fit the X-ray crystallography data; such a helix would have been wider across pairs of the pyrimidine bases and narrower across the places on the helix where smaller purine molecules linked the two strands of DNA. Accordingly, Watson and Crick reasoned that a purine was paired with a pyrimidine, and vice versa. Thus A was always paired with T, and G with C (not A with C, or G with T) (see Figure 3.8).

In 1953 Watson and Crick sent, to the science journal *Nature*, a one-page letter in which they announced their ideas about how the sequence of bases in DNA carried the genetic code. They ended their letter by commenting, "It has not escaped our notice that the specific pairing we have postulated immediately suggests a possible copying mechanism for the genetic material" (Watson and Crick 1953:737). The elegance of their solution was that if the two component strands of DNA were peeled

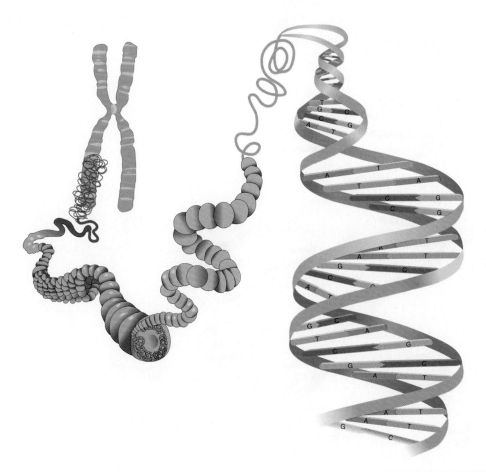

FIGURE 3.8
Nuclear DNA is coiled and packed tightly with proteins to form the chromosomes in each nucleus.

apart, as they are in cell division, then each one provides a template that, because of the A:T and G:C rule, will specify the correct order for the base pairs in any DNA copies. But how does the copying work? How is the genetic information in a single human fertilized egg copied again and again so that each of the billions of cells in our bodies has its own copy of our genetic code? When a cell divides, be it the fertilized egg, or a sex cell, or one of the cells in your skin, the DNA in each of the two daughter cells is a faithful copy of the DNA of the parent cell. The process that makes the DNA copies in the two daughter cells is known as DNA replication.

DNA replication works as follows. First, special proteins move down the double helix, unzipping it in much the same way as a closed zipper parts when you pull down the handle. Then the bases exposed on the now single strands of parental DNA specify the bases that are assembled to make the complementary strand of DNA. Wherever the parental strand has an A, the cell's machinery will insert a T into the growing strand. Wherever there is a G, a C will be inserted. This A:T and G:C assembly "rule" means that each of the two daughter cells should have a perfect copy of the DNA in the parental cell (see Figure 3.9).

DNA replication, like all processes, is not 100 percent reliable. Occasionally, the wrong base is added to the daughter DNA molecule. If the dividing cell is a skin cell, then there is always a risk that the single-base change will affect the behavior of the daughter cell such that it lacks the means to respond to the message to stop dividing.

FIGURE 3.9

As soon as the parental DNA is unzipped into single strands, complementary DNA is assembled to make two double-stranded daughter DNA molecules.

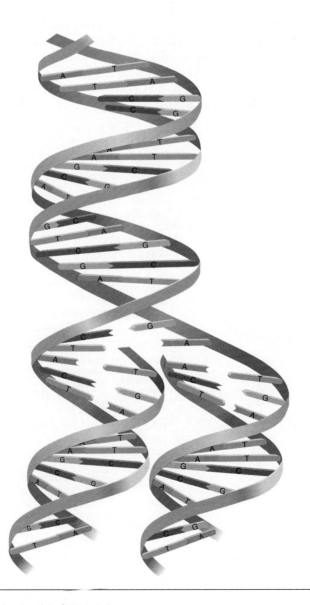

 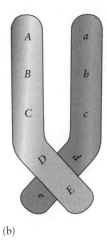 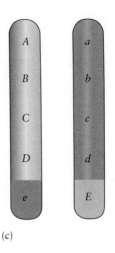

(a)   (b)   (c)

FIGURE 3.10
Recombination, the exchange of short pieces of parental chromosomes during meiosis, is one of the reasons why offspring differ genetically from their parents.

When this happens the cell becomes malignant, and the result is a potentially life-threatening cancer. When a replication error occurs in a sex cell, it does not always have a negative effect. In fact, most **mutations** (errors made when DNA is copied at the time of cell division) are neutral, and some are positive. If a sex cell bearing a positive mutation is involved in fertilization, then the offspring will have a slight advantage over others belonging to the same species. Geneticists refer to this advantageous behavior in the offspring as conferring greater genetic fitness on that individual.

Mutations occur constantly but not randomly. Most mutations occur in "hot spots" on chromosomes. Most have no effect on an individual's genetic fitness; these are called neutral mutations. Because mutations occur at a constant rate, the amount of accumulated genetic difference caused by mutations reflects how much time has elapsed since two daughter species evolved from an ancestral species. This is the principle of what scientists call the molecular clock. Mutations in sex cells, or gametes, are one source of the evolutionary novelties referred to as genetic variation. The other reason why "daughter" DNA may be subtly different from that of the parent is the recombination that occurs during sexual reproduction.

During meiosis, each of a component pair of chromosomes should remain intact. But sometimes, a section of a chromosome becomes detached and switches from one member of the pair to the other, a process called recombination (see Figure 3.10). The result of recombination is that offspring in the new generation have chromosomes that are not seen in either parent. The chances that the pieces switched between chromosomes would be the same in two offspring of the same parents are extremely small. This means that two offspring of the same parents are unlikely to have exactly the same chromosomes. These small differences do not necessarily have any effect on phenotype. But in some situations they lead to subtle, adaptively important phenotypic differences among the offspring. Of the two sources of genetic variation, mutations and recombinations, the latter provide most of the variation on which natural selection operates.

There is another reason why offspring of the same parents are different. Recall Mendel's Second Law, the Law of Independent Assortment, which says that when offspring inherit one of their 22 pairs of autosomal chromosomes from their parents, they do so randomly. The likelihood that this mix will be exactly the same in any two offspring of the same parents is extremely small. Thus the independent assortment of chromosomes is yet another reason why offspring of the same parents differ. However, unlike mutations and recombinations, which endure from generation to generation, the differences due to the independent assortment of chromosomes are ephemeral. Imagine shuffling two sets of 22 colored playing cards. The chances that you will end up with same combination the next time you shuffle them are very small. So it is with chromosomes. When they are reshuffled in the next generation, the chromosome combinations will be different. The genetic variation due to independent assortment has no staying power.

Linking Genes with Phenotypes

Selection, natural and artificial, acts on the phenotype. But you inherit your parent's genes, not their ability to see further, or to hear danger before others do, or to flee more rapidly from predators. How does the genetic message of an individual get translated into its phenotype? The short answer is that the genetic message and the phenotype are linked by proteins. Proteins are the components of the cellular machinery that constructs other molecules, such as sugars and fats, and ultimately the tissues that make up our bodies, such as muscles, nerves, bones, and teeth. Proteins consist of sequences of 20 types of amino acids. Although Watson and Crick's proposals for the structure of DNA explained how DNA could be replicated, they did not explain how the order of the nucleotide bases in a ribbon of DNA could provide blueprints for all the protein molecules that each of us can make.

A code in which two nucleotides coded for an amino acid (for example, AA, AT, AG, AC, TA) would not work. It would provide for only 4^2, or 16, of the 20 amino acids. But a code based on three nucleotides (for example, AAA, AAT, AAG, AAC, TAA), which is called a triplet code, would provide more than enough specificity, for it would result in 4^3, or 64, available combinations. In 1966, little more than a decade following Watson and Crick's letter to *Nature*, scientists confirmed that the genetic code is a triplet code. Sixty-one out of a possible 64 triplets, or triplet codons, specify an amino acid. The code is not ambiguous, because each triplet codes for only one amino acid (for example, GAA only codes for glutamic acid). However, it is redundant, for some amino acids are specified by more than one codon (for example, GAA and GAG both code for glutamic acid, so a switch from GAA to GAG would be a neutral mutation).

Thus the base component of a nucleotide is what makes it distinctive. A sequence of three nucleotides, or a triplet codon (for example, GAA or GAG), determines the type of amino acid, and the order of the amino acids determines the nature of the protein. This is the essence of the genetic code. The first part of the journey from DNA to a protein is called *transcription* because the DNA is read, or transcribed, into a type of ribonucleic acid, or RNA, called messenger RNA (see Figure 3.11). Then comes *translation,* when the messenger RNA moves to another part of the cell where its sequence of bases is translated into a string of amino acids that makes up the protein specified by that particular gene.

The scale of the system devoted to carrying the genetic code is awesome. Human nuclear DNA consists of 3 billion ($3 \cdot 10^9$) complementary pairs (called base pairs) of nucleotides (for example, A matched with T, or G with C). In modern humans, nuclear DNA is arranged in 23 pairs of DNA molecules that vary in length by a factor of five. Each of these DNA molecules is a double helix that consists of two strands of DNA joined at each pair of complementary bases by chemical bonds. The short-

FIGURE 3.11
Proteins are produced within a cell by a combination of transcription and translation.

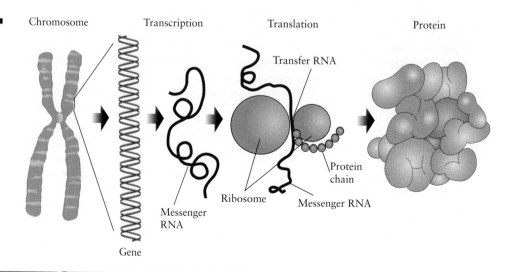

Chromosome   Transcription   Translation   Protein

Transfer RNA

Protein chain

Ribosome   Messenger RNA

Messenger RNA

Gene

est of these long and highly coiled DNA molecules contains 50 million (5.10^6) base pairs, the longest 250 million (250.10^6) base pairs. Together with its protein superstructure, each pair of these helical DNA molecules makes up one of our chromosomes. The DNA in a mammalian cell contributes barely 0.25 percent of its total weight, yet the total length of the uncoiled DNA in the longest chromosome would be close to 4 inches. A typical animal cell contains more than a yard of tightly coiled DNA. However, only about 5 percent of our DNA codes for genes. The function of the remaining 95 percent is largely unknown, but scientists do know that some of it is involved in controlling when genes are switched on and off.

Each nucleated cell in the body, except for a sperm or an egg, no matter whether it is in the brain or in the skin, has a complete set of nuclear genes called the nuclear genome. What type of cell it becomes, and what functions it subsequently carries out, however, are determined by the particular mix of genes activated in that cell. Active genes are those that are switched on, or expressed, in that cell. Genes are turned on and off during development, and the functions of an adult cell can also be switched on and off by some of the non-gene DNA.

Male germ cells consist almost entirely of chromosomes from the nucleus, whereas the egg contains chromosomes and some cytoplasm. The importance of this difference emerges when we consider the inheritance of the portion of the DNA that is found in small organelles, called mitochondria, within the cytoplasm of all cells, including the egg. Scientists call this mitochondrial DNA, or mtDNA, to distinguish it from the DNA in the nucleus, which is called nuclear DNA. There are many more maternal mitochondria in the egg than paternal mitochondria in the sperm, so mtDNA is essentially inherited entirely via the maternal line.

Unlike nuclear DNA, mtDNA is not bound to proteins. It exists in the form of small loops that are only about 16,800 base pairs in length. Each mitochondrion has between 5 and 10 of these loops, and each cell may have as many as 1000 mitochondria, yet mtDNA still makes up only about 1 percent of the total DNA within a cell. The genes in mtDNA mostly specify proteins involved in the basic activities that are required for the care and maintenance of any cell, no matter what its special function is. The functioning of mtDNA seems to be resistant to minor differences in the sequence of the bases, so this makes mtDNA a good place to look for variations in DNA sequences that accumulate purely as a function of time, with little or no selection effect.

A gene determines the nature of a particular protein molecule. Genes occupy discrete segments of DNA, either on a chromosome or in the mtDNA. These segments are referred to as a gene's *locus*, or place (plural, *loci*). In the nuclear genome, chromosomes come in pairs, so nuclear genes have two loci. Mitochondrial genes have a single locus. Human beings are estimated to have about 25,000–30,000 genes. Some, called *structural genes,* code for proteins that are the components of things like muscle and bone. Others, called *regulatory genes,* code for proteins that control processes. Genes vary in size from fewer than twenty base pairs to many thousands of base pairs. Sometimes there is a simple one-to-one link between a gene and a biological effect; such an arrangement is called a single-gene, or monogenic, system. Most of the traits that vary among individual modern humans, such as stature, are controlled by many genes and hence are called polygenic systems (see Figure 3.12 on p. 88).

DNA is central to animal and plant life. DNA determines the nature of the proteins, and proteins determine what types of cells we have in our bodies and also, to a large extent, control what size and shape we are. The environment, including culture, influences human growth and development, but many of those influences are mediated by DNA.

DNA is also the basis of heredity. Offspring resemble their parents because each parent contributes half of the offspring's DNA. DNA is the thread that runs through and connects generations of the same family. DNA also connects us to the rest of the Tree of Life. Modern humans share approximately 99 percent of our DNA with a chimpanzee, 90 percent with a mouse, and 40 percent with a banana. Why? The reason is that all of us (even the banana!) shared a common ancestor in the distant past.

THINKING OUTSIDE THE BOX

Come up with some ideas about what modern humans share with bananas, mice, and chimpanzees other than DNA.

FIGURE 3.12
A plot of the expressions of a trait that is determined by many genes, such as stature, produces a smooth curve.

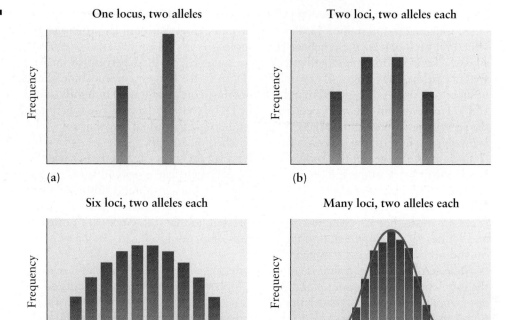

One locus, two alleles

(a)

Two loci, two alleles each

(b)

Six loci, two alleles each

(c)

Many loci, two alleles each

(d)   Stature

Genes that are located near each other on the same chromosome tend to change, and to be selected for, as a group rather than individually. These are called linked genes. A group of genes that consistently appears together is called a haplogroup, and organisms that share the same groups of genes are said to have the same *haplotype*. Haplotype variation is an important tool for studying the evolutionary basis of the modern human variation that we consider in Chapter 10 (see Methods Close-Up box on p. 90).

Evolution within Populations

So far, we have been discussing how genetics works at the levels of the cell and within individuals and their immediate offspring, subjects known as biochemical or Mendelian genetics. We now shift to considering how evolution works at the level of a **population,** which is defined as a group of potentially interbreeding individuals within a species, a subject area called population genetics. What matters within populations is the frequency and distribution of individuals with particular versions of genes.

In theory, it is possible for a population to be in a steady state with respect to evolution. In other words, the frequency of alleles does not change over time. This state is called the Hardy-Weinberg equilibrium. Such a steady state would exist if the alleles did not change (that is, there were no mutations), if individuals in the population mated randomly, if there were no selection, if the population were large enough to be theoretically infinite, *and* if no alleles were lost or gained. This ideal steady state, though, never exists in reality. Variation is regularly and randomly introduced into the system by mutations, which alone have little impact unless they spread within a population. Two processes encourage the spread of mutation: selection and genetic drift.

Selection, as we have seen, can be artificial or natural. In artificial selection, breeders accelerate the pace of evolution by deliberately bringing about the opposite of random mating. Think of the trouble that breeders of prize animals take to ensure that their strain of dog, cat, or horse is strengthened by choosing the right mate. Stallions that sire champion racehorses are sold for millions of dollars because their genes have a high probability of producing a race-winning phenotype.

For over three hundred years, the English racehorse has been selectively bred to produce the fastest breed of horse in the world over any distance greater than one-quarter of a mile. Descended from three imported Arabian stallions and some domestic mares, the present generation is the result of "selective breeding"; every mating since 1791 has been recorded in the *General Stud Book*. Along with this process, English racing society emerged and evolved as well (Cassidy 2002).

Cultural anthropologist Rebecca Cassidy conducted fieldwork related to thoroughbred breeding and racing in Newmarket, England, the center of British thoroughbred racing. She comments, "Riding across Newmarket Heath on some shiny specimen of thoroughbred perfection I often thought to myself, 'I must be the luckiest anthropologist ever' " (Cassidy 2002:vi). Studying horseracing as an anthropologist enabled her to make several dreams come true: riding racehorses, taking a yearling through the sales ring, seeing a thoroughbred foal born, and leading a victorious horse into the winner's circle.

Cassidy's relationship with her informants in Newmarket was influenced by the passion for horses that she shared with them, and her research would not have been possible without this shared passion. She learned about the thoroughbred world by participating in it in diverse ways—as a guest of an owner at events, as a trainer's assistant, as a "lass" (jockey), and as a lowly hand in the stable yard. She recalls that as she was mucking out a stall one cold morning, covered with various kinds of horse secretions and wondering why she was there in the first place, her boss yelled, "Rebecca! Get your anthropological arse out here!" (p. ix).

In her research, Cassidy paid attention to how people's perceptions of the "nature" of horses was related to their breeding, the process of training and racing thoroughbreds, bloodstock auctions, and the huge industry of betting on horses. In addition, it involved the study of a particular class system consisting of owners, breeders, trainers, racing administrators, lads, farriers (blacksmiths), stud-workers, and work-riders.

CROSSING THE FIELDS

Breeding and Culture in "the Sport of Kings"

A horse race at Ascot, England, attended by members of the elite. Rebecca Cassidy's research shows parallels between English perceptions about breeding and quality in race horses and in humans. ■ Consider how these perceptions might be affected by the fact that increasing numbers of non-English people, notably people from the Middle East, are becoming involved in "the sport of kings." (Source: © 2004 Getty Images)

Using DNA Evidence to Trace the Origins of the Indigenous People of the Andaman Islands

THE ANDAMAN ISLANDS are a string of islands in the Bay of Bengal that belong to India. Available archaeological data do not provide clear evidence of when modern humans first settled there. For unknown numbers of centuries, though, many of the islands were inhabited by people who fished, gathered, and hunted for their livelihood. In the early stages of European exploration and colonization, descriptions of the indigenous people of the Andamans included mention of their having tails and being cannibals who would kill and eat anyone who landed on their islands. During the eighteenth century, when European countries were expanding trade routes to the Far East, the Andaman Islands were of major strategic importance as a stopping place. Colonization of the islands was not easy, however. The seas around the islands are treacherous, and much of the islands' coastline is densely covered with mangrove trees. In addition, the indigenous people were highly skilled with their bows and arrows and could easily pick off new arrivals as they attempted to land.

European attempts to establish colonies failed until the later eighteenth and early nineteenth centuries, when the British first managed to colonize localized parts of one or two islands. In addition to securing the Andamans as a haven for British ships, they established a notorious prison there for insurgents in India fighting against British rule. The image of the indigenous people as murderous cannibals added to the dread of being imprisoned in the Andamans, because any prisoner who tried to escape would be likely to meet a worse fate in the jungle.

In 1789, when the British made their first attempt to establish a settlement, the total indigenous population was estimated at about 6000 people, and the islands were theirs alone (Miller 1997). Now, more than 200 years later, over 400,000 people live on the islands as a result of migration from the Indian mainland. And the total number of indigenous people is

A cultural anthropologist, Cassidy was interested in studying people, their perceptions, and their social relationships. She learned that in Newmarket, all of these are intimately related to horses and to breeding. A pervasive explanation for ability or talent in both horses and people is breeding and pedigree. Breeding and pedigree are used to explain a successful horse—it has "good blood." They are also used to explain a well-bred horse's failure—it was an accident, a flaw, even too much fine blood perhaps requiring more "rough" blood in future matings. In the realm of humans, blood is the explanation for a connection to the racing world. Some of Cassidy's informants invented a blood connection between her and racing through an imagined Irish line.

The social aristocrats of the racing world are the owners, and their position is thought to be based on superior blood and breeding. But not everyone born into an elite racing family is necessarily considered a member of the racing community. If such people fail to maintain a connection to racing, their blood relatives draw a line through their place on the family tree. Again, the explanation for this failure would be found in blood: an accident, a flaw, or too much fine blood.

This system of blood explanations for both horses and humans is now being challenged. In terms of horses, the possibility of cloning may destroy the traditional concept of pedigree, because individual horses would no longer be unique. In terms of the human aristocracy of horse owners, the increasing trend toward ownership by foreigners, especially wealthy oil sheikhs from the Middle East, also threatens the meaning and stability of blood as the explanation for success or failure. ■

FOOD FOR THOUGHT

- In your cultural experience, is "breeding" or individual agency and experience more likely to be mentioned as an explanation for the success or failure of an individual human? Would the same apply to a nonhuman?

about 400. This dramatic decline is both the direct and the indirect result of British colonialism, which brought contagious diseases, increased violence among groups, and prompted outright killing by the British of Andaman people who resisted their land being taken from them.

From the time of earliest observation of Andamanese people by outsiders, they have been objects of curiosity because of their physical appearance. They are much shorter than the majority populations of neighboring South and Southeast Asia. In addition, their hair forms small, tight curls close to their head. They look more like members of indigenous populations of southern Africa and of remote and hilly regions of southern India and Southeast Asia, including Malaysia and the Philippines. These groups have been referred to by outsiders as "pygmies" and "negritos."

Their languages, which also seem to be distinct from languages elsewhere in Asia, are another focus of anthropological inquiry. As noted in a government survey of the people and their customs, "The Andamanese languages are extremely interesting . . . on account of their isolated development. No connexion with any other group has yet been traced" (Temple 1909 [1994]:13).

There are now four surviving clusters of indigenous Andamanese. The smallest group, just a few dozen people, is made up of the last members of the so-called "Great Andamanese" populations. They live on a small island near the Port Blair capital area and in what is essentially a reservation area. North and Middle Andaman Islands were formerly populated by several different groups of "Great Andamanese" peoples, but there are no indigenous people on these islands any more. The so-called Jarawa, numbering perhaps 200, live in a reserved area on the southwest portion of South Andaman. The Onge, around 100 in number, live in one corner of Little Andaman. Another 100 people or so live on Sentinel Island, and they are called the Sentinelese. There has been the least contact with these people; no one from the outside has gotten much closer than arrow-range of their shore in the past century.

Anthropologists have recently used genomic evidence to trace the spread of modern humans out of Africa throughout the rest of the world (the topic of Chapter 8). An intriguing part of this story is the settlement of the Andaman Islands. Where, anthropologists ask, did the Andamanese people fit into the picture of modern humanity's global migrations? Is their similarity in appearance to southern African indigenous peoples due to a shared recent common ancestor or was it independently acquired?

A second area of inquiry is related to reports from the colonial era indicating both physical (phenotypic) differences and cultural differences within the indigenous populations at that time, the main differences being between those living in North and Middle Andamans and those living in the southern islands. Two hypotheses have been proposed to explain these differences: they result from divergent evolution of a single immigrant stock, or they result from two different waves of in-migrating people.

If DNA could be obtained from the indigenous people of the Andamans, it might be possible to address both issues. We could answer the question about their links with African populations, and we would learn whether the north/south variations within the indigenous populations are the result of variation that has accumulated following a single colonization or result from several waves of settlement of different populations.

Access to the indigenous people, however, is restricted by the Indian gov-

Andaman Islands

North Andaman

Middle Andaman

South Andaman

Sentinel Island ● Port Blair

Little Andaman

One of the many uninhabited islands in the Andamans, with typically dense coverage of mangrove trees. The Indian government is encouraging people from the mainland to settle in the Andamans. One result is widespread deforestation. ■ Visit the web site *www.andaman.org* for information on the Andaman Islands. (Source: Barbara Miller)

ernment. Thus, collecting blood or even hair from living Andamanese people for sampling DNA is not possible at this time. An alternative approach is to use skeletal evidence housed in museum collections. Some nineteenth-century anthropologists collected skeletons of the Andamanese, and the remains of more than fifty individuals are in the Natural History Museum in London. Recently, scientists selected eleven relatively well-preserved Andamanese skeletons from this collection for analysis (Endicott et al. 2003). They examined the teeth from these skeletons to see whether there was sufficient DNA to enable them to be compared with the DNA from living populations. They concentrated on two parts of the mitochondrial genome (mtDNA), the hypervariable (HRV1) and the protein-coding regions.

First, the results suggest that any phenotypic resemblance between the indigenous Andamanese people and modern African populations was independently acquired and not due to a recently shared evolutionary history. Evidence from the protein-coding region of the mtDNA suggests that the Andamans were colonized by people from the eastern part of the Indian subcontinent. Second, the evidence suggests that indigenous Andamanese people are the survivors of a single immigration event that probably took place no earlier than 40,000 years ago.

Ethnographic research in the early twentieth century often involved photography. This girl wears the skull of her deceased sister. Indigenous people of the Andamans revere the bones of their dead relatives and would not want them to be taken away, studied, or displayed in a museum. (Source: A. R. Radcliffe-Brown, *The Andaman Islands*. Cambridge: Cambridge University Press, 1992)

FOOD FOR THOUGHT

- At this time, the indigenous people of the Andaman Islands are not able to protect their cultural property rights, including their ancestors' skeletal material that is housed in collections overseas. Should scientists be able to study the Andamanese people's ancestors' bones without their knowledge or consent?

Natural selection is a process that constantly screens new and existing genetic variation. It cannot, by itself, generate novel variation; only mutations and the recombination of genes can do that. Natural selection works because "fitter" individuals are selectively advantaged, with the result that their pattern of alleles is represented in greater numbers in subsequent generations. Fitness, in this technical sense, is the probability that animals of a particular genotype will survive and reproduce. For example, if the expression of the A molecule in the ABO blood group system increases genetic fitness, then both the AA and AO genotypes should be equally favored by natural selection. Natural selection cannot discriminate between different genotypes if they result in the same phenotype.

Natural selection does not always result in the characteristics of the population shifting away from the average. For example, one version of natural selection, *stabilizing selection*, consists of selection against the extremes of the range of values for that species. Stabilizing selection is probably the mechanism that maintains stasis in one of the two varieties of macroevolution (discussed in the next section), called the punctuated equilibrium model.

Not all evolution within a population is due to selection, either natural or artificial. Much is due to chance, and chance is particularly important in small groups.

When an epidemic or famine, for example, causes a population to decline in number, some genotypes, by sheer chance, will get through the "bottleneck" in larger numbers than others. If the population subsequently expands, these survivor genes will be at a higher frequency than before. This process is called the *bottleneck effect* (see Figure 3.13). A similar change in gene frequency occurs when a small part of the original population becomes isolated. Again by chance, some genes will be at higher frequency in these isolates than in the original population. The general effect is called *genetic drift*; the particular influence of chance on isolates is called the *founder effect*.

Macroevolution

Macroevolution is the large-scale evolutionary history of any group of organisms. We discuss three examples of macroevolution in this section: speciation, adaptive radiations, and extinction.

Speciation

Speciation is the production of new species either by the splitting of an existing species into two new species or by the transformation of an existing species into a different descendant. Among mammals, including primates, there are two main ways in which a new species can be generated: allopatric and parapatric speciation. In allopatric speciation, a small part of an existing species undergoes so much microevolution—usually with the help of some isolating mechanism such as a change in the course of a large river or a change in climate that eliminates forests between the isolated population and the main population—that it eventually becomes distinct from the parent species. In parapatric speciation, speciation occurs at the boundary between two distinct regional populations. Although interbreeding occurs within the boundary zone (the resulting offspring are called hybrids), on either side of the boundary each group behaves as though it were a reproductively isolated species.

Some researchers think that new species are the result of gradual change involving the whole population. This point of view is called the phyletic gradualism model of evolution, and the form of gradual speciation associated with it is termed anagenesis. Others see speciation as being due to bursts of rapid evolutionary change concentrated in a subset of the population. In this model, most morphological evolution occurs at the time of allopatric speciation. This rapid-change model also suggests that between these bursts of evolution there should be no sustained trends in the

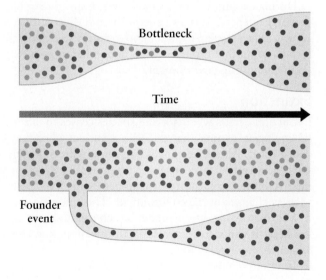

FIGURE 3.13
When a population declines dramatically, the genes that make it through the bottleneck are not a random sample. The same process applies, when a small number of individuals are separated from the main population through a founder event.

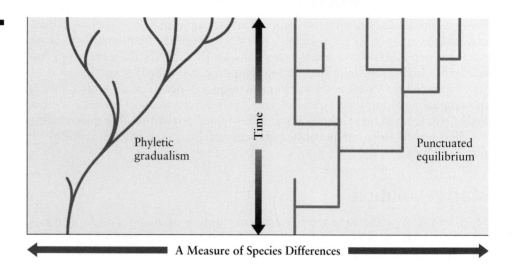

FIGURE 3.14
The phyletic gradualism and punctuated equilibrium models for evolution.

direction of morphological evolution, just "random walk" fluctuations in morphology (see Figure 3.14).

The term *stasis* is used to describe these periods of morphological stability. The pattern of long periods of stasis separated by episodes of species generation is called the punctuated-equilibrium model. Species formation in the rapid-change model is called cladogenesis—literally, "speciation by splitting." In some circumstances, speciation may be due to large-scale changes in the genotype brought about by rearrangements in the chromosomes. Researchers think that such large-scale changes may have occurred when modern humans split off from the other apes (Navarro and Barton 2003), a topic we discuss in Chapter 6.

Adaptive Radiations

One way in which taxa differ is in whether their members are *generalists* or *specialists*. Generalists use and tolerate a wide range of environments, and they eat a variety of foods. Specialists are restricted to a narrow range of habitats, and their diet is usually limited to certain kinds of foods, such as leaves or fruits. Given these differences, generalists and specialists are likely to have different evolutionary histories. When climate change affects the habitat, specialist taxa, occupying their narrow niches, are more likely to become extinct, yet they are also more likely to respond to changes in the paleoenvironments by speciating. Generalist lineages tend to speciate less.

During evolutionary history, some groups of taxa have undergone periods of particularly intensive species generation and diversification. These **adaptive radiations** appear to be associated with an opportunity to exploit a new environment. For example, when another group declines in number or goes extinct, new opportunities open up in an existing environment.

Extinction

Extinction occurs when a living species ceases to exist. In the fossil record, paleoanthropologists assume that a species is extinct when they can no longer find fossil evidence for it. All species, including ours, will ultimately become extinct. What is at issue is whether the causes of a species's extinction are to be found within its microevolutionary history or whether extinctions are determined by external events such as changes in the environment. This question can be studied in the laboratory by varying the conditions under which rapidly evolving organisms such as fruit flies are kept. It can also be investigated by comparing changes in the fossil record with evidence about past climates.

In later chapters, we will discuss examples of species of early human ancestors that are now extinct. We will also consider the possible role of humans in leading to the extinction of other animals, especially large game animals. This topic returns us in an interesting way to the biblical narrative discussed earlier in the chapter. According to the Bible, God would not have created animals that would become extinct. The fact of species extinction, established in the nineteenth century, was one more reason why doubt was cast on the Biblical narrative about the origin of humanity.

Alternative Explanations for Humanity

This chapter has presented scientific explanations for the Tree of Life and humanity's place on it. It does not address or make judgments about matters of religious faith held by people who, for one reason or another, are opposed to a scientific, evolution-based explanation for humanity. Among North American Christians, some people support what is called **creationism,** the Bible-based belief that all species date from the Day of Creation and have always been the way they are now. The roots of creationism are in the biblical literalism that flourished in Europe until the mid-nineteenth century. Creationism has many manifestations. We consider one historical instance and then the modern transformation.

The Argument from Design

Earlier in this chapter, we mentioned William Paley as a writer who inspired Darwin to come up with a scientific alternative to his interpretation. Published in 1802, Paley's *Natural Theology* was a defense of the biblical version of creation. Paley used the example of a watch and employed a method of argument called teleology. A teleological argument explains a future outcome by what has happened in the past.

Paley suggested that an elaborate outcome, such as a watch, means that there must have been a watch designer and a watchmaker in the past. An example from the living world would be that an elaborate outcome such as the complex eye of a mammal means there must have been a designer of the mammal eye and a maker of that eye in the past. Philosophers call this an "argument from design" (Ruse 2003:41).

Science and Intelligent Design

Recently, the argument against scientific evolution has changed its focus and is now framed as scientific, not religious or philosophical. Some opponents of Darwinian evolution claim that "intelligent design" is a scientific theory that should be placed alongside, and even displace, evolution as the most probable explanation for the Tree of Life.

Supporters of intelligent design emphasize a principle called *irreducible complexity.* This approach suggests that some parts of life are so complex that they would not function unless all the parts were present. Their complexity also means that a process such as evolution, which depends on chance events, could not have resulted in a sophisticated structure like the mammalian eye.

Biological anthropologists who accept the scientific approach agree that organisms are complex. They point out, however, that the fossil record suggests that organisms did not become complex instantly. Instead, organisms accumulated complexity over time—sometimes immense periods of time—under the influence of processes such as natural selection. Natural selection, they say, is sufficient to explain the diversity and complexity of modern humanity. The natural world, including humanity, did not need a designer.

In the United States, supporters of what is called creation science claim that it provides a serious scientific alternative to evolutionary interpretations of our origins. No one doubts the religious sincerity of creation scientists, but their explanations are not convincing as science. Evolution is consistent with scientific facts, but creation science is not. Creationism is a faith-based alternative to evolutionary interpretations of human origins, but despite the name of one of its manifestations, it is not science.

▪ WHAT is the scientific view about humanity?

The links between humanity and the rest of the natural world have been recognized at least since the time of the classical Greek and Roman philosophers, but the scientific evidence for this view has accumulated largely in the past two centuries. In Europe, a literal interpretation of the Bible was the predominant view between the fifth and nineteenth centuries. Humanity was thought to have arisen through divine creation, and humans were viewed as being at the top of the Great Chain of Being. This view made no allowance for extinct creatures or for any evolutionary change within species. The Renaissance and the age of exploration provided the foundation for scientific thinking, which relies on observation, hypothesis formation and revision, and further observation in order to understand phenomena. From the fifteenth century onward, accumulating evidence led scientists to question the validity of an explanation for human origins that relied on a literal interpretation of the Biblical narrative.

▪ HOW does the concept of evolution explain humanity?

By the middle of the nineteenth century, substantial evidence had accumulated to support the theory of evolution. Evolution needs three things: natural selection, variation, and heredity. Variation occurs because mutation and recombination ensure that no two individuals are exactly alike. Mendelian genetics provided the basic rules about heredity and the inheritance of variation. The mechanism of inheritance is the genetic code that is encrypted within DNA. The extent to which modern humans and other animals share the same DNA provides the best evidence that humanity is part of the Tree of Life. The genomes of a modern human and a chimpanzee are more similar than those of a chimp and a gorilla. Thus, just as DNA is the thread that connects different generations of the same animal, it also connects humanity to the rest of the natural world.

▪ HOW does evolution work?

Evolution works at two levels: microevolution and macroevolution. Microevolution works at the level of the individual and includes short-term changes within local populations. Macroevolution consists of long-term processes that have occurred in evolutionary history, such as the emergence of new species, adaptive radiations, and extinction. Starting in the 1950s, discoveries about DNA showed how small changes in the structure and function of molecules can produce changes in the structure and function of an animal. These small changes in the structure of DNA, when reflected in the phenotype, provide the differences in performance upon which natural selection can act.

KEY CONCEPTS

Peter J. Bowler. *Life's Splendid Drama*. Chicago: Chicago University Press, 1996. This book is the story of the efforts of the scientists who have tried to reconstruct the Tree of Life—in other words, the history of life on earth. The first hundred pages deal with the history of the general ideas about the Tree of Life, and the rest of the book traces the history of the ideas about the major groups of animals. It includes a review of the history of biogeography.

Robin M. Henig. *The Monk in the Garden*. Boston: Houghton Mifflin, 2000. Gregor Mendel has received relatively little attention from historians of science. This book is based on careful research about Mendel and his famous experiments. The second half of the book deals with how Mendel's work was rediscovered and became the basis for modern genetics.

Evelyn Fox Keller. *The Century of the Gene*. Cambridge, MA: Harvard University Press, 2000. Keller chronicles the history of the research that culminated in the discovery of the chemical basis for genes. The book assumes some knowledge of science.

Horace F. Judson. *The Eighth Day of Creation*. New York: Simon and Schuster, 1980. This book traces the discovery of the basis for the genetic code. Judson interviewed many of the leading scientists, and the book provides a detailed account of the research that preceded the unraveling of the structure and function of DNA.

Ernst Mayr. *What Evolution Is*. New York: Basic Books, 2001. This text, which assumes some knowledge of biology, provides an introduction to the principles of, and evidence for, evolution.

John A. Moore. *From Genesis to Genetics*. Berkeley, CA: University of California Press, 2002. This book explains the controversy between scientific evolution and creationism. The author encourages science and religion to do the work for which each is uniquely qualified.

John A. Moore. *Science as a Way of Knowing*. Cambridge, MA: Harvard University Press, 1993. A history of how biological thinking and research developed, this book begins with the Greeks and then sets out the major developments in biological research.

Mark Pagel. *Encyclopedia of Evolution*. Oxford: Oxford University Press, 2002. This encyclopedia contains detailed articles about the main elements of evolution. It covers all the major topics, including Mendelian and population genetics, natural selection, and micro- and macroevolutionary mechanisms.

Robert T. Pennock, ed. *Intelligent Design: Creationism and Its Critics*. Cambridge, MA: MIT Press, 2002. The author presents the arguments for and against Intelligent Design Creationism.

Mark Ridley. *Evolution*. Oxford: Blackwell, 2003. This widely used textbook for courses about evolution includes both evolutionary theory and the evidence for evolution.

Michael Ruse. *The Darwinian Revolution*. Chicago: Chicago University Press, 1999. This history of evolutionary thought begins by describing the state of ideas about evolution before Darwin. Then it reviews the impact of Charles Darwin's ideas about evolutionary mechanisms on his contemporaries and those that followed.

P. Tort. *Darwin and the Science of Evolution*. New York: Abrams, 2001. This short, illustrated book provides an introduction to Darwin's life and explains how he developed the ideas that shape current scientific thinking about evolution.

Christopher P. Toumey. *God's Own Scientists: Creationists in a Secular World*. New Brunswick, NJ: Rutgers University Press, 1994. A cultural anthropologist reports on the results of his long-term research project among contemporary Christian creationists in North Carolina in the 1980s. The book includes historical context on reactions to evolutionary theory in the United States during the nineteenth and early twentieth centuries. Most of the book, though, focuses on the variety of creationist groups and thinking in North Carolina and includes disputes with schools about the teaching of evolution.

THE BIG QUESTIONS

- HOW do anthropologists study humanity's past?
- HOW do anthropologists study contemporary people?
- WHAT challenges do anthropologists face in their research?

CHAPTER 4

Research Methods in Anthropology

*Anthropologists Robert Bailey and Nadine Peacock, members of a Harvard
University fieldwork team, conversing with some Ituri people who live in the
rainforests of the eastern part of the Democratic Republic of Congo. (Source:
© Tronick/Anthro-Photo File)*

Many people have an interest in the site of Çatalhöyük in central Turkey (see the photograph on p. 260), an important site of early farming, urbanization, and mural art, dating between the seventh and sixth millennia BCE. Some are collectors of Turkish kilims (woven carpets) who want to know about past cultures in the region. Others are fascinated by the paintings and sculptures. Members of the so-called "Goddess Movement" believe the site was important in the emergence of Goddess worship. Local people who live in nearby villages are curious about what the site can reveal about their past, but they are generally more concerned about making an everyday living.

Archaeologist Ian Hodder, formerly of Cambridge University and now at Stanford University, heads the archaeological work at Çatalhöyük. He is increasingly convinced that archaeologists need to be engaged with the diverse social groups interested in the site, rather than concentrating only on the excavation and the artifacts. To that end, he tries to keep communication lines open about the archaeological work going on at Çatalhöyük through a web site (*http://catal.arch.cam.ac.uk/catal/html*). This web site provides a virtual tour of Çatalhöyük and other information.

We urge you to visit the site and take a look at a 1998 interchange in which a woman involved in the Goddess Movement, one Anita Louise from the southwest United States, questions Hodder about certain interpretations of Çatalhöyük. She asks whether distinct groups of people lived there and, if so, whether they had different patterns of spiritual beliefs. Noting that one report distinguishes between sacred spaces and domestic spaces, she raises the possibility that the people may have made no such distinctions—that perhaps sacredness permeated all domains. She offers some interpretations of her own about various artifacts and what they might mean. She asks for any information that would shed light on women's lives and roles. And she expresses her deep appreciation to Hodder for making information about the site available to the public through the web site. In reply, Hodder attempts to respond to her several points and he thanks her for her comments.

Anthropologists use many different methods to explore the breadth of humanity's past and present. In each of anthropology's four fields, research covers the domains of data collection, analysis, and representation or interpretation (see Figure 4.1). In some fields, research may also involve preservation of one's findings.

A core method used in all four fields of anthropology for collecting information is **fieldwork,** or research at a site where humanity lived in the past or lives in the present. Anthropologists also conduct research in laboratories, with museum collections, and in historical archives (see Figure 4.2). In addition to the many methods used for collecting data, anthropologists use a variety of methods for data analysis and preservation. Whether they are collecting, analyzing, or preserving data, and whether they are using a more scientific or a more humanistic approach, all anthropologists must follow ethical guidelines set out by the discipline.

This chapter discusses many of the research methods anthropologists use. Separate sections consider research on humanity's past and research on contemporary humanity, because there are major differences between learning about humanity through remains and studying living people. (Discussion of methods in paleoanthropology is

FIGURE 4.1
Research activities in anthropology.

Data collection
Analysis and interpretation
Representation
Preservation
Community participation

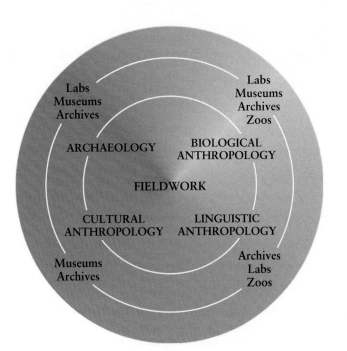

FIGURE 4.2
Data collection in the four fields.

included in Chapter 6 and on linguistic anthropology in Chapter 17; Methods Close-Up boxes in each chapter offer in-depth information about particular methods). In the last section of this chapter, we address two challenges that anthropologists face in doing research: danger in the field and linking research to the communities where it takes place.

STUDYING HUMANITY'S PAST

In this section, we discuss techniques for obtaining evidence about humanity's past, from several million years ago to the recent past. We discuss the major forms of evidence, how to retrieve the evidence, methods for dating the evidence, and ways of preserving the evidence.

Types of Data about Humanity's Past

Paleoanthropologists and archaeologists collect, analyze, interpret, represent, and preserve evidence of many varieties in their study of humanity's past. They rely mainly on seven types of data (see Figure 4.3). Fossils and artifacts are the two most important.

FIGURE 4.3
Seven types of data for studying humanity's past.

Fossils
Artifacts
Features
Sites
Documents
Genetic and molecular remains
The present

Fossils

A **fossil,** as defined in Chapter 2, is the preserved remains or trace of a plant or animal of the past. Fossils are usually, but not always, preserved in rocks. There are two major categories of fossils. The larger category, *true fossils,* consists of the actual remains of animals or plants. Animal fossils usually consist of hard tissues such as bones and teeth, because hard tissues are more resistant to being degraded than are soft tissues such as skin, muscle, or gut. Soft tissues are rarely preserved in the fossil record of humanity, and only in the later stages of that record. Examples of soft-tissue fossils include the preserved bodies of the Bog People of Northern Europe and the so-called Ice Man who died in the Alps around 5000 years ago (review the photograph and map on p. 5). *Trace fossils,* the smaller category, offer indirect evidence that animals and plants were there. Examples of trace fossils include coprolites (fossilized feces), footprints, and the impressions of leaves.

Chances are extremely small that an early human skeleton will be preserved in the fossil record. In order to be fossilized, bones need to be covered quickly by sediment from a stream, sand, or soil. This covering protects the fossil from scavengers and makes fossilization possible. Deliberate burial greatly increases the chance that a skeleton will be preserved in good condition, and it is one reason why the human fossil record begins to improve around 90,000 years ago when some early human ancestors started to place the remains of the dead under ground.

Fossilization begins when chemicals from the surrounding sediments replace first the organic material and then the inorganic material in bones and teeth. These chemicals permeate the bones and teeth and gradually replace the naturally occurring ones. Over many thousands of years, a bone or tooth turns into a fossil. Variations in the chemical environment may mean that bones of the same age from different places, or even bones from different areas of the same location, fossilize differently.

Most early human fossils are found in rocks formed from sediments laid down by rivers, or on lakeshores or in the floors of caves. These sediments form layers, or *strata.* Generally, older rocks and the fossils they contain are in the lower layers of sediment, and younger ones are nearer the surface. The movement of rocks, however, through tension and compression in the earth's crust, may tilt the layers and upset this general rule. A fossil found embedded in a rock is described as being found *in situ,* and the layer of rock the fossil appears in is referred to as its **horizon,** or **stratigraphic layer.** Most fossils that are discovered, however, have been displaced through erosion from their original horizon and are therefore found exposed on the ground; such fossils are called **surface finds.**

Artifacts

An **artifact** is any object made, modified, or transported by humans. Artifacts are portable and include objects such as stone tools, pots, jewelry, and furniture. Depending on the context, artifacts are made from raw materials such as bone, stone, wood, plant fiber, metals, and clay. A *mummy,* the corpse of a human or other animal with soft tissue deliberately preserved to resemble the once-living animal (Aufderheide 2003), can be considered an artifact because most mummies have been created by human modification. The analysis of mummified remains reveals details about past diet, health, and environment (see the Methods Close-up box). Artifacts are distinguished from *ecofacts,* or objects made, modified or transported by nature. Sometimes it is difficult to distinguish artifacts from ecofacts; for example, some early stone tools look much like stones that might have been chipped by natural processes.

Artifacts are the key marker of humanity and culture. Stone tools, dating from 2 to 3 million years ago, are the first preserved evidence of human culture. Not much else of human life from that early era is preserved. For example, we have no evidence of settlement sites. Thus stone tools are the major "voice" for the early phases of human culture. Later, many other types of artifacts become increasingly common in the archaeological record. They include bone tools, carvings, ornaments, settlement sites, and burials. Later still, we encounter fuller ranges of human artifacts as cities

Studying Egyptian Mummy Tissue for Clues about Ancient Disease

MANY ANTHROPOLOGISTS pursue research on human diseases of the past in order both to reconstruct this aspect of humanity and to shed light on contemporary disease patterns. The Manchester Egyptian Mummy Research Project was established in 1973 at the University of Manchester, northern England, to stimulate research on mummified remains (Lambert-Zazulak, Rutherford, and David 2003). One goal was to establish the International Ancient Egyptian Mummy Tissue Bank in order to store information about the diseases discovered in the mummies and to give researchers access to that information. A second goal was to develop new methods for studying the mummies. Mummies are a finite resource and must be preserved for future study.

An important development in the 1980s was the use of *endoscopy* (using a small camera or other instrument to see into a body cavity) as an almost nondestructive method for examining mummies and obtaining tissues samples from them for further examination. Endoscopy replaced the earlier practice of unwrapping the mummies and performing autopsies on them.

In the 1990s, a comprehensive study of the past and present distribution of schistosomiasis in Egypt was launched, in collaboration with researchers in Egypt and the United States. Schistosomiasis is an infectious tropical disease affecting over 300 million people today. Schistosoma worms are parasites that infect humans through contact with water that carries the eggs. Once inside the human bloodstream, larva can damage the lungs and renal and neural tissue. Reaction to the eggs produces inflammation, fibrosis, cirrhosis of the liver, diarrhea and abdominal swelling, enlargement of the liver and spleen, and hemorrhage.

As part of this project, researchers analyzed mummy tissue to learn about the antiquity of the disease. They needed a reasonably inexpensive, robust, and reproducible method in order to examine a large sample of mummy tissue. They turned to a

An Egyptian mummy that is part of the University of Manchester's Mummy Tissue Bank undergoes endoscopy to obtain tissue samples for testing. (Source: © The Manchester Museum, The University of Manchester)

method called *immunostaining* in which chemicals applied to tissue reveal either the presence or the absence of antibodies. For the first time, this method was successful in diagnosing schistosomiasis in any population, either ancient or modern. It revealed the presence of the infection in at least one-fourth of the sample, suggesting wide prevalence of the disease as far back as 5000 years ago.

The International Ancient Egyptian Mummy Tissue Bank project demonstrates progress in tissue collection, storage, and analysis. The databank widens access to mummies for research internationally. In developing new, nondestructive methods for tissue analysis, researchers have been mindful of the ethical issues that working with irreplaceable ancient tissue raises.

FOOD FOR THOUGHT

- Be prepared to discuss why it is important to know about the prehistory and history of diseases. If you do not agree that it is important, defend your position.

develop, trade and transportation networks increase, and people's material culture expands.

Whereas paleoanthropologists concentrate on fossils, archaeologists focus on artifacts. They classify artifacts first on the basis of their *attributes*, or descriptive features. These include the raw material used to create them and their shape, color, and material decoration. A second principle of classification is the artifact's *provenance*. Provenance information includes the artifact's age, where it was found, what it was found with, and the number of such artifacts found in a location.

Using information about both attributes and provenance, archaeologists organize artifacts into **assemblages,** or clusters of similar artifacts that are interpreted as representing the work of a cultural group. Most assemblages consist of stone tools or ceramics. Many long-standing debates surround some of the more prominent assemblages. For example, the "Mousterian debate" involves three competing views about the interpretation of Neanderthal stone tools from southwest France dating between 100,000 and 40,000 years ago (Gamble 2001:57):

> View 1: Five distinct cultural groups lived in the region, each with distinct tool assemblages.
>
> View 2: One homogeneous group lived in the region that possessed five different *functional toolkits* for different purposes.
>
> View 3: The five assemblages represent five different chronological stages.

All the archaeologists agree that five patterns exist in the tools. They disagree, however, on how to interpret the different patterns. Perhaps, as more evidence is found and better techniques for analysis are developed, the debate will be resolved. It may turn out that only one view is correct or that elements of more than one view are accurate.

Other Types of Data

- Features. A **feature** is an artifact that is not portable, such as a hearth, a building, or rock art.
- Sites. A **site** is a location containing remains of humanity's past. A site may have structures such as settlements, burial areas, and ceremonial centers. Or a site may include only scattered bones or tools.
- Documents. Written materials are a source of information about past cultures that had written language.
- Genetic and molecular materials. Genetic and molecular information can be recovered from soil, fossils, artifacts, and living people. The analysis of molecules found on artifacts help reveal what their uses might have been. DNA from living people shows how people were biologically related to each other, where their ancestors lived, and what bacteria they may have hosted.
- The present. Information from contemporary people can provide insights about the past. For example, oral histories of living people provide information about their ancestors. **Ethnoarchaeology** is a research method that involves studying contemporary people to gain insights about past cultural patterns. For example, in order to understand how prehistoric pottery may have been made at a site, one would determine how current inhabitants of the area make pottery, on the assumption that there may be cultural continuities between the past and the present. Similarly, one might study contemporary patterns of trash disposal to help generate interpretations of prehistoric refuse areas.

Discovering Fossils and Artifacts through Fieldwork

In the search for evidence of humanity's past by collecting fossils and artifacts, the first step is to identify a location for field research. Next come testing and surveying of the site to determine where more intensive research should take place. The next step involves recovering the evidence from the site, often through excavation. **Excavation** is a method for fossil or artifact recovery in which the material surrounding the evidence is removed both vertically and horizontally.

Identifying Sites

Where to search for evidence of humanity's past depends on what stage of the past is being researched. If you are interested in the earliest stages of human evolution, then you will look for promising locations in Africa (discussed in Chapter 6). Anthropol-

Aerial view of Mittelberg, Germany, a Bronze Age site in central Germany where many artifacts from around 1500 BCE attest to the site's importance. One of the most remarkable finds is a bronze disc, called the Sky Disc of Nebra, with gold-leaf appliqués representing the sun, moon, stars, and a ship. This aerial view shows the site surrounded by forest, which would not have been the case during the Bronze Age. ■ Generate a hypothesis as to why the region is more tree-covered now than then. (Source: © National Geographic Image Collection)

ogists who study the remains of sunken ships consult archival information to learn about where missing ships may be located. Aerial photography and satellite imagery have greatly enhanced anthropologists' abilities to learn about possible sites.

Many sites have been found through sheer accident, often as a result of construction projects. As bulldozers clear the way for roads, buildings, or airports, their earth moving has exposed such important sites as the one at Atapuerca, Spain, that is discussed in Chapter 7 (see the Lessons Applied box, p. 210). Such discoveries continue today. The recent expansion of Heathrow airport near London resulted in the unearthing of prehistoric remains, and the remains are being studied and preserved. Although construction and building have led to many discoveries, they have probably destroyed more sites than they have exposed for study and preservation.

Excavation

The first step in any excavation project is to map the site. The map provides the basis for dividing the site into smaller units, usually squares defined as a grid pattern or as three-dimensional cubes. These units help the archaeologists locate trenches and record data from the trenches. Trench location is usually determined by selecting a **sample**, or a selected set of units from a larger "universe" that consists of the entire site of the excavation project. Thus, instead of excavating completely a site of ten acres, the researchers will excavate only certain portions. Sometimes researchers will use a *random sample* technique in which each section has an equal chance of excavation. Alternatively, the excavation plan may involve *cluster sampling* that provides a way of focusing on excavation of areas of particular interest, such as a settlement area or a temple. Or sampling may be designed to ensure that researchers will collect evidence from different environmental zones within the site, such as wet areas and dry areas.

After decisions have been made about where to dig, excavating can begin. Digging tools include small trowels and brushes for soft sediments, chisels and picks for firmer sediments, and drills and explosives for hard sediments. Sieves are used for sifting sediment containing small fossils or pieces of artifacts. Certain sites may require specialized excavating equipment and techniques. No matter which methods are used, the researchers carefully record everything found, along with environmental data.

Excavation is time-intensive, costly, and damaging to the site. Even when the researchers take pains to rebury their finds, excavation inevitably alters the site. For these reasons, nondestructive methods of locating fossils and artifacts are increasingly used. Aerial photography and satellite remote sensing are powerful sources of

Archaeological research often requires detailed work and the use of small, fine tools. Lisa Nevell, student in the doctoral program in Hominid Paleobiology at George Washington University, is shown working on an excavation at Dmanisi, Georgia. ■ Besides patience, what other personal characteristics might be required for this kind of work? (Source: Courtesy of Lisa Nevell)

information about a site's layout, including buried walls, roads, and fields. Ground-penetrating radar and metal detectors make possible the plotting of buried artifacts. Often, discoveries made in these ways are left *in situ* rather than taken to a lab. Their locations are recorded on a computer. If excavation is still thought to be merited, these non-destructive sources of information can be used to minimize exploratory digging, to devise better sampling, and thus to ensure more precise excavation.

Dating Fossils and Artifacts

Accurate dates for fossils, artifacts, and the sites they come from are essential for their interpretation. Anthropologists can often determine the sequence of fossils and artifacts excavated from a site, from oldest to youngest, if there is a clear and undisturbed stratigraphic pattern. Stratigraphy is the study and description of the various layers of sediment at a site. If there have been no natural or human disturbances of the site, one can assume that objects found at lower levels are older than those found at higher levels. Many of the scholarly arguments about dating concern the question of whether objects found in a particular stratum were actually from that time period or had been displaced into the earlier stratum through upheavals in the earth, cave ceiling collapses, or intentional human action such as burial. Sometimes fossils and artifacts are discovered with little contextual information. These objects are more difficult to date than fossils within a stratigraphic sequence.

The following discussion covers only a few of the many methods available. If you take a separate course in archaeology or paleoanthropology, you will learn about many more, and in more detail. For our purposes, you should know that methods vary in terms of the materials they use and in terms of the time range for which they are appropriate. Keep in mind, also, that dating methods are constantly improving in accuracy and precision. These advancements have often meant that earlier interpretations of artifacts and sites have had to be revised. Two major categories of dating exist: absolute dating and relative dating.

Absolute Dating Methods

Absolute dating methods are methods of determining the age of a fossil, artifact, or site on the basis of a specific time scale, such as years before the present, or any other fixed calendrical system. Absolute dating methods rely on either knowing the time it takes for natural processes, such as atomic decay, to occur, or relating the horizon to precisely calibrated global events, such as reversals in the direction of the earth's magnetic field. Absolute dates are given in calendar years. A variety of absolute dating methods have been developed, especially since the middle of the twentieth century. More recent methods have extended the time range that can be dated (see Figure 4.4), but they often have wider margins of error than some of the earlier methods. Different methods work best for different materials and contexts.

One of the earliest absolute dating methods is *dendrochronology*, or tree ring dating. Most trees produce a new ring of wood every year. Differences in temperature and rainfall affect the width of the ring, as does the age of the tree itself because rings become narrower as the tree gets older. Dendrochronologists count the rings (they can obtain the data they need from standing trees by taking a small core that does not harm the tree), measure their thickness, and compare them to other trees in the area to construct a chronology for the region going back thousands of years. Then they can compare this information to, for example, a beam in a house to see when it was

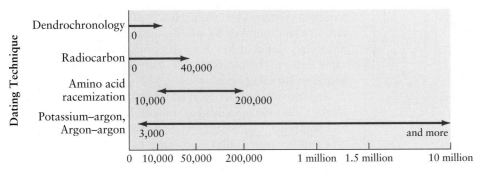

FIGURE 4.4
Some absolute dating methods.

cut. This method has been highly effective in the American southwest where wood is well preserved—for example, in Pueblo Indian villages.

Radiocarbon dating is based on measuring the amount of ^{14}C, a radioactive isotope of carbon, in organic remains such as bone and wood. The radiocarbon absorbed by all living organisms decays at a rate such that half of the amount of the parent isotope (^{14}C) present when the organism died is converted to its daughter isotope (^{14}N) after 5730 years, plus or minus 40 years (see Figure 4.5 on p. 108). This period of time is called the isotope's *half-life*. Radiocarbon dating is an extremely important dating method for archaeologists, but it can be used only for the more recent stages of human evolution. This limitation is due to the fact that the amount of radiocarbon left in fossils older than 40,000 years ago is so small that it cannot be measured precisely.

Working on the same principle as radiocarbon dating, **potassium–argon dating** (K–Ar) is based on measuring the decay rate of ^{40}K, a radioactive isotope of potassium, as it forms argon (^{40}Ar). The half-life of ^{40}K is 1250 million years. Because the half-life of ^{40}K is much longer than that of ^{14}C, the potassium–argon method can be used to date rocks that contain fossils and stone tools that are millions of years old. At this time, however, many of the dates yielded by this method have wide margins of error. Related to K–Ar dating is *argon–argon dating* (Ar–Ar), which measures the ratio of ^{40}Ar to ^{39}Ar. Ar–Ar dating has the same range as K–Ar dating but has the advantage that it can be used on very small samples, such as a single mineral grain.

Amino acid racemization (AAR) is one of the newest absolute dating methods. It relies on the fact that most complex chemicals in nature exist in two forms, an L-form and a D-form. For example, this is the case with an amino acid called leucine, which is a component of eggshell. Over time, leucine is converted from the L-form to the D-form. Scraps of ostrich eggshell are commonly found in African and Asian fossil sites as a natural occurrence or, at later sites, made into bead ornaments. Amino acid racemization dating of ostrich egg shells provides reliable ages for fossil sites from about 10,000 to 200,000 years ago in warm regions (less long ago in cold regions) and thus fills a gap in the age ranges of radiocarbon and potassium–argon dating

A San girl of southern Asia using an ostrich egg shell for carrying water. ■ Ostrich egg shells appear more than once in this book. Keep track of their importance in human evolution. (Source: © SVT Bild/DAS FOTOARCHIV/ Peter Arnold, Inc.)

Relative Dating Methods

Relative dating methods determine the age of a fossil or artifact by placing it in a chronological sequence or by matching evidence found at one site with equivalent evidence from another site that has been dated using an absolute method. For example, if human fossils found at Site A are similar to those at Site B, then Site A can be assumed to be approximately the same age as Site B.

The use of animal remains for dating, which is termed *biochronology*, is especially important for dating fossils from

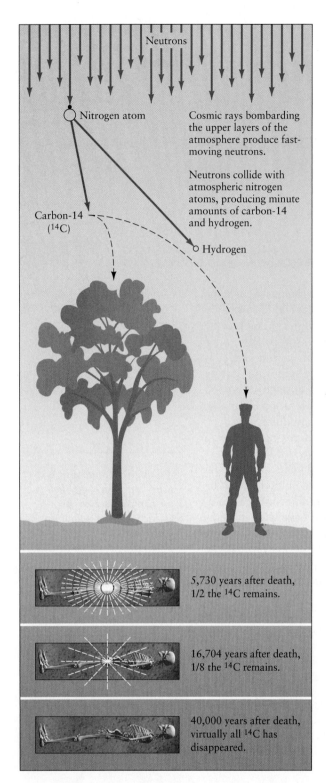

Neutrons

Nitrogen atom

Cosmic rays bombarding the upper layers of the atmosphere produce fast-moving neutrons.

Neutrons collide with atmospheric nitrogen atoms, producing minute amounts of carbon-14 and hydrogen.

Carbon-14 (^{14}C)

Hydrogen

5,730 years after death, 1/2 the ^{14}C remains.

16,704 years after death, 1/8 the ^{14}C remains.

40,000 years after death, virtually all ^{14}C has disappeared.

FIGURE 4.5
Steps in the life cycle of radiocarbon.

southern African cave sites. Nearly all of these sites contain antelope and monkey fossils. Because these fossils have been absolutely dated at key East African sites, we can apply the same dates to the layers that contain equivalent fossils in the southern African caves.

Another relative dating method using small meteorites, or *tektites*, has been employed at some early human sites in China and Southeast Asia. Scientists know when these tektites landed on earth because similar meteorites have been found in well-dated cores from the ocean floor.

Seriation is a relative dating method for prehistoric cultures that arranges artifacts, assemblages, or sites in a sequence based on their similarity or frequency (in the case of artifacts) and therefrom generates a rough chronology. Computer analysis has helped to refine this method, but it is still a subjective approach.

Reconstructing the Environment

Paleoanthropologists and archaeologists seek to understand fossils, artifacts, features, sites, and other data in relation to the wider environmental context in which they are found. Environmental factors offer different kinds of opportunities and impose various constraints that have shaped human biological and cultural evolution. The specialized subfield devoted to the study of past environments is called *paleoenvironmental studies*. Scientists working in this area study aspects of the environmental context in which fossils and artifacts are found, such as natural features and resources (water, soil type, minerals, altitude, caves, rock shelters), climate, plants (flora), and animals (fauna), as well as the influence of human ancestors.

Natural Features and Resources

The amount of land on which humans can live is a basic natural resource. During human prehistory, expansion and contraction of continental glaciers altered the area of land that could be occupied, created or removed land bridges between regions, and changed the shape of coastlines (see the map on p. 109). When water levels were lower than they are today, there was more land available for occupation, and more of the earth's landmass was connected, allowing settlement by people without boats.

Assessing the resources available at a site includes paying attention to water sources such as rivers and springs as well as to shelters such as caves. The soil and its mineral content are also important in understanding how early humans may have survived in particular locations.

An increasingly important part of site analysis is *soil structure*, which involves the use of microscopic techniques to study the components of soils. Examination of a block of soil reveals the source of the sediment, the process of soil formation over time, and possible human modification (Renfrew and Bahn 2004). Soil can contain evidence of human activity such as the use of fire, food storage, farming activities, and deforestation, thus providing important contextual information in light of which fossils and artifacts can be better interpreted.

Climate

The first step in learning about past climatic conditions is to take a global look in order to provide the broadest possible context. Water now covers about three-fourths of the earth's surface, and scientists who study paleoclimate often examine evidence from underwater. Sediments in the oceans and other bodies of water have accumulated over time. Analysis of cores taken from ocean and sea beds yields evidence about climate change. One core from the Pacific Ocean provides a climatic record of over 2 million years. The analysis of these cores reveals how temperature has changed through time. Similarly, ice cores can be studied to gain insight into temperature changes over time. Ice cores also offer information about rainfall, storminess, and windiness. Paleoanthropologists hypothesize that increases in storms and wind may have prompted populations to migrate out of such areas and discouraged others from migrating into them.

Prehistoric continental land mass. For most of human prehistory, what are now called the British Isles and Ireland were connected to the continent of Europe. The change from a peninsular to an island landmass began in the seventh to sixth millennia BCE. The dark color in the map represents what was land.

Plants

The vegetation that early humanity would have encountered in particular times and places is an important aspect of their environment. Some of our most important information about plants comes from the analysis of pollen grains, called *palynology*. Pollen analysis reveals changes in vegetation over time. It has shown, for example, that some contemporary regions that are very dry, such as the Sahara, were wet and green 3 million years ago.

Another method that helps us reconstruct plant life in prehistory is *phytolith analysis*. Phytoliths are tiny particles of silica (plant opal) that reside in plant cells and survive long after the plant has decomposed or been burned (Renfrew and Bahn 2004:225). Phytoliths are found in hearths, inside vessels, and even on stone tools.

Turning from microbotany to macrobotany, researchers sometimes are able to find whole seeds and fruits that have been preserved either through desiccation (drying out) or soaking. Remains of wood, such as charcoal, waterlogged wood, or parts of houses, provide insights into the flora of a particular period.

Animals

Both large animals (*megafauna*) and small animals (*microfauna*) were present throughout humanity's past. Early archaeologists recognized the importance of certain animals in particular times and gave past eras names such as the Mammoth Age. Microfaunal analysis is especially important to reconstructing past environments, because small animals have smaller ranges than large animals and are more sensitive to climate change. During excavation, sieving is the method used for recovering microfaunal remains. Common microfauna in the fossil record are insects, rodents, and bats. Birds and fish, being more fragile, are less widely represented in the fossil record.

Mollusks (shellfish) are useful because early humans often deposited the shells in **middens,** or mounds. As the mounds built up, they left a record of older mollusk shells at the bottom and of more recent ones higher up. The percentages of types of mollusks in the midden reveal different survival patterns that may have been related to climate change. For example, a decline in the frequencies of particular mollusks would be an indicator of a change in temperature. Growth patterns in the shells reveal information about the seasons that the particular animal experienced in its lifetime.

Many species of megafauna, including mastodons and mammoths, have become extinct. Scholars argue about whether these extinctions were due to extensive killing by early humans, climate change, or a combination of the two. The middle-ground theory suggests that human overexploitation may have led to extinctions of megafauna, especially herbivores. With the demise of these creatures, vegetation changes occurred that negatively affected the survival of mid-sized herbivores. Contemporary elephants damage and destroy large trees, thereby opening up clearings for smaller animals. In game reserves without elephants, some species of antelope have become extinct over the past 100 years, and other herbivores have declined in number.

Given what you know about current trends in technology, imagine what kinds of methods for studying the paleo-environment may be available in 2020.

THINKING

OUTSIDE THE BOX

A shell midden at Edisto Beach State Park, on Scotts Creek in South Carolina, is dated to about 4500 years ago. The state Department of Parks, Recreation, and Tourism hopes to build a seven-foot-high retaining wall to protect it from further erosion. ■ What is your position on the responsibility of U.S. taxpayers to support such conservation projects? (Source: AP/Wide World Photos)

New techniques for gathering and analyzing all types of environmental data promise to provide more insight into debates about the causes of extinction.

Analysis, Interpretation, and Representation of Findings

Anthropological research on humanity's past generates a wide variety of evidence, from molecular data that cannot be seen by the human eye to urban sites covering many square miles. The focus of the research might be to excavate centuries of human habitation or to understand what the condition of a single tooth from an early human ancestor indicates about that individual's health and lifestyle. Many research projects generate vast amounts of quantitative data that are analyzed using computers. Computers also allow for virtual analysis, reconstruction, and representation. Computer-generated visualization of sites, fossils, and artifacts aids in their analysis by scholars and in their appreciation and understanding by the general public.

In trying to understand the life of prehistoric ancestors on the basis of fossil evidence, or that of early humans on the basis of archaeological artifacts, anthropologists sometimes fall into the trap of uncritically seeing the past from the perspective of the present. One of the most problematic areas is that of interpreting and representing gender roles (Nelson 1997). Most paleoanthropologists and archaeologists in the past have been men from Euro-American cultures in which men are largely dominant. They rarely included women as their students or in fieldwork projects. Similarly, their **androcentrism,** or male-centered bias in research, often produced findings that emphasized the status and roles of males and relegated females to a marginal or passive position. For example, if a burial was accompanied by elaborate grave goods, it was considered a king's burial (Nelson 2003). The recent development of feminist anthropology, among both men and women researchers, has helped to correct many faulty interpretations and to open exciting new areas of inquiry less burdened by androcentrism.

Research findings are generally first published in academic outlets, such as in brief pieces called articles that are published in scholarly journals, or as book-length reports (sometimes called monographs). When a new fossil related to human evolution is discovered, it is appropriate for a formal description of the find to appear quickly in an international journal such as *Science* or *Nature,* so that the rest of the scholarly community can learn the details. Archaeologists often write a book-length *site report* that describes and catalogues the findings from one site in detail.

Many popular publishing outlets also exist, such as *National Geographic* and *Archaeology.* Publishing articles in these magazines helps ensure that research findings reach a more general readership. New research findings on humanity's past also reach the public through media such as radio and television shows, the Internet, and museum exhibits. Much of the research conducted on the human past is supported by government grants. Anthropologists who receive government funding have a special responsibility to make sure their findings are shared with the public.

Preservation of Fossils, Artifacts, and Sites

Anthropologists who study the past are responsible for contributing to the preservation of the fossils, artifacts, and sites on which their research is based. They try to do their best, given the state of knowledge in their times, to protect and preserve the heritage of humanity. Nevertheless, in hindsight, we sometimes learn that certain procedures or practices have had, and still have, undesirable side effects that must be addressed (see the Lessons Applied box on p. 112).

Fossil and archaeological sites require protection from the natural elements and from human damage related to construction, war, and looting. Protecting them from the natural elements may require building a shelter over parts of the site. But even this effort may not be as protective as the several feet of earth or water that formerly covered the remains. For example, following the discovery of the prehistoric footprints at Laetoli, Tanzania (see the photograph on p. 164), scientists sought to protect them by covering them with heavy black plastic. This plan did not work, because the plastic served to help incubate tiny seedlings that sprouted and grew in the footprints. A better form of covering has been devised.

Whenever a new site is discovered, there is the simultaneous risk of looting at the site and illicit commercialization of fossils and artifacts. Often, the exact location is kept secret until plans are in place for protecting the site from looting. Even well-protected sites have been damaged by looters. Paleoanthropologists and archaeologists are beginning to work harder to protect sites, fossils, and artifacts from such exploitation because looting destroys irreplaceable information about humanity's past. British archaeologist Colin Renfrew points out that since the 1970 adoption of UNESCO's *Convention on the Means of Prohibiting and Preventing the Illicit Import, Export, and Transfer of Ownership of Cultural Property,* the looting of sites has actually increased (2001). Many anthropologists are working with local community members to engage them in managing and protecting sites in their region (we discuss this topic in more detail in the last section of this chapter).

Looting is obviously linked to an interested market: looters would not pursue their work if there were no buyers. Buyers include individual collectors, antiquities dealers, and museums. Some discussions of cultural heritage destruction through looting suggest that we need to shift our attention from the often impoverished looters and overburdened bureaucracies in developing countries (where much, but not all, looting takes place) to the wealthy collectors (Brodie and Doole 2001). Trying to control the consumption patterns of powerful elites will prove difficult. Besides individual collectors, museums are also involved in collecting fossils and artifacts. Several prominent museums, following the lead of the University Museum of the University of Pennsylvania, now have a policy of not acquiring *unprovenanced antiquities*—objects without a "pedigree," including information on place of origin and legality of export. But many museums have not adopted this policy and continue to acquire unprovenanced objects.

This Moche site in Peru is riddled with looters' holes. Moche civilization preceded the Incas. It is noted for, among other things, beautiful pottery (see the photograph on p. 280). ■ If you were hired by the government of your home country to protect its antiquities from looters, what would be some of your main concerns, and how would you proceed? (Source: © Ira Block/National Geographic Image Collection)

Defining Guidelines Regarding the Chemical Contamination of Native American Objects

MUSEUMS HAVE LONG used a variety of chemicals to protect organic objects from damage by rodents, insects, and microorganisms. Arsenic and mercury were used in earlier years, followed with pesticides such as DDT. Some objects were subjected to multiple treatments. Museum records, historical documents, interviews with museum employees, and the available laboratory test results indicate that most or all museum collections of organic materials have been treated with hazardous materials (Davis, Caldararo and Palmer 2001). Since the 1980s, conservators have begun to question the widespread use of pesticide chemicals and have adopted approaches that emphasize prevention of damage.

In 1990, the United States passed the Native American Graves Protection and Repatriation Act (NAGPRA), which requires museums to return certain Native American materials to federally recognized tribes (Bray 1996). The process of repatriation has elevated concern about chemical contamination to an urgent level (Odegaard and Sadongei 2001). It appears that when the NAGPRA bill was signed the extent of health hazards that might be related to repatriation were not recognized. Only one statement about pesticides is made in the statute's implementation regulations: "The museum official or Federal agency official must inform the recipients of repatriations of any

presently known treatment of human remains, funerary objects, sacred objects or objects of cultural patrimony with pesticides, preservatives, or other substances that represent a potential hazard to the objects or to persons handling objects" (pp. 13–14). Given the lack of detailed records about various objects' museum history, providing such information is difficult if not impossible at the present time.

The Hoopa (Hopi) Tribe of Arizona first raised concerns about the health threat of repatriated objects in 1997 in response to a report it received from Harvard University's Peabody Museum of Archaeology and Ethnology. Since then, many workshops and conferences have been organized among tribal representatives, and among tribes, scientists, and museum staff. Progress thus far includes laboratory testing of many objects undergoing repatriation and the implementing of steps to improve museum records on the history of artifacts, especially of repatriated objects. In 1998, the Arizona State Museum (ASM) proposed the use of a repatriation check sheet with the following questions:

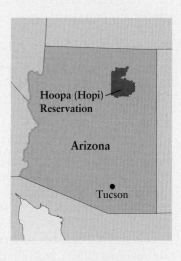

STUDYING CONTEMPORARY HUMANITY

Each of anthropology's four fields may involve study of contemporary people, but the field that is exclusively devoted to living people is cultural anthropology. For example, archaeologists sometimes conduct ethnoarchaeological research, biological anthropologists who study contemporary human variation work with living people, and many linguistic anthropologists conduct research that is similar to that of cultural anthropologists. All of these endeavors involve fieldwork. The *field* is anywhere that people are: a village far from the anthropologist's home, or a clinic or school in the anthropologist's own country.

When cultural anthropologists do fieldwork, their main method is **participant observation,** in which the researcher lives in and studies a culture for an extended period of time. The method was invented by cultural anthropologists and is still their primary means of learning about living people. Archaeologists work mainly with artifacts from past cultures, so they cannot truly participate in those cultures. Many biological anthropologists, especially primatologists, live in nonhuman primate habitats

- Is there evidence of prior infestation?
- Are residual particles indicated?
- Is there evidence of museum repairs, restorations, and alterations?
- Are there any written records that suggest the use of pesticides?
- Based on past storage locations, what pesticides might have been used on or near this object?

Museum environments, as well as artifacts, may contain contaminants. Contaminants in the air of storage areas and on working surfaces may spread throughout buildings via air conditioning systems to exhibit areas, offices, and other areas that do not house collections. Thus museum environments themselves may pose a risk for workers. Museum workers share with tribal members confusion and dismay about the lack of information on preservatives used and the possible health hazards resulting from exposure to contaminated objects (Caldararo, Davis, and Palmer 2001).

In addition to improving testing and records on artifact history, the following other recommendations have been made:

- An educational program for the tribes, explaining the risks of pesticide exposure during the repatriation process, should be instituted. This program should include detailed information on how to store repatriated items and on the importance of limiting handling and use of these materials. Tribal members are advised not to wear repatriated objects in ceremonies.

Through meetings and workshops, Native American tribes should work to increase, within their communities, awareness of the health risks associated with handling repatriated objects.

- Safety guidelines for museum employees should be posted and enforced. These guidelines include wearing a lab coat and special gloves when handling materials, working in a well-ventilated area, and in some cases wearing a mask or respirator. New museum employees should have a baseline medical examination and should undergo regular health monitoring during their employment. Health studies of museum workers past and present should be conducted, with special attention to pesticide poisoning.
- Basic medical research should be conducted to assess short-term and long-term effects on human health from chronic exposure to the kinds of pesticides used on museum materials.
- Greater national attention should be given to the entire issue of health risks from artifact contamination, and federal funding should support further research, dissemination of information, and education programs.

FOOD FOR THOUGHT

- Consider how this issue might extend beyond the United States and what lessons might usefully be shared more widely.

for long periods of time, but the limited degree to which humans and nonhuman primates can communicate with each other constrains true participation on the part of the researcher. Linguistic anthropologists who work with contemporary humans most resemble cultural anthropologists in their use of participant observation. They are able to observe and participate in the same ways that cultural anthropologists do.

Because of the centrality of fieldwork and participant observation to cultural anthropology, this section focuses on cultural anthropology research, but many of the points discussed apply to any anthropologist conducting research about living people.

Learning about Contemporary Culture through Fieldwork

This section explores how cultural anthropologists learn about culture through fieldwork and the overarching fieldwork tool, participant observation. We consider the process of fieldwork from the first step of getting an idea for a research project, to entering the field, leaving the field and writing up the results.

The first step is choose a research topic. One may find a topic by doing library research, or *secondary research*, to see what has already been done and identify a

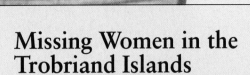

Missing Women in the Trobriand Islands

A LASTING CONTRIBUTION of cultural anthropologist Bronislaw Malinowski's ethnography, *Argonauts of the Western Pacific* (1961 [1922]), is its detailed description of the *kula,* a trading network linking many of the Trobriand Islands. Men from different islands have long-standing trading partnerships with each other for the exchange of goods such as food and also shell necklaces and armlets, which are highly valued personal decoration items. The necklaces and armlets circulate in a regular pattern, and no man may keep any particular item forever. Some of the necklaces and armbands are especially sought after and treasured by their temporary owners. Men risk dangerous waters in their canoes to maintain their trading relationships and give and receive shell ornaments. For decades, the kula system stood as the definitive example in cultural anthropology of the importance of exchange in nonmarket societies.

More than half a century after Malinowski's publication, Annette Weiner traveled to the Trobriands to study wood carving (1976). She settled in a village less than a mile from where Malinowski had done much of his research. She soon started observing some surprising behavior: "On my first day in the village, I saw women performing a mortuary [death] ceremony in which they distributed thousands of bundles of strips of dried banana leaves and hundreds of beautifully decorated fibrous skirts. Bundles of banana leaves and skirts are objects of female wealth with explicit economic value" (p. xvii).

She decided to abandon her original project and investigate women's exchange patterns. Weiner discovered a women's world of production, exchange, social networks, and prestige that Malinowski had overlooked. Men, as Malinowski described, exchange shells, yams, and pigs. Women, as Weiner discovered, exchange bundles of leaves and skirts. Both men

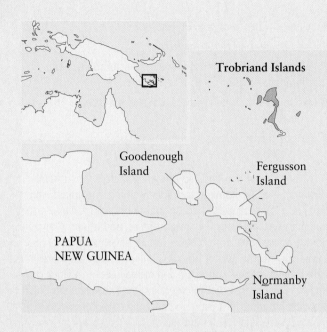

and women have access to power and prestige through exchange. Reading Malinowski provides only half of the picture. Reading Weiner's account, *Women of Value, Men of Renown,* provides the other half, as well as showing how the men's and women's exchange systems are linked and demonstrating that one must understand both systems to gain a full picture of Trobriand social life.

CRITICAL THINKING QUESTIONS

- Can you think of an explanation why Malinowski overlooked women's exchange systems?
- Do Annette Weiner's findings simply provide another one-sided view?

gap in current knowledge to date. Historical events often prompt new research ideas. The appearance of the HIV/AIDS virus has stimulated interest among many cultural anthropology researchers. Conflict situations in Ireland, Rwanda, the former Yugoslavia, and other places have prompted cultural anthropologists to ask what keeps states together and what inspires internal violence (Harris 1992). Following the 9/11 attacks on the United States, many cultural anthropologists have devoted their efforts to studying the bases of international conflict. The rising number of immigrants worldwide has stimulated research into migrants' adaptation patterns. Another approach is to conduct a **restudy,** in which an anthropologist goes to a previously studied site to look at the same topic again at a later period to see what has changed, or to look at a different topic in the same location (see the Critical Thinking box).

Unanticipated events can lead to a research topic. Spanish anthropologist Maria Cátedra stumbled on an important discovery during exploratory fieldwork in rural northern Spain. A person committed suicide in a hamlet in the mountains near where she was staying. She learned that the area had an extremely high rate of suicide and that the local people did not consider suicide strange. She decided to conduct her research on the social dynamics and meaning of suicide in the area.

Selecting a location may go hand in hand with deciding on the topic, as in Maria Cátedra's study. In the early days of cultural anthropology, over a hundred years ago, there was a definite preference for locations far from North America and Europe, such as Pacific islands and remote regions of Africa and Latin America. Another early preference was to study small groups with the goal of gaining a comprehensive, or holistic, view of the culture. An underlying goal was to study cultures that were "uncontaminated" by the outside world and thus represented "primitive" society. Things are much different now. Although many cultural anthropologists still conduct research on remote (to those of us in North America) tropical islands, many others conduct research in urban areas worldwide and in international institutions such as the United Nations. And many cultural anthropologists increasingly conduct research in their own countries.

After a topic and a location have been decided upon, other preparatory steps need to be taken, depending on the research context. The researcher needs to get approval of the project from the sponsoring university's or institution's committee that oversees the protection of "human subjects." Depending on the host country's rules, a visa or other kinds of permits may be required. Some countries restrict work in particular regions within their boundaries or on particular topics. Some countries have been completely closed to foreign researchers. China only recently relaxed the restrictions it imposes on American researchers, and Russia's policies changed even more recently. Issues of safety in the research locale have to be given serious thought (we return to this topic in the last section of the chapter).

Equipment may include data collection tools such as a laptop, cameras, and audio recorders. Special clothing may be required, such as long-sleeved garments for women researchers in the Middle East. Health preparations may involve a series of shots for immunization against contagious diseases such as yellow fever. A well-stocked medical kit may be essential if the research project is located far from a clinic or hospital.

A researcher who is not fluent in the local language must pursue intensive language training before undertaking fieldwork. Even with substantial language training in advance, many cultural anthropologists have found that they need to learn a local dialect of the standard version. Many researchers rely on the assistance of local interpreters.

Cultural anthropologist Jennifer Robertson (far left) celebrates the publication of her ethnography about cultural change in Kodaira, Japan, entitled Native and Newcomer. *With her are administrators from Kodaira city hall. They are relaxing after attending a large, formal ceremony at which she presented a copy of her book to the mayor.* ■ What cultural features are noteworthy about this gathering? (Source: Jennifer Roberston)

Establishing Rapport

Acceptance of the anthropologist by the people is crucial for successful research in cultural anthropology. A primary goal of the anthropologist is to establish **rapport,** or a trusting relationship between the researcher and the study population. The basic foundation of rapport is an open and honest presentation of goals by the anthropologist. When entering the field area, anthropologists should attempt to explain their interest in learning about the people's lives. This seemingly simple goal may be incomprehensible to the local people, especially those who have never heard of cultural anthropology and who cannot imagine why someone would want to study them.

Many stories exist about misunderstandings and *false role assignments*. For example, Richard Kurin reports that in the earliest stage of his research among the Karan people in northwest Pakistan, the villagers first thought he was a spy from the United States, Russia, India, or China (1980). After he convinced them that he was not a spy, the villagers thought he was a teacher of English because he was tutoring one of the village boys, next a doctor because he was giving out aspirin, and then a lawyer who could help them in negotiating local disputes because he could read court orders. Finally, they decided that he was a descendant of a local clan—thanks to the similarity of his last name to that of their ancestral king. The crowning touch for him was being considered a true "Karan."

An anthropologist's class, "race" or ethnicity, gender, and age may affect how she or he will be welcomed and interpreted by the local people. These factors may influence the success of fieldwork by paleoanthropologists and archaeologists, but they are likely to be more significant for cultural anthropologists who are conducting research among living people.

- Class. Cultural anthropologists often appear to be relatively wealthy and powerful to the people they study. They know that the anthropologist must have spent hundreds of dollars to travel to their village. They see the expensive equipment. This apparent wealth differential may mean that the people treat the researcher more like a high-status person than an average person or that they alter their normal behavior as a sign of respect.

  Laura Nader has urged anthropologists to depart from the tradition of studying people who are less wealthy and powerful by "studying up" (1972). In other words, she advocates doing research on the cultures of business elites, political leaders, policy makers, and government officials. In such situations, cultural anthropologists may find it difficult to get their prospective participants to talk with them. Research on the high-fashion industry of Japan placed a cultural anthropologist in touch with many members of the Japanese elite (Kondo 1997). These influential people made it clear to her that they would take her to court if they felt she wrote anything defamatory about them.

- "Race" and ethnicity. For most of its history, cultural anthropology has been dominated by Euro-American, White researchers who have studied people who are most often non-Euro-American and non-White. The effects of "Whiteness" on role assignments range from the anthropologist being labeled as a god or ancestor spirit to his or her being reviled as a representative of a colonialist past or imperialist present.

  While doing research in rural Jamaica, Tony Whitehead learned how perceptions of his "race" interacted with social class and status. An African American born in a family of poor sharecroppers, Whitehead thought that his heritage would lead to solidarity and rapport. Instead, the people assigned him to a high social position and referred to him as a "pretty talking man" because of his North American English. They also referred to him as "brown"—not on the basis of his skin color but because of his assumed high status. The status assignment did not impede Whitehead's fieldwork, but it did give him food for thought about the complexities of "race," class, and social status.

- Gender. Depending on the culture, gender roles and spatial boundaries may have a serious impact on research access. The very arrival of a young, unmarried woman may raise problems. A woman on her own may be considered weird or even unacceptable. On the other hand, where a public–private divide exists, some women researchers have been able to gain access to both men's public worlds and women's domestic worlds because they are assigned a gender-neutral role. In general, it is easier for men to gain rapport with men and for women to gain rapport with women. A woman researcher who studied a secretive gay community in the United States found that she could conduct research in settings dedicated to sociability and leisure, such as family gatherings, parties, and bars (Warren 1988:18). But she was not able to observe in domains dedicated to sexuality, such as homosexual bath houses.

- Age. Typically, anthropologists are adults, and they may therefore find it difficult to gain rapport with members of other age groups. Margaret Mead once commented that the ideal research team would consist of a three-generation family including children trained to understand what they are experiencing (1986:321). She knew that this ideal would not be practical. The best that researchers can do is to be aware of their limits and use imagination in establishing rapport across age groups. This challenge may require learning to understand and use age-specific language.

Culture Shock

Culture shock consists of the deep feelings of uneasiness, loneliness, and anxiety that often occur when a person has shifted from one culture to another. Culture shock can affect any anthropologist who conducts fieldwork, not just cultural anthropologists. It can involve negative reactions to the new culture's food, language, and social rules about privacy, for example. Food differences were a major source of adjustment difficulties for a Chinese anthropologist who came to the United States (Huang 1993). He could never get a "full" feeling from American food. Salads were especially unsatisfying. An American anthropologist who went to a Pacific island named Pohnpei found that her lack of fluency in the local language was the most serious cause of anxiety for her (Ward 1989). She bemoaned the fact that even the dogs of Pohnpei understood more than she did.

American cultural anthropologist Liza Dalby in full geisha formal dress. ■ Besides learning to dress correctly, what other cultural skills did Liza Dalby probably have to learn? (Source: Liza Dalby)

Sooner or later, depending on the researcher's adaptability and the nature of the challenges in the new context, culture shock usually passes. In time, the new culture becomes so familiar that the end of fieldwork and the return home may result in *reverse culture shock*. An anthropologist from California who spent a year in South India experienced reverse culture shock when he returned home (Beals 1980:119). Trust and warmth seemed to be replaced by inhumanity and coldness. He could not understand why people moved so quickly. He could not understand the babble on the television set, and he missed the soft sound of lowing cattle. Everything seemed wrong.

Data Collection Methods

Cultural anthropologists rely on participant observation as their cornerstone method. They also rely heavily on asking people questions either formally or informally. In addition, a range of other methods allow for more specialized data collection.

Participant Observation

The basic fieldwork technique of participant observation provides insights about the regular patterns that characterize the daily, weekly, and seasonal round of life, as well as about special events such as celebrations and about irregular, unexpected events such as arguments or intergroup violence. Being a participant means that, as much as possible, the anthropologist adopts the lifestyle of the people, living in the same kind of housing, eating the same food, speaking the local language, and participating in the study group's activities. Long-term participation is critical to the quality of the data. It improves the likelihood that the people in the study will not alter their behavior in response to the presence of the anthropologist. A minimum of a year is typical, because that period allows the anthropologist to see how the pattern of life changes over the seasons.

While participating in the culture, a cultural anthropologist seeks to observe carefully what is going on: who lives with whom, who interacts with whom, who the

Think of situations in which you have experienced culture shock, how it made you feel, and how you coped with it.

THINKING

OUTSIDE THE BOX

American cultural anthropologist Marjorie Shostak (right) during fieldwork among the Ju/wasi of Botswana in 1975. Shostak focused her research on women's lives and wrote Nisa, *a life history of a Ju/wasi woman.* ■ What would an anthropologist study about your everyday life? (Source: © Mel Konner/Anthro-Photo)

leaders are, and what seems important to people. The range of topics is vast, and a single anthropologist cannot hope to observe everything.

Asking Questions

Observation needs to be supplemented by asking questions. The most informal way to ask questions is through conversations with people while conducting participant observation. A more formal method is an **interview,** which is the gathering of verbal information through questions. Interview questions are often open-ended, which means that the respondent is asked to reply without any limits set on the response. These questions provide information that is **qualitative,** or descriptive. In contrast, **surveys,** or questionnaires, may be administered in a written format. Either the anthropologist or the person being questioned fills in answers on a paper form. Surveys often use closed-ended questions, which means, for example, that respondents must answer a question about whether they eat fish by saying "never," "rarely," "sometimes," or "often." Closed-ended questions provide **quantitative** or numeric data. Each of these kinds of data-collecting methods may be appropriate, depending on the context and kind of information sought. Cultural anthropologists tend to favor more open-ended formats because these provide what are called *emic* (insiders') views rather than *etic* (outsiders') views. Surveys, if used at all, should be carefully tested before use to be sure they make sense within the cultural context.

Like anthropologists studying humanity's past through site excavation, cultural anthropologists may employ sampling techniques because they realize they cannot talk to everyone in their field site or observe every activity. Random sampling may, in some contexts, be an appropriate and effective way to add breadth to one's study. For example, the anthropologist might visit and interview members of one household on each city block in a given zone, and that household would be determined in random fashion (say, the third house on the left side of the street). Cluster sampling is also used to provide more targeted information. Thus the anthropologist might visit twenty households in a poorer neighborhood and the same number in a richer neighborhood. A special kind of nonrandom sampling that cultural anthropologists often use is called *snowball sampling* (Bernard 1995). In this method, the sample grows through having research participants suggest other people who would be useful to interview. Although it is less scientifically representative than a random sample, using a snowball sample is often the only feasible way to proceed and will provide qualitative findings of value.

THINKING Imagine that a cultural anthropologist has come to spend a year with you and your **OUTSIDE** microcultural group. **THE BOX** What reactions would you have to being studied through participant observation?

Specialized Methods

Several specific methods provide in-depth information on certain aspects of culture.

- A method that provides quantitative data about people's behavior is called *time allocation study*. Recording, or asking the people themselves to record, daily activities provides rich insights into what people do (Gross 1984). Daily time allocation data about people's work, leisure, and special activities have shown, for example, how the patterns of men's and women's lives differ. Anthropologists using this method have sometimes been surprised at how much activity (such as hunting parties on moonlit nights, certain rituals, and social activities of a private nature) goes on at night.

- Another useful method is called the *life history*. A life history, collected through extensive interviewing, is a qualitative, detailed narrative of a single person's life experience as told to the researcher. It provides the most "micro" view of a culture. In the earlier days of the discipline, anthropologists who used this method tried to choose a "typical" or representative person. Because we now recognize that no single person is ever representative (in the scientific sense) of an entire culture, anthropologists focus on people who are particularly interesting. A life history study of four Hindu ascetics in Sri Lanka found that their long, matted hair had deep connections with their life history (Obeyesekere 1981). The ascetics say that their matted hair is a sign of a deity's presence.

Looking more closely at these people's lives, the anthropologist saw that they had all experienced psychological, personal afflictions, including sexual anxieties in their married life. In his interpretation, their matted hair symbolizes this suffering and provides them with a special status as holy and, thus, beyond the rules of married life and sexual relations.

- Cultural anthropologists also use texts and historical archives. The category of *texts* includes written or oral stories, myths, plays, sayings, speeches, jokes, and recordings of **discourse,** or language in use. In the early twentieth century, Franz Boas collected thousands of pages of texts from Native American groups of the Northwest Coast of Canada. This collection has proved valuable to contemporary tribal members as a repository of now-forgotten stories, songs, and rituals. Government and other official archives also are rich sources of data on the recent history of cultures. Ann Stoler has been a pioneer in the use of colonial archival data in her study of the role of the Dutch in Java (1985, 1989). She found information on colonial objectives and strategies of domination, the culture of the colonial Dutch people, and the impact of the Dutch on Javanese culture. Most countries have national libraries and archives. Localized collections are also important. Parish churches throughout Europe have detailed records of births and deaths. In Japan and China, government records provide information on land ownership and family histories. Photograph archives are another important source of data on recent cultural history.

A Sri Lankan woman whose life story Gananath Obeyesekere analyzed. A priestess to the deity Kataragama, she stands in the shrine room of her house, holding her long matted hair. ■ Think of how hairstyles in a culture that you know express a person's religion or marital status. (Source: Gananath Obeyesekere)

Teamwork

It is clear that a single anthropologist faces a major challenge in trying to participate, observe, ask, and otherwise learn about a huge range of topics. Whereas paleoanthropologists and archaeologists usually work in teams, cultural anthropologists have

A multidisciplinary team comprising anthropologists, engineers, and agricultural experts from the United States and Sudan meet to discuss a resettlement project. ■ Have you ever carried out research as part of a team? If so, what are the pros and cons? (Source: Michael Horowitz)

generally worked alone. Increasingly, though, cultural anthropologists are participating in team projects either with other anthropologists or with professionals in other specialties. A research project designed to assess the environmental and social affects of building a dam in the Senegal River Valley in West Africa involved a team consisting of cultural anthropologists, hydrologists, and agronomists (Horowitz and Salem-Murdock 1993).

Recording and Analyzing Contemporary Culture

While conducting participant observation and using more specific research methods such as those we have noted, cultural anthropologists must record their findings carefully and thoroughly, keeping track of dates, context, and the anthropologist's own impressions and queries as life proceeds. In addition, care must be taken to keep fieldwork records secure from damage, loss, or possible theft.

Field Notes

The primary method for recording findings that cultural anthropologists have used, for over a hundred years, is the taking of field notes. In earlier times, field notes were handwritten in journals by kerosene light on a crude wooden table in an "exotic" setting. Today, cultural anthropologists sometimes record their observations in handwritten notes, but more often in computer files, tape recordings, and video recordings. The age-old rule that "sooner is better" in recording observations and events still applies. Daily recordings are essential because human memory is so frail. Many anthropologists make "scratch notes" during the day, on small pieces of paper kept in a shirt pocket, to enhance their memory. Even a relatively uneventful day may result in dozens of pages of typewritten notes, and a busy or special day will yield much more.

Tape Recording and Photography

Various recording methods are important supplements to handwritten and computerized notes. These recording techniques require ethical care. They must be protected from improper use—perhaps kept in a locked trunk or closet. The recording of individual voices on tape or faces on film must not proceed without the permission of the people themselves. Given the multiple technical aids now available for recording culture, teamwork is again important. For example, if you are making a video recording of a ritual, you cannot simultaneously be asking people to explain what is going on and taking notes. Film recording has proved useful in all of anthropology's fields.

V isual anthropology encompasses a variety of methods such as still photography, film, and hypermedia. In the early years of anthropology, still photography was the only method available, and equipment was large and cumbersome. Now, increasing technological capabilities offer far more potential for using visual methods for collecting, analyzing, and presenting anthropological evidence. As noted earlier in this chapter when we considered methods for studying humanity's past, aerial photography aids in site location and can help pinpoint excavation work to make it more effective and less destructive.

Past, present, and potential uses of visual media vary across the four fields of anthropology, given the fields' differing objectives and sources of data. Yet similarities exist as well. We invite you to discover examples of past, present, and potential uses of visual media in the four fields. To spark your thinking, we provide a few examples here.

Using still photography and film for data collection has long been a core method in cultural anthropology. Early in the twentieth century, Franz Boas was a pioneer in filming rituals of Native American peoples as a kind of *salvage anthropology* project. Later, his student Margaret Mead pursued the use of film as a way of collecting data and documenting cultural practices in everyday life. One of her best-known filmmaking projects was the recording of how mothers bathed their babies in several cultures. These short films provided her with material for comparing child care and psychological development of children across cultures.

New forms of computer software allow data analysis and representation of archaeological evidence through simulations and reconstructions (Forte and Siliotti 1997). A recently developed graphics language called Virtual Reality Mark-up Language (VRML) can describe three-dimensional objects and allow the user to move into three-dimensional space via hypermedia links. Information and objects can be rotated and observed from any angle. Computer simulations can now generate reconstructions of temples and cities from their architectural remains and generate reconstructions of whole fossils from fragments. ■

FOOD FOR THOUGHT

■ Think of a small research project in any of anthropology's four fields that you would like to conduct. Consider how visual media could help improve data collection, analysis, interpretation, or preservation.

CROSSING
THE FIELDS

Visual Anthropology Methods
for All Four Fields

A computer reconstruction of the Great Temple at Tenochtitlan (Mexico City), Mexico. Computers are proving to be invaluable in many areas of research in anthropology, including architectural reconstructions such as this one. (Source: © Photoservice Electa)

Analysis, Interpretation, and Representation of Findings

Most cultural anthropologists return from the field with more data than they will ever be able to write up completely. Most also have collected a variety of types of data—written and visual, qualitative and quantitative. It is often daunting to contemplate analyzing the richness of the fieldwork experience.

Qualitative data include descriptive field notes, narratives provided by research participants such as myths or life histories, and video recordings of events. No set guidelines exist for the analysis and representation of qualitative data; this is an area where the "art" of cultural anthropology comes to the fore. One procedure is to search, either by hand or with the aid of a computer, for recurrent themes in the data. The anthropologist becomes immersed in the data, poring over it, until patterns of words and actions emerge that are then taken to be keys to understanding the culture under study. New forms of software allow for thematic searching, but this method depends, first, on computerizing all the data and, second, on devising a good coding scheme to guide the search.

Analysis of quantitative, or numeric, data is usually done with the aid of a computer. For example, in a study of household expenditure patterns using a sample of 120 households in Jamaica, the weekly expenditure data collected over a year were entered into a computer (Miller and Stone 1983). The data were sorted into urban and rural groups and, within those groups, into three expenditure groups (lower, medium, higher). The last step was to compute and compare mean (average) expenditures on food, housing, and transportation for the various social groups (see Figure 4.6).

Fieldwork results are usually written up in an **ethnography,** a book-length description of a culture or cultures studied for an extended period of time. Ethnographies

FIGURE 4.6

Mean weekly expenditure shares (percentage) in eleven categories by urban and rural expenditure groups, Jamaica, 1983–1984.

Item	Urban				Rural			
	Group 1	Group 2	Group 3	Total	Group 1	Group 2	Group 3	Total
Number of Households	26	25	16	67	32	30	16	78
Food	60.5	51.6	50.1	54.7	74.1	62.3	55.7	65.8
Alcohol	0.2	0.4	1.5	0.6	0.5	1.1	1.0	0.8
Tobacco	0.8	0.9	0.9	0.9	1.1	1.7	1.2	1.4
Dry Goods	9.7	8.1	8.3	8.7	8.8	10.2	14.3	10.5
Housing	7.3	11.7	10.3	9.7	3.4	5.7	3.9	4.4
Fuel	5.4	6.0	5.0	5.6	3.7	3.9	4.1	3.9
Transportation	7.4	8.2	12.4	8.9	3.0	5.3	7.6	4.9
Health	0.3	0.6	0.7	0.5	1.5	1.4	1.7	1.5
Education	3.5	2.8	3.1	3.2	1.2	2.1	3.0	1.9
Entertainment	0.1	0.9	1.1	0.6	0.0	0.1	0.3	0.2
Other	5.2	8.3	6.9	6.8	2.1	6.0	6.9	4.6
Total*	100.4	99.5	100.3	100.2	99.4	99.8	99.7	99.9

*Totals may not add up to 100 due to rounding.

(*Source:* From "Social Patterns of Food Expenditure Among Low-Income Jamaicans" by Barbara D. Miller in *Papers and Recommendations of the Workshop on Food and Nutrition Security in Jamaica in the 1980s and Beyond,* ed. by Kenneth A. Leslie and Lloyd B. Rankine, 1987.)

vary in style and content. In *realist ethnographies,* the anthropologist presents the findings of the study in a scientific way, adopting an objective view of the culture and incorporating little first-person voice. These ethnographies focus on the culture and its members' practices and beliefs. Most classic ethnographies, such as those by Margaret Mead and Bronislaw Malinowski, are realist ethnographies, and many contemporary ethnographies fit in this category, too.

In contrast, *reflexive ethnographies* tell the story of the research interaction between the anthropologist and the members of the culture studied. The word *reflexive* refers to the position of the ethnographer as constantly reflecting on his or her role in affecting the very findings of the project. Reflexive ethnographies explicitly seek to present a personalized account, with the anthropologist squarely in the picture. An example of such an ethnography is Vincent Crapanzano's book *Tuhami,* which explores the life history of a Moroccan man who believed he was possessed by spirits (1980). Crapanzano interweaves the effects of his presence in Tuhami's life and thinking, showing how cultural anthropology research is an iterative (two-way) process. As Crapanzano notes, "As Tuhami's interlocutor, I became an active participant in his life history . . . . Not only did my presence, and my questions, prepare him for the text he was to produce, but they produced what I read as a change of consciousness in him. They produced a change of consciousness in me, too" (p. 11).

Many of the newest ethnographies strike a balance between realism and reflexivity. Cultural anthropologists know very well that no one can spend a long period of time immersed in a culture without affecting it and also being affected by the experience. They realize that their research does not conform completely to the traditional scientific method, nor can it because they study living people in their everyday lives. Instead of the observation-hypothesis-observation conducted in a laboratory situation, good cultural anthropology requires sensitivity to the researcher's position and impact in the field and honest reporting about these matters.

In addition to writing ethnographies, cultural anthropologists write short articles for scholarly journals. Just like anthropologists who study humanity's past, cultural anthropologists share their findings with the public through radio, television, the Internet, and articles in popular magazines. Many cultural anthropologists work in museums creating exhibits for public education. In this work, they seek to build collaborations with the people whose culture is being represented in order to avoid possible misinterpretations.

Protection of Research Participants and Informed Consent

As noted in Chapter 1, anthropologists' primary obligations are to avoid any kind of harm to the people in the research project, to make sure they understand the scope and goals of the project, and to allow them to remain anonymous or receive recognition, depending on their wishes. Cultural anthropologists led the way in promoting ethical guidelines for fieldwork among living people. (This is a good time to review the Code of Ethics of the American Anthropological Association; see p. 25).

In the United States, since the 1990s, universities and other institutions that support or conduct social science research with living people have been brought under close review by institutional review boards (IRBs). IRBs are committees at each institution charged with monitoring the ethicality of projects that are conducted by affiliated researchers and involve living humans. The IRB guidelines were formulated on the basis of a medical model with the goal of protecting subjects in medical research by making sure they are fully informed of any possible consequences. IRB guidelines normally require written consent of the participants, and thus they involve the assumption that participants are literate members of a writing-based culture. Although obtaining the informed, written consent of research participants is reasonable and feasible in many anthropology research projects, it is not reasonable or feasible in many contexts, especially in largely oral-based cultures. Fortunately, IRBs are beginning to have a better understanding of the particular circumstances in which many anthropologists conduct fieldwork, and it is possible to request a waiver of written consent.

Student research projects that involve living people are also subject to IRB oversight. Failure to gain IRB approval means that findings from the project cannot be published. Because IRB guidelines are subject to modification, it is always best to check your institution's web site for the latest rules.

The basic message in this discussion is that researchers have a serious responsibility to avoid causing harm to anyone through a research project. Just as an archaeologist's work never leaves a site in exactly the same condition, the presence of an anthropologist doing research with living people inevitably brings about change. Anthropologists do not leave a physical mark such as a trench, but they may leave psychological marks through their very presence, their questions, their interactions, and their material exchanges with participants. The "field" is never quite the same again, and one must make one's best effort to ensure that the changes that occur are changes that the research population welcomes.

RESEARCH CHALLENGES

Both the objectives of anthropology and the conditions under which anthropologists work mean that anthropologists face some unusual challenges. Danger during fieldwork is an issue that was rarely discussed in the past but is gaining more attention now, especially in these times of increasing levels of violence worldwide. Certainly, anthropologists are not unique in having to pay attention to safety during their research, and we do not mean to portray anthropology as an especially dangerous field. Rather, we seek to counter the false image of anthropology as pure adventure.

A second major challenge arises from the history of anthropology as an "extractive" endeavor, in which anthropologists went to the field and collected data for themselves or for their country, giving little thought to their responsibility to communities from which the data came. It is only right, and increasingly urgent, to develop and implement collaborative models of research, preservation, and representation that link anthropologists and communities.

Danger in the Field

In this section, we consider the physical and psychological risks that fieldwork poses to researchers and to any members of their family who are also in the field. A long-standing romantic image of "the anthropologist as hero/heroine" or, more modestly, of the "anthropologist as intrepid adventurer" has had the effect of camouflaging the actual dangers and risks of fieldwork. Dangers from the physical environment are often serious and can be fatal. In the 1980s, the slippery paths of the highland Philippines claimed the life of Michelle Zimbalist Rosaldo, a major figure in cultural anthropology of the later twentieth century. Disease is frequently experienced. Many anthropologists working in tropical areas have contracted infectious diseases, such as malaria and typhoid, that persist for their entire lives, and some cases have been fatal. People who search for fossils in hot and dry areas risk exposure to heat and dehydration. There have been a few times when inexperienced researchers have lost their bearings, become dehydrated, and perished.

Social violence in the field figures prominently in some recent research experiences of cultural anthropologists. During the five years that Philippe Bourgois lived in East Harlem, New York, researching crack culture and poverty, he witnessed a shooting outside his window, a bombing and machine-gunning of a numbers joint, a shoot-out and police car chase in front of the pizza parlor where he was eating, the aftermath of a fire-bombing of a heroin house, a dozen serious fights, and "almost daily exposure to broken-down human beings" (1995:32). Additionally, the police rough-handled him several times because they did not believe he was "just a professor" doing research, and he was once mugged.

Canadian anthropologist Nancy Howell conducted the first—and to date the only—comprehensive study of health risks and other hazards involved in anthropological fieldwork (1990). After more than twenty years of fieldwork in southern Africa, she was suddenly confronted with the issue of danger in the field. One of her teenage sons was killed and another one injured in a truck accident in Botswana. While grieving, she heard, from anthropological friends and acquaintances, stories of other fieldwork accidents. She approached the American Anthropological Association (AAA) and pointed out the lack of attention to fieldwork safety in the discipline. The AAA responded by providing financial support for Howell to undertake a detailed inquiry into hazard types, regional variations, and variations across the four fields within anthropology. Her methods included drawing a random sample of 311 anthropologists from among those listed in the AAA's *Guide to Departments of Anthropology*. She sent these 311 people a questionnaire asking about their gender, age, work status, health status, and work habits in the field. She asked for reports of health risks and other hazards they had experienced in the field.

Of the 311 people in the sample, 236 completed the questionnaire—a good response rate for a mail survey. Survey questions asked about living conditions, including housing, water, sanitary facilities, food, transportation, health facilities, and safety equipment taken to the field. The responses provided rich information on many unstudied occupational hazards, including such rarely discussed topics as mental health problems while in the field. One of the major findings was that anthropologists in all four fields have equal patterns of hazard frequency, and this finding applies to both men and women. Regional variations did appear. Africa had the highest hazard rates, followed by Asia and the Pacific and then Latin America. Many anthropologists make inadequate health preparations beyond having the required inoculations. Only about one-fourth of the respondents, for example, reported taking a first-aid course before they went to the field. Major categories of hazards experienced include exposure to the elements (cold, sun, and high altitude), vehicular accidents on land and water, dietary deficiencies and weight loss, animal hazards such as snakebite, and social violence such as rape or attempted rape, assault, or military attack.

In spite of the general similarities in exposure to risk across the four fields, two types of hazards are specifically related to fieldwork involving excavation. The first category involves injuries from equipment and tools. In one case, a backhoe being used to move earth tipped over and fell on an archaeologist, injuring him seriously. Cuts from shovels and pickaxes occur, and one person lost an eye when a piece of equipment was tossed rather than handed from one worker to another. The second category of excavation injury is related to cave-ins. Several reports of injuries from cave-ins emerged from the sample, but no such injury was serious. Howell's study yielded numerous insights about hazards and a set of recommendations based on her findings (see Figure 4.7 on p. 126).

THINKING OUTSIDE THE BOX

Howell's study was conducted more than twenty years ago. What do you think a similar study would reveal about major fieldwork hazards now?

Linking Research to Communities

Anthropology is definitely making progress in moving beyond its colonial heritage of collecting objects and information from places and peoples in the interest of promoting the knowledge and status of the colonizing powers. For example, the earliest anthropologists would be quite intrigued by the concept of informed consent. Yet this progress is neither rapid nor easy. Collaboration and teamwork take time and require more social commitment and skills than extractive research methods do. The benefits, however, far outweigh the costs. Specifically, a collaborative model promotes

- fairness in terms of reciprocity.
- better data.

FIGURE 4.7

Recommendations for improving fieldwork safety.

General
Raise awareness of the dangers of fieldwork: ■ Overcome the tradition of denial of problems. ■ Share information on risks and strategies for risk reduction more widely.
For fieldworkers
Anticipate potential risks at the chosen site. Obtain appropriate medical training. Locate medical care facilities in the country and region.
For colleges and universities
Train anthropology students in fieldwork safety. Ensure that university policies on safety extend to fieldwork situations.

(*Source:* Adapted from "Recommendations for Improving Fieldwork Study," Chapter 15 in *Surviving Fieldwork: A Report of the Advisory Panel on Health and Safety in Fieldwork* by Nancy Howell. Copyright © 1990 by American Anthropological Association. Reprinted by permission of the American Anthropological Association.)

- more accurate and fair representations of peoples and their cultures.
- care and protection of cultural heritage.
- education and empowerment of local people.

In Research on Humanity's Past

In the early days of excavation, a research team would simply arrive at a site and start digging. At best, they would make contact with local residents to establish a source of cheap labor and arrange for food and water supplies. The researchers had little sense that local people could contribute anything of intellectual value to the project or that collaboration could even transform the entire project. Indigenous peoples of Australia have been pioneers in promoting collaborative archaeological research about humanity's past (Moser et al. 2002). Working with the Australian Institute of Aboriginal Studies, they have transformed research agendas, become involved as indigenous archaeologists, contributed oral histories that enhance material discoveries, and helped educate archaeologists about their concerns and interests. The collaborative model is spreading to all parts of the world with positive results.

One model project has been established in Quesir, Egypt. This site is one of the great trading centers of the ancient world, first linking Rome with the eastern world, declining in the third century, and then regaining prominence in the thirteenth and fourteenth centuries due to Muslim pilgrimage to Mecca and Medina and trade with the Arabian peninsula and India. In 1998, the Community Archaeology Project at Quesir was initiated between the British research team and local community members. Many local leaders were involved, including the mayor, who was concerned about the potential impact of tourism on the city. Others were simply interested in learning more about their heritage. This project has yielded insights about community relations that are relevant to research relations in all four fields (see Figure 4.8 on p. 128).

In Research on Humanity's Present

The earlier freedom of a cultural anthropologist to represent a culture as he or she perceived it is increasingly questioned and rejected. Many of the people whom anthro-

pologists traditionally studied—non-elites of Africa, India, and Asia—can now read what anthropologists have written about them. Many are not pleased and believe they have been misrepresented. For example, when Annette Weiner was doing her fieldwork in the Trobriand Islands, she was told by several people there that Malinowski had gotten some things wrong about their culture (1976:xvi). Even if members of researched cultures could not read the books written about them or see the exhibits which display their culture, anthropologists should still be concerned about what they say and display.

An emerging direction in cultural anthropology research, writing, and other forms of representing cultures is the attempt to collaborate with members of the study population as active participants rather than interacting with them as research subjects alone. A reflection of this change is the increasing discomfort with, and rejection of, the older term *informant.* The term sounds hauntingly and negatively related to espionage or war, in the first place, and it also implies the passive handing over of information sought by someone else. IRBs use the term *human subjects,* which cultural anthropologists reject for similar reasons. Many cultural anthropologists now use the term *consultant,* which seems to imply work for hire that is remunerated financially. We prefer the more neutral term *research population* or *research participants* to refer to the study group and the term *member of the research population* or *research participant* for an individual.

Cultural anthropologist Luke Eric Lassiter sets a good example of how to do collaborative research (2004). During his doctoral studies at the University of North Carolina at Chapel Hill, he began to explore how to conduct his dissertation research as a collaborative project. During his research with the Kiowa community of Oklahoma, he developed a close working relationship with about a dozen Kiowa people who especially helped him understand and write about Kiowa songs. For his Kiowa

FIGURE 4.8
Strategies for community collaboration in anthropological fieldwork.

Communication and partnership

Community participation in problem setting
Communication with local organizations and councils
Interviews and oral histories
Work updates
Openness about problems
Shared ownership of findings
Shared authorship

Employment and training

Full-time employment of local people
Basic training
Formal training

Public presentation

Reports written in plain language
Periodic temporary exhibits
Photographic and video archive
Establishing a web site
Making international connections

Education resources

Site visits
Children's books
Artifact database
Genealogy, oral history database

Community-controlled enterprises

Management of exhibits, learning center, or local museum
Publication royalties
Spin-off products such as t-shirts, project logo

(*Source:* Figure, "Strategies for Community Collaboration in Anthropological Fieldwork" from "Transforming Archaeology through Practice: Strategies for Collaborative Archaeology and the Community Archaeology Project at Quesir, Egypt" by Stephanie Moser et al., in *World Archaeology* 34, pp. 220–248, 2002. Reprinted by permission of Taylor & Francis, Ltd.)

collaborators, it was essential that the book not be just another academic dissertation but be accessible to "normal" people. Thus Lassiter's audience included both his academic advisors at the university and the Kiowa people. Throughout the write-up, he and his Kiowa collaborators pored over every page together, making sure that the material was accurate and that it reflected the Kiowa people's perceptions. The process of collaboration provided Lassiter with deeper insights into Kiowa culture, because the emerging text became a "centerpiece of a larger ongoing conversation" (p. 7). Beyond learning are the benefits of sharing. As Lassiter put it: "A collaborative ethnography opens up the possibility that ethnography can matter for people beyond the academy. This was brought home to me most powerfully when a sixteen-

The collaborative research team led by Luke Eric Lassiter includes Muncie community members, and students and faculty from Ball State University. ■ Consider the implications of collaborative fieldwork compared with fieldwork conducted by an individual researcher. (Source: © Danny Gawlowski)

year-old Kiowa singer revealed to me that *The Power of Kiowa Song* was the first book he had actually read from cover to cover" (p. 8).

Lassiter's next project was collaborative in an even wider sense. He involved students in his anthropology classes at Ball State University in ethnographic collaboration with many members of the African American community of Muncie, Indiana. This project generated a wide base of participation and resulted in a book with shared authorship (2004).

In all four fields of anthropology, adherence to research ethics and collaboration in writings and representations yield better insights about humanity and protect humanity's heritage. Methods are not a minor part of anthropology but are, in fact, central. Accordingly, we will not drop the subject here but will continue to discuss it throughout the book.

Listen to some Kiowa songs at *www.uspress. arizona.edu/extras/ kiowa/kiowasng.htm.*

THINKING

OUTSIDE THE BOX

THE BIG QUESTIONS REVISITED

■ HOW do anthropologists study humanity's past?

Paleoanthropologists and archaeologists collect, analyze, interpret, represent, and preserve evidence of many different kinds in their study of humanity's past. They rely mainly on seven types of data, fossils and artifacts being the most important. The anthropologist's first step in searching for evidence of humanity's past by collecting fossils and artifacts is to identify a location for field research. The second step involves recovering the evidence from the site, often through excavation. Excavation is a method for fossil or artifact recovery in which the material surrounding the evidence is removed both vertically and horizontally. Excavation is time-intensive, costly, and damaging to the site. Therefore, nondestructive methods of locating fossils and artifacts are increasingly used.

Accurate dates for fossils, artifacts, and the sites they come from are essential to their interpretation. Two major types of dating exist: absolute dating methods and relative dating methods. Research projects generate vast amounts of quantitative data that are analyzed using computers. Computers also allow for virtual analysis, reconstruction, and representation. Computer-generated visualization of fossils and artifacts aids in their analysis by scholars and in their appreciation and understanding by the general public.

■ HOW do anthropologists study contemporary people?

Cultural anthropologists gather data on contemporary people by conducting fieldwork. The field is anywhere that people are. It might be a village far from the anthropologist's home or a clinic or school in the anthropologist's own country. The main method of anthropological investigation in the field is participant observation, in which the researcher lives in and studies a culture for an extended period of time. A primary goal of the anthropologist when entering the field is to establish rapport, or a trusting relationship between the researcher and the study population. Fieldwork—and, later, returning from fieldwork—usually causes some degree of culture shock for the anthropologist. In addition to participant observation, anthropologists rely on asking people questions either formally or informally. The most informal way to ask questions is through simple conversations. A more formal method is through an interview. A range of other methods, such as time allocation studies and life histories, allow for more specialized data collection. Most cultural anthropologists collect several types of data—written and visual, qualitative and quantitative. They analyze their data by hand and/or by computer, depending on the kind of data. The customary way to present the results of fieldwork is to publish an ethnography.

■ WHAT challenges do anthropologists face in their research?

The objectives of anthropology and the working conditions that often prevail mean that anthropologists face some unusual challenges. Danger during fieldwork is one issue. Danger comes from physical sources, such as working at excavation sites and driving on rough roads, and from social sources such as political violence. A survey of anthropologists in the 1980s revealed that dangers are similar for all four fields of anthropology. Recommendations from the study include the need to raise awareness of possible risks, make sure field researchers receive appropriate medical training, promote teaching about fieldwork safety in anthropology classes, and urge funding agencies to provide financial support for special safety needs. A second major challenge arises from the history of anthropology as an "extractive" endeavor with little sense of responsibility to communities. Anthropologists sensitive to this problem have recently developed strong collaborative relationships with the communities they have studied. Some lessons that can be generally applied include the need to promote communication with the community members, to provide employment and training, to ensure that research results are shared with the public through a variety of presentations, to generate educational resources for the public, and to develop community enterprises that contribute to the economic welfare of the people. A collaborative model has many advantages over an extractive model, including fairness in terms of reciprocity, capacity to yield more accurate representations of people and their cultures, care and protection of people's cultural heritage, and the education and empowerment of local people.

KEY CONCEPTS

absolute dating method, p. 106
androcentrism, p. 110
artifact, p. 102
assemblage, p. 104
culture shock, p. 117
discourse, p. 119
ethnoarchaeology, p. 104
ethnography, p. 122
excavation, p. 104

feature, p. 104
fieldwork, p. 100
fossil, p. 102
horizon, or stratigraphic layer, p. 102
interview, p. 118
midden, p. 109
participant observation, p. 112
potassium–argon dating, p. 107
qualitative, p. 118

quantitative, p. 118
radiocarbon dating, p. 107
rapport, p. 115
relative dating method, p. 107
restudy, p. 114
sample, p. 105
site, p. 104
surface find, p. 102
survey, p. 118

SUGGESTED READINGS

Arthur C. Aufderheide. *The Scientific Study of Mummies*. New York: Cambridge University Press, 2003. This guide to the collection, study, and preservation of mummies also provides an overview of the world's mummies, a history of mummy studies, and a final chapter on the use and abuse of mummies.

H. Russell Bernard. *Research Methods in Anthropology: Qualitative and Quantitative Approaches*. Walnut Creek, CA: AltaMira/Sage, 1995. This book is a guide to a variety of research methods in cultural anthropology from start to finish: designing a research project, data collecting, analysis and presentation.

Kathleen M. DeWalt and Billie R. DeWalt. *Participant Observation: A Guide for Fieldworkers*. New York: AltaMira Press, 2002. This book is a comprehensive guide to doing participant observation. It covers research design, taking field notes, data analysis, and theoretical issues.

Maurizio Forte and Alberto Siliotto, eds. *Virtual Archaeology: Re-creating Ancient Worlds*. New York: Harry N. Abrams, 1997. Several hundred illustrations demonstrate the value of computer applications to re-creating and visualizing artifacts and sites from humanity's past. Reconstructions include Maya temples, Mongol herder camps, the city of Beijing, the face of an Egyptian prince, and domestic architecture in Çatalhöyük.

Peggy Golde ed. *Women in the Field: Anthropological Experiences*. 2nd ed. Berkeley: University of California Press, 1986. This classic collection provides 15 chapters on fieldwork by women cultural anthropologists including Margaret Mead, Laura Nader, Ernestine Friedl, and Jean Briggs.

Bruce Grindal and Frank Salamone, eds. *Bridges to Humanity: Narratives on Anthropology and Friendship*. Prospect Heights, IL: Waveland Press, 1999. Fourteen essays explore the mystery of the ethnographic relationship in which a stranger arrives as an observer but develops a personal relationship with those observed. The narratives provide insight into how cultural barriers are crossed in settings such as Nigeria, the Himalayas, and Mexico. The authors reflect on the friendships they established in the field, how friendship contributed to the research, and how or whether fieldwork friendships can be continued after the anthropologist leaves the field.

Joy Hendry. *An Anthropologist in Japan: Glimpses of Life in the Field*. London: Routledge, 1999. A first-person account by a cultural anthropologist, this book describes the author's third research project in Japan, revealing how her focus changed in the course of the research and how she reached unexpected conclusions.

D. Ann Herring and Alan C. Swedlund, eds. *Human Biologists in the Archives: Demography, Health, Nutrition and Genet-ics in Historical Populations*. New York: Cambridge University Press, 2003. The first and last chapters provide overviews about archival data for understanding important questions in the human biology of historic populations. Twelve case study chapters examine topics including population change among Chumash Indians at the Alta California missions, growth patterns of children in a New England middle school in the first half of the twentieth century, the Gibraltar cholera epidemic of 1865, and malnutrition among northern peoples of Canada in the 1940s.

Martin Jones. *The Molecule Hunt: Archaeology and the Search for Ancient DNA*. New York: Arcade Publishing Company, 2001. The author discusses how DNA analysis sheds new light on human prehistory.

Ann T. Jordan. *Business Anthropology*. Prospect Heights, IL: Waveland Press. This book provides material on methods in cultural anthropology and presents examples of how these methods have been used in business organizations to analyze consumer behavior, marketing, product design, organizational change, globalization. and diversity.

Choong Soon Kim. *One Anthropologist, Two Worlds: Three Decades of Reflexive Fieldwork in North America and Asia*. Knoxville: University of Tennessee Press, 2002. The author reflects on his fieldwork, conducted over thirty years, on Japanese industry in the American South and, in Korea, on families displaced by the war and partition. Korean-born and educated in the United States, Kim himself is of multiple cultural worlds.

Carolyn Nordstrom and Antonius C. G. M. Robben, eds. *Fieldwork under Fire: Contemporary Studies of Violence and Survival*. Berkeley: University of California Press, 1995. An introductory chapter presents general themes considered in the book. Case studies describe fieldwork in politically dangerous settings, including Palestine, China, Sri Lanka, the United States, Croatia, Guatemala, and Ireland.

Sarah Pink. *Doing Visual Ethnography: Images, Media and Representation in Research*. Thousand Oaks, CA: Sage Publications, 2001. The author considers a range of topics in visual ethnography, including the role of reflexivity and subjectivity, the usefulness of visual methods, ethics, photography, video, and electronic texts.

Carla M. Sinopoli. *Approaches to Archaeological Ceramics*. New York: Plenum Press, 1991. Ceramics are a major source of information about humanity's past, and this book provides an overview of how ceramic vessels are made, how archaeologists study their remains, how ceramics answer key questions about production and trade, and the relationship between ceramics and social organization.

PART II Biological and Cultural Evolution

YOHANNES HAILE-SELASSIE, a paleoanthropologist, is curator and head of the physical anthropology department at the Cleveland Museum of Natural History. His position has afforded him the opportunity to continue research on human evolution that he began as a graduate student at the University of California-Berkeley in the 1990s. An Ethiopian, Haile-Selassie participated in Berkeley's program as part of its mission to train students from developing countries in paleoanthropology.

Haile-Selassie has made significant discoveries in the Middle Awash valley of the Afar Region of Ethiopia, about 140 miles northeast of the capital Addis Ababa. His findings challenged scientific thinking about the ancestors of the human species. Scientists have now accumulated enough evidence to establish a potential new hominin species, which Haile-Selassie has named *Ardipithecus kadabba.*

ANTHROPOLOGY
in the Real World

■ **Yohannes Haile-Selassie, Paleoanthropologist**

Haile-Selassie has described the frustrations and joys of paleoanthropological expeditions. He notes that when he works without finding anything, it feels as if each hour is a day, but when he finds real evidence, he doesn't "even want night to come."

His long days have been successful. Between 1997 and 2000, he discovered 11 bone and teeth specimens from at least five individuals that date back to between 5 and 6 million years ago, the time when the human ancestral line is believed to have diverged from that of chimpanzees. In 2001, more dental fragments were recovered. Scientists disagree about whether their shape and wear patterns prove a hominin connection.

The form of a recovered toe bone and fragments of a leg bone are likewise important. Some scientists think that these hominins, who may have been about the size of a modern chimpanzee, walked upright. Current geochemical analysis of the sedimentary soils present when *Ardipithecus kadabba* lived indicate that the area was a rift valley with lakes and dense forests that provided woody plants as food for the species.

Haile-Selassie explains the importance of these scientific recoveries: "*Ardipithecus kadabba* may . . . represent the first species on the human branch of the family tree just after the evolutionary split between lines leading to modern chimpanzees and humans."

The Awash region of Ethiopia today is a hot, dry scrubland that presents a serious challenge to scientific research expeditions, but it has also proved to be rich with fossils. It was here that "Lucy" was discovered three decades ago and that the first stone tool used by human ancestors was uncovered in 1997. Haile-Selassie's discovery of *A. kadabba* may not be the "missing link" between humans and apes, or the first hominin, but it has brought us much closer to it.

THE BIG QUESTIONS

- WHAT are the general characteristics of primates?
- WHAT are the varieties of primates?
- WHAT can nonhuman primates reveal about humanity's past and what is their future?

The Nonhuman Primates

A chimpanzee termite-fishing. Recent research has revealed differences between males and females in how they learn to termite-fish. (Source: © James Balog/ Getty Images/The Image Bank)

Chimpanzees use tools more than any other nonhuman primate. Primatologists want to know how chimpanzees learn to use tools. A four-year study carried out in Gombe National Park, Tanzania, used videotape recordings of termite-fishing to provide a large dataset of observations (Lonsdorf and Eberly 2004). The researchers focused on fourteen wild chimpanzees under the age of eleven years and their mothers. The cameras were located at termite-fishing sites.

Termite-fishing consists of the extraction of termites from a termite mound through tool use. Typically, a chimpanzee selects a flexible twig, removes the leaves and side branches, and dips it into a hole in a termite mound. The termites cling to the dipping tool. The chimpanzee then removes the twig from the mound and, drawing the twig across its mouth, consumes the termites.

Analysis of many hours of observations revealed that young females quickly learn how to fish for termites, whereas young males prefer to spend their time playing. Young females termite-fished more often, and at a younger age, than males did. Females gathered more termites per dip than males did. Young females spent more time watching their mothers than young males did. Each of the young females adopted techniques that resembled those of her own mother. For example, an individual mother tends to select twigs of a particular length, and a daughter's tool length tends to be the same as that of her mother. Even so, no instance of active "teaching" by mothers was observed.

This evidence is the first to reveal clear differences in learning patterns between male and female chimpanzees. Scientists now wonder whether these differences are examples of sex-based differences in learning processes that are widely shared among primates, including humans, or whether they are largely due to group cultural patterns that "track" females into a particular strategy of resource acquisition and related learning.

This chapter introduces the main groups of living nonhuman primates. The first section provides an overview of general characteristics of the primate order. The second section describes the living primates. The last section considers the relevance of nonhuman primate studies for understanding humanity's past and the impact of contemporary humanity on the future survival and welfare of nonhuman primates.

 INTRODUCING THE PRIMATES

The **primates** make up an order of mammals that includes two suborders, *prosimians* ("pre-apes") and *anthropoids* (monkeys and apes). Modern humans are a variety of ape and thus are part of the primate order. Nonhuman primates are of great interest to the general public because of their (often amusing) similarities to humans. They are the focus of study of many scientists, including primatologists (as noted in Chapter 1).

Primatologists often spend weeks, even years, observing nonhuman primates in the wild and in captivity. They study where the animals live, what they eat, their social structure, and how they communicate. They do this for two main reasons. The first is the same as the reason why other biologists study carnivores, bats, or whales. These animals are all part of the living world, and modern humans are naturally curious about other living creatures.

The second reason is that primates are not just any other part of the living world; they are the group of animals to which modern humans belong. This close relationship to humans means that nonhuman primate studies are closely linked to the research questions of human evolution. Such studies reveal things about more than just these animals themselves. In this case, they also tell us about ourselves (Sperling 1991). For example, studying how living nonhuman primate morphology correlates with their behavior can help anthropologists generate hypotheses about the behavior of human ancestors. This approach uses living nonhuman primates as an *analogue,* or parallel, for early human ancestors. However, analogies cannot be taken too literally, because like modern humans, contemporary nonhuman primates have undergone their own evolution. Modern humans did not evolve from any living primate. Rather, modern humans and closely related African apes shared a common ancestor just a few million years ago.

The Primate Order

The fossil record of the primates begins around 65 million years ago with small shrew-like animals. The primate order has evolved into a group of animals that now range in size from several ounces to over 400 pounds. Some inhabit limited areas, and others range more widely. Humans are the most wide-ranging primate, and, as the last section of this chapter shows, this extensiveness is largely responsible for the shrinking ranges of nonhuman primates in the wild.

Morphology

In spite of the vast range in size among different nonhuman primate species, members of the primate order have a characteristic form, or *generalized morphology* (see Table 5.1). For example, compared to the faces of cows or dogs, most primate faces are nonprojecting with relatively little in the way of a snout. Primate eyes face forward and allow for stereoscopic vision that makes possible greater depth perception. Primates have five digits on their hands and feet, and they can grasp with both hands and feet. Primate brains are large in relation to body size.

This shared morphology, or physical form, is related to several characteristics of primate behavior. Most primate species are **arboreal** (tree-dwelling), **quadrupedal** (moving on all fours), and **diurnal** (active during the day). Primates are also distinct in terms of how much they rely on sight for dealing with their environment. Last but not least, most primates have a high degree of **sociality,** or the tendency to live in groups.

Not every primate has all the primate characteristics listed in Table 5.1, and some nonprimate animals also have some of these characteristics. Dolphins, for example, are extremely social. When considered together, however, these features help scientists to differentiate primates from other mammals. Also, because modern humans are primates, these general primate patterns shed light on human evolution and on modern human anatomy and behavior.

TABLE 5.1
General primate characteristics.

Morphology	Behavior
nonprojecting face	arboreal
large brain relative to body size	diurnal
three or more types of teeth	quadrupedal
forward-facing eyes	visual
eye sockets completely surrounded by bone	social
ear bones inside skull	
collarbones	
five digits on hands and feet	
nails at the end of digits	
grasping hands and feet	

Regions of the world where nonhuman primates live today.

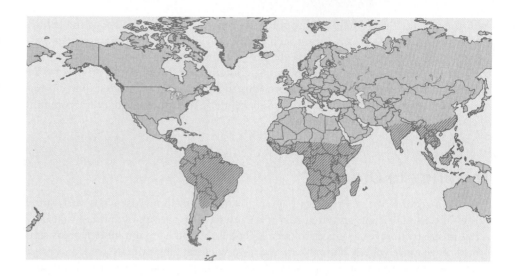

We now review four important features of primate life, with particular reference to nonhuman primates. These features are environment, diet, social behavior, and communication.

Environment

When studying and interpreting primate behavior, primatologists first consider the environmental context in which the primates live. In this work, they gain insights from the scientific discipline of *ecology,* which is the study of the relationships of living systems to the natural environment and to other living systems within that environment. Primate ecologists are interested in particular primate species and how they interact with aspects of their *ecological niche,* or environmental context, which includes the trees in which they live, their food sources, **conspecifics** (members of the same taxon), and other primate and nonprimate species. Primate ecologists ask how, within their ecological niches, particular primate species survive, reproduce, and maintain social relationships.

Most living nonhuman primate species live in forest environments in low-altitude areas of the tropics or subtropics. A few species live at high altitudes in Africa, Nepal, and Japan. Within these environments, especially in forest environments, a range of habitats often exist within the same area, allowing for the coexistence of several primate species in the same region. By evolving different adaptations in morphology (for example, size), diet, and social behavior, these coexisting primate species avoid competing for resources.

Diet

The search for food affects how animals move around, the size of the area they live in, and their social behavior. The term **foraging** refers to obtaining food that is available in nature through gathering, hunting, or scavenging. All nonhuman primates are foragers, but they vary in the kinds of foods they collect (Strier 2003). Several factors are involved in primate food choice:

- what is available in the environment.
- the need for energy for growth, reproduction, and survival.
- nutrients for physiological functioning.
- morphological constraints of the digestive system.
- competition for food within and across species.
- risk of predation (being injured or killed by other animals) while foraging.

Primate species fit into five feeding categories (see Table 5.2). These categories are based on what forms the majority of a species's diet, on average, throughout the year.

TABLE 5.2
Primate dietary categories.

Category	Primary Food	Morphological Characteristics	Advantages	Disadvantages
Frugivores	fruit	large incisors low, rounded cusps on molars long small intestine	good source of carbohydrates easy to digest	trees widely distributed fruits highly seasonal much competition
Folivores	leaves	high, sharp cusps on molars complex stomach or expanded large intestine	plentiful in forested environments little competition	low energy difficult to digest secondary compounds
Insectivores	insects	high, sharp cusps on molars short, simple guts	high in protein and energy little competition	variable distribution difficult to harvest low mass yield per time input
Gumnivores	gums and saps	protuding lower incisors expanded large intestine	plentiful in forested environments high in nutrition little competition	difficult to digest
Omnivores	no specialization	generalized tooth morphology generalized gut morphology	can adapt to habitat changes	cannot consume difficult-to-digest foods

Seasonal variation in diet does occur, of course, and within-species exceptions to general patterns exist (Harding 1981). We discuss some of these exceptions later.

Frugivores mainly eat fruits. They have large front teeth, or incisors, that allow them to get pieces of a large fruit into the mouth (as when you bite into an apple). Frugivores have low, rounded cusps on their molars because most fruit is soft and does not require substantial chewing before being swallowed. Most digestion of carbohydrates occurs in the small intestine, so frugivores have a long small intestine compared to the rest of their digestive tract.

Fruits are a good source of carbohydrates, but they are low in fiber and protein, and there are other limitations to a frugivorous diet. Fruit trees in the wild are often far apart, so frugivory may require an individual primate to travel long distances. Fruit trees are also highly seasonal, most bearing fruit for only a few weeks or months out of the year. Finally, because fruit is such a high-quality food, it attracts insects, birds, and other animals, so primate frugivores face stiff competition.

Folivores eat primarily leaves. Leaves are an extremely difficult food to digest because of the chemicals (such as cellulose) in their cell walls. Folivores' chewing teeth (premolars and particularly molars) have high, sharp, shearing crests that help them break leaves into small pieces before swallowing them; the smaller the particle, the easier it is digested. Primate folivores, like many other folivorous animals, rely on bacteria in their digestive system to break down the cell walls of leaves. Leaves require more time to ferment in the digestive tract than other foods (Milton 1984). Some primate folivores have complex stomachs to provide for a long fermentation process, whereas others have an expanded large intestine.

The major benefit of a folivorous diet is that leaves are plentiful in forested environments, and other organisms do not compete heavily for them. The major limitations of a folivorous diet are that leaves are a low-energy food and that leaves require

If you were a folivore, what food would you look for in your home range?

THINKING

OUTSIDE THE BOX

a long digestion time. In addition, some mature leaves contain secondary compounds such as caffeine and nicotine, which can be toxic if consumed in large quantities.

The diet of **insectivores** consists mainly of insects and other invertebrates. Insectivorous primates have high, sharp cusps on their molars to puncture and break up the hard outer covering of these food sources. The contents of the insects are easy to digest, so compared to other primates, insectivores have short, simple guts.

Insects are high in protein and energy, but most are small, they are often hidden, and many are fast-moving and difficult to catch. There is thus a limit on the number of insects that can be captured in a day. These factors constrain the body size of insectivores. All primates that rely on insects for most of their diet during some part of the year are smaller-bodied than other primates.

Gumnivores focus their diet on tree *exudates,* the gums and saps of trees. Some gumnivores use protruding lower incisors to gouge the outer layer of trees to start the flow of exudates. Most gumnivores have an expanded large intestine because gums are difficult to digest. The benefits of eating tree exudates include their abundance in forested environments, their high nutritional content, and the lack of competition from other organisms.

Omnivores, or multivores, do not specialize in any one type of food. Omnivorous primates are species in which no one food type makes up more than half of their diet. These primates do not have any special dental or gut morphology. The advantage of being an omnivore is that because omnivores eat a variety of foods, they can cope more easily than other primates with environmental and dietary changes. The disadvantage of being an omnivore is that at times of food shortage, omnivores are unable to fall back on plentiful but difficult-to-digest resources such as leaves.

Social Behavior

As with primate size, there is variation in nonhuman primate social behavior. And like dietary variation, this variation is considered adaptive because it provides flexibility in response to changing environmental conditions. In this section we consider some variations in social behavior; the following section offers more detail. Underlying this variation, though, is primate sociality, or the strong tendency to live in groups (Sussman and Chapman 2004).

Most primates live year-round in a **social group,** a group of animals that interact regularly and spend most of their time nearer to other group members than to non-

Members of a group of Hanuman langurs in India involved in social behavior. Most primates are highly social and interact with their group-mates in complex ways. ■ Think of ways that you regularly interact with other members of your social group. (Source: © Cyril Ruoso/Minden Pictures)

members. Social group membership among primates is generally stable, but it inevitably changes over time as a result of birth, death, and migration. Social groups typically occupy a particular geographic area throughout the year. Primatologists distinguish three types of areas in relation to social groups:

- *day range:* the area or distance traveled by a social group in a day.
- *home range:* the area used by a group but not necessarily defended by it.
- *territory:* a group's area that is defended from conspecifics of other social groups.

Primate areas are typically large and complex. A home range or territory must contain all of the resources that primates need: food, water, sleeping sites, and mates.

In many species, a group's home range or territory remains stable over several generations. Resource availability changes seasonally within a home range, and in their effort to keep track of resources, primates benefit from repetitive use and memory. By staying in the same area for generations, they accumulate knowledge about it (such as the location of the best fruit trees and water sources). Elders can pass this information down to younger group members, thus enhancing individual and group survival.

Reasons for Primate Sociality. Primatologists propose different theories to explain why primates generally live in social groups. Many explanations are Darwinian in that they point to the role that sociality plays in group survival and reproductive success. One theory says that group living improves access to food and thus improves the chances of individuals and groups surviving (Jolly 1985). At first glance, this idea seems counterintuitive, for if an individual lives with others who eat the same food, competition for food will be inevitable and constant. However, the disadvantages of this competition are outweighed by the benefits of increased access to resources. Individuals within a group help other group members find food, and larger social groups can gain access to food sources by displacing smaller social groups. For example, most primates spread out when they forage, and when an individual finds a good food site, he or she announces it to the rest of the group. This announcement, which is termed a *food call,* is a characteristic form of communication in such situations.

Another position, also Darwinian, says that social group life is adaptive because it provides protection from predators (van Schaik 1983). The more members in a group, the more eyes and ears there are to detect potential predators. Groups help provide defense by ganging up, mobbing, and driving away predators more effectively than a single primate can. There is also safety in numbers in that larger group size reduces the risk of an individual being attacked. One disadvantage of a larger group, however, is that it is more conspicuous than a smaller group.

Whatever the causes for group living, the consequences of group life are many. Members of groups need to have ways to organize themselves, form relationships with each other, and solve problems related to potential conflict and risks to security.

Organization of Social Groups. Nonhuman primate groups generally include adults and juveniles. They differ in form in their size and in the gender composition of the adults (Fedigan 1992). We outline here the three types of social groups, although many more variations exist across primate species (see Figure 5.1 on p. 142).

- By far the most common social group is the *multi-male/multi-female (MM/MF)* group. This type of group contains adults of both sexes and their offspring. Females make up the core of these groups, often forming strong alliances with each other and influencing the male social hierarchy by befriending males. Adult males are often unrelated and compete with each other for sexual access to females.
- Another type is the *one-male/multi-female (M/MF)* group, which contains one adult male, more than one adult female, and their offspring. The single male typically defends the group from males outside the group.
- A rare subvariety of the multi-male/multi-female group is referred to as a **fission–fusion group,** a large group that regularly breaks up into smaller subgroups for

What are the main forms of social groups in your microculture?

THINKING

OUTSIDE
THE BOX

Multi-male/multi-female group	One-male/multi-female group	Fission-fusion group

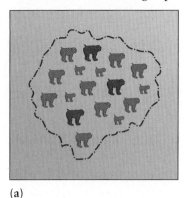      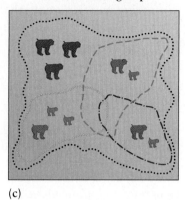

(a)   (b)   (c)

FIGURE 5.1
Three types of nonhuman primate groups.

(*Source:* Figure from p. 60 in *Primate Adaptation and Evolution,* 2nd ed., by John Fleagle. Copyright © 1999. Reprinted by permission of Elsevier.)

foraging and travel. This type of social group, though rare, is important because it is found in some of our closest primate relatives, the chimpanzees and bonobos.

An important factor that shapes primate social organization, and one that is related to the patterns of group formation just mentioned, involves what happens to individuals at or around the time of sexual maturity (Strier 2004). In most nonhuman primate species, females remain with their birth group throughout their lives, whereas males disperse to other groups upon reaching sexual maturity. This residence pattern is referred to as **matrilocality.** Less typical is **patrilocality,** in which males remain with their birth group throughout their lives and sexually mature females disperse.

Like other social animals, nonhuman primates have complex rules and communication systems that enable them to coexist in stable social groups. Three important areas of primate social behavior are the formation of inter-individual social relationships, patterns of dominance, and conflict resolution.

Inter-individual Relationships. Factors that affect how individuals within a group interact with each other include age, sex, kinship, reproductive status, personality, and degree of familiarity. An example of age as a factor is that adult primates are more tolerant of *immatures* (a term that refers to infants and juveniles) than they are of other adults. An example of kinship playing a role is that mothers are more disturbed by the death of their own offspring than by the death of the offspring of other females.

Enduring social ties between and among nonhuman primate individuals exist and are apparent in that some individuals spend more time with or near other individuals than would be predicted if chance alone were operating (Hinde 1983). Such relationships may involve more frequent grooming, sleeping and resting near each other, and supporting each other in aggressive encounters. Some associations last for many years, while others are brief. Some involve pair-bonding, while others include more than two individuals.

The dispersal of sexually mature individuals affects the likelihood of long-term associations, increasing the chances of relationships among individuals that remain in the birth group. In the many matrilocal/**matrifocal** (characterized by females forming the core of the group) species, the most enduring relationships exist among females. These relationships are often based on kinship, but non-kin relationships among nonhuman primate females also exist. The same applies for males in patrilocal species in which enduring social ties among males are prominent.

During the breeding season, short-term relationships lasting from hours to days develop between adult males and females. Some studies suggest that male–female bonding patterns are affected by female hormonal levels, although this hypothesized relationship is difficult to study in the wild (see the Methods Close-Up box). Additionally, individuals often form short-term alliances against others in aggressive or competitive situations.

Using Fecal Samples to Study the Effect of Female Hormones on the Behavior of Free-Ranging Spider Monkeys

ALL FEMALE PRIMATES, when they are not pregnant or lactating, have regular hormonal cycles associated with ovulation. A pattern of higher amounts of estrogen during pre-ovulation and higher amounts of progesterone during post-ovulation prevails among all female primates. But variation exists in the amount of each hormone released, in the timing of hormone release, and in the length of the hormonal cycle.

The relationship between reproductive hormones and behavior is a matter of scientific inquiry and popular concern. Evidence from studies of hormonal levels in captive populations demonstrate that, although most nonhuman primate females are receptive to mating throughout their cycle, they are most willing to mate during or near ovulation. Males appear to be more attracted to females at this time. Most of these studies are conducted using urine samples.

Few comparable studies for free-ranging primates have been conducted to link female reproductive cycles and hormonal profiles to behavior. The main factor constraining research is the difficulty of measuring hormone levels in wild primates. Urine samples are difficult to collect from free-ranging primates. New techniques enable primatologists to use fecal samples, instead, for measuring hormones. Fecal samples can be collected relatively easily and noninvasively (that is, without bodily penetration) from free-ranging primates. Christina Campbell and her colleagues used this technique to study the reproductive behavior and ovarian cycles of free-ranging spider monkeys in Panama (Campbell et al. 2001). To make sure that female hormones could be measured as accurately from feces as from urine, the researchers first compared

hormone levels found in the urine and feces of captive spider monkeys at the San Diego Zoo. The preliminary project confirmed that adequate hormone measures could be obtained from spider monkey feces.

Next, Campbell went to Panama to study free-ranging spider monkeys. She spent over a year patiently watching and waiting for specific females in her study group to defecate. Most of the time, feces were released from high in the trees, so she had to keep her eye on where they fell. Each collected sample was placed immediately in an airtight freezer bag and was frozen at the end of the day. While collecting fecal samples, she and others also collected ecological and behavioral data on the monkeys.

Campbell and her colleagues found that the ovarian cycle for free-ranging spider monkeys has an average length of 20 to 23 days, somewhat shorter than the average human cycle of 28 days. They were able to detect pregnancies in four of the animals during the study and noted one early fetal loss. The data analysis revealed that female spider monkey behavior was not influenced by the stage of the female's cycle but that it was influenced by a female's reproductive state—that is, whether or not she was pregnant. For example, pregnant females travel with more individuals than nonpregnant females. Pregnant females copulate less and are attacked less frequently by males than are nonpregnant females. Campbell's major finding about nonpregnant females is that they are receptive to copulations throughout their ovulatory cycle. This finding suggests that levels of estrogen and progesterone during the ovarian cycle do not significantly influence reproductive behavior in spider monkeys.

FOOD FOR THOUGHT

- How is human female behavior influenced by hormones?
- How is human male behavior affected by hormones?

Primatologists also study inter-individual relationships in terms of the degree of equality among members or, by contrast, any patterns of dominance that are observed. **Dominance** is an individual's priority in access to key resources, such as food and water, and in key relationships, such as mating and grooming. An individual with priority of access to such resources and relationships is said to be dominant over other individuals, who are termed subordinate. Primatologists assess dominance by observing interactions involving resource acquisition, aggression, supplanting behaviors (where one animal moves out of the way of another group member), grooming interactions, and attempts to mate with another group member.

Early studies in primatology focused on studying dominance rather than equality, cooperation, or affiliation. This focus arose because early studies involved mainly macaques and baboons. These species are atypical of nonhuman primates in two ways. First, they have unusually high rates of aggression, especially among adult males, and fights are dramatic, involving screaming, biting, and hair-pulling. Second, most macaque and baboon groups exhibit clear dominance hierarchies (*clear dominance hierarchies* are those in which a trained observer can predict the way individuals will interact with one another). In light of recent research, many theories and findings from early studies of dominance have been modified. The following propositions are *no longer accepted*.

Discredited Early Assumptions

- All primate species exhibit clear dominance hierarchies.
- Size and aggression alone determine rank and dominance.
- The most dominant group member is always a male.
- Males always dominate females.
- The most dominant male in a group fathers more offspring than other males.

Primatologists now recognize that the issue of dominance is much more complex than earlier researchers thought. This change in thinking is related to changes in ways of studying and measuring dominance. The choice of research method and the types of interactions observed both have significant effects on the results (see the Critical Thinking box). In early studies, dominance was assessed by observing *dyadic interactions*—interactions between two individuals. Most interactions within a group, however, involve more than two individuals. Thus current research focuses more on group dynamics. New findings show, for example, that a coalition of small females can dominate a large male. Recent studies also demonstrate that the dominant individual in a group is not always the largest or most aggressive individual, whether that individual is male or female. The existence of social alliances or individual personality may determine who is dominant. Another faulty assumption was overturned by the ability to detect biological kin relationships through DNA tests. This information revealed that dominant males do not always have the most offspring. Furthermore, females often choose their mates rather than being chosen.

Another impetus for the change in thinking came from feminist anthropologists who have questioned the validity of earlier generalizations about nonhuman primates, especially the image of the "dominant male" as a key feature of primate life. A survey of all living nonhuman primate species indicates that in forty percent of them, either females dominate males or males and females are co-dominant (Wright 1993). Thus males are dominant in about 60 percent of all living primate species—a majority but not by a huge margin.

An adult male Hamadryas baboon from Northern Africa yawns as a threat display that shows off his large canines. ■ Most primates are social, and they have evolved complex communication systems that involve visual, tactile, olfactory, and vocal components. What are some ways that you communicate with someone else without using verbal language? (Source: Sohns, Juergen & Christine/Animals Animals)

Conflict and Conflict Resolution.
Group life inevitably involves some conflict and, hence, the need for conflict resolution. Conflicts can occur when two or more individuals want the same thing at the same time. Conflicts among nonhuman primates may arise from misunderstandings. Misunderstanding occurs when an individual anticipates receiving something from another individual and fails to get it—for example, in relation to grooming, copulation, or access to the mother's nipple. Conflicts may also arise when previously established social expectations can no longer be relied on, as may occur upon the birth of a new infant or a change in the adult composition of the group.

Nonhuman primates have a variety of mechanisms to prevent and resolve conflict (de Waal 2000). Postconflict reconciliation behaviors include embracing others, grooming, and reciprocal copulation behaviors such as presenting

Infanticide in Primates and the Sexual Selection Hypothesis

DURING HER FIELDWORK on Hanuman langurs in Jodhpur, northern India, in the 1970s, primatologist Sarah Hrdy recorded a large number of infant deaths (1977). She concluded that these deaths were probably due to infanticide. **Infanticide,** the deliberate killing of offspring by conspecifics, has been reported in a variety of mammals, including lions and some primates. Phyllis Dolhinow, however, who studied Hanuman langurs in other parts of India, found no evidence of infanticide (1977). These contrasting findings launched a major debate in primatology: Does infanticide exist in primates, and if so, is it an adaptive behavior pattern? Since this debate began, several reports have been published documenting infanticide in a variety of primate species, including chimpanzees, gorillas, capuchin monkeys, colobus monkeys, baboons, and humans.

Many of those who argue that infanticides are a normal part of primate behavior support a position referred to as the *sexual selection hypothesis.* According to this hypothesis, infanticide is an adaptive behavior performed by males that evolved because it increases their reproductive success. The logic is as follows: When a new male joins a group, he may kill an infant (or infants) in the group in order to shorten the inter-birth interval of the dead infant's mother (lactating females normally do not ovulate). Thus the new male gains a mate sooner than he otherwise would. The infanticide also eliminates a male competitor's offspring, thereby increasing the infanticidal male's reproductive fitness in the population. Supporters of the sexual selection hypothesis argue that the small number of observed infanticides does not lessen the potential importance of the behavior. In this way, infanticide events are like predation events in that both are seldom directly observed among primates. Nonetheless, primatologists accept the importance of predation in primate behavior.

Few primatologists deny that infant primates are sometimes killed by adults of their own species. But not all are convinced that infanticide is common among nonhuman primates. They say that a close look at the published data reveals that only a handful of infanticides have been directly observed in primates (Bartlett et al. 1993). Most cases of infanticide have been inferred after the disappearance of an infant. Researchers who reject the sexual selection hypothesis claim that the lack of support with direct, empirical data is serious and cannot be brushed aside. With infant mortality rates among free-ranging primates often reaching 50 percent, the death of an infant after a male takeover cannot be assumed to be the result of infanticide. Infants are highly likely to die as a result of predation, disease, or congenital abnormalities.

Opponents of the hypothesis marshal evidence about infanticide to contradict its supposed function in enhancing male reproductive success. They cite the following cases of infanticide: males killing their own offspring, males killing infants long after taking over a group, and females killing infants. This evidence convinces them that the killing of infants in primates is not adaptive but is better viewed as the result of pathological behavior or sheer accident during general aggressive encounters.

CRITICAL THINKING QUESTIONS

- What further data are needed to support or refute the sexual selection hypothesis?
- What evidence do you have that humans do or do not commit infanticide?
- Develop your own hypothesis for infant killing among humans or nonhuman primates.

and mounting. These behaviors are interpreted as attempts to re-establish peaceful relationships, reduce physiological stress, and minimize social disruption.

Biological anthropologists have long debated whether conflict and aggression are part of the biological primate heritage of humanity and thus are inevitable. Those who support the proposition that all primates are innately violent present examples from many primate species, including humans, of conflict and aggressive encounters such as intergroup attacks and infanticide (Wrangham and Peterson 1996). Others argue that these examples of violence are numerically insignificant and do not support a view of primates as generally prone to violent behavior (Sussman 1997, Sussman and Garber 2004). Moreover, they point out that some examples of violent behavior are anthropogenic—caused by human intervention. For example, increases in violent episodes among chimpanzees are associated with the establishment of feeding stations in research areas and habitat destruction.

A white-faced capuchin monkey in Central America threatens another individual. ■ Do some Internet research to find out about the distribution of this variety of primate. (Source: © Gerry Ellis/Minden Pictures)

Whether or not violence is an innate primate tendency, there is much evidence that nonhuman primates have ways of preventing conflict and dealing with postconflict situations. These patterns are part of the primate heritage, though whether they are innate or learned is another question.

Communication

Complex communication and signaling systems are key features of nonhuman primate behavior that enable individuals to coexist in stable groups. Primate communication can involve olfactory (smell), tactile (touch), visual, and vocal communication. The complex facial muscles of all primates, especially around the eyes and mouth, allow for a greater range of facial expression compared to other mammals. Primates also use facial expressions and body language to communicate threats and fear and to facilitate courtship, play, grooming, and reconciliation.

Vocal communication is most highly developed among arboreal primates, because the dense vegetation makes it difficult for them to communicate visually. The wide range of vocalizations have been interpreted as including food calls, territorial calls, contact calls, lost calls, aggressive vocalizations, and warning barks (Cheney and Seyfarth 1996).

Although nonhuman primates have extremely complex vocal communication systems, they differ in several ways from human *language* (defined in Chapter 1). Human language is processed in specialized areas of the cerebral cortex, whereas nonhuman primate vocalizations are processed in the brain's limbic system (Joseph 2000). The **limbic system** comprises the olfactory cortex, the amygdala, and the hippocampus (see Figure 5.2). The limbic system is the part of the brain associated with emotion. Therefore, it is not surprising that most primate vocalizations are tied to their emotional state.

Two major differences distinguish nonhuman primate communication from human language. First, nonhuman primate communication is mostly context-specific. That is, nonhuman primates seem incapable of communicating about things that are not present in either space or time. In contrast, modern human language is devoted largely

Primatologist Sue Savage-Rumbaugh, working with Kanzi, an adult male bonobo. Kanzi has been involved in a long-term project studying ape language. He has learned to communicate with researchers using a variety of symbols. Some chimpanzees, bonobos, orangutans, and gorillas have learned to communicate using American Sign Language and symbols on computer keyboards. (Source: © Frans Lanting/Minden Pictures)

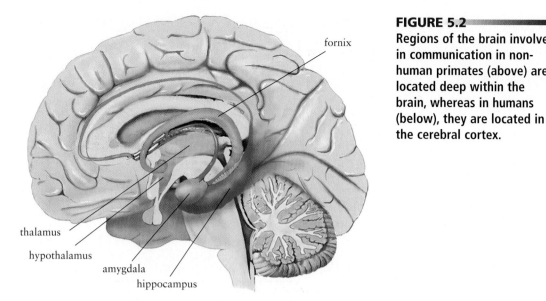

FIGURE 5.2
Regions of the brain involved in communication in non-human primates (above) are located deep within the brain, whereas in humans (below), they are located in the cerebral cortex.

fornix

thalamus

hypothalamus

amygdala

hippocampus

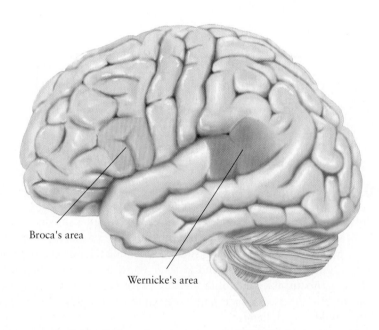

Broca's area

Wernicke's area

to conveying information about the past, the future, and events that have never happened and never may happen (consider science fiction). Second, nonhuman primate communication relies on a limited set of specific sounds, such as a food call, each having a particular meaning for sender and recipient. It is referred to as a *closed system*. Human language relies on a limited, or finite, set of sounds, but it can communicate an infinite set of meanings. Hence it is referred to as an *open system*. Chimpanzee communication as investigated in the laboratory seems to have limited aspects of an open system.

VARIETIES OF PRIMATES

This section describes the different primate species, paying special attention to their morphology and behavior. It first reviews a basic taxonomy of the primate order, using English names for the species discussed (see Figure 5.3 on p. 148), beginning with the category of prosimians, at the upper left of the diagram.

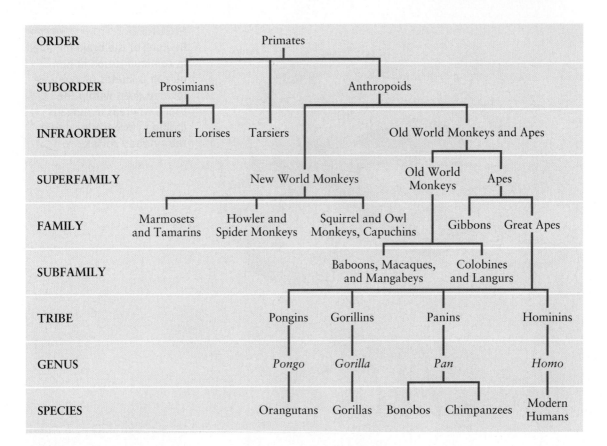

ORDER	Primates						
SUBORDER	Prosimians		Anthropoids				
INFRAORDER	Lemurs Lorises	Tarsiers		Old World Monkeys and Apes			
SUPERFAMILY		New World Monkeys		Old World Monkeys	Apes		
FAMILY		Marmosets and Tamarins	Howler and Spider Monkeys	Squirrel and Owl Monkeys, Capuchins		Gibbons Great Apes	
SUBFAMILY				Baboons, Macaques, and Mangabeys	Colobines and Langurs		
TRIBE			Pongins Gorillins		Panins		Hominins
GENUS			*Pongo* *Gorilla*		*Pan*		*Homo*
SPECIES			Orangutans Gorillas		Bonobos Chimpanzees		Modern Humans

FIGURE 5.3
Simplified basic primate taxonomy.

Examples of living prosimians from left to right: a lemur; a bushbaby, sometimes referred to as a galago; a loris; and a tarsier. ■ How are these primates similar to and different from monkeys and apes in physical form? (Sources: © Frans Lanting/Minden Pictures, two left most; © Dani/ Animals Animals; © Frans Lanting/Minden Pictures, right most)

Prosimians

Prosimians are found in Southeast Asia and sub-Saharan Africa, including the island of Madagascar. Prosimians are the most distant primates from humans in terms of evolution, and they are thus considered most like the earliest fossil primates. They are divided into lemurs, lorises, and tarsiers. Most prosimians are small, arboreal, insectivorous, **nocturnal,** and solitary. They groom each other using a comb-like row of lower teeth rather than their hands. Given their lifestyle and small size, studying them in the wild is a challenge.

Lemurs are an important exception to this general prosimian pattern. Some lemurs are large-bodied, diurnal, and **terrestrial;** have a variety of diets; and live in stable social groups. The distinctiveness of the lemurs among prosimians is probably related to their unique environmental context: Madagascar, which has been separated from mainland Africa for at least 100 million years. Lemurs have been the only primates on the island throughout most of their evolutionary history (Tattersall 1993). There-

fore, lemurs have been able to fill ecological niches normally filled by monkeys and apes in other parts of the Old World. Their survival, however, is now seriously threatened by human encroachment.

Anthropoids

Anthropoids (the monkeys, apes, and humans) differ from prosimians in several ways. Most anthropoids have nails instead of claws on all their digits. They have forward-facing eyes, larger brains, dry noses, jaw bones that are joined in the midline, and a flatter face instead of a snout (baboons are the exception). They use their hands rather than their teeth for grooming. This discussion of the anthropoids begins with New World monkeys.

New World Monkeys

New World monkeys are found only in Central and South America. They are now limited to the tropics, but the distribution of fossil monkeys shows that their range once extended close to the southern tip of South America.

All New World monkeys are arboreal. Distinctive anatomical features of New World monkeys include their small size and rounded nostrils. Some have prehensile (gripping) tails. Beyond these shared characteristics, the long evolutionary heritage of New World monkeys has brought diverse patterns of adaptation (Fleagle 1999). Because New World monkeys evolved without competition from either prosimians or apes, they were able to occupy ecological niches that, in the Old World, are occupied by a range of other primates. Some New World monkey species are prosimian-like in behavior, others are more ape-like, and yet others defy classification.

Consider the distinctive features of the marmosets. They are small and brightly colored, and males and females are the same size. Their diet is a combination of gumnivory and insectivory. Marmosets have specially adapted teeth and claw-like nails to help them extract tree sap and gouge out insects from trees. Marmosets are the only anthropoids that regularly give birth to twins. This pattern may be related to reproductive fitness in that the twin births involve very small infants, thus reducing maternal risks associated with birth of a single large infant. Perhaps also related to the high rate of twinning is the common practice of **allocare,** shared care of infants among group members (Goldizen 1987). Social groups usually contain one breeding female who is responsible for nursing all the infants. Other adult group members, both males and females, help care for the infants, carrying them and grooming them.

In terms of behavior, two groups of New World monkeys, the atelines and the capuchins, resemble some of the Old World apes (discussed next). Atelines are the only New World monkeys that have fission–fusion grouping patterns, like Old World chimpanzees. Atelines are also the only New World monkeys that brachiate. Capuchins, like Old World apes, regularly use tools, but they are the only New World monkeys that do so.

Old World Monkeys

Old World monkey species, as a group, are more uniform morphologically and behaviorally than New World monkeys. They comprise two main subgroups, the cercopithecines and the colobines (see Figure 5.3):

- Cercopithecines are omnivores. They are unique in using cheek pouches to store and transport food. Most live in Africa. Macaques are the only Asian cercopithecines.

- Colobines are folivores with complex stomachs. They live in Africa and Asia.

New World monkeys have round, outward facing nostrils (left) while Old World monkeys have narrow, downward facing nostrils (right). Old world monkeys also have ischial callosities (middle).

Bottom: An adult pygmy marmoset monkey carrying an infant. Caring of infants by non-mothers, known as allomothering, is common among marmosets. ■
Is allomothering common in your cultural experience? (Sources: © Frans Lanting/ Minden Pictures, left; © Yva Momatuik/John Eastcott/ Minden Pictures, right; © M. Harvey, middle; © Ken Lucas/Visuals Unlimited, bottom)

An adult spider monkey uses its prehensile tail to help support its weight in the trees. ■ What advantage does a monkey with a prehensile tail have over one that does not have a prehensile tail? (Source: © Frederick D. Atwood)

Among the cercopithecines, baboons stand out as the largest and most terrestrial. They comprise three main groups: the savannah baboon, which is pan-African in distribution; the mountain baboon, which is confined to Ethiopia; and the forest baboon of West Africa. Baboons live in large social groups of 15 to 200 members. They have marked sexual dimorphism in body size.

Apes

We now turn to the **hominoids,** which is the primate superfamily of apes, including humans. Apes differ from other primates in several morphological features: absence of a tail, distinct patterns of cusps on their lower molars, and large brains relative to body size. A characteristic form of ape travel that distinguishes them from most other primates is **brachiation,** in which the forelimbs are used to swing from branch to branch (see Figure 5.4). Most hominoids do not habitually brachiate, but all (including humans) are capable of brachiation. Morphological changes related to brachiation include a flat, broad thorax; a short trunk; flexible shoulders, elbows, and wrists; shoulder blades (scapulas) on the back and not the side of the chest; a long and strong collarbone (clavicle); and long forearms and fingers. The hominoid evolution from quadrupedal locomotion to brachiation involved a trade-off of stability for mobility in their upper body. Hominoids have more flexible upper bodies than other primates.

The four genera of living nonhuman apes are gibbons and siamangs, orangutans, gorillas, and chimpanzees and bonobos. The smaller apes (gibbons and siamangs) are called the lesser apes. The term **great ape** refers to the larger apes—orangutans, gorillas, chimpanzees, and bonobos—which are also the apes most closely related to humans. Our description of the apes starts with the lesser apes and proceeds to those most closely related to humans (see Figure 5.5).

Gibbons and Siamangs. Gibbons and siamangs are the smallest of the apes and the most distantly related to humans. All are frugivores, and all live in the tropical forests of Southeast Asia. They are the only habitual brachiators among the hominoids. Gibbons normally live in small, pair-bonded groups consisting of one adult male, one adult female, and immature offspring (see Table 5.3). Sexual dimorphism in body shape or size is not marked, although males and females differ in skin color.

Orangutans. Orangutans are the only Asian great ape. They live on the island of Borneo and the nearby island of Sumatra. Sexual dimorphism in body size in orangutans is marked, with adult male weight (175–200 pounds) roughly double that of adult female weight (73–99 pounds). In spite of their large size, orangutans are mainly arboreal, although adult males often travel long distances on the ground. In the trees,

FIGURE 5.4
Brachiation in action.

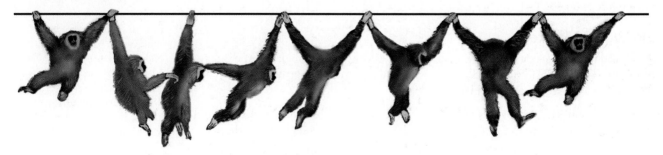

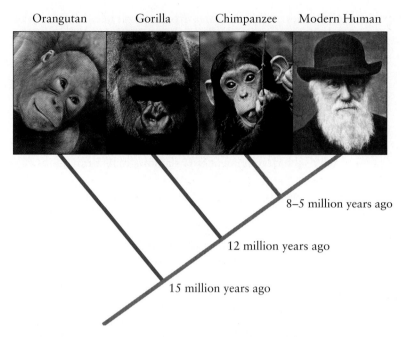

Orangutan   Gorilla   Chimpanzee   Modern Human

8–5 million years ago

12 million years ago

15 million years ago

FIGURE 5.5
Cladogram of the great apes including modern humans.

An adult gibbon in Malaysia. Gibbons are the smallest of the living apes and are sometimes referred to as "lesser apes." ■ Do you think this is a good way to refer to them? (Source: © Gerald Cubitt)

orangutans move slowly and cautiously, using a four-handed form of locomotion that enables them to distribute their weight among several branches. For ground travel, they use a four-footed pattern, walking on the outsides of their feet and on their fists. Orangutans are frugivorous and spend substantial amounts of time each day locating and consuming food.

Orangutans are the most solitary of the great apes. The only enduring social unit is that of a mother and her offspring (see Table 5.3). Adult males and females sometimes come together at choice feeding sites and occasionally for mating. Adult females have a smaller home range than males, sharing it with their offspring, who remain with them for many years. An adult male's territory overlaps the home ranges of

TABLE 5.3
Ape social groups.

Gibbons and siamangs	Small, pair-bonded family groups of one adult male and one adult female with offspring
Orangutans	No enduring groups of multiple adults; mother–offspring units
Gorillas	Small, cohesive groups of multiple adults, either SM/MF or MM/MF with offspring
Chimpanzees	Large, fluid communities with smaller groups formed through fission–fusion, male gangs, mothers–offspring
Bonobos	Matrifocal social groups that are MM/MF with offspring. Large fluid communities with smaller groups formed through fission–fusion

(*Source:* Table, "Ape Social Groups" from "Rethinking Sociality: Cooperation and Aggression among Primates" by Robert W. Sussman and Paul A. Garber in *The Origins and Nature of Sociality*, ed. by R. W. Sussman and Audrey R. Chapman. Copyright © 1994. Published by Aldine de Gruyter. Reprinted by permission of Copyright Clearance Center.)

Orangutans are the only great apes that live in Asia.
■ Besides geographic distribution, how do orangutans differ from the other great apes? (Source: © John Chellman/Animals Animals)

several females and is defended from other males. Adult males use air sacs on their necks to make loud bellowing noises so that they can locate, and usually avoid, each other. Around the age of ten years, most adult males increase in body size, and they develop large cheek pads around the sides of their faces. These pads may help produce locating calls and make the males look larger. Some males, though, do not increase in body size and do not grow cheek pads until they are around twenty years old (Knott 1999). At the present time, primatologists do not understand why such development exists among male orangutans.

Gorillas. The largest of the living primates, gorillas, live in sub-Saharan Africa. They are divided into three groups: western lowland gorillas, eastern lowland gorillas, and mountain gorillas. The subspecies differ in diet and morphology—specifically, in body size, limb length, and hair color and length. Gorillas eat a wide variety of plants, up to 200 species. They sometimes supplement their plant diet with termites and ants. An adult male can eat up to 50 pounds of vegetation in one day. The three gorilla subspecies have somewhat different diets. Mountain gorillas are mainly folivores, western lowland gorillas are mainly frugivores, and eastern lowland gorillas combine folivory and frugivory (Goldsmith 1999).

Like orangutans, gorillas have a high degree of sexual dimorphism in body size. In the wild, adult male gorillas weigh between 350 and 400 pounds, whereas adult females weigh between 150 and 200 pounds. Although they live primarily in dense forests, gorillas are terrestrial, adult males especially so because of their large body size. They are quadrupedal and travel using a locomotor pattern called **knuckle-walking.** Knuckle-walking is a form of terrestrial travel that involves walking flat-footed while supporting the upper body on the front of fingers bent beyond the knuckle.

Gorillas live in small, cohesive social groups of about a dozen individuals that are single-male/multi-female with offspring (see Table 5.3). Multi-male groups, however, are also known. Adult male gorillas often develop a graying saddle of hair on their backs as they reach adulthood. Not all such "silverbacks" are dominant; as with human hair, graying signals age more than rank.

Chimpanzees and Bonobos. There are two living species of chimpanzees: one called the chimpanzee (*Pan troglodytes*) and the other called the bonobo (*Pan paniscus*). All live in sub-Saharan Africa. Chimpanzees are found in several locations in West and Central Africa. Bonobos live only in the Democratic Republic of Congo. Several chimpanzee populations live in conservation areas and are somewhat protected from hunting. No bonobo population has such protection, and they are more heavily hunted.

Current genetic information does not show whether chimpanzees or bonobos are closer to humans. Because more is known about chimpanzees, we begin with them. Compared to orangutans and gorillas, chimpanzees are smaller and exhibit less sexual dimorphism in body size. In the wild, adult males weigh between 75 and 150 pounds, adult females between 60 and 100 pounds. Chimpanzees live primarily in humid tropical forests, but sometimes also open woodland. They are more arboreal than gorillas, but like gorillas, they are knuckle-walkers when on the ground. They are frugivores but occasionally eat other food, including vegetation and small animals such as monkeys.

Chimpanzees live in large, fluid groups of 50 to 60 individuals (see Table 5.3). The entire group is rarely, if ever, together in one area. Subgroups form, dissolve, and reform, often with different members. Adult males often travel together, while adult females travel with their offspring. In contrast to many other primate species, chimpanzees are patrilocal, with males staying in their birth group throughout their lives. Females leave their birth group at reproductive age, between 10 and 15 years. Therefore, the core of the large social group is biologically related males. Young males often form "gangs" that, as a group, seek food or defend territory.

Chimpanzees and bonobos spend 25 percent of their time in social interactions, compared with 10 percent for the other great apes. Most of the interactions occur between mothers and offspring, and grooming is the major form of interaction (Sussman and Garber 2004).

Jane Goodall's pioneering, long-term fieldwork among chimpanzees in Gombe, Tanzania, established a strong tradition of chimpanzee studies (1968). The rich literature on chimpanzees has had a major influence on theories about human evolution, and chimpanzees are often taken as the best model for early humans. Much less is known about the bonobos, but thanks to the research of Japanese primatologists, a growing tradition of bonobo studies now provides rich insights into the "forgotten ape" (Kano 1992, de Waal and Lanting 1997). Primatologists are especially interested in the differences and similarities between chimpanzees and bonobos (see Table 5.4) and which, if either, is the better model for human evolution.

In size, bonobos are similar to living chimpanzees, but they have less sexual dimorphism in body size. Bonobos live mainly in rainforests. Like the other African apes, bonobos are knuckle-walkers. They are frugivores but also sometimes hunt and eat small animals. They hunt less frequently than chimpanzees.

Compared to chimpanzees, bonobos have more stable social groups, although, like chimpanzees they are patrilocal. Outmigrating females gradually build strong alliances in their new group with non-kin females. Females dominate the control of food distribution, and males solicit their attention by offering them choice food items. Compared to other nonhuman primates, bonobos have the highest rates of sexual contact. Sexual contact occurs among all possible sex and age combinations, although sexual contact between close relatives is not common. Bonobo reproductive rates, nonetheless, are similar to those found among chimpanzees.

An adult male silverback gorilla knuckle-walking. ■ Compare the length of the gorilla's arms and legs, and then think about the relative length of arms to legs in humans. Practice knuckle-walking across a room and consider the role of arm-to-leg length in this form of locomotion. (Source: © Jim Tuten/ Animals Animals)

TABLE 5.4
Chimpanzee-bonobo differences.

Chimpanzees	Bonobos
Terrestrial and arboreal	Terrestrial, more erect posture
Frequent tool users	Little observed tool use
More hunting and meat-eating	Occasional hunting and meat-eating
Hunting by males	Hunting by males and females
Male dominance over females	Female dominance over males
Males share meat only	Females share fruit and sometimes meat
Infanticide documented	No infanticide observed
Frequent intergroup aggression	Infrequent intergroup aggression
Less frequent sexual behavior	Frequent sexual behavior
Male–female sexual interactions	Prolific sexual interactions between and among males and females

(*Source:* Stanford 1998 and comments by Frans B. M. de Waal, Barbara Fruth, Kano Takayoshi, and William C. McGrew.)

Chimpanzees and bonobos are humans' closest living relatives. Here is an adult female chimpanzee with her offspring (left) and an adult female bonobo with her young (right). ■ What are some similarities and differences between chimpanzees and humans, both in terms of appearance and behavior? (Sources: © ANUP SHAH/NATUREPL.COM, left; © OSF/Colbeck, M./Animals Animals, right)

In general, bonobos are more social and less violent than chimpanzees, although they also have their share of conflict. Bonobos frequently use sexual contact to prevent conflict and to resolve post-conflict situations. Attractive food, or almost anything of interest to more than one bonobo, sparks sexual interest. The two bonobos will suspend potential competition for the item of interest and briefly mount each other or participate in what primatologists refer to as *G-G rubbing,* or genital–genital rubbing (de Waal and Lanting 1997:109). G-G rubbing is unique to bonobos. This sexual activity appears to distract possible competitors and reframe the relationship as one of alliance and cooperation. In another example of sexuality in conflict prevention, after one mother struck another mother's infant, intense G-G rubbing between the two females—rather than hostility—was the outcome. The "art of sexual reconciliation" may exist in other animals, even humans, but it seems to have reached a peak among bonobos.

No genetic evidence suggests that bonobos are closer to modern humans than are chimpanzees, although many primatologists argue that they are a better model for human evolution. Notably, a bonobo model weakens the chimpanzee-based claim that the human biological heritage necessarily includes male dominance and violence. The bonobo model suggests, in contrast, that humanity's biological heritage includes a biological propensity for being peaceful, female-centric, and sexually active.

 # NONHUMAN PRIMATES: WINDOWS TO HUMANITY'S PAST FACE A FRAGILE FUTURE

We now address two topics of special interest in primatology. We first discuss two examples of how studies of nonhuman primates provide insight into human evolution. Then we consider a topic of direct importance to nonhuman primates themselves: their survival into the future and the question of their rights as humanity's closest living relatives.

Windows to Human Evolution

Information about nonhuman primates can help us understand the evolution of modern human behavior. Primatologists regularly use the great apes, especially chimpanzees and bonobos, as living analogues. This section demonstrates that insights into the evolution of modern human behavior can also come from investigating other primate species. We will first consider tool use and then nonhuman primate culture more generally.

Tool Use

For a long time, anthropologists viewed tools as a distinctive feature of human behavior, but we now know that tool use and tool-making are not unique to humans (Beck 1980). Among free-ranging primates, tool use is found in all known chimpanzee populations, some orangutan populations, and some populations of capuchin monkeys. No other wild anthropoid and no wild prosimian regularly uses or makes tools. In captivity, however, all the great apes and capuchin monkeys can be trained to make and use tools.

The presence of wild capuchin monkeys on the list of tool-makers and users presents us with an interesting situation. The great apes, including humans, are very distantly related to capuchin monkeys. None of the primates that are more closely related to the great apes, such as the Old World monkeys, use or make tools. Thus capuchin tool use is not due to genetic relatedness. Instead, tool use and tool-making behavior must have evolved independently in the great apes and capuchins.

Because all the great apes are capable of making and using tools, it is likely that the ability to use tools evolved before the time when the great apes and modern humans shared a last common ancestor (Panger et al. 2002a). In other words, modern humans and their ancestors almost certainly inherited the ability to use and make tools from even earlier ancestors.

Free-ranging chimpanzees use and make a wide range of tools. Materials include sticks, bark, branches, grass, other vegetation, and stone. For example, chimpanzees use sticks to fish for ants, and they make sponges from chewed leaves to soak up water from rock crevices and tree holes for drinking. Several West African chimpanzee populations use stone and wooden hammers and anvils to crack open nuts (Boesch and Boesch-Achermann 2000). Some free-ranging orangutan populations regularly manufacture and use hammers, probes, and scrapers made of sticks (Fox et al. 1999). Capuchin monkeys in the wild use wooden clubs, wooden probing tools, hammers and anvils, and leaf containers (Panger 1998).

Given what we know about ape and monkey tool use and tool-making, we can infer that early human ancestors used similar tools. Most such tools, however, are very unlikely to be preserved in the archaeological record. Even if they were, it would be difficult to recognize them as tools. In spite of these challenges, recent research that combines archaeology and primatology offers insights into tool use of early human ancestors (Mercader et al. 2000).

C himpanzees in the wild crack a variety of nut species using stone and wooden hammers and anvils. Chimpanzee nut-cracking behavior has been extensively studied at Taï, Côte d'Ivoire, Africa (Boesch and Boesch-Achermann 2000) (see the map on p. 156). The chimpanzees at Taï crack nuts of five different species. One, *Panda oleosa,* is extremely hard, and the chimpanzees nearly always use stone hammers to open them. For anvils the chimpanzees normally use the exposed root systems of hardwood trees. The chimpanzees often take stone hammers with them from tree to tree, but the anvil systems are stationary. During the nut-cracking season, adult chimpanzees spend up to three hours a day cracking nuts. They use the same anvils year after year, and large mounds of debris form around them. Although the chimpanzees have

CROSSING THE FIELDS

Learning about Chimpanzee Tool Use through Archaeology

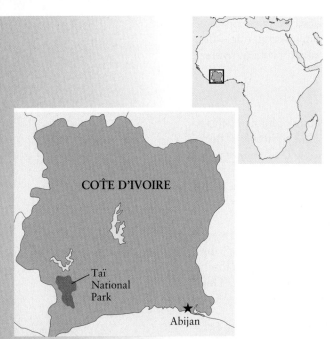

never been seen to modify their stone tools intentionally, the stone hammers sometimes break during use.

The research team of Julio Mercader (archaeologist), Melissa Panger (primatologist), and Christophe Boesch (primatologist) hypothesized that chimpanzee stone tool use might leave signals in the archaeological record at Taï. They went to Côte d'Ivoire in 2001 to conduct the first archaeological excavation of a chimpanzee stone tool site (Mercader et al. 2002). Their hypothesis was confirmed. They found that chimpanzee nut-cracking behavior does leave clear signals in the archaeological record in the form of buried nut debris and broken pieces of stone hammers. At six chimpanzee anvil sites associated with one *Panda* nut tree, the researchers recovered about 40 kilograms of buried nut shells and 479 pieces of buried stone. The stone pieces were buried as deep as 20 centimeters below the surface, at a level dated to a few hundred years ago. Thus chimpanzees have been cracking nuts at this site for at least that long. Most of the stone pieces recovered were small, about half of them between 1 and 10 millimeters. All of the buried stone had been brought in from other locations. Most of the stone pieces were flaked and showed evidence of having broken off from larger stones.

Through this pioneering project, the team created a new area of research called *chimpanzee archaeology* that combines the anthropological fields of primatology and archaeology. Just as traditional archaeology tells us about the cultures of past humans, chimpanzee archaeology tells us about the culture of past chimpanzees. For example, it indicates that chimpanzee nut-cracking behavior in West Africa is at least several

A chimpanzee using a stone hammer to crack open a nut. ■
Choose a tool you use everyday, such as a pen, toothbrush, or fork, and reconstruct how you probably learned to use it.
(Source: © Minden Pictures)

hundred years old. In addition, chimpanzee archaeology provides scientists with ideas about the origins of tool use among the human ancestors before 2.6 million years ago, when intentionally made stone tools first appear in the archaeological record (Chapter 6). ■

FOOD FOR THOUGHT
■ Compare the trash you produce in a week to the trash that chimpanzees would leave behind in a week.

Many anthropologists ask why tool use evolved. Most of the tool use observed in free-ranging chimpanzees, orangutans, and capuchins involves tools that enable individuals to retrieve nutritionally valuable foods that are difficult to access. For example, chimpanzees use probing tools to capture termites within their hard mounds, orangutans use probing tools to remove the pulp from fruits that have prickly outer husks that are painful to handle, and capuchin monkeys use hammers to open hard-shelled nuts. Thus tool use may have evolved because it allowed for increased access to highly nutritious food resources that would otherwise have been inaccessible. Tools were probably made and used to access *fall-back foods*—foods that are not primary sources of nutrition for a species but are accessed when the usual food sources are unavailable. In this scenario, the creativity and innovation involved in tool-making and tool use are driven by survival stress and physiological necessity.

Nonhuman Primate Culture

Culture itself, like the more specific cultural activities related to tools, has long been thought to be unique to humans and their direct ancestors. Most anthropological definitions of culture make some reference to modern human behavior. For a primatologist, *culture* is defined as behavior that is learned (not innate) and that is shared (not individual). Not all primatologists agree that nonhuman primates have *culture*, but examples of something like culture are increasingly documented in the primatological record. Many primatologists prefer to use the term *tradition* to refer to the kinds of behavior that we now discuss (Zihlman and Bolter 2004).

A team of Japanese primatologists, writing in the 1950s, first raised the possibility of nonhuman primate culture (Kawamura 1959). Their findings emerged from a long-term study of macaques on the island of Koshima, Japan. In order to draw the monkeys into areas where they could be observed easily, the researchers provided food on some of the island's sandy beaches. Sweet potatoes were among the first foods introduced to the monkeys. Soon, the researchers noticed that an adult female monkey, whom they named Imo, regularly carried the potatoes from the sandy beach to pools of fresh water to wash the sand from the potatoes before eating them. Some of Imo's relatives began to do the same thing, and over time, the behavior spread throughout much of her group. Others, however, exhibited a preference for potatoes washed in salty water, and they took theirs to the sea.

Later, the primatologists started provisioning the monkeys with rice in order to keep them in open areas for longer periods of time. They thought it would take the monkeys a long time to work out how to sort rice grains from beach sand. But Imo started dropping handfuls of sandy rice into the fresh water pools. The sand sank and the rice floated, making it possible for her to collect sand-free rice grains. This practice, too, spread throughout much of the group, especially among younger individuals.

These behaviors of Imo and her group appear to meet the two criteria for the basic definition of culture: They were learned and then were copied by many members of the group. Some scholars, however, question whether the sweet-potato-washing and rice-sieving behaviors were learned by watching other monkeys or were independently invented through trial and error (Galef 1992). In any case, leaving aside

A Japanese macaque washing a sweet potato. Sweet-potato-washing was an early example of a nonhuman primate cultural behavior studied by primatologists. ■ Take a position on why it does or does not make sense to term this behavior as culture. (Source: © Heather Angel/ Natural Visions)

questions about how the actual transmission occurred, this study established the possibility that nonhuman primates exhibit basic aspects of culture.

Today, more than fifty years later, primatologists approach the question of primate culture comparatively (McGrew 1992, Nashida 1987, Perry et al. 2003). They look for behavioral differences among primates of the same species at different field sites, particularly behavioral patterns not accounted for by genetic or environmental factors. For example, if chimpanzees at one site eat bananas and those at another site do not, but the difference is due to bananas being available at one site and not at the other, then this is an environmental difference, not a cultural difference.

Comparison of data from seven chimpanzee research sites in various parts of East and West Africa revealed 39 differences in tool use, grooming, and other social behaviors that can be explained only as the result of cultural differences and social learning (Whiten et al. 1999). The tools used included hammers and anvils for cracking open nuts, probes for ant-fishing, leaves to sit on, and sticks to fan away flies. Social behaviors included holding the arm of another individual over his or her head while grooming, knocking an individual with a knuckle to get his or her attention, and doing a slow bodily display dubbed a "rain dance" at the start of rain.

Comparative research has been conducted on capuchin monkeys and orangutans, with similar results. Among capuchins, researchers found that four study populations in Costa Rica differed in how they processed one-third of the foods common to all sites (Panger et al. 2002b). At some sites the monkeys pounded open certain fruits, whereas at other sites the same fruits were bitten open. Researchers studying orangutans found that tool use occurred at some but not all sites, and that when tool use did occur, it differed across sites (van Schaik et al. 2003). It appears increasingly likely that culture, defined basically as learned and shared behavior, is an important part of the adaptation of higher primates and of some monkeys.

Most scientists agree that human culture is more complex than the basic forms of culture of nonhuman primates and other animals. And most agree that studying culture in other animals, mainly primates, can shed light on the evolution of culture in our early human ancestors. A complex attribute such as human culture probably had a simpler evolutionary predecessor, perhaps like the culture of contemporary chimpanzees and orangutans.

Endangered Nonhuman Primates

Primate studies provide valuable insight into human behavior, but we can study them only if they survive. Of the over 300 species of living nonhuman primates, more than half are either threatened or endangered with extinction. During the 1990s a new primate species was discovered (Nowak 1999), but the same decade saw the first confirmed primate extinction in 100 years: Miss Waldron's red colobus (*Procolobus badius waldronii*), in West Africa.

Given the rapid pace of economic globalization, nonhuman primate habitats will experience increasing threats this century—even in the next few decades—and more cases of primate extinctions are likely. Strong measures are needed to protect the world's surviving nonhuman primates. This section explores the leading causes of population decline in nonhuman primates, the main elements involved in successful attempts to conserve nonhuman primates, and the possibility of extending "rights" to the great apes.

Threats from Humans

Human activities are now a major threat to nonhuman primate survival (Mittermeier et al. 1986). Most nonhuman primates live in tropical forests within developing nations that have limited financial resources and growing human populations. Human population growth and increasingly consumerist lifestyles create more pressure on the available land, trees, and other natural resources. Global and state commercial interests, though, are the major factor in habitat destruction. They are responsible for tropical forests being cut at a rapid and unsustainable rate. Some estimates indicate that 30 million acres of tropical forest are lost each year.

The distribution of habitat loss is as important as the sheer amount of loss. Although some habitat destruction involves huge expanses of land, much habitat destruction is patchy, involving smaller, scattered areas. This fragments and isolates primate populations, reducing the size of their breeding pool and increasing the likelihood of extinction.

Hunting is another threat to nonhuman primates. Early human ancestors may have hunted primates for food, and such hunting was sustainable. However, with increasing human population density, hunting pressure has increased and is now a threat to several nonhuman primate species. In recent years, there has been significant growth in the *bush meat trade* in Africa and Asia. Bush meat is meat procured from wild animals, and increasingly monkeys and apes are targets. Hunters sell the meat for family income to traders from cities where eating bush meat is fashionable. Hunting bush meat is an important source of money for the hunters, but it is merely a food fad for the rich urban consumers. Where primate hunting occurs, it affects species unequally. Factors such as the relative ease of hunting a species, population density of the potential prey, and local traditions influence hunting pressure. In general, people tend to hunt larger monkeys and apes, putting them at greater risk of extinction. Hunting nonhuman primates is illegal in many countries, but the laws are rarely enforced. They are not traditionally hunted in India because of Hindu religious beliefs (Richard et al. 1989).

Hunting is linked with commercial logging. Lumber companies cut roads in order to move equipment in and lumber out. These roads open up previously inaccessible areas to local populations. Additionally, the lumber companies' main source of meat in tropical areas is from hunting (Strier 2003). When logging and hunting occur together, their combined effect is even more rapid decline in wild primate populations.

Another threat to primates is live capture for international and local trade. Thousands of primates each year are sold as pets, for biomedical research, and to zoos. Some of these transactions are legal, but smuggling is common. This type of trade puts many species in danger of extinction, even those not routinely hunted. For example, rhesus monkeys of South Asia are some of the most commonly used monkeys in biomedical research because they survive the harsh conditions of captivity better than many other species. During the 1960s and 1970s, so many rhesus monkeys were exported from India for biomedical research in Western countries that the species was in danger of extinction. In the 1970s, the government of India banned the export of these monkeys. Laboratories in the United States and elsewhere were forced to establish their own breeding colonies, many of which still exist today. This practice eased the pressure on wild rhesus populations, but it has not stopped the worldwide sale of live primates for research. The emergence and spread of HIV/AIDS increased demand for nonhuman primates for medical research, prompting scientists to increase the breeding of rhesus monkeys and to consider alternatives to rhesus monkeys (National Academy of Sciences 2002).

Deforestation is one of the leading threats to living nonhuman primates. This photograph shows an area of a tropical forest in Panama that has been clear-cut for lumber and agriculture. ■ Do Internet research on an endangered nonhuman primate population and try to learn what deforestation has to do with the situation. (Source: © Danny Lehman/ CORBIS)

Primate Conservation and Primate Rights

Even though we know the causes of nonhuman primate population decline, it is difficult to stop that decline through primate conservation programs. There are several reasons why. First, because primates live in diverse environments and face different challenges to their survival, no "one size fits all" conservation program will work for all primates, or even for one species in all situations. Second, conservation programs must be cost-effective and supported by the local human populations. Nonhuman primates live in developing countries where finances are limited and where other priorities have stronger claims. Therefore, new approaches and incentives are needed to encourage governments and local people to support saving nonhuman primates and their habitats. Third, international commercial interests constitute the greatest challenge to primate conservation, and these powerful companies are often ruthless in pursuing their goals. Even so, some hope emerges from four directions: ecotourism, primate rehabilitation, selective logging practices, and the granting of rights to primates, especially the great apes.

Ecotourism. One avenue for promoting primate survival is through ecotourism, a variety of leisure travel in which tourists seek "natural" experiences, such as seeing rainforests and wild animals and plants in undisturbed locations. Ecotourism has succeeded in protecting nonhuman primate habitats in some areas, especially where it generates as much revenue as, or even more revenue than, logging or hunting. But ecotourism is successful only with species that are easy to see and charismatic, such as mountain gorillas. In addition, habituating animals for close human contact entails potential risk to the animals. It can make them easier prey for hunters. It can expose them to diseases to which they have no natural or acquired immunity, such as measles. Furthermore, tourism is a fickle industry that depends on the stability of the local government, the health of the world economy, and other factors that make it an unsound foundation for nonhuman primate survival (Strier 2003).

Rehabilitation and Relocation. Other conservation programs that have met with some success are rehabilitation and relocation programs. Rehabilitation involves training captive animals, either wild caught or captive bred, to survive in the wild and then releasing them into natural environments. Rehabilitation has had some success with chimpanzees in Africa and lion-tailed tamarins in Brazil (Kleiman et al. 1986). Relocation involves moving endangered primates from an area with heavy hunting pressure or rapid habitat loss to safer areas. This process requires extensive knowledge both of the population levels of the primates (see the Lessons Applied box) and of their ecological niche and social behavior. There are many potential risks, including the death of animals during trapping and transportation, the possible exposure of the primates to dangerous pathogens, and the risk of upsetting the ecological balance of the new area. Furthermore, both rehabilitation and relocation require secure and appropriate habitats. It does no good to rehabilitate or relocate endangered animals if there is no safe habitat available for them.

Selective Logging. Selective logging means that loggers are allowed to cut only a certain percentage of the trees in a particular area. This practice differs significantly from clear cutting, which involves cutting all the trees in an area. Although selective logging does not generate as much profit as clear cutting, it is far less environmentally destructive and thus more sustainable. An added benefit of selective logging is that some primate species actually increase in population density when the forests are logged selectively.

Rights for Great Apes. Alongside the growing awareness of the plight of free-ranging primates, ethical concern is increasing for primates in captivity. The same reasons that make nonhuman primates important research subjects for anthropologists make them models for biomedical research. Several national and international laws have been passed with the goal of ensuring the well-being of captive animals. An example is the United States Animal Welfare Act of 1986. These laws have improved living conditions for many captive animals. But according to many people, they fail to eliminate animal suffering in the name of scientific research. This suffering has led animal rights activists to weigh more heavily the moral costs of any potential benefits that might be gained through animal testing.

Using Primatology Data for Primate Conservation Programs

MANY PRIMATOLOGISTS conduct basic research, which simply means that they collect information for its own sake. Some also collect data with the goal of helping to solve real-world problems. The motivation for much applied research in primatology is to help save endangered primates from extinction. For primatologists and many other people, extinction of a primate species is a serious loss to humanity because we lose some of the biological richness of the world's living creatures. A recent example of applied primatology research for primate conservation is a study of the chimpanzee and gorilla populations in western equatorial Africa conducted by Peter Walsh and colleagues (2003).

Both chimpanzees and gorillas are endangered animals, and their populations are declining at alarming rates in Africa. Programs for conserving these great apes require detailed information on their population sizes, rates of population change, possible reasons for any declines noted, the locations of populations with stable numbers, and possible areas of refuge for endangered populations.

With these questions in mind, Walsh and his team decided to conduct fieldwork in West Africa because that region is considered a *refuge area* for chimpanzee and gorilla populations. It is estimated that Gabon and the Democratic Republic of Congo (DRC) are home to up to 80 percent of the world's gorillas and to more than half of the world's chimpanzees. In contrast, East Africa has much higher human population densities, higher rates of loss of nonhuman primate habitat, and far smaller nonhuman primate populations.

Chimpanzees and gorillas are shy, so it is difficult for researchers to find them in the forest. Every day, however, both gorillas and chimpanzees fabricate nests out of branches and leaves in which they rest and sleep. These nests are readily recognizable and persist in the forest for days or even months. Therefore, the researchers systematically surveyed the nests left behind by gorillas and chimpanzees in the year 2000 to get an indication of their population size and density. Then they compared the results of this survey with results of a similar study conducted in 1983. They found that the ape population in their survey area had declined by over 50 percent since 1983, a decline that the researchers aptly term catastrophic. The greatest population decreases occurred in areas near large towns and, more specifically, in areas where Ebola fever had spread.

The main reasons found for the rapid decline in the ape populations were increased human hunting, human settlement and other encroachment on primate habitats, and commercial logging. All these factors were exacerbated by the spread of Ebola, which affected humans and nonhuman primates. This information on patterns of population decline, and reasons for the decline, can be used to help conservationists design more effective programs for combatting further population decline and preventing the potential extinction of gorillas and chimpanzees in Africa.

FOOD FOR THOUGHT

- Should humans be responsible for preserving wild primates? Find an example of a primate conservation program and assess its effectiveness.

Since the early 1990s, global and local movements have promoted granting the great apes some sort of legal status and/or certain rights that are normally reserved for humans. The *Great Ape Project* is an international movement devoted to providing great apes with the right to life, protection of freedom, and prohibition of torture. Underlying this movement is the premise that being human, in contrast to being a nonhuman animal, entails self-consciousness and rationality. Research indicates that the great apes have problem-solving abilities, self-awareness, knowledge and memory of others as individuals, complex relationships, and a high order of intelligence. Therefore, the Great Ape Project argues that apes are like humans in morally significant ways and hence deserve many rights normally granted only to humans.

The work of the Great Ape Project and of related animal rights groups takes us a long way from the study of nonhuman primates as "lower animals" that are useful as keys to humanity's past or as medical research subjects. They point us in a new direction that recognizes great apes (and perhaps other primates) as important members of a single community along with humans.

▪ WHAT are the general characteristics of the primates?

Primates are an order of mammals that includes prosimians and anthropoids (monkeys, apes, and humans). All primates share a set of morphological characteristics (including prehensile hands, a large brain, binocular, stereoscopic vision) and a high degree of sociality. Primates live in a variety of different ecological niches, but most are arboreal and diurnal. Primate species eat an assortment of foods but tend to focus on particular food types. Frugivores eat primarily fruits, folivores focus on leaves, insectivores eat mainly insects, and gumnivores focus on tree exudates. Omnivores, or multivores, are dietary generalists, a characteristic that gives them more flexibility in where they can live.

Primates are social animals. Nonhuman primate social groups vary in structure, depending on the proportions of adult males and females. Factors such as age, sex, reproductive status, personality, past experiences, degree of kinship, and familiarity influence how primates interact with each other. Nonhuman primates have complex social rules and communication systems that rely on vision, scent marking, calls, and grooming.

Primatologists do not agree on whether primates are naturally aggressive and violent or are more inclined to cooperation and affiliation. Most agree, however, that earlier models of primate social relations that focused on male dominance need to be modified in view of findings emerging from the studies of more species and species closer to humans.

▪ WHAT are the varieties of primates?

The prosimians include lemurs, lorises, and tarsiers. Most are small, nocturnal, and solitary. Lemurs are unusual prosimians in that some are large, diurnal, and social. Their distinctiveness is related to their location on Madagascar and to its unique environment.

The anthropoids are the monkeys, apes, and humans. Monkeys are divided into New World and Old World monkeys, the latter being more closely related to humans. All New World monkeys are arboreal; Old World monkeys are both arboreal and terrestrial, depending on the species.

Apes include the physically smaller "lesser apes" (gibbons and siamangs) and the "great apes," which are larger (orangutans, gorillas, chimpanzees, and bonobos). Scholars debate which of the great apes provides the best model for early human evolution. Orangutans and gorillas have marked sexual dimorphism in size. Orangutans are solitary, whereas gorillas live in large groups. Chimpanzees and bonobos, though similar in many ways, exhibit important differences. Chimpanzees, for example, are male-dominated and more violent than bonobos, and they do more hunting.

▪ WHAT can nonhuman primates reveal about humanity's past and what is their future?

Nonhuman primates have long been valued by researchers as analogues for the human past. Primatologists have recently pointed to an important similarity that had been previously neglected: the likelihood that many nonhuman primates have basic features of culture in the form of learned and shared behaviors. Humans are not the only animals that use and make tools. Findings from the new research field of primate archaeology show that some nonhuman primates have been using stone tools for at least several hundred years. Although they do not intentionally fashion stone tools, they do selectively import certain kinds of stone—a behavior that indicates intentionality. Other aspects of nonhuman primate culture include certain group-specific forms of foraging, greeting, and grooming.

Even though nonhuman primates are valued as windows to humanity's past, more than half of known primate species are currently threatened or in danger of becoming extinct. Humanity itself is the leading threat to nonhuman primate survival. We know the causes of primate population decline, but it is difficult to implement conservation programs for several reasons. Primates are a diverse order, so no single approach works everywhere. Commercial interests in logging and other economic activities that destroy primate habitats are often ruthlessly pursued and difficult to stop. Countries where nonhuman primates live are not financially well off, and their governments face many demands on their resources. In addition, local people compete with nonhuman primates for land and often hunt them for sale as bush meat. Conservation laws are difficult to enforce. New approaches and incentives are needed. Some promising strategies include ecotourism, rehabilitation, selective logging, and promotion of basic rights for certain nonhuman primates, especially the great apes, as humanity's closest relatives.

KEY CONCEPTS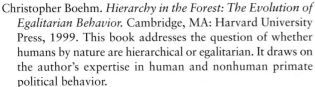

allocare, p. 149
anthropoid, p. 149
arboreal, p. 137
brachiation, p. 150
conspecific, p. 138
diurnal, p. 137
dominance, p. 143
fission–fusion group, p. 141
folivore, p. 139
foraging, p. 138

frugivore, p. 139
great ape, p. 150
gumnivore, p. 140
hominoid, p. 150
infanticide, p. 145
insectivore, p. 140
knuckle-walking, p. 152
limbic system, p. 146
matrifocal, p. 142
matrilocality, p. 142

omnivore, p. 140
nocturnal, p. 148
patrilocality, p. 142
primate, p. 136
prosimian, p. 148
quadrupedal, p. 137
social group, p. 140
sociality, p. 137
terrestrial, p. 148

SUGGESTED READINGS

Christopher Boehm. *Hierarchy in the Forest: The Evolution of Egalitarian Behavior.* Cambridge, MA: Harvard University Press, 1999. This book addresses the question of whether humans by nature are hierarchical or egalitarian. It draws on the author's expertise in human and nonhuman primate political behavior.

P. Cavalieri, Peter Singer, Douglas Adams, and Jane Goodall, eds., *The Great Ape Project: Equality beyond Humanity.* New York: St. Martin's Press, 1995. This collection of 30 essays includes writings of field biologists, psychologists, lawyers, philosophers, and anthropologists. The overarching theme is the question of the rights of the great apes.

Frans de Waal and Frans Lanting. *Bonobo: The Forgotten Ape.* Berkeley: University of California Press, 1998. The book describes the behavior and ecology of bonobos. It covers social relationships, leadership, parent–offspring ties, sexuality, and the relevance of bonobos as the best model for humans.

Phyllis Dolhinow and Agustin Fuentes, eds. *The Nonhuman Primates.* Mountain View, CA: Mayfield Publishing Company, 1999. Thirty-four chapters by primatologists provide brief overviews of a variety of subjects related to primates, such as primate evolution, taxonomy, conservation, behavior, and cognition.

John G. Fleagle. *Primate Adaptation and Evolution,* 2nd ed. San Diego: Academic Press, 1999. This textbook covers fossil and living primates.

William C. McGrew. *Chimpanzee Material Culture.* Cambridge: Cambridge University Press, 1992. McGrew discusses the behavior of chimpanzees as observed at several long-term field sites. Topics include chimpanzee culture

and similarities and differences between humans and chimpanzees.

Mary Ellen Morbeck, Alison Galloway, and Adrienne L. Zihlman, eds. *The Evolving Female: A Life-History Perspective.* Princeton, NJ: Princeton University Press, 1997. This book includes chapters written by anthropologists who examine life history from a biological, cultural, evolutionary, and female-centered perspective.

Ronald M. Nowak. *Walker's Primates of the World.* Baltimore, MD: Johns Hopkins University Press, 1999. A guide to the living and recently extinct primates, this book details their distribution, ecology, physical traits, life history, and behavior.

Sue Savage-Rumbaugh, Stuart G. Shanker, and Talbot J. Taylor. *Apes, Language, and the Human Mind.* Oxford: Oxford University Press, 2001. This book discusses the upbringing of Kanzi, a bonobo who learned to understand spoken English and to communicate using pictorial symbols called lexigrams. It explores whether or not linguistic skills are limited to humans.

Karen B. Strier. *Primate Behavioral Ecology,* 2nd ed. Boston: Allyn and Bacon, 2003. This textbook treats the ecology and behavior of the living nonhuman primates.

Robert W. Sussman, ed. *The Biological Basis of Human Behavior: A Critical Review,* 2nd ed. Upper Saddle River, NJ: Prentice-Hall, 1999. This collection of previously published papers and essays from scientific and popular media sources addresses the question of why humans behave the way we do. Chapters cover a variety of topics related to primates, the evolution of human behavior, the new biological determinism, and contemporary human behavior.

THE BIG QUESTIONS

- HOW do paleoanthropologists study human evolution?
- WHO were the early hominins?
- WHAT was life like for early hominins?

CHAPTER **6**

The Earliest Human Ancestors

The hominin footprints preserved at Laetoli, Tanzania, are about 3.6 million years old. The size of the better-preserved set on the left indicates that these individuals were between 3 and 4 feet tall when standing upright. (Source: © John Reader/Science Photo Library/Photo Researchers, Inc.)

165

Footprints are intriguing. Left in sand or snow, they soon disappear. Amazingly, however, the tracks of some extinct animals have lasted for millions of years. It takes unusual conditions for such preservation to occur—and equally unusual circumstances are often required for us to discover them.

On a typically hot day in the summer of 1976, some scientists visiting the expedition to Laetoli (in Tanzania) led by Mary Leakey decided to take a break from looking for fossils. Andrew Hill and David Western started tossing dried pieces of elephant dung to each other in an impromptu game of catch. As Andrew Hill ran to gather more missiles from a dried-up river bed, he noticed depressions in the surface of an exposed layer of hardened volcanic ash. Bending down, he realized that they were animal footprints. Mary Leakey's team began a series of careful excavations of the prints of a remarkable menagerie that ranged in size from large elephant and giraffe ancestors to small birds and hares. The real surprise came in 1978 when they excavated what looked like a **hominin** (a species more closely related to modern humans than chimpanzees or bonobos) heel print. More careful excavation revealed three hominin footprint trails at locality G (Leakey and Hay 1979). The public reaction to this discovery was one of widespread and intense interest.

The footprints were preserved because the hominins, and other animals, happened to walk across this area when its cover of volcanic ash had recently been moistened by a rainstorm. The moistened ash acted like wet cement, absorbing the impressions of the feet of the hominins and animals. When the sun dried the dust layer, it became hard as rock. The G site consists of 54 hominin footprints in two parallel trails about 80 feet long. Left by two indisputably **bipedal** (walking or running on two feet) individuals, they are a unique part of the early hominin fossil record.

The Leakey team recorded the footprints by photographing and making molds of them (Agnew and Demas 1998). Over time, concern grew that exposure was leading to deterioration of the trails. In 1979 they were reburied in order to preserve them. Given the site's remote location and difficulty of access, subsequent visits to it were infrequent. By the early 1990s, the few scientists who did visit the site raised concern that the trails were deteriorating because of root growth, especially from acacia trees. When a team opened a section, their fears were confirmed. Conservation efforts began in 1993 and continued for several years. With support from the Getty Conservation Institute, the root-infested covering was removed, the trail condition was stabilized as much as possible, and the trails were reburied using special materials to prevent root penetration.

A variety of opinions exist on how the footprints should be conserved. Some say it would be best to lift the entire trail and put it in a museum. Others say that such an idea violates the principle of trying to keep fossils in context. A replica of part of the trail is on display at the Museum at Olduvai Gorge in Tanzania, where it is viewed by thousands of visitors every year.

Genetic analysis indicates that modern humans and chimpanzees diverged, between 8 and 5 million years ago, from a **common ancestor,** a now extinct primate species from which both chimpanzees and humans evolved (Ruvolo 1997). Africa is the one place where both chimpanzees (panins) and modern humans (hominins) live today, so it is logical to assume that Africa is the place where the two separate lines evolved. It was not until the mid-twentieth century that enough evidence had accumulated to prove that Africa is where humanity first emerged. The fossil evidence for that time period, however, is both sparse and difficult to interpret in terms of whether a particular fossil represents the common ancestor, an early chimpanzee ancestor, or early human ancestors.

This chapter covers the evidence for the earliest phases of human evolution. It first discusses methods used to study human evolution, paying special attention to fossil hominins. It then traces the emergence of the hominins (review Figure 5.3, p. 148), starting with the evidence for the divergence of humans from the ancestor humans share with chimpanzees and bonobos. This section covers fossil and archaeological evidence for the period extending from roughly 7 to 1.3 million years ago. The last section reviews what the "bones and stones" indicate about the behavior and capabilities of the early hominins.

FINDING AND INTERPRETING HOMININ FOSSILS

This section looks at how paleoanthropologists discover fossil evidence about human evolution, how they determine the age and sex of the fossils they find, and how they make decisions about the relationships among hominin species, especially where ancestry is concerned.

Finding Hominin Fossils

Paleoanthropologists searching for evidence of early hominins focus their attention on Africa. Africa is where chimpanzees and bonobos, the closest living primate relatives of modern humans, are found. It is reasonable to assume that the ancestors of chimpanzees and bonobos lived on the continent where their descendants are now located, so paleoanthropologists search for early hominin evidence in Africa in places that might contain fossils from the relevant time period. Since the first quarter of the twentieth century, thousands of hominin fossils and artifacts have been found in Africa, many of them simply astounding in their character and quality. Unfortunately, many of these objects are highly sought after by international museums and even by private collectors (see the Lessons Applied box on p. 168.)

It may sound easy to look for hominin fossils in Africa, because that rules out much of the rest of the world. But Africa is a big continent. Where would you start to look for fossils? The fossils you are looking for are millions of years old and are likely to be deposited in rock layers buried beneath sediments accumulated over time or in caves deep beneath the ground. Usually, researchers rely on finding fossils in **exposures**, places where rocks of the right age have been revealed by water and wind erosion. Fossils in such locations are sometimes found by sheer chance—true "ah hah!" moments. In some cases, as noted in Chapter 4, mining or construction projects reveal hominin fossils. And sometimes, as we shall see, ingenuity and creative thinking lead to discovery.

Erosion by water and wind is particularly likely in places where the surface of the earth's crust has buckled and cracked through movement of the earth's plates, or tectonic action. Where the earth's plates meet, sections of the earth's crust between major faults (cracks) are forced downward and the earth's crust outside the faults is thrust upward, forming what are called **rift valleys,** geological formations that consist of sunken floors and elevated walls created by tectonic action. Sometimes, the cracks go so deep into the earth's crust that the earth's liquid core escapes through them. When under high pressure, the molten core escapes as a volcanic eruption. Volcanic eruptions result in showers of ash, and over time, this ash forms rocks called **tuffs** that are rich in potassium and argon.

Geologically, the African plate is quite stable. The one notable exception is called the African Rift. It has various subsections. One of these, the Great African Rift Valley, is a major exposure area and an important region for paleoanthropological research (see the map on p. 169). It runs from the Gulf of Aden, down through East and Central Africa, to Mozambique. The cracks and buckles in the earth's crust made in and around the East African part of the Great African Rift Valley divided the earth's surface into a series of giant puddles called lake basins.

During between roughly 8 and 5 million years ago, these lake basins provided environments where early hominins lived. During

The fossil-rich sediments at Koobi Fora, near Lake Turkana, Kenya. In some East African sites the height of the exposed rock layers is 100 feet or more whereas in Chad, in West Central Africa, the exposures are only 20 to 30 inches thick and there are no tuffs. ■ What kind of dating methods are useful in East African sites that cannot be used in Chad? (Source: Bernard Wood)

Paleoanthropologists Advocate for Museums in Africa

THE FOSSIL EVIDENCE for the early stages of human evolution is found in Africa in countries close to the equator. Nearly all of the countries where hominin fossils have been found so far—Tanzania, Kenya, Ethiopia, Malawi, and Chad—have national and even regional museums. For example, in Kenya, the National Museum in Nairobi houses most of the fossils, and some are kept in a Community Museum. These countries, though rich in fossils and ancient and modern biodiversity, typically have limited economic resources. Public finance for museums is a low priority compared to other needs, such as transportation, security, health, and education.

Rarely, though, are the original fossils on display in their home countries. The original fossils are, of course, irreplaceable. Putting them on display would subject them to risk of theft or damage; secure display cases and alarms are very expensive. In addition, the museums feel obligated to store the fossils in secure rooms where visiting scientists, who are nearly always from wealthy countries, can study the original fossils.

International interest in original fossils extends beyond researchers. Museums in developed countries would like to be able to display the original hominin fossils, because they know that original fossils, not copies, draw crowds. Bernard Wood has experienced the special thrill of holding many of the original fossils in his own hands and can understand the public interest in at least being able to *see* the "real thing," even though most people would not be able to distinguish the original from a copy. Thus wealthy museums in developed countries seek to borrow the original fossils. They induce museums in Africa to lend their fossils by offering them substantial amounts of money. Such schemes seem to make sense: African museums have a new source of income, museums in developed countries attract more visitors and promote wider public understanding of human evolution, and scientists living outside Africa can study the original fossils using modern imaging equipment not currently available in Africa.

In spite of these possible benefits, several paleoanthropologists, including Wood, raise serious questions about the wisdom of African museums' lending their hominin fossils. First, a one-time injection of cash is no substitute for adequate long-term financing for museums in developing countries. Second, if hominin fossils are allowed to move freely around the world, there will be no compelling reasons to install modern analytical equipment in African museums. Third, packing and unpacking the fossils and the international travel itself involve a range of risks to the fossils through damage, loss, or even theft.

Most of the hominin fossils that have been found in Kenya are kept at the National Museum of Kenya in a secure vault. The Museum has excellent facilities for researchers, who are mostly non-Kenyan, to study the original fossils. (Source: Bernard Wood)

In 1998, the Permanent Council of the UNESCO-affiliated International Association for the Study of Human Paleontology responded to news that an African museum and a museum in the United States were close to finalizing a deal that was to bring important fossil hominin evidence to the United States as the centerpiece of an exhibit. Wood, along with others, drafted a resolution expressing strong opposition to the proposed deal and to any similar "fossils for cash" arrangements (Permanent Council Resolution, 1999). The researchers also called upon their colleagues in developed countries to lobby their governments to provide financial aid for museums in those countries. The group further recommended that in the absence of compelling reasons to move a fossil, fossils remain in the home country.

The resolution has been less than completely effective. As of 2004, there is a plan to ship some original fossils from Ethiopia to Texas for an exhibition that will then move on to other museums in the United States. No doubt the museum in Texas will pay a substantial amount of money for the privilege of displaying fossils that had no need to leave their country of origin, but the Government of Ethiopia is eager to encourage tourism and believes that a U.S. exhibition that includes the "real" Lucy will be more impressive than one with just a model.

FOOD FOR THOUGHT

- What is your position on whether fossils should remain in their home countries?

Nearly all of the hominin fossils found in East Africa come from sites either in or along the edges of Rift Valleys.

that time, eruptions of volcanoes periodically spewed ash into the atmosphere, and each volcanic eruption left a distinctive tuff layer. The dates of the tuffs can be determined by either potassium–argon dating or argon–argon dating, and paleomagnetic dating is used to date the rocks between the tuff layers.

Cave sites in southern Africa are another important source of fossil evidence about the early stages of hominin evolution. The circumstances in which we find hominin fossils in southern Africa contrast markedly with those in and around Rift Valleys. Here, the fossils are found in sediments in caves that were formed within much older limestone rocks (see Figure 6.1 on p. 170). Limestone is made of chemicals that dissolve in water. When rainwater runs through cracks in the limestone, small cracks become big ones, big cracks become cavities, and cavities become caves. Later, soil is washed into the caves, where it forms layers of sediment. When pieces of rock fall from the roof of the cave and mix with the sediments, a cement-like substance called **breccia** is formed.

The southern African fossil hominins are accessible to researchers for two reasons. First, erosion by water has worn down the limestone plateau and exposed the contents of the caves. Second, access to the caves was created by miners seeking to extract lime from the caves. Although mining inevitably damaged some fossils, it enabled paleoanthropologists to investigate fossil-bearing sediments that otherwise would have been inaccessible.

Accurate dating of fossil hominins from southern African cave sites is much more difficult than dating such fossils in the East Africa Rift Valley, because there were no ash-producing volcanoes nearby. Therefore, fossil hominins found in the southern cave sites are dated by biochronology, a relative dating method that matches the fossil

Early hominin fossils from southern Africa are found within limestone caves such as this one at Sterkfontein. South African paleoanthropologist Phillip Tobias, standing on the rock-hard cave filling, lectures to visiting scientists. ■ Review which important hominin fossils have been found at Sterkfontein and why they are more difficult to date than East African hominin fossils. (Source: Bernard Wood)

evidence of animals found in association with the hominin fossils with similar fossil evidence from sites in East Africa that have been dated with absolute methods.

For many decades, the hominin fossils from East and southern Africa were the basis for our understanding of the earliest hominins. Until recently, most paleoanthropologists assumed that the earliest hominins were limited to these regions (see the map on p. 172). Most had not considered any region west of the Rift Valley as a likely site of hominin occupation, especially not the Sahara desert with its extreme heat and lack of water and food resources. But 7 to 6 million years ago, what is now the Sahara desert was grassy woodlands interspersed with lakes and rivers. Fauna included freshwater fish, turtles, crocodiles, snakes, and primitive horses (Vignaud et al. 2002). Thanks to the French paleoanthropologist Michel Brunet, we now know that the geographic range of the earliest hominins was much larger than was previously believed. The discovery of hominin fossils in Chad in 2002 by Brunet and his team shifted anthropologists' thinking about hominin evolution from what has been nicknamed the "East Side Story" to include a new version, the "West Side Story." The

FIGURE 6.1

Stages in southern African cave formation: (a) no opening between the cave and the surface; (b) sediment enters the cave through surface openings; and (c) the cave stratigraphy becomes increasingly complex.

(Source: Adapted from "Swartkrans: A Cave's Chronicle of Early Man," ed. by C. K. Brain. Transvaal Museum Monograph no. 8. Transvaal Museum, Pretoria, 1993. Reprinted by permission of Transvaal Museum.)

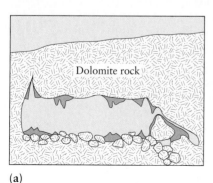

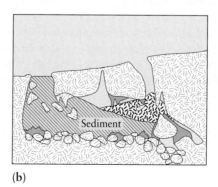

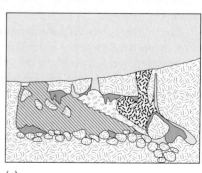

(a) (b) (c)

"West Side Story" demonstrates that the previous search for fossils was too narrowly focused on East and southern Africa. This kind of scientific surprise comes from being prepared to question preconceived notions and to approach things with an open mind.

Gaps and Biases in the Hominin Fossil Record

Over many decades, paleoanthropologists have accumulated hominin fossils from thousands of individuals going back to 7 million years ago. Most of the fossils, however, are from the later part of the hominin fossil record, starting around 500,000 years ago (we cover this material in later chapters). In addition to the temporal bias in the fossil evidence for human evolution, there is also a spatial bias. Some environments are more likely than others to result in the fossilization, and subsequent discovery, of hominin remains. Therefore, we cannot assume that the existence of more fossil evidence from a particular place or time necessarily means that more individuals were present there and then. It may simply be that the circumstances at that place and time were more favorable for fossilization.

The hominin fossil record is affected by how particular organisms, and parts of them, tend to be preserved. **Taphonomy** is the scientific study of the process of preservation and decay of organisms after their death and how these processes affect the fossil and archaeological records. Taphonomic studies reveal patterns of **differential preservation**—some types of organisms and some parts of organisms being more likely than others to be preserved in the fossil record. For example, animals that spend more time around places where sediments are being laid down are more likely to be fossilized than those that live in drier areas. The hardest parts of the skeleton, such as the teeth and the mandible, are better represented in the hominin fossil record, whereas more easily damaged regions, such as the vertebral column, the ribs, and the hands and feet, are poorly represented. Differential preservation is also affected by

THINKING OUTSIDE THE BOX

It is possible that there are other versions of hominin evolution to be added to the "East Side Story" and the "West Side Story." If you were given a grant of $1 million to search for early hominins, where would you take your team and why?

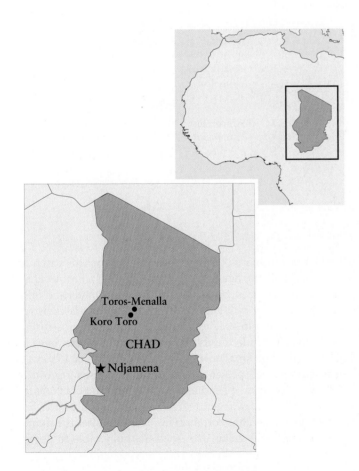

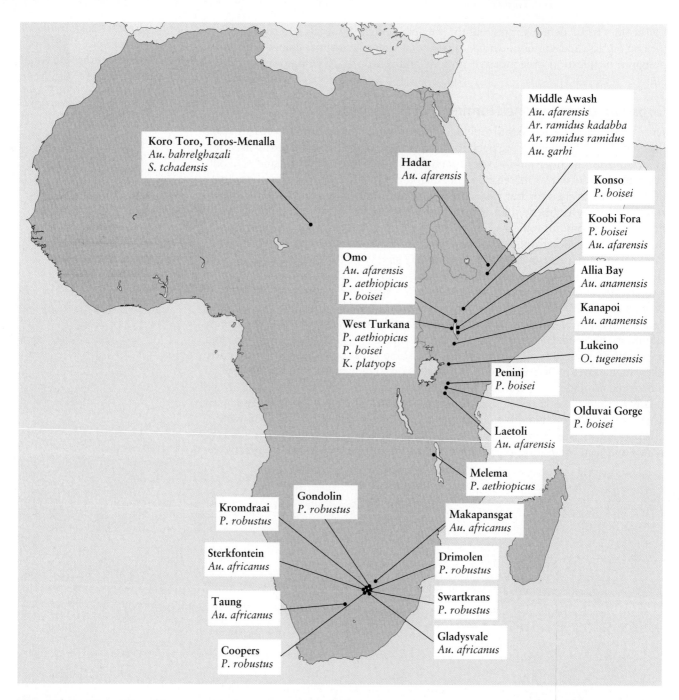

Sites and species mentioned in this chapter.

the eating preferences of predator carnivores. When modern-day leopards catch a monkey, they go for the limbs, especially the hands and feet (Brain 1981). Extinct carnivores seem to have had similar preferences, because fossil hominin hands and feet are scarce. Body size also has a significant influence on whether a species is likely to have a fossil record. Large-bodied hominin species are more likely to be fossilized than those with small bodies, and larger individuals within a hominin species have a greater likelihood of being fossilized than smaller members (Behrensmeyer 1991).

Very few early hominin fossils are well preserved or complete. Fossils are often deformed or abraded (worn). For example, if sand and soil get into the cracks in a fossil, the size of the bone or tooth will be exaggerated. When a bone is abraded, its size is reduced. Pressure on sediments, which is common in caves, can alter the shape of bones. The thin bones of the skull and pelvis are especially vulnerable to being deformed in this way.

Consider the fact that an adult hominin skeleton, just like a modern human adult skeleton, comprises 206 bones and a total of 32 teeth. Yet many early hominin fossil specimens include just one of these 238 elements, and most consist of less than a handful of them. Sometimes researchers come across a fossil cranium, but many of its component bones are usually missing. Even when the researchers find part of an early cranium, it is likely to be in fragments, and rarely are both sides preserved. Reconstructing a fossil from fragments is a major challenge for paleoanthropologists, although computers are now helping with the task (see the Methods Close-Up box on p. 174).

Even though the hominin fossil evidence discovered thus far is plentiful and exciting, it is just a small and biased sample of the original hominin population. Hominin species no doubt existed before our earliest fossil evidence of them, and they no doubt survived beyond the time of our most recent fossil evidence of their existence. Thus the *first appearance datum* (or *FAD*), and the *last appearance datum* (or *LAD*) in the fossil record are conservative statements about the dates of origin and extinction. Similarly, it is likely that early hominins lived in places other than where we have thus far found their fossil remains. Thus, the fossil data provide conservative estimates of the spatial *and* temporal distribution of early hominins.

Interpreting Hominin Fossils

We begin with the issue of identifying the age at death and the sex of a particular fossil. We then discuss how researchers decide whether they have found a new hominin species or more evidence about one that is already recognized and how researchers figure out how the different sorts of early hominins are related to each other and to later hominins.

Determining Age and Sex

Ideally, paleoanthropologists would like to know the age at death of every fossil they have, as well as other information about the individual, especially whether it was male or female. For the early stages of hominin evolution, this kind of information is difficult to obtain with certainty. Even if one has a nearly complete skeleton, determining the age and sex of hominin fossil remains is difficult. The problems are compounded when all that remains are small fragments of a cranium or a tooth or two.

Forensic anthropology tells us that ribs provide dependable information about the age of mature individuals. Ribs, however, are some of the most fragile bones in the body, and few are preserved in the hominin fossil record. Dental development can help determine the age of immature individuals, but once all the teeth are erupted and the roots of the teeth are formed, dental evidence is less useful. Age is then estimated from the of amount wear on the teeth and from the condition of the joints between the bones. These estimates are imprecise because, for obvious reasons, we have no reference populations with an independent record of the individual's age.

Sex is usually determined on the basis of the size of the bones and teeth, the extent of muscle markings, and (especially) the size and shape of the pelvis. Analogies from living nonhuman primates, especially chimpanzees, are the basis for this thinking. Sexual dimorphism in living chimpanzees is evident in both overall body size and weight and in skull size. Skulls of adult male chimpanzees are usually larger than those of females, and they often have a midline, or sagittal, crest for the main jaw-closing muscle. This pattern of size dimorphism is used as a rough guide for early hominins.

Paleoanthropologists hope that a recent methodological development may offer a dependable way to determine the sex of fossil hominins, although it has yet not been tested enough for them to be sure it will work (Brookes et al. 1995). This method is based on *amelogenin*, a protein in dental enamel that takes different forms in males and females. Amelogenin may be preserved in the enamel of fossil hominin teeth. If enough amelogenin could be recovered, it would help determine, with a high degree of accuracy, the sex of a fossil hominin.

Reconstructing Whole Fossils from Fragments

HOMININ FOSSILS that are several million years old are seldom found in good condition. The brain case and the face are particularly fragile and are easily damaged by being trampled by hoofed animals, crushed by rocks falling on them from the roof of a cave, or smashed by contemporary human construction activities.

Sometimes all that is left of a cranium is a single fragment of the brain case. In some instances, when more is preserved, one can attempt to put together the tiny pieces. Such work is a challenge because it is like doing a three-dimensional jigsaw puzzle without all the pieces and with no picture to help you figure out what piece is more likely to go where and what the final picture should look like. In the past, paleoanthropologists have painstakingly assembled fossil fragments by hand, a process that can take hundreds of hours even when a skilled anatomist is involved who knows every detail of a skull.

Marcia Ponce de Leon and Christoph Zollikofer have developed an alternative approach that takes advantage of recent advances in computer power and software (Ponce de Leon 2002, Zollikofer 2002). The fossil fragments are first scanned using a laser. Then a virtual version of the fragmented skull is displayed on the computer screen. Researchers can then rotate the scanned images of each piece to see whether and where it fits. The software also makes it possible to replace a missing piece on one side of the skull by a virtual mirror image of the

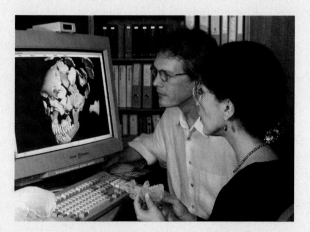

European scientists Marcia Ponce de León and Christoph Zollikofer reconstruct incomplete and fragmented fossils using virtual skulls based on CT images. (Source: © University of Zurich, Switzerland)

preserved piece from the other side. Similar software, in conjunction with CT scans, enables structures buried deep in the bone, such as bony canals of the inner ear or roots of the teeth, to be seen clearly.

FOOD FOR THOUGHT

- How much imagination should researchers use when reconstructing fossils—a lot, some, or none?

Assigning Fossils to Species and Determining Relationships among Species

Field researchers who find new hominin fossils need to determine how many sorts of animals are represented in their fossil collection. This work involves sorting the fossils into species (review Chapter 3) and then determining the relationships among the fossil species.

Measuring and Describing Hominin Fossils

The first step is to make a detailed assessment of the morphology (physical form) of the new fossil evidence. Morphology is what the fossil looks like both externally and internally. It includes both *gross morphology,* what the eye can see unaided, and *microscopic morphology,* what can be seen with a use of various types of microscopes. Laser beams enable researchers to capture precise details of the external morphology of fossils in three dimensions (3D).

A first step in the assessment of a new fossil is its *description*. This description is part of the formal announcement of a new discovery in a scientific journal. It includes information on the qualitative characteristics of the fossils, such as whether or not a cranium has a crest on the top of the braincase, and it also includes measurements, which make up the quantitative description. The quantitative description usually includes distances, called linear measurements, between defined anatomical *landmarks*. Researchers are increasingly using 3D data to provide information about the location of landmarks, the volumes of structures, and the shapes of curved surfaces—all things that are difficult to capture via conventional two-dimensional methods.

Sorting Fossils into Species

The measurements of the newly recovered fossils are then compared with those of specimens that represent existing fossil species. Analysts use living African apes and modern humans as models to help decide how much variation could have existed within a fossil species before researchers should conclude that their sample consists of more than one species.

Deciding how many species are represented in a collection of early hominin fossils is a difficult task because biological variation among hominins, including fossil hominins, is *continuous*. Therefore, the boundaries between taxa are arbitrary, and where boundaries are drawn is a matter of scientific judgment and debate. New methods often mean that boundaries have to change. New fossil discoveries prompt paleoanthropologists to consider the accuracy of their categories and labels. If new fossil evidence does not seem to belong to an existing species, then there is reason to establish a new species—perhaps even a new genus—with a new Linnaean name.

Relating Species to Other Species

The next step in fossil analysis is **cladistic analysis,** which in paleoanthropology means the use of morphology to determine how a fossil hominin taxon is related to other fossil hominin taxa. The term *clade* refers to all the descendants, no more and no less, of a common ancestor. Logically, then, the smallest clade consists of just two taxa, and the largest includes all living organisms. The branching diagram that results from cladistic analysis is called a *cladogram* (for an example, see Figure 5.5, p. 151). Cladograms depict the pattern of branches in the Tree of Life. A phylogeny has to be consistent with the cladogram for those taxa, but unlike a cladogram, it includes time and specific information about ancestors and descendants. And just in case you are not confused enough already, another name for cladistic analysis is *phylogenetic analysis,* even though cladistic analysis results in a cladogram, not a phylogeny.

Cladistic analysis works on the assumption that if members of two taxa share the same morphology, they must have inherited it from the same recent common ancestor. This assumption is often sound, but not always. Primates, like other animals, may experience **convergent evolution,** in which different lineages evolve similar morphology independently. The term **homoplasy** refers to similar morphology that appears in two species and is not inherited from a recent common ancestor. For example, it is likely that thick tooth enamel evolved more than once in human evolution, so its appearance in species that are not closely related represents homoplasy.

DNA analysis has much potential for helping solve the problem of how to detect homoplasies (Collard and Wood 2000). Individuals correctly grouped within a taxon should share more DNA with each other than two individuals drawn from different taxa, and taxa in the same clade should exhibit more DNA similarity than two taxa from different clades. DNA, though, is not readily available in early hominin fossils. Fossilization quickly causes nucleic acids such as DNA to degrade. From even as recently as 50,000 years ago, only small, fragmented amounts of DNA survive. Another problem with DNA analysis is the high probability of contamination. When people handle fossils, they inevitably leave hair and skin cells on the fossil, which are sources of contamination.

As noted in Chapter 3, grades are categories based on what an animal does rather than on what its phylogenetic relationships are. The category *folivorous monkey* is a grade that includes monkeys from both Old World and New World monkey clades. Grades may also be clades, but they are not necessarily so. For example, folivorous monkeys are not a clade because folivorous monkeys from the Old and New World are, respectively, just one component of larger Old and New World monkey clades. A clade must comprise *all* the descendants of a common ancestor, not just some of them.

Homoplasy complicates attempts to sort early hominins into clades. Therefore, paleoanthropologists are more likely to agree about grades than about clades. The two categories of hominins (primitive and archaic) that we discuss in the next section are both grades.

THE EARLY HOMININS

Here we describe what we know about the first stage of human evolution, around the time our earliest ancestors separated from the common ancestor that humans share with chimpanzees and bonobos. The scientific narrative of human evolution that we present is informed by Darwinian principles. However, as noted in Chapter 3, not everyone, either throughout history or today, subscribes to this narrative about human origins. Insights from cultural anthropology show how different groups in recent and contemporary times explain human origins and change. All narratives about human origins are influenced by cultural factors, including the scientific version.

CROSSING THE FIELDS

Cultural Variations on the Narrative of Human Origins and Evolution

It is likely that people in all past and present cultures have had ideas about what a person is, about the emergence of people, and about why some groups of people appear to be different from others. So-called *origin stories* sometimes also account for differences between men and women. For example, among the Mundurucu, an indigenous group of the Brazilian Amazon, the story goes that both men and women existed at the beginning of time (Murphy and Murphy 1985: 129). The women defied a prohibition and had sex with a certain man, and they all turned into fish. The world then had only men and fish, no women. The creator made new women out of clay, but these women were not equal to men, as the first women had been. And that is why, according to the Mundurucu people, Mundurucu men dominate women today.

On the other side of the globe, we find a different cultural construction of human evolution. Frank Dikötter, a British cultural anthropologist, has researched Chinese models of human evolution, beginning in late imperial China (the seven-

A depiction of an Ainu (indigenous) person of Japan in a Chinese anthropology textbook published in 1918.

teenth century) and continuing up to and including the present era, wherein a Western scientific view largely holds sway (1988). In the early period, a thin line was assumed to separate apes from modern humans, and the term *human* referred only to Chinese people. The Chinese classified Europeans and Africans as nonhuman beasts that did not understand human language. They pictured the nonhumans as hairy, often with tails.

By the early twentieth century, Darwinism had made a major impact on Chinese evolutionary thinking, though with some distinctive twists. According to the Chinese interpretation of Darwinism, the pathway of human evolution began with lower, hairy species whose members were "half-civilized," forest-dwelling, barbaric ape–people. The ascent to humanity was characterized by decreasing hairiness. For Chinese evolutionists, hairiness was one of the most important markers of "race." One textbook, for example, classified populations into five categories on the basis of hair texture. Today, these ideas continue in popular thinking about "hairy men" and "hairy monsters." For example, in China in 1981, the "Wild Man" Research Society was founded with the support of some highly regarded Chinese anthropologists. ■

FOOD FOR THOUGHT

■ Compare the narratives of the Mundurucu, historic Chinese, and historic Europeans (Chapter 3) in terms of how they may reflect social conditions and may shape social behavior through their definitions of superior and inferior beings.

This section describes the environmental context in which early hominins lived. Next, we note the general characteristics of the early hominins, and we explore the issue of whether it makes more sense to divide them into many species or into just a few. We then turn to the fossil evidence for the early hominins, dividing them into two groups. We first look at evidence for the species that have been put forward as **primitive hominins.** This category includes creatures that are ape-like in many ways but are probably more closely related to modern humans than to chimps and bonobos. In terms of time, they are close to the branching point between the chimpanzee and modern human lineages. Next we consider the **archaic hominins,** creatures that are certainly hominins but which retain some ape-like characteristics.

The Environmental Context in Africa

The time covered in this chapter is referred to by geologists as the Miocene and Pliocene epochs (see Figure 6.2 on p. 178). During the time of the common ancestor, around 8 million years ago during the Late Miocene, much of Africa was covered with thick forests interspersed with rivers and lakes, with their associated plant and animal life. During the period from 8 to 5 million years ago, substantial global and regional changes in climate occurred that had major effects on early hominins. Changes in rainfall and temperature were the most important. Over this period, the earth experienced a long-term drying and cooling trend. Drying occurred because the earth's moisture was increasingly locked up in ice around the north and south poles. Daytime temperatures in Africa were warm to hot, the nights cool or even cold at higher altitudes, especially in southern Africa.

Because of the increasing dryness, the dense forests declined. Open woodlands (patches of trees interspersed with patches of grassland) began to appear. The common ancestor of modern humans and chimpanzees probably lived in the dense forests. Some, though, began to adapt to life on the ground in more open conditions.

The fossil evidence for the early hominins comes from open woodland sites (Reed 1997). In fact, no early hominin fossils have been found in a dense forest. This pattern suggests that early hominins used resources associated with both forests and grassland. Trees would have provided fruit, nesting sites, and protection from predators.

FIGURE 6.2
Time periods of human
biological and cultural
evolution discussed in
Chapters 6–9.

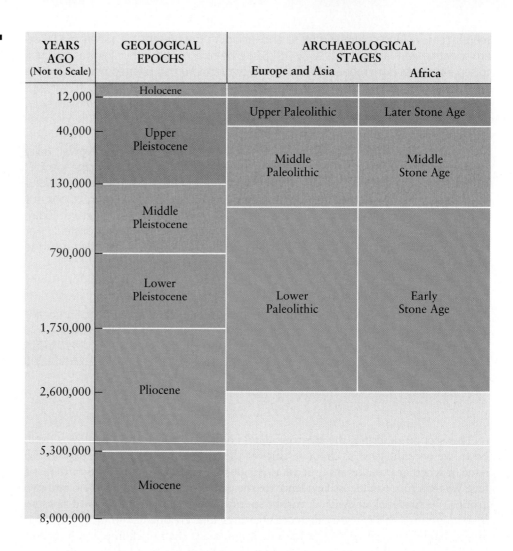

YEARS AGO (Not to Scale)	GEOLOGICAL EPOCHS	ARCHAEOLOGICAL STAGES	
		Europe and Asia	Africa
12,000	Holocene		
	Upper Pleistocene	Upper Paleolithic	Later Stone Age
40,000		Middle Paleolithic	Middle Stone Age
130,000			
	Middle Pleistocene		
790,000		Lower Paleolithic	Early Stone Age
	Lower Pleistocene		
1,750,000			
2,600,000	Pliocene		
5,300,000			
	Miocene		
8,000,000			

THINKING Diurnal nonhuman primates build nests in
trees where they sleep
at night. Generate some
OUTSIDE hypotheses about how
THE BOX early hominins living in
open woodlands spent
their nights.

Grasslands would have provided new food sources such as tubers, whereas lakes and rivers would have offered fish and mollusks. No evidence exists to indicate that early hominins lived in caves. Hominin bones are found in caves, but it is likely that hominins were either dragged there by carnivores or fell into the cave. Early hominins did not have a way of making controlled fires to discourage other animals from occupying caves, and they lacked weapons to help them compete with animals such as leopards.

Hominin Characteristics and Species

The general characteristics that distinguish hominins from panins include morphological features related to an increasingly upright posture, more emphasis on bipedal locomotion, a larger brain, and a change in diet. They include a larger brain case, a smaller face, smaller canines, larger chewing teeth, and longer legs. As you will read in the next section, not all of these characteristics were present in the earliest hominins, although we can see signs of some of them.

The classification scheme the authors of this book use recognizes a large number of archaic hominin species (see Table 6.1, Figure 6.3). Not all researchers recognize this many species (see the Critical Thinking box on p. 180). Because our perspective recognizes many species, we are called "splitters." Those who recognize few species are called "lumpers." Because anthropologists all use the same Linnaean taxonomic system, we can understand each others' point of view even though our taxonomies differ in certain details.

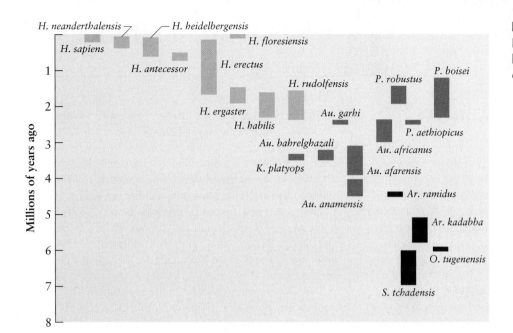

FIGURE 6.3
Primitive and archaic hominins discussed in this chapter.

TABLE 6.1
Early hominin species with dates and sites.

Hominin Category	Age (millions of years)	Sites
Primitive Hominins		
Possible		
O. tugenensis	6	Lukeino, Kenya
Ar. kadabba	5.8–5.2	Middle Awash, Ethiopia
Probable		
S. tchadensis	7.0–6.0	Toros-Menalla, Chad
Ar. ramidus s.s.	4.5–4.2	Middle Awash and Gona, Ethiopia
Archaic Hominins		
Kenyanthropus		
K. platyops	3.5–3.3	West Turkana and perhaps Allia Bay, Kenya
Australopiths		
Au. anamensis	4.5–4.0	Allia Bay and Kanapoi, Kenya
Au. afarensis s.s.	4.3–3.0	Laetoli, Tanzania; White Sands, Hadar, Maka, Belohdelie, and Fejej, Ethiopia; Allia Bay, West Turkana, and Tabarin, Kenya
Au. bahrelghazali	3.5–3.0	Koro Toro, Chad
Au. africanus	3.0–2.4	Taung, Sterkfontein, Makapansgat, and Gladysvale, South Africa
Au. garhi	2.5	Bouri, Middle Awash, Ethiopia
Paranthropus		
P. aethiopicus	2.5–2.3	Shungura Formation, Omo region, Ethiopia; West Turkana, Kenya
P. boisei s.s.	2.3–1.3	Olduvai and Peninj, Tanzania; Omo Shungura Formation and Konso, Ethiopia; Koobi Fora, Chesowanja, and West Turkana, Kenya; Melema, Malawi
P. robustus	2.0–1.5	Kromdraai, Swartkrans, Gondolin, Drimolen, and Coopers caves, South Africa

"Lumpers" and "Splitters"

ASSUME THAT YOU have a magic wand and that you use it to bring all the fossil evidence for human evolution together and put it on a large table. You sort out all the lower jaws, or mandibles, and then order them so the oldest are at one end of the table and the youngest are at the other. You then invite ten of the world's top paleoanthropologists, supply each of them with the same unlimited technical resources, and tell them that by the end of the day each must come up with a taxonomy. This means sorting individual fossils into species and then sorting species into genera. Would all ten recognize the same number of species and sort them in the same way? The short answer is no. Why? Because decisions like this are subjective and depend on the criteria you apply to make them. But surely, in science the criteria used to make decisions are agreed and accepted by all? That is what science aims for, but it cannot always be achieved. If you gave all ten scientists identical thermometers and asked them to record the temperature of boiling water, they would all give the same answer. Why not for the fossils?

There are two main reasons. The first is that there is no magic formula for working out how much variation can be tolerated in sample of twenty fossil hominin mandibles before it becomes clear that the sample includes fossils from more than one species. You might think that you could solve this problem by going to a museum and looking at twenty modern human and twenty chimpanzee mandibles, recording how they vary in size and shape, and then seeing whether your fossil mandibles are more variable or less variable than the museum specimens. Unfortunately, this would not work because the fossil sample and the museum sample are not equivalent. All the museum chimpanzee specimens were collected over the course of six years in the same forest in Uganda, whereas the fossils are half a million years different in age and come from sites that are thousands of miles apart. Obviously, even the same species is going to vary over that amount of time, but we do not know how much "extra" variation to allow for half a million years of time, so we have to combine reason and judgment with science.

The second reason why those ten paleoanthropologists would not all sort your fossils the same way is related to what might be called scientific philosophy. We noted in Chapter 3 that there are two basic models of how evolution occurred. In the *punctuated-equilibrium* model, a new species stays much the same until it either goes extinct or splits into two new species by a process called cladogenesis. In the *phyletic gradualism* model, species are longer-lived and change through time, until, eventually, a point comes when the changes are so profound that they merit a new species name.

Researchers who subscribe to the punctuated-equilibrium model of evolution and to a branching, or cladogenetic, interpretation of the fossil record will expect species to show relatively little variation, even over half a million years, and they will expect to see more rather than fewer species. They are thus likely to divide the hominin fossil record into a larger rather than a smaller number of species, and because of this they are called "splitters." Some splitters divide the early hominin fossil record into twelve species (see Figure 6.4).

Conversely, researchers who favor the phyletic gradualism model of evolution will expect species to be longer-lived and more prone to substantial changes in morphology through time. Instead of looking, as the splitters do, for morphological discontinuity, they will look for morphological continuity and place more emphasis on it. These researchers inevitably sort the hominin fossil record into fewer, more inclusive species, and accordingly they are called "lumpers." Lumpers recognize about half as many early hominin species as splitters do (see Figure 6.4). Some lumpers go to the extreme of recognizing only one species, *Homo sapiens,* for the entire hominin fossil record.

We use the more complex taxonomy for two reasons. First, a glance at the taxonomy of most other mammals over the same time period shows that their taxonomy is also complex. Second, one of the many factors that paleoanthropologists must take into account when making these judgments is that the fossil record is limited to bones and teeth. Consider

Primitive Hominins

Paleoanthopologists hypothesize about the nature of the earliest hominins by using what we know about the nonhuman primates most closely related to us and what the environment in Africa was like around 8 million years ago. Compared to the common ancestor of panins and hominins, the earliest hominins would probably have had smaller canine teeth, larger chewing teeth, and thicker lower jaws. There would have been some changes in the skull and skeleton linked with a more upright posture

FIGURE 6.4
Early hominin species according to "splitters" and "lumpers."

"Splitters" List	"Lumpers" List
Primitive Hominins	
Possible	
O. tugenensis	
Ar. kadabba	*Ar. ramidus s.l.*
Probable	
S. tchadensis	
Ar. ramidus s.s.	
Archaic Hominins	
Kenyanthropus	
K. platyops	
Australopiths	*Au. afarensis s.l.*
Au. anamensis	
Au. afarensis s.s.	
Au. bahrelghazali	
Au. africanus	*Au. africanus*
Au. garhi	
Paranthropus	*P. boisei s.l.*
P. aethiopicus	
P. boisei s.s.	
P. robustus	*P. robustus*

this example: We know that some living species of Old World monkeys (for example, *Cercopithecus* species) differ in coat and skin color, but we would not know about this difference if the only evidence we had of them was their bones and teeth. For this reason, some researchers think there are sound, logical reasons to suspect that a fossil record restricted to the hard tissues is likely to underestimate rather than overestimate the number of species.

CRITICAL THINKING QUESTIONS

- What evidence other than a fossil's appearance could be used to make judgments about how many species are represented in a fossil sample?
- If you had to be a "lumper" or a "splitter," which would you be and why?
- How might the state of preservation of the fossils affect decisions about how many species to recognize?

and the beginnings of a greater dependence on the hind limbs for bipedal walking. These would be likely to have included a forward shift of the *foramen magnum* (the place where the brain connects with the spinal cord), straighter knees, and a more stable foot—all changes related to bipedalism.

Researchers have put forward four species as primitive hominins (Table 6.1, Figure 6.4). One of the main problems in determining whether the fossils are actually primitive hominins is the small amount of fossil evidence for them. In fact, the fossil evidence for all four could fit in a carry-on suitcase. Furthermore, the carry-on suit-

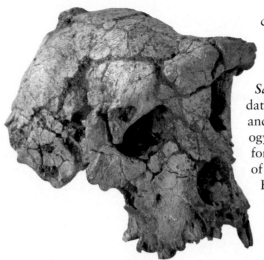

case does not contain the same parts of each contender: a toe bone of one, some teeth of another, and the thigh bone of a third.

Sahelanthropus tchadensis

Sahelanthropus tchadensis is the oldest of the primitive hominin candidates. It is known from six hominin fossils discovered by Michel Brunet and his team in 2001–2002 (Brunet et al. 2002). Dated using biochronology to between 7 and 6 million years ago, this fossil hominin is important for two reasons in addition to its age. First, it was found in Chad, in a part of Africa far from the main body of fossil evidence of early hominins in East and southern Africa. Second, the fossils have a puzzling combination of traits. The cranium exhibits a chimp-sized brain but has heavy brow ridges like those of later hominins. The mandible is thicker than the jaw of living chimpanzees. The canines are not ape-like because they are worn down only at the tip, not also on the sides as in chimpanzees. The brow ridge, jaw, and canines are the bases for the claim that *S. tchadensis* is a primitive hominin and neither the common ancestor of chimpanzees and humans nor a member of the panin line.

This fossil, discovered by the Chad-French team, is nicknamed "Toumaï," which means "a much-wanted child born after a long wait." ■ While doing Internet research on the latest discoveries in Chad, see if you can find out where the original fossil cranium is now. (Source: © Michel Brunet/Mission Paleoanthropologique francotchadienne [M.P.F.T.])

Not all paleoanthropologists are convinced that *S. tchadensis* is a hominin. One view, almost certainly wrong, is that it is a fossil gorilla. If *S. tchadensis* is an early hominin, as we believe it is, then the location of the site of its discovery in West Central Africa means that the earliest hominins occupied a much wider area of Africa than paleoanthropologists previously thought.

Orrorin tugenensis

The second oldest potential primitive hominin species is **Orrorin tugenensis,** the name given to fossils found in sediments in the Tugen Hills of northern Kenya. These fossils have been dated, via potassium–argon dating, to around 6 million years ago (Senut et al. 2001). One specimen, a lower molar tooth crown, was discovered in 1974, and twelve other specimens have been discovered since 2000. The main claim that this fossil evidence represents an early hominin is that its femur, thighbone, has features seen only in bipedal hominins (Pickford et al. 2002, Galik et al. 2004). In climbing animals the thighbone is thickened all around the neck, but in bipeds the thickening is greatest at the top and bottom of the neck. Critics of the view that these fossils are from an early hominin make two points. They say that the morphology of the *O. tugenensis* femur is not much different from that of an animal that moves around in a tree like a chimpanzee. And they maintain that the teeth of *O. tugenensis* are "ape-like."

Ardipithecus

The other two collections of fossils that might be from a primitive early hominin are both in the same genus, *Ardipithecus.* The older fossil collection, dated to between

Scientists from France and Chad are collaborating in the search for hominin fossils in Chad. The Sahelanthropus *cranium was discovered by Ahounta Dlimoumalbaye (center) who was an undergraduate student at the time of his discovery. He is seen here holding the cranium, along with two fellow students who were on the team.* ■ In addition to involving students in fieldwork, what else would you do to support in-country students and scientists? (Source: © Michel Brunet/Mission Paleoanthropologique francotchadienne [M.P.F.T.])

5.7 and 5.2 million years ago, is assigned to *Ardipithecus kadabba* and comes from the Middle Awash region of Ethiopia (Haile-Selassie 2001, Haile-Selassie et al. 2004). The fossils include a mandible, teeth, and some postcranial bones. Many aspects of the fossil evidence (such as the tall, pointed upper canines) resemble chimpanzees. Little of the morphology of the fossils in this collection resembles that of the early hominins we discuss next. The case for regarding *A. kadabba* as a hominin is not strong.

The *Ardipithecus* fossils in the second collection also come from the Middle Awash region. They date from around 4.5 million years ago. This fossil collection includes teeth, a small piece of an infant jaw, and part of the underside of a cranium. It is assigned to the genus *Ardipithecus* but is placed in a separate species called *Ardipithecus ramidus*—because its discoverers think that its canines are less ape-like than those of *Ar. kadabba* (White et al. 1994, Haile-Selassie et al. 2004). Several features link *Ar. ramidus* with hominins, the strongest evidence being the position of the foramen magnum. In *Ar. ramidus* this opening is further forward than in chimpanzees, though not so far forward as in modern humans.

We currently lack information about the size of the brain of *Ar. ramidus*, and evidence for its posture and locomotion is meager. In terms of size, both *Ar. kadabba* and *Ar. ramidus* were similar to a small adult modern chimpanzee, around 70–80 pounds. In spite of changes in the teeth and base of the skull that link *Ar. ramidus* with archaic hominins (discussed next), the overall appearance of *Ar. ramidus* would have been more like a chimpanzee than like a modern human.

Archaic Hominins

Compared to the primitive hominins, all the archaic hominins have larger chewing teeth and larger, wider faces. The larger teeth of this group of hominins are related to their more diverse diet. Most, but not all, archaic hominin species are included in the genus *Australopithecus*, and we use the term **australopiths** for these. Some of the archaic hominins have especially large chewing teeth, and they are included in a separate genus, *Paranthropus*. One archaic hominin species has been allocated its own genus, *Kenyanthropus*.

Australopiths in East and Central Africa

Three archaic hominin species have been found in East Africa and one in West Central Africa. We present them as separate species, although some researchers view them all as part of a single, evolving lineage.

Australopithecus anamensis. Fossils from sites in Kenya that date from around 4.5 to 4 million years ago belong to *Australopithecus anamensis*. The canines of *A. anamensis* are more chimp-like than those of *A. afarensis*, yet the chewing teeth are larger and more rounded than those of chimpanzees. This species may be ancestral to *A. afarensis*.

Australopithecus afarensis. The best known of the species discussed in this section is *Australopithecus afarensis*. The fossil evidence comes from sites including Laetoli, in Tanzania, and Hadar, in Ethiopia (see the map on p. 172). They are dated between 4 and 3 million years ago. The fossil collections include a skull, several well-preserved crania, many lower jaws, and enough limb bones to generate reliable estimates of its size and body weight.

The Hadar part of the collection contains "Lucy," probably the most famous fossil in the world. The 1974 discovery of Lucy by paleoanthropologist Don Johanson and his team made headlines because it was the first time researchers had recovered such a well-preserved early hominin. The team recovered about 40 percent of Lucy's skeleton. Knowing that the bones come from a single individual, researchers can make more accurate estimates about the hominin's stature, body weight, and other characteristics.

French paleoanthropologist Michel Brunet, leader of the joint Chad-French team, holds the Sahelanthropus *cranium.* ■ Do some Internet research to find out about the latest hominin fossil discoveries in Chad. (Source: © Michel Brunet/Mission Paleoanthropologique franco-tchadienne [M.P.F.T.])

At the time when the early hominins were evolving in Africa, the environment was changing from dense forest to patches of woodland interspersed with open grasslands. ■ How is this type of environment likely to be related to the evolution of bipedalism? (Source: © 2004 Frans Lanting)

Paleoanthropologists Meave Leakey (left) and Alan Walker (right) discuss fossils found at Kanapoi, Kenya, an important site with hominin fossils dating to 4.5 million years ago. They are examining a jaw bone that belongs to Australopithecus anamensis *and concentrating on one tooth whose size and shape is distinctly different in modern humans and chimpanzees.* ■ *Which tooth is that?* (Source: © Kenneth Garrett/National Geographic Images)

The skeleton of Lucy with American paleoanthropologist Don Johanson, the leader of the team that discovered it. Most indications are that the skeleton is of a female, though not all scientists are convinced. ■ If you had only one bone from a skeleton and you had to determine the skeleton's sex on that basis, which bone would be most useful and why? (Source: Donald Johanson/Institute of Human Origins)

Australopithecus bahrelghazali. Hominin fossils three and a half million years old collected in Chad, near the site where *S. tchadensis* was found, are assigned to *Australopithecus bahrelghazali.* The sample consists of only two jaws and some teeth. Its discoverers suggest that it can be distinguished from *Au. afarensis* on the basis of its tooth morphology (Brunet et al. 1995), but others regard it as a geographic variant of *Au. afarensis.*

Australopithecus garhi. The fourth East African australopith is *Australopithecus garhi,* which has been determined to be 2.5 million years old, and fossil evidence of which was found in the Middle Awash, Ethiopia. Its limb bones suggest it was bipedal, but its chewing teeth are much larger than those of other East African australopiths.

We have evidence that *Au. garhi* must have made sophisticated stone tools. Stone tools themselves have been found with the *Au. garhi* fossils, and marks on animal bones nearby indicate that the flesh was removed from them through the action of a sharp-edged tool. Only razor-sharp stone flakes would have allowed the flesh to be removed so neatly. These cut-marked bones are currently the oldest evidence of tool use among hominins, and they thus mark the beginning of the **Paleolithic period,** or Old Stone Age (see Figure 6.2 on p. 178).

Stone tools dating to 2.6 million years ago have been found at Gona (Semaw et al. 2003). At this site, we have stone tools but no fossil evidence as yet to help us understand what kind of hominin made and used them.

Australopiths and *Paranthropus* from Southern Africa

In recent years, the news-making fossil finds have come mainly from East Africa, with the exception of Chad. Southern African sites, however, were the first ones to be in the fossil limelight. In 1924, a landmark discovery occurred. A hominin child's skull was found in a small cave in Taung, southern Africa, which was exposed as a result of mining operations (see the map on p. 186). The Taung skull was brought to the attention of Professor Raymond Dart of the University of The Witwatersrand in Johannesburg, who recognized its significance.

Dart named the fossil *Australopithecus africanus* and published his findings on it in 1925. His report met with a frosty reception. Most researchers were ignorant of, had forgotten, or disagreed with Darwin's prediction that Africa was the cradle of humanity. Dart recruited a distinguished ally, paleontologist Robert Broom, who had made a name for himself by collecting fossils of mammal-like reptiles. Broom was convinced that Dart had found an important link between our ape ancestors and modern humans. He began to look for other caves that might contain similar fossils. More than a decade later, in 1936, Broom found a second cave, Sterkfontein, containing remains that are now interpreted as belonging to *Australopithecus africanus,*

This fossil bone from Olorgesailie, Kenya, is 990,000 years old. It provides evidence about the behavior of early hominins. The scratch marks are straight with clean edges, ruling out the possibility that they were made by accident, such as animal trampling. Instead, they were made by hominins who used stone flakes to remove flesh from the bones. The broken edge was due to intentional hammering with a stone tool. ■ Why would hominins have broken the bones? (Source: Human Origins Program, Smithsonian Institution)

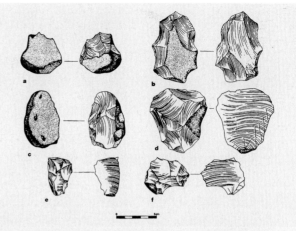

Stone tools, 2.6 million years old, from the Ethiopian site of Gona (see the map on p. 199). Their sharp edges can cut into the hide of an animal and remove the flesh from the bones. ■ Think of other materials that early hominins in Ethiopia could have used to make tools. (Source: Reprinted with permission from *Nature,* © 1977 Macmillan Publishers Ltd/Courtesy of Dr. Sileshi Semaw/"Semaw, S., Renne, P., Harris, J.W.K., Feibel, C., Bernor, R., Fesseha, N. & Mowbray, K., 2.5-million-year-old stone tools from Gona, Ethiopia. *Nature* 385:333–338.")

an australopith archaic hominin dated to between 3 and 2.4 million years ago. A decade later, similar-looking fossil hominins were discovered at a third cave, Makapansgat, and more were found in the 1990s at a cave called Gladysvale.

Fossil evidence of a hominin with a flatter face and larger jaws and chewing teeth than *Au. africanus* was discovered at Kromdraai, another cave site in southern Africa. Later on, more fossil evidence like that at Kromdraai was found at a nearby cave at Swartkrans. The fossils from Kromdraai and Swartkrans were allocated to their own genus and species, *Paranthropus* ("beside Man") *robustus.* More evidence of *P. robustus* has come from caves called Drimolen and Coopers. All these sites are thought to be younger than those where *Au. africanus* fossils have been found.

Thus the southern African cave sites have produced fossil evidence of two kinds of archaic hominins: *Au. africanus* and *P. robustus.* The major problem with interpreting all the early hominin fossils recovered from the southern African caves, as noted earlier in this chapter, is that they cannot be dated as reliably as those from sites in East Africa. Researchers are trying to find absolute dating methods that will work on the cave breccias. In the meantime, we must work with relative dates. The *Au. africanus*-bearing breccias have been dated to between 3 and 2.4 million years ago. The remarkably complete hominin skeleton, Stw 573, from deep in the Sterkfontein cave may be considerably older, dating from 4 million years ago, but it is too early to tell whether it belongs to *Au. africanus* or to a more primitive species (Clarke 2002). Other hominin fossils resembling *Au. africanus* have been recovered from even deeper in the Sterkfontein cave and are also likely to be around 4 million years old (Partridge et al. 2003). The *P. robustus* fossils are all from cave sediments that date to between 1.9 and 1.5 million years ago.

Two early hominin crania from southern Africa. On the right is Sts 5, Australopithecus africanus, *which is 3-2.5 million years old. At the lower left is SK48,* Paranthropus robustus, *which is 1.5 million years old.* ■ Locate these two species on Figure 6.3, p. 179. (Source: © John Reader/Science Photo Library/Photo Researchers, Inc.)

Paranthropus in East Africa

Additional evidence for *Paranthropus* emerged in 1959 when Mary and Louis Leakey discovered a *Paranthropus* cranium, dated to 1.8 million years ago, at Olduvai Gorge. The OH 5 cranium had larger chewing teeth

Cave sites in the Blauuwbank Valley, South Africa.

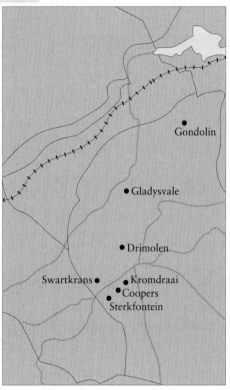

South African paleoanthropologist Ron Clarke with the skull belonging to a nearly complete hominin skeleton, dated to 3.3 million years ago. Found deep in the complex of caves at Sterkfontein, the individual may have been exploring the cave or accidentially fell into it, and then could not get out.

■ What are other reasons why hominin remains are found in the southern African cave sites? (Source: Bernard Wood)

and jaws than any other hominin taxon known at the time, but these were combined with small incisors and canines. This evidence suggests that these hominins were eating hard or tough foods as well as other foods and that they were not frugivores. The cranium became the type specimen of *Zinjanthropus boisei*, but most researchers have dropped the genus name *Zinjanthropus* and place the East African taxon into either *Australopithecus* or *Paranthropus*. We refer to it here as **Paranthropus boisei**.

Further evidence of *P. boisei* came with the discovery of a mandible with a large, robust body, large chewing teeth, and small incisors and canines at the Peninj River on the shores of Lake Natron, in Tanzania. Since then, more fossils belonging to *P. boisei* have been found at Olduvai and at sites in Ethiopia, Kenya, and Malawi.

The morphological features that set *P. boisei* apart are found in the cranium, mandible, and dentition. It is the only hominin to combine a massive, wide, flat face with very large chewing teeth and small incisors and canines. Despite its large jaws and chewing teeth, the brain of *P. boisei* is similar in size (about 480 cubic centimeters) to the brains of australopiths such as *A. africanus*. The earliest evidence of *Paranthropus* in East Africa is a variant with a more projecting face, larger incisors, and a more ape-like underside to the cranium. Some researchers assign these fossils from before 2.3 million years ago to a separate species, *P. aethiopicus*. Despite the richness of the cranial evidence for *P. boisei*, no postcranial remains have been found in association with cranial remains that are sure to belong to *P. boisei*. Therefore, regrettably, we have no good evidence about its posture or locomotion.

For the next half-century, paleoanthropologists interpreted the very large premolar and molar tooth crowns of *Paranthropus*, and especially *P. boisei*, as a specialization that enabled them to consume large quantities of low-quality plant food. A recent review of the evidence has led to a very different conclusion (Wood and Strait 2004). This is the view that although the large chewing teeth and mandibles of *Paranthropus* are specialized morphologically, they do not necessarily indicate a specialized diet. Instead, the large chewing teeth may have enabled it to consume a wide range of dietary items, including meat, plant foods, and perhaps insects. On the basis of this rethinking, then, *Paranthropus* would have been a dietary generalist, not a specialist. Conventional wisdom suggests that *Paranthropus* became extinct because it had become so specialized that when the climate began to fluctuate, it could not adapt to the new conditions. But if it was a generalist rather than a specialist, scientists will have to seek another explanation for the extinction of *Paranthropus*. In any event, we should not regard *P. robustus* or *P. boisei* as "second-class" hominins. *P. boisei* lasted a million years, from 2.3 to 1.3 million years ago.

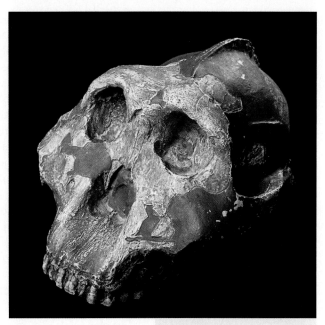

A cranium of P. boisei *from Olduvai Gorge, Tanzania, 1.8 million years old. Compared with a living ape it has a wide, flat face with small incisors and canine teeth. Living male apes use their large canines to threaten fellow males and to attract females. The small canines of* P. boisei *would have been ineffective for this kind of communication.* ■ Generate a theory about the implications of this species' small canines. (Source: © Photo Researchers, Inc.)

Kenyanthropus

The most recently discovered archaic hominin has been assigned to a new genus and species, **Kenyanthropus platyops**. This is the name Meave Leakey and her colleagues (2001) have given to a collection of fossils recovered from sediments with absolute dates of 3.5 to 3.3 million years ago. The best specimen is a nearly complete cranium, but it is deformed by many matrix-filled cracks that permeate the face and the rest of the cranium. Despite the cracking, it is apparent that some features of the face do not match the face of *Au. afarensis*, the best-known hominin from this time period. Meave Leakey's team is convinced that their find is distinct from *Au. afarensis*. They also point to the similarities between it and a taxon we will discuss in the next section, *Homo rudolfensis*. At this stage of their investigation, however, they are unsure whether the facial similarities with *H. rudolfensis* are inherited from a recent common ancestor or are homoplasies.

EARLY HOMININ ADAPTATIONS

Imagine you were a field primatologist and were lucky enough to find a living primate no scientist had ever seen before. First, you would need to prepare a formal description of the new taxon. Next, you and your colleagues would observe it in the wild to try to gather as much information as possible about what individual members of the taxon look like, how large they are, where they live, what they eat, how they move around, their social patterns, how intelligent they are, any possible tool use, and how they communicate with one another, among other topics.

Paleoanthropologists try to answer the same questions about extinct hominins, but they have only fragmentary evidence. Their task is much like that facing forensic scientists when they try to reconstruct the circumstances surrounding a crime.

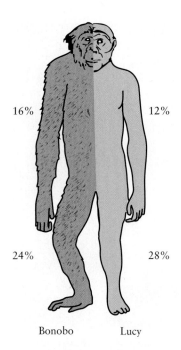

16%   12%

24%   28%

Bonobo   Lucy

FIGURE 6.5
Primatologist Adrienne Zihlman of the University at Santa Cruz compared Lucy's likely body weight proportions to those of living apes. She found that bonobos are most similar to Lucy. Lucy's arms are 12 percent of her body weight and her legs are 28 percent. In bonobos, arms are 16 percent of body weight and legs 24 percent. This pattern of weight distribution indicates a partial adaptation to bipedal locomotion. ■ Review Chapter 5's discussion of bonobos. (*Source:* Adapted from an original drawing by Carla Simmons in Sussman 1984:197.)

Both kinds of researchers have to search for clues and make the best of the scant and fragmentary information they have. In this section, we present what can be deduced from the fossil record about the habitat, appearance, and behavior of early hominins.

Paleoanthropologists use **functional morphology** and **behavioral morphology** to inform them about what early hominin life was like. In functional morphology, they look at a fossil bone or tooth and consider what functions it would have performed best and most frequently. For example, the shapes of finger bones and finger joints and the length of the fingers and thumb provide clues about manual dexterity. Holding the shaft of a hammer requires a *power grip*, whereas the ability to hold and use a small, sharp stone tool demands a *precision grip* and a different combination of arm, forearm, and small hand muscles. The thighbones of bipedal animals, which bear all their weight on their hind limbs, are differently shaped and have larger heads than those belonging to quadrupedal animals, which spread their weight over four limbs. Behavioral morphologists look at morphology in terms of what it suggests about behavior more widely. For example, they ask how sexual dimorphism in body size may have influenced relations between males and females. The following discussion presents what we can reasonably infer about various aspects of early hominin life on the basis of functional and behavioral morphology.

Body Shape and Locomotion

Primitive and archaic hominins were about the same size as an average living chimpanzee but smaller than later human ancestors and most modern humans. Most would have been around four feet tall when standing upright and would have weighed around one hundred pounds. In some, the presumed males were 50 percent larger than the presumed females.

Primitive and archaic hominins had arms slightly longer than those of modern humans, and the shortness of their lower limbs would have made them look more chimpanzee-like than human-like (see Figure 6.5).

It is likely that around 8 million years ago, the common ancestor of chimpanzees and modern humans was a knuckle-walker with occasional episodes of being upright, like modern chimpanzees. It is not known when our early ancestors abandoned knuckle-walking for bipedalism. Some think that the wrist bones of *Au. afarensis* still show signs of knuckle-walking (Richmond and Strait 2000), but others are unconvinced (Lovejoy et al. 2001). The oldest uncontested evidence of hominin bipedal walking is the trails of hominin footprints at Laetoli, Tanzania, which date from 3.6 million years ago (Leakey and Hay 1979, Schmid 2004).

For the early hominins with fairly good fossil records (such as *Au. afarensis*), it is clear that they had the ability to move bipedally. However, it is not clear to what degree bipedalism was replacing arboreal locomotion. A complicating factor is that a common-sense view of bipedal walking as an efficient, low-energy form of moving from one place to another needs some critical thinking. Compared to running, walking is more difficult in terms of maintaining body balance. Also, the energy requirements of walking need to be compared to running. Computer models of the lower limbs of archaic hominins show that running would have used less energy than walking (Crompton et al. 2003). Thus, early hominins may have been able to both walk and run on the ground, while still being capable of seeking shelter and protection in trees—a combination that gave hominins a decisive advantage.

Many theories have been proposed for the evolution of upright posture and bipedalism. Some are related to the conditions of living in an open woodland environment rather than a dense forest. For example, one proposition says that upright posture and bipedalism evolved because they enabled hominins to see other animals over the tall grasses in the more open areas. Another theory involves the possible decline in hair covering the body, which made it more difficult for an infant to cling to its mother. Thus, it is suggested, bipedalism emerged because it freed the arms for carrying infants. Although these propositions are intriguing, they cannot be proved with the current evidence. It is possible, as well, to conjecture about the adaptive compromises (Chapter 2) involved in upright posture and bipedalism. Just as upright posture meant that hominins could see further across the grasslands, they simultaneously became more visible to possible predators. This new vulnerability may have prompted early hominins to use and throw objects for defensive purposes, a behavior that again ties into the greater use of the upper limbs. An additional risk with upright posture is that it exposes the belly. Furthermore, the abdominal wall and internal abdominal organs of modern humans are still adjusting to an upright posture. The prevalence of varicose veins and back problems among modern humans are examples of our incomplete adjustment to being upright and bipedal.

What other hypotheses can you generate about the causes and consequences of upright posture and bipedalism?

THINKING OUTSIDE THE BOX

Diet

The general pattern of early hominin food acquisition, like that of free-ranging chimpanzees today, is foraging—that is, collecting wild food available in nature. Given the changing environmental conditions in Africa during the period covered in this chapter, we find some changes in the content of the diet from primitive to archaic hominins, and these changes had important implications for hominin adaptability.

Insights about early hominin diets come from looking at the size, shape, and condition of the fossil teeth of each hominin species and at the chemical composition of their teeth and bones. Teeth with large, flat crowns covered by thick enamel are likely to have evolved to cope with a diet that included tough food or food enclosed in a hard outer coating, such as the shell of a nut, that must be broken before the contents could be eaten. Different types of foods leave different patterns of minute scratches on teeth called *microwear*, which are visible only with microscopes. For example, foods such as tubers that grow in the ground may contain grit, and eating such food leaves marks on the surface of the tooth enamel (Teaford and Ungar 2000).

The chemical evidence about diet comes from *stable isotope analysis*, which measures the levels of different carbon isotopes in fossil teeth and bones and then matches the pattern found in the fossil evidence with patterns seen in living animals whose diets are known. This method indicates that two of the archaic hominins, *Au. africanus* and *P. robustus*, ate at least some meat from grazing animals (Lee-Thorp et al. 2003).

Overall, the fossil evidence suggests that the diet of the early hominins was mixed, not specialized, and included a wide variety of fruits, nuts, tubers, and insects and some animal meat. The diet of the primitive hominins was likely to have included a higher proportion of fruits than that of the archaic hominins, which ate a wider range of foods. The greater dietary breadth of archaic hominins allowed them to inhabit more diverse environments. It was the beginning of a trend that eventually enabled later hominins to colonize even more varied environments around the world.

Sociality

The fossil evidence provides little that can enlighten us about early hominin social groups and relations. Relying on information about presumed male–female differences in body size and shape, and on assumptions about their possible social correlates based on living chimpanzees, puts us on shaky ground. As noted in Chapter 5, sexual dimorphism in body size among some species of living monkeys and apes is associated with male competition for the sexual attention of females. In such groups, males develop a ranking order among themselves, and in some cases males appear to dominate females. We also saw that larger size is not always linked to dominance, because smaller animals can form coalitions and dominate larger individuals through group action. Thus it is impossible to make definitive statements about social roles and social interaction of the early hominins on the basis of sexual dimorphism in size and shape.

Chewing has left many pits and scratches, called microwear, on the surface of this tooth from Paranthropus robustus *from Swartkrans.* ■ Think of some foods that you eat which are likely to leave pits and other foods which are likely to leave scratches. (Source: Courtesy of Peter Ungar and Robert Scott)

Using analogies from living chimpanzees and bonobos about sociality more generally, we can say that early hominins probably had a high degree of sociality that was expressed in mother–infant care and inter-individual grooming patterns. Given patterns of social group formation among living chimpanzees and bonobos, it is likely that early hominin groups were multi-male/multi-female with offspring. Again, judging by analogy with the living primates most like humans, it is probable that mature females left their birth groups and joined other groups.

Intelligence

No solid evidence exists about the intelligence and creativity of the early hominins. The fossil record includes fossil crania, and we can measure the size of the brain case. The only fossil cranium of a primitive hominin belongs to *S. tchadensis*. Its volume has been estimated to be around 350 cubic centimeters (cc), and it is thus similar in average size to the brain of both chimpanzees (380 cc) and bonobos (340 cc). The earliest archaic hominin for which there is a reasonable set of fossils indicating brain size (from four individuals) is *Au. afarensis*. Their average brain size is 450 cc, about one-third larger than the average brain size of *S. tchadensis*.

In addition to absolute brain size, it is important to consider brain size in relation to body size. For example, blue whales have larger brains than modern humans, but they also weigh more than humans, so they have a lower ratio of brain size to weight. The brain-size-to-body-weight ratio of *Au. afarensis* is not much greater than that of a chimpanzee. But does this finding necessarily mean that *Au. afarensis* was about as intelligent as a chimpanzee?

Researchers cannot explain what this evidence about brain weight and body size means in relation to the behavior and intelligence of the primitive and archaic early hominins. In modern humans, there is no relationship between individual brain size and intelligence. It is likely, therefore, that no such correspondence occurred in early hominin species. However, the generally higher level of demonstrated intelligence of monkeys compared to prosimians (review Chapter 5), and of living apes compared to living monkeys, is paralleled by larger brain size, both absolute and relative. The safest conclusion we can reach about intelligence of the early hominins is that they are likely to have been at least as intelligent as chimpanzees. Primitive and archaic hominins show little evidence of significant increases in brain size over time. The one species whose brain did exhibit a modest increase is *P. boisei* from East Africa, although its body size apparently did not increase (Elton et al. 2001).

Tools

Primitive and archaic hominins were able to make and use tools, certainly at the level of living chimps, gorillas, and orangutans. To that extent, they possessed culture. The earliest hominin stone tools, from Gona, are dated to around 2.6 million years ago, roughly the same time as the earliest evidence for cut marks on animal bones found with the remains of *A. garhi*.

Going further into the past, to between 3 and 4 million years ago, the hand morphology of *Au. afarensis* indicates that they would have been capable of making and using sharp stone flakes. Similarly, *P. robustus* was physically capable of making and using primitive stone tools, and we have good evidence that they made bone tools. Pointed bone fragments found with *P. robustus* at the cave site of Swartkrans, dated between 1.9 and 1.5 million years ago, show wear indicating that they may have been used to break into termite hills to fish for termites (Backwell and d'Errico 2003).

Language

Paleoanthropologists have long thought that a swelling on the surface of the part of the brain that controls the muscles used in speech indicated the ability to use verbal language. Functional studies of the brain made when people are speaking or thinking about words now show that many other parts of the brain are used in speech.

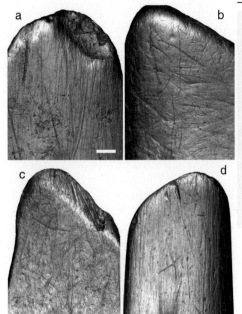

Four images showing the tips of bone tools. (a) Fossil bone tool from Swartkrans, dating to 1.5 million years ago. (b) Recent bone tool used to dig up bulbs such as onions. (c) Recent bone tool used to dig up tubers and insects. (d) Recent bone tool used to dig into a termite mound. ■ Study all four images and then decide what is the most likely use of the Swartkrans bone tool. (Source: Lucinda Backwell)

Thus there is no simple way of using the shape of the brain to determine whether early hominins could speak. It is highly likely, however, that they had effective ways of communicating much as living nonhuman primates do—through sounds and body language that may have been learned and shared.

One solid conclusion about the primitive and archaic hominins is that they were neither fossil chimpanzees nor just small versions of modern people. They are interesting and important in their own right, and they evolved diets and locomotor behaviors that were distinct. The fossil evidence for several early hominin species spans over a million years. In evolutionary terms, they were "successful" animals in that they lasted as long as the average mammal species lasts in the fossil record.

THE BIG QUESTIONS REVISITED

■ HOW do paleoanthropologists study human evolution?

Evidence about human evolutionary history comes from two sources. The first source is a combination of genetic and fossil evidence. The genetic evidence tells us about relationships, the fossil evidence about time. In terms of human evolution, the genetic evidence tells us that modern humans and chimpanzees (including bonobos) are each other's closest relatives. The fossil evidence about primate evolution suggests that humans shared a common ancestor with chimpanzees between 8 and 5 million years ago.

Paleoanthropologists assume from this genetic evidence that Africa is where the common ancestor lived, so that is where researchers look for the earliest fossil evidence of hominins. Over the years, they have found many important early hominin fossils, especially in East and southern Africa, but most recently in Chad, in West-Central Africa. In spite of the rich collections of fossils, many gaps and biases exist. Taphonomy is the study of how organisms are preserved depending on the their size, location, and other factors, and it helps scientists to adjust for the biases in the fossil record. Determining the age at death and the sex of early hominin fossils is extremely difficult. New methods promise to help in these areas. When a new fossil species is discovered, the international scientific community provides rules about how it is to be named.

▪ WHO were the early hominins?

The early hominins occupied open woodland, rather than forests like most panins. They were recognizably ape-like in their body size and shape, but they were partially bipedal and consumed a more diverse diet.

The early hominins can be divided into two groups: primitive hominins and archaic hominins. Four species are claimed to be primitive hominins: *S. tchadensis*, *O. tugenensis*, *Ar. kadabba*, and *Ar. ramidus*. The two species that are the most solid candidates as primitive hominins are *S. tchadensis* and *Ar. ramidus*.

Archaic hominins are almost certainly more closely related to modern humans than to chimpanzees. They form a large group of australopiths, two species of *Paranthropus*, and one species belonging to the genus *Kenyanthropus*.

▪ WHAT was life like for early hominins?

Early hominins were unique. They were neither human-like chimpanzees nor chimp-like modern humans. They evolved in an open woodland habitat—groves of trees with patches of grassland between them. The first hominins walked and climbed on all fours some of the time and walked bipedally some of the time. They ate a largely vegetarian diet but occasionally consumed insects and small animals. They used simple tools made by modifying natural objects. They were social and probably lived in groups that resemble modern-day extended families. They matured relatively quickly, and individuals were capable of operating independently at a young age. They communicated with each other in ways that more resemble chimps than modern humans; complex spoken language almost certainly evolved relatively late in human evolution.

KEY CONCEPTS

archaic hominin, p. 177
Ardipithecus kadabba, p. 183
Ardipithecus ramidus, p. 183
Australopithecus afarensis, p. 183
Australopithecus africanus, p. 184
Australopithecus anamensis, p. 183
Australopithecus bahrelghazali, p. 184
Australopithecus garhi, p. 184
australopith, p. 183
behavioral morphology, p. 188

bipedal, p. 166
breccia, p. 169
cladistic analysis, p. 175
common ancestor, p. 166
convergent evolution, p. 175
differential preservation, p. 171
exposure, p. 167
functional morphology, p. 188
hominin, p. 166
homoplasy, p. 175

Kenyanthropus platyops, p. 187
Orrorin tugenensis, p. 182
Paleolithic period, p. 184
Paranthropus boisei, p. 186
Paranthropus robustus, p. 185
primitive hominin, p. 177
rift valley, p. 167
Sahelanthropus tchadensis, p. 182
taphonomy, p. 171
tuff, p. 167

SUGGESTED READINGS

Eric Delson, Ian Tattersall, John van Couvering, and Alison Brooks, eds. *Encyclopedia of Human Evolution and Prehistory.* 2nd ed. New York: Garland, 2000. This encyclopedia contains hundreds of brief articles covering the entire range of fossil and archaeological evidence for human prehistory.

Donald Johanson and Blake Edgar. *From Lucy to Language.* New York: Simon and Schuster, 1996. This book offers an account of human evolution with abundant photographs of the fossils.

Alison Jolly. *Lucy's Legacy: Sex and Intelligence in Human Evolution.* Cambridge, MA: Harvard University Press, 1999. This account of human evolution focuses on the evolution of sex and intelligence in humans and other primates, paying explicit attention to a female perspective on the subject. This interpretation favors the role of cooperation over competition.

Jon Kalb. *Adventures in the Bone Trade: The Race to Discover Human Ancestors in Ethiopia's Afar Depression.* New York: Springer-Verlag, 2001. The author recounts his experiences as part of the scientific exploration of the Afar Depression, Ethiopia. He describes the competition among scientific expeditions.

Jeffrey K. McKee. *The Riddled Chain: Chance, Coincidence, and Chaos in Human Evolution.* New Brunswick, NJ: Rutgers University Press, 2000. The author offers a provocative rethinking of hominin evolution, maintaining that the evidence for linking events in hominin evolution with changes in the paleoclimates is weak. He suggests that paleoanthropologists should pay more attention to the role of chance in hominin evolution.

Robert J. Meier. *The Complete Idiot's Guide to Human Prehistory.* New York: Alpha Books, 2004. This book covers a wide range of topics, including methods of dating, taxonomy, the various stages of human evolution from the early hominins to modern human global colonization, Darwinian evolution, creationism and intelligent design, and the challenges facing humanity in the future.

Virginia Morrell. *Ancestral Passions.* New York: Simon and Schuster, 1996. In this book, a journalist provides a detailed account of the many fossil hominin discoveries made by the Leakey family.

Richard Potts. *Humanity's Descent: The Consequences of Ecological Instability.* New York: Avon, 1997. The author reviews humanity's ancestors, focusing on the role that rapidly changing environments played in human evolution. The book concludes by linking hominin–environmental interactions of the past to current issues of modern human–environmental interaction, such as global warming.

Bernard Wood. "Hominid Evolution," "Hominid Radiations: Early." In *Nature Encyclopedia of Life Sciences.* London: Nature Publishing Group, *www.els.net.* This web-based encyclopedia contains many articles on hominin evolution.

THE BIG QUESTIONS

- WHAT are the earliest forms of *Homo*?
- WHEN did archaic *Homo* leave Africa and where did they go?
- WHAT were key features of archaic *Homo* behavior and culture?

Emergence and Evolution of Archaic *Homo*

Georgian paleoanthropologist David Lordkipanidze with the 1.7-million-year-old skull of a hominin from Dmanisi, Georgia, which his research team discovered. This slightly built individual belongs to a species of hominin with a small brain. Nevertheless, it was able to migrate out of Africa as far as the Caucasus region. (Source: © Reuters/CORBIS)

The word *Neanderthal* means "Neander's Valley" in Old German. It refers to a valley cut by the river Düssel into limestone hills a few miles east of the modern city of Düsseldorf. In August 1856, commercial limestone quarrying exposed the contents of a cave, called the Kleine Feldhofer Grotte, on the south wall of the valley (Schmitz et al. 2002). Workers cleared the cave of its contents, which they threw onto a dump pile. By chance their supervisor noticed some unusual bones in the dump pile and showed them to the local schoolteacher, who identified them as human bones. Eventually, a skullcap and a total of fifteen limb bones were recovered from the dump. This collection of bones formed the basis for the first description of *Homo neanderthalensis*.

After some time, quarrying ceased. No surveys were done of the site, and by 1900 the exact location of the cave was no longer known. Most scientists assumed that the hominin fossils stored in the local museum were the full extent of the type specimen of *H. neanderthalensis* from the Kleine Feldhofer Grotte.

But two German researchers, Ralf Schmitz and Jürgen Thissen, recently decided that the cave and its contents were worth some hard searching. Archival research led to their rediscovery, in 1997, of the cave and the area where its contents were dumped. They soon began to recover Paleolithic fossils and stone tools. The fossils included parts of a face and mandible and some pieces of limb bones. To their delight, one of the small pieces of limb bone fit exactly into the lower end of the left femur of the type specimen housed in the museum. They also found pieces that fit onto the Neanderthal skullcap, including parts of the face and the cranial vault. The Neanderthal fossils, which had been damaged by quarrying and flung into a dump 150 years ago, were finally reunited.

This chapter includes the fossil and archeological evidence for species sufficiently like modern humans to be included in the human genus, *Homo.* But they are not enough like us to be included in our own species, *Homo sapiens,* so they are called **archaic** *Homo.* Archaic *Homo* species spanned nearly 2 million years. They migrated into much of the Old World and left a legacy of fossils and artifacts that records an important period in the evolution of humanity.

THE FIRST HUMANS

The term *archaic Homo* refers to five extinct human species (see Figures 7.1, 7.2, and 7.3). Compared to the archaic hominins discussed in Chapter 6, these species have a modern human-like body shape and small teeth and jaws. However, despite the similarities in body shape, the postcranial skeleton of all five species is more robust than that of modern humans, and four of the species—the Neanderthals are the exception—have smaller brains than modern humans.

Environment and Time

The time period covered in this chapter extends from about 2 million years ago to just less than 30,000 years ago, the date of the last fossil evidence for archaic *Homo.* In Africa, this period is divided into the **Early Stone Age,** or ESA, and the **Middle Stone Age,** or MSA (review Figure 6.2, p. 178). In Europe and Asia, the same time span is divided into the **Lower Paleolithic,** or LP, and the **Middle Paleolithic,** or MP. Archaeologists use two different sets of names to indicate that distinctive developments occurred in the two regions.

The long-term cooling of the world's climate continued from 2 to 1 million years ago, and the climate continued to fluctuate in approximately 40,000-year cycles. But around 1 million years ago, for some unknown reason, 100,000-year cyclic changes in the shape of Earth's orbit began to be the major influence on world climate. During

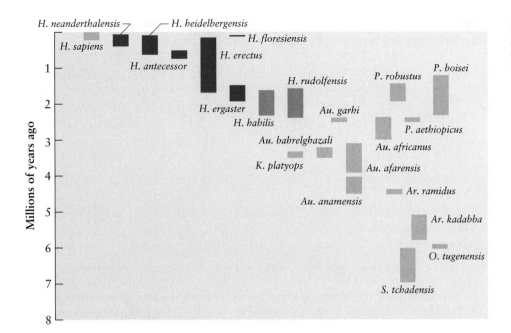

FIGURE 7.2
Archaic *Homo* and transitional species with dates and sites.

Hominin Category	Age (millions of years)	Sites
Homo		
H. habilis s.s.	2.4–1.6	Olduvai Gorge, Tanzania; Koobi Fora and perhaps Chemeron, Kenya; Omo (Shungura) and Hadar, Ethiopia; perhaps also Sterkfontein, Swartkrans, and Drimolen, South Africa.
H. rudolfensis	1.8–1.6	Koobi Fora, and perhaps Chemeron, Kenya; Uraha, Malawi
H. ergaster	1.9–1.5	Koobi Fora and West Turkana, Kenya; possibly Dmanisi, Georgia
H. erectus s.s.	1.8–0.2	Sites in Indonesia (Trinil, Sangiran, Sambungmachan), China (Zhoukoudian, Lantian) and Africa (Olduvai Gorge, Melka Kunture).
H. antecessor	0.7–0.5	Gran Dolina, Atapuerca, Spain
H. heidelbergensis	0.6–0.1	Sites in Europe (Mauer, Petralona); Middle East (Zuttiyeh); Africa (Kabwe, Bodo); China (Dali, Jinniushan, Xujiayao, Yunxian) and possibly India (Hathnora).
H. neanderthalensis	0.4–0.03	Fossil evidence for *H. neanderthalensis* has been found throughout Europe, with the exception of Scandinavia, as well as in the Levant and Western Asia.
H. sapiens s.s.	0.19–present	Fossil evidence of *H. sapiens* has been recovered from sites on all continents except Antarctica. The earliest absolutely dated remains are from Herto, Ethiopia.

FIGURE 7.3
Early *Homo* species according to "splitters" and "lumpers."

"Splitters" List		"Lumpers" List
Homo		
H. habilis s.s.	}	H. habilis s.l.
H. rudolfensis		
H. ergaster	}	H. erectus s.l.
H. erectus s.s.		
H. floresiensis		
H. antecessor	}	
H. heidelbergensis		H. sapiens s.l.
H. neanderthalensis		
H. sapiens s.s.		

long periods when Earth's orbit was farther away from the sun, global temperatures fell. The ice accumulation at the South Pole was so deep that it buried even the highest mountains of Antarctica. Because so much water was locked up in ice sheets, the level of the seas fell. During the other part of the cycle, when Earth's path was closer to the sun, temperatures rose, and the ice sheets decreased in size. These 100,000-year changes were responsible for the series of major and minor ice ages that have affected Europe and North America during the past million years. These climate changes affected the entire globe. During this period, open woodlands in Africa expanded into a type of environment called a **savannah,** an open plain with tall grasses and sparse patches of trees.

Distinctive Features of *Homo*

This section first reviews the criteria for including particular hominin fossils in the genus *Homo*. We explain why we regard most of the longstanding reasons for including taxa in *Homo* as either impractical or unreliable, and we propose a different set of criteria. We then look at two forms of early *Homo* that appear to be transitional between the archaic hominins and species that are properly treated as human.

Until recently, anthropologists used six main criteria for deciding which hominin fossils should be included in the genus *Homo* (see Figure 7.4). These criteria are related to anatomical features and behaviors that scientists for most of the twentieth century thought made modern humans distinct from the other great apes. Our knowledge and understanding have advanced, however, and have shown many of these criteria not to be scientifically valid. Some involve capabilities that are difficult or impossible to determine or infer from the fossil and archeological records. For example, researchers have traditionally based inferences about the capacity for spoken language on the shape of the parts of the brain that were thought to be the sole control centers for language production. Scientists now know that many more parts of the brain than the classic motor language centers are involved in language production (Gannon et al. 1998). Furthermore, the brain size criterion of 750 cubic centimeters (cc) is problematic because it is arbitrary and because it was based on observations about the size of gorilla brains. Molecular and morphological evidence now confirms that gorillas are not our closest living relatives, so their brain size should not be used to generate a yardstick for human brain evolution.

The precision grip and stone tool making criteria are impractical as criteria for two reasons. First, fossil hand

During this stage of human evolution, dry conditions transformed much of Africa's woodlands into open grasslands, called savannahs. ■ What would have been some major challenges to survival in a savannah environment compared to a dense woodland environment? (Source: © Paul A. Souders/CORBIS)

FIGURE 7.4
Earlier criteria for classification as *Homo*.

Brain size larger than 750 cc
Ability to generate and understand spoken language
Ability to use the hand in a *precision grip*
Ability to make stone tools
Upright posture
Bipedal locomotion

bones are rare, so little can be said about the manual dexterity of early hominins. Second, the first simple stone tools are found in East Africa at sites dated to around 2.6 million years ago (Chapter 6). Several sorts of hominins have been found at such East African fossil sites, and it is presently not possible to be sure which ones made the tools and which ones did not.

The authors of this textbook believe that, instead of these earlier criteria, the inclusion of early hominin taxa in *Homo* should be based on (1) parts of the body that are well represented in the fossil record—that is, jaws and teeth, and (2) behaviors that can be reliably inferred from the fossil record.

Sites mentioned in this chapter.

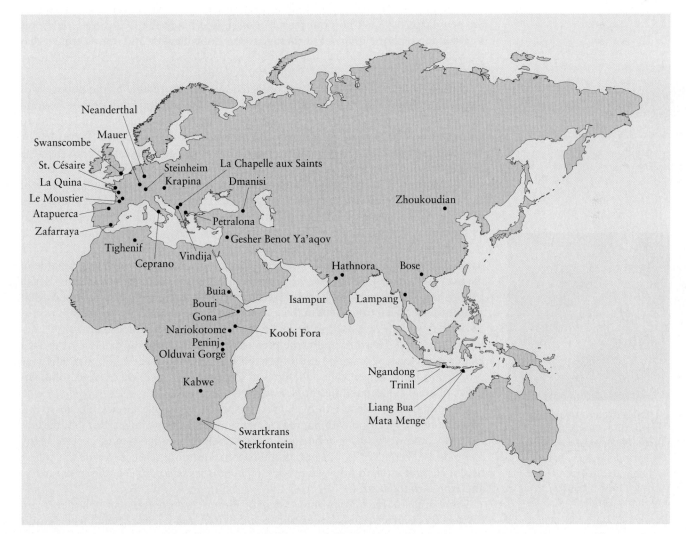

According to this view, the genus *Homo* would include only hominin species with jaws and chewing teeth similar in size to those of modern humans and with limb morphology and limb proportions consistent with an upright posture and modern human-like bipedalism (Wood and Collard 1999a). This brief review of old and new criteria should help readers make sense of the following discussion about "contested" hominin fossils.

A Contested First Human: *Homo habilis*

In Olduvai Gorge, Tanzania, Louis and Mary Leakey made the first of a series of discoveries of fossils representing a form they thought much more human-like than *P. boisei*. This occurred in 1960. Half a century later, scientists are still debating whether these remains represent a primitive human—that is, a member of the genus *Homo*—or are from an advanced australopith.

Fossil Evidence for *Homo habilis*

The collection of new fossils included evidence from the cranium and some hand, leg, and foot bones. The cranial remains showed no sign of the bony crests characteristic of large-bodied *P. boisei* individuals, and the premolar and molar teeth were substantially smaller than those of *P. boisei*. At the time, the scientific consensus was that all *Homo* species should have a brain size of at least 750 cc. The brains of the new Olduvai discoveries, however, were only about 600–700 cc. Nonetheless, Louis Leakey and his colleagues argued that the Olduvai evidence should be included in *Homo* because the new evidence satisfied the functional criteria for *Homo*: manual dexterity, upright posture, and fully bipedal locomotion. They were convinced that the new larger-brained hominin, not *P. boisei*, had made the Oldowan stone tools found along with the fossils. For these reasons, Louis Leakey and others argued that the material justified establishing, within the genus *Homo*, a new species called **Homo habilis** (literally "handy man") (Leakey et al. 1964).

Placing these fossils in *Homo* was rendered more questionable by the discovery of many other fossils like those of *Homo habilis* from Olduvai and from sites in East and southern Africa, such as Koobi Fora and Sterkfontein. The single largest addition to the collection of *H. habilis* comes from the site of Koobi Fora in Kenya (Wood 1991). When researchers examined this new evidence carefully, and when they looked at the original Olduvai evidence with fresh eyes, they found little in any of it that distinguished *H. habilis* from archaic hominins. Relating the size of the jaw and teeth of *H. habilis* to its body size reveals that *H. habilis* is more like archaic hominins than like later *Homo* species. Limb bones found with *H. habilis* cranial remains show that its skeleton was australopith-like. In fact, its limb proportions cannot be distinguished from the best-known australopith species, *Au. afarensis* (Richmond et al. 2002). If the hand bones found at Olduvai do indeed belong to *H. habilis*, then it was capable of the manual dexterity involved in the manufacture and use of simple stone tools. Recall from Chapter 6, however, that *Au. afarensis* and *P. robustus* also had hands that appear to have been capable of making and using crude stone tools, and that *P. robustus* probably made and used stone and bone tools. Yet neither of these taxa is classified in the genus *Homo*. Finally, the premise that *H. habilis* was capable of spoken language because of assumed links between Broca's area in the brain and language production is no longer valid, as noted in Chapter 6. Hence, there is no solid evidence of language capabilities in *H. habilis*.

An additional problem with *H. habilis* is its status as a single species. The fossil evidence has more variation within it than scientific classification allows. Notably, the crania, jaws, and teeth of *H. habilis* are more variable than one would expect. Many researchers (Wood 1992), but not all, think it makes more sense to divide the collection of *H. habilis* fossils into two species, *H. habilis sensu stricto* ("in the strict sense") and *Homo rudolfensis*.

Compared to *H. habilis sensu stricto*, **Homo rudolfensis** has a larger brain (700–800 cc); a face that is larger, wider, and flatter; and larger chewing teeth. Noth-

This core tool is one of the major tool types associated with the Oldowan tradition.
■ How do archaeologists attempt to discover the use of such tools? (Source: Bernard Wood)

ing is known for certain about the limbs and the locomotion of *H. rudolfensis*. The larger chewing teeth of *H. rudolfensis* suggest that its diet may have been similar to that of the archaic hominins—in other words, mixed. The evidence for *H. rudolfensis* indicates that it, too, should not be included in *Homo*. Both *H. habilis s.s.* and *H. rudolfensis* and best regarded as transitional hominins with some signs of the features we see in later *Homo*.

Oldowan Stone Tools

Associated with *H. habilis* are distinctive stone tools that have been given the name **Oldowan**. The Oldowan toolkit is characterized by core tools and flake tools. The earliest evidence, thus far, of Oldowan stone tools are the ones found at Gona, Ethiopia, dated to 2.6 million years ago (Chapter 6). Similar toolkits found throughout the Old World are described as Oldowan. **Core tools** are made from *cobbles* (rounded stones of a certain size) that have had flakes chipped off them, either at one end or along one side. A **prepared core** is a specially selected and prepared stone cobble from which tools such as flakes are made. Any kind of stone that is used to make a stone tool is said to be a **blank,** so in the Oldowan tradition, the blanks are cobbles. Tools called flakes are more numerous than core tools. **Flakes** are stone tools that consist of the sharp pieces of stone that break off a cobble when it is struck. A **biface** is a stone tool that has been flaked on both sides. Oldowan flake tools have a blunt end and a sharp end. A third Oldowan tool type is the **scraper,** a large (several inches long) flake with a sharpened edge along one side. Finally, some cobbles, both natural and shaped, were used as hammers; they are called *hammerstones*.

Oldowan stone tools are highly effective. Razor-sharp flakes can easily cut through animal hide, core tools can be used to smash limb bones to extract the marrow, and scrapers are effective for removing flesh from bones. The flakes are so sharp that they leave marks on the surface of animal bones where they have been used to remove flesh. Archaeologists Kathy Schick and Nicholas Toth have conducted *experimental studies* in order to understand better the manufacture and functions of stone tools. With their team of researchers, they have made and used stone tools (Schick and Toth, 1993; Stout et al. 2000). From such studies, it is clear that Oldowan stone tools could serve a variety of purposes, such as butchering animals, breaking bones to extract the marrow for eating, making wooden tools, cracking nuts and other hard foods, making other stone tools, and use for defense or offense as *projectiles* (throwing objects).

Hundreds of Oldowan tools have been found in Africa and Asia. Starting with the oldest known stone tools from Gona, Oldowan toolkits persisted in Africa until 500,000 years ago, and they were made in Asia until 200,000 years ago. It is unlikely that Oldowan stone tools were the only tools used by their makers. Rather, they were the tools that survived in the archaeological record because they were made of hard stone (see the Critical Thinking box on p. 202).

The link between *Homo* and the use and manufacture of stone tools is a strong one, because all archaic *Homo* taxa are associated with stone tools. Nevertheless, the stone tools at Gona

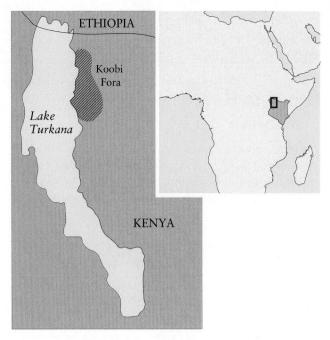

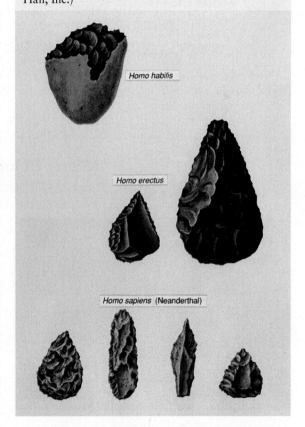

Starting at the top is an example from the oldest stone tool tradition, the Oldowan. In the middle is an Acheulian stone tool. The bottom tool is a Mousterian tool. ■ Assume that scientists decide to abandon the type-site names for these traditions in favor of names that describe the tools themselves. What names would you suggest for each tradition? (Source: Howard S. Friedman/Prentice Hall, Inc.)

Homo habilis

Homo erectus

Homo sapiens (Neanderthal)

What Is Really in the Toolbox?

IT IS REASONABLE to assume that stone tools were not the only tools that archaic *Homo* used, given that it is likely that other materials were available for tools and that a wider variety of uses existed than the probable functions of core tools, flakes, and scrapers. This exercise asks you to do a mini-experimental study by imagining that you are living in an environment like that of archaic *Homo*—open woodland. Imagine your daily life, including how you obtain food and sleep at night.

CRITICAL THINKING QUESTIONS

- Make a list of the activities you would you perform, over a 24-hour period, and what tools you might need for those activities.
- What materials in the forest would provide useful tools for performing these activities?
- Assume you have ten tools in your toolkit. Three of them are made from stone: one core tool and two flakes. What are the other seven tools? What is the likelihood that these other seven tools would be preserved in the archaeological record available to future ages?

THINKING OUTSIDE THE BOX Review the Crossing the Fields section in Chapter 5, pp. 155–157, and think about the significance of seeking out particular types of stones from a distance as an indication of human-level intelligence.

An experimental archaeologist uses a newly made stone tool to cut raw meat.
■ Do some Internet research on the experimental stone tool research projects of archaeologists Nicholas Toth and Kathy Schick. (Source: © Lowell Georgia/CORBIS)

predate the advent of archaic *Homo* by several hundred thousand years. Thus the phrase "Man the Tool-Maker" is misleading, because humans share the capability of making and using tools with nonhuman primates and share the ability to make stone tools with their archaic hominin ancestors (Wood and Collard 1999b). It is also inappropriate because it uses the word *man* generically, implying that there was no such hominin as "Woman the Tool-Maker." In short, if one insists on maintaining the linkage between *Homo* and tool-making, then one must redefine *Homo* to include nonhuman primates and archaic hominins.

Homo ergaster

Fossils from Koobi Fora, Kenya, dated to around 1.9 million years ago, provide the first evidence of hominins more clearly like modern humans than any of the hominins considered so far. The Linnaean name for this fossil evidence is *Homo ergaster*. Some researchers (lumpers—recall the Critical Thinking box in Chapter 6, p. 179) do not recognize it as a separate species. They refer to it as "early African *Homo erectus*."

A Better Fit for *Homo*

Homo ergaster is the first hominin with a body size and shape much like those of modern humans. Its brain, with an average size of around 800 cc, is larger than that of all the archaic hominins but still well below the average brain size of modern humans. The cranium of *H. ergaster* has heavy brow ridges in the upper part of the face, but the rest of the face shows more advanced characteristics in that it is narrower, less projecting, and smaller than in archaic hominins. Likewise, its teeth and jaws are smaller than in an archaic hominin of equivalent size. Its body size and shape, especially its chest shape and limb proportions, are also more like those of modern humans than like any archaic hominin or *H. habilis*. *H. ergaster* crania, however, show little advance in brain size over *H. rudolfensis*, one of the transitional hominins that may not belong to *Homo*. Why large brains do not appear until much later in human evolution is still a puzzle to paleoanthropologists.

Acheulian Stone Tools

Around 1.7 million years ago, quite soon after the fossil evidence of *H. ergaster* dated at 1.9 million years ago, a new tradition called the **Acheulian** appears, a stone toolkit characterized by the prevalence of stone tools called handaxes (Toth and Schick 1993). The Acheulian tradition is named after a site in St. Acheul, France, where European archaeologists first discovered handaxes. The oldest Acheulian stone tools are from Ethiopia and Kenya.

A **handaxe** is a bifacial (two-sided) stone tool that is flat, pear-shaped, and flaked on all its edges and on both surfaces. Two other important types of Acheulian tools are *cleavers* (large tools about 12 inches long with a broad, flaked, cutting edge) and *picks* (long and thick pointed tools that are flaked on one or both sides). Acheulian tools differ from Oldowan tools in several ways. First, they are more bifacially worked than Oldowan tools. Second, the edges of Acheulian tools are more finely worked. And third, Acheulian tools are more symmetrical. Early Acheulian tools, like the Oldowan tools, were made using hammerstones. Later, use of the hammerstone was complemented by the use of "soft hammers," such as bone, to achieve more precise bifacial chipping. Overall, Acheulian tools indicate a greater degree of forethought and planning, as well as more skill and dexterity.

Acheulian tools probably served multiple functions, and the handaxe was probably the Swiss Army knife of the Lower Paleolithic. Studies of **use wear,** or evidence of patterns of use, show that handaxes were used for digging up tubers (edible roots), processing plant fibers, and scraping animal skins. There is no evidence that Acheulian stone tools were hafted (attached to a handle). Hafting leaves signs of wear on stone tools, and these tools bear no such signs. But even without hafting, they could have been used for cutting wood or as missiles.

The earliest Acheulian stone tools in Africa are dated to about 200,000 years after the earliest fossil evidence for *Homo ergaster*. It is tempting to credit *H. ergaster* with their invention, but as the next section of this chapter shows, discoveries at a site far from Africa, in the country of Georgia, complicate this attribution. Although perhaps it was not the inventor of stone handaxes, some evidence indicates that *H. ergaster* may have been the first hominin to use controlled fire for cooking food (Wrangham et al. 1999). Around the time when *H. ergaster* first appears in the fossil record, archeologists have found evidence of burned earth close to where stone tools have been found (Harris 1978, Gowlett et al. 1981). Such evidence may indicate the deliberate use of fire, but a more cautious interpretation is that the burned earth is an ecofact, something that is caused by nature (Bellomo 1994). When lightning sets a tree on fire, the remains of the burned tree stump resemble the remains of a controlled fire in a hearth. More convincing early evidence for the use of fire comes from an Acheulian site in Israel, Gesher Benot Ya'aqov, dating to 790,000 years ago (Goren-Inbar et al. 2004).

An Acheulian stone handaxe from Olduvai Gorge, Tanzania, made around 700,000 years ago. ■ Think of some functions for which this handaxe might have been used. (Source: Bernard Wood)

 ## ARCHAIC *HOMO* MOVES OUT OF AFRICA

Until just less than 2 million years ago, the hominin fossil and the archaeological records are confined to Africa. But the adage "Absence of evidence is not evidence of absence" reminds us that it is still possible that archaic hominins and archaic *Homo* existed outside of Africa before 2 million years ago. In this as in every other aspect of the study of human evolution, new discoveries may well bring surprises. Until then, it makes sense to accept the working assumption that hominins did not leave Africa until around 2 million years ago.

This section considers where these first hominin migrants went and what we know about them from the fossil and archaeological records. At this point, the question of "why" archaic *Homo* left Africa remains unanswered. Different hypotheses exist, such as the following three:

- Hominins had become meat-eaters, and their preference for meat led them to follow herds of animals as these moved out of Africa to new areas.
- They were attracted by the cool and arid northern climate, where their ability to adapt to varied conditions gave them an advantage over other species.
- Humans are "natural" migrants—they just have to keep moving on.

Although we do not know why hominins began to spread throughout the Old World, there is evidence about where they went and when. The general direction of migration was north and east out of Africa toward the Middle East and then on into Asia. It is likely that they had arrived in Java, in Southeast Asia, by 1.8 million years ago. If so, they must have lived in other parts of the Middle East and Asia several thousand years before then.

First Evidence of Humanity in Eurasia: Dmanisi

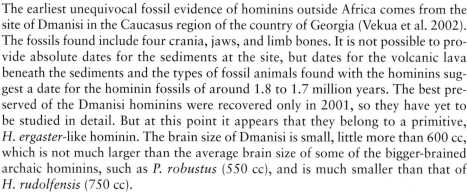

The earliest unequivocal fossil evidence of hominins outside Africa comes from the site of Dmanisi in the Caucasus region of the country of Georgia (Vekua et al. 2002). The fossils found include four crania, jaws, and limb bones. It is not possible to provide absolute dates for the sediments at the site, but dates for the volcanic lava beneath the sediments and the types of fossil animals found with the hominins suggest a date for the hominin fossils of around 1.8 to 1.7 million years. The best preserved of the Dmanisi hominins were recovered only in 2001, so they have yet to be studied in detail. But at this point it appears that they belong to a primitive, *H. ergaster*-like hominin. The brain size of Dmanisi is small, little more than 600 cc, which is not much larger than the average brain size of some of the bigger-brained archaic hominins, such as *P. robustus* (550 cc), and is much smaller than that of *H. rudolfensis* (750 cc).

The stone tools at Dmanisi are all core and flake tools, similar to the toolkit found with *P. boisei* and *H. habilis* at Olduvai Gorge. No handaxes have been found at Dmanisi. The Dmanisi evidence is thus of a small-brained hominin with a core and flake toolkit who lived more than a thousand miles outside of Africa. The Dmanisi finds have forced researchers to rethink the accepted view of this stage of hominin evolution in two ways. First, conventional wisdom had suggested that in order to survive in the harsher, more seasonal environments outside of Africa, hominins would need a large brain and, at the least, an Acheulian toolkit. Apparently this assumption is incorrect. Second, the Dmanisi discoveries mean that anthropologists have to think anew about which kinds of hominins made Oldowan tools. They may have been made by *Homo ergaster*-like migrants who left Africa before the Acheulian tradition developed in Africa. If the Dmanisi evidence turns out to confirm the existence of *Homo ergaster* without the Acheulian tools typically associated with them, then the link between handaxes and *H. ergaster* will need to be loosened.

Homo erectus in Asia

Homo erectus is the first human species that is widely distributed across the Old World. It is the species name given to fossils that Dutch anthropologist Eugene Dubois discovered in the 1890s in Java. His finds came from a site called Trinil on the banks of the Solo River. Some of the best-known fossil evidence of *H. erectus* comes from other sites along the Solo River dating from as early as 1.8 to less than 1 million years ago. For some periods during that time span, Java was connected to the Asian mainland.

If you met an individual representing *H. erectus* in the street, you would be unlikely to confuse it with a modern human. Its head would be smaller, its forehead would be lower, and no modern human would have such a pronounced brow ridge. Its average brain size was about 1000 cc, or two-thirds the size of the average modern human brain. Its jaws and skull bones were thicker than those of modern humans. Its limb bones were similar in size to those of modern humans, but the shafts of the long bones had a thick covering of outer bone. These differences suggest that *H. erectus* individuals were more muscular than most modern humans.

Most of the hominin fossils from the Javan sites were found by accident in the 1930s and 1940s as farmers plowed their fields. Researchers had to rely on descriptions from the farmers about the locations of the finds. Thus, little contextual evidence exists for the fossils. There is also relatively little volcanic ash in the Javan sediments, so the dates of the Javan hominins are less precise and accurate than the dates for sites in East Africa.

The question of when *Homo erectus* arrived in Asia is unanswered at this point. Some researchers think that *H. erectus* reached Java as early as 1.8 million years ago (Swisher et al. 1994). If so, then *Homo erectus* would probably have been established on the Asian mainland well before that. But the earliest reliable evidence of hominin activity in China comes from stone tools dated to 1.5 million years ago (Zhu et al. 2001). There are several possible explanations for this time gap:

- The date of 1.8 million years ago and other early dates for *H. erectus* in Java are inaccurate.

- The fossils in Java represent a more primitive form of hominin than *H. erectus*.

- Hominins were on the mainland before 1.8 million years ago, but evidence of their occupation has not yet been found.

More reliably dated evidence from mainland Asia is crucial if we are to fill in this gap in our knowledge.

In addition to the many sites in Java, there are many other *H. erectus* sites elsewhere in Asia. The most important of these is Zhoukoudian, near present-day Beijing, China (Etler 1996). Excavations began there in the 1920s, but most of the fossils

The earliest evidence for fossil hominins in Southeast Asia comes from sites along the Solo River in Java. These sites have been exposed through erosion caused by the river flow. ■ What is the current population density of Java? (Source: © National Geographic Image Collection)

Dr. John de Vos, a curator at the Leiden Museum, holding Trinil 2, the type specimen of Homo erectus, *found in Java in 1891. This original fossil is in a museum in Holland.* ■
What is your position on whether or not it belongs there? (Source: Bernard Wood)

THINKING OUTSIDE THE BOX How does this discussion of bamboo as a material for many types of tools prompt you to rethink your responses to questions in this chapter's Critical Thinking box? What can you find out, through independent research, about contemporary people's use of bamboo in Asia?

collected in this early work was mysteriously lost during World War II. However, an excellent set of plaster casts of many of the fossils survived. Excavations at Zhoukoudian conducted by Chinese and international researchers are providing new evidence about hominin adaptations at this site.

In the 1930s, archaeologists speculated about cannibalism at Zhoukoudian, noting that the bottoms of the skulls were missing. Because of the loss of the original fossil material in the Second World War, however, it is impossible to explore, with current methods, whether the marks were made by stone tools (and thus constitute evidence of cannibalism) or were made by hyenas or other predators. Some researchers claim there is evidence that *H. erectus* used fire at Zhoukoudian (Boaz et al. 2004); others are not convinced (Goldberg et al. 2001). Those who support the controlled use of fire say that there is evidence of charred bones and that the burning occurred within the cave. Others say that the bones and stones were burned elsewhere (through natural fire) and then brought into the cave. Still others say that the bones and lithics were not burned at all but are discolored from chemicals in the sediment. There are no signs of any kind of hearth or banked stones—the sort of direct evidence that would most strongly support the argument that *H. erectus* at Zhoukoudian used fire (Gamble 1996:133). The indirect evidence is mainly that of cave occupation itself, which is often assumed to depend on the use of fire to drive other animals out and to provide light.

Anthropologists sometimes refer generally to "Asian" patterns of *H. erectus*, but doing so neglects the fact that significant differences existed between *H. erectus* in China and in Java, regions separated by thousands of miles. A recent comparison of the Chinese and Javan fossils emphasizes differences in cranial morphology between the two fossil collections (Anton 2003). Behavioral differences may also have existed, and further research may shed light on them.

Debate is vigorous about whether regional populations of archaic *Homo* evolved in Asia and elsewhere in the Old World into modern humans (discussed in Chapter 8). At Ngandong, Java, the date of occupation of *H. erectus* may be as recent as 30,000 years ago (Swisher et al. 1996). If this date is correct, this population would be the most recent surviving group of archaic *Homo,* persisting in Asia up to the time when modern humans are likely to have been in Asia. But most researchers doubt that later *H. erectus* in Asia made a significant contribution to the modern human gene pool.

In the Asian fossil evidence, there is a mismatch between brain size and tool-making style. *H. erectus* in Asia had relatively large brains, but they had an Oldowan stone toolkit. One explanation for this discrepancy suggests that *H. erectus* may have had a more sophisticated bamboo toolkit (Pope 1989). This idea is based on the geographic distribution of bamboo in the Old World. Sixty percent of the world's species of bamboo are found in East and Southeast Asia, whereas only 16 percent are found in Africa. Thus the Asian environment offers a rich source of raw material for non-stone tools. Many tools can be produced from bamboo, including knives, spears, projectile points, traps, rope, clothing, and containers for cooking and storage. This idea offers a plausible explanation for the apparent mismatch between the simplicity of the stone tools found along with *H. erectus* and their obvious ability to thrive in a temperate climate and in a wide variety of habitats, including temperate grasslands and tropical forests. It cannot be proved, however, because it is an explanation that relies on reasoning but no direct evidence. Furthermore, new research reveals that some sites in bamboo-rich regions, such as Bose in China (Yamei et al. 2000), Lampang in Thailand (Schick and Zhuan 1993), and Isampur in India (Petraglia et al. 1999), also had Acheulian-like stone tools.

Homo erectus in Africa and Europe

Compared to the fossil and archaeological records for *Homo erectus* in Asia, there is far less information for this species elsewhere in the Old World. In Africa, crania similar to those found in Asia have been found at Buia in Eritrea (Abbate et al. 1998) and Bouri in Ethiopia (Asfaw et al. 2002). Olduvai Gorge and Swartkrans are also important *H. erectus* sites in Africa. From the Algerian site of Tighenif, two jaws may represent *H. erectus*.

In Europe, the only good evidence for a *H. erectus*-like hominin is the 600,000-year-old cranium from Ceprano, Italy (Manzi et al. 2001). But this cranium was discovered in the course of excavations for a road, and no contextual evidence was found with it. It is not clear why *H. erectus* remains are not more common in Europe. Perhaps they were there, but the evidence is still undiscovered, or perhaps they were infrequent visitors. More likely, the cold and harsh climate that gripped Europe intermittently during the last million years prompted *H. erectus* to avoid the region. Overall, *H. erectus* was a highly successful species in terms of duration, almost 2 million years, and geographic distribution throughout much of the Old World.

Late-Surviving Archaic *Homo* Species

A new species of *Homo*, *H. floresiensis*, appears to be a dwarfed form of either *H. ergaster* or *H. erectus* (Brown et al. 2004). The fossil evidence for this species consists of a well-preserved skeleton from one individual, dating to 18,000 years ago, and a single tooth from another individual, dating to 40,000 years ago. The hominin was just over three feet tall, stood upright, and was probably bipedal. Its brain size was 380 cm. Its cranium and jaws look like a dwarf version of *H. ergaster*. Found with the fossils are varieties of stone tools that archaeologists associate with the emergence of *Homo sapiens*, fully modern human beings (Chapter 8).

It is not known how long *H. floresiensis* lived on Flores and to what degree it evolved in isolation from other hominins. Following the general theory that isolated island populations tend toward dwarfism, it is likely that *H. floresiensis* was larger when it first came to Flores. Over time, in response to the absence of large carnivore predators in the region, *H. floresiensis* became smaller. While its overall morphology and brain size did not evolve toward modernity, however, it possessed a capacity to make stone tools that are far in advance of its biology (Morwood et al. 2004).

Homo heidelbergensis

By 600,000 years ago, a new species of hominin appears in Africa, Asia, and Europe. This species is named **Homo heidelbergensis** after a jaw discovered at Mauer, near Heidelberg, Germany. *H. heidelbergensis* is a species of archaic *Homo* that lacks the thick, straight brow ridges found in *H. erectus* crania and has smaller teeth. The brains of *Homo heidelbergensis* were larger than those of the average *H. erectus*, around 1200 cc compared to 1000 cc. The oldest fossil evidence for *H. heidelbergensis* comes from Bodo, Ethiopia. Similar-looking fossils have been found at Kabwe in Zambia, Petralona in Greece, Hathnora in India, and Dali in China (Rightmire 2004). The stone tools found in Africa along with *H. heidelbergensis* fossils are mainly Acheulian. Three spruce spears, one more than 8 feet long, were found in a coal mine at Schöningen, Germany (Thieme 1997). Around 400,000 years old, they are the earliest complete hunting weapons. They were apparently used to hunt wild horses.

Paleoanthropologists disagree about where the boundary should be drawn between *H. heidelbergensis* and *H. neanderthalensis*. Some researchers think that hominin fossils recovered from the Gran Dolina Cave at Atapuerca in northern

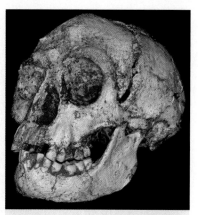

This skull of a Homo floresiensis *skeleton dated at 18,000 years ago was discovered in 2004 in a cave called Liang Bua on the island of Flores, Indonesia.* ■ Consider the possible reasons why this new hominin species is so small. (Source: © Peter Brown)

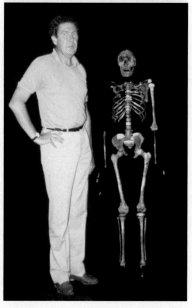

The skeleton of a 1.6-million-year-old H. ergaster *adolescent male from Nariokotome, West Turkana, Kenya. With it is Alan Walker of Pennsylvania State University who reconstructed the skeleton. So-called Nariokotome boy is an example of the first hominin to have a body shape and limb proportions like modern humans.* ■ Look ahead to the photo of a living adolescent Maasai male, on p. 300, and consider the long-term adaptiveness of a tall, thin body in a hot climate. (Source: Virginia Morell)

Researchers who work in the Sima de los Huesos cave at Atapuerca together with the remains of more than 30 individuals they have recovered from the cave. (Source: Javer Trueba/ Madrid Scientific Films S.L.)

Spain, dated at 750,000 years ago, belong to *H. heidelbergensis*. Others, who think these fossils are ancestral to *H. heidelbergensis*, assign an ancestral species name, *Homo antecessor* (Bermúdez de Castro et al. 1997). As with *H. heidelbergensis*, the fossil record for *H. antecessor* is so sparse that we cannot say much more about it.

Homo neanderthalensis

Homo neanderthalensis, known informally as **Neanderthals**, is morphologically the most distinctive archaic *Homo* species. Neanderthals were probably the first hominins to bury their dead regularly, so the quality and quantity of their fossil record are better than for other archaic *Homo* species. Neanderthals are known from more than a hundred sites spread across most of Europe, from Portugal to Western Asia.

Early Neanderthals

Lumpers and splitters disagree about the Neanderthal designation. Lumpers think *H. neanderthalensis* should include older fossils with any sign of a Neanderthal morphological specialization. The lumper definition includes evidence from sites such as Swanscombe in England and Steinheim in Germany, dated around 400,000–300,000 years ago. Some lumpers also think the fossils from the Sima de la Huesos, at Atapuerca (discussed next), should be assigned to *H. neanderthalensis*, not to *H. heidelbergensis*. According to this interpretation, the time range for Neanderthals would go back to at least 400,000 years ago. Splitters prefer not to include in the species *H. neanderthalensis* fossils from before 100,000 years ago that have only some Neanderthal morphology.

The oldest well-dated hominin fossils with some Neanderthal characteristics come from the site called the Sima de los Huesos at Atapuerca, Spain (see the map on p. 210). Here, a Spanish team led first by Emiliano Aguirre and later by Juan Luis Arsuaga has unearthed a treasure trove of hominin fossils (Arsuaga et al. 1993, Bermúdez de Castro et al. 2004). It is the largest collection of hominin fossils in the world to have come from a single site and a single time. So far, the team has found more than 4000 separate hominin fossils that represent more than 30 individuals. The fossil hominins include skulls, crania, teeth, and many limb bones, and most are in excellent condition. Given the importance of the Atapuerca cave complex, archaeologists and other scientists advocated its designation as a UNESCO World Heritage site, which would entail provision of resources for its scientific preservation and public use (see the Lessons Applied box on p. 210).

The oldest Neanderthal sites are in Western Europe, where Neanderthal remains are found mainly in rock shelters and caves. In addition to Sima de los Huesos, two other important early Neanderthal sites are Swanscombe, England, and Steinheim, Germany. The fossils at these sites exhibit some, but not all, of the morphological features of the "classic Neanderthals" of around 100,000 years ago (the later Neanderthals are discussed in Chapter 8).

Morphology

The distinctive morphology of Neanderthals includes a large nasal opening, a face that projects forward in the midline, a cranium that is rounded at the sides and top, teeth with distinctively shaped crowns, and limb bones with thick shafts and large joint surfaces. Neanderthals are the only hominin species whose brain is large as, or larger than, the brain of modern humans.

Another distinction of the Neanderthals is that they were the only hominin species able to tolerate, over thousands of years, the cold temperatures that intermittently affected Europe during their existence. It is possible that much of the distinctive morphology of the Neanderthals, including their prominent nose, swept-back face, and short, stocky limbs, are the result of biological adaptations to a very cold climate.

Mousterian Stone Tools

Most Neanderthal fossils are found in association with a stone toolkit referred to as Mousterian. This tradition is named after the site of Le Moustier, France, where such tools were first described. **Mousterian** toolkits, compared to the Acheulian, are characterized by the predominance of smaller, lighter, and more specialized flake tools such as points, scrapers, and awls. Mousterian tools are made from flakes produced from a specially prepared core (Boëda 1995). The tool-maker removes flakes from a suitable stone until it has a flat top and a round base, like half a grapefruit. Once this core has been prepared, the tool-maker strikes the edge of the flat top of the core against a stone anvil to detach precisely shaped flake tools. This process is called the **Levallois** technique. Not all Neanderthal populations used the Levallois technique, however. For example, at La Quina, Spain, horizontal slices were removed from a long stone core much as one would take a large slice off one end of a sausage. According to experimental studies, this technique was even more efficient than the Levallois technique because it produces more usable flakes from a core.

Mousterian stone-tool-making techniques are evidence that Neanderthals understood the mechanics of stone flaking and had a clear idea of a great many tool types and how to make them. They probably made and used tools other than stone tools, although we have little direct evidence of such tools. Wear on the front teeth of some Neanderthal fossils indicates that they used their teeth to grip hides, rope or other tough materials.

Expressive Culture

In addition to having a sophisticated stone toolkit, Neanderthals created other material items that demonstrate their relatively advanced way of thinking and behaving, compared to archaic hominins and to earlier species of archaic *Homo* (see Figures 7.5 and 7.6 on pp. 211–212). Recalling a definition from cultural anthropology of **expressive culture** as consisting of behavior and beliefs related to art and leisure, we can see elements of expressive culture among Neanderthals.

Distribution of Neanderthal sites.

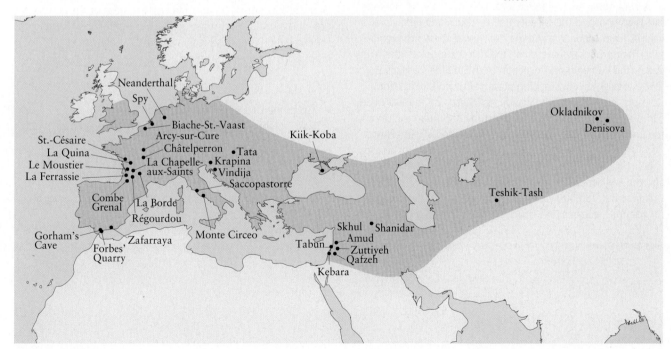

Anthropologists Advocate for World Heritage Status for Atapuerca, Spain

THE PROCEDURE for giving an archaeological site World Heritage status was adopted in November 1972 at the 17th General Conference of UNESCO. It was established that a World Heritage Committee "will establish, keep up-to-date and publish" a World Heritage list of cultural and natural properties considered to be of outstanding universal value. As of 2004, UNESCO had compiled a list of 754 World Heritage sites (582 cultural sites, 149 natural sites, and 23 mixed properties) in 129 countries.

A group of scientists played a key role in advocating for a Paleolithic site to become the cultural property of all humans. These scientists did so by highlighting the biological and cultural implications of Paleolithic material recovered from a complex of sites in Northern Spain.

Atapuerca is a complex of caves within limestone hills located between the Ebro and Duero basins in the interior of Spain. More than 2 million years of erosion created a vast system of caves used for shelter by both animals and archaic *Homo*. The caves at Atapuerca are classified in two groups:

- Trinchera del Ferrocarril, including sites such as Gran Dolina
- Cueva Mayor, including sites such as Sima de los Huesos

The team of Spanish paleoanthropologists and archaeologists who nominated Atapuerca for UNESCO's World Heritage status emphasized the exceptional biological and behavioral records from Atapuerca and their relevance for world prehistory. Their proposal centered on the following points: the large size of the human bone collection from Sima de los Huesos (2500 fossils), the outstanding preservation conditions (for example, cranium 5 from Sima de los Huesos is the most nearly complete cranium preserved in the study of human evolution), the unique biological information to be gained about extinct populations (for example, the groups from Sima de los Huesos had shorter life cycles and were heavier than modern humans), and the earliest existing evidence of cannibalism (from Gran Dolina about 750,000 years ago). The extraordinary potential for scientific research was coupled with the need for public dis-

semination of knowledge about Atapuerca through outreach and public discussions.

In 2000, through the combined efforts of Paleolithic archaeologists, paleoanthropologists, local authorities, and the Atapuerca Foundation, and with the support of UNESCO, Atapuerca was granted World Heritage status. Two criteria had special relevance in the final declaration and inscription of the Atapuerca complex in the UNESCO's World Heritage Site list:

- It offers the earliest and most extensive evidence of early humankind in Europe.
- It is an exceptional reserve of information about past lifeways and environments.

With this recognition has come greater worldwide appreciation of this Paleolithic site complex as an archaeological and natural resource for the use and enjoyment of all humanity. Gran Dolina, one of the most important areas of the complex, now has a protective infrastructure and scaffolding that allows for excavation and observation of the 17 meters of stratigraphic record preserved there.

FOOD FOR THOUGHT

- Go to the UNESCO World Heritage web site, *www://whc.unesco.org*. Review recent proposals for World Heritage status, and determine which sites have been granted this status in the past few years, paying special attention to those of anthropological relevance.

Source: The Atapuerca Foundation kindly provided background information for this box.

Mousterian stone tools from France. ■ Compare the crafting of these stone tools with the Oldowan and Acheulian stone tools shown on p. 201. (Source: American Museum of Natural History)

Neanderthals were able to survive in cold climates, were proficient stone tool-makers, and had culture. Nevertheless, they are often stereotyped as the quintessential "cave dwellers," living a brutish existence and not being very smart. A common insult hurled in English slang to imply bad manners or stupidity is calling a person a "Neanderthal"—not an "australopith." Neanderthals have also been the subject of many erroneous interpretations involving pathology. In one instance, fossils from an individual who was ill were taken to represent the species as a whole. The skeleton of an aged, arthritic male from La Chapelle aux Saints in France, discovered in 1908, led to the assumption that all Neanderthals, young and old, were stooped and round-shouldered. In other cases, pathology (evidence of illness) has been used to explain normal Neanderthal morphology. In one example of this kind of erroneous interpretation, Neanderthal morphology was said to be due to cretinism, a condition caused by a poorly functioning thyroid gland. This view was based of the general correspondence between the spatial distribution of Neanderthal sites and the contemporary *goiter belt,* a region extending across Europe to Central Asia and the Middle East, where there are high rates of people who have an enlarged, poorly functioning thyroid gland. This kind of thinking is an example of ignoring the difference between *correlation* (which occurs when two factors vary in the same way without either one influencing the other) and *cause and effect* (which occurs when one factor directly influences the other). Cretinism leaves distinctive marks on the skeleton that are not found on any Neanderthal fossils, so it cannot explain their body morphology.

In spite of their negative public image, Neanderthals have played an important role in attempts to understand human evolution. In the mid-nineteenth century, the recognition that Neanderthals were anatomically distinct from modern humans

FIGURE 7.5

Aspects of Neanderthal expressive culture and symbolic thought.

Artifact	Interpretation
Finely crafted stone tools	Suggests sense of style (crafting goes beyond necessity)
Incised bones	Possible form of symbolic, prehistoric art
Perforated teeth and bones	Possible personal ornaments
Strings of shells	Possible personal ornaments
Decorated burials	Suggests sense of afterlife

FIGURE 7.6

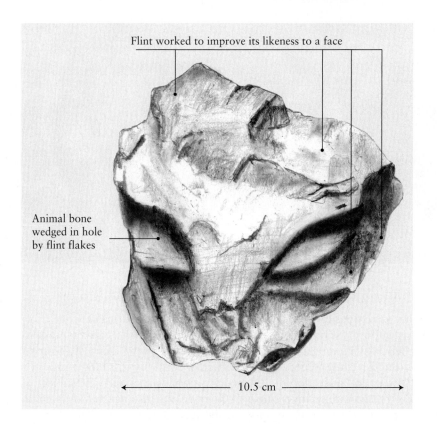

Flint worked to improve its likeness to a face

Animal bone wedged in hole by flint flakes

10.5 cm

contributed to the growing awareness of evolution as an explanation for humanity. For a long time after that, conventional wisdom had it that Neanderthals evolved into modern humans. New findings from DNA research indicate that such a scenario is not likely (discussed in Chapter 8).

BEHAVIORAL AND CULTURAL EVOLUTION

Compared to the archaic hominins discussed in Chapter 6, for archaic *Homo* there are far more sites and many more fossils and artifacts. As in any scientific endeavor, the more evidence one has, the more difficult it is to make simple generalizations. Nevertheless, this section attempts to provide an overview of what can be said with some confidence about the lifeways of archaic *Homo*.

Body Shape and Locomotion

It is impossible to know precisely how tall any individual extinct hominin was or how much it weighed. Among living animals, some parts of the skeleton, such as the length of the femur, are correlated with height, and others, such as the size of the eye socket and the size of the head of the femur, are correlated with weight. If you have enough such fossils for a species, you can use the information about living animals to generate a rough estimate of the height and weight of the fossil and the probable range of height and weight in that species. A well-preserved fossil skeleton provides a much more reliable estimate of height and weight. There are not many complete, or nearly complete, skeletons in the early human fossil record, which is why a find such as the one at Nariokotome, West Turkana, dated to 1.6 million years ago, was so important.

Estimates of height and weight for archaic *Homo* species, from *H. ergaster* onward, indicate that they are all larger than the archaic hominins and larger than the transitional species, *H. habilis* and *H. rudolfensis*. They weighed 150 pounds or more (compared to 100 pounds), and they were 5 feet or more in height (compared to between 4 and 4.5 feet). The larger and taller bodies of *H. ergaster* are better adapted to tolerate heat and better able to conserve water (Wheeler 1992, 1993). This change would have been advantageous if, as researchers think, *H. ergaster* was the first hominin to spend more time in savannah environments. Taller and heavier individuals are also better able to protect themselves from predators.

One of the main reasons why *H. ergaster* and subsequent archaic *Homo* species are taller than archaic hominins is that they have longer legs. Longer legs make a hominin less well adapted for living in the trees, but they make it better adapted for bipedal locomotion. The long legs and more stable foot of *H. ergaster,* and of all the later archaic *Homo* species, suggest that it and they were as bipedal as modern humans (Harcourt-Smith and Aiello 2004). When you walk bipedally, the longer your legs are, the longer the stride you can take; think of small children running to keep up with their larger siblings. A long stride means that you can cover the same distance with fewer steps—and thus with less energy expenditure (Alexander 2004).

Longer legs gave archaic *Homo* two advantages. First, they could travel longer distances, and because they did not need their arms and hands for locomotion, they could carry the resources they needed, whether bundles of roots and tubers, or stones for making stone tools (Wang and Crompton 2004). Second, people with longer legs can run faster than those with shorter legs, and this, along with a larger body, helped archaic *Homo* evade predators.

Evidence from Mata Menge, on the island of Flores in Southeast Asia suggests that around 800,000 years ago, *H. erectus* had devised a way to travel by water, presumably using some sort of raft or boat (Morwood et al. 1998). Flores is one of the eastern islands of present-day Indonesia and has never been connected by a land bridge to neighboring islands. Migration required the crossing of substantial distances, at least fifteen miles, on open sea. The ability to do so marks a major locomotive advance, enabling archaic *Homo* to migrate to and settle in a far wider range of places than are available by foot.

A bonobo brandishing large branches as part of a threat display. Partial bipedalism of bonobos allows them to use their arms more like humans do, for example, to throw objects. The ability to throw objects at a target with a high degree of accuracy is a uniquely human ability. ■ Consider how this ability contributed to human adaptation during evolution. (Source: © Gallo Images/CORBIS)

Diet

The smaller chewing teeth and the smaller and more slender jaws of *H. ergaster,* compared to archaic hominins, suggest that *H. ergaster* was either eating different kinds of food or was eating the same food but was processing it outside the mouth, possibly by cooking. The small teeth and jaws of *H. ergaster* suggest that it probably had a *higher-quality diet* (a diet that provides more energy for each mouthful of food) than archaic hominins. The shape of the chest of the *H. ergaster* skeleton from Nariokotome is another indication that the diets of *H. ergaster,* and by implication of later archaic *Homo* species, differed from those of archaic hominins. Its chest is not cone-shaped like the chests of living apes and *Au. afarensis* but, rather, has straight sides like a modern human chest. This shape suggests that *H. ergaster* had a small, modern-human-sized gut rather than the larger gut needed to digest a mostly vegetarian diet.

One way to improve dietary quality would have been to eat more meat or fish, because these food sources provide large amounts of energy-rich protein and fat.

Food sources such as eggs, worms, and insects can also provide protein and fat, but in smaller quantities per mouthful. Evidence that *H. ergaster* or *H. erectus* was probably eating meat has come from an unlikely source: tapeworms (Hoberg et al. 2001). The first evidence of tapeworm infection in hominins coincides with the emergence of archaic *Homo* in Africa, a finding that points to the likelihood that archaic *Homo* ate substantial amounts of meat.

The sites where stone tools were found were first interpreted as hunting camps—bases from which men would go out to seek and hunt game. Beginning in the 1970s, a different interpretation emerged, inspired by the field research of archaeologist Glynn Isaac and his students at Koobi Fora (Isaac 1978). Their findings suggested that archaeological sites were places where plant foods such as tubers and nuts were shared among a group of hominins, along with occasional inputs of meat. This interpretation was based on analogies with living people, especially observations made by cultural anthropologists about some groups of living foragers.

Another enduring research question is whether hominins obtained meat by their own efforts or by scavenging from carnivore kills (Potts 1984, Dominguez-Rodrigo 2002). Researchers have shown that bones broken and chewed by the powerful jaws of carnivores have different patterns of breaks and scratches than bones that have been defleshed and then broken open via stone tools. By noting whether the carnivore or hominin marks came first, it is possible to tell whether hominins or carnivores had initial access to the carcasses. Studies of animal bones found at archaeological sites at Koobi Fora and Olduvai Gorge suggest that archaic *Homo* probably did not hunt large mammals but, instead, gained access to them by chasing carnivores from the kills. Then they either cut meat from the carcass at the site of the kill or removed a limb and took it back to where they had stored the stone tools needed to break open the bones (Bunn 1981, Blumenschine 1987) and gain access to the nutritious marrow. Animal fat in bone marrow is an excellent source of energy and also provides, in an accessible form, the essential nutrients that hominins needed to grow and support their relatively large brains (Cordain et al. 2001).

Archeologists can infer what sorts of meat were eaten by examining the animal bones at living sites. They can also use chemical methods to analyze the hominin bones themselves for further insights into hominin diet. For example, analysis of the bone chemistry of some *H. neanderthalensis* fossils from Vindija Cave, Croatia, showed that most of their protein came from meat. Their bones had a chemical profile similar to those of a wolf and an Arctic fox found in the same cave (Richards et al. 2000). DNA analysis of microscopic food particles left on the edges of stone tools also provides information about the diet of archaic *Homo* (see the Methods Close-Up box).

The first known case of pathology (sickness) in the human evolutionary fossil record is perhaps related to an increase in the consumption of animal meat by *H. ergaster*. The partial skeleton of KNM-ER 1808, found at Koobi Fora in Kenya, exhibits abnormalities that are clearly related to health problems (Walker and Leakey 1982). The fossils are the remains of a presumed female who lived about 1.4 million years ago. The skeleton shows signs of abnormal bone growth consistent with a diagnosis of hypervitaminosis A, or too much vitamin A. Researchers are uncertain what could have led to this condition. One possibility is that KNM-ER 1808 consumed large quantities of organ meat—especially fresh carnivore liver, which contains very high levels of vitamin A. Similar bone changes have been seen in some circumpolar people who have consumed too much polar bear liver. The thinking goes like this: As early hominins' diets shifted more toward meat around 2 million years ago, it may have taken them some time to learn which parts of animals should be avoided—and thus to develop a sense of preventive health through dietary control. Of course, it is not possible to say for sure what kind of food avoidances were practiced at that time, and KNM-ER 1808 is our only example of such pathology for many thousands of years. Perhaps the most significant point is that, among the many, many specimens in the fossil record of human evolution, nutritional and disease problems are rare until recent times.

Recovering Mammalian DNA from Neanderthal Stone Tools

STONE TOOLS are the most abundant cultural remains for most of human prehistory, so they are the basis for most of our thinking about human cultural evolution. Archaeologists use a range of techniques, including use-wear analysis, ethnographic analogy, and experimental replication, to make inferences about how stone tools were used. Then they use evidence gleaned from all these methods to generate plausible hypotheses about how stone tools were used. Even so, none of these methods provides direct evidence of what the tools were used for (Hardy and Raff 1997). The relatively recent use of DNA analysis to identify the source of the tissues left on stone tools can help fill this gap in our knowledge about actual tool use.

One DNA-based study examined stone tools and soil from the Middle Paleolithic site of La Quina, a rock shelter in southwest France. Its archaeological deposits date from 65,000 to 35,000 years ago and include Neanderthal remains and Mousterian stone tools. Recent excavations at La Quina have been conducted under controlled conditions to reduce to a minimum the chance of contamination with DNA from modern sources. For example, as soon as a stone tool to be used in DNA analysis was uncovered and its position was recorded, it was placed in a new, clean, self-sealing plastic bag. Soil samples were handled in the same way.

DNA extraction was performed at the field laboratory in La Quina, and then the samples were transferred to the United States for amplification (the amounts of DNA on the tools are very small) and sequencing.

To date, eight stone tools and their corresponding soil samples have been studied, and five of them have yielded mtDNA

from the part of the mitochondrial genome that codes for the enzyme cytochrome b. If a DNA sequence was recovered from the tool but not from the soil, the DNA was assumed to be related to its use. Checks for contamination with modern DNA were negative. Three different sequences were detected on the tools, one tool had a sequence from a wild boar, all five of the tools with detectable mtDNA had a sequence that could have come from either a deer or an antelope, and one tool had mtDNA that was indistinguishable from modern human mtDNA.

The researchers offered the following advice to other researchers who seek to use DNA in this manner:

- Choose a site in a primary, undisturbed context.
- Excavate with new, disposable surgical gloves.
- Seal all the specimens immediately in new, self-sealing plastic bags.
- Use brushes with synthetic bristles.
- Sample the surrounding soil and any nonartifactual material.
- Work in a laboratory where samples of modern animals have not been studied.
- Use equipment that is dedicated to work with ancient DNA.

FOOD FOR THOUGHT

- Given the fact that most earlier excavations and handling of artifacts have been done without safeguards against contamination with modern DNA, do you think that efforts to learn about the ancient DNA of those specimens will always be useless? Or is there a chance that a method can be developed to sort ancient from modern DNA?

Stone Tools and Cultural Evolution

Archeologists have recovered thousands of stone tools from hundreds of sites throughout the world. Like other scientists, they need to find some way of organizing this material in order to make sense of how the tools were used and whether they had a broader meaning for human evolution. They use morphology (size, shape, and appearance) to classify particular stone tools in terms of their assumed function. Another way of organizing stone tools is on the basis of distinctive *toolkits* or tool *assemblages*.

Defining stylistic distinctions among toolkits is a matter of debate among archaeologists. Some researchers classify stone tools on the basis of their shape, whereas others emphasize the way they were produced. Those who emphasize the form of the tools are the archaeological equivalent of "lumpers." For example, they interpret the period between 2.6 and 1.6 million years ago, the span of Oldowan technology, as evidence for behavioral stasis. Others argue that the Oldowan category includes too much variety, from unskilled tool-making to much more sophisticated tool-making

(Roche et al. 1999). Recent excavations at the Peninj site in Tanzania recovered so-called Oldowan stone tools that, if they had been found in Europe, would have been interpreted as Mousterian prepared cores (de la Torre et al. 2003).

Anthropologists wonder why the stone tools of archaic *Homo* changed so little over this million-year period, and by implication, they assume that behavior and culture may have changed little. This kind of thinking is probably erroneous, however, for two reasons. First, the evidence is incomplete. Even though a stone toolkit does not change much, the hominins may have used the tools for different purposes and in different ways. Second, it is most unlikely that stone tools were the hominins' only tools (Backwell and d'Errico 2003), and they may have applied more creativity to other tools, which have not been preserved. Third, tools are only a limited part of human life. Other aspects of life, preserved in neither the fossil nor the archaeological record, may have changed.

Settlement Patterns

Unlike the archaic hominins discussed in Chapter 6, some of the archaic *Homo* species discussed in this chapter lived in caves. This change could have been accomplished only by having a way to see once deep inside the caves and by having a way to scare off the dangerous animals (such as large cats) that had previously occupied them. The only possible explanation is the controlled use of fire, a behavior that cave dwelling strongly implies.

Whereas many different-looking archaic hominin species all lived in a woodland environment, archaic *Homo* species, which are relatively homogeneous morphologically, inhabit a wide range of habitats, ranging from the open country to which *H. erectus* adapted to the cold weather tolerated by *H. neanderthalensis*. An increasingly complex culture was the key to exploring and surviving in new environments.

Sociality and Gender Relations

There is no direct evidence about the social organization of archaic *Homo* species. Anthropologists make inferences on the basis of archaeological evidence and analogies to living chimpanzees and ethnography. Analogies, as we have noted before, must be treated with caution. Most anthropologists would find it plausible that social groups among archaic *Homo* species were roughly like those of twentieth century foraging groups. In terms of group size, they may have ranged between 10 and 20 people, with flexible membership depending on the season. Such groups would probably have been egalitarian in terms of access to valued resources and would have exhibited little formality in terms of leadership.

Statements about gender roles and relations must be made with similar caution. Compared to archaic hominins, *H. ergaster* and all subsequent archaic *Homo* species exhibit less sexual dimorphism in body size. According to the reasoning outlined earlier in this book about sexual dimorphism in body size and male–female social relationships, it is possible that competition among males for sexual access to females was less intense among *H. ergaster* than among archaic hominins. The reduction in sexual dimorphism in size is a step, anatomically, in the direction of modern humans. What this might indicate about relationships among males and females is, however, impossible to infer on the basis of the anatomical evidence.

Cognition and Intelligence

Stone tool-making has implications for the cognitive abilities of the tool-makers. Some researchers see continuity between the stone tools made by chimpanzees and the Oldowan culture (Wynn and McGrew 1989). Others say that human stone tool-making marks a major dividing line between humans and nonhumans. In this latter view, the task of making a scraper (striking a large flake from a cobble and then shaping the flake by taking smaller flakes from it) is a much more sophisticated activity than the tool-making efforts of nonhuman primates (de Beaune 2004).

The logic in the latter view proceeds from the fact that stone tools can be made only from rocks that fracture in predictable ways when they are struck with another rock. Forethought is involved in knowing which rocks to use and where to aim the blows. Further planning is implied in that archaeological sites are often close to streambeds where rocks of the right sort are found. Hence, early humans were selective about their campsites on the basis of their tool-making needs. Even more forethought is evident at some sites, such as Olduvai Gorge, where the hominins would have had to make round trips of several miles to get the stones they used for tool-making. Selectivity in stone use and intentional travel to gather particular kinds of stones are considered by some researchers to be an important dividing line between nonhuman primate tool-making and hominin and human tool-making. This claim is countered by primatologists, who point out that Tai Forest chimpanzees also travel to get preferred stones to use for nut-cracking.

Further, in order for individuals to pass tool-making techniques on to other individuals, the sequence would need to be explained, which would require verbal language. Thus, for some archaeologists, the ability to manufacture complex tools is sufficient evidence to support the inference that a particular hominin could talk (Wynn 1993). Experimental studies with some nonhuman primates shed light on some of the capabilities of great apes related to stone tool production. This research supports the middle-ground position that there are both continuity and important differences between nonhuman and human tool-making.

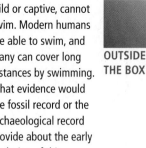

THINKING OUTSIDE THE BOX

Nonhuman primates, wild or captive, cannot swim. Modern humans are able to swim, and many can cover long distances by swimming. What evidence would the fossil record or the archaeological record provide about the early evolution of this activity?

CROSSING THE FIELDS

From Kanzi to Olduvai, But Not Quite

Kanzi is a 160-pound bonobo that lives at the Language Research Center in Atlanta, Georgia. The Language Research Center is jointly sponsored by Georgia State University and the Yerkes Regional Primate Research Laboratory of Emory University. A research team including Atlanta-based primatologists/psychologists Sue Savage-Rumbaugh, Duane Rumbaugh, and Rose Sevcik, and two archaeologists from Indiana University, Kathy Schick and Nick Toth, decided that if they could teach Kanzi to make crude stone tools, they might gain some insight into the evolution of early hominin stone tool manufacture and related behavior (Schick and Toth 1993:135–140). Kanzi had long been involved in primate communication research (see Kanzi's photograph on p. 146), but he had never seen stone tools used or seen them being made.

First, the researchers showed Kanzi how stone tools can be useful. They used a stone flake to cut a cord and open a box containing a favored treat of Kanzi's, such as a bunch of grapes, a slice of watermelon, or a cold fruit juice drink. By the end of the day, Kanzi was readily using flakes that the researchers had made to gain access to his treats. By the end of the second day, he had become an excellent judge of the quality of the tools offered to him. Nine times out of ten, he chose the sharpest of the tools. He was also making casual attempts to hit rocks together to make a tool on his own.

Kanzi's involvement in ongoing research projects about communication meant that he could participate in the tool study only occasionally, and sometimes with weeks intervened between experiences. Nevertheless, within a month he was striking flakes from cores with hard-hammer percussion. The researchers had shown Kanzi the basic technique of simple stone tool manufacture. Over time, he developed his own flaking style and gained precision. Several months into the study, he invented a way to make flakes by throwing a stone on a hard floor. Within a few throws, he was able to produce a flake that could cut the cord of the treat box. From this process, he appeared to learn that there is a connection between force and successful flaking, and his throwing became more forceful and more efficient.

Nine months into the study, he could remove flakes from cores, but these were not as well made as flakes from the Oldowan toolkit. Kanzi's methods were less controlled, and he did not appear to understand flaking angles. Thus, even the Olduvai tool-makers had more competence than bonobos. ■

FOOD FOR THOUGHT

■ Go to the Web and find an update on Kanzi and related studies of tool-making by primates in captivity.

Cognition and Intelligence

As we saw in Chapter 6, scientists have been searching for ways to infer the capability for complex verbal language from either the fossil or the archaeological record. But the fossil record has not lived up to its early promise as a source of evidence about language. Two things are required for spoken language: a brain that knows what to say and a vocal tract—a mouth, tongue, pharynx, and larynx (the voice box)—capable of making a variety of precise sounds. Neanderthals, initially credited with an ability to talk somewhat comparable to that of modern humans, are now thought to have been incapable of complex verbal speech. The base of the cranium is flatter in *H. neanderthalensis* than in modern humans, and computer models devised to reconstruct the Neanderthals' vocal tract suggest that the sounds they could utter were not as varied as those that modern humans produce.

Some archaeologists use stone tool-making as a proxy for verbal language abilities. The problem those researchers face is how to test their hypothesis. So far no one has been able to do more than put forward a strong circumstantial case for a link between language and tool-making. Yet intuitively, as tool-making becomes ever more sophisticated, a link between language and tool-making seems more likely. Similar logic is applied with respect to archaeological sites where early hominins hunted for large game. Ethnographic research on southern African hunter–foragers shows that knowledge is shared verbally among hunters before, during, and after the hunt (Lee and DeVore 1968). By analogy, researchers argue, archaic *Homo* hunters must have had an effective means of communicating verbally in order to organize such hunting.

Other researchers use genetic methods to study the evolution of language. They reason that if they could demonstrate a link between a particular gene or genes and language, then they could try to discover when that gene became active in early humans. The search for evidence of a genetic basis for the predisposition for modern humans to acquire language has focused on a family that shows a severe speech and language disorder. Affected members of the family have a defect in chromosome 7 that directly affects the gene *FOXP2* (Lai et al. 2001). Apparently, two copies of the gene are needed for the individual to develop language, and what seems to be crucial is a difference in just 2 of the 715 amino acids involved in constructing that particular small protein (Enard et al. 2002). The researchers have also shown that the difference between the *FOXP2* genes of modern humans and chimpanzees may have begun to take effect within modern humans only during the last 200,000 years (Chapter 8).

Most researchers are skeptical about the claim that the facility for human language is due to changes in a single gene, and it will be important to learn more about why language acquisition is problematic for the affected members of this family. This kind of research may, however, shed light on why modern human language is so much more complex than chimpanzee communication.

■ WHAT are the earliest forms of *Homo*?

The earliest forms of *Homo* are called archaic *Homo* and they include five extinct species. These species existed over a period from about 2 million years ago to less than 30,000 years ago. Criteria for including fossils in the genus *Homo* include jaws and teeth more like those of modern humans than like those of archaic hominins, and limb morphology and proportions consistent with upright posture and bipedalism. Some paleoanthropologists believe that fossils of *Homo habilis*, found in Olduvai Gorge, are the earliest example of *Homo*, whereas others maintain that these fossils are more advanced australopiths. Like another species, *Homo rudolfensis*, *H. habilis* is perhaps best understood as transitional between the australopiths and *Homo*. The Oldowan stone-tool-making tradition is characteristic of early archaic *Homo*. This toolkit consists of core tools and flake tools.

On the basis of its jaws, teeth, and limb morphology, *H. ergaster* is an undisputed member of the genus *Homo*. *H. ergaster* is associated with a more advanced stone-tool-making tradition called the Acheulian, in which the most distinctive tool type is the handaxe. Acheulian tools are bifacially worked, indicating a new level of dexterity and mental forethought.

■ WHEN did archaic *Homo* leave Africa and where did they go?

Starting around 1.8 million years ago, members of archaic *Homo* began to leave Africa. The earliest evidence for *Homo* outside Africa comes from Dmanisi, Georgia. Many fossil and archaeological sites in Asia attest to the early presence of *H. erectus* there. The earliest dates come from Java, implying that *H. erectus* must have been in mainland Asia before then. Sites in China and Southeast Asia shed light on diet, which often included meat, and the new ability to inhabit caves, which strongly suggests the use of controlled fire. *H. erectus* in East and Southeast Asia had a stone toolkit of the Oldowan tradition, even though they were more biologically advanced than *H. ergaster*. *H. heidelbergensis* may be directly related to modern humans, but more evidence is needed before that claim can be established. The last species of archaic *Homo* is *H. neanderthalensis*, or the Neanderthals. There is abundant evidence for this species across mainland Europe from Portugal to Western Asia and existed from 400,000 to 30,000 years ago.

Neanderthals were biologically adapted to cold climates and developed a set of cultural adaptations, including advanced stone tool-making and some ability for symbolic thinking. Their stone-tool-making tradition is called Mousterian, and they developed the Levallois method of detaching many flakes efficiently from the same core. Most evidence suggests that Neanderthals contributed little, if anything, to the gene pool of modern humans.

■ WHAT were key features of archaic *Homo* behavior and culture?

Members of all archaic *Homo* species were larger than the archaic hominins discussed in Chapter 6. Their greater height is related to having longer legs, a morphological adaptation to bipedalism that freed the arms for nonlocomotive tasks. Another locomotive advance was the seafaring ability of *H. erectus* in island Southeast Asia. Diet quality and variation increased in this phase of human evolution, and there was a general shift from reliance on a vegetarian diet to one that included meat. It is unlikely that archaic *Homo* hunted large game animals. They probably gained access to carcasses by chasing carnivores away from the kill.

Oldowan, Acheulian, and Mousterian stone tool traditions enabled archaic *Homo* to access and process new kinds of food, including meat, and to construct shelters and (in some cases) build rafts or boats. Later, many archaic *Homo* populations occupied caves, which suggests the controlled use of fire to drive animal competitors out of the space and to provide light while inside.

Social group formation, on the basis of ethnographic analogy indicates that archaic *Homo* may have lived in small groups whose flexible membership depended on the season. Reduction in sexual dimorphism in body size in archaic *Homo* may indicate less competition among males for access to females. Although it is hard to speculate about the cognitive and communication abilities of archaic *Homo*, these skills were probably more advanced than those of living chimpanzees and bonobos. The bonobo Kanzi can make and use stone tools, but he has no concept of producing flake tools with any precision. The fossil record provides no direct evidence either for or against the capacity for verbal language.

KEY CONCEPTS

SUGGESTED READINGS

Juan Luis Arsuaga. *The Neanderthal's Necklace: In Search of the First Thinkers*. Andy Klatt, trans. New York: Four Walls Eight Windows, 2001. The author, co-director of excavations at Sierra de Atapuerca, discusses how the Neanderthals lived and why they disappeared. He includes a chapter on the flora and fauna of the time.

Eric Delson, Ian Tattersall, John van Couvering, and Alison Brooks. *Encyclopedia of Human Evolution and Prehistory*. 2nd ed. New York: Garland, 2000. This comprehensive encyclopedia includes many entries related to this chapter.

Donna L. Hart and Robert W. Sussman. *Man the Hunted: Primates, Predators, and Human Evolution*. New York: Westview Press, 2005. In contrast to theories dating from the 1960s, the authors take the position that hominins evolved as vulnerable prey rather than as aggressive hunters. They marshal fossil evidence and their own eyewitness accounts of living primates. They conclude that primates have been prey for millions of years, and this fact influenced the morphology and behavior of early human ancestors.

Clark Spencer Larsen, Robert M. Matter, and Daniel L. Gebo. *Human Origins: The Fossil Record*, 3rd ed. Prospect Heights, IL: Waveland Press, Inc., 1998. Many hominin fossils are illustrated by careful line drawings.

Jeffrey K. McKee. *The Riddled Chain: Chance, Coincidence, and Chaos in Human Evolution*. New Brunswick, NJ: Rutgers University Press, 2000. The author provides a rethinking of hominin macroevolution, suggesting that the evidence for linking events in hominin evolution to changes in the paleoclimates is weak. He argues that paleoanthropologists should pay more attention to the role of chance in hominin macroevolution.

Richard Potts. *Humanity's Descent: The Consequences of Ecological Instability*. New York: Avon, 1997. The author reviews humanity's ancestors, focusing on the role that rapidly changing environments have played in human evolution. The book concludes by linking hominin/environmental interactions of the past to current issues of modern human/environmental interaction, such as global warming.

G. Philip Rightmire. *The Evolution of* Homo erectus: *Comparative Anatomical Studies of an Extinct Species*. New York: Cambridge University, 1990. Nine chapters provide descriptions of *Homo erectus* fossils in Africa and other regions of the Old World with details about individual crania, jaws, and postcranial remains. The evidence attests to the fact that this species was widely dispersed and long lasting.

Kathy D. Schick and Nicholas Toth. *Making Silent Stones Speak: Human Evolution and the Dawn of Technology*. New York: Simon and Schuster, 1993. The authors trace the prehistory of stone tools from their earliest appearance in the archaeological record up to modern humans. They also include insights gleaned from their experimental research in making and using stone tools and from their research with Kanzi and his stone-tool-making abilities.

Pat Shipman. *The Man Who Found the Missing Link: Eugene Dubois and His Lifelong Quest to Prove Darwin Right*. New York: Simon and Schuster, 2001. Drawing on the personal archives of Dubois, the author provides a biography of the "father of modern paleoanthropology." Dutch physician-scientist Eugene Dubois, born in 1858, dreamed of finding the "missing link" between apes and humans. His discovery of so-called Java Man, however, met with skepticism from European scientists. He spent the rest of his life working to achieve what he thought was proper recognition for the fossils that he discovered.

Carl C. Swisher III, Garniss H. Curtis, and Roger Lewin. *Java Man: How Two Geologists' Dramatic Discoveries Changed Our Understanding of the Evolutionary Path to Modern Humans*. New York: Scribner, 2000. Garniss Curtis and Carl Swisher, both geologists who specialize in dating volcanic rocks, were determined to date the Javan *Homo erectus* remains. They collaborated with the science writer Roger Lewin to tell the story of how they found and dated layers of volcanic ash linked with the oldest and youngest of the Javan hominins.

Ian Tattersall. *The Fossil Trail: How We Know What We Think We Know about Human Evolution*. New York: Oxford University Press, 1995. This book is a history of the study of human evolution from its beginnings with Lamarck and Cuvier, to the breakthroughs of the mid-nineteenth century, and up to modern theorists such as Niles Eldredge and Stephen Jay Gould. The narrative includes descriptions of important fossil finds such as Lucy. The author provides information about methods, for example, radiocarbon dating and the analysis of human mitochondrial DNA. The discussion is situated within the context of the times, showing how received wisdom shapes scientific research and interpretation.

Ian Tattersall and Jeffrey H. Schwartz. *Extinct Humans.* Boulder, CO: Westview Press, 2000. Eight chapters (including Chapter 4 on *Homo habilis,* Chapters 5 and 6 on *Homo ergaster* and *Homo erectus,* and Chapter 7 on the Neanderthals) cover human evolution from the australopiths to modern humans. Emphasis is on the fossil record, and the discussion is accompanied by many photographs of the fossils that Jeffrey Schwartz took.

J. S. Weiner. *The Piltdown Forgery.* Fiftieth-anniversary edition with new introduction and afterword by Chris Stringer. New York: Oxford University Press, 2003 [1955]. This book is a republication of the scientific investigations surrounding the fossil discovery of so-called Piltdown Man in England in 1912. The research revealed that, instead of representing a species of early human living in England a million years ago, the fossils were partly from an orangutan and had been stained to make them look ancient.

Melanie G. Wiber. *Erect Men and Undulating Women: The Visual Imagery of Gender, "Race" and Progress in Reconstructive Illustrations of Human Evolution.* Waterloo, Ontario: Wilfrid Laurier University Press, 1997. This book offers a critique of human evolution as a field, narratives of human evolution, theories about male and female foraging roles ("Man the Hunter," "Woman the Gatherer") and the ways in which males, females, and "primitives" have been depicted and are depicted in human evolution publications and anthropology textbooks.

Bernard Wood. *"Homo erectus," "Homo neanderthalensis," "Hominid radiations: early."* In *Nature Encyclopedia of Life Sciences,* Nature Publishing Group, London, *www.els.net.* In addition to the entries listed here, this encyclopedia includes useful background articles about human evolution.

THE BIG QUESTIONS

- WHAT are the origins of modern humans?
- WHAT was modern human life like during the Upper Paleolithic?
- WHAT changes occurred during the Holocene era?

CHAPTER **8**

Modern Humans: Origins, Migrations, and Transitions

A human head carved in mammoth ivory, called the Venus of Brassempouy, is 3.6 centimeters high (an inch and a half). Found in France, it is dated to between 30,000–26,000 years ago. Its stratigraphic position was not carefully documented at the time of its discovery. Because of the lack of details about its discovery and its lack of surface corrosion, some archaeologists question its authenticity. (Source: © Réunion des Musées Nationaux/Art Resource, NY)

usic, a universal feature of contemporary human cultures, has deep prehistoric roots. Like many other human behaviors that evolved during prehistory, music must predate the first archaeological evidence of it. Singing or humming can be musical, for example, but like vocal communication, they leave no traces in the archaeological record.

Bone flutes in Europe are the earliest archaeological evidence of musical instruments. The oldest bone flutes are from Isturitz cave, France (d'Errico et al. 2003). Discovered in 1921, the flutes are dated to around 25,000 years ago. Two complete flutes made of bird bone were found, along with more than twenty fragments.

These ancient flutes continue to attract the interest of archaeologists as well as of professional musicologists because of their design. The pipes have three to four finger holes. They also display marks that may have been used as notational codes. The end where the player's mouth would be placed has no sharp edge to blow against, suggesting the use of a vibrating reed. This is a sophisticated feature because the form and tensile strength of the reed would have affected the frequency of the sound made by the player. Bone flutes are just one of the many aspects of the *cultural revolution* in Europe during the Upper Paleolithic.

The species discussed in Chapter 7 belong to the genus *Homo,* but none of them belongs to the category of modern humans, or *Homo sapiens.* This chapter first considers the characteristics—morphological and cultural—of modern humans, the major theories about the origins of modern humans, and the fossil and archaeological evidence about early modern human origins in Africa. The second section follows the dispersal of modern humans into the Old and New Worlds. The last section provides examples of changes in modern human life during the Holocene era, when new ways of providing food and new social arrangements began to emerge.

This chapter's time span extends from 300,000 years ago to just a few thousand years ago. In terms of the human skeleton, it is the last period during which there is any evidence of significant change. After this time, human biological evolution consists mainly of changes in gene frequencies. Culture, in contrast, continues to become more elaborate and complex, as people alter how they interact with nature and with each other. In this relatively short period, modern humans changed from being a rare and insignificant creature to being the only form of human life on the earth. For the first time, the number of human species is reduced to one: *Homo sapiens,* modern humans.

This bone flute from Isturitz, France, is the oldest flute known with secure dating. Older examples of bone with flute-like holes are contested as being human-made because the holes may have been the result of carnivore activity.
■ What do you know about the origins of other contemporary musical instruments? How would you find out about the first harp or piano? (Source: Réunion des Musées Nationaux/Art Resource, NY)

 ## THE ORIGINS OF MODERN HUMANS

This section begins with a discussion of what anthropologists mean by *modern human,* first in terms of morphological and genetic criteria and then in terms of the cultural features that archaeologists consider to be signs of modernity. It then presents a major debate about how to interpret the fossil, archaeological and genetic evidence for the origin of modern humans. Finally, it reviews fossil, genetic, and archaeological evidence about the earliest modern humans.

Modern Human Biology and Culture

Biological anthropologists use the term **anatomically modern humans** (**AMH**) to refer to *Homo sapiens,* the species to which modern humans belong; this chapter uses the short version, **modern humans.** Modern humans differ morphologically from archaic *Homo* species in several ways. For example, compared to the Neanderthals (see Figure 8.1), they have a steeper forehead with smaller brow ridges, a smaller face, smaller incisor teeth, thinner limb bones, smaller limb joints, and a shorter, thicker, pubic

FIGURE 8.1

Main anatomical differences between Neanderthals and modern humans.

	Neanderthals	Modern Humans
Brain size	Very large, average 1450 cc	Large, average 1350 cc
Brow ridges	Thick and arched	Weak
Nose and mid-face	Projecting	Flat
Incisor teeth	Large	Small
Rib cage	Broad	Narrow
Pelvis	Wide	Narrow
Limb bones	Curved	Straight
Joints	Large	Small
Thumb	Long	Short

bone. Changes in the shape of the cranium may reflect enhanced abilities to think creatively and innovatively. The less robust and smaller body of anatomically modern humans may reflect increasing reliance on culture rather than on physical strength. Reduced body size means less demand for food, thus freeing modern humans for activities other than food gathering and resting.

Human *culture*, defined in Chapter 1 and discussed further in Chapter 2, consists of learned and shared behaviors and beliefs. It is thus distinguished from nonhuman primate culture, discussed in Chapter 5, which consists of shared behavior but not, as far as we know, shared *beliefs*. Chapter 6 and Chapter 7 present evidence that early hominin culture was becoming more complex and varied. For example, indications of advanced cognition (thinking) appear in complex tool-making, such as the Levallois technique of the Neanderthals.

Modern human culture consists of even more complex systems of symbols and meaning. Modern humans have highly elaborate, learned forms of communication that are both vocal and visual, and they have seemingly infinite ways of creating new culture. Archaeologists see evidence of such cultural modernity and complexity in new tool types and materials, different diets, new forms of social organization, and the increasing importance of symbolism in language, religious beliefs, art, and music.

Two Opposing Models for Modern Human Origins and a Middle Position

No one has a good explanation "why" modern humans evolved. Anthropologists are on somewhat firmer ground in responding to the questions about "where" and "when" modern humans appeared, but even these questions can inspire vigorous debate. New fossil discoveries and improved dating methods continue to prompt anthropologists to adjust their thinking about where and when modern human originated. And new finds and methods will continue to provide opportunities for further debate and rethinking about the "why" question.

Since the 1980s, three models have been proposed in an attempt to explain the origins of modern humans (see Figure 8.2 on p. 226). The first model is associated with American biological anthropologist Milford Wolpoff. Called the **Multiregional Model,** it proposes that modern humans evolved from local archaic *Homo* populations in several regions of the Old World (Wolpoff et al. 1984). This model says that the most recent common ancestor of modern humans was an early form of *H. erectus* that emerged in Africa around 2 million years ago. Regional transformations in the Old World to modern humans did not take place in complete isolation from each other, however. Social contact among regional groups meant that genes were

FIGURE 8.2

Two opposing models of modern human origins and a model that draws on both.

Multiregional Model	Recent African Replacement Model	Diffusion Wave Model
Modern humans evolved in various locations from regionally distinct archaic *Homo* populations, with some gene flow across groups.	Modern humans evolved in Africa 300,000–200,000 years ago. From there they migrated to the rest of the Old World and the New World. They replaced regionally distinct archaic *Homo* populations wherever they met them.	Biologically and culturally modern humans evolved recently in Africa.
H. erectus populations are in the direct evolutionary line to humans, and Neanderthals are ancestral to modern humans.	*H. erectus* and *H. neanderthalensis* populations are not ancestral to modern humans; their extinction may have been influenced by contact with modern humans.	Interbreeding and cultural exchange between modern humans and earlier regional populations of archaic *Homo* are possible in some instances but are not likely to have been significant in the case of the Neanderthals.

exchanged across the boundaries between different regional populations to the extent that after the evolution from *Homo erectus*, our ancestors always belonged to a single species (review the definition of a species in Chapter 3). Because that species is seen as continuous with contemporary modern humans, Wolpoff proposes that it should be called *Homo sapiens*. Thus the Multiregional Model lumps the species of archaic *Homo* covered in Chapter 7 into *Homo sapiens*. Yet, according to the Multiregional Model, regional groups of *Homo sapiens* kept enough of their own characteristic morphology to make contemporary regional populations of modern humans physically distinctive.

The second approach is associated mainly with British biological anthropologists Chris Stringer and Peter Andrews (Stringer and Andrews 1988). The **Recent African Replacement Model** proposes that modern humans evolved from archaic *Homo* in Africa around 200,000 years ago. This model argues that Africa has always generated morphological and behavioral novelties. The dispersal of *H. ergaster* was just the first of many hominin migrations that originated in Africa (Templeton 2002). According to the Recent African Replacement Model, modern humans began to migrate out of Africa between 200,000 and 100,000 years ago. Throughout the Old World, they so thoroughly replaced local populations of archaic *Homo*, including Neanderthals, that there are no traces of the genomes of any of the regional archaic populations in the genome of modern humans. In this model, morphological differences among contemporary regional modern human populations are recent, most having evolved in the last 50,000 years or so.

A third model incorporates some features from each of the first two models. The **Diffusion Wave Model** recognizes the recent origin of modern humans in Africa and the probability that there were biological and cultural interactions between modern humans and regional archaic *Homo* populations (Eswaran 2002). The authors of this book favor the third model. We agree with the Recent African Replacement Model that modern humans migrated out of Africa to the rest of the Old World and then the New World. We diverge from it, however, when it discounts possible interactions and significant interbreeding among modern humans and surviving regional populations of later *H. erectus, H. heidelbergensis,* and Neanderthals. We think that social contact, such as exchange, between modern humans and local groups was probable and that such contact must inevitably have involved the transfer of genes and ideas.

One highly contentious area of dispute between the Multiregional Model and the Recent African Replacement Model concerns the relationship between later Neanderthals and modern humans. The Multiregional Model considers the morphological differences between the Neanderthals and modern Europeans to be trivial. It argues that, over 50,000 to 10,000 years of coexistence in Europe, interbreeding between Neanderthals and modern humans occurred to such an extent that Neanderthals made a genetic contribution to the modern human lineage. The Recent African Replacement Model says that the Neanderthals were morphologically distinct and made no significant contribution to the modern human gene pool (Stringer 2002). Those scientists who take the first position favor including Neanderthals in *H. sapiens*. Those who take the second position favor classifying Neanderthals and modern humans in separate species. The authors of this book consider that despite probable biological and cultural interchange between modern humans and Neanderthals, the latter are distinctive enough to be considered a separate species.

An emerging body of DNA evidence taken from Neanderthal fossils supports a species-level distinction between Neanderthals and modern humans. Scientists first extracted short fragments of mitochondrial DNA (mtDNA) from the humerus recovered from the original Neanderthal site in Germany (Krings et al. 1997, 1999). The analysis indicated that the fossil mtDNA sequence was outside the range of variation of a diverse sample of modern humans, suggesting that it belonged to a separate species from modern humans. Subsequently, Neanderthal mtDNA was recovered from the fossil of a second individual found at the same site (Schmitz et al. 2002), from another fossil found in Russia (Ovchinnikov et al. 2000), and from another from Croatia (Krings et al. 2000). The differences between the four Neanderthal fossil samples of mtDNA and living modern human mtDNA are substantial and significant (Knight 2003). Analysis of mtDNA from four more Neanderthals and five modern human fossils from Europe confirms that Neanderthals and modern humans should be in two separate species (Serre et al. 2004). Admittedly, the DNA recovered from the Neanderthal fossils consists only of short fragments of mtDNA. Future studies using more substantial fragments or nuclear DNA will provide further insights.

Fossil and Genetic Evidence for Modern Human Origins in Africa

Fossil discoveries in Africa during the 1960s startled the world with the idea that Africa, not Europe or Asia, was where modern humans originated. These new finds were of modern human-like fossils from sites at Klasies River Mouth, South Africa (Rightmire 1979), and in the Omo Valley, Ethiopia (Day 1969) (see the map and Figure 8.3 on p. 228). Although none of the remains were in circumstances that allowed for absolute dating methods, researchers felt sure they were substantially older than the fossil evidence for modern humans in other parts of the world.

Subsequent fossil finds in Africa added further support for the new idea. At Herto, Ethiopia, the discovery of well-preserved crania dated to 160,000 years ago left little doubt that there were populations of hominins in East Africa during the Middle Stone Age whose remains are difficult to distinguish from modern humans (White et al. 2003, Stringer 2003). They have physical features seen in all living modern humans, such as rounded brain cases and small faces tucked beneath the brain case (Lieberman et al. 2002).

Support for the African origin of modern humans also comes from reconstructing human evolutionary history through analysis of modern human genes. The genetic evidence indicates that all modern humans are descended from a common ancestral population that lived in Africa between 200,000 and 100,000 years ago (Cann, Stoneking and Wilson 1987, Quintana-Murci et al. 1999, Ingman et al. 2000). Many novel versions of genes have their origin in African populations and then appear to have spread into the Middle East, Asia, and Europe (Pääbo 2003). There are more

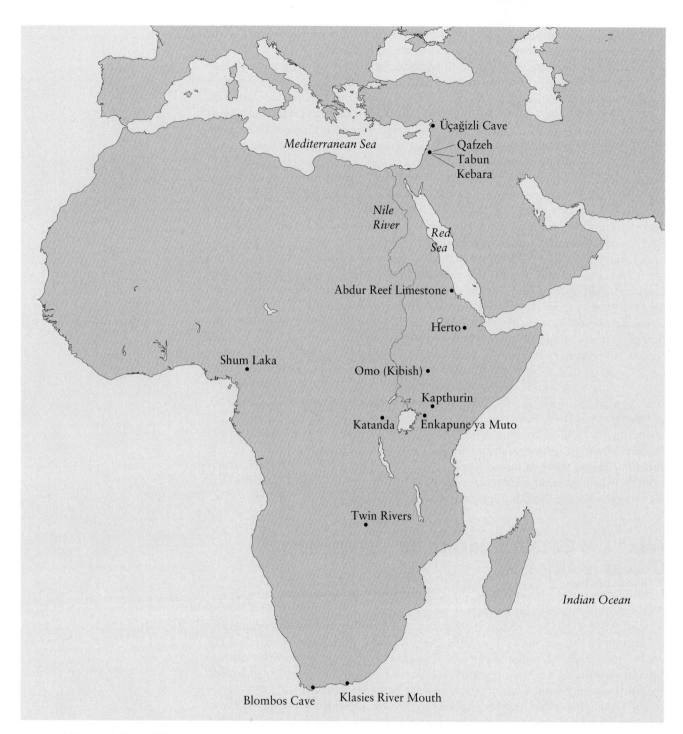

Sites in Africa and the Middle East mentioned in this chapter.

FIGURE 8.3

Middle Stone Age sites in Africa with evidence of modern humans.

Site Name and Location	Date
Kapthurin, Kenya	300,000 years ago
Twin Rivers, Zambia	300,000 years ago
Omo (Kibish), Ethiopia	130,000 years ago
Katanda, Democratic Republic of Congo	90,000 years ago
Blombos Cave, South Africa	75,000 years ago

different versions of genes in contemporary modern human populations in Africa than in all the rest of the world put together (Tishkoff and Verrelli 2003). This finding is consistent with the view that Africa has been the dominant source of the novel genes and gene combinations of modern humans.

Archaeological Evidence for Modern Human Origins in Africa

A growing number of archaeological discoveries also support the view that modern humans originated in Africa. This evidence comes from the Middle Stone Age (MSA), a period of time in Africa between 300,000 and 40,000 years ago (review Figure 6.2, p. 178).

The Middle Stone Age

The MSA is characterized by *blade technology*. A **blade** is a long, parallel-sided flake made from hard stone such as flint or obsidian. In order to be termed a blade, the flake must be at least twice as long as it is wide. Blade manufacture involves several steps, beginning with selecting the right shape core, shaping the core, and then striking the core at precisely the right places to produce a blade of the desired size.

This description may not sound so different from that of the Levallois technique (Chapter 7), but it involves distinctive features that are further evidence of the complex thinking associated with modern humans. First, during the MSA there is increased standardization in the size and shape of the blades, which implies more intentionality and control on the part of the tool-maker. Second, some blades, called **projectile points,** are specially shaped for use on the tips of spears or arrows. MSA projectile points are the first evidence of a **composite tool**—a tool made by combining separate pieces of stone, bone, or any other suitable material into a single tool. Spears and arrows, made of stone tips attached to a shaft, are early examples of composite tools. The making of composite tools involves complex stepwise planning and a sophisticated sense of design.

Blades from Kapthurin, Kenya, dated at 300,000 years ago. Many archaeologists say that these blades, and other early tools, indicate that humans had features of modern behavior far in advance of modern anatomy.
■ Speculate on the possible uses of these blades. (Source: Sally McBrearty)

Bone harpoon from Katanda, Democratic Republic of Congo, dated at 90,000 years ago. ■ What advantages do such weapons have? (Source: Chip Clark/NMNH/Smithsonian Institution)

Some evidence of modern tool-making is dated to 300,000 years ago. This evidence includes blades found at Kapthurin, Kenya (McBrearty and Brooks 2000) and components of composite tools found at Twin Rivers, Zambia (Barham 2002). The date of 300,000 years ago creates a puzzle because it is at least 100,000 years earlier than the fossil evidence for anatomical modernity. This apparent time gap has led some anthropologists to subscribe to the "brains before body" view of modern human evolution.

Several other features of modernity make an appearance during the MSA. Evidence of modern behavior comes from several sites in the Democratic Republic of Congo (Yellen et al. 1995). For example, bone harpoons found at Katanda, tentatively dated to 90,000 years ago, substantially predate the use of similar harpoons by European populations. Regionally distinctive styles of stone tool production appear for the first time, implying creativity, originality, a sense of style, and identity expressed through objects.

An important site of early modern humans, Blombos Cave in South Africa, dated to about 75,000 years ago, provides the earliest evidence of abstract imagery and personal ornamentation. The evidence consists of carved pieces of *ochre* (earth that contains iron and is pale yellow to red in color) and shell beads (Henshilwood et al. 2002, 2004). The use of ochre, at an earlier date in Africa than in Europe, places it as the first instance of ritual body decoration (see the Crossing the Fields section on p. 526). Use wear on the shell beads indicates that they were probably strung on some kind of thread and worn as ornaments. They are the earliest ornamental beads.

The MSA also provides the earliest archaeological evidence of behavioral modernity in the form of more complex economic strategies such as adaptations to seasonal changes. In Egypt, for example, people harvested Nile catfish and tilapia stranded in ponds left by the annual flooding (Wendorf, Close, and Schild 1994). Food-getting practices indicate modernity in tool use, as evidenced by the acquisition of very large animals and fish. As early as 90,000 years ago, people at Katanda were using the oldest known harpoons to catch catfish up to 6 feet long (Yellen et al. 1995). Catching fish of this size probably involved group coordination and knowledge that was passed down over generations. Given that the catch was so large, its consumption probably involved group sharing and perhaps some form of preservation (drying) and means of storage. Food storage, another important marker of behavioral modernity, implies that people have evolved beyond a basic concern with the "here and now." It implies planning. Coordinated group behavior involved in catching the fish and dividing it up, by extension, suggests the existence of complex verbal language.

Exchange, the transfer of goods or services between two or more people, was probably occurring within groups occupying campsites as well as among different regional groups. Ethnographic analogy suggests that such exchanges probably were balanced and **egalitarian.** Within groups, all members would have received equal shares of food and other resources. In addition to shedding light on possible exchange patterns, ethnographic analogy also helps expand our understanding of possible food consumption and preparation practices during the MSA (see the Methods Close-Up box).

The question of what kinds of humans lived during the MSA has not been fully answered. The archaeological evidence suggests the existence of technological and social modernity 300,000 years ago. But is the archaeological evidence the product

Cultural Clues from South Africa about Modern Human Diet

ARCHAEOLOGY AND CULTURAL anthropology join forces in the area of ethnoarchaeology (defined in Chapter 4) to shed light on important questions in human evolution, including issues relating to diet and tool use. This example shows how ethnoarchaeology provides insights about particular features of early modern humans' diet in southern Africa. It concerns the use of fire and a creature called the Cape dune mole-rat.

Fossil evidence of the Cape dune mole-rat is common in many prehistoric sites along the southwestern coast of South Africa (Henshilwood 1997). At some sites, mole-rats are the most common faunal species, constituting up to 90 percent of the faunal remains. This concentration of mole-rats suggests to some researchers that our human ancestors collected them and brought them back to their base, where they ate them. Other researchers claim that predators, probably eagle owls, accumulated the mole-rat fossils. A third view attributes the concentration of dune mole-rats to a combination of human and eagle owl activity.

The way in which contemporary people catch, cook, and consume mole-rats offers insights into the role that the prehistoric mole-rats may have played in prehistoric diets in southern Africa. Mole-rats are large rodents, males averaging about 900 grams (2 pounds) and females about 670 grams (1½ pounds). They excavate deep burrows, digging with their large, strong, clawed forefeet. Common predators of mole-rats these days include snakes, various birds, and carnivores, including wildcats, jackals, and hyenas. In addition, some people today consider mole-rat meat a delicacy, and families are known to consume four to five weekly.

In order to learn more about how contemporary modern humans who live near Blombos Cave (see the map on p. 228) collect and consume mole-rats, Christopher Henshilwood conducted ethnographic research with several South African farm workers. He learned that the method they use to capture mole-rats is to scoop away the sandy mound formed by the mole-rat in order to open up its burrow. Then one person sits at the entrance and waits. The mole-rat senses that its burrow has been opened and attempts to close the entrance. When the animal's head appears at the burrow opening, it is "hooked out of the hole using a fishing gaff and its throat slit" (Henshilwood 1997:661). The mole-rat is cooked by placing it, on its back, in a bed of coals. It is baked for about 30 minutes. The thick fur protects the meat except at the front of the upper and lower jaws, where charring around the mouth occurs.

Most of the fossilized mole-rat bones found at Blombos have charred bone on the face that is similar to that on the contemporary mole-rat bones. This indirect evidence suggests that early humans collected, cooked, and ate the mole-rats at Blombos Cave. Without the ethnographic data, researchers would have found it much more difficult, if not impossible, to solve the problem of who, or what, accumulated the Blombos Cave mole-rats.

FOOD FOR THOUGHT

■ Given that mole-rats were an important food in prehistory, what other small animals might also have been important food sources then?

---

of modern humans, *Homo sapiens?* This question cannot yet be answered because the earliest fossil evidence of anatomically modern humans, from Omo, Ethiopia, is dated at 195,000 years ago. The archaeological evidence thus challenges the fossil hunters to fill the gap in the fossil evidence.

Given the thinness of the evidence for human modernity in Africa between 300,000 and 160,000 years ago, it is not surprising that not all researchers accept it. One critic is Richard Klein, an archaeologist at Stanford University (Klein 2000). He rejects the examples of human modernity before that time, such as the Katanda harpoons and Blombos Cave ochre use, by saying that, first, they are not much different from examples from the same time period in Europe, which are not classified as modern, and second, are too rare to constitute definite evidence of modernity. According to Klein, a major turning point toward modernity occurred in Africa but much later, around 40,000 years ago, when there is evidence of the sudden appearance of small, specialized bone tools such as arrow points, needles, and fish hooks. Klein suggests that this radical change corresponds to the fossil evidence for the emergence of a more

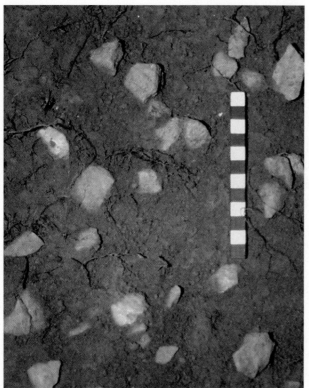

Later Stone Age microliths from Isak Baite in the Democratic Republic of Congo. ■ If you were an archaeologist, what clues would indicate that they were made intentionally, rather than by accident, and by humans, rather than by nonhuman primates? (Source: Julio Mercader)

slender skeleton. He also speculates that the toolkit changes coincided with the acquisition of the ability to communicate complex ideas through spoken language.

The authors of this book accept the examples of harpoon use, ochre use, and other evidence from the Middle Stone Age as important enough to be counted as evidence for cultural modernity in Africa that substantially predates similar evidence elsewhere in the the Old World. We also accept the possibility that aspects of cultural modernity occurred before anatomical modernity.

The Later Stone Age

The **Later Stone Age,** or **LSA,** is a time period in Africa that begins between 40,000 and 20,000 years ago and is characterized by **microliths,** very small stone tools whose edges have been retouched, and by increasing standardization of stone tools (Brooks and Robertshaw 1990). Microliths are usually less than 5 centimeters (2 inches) long and have geometric shapes such as triangles and trapezoids. They are made from blades that are snapped and broken into smaller pieces, which are then *retouched* (that is, small flakes on the surface and edges are removed). Microliths were used on spear and arrow tips, or several microliths were set in rows, like the teeth on a saw, to make composite tools for cutting. Marked regional differences in LSA toolkits suggest that LSA stone tool-makers were creative and had a sense of identity and style.

LSA sites are found in a wide range of African environments, including savannahs, woodlands, and rainforests (Mercader and Brooks 2001). The earliest LSA sites (such as Enkapune ya Muto, Kenya, dated around 40,000 years ago, and Shum Laka, a rock shelter site in Cameroon, dated at 30,000 years ago) are located in tropical latitudes. Most LSA sites beyond the tropical regions, in southern and North Africa, date to 18,000 years ago or later. Archaeologists are puzzled as to why the earliest evidence for the LSA is found in the tropics rather than in the temperate zones. A possible explanation is that population size was greater in tropical Africa, which led to more social interaction, which in turn promoted more creativity and innovation.

The diets of LSA people varied according to the environmental context. Scavenging meat was probably important for many LSA groups, along with gathering smaller food sources such as eggs and insects. Some LSA coastal sites reveal continuity of the MSA tradition of exploiting the rich resources of shellfish. For example, at Klasies River Mouth, shell middens (piles of discarded shells) are evidence of the importance of shellfish consumption. Evidence at other LSA sites of the remains of large fish and of large and dangerous terrestrial animals suggests that social changes involving increased cooperation occurred along with the development of new kinds of tools.

The time of the end of the LSA varies across Africa. In parts of sub-Saharan Africa, the LSA persisted into recent times, and some anthropologists argue that twentieth-century African foraging lifestyles are directly descended from prehistoric LSA lifestyles. Thus they consider contemporary African foraging groups relevant ethnographic analogies for prehistoric peoples. On the basis of such analogies, the lifestyle of the early LSA people would have been characterized by the features listed in Figure 8.4. Ethnographic analogy, complemented by archaeological evidence, suggests that social organization within local groups was egalitarian, characterized by an even distribution of material goods, status, and quality of life. In resource-rich areas, it is possible that some degree of social ranking and inequality was beginning to develop as food surpluses and luxury goods accumulated.

Other anthropologists are more cautious about the use of analogies based on recent and contemporary foragers for interpreting the lifestyles of prehistoric populations. They say that, first, modern-day foragers' territories are smaller than those in pre-

FIGURE 8.4

Later Stone Age cultural features.

Diet: Varying food sources depending on environment
  Low altitudes: more seeds, nuts
  Middle altitudes, steppes: more game
  Emergence of fishing and fowling

Technology: More innovations at a faster pace
  Innovations for cold environments (clothing, shelter)
  Wide variety of bone points
  Harpoons, some with barbs
  Bow and arrow
  Fire-hardened clay pottery

Social organization (indirect evidence)
  Increased social contact among distant groups through trade
  Generally egalitarian within groups
  Possibility of social ranking in resource-rich areas

Ideology (indirect evidence)
  Modern symbolic thinking: body ornaments
  Wall art
  Portable art
  Group burials, many with elaborate grave goods

Health and population
  Longer lifespan
  Rare evidence of pathology
  No evidence of infectious disease
  Rare evidence of interpersonal violence
  Increased proportion of aged people

historic times. Second, even though contemporary foragers use some tools that are similar to those of the LSA, other aspects of their lifestyle have changed. Note that these anthropologists do not reject the use of analogies, but they instead urge caution.

 ## MODERN HUMANS DURING THE UPPER PALEOLITHIC

This section follows the migrations of modern humans out of Africa in roughly chronological order, starting with the Middle East, then moving toward Asia, then Europe, and finally the New World. The fossil and archaeological records for modern humans are uneven, with rich evidence and reliable dating in some places but sparse evidence and insecure dates in others. Generally, the data are better for Europe and the Middle East than for East Asia. Some regions have been more intensively studied than others, for various reasons. More sites have been found close to cities, simply because most researchers work at universities in cities and tend to conduct fieldwork in nearby areas. As anthropologists openly admit, the preponderance of sites in southwest France may have as much to do with the excellent fieldwork conditions as with the scientific value of sites in the region compared to elsewhere. Increasingly, paleoanthropologists and archaeologists are studying sites in more physically challenging places such as Siberia and tropical rainforests, filling gaps in knowledge of this period of humanity's prehistory.

The **Upper Paleolithic, or UP,** is the period of modern human occupation in the Old World (other than Africa) from approximately 45,000–40,000 years ago to around 12,000 years ago, during which microliths and other small, finely made stone and bone tools are the defining elements of technology. During this period, modern humans also increased their ability to make and use tools made of organic materials such as nets and baskets. In many places, they created impressive works of art.

Migrations into the Old World

Following the model that modern humans originated in Africa, their first migration destination out of Africa would have been the Middle East, given its proximity. The most logical path was from northeast Africa to the Levant, a narrow coastal region running along the eastern edge of the Mediterranean Sea from the Sinai Peninsula in the south to Turkey in the north. Evidence of probable occupation by modern humans is found in stone tools at the Abdur Reef Limestone, an emerged reef terrace on the Red Sea coast of Eritrea, dated to 125,000 years ago (Walter et al. 2000). The stone tools are a mixture of MSA-style blades and flakes and more modern-looking bifacial tools. This transitional assemblage fits with the time frame of modern human migrations out of Africa.

Transitions in the Levant

The oldest modern human fossils outside Africa, found in the Levant, are dated at around 100,000 years ago (Hublin 2000). Levant sites indicate that both modern humans and Neanderthals lived there for some time. Modern human fossils from sites such as Qafzeh are substantially older than Neanderthal fossils from nearby sites, such as Tabun and Kebara. Thus modern humans arrived in the Levant before the Neanderthals (Lieberman and Shea 1994). Increasing aridity in Africa may have prompted modern human groups to move north, whereas increasing cold in Europe may have prompted Neanderthals to move south. An intriguing feature of the early modern humans in the Levant is that their toolkits closely resemble Mousterian toolkits found at many Neanderthal sites in Europe. Thus, although the early modern humans in the Levant were anatomically modern, and probably culturally modern in some ways, their stone toolkit was not modern. Modern humans in the Levant developed a distinct stone tool-making technique called *recurrent Levallois reduction*, which was an efficient way of producing many flakes from the same core.

Major research questions about the Levant during this period concern its simultaneous occupation by modern humans and Neanderthals. There was probably a geographic demarcation between Neanderthals and modern humans in the Levant, modern humans being concentrated in the coastal lowlands and Neanderthals in the uplands of the interior. The two populations appear to have used the landscape differently. Modern human groups moved to different locations as the seasons changed. Neanderthals were mainly stationary. When they traveled, they moved out in a spoke-like fashion, later returning to the same location (Lieberman and Shea 1994).

From the Levant, modern humans migrated toward Asia, probably taking a coastal route around the Arabian peninsula and then traveling along the coastline of India and on to Southeast Asia and the Pacific (Stringer 2000). Others dispersed north to Anatolia (present-day Turkey). From there, some modern humans migrated into Eastern and Central Europe, and others moved into Central Asia and beyond to Siberia and eventually the New World. The oldest fossil evidence is in Southeast Asia and Australia.

Southeast Asia, Australia, and the South Pacific Region

There is evidence of modern humans in Southeast Asia by 40,000 years ago and some evidence in Papua New Guinea and Australia well before that (O'Connell and Allen 2004; Thorne et al. 1999). During the last glacial period, when water from the ocean was locked up in the polar ice caps and in glaciers that covered the higher latitudes of the Old and New Worlds, many areas that are now submerged were above water

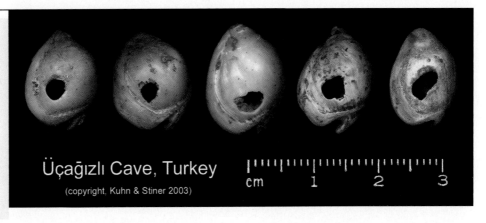

Shell beads from Üçağizli (pro-nounced "euch auhzluh") Cave, Turkey. The beads were found in the oldest layers, which date beginning 41,000 years ago. More than 2000 marine shells have been recovered from all Upper Paleolithic levels combined. ■ Why might shells have been the earliest material used for jewelry? (Source: Courtesy of Steven L. Kuhn and Mary C. Stiner)

Üçağızlı Cave, Turkey
(copyright, Kuhn & Stiner 2003)

cm   1   2   3

level. Land bridges connected areas now separated by water. Two paleoregions relevant to this section are

■ *Sunda:* the geographic platform supporting the present-day islands of Southeast Asia, such as those in the Indonesian archipelago.

■ *Sahul:* the geographic platform supporting present-day Papua New Guinea, Australia, Tasmania, and nearby islands.

It seems logical that early humans would have arrived in Sunda before Sahul, but the dates for fossil sites in Sahul are, thus far, earlier than those for sites in Sunda. Controversial findings of flake-based stone technology from the cave site of Song Terus, Java, point to a modern human presence there between 185,000 and 80,000 years ago (Semah et al. 2003). If dates as early as 185,000 years ago are confirmed, they will raise new questions about how modern humans arrived in Sunda so early.

It is unclear whether, or how much, modern humans overlapped and interacted with archaic *Homo* in this region. As noted in Chapter 7, the dates of the last *H. erectus* fossils in this region, from Ngandong, Java, are not firm (Swisher et al. 1996). The later dates from Ngandong, if correct, would make temporal overlap between the two populations highly likely. Temporal overlap, as in the Levant, does not necessarily mean physical contact. The recently discovered "dwarf" form of *H. erectus* that lived until 18,000 years ago on the relatively isolated island of Flores is an example of how separate species may have existed simultaneously in the region without any contact with each other (Brown et al. 2004).

Another conceptual challenge concerning modern humans in this region is that most of the stone tools associated with early modern humans in Sunda and Sahul are, by African standards, not modern. Most are pebble and flake toolkits, with little or no signs of core preparation and little standardization (Bulbeck 2003). Blades and microliths are rare. Yet the humans who made these tools were anatomically modern humans. Further, these modern humans with simple stone tools successfully met complex behavioral challenges. Like archaic *Homo* before them, they were able to travel long distances over water and to navigate difficult sea passages. They must have had rafts or boats capable of maintaining buoyancy for several days in order to cross the open water between Sunda and Sahul. Like those of their archaic *Homo* predecessors, the boats or rafts made by modern humans have not been preserved. The places where they lived and built their watercraft are now submerged under water. Their boats, and their tools and dwellings, were probably constructed of bamboo or wood, materials that would rarely be preserved in the archaeological record.

By 35,000 to 30,000 years ago, modern humans in Southeast Asia and the Pacific region were skilled enough as seafarers to reach many islands, including Timor, the Moluccas, New Britain, and New Ireland. Archaeological evidence of stone tools is limited in these island sites, with assemblages often containing between 15 and 30

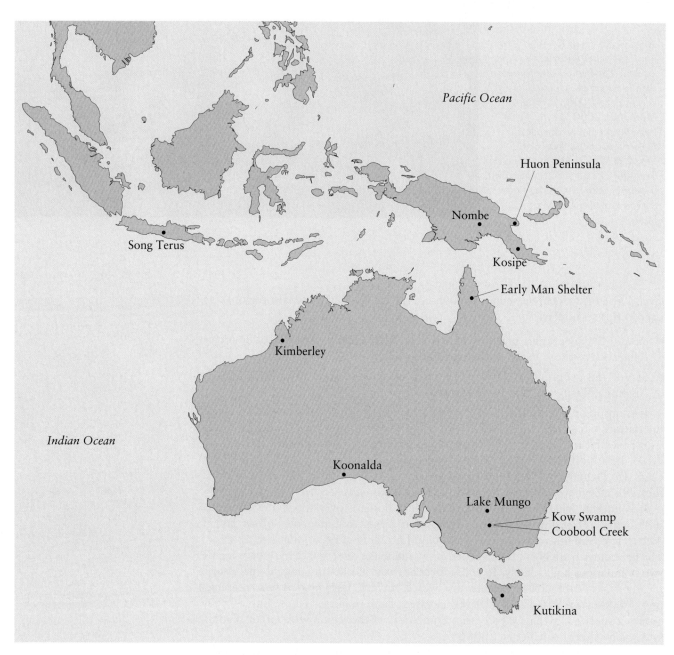

Sites in Southeast Asia and Australia mentioned in this chapter.

stone objects (Pavlides and Gosden 1994). Fish bones are prominent, suggesting the dietary importance of fish.

Sahul was occupied by modern humans perhaps as early as 50,000 years ago (O'Connell and Allen 2004) and certainly by 40,000 to 35,000 years ago. Most evidence indicates that modern humans were the first hominins to enter this region, so there is no question of overlap with earlier groups. In Papua New Guinea, the earliest evidence of modern humans comes from the coastal lowlands of the Huon peninsula, dating between 50,000 and 40,000 years ago (Groube et al. 1986). From the lowlands, modern humans expanded into the highlands, beginning around 30,000 years ago. A special kind of axe called a *waisted axe* has been found at two highland sites in Papua New Guinea: Nombe and Kosipe. These axe-shaped flakes are large, about 30 cm (12 inches) across and 25 cm (10 inches) long. They are grooved in their middle sections, or waisted (just as the middle part of the human body is narrower than the rest), which may have facilitated mounting them on wooden handles. Waisted axes are partially flaked and partially polished. They are the earliest polished stone tools, preceding similar examples elsewhere in the world by thousands of years.

When modern humans arrived in Australia, the climate was wetter than it is today. Regions that are now parched and dry were then green and lush, full of plant and animal life. Fossils of early modern human populations in Australia exhibit wide anatomical variation. People living at sites around Lake Mungo had steep foreheads, taller brain cases, and flat faces, whereas those at Kow Swamp and Coobool Creek had more sloping foreheads, lower brain cases, and projecting faces. This variation may be evidence of successive waves of immigration by distinctly different groups of people, possibly including archaic *Homo*. Or the variation may be due to the effects of a single species moving into a large land mass. Population density would have been low and breeding groups isolated, leading to the emergence of distinctive morphologies that persisted until they were erased by later gene flow.

The diet of modern humans living at sites around Lake Mungo included mussels, crayfish, frogs, kangaroos, wallaby, wombats, and emus. This mixed-game diet is probably typical of people living elsewhere on the continent. Using ethnographic analogies based on twentieth-century Australian foragers, anthropologists suggest that the gender division of labor included overlapping male and female roles for procuring small game and other everyday food items, and men being more responsible for hunting large game. Large-game hunting, not prominent as a food-procuring method, was probably resorted to when more accessible food sources were scarce, just as is the case among early-twentieth-century foraging groups (Hiatt 1970).

An important question is whether the growth and expansion of modern human populations had negative effects on the survival of megafauna (large animals) such as giant kangaroos, wombats, and flightless birds. Around 46,000 years ago in Sahul, many large marsupials and reptiles disappeared abruptly (Roberts et al. 2001). Between 40,000 and 15,000 years ago, another fifty species became extinct. These extinctions cannot be attributed to climate change, and there were few natural predators before the arrival of humans. Therefore, one theory argues that human hunting caused the extinctions. At this point, there is not enough evidence about the timing of the extinctions in relation to the timing of human settlement to prove or disprove this theory (Barnosky et al. 2004). It is possible that human hunting was implicated in the extinctions in some places but not in others. For example, megafauna in Tasmania appear to have gone extinct before humans arrived. At some Australian sites, however, evidence of overlap between modern humans and now-extinct megafauna points to a possible human impact (Field et al. 2001).

As in Sunda, the archaeological evidence associated with modern humans in Sahul is mixed. Crude stone tools are found along with bone tools, art, and burials. Lake Mungo has yielded the earliest evidence of ritual cremation and the application of pigment to corpses. Modern humans in Sahul were prolific artists. A rock painting dated to about 25,000 years ago at the site of Laura, northern Australia, is as old as many of the world-famous Paleolithic cave paintings of Europe. Prehistoric art in Sunda is found in a variety of forms. At Koonalda, linear engravings were made by applying finger pressure on soft clayey walls. At the Early Man Shelter, schematic designs were painted and engraved on large stone panels. Naturalistic representations are found at caves sites in Tasmania such as Kutikina.

Today, many Aboriginal Australian groups are reaffirming their connections to these artistic sites, some of which have become important tourist destinations and archaeological research sites. A recent conflict that erupted over a gallery of cave painting in the Kimberley region involved a museum anthropologist (see the Lessons Applied box on p. 238).

A member of the Dani people, Irian Jaya, holding a stone adze, photographed in the 1990s. ■ How long do you think it would take you to make such a tool? (Source: © Lindsay Hebberd/CORBIS)

Find out where the site of Laura is located and learn more about the paleoart there.

THINKING

OUTSIDE THE BOX

Helping to Resolve Conflicts about Repainting Australian Indigenous Cave Art

NEWSPAPER HEADLINES across Australia announced "Ancient Rock Defaced" (Bowdler 1988). The rock art in question was paintings on the walls of rock shelters in the Kimberley area, in northwest Australia. The accused defacers were Aboriginal people of the region. The case was first raised by a White Australian rancher who owns property on which the paintings are located. Other elements add to the complexity of this case. The repainting was done with funding from an Australian Commonwealth agency under a program called the Commonwealth Employment Programme. The statutory authority responsible for the sites is the Aboriginal Sites Department of the Western Australian Museum.

One of the major issues underlying the accusations was whether "defacement" or "desecration" of "age-old" paintings had occurred. Another concerned whose heritage was involved—that of the Aboriginal people or "humanity" more widely. Archaeologists from the museum became involved in trying to address these questions.

The Kimberley region is noted for its rich rock art. Of the many examples of art in the area, the most famous are the Wandjina, large anthropomorphic figures, round-eyed and mouthless, with radiating headdresses. The term *Wandjina*

refers to ancestral spirits who control the weather. A series of myths about the Wandjina are part of the living tradition of the Wanang Ngari people of Kimberley. Ethnographic research from the first half of the twentieth century documents that, on certain occasions, some individuals had the right and obligation to repaint the figures. Aboriginal elders retain the knowledge about appropriate forms of repainting, which can include the addition of new motifs. Repainting often involves superimposition (painting over) and even obliteration of older motifs.

The Wanang Ngari people say that they inherited the Wandjina paintings from the spirits themselves. Archaeological evidence indicates that the paintings date from some time earlier than 3000 years ago. They have been continuously repainted since then.

The Commonwealth Employment Programme initiated a repainting project to train Wanang Ngari youth to continue the repainting process and to participate in other projects such as the recording of oral histories and conservation of the site. Part of the impetus for the project was from older Aborigines who thought the younger people were losing touch with their traditional heritage. Young people of both genders were involved and received training from a technical specialist associated with a museum and from a group of elders.

In June 1987, a White Australian rancher lodged a complaint about "desecration" and "irreparable damage" to "age-old" paintings. The complaint noted that the paintings had been "trivialized" by the addition of inappropriate graffiti and

THINKING OUTSIDE THE BOX Listen to the interview on the Web with French paleoanthropologist Jean-Jacques Hublin about Neanderthals and their fate: *www.pbs.org/wgbh/evolution/library/07/3/text_pop/1_073_02.htm*. What is Hublin's position in the debate about Neanderthal extinction or continuity?

Europe

The arrival of modern humans in Europe marks the beginning of a period of rapidly increasing cultural complexity that is often referred to as a *cultural revolution* or "Golden Age" (Roebroeks et al. 2000, Bar-Yosef 2002a). Cultural changes during the European Upper Paleolithic include increased economic specialization, more complex social relations, technological innovations, probable verbal language, and a leap forward in symbolic thinking.

When modern humans arrived in Europe, the Neanderthals had already been living there for many thousands of years, although their population was sparse and scattered (Hublin 1998). The transitional phase, during which Neanderthals and modern humans both occupied the same region, lasted 10,000 years or less, depending on the location. The most recent evidence for Neanderthals comes from sites such as St. Césaire in France, Zafarraya in Spain, and Vindija in Croatia, all dated to just less than 30,000 years ago. As noted earlier, anthropologists disagree on several issues related to the Neanderthals, including why they died out, whether they contributed to the modern human line, and how advanced their culture was (see the Critical Thinking box on p. 240).

During the European Upper Paleolithic, a more varied diet among modern humans is evident at many sites (Richards et al. 2001). Compared to the Neanderthal populations, who obtained most of their protein from large animals such as deer, modern

Wandjina figures in the Kimberley area, northwest Australia. Australia has the longest continuing tradition of rock art in the world. (Source: Ted Mead/Photolibrary.Com)

that including young people of both genders was an offense to "traditional Aboriginal culture." As a result of this letter, the grant was suspended with no discussion with the Aboriginal people involved.

The Museum's Department of Aboriginal Sites decided to investigate the case. An anthropologist consulted with all individuals whose views were relevant. The conclusions were the following: There was no evidence of desecration, because repainting is a traditional practice. There is evidence that women have traditionally been involved in repainting. With regard to the presence of young people, an elder was always present at the site during the repainting. In sum, the complaint lacked substance.

In spite of these findings, this case did not have a happy conclusion. The Wanang Ngari returned the money to the Commonwealth Employment Programme. They explained that they felt "abused" and that decisions about their site should not have been made by outsiders, including the anthropologist.

FOOD FOR THOUGHT

- What difference might it have made if the anthropologist that the department sent to investigate had been a member of the indigenous people of the Kimberley region?

humans ate significant amounts of birds, small game such as hares, and aquatic animals such as fish and mollusks (Stiner et al. 2000). This pattern of wider diversity in food items is referred to as a **broad-spectrum diet.** Archaeologists think it emerged in the Upper Paleolithic as a response to increased population density. At several sites, however, especially in southwestern France during a time called the Magdalenian period (discussed below), modern humans ate mainly one animal species: reindeer (Grayson et al. 2001). To explain this pattern, archaeologists propose that, in response to climate changes that promoted the increase of reindeer in the region, modern humans had developed more effective ways of capturing reindeer. The fact that modern humans had dietary breadth in some regions and relied on a single species in others suggests flexibile economic strategies.

If sophisticated blade technology is used as an indication of modernity, the first evidence of modern humans in Europe comes from sites in Central Europe, around 40,000 years ago. By around 36,000 years ago, modern humans reached Western Europe. Archaeologists first discovered fossil evidence for modern humans at Cro-Magnon, a rock shelter site in Les Eyzies, France. This site provides the type name for the first modern humans in Europe, the **Cro-Magnon** people.

For several thousands of years after the arrival of modern humans in Europe, the archaeological record displays a complex array of tool assemblages that have been

Unfair to Neanderthals?

PALEOANTHROPOLOGISTS HAVE BEEN conducting research on Neanderthals since the mid-1800s, and for most of that time the interpretation of Neanderthals has been that they are distinctly subhuman and definitely not a direct part of our human ancestry. The consensus about Neanderthals has its roots in the work of prominent experts. They contrast the Neanderthals' archaeological record, called the Mousterian, with that of the later archaeological period, called the Aurignacian, that replaced the Mousterian in Europe and Central Asia. They point to the presence in the Aurignacian of **art** (the application of imagination, skill, and style to matter, movement, and sound in a manner that goes beyond the purely utilitarian) and to a complex tool inventory that includes fine, specialized artifacts such as carved bone needles. They assert that the Mousterian tool inventory is markedly more limited and that almost no art is associated with the Neanderthals. Finally, although they credit Neanderthals with some minimal language ability (vowels but not consonants), they believe that the full complexity of verbal language came later with modern human language.

In sum, they see the culture of the Aurignacian people as sophisticated and that of the Neanderthals as unsophisticated. On these grounds, they argue for a wide and deep gulf between the culture and mind of the so-called "ancients" of the Mousterian and the "moderns" of the Aurignacian (Mellars 1996).

Other researchers come to different conclusions. Some argue that the contrasts between the two periods have been exaggerated. They point out that there is evidence of "advanced" behavior and culture at many Neanderthal sites, especially later ones. At a site in Gibraltar, Neanderthals exploited marine resources, an economic strategy usually associated with modernity (Stringer 2002). At Arcy-sure-Cure, France, Neanderthals are found with Aurignacian-like personal ornaments (Hublin et al. 1996). Some Neanderthals carved bone and ivory with designs that appear to have symbolic content. Variation in modern humans' Aurignacian technology, these anthropologists point out, should also be taken into account. Many modern human sites lack key features of modernity, such as fine bone tools, thus bringing them closer to the Neanderthals in cultural evolution (Clark 2002).

Others say that if the criteria used to reject the Neanderthals as modern were applied to some contemporary modern human populations, they might not qualify. For example, how would the Turkana people of Northern Kenya fare? The Turkana make an adequate, though basic, livelihood around the shores of Lake Turkana. They fish, hunt crocodiles, and herd goats. The environment is harsh: temperatures are high and relieved only by a strong wind. The lake water is not drinkable, and people have to get fresh water by digging water holes. Infectious diseases are common. The Turkana have no art in the sense that the term is used when Neanderthals are found lacking, and the stone tools they make conform to relatively simple designs. The Turkana, however, are undoubtedly modern humans.

Thus the criteria used to dismiss the Neanderthals as modern may also be inappropriate, biased, and even unfair. The Neanderthals survived for tens of thousands of years in cold and harsh environments, in conditions that would be challenging to most humans living today. Their ability to do so was the result of sophisticated biological and cultural adaptations.

CRITICAL THINKING QUESTIONS

- What criteria should be used to determine whether populations are modern?
- How important was the physical environment in shaping early modern human culture?
- Think of characteristics of cultural modernity that Neanderthals might have possessed but that might not appear in the fossil record.

given several stylistic names (see Figure 8.5). This rapid and regionally varied diversification in tool styles is probably related to the introduction of the blade, from which many varieties of tools can be crafted. The early part of the Upper Paleolithic associated with modern humans in Europe, beginning around 40,000 years ago, is referred to as the **Aurignacian period.** Aurignacian stone tools, made using blades as blanks, included scrapers and *burins* (a burin is a chisel-like stone tool used to make other tools from wood or bone). Aurignacian tools have a distinctive style of retouching around the edges. Another characteristic aspect of the Aurignacian period is the increased use of bone for tools including points and awls. Most archaeologists agree that Aurignacian tools were produced solely by modern humans.

The **Gravettian period,** beginning around 28,000 years ago, is characterized by small, narrow, stone blades sometimes with tanged (pronged) points. The Gravettian stone tool tradition was centered in France and Germany, but it extended eastward into Central Europe and parts of Russia and southward into Italy and Spain. An important site in Central Europe is Dolní Věstonice, in the Czech Republic, dated at 26,000 years ago. A distinctive feature of this site is the numerous small female figurines made of *terracotta* (baked clay), many of which were intentionally placed in the hottest part of the fire and thus cracked during the process. No one knows the purpose of such intentional breakage. During the Gravettian period, modern humans made tools made of material other than stone and bone, including perishable nets woven from plant fiber probably used to capture hares, foxes, and other small mammals (Soffer et al. 2001). By extension, these people's ability to knot fibers into nets for capturing small animals may mean they were also able to weave larger nets and trap bigger animals.

Upper Paleolithic sites in Europe mentioned in this chapter.

The third phase of the European Upper Paleolithic is the **Solutrean period,** found mainly in France and Spain and beginning around 21,000 years ago. It is characterized by finely made, leaf-shaped stone points. While many of these delicate points were used for hunting, some may have been objects of beauty and exchange.

The fourth major cultural phase of the European Upper Paleolithic, beginning around 18,000 years ago, is the **Magdalenian period.** During this time, there is a major development of composite, hafted stone tools, harpoons made from bone and antler, borers, and fine bone needles and beads. Some German and Russian sites offer evidence of domesticated dogs, with the earliest evidence for this innovation from sites in Russia (Vilà et al. 1997). The first domesticated dogs were probably used for hunting.

During the Upper Paleolithic, two main categories of art appear and become widespread (Bahn and Vertut 1997). The first is **portable art**—small, movable objects that are engraved or sculpted. Portable art includes sculptures of animals, humans, and creatures that are part animal and part human, such as a standing lion–man figure from Germany. A tradition of sculpting small female figurines begins in the Aurignacian period and is prominent during the Gravettian phase. These statues, of which

FIGURE 8.5
European stylistic periods of the Upper Paleolithic.

Period	Dates (approximate)	Characteristics	Type Site
Aurignacian	40,000–28,000 BCE	Blade stone technology with distinctive retouching; bone tools; cave art	Aurignac, France
Gravettian	28,000–20,000 BCE	Backed stone blades, end scrapers and distinctive points; carved figurines	La Gravette, France
Solutrean	21,000–17,000 BCE	Leaf-shaped stone points, delicate retouching; perforated bone needles	Solutré, France
Magdalenian	18,000–12,000 BCE	Bone, ivory, and antler tools; cave paintings, domesticated dogs	La Madeleine, France

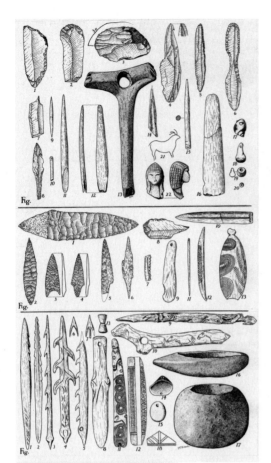

Upper Paleolithic artifacts. These artifacts were made by the earliest modern humans in Europe. ■ How do they differ from Neanderthal artifacts? (Source: American Museum of Natural History)

THINKING OUTSIDE THE BOX   Generate a theory about why Gravettian people carved mainly female figurines and only rarely carved male figurines.

the earliest date to 30,000 years ago, are found across Europe, from the Pyrenees mountains in southern France to as far east as Siberia (Nelson 1997). Nearly 200 statues have been found so far, ranging from those that are quite realistic to those that are so abstract that they are difficult to identify as human figures. Most theories about who made these statues and their use suggest a possible connection to fertility magic or rituals, because many have exaggerated breasts and enlarged abdomens. If so, it is still not known whether the statues were more important to women or to men or both. More imaginative theories propose that the statues were the first erotic art made by men, or were self-portraits of women, possibly even pregnant women.

The second type of art is **cave art,** which includes painting and engraving on cave walls. Painting is the main form of cave art in Upper Paleolithic Europe. The oldest examples of cave painting are found deep in caves at Chauvet and Cosquer, southern France. The paintings depict horses, bears, and other large mammals. They were created between 32,000 and 27,000 years ago (Clottes 2000). Somewhat later, the region of southern France and northern Spain was home to a sophisticated cave art tradition, especially during the Magdalenian period (Clottes 2001). The major subjects painted were large mammals, such as mammoths and bison. The important cave art sites of this era include Lascaux, painted between 15,000 and 10,000 years ago, and Altamira, painted between 16,000 and 11,000 years ago.

Archaeologists have proposed many theories to explain why Upper Paleolithic people created these cave paintings and what the images and motifs meant. One of the earliest theories proposed is that the drawings were *imitative magic,* in which a likeness of something has a connection to the real object. For example, if a person drew an arrow shooting a painted image of a bison, this artistic act would magically ensure that a real arrow during a hunt would strike its real target. Another functional interpretation says that the paintings marked places of community ritual. However, many of the painted areas are difficult to reach and too small to allow many people to congregate, so this explanation cannot apply to all cave paintings.

Other interpretations attempt to find social meanings in the images and symbols. For example, wide or rounded designs might symbolize females while long or pointed designs might symbolize males. Most contemporary anthropologists consider such a view too simplistic. More fruitful directions of interpretation might come from considering why European cave art does not include recognizable images of human females, whereas they do include figures that appear to be human males.

Another interpretation is that the functions and meanings of the images may have changed over time. Thus it would be wrong to attribute one single meaning or function to all of them. Like the Australian rock paintings mentioned earlier, many European cave paintings were overpainted several times, over many thousands of years.

Central Asia and Siberia

Survival in cold and barren areas requires cultural innovations such as long-term planning for food security and shelter and clothing (Davis and Ranov 1999). The modern humans who settled in these regions did not have a morphology adapted to extreme cold as the Neanderthals did (Hoffecker 2002). Thus modern culture, not biology, must have been the adaptive mechanism that made modern human occupation of cold regions possible. The lack of plant food and the scarcity of wood and other fuel sources were additional challenges (Rhode et al. 2003).

At the time of modern human migrations into Europe and Western Asia, Neanderthals may still have been there, so some overlap between the two populations may have occurred. Several Siberian sites provide archaeological evidence of a transition from the Middle to the Upper Paleolithic, with mixed assemblages of bifacial stone points, stone blades, and bone tools (Pavlov et al. 2001).

Evidence for modern human occupation in southern Siberia is followed by evidence for modern human settlement farther north, within the Arctic Circle, by 27,000 years ago (Pitulko et al. 2004). Between 17,000 and 11,000 years ago, there is evidence of long-term occupation by modern humans in this cold and harsh environment. Tools at Arctic Circle sites include microliths and *microblades* (Goebel 1999). Adaptations included the ability to hunt large animals, such as mammoths. During this period, the so-called *mammoth steppe* extended across Eurasia into the New World. Most anthropologists agree that modern humans migrated into the New World from Siberia, on foot, through the paleoregion of *Beringia*, the land bridge that linked Asia with the New World at that time. It is possible that modern humans followed migrating herds of mammoths from the Old World to the New.

Migrations into the New World

The fossil and archaeological evidence from Siberia establishes that modern humans were in position to migrate into present-day Alaska and then the Americas as early as 30,000 years ago. Early Siberian–Alaska peoples had similar toolkits dominated by microblades, which are used as insets on points, producing a hunting weapon that is both strong and lethal (Elston and Brantingham 2002). An innovation of Alaskan people, in contrast to Siberian peoples, is the exploitation of sea mammals and fish.

How did these people make their way from Alaska into the rest of the New World? The most widely accepted scenario of settlement of the Americas says that from Beringia, they migrated south through the *ice-free corridor* in Alaska and western Canada. People populated all of North, Central, and South America in quite a brief time period. This scenario makes sense because people in Siberia were always on the move, and, logically, they would follow bison herds east into Alaska and then down through the ice-free corridor.

A so-called Venus figurine, found at Willendorf, Austria, is carved from fine limestone and is 11 centimeters tall (around 4 inches). Discovered in 1908, this figurine is around 25,000 years old. (Source: © Erich Lessing/ Art Resource, NY)

Left: An upper Paleolithic wall painting at Lascaux, France, depicting a variety of animals. Of the hundreds of figures painted in Lascaux's several galleries, only one depicts a human form, and it has a bird head. Right: Later, during the Mesolithic, rock art increasingly depicted scenes including both humans and animals, as in this painting in Bhimbetka, central India. ■ Consider why human figures are relatively rare in Upper Paleolithic rock painting compared to that of later times. (Source: Réunion des Musées Nationaux/Art Resource, left; Kenneth A. R. Kennedy, right)

Most of the archaeological evidence indicates that the first settlers arrived in the New World sometime after 17,000 years ago. The major body of archaeological evidence about the first modern humans in the New World is that of the **Clovis** culture, characterized by the Clovis point (Haynes 2002). First discovered in New Mexico, a Clovis point is distinct in that it is bifacial and *fluted,* meaning that it has a long, vertical flake chipped from its base. This kind of fluting is found only in the New World. The oldest Clovis sites are dated to slightly before 11,000 years ago, and shortly thereafter there is evidence of Clovis people and their fluted points over most of the unglaciated regions of North America. So far, around 12,000 fluted points have been found, some of them in *caches* (intentionally placed clusters) far from the source of the stone.

Clovis people made similar artifacts and left similar settlement patterns all across the continent (Haynes 2002). The consistency of Clovis culture across such a wide area is an indication of social interactions among the regional groups. It is likely that the Clovis people had a flexible gender division of labor in which both men and women gathered and hunted, including joint participation in the communal hunting of megamammals.

In contrast to its wide range, Clovis culture lasted only a short while. No one has a good explanation for the sudden rise, rapid spread, and sudden demise of Clovis culture. Another mystery about the Clovis people is their possible relationships with megafaunal extinctions and changes in the natural environment. Perhaps their success as hunters contributed to the extinction of megafauna such as mammoths and saber-tooth tigers. Or they may have been altering the environment in ways that indirectly led to megafauna extinction, such as using fire to clear brush to enhance hunting and preferentially cutting certain kinds of trees for bows (Haynes 2002:270ff).

For a long time, archaeologists accepted Clovis sites as the earliest human sites in the New World. Recently, however, several claims for pre-Clovis sites have been made. In North America, they include Meadowcroft, Pennsylvania; Cactus Hill, Virginia; and Topper, South Carolina. In South America, they include Taima-Taima, Venezuela; Pedra Furada, Brazil; and Monte Verde, Chile. Most are problematic because of imprecise and unreliable dating and stratigraphic disturbance. In North America, Meadowcroft is the strongest contender as a pre-Clovis site. Monte Verde, in South America, has established pre-Clovis dates.

The rock shelter site of Meadowcroft, in southwest Pennsylvania, has been excavated over many years (Adovasio and Page 2002). Radiocarbon dates provided by the Smithsonian Institution indicate that it was inhabited by modern humans at least 14,000 years ago. Fragments of a basket, if the dating is verified, would push that date back to around 20,000 years ago, making Meadowcroft the oldest human site in the United States. Meadowcroft thus poses a strong challenge to the *Clovis First* theory that the Clovis people were the first inhabitants of the New World.

Monte Verde is the most convincing pre-Clovis site in the New World. It suggests a human presence in South America 12,500 years ago and thus also poses a conflict with the Clovis First theory (Dillehay 2000). Located in Chile between the Pacific coast and the Andean highlands, Monte Verde was an open-air site near a river, and the boggy conditions promoted excellent preservation of a wide range of remains. Even the cords used to tie hides to poles have been preserved, as have the remains of a dwelling which may have housed 20 to 30 people. The people at Monte Verde used stone tools, including unifacial and bifacial stone points, and bone tools. Cooking pits, mortars, and grinding stones have also been recovered, as well as spilled seeds, nuts, and berries. In one location, what appear to be medicinal herbs have been found. Monte Verde was occupied year-round and thus is the earliest known site of semipermanent (or semisedentary) occupation in the New World.

Ongoing research elsewhere in South America is providing evidence of other possible pre-Clovis sites (Scheinsohn 2003). If, as Monte Verde and other sites indicate, South America was settled 12,500 years ago, and if settlers came to the Americas via Beringia as is generally assumed to be the case, then the occupation of North America must have taken place several thousand years earlier.

An example of a Clovis point. ■ Do research on the Internet to learn about a museum exhibit in which you would be able to learn about Clovis culture. (Source: © Jacka Photography)

Another problem with the Clovis First model is that many of the important Clovis sites are in the eastern part of the United States and Canada. How, researchers ask, if Clovis people came from the northwest, can one explain this pattern? An archaeologist and a biologist have proposed that circumpolar navigation along the north Atlantic ice cap brought Solutrean groups from Spain to the North American eastern seaboard (Stanford and Bradley 2002). They point to similarities in Solutrean and Clovis toolkits as supporting an "Iberian" rather than a "Siberian" source for modern human settlement of North America. This theory, though intriguing, is not widely accepted. Most archaeologists do not see a strong similarity between Clovis and Solutrean tools.

It is likely there were several migrant streams of modern humans into the New World. Different groups arrived and settled over different periods and each made its own contribution to the genetic and cultural diversity of New World populations. No matter when, where, and how modern humans arrived in the New World, they spread rapidly over a diverse range of environments.

The modern human populations in the New World were generalized foragers, exploiting a wide range of food that included plant materials, animals, and marine sources. As in Australia, extinctions of megafauna occurred around the time of human occupation, suggesting overhunting by humans. A lack of conclusive evidence about the possible human role in the extinctions means that this issue is still unresolved. Humans may have played an important role directly through hunting, indirectly through habitat alterations, or through a combination of these activities (McKee 2003). Such anthropogenic effects may have co-occurred with environmental changes during this period.

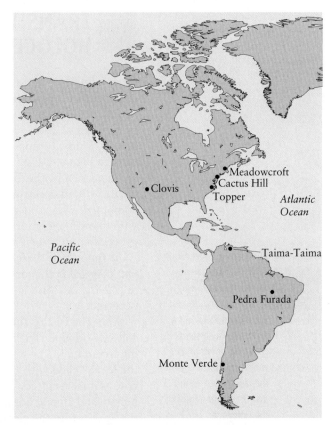

Sites in the New World mentioned in this chapter.

A group of archaeologists visited Monte Verde to inspect the site and its artifacts. Their research report confirmed the early age and authenticity of this site in Chile. ■ Compare the various explanations for how modern humans reached Chile so early, and decide which one you support and why. (Source: © Kenneth Garrett/National Geographic Image Collection)

TRANSITIONS DURING THE HOLOCENE ERA

During the later phases at many LSA/UP sites, people began to move beyond foraging toward **food production,** an economic strategy in which people manage or control plants and animals in order to enhance the supply of these food sources. These first stages of food production became more marked during the Holocene era, a period of time beginning about 12,000 years ago, after the last glacial period ended (review Figure 6.2, p. 178). In Europe, this period is termed the **Mesolithic,** and it is characterized by the increasing importance and variety of microlithic stone and bone tools, a broad-spectrum diet, and a semisedentary (partially settled) life. Foraging is combined with food production techniques including the harvesting of wild foods with more efficient tools, the managing of animal herds, and new forms of plant food processing such as grinding and roasting.

In spite of all these important changes, this period is sometimes described as the Dark Age of prehistory because the artistic activity of the Upper Paleolithic declines markedly. No one is certain why the decline of both portable art and cave art occurred.

After the end of the last glaciation, environmental conditions changed dramatically worldwide. The massive glaciers melted and retreated in response to a warming trend. Land masses gained elevation as a result of being freed from the weight of the ice. Swelled with increased water from the melted glaciers, ocean and sea levels rose, submerging coastal and low-lying areas and reducing the land available for human and animal occupation. For example, what is now the Persian Gulf was above sea level before the glaciers melted and would have been a favored environment for humans, animals, plants, and riverine life (Tudge 1998:36). Paleogeographer Juris Zarins proposes that the flooding of the Persian Gulf and subsequent events underpin the biblical story of the Garden of Eden and its demise (Hamblin 1987). Other environmental changes included the growth of dense forests as a result of increasing moisture.

Old World Transitions

This section discusses examples of the earliest transition to managing wild plants and animals by people at the beginning of the Holocene era. It starts with the Levant region where the oldest archaeological evidence for food production has been found.

Eurasia: First Steps toward Managing Wild Foods

For about 5000 years following the end of the Magdalenian period, Eurasia provides many examples of transitions in food-providing strategies, social organization, shelter, treatment of the dead, and artistic expression. Climatic changes and increasing human populations probably both contributed to the extinction of megafauna. People began to turn to alternative food sources. At the same time, new food sources became available as changes in water temperatures led to increased marine resources such as fish and shellfish.

Natufian culture is the primary example of the Mesolithic transition (Bar-Yosef 2002b). Termed *complex foragers,* the Natufians are known from many Levantine sites, such as Shubakh Cave, El-Wad Cave, and El-Wad Terrace. Natufian culture emerged around 15,000 BCE and constitutes a major turning point in human prehistory because it provides the earliest signs of food production. Natufian sites range in size from small base camps to villages. The villages contain dwelling structures, stone tool industries including new tool types of picks and sickles, animal bone tools, and stone grinding tools. Graves are found in all the larger settlements. They often contain more than one individual and thus provide the first evidence of cemeteries (formalized group burials). Several burials with the skull removed have been found,

THINKING OUTSIDE THE BOX Read, in the Bible, Genesis 2:10–14, and see whether you are convinced that the description of Eden's location makes sense in terms of changing environmental conditions at the end of the last glacial period and the beginning of the Holocene.

and many skeletons are decorated with shells, bones, and animal tooth pendants. This evidence indicates a social pattern of treatment of the dead, perhaps involving beliefs about an afterlife or supernatural realm.

At this time, the Levant was rich in plant species but not in maritime resources. The seasons would have been marked by alternating dry and cold periods, inflicting considerable stress on humans. One way of dealing with such environmental stress is the adoption of partial sedentariness, or semipermanent residence in one place, with more substantial dwellings. Deliberate management of plant and animal food resources would have supported a sedentary lifestyle by providing more dependable, local food sources. Microscopic studies of the edges of Natufian sickles show that they were used to harvest wild cereals. The use of a sickle increases the yield of seeds from grain plants. Natufian people used large stone mortars to grind wild grains—the first evidence of cereal processing.

One of the many mysterious stone sculptures found at Lepenski Vir, a Mesolithic site in eastern Europe. ■ Go to the Internet and find a reconstruction of the site and information on where its artifacts are now housed. (Source: © Erich Lessing/Art Resource, NY)

In the Zagros mountains in the northern Levant region, Mesolithic people began to manage animal populations through selective hunting practices (Zeder and Hesse 2000). Selective killing of adult male gazelles indicates that people were deliberately removing nonreproductive members of the herd to ensure that herd size and survival would not be jeopardized.

Beyond the Levant, in northwestern Europe, hazelnuts were one of the most important new food resources of the Mesolithic. With the warmer and moister conditions of the Holocene, dense woodlands with heavy concentrations of hazelnut trees emerged. Staosnaig, on the Isle of Colonsay, Scotland, provides evidence of the central role of hazelnuts in people's diets (Mithen et al. 2001). Charring indicates that Mesolithic people roasted the hazelnuts. Similar to changes in the Levant, people had devised new forms of food processing that allowed for consumption of new kinds of plant foods.

Expressive culture and art were not entirely absent, as evidenced by many examples of rock paintings and engravings. The first form of monumental stone sculpture was created during the Mesolithic. Lepenski Vir, Serbia, is a site of complex foragers with a unique tradition of stone sculpture. Located on the banks of the Danube River, Lepenski Vir is now completely submerged because of a dam construction project. Around 8000 years ago, and for about 600 years, a cultural mosaic existed: a foraging economy combined with permanent settlement and **monumental art**—that is, large-scale, permanent art works (Srejović 1972). People at Lepenski Vir occupied a flat area by the river, living in trapezoidal huts that faced the river (see Figure 8.6 on p. 248). The huts had stone-paved floors and hearths with spits (devices for elevating food to be cooked above the fire), probably for grilling fish caught in the Danube. The monumental art consists of small boulders carved to look like fish–human heads. These sculpted boulders are usually found within the domestic structures and may have been memorials to an ancestor or representations of a fish-type deity.

FIGURE 8.6

Lepenski Vir settlement pattern. During the first phase of settled life at Lepenski Vir, more than 80 houses were built on a ledge overlooking the Danube River. All were made of local wood and stone. The people must have had mathematical skills in order to design houses with geometric proportions, which are strictly maintained in each structure regardless of size.

(*Source:* Adapted from *Europe's First Monumental Sculpture: New Discoveries at Lepenski Vir,* p. 68, by Dragoslav Srejović. New York: Stein and Day, 1972.)

Africa: Flexible Adaptations to Varied Environments

During the early Holocene in Africa, environmental conditions across the continent generally became drier and cooler. At least two patterns of adaptation to these changes emerged. In drier areas, people became more mobile in order to follow herds of large animals. In wetter areas, people became more sedentary, concentrating on plant and marine resources.

Many people migrated to areas with more dependable water and food supplies, such as the Nile River valley, where population density increased and settlements became more permanent (Kusimba 1999). From 10,000 to 7000 years ago, people across tropical Africa, from Senegal to Kenya, clustered near rivers and lake resources. The general term for people whose lives revolved around lakes and rivers is *aqualithic.* Aqualithic cultures are associated with bone harpoons, pottery (low-fired clay) vessels, and a diet of porridge (cooked wild grains) and fish stew (Sutton 1977).

Major population movements continued to occur throughout Africa during the late Holocene. Anthropologists use a variety of methods in their attempt to reconstruct such population movements and the changing regional distributions of various ethnic groups in order to provide insights into human cultural evolution during this era.

The phenomenon known as the *Bantu expansion* is the single most important factor that shaped the configuration of late prehistoric societies living in Africa south of the equator during the last 5000 years (Afolayan 2000). Today, Bantu culture provides a shared socioeconomic and linguistic context for over 100 million people in Africa.

The classic view of the Bantu expansion is that it involved a large population movement that encompassed most of sub-Saharan Africa. Because Bantu speakers were farmers and had advanced technology, archaeologists long assumed that they displaced Later Stone Age foragers and colonized their territory. New linguistic and archaeological data support a different and more complex view. According to this new perspective, although migrating Bantu people may have sometimes displaced the indigenous foragers, in other cases there were significant forager–farmer interactions and cultural interchange.

Linguistic anthropologists can trace some of the changes involved. Over 600 contemporary African languages are derived from an ancestral language called *proto-Bantu,* which means that the speakers of those 600 languages were once related and shared a common cultural ancestry. All languages are constantly changing, and the separation

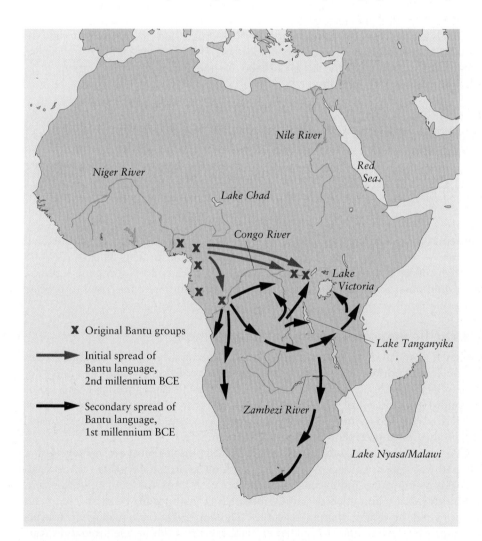

Original Bantu groups

X Original Bantu groups

→ Initial spread of
Bantu language,
2nd millennium BCE

→ Secondary spread of
Bantu language,
1st millennium BCE

Diffusion of Bantu groups and languages.

and differentiation from a mother language is often affected by borrowing from other languages. By taking a set of related words and examining them within a known period, it is possible to calculate the fraction that have retained their original form and meaning and the fraction that have changed. This rate of divergence serves as a clock with which to estimate how much time has passed since the languages diverged from the mother language. Historical linguists call this method *glottochronology*. The formal analysis of *sound shift* is one aspect of glottochronology (Ehret 1998). According to this principle, changes in languages, such as from a *b* sound to a *p* sound in a word, occur in regular ways, following sound shift rules.

There are 2000 common linguistic roots in 28 zones of equatorial Africa, and from this information it is possible to trace 455 roots of proto-Bantu, aspects that all Bantu languages once shared (Guthrie 1967–1972). This core can still be found in the languages spoken by people in Cameroon and Nigeria, such as the Tiv, Efik, Ekoi, and Duala. Thus, this region is presumed to be the homeland of proto-Bantu. Glottochronology indicates that 5000 years ago, Bantu culture began to spread east of this homeland. Around 2000 years ago, continued Bantu expansion went in two directions: a western branch moved along the Atlantic coast, and another moved eastward and then southward through the Great African Rift Valley.

The archaeological evidence, however, does not match the narrative from glottochronology. Linguistic and archaeological data sometimes provide complementary, and sometimes contradictory, evidence about human cultural evolution. Changes in material culture studied by archaeologists are not as easily traced as linguistic changes. Technologies may remain unchanged for centuries, while language changes more rapidly. Furthermore, archaeologists and linguistic anthropologists measure time differently. Thus absolute ages obtained through ^{14}C testing often do not correspond with estimates from glottochronology. Archaeologists say it is possible that the Bantu expansion was simply an imported cultural package, without much actual Bantu population migration or genetic contribution. ■

FOOD FOR THOUGHT

- Consider a case where a language expands its territory without actual migration of its original speakers. What are the political and social consequences of such expansion?

Several North African sites exhibit an intensified pattern of wild plant collection and use. At Nabta Playa, in southern Egypt near Sudan, foragers as early as 8000 years ago collected a wide variety of wild plants, including millet, sorghum, legumes, tubers, and nuts. Some North African sites contain grinding stones used to process wild grains, and some have ceramic vessels.

The Pacific Region: Landscape Management

In what is now Papua New Guinea, by 9000 years ago, highland foraging groups manipulated important food species through selective digging, replanting, and relocation of plant species across the landscape (Latinis 2000, Denham et al. 2003). Some highland staples today, such as *taro* (a starchy root crop), originated in the lowlands and were transferred to the highlands during the Holocene. These initial steps toward food production supplemented generalized foraging.

In Australia, for thousands of years, foragers used fire to burn off dry vegetation, keep pathways open, and encourage the growth of favored food items such as seed-bearing grasses, yams, and cycads (plants in between ferns and palms). In this way, they created and maintained culturally modified landscapes in which specific plant species would thrive with human assistance (Hallam 1989). Such management practices improved the amount and quality of plant resources. Holocene foragers in Australia also began to concentrate on parts of the landscape where yams naturally clustered. In such places, they extracted the tubers and then placed part of the reproductive tissue back into the ground. Regular revisiting of the same gathering grounds became part of a schedule of seasonal rounds for collecting food.

New World Transitions

Plant resources, like other organic remains, are extremely difficult to find in the archaeological record. In the New World as in the Old, evidence of plants as food resources, and of their use in making tools such as nets and baskets, increases. Given its environmental distinctiveness and separate evolution for many thousands of years, the New World offered some unique resources for modern humans.

Pine nuts (or pinyon), for example, played an important role in the emergence of settled life in the southeastern area of the United States in a region called the Great Basin (Zeanah 2002). The Great Basin covers the state of Nevada and extends into southern California, western Utah, and southern Oregon. Just as hazelnut trees proliferated in Europe, Holocene conditions in the New World led to the spread of pinyon woodlands. At the site of Danger Cave, on the border between Nevada and Utah, hulled pinyon nuts have been recovered that date to 6700 years ago. Small but nutritious, pinyons store well. They thus provided winter food and encouraged permanent settlements. Their widespread use also implies the development of food-processing tools to hull the nuts. Stone grinding tools are found at several base camps, while more mobile groups probably used wooden grinding tools.

The Andean region of South America offers insights about the transition to the management of animal herds (Aldenderfer 2002). Findings from three sites in southern Peru indicate that the transition from foraging to managing llama herds around 4500 years ago took place within just a few hundred years. During this short time, people's mobile foraging patterns changed to a semisedentary lifestyle. The rapidity of the transformation suggests that llama management practices were imported from elsewhere, rather than independently invented, reflecting the existence of extensive and strong regional social networks.

Throughout the Old and New Worlds, the changes during the Holocene foreshadow what comes next in the evolution of humanity. Instead of reacting and responding to environmental conditions and the varying availability of certain food sources, humans began to shape their environment and attempt to control and manage food sources. At the same time, social groups increased in size, and expressive culture became more important in establishing and maintaining connections between humans and nature, between humans and other humans, and between humans and the supernatural world.

THE BIG QUESTIONS REVISITED

▪ WHAT are the origins of modern humans?

Anatomically modern humans, or *Homo sapiens,* differ morphologically and culturally from archaic *Homo* in several ways. Their crania are shaped differently, and their bodies are smaller and less robust. Culturally, they are distinguished by greater emphasis on blade technology, in their early stages, and later by an increasing trend toward microlithic technology. Two opposing models for the origin of modern humans, the Multiregional Model and the Recent African Replacement Model, differ in their view about when and where modern humans originated. A third perspective, the Diffusion Wave Model, incorporates some aspects of the first two models; it is the model accepted by the authors of this book. We accept evidence of signs of modern human behavior in the form of stone blades and composite tools dated to 300,000 years ago. Other evidence of cultural modernity includes the catching of large fish, bone harpoons, the ritual use of ochre, and shell bead ornaments.

▪ WHAT was modern human life like during the Upper Paleolithic?

The Upper Paleolithic is the period when modern humans migrated out of Africa into the rest of the Old World and then to the New World. Modern humans in Africa migrated first toward the Levant region. Later, modern humans probably followed a coastal route around India to the paleoregions of Sahul and Sunda, present-day island Southeast Asia and Australia. Modern humans occupied Sahul by 50,000 years ago, or earlier. The extinction of megafauna in Australia, starting around 40,000 years ago, may be related to anthropogenic causes. Stone toolkits in Sunda and Sahul are not modern by African standards. Other aspects of behavior, such as ritual cremation and a rich tradition of rock art, are clear markers of modernity.

Modern humans arrived in Europe around 40,000 years ago, thus overlapping with the Neanderthals, who, though sparsely distributed, continued to exist in Europe for another 10,000 years. Modern human dietary breadth increased, and population density rose. The first stone tool tradition of modern humans in Europe is the Aurignacian tradition. Archaeologists have named other regional traditions, all having type sites in France. Along with a trend toward microlithic tools of stone and bone, the European Upper Paleolithic was a time of artistic creativity, as seen in both portable art and cave art. Population movements into the cold and harsh environments to the east resulted in evidence of human occupation of Siberian sites by 36,000 years ago. Unlike the Neanderthals, modern humans lacked biological adaptations to the environment and relied on cultural innovations instead. Their technology emphasized microblades, and they hunted megafauna.

Modern human settlement of the New World is a contested topic. Most anthropologists accept that modern humans crossed over the land bridge, Beringia, quickly spread throughout the rest of the North America, and then into Central and South America. Evidence of the Clovis culture is widespread in North America, yet some sites show human occupation earlier than Clovis culture. It is likely that several waves of migrating people were involved. Megafauna extinctions in the New World following the arrival of humans suggest anthropogenic effects.

▪ WHAT changes occurred during the Holocene era?

Throughout the Old and New Worlds, with the end of the last glacial age and the beginning of the Holocene, foraging people began to practice various forms of food production. In the Levant, people began to use new tools, such as sickles to harvest wild grain and stone mills to grind grain. These processes supported settled populations. People started to manage animal herds. In northwestern Europe, forest growth provided new food sources, particularly hazelnuts. The first evidence of monumental art comes from a mixed foraging community in Serbia, Lepenski Vir. In Africa, people responded to environmental variations across the continent by establishing settlements in water-rich areas such as the Nile River valley and around inland lakes. In the Pacific region, people began to manage forests by selectively protecting certain plants and transferring plant stocks from one region to another. In Australia, people used fire to burn off unwanted vegetation and promote the growth of favored plants. Resources important in the New World, such as pine nuts and llamas, became part of new economic strategies.

KEY CONCEPTS

anatomically modern humans (AMH), or
    modern humans or *Homo sapiens*,
    p. 224
art, p. 240
Aurignacian period, p. 240
blade, p. 229
broad-spectrum diet, p. 239
cave art, p. 242
Cro-Magnon, p. 239
Clovis, p. 244

composite tool, p. 229
Diffusion Wave Model, p. 226
egalitarian, p. 230
exchange, p. 230
food production, p. 246
Gravettian period, p. 241
microlith, p. 232
Later Stone Age, or LSA, p. 232
Magdalenian period, p. 241
Mesolithic, p. 246

monumental art, p. 247
Multiregional Model, p. 225
portable art, p. 241
projectile point, p. 229
Recent African Replacement Model,
    p. 226
Solutrean period, p. 241
Upper Paleolithic, or UP, p. 234

SUGGESTED READINGS

Jean Clottes. *Chauvet Cave: The Art of Earliest Times*. Paul G. Bahn, trans. Salt Lake City: University of Utah Press, 2003. Chapters in this oversize volume cover the environmental context of the cave, traces of humans and animals in the cave, the cave drawings throughout several chambers, the techniques of cave art used, and a review of the animals and signs drawn. A conclusion provides an anthropological view. Over 200 color photographs are included.

Thomas Dillehay. *The Settlement of the Americas: A New Prehistory*. New York: Basic Books, 2000. This book focuses on efforts to determine who the first modern humans in the Americas were. It reviews dating, paleoenvironments, stone tools, and cultural and linguistic traditions from Paleoindian sites, with emphasis on South America and the site of Monte Verde, Chile.

S. Boyd Eaton, Marjorie Shostak, and Melvin Konner. *The Paleolithic Prescription: A Program of Diet and Exercise and a Design for Living*. New York: Harper & Row, 1988. The authors argue that modern human biology is adapted to a Paleolithic lifestyle, so our bodies today are not well suited to a Westernized, urban lifestyle and diet. According to the "Paleolithic prescription," we should eat less fat and get more exercise.

Clive Gamble. *The Paleolithic Societies of Europe*. New York: Cambridge University Press, 1999. This book reviews the Paleolithic archaeology of Europe and offers insights into the social life of European foragers over 500,000 years of human cultural evolution.

Joan M. Gero and Margaret W. Conkey, eds. *Engendering Archaeology: Women and Prehistory*. Cambridge, MA: Basil Blackwell, 1991. Fourteen chapters explore topics in prehistory from a gender perspective, including analyses of gender and power in the Magdalenian, gender and architectural remains, gender and food in prehistory, women and stone tool-making, women and prehistoric pottery making, and women and art at Lepenski Vir.

Kenneth A. R. Kennedy. *God-Apes and Fossil Men: Paleoanthropology in South Asia*. Ann Arbor: University of Michigan Press, 2003. This book provides an overview of the prehistory of South Asia, from the earliest times to the megalith builders. The last chapter discusses Indian "races" and current DNA evidence about biological diversity on the subcontinent.

B. Kooyman. *Understanding Stone Tools and Archaeological Sites*. Calgary: University of Calgary Press, 2000. The author describes prehistoric technology, lithic reduction and form, sources of raw materials, use-wear, and residue analysis on stone tools.

Sally McBrearty and Alison Brooks. "The Revolution That Wasn't: A New Interpretation of the Origin of Modern Human Behavior." *Journal of Human Evolution*, 39(5), 2000. Two archaeologists discuss differences between the African Middle Stone Age and the European Middle Paleolithic. They provide evidence of modern behavioral innovations of the Middle Stone Age that predate similar evidence in Europe.

Julio Mercader, ed. *Under the Canopy: The Archaeology of Tropical Rainforests*. New Brunswick, NJ: Rutgers University Press, 2003. The essays in this collection address many aspects of the Paleolithic archaeology of the wet tropics. Evidence supports an early prehistoric occupation of rainforests worldwide.

John Mulvaney and Johan Kamminga. *Prehistory of Australia*. Washington, DC: Smithsonian Institution, 1999. This overview of Australian prehistory devotes over half its length to Pleistocene archaeology and the rest to findings from the Holocene.

Christopher Stringer and Clive Gamble. *In Search of the Neanderthals: Solving the Puzzle of Human Origins*. London: Thames and Hudson Ltd, 1993. This book addresses the debate between those who support the Replacement Model for modern human origins and those who favor the Multiregional Model.

David Whitley, ed. *Handbook of Rock Art Research*. Walnut Creek, CA: AltaMira Press, 2001. An overview of prehistoric rock art worldwide, this volume addresses a wide range of topics from analysis of the meaning of rock art depictions to questions of conservation.

THE BIG QUESTIONS

- WHAT major changes occurred during the Neolithic Revolution?
- WHAT were the earliest cities, states, and empires like?
- WHAT lessons do the Neolithic and later times provide about our world today?

The Neolithic and Urban Revolutions

Located high in the Peruvian Andes, the fifteenth-century palace complex at Machu Picchu is among the most spectacular archaeological sites in the world. Machu Picchu was designated a World Heritage site in 1983. (Source: © Robert E. Barber)

f you thought civilization began when beer was invented, you would be right, at least according to some scholars. A theory that foragers settled down in early Neolithic times in order to turn barley into beer is intriguing—though not correct because the earliest direct evidence for beer-making in antiquity comes much later.

At Godin Tepe, a trading post in the Zagros Mountains of Iran dating to 3500 BCE, archaeologists have found the first evidence of beer-making from fermented barley (Michel et al. 1992). Residues in several large clay vessels contain calcium oxalate, a component of the residue known as "beerstone," typical of barley beer, that settles to the bottom of fermentation and storage vats. The pots have a criss-cross pattern of grooves on their interiors, resembling the Sumerian symbol for beer. Other clay jars in the same room at Godin Tepe, containing residues of fermented grapes, provide the earliest direct evidence of wine-making.

By 1800 BCE, drinking beer was apparently popular in Mesopotamia. The Code of Hammurabi, dated to that time, prescribed stiff penalties for bad behavior in drinking establishments. Owners who overcharged customers were condemned to death by drowning. High priestesses caught in such places were executed by burning (Katz and Maytag 1991).

Did people make beer before they made bread? It is still not certain whether beer-making and wine-making preceded other aspects of settled life. One thing is clear: alcohol was probably the catalyst for many a wild night at the lonely outpost of Godin Tepe.

This chapter takes the narrative of humanity's cultural evolution to the time when the foundations of modern life, as experienced by most of us, are established—surplus food production, cities, writing, and complex rituals. The first section discusses the transition to settled life in permanent villages and related developments. The second section reviews examples of early cities, states, and empires. For the first time, historical records now join artifacts as evidence. The third section considers the relevance of changes that occurred during and after the Neolithic to our contemporary lives and the future of humanity.

 ## THE NEOLITHIC REVOLUTION AND THE BEGINNINGS OF SETTLED LIFE

Beginning with the advent of the Holocene era around 12,000 years ago, people in many places across the world started changing their lives in ways that differed fundamentally from previous times. Many began to live in small, permanent settlements, a lifeway called **sedentism**. They started to eat different foods, and they used new ways of obtaining, processing, and storing food. Instead of relying on only wild foods, people turned to plant and animal domestication. **Domestication** is the process by which human selection causes changes in the genetic material of plants and animals. Through human selection, new species form that sometimes bear little resemblance to their ancestors. The earliest methods of selection could have been as simple as removing undesired plants from around desired plants. Later, more intensive kinds of selection took place, with intentional relocation of desired plants into garden areas. The experiments in domestication discussed in this chapter are a major defining feature of humanity's last several thousand years.

V. Gordon Childe, a British archaeologist of the early twentieth century, coined the phrase *Neolithic revolution* to describe the emergence and spread of farming in the Old World (1934). **Neolithic**, which means "New Stone," refers to changes in stone tool technology that became widespread with the first sedentary farmers. This technology included sickle blades made of stone, which were used for harvesting grain, and grinding stones used to process seed crops for consumption

(Piperno et al. 2004). More people started living in permanent houses, using pottery and ceramic vessels for cooking and storage, and burying their dead in cemeteries. These changes are foreshadowed during the Mesolithic, but during the Neolithic they become widespread.

This section reviews the archaeological evidence for the Neolithic era, first in the Old World and then in the New World. Everywhere, the consequences of Neolithic practices were profound, and the era was indeed revolutionary in its long-term effects.

The Neolithic in the Old World

The story of the Neolithic begins in Mesopotamia, especially the region called the Fertile Crescent and the nearby Zagros mountains. Rye, wheat, barley, and other important food crops were first domesticated here, along with animals such as sheep, goat, cattle, and pigs (see Table 9.1 on p. 258). Domestication of plants and animals occurred in several places in the Old and New Worlds. Some of these events resulted from independent invention. In others, **diffusion**, or the spread of culture through contact, was responsible for the Neolithic transition. Further, in considering diffusion, archaeologists seek to learn whether change was brought about by the diffusion of populations (through migration and colonization), or through the spread of ideas, or through a combination of the two (Bellwood 2001).

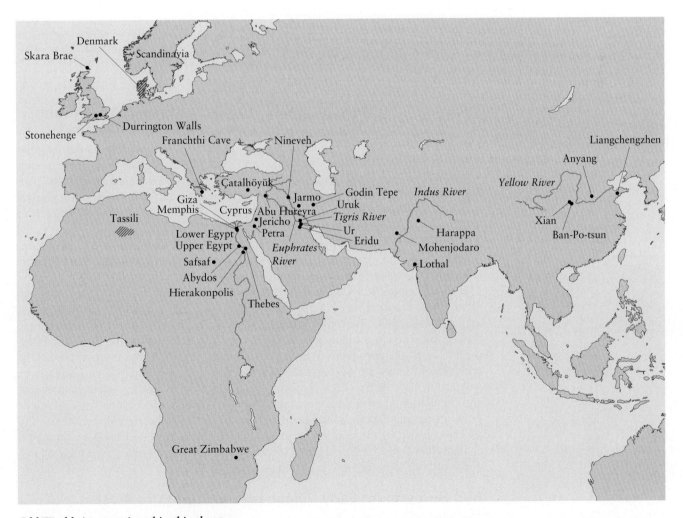

Old World sites mentioned in this chapter.

TABLE 9.1

The origins of selected plant and animal domesticates.

Plants	Region	Approximate Date BCE
Barley, wheat	Middle East	8000–7000
Squash, gourd, maize	Middle America	7000–6000
White potato, chile pepper	South America	7000–6000
Rice, millet, water chestnut	East Asia	6000–5000
Pearl millet, sorghum,	Africa	3000
African rice	Africa	3000
Animals		
Dog	Russia, Eastern Europe	10,000
Sheep, goat	Middle East	7000
Pig, cattle	Middle East	6000
Chicken	China	6000
Horse	Central Asia	4000
Llama, alpaca	South America	4000
Donkey	Middle East	3500
Bactrian camel	Central Asia	2000
Dromedary camel	Middle East	2000
Turkey	Middle America	Unknown

(*Source:* Adapted from pp. 24–25, "The Origins of Selected Plant and Animal Domesticates" from *The Human Impact on the Natural Environments*, 5th ed., by Andrew Goudie. Copyright © 2000. Reprinted by permission of The MIT Press.)

Theories about the Origin of Plant and Animal Domestication

Why did people start to domesticate plants and animals? One prominent theory was advanced by Lewis R. Binford, an American archaeologist (1968). His model says that domestication was an adaptation to new and stressful environmental conditions combined with population growth. Environmental changes were caused by global warming and the consequent rise in the sea level. These factors put pressure on coastal resources and forced people to move inland, into the habitat zone of wild grasses. In confirmation of his theory, many of the earliest villages, such as Jarmo, are located where wild forms of rye, wheat, and barley are found (Braidwood 1960). With continued population growth, these resources, too, were exhausted. Some people responded to this pressure by migrating to even more marginal zones of wild grasses.

Binford's model is called the **Edge Hypothesis,** because it posits that the place where plant domestication first occurred was outside—at the edge of—the areas of greatest natural productivity. Forced by necessity to find alternative sources of food, people concentrated on a few highly productive plants. Through human selectivity and intervention in plant reproduction, certain plants eventually became domesticated. One criticism of Binford's model is that it allows little scope for human agency, creativity, or decision making. The Edge Hypothesis is a *structurist model* in which environment and population growth determined new forms of human adaptation.

More recent theories of the transition to farming emphasize *human agency* and selectivity, within the context of larger structural factors such as environmental change (Bar-Yosef 1998, Flannery 1999). The examples discussed here provide evidence of both structure and human agency at work.

Abu Hureyra: An Early Village on the Euphrates River

Abu Hureyra was a Natufian site located near the floodplain of the Euphrates River (Moore et al. 2000). The Natufians lived in the Levant at the time of the transition from foraging to settled life (review Chapter 8 on the Mesolithic Natufians). At this time, the beginning of the Holocene era, the region was rich in forest resources and wild grasses, and the climate was warmer and wetter than today. Abu Hureyra, like many Neolithic sites in the region, is a **tell,** a human-made mound resulting from the accumulation of successive generations of house construction, reconstruction, and trash. Over thousands of years, tells gradually rose above the surrounding plain. The tell at Abu Hureyra is 8 meters high (about 25 feet).

Abu Hureyra was occupied from 10,500 to 6000 BCE (Moore et al. 2000). The first occupants were sedentary foragers, living in a village of between 200 and 300 people. They hunted gazelle and collected wild plants, including cereals, lentils (pulses), fruits, nuts, and berries. Earliest levels at the site show the stages in the transition to plant domestication. By 10,000 BCE, the occupants had domesticated rye. After 9000 BCE, they had domesticated wheat and barley, though hunting gazelle was still important and gazelle constituted 80 percent of the animal food that people ate. The first domestic grains were probably produced on a small scale, through gardening or **horticulture,** the growing of domesticated plants by using hand-held tools and relying on natural sources of moisture and soil enrichment.

Later levels provide evidence of a fully Neolithic lifestyle combining sedentism and domesticated plants and animals, including two herd animals—goats and sheep. Perhaps because of an increasingly arid environment and human over-hunting, the gazelle population had declined, and domesticated animals gradually took their place as sources of animal meat. The scarcity of wild animal resources, thus, appears to have prompted people to domesticate replacements.

The village grew to 6000 inhabitants by 7000 BCE, when sedentary life was combined with a more intensive form of domesticated grain production called farming or **agriculture,** the growing of crops on permanent plots of land by using the plow, irrigation, and fertilizer. The series of sequential transitions at Abu Hureyra is typical of those at other sites in the Middle East (see Figure 9.1).

Houses at Abu Hureyra were rectangular and made of mud-bricks. Mud-bricks, also called sun-dried bricks, are made of clay mixed with straw or some other tempering material, formed into molds, and dried in the sun (Pollock 1999:53). People at Abu Hureyra participated in long-distance trade, especially of **obsidian,** a prized volcanic glass brought from Turkey and used to make razor-sharp cutting tools. Shell, turquoise, and other rare stones came from throughout the Mediterranean area.

How rapidly did plant and animal domestication proceed? This question is important in terms of explanations for the transition to settled village life and farming. Experimental studies have been conducted, crossing wild plants in the lab and in the field, to see how long it takes to create genetic changes (Hillman and Davies 1990). These studies suggest that the process of plant domestication can be very fast, requir-

Learn more about Abu Hureyra by visiting a web site developed by the primary excavator, M. T. Moore: *www.rit.edu/ ~698awww/statement. html.*

THINKING

OUTSIDE THE BOX

FIGURE 9.1
Stages in the transition to the Neolithic at Abu Hureyra.

- In Natufian times, foragers began to adopt a semisedentary lifestyle.
- Later, they began to domesticate several wild plant species, including barley, wheat, and rye.
- The early experiments in food production took place in zones where the wild ancestors of domesticated plants grew in abundance.
- By the Neolithic, farming was established, followed by the domestication of animals, including sheep and goats.

But why did the Natufians settle down in the first place? Early Holocene environmental changes may have altered the availability of wild animals, making foraging riskier than establishing permanent settlements near abundant wild plant resources.

Neolithic blades made from obsidian, a dense form of volcanic glass. Obsidian tools are as sharp as surgical scalpels. These tools were found at Jericho. The closest source of obsidian is in Anatolia, so extensive trade networks must have existed. ■ What cutting tools do you use in your daily life, what are they made of, and where were they made? (Source: © Pictures of Record, Inc.)

ing no more than a single human generation. This finding opens the possibility of a greater role for human agency and intentionality in models of farming origins, because such a short time frame would allow people to see the results within their own lives.

Çatalhöyük: A Center of Trade and Ritual

Çatalhöyük, a tell site located in central Turkey, was occupied from about 7000 to 6000 BCE. It was a large settlement for its time, measuring about 13 hectares (one hectare is 10,000 square meters, or 0.039 square mile). The tell is nearly 20 meters (over 60 feet) high. The population reached 10,000 at its peak, so Çatalhöyük can be considered either a very large village or a small city.

Located near one of the few obsidian sources in the Middle East, Çatalhöyük probably controlled the regional trade of obsidian, which may explain its prominence. Obsidian nodules were brought to Çatalhöyük, where they were crafted into finished objects and tools. Copper was another important trade item. Brought to Çatalhöyük from the Zagros mountains, it was fabricated into beads for personal adornment. People had other luxury goods in the form of jewelry made of stone and shell, some brought in through trade. Burials, placed under the house floors, often contained exotic and expensive *grave goods*—items interred with the individual. House styles and burials are generally similar, indicating that residents had roughly equal wealth and status.

British archaeologists discovered Çatalhöyük in 1958. Since that time, only a small portion of the tell has been excavated. Current excavations are being carried out by an international team of over one hundred experts including archaeologists, biological anthropologists, cultural anthropologists, paleoenvironmentalists, climatologists, botanists, architects, geologists, geophysicists, chemists, computer experts, and a psychoanalyst. ■ Does this range of expertise leave out any possibly useful area of inquiry? (Source: © Yann Arthus-Bertrand/CORBIS)

During Neolithic times, Çatalhöyük was surrounded by marshy wetlands that were probably flooded for two or three months during the year (Balter 2001). The site was several miles from the wheat and barley fields and the goat and sheep herds on which its residents depended for food. Çatalhöyük's food supplies must have been obtained through trade networks with food producers who lived in outlying areas. Archaeologists suggest that one reason why Çatalhöyük was located where it was is that the wetlands provided a rich supply of limey clay that people used for plastering their walls, floors, and ovens. The plastered walls contain abundant artwork, including sculptures and murals (wall paintings).

Çatalhöyük offers evidence of the existence of **religion**—beliefs and actions related to supernatural beings and forces. Many structures contained rooms decorated with bull and ram skulls that were plastered and painted. Some have enigmatic mural paintings showing vultures, bulls, and people. In a scene repeated in several locations, a woman is shown giving birth to a bull. This image has given rise to considerable speculation about fertility cults and the worship of female supernatural beings. The function of these rooms is also the subject of recent rethinking. An earlier interpretation was that their sole purpose was for religious activity (Mellaart 1967). Ian Hodder offers a reinterpretation of the shrines, proposing that few, if any, were used only for ritual purposes (1999). Instead, Hodder believes they were dual-use domestic and ritual space. This new interpretation does not reduce the importance of religion and ritual at Çatalhöyük; rather, it implies that religion and ritual were integral parts of people's everyday life.

Cattle Before Crops in the Sahel

An independently developed pattern of African domesticates emerged in the Sahel, the grassland regions south of the Sahara desert. For thousands of years, foragers had occupied this region of rich lakesides and abundant wild grasses. Their economy combined fishing, hunting herd animals, and harvesting wild grasses such as millet, sorghum, and African rice. During the Holocene, the Sahel offered more seasonally available food sources than it does now.

The domestication of cattle was the first step in the transition to the Neolithic in Africa (Marshall and Hildebrand 2002). It is likely that people domesticated cattle in order to ensure their availability as food resources. The ritual sacrifice and consumption of cattle may have provided a scheduled pattern of herd thinning. The domestication of wild cattle supported the emergence of **pastoralism,** an economic strategy in which people depend on domesticated animals for most of their food.

Dating of the earliest domesticated cattle herding is difficult because pastoralists have few material possessions and leave few traces on the environment (MacDonald 1999). Direct evidence for domesticated cattle in Chad is dated at 5900 BCE, although other studies suggest a much earlier date, also in Chad, of 9000 BCE. A study of cattle DNA sought the genetic origins of modern cattle (Bradley 2003). Daniel Bradley traveled from his home in Britain to South Asia and then the Sahara, following "the signposts of DNA" back in time to when people first domesticated the wild ox, a dangerous and fearsome beast. His study confirms that domesticated cattle had an early origin in Africa.

Indirect evidence also supports an early origin of cattle domestication in Africa. Rock art paintings in Libya, dated to 5000 BCE, depict people herding animals. Rock art in Egypt depicts cattle carrying burdens, indicating that domesticated animals were used for load-carrying. Another, even more indirect form of evidence for domesticated cattle is related to their use as pack animals. Throughout the Sahara, foragers used stone tools. But the Sahara lacks stones from which tools can be made. At Safsaf, a site in southern Egypt, archaeologists have found unworked stone blocks weighing 40 kilograms (around 100 pounds), a weight that few people could manage to carry (Close 1996). These stone blocks must have been carried in, but probably not by people.

The first domesticated plants in Africa were grown in Egypt and date to 5500 BCE (Fowler 2004). These crops, diffused from the Middle East, required regular moisture

---

and so were limited to the Nile Valley. Several indigenous wild plants, including millet, sorghum, and African rice, were independently domesticated in Africa around 3000 BCE (Harlan 1992). In contrast to the crops planted along the Nile, the indigenous domesticates are drought-resistant savannah plants. The stages of their domestication may have involved a first step of planting wild grasses near lakeside settlements at the beginning of the dry season. Then the foraging groups would move to areas where wild food resources were abundant, returning later to the lakeside areas and harvesting the grasses. This pattern of seasonal migration, and the use of variable food resources at each stopping place, established what would become a regular annual round for many groups across Africa.

The Sahelian sequence of domestication differed from that in the Fertile Crescent in two important ways. The first difference is that, in the Sahel, animal (cattle) domestication preceded plant domestication. People first incorporated domesticated herds of cattle into their foraging pattern and only later incorporated domesticated plants. Second, people in the Sahel did not live in settlements year-round. This mixed pattern of a foraging–herding–farming economy that is semisedentary is unique to Sahelian Africa.

Europe's First Farmers Borrow from the Middle Eastern Package

The transition to the Neolithic in Europe is a story of the introduction of plant and animal domesticates, originally from the Middle East. People adopted selected aspects of the Middle Eastern Neolithic package and adapted them to fit local circumstances and needs. The first plant and animal domesticates appeared in southeastern Europe around 6000 BCE (Richards 2003). By 4000 BCE, farming lifeways had spread across most of Europe (Price et al. 1995).

Early evidence for domesticated plants in Europe comes from Franchthi Cave in southern Greece (Jacobsen 1976). A large collection of preserved plant remains from this site has been obtained using the method called **flotation,** which uses water to recover lighter charred or dried plant remains from heavier soil. Analysis of the remains revealed a sequence of cave use from 18,000 to 3000 BCE. Until 6000 BCE, the cave's occupants were foragers whose diet consisted of wild plants and animals, including shellfish, deep water fish, and terrestrial animals. After 6000 BCE, they began to add domesticated crops such as wheat, especially, and barley to their foraging activities. Over time, reliance on domesticated plants and animals, especially sheep but also goats, increased at Franchthi Cave. Sheep prefer open environments, so they may have been kept in cleared fields. They are more resistant than goats to dry conditions (Perlès 2001).

Lentils (pulses) were an important food plant in the Neolithic in Greece (Perlès 2001). Their drought resistance would have provided a back-up to wheat, which is less drought-tolerant. Some members of village populations may have been semi-sedentary, moving with their animal herds on a seasonal basis. Pottery and ceramic production increased, as did village size, and cave occupation decreased.

Compared to the Middle East, a distinct feature of the Greek Neolithic is the presence of the domesticated dog. Dogs were domesticated in Russia and Central Europe long before herd animals (review p. 241), and their domestication probably spread from there to Greece. Domesticated sheep and goats were introduced from the Middle East, followed by cattle and pigs. Domesticated cattle and pigs spread to the rest of Europe, where they adapted well because they prefer forest living and can adapt to cold temperatures. (Sheep and goats, as noted earlier, prefer an open environment.)

Many questions remain about exactly how the Neolithic spread across Europe: Was it spread through trade, or by the migration of farming people, or by a combination of the two? Was it gradual or rapid? Did Mesolithic foragers choose to become farmers or were they forced to do so by economic necessity? (For recent examples of findings and debates, see Colledge et al. 2004, Pinhasi and Pluciennik 2004, Rowley-Conwy 2004.) It is probably safe to say that no single explanation applies to the entire continent of Europe. Contact through trade probably brought the first domesticated plants and animals into southeast Europe. But migration appears to have played a part in other cases. A study of the early Neolithic on the island of Cyprus indicates the likelihood of migration of Neolithic people from the Levant (Simmons 2004).

During the Neolithic transition in northwest Europe, foragers continued to occupy the coastal margins. By 4000 BCE, these groups had either died out or had become farmers. The prevailing model for northwest Europe's transition to the Neolithic is that there was a rapid transition involving the abandonment of wild marine sources (marine mammals, fish, and shellfish) in favor of terrestrial domesticated food sources (meat and vegetables). The underlying message in this transition model is that people exercised agency and choice, opting to abandon a more "primitive" lifestyle in favor of a more "advanced" lifestyle. Study of people's diets is one way of learning

Interior of a Neolithic house at Skara Brae, the Orkney Islands, northern Scotland. Several such houses, clustered together and dating from 3100–2500 BCE, all have a similar layout and furnishings. ■ Do some research to find out more about the Neolithic in the Orkney Islands. (Source: Mick Sharp Photography)

Reconstructing Prehistoric Diets during the Early Neolithic in Denmark

THE DIETS of the last foragers in northwestern Europe have been studied using a method called stable isotope analysis (*isotopes* are forms of the same chemical element that differ in atomic weight). There are several varieties of stable isotope analysis, depending on which chemical element is used. One form of stable isotope analysis uses the carbon isotopes preserved in an individual's collagen to reconstruct the diet of that individual. Bone has both an inert inorganic component and an organic component, and much of the organic component consists of a complex molecule called collagen.

Plants get their energy through photosynthesis. There are two main forms of photosynthetic pathways: C_3 and C_4. Trees and temperate-climate grasses use the C_3 pathway, whereas tropical and savannah grasses use the C_4 pathway. Marine plants use a mixture of the two pathways. The different pathways result in different proportions of two isotopes of carbon: ^{13}C, which is heavier, and ^{12}C, which is lighter:

- C_4 pathway plants have a higher proportion of ^{13}C.
- C_3 plants have a lower proportion of ^{13}C.
- Marine plants have an intermediate level of ^{13}C.

The important point for archaeologists is that ^{12}C and ^{13}C are *stable isotopes*, which are passed along the food chain and which leave distinctive isotopic signatures. Any animal that a person eats will carry the carbon isotope signatures of the plants it consumed. Thus, when applied to fossil bone, this method reveals whether a person ate fish or terrestrial animals.

In a classic study, Henrik Tauber measured carbon isotopes in fossil remains of late foragers in Denmark (1981). The isotopic signatures show that before farming was introduced, Danish populations ate primarily marine foods such as deep-water fish and shellfish. After the introduction of farming, in Tauber's view, people totally abandoned marine foods and began to eat only terrestrial foods such as meat and vegetables. Thus the shift from a Mesolithic marine food diet to a terrestrial one was a sudden event.

Recent analyses of stable carbon isotopes extracted from human bone recovered from coastal sites in Denmark suggest that the shift from marine to terrestrial resources was not as clear-cut or sudden as Tauber suggested (Richards et al. 2003). Some of the Mesolithic foragers had isotope signatures indicating a mixed diet of marine and terrestrial resources, the latter most likely being domesticated plants and animals. Later, during the early Neolithic, however, diets became dominated by terrestrial species, and this change was quite sudden, around 4000 BCE.

FOOD FOR THOUGHT

- What factors might have prompted the transition in Denmark to completely terrestrial foods and the abandonment of marine resources?

more about the transition period from the late Mesolithic to the early Neolithic (see the Methods Close-Up box).

Europe's later Neolithic brought new developments in food procurement and processing and increased social *complexity* (the emergence of distinct group identities and inequality). Across the continent, abundant archaeological evidence documents social status differences, group ceremonies and feasts, and religious sites that drew thousands of pilgrims from wide areas. The most well-known late Neolithic monumental site is Stonehenge, in southern England. It is one of many similar, though smaller, *henge monuments* in the British Isles, France, and elsewhere (review the Crossing the Fields section in Chapter 1, pp. 21–23). A henge monument is a construction in the shape of a circular enclosure with an opening at one point in the circle. European henge monuments have generally been interpreted as ceremonial sites, some of which also had secular functions such as serving as residential areas.

Although it may also have had some secular use, the henge site of Durrington Walls was clearly a site of ceremonial feasting (Albarella and Serjeantson 2002). Excavations at this site in southern England have yielded a uniquely rich collection of animal bones. Cattle and pig bones were by far the most common animal bones found, and pig bones were far more abundant than cattle bones. The question arises whether the prevalence of pig bones reflects the importance of pigs at the time in people's everyday economy or whether it is due to the ceremonial nature of the site, which may have involved pig sacrifices and pig feasts. Study of the pig remains indicates that most were killed while immature. The pig carcasses were not intensively butchered, but instead the meat must have been cooked and consumed in large chunks. Other evidence suggests episodes of preparing large amounts of meat consumed at one time in a ceremonial feasting situation. An additional indication of ritual or ceremony comes from the unusual finding of embedded flint in several of the bones. The flint is embedded in a way that suggests hunting, although the pigs involved were domesticated, penned animals. Possibly their death was somehow ritualized as part of the ceremonies.

Throughout the Neolithic in Europe, the *built environment,* such as houses and monuments, became more permanent and large-scale (Earle 2004). This trend is related to population growth and the emergence of larger social groups and identity, greater attachment to group-held permanent property, and greater wealth for elites. Attention to burials increased and is evident in the greater inputs of labor and construction materials. Massive chamber graves, built at many places across northern Europe, were constructed using large boulders for the walls and roof. These graves could be reopened, and over time, they contained individuals from many generations. Such massive, stone-marked burials, and permanent attachment by a group to a place is an innovation of the Neolithic.

The Neolithic in the New World

The Neolithic transition in the New World first began in Middle America (or *Mesoamerica*), the region between North and South America. Later transitions in South America and North America occurred partly through independent invention and partly through diffusion, the spread of maize being the most significant factor leading to sedentism in the hemisphere.

Maize and Middle American Transitions

Several features distinguish the pattern of plant and animal domestication and sedentism in Middle America. First, early experiments with domesticated plants took place long before the sedentary pattern evolved, the opposite of the sequence in the Middle East. Second, the wild plants and animals that were potential domesticates were different. Gourds, squash, beans, and maize were prominent plant domesticates, and animal domesticates were dogs, turkeys, and honey bees. Third, the transition to an entirely agricultural way of life was slow, taking thousands of years from 8000 to 2000 BCE. Called the **Archaic,** this period was a time when small bands of mobile foragers, or *Archaic foragers,* gradually incorporated domesticated plants, and later animals, into their mixed economies.

In the 1960s, Richard S. MacNeish of the National Museum of Canada initiated a field study in the Tehuacán Valley, Mexico (1967). Seeking to discover the origins of maize farming, he chose the Tehuacán Valley because dry caves in the arid highlands were ideal places for preserving plant remains. The project generated a collection of over 40,000 plant remains. This research convinced MacNeish that Tehuacán was the site of the first domesticated maize, dated at 5000 BCE.

Later, improved dating techniques showed that the correct date for the corncobs was much later, around 3500 BCE (Long et al. 1989). Thus Tehuacán was displaced as the first center of maize domestication. Now, half a century after MacNeish's first attempt, archaeologists are still searching for the origins of maize. Analysis of plant microfossils suggests that it originated in the Central Balsas River Valley in southwestern Mexico around 5000 BCE (Piperno 2001). The wild ancestor of maize is probably **teosinte,** a wild grass found in highland Mexico.

Even though it is not the place where maize was first domesticated, Tehuacán is an important site in the New World Neolithic. It was first occupied before 10,000

A cob of teosinte and its leaves, center and right, with a cob of modern maize on the left. The location of the earliest domestication of maize is likely to be in southern Mexico. ■ How do you think people first prepared teosinte as a source of food? (Source: Andrew McRobb © Dorling Kindersley)

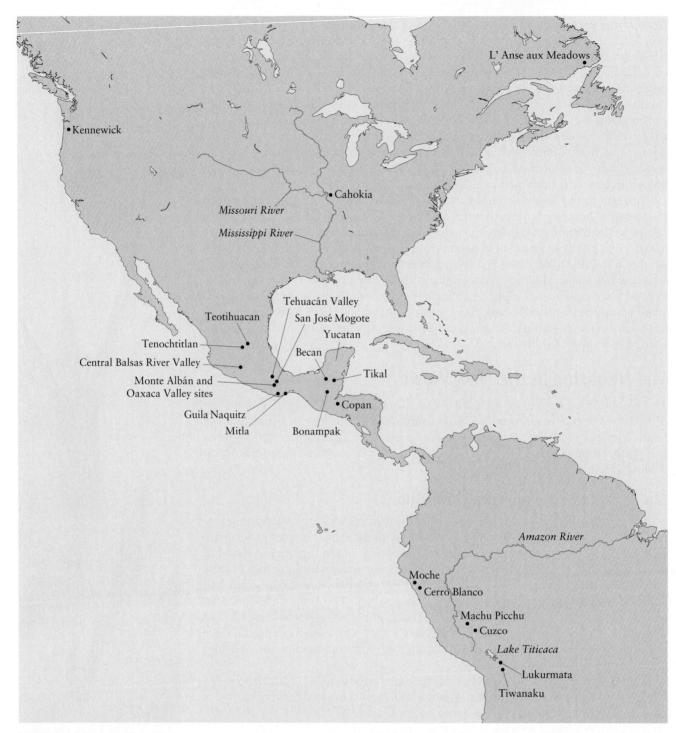

New World sites mentioned in this chapter.

Note: The authors follow the general rule that accents are mainly used in names of Spanish derivation and not for indigenous names.

BCE. At that time, foragers' staple food sources included wild horses and other large game animals. With the extinction of these megafauna, people switched to hunting smaller species such as deer, rabbit, and turtle. They increasingly supplemented their diets with seasonally abundant and highly nutritious wild plant foods such as cactus fruit, acorns, and mesquite pods (these pods, when green, can be eaten whole; when dried, they can be ground into flour for making bread or a beverage). Domesticated plant species became significant parts of the diet after 5000 BCE. The most important domesticated plants were the so-called **Mesoamerican triad,** a consistently found group of three foods: maize (corn), squash, and beans.

Dry cave settings in the Oaxaca Valley have also preserved many plant varieties and other evidence of human activities. During the 1960s, Kent Flannery and a University of Michigan team excavated the cave site of Guila Naquitz (Flannery 1986). The earliest domesticated plants at this site were gourds and squash, dated to 8000 BCE (Smith 1997). There is no evidence of the domestication of maize at this site. The contribution of gourds to the diet was minimal, so perhaps they were domesticated for their value as containers.

Flannery argues that the origin of agriculture in Middle America was an outgrowth of foraging in which many kinds of wild plants and small animals contributed to the diet (1986). It was not possible for foragers to settle down and become full-time farmers until maize was domesticated and sufficiently abundant to support sedentism. That development, according to Flannery, was a matter of human agency and choice; there is little evidence that rapid climate change or population pressure was a significant factor.

Do some Internet research on contemporary uses of bottle gourds.

THINKING

OUTSIDE THE BOX

Potatoes and Other Domesticates in South America

People in the Andes mountains first domesticated the potato, a member of the tuber family of root crops (Ochoa 1991). Tubers are difficult to find archaeologically because they spread by sending out shoots underground rather than by seeds. Thus the date of 5000 BCE for potato domestication is conjectural, based on the assumption that it occurred around the time of other Andean domesticates, including beans, quinoa (an indigenous seed crop), llamas, alpacas, and guinea pigs. Some ancient potatoes have been dated to as old as 8000 BCE, but too few examples from this period have been found to provide a definitive date (see the photograph on p. 327 of some indigenous Andean potato varieties).

Studies of **phytoliths,** or microscopic plant remains, from coastal Ecuador shed light on the origins of plant domestication in lowland areas of the Americas (Piperno and Stothert 2003). In humid conditions, phytoliths survive and can be extracted from soils and even from the surfaces of pots and other artifacts. Phytolith studies show that gourds and squash were also domesticated in Ecuador by 10,000 BCE, pointing to independent domestication.

Imported Maize in North America

By 4000 BCE, people in eastern North America were experimenting with various plants as part of a mixed economic strategy of hunting, collecting wild plants, and cultivating a few domesticated species of seed crops (Smith 1995, 1998). The most important indigenous domesticates were seed crops such as goosefoot (similar to spinach, but also grown for its seeds, related to quinoa of South America), sunflowers, and possibly squash. None of these plants, however, could support a sedentary farming population. Between the first and third centuries of the present era, the introduction of maize led to the emergence of farming communities throughout North America into Canada.

Consider the different contexts of domesticated guinea pigs: first, as a major food source in the Andean region, and second as pets in the United States and Canada. Generate some hypotheses about these different patterns and about the likelihood that guinea pigs will become a major food source in North America and a popular pet in the Andes.

THINKING

OUTSIDE THE BOX

CIVILIZATION: THE URBAN REVOLUTION, STATES, AND EMPIRES

The word *civilization* literally means "living in cities." V. Gordon Childe contributed the notion of the *urban revolution* (1950). Of the several traits that Childe listed as defining early civilizations, one was cities. A city is distinguished from a village or town by having a larger population (say, more than 10,000 people as a rough guide) and by having more specialization, more elaborate architecture, and central services such as temples, government agencies, and trade organizations.

Another characteristic of civilizations according to Childe was a state-level political system. A **state** is form of centralized political organization encompassing many communities. States are typically bureaucratic—that is, they have specialized units with authority over limited areas of governance, with trained personnel and usually written records. States have the power to levy taxes, keep the peace through use of legitimate force, and wage war. The question of the origins of state-level political organization has inspired archaeological thinking and research for many decades. Archaeologists have gained insights about state origins from anthropologists in the other fields, notably cultural anthropologist Robert Carneiro.

CROSSING THE FIELDS

A Theory from Cultural Anthropology about How Early States Formed

Cultural anthropologist Robert Carneiro of the American Museum of Natural History has worked for many years among the living peoples of South America. He is especially interested in the evolution of political authority and in why some societies become more complex than others. Although Carneiro is a cultural anthropologist, his work on the evolution of the state has had a major, though controversial, impact on the thinking of archaeologists.

Carneiro argues that under conditions of **circumscription,** or the tight bounding of societies in small areas, along with population growth, one group will eventually take over another through conquest warfare (1970). These groups evolve into a form of political organization called a **chiefdom,** or cluster of villages under one leader. When one chiefdom conquers another, it is possible that a state will form through the pressure to integrate an even larger population over an even wider area (see Figure 9.2). This idea has stimulated much archaeological research on ancient states and how they formed.

Carneiro developed his model to explain the origins of Andean states, but archaeologists have found evidence for similar patterns of political evolution and warfare among chiefdoms elsewhere in the New World.

The circumscription model may apply to the evolution of Old World States as well. Most Old World archaeologists, however, emphasize the role of trade in state formation. ■

FOOD FOR THOUGHT

■ Choose an example of inter-state warfare in contemporary times, and consider to what extent the circumscription model applies to it.

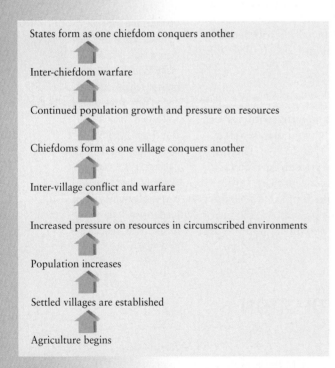

States form as one chiefdom conquers another

⬆

Inter-chiefdom warfare

⬆

Continued population growth and pressure on resources

⬆

Chiefdoms form as one village conquers another

⬆

Inter-village conflict and warfare

⬆

Increased pressure on resources in circumscribed environments

⬆

Population increases

⬆

Settled villages are established

⬆

Agriculture begins

FIGURE 9.2
Carneiro's model of the origin of the state, based on coastal Peru.

Other characteristics of states include **social stratification** (hierarchy and inequality among different groups), surplus production, full-time craft specialization, and some form of recordkeeping, usually writing. Given the cumulative effects of these changes, the urban revolution was, in Childe's sense, indeed revolutionary over the long term.

Cities, states, and empires (an **empire** is a form of political organization that involves rule over multiple states and territories) emerged, in several places throughout the world. There is no explanation for the development of cities, states, and empires that fits all cases. Broad similarities exist in the process, but the precise sequence of changes that brought about their emergence differed in each region. This section looks at cities, states, and empires in first the Old World and then the New.

Underlying the discussion that follows is the importance of two complementary research approaches to understanding ancient civilizations (Pollock 1999:45–46, Balkansky 1998). The first approach is to focus on individual sites themselves through intensive surface studies and excavations. The second, **settlement pattern research,** emphasizes the relationships of settlements in a region with their environment and each other. This approach is informed by settlement surveys that record the distribution and size of sites over a wide area and surface remains, such as architecture, pottery, and other debris. Settlement surveys are done using a combination of aerial photography and on-the-ground mapping and measurement while walking across a particular region (a *pedestrian survey*) or traveling in a vehicle. Settlement pattern research has provided valuable information on primary urban centers, neighboring and satellite cities, and earlier sites within the region.

Old World Cities, States, and Empires

Many theories seeking to explain the causes of urbanization come from archaeologists who work in the Middle East where the management of surplus production and increasing trade are key factors in launching the urban revolution. This section starts with Mesopotamia, home of the world's first cities.

Mesopotamia and the World's First Cities

Mesopotamia, which means "the land between two rivers" (referring to the Tigris and the Euphrates), is the home of the world's earliest cities, dated to 3500 BCE. Important early cities in Mesopotamia include Uruk, Ur, Eridu, and Nineveh, all of which were pre-eminent at different times.

The remains of Uruk in southern Mesopotamia. Occupied starting around 5000 BCE, Uruk had the earliest, grandest, and most numerous monumental buildings in Mesopotamia. The Uruk period saw many innovations including the potter's wheel and the development of cuneiform writing. ■ Do research to learn about the current status of archaeology and cultural heritage preservation in Iraq. (Source: © Nik Wheeler/CORBIS)

An artist's reconstruction of Anu Ziggurat and the White Temple at Uruk, around 3100 BCE. No written documents exist to indicate the amount of labor involved in constructing such monuments, but it was obviously substantial. It is also unclear whether or not the labor was voluntary. ■ In your culture, what are some important urban monuments, who built them, and for what purpose? (Source: © The Granger Collection, New York)

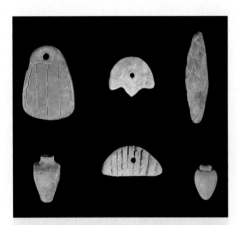

Clay tokens from Susa, southern Mesopotamia. They are dated at 3300 BCE and are probably precursors of later forms of money. The top left token represents one garment. ■ What might the others represent? (Source: © Réunion des Musées Nationaux/Art Resource)

Uruk is a well-studied Mesopotamian city. By 3500 BCE, it covered over 100 hectares (10 soccer fields) and its population was around 10,000 people (Adams 1972, 1981). During the next period, it grew to 400 hectares and 50,000 inhabitants. People lived in houses, made of dried mud-brick, which were packed tightly together and interspersed with narrow, winding streets (Pollock 1999). There is little indication of urban planning in the layout of streets or houses. Surrounding Uruk was a massive brick wall 7 meters (23 feet) high, its numerous gates and guard towers suggesting the need for defense. Monumental architecture included a prominent feature called a **ziggurat,** a massive stepped platform that supported temples and administrative buildings. Government and religion were closely connected, so temples served both sacred and secular purposes, including storage and redistribution of agricultural surpluses, craft production, and economic management and recordkeeping.

Rulers held powerful and privileged positions, and they were believed to be descended from the gods (Pollock 1999:117). Beneath them in the status hierarchy came priests and priestesses, then bureaucrats and military leaders, merchants, craftspeople, agricultural and other commoner laborers, and, last, slaves. Many of the slaves were women and children who worked as weavers, grain grinders, and oil pressers (Wright 1996). It is likely that the commoners and slaves lived outside the city walls in houses made of perishable materials such as reeds. Commoner laborers and slaves built and maintained the monumental buildings in which state rule and commerce were managed, they wove the fine linen garments that elite men and women wore, and they pressed the high-quality oils consumed at royal feasts. The greatness of the early cities was thus based on exploitation of the labor of many commoners and slaves.

Early Mesopotamian cities were centers of regional trade, a feature that some archaeologists view as the primary catalyst for the urban revolution (Algaze 2001). Trade is also seen as the catalyst for the development of the world's earliest writing. Most scholars agree that writing was first invented between 3500 and 3000 BCE in southern Mesopotamia for economic recordkeeping (Lawler 2001). Two other early writing systems emerged at roughly the same time in Egypt and the Indus Valley. So far, though, Mesopotamia retains its claim as home of the oldest writing, though perhaps by only a few hundred years.

Mesopotamian writing, referred to as *cuneiform,* used around 1500 signs, many of which referred to specific goods, such as bread and oil. Specially trained scribes worked in administrative roles in what was an early sort of **bureaucracy,** a form of administration that is hierarchical, specialized, and relies heavily on recordkeeping. The hundreds of thousands of cuneiform tablets that archaeologists have found in early Mesopotamian cities provide a wealth of information about life at the time.

After 2700 BCE, Uruk declined and rival political centers arose. This was a time of intense political competition and warfare in the region. Cities had thick defensive walls, and metal weapons became more common. Militarism was a major means to political power, and armies numbered in the thousands of soldiers. Military leaders conducted campaigns, aided in their mobility by the use of horse-drawn chariots (the wheel was probably invented first in Mesopotamia around 5000 BCE). Successions of city–state rulers rose and fell.

In 2350 BCE, the world's first empire was formed by Sargon of Akkad, whose conquests united southern Mesopotamia. Great as it was, however, the Akkadian empire lasted only 100 years, brought to an end by the misrule of Sargon's grandson. The existence of the empire's capital city, Akkad, is known from textual references but the city has yet to be located by archaeologists.

Egypt's Pharaohs and Imperial Designs

Hieroglyphic inscriptions provide rich information on the emergence of cities and states in Egypt (Brewer and Teeter 1999). In Egypt, as in Mesopotamia and the Indus Valley, the evolution of writing co-occurred with the rise of the state, also around 3300 BCE. Egyptian hieroglyphic writing combines **pictographic** elements (a sign stands for a concept) and phonetic elements (a sign stands for a sound or sounds).

The earliest example of hieroglyphic writing is the Narmer Palette, which depicts the unification of Egypt under King Narmer around 3050 BCE. King Narmer ruled Hierakonpolis, the capital of Upper Egypt (in the south, near the source of the Nile River). Through strategies of alliance formation and warfare, he unified Lower and Upper Egypt, becoming its first king. He established his new capital at Memphis, located between Lower and Upper Egypt, and it became the major urban administrative center of Egypt. At Memphis, a vast walled palace was used for administrative purposes. The ruler's residence was elsewhere, setting a precedent followed by later kings of having palatial residences in several locations. Like other Egyptian cities, Memphis shows no evidence of urban planning.

Many of the best-known monuments in Egypt, such as the Great Pyramids and Great Sphinx at Giza, were built around 2500 BCE. No one knows exactly how the pyramids were constructed, but they clearly involved a massive labor force working over long periods of time. Archaeological research near Giza reveals the presence of bakeries and other services for the laborers. The pyramids were meant to be burial chambers that would protect their inhabitants in their life in the afterworld. Unfortunately, most were looted or dismantled in the distant past. Many royal burials are of queens. A queen might rule as a regent (guardian of a young son who would later become king), as a partner of the king, or in her own right associated with divine powers (Troy 2003). Famous Egyptian queens include Hetshepsut, who reigned in her own right for about ten years; Nefertiti, who reigned as royal wife of Akhenaten; and, much later, Cleopatra, who was Greek and reigned as co-regent with her half-brother.

A phase of empire began between 1550 and 1070 BCE, when pharaohs viewed themselves as rulers of an empire, as evident in such terms as "ruler of the rulers" and "king of the kings" (Morkot 2001). Egyptian pharaohs used military force to conquer and control much of Nubia, the land to their south. Nubia was rich in gold, ivory, ostrich feathers, ebony, and humans, as slaves. Most of the indigenous Nubians were driven out of the Nile Valley, and they took up pastoralism in the surrounding semidesert region. The Egyptians built a small number of urban centers for residential, administrative, and ritual purposes, and the land was devoted to agriculture. Reasons for the end of Egyptian rule in Nubia are unclear, but one factor may be that the gold supplies had been exhausted.

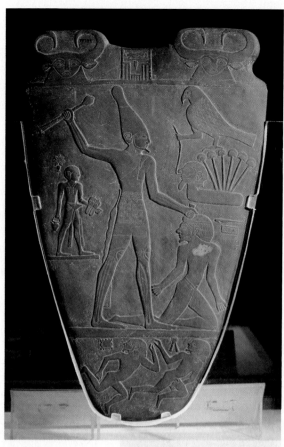

The Narmer palette, made of slate in 3168 BCE, shows Pharoah Narmer wearing a crown and subduing Lower Egypt. ■ How do contemporary world leaders publicize their power? (Source: © Erich Lessing/Art Resource, NY)

The Indus Valley Civilization

A distinct civilization formed in the Indus River valley, in Pakistan and northwestern India. The Indus Valley was home to an urban-based civilization from 2800 to 1700 BCE, although it was first occupied much earlier (Kenoyer 1998). This civilization included several major cities surrounded by lower-order cities. The largest were Harappa and Mohenjodaro. Lothal, a smaller city, was a trading port on the Arabian Sea. Because of the build-up of riverine silt deposits, it is now several miles inland.

Harappa was the first Indus Valley city studied by archaeologists, including the renowned British archaeologist Sir Mortimer Wheeler (Wheeler 1953). At its peak it was over 150 hectares in size and had more than 50,000 residents. Harappa's several

Egyptology, the study of Egypt, is a widely popular hobby as well as a formal academic subject. Visit various Egyptology web sites and learn about the range of interests and opinions involved.

THINKING

OUTSIDE THE BOX

Petra (or Khazneh) is located in present-day Jordan. During the fifth century BCE it was the capital city of the Nabataean people and a powerful commercial center. The site includes many rock-cut tombs, temples, palaces, and houses. It is approached via a narrow gorge known as the Sik. ■ Assume that you have just received funds for a one-week trip to Petra and the surrounding area; plan your flight, domestic travel, and accommodations. (Source: © Andy Chadwick/Getty Images/Stone)

neighborhoods were separated by walls. A massive mud-brick wall surrounded the oldest part, with a main gateway large enough to allow the passage of an ox cart. The gateway opened into a public space that may have been a market or a place for tax collection, or both. The hallmarks of Harappa and other major Indus Valley cities were urban planning, a high degree of craft specialization, and writing.

Advanced urban planning is one of the most distinct features of the Indus Valley civilization. City streets were laid out in a grid pattern, at right angles to each other, with areas for public structures, residences, public baths, granaries, pottery making and grain threshing (Possehl 2002). A reservoir was located in the center of the city, and wells were dispersed throughout the neighborhoods. Many houses contained bath rooms (toilet facilities). Waste water from homes was channeled into the streets and carried away in fired brick drains connected to larger underground drains that carried the sewage beyond the city walls. The city of Harappa is the world's first example of urban planning involving waste management.

People in the rural areas grew wheat and barley and had domesticated cattle, goats, pigs, and chickens. Indus Valley farmers were the first in the world to grow domesticated cotton. Indus Valley people's diets varied depending on their occupation, status, and gender. Studies of the dentition of males and females reveal that females had more *caries* (cavities) and *enamel hypoplasia*, marks in tooth enamel indicating nutritional or health problems during growth (Lukacs 1996). This pattern shows that girls and women had poorer diets than boys and men, perhaps including low-quality roots, tubers, and grains and less high-protein foods.

Full-time craft specialists were an important part of the population of Indus Valley cities. In Harappa, potters, bead makers, shell workers, and copper workers lived and worked in separate districts. Raw materials were brought into the city, where the specialists crafted them into tools, ornaments, and ritual objects. Trade in Indus Valley products extended by sea to Mesopotamia and overland to Central Asia.

The first evidence of Indus Valley writing, dated to 3300 BCE, is a stamp seal (see the photograph on p. 504) (Lawler 2001). Still undeciphered, the Indus script contains over 400 signs and was probably a mainly **logosyllabic** system, in which a sign indicates a word, syllable, or sound, but some signs are pictographic (the sign stands for a concept). Like regional trade, writing served to integrate the hundreds of Indus Valley settlements. Disappearance of the script after 1700 BCE coincides with the decline of the Indus Valley civilization. Around this time, many Indus Valley cities were abandoned, and the civilization came to an end.

Many small terracotta figures have been found at Indus Valley sites, including this cart, which may have been a toy. Animals and humans were the most frequent subjects. Female figurines often have large and elaborate headdresses. ■ What modern children's toys most resemble such Indus Valley artifacts? (Source: © CORBIS)

Scholars disagree about the reasons for the decline of the Indus Valley civilization. One possible cause was a change in the Indus River's path to the sea, which may have damaged the agricultural base of the economy and disrupted trade networks. Another theory proposes that increased rates of malaria were a contributing factor that, along with others, decreased the overall ability of Indus Valley peoples to maintain production levels and trade links. A convincing scenario for its decline has yet to be proposed.

From Dynasty to Empire in China

Early Chinese cities and states developed mainly in two large areas: the northern region along the Yellow River and the southern region along the Yangtze River (see the map on p. 274). One early Neolithic settlement is Ban-po-tsun, located on the Yellow River (Watson 1966). Dated to between 6000 and 5000 BCE, it equaled in size the early urban centers in Mesopotamia. It was divided in separate areas for residences, pottery making, and burials. The staple food, typical of the region, was millet. People had an unusually large number of dogs, perhaps as food sources. This site boasts the excellent preservation of house foundations. Nearly all houses had a square plan, with four pillars supporting a peaked thatch roof (see Figure 9.3 on p. 274).

The transition in China to urbanism and states began around 3000 BCE with the Longshan period, which lasted until 2205 BCE (Chang 1986). Longshan elite burials include rich grave goods such as finely carved jade objects and other luxury items, indicating social stratification. Over time, settlements increased in size and population, and some may have been regional capitals.

Until recently, archaeologists had little information on the transition from Neolithic farming settlements to urban centers and the state in China. Since 1995, archaeologist Anne Underhill has been conducting a large-scale pedestrian settlement survey in northern China to address this gap (Underhill et al. 2002). Working near Liangchengzhen, a Longshan period settlement, she and her team have collected data on hundreds of sites. Results indicate that Liangchengzhen was much larger than previously thought, over 2 square kilometers, and it probably controlled subordinate sites in its region. The survey also shows that Chinese urbanization and state-level political organization were local innovations.

Following the end of the Longshan civilization, northern China entered a period called The Three Dynasties. Starting with the Xia dynasty (2205 to 1766 BCE), China's first written dynastic records were produced. By the Shang period (1766 to 1122 BCE), the Chinese state was established. The Shang dynasty is distinguished by its elaborate bronze work (ritual cooking and drinking vessels, and weapons), high-fired ceramic ware, royal cemeteries, human sacrifice, and *oracle bones* (animal bones and turtle shells used for foretelling the future, with symbols written or incised on them). Shang rulers were considered semidivine beings, and their burials contain rich grave goods and numerous human sacrificial burials. Queens did not rule in their own right but, upon their death, were revered as divine mothers of future kings (Linduff 2003). Society was markedly stratified, from rulers and royal households at the top to the rest of the nobility, to tribute-paying commoners, and, finally, slaves. Warfare was frequent. The Zhou dynasty (1027 to 223 BCE), which replaced the Shang, was a period of population growth, increased urbanization, and intensification of agriculture. **Intensification** refers to the use of inputs of increased human labor and technology such as plowing, irrigation, and fertilizer to improve the agricultural productivity of a given plot of land. The Three Dynasties were characterized by multiple capital cities; some were important for administration, and others were ancestral cult sites. The king, with his court, traveled frequently throughout the kingdom, trans-

The abundance of beads found at Indus Valley sites indicates the popularity of jewelry among men and women. They wore headbands, earrings, necklaces, bracelets, bangles, and waistbands. Beads were made from locally available semiprecious stones such as agate, jasper, and carnelian. Pottery beads were probably worn by people of lower economic standing. ■ What do different kinds of jewelry signify about the wearer in your culture? (Source: © Archivo Iconografico, S.A./CORBIS)

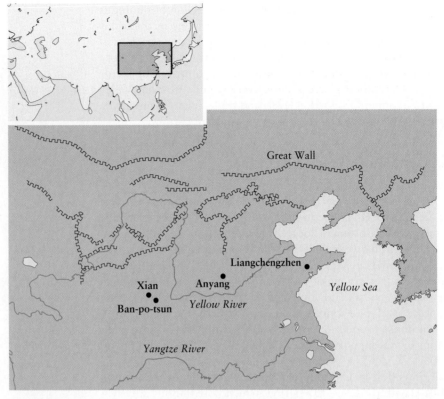

Sites in China mentioned in this chapter. Construction of the Great Wall began in the seventh century BCE and was significantly expanded during the Chin Dynasty. Later dynasties continued building sections throughout subsequent centuries.

acting business, conducting sacrifices, feasting with local officials, and waging war (Keightley 1983).

The Qin (pronounced Chin) dynasty, which lasted only from 221 to 207 BCE, established the first unification of north and south China. The reign of emperor Qin Shi Huangdi is associated with the empire-wide standardization of writing, coinage, and law. The Great Wall across the northern frontier was expanded. The emperor's tomb at Xian (pronounced Shee-An) contains the famous "Terracotta Army," a life-size army of over 7000 soldiers with horses, weapons, and chariots, all meant to serve the emperor through eternity.

FIGURE 9.3

Reconstruction of a Neolithic house at Ban-po-tsun, China. The pattern of the supporting pillars, with interlocking beams over the pillar heads, prefigures later Chinese architecture.
(Source: Adapted from p. 218 in *Atlas of Ancient Archaeology* by Jacquetta Hawkes, ed. New York: McGraw Hill, 1974.)

Great Zimbabwe and Cities without Citadels

Great Zimbabwe and other sites in Africa are known for metalworking in iron, bronze, and gold and for ocean-going trade in these items that extended from East Africa to China (Garlake 1973, McIntosh 1999). Great Zimbabwe was the center of the Shona kingdom during the fourteenth century, but its origins are much earlier, in the Bantu migrations (review the Crossing the Fields section in Chapter 8, p. 249). The word *zimbabwe* means "stone enclosure," and many settlements in this region are distinguished by stone enclosures (Sinclair et al. 1993). But they do not have citadels or any evidence of militarism. Great Zimbabwe is surrounded by the most massive stone enclosures of any African settlement of this time. The walls of the Elliptical Enclosure, the largest single structure at the site, are 10 meters (over 30 feet) high and 5 meters (over 15 feet) thick. Enclosed within the walls are many dwellings, large food storage areas, and ritual buildings. At its peak, Great Zimbabwe was 700 hectares in size and had 20,000 residents.

Trade was an important part of Great Zimbabwe's economy. Trade items included ceramics from China and shell from the Indian Ocean. Great Zimbabwe controlled a vast territory, thousands of square kilometers, although the means of political integration are unknown. Another distinct feature of the economy of Great Zimbabwe and other African sites was the importance of cattle herding in the economy. At the time, the environment was not favorable to intensive agriculture. Pastoralism of cattle, sheep and goats, combined with cultivation of sorghum, millet, and rice, provided food for rural and settled people and surpluses to support the elite.

Great Zimbabwe, along with many other sites throughout sub-Saharan Africa, challenges theorists because these kingdoms differ from prevailing models. They grew in size and complexity without a central administration and military control of large areas. Networks of traders may have created regional economic integration, and centers may have sponsored elaborate ritual events leading to regional social and political identity.

The Vikings and a Failed Colony in the New World

The existence of Viking colonies in North America about 1000, five centuries before Columbus sailed, is confirmed by excavations at the site of L'Anse aux Meadows in Newfoundland, Canada (Ingstad 1977). Still earlier Viking voyages are mentioned in the Icelandic sagas (*eddas*). Viking colonists had left their homelands in Scandinavia and had occupied parts of the British Isles before founding colonies on Iceland and Greenland during the Viking Age, from 800 to 1100—a time of expansion, trading, and raiding as far as the Mediterranean and Caspian Seas (Fitzhugh and Ward 2000).

Given the success of the Vikings in establishing colonies in the British Isles, the question of why their New World colonies failed remains a puzzle. One view is that the failure was due to a combination of environmental circumstances and bad timing (McGovern and Perdikaris 2000). The early Vikings transplanted a farming economy that worked in Scandinavia to Iceland and northern North America, where the environment was unsuitable. Cold winters and short growing seasons made life in North America more difficult than expected. Extensive tree-cutting and the introduction of domesticated animals such as cattle and pigs quickly stripped the vegetative cover and led to catastrophic soil erosion. Conflict with indigenous people may have made matters worse for the Viking settlers. L'Anse aux Meadows lasted just a few years, and the Greenland colonies were abandoned by 1450.

New World Cities, States, and Empires

New World cities, states, and empires formed later than those in the Old World. Their pattern of development is distinct in several ways, including the fact that some did not have writing. Many, however, rival or surpass their Old World counterparts in size, power, wealth, and duration.

Teotihuacan, Mexico: City of the Gods

Teotihuacan is located near modern Mexico City and, like it, was the largest city of its time in the Western Hemisphere. Teotihuacan had over 100,000 residents at its height, many of whom came from other parts of Middle America. Teotihuacan was cosmopolitan in every sense, and it remains the premier example of the Middle American urban tradition (Sanders and Webster 1988). Ritual was a prominent aspect of Teotihuacan life, and it was related to state power. In the words of one archaeologist, the temples and other monuments are "overwhelming" in scale and mass (Cowgill 1992:87).

Few visitors today who walk down the Street of the Dead toward the Sun and Moon Pyramids, amid the monuments (see the photograph on p. 123), are aware of what archaeologists have found in the ruins beyond the center of the city. During the 1960s, archaeologist Rene Millon led an urban survey called the *Teotihuacan Mapping Project* that provided the first systematic data from outside the central monument area (1973). He and his team discovered residential *barrios* (neighborhoods) and mapped over 2000 apartment compounds, many of which had been occupied by members of the same kin groups for decades (see Figure 9.4). Craftwork, especially

FIGURE 9.4

Archaeologist Rene Millon's mapping project revealed that many people living in the residential barrios within Teotihuacan had ties to regions outside the Valley of Mexico. Ongoing research seeks to learn more about the ethnic composition of these barrios, people's social status, and their economic roles within the city.

(*Source:* Adapted from "Plan of the Central Area of Teotihuacan" from *Urbanization at Teotihuacan, Mexico,* Volume I, Part One by Rene Millon. Copyright © 1973 by Rene Millon. Published by University of Texas Press. Reprinted with permission of the author.)

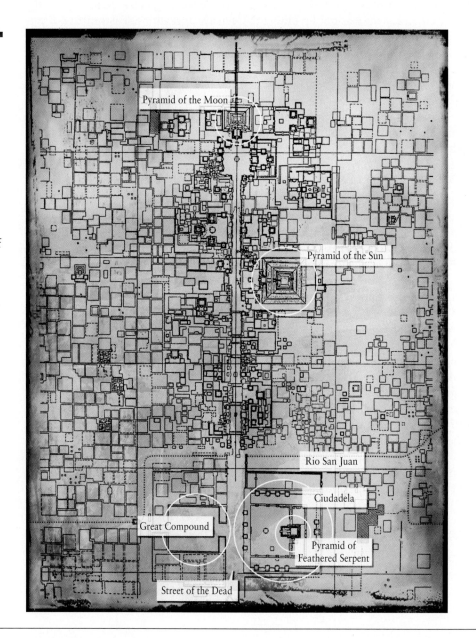

production of obsidian tools and ritual items, was an important part of the economy. Many residents of the city were at least part-time craft specialists.

Teotihuacan's political ties extended far beyond its local region, but the extent and nature of these ties are debated. Did Teotihuacan establish colonies and conquer cities elsewhere in Middle America (Braswell 2003)? The evidence for far-flung conquests is unclear, although economic alliances, as with some sites in the Maya area, were established. Political ties may have been created through regional intermarriages among the class of ruling nobles.

Teotihuacan was destroyed by fire and partially abandoned by 700. Buildings on the Street of the Dead were intentionally set ablaze, but archaeologists do not know why or by whom. Many of the residents left for neighboring cities. The reasons for Teotihuacan's collapse are, like those for most civilizations, debated. Contributing factors included internal political instability, intensified regional competition and warfare, and changing trade routes. The decline of the civilization did not lead to the total abandonment of Teotihuacan. It retained a significant population, at least for a short period, although it was no longer dominant.

Zapotec Civilization and Monte Albán

Zapotec civilization emerged in the Oaxaca Valley, southern Mexico, with its center at Monte Albán (Marcus and Flannery 1996) (see Table 9.2). Monte Albán, established in 500 BCE, is located on a mountain overlooking the valley. On the mountain top, a great plaza, larger than an American football field, was surrounded by monumental public buildings. There the rulers and the elite lived. Other residents occupied hundreds of houses built on terraces cut into the hillside and supported with stone walls. By the year 500, 35,000 people occupied the terraces.

Excavations began in the 1930s at Monte Albán, led by Mexican archaeologist Alfonso Caso. From 1971 to 1980, an American team led by Richard Blanton and Steve Kowalewski conducted a regional settlement study, and this project has since been extended into outlying regions beyond the valley, covering more than 7000 square kilometers (Blanton et al. 1999). Other excavations at several sites in the Oaxaca Valley provide further details about periods immediately prior to Monte Albán's foundation (Marcus and Flannery 1996).

The Monte Albán state emerged in a period of great conflict among competing chiefdoms (Balkansky 2002). It may have been formed through a confederation of such competitors. Or the most powerful of the competing chiefdoms, San José Mogote, may have founded Monte Albán and then begun to conquer its neighbors. Along the lines of Carneiro's model (see Figure 9.2, p. 268), warfare played a key role in state formation in this region. Monte Albán conquered and colonized many areas outside the Oaxaca Valley, and its expansion continued for several hundred years. More than fifty locations, recorded in stone monuments on the city's grand plaza, are claimed as conquered territories.

TABLE 9.2
Selected early new world civilizations.

Name	Location	Approximate Dates	Noteworthy Feature
Zapotec	Southern Mexico	500 BCE–1520s	Capital city of Monte Albán, one of the first New World cities
Classic Maya	Mexico, Middle America	200–900	Most complex New World writing system
Aztec	Central Mexico	1300–1521	Tenochtitlan, the largest imperial city of its time; ruins now buried under Mexico City
Inca	Peru, Andes region	1300–1532	Largest New World empire

Ruins at Monte Albán, the predominant urban center of the Zapotecs. Archaeological research in the Oaxaca Valley shows how, over a 12,000-year period, the valley changed from being populated by foragers with an egalitarian social organization to a state with class-based inequality. Along with changes in social organization came changes in religion with plain-floor ceremonial areas evolving into men's houses and, later, formal temple structures. (Source: © Danny Lehman/CORBIS)

Writing in Oaxaca had its origin in elite competition and warfare (Marcus 1992). It developed into an elaborate mixed system of pictographic and logosyllabic signs. Zapotec writing was concerned with place names and genealogical descent among elites—both important factors in the rulers' claims to political legitimacy and territorial control.

The city of Monte Albán was a major center of political power and a cultural force in a large region for more than 1000 years. The arrival of the Spanish added another layer to its history. Now, its hillsides are being recolonized by the modern inhabitants of the Oaxaca Valley. Along with many other archaeological sites in Mexico, it is a zone where influence is sought by many interest groups, not least the government of Mexico, which seeks to promote expanded tourism based on its rich archaeological heritage. Archaeologists sometimes find themselves in the midst of conflicts about site use and heritage preservation, and some archaeologists are working to devise strategies to resolve conflicting interests (see the Lessons Applied box).

The Maya: An Enduring Civilization in the Tropics

In 1839, explorers John Lloyd Stephens and Frederick Catherwood made the first systematic survey of the Maya civilization in the jungles of Guatemala, and adjacent regions of Mexico and Central America, and their findings raised scientific curiosity about the ancient Maya (Stephens 1969 [1841]). They argued that the ruins of Copan and other Maya centers were remains of true cities. Later scholars disagreed, saying they were vacant ceremonial centers with only small residential populations (Thompson 1954). The notion that a literate civilization could arise in the wet tropics was alien to many scholars whose expectations were shaped by findings in Mesopotamia and Egypt.

Contemporary views of the ancient Maya are very different (Sabloff 1990). Two major factors prompting this change are continued work translating Maya written records and the contribution of settlement pattern studies that reveal relationships among elites and non-elite populations. Many Maya sites, such as Tikal, were vast urban centers with populations numbering in the tens of thousands and with marked social stratification. Elites lived in the city center, and lesser nobles and commoners lived outside the center. Members of the elites were fully literate, and they recorded extensive information about their exalted lineages, life histories, marriages, and ties with neighboring groups. These records provide insight into Maya political dynamics, urban history, and the lives of individual rulers with names such as Curl Nose, Stormy Sky, and Jaguar Paw of Tikal. Like the Zapotecs, the Maya elite wrote about themselves.

Scholars have abandoned a long-prevailing view of the "peaceful Maya," given the discovery of fortified settlements such as Becan and depictions of war captives on the

Archaeologists, Government, and Communities Learning to Work Together in Mexico

NELLY M. ROBLES GARCÍA is an archaeologist who works for the National Institute of Anthropology and History in Mexico. She has participated in many archaeological field projects, but she is especially interested in the complicated relationships among archaeologists, the government, and local communities. All of these groups have strong and differing interests in Mexico's prehispanic sites (Robles 2003).

Today, Mexico's archaeological heritage is in greater jeopardy than ever before because of a combination of factors: dwindling research budgets and administrative cutbacks, urban growth that is rapidly destroying prehistoric and historic sites and monuments, and pressure to promote tourism at archaeological sites in order to generate foreign revenue. This situation is not unique to Mexico. It is shared by all low-income countries faced with the demands of economic growth and competing interest groups. One result of these competing demands is that the preservation of many archaeological sites is in jeopardy.

Robles's difficult job is to balance competing local and national interests and preserve Mexico's cultural heritage for the future. In 1987 she was working with an archaeological team to reinforce the foundations of a colonial-period church in Mitla. The church had been built on top of the foundations of a prehispanic temple platform. She and her crew were approached by a group of people from the local community, shouting and demanding that the crew leave. These angry people told the archaeologists that they had no right to be excavating and accused them of being thieves who wanted to steal from the church.

Robles tried to calm the people down by explaining that the purpose of the excavation work was to reinforce the church and that her team had the permission of the municipal authorities. Her explanation was not well received: "In the midst of all the shouting I suddenly felt a gun barrel pressed against my head. One of the crowd threatened to kill me right there, stating bluntly that the mayor had no right to give permission to work in the church and that I headed a group of thieves." (Go to *http://www.saa.org/publications/oaxaca/cover.html* to read the full case study.)

The team's boss intervened. Speaking in Zapotec, he thrust himself in front of the crowd and, machete in hand, dragged Robles away. For the rest of the excavation in Mitla, the protection of a bodyguard was required. On the basis of this experience, Robles emphasizes that archaeologists tend to ignore the social context and the community relations aspect of their field research until a crisis occurs. Instead, collaborative relations with the community have to be established from the start.

At another level are the Mexican government and its interests. Current government policy in Mexico promotes tourism as the single use for the most prominent archaeological sites. This policy often runs counter to local people's land tenure claims, to the religious practices of indigenous communities, and to the everyday economic interests of families living near archaeological remains. Robles argues that archaeologists and governments must realize that archaeological zones are collective resources spanning multiple levels of interest, including global, state, and local communities. She advocates an approach to archaeological heritage conservation called the *Site-Society Interface*. Thus Robles considers it important first to conduct research about, and with, local communities. The next step is to integrate that research into socially grounded heritage management programs. Only then should archaeological work begin. This approach should have the multiple benefits of ensuring community participation, preventing conflict, and preserving the site's—and people's—archaeological heritage.

FOOD FOR THOUGHT

- Who should determine the fate of archaeological heritage: the local people whose ancestors may have built a site and may be buried in it, the country in which the site is located, or an international body such as UNESCO?

---

murals of Bonampak (Webster 1977, 2000). Studies of the images depicted on carved stone monuments reinforce the new view that warfare and violence were basic facts of Maya life. The importance of blood rituals and human sacrifice in Maya religion further contradict a view of the Maya as mainly peaceful (Marcus 1974, Schele and Miller 1986).

An ongoing debate over the Maya concerns what happened to the Maya cities during the ninth century (Demarest et al. 2003). The Maya urban decline is marked by the end of monument construction and of elite writing on carved stone monu-

Moche portrait vessels, considered a brilliant art style, flourished on the northern coast of Peru around the year 500. Many of the pieces depict high-status males with elaborate headdresses and face painting. This piece of Moche pottery depicts a woman carrying a load. ■ Do research to learn whether the vessels are portraits of actual people or represent generic social categories. (Source: Dave Rudkin © Dorling Kindersley, Courtesy of the Birmingham Museum and Art Galleries)

ments and by dramatic population decline in the major cities. As always, it is difficult to determine why the sudden decline occurred. Little direct evidence exists to support a theory of invasion by outsiders. Current views focus on the fragility of the tropical ecosystem and on the possibility that the Maya had pushed their agricultural system to its limits through overpopulation and deforestation. In such a fragile situation, any short-term perturbation, such as drought or warfare, could have dealt the final blow.

Andean Civilizations: From the Moche to the Inca Empire

The Moche or Mochica civilization emerged around 200 BCE in the deserts of Peru's north coast. Rivers descending from the Andes Mountains fed irrigation works that supported agricultural production to supply dense urban populations (Billman 2002). The Moche civilization is known for distinctive artistic styles and craftwork, especially mold-made portrait vessels and copper, silver, and gold metalwork (Quilter 2002, Shimada 1994). Warfare was an important component of state formation in the Andes, and Moche ceramics often depict warfare and human sacrifice.

Moche civilization reached its height during the first few centuries of the Common Era, although whether it was composed of competing states or constituted a single conquest state is debated. Multi-level adobe platforms, or *huacas*, supported the palaces and burial grounds of rulers. The Huaca del Sol (Pyramid of the Sun) at the site of Cerro Blanco was a solid platform constructed of more than 100 million adobe bricks, each of which had maker's marks. The bricks are probably evidence of communal labor gangs whose contribution to the pyramid was a form of labor tribute called *mit'a*, a practice also found among the Inca (Moseley 1975).

Around the year 500, another early Andean state formed at Tiwanaku, an urban center located on the shores of Lake Titicaca (Stanish 2003). Tiwanaku dominated a large region in the south-central Andes from Peru to Bolivia for the next 500 years. It was the largest city in the Andes, with a population numbering between 40,000 and 80,000 people at its peak. Like other capital cities of complex societies, Tiwanaku dominated many subsidiary centers through an administrative hierarchy (Bermann 1994). Lower-order sites, such as Lukurmata, were *cultural microcosms* of the capital city, containing smaller-scale versions of Tiwanaku-style architecture, such as a platform, temple, and ceremonial burial area.

At the time of the Spanish Conquest in 1532, the Inca had formed the largest empire in the world (Moseley 1992). Tahuantinsuyo is the indigenous term for the Inca Empire and means "the land of four quarters" (MacCormack 2001). The empire was vast, stretching from Colombia in the north to Chile in the south. The city of Cuzco was the empire's capital, and it was linked to distant provinces by a network of roads and bridges (D'Altroy 2002, Hyslop 1990). Llamas and alpacas were important domesticated animals, used for their wool and meat and also as pack animals. The most important food crop was the potato; hundreds of varieties were grown on terraced hillsides. The varied ecological niches in the empire included desert coast, high mountains, and Amazonian rainforest. Andean peoples exploited these niches through colonization and trade. They exchanged products particular to local altitudinal zones, a practice called *zonal complementarity* (Murra 1985).

Administrative strategies included forced resettlement of entire communities, building storehouses and shrines along the highways, and establishing military garrisons in conquered provinces (Morris 1998). The Inca state controlled many aspects of the economy. Its revenues included payments in tribute, often in labor for harvesting food crops and for building and maintaining roads. The Inca never developed a writing system. Instead, state administrators used a system of knotted cords called *quipu* for recordkeeping (see the photograph on p. 505).

North American Chiefdoms: Civilizations without States

As noted in the first section of this chapter, maize spread from its place of origin in southern Mexico to North America. Along with other plants (such as squash and beans) and hunting and fishing, maize cultivation supported the emergence of sedentism and large villages. From the pueblo sites of the United States southwest to the Iroquois nation of the northeast into Canada, many complex societies emerged, developed extensive trade networks, engaged in extensive warfare, and built massive and enduring earthwork monuments. Politically, these societies did not develop state-level institutions but, rather, remained as complex chiefdoms, some of which verged on having urban centers (Earle 1997, Smith 1990).

Many large chiefdom centers contain monumental earthworks and other forms of ritual structures that attracted pilgrims from wide areas, but whose own polities remained autonomous. Dating from the beginning of the present era to about the year 500, hundreds of sites of monumental earthworks were constructed throughout the east-central region of the United States, termed the Hopewell culture (Bernardini 2004). Monuments comprising one square and two circular structures are found dispersed across this wide area, but with remarkable similarity in form. The interpretation is that the monuments were important to the mobile foragers as ceremonial centers.

Later, in the same large region, chiefdoms now called Mississippian cultures emerged, dating to between 900 and 1550. Many large villages were located on or near the floodplains of rivers. They were established after the introduction of domesticated corn made it possible to generate large agricultural surpluses and support a sedentary lifestyle. Annual flooding of the rivers deposited rich soil and supplied moisture, providing ideal conditions for growing maize. The rivers were also important for trade.

Mississippian centers had earthen platform mounds that supported elite residences, ceremonial areas, and burial mounds. Settlement pattern research indicates that these centers are located about 30 kilometers apart from each other. Local leaders gained status through the exchange of prestige goods, in which exotic materials and finished goods were traded over large distances (Peregrine 1992). Chiefdoms formed alliance networks with each other over much of the region.

One of the largest North American chiefly centers was Cahokia, in Illinois (Fowler 1975, Pauketat 2004). Cahokia reached regional prominence around the year 1000. It is located on a vast floodplain where the Mississippi, Ohio, and Missouri Rivers meet. Fish and waterfowl were plentiful, and maize could be grown in abundance in the fertile and well-watered soil of the floodplain. Terrestrial game was available in the forested uplands. Control over the intersection of several major exchange routes was a key factor in Cahokia's rise to prominence. Enormous for its time and place, Cahokia covered an area of 13 square kilometers with a peak population of several thousand people. The site contains a large rectangular plaza surrounded by earthwork mounds.

There were more than 100 earthen mounds at Cahokia. The largest, Monk's Mound, was 30 meters (over 90 feet) high and is the largest earthwork in North America. Monk's Mound, at the center of the site, was built in stages between 900 and 1200. The extent of mound construction at Cahokia is a testament to the organizational capacity of the Cahokian political system to harness labor for construction on a grand scale.

Like other powerful chiefdoms throughout the world, Cahokia had marked social inequality. This inequality is evident in burials, with abundant prestige goods marking high-status burials. Status and gender differences in diet confirm that high- and low-status people had significantly different diets and health (Ambrose et al. 2003). High-status people ate more animal protein and less maize, whereas low-status

THINKING
Develop a theory to explain why elites in many civilizations tend to occupy areas of high elevation.
OUTSIDE THE BOX

Top: A view of the site of Cahokia, located in East St. Louis, Illinois The large mound, Monk's Mound, dominates the site. Bottom: An artist's reconstruction of Cahokia showing thatch-roofed houses and massive earthworks. The site reached prominence around the year 1000 and was largely abandoned by 1400. ■ Visit the web site *www.cahokiamounds.com/cahokia.html.* (Source: © Otis Imboden Jr./National Geographic Image Collection, top; Cahokia Mounds State Historic Site, bottom)

people's diet was more dependent on maize. Low-status females' diet had the highest proportion of maize, about 60 percent. Other paleodiet studies have examined the percentage of maize in the diet and its health effects, from southern California to Canada (Harrison and Katzenberg 2003, van der Merwe et al. 2003). Results show that dietary dependence on maize, in the absence of sources of high-quality protein such as meat, fish or beans, resulted in lowered health status compared to a foraging diet. Low-status groups, usually women and slaves, tended to have higher proportions of maize in their diets.

The site of Cahokia suffered substantial damage in the late 1800s and early 1900s as a result of urban development, construction of roads and railways, expansion of farmland, and amateur collecting (Young and Fowler 2000). Many mounds were bulldozed, and their contents, including human bones and artifacts such as copper goods and shell beads, were used as land fill. Concern expressed by a few archaeologists gradually raised public awareness and put a halt to the destruction and neglect. Cahokia is now a World Heritage Site, and Native American groups from across the United States hold regular ceremonies there. Such collaboration among Native Americans, archaeologists, and government contrasts markedly with what has occurred since the discovery of Kennewick Man (see the Critical Thinking box).

Kennewick Man and Native American Reburial

IN 1996 in Kennewick, Washington, the remains of a 9000-year-old skeleton were discovered in an eroding riverbank. At first, people thought the remains were those of a missing person or murder victim. Closer examination revealed a Cascade-style spear point embedded in the hip, indicating that the individual was an early Native American.

Because few skeletons of this antiquity exist in North America, archaeologists wanted access to the skeleton to study it and gain insights about the first Americans. But Native Americans in Washington state wanted the remains reburied. In accordance with the 1990 protocols of NAGPRA (the Native American Graves Protection and Repatriation Act), the U.S. Army Corps of Engineers confiscated the skeleton, referred to as Kennewick Man, with the intent of returning it for reburial. Several archaeologists brought a lawsuit against the Army Corps. They argued that NAGPRA was being misapplied in this case. The legal wrangling is still ongoing (for a personal account of the episode, see Chatters 2001).

The Kennewick case is the latest manifestation of ongoing debates about Native American reburial. It is part of a long history of conflict and mistrust between archaeologists and native communities (Echo-Hawk 1997, Thomas 2000). Archaeologists who brought the lawsuit against the Army Corps consider Kennewick Man to belong to all of humanity. According to these scholars, the remains are not clearly ancestral to the living tribes of Washington, and any such link between Kennewick Man and modern Native Americans has to be determined through scientific study. Native American groups in Washington and elsewhere consider the skeletal material sacred. They argue that the scientific study of ancient skeletons is both insulting and a sacrilege against their ancestors (Riding In 1992).

Beyond scientific study, displaying skeletal remains is especially offensive, and most museums in the United States no longer do so. As part of the NAGPRA legislation, the Smithsonian Institution and other museums are required to inventory Native American artifacts and skeletal remains, some of which are being returned to the tribes. Yet the debates continue, and scientists and Native Americans are divided among themselves on the issues. Some characterize reburial as a conflict between

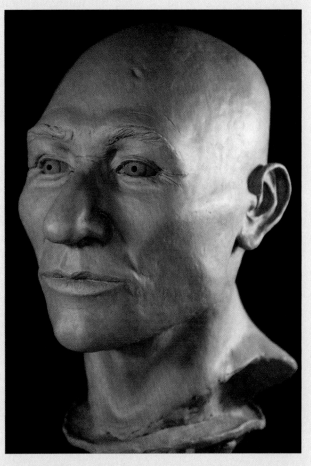

A reconstruction of the head of Kennewick Man. (Source: AP/Wide World Photos)

science and religion. Others assert that the argument is really about the telling of history and about who holds the power to control what is written about the past.

CRITICAL THINKING QUESTIONS

- Should Native American remains that are in museums be returned and reburied?
- Should Native American remains be studied by scientists?
- Is there a middle-ground position that would satisfy all groups?

LESSONS FROM THE NEOLITHIC AND LATER TIMES ABOUT OUR WORLD

Popular opinion tends to take a positive view of the Neolithic innovations of farming and sedentism compared to the life of mobile foragers. But studies of living foragers in the mid-twentieth century yielded some surprising findings (Lee and DeVore 1968). Many foragers were healthy and lived into old age. Their average work week involved far fewer hours of labor than the typical farming family invests today. Archaeology also shows that agriculture and settled life in cities were accompanied by several negative social consequences (Cohen 1977, 1989).

Agriculture as an Adaptive Compromise

Agriculture, first, brought with it much higher rates of population growth (Cohen 1989). This growth was related both to increased food supplies and to the need for family labor to work on the farm (discussed further in Chapter 12). Second, agricultural populations experienced new health and nutrition problems, such as caries (dental cavities) and infectious diseases. Life expectancy declined, and in many areas people's height declined.

These two changes are related to the fact that farming people's diets were more starch-based and less varied and nutritious than those of foragers (Lovell and Whyte 1999). This decline in health is more significant in early New World farming populations who were dependent on maize-based diets than in Asian populations whose diets were based on rice (Tayles et al. 2000).

The Paradoxes of Domestication: Consider the Potato

The potato is a good example of the mixed blessings of plant domestication. From their original home in the Andean region of South America, white potatoes have spread throughout the world (Messer 2000). In Europe, potatoes first gained appeal as a famine food, a fall-back item eaten by the poor during times of food scarcity. In the British Isles, potatoes became a staple food, especially of the poor. In the nineteenth century, potatoes fed workers during the Industrial Revolution. At the same time, dependence on potatoes contributed to the Irish famine.

In the twentieth century, potatoes continued to gain popularity. They are now a standard part of industrialized food production in the form of frozen "French" fries and packaged potato chips. Along with burgers and soft drinks, they are one of the components of what could be called the *McDonald's Triad*.

Human intervention in potato breeding did not stop with initial domestication, many thousands of years ago, in the Andes. "Improved" potato varieties include factors such as size, shape, shelf life, disease resistance, and stress tolerance. For example, in 1995, a genetically engineered potato was developed that was resistant to the potato beetle.

Some food scientists are now concerned that indigenous, heritage varieties of potatoes are being lost and, with them, potentially important biological diversity (see the photograph on p. 327). Efforts are underway worldwide to protect and conserve potato biodiversity. The prehistory, history, and present status of the potato illustrate three paradoxes:

- A mountain food is now grown almost everywhere.
- A poor people's staple is now part of the globalized McDonald's Triad.
- Small, irregular, ancient varieties of heritage potatoes are the focus of scientific attention at international levels.

Civilizations Are Not Forever

Case studies of states have revealed a variety of causes that lead to their rise and decline (Yoffee and Cowgill 1988, Tainter 1988). Archaeologist Joyce Marcus has conducted a comparative analysis of many early states (1998). On the basis of the findings, she maintains that all past states have gone through cycles of expansion and decline followed by regional reorganization and the rise of new states. Marcus's **Dynamic Model** fits well with many individual cases discussed in this chapter, including the Mesopotamian states, the Zapotec civilization, and the Maya civilization. Although each case has unique features, three common patterns emerge:

- In their earliest stages, states tend to reach their maximum territorial extent quickly by conquering neighboring regions and establishing colonies.
- Eventually, even the most powerful states and empires collapse. These periods of decline and eventual dissolution can last many centuries.
- Periods of decline, rather than the more archaeologically visible episodes of powerful territorial states, are the norm. During these periods, former subject provinces gain independence and strength. If they succeed in conquering and integrating territories, the building of a successor state begins.

Why do even the most powerful states inevitably collapse? Marcus suspects that the main reason is the difficulty of maintaining extreme social inequality over long periods. Nonegalitarian structures are inherently fragile and unstable. Because they were the most hierarchical and stratified, the most powerful and wealthy states and empires were often the most short-lived.

Study of the changes during the Neolithic and urban revolutions sheds light on humanity's prospects in the future. Many archaeologists think that anthropogenic effects on the environment contributed to the collapse of many great and powerful civilizations. The Maya civilization is an important case, because the Maya were highly successful at harnessing the productivity of a tropical forest environment for two thousand years. Nevertheless, their civilization, like all others, declined. Maya civilization teaches two lessons: even long-term success does not last forever, and actions taken in the interest of the present may have negative long-term consequences.

The material in this chapter demonstrates that patterns of change in the past can be considered high-risk experiments. Niles Eldredge, of the American Museum of Natural History in New York City, is a paleontologist who has applied lessons from the study of animal fossils to thinking about humans. In his book *Dominion,* which considers humanity's impact on the natural environment, he says that ". . . our cultural heritage proclaims us to be something apart from, even over and above, the beasts of the field. But we have now reached the next crucial phase: *We have become the first species on earth to interact as a whole with the global system . . .*" (italics in the original) (Eldredge 1995:xv). Eldredge is concerned about changes that began with the Neolithic and have since accelerated. He is not alone in his concern. Other scholars have gone so far as to argue that the collapse of our current, globalized civilization is imminent (Sanderson 1999). But try telling that to Sargon of Akkad or Jaguar Paw of Tikal!

- ## What major changes occurred during the Neolithic Revolution?

During the Holocene, many people in the Old and New Worlds began to domesticate a variety of plants and animals as new sources of food. In some places, this transition to domesticated foods preceded settled life in villages; in other cases, people continued to pursue mobile lifeways along with developing domesticates. The earliest plant and animal domestication occurred in Mesopotamia, especially in the Fertile Crescent and the Zagros mountains. Rye, barley, and wheat were the first plant domesticates; sheep and goats the first animal domesticates. In Africa, cattle domestication preceded crop domestication. The Neolithic in Europe was the result of diffusion, either of ideas through trade or of population migration, or both. In northwestern coastal Europe, diets changed from marine-based to terrestrial-based. A different set of domesticates is found in the New World Neolithic. The important domesticated plants are maize, squash and gourds, beans, and potatoes. The important animal domesticates are llamas, alpacas, and guinea pigs.

Theories about why people began to domesticate plants and animals and live in permanent villages tend to emphasize the role of environmental change, loss of reliable foods sources, and population growth. These theories imply that people were forced into new adaptations. Some theories, however, emphasize human agency in bringing about these changes.

- ## What were the earliest cities, states, and empires like?

The increased use of domesticated plants and animals supported larger populations, and population growth itself may have contributed to regional conflict. These and other reasons, including trade and the exchange of ideas, led to the emergence of what are called civilizations, or large-scale societies characterized by residential life in urban centers, development of the state as the prevailing form of political organization, the independent invention of writing in many places, social stratification, trade, and warfare.

Mesopotamia is where the earliest civilizations emerged, first in the southern region, around the city of Uruk. Uruk was a major center of trade, and its writing system—cuneiform—was devoted to recording economic transactions. In Egypt, kings established control over wide areas of the Nile Valley and also had a system of writing—hieroglyphics—that documented the political control of the pharaohs. Around the same time, the Indus Valley civilization developed, with its unique writing system and urban planning. Later examples in the Old World of powerful cities, states, and empires emerged in northern China, sub-Saharan Africa, and Europe.

The earliest New World civilizations are found in Mexico and Middle America, and later on in the Andes mountains of South America and the central riverine floodplains of North America. Most of these civilizations had writing systems, but some did not, even though they administered vast empires.

- ## What lessons do the Neolithic and later times provide about our world today?

Studies of the health and nutritional status of human remains from the time of the transition to agriculture and sedentism show fairly consistent evidence of declines—in some cases for the entire population, and in others for females in particular. The adoption of a mainly starch-based diet with reduced intakes of high-protein food sources resulted in reduced height, increased dental cavities, and more evidence in teeth enamel of growth disruptions in childhood due to malnutrition or disease. Thus, although plant and animal domestication provided more food and more reliable food supplies, the nutritional quality was often lower. In addition, growing social inequality meant that certain segments of the population consistently received lower-quality food. Potatoes are a good example of the paradoxes of crop domestication and agriculture. This indigenous domestic of the Andes has been involved in the Irish famine, in McDonaldization, in genetic modification, and (today) in concern about the loss of ancient varieties.

Comparative study of many examples of state formation and decline indicates that no state or empire lasts forever. One theory suggests that the association of advanced state formation with extreme social inequality is the key to the decline of states. The archaeological lessons for our contemporary world and its complex, dense, and intricate social linkages will be played out in our lifetime and demand urgent attention.

KEY CONCEPTS

agriculture, p. 259
Archaic, p. 265
bureaucracy, p. 270
chiefdom, p. 268
circumscription, p. 268
diffusion, p. 257
domestication, p. 256
Dynamic Model, p. 285
Edge Hypothesis, p. 258
empire, p. 269

flotation, p. 262
horticulture, p. 259
intensification, p. 273
logosyllabic, p. 272
Mesoamerican triad, p. 267
Neolithic, p. 256
obsidian, p. 259
pastoralism, p. 261
phytolith, p. 267
pictographic, p. 271

religion, p. 261
sedentism, p. 256
settlement pattern research, p. 269
social stratification, p. 269
state, p. 268
tell, p. 259
teosinte, p. 265
ziggurat, p. 270

SUGGESTED READINGS

Richard L. Burger and Lucy C. Salazar, eds. *Machu Picchu: Unveiling the Mystery of the Incas.* New Haven, CT: Yale University Press, 2004. This book includes seven chapters, the first of which is a reprinted version of the 1913 article on the site's discovery by Hiram Bingham III. Other chapters discuss Machu Picchu's status as a royal estate, everyday life at Machu Picchu, and the site's contemporary significance, including its role in people's political identity and links to conservation efforts.

Mark Nathan Cohen. *Health and the Rise of Civilization.* New Haven, CT: Yale University Press, 1990. Cohen argues that civilization brought disease and malnutrition. He presents three types of evidence: recent biomedical studies on causes of various illnesses, patterns of health and nutrition among modern foragers, and bioarchaeological data (derived from skeletal remains) on the health and nutrition of prehistoric populations.

Jared Diamond. *Guns, Germs, and Steel: The Fates of Human Societies.* New York: Norton, 1997. The author examines humanity's varied evolutionary trajectories, from the rise of food production and the origins of states to contemporary social transformations. Case studies are drawn from around the globe.

Timothy Earle. *How Chiefs Come to Power: The Political Economy in Prehistory.* Stanford, CA: Stanford University Press, 1997. An expert on chiefdoms compares case studies from Denmark, Hawaii, and Peru, examining the varied political strategies and economic arrangements in this form of organization.

Gary M. Feinman and Joyce Marcus. *Archaic States.* Santa Fe, NM: School of American Research, 1998. This volume is a collection of essays written by leading experts on prehistoric states, emphasizing varied forms and long-term patterns of change. The case studies are drawn from all parts of the globe and underscore the importance of the comparative approach to studying early civilizations.

Clark Spencer Larsen. *Skeletons in Our Closet: Revealing Our Past through Bioarchaeology.* Princeton, NJ: Princeton University Press, 2000. This book focuses on what human skeletal remains reveal about the lives, health, and diet of New World peoples from the Archaic period through European colonialism. Chapters address what the author calls the "population collapse" in the Americas following contact, population decline and extinction in Spanish Florida and in frontier North America.

Katheryn M. Linduff and Yan Sun, eds. *Gender and Chinese Archaeology.* New York: AltaMira Press, 2004. This book's several chapters cover the influence of Marxist political theory and Chinese state values on archaeology in China, data on burial contents, divinities, and textile production. Case studies address gender in the Neolithic, Shang, Zhou, and Han periods.

Joyce Marcus and Kent V. Flannery. *Zapotec Civilization: How Urban Society Evolved in Mexico's Oaxaca Valley.* London: Thames & Hudson, 1996. The authors discuss 12,000 years of prehistoric change, from the earliest occupants of the Oaxaca Valley to the urban revolution.

Patrick E. McGovern. *Ancient Wine: The Search for the Origins of Viniculture.* Princeton, NJ: Princeton University Press, 2003. The author explores the origins of wine, reviewing the evidence from the Neolithic and proceeding to Egypt, Mesopotamia, the biblical Holy Land, and Greece. The last chapter considers the molecular study of wine and what the future of wine studies may hold.

A. M. Moore, G. C. Hillman, and A. J. Legge. *Village on the Euphrates: The Excavation of Abu Hureyra.* Oxford: Oxford University Press, 2000. The authors present a site report describing the discovery of the world's oldest evidence for farming of domesticated grain. Also included are discussions of the innovative field methods used during the early 1970s and an explanation for the transition from foraging to farming.

Bruce D. Smith. *The Emergence of Agriculture.* New York: Scientific American Library, 1998. This volume offers an account of the rise of food production in eight world regions, seeking the common processes at work in this transition.

Bruce W. Trigger. *Understanding Early Civilizations.* New York: Cambridge University Press, 2003. This book examines the development of seven of the best-documented early civilizations: ancient Mesopotamia, ancient Egypt, Shang China, the Aztecs, the classic Maya, the Inca, and the Yoruba. Material is organized in chapters devoted to the topics of political organization, economy, and cognitive and symbolic life.

Norman Yoffee and George L. Cowgill, eds. *The Collapse of Ancient States and Civilizations.* Tucson: University of Arizona Press, 1988. This collection of essays examines notable cases of collapse and highlights the debates about what causes the collapse of civilizations. Case studies include both Old World and New World examples.

PART III Contemporary Human Social Variation

CHAPTER 10
Contemporary Human Biological Diversity

CHAPTER 11
Economic Systems

CHAPTER 12
Reproduction and Human Development

CHAPTER 13
Illness and Healing

CHAPTER 14
Kinship and Domestic Life

CHAPTER 15
Social Groups and Social Stratification

CHAPTER 16
Political and Legal Systems

LARA TABAC, medical anthropologist, works at the New York City Department of Health and Mental Hygiene, along with another cultural anthropologist and 6000 other employees. Her responsibilities with the DOHMH's Epidemiology Services require that she collect qualitative information from New Yorkers about how certain health issues affect their lives.

Tabac describes her job as an "unusual joint venture of words and numbers." She explains that the department is traditionally highly quantitative; it uses statistics to determine health-action agendas. The numbers "tell how many, but they do not tell why. In order to be responsive to the health needs of New Yorkers, the DOHMH needs to know why. This is where I come in."

Formal anthropological training reinforced and shaped Tabac's natural tendency to observe and ask questions. She now puts these skills and interests to work by listening to and talking with people who are affected by various health initiatives.

ANTHROPOLOGY
in the Real World

■ **Lara Tabac, Medical Anthropologist**

"I do a lot of listening on a wide range of topics, and I need only a MetroCard to reach far-flung and eclectic neighborhoods peopled with individuals who share their health dilemmas and life struggles with me, as well as their suggestions for improving the services and programs that will ultimately affect them."

One project that Tabac has been working on analyzes the sexual behaviors of men who have sex with men. Noting an increase in recent years of syphilis cases in this population, the DOHMH believes that the safe-sex message has lost its urgency. Tabac is consequently trying to determine what situations affect whether individuals in this group use condoms and for what reasons they do or do not do so.

To gather qualitative information about the issue, Tabac has spent many hours in Internet chat rooms and conducting open-ended, face-to-face interviews. "As a technique, interviewing is crucial for gaining a deep understanding of sensitive issues. . . . [P]eople tend to be more honest when they don't feel as though they are going to be judged by their peers." She notes that every interview for this project has been valuable.

Another project she has collaborated on involves interviewing injection drug users about unsafe injection practices, which often cause HIV, and other sexually transmitted diseases. Many public health experts believed that if people know how to protect themselves, they will do so, and considerable effort was put into educating individuals at risk. But recent research has disproved this assumption. Tabac's assignment was to discover when and why this assumption fails and to create alternative programs that might have more success in encouraging individuals to protect themselves from infectious disease.

Tabac finds her job with the DOHMH challenging and socially relevant. She took it because she wanted to contribute to improving the quality of people's lives. She has not been disappointed.

THE BIG QUESTIONS

- HOW do contemporary humans vary genetically?
- HOW do contemporary humans vary physically?
- WHAT are some urban challenges to human biology and health?

CHAPTER 10

Contemporary Human Biological Diversity

Biochemical threats to human health and survival have reached a new level of concern. But biochemical weapons, or weapons that employ natural elements, are not new. The English word toxin is derived from the Greek word toxik for poison arrow. Poison arrows may have been decisive in the Trojan War.
(Source: AP/Wide World Photos)

The dark eyes and red hair of many Icelanders have long suggested the possibility of a non-Nordic genetic contribution to the population. The technique most recently used to explore the question of who first settled Iceland is **genome analysis,** the sequencing of an individual's DNA. The results have been inconsistent. At one extreme, a recent study suggests that 86 percent of the genetic markers examined were typical of Scandinavians and thus supports the view that modern Icelanders are genetically homogeneous and mainly Nordic in origin (Helgason et al. 2003). Another study has come to what appears to be a quite different conclusion: that Icelanders are genetically a more or less equal mixture of Celtic and Nordic stock (Árnason 2003). A review of these and other studies reveals that the various researchers are arriving at different conclusions from the same data (Thorgeirsdottir 2004). In other words, there is heterogeneity in the Icelandic population, but from some angles it looks minor and from others significant.

Genetically, Icelandic women are most similar to the Welsh and British, but they also share mtDNA with other groups such as Scandinavians, Russians, Germans, Austrians, and Turkish people. Their phenotype reflects this genetic heterogeneity. Yet when companies market Iceland and Icelandic products, including its genomic database and its national airline, Icelandair, the image they incorporate is usually a young, blonde woman.

This chapter serves as a bridge between the preceding chapters that address the biological and cultural evolution of humanity before the present, and the following chapters that focus on contemporary humans from a cross-cultural point of view. This chapter looks at human diversity mainly from a biocultural perspective.

Humans are one species, yet scientists and nonscientists alike acknowledge that there are differences among individuals, groups, and regional populations, and they apply and use labels for the differences they perceive. This chapter considers which kinds of differences are significant and which are not. It demonstrates that some biologically based differences do "make a difference," either positive or negative, in terms of health, survival, and social success. It also points out that some categories that purport to describe differences among people, such as "race," have little biological reality.

The first section discusses what genomic research reveals about the genetic characteristics of contemporary humans, describes the Human Genome Diversity Project, and addresses the now outmoded concept of "race." The second section provides examples of biological adaptations in response to external factors, such as environmental influences, and takes a look at three genetic diseases. The last section considers how urban life challenges the biology and health of contemporary humans.

CONTEMPORARY HUMAN GENETIC VARIATION

This section first considers what the human genome—the genetic information encoded in the DNA of each individual—reveals about variation across and within contemporary human populations. Every living human has a unique genome yet shares 99.9 percent of their genome with all other contemporary humans, 99.99 percent of it with contemporary humans who share the same recent evolutionary history, and nearly all of it with parents and siblings. (Bear in mind that humans share 90 percent of their DNA with mice, so small percentage differences can be significant.)

Variation in the Genome

It is still too expensive and time-consuming to compare all of the 3 billion or so nucleotides in the human genome, so comparisons are restricted to selected parts of the genome. As noted in Chapter 3, 99 percent of the human genome consists of nuclear DNA, the remaining 1 percent being the mtDNA in mitochondria. The vast majority of the nuclear DNA is in 22 pairs of *autosomes*, the chromosomes common to both sexes, and the rest is in a pair of *sex chromosomes* that differ between the sexes, with females having two X chromosomes (XX) and males an X and a Y (XY). The DNA in the 22 chromosomes common to both sexes and in the X chromosome evolves relatively slowly, whereas changes occur more quickly in the DNA of the Y chromosome and in the mtDNA. Also, because neither the mtDNA nor a substantial part of the Y chromosome (NRY) can have their genetic material shuffled by a process called *recombination* during meiosis (review Chapter 3), small changes in the nucleotides of these parts of the genome are likely to persist.

Thus, if researchers are interested in genetic differences that occurred before 200,000 years ago, for example, they look at the sequence of the nucleotides in the autosomes and in the X chromosome. If they are interested in more recently acquired differences, they focus on nucleotide sequence differences in the Y chromosome and in the mtDNA.

An Ainu woman of northern Japan, with tattooes on her face. The origins of the Ainu people of Japan have long been a puzzle. ■ Do some research to find out if recent DNA studies have shed light on the genetic relationships of the Ainu people to other groups. (Source: © Morton Beebe/CORBIS)

Genetic Variation at Three Levels

Variation in the human genome exists at three levels: *global, regional,* and *individual.* Because scientists cannot possibly investigate the DNA of all 6 billion people in the world, they rely on analyzing population samples at the global and regional levels. They try to select these samples in a random manner—that is, without any bias—to ensure that insofar as possible the samples faithfully reflect the characteristics of the larger populations from which they were drawn. When scientists investigate variation among individuals, these individuals are also selected randomly.

Global Genetic Variation

When exploring the genomic variation of the world's population by analyzing the mtDNA of several hundred contemporary humans from around the globe, scientists found remarkably little genetic diversity. Despite what are often perceived as significant differences among the phenotypes of contemporary humans, there is as much genetic variation within a single group of chimpanzees in West Africa as was found

A mural (wall) painting in an Etruscan tomb, Rome, dating to 700 BCE. The Etruscans, who had dominated northern Italy, were conquered by the Roman Empire. After that, their population declined dramatically, producing a population bottleneck. DNA sequences from 80 prehistoric Etruscans differ enough from that of modern Italian people to confirm the bottleneck model. (Source: © Charles & Josette Lenars/CORBIS)

in the global sample of contemporary humans (Gagneux et al. 1999, Stone et al. 2002).

The variation within the West African chimpanzees is not unusually high, so it must be that the genetic variation among the contemporary humans is unusually low. A probable explanation for the low level of genetic variation in contemporary humans is that within the past few hundred thousand years, there was at least one major population bottleneck when the human population shrank, perhaps to as few as 5000 individuals (Hammer 1995). Such a bottleneck would have screened out most of the existing neutral genetic variation that had accumulated over time and would mark the beginning of the accumulation of neutral genetic differences again.

Another significant aspect of contemporary human global genetic variation is how it is distributed across the globe. Common sense suggests that a person's DNA would be more like that of someone who lives in a nearby town than like that of someone who lives on the other side of the globe. But that is not the case. Between 85 and 95 percent of the overall genetic variation is due to differences within local populations (Owens and King 1999, Rosenberg et al. 2002). The remaining 15 to 5 percent of the genetic variation occurs among contemporary humans on the same continent or on different continents.

Regional Genetic Variation

Most of the evidence for regional contemporary human genetic variation comes from the Y chromosome (Hammer et al. 1997, Jobling and Tyler-Smith 2000) and from mtDNA (Wallace et al. 1999, Mishmar et al. 2003). The Y chromosome is found only in males, so this evidence provides evidence about variation from the male perspective. Because you inherit nearly all your mitochondria from your mother, the mtDNA provides information about genetic variations from the female perspective. Evidence from the Y chromosome and evidence from the mtDNA show similar overall patterns (Tishkoff and Verrelli 2003). Both sets of data suggest that there was and is more human genetic variation within the people sampled from African populations than in the samples drawn from the rest of the world—and this finding is even more striking, given that the continent of Africa has only about 13 percent of the world's population (see map). Two reasons for this finding have been proposed. One is that modern humans have been in Africa longer than in other parts of the world, and that because most of the mutations responsible for differences in nucleotide sequences are neutral, the degree of difference is a simple reflection of the duration of time that the population has been in existence. In other words, the genome of contemporary Africans is likely to be the one that is closest to the ancestral genome of *H. sapiens*. The second reason is related to population size. The smaller amount of genetic diversity outside Africa is due to the fact that non-African populations have, in the past, experienced greater declines in numbers than African populations have (Relethford and Jorde 1999; Eller 2001). For example, many indigenous groups in Asia and the Americas suffered massive population declines during Western colonial expansion.

A comparison of the amount of estimated modern human genetic variation in Africa and the rest of the Old World. ■ (Note: BP means "before present") (Source: © 1999 Kenneth K. Kidd, Yale University. All rights reserved.)

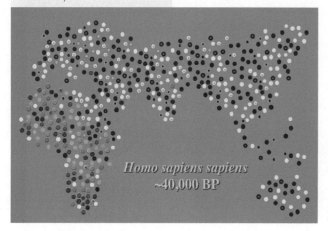

Homo sapiens sapiens
~40,000 BP

Individual Genetic Variation

Comparison of the genomes of individuals focuses on short nucleotide sequences that take different forms. These alternative forms, or "morphologies," are called *polymorphisms*. Differences in DNA that are restricted to one nucleotide, which are called **single nucleotide polymorphisms**, or **SNPs**, have proved to be particularly useful for comparing individuals. The SNP category includes insertions (extra nucleotides) and deletions (the loss of a single nucleotide).

So far, scientists have identified around 6 million SNPs among the 6 billion nucleotides in the human genome. Some are within functional genes, but most are in the 95 percent of the genome that is not directly involved in coding for proteins. Medical researchers are interested in seeing whether people who are prone to particular diseases have distinctive patterns of SNPs. If so, they can then advise people to avoid certain risk factors, and perhaps they can even change the person's DNA (Chakravarti 2001). Ethical problems arise, however, because companies may be instructed by their medical insurers not to employ individuals with particular SNPs. Thus, protecting the privacy of information about an individual's genome is important in order to prevent social discrimination.

The Human Genome Diversity Project

In 2001 it was announced that scientists had produced a draft of the human genome (IHGSC 2001, Venter et al. 2001) based on the genome analysis of between five and ten contemporary human individuals. Since then, scientists working with the *Human Genome Diversity Project* (HGDP) have sought to collect and analyze human genomes from many more people around the world in order to look in more detail at genomic diversity among modern humans. Human genome diversity research focuses on the distribution of differences in nucleotide sequences within and among populations of *Homo sapiens*. It involves collecting biological samples (for example, cells scraped from the inside of the cheek, hair, or blood) from individuals and groups worldwide, and it brings with it important questions about research ethics (see the Methods Close-Up box on p. 298).

Iceland became the first country in the world to have many of the genes of its entire population sequenced, or *mapped*. Following several years of controversy and then vigorous public debate from 1996 to 1999, the government contracted with DeCode Genetics, a private genetics research company, to undertake a comprehensive genetic survey of the Icelandic population, past and present. The project will include using clinical records going back to 1915 to trace the incidence of diseases that have a complex genetic basis, and a genealogical database that seeks to locate all living Icelanders and many of those now dead. The medical and other information about each individual, together with their gene sequences will be stored in a massive database.

Go to the web site *www.oxfordancestors* to learn how individuals can obtain information on their own genetic heritage.

THINKING

OUTSIDE THE BOX

A fter months of public debate, in December 1998, the Icelandic Parliament passed a bill allowing the construction of an Icelandic National Health Sector Database (Pálsson and Harðardóttir 2002). The goal of the project, and the cause of much of the controversy, was to compile medical records for the entire Icelandic population and, from these records, to trace the role of genes in diseases not known to be caused by changes in a single gene.

The license to construct the database was open to competition. The licensee would have to finance the project, but in return, it would for 12 years have the exclusive right to use the data collected for commercial purposes. The database, however, would belong to the Icelandic National Health Service. DeCode Genetics, which was already compiling genetic data in Iceland, outlined the original plans for the health database, and won the contract. DeCode Genetics is financed by venture capital funds coordinated in the United States. The Icelandic National Health Sector Database is just one component of the much larger Icelandic Biogenetic Project (see Figure 10.1 on p. 296).

It is important to consider why the Icelandic gene pool is such an important commodity. First, because Iceland is relatively isolated, its gene pool is more homogeneous

CROSSING
THE FIELDS

Popular Opinion in Iceland on the National Human Genome Project

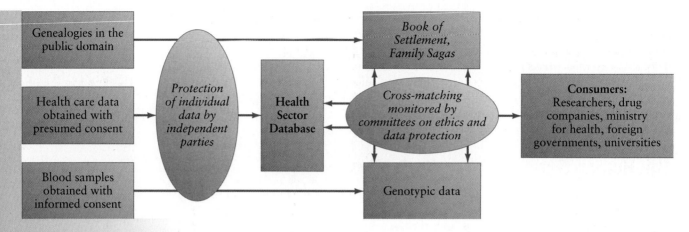

FIGURE 10.1

Components of the Icelandic Biogenetic Project.

(*Source:* Adapted from p. 275 in "For Whom the Cell Tolls: Debates about Biomedicine" by Gísli Pálsson and Kristín E. Harðardóttir. *Current Anthropology* 43, 2002.)

than that of many other countries. Second, its population of around 280,000 provides a database of manageable but scientifically useful size. Third, Iceland has remarkably detailed genealogical records. These include the *Book of Settlement* (written in 1125) and the *Family Sagas,* which are both computerized. Furthermore, Iceland's national census conducted in 1703 was the first of its kind in the world. Finally, Iceland's centralized national medical service has detailed medical records of the islanders that help researchers track disease.

Cultural anthropologists are studying the public reaction in Iceland both to the wider Icelandic Biogenetic Project and to the Health Sector Database. In coordination with researchers at the University of Iceland and the University of Oslo, the University of California at Berkeley has established a web site dedicated to the Human Genome Diversity Project and the Icelandic projects: *http://sunsite.berkeley.edu/biotech/iceland.* Viewers are invited to send their comments to the web site.

One analysis was conducted using several hundred newspaper articles and op-eds published in Iceland that mentioned either the Biogenetic Project or the Health Sector Database (Pálsson and Harðardóttir 2002). The goal of the study was to learn how the public discourse changed over time—either positively or negatively. The newspaper chosen for analysis was the *Morgunblaðið,* which, with a circulation of about 55,000 copies a day, is Iceland's most widely read newspaper. About 64 percent of Icelanders read it daily; an even higher 71 percent read it daily in the capital city, Reykjavik. It prints almost every article sent to it.

From April 1998 through June 2000, the researchers collected a total of 569 news reports and op-ed pieces (including letters to the editor) related to the subject. They classified all these items in terms of whether they were "for," "against," or "neutral" in terms of either the Biogenetic Project or the Health Sector Database.

There have been dramatic changes in the volume of public discourse, with a major peak in October 1998, when the newspaper emphasized the need to clarify issues with detailed analysis and reporting. Over time, most of the news items have been neutral, whereas most of the op-ed pieces have been negative. The op-ed items, which represent the voices of some of the public, are the more interesting set of material. The writers of op-eds fell into five groups: physicians, professional writers (journalists, creative writers), politicians, spokespersons for companies or associations, and the general public. Physicians wrote 29 percent of the op-eds, and their comments were overwhelmingly negative. But only a small number of physicians were responsible for the many op-eds: One physician was the author of 15 of the 54 items

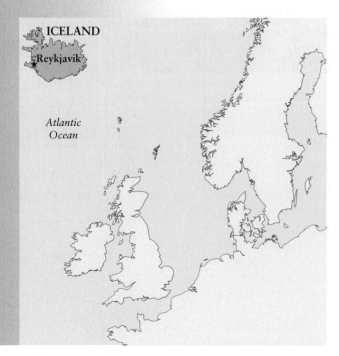

Bathers in the Blue Lagoon, a run-off pond at a geothermal power plant in Iceland. ■ Go to the Web to learn more about Iceland's population. (Source: © Roger Ressmeyer/CORBIS)

in this category. Only in the op-eds written by the general public did positive views out-number negative views.

Many of the concerns about the Health Sector Database involved the confidentiality of personal information. Another was the question of informed consent: The Health Sector Database operates on the principle of *presumed consent.* That is, people can refuse to be included in the database, but if they do not formally refuse, information on them will automatically be entered. A third concern was the issue of property, ownership, and control. A physician commented that the medical records he had kept should not be turned into scientific data. People were also unsure what the appropriate return, or fee, should be for health information. The dominant theme that it is wrong to commoditize and commercialize medical data was expressed in comments such as "The nation is being sold" and in references to "biopiracy."

Supporters emphasized the medical advances the projects would promote and the new employment opportunities they would provide in a stagnating or declining economy based mainly on fishing. Opponents expressed concerns about how to protect the new forms of property that biogenetics research highlights: one's blood and DNA, one's personal identity, and one's life history. ■

FOOD FOR THOUGHT

■ Is the commoditization of DNA, blood, and medical records any different from the commoditization of one's labor (working for pay), the sale of one's land, or the sale or licensing of an idea?

Genetics and "Race"

As noted in Chapter 3, the term *race* was traditionally defined by Western science as a group of people with shared physical traits that were thought to be distinct from those of other groups. But findings about regional and global variation in the human genome show that there are no clear boundaries between and among groups of people according to the traditional notion of "race" (Long and Kittles 2003). Thus science has shown that this old-fashioned concept has no validity. As two anthropologists

Ethics in Genetic Diversity Research

IN 1999 a workshop was held at the University of Wisconsin-Milwaukee to discuss ways of improving ethics in genetic diversity research (Turner 1999). The fifty attendees at the workshop included biological anthropologists, archaeologists, cultural anthropologists, ethicists, attorneys, and members of study populations from across the United States. Discussions focused on:

- the relationship among researchers and study group members.

- group consent for use of biological material.

- the need to protect the financial benefits, health, and privacy of the study groups and their members.

In terms of the first topic, several cases of long-term research relationships were mentioned as good examples. In India, scientists from the United States helped to set up a laboratory at Andhra University to train local scientists in **PCR** technology (PCR is short for *polymerase chain reaction,* the method used to make the large quantities of DNA that are needed for sequencing, or genomic analysis). In the United States, a successful study of prostate cancer among African Americans involved African American physicians in collecting samples and analysis at Howard University in Washington, DC, one of the oldest traditionally African American universities in the country.

Group consent for genetic research is a complex and sensitive issue. Some local populations find it troubling that blood and DNA samples can be stored or transformed into cell lines. When a group gives consent for a particular project, long-term storage may mean that samples are later used in ways not originally described and approved. This problem led to establishment of the principle that the local community must be consulted in all projects involving their biological materials. Another possible solution is to return samples or dispose of them in culturally appropriate ways after the study has been completed.

Protecting the interests of the study population involves several issues, such as providing for biological property rights through patents and preventing social and psychological harm to the study population. A participant at the workshop who is both a geneticist and an attorney explained some of the details of the U.S. patenting process. Apart from concern about their property rights, some members of study populations felt that disease-related studies might expose them to public stigma, and others reported that findings of genetic studies run counter to their own beliefs about their origins. From these discussions, it was clear that in some cases, genetic research will simply not be possible.

The major conclusion was that successful genetic research needs to be based on trust between researchers and study populations. Such trust requires a long-term relationship, participation by study group members in the planning of the research, and explicit agreements to safeguard the financial rights and health of the study population and to discourage undesirable social effects.

FOOD FOR THOUGHT

- If a scientist wanted to conduct a genetic study on your "group," what would that group be and from whom would group consent be obtained? As an individual member of the group, would you be willing to give your consent? If not, why not? If yes, under what conditions?

---

have commented, "More definitions of race or denials of its existence are unnecessary . . ." (Weiss and Mann 1981:483). The authors of this book agree with that statement.

Nonetheless, anthropologists study and describe the biological characteristics of people who belong to particular ethnic groups or *populations*, paying attention to features that group members share, to variation within the group, and to differences that distinguish the group from other populations. An ethnic group, as defined in Chapter 2, is constituted on the basis of a shared history, region, or sense of cultural identity. A **population** is a group of humans who share more genetic material with other group members than they do with members of other populations. Compared to the discredited concept of "race," the definition of a population allows for the recognition of within-group variation in genetic patterning and for the recognition that people who are not part of the population may share some of that patterning. In other words, the perceived boundaries between and among populations are recognized as culturally constructed and to some extent arbitrary and fuzzy.

CONTEMPORARY HUMAN PHYSICAL VARIATION

Throughout human evolution, several major physical adaptations have occurred, such as the shift to bipedalism, larger brains, and a more diverse diet (discussed in Chapter 6). The following discussion describes several adaptations of contemporary humans. We first consider some positive examples of adaptation to environmental factors. Then we turn to diet and show that diets are sometimes adaptive and sometimes maladaptive. Last, we discuss three examples of genetic disease.

Before we proceed, it is useful to review the concept of adaptation. An adaptation is a feature of an organism that enables it to survive and reproduce in its natural habitat more effectively than it could if it lacked that feature. Human adaptations can be divided into three categories:

- Genetic: A **genetic adaptation** is one that, over a long period of time, has been selected for and thus becomes part of the genetic heritage of a population. One example is the evolution of sweating to cool the body in hot climates.

- Phenotypic or physical: These include, first, **developmental adaptation,** the gradual physiological changes that occur during human growth. Second is the *short-term acclimatization* that people undergo when they move from a hot to a cold climate (or vice versa) or from a low-altitude to high-altitude location. Most people unconsciously adjust physiologically to the new conditions in a few weeks.

- Cultural: In many instances, the primary response is a *cultural adaptation,* which is a learned and shared response to environmental stresses. Examples include the use of fire, the construction of housing, and the preservation of food.

Adaptations to the Environment

Over the course of human evolution, populations have adapted to a wide range of environments, each of which is characterized by specific challenges and resources. These adaptations have led to considerable human biological variation, but not so much that speciation has occurred. Living humans are all one species, with different populations sharing different biological characteristics.

Climate

Adaptations to Hot Climates.   Scientists hypothesize that our evolutionary heritage in tropical areas provides contemporary humans with an adaptive advantage in relation to heat. Several studies confirm this hypothesis. Comparisons of different ethnic groups in Malaysia—Chinese Malays, South Indian Malays, and indigenous Malays—reveal that the indigenous Malays experience the least heat stress, a result consistent with their longer-term adaptation to the hot and humid climate (Duncan and Horvath 1988).

Normal body temperature is around 37 degrees Celsius (98.6 degrees Fahrenheit). The highest tolerable levels of body heat are between 40 and 42 degrees Celsius (104–107 degrees Fahrenheit). Stress from excess heat, or **hyperthermia,** is produced by the external environment and by heat generated by the body's metabolism (Beall and Steegman 2000). Extreme heat is one of the most dangerous climatic stressors. In extreme cold, a person can exercise or work to increase body temperature, but engaging in such activities in extreme heat only aggravates the situation. The challenge of surviving heat stress is to maintain the body temperature low enough to allow for operation of the brain, heart, and liver. Sweating is the most important bodily mechanism for removing excess body heat and keeping tissues cool. Among mammals, humans are the best sweaters.

Excess heat causes heat exhaustion, which is marked by weakness, fatigue, headache, impaired judgment, dizziness, faintness, thirst, nausea, vomiting, and mus-

Maasai tribe members, with a male adolescent in the center and two young girls. The Maasai people live in East Africa. Their tall and slender bodies help them to remain cool in an open tropical environment. ■ Consider, in contrast, the adaptive significance of African tropical rainforest people who are typically short in stature. (Source: © Hinsta Haga/HAGA/The Image Works)

cle cramps (Beall and Steegman 2000:184). It is brought on by dehydration and salt loss through sweating. Excess heat also causes heat stroke, a serious illness that may rapidly result in death. Heavy sweating leads to a reduction in plasma volume, which reduces blood flow to the skin. The body's core temperature rises, blood coagulates, and ultimately the brain is damaged and death occurs.

Periods of extreme heat in various parts of the world have caused many deaths throughout history as well as in contemporary times. Most heat stroke fatalities occur among infants, the aged, and the poor during severely hot and humid weather. Infants and elderly people are more vulnerable to extreme heat because they have less heat resistance. Heat resistance is defined as the ability to maintain deep body temperatures below dangerous levels when exposed to excess heat (Beall and Steegman 2000:186). Economically disadvantaged people suffer disproportionately from excess heat because they may be unable to afford more protective forms of shelter and technological aids such as fans and air conditioners.

Another form of health risk from excess heat is *exertional heat stroke,* which occurs among industrial workers, military personnel, and athletes. The threat to life from heat stroke is poorly understood, and no genetic bases have been detected for it. A recent review concludes as follows: "Either heat stroke resistance is not genetically based (removing it from the action of natural selection), or it is genetically based and found in all populations" (Beall and Steegman 2000:184).

Adaptations to Cold Climates.   Life in a cold climate requires the maintenance of internal body temperatures high enough to allow for muscle and joint mobility as well as physical and mental processes. Hands and feet are especially vulnerable to cold. If they get too cold, they will fail to function and may freeze. Adaptations to cold stress include the development of a wide range of responses that maintain internal body temperature and prevent **hypothermia,** or low body temperature.

Indigenous peoples of the Arctic region have evolved some biological protections to extreme cold that are genetic. Genetic defenses against hypothermia include layers of subcutaneous fat (located immediately below the skin), more muscle tissue, and body shape. Members of cold-climate-adapted populations tend to have wider and shorter bodies than members of tropical-climate-adapted populations, a generalization called **Bergmann's Rule** (see Figure 10.2). Bergmann's Rule is based on the principle that heat is lost on the surface of the body through the skin, and thus heat conservation improves with a lower ratio of body surface area to body mass. Humans from cold climates tend to have broader hips than those from hot climates (Ruff 1994). Bergmann's Rule, however, is complicated by other factors, such as the amount of subcutaneous fat, so scientists treat it with caution.

Members of cold-climate-adapted populations also tend to have short arms and legs relative to their height, a generalization called **Allen's Rule.** The logic is the same as that for Bergmann's Rule: shorter limbs reduce surface area and therefore heat loss. Neanderthal body proportions have been termed "hyperpolar" (Trinkaus 1981, Holliday 1997) because they appear to conform to both Bergmann's Rule and Allen's Rule even more than do contemporary Arctic peoples' bodies.

Shivering—a combination of "goosebumps" and involuntary, uncoordinated contraction of the skeletal muscles—is a poorly understood adaptation to cold. A study of Canadian soldiers' frequency of shivering over several very cold months revealed that their shivering declined and their metabolic rate decreased (LeBlanc 1975). Scientists do not really know how shivering works as part of acclimatization to extreme

FIGURE 10.2
Two rules about cold climate and body shape and size.

Bergmann's Rule	Cold-climate-adapted populations tend to have larger bodies than populations adapted to the tropics
Allen's Rule	Cold-climate-adapted populations tend to have shorter arms and legs relative to height than populations adapted to the tropics

cold. It may be that shivering temporarily boosts metabolism. With acclimatization, less shivering may be required as the body establishes a different pattern of ther-moregulation that may include hormonal adjustments.

Another relationship between anatomy and climate involves the nose. Noses are narrower and project more in climates that are colder and dryer. A long and narrow nasal passage increases the surface area of the nasal passage and creates more tur-bulence of incoming air, thus increasing the capacity of the warm nasal passage to heat the incoming air. Again, though, the relationship between nose width and adapta-tion to climate is not clear and simple. For example, variation in nose width may be related more to humidity than to temperature.

The primary defense against hypothermia, however, is cultural (Beall and Steegman 2000:165). Behavioral adaptations include avoiding high-risk situations, wearing appropriate clothing, building shelters, developing technology that provides heat, and avoiding alcohol. Diet is also important. Indigenous Arctic peoples' diets include substantial quantities of fish and marine mammals, which are high in polyunsatu-rated fats (Shephard and Rode 1996). These fats provide the significant amounts of energy needed in cold climates where people burn energy more rapidly.

Altitude

Oxygen pressure is lower at high altitudes than at sea level. The percentage of oxy-gen in the air is the same as that at sea level, but the lower pressure at high altitude means a decrease in the force that pushes oxygen across the lining of the lungs and into the blood vessels (Weiss and Mann 1992). People who are not used to living at high altitudes experience **hypoxia,** or oxygen deprivation. Acute mountain sickness

A member of an indigenous group of the circumpolar region in Canada with a typically short and wide body. Circumpolar people's body shape helps con-serve heat. Cultural adaptations help, too. ■ Make a list of the cultural adaptations that you would want to have with you if you were going to do fieldwork in the Arctic. (Source: © Bryan & Cherry Alexander Photography)

(AMS) is due to hypoxia. People affected by AMS experience headaches, nausea, vomiting, shortness of breath, and severe fatigue.

The capability of highland peoples to tolerate lower oxygen pressure is part of a universal genetic ability to adapt to high-altitude conditions, but an individual has to be exposed to high-altitude conditions as a child in order for the tolerance to shape physiological features. A comparative study of lowland and highland peoples of Peru found that people who were born and raised in the mountains had greater aerobic capacity than those born and raised in the lowlands (Greksa 1991, 1996). The highland people have more red cells in their blood, so their blood has increased capacity to transport oxygen from the lungs to the tissues. Highland children in this study had larger chests at all ages than lowland children. Low oxygen pressure during the growth years may stimulate growth in the chest cavity and lungs. Because both groups are from the same or very similar gene pool, the difference in oxygen consumption is a result of the highland peoples' undergoing developmental adaptation to the environment during growth and development.

Other comparative studies generally confirm the finding that the capacity to tolerate low oxygen pressure at high altitudes is a developmental adaptation. Exactly how this ability is achieved is still unknown, but the fact that it develops within the short period of human growth is a clear example of human physiological, or phentypical, plasticity.

THINKING OUTSIDE THE BOX How do people who have been living at low altitude adjust to high-altitude conditions for activities such as leisure mountain climbing, scientific research, or military activities?

Sunlight

Sunlight contains ultraviolet radiation (UVR), which can damage bare skin. Contemporary humans have lost most of their body hair. This adaptation makes sweating more efficient and improves their capacity to work in warm environments, but it exposes them to sunlight-borne UVR. Anthropologists have suggested that skin color is a way in which our relatively hairless ancestors adapted to sunlight and UVR. Darker skin has more **melanin,** the major pigment responsible for human skin color, than lighter skin. Melanin provides powerful adaptive protection against UVR damage.

Skin color has a nonrandom spatial distribution, if one considers indigenous populations (Jobling et al. 2004:407ff). Indigenous populations with more melanin and hence darker skin tend to be located in the tropics, whereas populations with less melanin and hence lighter skin are found more in northern latitudes. The most plausible adaptive hypothesis for this broad regional pattern is that modern humans are descended from a forest-dwelling ancestor who, like chimpanzees, had light skin covered with dark hair (Jablonski and Chaplin 2000). Thereafter, as human ancestors spread into more open areas with strong sunlight, natural selection would have operated to favor genotypes with more melanin.

Dietary Adaptations

Humans are primates, but unusual primates in terms of their generalized diets. Humans can eat and digest a wide range of items, from insects to blood. In times of famine, people have eaten tree bark and earth to stay alive. Given the basic importance of food intake to individual survival and health, the following discussion concerns aspects of dietary adaptations and dietary trends.

Dietary Quality

To sustain life, humans require a range of nutrients that scientists classify into six broad groups: carbohydrates, protein, fats, vitamins, minerals, and water. The first three, which are termed *macronutrients,* are critical for providing energy for the body and thus are required in relatively large amounts (Leonard 2000). Of these, carbohydrates are the largest source of energy for most humans. Proteins, in addition to providing energy, are critical for growth and replacement of living tissues. Vitamins and minerals are required only in small amounts, so they are called *micronutrients.* Vitamins help the body use energy, and minerals help the body maintain physiological functions. The body cannot function for long without an adequate supply of water. Water accounts for between 60 and 70 percent of adult body weight. A person loses a minimum of several pints of water a day in urine, feces, and perspiration. Unless at least that much water is taken in to replace what is lost, the result is dehydration, and dehydration can be fatal.

Around the world, nutritional scientists and policy makers are involved in determining standards for nutrient requirements. National research organizations set guidelines for their citizens, and international bodies such as the World Health Organization make recommendations that apply worldwide. Standards are usually defined as *recommended daily allowances* (RDAs), or basic levels of intake. RDAs have been developed for every major nutrient. Standards are often determined for an "average" adult, but increasingly, more fine-grained standards have been developed for different age groups and for males and females. Obviously, an individual's daily energy and nutrient needs vary greatly depending on body size, age, and activity pattern. So no single standard can be taken as a hard and fast rule for everyone.

Body size affects nutritional requirements through its effect on metabolism. Larger bodies have proportionally lower metabolic rates than smaller ones, a relationship known as **Kleiber's Law.** This principle applies across all the primate species. Smaller primates' diets must supply proportionately more nutrients and energy than those of larger primates (Leonard 2000:312). Smaller primates consume nutrient-rich foods such as insects, whereas larger primates eat leaves that provide fewer macronutrients per unit weight. Thus the diets of smaller primates are said to be of "higher quality," because they include a higher ratio of animal foods to nonanimal foods.

Humans, however, diverge from Kleiber's Law. Humans are a large primate, yet they generally eat a high-quality diet in terms of nutrient density (Leonard 2000:314). For example, data from several contemporary foraging groups reveal a higher proportion of animal food in their diets than what would be predicted on the basis of their size. Something about human evolution may have prompted a shift toward inclusion of more nutrients and protein in the diet, and a likely candidate is the high metabolic costs of a large brain. Humans devote a large proportion of their daily energy expenditures, around 25 percent, to brain metabolism. A comparative study

This boy lives in Kenya, in the region where Nariokotome boy (see the photograph on p. 207) lived. This boy, though, has rickets, a condition caused by an inadequate diet which produces bone deformities. (Source: © Jeffrey L. Rotman/CORBIS)

In West Darfur, Sudan, over 60,000 refugees live in camps where water and food supplies are inadequate. (Source: © Hartmut Schwarzbach/Peter Arnold, Inc.)

THINKING

OUTSIDE THE BOX

Assume that your job is to promote the consumption of dairy products in China. How will you proceed?

of brain size and diet quality across twenty-five primate species confirmed that relative diet quality is associated with brain size.

Lactase Impersistence and Lactase Persistence

In the majority of the world's populations, the ability to digest *lactose,* the major sugar in fresh milk, is lost shortly after infancy. The inability to digest raw milk and raw milk products is related to a decline in the level of the enzyme *lactase* in the small intestine—something that happens in all mammals and perhaps encourages young animals to accept weaning from their mother's milk to an adult diet. These people, who are referred to as exhibiting **lactase impersistence** (LI), tend to avoid consuming fresh milk and other raw dairy products because eating these foods induces cramping and diarrhea.

In contrast, a minority of the world's people retain intestinal lactase into adulthood and thus remain able to digest lactose throughout their lives. This **lactase persistence** (LP) is a specialized genetic adaptation. Members of LP populations can consume the fresh milk of cows, goats, and camels without having negative reactions. Lactase persistence is especially prevalent, over 70 percent, in people of Northern Europe, Euro-Americans, and some African herding groups (Swallow and Hollox 2000, Swallow 2003). It is intermediate among people in the Middle East, the Mediterranean region, and Central and South Asia. It is low among people of East Asia, Southeast Asia, the Pacific, and Native North America.

The regional distribution is thought to be an adaptation related to the Neolithic shift to animal domestication and dependence on herding and dairy products. This transformation may have prompted the natural selection of people with lactase persistence. A recent study confirmed this possibility through an analysis of population genetic evidence. This analysis revealed strong genetic selection acting on the lactase gene in Northern-European-derived populations 10,000–5,000 years ago, a place and time consistent with the spread of dairy farming (Bersaglieri et al. 2004). Yet although this explanation is generally convincing, it sheds no light on the fact that among neighboring groups in Africa that all depend on animal herds for their livelihood, not all are LP.

In the United States, where the dairy industry is a powerful part of the economy, fresh milk is vigorously promoted as a universally important key to good health (Wiley 2004). All government-recommended healthful diets include dairy products as critical. But the U.S. population includes substantial numbers of LI people, for whom fresh milk consumption causes negative reactions. Agencies charged with educating the public about nutrition make little attempt to devise and promote a more diversified approach to dairy product marketing. Instead, there is a tendency to "pathologize" lactase impersistent people and prescribe medications and other treatments to help them digest fresh milk. A small but growing anti-milk movement protests the ubiquity of messages promoting the consumption of fresh milk.

Genetic Diseases

Some biological anthropologists study the possible associations between specific genotypes and diseases. One common approach is the *cohort study,* in which groups of individuals, usually contemporaries, are identified as possessing or as not possessing specific genetic risk factors (Weiss 1995). Then their medical history is tracked *prospectively,* over time. The analysis determines what percentage of the at-risk and of the not-at-risk individuals have developed the disease. Another approach is to collect family history data. This approach is *retrospective* because it relies on a reconstruction of the past. In either approach, the overall objective is to learn about the distribution of genetic diseases across various populations, a goal of the field called *genetic epidemiology.*

The ABO blood groups were the first human genetic system to be typed on a wide scale (Weiss 1995). Many noninfectious diseases are associated with ABO genotypes, including several forms of cancer (of the stomach, pancreas, colon, cervix, ovary, and breast) and other diseases such as ulcers, diabetes mellitus, and gallstones. The exact mechanisms through which blood genotype affects susceptibility to disease are not known, but current thinking points to links between ABO substances and the human immune system. Three genetic diseases are reviewed here as examples of various ways in which genes are implicated in health problems.

Sickle-Cell Syndrome

Knowledge about the hereditary nature of sickle-cell syndrome marked the emergence, in the mid-twentieth century, of the molecular model in biology and medicine. **Sickle-cell syndrome** is a group of inherited disorders that result from an abnormality in a person's hemoglobin, the part of the red blood cell that contains iron and transports oxygen (Halberstein 1997). The protein component of hemoglobin (Hb) is made up of two chains of amino acids, the alpha and the beta chains. A difference in the sixth amino acid out of 146 in the beta chain is what causes the change from the normal Hb A to Hb S.

The severe, homozygous form of the syndrome is called sickle-cell disease, and the milder, heterozygous form is known as sickle-cell trait (review Chapter 3's discussion of homozygous and heterozygous traits). Sickle-cell disease is a potentially life-threatening condition with symptoms ranging from joint pain to spleen damage. Early childhood growth is impaired. Sickle-cell disease predisposes people to bacterial infections, and affected women are prone to spontaneous abortion. Neonatal and childhood mortality rates are high. At this time, there is no cure for sickle-cell disease. Some drug treatments can reduce symptoms, and blood transfusions and bone marrow transplantation have been successfully used. By contrast, individuals who carry the sickle-cell trait are usually unaware of it.

The first case of sickle-cell disease was diagnosed and reported in 1910 by a Chicago doctor who noted "crescent-shaped" red blood cells in a patient from Grenada, in the Caribbean (Halberstein 1997). More cases were diagnosed, thereafter all in people of African descent. Further research among Bantu peoples in Africa revealed that whereas the sickle-cell trait could be inherited from one parent, sickle-cell disease occurs only when the abnormality is inherited from both parents. The particular geographic/ethnic distribution of the gene in African populations suggests that the sickle-cell trait probably originated in sub-Saharan Africa and then spread through population migration. Adaptationist arguments note that the reduced oxygen caused by the abnormal hemoglobin inhibits malarial infection, and thus natural selection has favored the sickle-cell trait, especially in malaria-endemic areas.

This hypothesis is supported by the difference between the frequency of HbS in indigenous Africans exposed to malaria, which is 8–15 percent, and its frequency in African Americans not exposed to malaria, which is 2–6 percent (Weiss and Mann 1981:82). In the United States, the incidence of sickle-cell trait is highest among African Americans; about 1 of every 400 African Americans has some version of sickle-cell syndrome (The Sickle Cell Information Center 1997). But it is also found among people, and descendants of people, from the Mediterranean area, the Middle East, and India. The high proportion of people of African descent in the Caribbean means that both the sickle-cell trait (Hb AS) and sickle-cell disease (Hb SS) are common there. Sickle-cell trait reaches a level of 10 percent in some of the islands, whereas the prevalence of sickle-cell disease is 0.1 or 0.2 percent.

Most people with Hb AS exhibit no physical symptoms. In contrast, people with Hb SS have slower skeletal development; girls reach menarche 2 to 3 years later; the trunk of the body is shorter; bone infections, called *osteomyelitis*, are common; and cardiovascular effects include an enlarged heart and increased blood pressure.

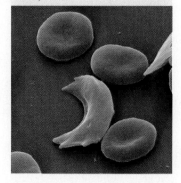

Normal round red blood cells and sickle cells. ■ What other hereditary conditions affect red blood cells? (Source: © Eye of Science/Photo Researchers, Inc.)

Scientists wonder why the sickle-cell trait persists at such high frequencies. In areas where malaria is endemic, the trait is highly adaptive because it promotes resistance to the disease. But why does the trait thrive in nonmalarial areas? One theory is that adult males with the sickle-cell trait are more fertile than males without it (Eaton and Mucha 1971). Subsequent studies have not confirmed this hypothesis, and so the question of the trait's persistence remains unanswered (Ezeh and Modebe 1996).

Like many diseases that affect some ethnic groups more than others, especially underprivileged minority groups, sickle-cell syndrome has ramifications related to social power and control and group identity (Tapper 1999). Genetic information—including the lack of it and the existence and use of it—can be either helpful or hurtful to particular groups. In the United States, controversy related to sickle-cell syndrome arose in the 1970s when four African American army recruits died suddenly during training in Fort Bliss, Texas (Nickens 1996). The men were heterozygous for the sickle-cell gene and, under normal circumstances, would have shown no symptoms. Fort Bliss, where they were training, however, is more than 4000 feet above sea level. At this altitude, less oxygen is available. Like all the other recruits, the recruits who died were subjected to intensive physical exercise within the context of oxygen scarcity, but for them it was a lethal combination. Subsequent public outrage, especially among African Americans, about neglect of the actual and potential dangers of sickle-cell syndrome prompted more research and widespread testing. At the same time, charges of racial discrimination were leveled at proposals to screen couples before marriage, exclusion of sickle-cell carriers (those heterozygous for the trait) from certain occupations, and the possibility of increased insurance rates. Along with vigorous advocacy for research and the development of treatment programs came claims of racism. This two-sided problem—unfair inattention versus unfair attention—links the genetics lab to cultural issues and health policy.

THINKING OUTSIDE THE BOX

What percentage of the world's major diseases are hereditary? Which hereditary diseases are the most prevalent?

Down Syndrome

Down syndrome, which is also known as DS and trisomy 21, is a disorder caused by an error during meiosis that produces an additional third chromosome 21. Thus individuals with Down syndrome have 47 chromosomes instead of the usual 46. Down syndrome is the most common congenital condition in humans, found in 1 of every 800 births in the United States (Benke et al. 1995). One-half to three-quarters of DS fetuses are spontaneously aborted, making DS the most common abnormality in aborted fetuses. Down syndrome is associated with distinctive skeletal features, including a short skull and slowed growth of the base of the skull and face (German 1991). Accompanying problems are short stature, congenital hip dysplasia, deformed fifth fingers, and increased risk of infection and childhood leukemia.

All individuals with DS have extra chromosome 21 material. Children with DS are, however, born to cytogenetically normal parents. Three genetic mechanisms account for trisomy 21 (Benke et al. 1995). The first and most common (over 90 percent of DS births) results from the error in cell division mentioned above, which is called disjunction. The second form (3–5 percent of DS births) is due to another error in cell division called translocation, which occurs when part of a chromosome is translocated to another chromosome. Children with translocation DS have the same appearance and symptoms as those with the first, predominant form of DS. The third form (2–4 percent of DS births) is mosaic Down syndrome, in which trisomy 21 cells are mixed with a second, normal cell line. People with this form of DS have milder symptoms, especially when the proportion of normal cells is large. No matter what form of DS is involved, some of these children fare better than others. The reasons for such differences are not precisely known, but there is some evidence that the variations are due to the kind of care given to the child.

No clear association exists between Down syndrome and ethnicity or lifestyle (Olsen et al. 2003). The only clear association is with maternal age; the highest rates occur among births to mothers over the age of thirty years. But more children on average are born to younger women, so a significant proportion, between 30 and 60 percent, of babies with Down syndrome are born to relatively young women. Some theories suggest links between DS and such maternal behaviors as alcohol or tobacco consumption, use of hormonal or nonhormonal contraceptives, drinking fluoridated water, and exposure to radiation. So far, none of these possible connections has been proven. The role that maternal age plays has not been adequately explained either.

The origins of Down syndrome are unknown. The earliest skeletal evidence of Down syndrome is from Germany, around 350 BCE (Roberts and Manchester 1997:41). The next earliest case is that of a child who lived in the Saxon period in England, between the tenth and eleventh centuries. The child was about nine years old at the time of death. The interpretation is that the child lived that long because of the care it received in the Saxon monastery. Although they are few, these instances of Down syndrome in the past call for explanatory theories that are not narrowly contemporary.

Cystic Fibrosis

Cystic fibrosis is an autosomal recessive disease that affects people who are homozygous; that is, it appears in people who carry two copies of the cystic fibrosis gene (Jobling et al. 2004:441–443). Its frequency is highest in white Europeans and Euro-Americans (40 per 100,000 people). People who do not have cystic fibrosis produce a protein that reduces the stickiness of the mucus produced by the lining of the lung. Individuals with the disease do not produce that protein, and they have sticky mucus that makes them more vulnerable to infections such as pneumonia. In addition to causing increased morbidity (illness), the frequent infections suffered by cystic fibrosis victims mean that they also have stunted growth.

Scientists are trying to determine how the disease got established and why it persists. As with sickle-cell disease, it is possible that people with just one cystic fibrosis gene, so-called heterozygotes, are protected from certain diseases. Research is illuminating the role of one cystic fibrosis gene in relation to the lining of the small intestine and typhoid. In order to infect people, the bacterium that causes typhoid, *Salmonella typhi,* has to enter the cells lining the small intestine (Slatkin and Bertorelle 2001). It does so by linking up with a special type of protein called a receptor. When exposed to *Salmonella typhi,* people without a cystic fibrosis gene absorb substantial amounts of the bacterium. But when people with one copy of the cystic fibrosis gene are exposed to *Salmonella typhi,* they take up very few of the typhoid bacteria. Again, as in sickle-cell disease, being heterozygous is a positive adaptation, whereas being homozygous carries new risks.

Urban Life's Challenges to Human Biology and Health

As noted in Chapter 9, the emergence of sedentary (settled) life in villages and cities occurred only a few thousand years ago. Thus, contemporary humans have not had much time to develop genetic adaptations to the novel stressors of urban life (Schell and Denham 2003). New challenges include changed activity patterns, different diets, often extreme social inequality, psychosocial stress, crowding, pollution, and crime. The **discordance hypothesis** says that contemporary humans are biologically adapted to Paleolithic lifestyles (Boyd Eaton, Shostak, and Konner 1988). This hypothesis is relevant to the question of whether modern humans are suited for urban life.

This section provides examples of urban challenges to human biology and health. Although urban life presents many positive opportunities for people, biological anthropologists are more concerned with the *stressors* involved and with how people, given

In the areas surrounding La Paz, Bolivia, people live in makeshift houses and most do not have access to clean water. (Source: © Chris Lisle/CORBIS)

Learning from the 1865 Cholera Epidemic in Gibraltar

DURING MUCH of the nineteenth century, Gibraltar was a garrison town where several thousand military families lived for up to two years, coming and going in sometimes large-scale and rapid relocations dictated by military needs (Sawchuk and Burke 2003). It was also an important market town, daily attracting a variety of marketers and buyers. Thus Gibraltar was a place of constant population movement and intermingling. It was crowded, with a poorly administered colonial (British) hospital. The residents of nineteenth-century Gibraltar had a higher than normal mortality rate. In 1865, an outbreak of cholera added to the health problems of Gibraltar.

Gibraltar is located on a peninsula, connected to the southern tip of Spain by a flat, sandy strip of land. It is slightly more than 3 miles long and 3.6 square miles in area. Its history has been shaped by its strategic location at the western entrance to the Mediterranean. With no natural resources and little agricultural land, it is dependent on other countries for food and supplies. Most of the territory available for housing has been occupied, in historic times, by military and naval forces. Civilians have had a difficult time finding affordable housing. Compared to other colonial ports and garrison locations, such as Malta and Hong Kong, Gibraltar is unique because of its extremely limited and inhospitable terrain.

The health situation in Gibraltar in the 1860s was dire. The **infant mortality rate (IMR),** or number of infant deaths per 1000 live births, was around 180—a rate similar to the current

IMR in poor countries such as Angola, Sierra Leone, and Mozambique (United Nations 2004). Life expectancy at birth for most years of the 1860s was around thirty years; it dropped to nineteen years in 1865. During the 1860s, several epidemics spread throughout the population (see Figure 10.3). Of all of these epidemics, the cholera epidemic of 1865 had the most damaging effects on life expectancy. Cholera, widely feared throughout the nineteenth century, can kill a person within a few hours with rapid dehydration accompanied by violent

FIGURE 10.3
Epidemics in Gibraltar in the 1860s

Year	Epidemic
1860	Cholera, smallpox
1862	Scarlet fever
1864	Measles
1865	Cholera, smallpox
1867	Scarlet fever
1868	Measles

(*Source:* Table 9.6, "Epidemics in Gibraltar in the 1860s," p. 199, from "The Ecology of a Health Crisis: Gibraltar and the 1865 Cholera Epidemic" by L. A. Sawchuk and S. D. A. Burke in *Human Biologists in the Archives: Demography, Health, Nutrition, and Genetics in Historical Populations,* ed by D. A. Herring and A. C. Swedlund. Copyright © 2003. Reprinted by permission of Cambridge University Press.)

THINKING OUTSIDE THE BOX Name as many sources of social support that you can think of that may be available in urban areas but not in remote rural areas. How successful do you think these sources of support are in helping people cope with prominent urban stressors? How would a biological anthropologist try to measure the effects of social support on human health and well-being?

their Paleolithic bodies, react to them (Schell and Ulijaszek 1999). Stressors are elements in any environment that may be deleterious to health and well-being. Urban environments vary substantially, as do the stressors they present. Cities are built environments that vary cross-culturally and intraculturally in population density, the extent and distribution of open and green spaces, pollution, lighting, noise, sanitation, safety and personal security, transportation, accessibility to services, entertainment, and interpersonal and community ties. Urban populations are also social entities, sometimes comprising people from many different ethnic groups and regions as a result of immigration. Most cities also contain a range of economic classes. Members of these various groups are likely to experience the opportunities and stresses of urban life differently, depending on their access to jobs, housing, sanitation, schools, health care, social organizations, and other support systems.

Sanitation and Water Supply

Unlike small groups of migratory foragers, permanently settled, dense clusters of people living in cities face the serious problems of securing clean drinking water, vomiting and diarrhea. Cholera was not endemic to Gibraltar but was brought in from the outside because so many people entered the area daily.

The major mode of cholera transmission in Gibraltar was through the high degree of interpersonal contact in the small, crowded settlement (Sawchuk and Burke 2003:201). Deaths from the 1865 cholera epidemic, however, were unequally distributed across the population. Male prisoners experienced by far the highest death rate, given the rapid transmission of the disease in the overcrowded and unsanitary prison. In stark contrast, the military community fared the best—better than ordinary civilians and far better than prisoners. Two factors explain this pattern:

- Favorable age distribution—The military community did not include many aged people, and among civilians, the old suffered the highest mortality of all age groups.
- Better nutritional status because of reliable supplies of rations.
- More dependable and cleaner water supply.

Thus, even in a small community with extremely high rates of interpersonal contact, a pattern of **differential mortality** emerged, in which people belonging to different groups experienced varying death rates. The differential mortality in Gibraltar was socially shaped rather than due to genetic differences. It clearly demonstrates how cultural patterns affect the biological experiences of illness and the death rate.

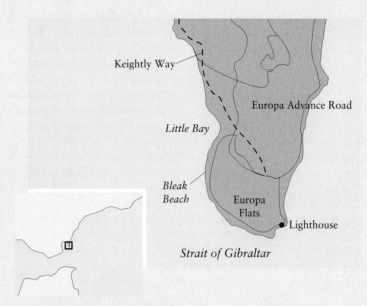

CRITICAL THINKING QUESTIONS

- How do the mortality rates of prisoners in your home country compare to the national average? Do male and female prisoners have the same or different mortality rates?
- Think of a current example of military life in which military personnel have better chances of maintaining good health than the civilian population.
- What is the current status of cholera in terms of its effects on global health?

disposing of human and animal waste, and having fresh air to breathe. These challenges are linked to the fact, evident in the prehistoric fossil evidence, that infectious disease first became significant with settled, urban life (Cohen 1989). In response to the health risks of urban living, some of the world's first major cities, such as Harappa (review Chapter 9), had well-designed sewer systems. Nonetheless, abundant examples throughout prehistory and history attest to frequent health crises and high mortality rates in urban areas. Like all features of urban life, sanitation interacts with other factors, such as housing quality, employment, and social inequality, to shape patterns of illness and death. Archival study of a cholera epidemic in Gibraltar in 1865 reveals such complex environmental/biological/cultural links (see the Critical Thinking box).

Crowding

High levels of population density, in combination with air pollution, low-quality housing, and lack of human services, place strains on human physical and mental health. Many diseases are essentially urban diseases.

In the United States, the incidence of tuberculosis has increased in recent years, and this increase has occurred mainly in urban areas (Di Ferdinando 1999). **Tuberculosis (TB)** is a mycobacterial infection of the soft or skeletal tissues. It is usually acquired from other infected humans, whose coughing spreads bacilli-carrying droplets into the air. In the United States, rates of TB are generally higher in southern states than in northern states (with the exceptions of New York and Illinois because of their large urban populations). They are much higher among males than among females and higher among low-income people than among other income groups. The risk of contracting TB is closely tied to poor housing, crowding, poverty, and lack of access to health care. Beginning in the 1980s, outbreaks of **multi-drug-resistant mycobacterium tuberculosis (MDRTB)**, one of several new strains of TB that are resistant to treatment by conventional drugs, alerted public health authorities to its seriousness as one of the "new infectious diseases." In New York City, outbreaks of MDRTB occurred in many hospitals and prisons, a pattern related to the crowded conditions of these institutions (Munsiff et al. 2002). In 1992, New York City implemented an enhanced Tuberculosis Control Program, and no new cases have been reported since 1994.

TB is now often seen as a complication of HIV/AIDS. In New York City, there are so many people with TB and HIV/AIDS that they cannot be accommodated in public hospitals. Shelters for the homeless are overwhelmed by new applicants, many of whom are chronically ill with infectious and other diseases. Overcrowding in health and other institutions increases the likelihood of the further spread of infection. Interventions aimed at addressing this health crisis include the earlier diagnosis of new cases, better management of air circulation in health care facilities, and prevention of new cases by trying to change behavior.

Pollution

Pollution comes in a variety of forms—in air, water, and food. Air pollutants are gases and particles emitted as by-products of combustion from industry, power generation, transportation, and the manufacture and use of chemicals (Schell and Denham 2003:113). In high concentrations, these pollutants undermine health in the short term by producing symptoms such as burning eyes and sore throats, and in the long-term, they cause life-threatening cancers and damage to the immune, reproductive, neurological, and respiratory systems. Worldwide, air pollution is far more problematic in urban than in rural areas. Air pollution inside homes and workplaces is becoming a greater threat than air pollution outdoors.

Lead is a form of pollution borne in dust, air, food, and water (Schell and Stark 1999). Lead poisoning affects human health and functioning in many ways, producing, for example, **anemia** (low numbers of red blood cells), cognitive impairment, and problems in neurobehavioral development. In the United States, public health concern about exposure to lead has been demonstrated since the 1970s in various programs designed to increase awareness of exposure risks, such as that from lead-based paint. Distinct class and ethnic patterns of exposure still exist (see Figure 10.4). Class and ethnic inequalities in exposure to lead emerged clearly in the 2004 news coverage of lead content in the drinking water of many Washington, DC, neighborhoods. The most severely affected neighborhoods are those where low-income residents, and mainly low-income African Americans, live. Children are especially vulnerable to the effects of lead, but prenatal growth may also be affected. Policy makers debate acceptable levels of lead in drinking water. In the United States the acceptable level was lowered in 1991, a change reflecting greater awareness of the danger lead poses to health. A more cautious position says that no level of lead in drinking water can be deemed safe.

It has been suggested that airborne particles may induce heritable mutations (Samet et al. 2004). A study of mice exposed to an industrial location on western Lake Ontario revealed that offspring of the exposed mice had an increased rate of genetic mutations and that these genetic changes were paternally derived. Scientists are still

Air pollution hangs over New Delhi, India. So-called Asian Brown Haze, according to a report from the United Nations Environment Programme, is endangering the health and lives of more than one billion people in Asia. It is also affecting the global climate, agriculture, and even the amount of daylight. (Source: © Pallava Bagla/CORBIS)

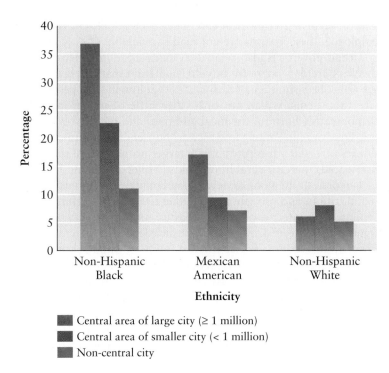

FIGURE 10.4

Percentage of 1- to 5-year-old children with elevated lead levels by ethnicity and urban status: United States, 1988–1991.

(*Source:* Adapted from p. 117 in "Environmental Pollution in Urban Environments and Human Biology" by Lawrence M. Schell and Melinda Denham. *Annual Review of Anthropology* 32, 2003.)

trying to determine how the pollutants induced genetic changes in the male mouse germ cells. A few studies of the effects of cigarette smoking suggest the possibility of smoking-associated germ cell mutations. However, none of these findings has yet offered firm evidence that certain pollutants adversely affect germ cells as well as somatic cells.

Poverty and Gender

Worldwide, it is the poor, both urban and rural, who are more likely to be exposed to inadequate sanitation, crowding, pollution, and violence. Women are more likely to be poor than men, so they constitute an especially important category of urban dwellers at risk of infectious disease, malnutrition, and other problems (Farmer et al. 1996). Access to decent jobs and a steady income empowers people to move to more healthful locations, to lobby for government policies that protect their health,

A sign warns of hazardous waste contamination at Love Canal, near Buffalo, New York State. Residents were evacuated in 1978 when levels of toxic chemical waste were found to be related to high levels of infant and other health problems. (Source: © Galen Rowell/ CORBIS)

and to secure better medical care when they are ill. For the unemployed and underemployed, these options are not readily available.

Urban poverty is also related to inadequate diet. Throughout the world, urban dwellers are dependent on buying food from markets because urban garden spaces are rare. Sheer shortage of cash means that low-income people opt for the least expensive food items, which not only offer little of nutritional value but also contain demonstrably harmful chemical additives and high levels of saturated fats and sugars. For example, among low-income households in rural and urban Jamaica, expenditures on sugar constitute a much larger proportion of the weekly budget for urban households than for rural households (Miller and Stone 1983).

Children of the poor in developing countries experience higher rates of mortality, malnutrition, and growth stunting due to undernourishment. Malnutrition exists in synergy with infectious disease, because a poorly nourished child has less ability to fight off infectious diseases such as measles and tuberculosis. Undernourished girls grow up to become undernourished mothers, often bearing low-birth-weight babies whose chances of survival are reduced. In spite of abundant global food supplies, millions of the world's children are currently undernourished, especially in poor countries.

The major underlying cause of widespread childhood malnutrition is social inequality and unequal access to adequate food by the poor. This underlying cause is exacerbated by unequal access to clean water, health care, and other services. The more inequality there is within a country, the higher its rate of childhood malnutrition (Castilho and Lahr 2001). A study conducted in Brazil, which has the highest rates of income inequality in the world, shows how wealth is correlated with child growth and health. Anthropometric measurements of nearly 8,000 middle- and upper-class children of the city of São Paulo (see the map on p. 313) between 1979 and 1998 indicate that these privileged children showed dramatic increases in weight and height over the period, reflecting their improved material conditions. By the end of the study, their growth rates matched international standards. There is no parallel study of poor children's growth rates over the same period, unfortunately.

Percentage of children with malnutrition, by country, 1993–1999.

Less than 10%

10–19%

20–29%

30–39%

40% or more

No data

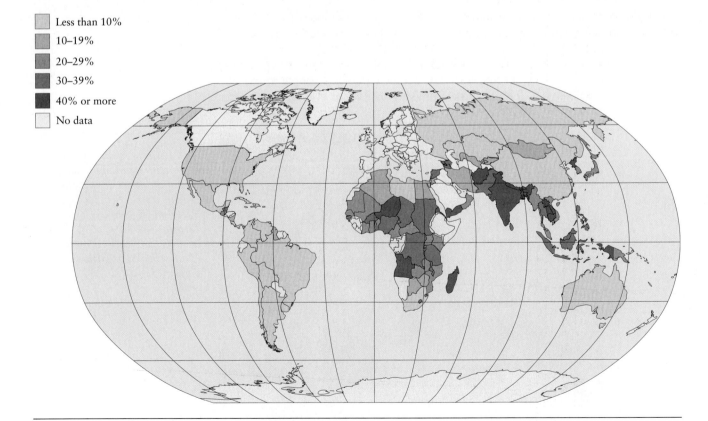

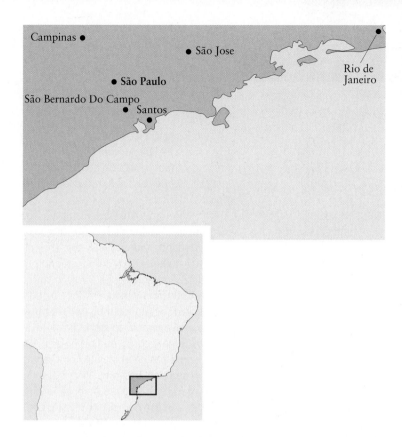

Southern Brazil showing location of São Paulo.

In the United States, by contrast, a major public health concern is the increasing prevalence of obesity. Some of the highest levels of obesity are found among teenagers and young adults (Johnston and Gordon-Larsen 1999). There is increasing evidence that the fetus receives cues about the nutritional status of the mother (Gluckman and Hanson 2004). For example, even when low-birth-weight babies born to malnourished mothers grow up in contexts where food is more abundant than what their mothers had, they are more vulnerable to obesity and to the diseases associated with it than are normal-birth-weight babies in the same environment (Bateson et al. 2004).

In spite of many studies and public programs, obesity is rising in the United States and the United Kingdom, especially among children. Students at the University of Pennsylvania decided to get involved in improving the diets of West Philadelphia teenagers by using an approach that had been successful in international development projects: community participation (see the Lessons Applied box on p. 314).

The challenges that urban life poses for human health and biology are many and varied, but so is the potential for change through urban services and such social institutions as neighborhood organizations, churches, and the media. Anthropologists from all four fields contribute to better understanding of urban risks and coping strategies by conducting research and participating in applied programs.

Fruits 'R' Us: A Participatory Action Research Project to Improve Nutrition among Youth in West Philadelphia

THE TURNER NUTRITIONAL AWARENESS PROJECT (TNAP) is a research and service project carried out among eleven- to fifteen-year-old students from the John B. Turner Middle School in West Philadelphia. The project promotes community participation through a partnership between the University of Pennsylvania and the surrounding West Philadelphia community (Johnston and Gordon-Larsen 1999). Its goals are as follows:

- Describe and analyze nutritional patterns of the students at Turner school.

- Enhance the ability of Turner students and their families to make informed decisions about food habits.

- Increase the diet quality and nutritional status of the Turner community.

- Establish community structures to maintain dietary awareness.

- Monitor and evaluate dietary quality and nutritional status of the Turner community.

- Disseminate results of the project to scholars and policy makers.

- Enhance the education of students at the University of Pennsylvania through problem solving and community service.

TNAP was launched in 1992. The Turner School is a middle school in West Philadelphia. The neighborhood has high crime rates, and the housing infrastructure is deteriorated. Incomes in the neighborhood are low, and most families live in poverty. All students are eligible for free breakfast and lunch under federal funding, although most do not take advantage of this provision. Ethnically, 99 percent of the students enrolled in the school are African American.

Two undergraduate students at the University of Pennsylvania came up with an idea for an "intervention" to improve the Turner students' nutritional status. They planned it with other university students, sixty Turner students, and these students' teachers at Turner. Their idea was to start a food store called "Fruits 'R' Us (and Vegetables Too!)" at the school. As a group, they decided what would be the most practical and healthy foods to sell and how to stock the store, staff it, manage finances, keep records, and advertise it. The store became a reality, and it has been maintained even though the founding group of students has long since moved on.

Did the store make a difference in Turner student nutrition? Data on the number of visits to the store suggest that this program did increase the consumption of fruits and vegetables. More generally, this project shows how community participation helps encourage positive change. Those students who were more involved in the store (working in the store, for example), or visiting it more often, had the most improved diets.

FOOD FOR THOUGHT

- What foods and beverages were available at your high school? Would your school have benefited from the equivalent of the TNAP?

▪ HOW do contemporary humans vary genetically?

The discovery of the role that DNA plays in controlling inherited variation and the development of methods for sequencing DNA have provided the basis for performing genome analysis to learn about genetic variation globally and regionally as well as at the individual level. This information provides a much more precise idea of biological human variation than indicators, such as blood type and skin color. Modern humans in Africa have more genetic variation than the rest of the world's populations combined, supporting the hypothesis that modern humans evolved there. Results of genetic studies show that there are no clear boundaries among the traditionally conceived races and that there more genetic differences within each of such groups than among them. The term *ethnic populations* or simply *populations* is preferred, although even they do not completely avoid possible racial connotations.

Certain diseases related to heredity are of interest to anthropologists and medical professionals. One major hereditary disease is sickle-cell syndrome, a blood disorder that can have serious health consequences even though, in malaria-endemic areas, the presence of the sickle-cell trait confers some protection against that disease. Down syndrome is an example of a widespread nonadaptive chromosomal disorder that results from an error occurring during the formation of germ cells.

▪ HOW do contemporary humans vary physically?

Contemporary humans vary physically across and within populations in several important ways. Some of these variations are developmental; that is, they occur as part of the growth process in response to specific external factors. Environmental conditions—especially extreme heat and cold, high altitudes, and variations in sunlight—play an important role in shaping developmental adaptations. Variations in body shape and size appear to be physical adaptations to climate. Increased lung capacity is one adaptation to high altitude. The amount of melanin in the skin appears to be an adaptation to the amount of sunlight, because melanin provides protection against ultraviolet radiation.

Dietary adaptations have long been one of humanity's major ways of responding to different environments. Certain macronutrients and micronutrients, however, are universally important for sustaining life and health. Although international organizations suggest general guidelines, different human activity patterns, along with factors such as gender and age, make it impossible to set universal standards. One notable genetic adaptation to diet is the greater percentage of people who have lactase persistence into adulthood in populations where dairy products are important.

▪ WHAT are some urban challenges to human biology and health?

For thousands of years during the Middle and Upper Paleolithic, early modern humans adapted biologically and culturally to Paleolithic environments. Urban life, which emerged only a few thousand years ago, presents humans with new biological and health challenges for which they may not be adapted. The stresses of urban life create "discordances" with humanity's Paleolithic biology.

Urban stresses vary cross-culturally and also affect people differently depending on their social status, ethnicity, gender, and age. Aspects of city life related to stress include population density, the extent and distribution of green spaces, pollution, lighting, noise, sanitation, safety and personal security, transportation, accessibility to and quality of services, entertainment, and interpersonal and community ties. Class differences are of critical importance in shaping the health experiences of urban dwellers. The poor, everywhere, are more likely to suffer from nutritional problems (including obesity in developed countries and malnutrition in poor countries), infectious diseases, and lack of access to health services. And worldwide, women constitute a disproportionate proportion of the urban poor.

KEY CONCEPTS

Allen's Rule, p. 300
anemia, p. 310
Bergmann's Rule, p. 300
developmental adaptation, p. 299
differential mortality, p. 309
discordance hypothesis, p. 307
Down syndrome, p. 306
genetic adaptation, p. 299
genome analysis, p. 292
hyperthermia, p. 299
hypothermia, p. 300
hypoxia, p. 301

infant mortality rate (IMR), p. 308
Kleiber's Law, p. 303
lactase persistence, p. 304
lactase impersistence, p. 304
melanin, p. 302
multi-drug-resistant mycobacterium tuberculosis (MDRTB), p. 310
PCR, p. 298
population, p. 298
sickle-cell syndrome, p. 305
single nucleotide polymorphisms (SNPs), p. 294
tuberculosis (TB), p. 310

SUGGESTED READINGS

Laura Betzig, ed. *Human Nature: A Critical Reader.* New York: Oxford University Press, 1997. Following the Introduction, which is titled "People Are Animals," this book presents eighteen classic essays about the role of natural selection in shaping human behavior, with critiques and updates for each. The essays are organized in three sections: studies of traditional societies, studies of modern societies, and comparative and historical studies. Some of the topics included are warfare, fertility, sexuality, rape, marriage, child rearing, and despotism.

Cheryl Brown Travis, ed. *Evolution, Gender and Rape.* Cambridge, MA: M.I.T. Press, 2003. Seventeen chapters address questions concerning the role of biology and evolution in male sexual aggression and in conflict between men and women. Contributors include psychologists, biological anthropologists, and cultural anthropologists. The first section lays out evolutionary theories, the second provides critiques of simplistic evolutionary models of male rape of women, and the third offers culturally informed analyses of rape.

Donald E. Brown. *Human Universals.* New York: McGraw-Hill, 1991. The author takes the perspective that most anthropologists focus almost exclusively on cultural differences and do not pay enough attention to human universals, or what all people do. By ignoring universals, anthropologists downplay the importance of human biology and natural selection. The book presents examples of universals, some of which are biological adaptations and others cultural adaptations, including the use of fire, incest taboos, kinship terminologies, and language.

Nora Ellen Groce. *Everyone Here Spoke Sign Language: Hereditary Deafness on Martha's Vineyard.* Cambridge, MA: Harvard University Press, 1985. This book examines the genetic and social dynamics of an unusually high rate of hereditary deafness among the population of Martha's Vineyard, an island off the coast of Massachusetts. In nineteenth-century Martha's Vineyard, deafness was not considered a handicap. Both deaf and hearing people spoke Island sign language. Deaf people's lives on the Island were no different from those of hearing people: they did the same jobs, including fishing, went to the same churches, and intermarried.

The author based her findings on a combination of archival research and oral histories.

Stephen Molnar. *Human Variation: Races, Types and Ethnic Groups.* 5th ed. Upper Saddle River, NJ: Prentice-Hall, 2002. Chapters in this textbook cover the concept of race and racial variation in the past, human genetic variation, inherited traits both simple and complex, how human biological variation is related to behavior, and how contemporary human populations are changing in terms of population growth, disease, and the emerging effects of natural and cultural selection.

Elaine Morgan. *The Scars of Evolution.* New York: Oxford University Press, 1990. The author discusses some of the physical costs to humans of certain evolutionary adaptations such as disc problems and hernia attributed to upright posture and skin cancer resulting from the loss of body hair covering. She also considers how evolution is related to the distribution of fat on the body, breathing disorders, and sexuality.

Thomas H. Murray, Mark A. Rothstein, and Robert F. Murray, Jr., eds. *The Human Genome Project and the Future of Health Care.* Bloomington: Indiana University Press, 1996. The twelve chapters in this volume address many aspects of the Human Genome Diversity Project in relation to health, including effects on the patient–physician relationship, educating clinicians about genetics, genetic therapies, reproductive decision making, access to health insurance, and the social distribution of access to services.

Francisco M. Salzano and A. Magdalena Hurtado, eds. *Lost Paradises and the Ethics of Research and Publication.* New York: Oxford University Press, 2004. Eleven chapters explore aspects of the ethics of research among small, isolated indigenous populations. Some chapters address the controversy surrounding biological research among the Yanomami of the Venezuelan Amazon, others consider the question of whether genetic research should be done among small, indigenous groups, and still others review the health status of selected populations.

Vincent Sarich and Frank Miele. *Race: The Reality of Human Differences.* Boulder, CO: Westview Press, 2004. The authors maintain that the biological concept of race has validity and attempt to refute the arguments of those who deny it, including the late Stephen Jay Gould. They explain how they believe human evolution led to biologically distinct races and how, in their view, race is linked to physical and behavioral differences today. The last chapter discusses race in terms of contemporary policy issues, such as affirmative action and health care.

Melbourne Tapper. *In the Blood: Sickle Cell Anemia and the Politics of Race*. Philadelphia: University of Pennsylvania Press, 1999. The author looks at the history in the United States of public discourse about sickle-cell anemia as an important example of the multiple connections among disease, genetics, race, politics, and personal agency. The material that is included ranges from personal narratives of people with sickle-cell anemia to congressional statements, hearings, and legislation related to the disease.

Lewis Wolpert. *Malignant Sadness: The Anatomy of Depression*. New York: The Free Press, 1999. The author, a biologist who suffers from periodic depression, presents an account of the affliction that combines personal experience, current knowledge about the biology of depression, and cross-cultural perspectives.

THE BIG QUESTIONS

- WHAT are the five major modes of production and their characteristics?
- HOW are modes of production related to consumption and exchange?
- HOW are production, consumption, and exchange changing in contemporary times?

CHAPTER 11

Economic Systems

A woman pounding millet in Agadez in Niger, West Africa. Wild millet, a kind of grass, was first domesticated in Africa and is now, after sorghum, the second most important food grain in Africa. It is typically combined with meat and vegetables in a stew, and it is also used for brewing beer. (Source: © Charles Cecil)

319

An American woman living in Florida recently established the name of the Yanomami, an Amazonian tribe who live in the rainforests of Venezuela and Brazil, for a web site address. She was auctioning *http://www.yanomami.com* for $25,000. When leaders of the Yanomami people heard about this, they were not happy. In order to use their own tribal name for their site, they would have to buy it, at a very high price. This example demonstrates that it is possible to create virtual products and make money by selling them. If a group cannot afford to buy its own name for a web site, it is out of luck.

For thousands of years of human life in the past, everyone made their living by gathering food and other basic necessities from nature. Everyone had equal access to key resources. We now live in a very different world where most people work to earn cash to purchase food and shelter. Increasingly, people work to earn money for nonessential goods and services.

Anthropologists have long studied how people make a living in different contexts around the world. Today, in this rapidly shrinking world, they study much more than localized economic systems. They also do research on how globalization affects local economies, the social effects of e-commerce, the stock market as a cultural system, and more.

This chapter takes us into *economic anthropology,* a subfield of cultural anthropology that is devoted to the cross-cultural study of contemporary human economic systems. Economic systems include **production,** making goods or money; **consumption,** using up goods or money; and **exchange,** the transfer of goods or money between people or institutions. We focus on contemporary patterns and cultural variation, but readers should keep in mind that the material presented here has many links to humanity's biological and cultural past as well as to contemporary biological patterns.

Production is the subject of the chapter's first section. The second section looks at how production is related to consumption and exchange. Finally, we consider some examples of how production, consumption, and exchange worldwide are changing, especially as a result of capitalist globalization.

MODES OF PRODUCTION

The term **mode of production** refers to the dominant way people make a living in a particular culture. Anthropologists have delineated five major modes of production (see Figure 11.1). We discuss the five modes of production in order of their chronological appearance in the human record. The chart does not indicate that a particular mode of production necessarily evolves into the one following it. Nor does it imply any kind of judgment about level of sophistication or superiority of the more recent modes of production. Even the oldest system involves complex and detailed knowledge about the environment that a contemporary city dweller, if transported to a rainforest, would find difficult to in order to survive.

Most cultural anthropologists are uneasy about typologies because they never fully reflect the richness and diversity of reality. For every generalization or category, we can always find cases that do not fit. This scheme simply provides a way for us to organize and discuss the ethnographic information in this chapter and following chapters.

Foraging

Foraging was defined in Chapter 5 as a general primate economic pattern. It consists of acquiring food by collecting what is available in nature. It is the oldest way of "making a living" among humans and was the only mode of production for more than 90 percent of human existence. Today, only about 250,000 people worldwide are foragers. Contemporary foragers occupy what are considered marginal areas,

FORAGING	HORTICULTURE	PASTORALISM	AGRICULTURE	INDUSTRIALISM (CAPITALIST)
Reason for Production				**Reason for Production**
Production for use				Production for profit
Division of Labor				**Division of Labor**
Family-based				Class-based
Overlapping gender roles			High degree of occupational specialization	
Property Relations				**Property Relations**
Egalitarian and collective				Stratified and private
Resource Use				**Resource Use**
Extensive and temporary				Intensive and expanding
Sustainability				**Sustainability**
High degree				Low degree

such as deserts, the circumpolar region, and dense tropical forest regions. Ironically, and unfortunately for foragers, these marginal areas are often rich with mineral or other natural resources that outsiders want.

Depending on the environment, the main activities of foraging include gathering such food as nuts, berries, roots, honey, insects, and eggs; trapping or hunting birds and animals; and fishing. Successful foraging requires sophisticated knowledge of the natural environment—for example, how to find certain roots buried deep in the ground, how to follow animal tracks and other signs, and how to judge the weather and locate sources of water.

The tools used in foraging include digging sticks (for removing roots from the ground and for penetrating the holes dug by animals in order to get the animals out), bows and arrows, spears, nets, and knives. Baskets are important for carrying food items. For processing raw materials into edible food, foragers use stones to mash, grind, and pound. Fish and meat can be dried in the sun or over fire, and fire is used for cooking. Few fuel sources, beyond wood or other combustible substances for cooking, are required for obtaining and processing food.

Foraging is an **extensive strategy**—that is, a mode of production involving temporary use of large areas of land and much spatial mobility. The foraging mode of production varies depending on the environment. Major contrasts exist between foraging in warm, temperate areas and in cold areas, especially the circumpolar regions (see Figure 11.2 on p. 322).

In warm climates, shelters are casually constructed and require little maintenance. Before they were sedentarized (settled down) on reservations or in farming communities, San peoples of southern Africa, including local groups such as the Ju/wasi, migrated several times during a year, depending on the availability of water. Each cluster of families would return on a regular basis to "their" territory, reconstructing or completely rebuilding their shelters with sticks for frames and leaf or thatch coverings. The shelters might be attached to two or three small trees for support. The amount of investment of time, labor, and material in constructing shelters was modest.

In contrast, foragers of the polar regions of North America, Europe, and Asia have to devote more time and energy to obtaining food and providing shelter. The specialized technology of circumpolar foragers includes spears, nets, and knives, as well as sleds and the use of domesticated animals to pull them. Dogs or other animals that are used to pull sleds are an important aspect of circumpolar peoples' technology (Savishinsky 1974). Much labor is needed to construct and maintain durable igloos or permanent log houses, which are necessary adaptations to the cold temperatures.

THINKING OUTSIDE THE BOX

Plan a two-week camping trip for yourself to (a) a region in central or southern Africa and (b) a circumpolar region. What will you need to take with you on each trip?

FIGURE 11.2

Temperate and circumpolar foraging systems compared.

	Temperate-Region Foragers	Circumpolar-Region Foragers
Diet	Wide variety of nuts, tubers, fruits, small animals, and occasional large game	Large marine and terrestrial animals
Gender Division of Labor in Food Procurement	Men and women forage; men hunt large game	Men hunt and fish
Shelter	Casual construction, nonpermanent, little maintenance	Time-intensive construction and maintenance, some permanent

Protective clothing, including warm coats and boots, is another feature of circumpolar adaptation.

Division of Labor

Among temperate foragers, most people do most tasks, and these tasks are mainly related to gathering small food items. One gender difference is that when hunting is undertaken, men are more likely to go on long-range expeditions to hunt large animals. Such expeditions, however, are rare among temperate foragers, whose diet is based on small food items such as birds, insects, roots, nuts, and berries. Among circumpolar foragers, however, hunting large animals (including seals, whales, and bears) and capturing large fish is an important activity. Thus there is usually a marked gender division of labor, with men hunting and fishing and women spending much time processing meat, fish, and hides.

Age is a basis for task allocation in all societies. Children and the aged generally spend less time in food provision than adults. Both boys and girls perform various tasks that North Americans would label "work," particularly gathering food and taking care of younger siblings.

Property Relations

The concept of *private property*, in the sense of owning something that can be sold to someone else, does not exist in foraging societies. More appropriate is the term **use right,** which refers to socially recognized priority in access to designated resources such as foraging areas and water holes. This access, however, is always willingly shared with others who follow social conventions or directly ask for permission to share the resource. Among the Ju/wasi, for example, family groups control access to particular water holes (Lee 1979:58–60). Visiting groups are welcome and are given food and water. In turn, the host group, at another time, will visit other camps and be offered hospitality there. Use rights are invested in the family group and passed down equally to all children in the group.

Foraging as a Sustainable System

When untouched by outside influences, foraging systems are sustainable; that is, crucial resources are regenerated over time in balance with the demand that the population makes on them. Sentinel Island, one island in India's Andaman Islands (see the map in Chapter 3 on p. 91) provides a clear case of foraging sustainability. Its inhabitants have lived in a "closed" system for uncounted centuries. The few hundred Andamanese on Sentinel Island have maintained their lifestyle within a limited area since Westerners first observed them in the late nineteenth century (Pandit 1990).

THINKING OUTSIDE THE BOX The 2004 tsunami in the Indian Ocean damaged much of the coastline of Sentinel Island but was much more destructive on other islands in the Andaman chain where the mangrove trees have been cleared. Learn about the effect of the tsunami in the Andaman Islands by visiting the A&N News Section of the web site *www.andaman.org.*

Two additional reasons for the sustainability of foraging are that foragers have minimal needs (discussed later in this chapter) and that their population growth rate is low (discussed in Chapter 12).

Some anthropologists refer to foragers as the *original affluent society* because all their needs were completely met. This phrase also reflects the fact the foragers do not have to work many hours a week to maintain their lifestyle. In undisturbed foraging societies, people spend as few as five hours a week, on average, collecting food and making or repairing tools. They have much more time than we do for leisure activities such as storytelling, playing games, and resting. Foraging people also traditionally enjoyed good health records. During the 1960s, the age structure and health status of the Ju/wasi compared well with those of the United States around 1900—without any modern medical facilities (Lee 1979:47–48).

Horticulture

Horticulture is a production system based on the cultivation of domesticated crops in gardens via hand tools. Prominent horticultural crops include many kinds of tubers, corn (maize), beans, and grains such as millet and sorghum, all of which are rich in protein, minerals, and vitamins. Food crops are often supplemented by foraging for wild foods, fishing and hunting, and trading with pastoralists for animal products. Horticulture is currently practiced by many thousands of people mainly in sub-Saharan Africa; South and Southeast Asia, including the Pacific island of Papua New Guinea; Central and South America; and some Caribbean islands.

Horticultural technology includes hand-held tools, such as digging sticks and hoes, and baskets for carrying harvested crops. Rain is the sole source of moisture. Horticulture requires rotation of garden plots in order to allow used areas to regenerate; thus it is also termed shifting cultivation or fallowing. Anthropologists distinguish five phases in the horticultural cycle: clearing, planting, weeding, harvesting and *fallowing* (allowing the field to rest between plantings). Average plot sizes are less than 1 acre, and 2.5 acres can support a family of 5 to 8 members for a year. Yields are often sufficient to support semipermanent village settlements of 200 to 250 people. Horticulture is an extensive strategy because of the need to let fields lie fallow. Surpluses in food supply are possible in horticulture.

Division of Labor

Compared to foraging, horticulture is more labor-intensive because of the energy required for plot preparation and food processing. A family of husband, wife, and children forms the core work group for cultivation, but groups of men form for hunting and fishing expeditions, and women work in collective groups for food processing. Gender is the key factor in the organization of labor, and male and female work roles are often clearly differentiated. Most commonly, men clear the garden area of trees and brush, whereas both men and women plant and tend the crops. This pattern exists in Papua New Guinea, much of Southeast Asia, and parts of West and East Africa. Hunting, when undertaken by horticulturalists, is men's work. In rural Malawi, southern Africa, for example, hunting is strictly associated with men, whereas food crops are women's responsibility (Morris 1998).

Two horticultural examples illustrate unusual patterns of gender roles and status. The first is the pre-contact Iroquois Indians of central New York State (Brown 1975) (see the map on p. 324). Iroquois women cultivated maize, the most important food crop, and they controlled its distribution. This control meant that they were able to decide whether the men would go to war, because a war effort depended on an

Hare Indian children in Alaska use their family's sled to haul drinking water to their village. ■ In your everyday life, what is involved in obtaining drinking water? (Source: © Joel Savishinsky)

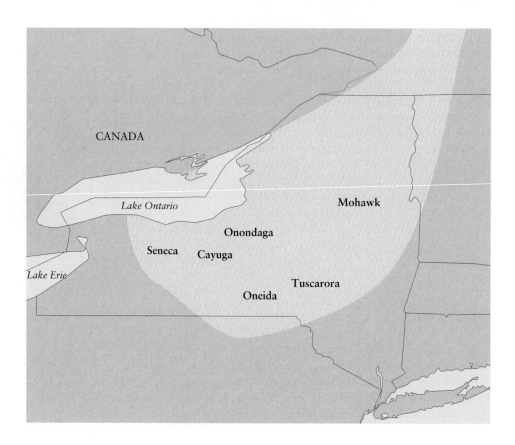

Iroquois area in the nineteenth century.

adequate supply of maize to support it. In contrast, among the Yanomami of the Venezuelan Amazon, men dominate in food production and distribution (Chagnon 1992). Yanomami men clear the fields and tend and harvest the crops. They also do the cooking for ritual feasts. Yanomami women, though, are not idle. They play an important role in providing the staple food that comes from manioc. Manioc is a starchy root crop that requires substantial processing work. It has to be dug out of the ground, soaked for a long time in water to remove toxins, and then processed by scraping it across a rough surface to give it a mealy consistency. Although manioc is the core of the Yanomami diet, and it requires arduous work by women, Yanomami women's social status is low while that of men is high.

Anthropologists disagree about what causes different gender divisions of labor in horticulture. The consequences of various divisions of labor on men's and women's status are more clear (Sanday 1973). Ethnological (comparative) analysis of many horticultural societies shows that women's contribution to food production is a necessary but not sufficient basis for high status. In other words, if women do not contribute to producing food, their status is low. If they do contribute, their status may or may not be high. The critical factor is control over the distribution of what is produced, especially its public distribution beyond the family. Slavery is a prime illustration of a contribution to production that does not bring high status because a slave has no control over the product.

Children do much productive work in horticultural societies, perhaps more than in

Current reserve area of the Yanomami people.

any other type of economy. A comparative research project, the *Children of Six Cultures* study, examined children's roles in different modes of production (Whiting and Whiting 1975). Children among the horticultural Gusii of Kenya were found to perform more tasks at younger ages than children in the other cultures. Both boys and girls were responsible for caring for siblings, collecting fuel, and hauling water. Horticultural societies involve children so heavily in responsible tasks because adult women's time allocation to work is very high, and children's labor serves as a replacement in the domestic domain.

Property Relations

As among foragers, the concept of private property does not exist in horticultural societies. Use rights, however, are more clearly defined than in foraging societies. Clearing and planting a parcel of land gives a family some claim to it and its produce, but no one can sell land to anyone else. With the production of surplus goods, inequality in access to resources sometimes emerges and some people gain higher social status than others.

Horticulture as a Sustainable System

Crop rotation and fallowing are crucial factors in the sustainability of horticulture. Crop rotation varies the demands made on the soil. Fallowing allows the plot to recover its nutrients. In general, seven years or more of fallow time are required for a year of cultivation. Reducing fallowing time quickly brings negative consequences, including depletion of soil nutrients and soil erosion. Several factors contribute to the overuse of plots that should be left fallow, including encroachment by ranchers, farmers, loggers, and tourists; government pressure to grow cash crops; and population pressure when out-migration is not possible (Blaikie 1985). Population growth is typically blamed as the sole culprit in soil overuse, but it is often not involved at all.

Sibling caretaking, as shown here in Ghana, is a common task of older children cross-culturally, but especially in nonindustrial societies. ■ What tasks do children in your microculture regularly do? (Source: © Roshani Kothari)

Pastoralism

Pastoralism is a mode of production based on the domestication of animal herds and the use of their products, such as meat and milk, for 50 percent or more of the diet. Contemporary pastoralists raise a variety of animals. The six most popular species are sheep, goats, cattle, horses, donkeys, and camels. Three others have more restricted distribution: yaks at high altitudes in Asia, reindeer in northern circumpolar regions, and llamas in highland South America. Many pastoralists keep dogs for protection and for help with herding. Pastoralism is geared to providing daily food, primarily milk and milk products. Given the limitations of animals as food sources, pastoralists often trade with other economic groups for food grains and manufactured items such as cooking pots. All pastoralists need fresh pasture for their animals, so pastoralism is an extensive mode of production.

Division of Labor

Families and clusters of related families are the basic unit of production. Gender is an important factor in the allocation of work. In many pastoralist cultures, male and female tasks are distinct. Men are in charge of herding, whereas women are responsible for processing the herd's products, especially the milk. A cultural emphasis on masculinity characterizes many pastoralist people. For example, reindeer herding among the Saami, indigenous people of Scandinavia, was connected to male identity

Review Chapter 8's discussion, p. 241, of the first evidence of the domestication of dogs. What kinds of biological/genetic changes have dogs experienced since then?

THINKING

OUTSIDE THE BOX

Among the Ariaal, pastoralists of Kenya, men are in charge of herding camels.
■ Why do you think an adult man is in charge of these baby camels? (Source: Elliot Fratkin)

(Pelto 1973). The very definition of being a man was to be a reindeer herder. As herding declined during the latter part of the twentieth century, men struggled to find new bases for identity. In contrast, women are the predominant herders among the Navajo of the American Southwest, whereas men craft silver jewelry. Children often have work roles in pastoralist economies, usually tending the herds. Among the cattle-keeping Maasai of Kenya and Tanzania, for example, parents want to have many children to help with the herds.

Property Relations

The most important forms of property among pastoralists are animals, housing such as tents or yerts, and domestic goods such as cooking ware and carpets. Use rights regulate pasture land and migratory routes. Some sense of private property exists, and animals may be traded by the family head for other goods. A family's tent is also its own. However, no private rights in land or travel routes exist. Many pastoral societies emphasize male ownership of the herds, and sons inherit herds from their fathers. In other societies, such as the sheepherding Navajo, herds pass from mother to daughter.

Pastoralism as a Sustainable System

Pastoralists have developed sustainable economies in resource-poor environments. As in other extensive systems (foraging and horticulture), overexploitation of the environment results when outside forces constrict the available space. Again, the pastoralists are often blamed for depleting the environment, rather than the outside factors.

Agriculture

Agriculture is an *intensive* strategy of production—that is, it focuses on a fixed area of land and applies more resources to that area rather than moving from place to place. Agriculture relies on domesticated animals for plowing, transportation, and providing organic fertilizer (manure). Elaborate terraces are often built to increase the amount of land available for cultivation. Key inputs that allow the same land to be farmed continuously without fertility decline include:

Girls are in charge of herding water buffaloes to the Ganges River, at Varanasi, India, for watering. ■ What knowledge might these girls have to possess in order to do their job? (Source: Barbara Miller)

The Global Network of Indigenous Knowledge Resource Centers

IN 1992, the United Nations Conference on Environment and Development, held in Rio de Janeiro, first brought to global awareness the complementary relationship between indigenous knowledge (IK) about the environment and biodiversity (Warren 2001). Scholars had recognized the importance of both indigenous knowledge and biodiversity for many years, but awareness of the links between them has led to action promoting IK in order to prevent further loss of biodiversity. Cultural anthropologists who study IK, especially in relation to nonindustrial production systems, have documented IK systems involving, for example, types of soil, what kinds of foods grow best in different contexts, and how to prevent pests from destroying food crops.

Now, an effort is under way to link universities and research laboratories worldwide that are repositories of IK documentation in order to support preservation of IK and to encourage continued research. Studies reveal that IK is socially differentiated—that is, there is microcultural variation in IK, and such variation is important to record. Men know some things, women know other things, the old and the young have different IK, and so do members of different economic niches within the same culture. Overall, though, IK differs from Western scientific knowledge in that it fosters mixed planting rather than mono-planting and promotes other practices that maintain biodiversity.

Over 30 IK resource centers exist around the world, housing computerized databases of case studies and reports. Coordination among the centers is leading to improved guidelines and recommendations for recording, archiving, and sharing IK. All of these practices are aimed at encouraging recognition of the importance of IK in promoting biodiversity.

FOOD FOR THOUGHT

- This global network will help inform policy makers. Do you think it will help the people whose knowledge is being recorded and preserved in the databanks?

Native American potatoes on sale in a market in Peru. Potatoes were domesticated in the Andean region of South America around 7000 BCE. Spanish conquistadores took potatoes back to Europe where they gained immediate popularity as a staple food of the poor. Globally, they are now the fourth most important food crop in the world, following rice, wheat, and maize. The number of "heirloom" varieties has substantially declined, leading to concern among food scientists that valuable biological diversity has been lost forever. (Source: © Anders Ryman/ CORBIS).

- substantial labor devoted to weeding
- natural and chemical fertilizers
- irrigation

Permanent houses, privately owned property, and increased crop yields all promote larger family size as a way of further increasing production through the use of household labor. Thus population density is high in agricultural societies.

Agriculture involves complex local forms of knowledge about the environment, including plant varieties, pest management, precipitation patterns, and soil types. Anthropologists refer to this knowledge as **indigenous knowledge** (IK) to distinguish it from Western, scientific knowledge. As long-standing agricultural traditions are increasingly displaced by methods introduced from the outside, indigenous knowledge is threatened with extinction, along with the cultures and languages associated with it. Many anthropologists are now actively involved in recording indigenous knowledge as a resource for the future (see the Lessons Applied box).

Agricultural systems are found on all continents except Antarctica. Because of the richness and complexity of farming systems cross-culturally, we will describe three different types (see Figure 11.3 on p. 328).

FIGURE 11.3
Characteristics of three forms of agriculture.

	Family Farming	Industrial Capital Agriculture	Industrial Collectivized Agriculture
Labor Inputs	Kin-based	Hired, impersonal	Communal
Capital Inputs	Low-moderate	High	Moderate-high
Sustainability	High	Low	Low-moderate

(*Source:* Reprinted by permission of Allyn & Bacon)

Family Farming

Over a billion people, or about one-sixth of the world's population, belong to households involved in **family farming** (sometimes termed *peasant farming*). In family farming, farmers produce most of their own food using family labor. Although it is found throughout the world, family farming is more common in less-industrialized countries such as Mexico, India, Poland, and Italy.

Family farmers exhibit much cross-cultural variety. They may be full-time or part-time farmers; they may be more or less closely linked to urban markets; and they may or may not grow cash crops such as coffee or sugar cane. Major tasks include plowing, planting seeds and cuttings, weeding, caring for terraces and irrigation systems, harvesting, processing, and marketing.

Division of Labor.   The family is the basic unit of production, and gender and age are important in organizing work. Most family farming societies have a marked gender-based division of labor. Cross-cultural analysis of gender roles in forty-six cultures revealed that men perform the bulk of the productive labor in over three-fourths of the sample (Michaelson and Goldschmidt 1971). The remaining one-quarter of the cultures includes those in which men's and women's productive roles are balanced and those in which women play the predominant role. In most family farm cultures, women's work is more often devoted to activities near the home, such as processing food and child care. Anthropologists have proposed different theories to explain why productive work on family farms is male-dominated (see Figure 11.4).

In family farms in the United States, husbands are primarily responsible for daily farm operations, and wives' participation ranges from minimal to equal to that of their husbands (Barlett 1989:271–273). Women do run farms in the United States, but generally only when they are divorced or widowed. Wives are usually responsible for managing the domestic domain. On average, women's daily work hours are 25 percent more than those of men. A new trend is for family farm women to take salaried jobs off the farm to help support the farm.

In some family farming systems, however, females play a more important role than males in agricultural production and distribution; such systems are referred to as *female farming systems*. Most female farming systems are found in southern India and neighboring Southeast Asia where wet rice agriculture is practiced. This is a highly labor-intensive way of growing rice that involves starting the seedlings in nurseries and transplanting them to flooded fields. Men do the initial plowing of the fields, but women's labor and decision making are the backbone of the operations. Why women predominate in wet rice agriculture is an intriguing question (Winzeler 1974). We have no explanation why this system came into being, but we can point to its consequences for women's status: where female farming systems exist, women are more likely to own land, to play a greater role in household decision making, and to have more autonomy (Dyson and Moore 1983, Stivens et al. 1994).

A third variation in the gender division of labor in family farming involves complementary and balanced task allocations between males and females, with males involved in agricultural work and females involved in food processing and marketing. This complementary of gender division of labor is common among highland communities of Central and South America. For example, among the Zapotec Indians of southern Mexico's state of Oaxaca, men grow maize, the staple crop, and cash crops such as bananas, mangoes, coconuts, and sesame (Chiñas 1992). Zapotec women sell produce in the town markets and make tortillas to sell from their houses. The family thus derives income from the labor of both genders working interdependently on different aspects of the production process. Male status and female status are balanced.

Children's roles in agricultural societies range from prominent to minor, depending on the context. The *Six Cultures Study*, mentioned earlier, found lower rates of child work in the North Indian and Mexican agricultural villages than in the horticultural village in Kenya. But in some agricultural societies, children's work rates are high, as shown through detailed observations of children's activities in two Asian villages, one in Java and the other in Nepal. In these villages, an important task of children, even those as young as six years old, is tending the farm animals (Nag, White, and Peet 1978), and children spend more time caring for animals than adults do. Girls aged six to eight spend more time than adults in child care. Some Javanese children in the six- to eight-year-old group work for wages. In general, girls work more hours each day than boys. Children in the United States are not formally employed in farm work, but many family farms rely on children's contributions on weekends and during summer vacations. Amish farm families rely on contributions from all family members (Hostetler and Huntington 1992).

A farming mother and daughter eat rice during a break from work in the rice fields of Vietnam's Mekong Delta. ■ What are the prospects that mechanization could replace these women farmers in producing wet rice? (Source: © Mark Henley/Panos Pictures)

FIGURE 11.4
Three hypotheses to explain male dominance in the gender division of labor in family farming.

Men and Plowing Hypothesis
This hypothesis is based on the importance of plowing fields in preparation for planting and on the fact that plowing is almost exclusively a male task (Goody 1976). Some anthropologists say that men plow because they are stronger than women and have the advantage of greater aerobic capacity. In southern India, for example, weather patterns require that plowing be accomplished in a very narrow time period (Maclachlan 1983). Assigning the task to the physically stronger gender ensures that the work is done more quickly and is thus an adaptive cultural strategy because it increases the chances for a good crop.

Women and Child Care Hypothesis
This hypothesis says that women are not involved in plowing and other agricultural field labor as much as men because such tasks are incompatible with child care (J. K. Brown 1970).

Women and Food Processing Hypothesis
This hypothesis notes that agriculture increases the demand for labor within and near the house (Ember 1983). Winnowing, husking, grinding, and cooking agricultural products are extremely labor-intensive processes. Linked to women's primary roles in child care and increased fertility in farm families, these new labor demands restrict women to the household domain.

This farmer works near the urbanized area of Kyoto, Japan, where farming combines elements of industrial mechanization with intensive labor. ■ Which features shown in this photograph fit with industrialized agriculture? Which do not? (Source: Barbara Miller)

Property Relations. Family farmers make substantial investments in land, such as the clearing, terracing, and fencing that are linked to the development of firmly delineated and protected property rights. Rights to land can be acquired and sold. Formal rules govern the inheritance of rights to land. Institutions such as law and police exist to protect private rights to land and to other resources. In family farming systems where male labor and decision making predominate, women and girls tend to be excluded from land rights and other forms of property control. Conversely, in female farming systems, inheritance rules provide for transmission of property rights through females.

Industrial Agriculture

Industrial capital agriculture produces crops through means that are capital-intensive, using machinery and inputs such as processed fertilizers instead of human and animal labor (Barlett 1989:253). It is most widely practiced in the United States, Canada, Germany, Russia, and Japan and is increasingly being adopted in developing nations such as India, Brazil, and China.

Industrial agriculture has brought the advent of **corporate farms,** huge enterprises that produce goods solely for sale and that are owned and operated by companies that rely entirely on hired labor. Four characteristics of industrial agriculture have major social effects (see Figure 11.5).

FIGURE 11.5
Three features of industrial agriculture and their social effects.

■ Increased use of complex technology (including machinery, chemicals, and genetic research) on new plant and animal varieties.

Social effects: displacement of small landholders and field laborers. For example, replacing mules and horses with tractors for plowing in the American South during the 1930s led to the eviction of small-scale sharecroppers from the land because the landowners could cultivate larger units. Similarly, the invention of mechanical cotton pickers displaced field laborers.

■ Increased use of capital (wealth used in the production of more wealth) in the form of money or property.

Social effects: The high ratio of capital to labor enables farmers to increase production but reduces flexibility. If a farmer invests in an expensive machine to harvest soybeans and then the price of soybeans drops, the farmer cannot simply switch from soybeans to a more profitable crop. Capitalization creates opportunities and risks for farmers. It is most risky for smaller farms, which cannot absorb losses easily.

■ Increased use of energy (primarily gasoline to run the machinery and nitrates for fertilizer) to grow crops. This input of energy often exceeds the calories of food energy yielded in the harvest. Calculations of how many calories of energy are used to produce a calorie of food in industrial agricultural systems reveal that some 2.5 calories of fossil fuel are invested to harvest 1 calorie of food—and more than 6 calories are invested when processing, packaging, and transport are taken into account.

Social effects: This energy-heavy mode of production creates farmers' dependence on the global market of energy supplies.

(*Source:* Adapted from "Industrial Agriculture" by Peggy F. Barlett in *Economic Anthropology*, ed. by Stuart Plattner. Copyright © 1989. Published by Stanford University Press.)

Corporate farms depend completely on hired labor rather than on family members. Much of the labor demand in industrial agriculture is seasonal, which creates an ebb and flow of workers, depending on the task and time of year. Large ranches hire seasonal cowboys for round-ups and fence mending. Crop harvesting is another high-demand point. Leo Chavez (1992) studied the lives of undocumented ("illegal") migrant laborers from Central America who work in the huge tomato, strawberry, and avocado fields owned by corporate farms in southern California. Many of the migrants are Indians from Oaxaca, Mexico. They illegally cross the border to work in the United States in order to provide for their families. In the San Diego area, they live temporarily in shantytowns or camps.

Members of this Romanian collective farm work team are sorting potatoes. Teams were composed of close friends, relations, and neighbors. ■ How might this form of organization contribute to productivity? (Source: David Kideckel)

Industrial collectivized agriculture is a form of industrialized agriculture that involves state control of land, technology, and goods produced. Collectivism's basic goal was to provide improved welfare for the masses and greater economic equality than exists under competitive capitalism. A variety of collective agriculture arrangements have been implemented, with varying degrees of success, in places such as Russia, countries of Eastern Europe, China, Tanzania, Ethiopia, and Nicaragua.

Cultural anthropology studies of collectivized agriculture are rare. Here we provide a brief summary of findings from research conducted in Romania's Olt Land region (Kideckel 1993). Romanian socialism, established through Soviet support, was Stalinist and involved highly centralized state planning. Romania had the most comprehensive and centralized system in Eastern Europe. The state oversaw nearly every aspect of society, from university enrollments to the production of steel and tractors. Romanian agriculture was organized into state farms and collective farms. With the completion of collectivization in the early 1960s, about 30 percent of the land was in state farms, 60 percent in collectives, and 10 percent privately held. Workers on state farms were paid wages and given a small garden plot. Organized like a rural factory, the state farm provided services such as child care facilities and shopping centers.

In spite of the socialist rhetoric proclaiming equality among all workers, economic distinctions remained between men and women. Women were relegated to agricultural and reproductive labor, whereas rural men moved into industry. Although women were the mainstay of collective farm labor, they were underrepresented among the leadership. Nevertheless, women's increased involvement in wage earning and their roles in cultivating plots for household use strengthened their influence in the household and the community.

After the Revolution of 1989, the policy to transfer land back to private citizens had mixed results. State farms gave up land reluctantly. Many collective farmers thought that privatized farming was not worth the effort now that other kinds of opportunities existed for making a living. In addition, they were accustomed to some of the benefits of collective farming, such as shared risk and shorter workdays. Some of the younger people welcomed the idea of private farming but felt they lacked the necessary knowledge to succeed.

The Sustainability of Agriculture

Agriculture requires substantial labor inputs, technology, and nonrenewable natural resources. Especially in its corporate form, agriculture is not sustainable. Furthermore, the spread of corporate agriculture is seriously undermining the sustainability of foraging, horticulture, and pastoralism. In its demand for increased farm land and fuel sources, it also has major negative effects on the natural environment. As noted in Chapter 9, the emergence of agriculture brought with it new levels of social inequality, conflict, and state-level mechanisms of social control.

FIGURE 11.6

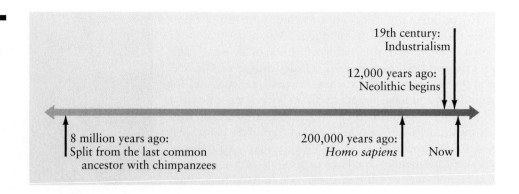

The industrial mode of production is a late arrival in human economic evolution. (Note: This figure is not to scale.)

Industrialism and Post-Industrialism

Industrialism is the production of goods through mass employment in business and commercial operations. Industrialism began only a short time ago, in the latter half of the nineteenth century (see Figure 11.6). Since that time it has spread, unevenly, to most countries. Compared to the other modes of production, which have been around much longer, industrialism has had an extremely brief test of time in terms of its social effects and sustainability.

In industrial capitalism, most goods are produced not to meet basic needs but to satisfy consumer demand for nonessential goods. Employment in agriculture decreases, while jobs in manufacturing and the service sector increase. In some industrialized countries, the number of manufacturing jobs is declining, and more people are finding employment in service occupations and in the growing area of information processing (such as computer programming, data processing, communications, and teaching). Some experts feel that the United States, for example, has moved out of the industrial age and into the post-industrial or *information age*.

THINKING OUTSIDE THE BOX How many countries have laws against child labor? Should children everywhere be prevented from working for wages?

MODES OF CONSUMPTION AND EXCHANGE

Imagine that it is the late eighteenth century and you are a member of the Kwakwaka'wakw tribe of British Columbia in Canada's Pacific region. Along with the rest of your local tribal group, you have been invited to a potlatch, a grand feast in which guests are served elaborate meals and receive gifts from the hosts (Suttles 1991). Be prepared to eat a lot, because potlatch guests are served abundant helpings of the most honorable foods: fish oil, high-bush cranberries, and seal meat, all presented in ceremonial wooden bowls. The chief will present the guests with many gifts: embroidered blankets, canoes, carefully crafted household articles such as carved wooden boxes and woven mats, and food to be taken back home. The more the chief gives, the higher his status will rise, and the more his guests will be indebted to him. Later, when it is the guests' turn to hold a potlatch, they will try to give away as much as—or more than—their host did, thus shaming him into giving the next potlatch.

Before the arrival of the Europeans, tribes throughout the Pacific Northwest were linked with each other through a network of potlatching relationships. The Europeans tried to stop potlatching because they thought it was wasteful and because it contained elements that ran counter to Christian principles they were trying to promote. In spite of the fact that the colonialists even made potlatching illegal, it has survived to the present day among some groups and is being revived by others.

This sketch demonstrates how closely linked production, consumption, and exchange are. Potlatches are related to levels of production; they are opportunities for consumption; and they involve the exchange of goods among groups. In this section, we look cross-culturally at **modes of consumption,** or the predominant patterns of using up goods and services within a culture, and **modes of exchange,** or the predominant patterns of transferring goods, services, and other items between and among people and groups within a culture.

Modes of Consumption

Consumption has two senses. First, it is a person's *intake* in terms of eating or other ways of using things; second, it is a person's *output* in terms of spending or using resources. Thus consumption includes eating habits and household budgeting practices. People consume many things: food, drink, clothing, and shelter are the most basic consumption needs. Beyond that, people may acquire and use tools, weapons, means of transportation, computers, books and other items of communication, art and other luxury goods, and energy for heating and cooling their residence.

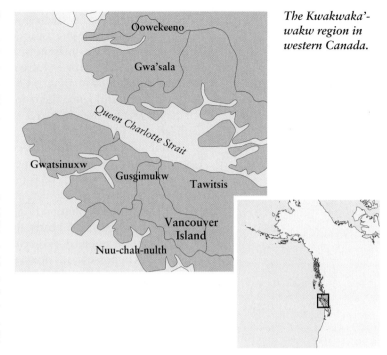

The Kwakwaka'-wakw region in western Canada.

The modes of consumption correspond generally with the modes of production (see Figure 11.7). At the opposite ends of the continuum, two contrasting modes of consumption exist, defined in terms of the relationship between demand (what people want) and supply (the resources available to satisfy demand). **Minimalism** is a mode of consumption that emphasizes simplicity and is characterized by few and finite (limited) consumer demands and by an adequate and sustainable means to achieve them. At the other end of the continuum is **consumerism,** in which people's demands are many and infinite, and the means of satisfying them are insufficient and become depleted in the effort to meet demands. Minimalism is most

FORAGING	HORTICULTURE	PASTORALISM	AGRICULTURE	INDUSTRIALISM (CAPITALIST)
Mode of Consumption				Mode of Consumption
Minimalism Finite needs				Consumerism Infinite needs
Social Organization of Consumption				*Social Organization of Consumption*
Equality/sharing Personalized products				Class-based inequality Depersonalized products
Primary Budgetary Fund				*Primary Budgetary Fund*
Basic needs				Rent/taxes, luxuries
Mode of Exchange				Mode of Exchange
Balanced exchange				Market exchange
Social Organization of Exchange				*Social Organization of Exchange*
Small groups, face-to-face				Anonymous market transactions
Primary Category of Exchange				*Primary Category of Exchange*
The gift				The sale

FIGURE 11.7
Modes of production, consumption, and exchange.

(*Source:* Reprinted by permission of Allyn & Bacon)

clearly exemplified in (free-ranging) foraging societies; consumerism is the distinguishing feature of capitalist industrial cultures. If we envision foraging societies at the far left of the continuum, then in between these two extremes we observe blended patterns, with a decreasing trend toward minimalism and an increasing trend toward consumerism as one moves from left to right. Changes in the mode of production influence the transformation in consumption. Notably, the increase of surpluses and the ability to store wealth for long periods of time enable a more consumerist lifestyle to emerge.

Minimalist and consumerist cultures also differ in the social organization of consumption. In foraging societies, everyone has equal access to all resources. As among the traditional Ju/wasi, food is not consumed by family members alone but is shared with a group of up to 30 or more people. Every member receives an equitable share (Lee 1979). The distribution of personal goods such as clothing, or of "luxury" items such as ostrich egg shell beads, musical instruments, or smoking pipes, is also equal. In horticultural and pastoral societies, group sharing is still a prevalent ethic, although inequalities in possessions do sometimes exist among individuals and among groups. It is the duty of leaders of horticultural and pastoral groups, however, to make sure that everyone has food and shelter.

At the other end of the continuum, social inequality in consumption is prominent. The United States is the major consumerist culture of the world (Durning 1993), but as globalization occurs, consumerism is spreading. Many countries have growing economies that allow people to demand consumer goods such as big cars, electrical appliances, and air conditioning. These countries include the rapidly developing nations of Asia, such as China, the Republic of Korea, and Vietnam, and many countries in Africa and Latin America. The amount of goods that the world's population consumed in the second half of the twentieth century is equal to what was consumed by all previous generations of humans. Some industrialized nations, such as Sweden, have taken steps to control consumerism and its negative environmental effects, especially through reducing the use of cars.

In small-scale societies, such as those of foragers, horticulturalists, and pastoralists, consumption items are mainly produced by the consumers themselves. If not, they are traded for among people with whom the consumer has a personal relationship. In such *personalized consumption,* everyone knows where products come from and who produced them. This pattern contrasts markedly with a rapidly growing pattern of consumption in our contemporary globalized world: *depersonalized consumption.* In depersonalized consumption, multinational corporations manage the production of most of the goods that people in industrialized countries consume. Many products are made of components produced in several different countries and assembled in diverse parts of the world by hundreds of unknown workers. Some anthropologists believe that depersonalized consumption is harmful to the actual producers (see the Critical Thinking box).

Consumption Microcultures

Distinct consumption microcultures are often defined on the basis of class, ethnicity, gender, and age. People's consumption patterns, though, are rarely the consequences of just one microculture. Rather, they are shaped by multiple and intersecting microcultures that determine one's ability to consume in certain ways, one's taste for certain consumption items, and the consequences of particular patterns of consumption on one's health and longevity.

Class

In cultures with class structures, upper-class people spend more on consumption than the poor do. The poor, however, spend a larger percentage of their total income on consumption, especially on basic needs such as food, clothing, and shelter. As noted in Chapter 10, income inequalities worldwide account for dramatic

Can the Internet Create Responsible Consumers?

ONE IMPORTANT FEATURE of increasingly globalized production is that the role of the producer is hidden from the consumer. In other words, commodities are no longer linked with particular producers. Furthermore, many products are assembled with parts from all over the world, created by many invisible workers. British culturalist anthropologist Daniel Miller says that such labor invisibility and product depersonalization make it all too easy for consumers unkowingly to support practices that are harmful to the distant, unseen laborers (2003). Most people are happy enough to blame multinational corporations for the poor treatment of producers. But Miller points out that the major responsibility should lie with us, the consumers. It is our search for the cheapest possible goods that drives the commercial competition that results in further exploitation of workers. It is consumers who must be persuaded to pay higher prices in order to provide better conditions for producers.

If consumers were educated about the actual dynamics of production and the role of the laborers, they would be more likely to make wiser and more responsible choices about which products to buy. For example, they would avoid products made by the more exploitative companies or by less ecologically responsible companies. And they might be willing to pay higher prices to discourage abuse of workers and of the environment.

Miller sees a major gap in the school curriculum in his home country, the United Kingdom. It is extraordinary, he says, that we call people "educated" who know more about ancient Rome or physics than about the products they consume every day. Most students will never use the higher math or physics that they study in school, but they will be consumers for the rest of their lives. So, he asks, why not provide consumer education for students?

To that end, Miller devised an Internet education project for school children that would teach them about the role of workers in relation to the products they consume and would put the human faces of producers behind commodities. Having discovered the importance of "interactivity" from his earlier fieldwork on people's use of the Internet in Trinidad, he created a plan for an interactive narrative about a product. The Internet could enable students to talk in "real time" with actual producers. To avoid a power differential between workers and viewers, the producers should be able to question the students (the consumers) about their lives as well. This interactive per-

Child labor is prominent in many modes of production. In this photograph, a girl picks coffee beans in Guatemala. (Source: © Sean Sprague/Stock Boston, LLC)

sonalization would include, in the case of a relatively simple product such as a banana, not just the plantation worker but also the wider system and process of banana production: plantation managers, packers, and transporters. The students would choose a banana company, web cams would be supplied to the workers, and both students and workers would be connected online once a week. In order to push the reality of production all the way, Miller hopes that the students would actually end up eating the same bananas that they saw being produced.

This is a big project, even for just a single commodity. Miller is well aware that we cannot, within reason, learn everything about the production of everything we consume. He suggests that three illustrative products be chosen for the education project, starting with the banana. The second product should be more complex to illustrate the multiple sourcing of most goods. The third product might be locally produced by a small-scale firm.

Miller sought government funding for his project but was denied. Undaunted, he published an article in a journal in order to share his idea and inspire others to develop similar consumer education projects elsewhere.

CRITICAL THINKING QUESTIONS

- Is Miller's idea of enhancing the school curriculum in this way important?
- Is it feasible?
- What suggestions do you have for products to study in addition to bananas?

Homeless children in Ho Chi Minh City, Vietnam. ■ Locate a web site that provides information on the numbers of homeless children by country. (Source: © Edward Keller III)

differences in nutrition and health. As discussed in Chapter 10, the urban poor are more likely to be exposed to various forms of pollution and to have less access to good social and health services.

Class differences in consumption in contemporary industrial societies may seem so obvious that they are scarcely worth studying. A team of French researchers, however, undertook a national sample survey with over 1000 responses to study class differences in consumer preferences and tastes (Bourdieu 1984). The results revealed strong class patterns in, for example, choice of favorite painters or pieces of music, that were most closely associated with people's level of education and their father's occupation. An overall pattern of "distance from necessity" in tastes and preferences characterized members of the educated upper classes, who were more likely to prefer abstract art. In comparison, tastes among the working classes were closer to "necessity," and their preference was for realist art. This study produced the concept of the *game of distinction,* in which people of lower classes take on the preferences of the upper classes in order to enhance their standing. Education, in this view, provides the means for lower-class people to learn how to play the game of distinction according to upper-class rules.

"Race" and Ethnicity

Racial apartheid was a matter of national policy in South Africa until 1994 and is a clear example of explicit racialized inequalities in consumption. Whites owned property, had wealth, and lived prosperous lives that included good food, good housing, and educational opportunities for their children. Blacks were denied all of these things. The current government in South Africa is now attempting to redress decades of deprivation linked to racial categories and is also facing the burden of widespread HIV/AIDS.

Overconsumption is a relative term that is linked to the issue in the United States and the United Kingdom of rising rates of obesity (review Chapter 10). In both countries, the obesity rate (as medically defined) is high and increasing, and within the general population, certain people are more likely to be obese than others. It appears that ethnicity is often relevant, and it interacts with other factors such as class, gender and age. Among Puerto Ricans in Philadelphia, the overall incidence of obesity is 20 percent higher for women than for men (Massara 1997). Puerto Rican women between forty and eighty years of age are 67 percent more likely to be obese than Puerto Rican women under the age of twenty-five. The culture of food in many American Puerto Rican families emphasizes strong links between a woman's being a good wife and mother and her role as food preparer and server. A married woman may eat dinner with her children and then, again, join her husband when he comes home later for his dinner. Some of the heavier women explained that their size made them appear asexual and allowed them to lead a more active social life outside the home without provoking their husbands' anger. Many women in the study thought that a certain amount of overweight, in medical terms, is acceptable. A deeper analysis, though, hinted that for many adult Puerto Rican women, overeating is a response to stress or to feelings of neglect in the family.

Gender

Consumption patterns, like obesity, are often gender-marked. Specific foods may be thought to be "male foods" or "female foods." In cultures where alcoholic beverages are consumed, the general pattern is that men drink more than women do. Gender differences in consumption have effects on growth and development, health, and even survival.

In all human populations, males on average are taller than females. But cultures vary in the degree of this aspect of sexual dimorphism (Holden and Mace 1999). To a certain extent, height is genetically influenced, but it is also affected by the environment and culture through diet.

From the perspective of biological anthropology, Darwinian theory suggests that sexual dimorphism in height—males generally being taller than females—is related to a primate-wide pattern of male competition for sexual access to females. In situations of male–male competition for females, larger males have an advantage over smaller males and therefore produce more offspring. This pattern eventually leads to the birth of more tall males, whereas no such selection pressure is exerted on females.

Such male–male competition, it has been hypothesized, would be especially strong in societies where *polygyny,* in which one man may have multiple wives, is practiced. Polygyny creates a scarcity of marriageable women. Biological anthropologists have investigated whether taller males are found in polygynous societies. They conducted a comparative study using data on seventy-six cultures. They found, however, no relationship in height differences between men and women in polygynous compared to nonpolygynous cultures.

Looking more closely at their data, they saw a different relationship: male height compared to female height is greater in cultures where women play a lesser role in production. The researchers suggest that where males provide the bulk of the productive labor, it is adaptive for parents to invest more food resources in their sons than in their daughters. Thus, boys are better able than girls to achieve their full growth potential.

This study affirms the importance of the environmental context and economic culture in affecting children's diet, growth, and, ultimately, their height. Such height differences would not be transmitted over generations through genes but are recreated in each generation through cultural preferences and actions. ■

FOOD FOR THOUGHT

■ How do the results of this cross-cultural analysis prompt possible reconsideration of the explanations given in Chapter 5 for sexual dimorphism in size among some of the great apes?

CROSSING THE FIELDS

Linking the Gender Division of Labor to Diet and Growth

Consider a dramatic case of gender differences in food consumption in highland Papua New Guinea (Lindenbaum 1979) (see the map on p. 338). This story begins with a mysterious epidemic, with the local name of *kuru,* among the Fore (pronounced FOR-AY), a horticultural group. Between 1957 and 1977, about 2500 people died of kuru. A victim of the disease would have shivering tremors, followed by a progressive loss of motor ability along with pain in the head and limbs. People afflicted with kuru could walk unsteadily at first but would later be unable to get up. Death occurred about a year after the first symptoms appeared. Deaths from kuru were not evenly distributed among the Fore: most victims were women.

The Fore believed that kuru was caused by sorcery. A team of Western medical researchers and a cultural anthropologist, Shirley Lindenbaum, showed that kuru was a neurological disease caused by consumption of the flesh of deceased people who were themselves kuru victims. Who was eating human flesh, and why? Among the Fore, it was considered acceptable to cook and eat the meat of a deceased person, although it was not a preferred food. Because of growing scarcity of the usual sources of animal protein in the region, some Fore women turned to eating human flesh. The

The area of the kuru epidemic in highland Papua New Guinea.

scarcity was related to increasing population density, more areas under cultivation and decreased forest areas, all of which reduced the numbers of local wild animals in the region. This scarcity acted in combination with the Fore's male-biased consumption pattern, which allocated preferred protein sources to men. Women turned to consumption of less-preferred food, including human flesh, and were at greater risk of contracting kuru.

Age

THINKING OUTSIDE THE BOX How do your consumption patterns compare with those of your parents? With those of your grandparents? What explains the variations? Are differences in age a factor?

Age categories often have characteristic consumption patterns that are culturally shaped. Certain foods may be believed to be appropriate for infants, young children, adolescents, adults, or the aged. This section looks at food consumption among the category of "the aged."

Biologically, the elderly have unique nutritional needs (Shifflett and McIntosh 1986–1987). In spite of these special needs, in many cultures, aged people experience declining quality of consumption. In the United States, the elderly tend to omit important food groups, especially fruits and vegetables. Among elderly Virginians, several factors related to dietary change were discovered, including lack of social support and loneliness. One respondent reported that she had been widowed for ten years and that she had undergone a negative change in her food habits soon after her husband died. For several years she felt she "had nothing to live for." She ate only junk food and food she could prepare with the least effort. She experienced a rapid weight gain up to 200 pounds, but "One day I realized what I was doing to my health and I went on a diet. I tried to eat a balanced diet and am still trying to eat better now" (10).

Aging affects everyone, regardless of class position, but wealth can protect the elderly from certain kinds of marginalization and deprivation. Income level is positively related to longevity (lifespan) around the world. Money can often buy better health care. Wealthier people can afford home care when they become infirm and

FIGURE 11.8
Items of exchange.

Category	Selected Examples
Material Goods	Food to family and group members Gifts for special occasions such as weddings Money
Nonmaterial Goods	Myths, stories, rituals Time, labor
People	Offspring in marriage Slavery

unable to care for themselves. In the United States, middle-class people may have to spend their last years in a nursing home, but the poor fare even worse. Park benches or shelters provided by local governments and volunteer organizations may be their only option (Vesperi 1985).

Modes of Exchange

Exchange, as defined in Chapter 8, is the transfer of something material or immaterial between at least two persons, groups, or institutions. In all economic systems, individuals and groups exchange goods and services with others, so exchange is a cultural universal. But variation arises in the mode of exchange, or the predominant pattern of exchange in a society. Variations also exist in terms of what items are important in exchange (see Figure 11.8).

Parallel to the two contrasting modes of consumption described earlier (minimalism and consumerism), two distinct modes of exchange can be delineated (see Figure 11.7 on p. 333). These are **balanced exchange,** a system of transfers in which the goal is either immediate or eventual balance in value, and **unbalanced exchange,** a system of transfers in which one party attempts to make a profit.

Balanced Exchange

The category of balanced exchange contains two subcategories based on the social relationship of the two parties involved in the exchange and the degree to which a "return" is expected (see Figure 11.9).

FIGURE 11.9
Keeping track of exchange.

	Balanced Exchange		Unbalanced Exchange	
	Generalized Reciprocity	Expected Reciprocity	Market Exchange	Theft, Exploitation
Actors	Kin, friends	Trading partners	Buyers/sellers	Non-kin, non-friends, unknown
Return	Not calculated or expected	Expected at some time	Immediate payment	No return
Example	Buying coffee for a friend	*Kula*	Internet shopping	Shoplifting

(*Source:* Reprinted by permission of Allyn & Bacon)

Generalized Reciprocity.   **Generalized reciprocity** is a category of exchange that involves the least conscious sense of interest in material gain or thought of what might be received in return. When or whether a possible return might be made is not calculated. Such exchanges often involve goods and services of an everyday nature, such as a cup of coffee. Generalized reciprocity is the predominant form of exchange between people who know each other well and trust each other. It is the predominant form of exchange in foraging societies, and it is also found among close kin and friends cross-culturally.

A **pure gift**, something given with no expectation of a return, is an extreme form of generalized reciprocity. Examples of a pure gift may include donating money for a food drive and making donations to famine relief, blood banks, and religious organizations.

Expected Reciprocity.   **Expected reciprocity** is the exchange of equally valued goods or services, usually between people of equal social status. The exchange may occur simultaneously between both parties, or an agreement or understanding may exist that stipulates the time period within which the exchange will be completed. This aspect of the timing contrasts with generalized reciprocity, in which there is no fixed time limit for the return. In expected reciprocity, if the second party fails to complete the exchange, the relationship will break down. The difference is that expected reciprocity is less personal than generalized reciprocity and, according to Western definitions, more "economic" in terms of profit-seeking.

The *kula* is an example of a system of expected reciprocity (review the Critical Thinking box in Chapter 4, p. 114). Throughout the Trobriand Islands, men exchange necklaces and armlets with their trading partners, who include close neighbors as well as people on distant islands. Trobriand men gain social distinction by having particular armlets and necklaces, some of which bestow more prestige than others. One cannot keep any trade item for long, though, because the kula code dictates that "to possess is great, but to possess is to give." Generosity is the essence of goodness, and stinginess is the most despised vice. Another rule is that kula exchanges should involve items of equivalent value. If a man trades a very valuable necklace with his partner, he expects to receive in return a very valuable armlet as a *yotile* (equivalent gift). At the time, if one's partner does not possess an equivalent item, he may have to give a *basi* (intermediary gift). The basi stands as a token of good faith until a proper return gift can be given. The *kudu* (clinching gift) will come later and will balance the original gift. The equality of exchange ensures a strong social bond between the trading partners and is a statement of trust. When a man goes to an area in which there may be danger because of previous raids or warfare, he can count on having a friend to receive him and give him hospitality.

Redistribution.   **Redistribution** is a form of exchange that involves one person collecting goods or money from many members of a group. Then, at a public event later on, that person "returns" the pooled goods to everyone who contributed, in the form of a generous feast. Ideally, over the long run, the returns should balance the original contributions. But compared to the two-way pattern of exchange involved in balanced exchange, redistribution involves a certain degree of centricity. And there is the possibility of institutionalized inequality, because what is returned to each individual may not always equal what that individual contributed.

The group of contributors may continue to give, in spite of perceived unfairness, because of the leadership skills of the person who mobilizes contributions. Political leadership throughout Papua New Guinea and many Pacific islands is based on redistribution through a system of contributions that lead to an impressive ritual feast that may take several years to organize (this topic is discussed in Chapter 16).

Unbalanced Exchange

Beginning mainly with the emergence of agriculture and settled life in the Neolithic is a different form of exchange, in which profit becomes the major goal, overriding concern with balance. Several forms of such unbalanced exchange exist.

In China, many marketers are women. These two women display their wares in a permanent neighborhood food market in a city near Shanghai. ■ Assume you are at this market and would like to cook a chicken for dinner. What steps do you take to make that happen? (Source: Barbara Miller)

Market Exchange. **Market exchange** is the buying and selling of commodities under competitive conditions in which the forces of supply and demand determine value (Dannhaeuser 1989). In market transactions, the people involved may not be related to or even know each other. They may not be social equals, and their exchange is not likely to generate social bonding. Many market transactions take place in a marketplace, a physical location in which buying and selling occur. Markets evolved from less formal contexts of trade into the formalized exchange of one thing for another according to set standards of value. In order for trade to develop, someone must have something that someone else wants. Specialization in producing a particular good promotes trade between regions. Particular products are often identified with a town or region. In Oaxaca, Mexico, for example, different villages are known for blankets, pottery, stone grinders, rope, and chili peppers (Plattner 1989:180–181).

The *periodic market*, a site for market transactions that is not permanently set up but occurs regularly, emerged with the development of agriculture and urban settlements. A periodic market, however, is more than just a place for buying and selling; it is also a place of social activity. Government officials drop in, religious organizations hold services, long-term acquaintances catch up with each other, and young

Well-stocked and brightly lit candy shops are a prominent part of urban night life in Valencia, southern Spain. Sugarcane was introduced into Spain by the Arabs. Later, the Spanish established the first sugarcane plantations on Madeira and the Canary Islands using enslaved laborers from Africa. ■ Log your food and drink consumption every day for a week and assess the role sugar plays in the results. (Source: Barbara Miller and Bernard Wood)

people may meet and fall in love. Worldwide, permanent markets situated in fixed locations have long served the everyday needs of villages and neighborhoods. *Permanent markets,* like periodic markets, often involve social relationships and enduring ties. More contemporary, less personalized forms of permanent marketplaces include shopping malls and stock exchanges.

Turning to other forms of unbalanced exchange, we find extreme instances in which no social relationship is involved and others wherein sustained unequal relationships are maintained over time. These forms can be found in any mode of production, but they are most likely to be found in large-scale societies.

Gambling. *Gambling,* or gaming, is the attempt to make a profit by playing a game of chance in which a certain item of value is staked in hopes of acquiring the much larger return that one receives if one wins the game. If one loses, that which one staked is lost. Gambling is an ancient practice and is common cross-culturally. Ancient forms of gambling include games such as dice throwing and card playing. Investing in the stock market can be considered a form of gambling. Although gambling may seem an odd category within unbalanced exchange, the gambler's goal of making a profit seems to warrant its placement here. The fact that gambling is on the rise justifies anthropological attention to it. In fact, some scholars have referred to the present stage of Western capitalism as *casino capitalism,* given the propensity of investors to play risky games on the stock market.

Native American gambling establishments in the United States and Canada have proliferated in recent years. The state of Michigan alone has nearly twenty Native American casinos. Throughout the country, Native American casinos are so financially successful that they are perceived as an economic threat to many state lotteries. The Pequot Indians of Connecticut, a small tribe of around 200 people, operate the most lucrative gaming establishment in the world, Foxwoods Resort and Casino, established in 1992 (Eisler 2001). The story of this success hangs on the creativity of one man: Richard "Skip" Hayward. An unemployed shipbuilder in the 1970s, he granted his grandmother's wish that he try to revive the declining tribe. Hayward used the legal system governing Native Americans to his advantage, forged links with powerful people such as Malaysian industrialist Lim Goh Tong and Bill Clinton (to whose campaign the Pequot donated half a million dollars), made powerful enemies such as Donald Trump, and became the chief of his now-rich tribe.

The Pequots, and many Native American groups, have become highly successful capitalists. Anthropologists and other social scientists are asking what impact these casinos will have on their Native American owners and on the surrounding area and what such newly rich groups will do with their wealth. In 1992, twenty-four Native American tribes formed an intertribal organization called USET (United South and Eastern Tribes), which is supporting a nationwide study of the social and economic effects of Native American gaming.

Theft. *Theft* is taking something with no expectation or thought of returning anything to the original owner for it. Thus it is the logical opposite of a pure gift. Theft has been neglected by anthropologists, perhaps because studying it might involve danger. One innovative research project considers food stealing by children in Sierra Leone, Africa (see the Methods Close-Up box).

Obviously, much theft that occurs in the world is motivated by greed, not economic deprivation or oppression. The world of theft in expensive commodities such as gems and art has not been researched by cultural anthropologists, nor has corporate financial malpractice been examined as a form of theft.

Exploitation. *Exploitation,* or getting something of greater value for less in return, is a form of extreme and persistent unbalanced exchange. Slavery is a form of exploitation in which people's labor power is appropriated without their consent and with no recompense for its value. Slavery is rare among foraging, horticultural, and pastoral societies.

Studying Children's Food Stealing

IN ORDER to learn about children's food stealing practices, Caroline Bledsoe first had to gain the trust of the children:

> I focused on eliciting information primarily from children themselves. This required careful effort, because children wanted to avoid getting in trouble. Most were reluctant at first to divulge their strategies. However, as children saw that I regarded their efforts as they themselves did—as almost an art—they disclosed some of their more creative techniques of "tiefing" (TEEF-ing), as petty stealing is referred to in Sierra Leone Creole (1983:2).

Bledsoe had the children participate in simulations of meal preparation and meal serving. In both situations, children revealed to her their subtle methods of tiefing. From an analysis of tiefing reports from many children, she found that fostered children (children temporarily placed in the care of friends or relatives) do more food stealing than children living with their own families. Food stealing can be seen as children's attempts to compensate for their less-than-adequate food shares at home. They do this by claiming, via tiefing, food that is not part of their rightful entitlement.

FOOD FOR THOUGHT

- Can you think of other research methods that could be used to provide data on these children's diet?

Social relationships that involve sustained unequal exchange do exist between members of different social groups. Unlike pure slavery, they involve no overt coercion and entail a certain degree of return by the dominant member to the subdominant member. Some degree of covert compulsion or dependence is likely to be present, however, in order for relationships of unequal exchange to endure. Relationships between the Efe, who are "pygmy" foragers, and the Lese, who are farmers, in Congo exemplify sustained unequal exchange (Grinker 1994). The Lese live in small villages. The Efe are seminomadic and live in temporary camps near Lese villages. Men of each group maintain long-term, hereditary exchange partnerships with each other. The Lese give cultivated foods and iron goods to the Efe, and the Efe give meat, honey, and other forest goods to the Lese. Each Efe partner is considered a member of the "house" of his Lese partner, although he lives separately. Their main link is the exchange of food, conceptualized by the Lese not as trade, per se, but as sharing of co-produced goods, as though the two partners were a single unit with a division of labor and a subsequent division or co-sharing of the goods produced. Yet there is evidence of inequality in these relationships, with the Lese having the advantage. The Efe provide much-wanted meat to the Lese, but this role gives them no status. Instead, it is the giving of cultivated foods by the Lese to the Efe that conveys status. Another area of inequality is marital and sexual relationships. Lese men may marry Efe women, and the children are considered Lese. Efe men cannot marry Lese women.

GLOBALIZATION AND CHANGING ECONOMIES

The spread of Western capitalism in recent centuries has had far-reaching effects on the modes of production it has met. The intensification of global trade created a global division of labor, or **world economy,** in which countries compete unequally for a share of the wealth (Wallerstein 1979).

The modern world economy is stratified into three major areas: core, periphery, and semiperiphery. Core areas monopolize the most profitable activities of the division of labor, such as high-tech manufacturing service and financial activities, and they have the strongest governments, which play a dominating role in the affairs of other countries. Peripheral areas are stuck with the least profitable activities, including the production of raw materials, foodstuffs, and labor-intensive goods, and they import high-tech goods and services from other areas. They tend to have weak governments and are dominated, either directly or indirectly, by core country governments and policies. Semiperipheral areas stand in the middle, exhibiting some characteristics of each.

According to this analysis, all areas are equally interdependent in the division of labor, but the benefits that accrue from their specialized roles are highly unequal. Core states, with about 20 percent of the system's population, control 80 percent of the system's wealth and emit 80 percent of world pollution. In the political sphere, the core states have increased their economic power and influence through international organizations such as the World Trade Organization (WTO), which forces "free trade" policies on peripheral countries and appears to be yet another mechanism that intensifies the unequal division of labor and wealth.

This chapter has examined five modes of production that, over many centuries, have been variously but increasingly affected by the capitalist logic of commodity production for markets in the service of ceaseless capital accumulation. In this section we draw attention to a few changes that have occurred in recent times in some of the modes of production. Note, though, that contemporary economic globalization is only the latest force of outside change to be exerted on local economies. European colonialism had major effects on indigenous economies, mainly by introducing cash cropping in place of production for household use.

In the later part of the twentieth century, rapid economic growth in Asia, the fall of socialism in the former Soviet Union, and the increasing economic power of the United States throughout the world combined to create the current pattern of globalization. New levels of interconnectedness among economic systems worldwide are found in raw materials, labor supply, transportation, finance, and marketing (Robins 1996). This interconnectedness is characterized by its instantaneity. Electronic forms of communication mean, more than ever, that when a world economic power center sneezes, the rest of the world will catch a cold.

Social scientists vigorously debate the effects of economic globalization on poverty and inequality (Ravaillon 2003). Economists, who rely on national-level statistics about income levels and distribution, tend to support the view that economic globalization is beneficial overall, because it increases economic activity and growth. Cultural anthropologists, who work with localized data and have a more "on the ground" view, tend to emphasize the negative effects of globalization. In terms of economic globalization specifically, anthropologists point to three major problems that rapid capitalist expansion has caused for local populations (Blim 2000):

- Increased cash cropping and other forms of commercial production in response to demands of the global market.
- Recruitment of former foragers, horticulturalists, pastoralists, and family farmers to work in the industrialized sector, and their exploitation in that setting.
- Dispossession of local people of their land and other resource bases, and substantial growth in the numbers of unemployed, displaced people.

Cash Cropping and Declining Nutrition: People Cannot Eat Sisal

Increasing numbers of horticultural and agricultural groups have been persuaded to switch from growing crops for their own use to cash crop production. Intuition might suggest that cash cropping should lead to a rising standard of living. Some studies show, to the contrary, that people's nutritional status often declines with the introduction of cash cropping. A carefully documented analysis of how people's nutritional status was affected by the introduction of *sisal* (a plant that has leaves used for making rope) as a cash crop in Brazil is one such case (Gross and Underwood 1971). Around 1950, growing sisal was widely adopted in arid parts of northeastern Brazil. The traditional economy was based on some cattle raising and subsistence farming. Many poor farmers gave up farming and went to work in the sisal-processing plants. They thought that steady work would be preferable to being dependent on the unpredictable rains in this dry region.

Processing sisal leaves for rope is an extremely labor-intensive process. One of the most demanding jobs is being a "residue man," whose tasks include shoveling soggy masses of fiber, bundling fiber, and lifting bundles for weighing. In families that included a "residue man," the amount of money required for food was as much as what the sisal worker earned. In one household studied, the weekly budget was completely spent on food. The greatest share of the food goes to the sisal worker himself because of his increased energy needs for sisal work. Analysis of data on the nutritional status of several hundred children in sisal-processing areas showed that some sisal workers were forced to deprive their dependents of an adequate diet in order to continue functioning as wage earners. The growth rates of children of sisal workers suffered in comparison to growth rates of other children.

The Lure of Western Goods

There is now scarcely any human group that does not engage in exchanges beyond its boundaries to acquire new consumer goods (Gross et al. 1979). As Katherine Milton, a biological anthropologist who has studied recently "contacted" indigenous groups in the Brazilian Amazon, puts it, "Despite the way their culture traditionally eschews possessions, forest-living people embrace manufactured goods with amazing enthusiasm. They seem to appreciate instantly the efficacy of a steel machete, ax, or cooking pot. It is love at first sight. . . . There are accounts of Indian groups or individuals who have turned their backs on manufactured goods, but such people are the exception" (1992:40). Their love for these goods has brought significant economic, political, and social changes in their lives.

In the early decades of the twentieth century, when the Brazilian government sought to "pacify" Amazonian groups, they placed pots, machetes, axes, and steel knives along Indian trails or hung them from trees. These techniques proved so successful that they are still used. Milton describes the process: Once a group has been drawn into the pacification area, all its members are presented with various trade goods—standard gifts include metal cooking pots, salt, matches, machetes, knives, axes, cloth hammocks, T-shirts, and shorts. After the Indians have grown accustomed to these new items, the Indians are told that they will no longer receive them as gifts but must work to earn money or produce goods for trade in order to obtain the new items. Unable to contemplate life without steel axes, the Indians began to produce more arrows or blowguns, weave more baskets, and hunt additional game in order to be able to have items for trade.

Adoption of Western foods has negatively affected the nutrition and health of indigenous Amazonian peoples. Milton reports that "The moment manufactured foods begin to intrude on the indigenous diet, health takes a downward turn" (1992:41). The Indians have begun to use table salt, which they were given by outsiders, and refined sugar.

A member of the Kayapo tribe of Brazil eats a popsicle during a break in a meeting of indigenous peoples to protest a dam-building project. The incidence of tooth decay, diabetes, and obesity is rising among indigenous peoples worldwide as a result of changing consumption patterns. ■ What makes sugar so appealing to people? (Source: © Wilson Melo/CORBIS)

Previously, they consumed small quantities of salt made by burning certain leaves and collecting the ash. The sugar they consumed came from wild fruits. Refined sugar tastes "exceptionally sweet" in comparison, and the Indians get hooked on it. As a result, tooth decay, obesity, and diabetes become new health risks.

Privatization's Effects in Russia and Eastern Europe

As the countries of the former Soviet Union have entered the market economy, income inequality has risen. The new rich enjoy unprecedented levels of comfortable living, including ownership of mansions and Mercedes-Benz cars. The influx of Western goods, including sugared soft drinks and junk food, nicknamed "pepsistroika" by an anthropologist who did fieldwork in Moscow (Lempert 1996), encourages people to change their traditional diets.

At the same time, consumption levels fell dramatically among the newly created poor. Historically, average reported levels of food intake in what are now Russia and Eastern Europe exceeded those of most middle-income countries (Cornia 1994). Between 1961 and 1988, consumption there of calories, proteins, and fats was generally above the level recommended by the World Health Organization. These countries were also characterized by full employment and low income inequality, so the high consumption levels were shared by everyone. This is not to say that diets were perfect. Characteristic weaknesses, especially in urban areas and among low-income groups, were low consumption of good-quality meat, fruits, vegetables, and vegetable oils, whereas people tended to overconsume cholesterol-heavy products (eggs and animal fats), sugar, salt, bread, and alcohol.

Now, there are two categories of poor people: the *ultrapoor* (those whose incomes are below the subsistence minimum, or between 25 and 35 percent of the average wage) and the *poor* (those whose incomes are above the subsistence minimum but below the social minimum, or between 35 and 50 percent of the average wage). The largest increases in the number of ultrapoor occurred in Bulgaria, Poland, Romania, and Russia, where between 20 and 30 percent of the population could be classified as ultrapoor and another 20 to 40 percent as poor. Overall calorie intake and protein consumption have diminished significantly. People in the ultrapoor category substitute less expensive sources of nutrients, so now they consume more animal fats and starch and less milk, animal proteins, vegetable oils, minerals, and vitamins. Rates of low-birth-weight babies have risen in Bulgaria and Romania, reflecting the deterioration in maternal diets. The rate of childhood anemia has risen dramatically in Russia.

An upscale car dealer in Moscow uses a cell phone to communicate with customers. His car lot stands on what was a sports ground during the Soviet era. ■ Conduct research on the social distribution of wealth in several post-Soviet countries. (Source: © Caroline Penn/CORBIS)

Credit Card Debt

Throughout the world, certain markets have long allowed buyers to purchase goods on credit. Such informal credit purchasing is usually based on personal trust and face-to-face interaction. Only recently, however, has the credit card made credit purchasing a massive, impersonal phenomenon in the United States and many other countries: "New electronic technology in the 1970s and deregulation in the 1980s offered retail bankers exciting opportunities to experiment with credit as a commodity, and they did experiment at "penetrating the debt capacity" of varied groups of Americans" (B. Williams 1994:351).

Among middle-class people in the United States, the use of credit cards is related to attempts to maintain a certain lifestyle. The primary users of credit cards are between twenty-five and forty-four years old with stagnant or falling incomes. Many use credit cards to support what they see as the appropriate life cycle stages, especially to acquire a college education or to set up a household and buy appliances. Maintaining (and paying monthly interest on) a running debt to credit card companies becomes an expected part of life and a habit that is not easily changed.

People's attitudes about their credit card debts vary. Some people express feelings of guilt similar to those prompted by a drug dependency. One woman reported, "Last year I had a charge-free Christmas. It was like coming away from drug abuse" (354). Others who are in debt feel grateful: "I wouldn't be able to go to college without my credit card" (355). No matter what people's attitudes are, credit cards are dragging many Americans deeply into debt. The cards buy a lifestyle that is not actually affordable, and therefore they "mask" actual economic decline in America. The culture of electronic credit is a subject that cultural anthropologists will no doubt be devoting more attention to in the future.

Continuities and Resistance: The Enduring Potlatch

As noted earlier in this chapter, potlatching among native peoples of the northwest coast of the United States and Canada was subjected to decades of opposition from Europeans and Euro-Americans (Cole 1991). The missionaries opposed potlatching as "un-Christian." The government thought it was wasteful, excessive, and not in keeping with their goals for the "economic progress" of the Indians. In 1885 the

A dance during a potlatch in the memory of a Tshimshian elder. The potlatch was held on the island of Metlakatla, southeast Alaska. ■ What kinds of social gatherings and exchange, if any, take place at death ceremonies of people in your microculture? Are there variations on the basis of the status of the deceased person? (Source: © Lawrence Migdale)

Canadian government outlawed the potlatch. Among all the northwest coastal tribes, the Kwakwaka'wakw resisted this prohibition most strongly and for the longest time. Potlatching among the Haida and Tlingit, in contrast, disappeared with relatively little resistance. Potlatches are no longer illegal, but a long battle was required to remove restrictions.

Contemporary reasons for giving a potlatch are similar to those in traditional times: naming children, mourning the dead, transferring rights and privileges, celebrating marriages, and raising totem poles (Webster 1991). However, the length of time devoted to planning a potlatch has changed. In the past, several years were involved in planning a proper potlatch. Now, about a year is enough. Still, much property must be accumulated to make sure that no guest goes away empty-handed, and the guest list may include between 500 and 1000 people. The kinds of goods exchanged are different today. Typical potlatch goods now include crocheted items (such as cushion covers, afghan blankets, and potholders), glassware, plastic goods, manufactured blankets, pillows, towels, articles of clothing, and sacks of flour and sugar.

THE BIG QUESTIONS REVISITED

■ WHAT are the five major modes of production and their characteristics?

The five modes of production among contemporary people are foraging, horticulture, pastoralism, agriculture, and industrialism. Each one involves factors of labor, property relations, and sustainability. In foraging societies, the division of labor is based on gender and age, and temperate foragers exhibit more gender overlap in tasks than circumpolar foragers. Property is shared, and all people have equal rights to resources such as land and water holes. Foraging has long-term sustainability when not affected by pressure from the outside world. Horticulture and pastoralism are also extensive strategies. Horticulture requires the fallowing of plots. Pastoralism requires the pastoralist to follow migrating animals to fresh pastures. The division of labor in these modes of production includes those in which men do most of the work, those in which women do most of the work, and those in which work loads are shared more evenly. Use rights are the prominent form of property relations, but increased levels of production through the domestication of plants and animals yield more food and goods, as well as heightened interest in protecting group rights to land. Like foraging, these modes of production have long-term sustainability when not limited by other economic systems.

Most family farming systems involve male labor in the fields and female labor in the domestic domain, although some examples of dominant female roles in field labor exist. In capitalist farm systems, access to the primary means of production—land—is unequal, and income gaps exist between the rich, landed people and the landless poor. Agriculture's sustainability is limited by the need to replenish the land, which is used continuously for crops and animals.

In industrialism, labor is highly differentiated by class as well as by gender and age. Widespread unemployment plagues many industrial economies. In capitalist industrial societies, private property is the dominant pattern. Given its intensive and expanding exploitation of nonrenewable resources, industrialism lacks long-term sustainability.

E-commerce is creating new ways of making a living, new labor patterns, new forms of property, and new questions about sustainability.

■ HOW are modes of production related to consumption and exchange?

Anthropologists contrast modes of consumption in non-market and market-based systems of production. In the former, minimalism is the dominant mode of consumption, with finite needs. In the latter, consumerism is the dominant mode of consumption, with infinite needs. Foraging societies typify the minimalist mode of consumption. Industrial capitalist societies typify the consumerist mode of consumption. The modes of production between foraging and industrialism exhibit varying degrees of minimalism and consumerism. In nonmarket economies, most consumers either produce the goods they use themselves or know who produced them. This is called personalized consumption. In market economies, consumption is largely depersonalized through globalized mass production. Consumers are alienated from producers, and the latter are thus more likely to be exploited by corporate management via low wages and poor working conditions.

Modes of exchange correspond to the modes of production and consumption. In foraging societies, the mode of exchange is balanced exchange, with the goal of keeping the value of the items exchanged roughly equal over time. The balanced mode of exchange involves people who have a social relationship with each other, and the relationship is reinforced through continued exchange. In market exchange, the predominant form of unbalanced exchange, the goal of making a profit overrides social relationships. In market exchange, the people involved in the transaction are less likely to know each other or to have a social relationship.

■ HOW are production, consumption, and exchange changing in contemporary times?

Economic globalization is changing production, consumption, and exchange around the world. Western goods, such as steel axes, are in high demand by people in non-Western, nonindustrialized contexts. Such goods must be purchased, a fact that impels people to work for cash so that they can buy things. The nutritional status of many nonindustrial groups has fallen with their adoption of Western-style foods; especially marked are increases in the amounts of sugar and salt in food.

The demand for cash has prompted many people to switch from growing food for their own use to growing crops for sale. This transition means that farmers put themselves at risk when a drop occurs in the market price of the crop they grow. Throughout the post-Soviet world, average health and nutrition levels fell after perestroika. Credit card shopping, in combination with middle-class values, is creating high levels of indebtedness in the United States.

In spite of the powerful effects of globalization on local economic patterns, many groups are rejecting Western economic incorporation and seeking to restore traditional patterns of production, consumption, and exchange. The revival of the potlatch tradition in the Pacific Northwest is one example of this trend.

KEY CONCEPTS

balanced exchange, p. 339
consumerism, p. 333
consumption, p. 320
corporate farm, p. 330
exchange, p. 320
expected reciprocity, p. 340
extensive strategy, p. 321
family farming, p. 328

generalized reciprocity, p. 340
indigenous knowledge, p. 327
industrial capital agriculture, p. 330
industrial collective agriculture, p. 331
industrialism, p. 332
market exchange, p. 341
minimalism, p. 333
mode of consumption, p. 333

mode of exchange, p. 333
mode of production, p. 320
production, p. 320
pure gift, p. 340
redistribution, p. 340
unbalanced exchange, p. 339
use right, p. 322
world economy, p. 343

SUGGESTED READINGS

Jans Dahl. *Saqqaq: An Inuit Hunting Community in the Modern World*. Toronto: University of Toronto Press, 2000. This ethnography of Saqqaq, a hunting community located on Disko Bay, eastern Greenland, is based on fieldwork carried out at several times since 1980 in order to provide a longitudinal perspective. Hunting beluga is a central community activity and still forms the basis of community identity, even though commercial fishing and other economic activities have gained importance recently.

Frances Dahlberg, ed. *Woman the Gatherer*. New Haven, CT: Yale University Press, 1981. The essays in this book examine the role of women in four different foraging societies, provide insights into human evolution from studies of female chimpanzees, and give an overview of women's role in human cultural adaptation.

Elliot Fratkin. *Ariaal Pastoralists of Kenya: Surviving Drought and Development in Africa's Arid Lands*. Boston: Allyn and Bacon, 1998. Based on several phases of ethnographic research among the Ariaal beginning in the 1970s, this book provides insights about pastoralism in general and the particular cultural strategies of the Ariaal. It focuses on social organization and family life.

Jane I. Guyer, ed. *Money Matters: Instability, Values and Social Payments in the Modern History of West African Communities*. Portsmouth, NH: Heinemann/James Currey, 1995. A collection of chapters by historians and cultural anthropologists examines topics such as why people in rural Gambia do not save money in banks, money as a symbol among the Yoruba, and the impact of colonial monetization in Nigeria and elsewhere.

Betsy Hartmann and James Boyce. *Needless Hunger: Voices from a Bangladesh Village*. San Francisco: Institute for Food and Development Policy, 1982. Evidence from fieldwork in rural Bangladesh shows that poverty and hunger in Bangladesh are caused primarily by severe class inequalities. The text includes a critique of the role of foreign aid in perpetuating inequalities, as well as suggestions for change.

Dwight B. Heath. *Drinking Occasions: Comparative Perspectives on Alcohol and Culture*. New York: Taylor & Francis, 2000. This book provides an ethnological review of drinking. The author focuses on several questions: When do people drink alcohol? Where do people drink? Who drinks and who doesn't? How do people drink? What do people drink? Why do people drink? He asks, in conclusion, where do we go from here with this topic?

David Uru Iyam. *The Broken Hoe: Cultural Reconfiguration in Biase Southeast Nigeria*. Chicago: University of Chicago Press, 1995. Based on fieldwork among the Biase people by an anthropologist who is a member of a Biase group, this book examines changes since the 1970s in the traditional forms of subsistence—agriculture, fishing, and trade—and the related issues of environmental deterioration and population growth.

Anna M. Kertula. *Antler on the Sea: The Yup'ik and Chukchi of the Russian Far East*. Ithaca, NY: Cornell University Press, 2000. Economic and social changes among two groups—sea mammal hunters and reindeer herders—in a Siberian village on the Bering Sea are the focus of this ethnography. The author explores adjustments in intergroup relations, conflict, identity, and cooperation that have taken place since the breakup of the former Soviet Union and the subsequent collapse of the local economy.

Christine Mullen Kreamer and Sarah Fee, eds. *Objects as Envoys: Cloth, Imagery, and Diplomacy in Madagascar*. Washington, DC: Smithsonian Institution Press, 2002. Six chapters explore the history and culture of Madagascar by focusing on textile arts and on textiles as items of exchange with deep social meaning and value. For centuries, Madagascar has used textiles to form and maintain social relationships internally and internationally.

Daniel Miller. *The Dialectics of Shopping*. Chicago: University of Chicago Press, 2001. This book reflects the author's interest in studying shopping as a clue to social relations. He discusses how shopping is related to kinship, community, ethics and identity, and the political economy. He draws on his own ethnographic research in several locations.

Sidney W. Mintz. *Sweetness and Power: The Place of Sugar in Modern History*. New York: Penguin Books, 1985. Combining historical and anthropological techniques, this book traces an important part of the story of world capitalism: the transformation of sugar from a luxury item to an omnipresent item of consumption worldwide.

Heather Montgomery. *Modern Babylon? Prostituting Children in Thailand*. New York: Bergahn Books, 2001. The author conducted fieldwork in a tourist community in Thailand where parents frequently commit their children to prostitution. She sought to gain a view of this system from the perspective of the children and the parents. She found that these insiders' views are far more complex than the monolithic "victim" picture painted by international agencies.

Brian Morris. *The Power of Animals: An Ethnography*. New York: Berg, 1998. This book is an ethnography of Malawi, southern Africa. It is based on in-depth fieldwork in one region, supplemented by travel and study throughout the country. It focuses on men's roles in animal hunting and women's roles in agriculture as crucial to understanding wider aspects of Malawian culture, including diet and food preparation, marriage and kinship, gender relations, and attitudes toward nature.

Katherine S. Newman. *Falling from Grace: The Experience of Downward Mobility in the American Middle Class*. New York: The Free Press, 1988. This book describes ethnographic findings on downwardly mobile people of New Jersey as a "special tribe," paying special attention to loss of employment by corporate managers and blue-collar workers and the effects of downward mobility on middle-class family life.

Richard H. Robbins. *Global Problems and the Culture of Capitalism*. Boston: Longman, 1999. Robbins takes a critical look at the role of capitalism and global economic growth in creating and sustaining many world problems, such as poverty, disease, hunger, violence, and environmental destruction. The last section includes case studies.

Lidia D. Sciama and Joanne B. Eicher, eds. *Beads and Bead Makers: Gender, Material Culture and Meaning*. New York: Berg, 1998. This book includes over a dozen articles on beads, including early international trade in Venetian beads, the relationship between beads and ethnicity in Malaysia, beads and power at the New Orleans Mardi Gras, and rosaries in the Andes. All the articles offer insights into gender roles and meanings.

Deborah Sick. *Farmers of the Golden Bean: Costa Rican Households and the Global Coffee Economy.* Dekalb: Northern Illinois University Press, 1999. This book is an ethnography of coffee-producing households in Costa Rica. It describes the difficulties that coffee farmers face as a consequence of unpredictable global forces and examines the uncertain role of the state as a mediator between the global and the local.

James L. Watson, ed. *Golden Arches East: McDonald's in East Asia.* Stanford, CA: Stanford University Press, 1997. This book contains five case studies, an introduction written by the editor, and an afterword by Sidney Mintz, noted cultural anthropologist of food and foodways. Case studies located in China, Taiwan, Korea, and Japan address topics such as how McDonald's culture becomes localized, dietary effects on children, eating etiquette, and how food choices are related to national identity.

Patsy West. *The Enduring Seminoles: From Alligator Wrestling to Ecotourism.* Gainesville: University Press of Florida, 1998. During the first half of the nineteenth century, Andrew Jackson and others fought against Native American groups and displaced them from their land. This book describes how a southern group of Seminoles began to develop tourist attractions that appeal to the growing numbers of visitors from the North. Calling themselves the *i:laponathli:*, they have built a thriving economy by marketing old and new aspects of Seminole life, and they are proud to consider their culture "unconquered."

THE BIG QUESTIONS

- HOW are modes of reproduction related to modes of production?
- HOW does culture shape fertility in different contexts?
- HOW does culture shape personality and human development over the life cycle?

CHAPTER 12

Reproduction and Human Development

An elderly woman out shopping in an urban market in central China. Throughout Asia, it is the responsibility of children to care for their parents in their old age. But the numbers of the elderly are growing, while reduced fertility means fewer family caretakers. (Source: Courtesy of Barbara Miller)

"Should I have been killed at birth?" asks disability rights lawyer Harriet McBryde Johnson, who practices in Charleston, South Carolina (2003). Born with a weakened respiratory system that, before antibiotics, would have resulted in her death from childhood pneumonia, Johnson now moves about via a power wheelchair, eats only soft food, and uses a bed pan instead of a toilet.

She was recently invited to speak at Princeton University by a professor there, Peter Singer, who supports "disability infanticide." He argues that if abortion is legal, selective infanticide should also be legal, allowing parents to choose to keep children whose chances of happiness are greater. Johnson, a member of a disability rights group called Not Dead Yet, disagrees, saying that nondisabled people should not be allowed to make judgments about the quality of life, or degrees of happiness, of people with disabilities.

Singer further claims that no infant is a "person" with a right to life. Personhood, he maintains, only comes later. Even though some of Johnson's friends, relatives, and colleagues were disappointed with her for consenting to spend time with Singer, she gained from the experience. She realized that if she were to demonize him, she would have to consider many other people as evil too. Instead, Johnson continues to work for legal protection of people with disabilities and to help them live rewarding lives.

The entire process of bearing and raising children into adults and the issue of defining humanity and the quality of life are the topics of this chapter. The first section provides an overview of reproduction in relation to modes of production. The second section focuses on **fertility**, or the rate of population growth derived from the numbers of births and deaths, and how culture shapes fertility. The third section provides insights into the cultural development of the person, and of personality, over the life cycle.

MODES OF REPRODUCTION

Cultural anthropologists have enough data to support the construction of **modes of reproduction** (the predominant pattern of fertility in a culture) that correspond roughly to three of the major modes of production (see Figure 12.1). The foraging mode of reproduction, which existed for most of human prehistory, had low rates of population growth because it was characterized by moderate birth rates and moderate death rates. The agricultural mode of reproduction emerged with sedentism (permanent settlements). As increased food surpluses became available to support more people, birth rates increased over death rates, and high population densities were reached in agricultural societies. In the industrialized mode of reproduction, exemplified in Europe, Japan, and the United States, population growth rates declined as birth rates fell faster than death rates.

Horticulturalists and pastoralists exhibit some features of both the foraging mode of reproduction and the agricultural mode of reproduction, depending on the context. Because anthropologists have done less research on reproduction than on production, it is impossible to provide as much detail for modes of reproduction in these economic systems.

The Foraging Mode of Reproduction

Archaeological evidence about prehistoric populations, from about 200,000 years ago to the Neolithic era of agricultural development starting 12,000 years ago, indicates that population growth rates among foragers remained low over thousands of years (Harris and Ross 1987). Foraging societies' spatial mobility calls for few children. It is simply not possible for an adult to carry several babies. The low population growth rates over thousands of years probably resulted from several factors:

FIGURE 12.1
Modes of production and reproduction.

(*Source:* Reprinted by permission of Allyn & Bacon.)

FORAGING	AGRICULTURE	INDUSTRIALISM (CAPITALIST)
Population Growth	*Population Growth*	*Population Growth*
Moderate birth rates Moderate death rates	High birth rates Declining death rates	Industrialized nations— negative population growth Developing nations—high
Value of Children	*Value of Children*	*Value of Children*
Moderate	High	Mixed
Fertility Control	*Fertility Control*	*Fertility Control*

Indirect means
  Low-fat diet of women
  Women's work and exercise
  Prolonged breastfeeding
  Spontaneous abortion
Direct means
  Induced abortion
  Infanticide
	Increased reliance
	on direct means
	  Pronatalist techniques
	  Herbs
	  Induced abortion
	  Infanticide
		Direct methods grounded
		in science and medicine
		Chemical forms
		of contraception
		In vitro fertilization
		Abortion

Social Aspects	*Social Aspects*	*Social Aspects*

Homogeneous fertility
Few specialists
	Emerging class differences
	Increasing specialization
	  Midwifery
	  Herbalists
		Stratified fertility
		(globally, nationally,
		and locally)
		Highly developed
		specialization

high rates of spontaneous abortion because of the heavy workloads borne by women, reproductive stress that seasonality of diets imposed on women, long breastfeeding of infants (which suppresses ovulation), induced abortion, and **infanticide,** the deliberate killing of offspring. Low birth rates appear to be more important than mortality in leading to population stability, or *homeostasis,* among foragers.

Research on the Ju/wasi sheds light on how population homeostasis is achieved (Howell 1979). Birth intervals (the time between one birth and a subsequent birth) among the Ju/wasi are several years long. Two factors account for long birth intervals: breastfeeding and women's low level of body fat. Frequent and long periods of breastfeeding inhibit progesterone production and suppress ovulation. A certain level of body fat is required for ovulation (Frisch 1978), and Ju/wasi women's diets contain little fat. Their body fat is also kept low through the physical exercise that their foraging work entails.

Thus, environmental factors (food supply and diet) and economic factors (women's workloads) shape a pattern of reproduction that is adaptive in the Ju/wasi environment. Among the Ju/wasi who have abandoned foraging and become farmers or laborers, fertility levels have increased. Important factors explaining the increase include dietary change—eating grains and dairy products—and reduced physical mobility.

The Agricultural Mode of Reproduction

Agriculture promotes and supports the highest fertility rates found in any mode of production. **Pronatalism,** an ideology promoting many children, is a key value of farm families. Pronatalism is related to the need for a large labor force to work the land, care for animals, process food, and do marketing. Thus, having many children is an adaptive reproductive strategy for a people engaging in the agricultural mode of production.

Members of an Amish household sit around their kitchen table in Indiana. ■ How many, if any, children do you want to have? How does that goal fit with your microculture and mode of production? (Source: © David & Peter Turnley/CORBIS)

In rural North India, sons are especially important, given the gender division of labor in farming communities. Men plow the fields and protect the family land when quarrels over land rights occur. When Western promoters of family planning first visited a village in North India in the late 1950s to spread the idea of reducing births, the villagers were puzzled (Mamdani 1972). The farmers equated a large family with wealth and success, not with poverty and failure. The Western family planning agents had assumed they could simply provide the rural Indians with modern contraceptive techniques that would be eagerly accepted. They failed to understand that having many children in a family farming system makes sense and that having few children does not. With mechanization and other changes that reduce the need for family labor, however, farm families respond by opting for fewer children.

The Industrial Mode of Reproduction

In industrial societies, either capitalist or socialist, reproduction declines to the point of **replacement-level fertility,** when the number of births equals the number of deaths, or **below-replacement-level fertility,** when the number of births is less than the number of deaths, a situation that leads to population decline (see Figure 12.2). Children in most industrialized contexts are not valued as workers, and mandatory school attendance further lowers their value as laborers. Parents respond to these changes by having fewer children and by investing more resources in them.

The industrial mode of production involves three additional distinct features:

■ Class variation in reproduction.

■ An increase in the numbers of senior people.

■ The role of science and technology in reproduction.

In terms of class variations, middle-class and upper-class people tend to have few children, and their children tend to have high survival rates. Among the poor, in contrast, fertility and **mortality** (death) rates are high. As noted in Chapter 10, Brazil has the most extreme inequality of income distribution in the world. It also has extreme differences in reproductive patterns between the rich and the poor.

Another characteristic of industrial countries is population aging. In Japan, for example, the total fertility rate declined to replacement level in the 1950s and later reached the below-replacement level (Hodge and Ogawa 1991). Japan is currently experiencing a decline in population growth of about 15 percent per generation. At the same time, Japan's population is rapidly aging. Many people are moving into the senior category, creating a population bulge not matched by population increases in younger age groups.

FIGURE 12.2

Nations with below-replacement-level fertility (fertility rates below two births per woman), late 1990s.

Country	Fertility Rate	Country	Fertility Rate	Country	Fertility Rate
Armenia	1.4	Dominica	1.9	Norway	1.8
Australia	1.7	Finland	1.7	Poland	1.4
Austria	1.3	France	1.8	Portugal	1.5
Azerbaijan	1.9	Germany	1.3	Romania	1.3
Barbados	1.8	Greece	1.3	Russia	1.2
Belarus	1.3	Hungary	1.3	Singapore	1.5
Belgium	1.6	Italy	1.2	Slovakia	1.4
Bosnia-Herzegovina	1.6	Ireland	1.9	Slovenia	1.2
Bulgaria	1.1	Japan	1.3	Spain	1.2
Canada	1.5	Kazakhstan	1.7	Sweden	1.5
China	1.8	Korea, South	1.5	Switzerland	1.5
Croatia	1.5	Lithuania	1.3	Taiwan	1.5
Cuba	1.6	Luxembourg	1.7	Thailand	1.9
Cyprus	1.9	Macedonia	1.9	Trinidad & Tobago	1.7
Czech Republic	1.1	Martinique	1.8	Ukraine	1.3
Denmark	1.7	Netherlands	1.6	United Kingdom	1.7

(*Source:* Table, "Some Nations with Below-Replacement-Level Fertility [Fertility Rates Below Two Births per Woman], Late 1990s" from *2000 World Population Data Sheet*, Population Reference Bureau. Copyright © 2000. Reprinted by permission of Population Reference Bureau.)

In industrial societies, there is a high level of scientific involvement in all aspects of reproduction. Technology now exists for preventing pregnancy, for becoming pregnant, and for terminating a pregnancy (Browner and Press 1996). The growing importance of the "new reproductive technologies," such as *in vitro* fertilization, is a major part of an expanding market in scientific reproduction. These forms of technology are accompanied by increasing levels of professional specialization in providing the new services.

CULTURE AND FERTILITY

Cultures shape human reproduction from its very beginning, if that beginning can be said to be sexual intercourse itself. Cultural practices and beliefs about pregnancy and birth also affect the viability of the fetus during its gestation and the infant's fate after birth.

Sexual Intercourse

Anthropological research on sexuality and sexual practices is particularly difficult to undertake because sexuality involves private—sometimes secret—beliefs and behaviors. The ethics of participant observation prevent intimate observation (and certainly rule out participation). Thus, information on sexual behavior can be obtained only indirectly. For several reasons, biases are likely in people's reports to an anthropologist about their sexual beliefs and behavior. They may be too shy to talk about sex, too boastful to give accurate information, or simply unable to remember the answers to questions such as "How many times did you have intercourse last year?" The gender of the anthropologist and the gender of the respondent may also affect the answers to questions about sexual behavior (see the Methods Close-Up box on p. 358).

Taking Gender into Account When Surveying Sexual Behavior

A COMMON ASSUMPTION in survey work about sexual behavior is that respondents will give more accurate information to interviewers of the same gender as the respondent (McCombie and Anarfi, 2002). This assumption was questioned and examined using survey results gathered in Ghana in 1991, during the early stages of the AIDS epidemic. The survey was conducted among people fifteen to thirty years old to establish baseline information before establishing a campaign to raise the awareness of AIDS and promote its prevention.

The assignment of interviewers to respondents was randomized by gender so that each male and female interviewer interviewed some men and some women. The questionnaire included one hundred questions on basic demographics, sexual behavior, and AIDS awareness. This discussion of potential gender bias in response considers only the questions on sexual behavior.

Did responses to male and to female interviewers differ? Results show that males responded similarly to male and female interviewers about their sexual behavior. But females did not. The most striking difference was among women aged 15 to 18 years, who were much more likely to report that they had had sex to a male interviewer than to a female interviewer. When the interviewer was male, 64 percent reported that they had had sex. When the interviewer was female, only 44 percent reported having had sex. This pattern confirms a local belief that "women won't tell other women anything."

The lesson about methods from this analysis of Ghanaian survey data is that gender matching in surveys is not necessarily the best approach. If the survey had been conducted by matching the gender of the interviewer with that of the respondent, severe underestimation of young women's sexual activity would have resulted. Matched-gender interviews may be appropriate and effective in some cultural contexts, but they are not always so.

FOOD FOR THOUGHT

- If an interviewer asked you questions about your sexuality, would the likelihood of your answering truthfully be affected by whether the interviewer was male or female?

When to Begin Having Intercourse?

Biologically speaking, sexual intercourse between a fertile female and a fertile male is normally required for human reproduction, although artificial insemination or embryo transplantation are options in some contexts. Biology also defines the time span within which a female is fertile: from *menarche* (the onset of menstruation) to *menopause* (the cessation of menstruation). Globally, the age of menarche varies. The average is fourteen years in industrial countries and sixteen years in developing countries. This difference may be due to variations in diet and activity patterns. Average age at menopause varies more widely, from the forties to the fifties; the later averages tend to occur in industrialized societies. This difference may be related to the higher fat content of diets in industrialized nations.

Cultures socialize children about the appropriate time to begin sexual intercourse. Guidelines for initiating sexual intercourse differ by gender, class, and ethnicity. Cross-culturally, rules more strictly forbid premarital sexual activity of girls than of boys. In Zawiya, a traditional Muslim town of northern Morocco, the virginity of the bride—but not of the groom—is highly valued (Davis and Davis 1987). Most brides conform to the ideal. Some unmarried young women do engage in premarital sex, however. If they wish to have a traditional wedding, they have to deal with the requirement of producing blood-stained sheets after their wedding night. How do they do this? The groom may assist in deception by nicking his finger with a knife and bloodying the sheets himself. Another option is to buy fake blood in the drugstore.

How Often to Have Intercourse

Cross-culturally, there is a wide range in frequency of sexual intercourse. This variation confirms the role of culture in shaping sexual desire. A classic study of reported frequency of intercourse for Euro-Americans in the United States and Hindus in India revealed that the Indians had intercourse less frequently (less than twice a week) than the Euro-Americans did (two to three times a week) (Nag 1972).

Several features of Indian culture limit sexual intercourse. The Hindu religion teaches the value of sexual abstinence and suggests that people should abstain from intercourse on sacred days, including the first night of the new moon, the first night of the full moon, the eighth day of each half of the month (the light half and the dark half), and sometimes Friday. As many as one hundred days each year could be observed as non-sex days. Another factor is Hindu men's belief in what cultural anthropologists term the *lost semen complex*. An American anthropologist learned about this complex during fieldwork in North India: "Everyone knew that semen was not easily formed; it takes forty days and forty drops of blood to make one drop of semen . . . . Semen of good quality is rich and viscous, like the cream of unadulterated milk. A man who possesses a store of such good semen becomes a super-man [and] every sexual orgasm meant the loss of a quantity of semen, laboriously formed" (Carstairs 1967, 83–86, quoted in Nag 1972: 235).

(*Source:* Reprinted by permission of Allyn & Bacon.)

Fertility Decision Making

This section explores decision making about fertility at three levels: family, state, and global. Family decision makers weigh various factors in deciding why and when to have a child. State governments define population goals in relation to labor needs, their tax base, and other factors. At the global level, powerful economic, political, and religious institutions influence the reproductive policies of states and, in turn, the practices of families and individuals within them.

Family-Level Decision Making

At the family level, parents' and other family members' perceptions about the value and costs of children influence reproductive decision making (Nag 1983). Assessing the value and costs of children is a complex matter involving many factors, the most important of which are

- children's labor value.
- children's value as old-age support for parents and other family members.
- infant and child mortality rates.
- the economic costs of children.

In the first three factors, the relationship is positive: when children's value is high in terms of labor or old-age support, fertility is likely to be higher. When infant and child mortality rates are high, fertility rates also tend to be high in order to "replace" offspring who do not survive. But in terms of costs—including direct costs (for food, education, and clothing) and indirect costs (employment opportunities

A bride wearing traditional wedding clothing in the city of Meknès, Morocco. ■ On the Web, find a detailed map of Morocco and locate the town of Zawiya. (Source: © Stephanie Dinkins/Photo Researchers, Inc.)

Girls participating in the Guelaguetza festival, Oaxaca. Oaxaca is a distinctive cultural region and the scene of a vigorous movement for indigenous people's rights. ■ Find a current events item about Oaxaca from a newspaper or the Internet. (Source: © Rose Hartman/CORBIS)

A family planning clinic in Egypt. Throughout much of the world, provision of Western-style family planning advice is controversial because it may conflict with local religious and other beliefs about the value of having many children and women's duty to be child bearers. ■ In your cultural experience, what is the prevalent attitude about family planning, specifically birth control and women's access to means of fertility management? (Source: © Barry Iverson/Woodfin Camp & Associates)

that the mother gives up)—the relationship is negative. In other words, higher costs promote a desire for fewer children. As mentioned earlier, industrialization reduces the labor value of children, and it greatly increases their costs.

Although these four factors are generally important, particular cultural contexts reveal internal variation in how they affect fertility decision making. In a highland village in the Oaxacan region of southern Mexico, men and women have different preferences about the number of children, with men more in favor of having many children than women (Browner 1986). One woman said, "My husband sleeps peacefully through the night, but I have to get up when the children need something. I'm the one the baby urinates on; sometimes I have to get out of bed in the cold and change both our clothes. They wake me when they're sick or thirsty; my husband sleeps through it all" (714).

At the State Level

State governments play important roles in affecting the rates of population growth within their boundaries. Governments are concerned about providing employment and public services, maintaining the tax base, filling the ranks of the military, maintaining ethnic and regional proportions, and dealing with population aging. Many countries, including Japan and France, are concerned about declining rates of population growth. Their leaders have urged women to have more babies.

At the Global Level

The most far-reaching layer that affects fertility decision making is the international level, where global institutions such as the World Bank, pharmaceutical companies, and religious leaders influence priorities about fertility. In the 1950s there was an initial wave of enthusiasm among Western nations for promoting family planning programs of many types. Recently, the United States has adopted a more restricted policy of limited advocacy for family planning and has withdrawn support for certain methods, such as abortion.

Fertility Control in Cross-Cultural Perspective

All cultures from prehistory to the present have had ways of influencing fertility, including ways to increase it, reduce it, and regulate its spacing. Some ways are direct, such as using herbs or medicines that induce abortion. Others are indirect, such as long periods of breastfeeding, which reduce the chances of conception.

Indigenous Methods

Hundreds of indigenous fertility control methods are available cross-culturally, and many of them were in existence long before modern science came on the scene (Newman 1972, 1985). A study in Afghanistan in the 1980s found over five hundred fertility-regulating techniques in just one region (Hunte 1985). In Afghanistan, as in most nonindustrial cultures, it is women who possess this information. Specialists, such as midwives or herbalists, provide further guidance and expertise. Of the total number of methods in the Afghanistan study, 72 percent were aimed at increasing fertility, 22 percent were contraceptives (preventing fertilization of the ovum by the sperm), and 6 percent were used to induce abortion. The methods involve plant and animal substances prepared and administered in a variety of ways, including herbal tea and pills.

Western scientific research confirms the efficacy of many indigenous fertility-regulating methods. For example, experiments on animals show that some 450 plant species worldwide contain natural substances that prevent ovulation or reduce fertility in some other way.

Induced Abortion

Induced abortion, in its many forms, is probably a cultural universal. A review of about four hundred societies indicates that it was practiced in virtually all of them (Devereaux 1976). Social attitudes toward abortion range from absolute acceptability to conditional approval (abortion is acceptable under specified conditions), tolerance (abortion is regarded with neither approval nor disapproval), and opposition and punishment for offenders. Methods of inducing abortion include hitting the abdomen, starving oneself, taking drugs, jumping from high places, jumping up and down, lifting heavy objects, doing hard work, and inserting sharp obects vaginally.

Economic and social factors largely explain why people induce abortion (Devereaux 1976:13–21). Women in foraging and pastoralist societies, for example, sometimes

In your microculture, is there a general preference about the desired number of children, if any? How does this pattern compare with that of your parents' generation?

THINKING OUTSIDE THE BOX

Given all the cultural pressures on people's fertility, from local cultural norms to state-level and international policies, consider how much agency an individual has in fertility decision making.

THINKING OUTSIDE THE BOX

Afghan women waiting for their turn at the clinic in Bazarak. Throughout Afghanistan, patriarchal norms prevent women from going to clinics, and the geographical terrain and distance make it impossible to get to a clinic in cases of emergency. Rates of maternal mortality in remote areas of Afghanistan are perhaps the highest in the world.
■ Consult the United Nation's *Human Development Report* for national statistics on maternal mortality worldwide. (Source: © Reza; Webistan/CORBIS)

In parts of Mongolia and Siberia, many pastoralists continue to herd reindeer as a major part of their economy. ■ Do some research to learn about the worldwide distribution of reindeer in the wild and the culture and fertility of the people who herd them. (Source: © Xinhua-Chine Nou/Gamma Press)

People regularly visit and decorate statues in memory of their "returned" fetuses in Japan. ■ In your cultural world, how do people define the fetus and how do they treat it? (Source: © Oliver Pichetti/Gamma Press)

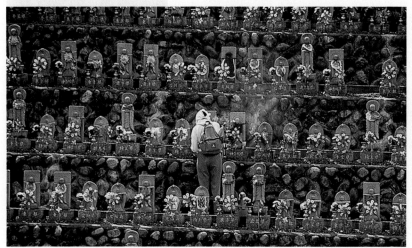

have to move over long distances and carry heavy loads. This lifestyle does not allow for the care of many small children at one time. Poverty is another motivating factor: When a family is faced with a birth in the context of limited resources, abortion may appear to be the best option. Culturally defined legitimacy of a pregnancy, along with possible social penalties for bearing an illegitimate child, has been a prominent reason for abortion in Western societies.

Governments have sometimes intervened in family decisions to regulate access to abortion, sometimes promoting it and at other times forbidding it. Starting in the late 1980s, China pursued a rigorous campaign to limit population growth (Greenhalgh 2003). Its one-child-per-couple policy allowed most families to have only one child. This policy involved strict surveillance of pregnancies, the use of peer disapproval directed toward women pregnant for the second time or more, and forced abortions and sterilizations. Inadvertently, this policy also led to an increase in female infanticide, as some parents, in their desire for a son, opted to kill or abandon any daughters born to them.

Some religions take a position against abortion, although what a religion teaches and what people actually do may diverge. For example, Catholicism forbids abortion, but thousands of Catholic women throughout the world have sought abortions. Islamic teachings forbid abortion and female infanticide, yet sex-selective abortion of female fetuses is practiced covertly by Muslims in Pakistan and in India. Hinduism teaches ahimsa, or nonviolence toward other living beings, including a fetus whose movements have been felt by the mother. Yet thousands of Hindus seek abortions every year, especially of female fetuses (Miller 2005).

In contrast, Buddhism includes no rules against abortion. Japanese Buddhism teaches that all life is fluid and that an aborted fetus is simply "returned" to a watery world of unshaped life and may later come back (LaFleur 1992). This belief fits well with the fact that in recent years, abortion has been the most commonly used form of birth control in Japan.

Infanticide

Deliberate killing of offspring has been widely documented cross-culturally, although it is not usually a frequent or common practice in any society. Infanticide can take the form of *direct infanticide* or *indirect infanticide* (Harris 1977). Direct infanticide is the intentional death of an infant or child resulting from actions such as beating, smothering, poisoning, or drowning. Indirect infanticide, a more subtle process, may involve prolonged practices such as food deprivation, failure to take a sick infant to a clinic, or failure to provide warm clothing in winter.

The most common motive for direct infanticide cross-culturally is that the infant was ill or "deformed" (Scrimshaw 1984:490–491). No general theory has been formulated to explain the relationship between resource constraints and perceived child "fitness." Not all people living in poverty practice infanticide, nor do all people practice infanticide when a child is born with certain disabilities. Other motives for infanticide include sex of the infant, an adulterous conception, an unwed mother, the birth of twins, and the family having many other children already.

Culturally accepted infanticide has long existed among the Tarahumara, a group of around 50,000 indigenous people who live in a dry and mountainous part of northern Mexico (Mull and Mull 1987). Most Tarahumara live in log houses with dirt floors and no running water or electricity. They grow corn and beans and raise sheep and goats, mainly for their own use. Human strength is valued in children as well as in adults, because quite young children help with herding and child care. The possibility of infanticide first became apparent to anthropologist Dennis Mull when he was working as a volunteer physician in a hospital. A twelve-month-old girl who had been admitted several months earlier developed a complication requiring the amputation of half her foot. During her recovery period, her mother's visits became less frequent. In conversations with the medical staff, the mother expressed a restrained but deep anger about the fact that her daughter had lost half her foot. After the child was dismissed from the hospital, she reportedly "failed" and died. One member of the community interpreted her death this way: "Well, after all, with only half a foot she'd never be able to walk right or work hard. She might never find a husband" (116–117).

Among the poor of northeast Brazil, there exists a similar pattern of indirect infanticide that is related to poverty (Scheper-Hughes 1992). Life is hard for the residents of the shantytown called Bom Jesus, in the state of Pernambuco. Life expectancy is low, although precise information on mortality is not available for these shantytown dwellers. Poverty forces mothers to selectively (and unconsciously) neglect babies that seem sickly or weak, sending them to heaven as "angel babies" rather than trying to keep them alive (see the photograph on p. 365). The people's religious beliefs, a form of Catholicism, provide ideological support for this practice of indirect infanticide because it allows mothers to believe that their dead babies are now safe in heaven.

When the infant's gender is the basis for infanticide, females are more likely to be the target (Miller 1997 [1981]). Among foraging groups, female infanticide is found

The states of Brazil.

mainly among some circumpolar groups of North America, where it is related to the importance of raising males who will provide food by hunting large game. Among horticultural societies, a correlation exists between the practice of female infanticide and the level of intergroup warfare (Divale and Harris 1976). Warfare places greater value on raising males, to the detriment of investing care and resources in females.

The generalization about females being the more common focus of infanticide applies to contemporary cultures, not to the distant past. Archaeological evidence about infanticide is difficult to interpret in terms of possible gender patterns, but there are cases from Mesopotamia and Biblical Egypt of preferential male infanticide, particularly among ruling elites (Scott 2001). These examples suggest that infanticide has not always been directed mainly at female offspring.

PERSONALITY, HUMAN DEVELOPMENT, AND THE LIFE CYCLE

This section describes how cultural anthropology has approached the study of the individual, especially how cultures shape **personality,** an individual's patterned and characteristic way of behaving, thinking, and feeling. The material is presented in the order of the stages of the life cycle, from birth through death in old age. The subject matter is referred to as **ethnopsychology,** the study of how different cultures define and create personality, identity, and mental health. The focus in this chapter is on "normal" human development. Problematic aspects of human development, including what Western psychology defines as mental illness, are discussed in Chapter 13.

Margaret Mead, during her later years of fieldwork, observes children's interactions in Sicily. ■ Have you ever attempted to observe small children's behavior for research purposes? How would such research differ from doing research among teenagers or adults? (Source: © Ken Heyman/Woodfin Camp & Associates)

Most cultural anthropologists think that personality is formed through enculturation, or socialization, the process by which culture is transmitted to infants and other new members. They seek answers to these questions: Do different cultures enculturate their members into different personalities? If so, how and why?

Birth, Infancy, and Childhood

In the United States, commonly accepted life stages include infancy, childhood, adolescence, middle age, and old age (psychologists and other experts concerned with human development construct even finer substages). Western life-cycle stages are based on biological features such as the ability to walk, puberty, and capacity for parenthood (Bogin 1988). These stages are not cultural universals. Whereas the biological model assumes that all its life-cycle markers would form the basis of universal stages, cultural anthropologists find striking variation in how different cultures construct life stages, and they have discovered that such stages may be quite unrelated to biology (Johnson-Hanks 2002). The cultural construction of life stages thus can ignore or override what Western biology would dictate. This section considers how cross-cultural findings on broad life stages provide insight into how people in different cultures are born, grow up, and move into old age.

Giving Birth

Cultural anthropologists have asked whether the cultural context of the event of birth itself has psychological effects on the infant. Cross-cultural research shows that variations in the birth experience affect an infant's psychological development. Brigitte Jordan (1983), a pioneer in the cross-cultural study of birth, conducted research on birth practices in Mexico, Sweden, Holland, and the United States. She studied the birth setting, including its location and who is present, the types of attendants and their roles, the birth event, and the post-partum period. Among Maya women in Mexico, the midwife is called in during the early stages of labor. One of her tasks is to give a massage to the mother-to-be. She also provides psychological support by telling stories, often about other women's birthing experiences. The husband is expected to be present during the labor so that he can see "how a woman suffers." The woman's mother should be present, along with other female kin (such as her mother-in-law, godmother, and sisters), and her friends. Thus a Maya mother is surrounded by a large group of supportive people.

In the United States, hospital births are the norm. The newborn infant is generally taken to the nursery, where it is wrapped in cloth and placed in a plastic crate under bright lights rather than being cared for by a family member. Some critics argue that the hospital-based system of highly regulated birth is extremely technocratic and too managed, alienating the mother—as well as other members of the family and the wider community—from the birthing process and the infant (Davis-Floyd 1992). Such criticism has led to widespread consideration of how to improve the way birth is conducted.

The Western medical model of birth and non-Western practices contrast sharply, and sometimes come into conflict. In a Western hospital birthing situation, a culturally informed perspective can help resolve conflicts between the medical model and families on the appropriate treatment of a newborn (see the Lessons Applied box on p. 366).

In Bom Jesus, a shanty-town in northeastern Brazil, this mother was told by a doctor at the local clinic that her son was dying of anemia and that she needed to feed him red meat. The mother said, "Now, where am I going to find the money to feed my hopeless son rich food like that?" ■ What is your perspective on Western bonding theory, and how did you come to have this view? (Source: Nancy Scheper-Hughes)

The Role of Cultural Brokerage in the Newborn Nursery

IN A SUBURBAN COMMUNITY in the United States with a rapidly growing immigrant population, a new hospital was built to respond to this growth (Deitrick 2002). Most of the nurses on staff were long-term residents of the community and had graduated from the local community college, where the training included no attention to cultural differences.

However, a situation of conflicting cultural views soon arose upon the birth of a baby to a Turkish immigrant family. The infant had not yet been brought to the mother's room, and members of her family arrived to welcome the new baby. Along with them came a Muslim religious leader to administer the usual honey blessing to the infant before his first feeding. This ritual ensures a sweet life for the newborn.

The nurse in charge denied the family access to the baby, saying that the baby had to have a medical examination first and that unpasteurized honey could not be given to the baby. The father was upset and claimed that the baby must be blessed with the honey because the first taste a baby experiences determines the quality of its life.

Fortunately, a nurse with training in cultural anthropology, Lynn Deitrick, entered into the discussion and was able to serve as a **cultural broker,** a person—often but not always an anthropologist—who understands the perceptions and practices of two different cultures and can promote cross-cultural understanding and conflict resolution. She listened to the views of the Turkish family and learned that only a tiny amount of honey would be placed on the infant's tongue for the blessing. She then suggested to the medical staff a compromise: the baby would be taken to the mother's room for ten minutes, where the family and Muslim cleric would be present and could administer the blessing. The attending physician agreed, saying that she was not "on record" as approving the honey blessing but that she could understand its importance. Deitrick took the baby to the family and went back ten minutes later to find a smiling mother and a happy father. The baby then underwent the blood tests and other medically mandated procedures and was discharged in good health two days later.

FOOD FOR THOUGHT

- Did Lynn Deitrick do the right thing by acting as a cultural broker, or should the medical model have been followed strictly?

Bonding

Many contemporary Western psychological theorists say that parent–infant contact and bonding at the time of birth is crucial for setting in motion parental attachment to the infant. Western specialists say that if this bonding is not established at the time of the infant's birth, it will not develop later. Explanations for juvenile delinquency and other child development problems often include reference to lack of proper infant bonding at birth.

Cultural anthropologist Nancy Scheper-Hughes, whose research in a Brazilian shantytown was discussed earlier, questions Western bonding theory (1992). She argues that bonding does not necessarily have to occur at birth to be successful. Her observations show that many poor Brazilian mothers do not exhibit bonding with their infants at birth. If the child survives infancy, bonding occurs later, when it is several years old. She proposes that this pattern of later bonding is related to the high rate of infant mortality among poor people of Brazil. If women were to develop strong bonds with their infants, they would suffer untold grief. Western bonding is adaptive in low-mortality/low-fertility societies in which strong maternal attachment is reasonable because infants are likely to survive.

Gender and Infancy

Cultural anthropologists distinguish between sex and gender. Sex is something that everyone is born with. In the view of Western science, it has three biological markers: genitals, hormones, and chromosomes. Males are defined as people who have a penis, more androgens than estrogens, and an X and a Y chromosome. Females have a vagina, more estrogens than androgens, and two XX chromosomes. Increasingly, however, scientists are finding that these two categories are not sufficient. In all populations, some people are born with indeterminate genitals, similar proportions of androgens and estrogens, and chromosomes with more complex patterns of sex chromosomes (XXY, and XXX, for example). Thus a continuum model of gender is more accurate than a strict binary model.

Gender, in contrast, reflects the learned behavior and beliefs associated with maleness and femaleness and thus varies culturally (Miller 1993). Individuals acquire their gender identity, roles, and status through learning, much of which is unconscious. From the moment of birth, an infant's life course is shaped by whether it is labeled male or female and what the defined roles and status of "male" and "female" are in a particular culture. Most cultural anthropologists believe in a high degree of human "plasticity" (or personality flexibility), as demonstrated by Margaret Mead's early work on gender roles and personality in Papua New Guinea, and are convinced that gender socialization can to a large extent override sex-linked features such as hormones.

Many other researchers continue to insist that a wide range of supposedly sex-linked personality characteristics are innate. A major problem arises in trying to test for innate characteristics. First, one needs data on infants before they are subject to cultural treatment. But culture starts shaping the infant from the moment of birth through handling and treatment by others (this shaping may even begin in the womb, through exposure to sound and motion). Second, studying and interpreting the behavior of infants is fraught with potential bias.

Studies of infants have focused on assessing the potential innateness of three major Euro-American personality stereotypes: that infant males are more aggressive than infant females, that infant females are more social than infant males, and that males are more independent (Frieze et al. 1978:73–78). Boy babies cry more than girl babies, and some people believe that this is evidence of higher levels of inborn aggression in males. An alternative interpretation is that baby boys on average tend to weigh more than girls. They therefore are more likely to have a difficult delivery from which it takes time to recover, so they cry more, but not out of aggressiveness. In terms of sociality, baby girls smile more often than boys. Does this mean girls are born to be people pleasers? Evidence of caregivers smiling more at baby girls shows that the more frequent smiling of girls is a learned, not an innate, response. In terms of independence or dependence, studies thus far reveal no clear gender differences in how upset babies are when separated from their caregivers. Taken as a whole, studies seeking to document innate gender differences through the behavior of infants are not convincing.

Socialization during Childhood

The concept of "the child" as a special age category may have emerged first in Europe in the last few centuries (Ariès 1962). In art, portraits of children became commonplace only in the seventeenth century. Other changes occurred at the same time: new interests in children's habits, more elaborate terminology about children and childhood, and special clothing for children instead of small-sized versions of adult clothing. The special focus on "the child" is associated with the emergence of industrial capitalism's need for an ever-expanding market. In nonindustrialized cultures, "the child" is not regarded as having such specialized needs. In these societies, children are expected to take on adult tasks at an early age. Different expectations about what a child is and should do have implications for personality formation.

The *Six Cultures Study,* mentioned in Chapter 11, is a cross-cultural study designed to provide comparative data on children's personalities in relation to their activities and tasks (Whiting and Whiting 1975). Researchers observed sixty-seven children between the ages of three and eleven years. They recorded many forms of behavior, such as being supportive of other children; hitting other children; and performing tasks such as child care, cooking, and errands. These behaviors were analyzed in the following personality dimensions: "nurturant-responsible" or "dependent-dominant." Nurturant-responsible personalities are characterized by caring and sharing acts toward other children. The dependent-dominant personality involves fewer acts of care-seeking and more acts that asserted dominance over other children. Six teams of researchers were trained in the methodology and conducted field research in six contexts.

Group A: Horticulture or family farming

- Gusii, Kenya
- Oaxaca, Mexico
- Tarong, Philippines

Group B: Intensive agriculture or industrial

- Taira, Japan
- Rajputs, India
- Orchard Town, United States

The Gusii children of Kenya had the highest rate of a nurturant-responsible personality type, whereas the children in Orchard Town had the lowest. Orchard Town children had the highest prevalence of the dependent-dominant personality type. The range of variation follows a general pattern correlating with the mode of production. "Group A" cultures all had more nurturant-responsible children. Their economies are similar: They are more reliant on horticulture and other forms of less intensive production. The economies of "Group B" cultures were based on either intensive agriculture or industry.

How does the mode of production influence child tasks and personality? The key underlying factor is differences in women's work roles. In Group A cultures, women are an important part of the labor force and spend much time working outside the home. In these cultures, children take on more family-supportive tasks and thereby develop personalities that are nurturant-responsible. When women are mainly occupied in the home, as in Group B cultures, children have fewer tasks and less responsibility. They develop personalities that are more dependent-dominant. Gusii children were responsible for a wider range of tasks and at earlier ages than children in any other culture in the study, often performing tasks that an Orchard Town mother does. Some children in all six cultures took care of other children, but Gusii children (both boys and girls) spent the most time doing so. They also began taking on this responsibility at a very young age, between five and eight years old.

This study has implications for Western child development experts. Consider, for example, what happens when the dependent-dominant personality develops to an extreme level—into a narcissistic personality. A narcissist is someone who constantly seeks attention and self-affirmation, with no concern for other people's needs. The Western consumer-oriented economy supports the development of narcissism by promoting identity formation through ownership of self-defining goods (clothing, electronics, and cars) and access to self-defining services (vacations, therapists, and fitness salons). The *Six Cultures Study* suggests that involving children more in household responsibilities might result in less self-focused personality formation.

An examination of how corporate culture shapes male personality formation reveals how child care patterns and the demands of the corporate business world fit together to create compliant workers. In Japan, salaried corporate employees work

THINKING OUTSIDE THE BOX Consider the factors in your childhood that contributed to shaping your personality. What were the most important and what were their results in terms of the kinds of traits the *Six Cultures Study* considered.

long hours and are nicknamed "7–11 men." Tokyo salarymen typically eat dinner with their families only a few times a year. After work they spend hours at expensive nightclubs with their co-workers, and the corporation pays the bill. The men relax, have fun, and are given lots of attention by attractive female hostesses who sit at each table. Cultural anthropologist Anne Allison conducted participant observation while working as a club hostess in Tokyo (1994). She found that the conversations between hostess and salarymen are loaded with derogatory comments about the hostess: her breasts are small, her hair is not right, and so on. Allison suggests that men's club behavior is a reaction to the tight maternal control exerted in childhood when, often as the only child in the family and with his father rarely present, the boy was the sole focus of his mother's attention. Club culture puts the man in control, reversing the power differences of his childhood. At the club, he has guaranteed control over a desirable woman who flatters him, flirts with him, and never criticizes him. Club culture, however, provides only temporary ego gratification for a salaryman. He needs to return again and again for reinforcement. This pattern keeps salarymen away from home, leaving their sons in the isolated care of the mother. From the corporation's point of view, club culture has the positive effect of creating strong bonds among the salarymen and fostering deep devotion to the corporation.

Adolescence and Identity

Puberty is a time in the human life cycle that occurs universally and involves a set of biological markers. In males, the voice deepens and facial and body hair appear; in females, menarche and breast development occur; in both males and females, pubic and underarm hair appear and sexual maturation is achieved. **Adolescence**, in contrast, is a culturally defined period of maturation that lasts from around the time of puberty until the attainment of adulthood, which is usually marked by becoming a parent, getting married, or becoming economically self-sufficient.

Is Adolescence a Universal Life-Cycle Stage?

Some anthropologists say that all cultures define a period of adolescence. To support their position, they point to cross-cultural studies that indicate the "ubiquity" of a defined phase of adolescence (Schlegel and Barry 1991). Cultures as diverse as the Navajo and the Trobriand Islanders, among others, have special terms comparable to the American term *adolescent* for a person between puberty and marriage. This apparent ubiquity has been taken as grounds for the theory that adolescence is a universal cultural response to the universal biological onset of reproductive capacity and that it is biologically adaptive because it provides "training" for becoming a parent (Schlegel 1995:16).

In contrast, other anthropologists view adolescence as culturally constructed. They dispute the claims that adolescence is universal and always functions as reproductive training. They point out that there is no recognized period of adolescence in many cultures. In others, recognition of an adolescent phase is recent and reflects Western influence or Western-style modernization. Moroccan anthropologist Fatima Mernissi (1987), for example, states that adolescence was not a recognized life-cycle phase for females in Morocco until the late twentieth century: "The idea of an adolescent unmarried woman is a completely new idea in the Muslim world, where previously you had only a female child and a menstruating woman who had to be married off immediately so as to prevent dishonorable engagement in premarital sex" (xxiv).

The length of adolescence, or whether it exists at all, is related to gender roles. In many horticultural and pastoral societies where men are valued as warriors, as among the Maasai, a long period between childhood and adulthood is devoted to training in warfare and to developing solidarity among males. Females, on the other hand, move directly from being girls to being wives. A Maasai girl learns her adult roles while she is a child, assisting in the care of cattle and doing other tasks. In other cultures, females have long periods of separation between girlhood and womanhood, marked by seclusion from general society, during which they learn special skills and lore. At the end of this period, they re-emerge into society as marriageable (J. Brown 1978). Such evidence of variation speaks against universality.

Corporate workers in Japan, who are mostly male, are nicknamed "7-11 men" because they leave home early in the morning and do not return until late at night.
■ Given your cultural experience, how do men's and women's work patterns relate to child-rearing patterns and their possible psychological effects on children? (Source: © Mark Henley/Panos Pictures)

Coming of Age and Gender Identity

Margaret Mead made famous the phrase "coming of age" in her book *Coming of Age in Samoa* (1961 [1928]). The phrase can refer generally to the period of adolescence or specifically to a ceremony or set of ceremonies that marks the boundaries of adolescence. What are the psychological aspects of "coming of age"?

Among the Sambia, a highland New Guinea group, people do not believe that a young boy "naturally" grows into a man (Herdt 1987). Instead, a boy's healthy maturation requires that he join an all-male initiation group. In this group, he becomes a partner of a senior male, who regularly transfers his semen to the youth orally. The Sambia believe that ingesting semen nourishes the youth. After a period in this initiation group, the youth will rejoin society, form a heterosexual relationship, and raise children.

Ceremonies that provide the transition from youth to adulthood often involve marking the body in some way as though to impress the person undergoing this treatment with a clear sense of gender identity and group identity. Such marking includes scarification, tattooing, and genital surgery. In many societies, adolescent males undergo genital surgery that involves removal of part of the skin around the tip of the penis. Without this operation, the boy would not become a full-fledged male. A young Maasai male, in a first-person account of his initiation into manhood, describes the "intolerable pain" he experienced following the circumcision, as well as his feeling of accomplishment two weeks later when his head was shaved and he became a warrior: "As long as I live, I will never forget the day my head was shaved and I emerged a man, a Maasai warrior. I felt a sense of control over my destiny so great that no words can accurately describe it" (Saitoti 1986:71).

For girls, the biological fact of menstruation is ritually celebrated in some cultures but goes unmarked publicly in others. In rural areas of Turkey, and throughout much of the Middle East, menstruation is not even mentioned to young girls, who are thus surprised and shocked at menarche (Delaney 1988:79). Turkish girls report feeling ashamed and embarrassed by menstruation. Their Islamic culture teaches them that menstruation is the result of Eve's disobedience against Allah. Eve allowed herself to be persuaded by Satan to eat a forbidden fruit, so she was punished by being made to bleed monthly. In India, Hindus in the southern part of the country have elaborate feasts and celebrations for girls on their first menstruation, but there are no such celebrations among Hindus in the northern part of the country (Miller 1997 [1981]). In the absence of studies on the psychological impact of these differences, one can only speculate that being honored at a celebration would have positive effects on a girl's sense of self-esteem, whereas ignoring menstruation or linking it with shamefulness would have the opposite effect.

The Western term **female genital cutting (FGC)** refers to several forms of genital cutting performed on females (Gruenbaum 2001). These practices may include the excision of part or all of the clitoris, part or all of the labia, and (the least common practice) infibulation—the stitching together of the vaginal entry, leaving a small aperture for drainage of menstrual blood. These procedures take place when the girl is between seven and fifteen years of age. Some form of genital cutting is most common in the Sahel region of Africa, from the west coast to the east coast. It is also found in Egypt, in some groups of the Middle East (particularly among Bedu tribes), and among some Muslim groups in South and Southeast Asia. Genital cutting occurs in many groups in which female labor participation is high, but also in others where it is not. In terms of religion, genital cutting is often, but not always, associated with people who are Muslim. In Ethiopia, some Christian groups practice it. Scholars have yet to provide a convincing explanation for the regional and social distribution of female genital cutting.

Many young girls have been reported to look forward to the ceremony so that they will be free from childhood tasks and can take on the more respected role of an adult woman. In other cases, anthropologists have reported hearing statements of resistance. Among the Ariaal, pastoralists of northern Kenya, a new bride's genitals are cut on the day of her wedding (Fratkin 1998:60). The Ariaal practice involves

Cultural Relativism and Female Genital Cutting

IN CULTURES that practice female genital cutting, it is regarded as a necessary step toward full womanhood. A woman must go through it to be considered marriageable—and these are societies in which marriage is the normal path for women. Fathers say that an "uncircumcised" daughter is unmarriageable and will bring no brideprice. Supporters also claim that removal of the labia makes a woman beautiful and that removing her "male" parts (clitoridectomy) makes her a complete woman.

The more prevalent, Western view, which is increasingly shared by many people who traditionally practiced female genital cutting (FGC), is that FGC is a sign of low female status, a health risk, and an unnecessary cause of suffering in women.

FGC has been linked to a range of health risks, including those related to the surgery itself (shock, infection) and future genito-urinary complications (Gruenbaum 2001). The stitching together of the vaginal entry causes scarring and malformation of the vaginal canal that obstruct delivery and may cause lacerations to the mother and even death of the infant and mother. The practice of having a new bride's husband "open" her, using a stick or knife to loosen the aperture, is both painful and a cause of infection. After giving birth, a woman is usually reinfibulated, and the process begins again. Health experts have suggested that this repeated trauma to the woman's vaginal area could increase the risk of her contracting HIV/AIDS. The Western view is that the effects of both clitoridectomy and infibulation on a woman's sexual enjoyment are highly negative—that clitoral orgasm, for one thing, is no longer possible. Some experts have also argued that FGC is related to the high level of infertility in many African countries. A study of fertility data from the Central African Republic, Côte d'Ivoire, and Tanzania, however, found no clear relationship between FGC and fertility level (Larsen and Yan 2000).

Although no one knows its precise beginnings, FGC has too often been viewed in oversimplified terms and modeled on the basis of its most extreme forms. What are the views of insiders? Is there any evidence for agency? Or is it all structure and should anthropologists support FGC liberation movements?

One new voice that transcends insider/outsider divisions is that of Fuambai Ahmadu, who was born and raised in Washington, DC. She is descended from a prominent Kono lineage in Sierra Leone and is getting a doctorate in anthropology for research on female genital cutting at Cambridge University (2000). In 1991 she traveled to Sierra Leone with her mother and several other family members for what she refers to as her circumcision. In a powerful and insightful essay, she describes

Kono culture as gender-complementary, with strong roles for women. She also describes her initiation and subsequent reflections. Although the physical pain was excruciating (in spite of the use of anesthetics), "the positive aspects have been much more profound" (p. 306). Through the initiation, she became part of a powerful female world. Her analysis addresses the effects of genital cutting on health and sexuality and argues that Westerners have exaggerated these issues by focusing on infibulation (which she says is rarely practiced), rather than on the less extreme forms. She adds, however, that if global pressures against the practice continue, she will go along with that movement and support "ritual without cutting" (p. 308).

CRITICAL THINKING QUESTIONS

- Why do you think that FGC is a prominent issue in human rights debates in the West, whereas other forms of initiation (such as male circumcision and fraternity and sorority hazing) are accepted?
- Where do you stand on the issue and why?
- Consider the widespread practice of extreme dieting and exercise, and high rates of eating disorders, among young North American females in comparison to FGC.

removal of the clitoris and part or all of the labia majora. At one wedding, a bride-to-be was heard to say, "I don't want to do this, I don't even know this man, please don't make me do this." The older women told her to be strong and that it would soon be over. The bride-to-be is expected to emerge in a few hours to greet the guests and join the wedding ceremony. Few issues have forced the questioning of cultural relativism more clearly than female genital cutting (see the Critical Thinking box).

Sexual Identity

Puberty is the time when sexual maturity is achieved and sexual orientation becomes more apparent. Scholars have long debated whether sexual preferences are biologically determined genetic or hormonal factors, or culturally constructed and learned. Biological anthropologist Melvin Konner (1989) takes a middle position, saying that both factors play a part, but simultaneously warning that no one has a simple answer to the question of who becomes gay.

A Maasai warrior's mother shaves his head during part of his initiation ceremony into adulthood. ■ Think of other rites of passage and how they do or do not involve changes in hair style or headdress. (Source: © Robert Caputo/National Geographic Image Collection)

Lesbian feminist poet Adrienne Rich's (1980) approach also combines biology and culture. She believes that all people are biologically bisexual but that patriarchal cultures try to mold them into being heterosexual. This "compulsory heterosexual project," she says, will never be completely successful in overcoming innate bisexuality, so some people will always opt out of the heterosexual mold and become either homosexual or bisexual.

The cultural constructionist position emphasizes socialization and childhood experiences as the most powerful factors shaping sexual orientation. Support for this position comes from a recent study in the United States suggesting that later-born male children are more likely than earlier-born children to be homosexual (Blanchard et al. 1995). For lesbians, fewer studies are available, but they also indicate that lesbians tend to be later-born and to have more sisters than heterosexual women. A hypothesis worth investigating is whether parents unconsciously promote "girl-like" behavior in a last-born boy when they already have several sons, in order to have a child to fulfill female roles, and whether they similarly promote "boy-like" behavior in a last-born girl who follows several sisters.

Another indication of the role of culture in sexual identity is that many people change their sexual orientation more than once during their lifetime. In the Gulf state of Oman, the *xanith* is a male who becomes more like a female, wearing female clothing and having sex with other men for several years, but then reverts to a standard male role by marrying a woman and having children (Wikan 1977). Similar fluidity, during the life cycle, between homosexuality and heterosexuality occurs among Sambia males (Herdt 1987). These examples indicate that, given the same biological material, some people can assume different sexual identities over time.

No matter what theoretical perspective one takes on the causes of sexual preferences, it is clear that homosexuals are discriminated against in contexts where heterosexuality is the norm. Homosexuals in the United States have frequently been victims of violence and discrimination in the law, access to housing, and problems in the work place. They often suffer from being stigmatized by parents, other students, and the wider society. The psychological damage done to their self-esteem is reflected in the fact that homosexual youths in the United States have substantially higher suicide rates than heterosexual youths.

A Zuni berdache, We'wha, wearing the ceremonial costume of Zuni women and holding a pottery bowl with sacred corn meal. ■ Generate a theory about why most cultural examples of cross-gender roles involve males assuming female roles and dress, rather than the other way around. (Source: © The National Anthropological Archive/Smithsonian Institution)

Some cultures explicitly allow for more than two strictly defined genders and permit the expression of varied forms of sexual orientation without societal condemnation. Most such "third genders" are neither purely "male" nor purely "female," according to a particular culture's definition of those terms. These gender categories offer ways for "males" to cross gender lines and assume more "female" behaviors, personality characteristics, and dress. In some Native American cultures, a **berdache** is a male (in terms of genital configuration) who opts to wear female clothing, may engage in intercourse with a man as well as a woman, and may perform female tasks such as basket weaving and pottery making (Williams 1992). The berdache constitutes an accepted and admired third gender role. A particular person may become a berdache in a variety of ways. Some people say that parents, especially if they have several sons, choose one to become a berdache. Others say that a boy who shows interest in typically female activities or who likes to wear female clothing is allowed to become a berdache. Such a child is a focus of pride for the family, never a source of disappointment or stigma. Throughout decades of contact with Euro-American colonizers, including Christian missionaries, the institution of the berdache became a target of disapproval and ridicule by the outsiders (Roscoe 1991). Under the influence of the negative reactions of the Euro-Americans, many Native American cultures began to suppress their berdache traditions in favor of mainstream White values and practices that promote less gender fluidity. In the 1980s, as Native American cultural pride began to grow, the open presence of the berdache and the **amazon** (a woman who takes on male roles and behaviors) has returned. Native American cultures in general remain accepting of gender role fluidity and the contemporary concept of being gay: "Younger gay Indians, upon coming out to their families, will sometimes have an elderly relative who takes them aside and tells them about the berdache tradition. A part-Choctaw gay man recalls that his full-blooded Choctaw grandmother realized he was gay and it was totally acceptable . . . . This respectful attitude eliminates the stress felt by families that harbor homophobia" (p. 225).

In India, the counterpart of the Native American berdache is termed a **hijira**. Hijiras dress and act like women but are neither truly male nor truly female (Nanda 1990). Many hijiras were born with male genitals or with genitals that were not clearly male or female. Hijiras have the traditional right to visit the home of a newborn, inspect its genitals, and claim it for their group if the genitals are indeterminate. Hijiras born with male genitals may opt to go through an initiation ceremony that involves cutting off the penis and testicles. Hijiras roam large cities of India, earning a living by begging from store to store (and threatening to lift their skirts if not given money). Because women do not sing or dance in public, the hijiras play an important role as performers in public events, especially as dancers or musicians. Given this public role and the hijira's association with prostitution, people in the mainstream do not admire or respect hijiras, and no family would be delighted to hear that their son had decided to become a hijira. In contrast to the berdache among Native American groups, hijiras are separate from mainstream society.

In Thailand, three gender categories have long existed: *phuuchai* (male), *phuuying* (female), and *kathoey* (transvestite/transsexual/hermaphrodite) (Morris 1994). Like the berdache and hijira, a kathoey is "originally" a male who crosses into the body, personality, and dress defined as female. The sexual orientation of kathoeys is flexible, including either male or female partners. In contemporary Thailand, explicit discussion and recognition of homosexuality exists, usually couched in English terms, conveying a sense of foreignness. The words for lesbian are *thom* (from the word *tomboy*) and *thut* (an ironic usage from the American movie *Tootsie* about a male transvestite). As in many parts of the world, reflecting the widespread presence of patriarchal norms, lesbianism in Thailand is a more suppressed form of homosexuality than male homosexuality.

Adulthood

Adulthood for most of the world's people means the likelihood of entering into some form of marriage or other long-term domestic relationship, and having children. This section considers how selected aspects of adulthood, such as parenthood and aging, affect mature people's psychological status and identity.

Becoming a Parent

Biologically, a woman becomes a mother when she gives birth to an infant and is transformed from a pregnant woman into a mother. Motherhood, the cultural process of becoming a mother, has been termed *matrescence* (Raphael 1975). Like adolescence, matrescence varies cross-culturally in terms of duration and meaning. In some cultures, a woman is transformed into a mother as soon as she thinks she is pregnant. In other cultures, such as in much of northern India, she is granted full maternal status only when she delivers a son.

Among the Beti people of Southern Cameroon, West Africa, motherhood is not necessarily defined by having a child (Johnson-Hanks 2002). The Beti are both an ethnic group and a social status group of educated professionals within the wider society. "School girl" is one category of young Beti women. If a school girl becomes pregnant, this is a matter of great shame, and the girl is not considered to have entered a phase of motherhood even though she has borne a child. In this case, a biological marker does not bring about movement into a new life stage but instead contributes to social ambiguity.

In nonindustrial cultures, matrescence occurs in the context of supportive family members. Some cultures promote prenatal practices, abiding by particular food taboos, which can be regarded as part of matrescence. Such rules make the pregnant woman feel that she has some role in helping to make the pregnancy successful. In the West, medical experts increasingly define the prenatal period as an important phase of matrescence, and they have issued many scientific and medical rules for potential parents, especially mothers (Browner and Press 1995, 1996). Pregnant women are urged to seek prenatal examinations, to be under the regular supervision of a doctor who monitors the growth and development of the fetus, to follow particular dietary and exercise guidelines, and to undergo a range of tests such as ultrasound scanning. Some cultural anthropologists think that such medical control of pregnancy leads to the greater likelihood of post-partum depression among mothers as a result of their lack of control in matrescence.

Patrescence, or becoming a father, is less socially noted than matrescence. The practice of *couvade* is an interesting exception to this generalization. Couvade consists of "a variety of customs applying to the behavior of fathers during the pregnancies of their wives and during and shortly after the births of their children" (Broude 1988:902). The father may take to his bed before, during, or after the deliv-

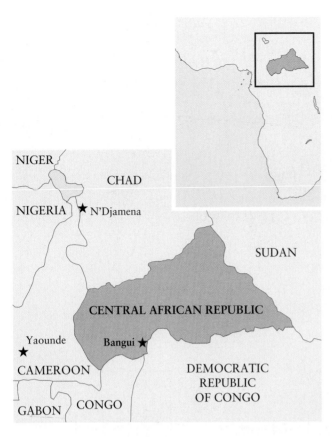

ery. He may also experience pain and exhaustion during and after the delivery. More common is a pattern of couvade that involves a set of prohibitions and prescriptions for male behavior. For example, an expectant father may not hunt a certain animal, eat certain foods, cut objects, or engage in extramarital sex. Early theories of why the couvade exists relied on Freudian interpretations that men were seeking cross-sex identification (with the female role) in contexts where the father role was weak or fathers were absent. But cross-cultural data on the existence of couvade indicate the opposite: Couvade occurs in societies where paternal roles in child care are prominent. This interpretation views couvade as one phase of men's participation in parenting: their proper behavior as expectant fathers helps ensure a good delivery for the baby. Another interpretation of couvade is that it offers support for the mother. In Estonia, a folk belief is that a woman's birth pains will be less if her husband helps by taking some of them on himself (Oinas 1993).

The widespread pattern of women being the major caretakers of infants and children has led many people to think that something innate in females causes them to assume care-taking roles. Most cultural anthropologists agree that child care is predominantly the responsibility of females worldwide—but not universally. They point to differences in women's degree of involvement and to other possible caretakers besides the biological mother. In many cultures of the South Pacific, child care is shared among several families, and women breastfeed other women's babies. Paternal involvement varies as well. Among the Aka pygmy foragers of the Central African Republic, paternal child care is prominent (Hewlett 1991). Aka fathers are intimate, affectionate, and helpful, spending about half of their time each day holding or within arm's reach of their infants. While holding their infants, they are more likely to hug and kiss them than mothers are. The definition of good fatherhood among the Aka means being affectionate toward children and assisting the mother when her workload is heavy. Among the Aka, gender equality prevails, and violence against women is unknown. The high level of paternal involvement in child care helps explain this pattern.

An Aka father and his son. Aka fathers are affectionate caregivers of infants and small children. Compared to mothers, they are more likely to kiss and hug children. ■ How does this compare with your microculture? (Source: Barry Hewlett)

Middle Age

In industrial countries, being of "middle age" is typically defined as being between thirty and seventy years of age (Shweder 1998). A major turning point is now the fortieth birthday. Stanley Brandes explores the meanings of turning forty to American middle-class men in a book entitled *Forty: The Age and the Symbol* (1985). The "forty syndrome" comprises feelings of restlessness, rebelliousness, and unhappiness that often lead to family breakup. One possible reason behind this emphasis on forty as a turning point for males is that it reflects the current midpoint of a "typical" life span for a middle-class American man. In cultures with shorter lifespans, a "midlife" crisis would necessarily occur at some point other than the age of forty years, if it were to happen at all. Such a "crisis" seems strongly embedded in contemporary U.S. culture and its pervasive fear and denial of death (Shore 1998:103).

Menopause is a significant aspect of middle age for women in some, but not all, cultures. A comparative study examined differences in perception and experience of menopause among Maya women of Mexico and rural Greek women (Beyene 1989). Among the Maya women, menopause is not a time of stress or crisis. They associate menstruation with illness and look forward to its end. Menopause among these women is not associated with physical or emotional symptoms. None of the women reported hot flashes or cold sweats. No role changes were associated with menopause. In contrast, the rural Greek women recognized menopause as a natural phenomenon that all women experience and one that causes temporary discomfort, *exapi*, which is a phase of hot flashes, occurring especially at night, that may last about a year. The women did not think exapi was terribly serious and certainly did not regard it as worthy of medical attention. Postmenopausal women emphasized the relief and freedom they felt. Postmenopausal women can go into cafes by themselves, something they would never do otherwise, and they can participate more fully in church ceremonies. In Japan, also, menopause is a minimally stressful experience and is rarely considered something that warrants medical attention (Lock 1993).

Whereas cultural anthropologists emphasize the cultural variability of menopause, from a positively anticipated stage to one associated with discomfort and requiring medical treatment, biological anthropologists view menopause as a universal experience among women and as an important adaptive feature of human life.

A mong all primates, including humans, fertility declines with age. But only among human females does reproductive capacity completely cease before the end of their life span. Among twentieth-century foragers in temperate regions, such as the Ju/wasi, women live an average of 20 healthy years following menopause (Blurton-Jones et al. 2002). Some biological anthropologists think that this long, infertile period merits study and explanation. When did it emerge in human evolution, and what adaptive role might it have played during human evolution?

According to the Darwinian perspective, menopause and the cessation of fertility may contribute to *inclusive fitness* (the reproductive success of individuals and their relatives, especially their offspring). According to this logic, menopause evolved because it allowed prehistoric postmenopausal females to devote their energy to caring for their grandchildren rather than to producing more offspring themselves. The more vigorous the grandmother, the more able she is to contribute to the reproductive success of her descendants. Over time, the offspring of women who led more vigorous lives following menopause are, in evolutionary terms, selected for in favor of the offspring of women who were less vigorous in later life.

This model, called the **grandmother hypothesis,** emphasizes the importance of the contribution of postmenopausal grandmothers to ensuring that the children of their daughters have adequate food (O'Connell et al. 1999). An extended postmenopausal period affects women's inclusive fitness in two ways:

- The woman's daughter's offspring are more likely to survive.
- The earlier infants are weaned, the more likely it is that the daughter will become pregnant again—and thus a vigorous postmenopausal grandmother increases her daughter's fertility.

CROSSING
THE FIELDS

**Menopause,
Grandmothering,
and Human Evolution**

The grandmother hypothesis provides insight into rethinking aspects of the evolution of modern humans. Conventionally, the emergence of modern humans has been linked to an emphasis on large game hunting by males and on new social bonds between males and females that form the basis of food sharing and family ties (Chapter 8). In Africa, however, where anatomically modern humans first emerged, the more likely scenario is that food provisioning in savannah environments was more dependent on collecting fruits, nuts, grubs, eggs, and (perhaps most important) tubers, dug out of the ground. Thus, the long-standing role of women in gathering such foods provided the foundation for survival. Specifically, the importance of tubers resulted in a productive role for grandmothers. Digging tubers takes quite a bit of work, and then they need to be cooked. If a mother is carrying and caring for a baby, she is at a disadvantage when collecting and preparing tubers. Enter the grandmother, with her free hands. Thus the grandmother hypothesis shifts the understanding of human evolution from "man the hunter" to "grandmother the tuber collector."

Why is there an emphasis on resource transfers through the female line in this model? The answer is that a grandmother can be certain of her genetic relationships only through her daughter's children, because her son's female partner may have had sexual relations with another man. Hence she cannot be sure that her son's children are related to her.

The grandmother hypothesis has sparked studies in many cultural contexts. One such study uses historical data from a village in central Japan, during the Tokugawa period from 1671 to 1871 (Jamison et al. 2002). The presence of a maternal grandmother had a positive effect on reducing mortality rates of the grandchildren, but, contrary to the grandmother hypothesis, her presence had a stronger effect on reducing the mortality of her grandsons than on reducing that of her granddaughters. The presence of grandfathers tended to be associated with higher mortality rates of grandchildren in general. ■

FOOD FOR THOUGHT

■ Why do you think grandfathers do not appear to have played a positive role in the survival and health of their grandchildren among either African foragers or the Tokugawa Japanese villagers?

The Senior Years

The "senior" life-cycle stage may be a development of contemporary human society because, like most other mammals, our early ancestors rarely lived beyond their reproductive years (Brooks and Draper 1998 [1991]). The category of the aged, like several other life-cycle stages we have discussed, is variably recognized, defined, and valued. In many cultures, elders are highly revered and their life experiences are valued as the greatest wisdom. In others, aged people become burdens to their families and to society. In general, the status and well-being of the elderly are higher when they continue to live with their families (Lee and Kezis 1979).

This pattern is more likely to be found in nonindustrialized societies than in industrialized ones, where the elderly are increasingly experiencing a shift to "retirement homes." In such age-segregated settings, people have to create new social roles and ties and find new ways of gaining self-esteem and personal satisfaction. Research in a rural central New York retirement home shows that being allowed to have pets has a positive effect on people's adjustment (Savishinsky 1991).

The Final Passage: Death and Dying

It may be that no one in any culture welcomes death, unless he or she is in very poor health and suffering greatly. The contemporary United States, with its dependence on medical technology, appears to play a leading role in resisting death, often at high financial and psychological cost. In many other cultures, a greater degree of acceptance prevails. A study of attitudes toward death and dying among Alaskan Inuits revealed a pervasive feeling that people are active participants in their death rather than passive victims (Trelease 1975). The person near death calls friends and neighbors together, is given a Christian sacrament, and then, within a few hours, dies. The author comments, "I do not suggest that everyone waited for the priest to come and then died right away. But the majority who did not die suddenly did some degree of planning, had some kind of formal service or celebration of prayers and hymns and farewells" (35).

In any culture, loss of a loved one is accompanied by some form of sadness, grief, and mourning. The ways of expressing such emotions vary from extended and public grieving that is expressively emotional to no visible sign of grief whatsoever. The latter pattern is the norm in Bali, Indonesia, where people's faces remain impassive at funerals and no vocal lamenting occurs (Rosenblatt, Walsh, and Jackson 1976).

No one knows how different modes of expression of loss are related to the actual experience of loss itself (Brison and Leavitt 1995). Does highly expressive public mourning contribute to a faster healing process, or does a quietly repressed sense of grief play an adaptive role? The domain of emotional suffering surrounding death is a relatively new area of study for anthropologists—one that promises to provide intriguing insights. The expression of grief surrounding death is also of interest to anthropologists who study religion (Bowen 1998). Research shows that beliefs about the dead, and about how the dead may affect the living, shape people's experience of death and mourning.

The Dogon people of Mali, West Africa, wrap their dead tightly in cloth and pull them up a cliff face to a burial cave. ■ Consider various burial traditions that you know about in contemporary times and what traces they would leave in the archaeological record 5000 years from now. (Source: © Carol Beckwith/Angela Fisher/Robert Estall Photo Agency)

THE BIG QUESTIONS REVISITED

■ HOW are modes of reproduction related to modes of production?

The mode of reproduction of a society—that is, its predominant pattern of fertility—is everywhere shaped by culture. More specifically, the various modes of production are basic structures to which reproduction is related. For thousands of years, foragers maintained a balanced level of population through direct and indirect means of fertility regulation. As sedentism increased and food surpluses became more available and storable, population growth increased, culminating in the highest rates of population growth in human prehistory and history among settled agriculturalists.

■ HOW does culture shape fertility in different contexts?

Cross-culturally, many techniques exist for increasing fertility, reducing it, and regulating its timing. There are hundreds of different methods, including the use of herbs and other natural substances for inhibiting or enhancing fertilization and for inducing abortion if an undesired pregnancy occurs. In nonindustrialized societies, the knowledge about and practice of fertility regulation are largely unspecialized and available to all women. In the industrial mode of reproduction, scientific and medical specialization increases, and most knowledge and expertise are in the hands of professionals rather than of women. Class-stratified access to fertility-regulating methods now exists both globally and within nations. Population growth is also shaped through the practice of infanticide, which, though of ancient origin, still exists today. It is sometimes performed in response to limited family resources, perceptions of inadequate "fitness" of the child, or preferences about the gender of offspring.

▪ HOW does culture shape personality and human development over the life cycle?

Cultural anthropologists emphasize the effects of infant care practices on personality formation, including gender identity. Other cross-cultural studies show that children's family and work roles correspond to personality patterns. Adolescence, a culturally defined time beginning around puberty and running until adulthood, varies cross-culturally from being nonexistent to involving detailed training and elaborate ceremonies. In contrast to the sharp distinction between "male" and "female" made in Euro-American culture, many cultures have traditions of third gender identities.

Cross-culturally, adult roles usually involve parenthood. In nonindustrial societies, learning about motherhood is embedded in other aspects of life, and knowledge about birthing and child care is shared among women. In industrialized cultures, science and medicine play a large part in defining the maternal role. The senior years are generally shorter in nonindustrialized societies than in industrialized societies, where life spans tend to be longer. Elder men and women in nonindustrial cultures are treated with respect, are assumed to know the most, and retain a strong sense of their place in the culture. Increasingly in industrialized societies, elderly people live apart from their families and spend may years in age-segregated institutions or living alone.

KEY CONCEPTS

adolescence, p. 369
amazon, p. 374
below-replacement-level fertility, p. 356
berdache, p. 374
cultural broker, p. 366
ethnopsychology, p. 364

female genital cutting (FGC), p. 371
fertility, p. 354
grandmother hypothesis, p. 377
hijira, p. 374
infanticide, p. 355
mode of reproduction, p. 354

mortality, p. 356
personality, p. 364
pronatalism, p. 355
puberty, p. 369
replacement-level fertility, p. 356

SUGGESTED READINGS

Anne Allison. *Nightwork: Sexuality, Pleasure and Corporate Masculinity in a Tokyo Hostess Club*. Chicago: University of Chicago Press, 1994. Based on the author's participant observation, this book explores what it is like to work as a hostess in a club that caters to corporate male employees and discusses how that microculture is linked to men's corporate work culture.

Kamran Asdar Ali. *Planning the Family in Egypt: New Bodies, New Selves*. Austin: University of Texas Press, 2002. This ethnographic study, conducted by a Pakistani doctor and anthropologist, examines the policies and practices of family planning programs in Egypt to see how this elitist, Western-influenced state creates demographically compliant citizens. His findings reveal the dilemma created for women as family planning programs pressure them to think of themselves as individual decision makers acting in their own and the nation's interest by limiting their fertility, even though they are still bound by their wider families and religion to pronatalism.

Evalyn Blackwood, ed. *The Many Faces of Homosexuality: Anthropological Approaches to Homosexual Behavior*. New York: Harrington Park Press, 1986. This text contains chapters on anthropological writings about lesbianism, as well as case studies of ritualized male homosexuality in Irian Jaya, the berdache in North America, hijiras of India, lesbian relationships in Lesotho, and Mexican male homosexual interaction patterns in public.

Caroline Bledsoe and Barney Cohen, eds. *Social Dynamics of Adolescent Fertility in Sub-Saharan Africa*. Washington, DC: National Academy Press, 1993. An anthropologist and a demographer examine national survey data on cultural factors related to high fertility rates among adolescents in sub-Saharan Africa. Attention is given to patterns of adolescent sexuality, attitudes toward marriage, women's status, knowledge and practice of contraception, and the role of education in change.

John D. Early and Thomas N. Headland. *Population Dynamics of a Philippine Rain Forest People: The San Ildefonso Agta*. Gainesville: University of Florida Press, 1998. This study of population dynamics of an Agta group living on Luzon Island in the Philippines draws on a forty-four-year quantitative database on fertility, mortality, and migration from the time when the Agta were forest foragers to the present (they are now small-scale farmers). It profiles a minority people without economic and political power and documents the impact of international logging interests on their lives.

Peter T. Ellison. *On Fertile Ground: A Natural History of Human Reproduction*. Cambridge, MA: Harvard University Press, 2001. This biological anthropology study covers male and female reproductive physiology and conception, early fetal development, childhood, sexual maturation, pregnancy, birth, lactation, menopause, and the post-reproductive life phase. It explains how all of these are related to human evolution.

Thomas E. Fricke. *Himalayan Households: Tamang Demography and Domestic Processes*. New York, Columbia University Press, 1994. This example of demographic anthropology is a local study of population patterns and change in one region of Nepal. The book includes chapters on the subsistence economy, fertility and mortality, the life course, household dynamics, and recent changes.

Ellen Gruenbaum. *The Female Circumcision Controversy: An Anthropological Perspective*. Philadelphia: University of Pennsylvania Press, 2001. The author draws on her more than five years of cultural anthropology fieldwork in Sudan and discusses how change is occurring through economic development, the role of Islamic activists, health educators, and educated African women.

W. Penn Handwerker, ed. *Births and Power: Social Change and the Politics of Reproduction*. Boulder, CO: Westview Press, 1990. An overview chapter by the editor is followed by accounts of studies of reproduction among the Inuit of Canada, the Bariba of West Africa, and the Mende of Sierra Leone; studies of Hungary and of Bangladesh; and studies from the United States addressing teen pregnancy. An essay on AIDS in Africa is also included.

Charlotte E. Hardman. *Other Worlds: Notions of Self and Emotion among the Lohorung Rai*. New York: Berg, 2000. The author conducted cultural anthropology fieldwork in a mountainous region of Nepal to learn about one community's perception of what it means to be a person.

Sarah Blaffer Hrdy. *Mother Nature: A History of Mothers, Infants, and Natural Selection*. New York: Pantheon Books, 1999. Drawing on anthropology, history, literature, and developmental psychology, the author critiques conventional stereotypes of female biology and provides a new view with attention to maternal attitudes, male–female tensions, and the role of women in human evolution.

Nancy Howell. *Demography of the Dobe !Kung*. New York: Academic Press, 1979. This classic study of the demography of a group of Southern African foragers describes their reproduction patterns before they were sedentarized. The text considers how anthropological methods contribute to demographic analysis of small-scale societies, causes of illness and death, fertility and sterility, and population growth rates.

Marcia C. Inhorn. *Infertility and Patriarchy: The Cultural Politics of Gender and Family Life in Egypt*. Philadelphia: University of Pennsylvania Press, 1996. Based on fieldwork in Alexandria, this book uses narratives from several infertile Egyptian women to show the different ways in which these women and their families deal with cultural pressures to bear children.

Lynn Meskell. *Private Life in New Kingdom Egypt*. Princeton, NJ: Princeton University Press, 2002. Archaeological, textual, and iconographic evidence from 450 years of the New Kingdom are combined to reconstruct the lives of ordinary people from birth to death.

Judith Schachter Modell. *Ruth Benedict: Patterns of a Life*. Philadelphia: University of Pennsylvania Press, 1983. This biography of a prominent psychological anthropologist provides insights into Benedict's development as an anthropologist, her research, and her writings.

Michael Moffatt. *Coming of Age in New Jersey: College and American Culture*. New Brunswick, NJ: Rutgers University Press, 1991. Based on a year's participant observation in a college dormitory at a university in the eastern United States, this study offers insights into sexuality, ethnic relations, and individualism.

Leith Mullings and Alaka Wali. *Stress and Resilience: The Social Context of Reproduction in Central Harlem*. New York: Kluwer Academic, 2001. In documenting the circumstances of poverty that shape reproductive behaviors and cause chronic stress for African American women in Harlem, the authors also present the voices of the community and the women.

Mimi Nichter. *What Girls and Their Parents Say about Dieting*. Cambridge, MA: Harvard University Press, 2000. The author conducted interviews with adolescent girls in the United States, focusing on perceptions of weight, attachment to dieting, and the influence of their mothers' views and comments on weight.

Richard Parker. *Bodies, Pleasures and Passions: Sexual Culture in Contemporary Brazil*. Boston: Beacon Press, 1991. This ethnographic study of contemporary sexual culture in Brazil addresses sexual socialization, bisexuality, sadomasochism, AIDS, prostitution, samba, the symbolism of breasts, courting, and carnival.

Joel S. Savishinsky. *Breaking the Watch: The Meanings of Retirement in America*. Ithaca, NY: Cornell University Press, 2000. Fieldwork at a nursing home in a small town in central New York state sheds light on the retirees through vivid portraits of several, along with their own words on friendship in the home, finding purpose in life, and dealing with finances.

Nancy Scheper-Hughes. *Death without Weeping: The Violence of Everyday Life in Brazil*. Berkeley: University of California Press, 1993. This book is a landmark "ethnography of death" based on fieldwork in a Brazilian shantytown over several periods of time. The author argues that poverty and inequality are key factors shaping the demographic system of very high infant mortality rates and high fertility.

John W. Traphagan. *Taming Oblivion: Aging Bodies and the Fear of Senility in Japan*. Albany: State University of New York Press, 2000. The author conducted fieldwork in a small town north of Tokyo to investigate people's attitudes and practices related to old age, especially as aging people attempt to prevent the onset of the *boke* condition, or what English-speaking Westerners would call senility.

Marlene Zuk. *Sexual Selections: What We Can and Can't Learn about Sex from Animals*. Berkeley: University of California Press, 2002. This book provides a current overview of knowledge of animal sexuality and its implications for human evolution.

THE BIG QUESTIONS

- WHAT is ethnomedicine?
- WHAT are three major theoretical approaches in medical anthropology?
- HOW are illness and healing changing as globalization occurs?

CHAPTER 13

Illness and Healing

Steven Benally, Jr., an apprentice medicine man, practices for a ceremony in his hogan on the Navajo Reservation near Window Rock, Arizona. An apprentice often studies for a decade or more. (Source: © Kevin Fleming/CORBIS)

Primatologist Jane Goodall witnessed a polio epidemic among the chimpanzees she was studying in Tanzania (Foster and Anderson 1978:33–34). A group of healthy animals watched a stricken member try to reach the feeding area but did not help him. Another badly paralyzed chimpanzee was simply left behind when the group moved on.

Humans also sometimes resort to isolation and abandonment, as in the Inuit practice of leaving aged and infirm people behind in the cold, the stigmatization of HIV/AIDS victims, and the neglect of the homeless and mentally ill in the United States. Compared to our nonhuman primate relatives, though, humans have created more complex and variable ways of interpreting health problems and highly creative methods of preventing and curing them.

This chapter on medical anthropology provides some of the strongest connections across anthropology's four fields. Biological anthropologists study health during human evolution and in contemporary populations, archaeologists document disease and healing practices in the past, linguistic anthropologists study healer–patient communication patterns, and cultural anthropologists address the range of contemporary practices and beliefs related to health. The study of how and why people become ill, how they perceive and understand illness, and how they attempt to prevent and cure illness can benefit from a four-field approach. This chapter, however, focuses mainly on the findings from cultural anthropology.

We first provide an overview of the field of **ethnomedicine,** or the health systems of particular cultural groups. This section describes various cultural approaches to health, illness, and healing from an emic perspective. In the next section we consider three important theoretical approaches in medical anthropology, each with a different view of how best to study and understand health systems and health problems. In the last section we consider selected topics in contemporary ethnomedicine, including new health challenges and changing ways of healing.

ETHNOMEDICINE

Medical anthropologists have long been interested in studying ethnomedicine, or cross-cultural health systems. A health system encompasses many areas: perceptions and classifications of illness, prevention measures, diagnosis, healing (magical, religious, and scientific), healing substances, and healers. In addition to these core topics, ethnomedicine has recently expanded its focus to new topics such as the anthropology of the body, culture and disability, and change in indigenous or "traditional" healing systems, especially change resulting from the effects of globalization and the growth of multiple and mixed healing systems.

When the term *ethnomedicine* first came into use in the 1960s, it referred only to non-Western health systems and was synonymous with *folk medicine, popular medicine,* and even the abandoned term *primitive medicine.* Two major problems exist with using the term *ethnomedicine* in this way. First, it is "totalizing"—that is, excessively generalizing. Labeling all non-Western medicine as "folk" or "popular," in contrast to "scientific" or "professional" Western medicine, overlooks such highly developed and specialized non-Western systems as those of India and China, to name just two examples. It is also totalizing in terms of implying that all Western health systems are "professional" and thus overlooks much thinking and practice in the West that could well be labeled "folk" or "popular." Second, the early meaning of *ethnomedicine* is ethnocentric, because Western medicine is an ethnomedical system too, intimately bound to Western culture and its values. We must nonetheless recognize that, especially since the 1950s and the increasing spread of Western culture and science globally, Western biomedicine is more appropriately termed a global or "cosmopolitan" system.

The current use of the term *ethnomedicine* thus embraces all cultural health systems. Within any of them, a range of variations may exist—from local practices and beliefs held by laypeople to more widespread practices requiring skills that must be learned over many years of training available to only a few.

Perceptions of the Body

Cultures have various ways of defining the body and its parts in relation to illness and healing. The highland Maya of Chiapas, southern Mexico, have a detailed vision of the exterior body but do not focus much attention on internal organs, a fact related to the nonexistence of surgery as a healing technique among them (Berlin and Berlin 1996). Separation of the mind from the body has long characterized Euro-American popular and scientific thinking. Thus Western medicine has a special category, "mental illness," that addresses certain health problems as though they were located only in the mind. In many cultures where such a distinction between mind and body does not exist, there is no such category as "mental illness."

Cross-cultural variation exists in perceptions of which bodily organs are most critically involved in the definition of life versus death. In the West, a person may be declared dead while the heart is still beating if the brain is judged "dead." In many other cultures, this definition of brain death is not accepted; perhaps this difference reflects the relatively great value assigned to the brain in Western culture (Ohnuki-Tierney 1994).

In Japan, attitudes against cutting the body explain the much lower rates of surgery there than in the United States. The Japanese concept of *gotai* refers to the value of maintaining the body intact in life and death to the extent that ear piercing is devalued: "Newspapers reported that one of the qualifications of a bride for Crown Prince Naruhitao was that she not have pierced ears" (Ohnuki-Tierney 1994:235). An intact body ensures rebirth. Historically, the warrior's practice of beheading the victim was the ultimate form of killing, because it violated the integrity of the body and prevented the enemy's rebirth. Gotai is also an important reason for the widespread popular resistance to organ transplantation in Japan.

Another topic related to the body is whether it is considered to be a bounded physical unit, in which case the treatment of disease focuses on just the body, or is considered to be connected to a wider social context, in which case treatment addresses the wider social sphere (Fabrega and Silver 1973). Western biomedicine typically addresses a clearly defined, individual physical body or mind. In contrast, many non-Western healing systems encompass the social context within which an individual's physical body is situated. Diagnoses that address the "social body" in nonindustrial, non-Western medical systems may include the family or community members as responsible for illness, or they may look to the supernaturals as being in some way unhappy. A cure is brought about by holding a family or community ritual that seeks to restore correct social relations or to appease the deities.

Defining Health Problems

Medical anthropologists often sound like philosophers, devoting much attention to defining concepts and delineating the object of study. Because medical anthropologists have conducted many studies of emic perceptions of health and health problems, they have found that their own (usually Western) concepts do not fit well with other cultural definitions. Cross-cultural knowledge forces us to broaden our own definitions. Consider, for example, the term *dore* as used by the Desana people of the Colombian rainforest, a group of forager–horticulturalists (Reichel-Dolmatoff 1971 cited in Hahn

An English Heritage advisor displays a skull with a hole dating to 1759 BCE. Discovered on the banks of the Thames River near London, this is the first skull from the area found with evidence of trepanation, a prehistoric surgical procedure in which a portion of the bone was removed from a living and probably conscious individual. ■ Do some research to learn more about prehistoric trepanation. (Source: © Reuters/CORBIS)

THINKING

In your microculture, what are the prevailing perceptions about the body and how are they related to medical treatment?

OUTSIDE THE BOX

Tshampa Xiganang, a practitioner of traditional Tibetan medicine living in Nepal. ■ Note similarities and differences between this setting and one that you might visit for a checkup or minor health complaint. (Source: © Macduff Everton/CORBIS)

1995:23). This term refers to a complex set of symbols related to the verb "to order" or "to send." Among the Desana, falling sick is the result of an order, a mandate, sent by or through a supernatural agent—a rather different definition from any found in Western biomedicine.

An approach commonly used in medical anthropology to help sort through the wide variety of cultural labels and perceptions is the **disease/illness dichotomy.** This dichotomy is parallel to etic and emic understandings of health problems. The term *disease* refers to a biological pathology that is objective and universal (Kleinman 1995:31). In this view, a virus is a virus no matter where it lands. Disease is thus a scientific, etic concept. In contrast, the term *illness* refers to the culture-specific understandings and experiences of a health problem or some more generalized form of suffering. A viral infection may be differently understood and experienced in different cultures. In some it may not be perceived as a health problem at all or may be thought of as "sent" by a supernatural force. Culture thus provides the framework within which disease and other forms of suffering become illness (Rubel, O'Nell, and Collado-Ardón 1984). Medical anthropologist and physician Arthur Kleinman suggests that Western biomedicine focuses too narrowly on disease and neglects illness (1995). He urges medical anthropologists to continue to do research on illness and bring its importance to the attention of biomedicine.

Another important concept, **structural suffering,** also known as structural affliction, reflects the attempt of medical anthropologists to broaden ethnomedicine and move it further from narrow biological definitions of health problems. The term *structural* refers to certain devastating forces that cause suffering, such as economic and political situations like war, famine, forced migration, and poverty. These conditions affect health in many ways, inducing effects that range from depression to death. They also include the negative effects of disrupting of one's family life, livelihood, and sense of home and security. The usual approaches in Western biomedicine are not designed to deal with the effects of structural suffering, and Western disease classifications do not encompass it. For example, following the attacks on the United States of September 11, 2001, medical personnel had to classify the health status of survivors and the causes of deaths. In many cases, their customary coding system was inadequate.

Medical anthropologists study how people of different cultures label and classify illness and suffering. The term *nosology* refers to the classification of health problems. The term **ethno-nosology** refers to cross-cultural systems of classification of health problems. Western biomedicine defines and labels diseases according to its diagnostic criteria and sets these guidelines down in thick manuals used by physicians when treating patients. In nonstate societies, verbal traditions are the repository of such information. A range of bases for classifications exist cross-culturally: causal agent, vector (the means of transmission, such as mosquitoes), the body part that is affected, symptoms, the pathological process itself, the stage of the disease, the victim's behavior, and combinations of any of these.

Locally specific disorders are referred to as **culture-bound syndromes** (see Table 13.1). A culture-bound syndrome is a collection of signs and symptoms that is restricted to a particular culture or a limited number of cultures (Prince 1985:201). Many culture-bound syndromes are caused by psychosocial factors such as stress or shock, but they may have physical symptoms. For example, *susto*, or "fright disease," is a widely distributed culture-bound syndrome of Latino cultures. People

TABLE 13.1
Selected culture-bound syndromes.

Syndrome	Cultural/Geographic Location	Symptoms
aiyiperi	Yoruba (Nigeria)	hysterical convulsive disorders, posturing and tics, psychomotor seizures
amok	Malaysia and Indonesia	dissociative episodes, outbursts of violent and aggressive or homicidal behavior directed at people and objects, persecutory ideas, amnesia, exhaustion
anfechtung	Hutterites (Manitoba, Canada)	withdrawal from social contact, feeling of having sinned, feeling of religious unworthiness, temptation to commit suicide
brain fag	Nigerian and East African students	pain, heat, or burning sensations, pressure or tightness around the head, blurring of vision, inability to concentrate when studying, anxiety and depression, fatigue and sleepiness
cholera	Guatemala	nausea, vomiting, diarrhea, fever, severe temper tantrums, unconsciousness and dissociative behavior
ghost sickness	Navajo of the southwestern United States	weakness, bad dreams, feelings of danger, confusion, feelings of futility, loss of appetite, feelings of suffocation, fainting, dizziness, hallucinations and loss of consciousness
koro	South China, Chinese, and Malaysian populations in southeast Asia; Hindus of Assam	in males, anxiety that the penis will recede into the body; in females, anxiety that the vulva and breasts will recede into the body.
latah	Malaysia and Indonesia	afflicted person becomes flustered and may say and do things that appear amusing, such as mimicking people's words and movements
mal de ojo (evil eye)	Mediterranean and Latin American; Hispanic populations	fitful sleep, crying without apparent cause, diarrhea, vomiting, fever in a child or infant
pibloktoq (Arctic hysteria)	Inuit of the Arctic, Siberian groups	brooding, depressive silences, loss or disturbance of consciousness during seizure, tearing off of clothing, fleeing or wandering, rolling in snow, speaking in tongues or echoing other people's words
windigo	Cree, Ojibwa, and related Native American groups of central and northeastern Canada	depression, nausea, distaste for usual foods, feelings of being possessed by a cannibalistic monster, homicidal or suicidal impulses
shinkeishitsu	Japan	fear of meeting people, feelings of inadequacy, anxiety, obsessive–compulsive symptoms, hypochondriasis

(*Source:* Adapted from "Selected Culture-Bound Syndromes," pp. 91–110, in *The Culture-Bound Syndromes: Folk Illnesses of Psychiatric and Anthropological Interest,* ed. by Ronald C. Simons and C. C. Hughes. Copyright © 1985. Reprinted by permission of Springer Science and Business Media.)

afflicted with susto attribute it to shock, such as losing a loved one or experiencing a frightening incident (Rubel, O'Nell, and Collado-Ardón 1984).

In the Oaxaca area of Mexico, a woman reported that her susto was brought on by an accident in which pottery that she had made was broken on its way to market, and a man said that his susto came on after he saw a dangerous snake. Susto symptoms include appetite loss, loss of motivation, breathing problems, generalized pain, and nightmares. Analysis of many cases of susto in three villages showed that the people most likely to be afflicted were those who were socially marginal or were experiencing a sense of role failure. The woman whose pottery had broken, for example, had also suffered two miscarriages (spontaneous abortions) and was worried that she would never have children. People with susto have higher mortality rates than the unafflicted population. This finding indicates that a deep sense of social failure places a person at a higher risk of dying.

THINKING OUTSIDE THE BOX

Learn about a culture-bound syndrome in your microculture and its possible connections to social success or failure.

Anorexia nervosa and a related condition, bulimia, are examples of culture-bound syndromes found predominantly among Euro-American adolescent girls of the United States (Brumberg 1988), although some cases have been documented among African American girls in the United States, and among girls in Japan, Hong Kong, and India (Fabrega and Miller 1995). Anorexia nervosa's cluster of symptoms includes self-perceptions of fatness, aversion to food, hyperactivity, and, as the condition progresses, wasting of the body and sometimes death. The association between anorexia and industrial culture suggests that as industrialism and westernization spread throughout the world, it is likely that the associated culture-bound syndromes will also spread.

No one has found a biological cause for anorexia nervosa, and thus it stands as a clear example of a culturally constructed affliction. It is difficult to cure with either medical or psychiatric treatment (Gremillon 1992), and this is a logical result of its cultural foundations. Pinpointing what the cultural causes are, however, has also not proved easy. Many experts cite the societal pressures on young girls in the United States toward excessive concern with their looks, especially body weight. Others feel that anorexia is related to girls' unconscious resistance to overly controlling parents. To such girls, their food intake may appear to be the one thing they have power over. This need for self-control through food deprivation becomes addictive and entrapping. Although the primary cause may be rooted in culture, the affliction becomes intertwined with the body's biological functions. Extreme fasting leads to the body's inability to deal with ingested food. Thus some medical treatments involve intravenous feeding to override the biological block.

Aspiring teenage models before a show in Florida. ■ As a research project on changing views of the ideal female body in the United States, choose a magazine or newspaper that has been in circulation since at least the 1950s. Analyze the size and shape of models' bodies in advertisements for women's clothing over time for possible changes. (Source: © Jeff Greenberg/PhotoEdit)

Preventive Practices

Many different practices based in either religious or secular beliefs exist cross-culturally for preventing misfortune, suffering, and illness. Among the Maya of Guatemala, one of the major illnesses is called *awas* (Wilson 1995). Children born with awas show symptoms such as lumps under the skin, marks on the skin, and/or albinism. Causes of awas are related to events that happen to the mother during her pregnancy: She may have been denied food she desired or have been pressured to eat food she didn't want, or she may have encountered a rude, drunk, or angry person (usually a male). In order to help prevent awas in babies, the Maya go out of their way to be careful around pregnant women. A pregnant woman, like land before planting, is considered sacred and is treated in special ways. She is always given the food she wants, and people behave with respect in her presence. In general, the ideal is to keep a pregnant woman in a state of contentment and optimism.

Common forms of ritual health protection include charms, spells, and strings tied around parts of the body. After visiting a Buddhist temple in Japan, one might purchase a small band to tie around the wrist to prevent future problems related to health and fertility. Wrist ties are commonly placed on infants in rural areas in India, especially by Hindus. Tying strings onto a tree or part of a shrine when undertaking a pilgrimage is another way that people attempt to secure their wishes for a healthy future.

An anthropologist working in rural northern Thailand learned of the display of carved wooden phalluses throughout a village as protection against a certain form of sudden death among men (Mills 1995). In 1990, fear of a widow ghost attack spread throughout the area. The fear was based on several radio reports of unexplained deaths of migrant Thai men working in Singapore. People interpreted these sudden deaths as caused by widow ghosts. Widow ghosts are believed to roam about, searching for men whom they take as their "husbands." Mary Beth Mills was conducting research in Baan Naa Sakae village at the time of the fear:

> I returned to Baan Naa Sakae village after a few days' absence to find the entire community of two hundred households festooned with wooden phalluses in all shapes and sizes. Ranging from the crudest wooden shafts to carefully carved images complete with coconut shell testicles and fishnet pubic hair, they adorned virtually every house and residential compound. The phalluses, I was told, were to protect residents, especially boys and men, from the "nightmare deaths" (*lai tai*) at the hands of malevolent "widow ghosts" (*phii mae maai*). (249)

In the study area, spirits (*phii*) are a recognized source of illness, death, and other misfortunes. One variety, a widow ghost, is the sexually voracious spirit of a woman who has met an untimely and perhaps violent death. When a seemingly healthy man dies in his sleep, a widow ghost is blamed. The wooden phalluses hung on the houses were protection against a possible attack:

> [I]nformants described these giant penises as decoys that would attract the interest of any phii mae maai which might come looking for a husband. The greedy ghosts would take their pleasure with the wooden penises and be satisfied, leaving the men of that household asleep, safe in their beds. (251)

As the radio reports ceased, villagers' concerns about the widow ghosts died down, and the phalluses were removed.

Throughout northern India, people believe that the tying on of strings provides protection from malevolent spirits and forces. This baby has five protective strings. ∎ What parallel forms of protection for infants would Western biomedicine require? (Source: Barbara Miller)

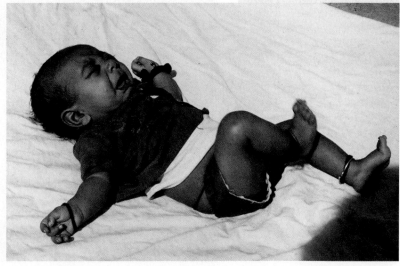

Diagnosis

If an affliction has been experienced and the person with the condition decides to seek help for it, diagnosis is the first stage in treatment. Diagnosis is the result of efforts to find out what is wrong and to label the affliction in order to determine the proper form of treatment. It includes magical–religious techniques such as **divination,** in which a specialist attempts to gain supernatural insights, and secular techniques such as asking the ill person to supply detailed descriptions of symptoms. Among the Navajo of the southwestern United States, hand trembling is an important diagnostic technique (W. Morgan 1977). The hand trembling diagnosis works this way: The specialist enters the home of the afflicted person and, with friends and relatives present, discusses the problem. The specialist sits facing the patient, closes his eyes, and thinks of all the possible causes. When the correct one comes to mind, the specialist's arm involuntarily shakes, revealing the diagnosis. In all three forms of Navajo diagnosis, the specialist goes into a trance-like state that lends authority to the outcome.

Among the urban poor of Bahia in Brazil (see the map of Brazil on p. 363), a flexible approach exists to ascertaining the cause of disease (Ngokwey 1988). In Feira de Santana, the second largest city in the state of Bahia, illness causation theories fit into the following domains: natural, socioeconomic, psychological, and supernatural. Natural causes include exposure to the environment. Thus "too much cold can provoke gripe; humidity and rain cause rheumatism; excessive heat can result in dehydration. . . . Some types of winds are known to provoke *ar do vento* or *ar do tempo,* a condition characterized by migraines, hemiplegia, and 'cerebral congestion'" (795). Other natural explanations for illness take into account the effects of aging, heredity, personal nature (*natureza*), and gender. Contagion is another "natural" explanation, as are the effects of certain foods and eating habits. Popular knowledge connects the lack of economic resources, proper sanitation, and health services with illnesses. "One informant said, 'There are many illnesses because there are many poor'" (796). In the psychosocial domain, certain illnesses are attributed to emotions: "Anger and hostile feelings (*raiva*), anxiety and worry are possible causes of various illnesses ranging from *nervoso,* a folk illness characterized by 'nervousness,' to heart problems and *derrame* (cerebral hemorrhage)" (796). In the supernatural domain, illness is caused by spirits and magical acts.

The African–Brazilian religious systems of the Bahia region encompass a range of spirits who can inflict illness, including spirits of the dead and devil-like spirits. Some spirits cause specific illnesses; others bring general misfortune. Spells cast by envious people with the evil eye (*ohlo grosso*) are a well-known cause of illness. People recognize multiple levels of causality. In the case of a stomach ache, for example, they might blame a quarrel (the ultimate cause), which prompted the aggrieved party to

Umbanda is a popular religion in Brazil and increasingly worldwide. Its ceremonies are often devoted to healing through spiritual means. In this session, tourists at the back of the room watch as Umbanda followers perform a dance related to a particular deity. ■ What is your opinion on the role of spirituality in health and healing, and on what do you base this view? (Source: © Ricardo Azoury/ CORBIS)

seek the intervention of a sorcerer, who cast a spell (the instrumental cause), which led to the illness. This multiple etiology then calls for a range of possible treatments.

Emic perceptions of symptoms and explanations for why illness occurs often directly contradict the teachings of Western biomedicine. This divergence may lead, on the one hand, to people's rejection of Western biomedicine and, on the other, to frustration among Western medical care providers who accuse such people of "noncompliance."

CROSSING THE FIELDS

Linguistic Anthropology and the Medical Interview

Differences in linguistic patterns that are quite subtle can lead to serious miscommunication. A linguistic anthropology study of doctor–patient communication in northern New York State provides a clear example of cross-cultural miscommunication (Woolfson et al. 1995). In this situation, health care providers who speak standard English often misinterpret the *linguistic cues* conveyed by speakers of Mohawk English. Linguistic cues are words or phrases that preface a remark to give the speaker's attitude toward what is being said, especially the speaker's degree of confidence in it. Some standard-English linguistic cues that serve this purpose are "maybe" and "in my opinion." Three functions of cuing exist in Mohawk English. They may indicate the speaker's unwillingness or inability to verify the certainty of a statement, respect for the listener, or the view of Mohawk religion that health is in the hands of the creator and any statement about health must acknowledge human limitations. Here are typical examples of Mohawk cuing (underlined) during an anthropological interview:

> Interviewer: What were the other kinds of diseases that people talked about in the past?
>
> Respondent: Hmm . . . That [tuberculosis] . . . was mostly, it well . . . they always said cirrhosis . . . . It seems like no matter what anybody died from . . . if they drank, it was cirrhosis. I don't know if anybody really knew a long time ago what anybody really died from. Even if the doctor requested an autopsy, the people would just say no . . . you know . . . it won't be done. So I don't think it was . . . you know . . . it was just what the doctor thought that would go down on the death certificate . . . . (p. 506)

Such linguistic cues, and their high frequency in Mohawk speech, appear to health care practitioners as signs of indecisiveness or reluctance to cooperate. These interpretations are incorrect. The speakers are following religiously grounded guidelines about humility and the extent of human knowledge. ▪

FOOD FOR THOUGHT

- Think of some examples of linguistic cues or other features of your speech when you meet with a doctor to discuss a health problem and its possible causes.

Ways of Healing

This section considers two ways of conceptualizing and dealing with healing: the public and participatory group healing of the Ju/wasi and the humoral system of bodily balance through food intake in Malaysia. We also consider healers and healing substances.

Community Healing Systems

A general distinction can be drawn between private and **community healing.** The former addresses bodily ailments more in isolation, and the latter emphasizes the social context as crucial to healing. Compared to Western biomedicine, many non-Western systems involve greater use of public healing and community involvement. An example of public or community healing comes from the Ju/wasi foragers of the Kalahari desert in southern Africa. Ju/wasi healing emphasizes the mobilization of community "energy" as a key element in the cure.

The central event in this tradition is the all-night healing dance. Four times a month on the average, night signals the start of a healing dance. The women sit around the fire, singing and rhythmically clapping. The men, sometimes joined by the women, dance around the singers. As the dance intensifies, *num* or spiritual energy is activated by the healers, both men and women, but mostly among the dancing men. As num is activated in them, they begin to *kia* or experience an enhancement of their consciousness. While experiencing kia, they heal all those at the dance . . . .

The dance is a community event at which the entire camp participates. The people's belief in the healing power of num brings substance to the dance. (Katz 1982:34–36)

Thus an important aspect of the Ju/wasi healing system is its openness—everyone has access to it. The role of healer is also open: There is no special class of healers with special privileges. In fact, more than half of all adult men and about 10 percent of adult women are healers.

A Ju/wasi healer in a trance, in the Kalahari desert, southern Africa. Most Ju/wasi healers are men, but some are women. ■ In your microculture, what are the patterns of gender, ethnicity, and class among various kinds of healers? (Source: © Irven DeVore/Anthro-Photo)

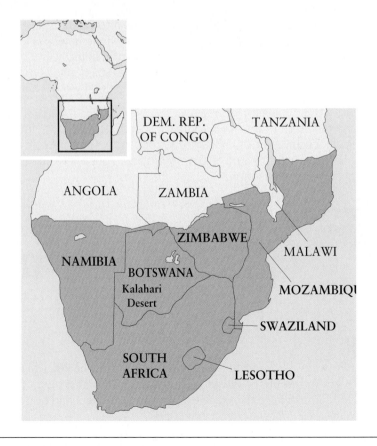

Humoral Healing Systems

Humoral healing systems are based on a philosophy of balance among certain natural elements within the body (McElroy and Townsend 1996). In such a system, food and drugs have different effects on the body and are classified as either "heating" or "cooling" (the quotation marks indicate that these properties are not the same as thermal measurements). Diseases are the result of bodily imbalances—too much heat or coolness—which must be counteracted through dietary changes or medicines that will restore balance.

Humoral healing systems have been practiced for thousands of years in the Middle East, the Mediterranean, and much of Asia, and they spread to the New World through Spanish colonization. They have shown substantial resilience in the face of Western biomedicine, often incorporating it into their own framework—for example, in the classification of biomedical treatments as either heating or cooling.

In Malaysia, several different humoral traditions coexist, reflecting the region's history of contact with outside cultures. Malaysia has been influenced by trade and contact between its indigenous culture and that of India, China, and the Arab–Islamic world for around two thousand years. Indian, Chinese, and Arabic medical systems all define health as the balance of opposing elements within the body, although each has its own variations (Laderman 1988:272). Indigenous belief systems may have been especially compatible with these imported models because they were also based on concepts of heat and coolness.

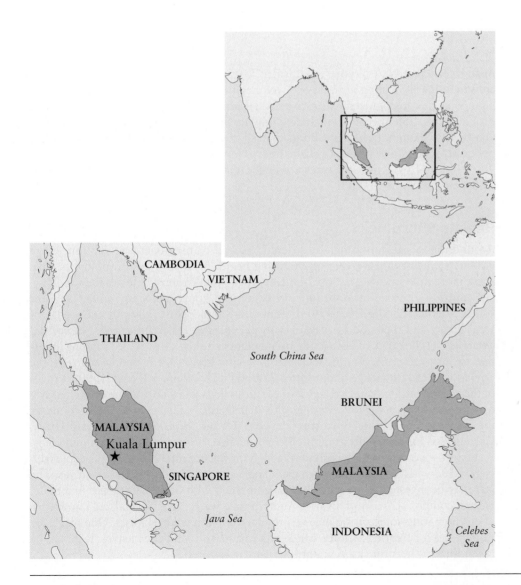

Insights about what the indigenous humoral systems were like before outside contact comes from ethnographic accounts about the Orang Asli, relatively isolated indigenous peoples of the Malaysian peninsula. A conceptual system of hot–cold opposition dominates Orang Asli cosmological, medical, and social theories. The properties and meanings of heat and coolness differ from those of Islamic, Indian, or Chinese humoralism in several ways. In the Islamic, Indian, and Chinese systems, for example, death is the ultimate result of too much coolness. Among the Orang Asli, excessive heat is the primary cause of mortality. Heat emanates from the sun and is associated with excrement, blood, misfortune, disease, and death. Humanity's hot blood makes people mortal, and their consumption of meat speeds the process. Heat causes menstruation, violent emotions, aggression, and drunkenness. Coolness, in contrast, is vital for health.

Among the Orang Asli, health is protected by staying in the forest to avoid the harmful effects of the sun. This belief justifies the rejection of agriculture by some groups, because that lifestyle exposes people to the sun. Treatment of illness is designed to reduce or remove heat. If someone were to fall ill in a clearing, the entire group would relocate to the coolness of the forest. The forest is also a source of cooling leaves and herbs. Healers are cool, and they retain their coolness by bathing in cold water and sleeping far from the fire. Extreme cold, however, can be harmful. Dangerous levels of coolness are associated with the time right after birth, because the mother is believed to have lost substantial heat. The new mother should not drink cold water or bathe in cold water. She increases her body heat by tying around her waist sashes that contain warmed leaves or ashes, and she lies near a fire.

Healers

In an informal sense, everyone is a "healer" because self-treatment is always the first consideration in dealing with a perceived health problem. Yet in all cultures, some people become recognized as having special abilities to diagnose and treat health problems. Notable specialists include: midwife, bonesetter (someone who resets broken bones), **shaman** (a healer who mediates between humans and the spirit world), herbalist, general practitioner, psychiatrist, acupuncturist, chiropractor, and dentist. Cross-cultural evidence indicates some common features of healers (Foster and Anderson 1978). See Table 13.2.

Healing Substances

Around the world, thousands of different natural or manufactured substances are used as medicines for preventing or curing health problems. Anthropologists have spent more time studying the use of medicines in non-Western cultures than in Western cultures, although a more fully cross-cultural approach is emerging (van der Geest, Whyte, and Hardon 1996). **Ethnobotany** explores the cultural knowledge of local plants and their use for a variety of purposes in different settings. Increasing awareness of the range of potentially useful plants worldwide provides a strong incentive for protecting the world's cultural diversity, because it is people who are the repositories of knowledge about different botanical resources (Posey 1990). Leaves of the coca plant, for example, have for centuries been a key part of the medicinal systems of the Andean region, although this plant has broader uses in ritual, in masking hunger pains, and in combatting the cold (Carter, Morales, and Mamani 1981). Coca is used for gastrointestinal problems and also for sprains, swellings, and colds. A survey of coca use in Bolivia showed a high prevalence rate: of the 3501 people who were asked whether they used coca medicinally, about 85 percent answered yes. The leaf may be ingested alone (chewed), or combined with other substances in a *maté*, a drink composed of any of a variety of herbs in a water base. Specialized knowledge about preparing some of the matés is reserved for trained herbalists. One maté, for example, is for treating asthma. Made of a certain root and coca leaves, it should be taken three to four times a day until the patient is cured.

TABLE 13.2
Criteria for becoming a healer.

- **Selection:** Certain individuals may show more ability for entry into healing roles. In Western medical schools, selection for entry rests on apparently objective standards, such as pre-entry exams and college grades. Among the Ainu of northern Japan, healers were men who had a special ability to go into a sort of seizure called *imu* (Ohnuki-Tierney 1980).

- **Training:** This often involves years of observation and practice, and the period of training may be extremely arduous, even dangerous. In some non-Western traditions, a shaman must make dangerous journeys, through trance or use of drugs, to the spirit world. In Western biomedicine, medical school involves immense amounts of memorization, separation from family and normal social life, and long periods of work without sleep.

- **Certification:** Legal certification or ritual certification, such as a shaman going through a formal initiation ritual announcing his or her competence.

- **Professional image:** One who plays the healer role is demarcated from ordinary people through behavior, dress, and other markers, such as the white coat in the West and the Siberian shaman's tambourine for calling the spirits.

- **Expectation of payment:** Compensation in some form, whether in kind or in cash, is expected for all formal healers. Payment level may vary depending on the status of the healer and other factors. In northern India, strong preference for sons is reflected in payments to the midwife for helping with the delivery; in rural areas, the payment is twice as great when a son is born. In the United States, medical professionals in different specializations earn markedly different salaries.

What kinds of medicines **THINKING** do you think the first modern humans used, and how might such medicines have varied **OUTSIDE** in Africa, Asia, Europe, **THE BOX** and the New World?

Ingredients for traditional medicines available in a shop in Singapore include deer and antelope horns, monkey gall bladders, amber, freshwater pearls, and ginseng. ■ Have you ever gone to a pharmacy in a non–Euro-American context? If so, what did you notice? Are there any similarities to Western pharmacies? (Source: © William & Deni McIntyre/Photo Researchers, Inc.)

Minerals are also widely used for prevention and healing. For example, bathing in water that contains high levels of sulfur or other minerals has wide popularity for promoting health and curing several ailments, including arthritis and rheumatism. About 40,000 people a year go to the Dead Sea, located between Israel and Jordan, for treating their skin diseases (Lew 1994). The adjacent sulfur springs and mud from the shore are believed to be helpful for people with skin ailments such as psoriasis. In fact, expenses for a therapeutic trip to the Dead Sea are tax deductible in the United States. German studies conclude that it is more cost-effective to pay for a trip to the Dead Sea than to hospitalize a psoriasis patient. Whereas these practices seem clearly to have therapeutic value, instances of people's eating dirt appear to be less understandable within the framework of therapy (see the Critical Thinking box on p. 396).

Western patent medicines have gained popularity worldwide. There are benefits to using these medicines, as well as detriments, including use without prescription and overprescription. Often, the sale of patent medicines is unregulated, and they are available for purchase from local markets by self-treating individuals. The popularity of capsules and injections has led to overuse in many cases. Medical anthropologists are assessing the distribution channels of medicines, the increased commodification of medicine, and cross-cultural perceptions of the efficacy of various types of medicines.

Why Do People Eat Dirt?

GEOPHAGIA, THE EATING of earth, is a special form of *pica*, or the "habitual consumption of items not commonly considered to be food or the compulsive consumption of otherwise normal food items" (Reid 1992). It presents a fascinating puzzle that has been studied by medical anthropologists, cultural geographers, historians, and medical experts. Geophagia has been documented in several Native American groups of South America and the American Southwest, in the Mediterranean region, among women and children in India, among pregnant African American women and children, and in some African cultures. There is typically a preference for certain kinds of earth or clay, and the clay is often baked before consumption, formed into tablets, or mixed with other substances such as honey.

Medical experts offer explanations based on pathology; in other words, they believe people eat earth or clay because there is something wrong with them. Some pathologies linked with geophagia are colon perforation, fecal impaction, severe tooth abrasion, and, especially, anemia. According to this view, anemic persons consume earth as an unconscious way of increasing iron levels. Therefore, geophagia can be "cured" through iron therapy. Other experts argue that the arrow of causation points in the opposite direction: clay consumption reduces the body's ability to absorb iron, so it causes anemia. The anemia arguments are complex and the data often inconclusive because of small samples or lack of good control groups. Thus, although an association between geophagia and anemia seems often (but not always) to exist, the direction of causation is undetermined.

Some medical anthropologists propose that geophagia has a positive adaptive value. Eating clay, they say, may function as a supplement to dietary minerals. Clay from markets in Ghana, for example, has been found to contain phosphorus, potassium, calcium, magnesium, copper, zinc, manganese, and iron. Another adaptive role for geophagia is in traditional antidiarrheal preparations. Many clays of Africa have compositions similar to that of Kaopectate, a Western commercial antidiarrheal medicine.

A third hypothesis is that consuming clay may act as a detoxicant, preventing the nausea or indigestion that would otherwise result from eating plant materials that contain certain toxins. This hypothesis receives support from the fact that clay is commonly eaten during famines to help people digest leaves, bark, and other unaccustomed and hard-to-digest foods. In addition, laboratory rats react to exposure to chemical toxins or new flavors by eating clay.

CRITICAL THINKING QUESTIONS

- Is it likely that only one of the above explanations for geophagia is correct in all cases? Why or why not?
- Could all of the above explanations be correct?
- Could none be correct? Why?

THEORETICAL APPROACHES IN MEDICAL ANTHROPOLOGY

Here we consider three theoretical approaches to understanding health systems. The first emphasizes the importance of the environment in shaping health problems and their spread. The second highlights symbols and meaning as key in people's expression of suffering and how healing occurs. The third underlines the need to look at economic and political structural factors as causes of health problems and as related to certain features of Western biomedicine.

The Ecological/Epidemiological Approach

The **ecological/epidemiological approach** examines how aspects of the natural environment interact with culture to cause health problems and to influence their spread throughout the population. According to this approach, research should focus on gathering information about the environmental context and social patterns that affect health, such as food distribution within the family, sexual practices, hygiene, and

A Quantitative Comparison of Health Problems of Pastoralist and Settled Turkana Men

PALEOPATHOLOGISTS STUDY health changes in prehistory using fossils. How can we learn about the health effects of changes in lifestyle among contemporary people? One approach is to compare the health status of two cultural subgroups, one in which the members maintain a nonsedentary way of life and one whose members have taken up life in a sedentary context such as agriculture or urban labor. A quantitative (numeric-based) study can provide insights into the heath problems of people in different environmental and social contexts.

One such study was conducted in the early 1990s as part of a larger research project called the South Turkana Ecosystem Project (Barkey, Campbell, and Leslie 2001). Researchers conducted interviews with 152 pastoralist men and 124 settled men. They used a health questionnaire that asked respondents to describe current health problems and problems experienced in the last month. In order to aid memory and improve reliability, the interviewer read a list of Turkana disease categories and asked the respondent whether he had suffered from them in the past month. Other information was also collected, such as the respondent's age, weight, and height; skin-fold measurements; and diet for the past 48-hour period. Two researchers independently coded responses to the health questions according to severity: no complaints, mild, moderate, or serious. The two coders' results were discussed, and any major discrepancies that occurred between their scores were reconciled.

Results showed significantly more serious health complaints among the settled Turkana than among the pastoral Turkana. Settled men reported more eye infections, chest infections, backaches, and cough/colds. For example, 50 percent of the settled men reported eye infections compared to 26 percent of the pastoral Turkana.

In terms of nutrition, the settled Turkana were shorter and had greater body mass than the pastoral Turkana. Diets were markedly different among the two groups, with the pastoral Turkana diet (milk, meat, animal blood) being high in protein and low in calories and the settled Turkana diet (maize, beans) being high in calories and low in protein.

FOOD FOR THOUGHT

- What might be done to improve the health and nutrition of the settled Turkana people?

population contact. Research tends to be quantitative and etic, although this approach is often combined with qualitative and emic methods to provide richer results.

The ecological/epidemiological approach yields findings relevant to public health programs by revealing causal links between environmental context and health problems. It also helps by providing socially targeted information about groups "at risk" for specific problems. For example, although hookworm is extremely common throughout rural China, researchers learned that rice cultivators have the highest rates of all. This pattern is related to the fact that the disease is spread through night soil (human excrement used as fertilizer) that is applied to the fields where the cultivators work.

Settled populations living in dense clusters are more likely than mobile populations to experience certain health problems, including malnutrition and infectious disease (Cohen 1989). Many contemporary studies in the ecological/environmental mode attest to the importance of this distinction. As more and more mobile populations choose, or are forced, to settle into agricultural or urban lives, it is increasingly urgent that the often negative health consequences of sedentism are recognized and mitigated. One recent study compared the health status of two groups of Turkana men in northwest Kenya (see the Methods Close-Up box). Some of the Turkana are still pastoralists, whereas others have settled into a town where they no longer keep animals.

These fossilized teeth are from a child who lived 1.6 million years ago, found at Koobi Fora, Kenya, and belonging to the species H. ergaster. *The grooves on the teeth reflect periods of nutritional stress, or illness, or both, when enamel growth slows down or stops. Of the many fossils from this period, very few show any form of pathology, making this fossil specimen a rare case.* (Source: Bernard Wood)

Colonialism and Disease

Anthropologists have applied the ecological/epidemiological approach to the study of the impaired health and survival of indigenous peoples as a result of colonial contact. A basic question is how the introduction of European pathogens (disease-producing organisms) varies in relation to the size of the indigenous population involved (Larsen and Milner 1994). Overall, findings about the effects of colonial contact are negative, ranging from the quick and outright extermination of many indigenous peoples to adjustment, among others, to drastically changed conditions.

In the Western hemisphere, colonialism brought a dramatic decline in the indigenous populations, although disagreement exists about the numbers involved (Joralemon 1982). In coordination with archaeologists and colonial historians, medical anthropologists have tried to estimate the role of disease in depopulation (relative to other factors such as warfare, harsh labor practices, and general cultural disruption) and to discover which diseases were most important. Research along these lines indicates that the precontact New World was largely free of the major European infectious diseases, such as smallpox, measles, and typhus, and perhaps also free of syphilis, leprosy, and malaria. The exposure of indigenous peoples to these infectious diseases, therefore, was likely to have a massive impact, given the people's complete lack of resistance. One analyst has compared colonial contact to a "biological war":

> Smallpox was the captain of the men of death in that war, typhus fever the first lieutenant, and measles the second lieutenant. More terrible than the conquistadores on horseback, more deadly than sword and gunpowder, they made the conquest by the whites a walkover as compared to what it would have been without their aid. They were the forerunners of civilization, the companions of Christianity, the friends of the invader. (Ashburn 1947:98, quoted in Joralemon 1982:112)

This quotation emphasizes the importance of the three major diseases in New World colonial history: smallpox, measles, and malaria. A later arrival, cholera, also had severe effects because its transmission through contaminated water and food is especially rapid in areas where sanitation is inadequate.

Women working in padi fields near Jinghong, China. Agricultural work done in standing water increases the risk of hookworm infection. ■ Is hookworm a threat where you live? What is the most common infectious disease in your home region? (Source: © Peter Menzel/Stock Boston, LLC)

The Interpretivist Approach

Some medical anthropologists examine health systems as systems of meaning. They study how people in different cultures label, describe, and experience illness and how healing modalities offer meaningful responses to individual and group distress. These interpretivist anthropologists have examined aspects of healing, such as ritual trance, as symbolic performances. Claude Lévi-Strauss (see his photograph on p. 41) established this approach in a classic essay, "The Effectiveness of Symbols" (1967). He examined how a song sung during childbirth among the Kuna Indians of Panama lessens the difficulty of childbirth. His main point was that healing systems provide meaning to people who are experiencing seemingly meaningless forms of suffering. The provision of meaning offers psychological support and courage to the afflicted and may enhance healing through what Western science calls the *placebo effect* or *meaning effect,* a healing effect obtained through the positive power of believing that a particular method is effective. Cross-cultural research suggests that between 10 and 90 percent of the efficacy of medical prescriptions lies in the placebo effect (Moerman 2002). Several features may be involved: the power of the person prescribing a particular treatment, the act of prescription, and concrete details about the medicine such as its color, name, and place of origin (van der Geest, Whyte, and Hardon 1996).

Margaret Trawick, in her study of Ayurvedic healing in India, follows the "healing is in the meaning" approach in interpreting some aspects of the efficacy and appeal of Ayurvedic treatments (1988). Ayurvedic medicine is a widely used Indian health system recorded in texts composed from the beginning of the present era and continuing over a period of about a thousand years. Based on humoral principles, Ayurvedic diagnoses take into account whether bodily "channels" controlling the flow of life in the human body are blocked or open and clear. An interview between an Ayurvedic physician and an old woman of a poor caste group in southern India reveals the themes of channels, processes of flow, points of connection (the heart is believed to be the center of all channels), and everyday activities that regulate the flow of life.

Here are some excerpts from the doctor–patient (D–P) conversation:

D: Let's see your eyes. Let's see your pulse. Is your age over sixty?

P: Probably.

D: . . . Is there chest pain?

P: A little.

D: Does your heart flutter?

P: It flutters . . . .

D: Is there pain in the joints?

P: Yes . . . .

D: Have you taken any treatment for this?

P: I have taken no treatment at all . . . . (138–139)

After the interview, the doctor offers dietary prescriptions to "quicken" the patient's body—such as avoidance of tamarind, because that causes "dullness," and consumption of light food so that it won't get crowded inside her. In addition to general advice about what to eat and what to avoid, he gives her a detailed daily regimen to follow: "Drink two coffees, in the morning a coffee and in the evening a coffee. Add palm sugar to the coffee, filter it and remove the dirt, add cow's milk and drink it . . . . Eat wheat grain made soft. At three o'clock drink only one cup of coffee. Eat more food than coffee" (138–139). Finally, he gently tells her that, basically, she is growing old:

> I will give you a medicine. In the time of age, at this age of sixty, if the strength of your body has diminished it is difficult for it to return. Therefore you must carry with you your existing strength without its diminishing still more quickly. You must

carry it without evils coming and without making room for other diseases. Don't show your head and mix in noisy places and take the air for too long. You must go to mountain places refreshing to the mind, and seeing the plants and trees there be happy. Or else go to the temple and worship God. From that your mind will be pure. A good refuge for your body will be found. (page 40)

In this interaction, the meanings conveyed through the interview offer the client a sense that she is being taken seriously by the caregiver and give her some self-efficacy in that there are things she can do to alleviate her distress, such as carefully following a dietary regime. The doctor also communicates that there will be no dramatic cure and that taking good care of herself and seeking peace of mind will do the most to promote her well-being.

THINKING OUTSIDE THE BOX How can the placebo effect, or meaning effect, be understood as both cultural and biological?

Critical Medical Anthropology

Critical medical anthropology is an approach that, like structurism (review Chapter 2, p. 61), focuses on the analysis of how economic and political power structures shape people's health status, their access to health care, and the prevailing healing systems. Critical medical anthropologists show how economic and political systems create and perpetuate social inequality in health status. They also take a cultural constructionist position, arguing that illness is more often a product of one's culturally defined position than of something "natural." Critical medical anthropologists have exposed the power of **medicalization**—that is, the labeling of a particular issue or problem as medical and requiring medical treatment when, in fact, the problem may be economic or political.

Critical medical anthropologists tend to look first at how larger structural forces determine the distribution of illness and people's responses to it. But they are also concerned to see how individuals may, through personal agency, resist such forces. Some critical medical anthropologists examine Western biomedicine itself, viewing it as a global power structure, critiquing Western medical training, and looking at doctor–patient relationships as manifestations of social control rather than social liberation.

The Role of Poverty

Broad distinctions exist between the most prevalent afflictions in the richer, more industrial nations and those of the poorer, less industrial nations. In the former, the major causes of death are circulatory diseases, malignant cancers, AIDS, alcohol consumption, and tobacco consumption (United Nations Development Programme 1994:191). In developing countries, tuberculosis, malaria, and AIDS predominate. There is substantial empirical evidence that poverty is a major cause of morbidity (sickness) and mortality (death) in both industrial and developing countries. It may be manifested in different ways—for example, by causing extreme malnutrition in Chad or Nepal and resulting in high death rates from street violence among the poor of affluent nations.

Throughout the developing world, rates of childhood malnutrition are inversely related to income (review the discussion and map on p. 312). As income increases, calorie intake as a percent of recommended daily allowances also increases (Zaidi 1988:122). Thus increasing the income levels of the poor may be the most direct way to influence health and nutrition. Yet, in contrast to this seemingly logical approach, many health and nutrition programs around the world have been focused on treating the outcomes of poverty rather than its causes.

The widespread practice of addressing the health outcomes of poverty and social inequality with pills or other medical options has been documented by critical medical anthropologists. An example is Nancy Scheper-Hughes's research in Bom Jesus, northeastern Brazil, mentioned in Chapter 12 (1992). The people who experienced symptoms of weakness, insomnia, and anxiety were given pills by a local doctor. Scheper-Hughes is convinced that the people were hungry and needed food. Such "medicalizing" serves the interests of pharmaceutical companies and, more generally, helps to maintain inequitable social systems. Similar critical analyses have shown how psychiatry insists on treating symptoms and serves to keep people in their places, rather than addressing the root causes of affliction, which may be powerlessness, unemployment, and thwarted social aspirations. High rates of depression among women in Western societies and their treatment with a range of psychotropic drugs and personal therapists, are an example.

Western Medical Training Examined

Since the 1980s, critical medical anthropologists have studied Western biomedicine as a powerful cultural system. Much of their work critiques Western medical school training and its emphasis on technology. They often advocate greater recognition of social factors in diagnosis and treatment, reduction of the spread of biomedical technology, and diversification of medical specialists to include alternative healing, such as massage, acupuncture, and chiropracty (Scheper-Hughes 1990).

Robbie Davis-Floyd examined the culture of obstetrical training in the United States (1987). She interviewed twelve obstetricians, ten male and two female. As students, they absorbed the technological model of birth as a core value of Western obstetrics. This model treats the body as a machine. The physician–technician uses the assembly-line approach to birth in order to promote efficient production and quality control. As one of the residents in the study explained, "We shave 'em, we prep 'em, we hook 'em up to the IV and administer sedation. We deliver the baby, it goes to the nursery and the mother goes to her room. There's no room for niceties around here. We just move 'em right on through. It's not hard to see it like an assembly line" (292). The goal is the "production" of a healthy baby. The doctor is in charge of achieving this goal, and the mother takes second place. One obstetrician said, "It is what we all were trained to always go after—the perfect baby. That's what we were trained to produce. The quality of the mother's experience—we rarely thought about that. Everything we did was to get that perfect baby" (292).

This goal involves the use of sophisticated monitoring machines. One obstetrician said, "I'm totally dependent on fetal monitors, 'cause they're great! They free you to do a lot of other things . . . . I couldn't sit over there with a woman in labor with my hand on her belly, and be in here seeing 20 to 30 patients a day" (291). In addition, use of technology conveys status: "Anybody in obstetrics who shows a human interest in patients is not respected. What is respected is interest in machines" (291).

How does obstetrical training socialize medical students into accepting this technological model? First, medical training involves a lengthy process of *cognitive retrogression* in which the students go through an intellectual hazing process. During the first two years of medical school, most courses are basic sciences, learning tends to be rote, and vast quantities of material must be memorized. The sheer bulk of memorization forces students to adopt an uncritical approach to it. Mental overload socializes students into a uniform pattern, giving them a *tunnel vision* in which the knowledge of medicine assumes supreme importance. One informant put it this way:

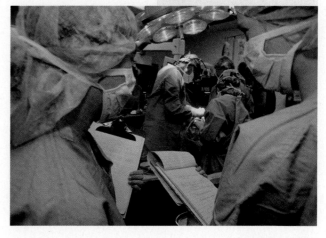

Medical students in training in a Western biomedical setting. These students are observing brain surgery. ■ What does this scene convey about values and beliefs of Western medicine? (Source: © Lara Jo Regan/Getty Images)

> Medical school is not difficult in terms of what you have to learn—there's just so much of it. You go through, in a six-week course, a thousand-page book. The sheer bulk of information is phenomenal. You have pop quizzes in two or three courses every day the first year. We'd get up around 6, attend classes till 5, go home and eat, then head back to school and be in anatomy lab working with a cadaver, or something, until 1 or 2 in the morning, and then go home and get a couple of hours of sleep and then go out again. And you did that virtually day in and day out for four years, except for vacations. (298–299)

The second phase, which could be termed *dehumanization*, is one in which medical school training succeeds in

THINKING
OUTSIDE
THE BOX

In recent years, many medical schools in the United States have reformed their training programs. On the Internet, visit two or three medical schools to see if you can find evidence of change. For a wider exploration, look at medical schools in other countries.

overriding humanitarian ideals through its emphasis on technology and objectification of the patient. One informant explained, "Most of us went into medical school with pretty humanitarian ideals. I know I did. But the whole process of medical education makes you inhuman . . . . by the time you get to residency, you end up not caring about anything beyond the latest techniques you can master and how sophisticated the tests are that you can perform" (299). The physical aspect of hazing through exhaustion intensifies during the residency years. The last two years of medical school and the four years of residency are devoted primarily to hands-on experience. The obstetrical specialization involves intensive repetition and learning of technical skills, including surgery. One obstetrician summed up the entire process of transformation: "It doesn't seem to matter—male or female, young or old, wealthy or poor—it is only the most unusual individual who comes through a residency program as anything less than a technological clone" (307).

This study emphasizes how biomedical caregivers are trained to become dependent on technology as the basis of their expertise. Similar studies of other biomedical specialists, such as surgeons, make the same point (Cassell 1991) and show how the power of physicians is correlated with the complexity of the technology they use.

GLOBALIZATION AND CHANGE

Globalization in the past decade has brought changes in both health problems and health treatment. In this section, we review some of the new and emerging health risks, as well as new and emerging treatment practices and options.

In recent decades new diseases have arisen, and some, such as HIV/AIDS, have spread rapidly. The promotion of agriculture, dam building, and other aspects of global economic change have also brought new health risks.

The New Infectious Diseases

The 1950s brought hope that infectious diseases were being controlled through Western scientific advances such as antibiotic drugs, vaccines against childhood diseases, and improved technology for sanitation. In North America, death from infections common in the late nineteenth and early twentieth centuries was no longer a major threat in the 1970s. In tropical countries, pesticides lowered rates of malaria by controlling the mosquito populations. Since the 1980s, however, we have entered an era of shaken confidence. Besides the spread of the HIV/AIDS epidemic, another challenge is presented by the fact that many infectious microbes have reappeared in forms that are resistant to known methods of prevention and treatment. New contexts for exposure and contagion are being created through increased international travel and migration, expansion of populations into previously uninhabited forest areas, changing sexual behavior, and overcrowding in cities. Several new and re-emerging diseases are related to unsafe technological developments. For example, the introduction of soft contact lenses has caused eye infections.

Many medical anthropologists are contributing their expertise to understanding the causes and distribution of the new infectious diseases by studying social patterns and cultural practices. Research about HIV/AIDS addresses factors such as intravenous drug use, sexual behavior, and condom use among different groups and how intervention programs could be better designed and targeted. For example, one study assessed attitudes toward condom use among White, African American, and Hispanic respondents in the United States (Bowen and Trotter 1995). Whites were most

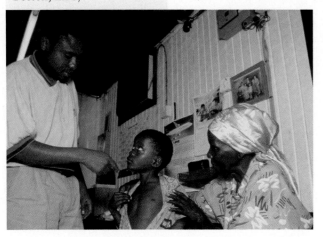

A woman takes her eight-year-old grandson, who has HIV/AIDS, to a clinic in Dar es Salaam, Tanzania. Throughout the world, increasing numbers of children are infected with HIV/AIDS and are also orphans because their parents have died of the disease. ■ In your culture, what is the prevalence of HIV/AIDS among children, and what services are provided for them? (Source: © Sean Sprague/Stock Boston, LLC)

likely to use condoms, followed by Hispanics, and then African Americans. Within all groups, people with "main partners" (as opposed to "casual partners") were more likely to use condoms, as were older people and people classified as having a higher level of personal assertiveness. Recommendations for increasing condom use include self-awareness programs and assertiveness training, especially for younger people in casual relationships.

Diseases of Development

Diseases of development are diseases that are caused or increased by economic development activities. Examples of diseases in this category are schistosomiasis, river blindness, malaria, and tuberculosis (Foster and Anderson 1978:27).

In many developing countries, dramatically increased rates of schistosomiasis (a disease caused by the presence of a parasitic worm in the blood system) have been traced to the construction of dams and irrigation systems. Over 200 million people suffer from this disease, which causes anemia and fatigue (Foster and Anderson 1978). The larvae of this particular form of worm hatch from eggs and mature in slow-moving water such as lakes and rivers. Upon maturity, they can penetrate human (or other animal) skin with which they come into contact. People who wade or swim in infected waters are likely to become infected. Once inside the human body, the adult schistosomes breed in the veins around the human bladder and bowel. They send fertilized eggs through urine and feces into the environment. These eggs then continue to contaminate water in which they hatch into larvae. Anthropologists' research has documented steep increases in the rates of schistosomiasis near dam sites over the past three decades of dam construction in developing countries (Scudder 1973). This increased risk is caused by the dams slowing the rate of water flow. Stagnant water systems offer an ideal environment for development of the larvae. Anthropologists have used this information to speak out against the construction of large dams.

Formerly unidentified diseases of development continue to appear. One of these is Kyasanur forest disease, or KFD (Nichter 1992). This viral disease was first identified in 1957 in southern India:

> Resembling influenza, at onset KFD is marked by sudden chills, fever, frontal headaches, stiffness of the neck, and body pain. Diarrhea and vomiting often follow on the third day. High fever is continuous for five to fifteen days, during which time a variety of additional symptoms may manifest themselves, including gastrointestinal bleeding, persistent cough with blood-tinged sputum, and bleeding gums. In more serious cases, the infection progresses to bronchial pneumonia, meningitis, paralysis, encephalitis, and hemorrhage. (224)

In the early 1980s, an epidemic of KFD swept through over thirty villages near the Kyasanur forest. Mortality rates in hospitals ranged between 12 and 18 percent of those admitted. Investigation revealed that KFD especially affected agricultural workers and cattle tenders, who were most exposed to newly cleared areas near the forest. In the cleared areas, international companies established plantations and initiated cattle raising. Ticks, which had long existed in the local ecosystem, increased in numbers in the cleared area and found inviting hosts in the cattle and their tenders. Thus human modification of the environment through deforestation and introduction of cattle raising caused the epidemic and shaped its social distribution.

Changes in Healing: Medical Pluralism

In terms of changes in medical care, Western biomedicine continues to spread throughout the world while some non-Western practices find increasing acceptance in the West. **Medical pluralism,** in which more than one health care system exists in a given culture, is increasing worldwide, thus offering people more choices.

Medical pluralism both provides options and introduces complications. First, a condition may be classified as a health problem in some health systems and not in others.

Among the many forms of medical treatment available to the Sherpa of Nepal, shamanic healing remains a popular choice. ■ Why might many Sherpa people continue to see a shaman for illness rather than a biomedical doctor? (Source: Vincanne Adams)

For example, spirit possession is welcomed in some cultures but might be diagnosed as schizophrenia by Western psychiatry. Second, the same issue may be classified as having a different cause (such as supernatural versus germ theories) and may therefore require different treatments. Third, certain treatment modalities may be rejected as violating cultural rules. All of these issues affect how a particular culture will react to exogenous (outside) medical practices.

The two cases discussed next illustrate, first, the coexistence of several forms of healing that offer clients a range of choices and, second, a situation of conflicting explanatory models of illness and healing that result in serious misunderstandings between healers and clients.

Selective Pluralism: The Case of the Sherpas

The Sherpas of Nepal offer an unusual example of a newly capitalizing context in which preference for traditional healing systems remains strong, along with the adoption of certain aspects of biomedicine (V. Adams 1988). Formerly pastoralist–farmers, the Sherpas now provide services for international tourism. They work as guides, porters, cooks, and administrators in trekking agencies and as staff at hotels and restaurants. The variety of healing therapies available in the Upper Khumbu region fall into three categories:

- Orthodox Buddhist practitioners, such as lamas, who are consulted for both prevention and cure through their blessings.
- *Amchis,* who practice a system largely derived from India's Ayurvedic medicine.
- Unorthodox religious or shamanic practitioners, who perform divination ceremonies for diagnosis.
- Biomedical practitioners, who first offered diagnostic and medicinal services mainly to tourists and later established a permanent medical facility in 1967.

In Khumbu, thriving traditional healers are in no way threatened by wider economic changes occasioned by the tourist trade and the attendant influx of wealth. The reason is that high-mountain tourism is a particular form of capitalist development that does not radically change the local social relations involved in production. This type of tourism brings in money but does not require large-scale capital investment from outside. Thus the Sherpas maintain control of their productive resources, their family structures remain largely the same, and wider kinship ties remain important in the organization of tourist business.

When Explanatory Models Conflict

The disjuncture between biomedicine and local cultural patterns has been documented by many anthropologists. In some instances, miscommunication occurs between biomedical doctors and clients in matters as seemingly simple as a prescription that should be taken with every meal. The doctor assumes that this means three times a day, but some people do not eat three meals a day and thus do not follow the regimen the doctor intended to prescribe.

One study of a case in which death resulted from cross-cultural differences shows how complex the issue of communication across medical cultures is. The "F family" are Samoan immigrants living in Honolulu, Hawai'i (Krantzler 1987). Neither parent speaks English. Their children are "moderately literate" in English but speak a mixture of English and Samoan at home. Mr. F was trained as a traditional Samoan healer. Mary, a daughter, was first stricken with diabetes at the age of sixteen. She was taken to the hospital by ambulance after collapsing, semi-conscious, on the sidewalk near her home in a Honolulu housing project. After several months of irregular contact with medical staff, she was again brought to the hospital in an ambulance, unconscious, and she died there. Her father was charged with causing Mary's death through medical neglect.

Medical anthropologist Nora Krantzler analyzes this case from the perspectives of the Western medical providers and Samoan culture. Here is the medical sector view, beginning with Mary's first admission to the hospital:

> At that point, her illness was "discovered" and diagnosed as juvenile onset diabetes mellitus. She was initially placed in the Pediatric Intensive Care Unit for 24 hours, then transferred to a pediatric ward for about a week until her diabetes was "under good control." She, her parents, and her older sister were taught how to give insulin injections, and Mary was shown how to test her urine for glucose and acetone. She was given a 1-month supply of insulin. . . . She was further "counseled" about her diet. . . . She was then to be followed up with visits to the outpatient clinic. Following the clinic's (unofficial) policy of linking patients with physicians from their own ethnic group, she was assigned to see the sole Samoan pediatric resident. (326–327)

Over the next few months, she was seen once in the clinic by a different resident (a physician at the stage of training following internship). She missed her next three appointments, came in once without an appointment, and was readmitted to the hospital on the basis of test results from that visit. At that time, she, her parents, and her older sister were once again advised about the importance of compliance with the medical advice they were receiving. Four months later, she returned to the clinic with blindness in one eye and diminished vision in the other. She was diagnosed with cataracts, and Dr. A, the Samoan physician, again advised her about the seriousness of her illness and the need for compliance. He wanted her to be admitted to the hospital to have the cataracts removed. Her father initially refused but then was persuaded. Dr. A wrote in Mary's chart:

> Her diabetes seemed to be very much out of control at the time but I was having a very difficult time with the patient and her father. . . . I consented to the father's wishes to have him supplement the insulin with some potion of his that he had prepared especially to control her sugar. . . . He did not believe that there was such an illness which would require daily injection for the rest of one's life and thanked me for my efforts but claimed that he would like to have total control of his daughter's illness at this time. (328–329)

The medical experts increasingly judged that "cultural differences" were the basic problem and that in spite of all their attempts to communicate with the F family, the family was basically incapable of caring for Mary. Legal sanctions were used to force her family to bring her to the hospital for surgery.

The family's perspective, in contrast, was grounded in *fa'a Samoa,* the Samoan way. Their first experience in a large hospital occurred after Mary's collapse:

> When Mr. F first arrived at the hospital, he spoke with different hospital staff (using a daughter as a translator) and was concerned that there was no single physician caring for Mary. (Since it was a teaching hospital, she was seen by residents as well as by attending physicians.) He felt that the hospital staff members gave him different interpretations of Mary's illness, including discrepant results, leading him to perceive her care as experimental and inconsistent. The family also observed a child die while Mary was in the Intensive Care Unit, further reinforcing this perception and instilling fear over Mary's chance of surviving in this hospital. Partly due to language difficulties, they felt they did not get an adequate explanation of her problem over the

course of her treatment. When they asked what was wrong with her, their perception was that "everyone said 'sugar.'" What this meant was not clear to the family; they were confused about whether she was getting too much sugar or too little. Mary's mother interpreted the explanations to mean she was not getting enough sugar, so she tried to give her more when she was returned home. Over time, confusion gave way to anger, and a basic lack of trust of the hospital and the physicians there developed. The family began to draw on their own resources for explaining and caring for Mary's illness, relying heavily on the father's skills as a healer. (330)

From the Samoan perspective, the F family behaved logically and appropriately. The father, as household head and healer in his own right, felt he had authority. Dr. A, although Samoan, had been resocialized by the Western medical system and alienated from his Samoan background. He did not offer the personal touch that the F family expected.

Clinical Medical Anthropology

Clinical or applied medical anthropology is the application of anthropological knowledge to further the goals of health care providers—for example, in improving doctor–patient communication in multicultural settings, making recommendations about culturally appropriate health intervention programs, and providing insights about factors related to disease that medical practitioners do not usually take into account. In their work, different clinical medical anthropologists draw on ethnomedical knowledge and on any of the three theoretical approaches or a combination of them.

Although critical medical anthropology and clinical medical anthropology may seem diametrically opposed to each other (the first seeking to critique and even limit the power and range of the Western biomedical establishment, and the second seeking to make it more effective), some medical anthropologists are building bridges between the two perspectives.

An example of a clinical medical anthropologist who combines the first two approaches is Robert Trotter (1987), who conducted research on lead poisoning among children in Mexican American communities. The three most common sources of lead poisoning of children in the United States are eating lead-based paint chips, living near a smelter where the dust has high lead content, and eating or drinking from pottery made with an improperly treated lead glaze. The discovery of an unusual case of lead poisoning by health professionals in Los Angeles in the early 1980s prompted investigations that revealed a fourth cause: the use of a traditional healing remedy, *azarcon*, which contained lead, by people of the Mexican American community. Azarcon is used to treat a culture-bound syndrome called *empacho*, which is a combination of indigestion and constipation that is believed to be caused by food sticking to the abdominal wall.

Trotter was called on by the U.S. Public Health Service to investigate the availability and use of azarcon. His research took him to Mexico, where he surveyed the contents of herbal shops and talked with *curanderos* (local healers). He learned about an alternative name for azarcon, *greta*, which helped him trace the distribution of this lead-based substance in the United States. His work led to U.S. government restrictions on azarcon and greta to prevent their further use, to recommendations about the need to provide a substitute remedy for the treatment of empacho that would not have harmful side effects, and to ideas about how to advertise this substitute. Throughout his involvement, Trotter played several roles: functioning as researcher, consultant, and program developer. In the end, he was able to apply anthropological knowledge to the solution of a health problem.

Much work in clinical medical anthropology involves health communication (Nichter 1996:327–328). Anthropologists can help health educators in the development of more meaningful messages through

- addressing local ethnophysiology and acknowledging popular health concerns.
- taking seriously all local illness terms and conventions.

Promoting Vaccination Programs

VACCINATION PROGRAMS, especially as promoted by UNICEF, are often introduced in countries with much fanfare, but they are sometimes met with little enthusiasm by the target population. In India, many people are suspicious that vaccination programs are clandestine family planning programs (Nichter 1996). In other instances, fear of foreign vaccines prompts people to reject inoculations. Overall, acceptance rates of vaccination have been lower than Western public health planners expected. What factors have limited the acceptance of vaccination?

Public health planners have not paid enough attention to broad reasons why certain innovations are accepted or rejected. There have been problems in supply (clinics do not always have vaccines on hand). Cultural understandings of illness and the role of inoculations have not been considered. Surveys show that many mothers have a partial or inaccurate understanding of what the vaccines protect against. In some cases, people's perceptions and priorities did not match what the vaccines were supposed to address. In others, people did not see the value of multiple vaccinations. In Indonesia, a once-vaccinated and healthy child was not considered to need another inoculation.

Key features in the overall communication strategy are promoting trust in the public health program and providing locally sensible understandings of what the vaccinations do and do not do. Another important role that applied medical anthropologists play in promoting more effective public health communication is to work with public health specialists in enhancing their understanding of and attention to local cultural practices and beliefs.

FOOD FOR THOUGHT

- Are all vaccines of unquestionable benefit to the recipients? Search the Internet for information on new vaccines—for example, the vaccine against hookworm—in terms of their pros and possible cons.

- adopting local styles of communication.
- identifying subgroups within the population that may be responsive to different types of messages and incentives.
- monitoring the response of communities to health messages over time and facilitating corrections in communication when needed.
- exposing possible victim-blaming in health messages.

These principles helped health care officials understand local responses to public vaccination programs in several countries of Asia and Africa (see the Lessons Applied box).

Since 1978, the World Health Organization has endorsed the incorporation of traditional medicine, especially healers, into national health systems (Velimirovic 1990). This policy emerged in response to increasing pride, among nations, in their own medical traditions and in response to shortages of trained biomedical personnel. Debates continue about the efficacy of many traditional medical practices as compared to biomedicine. For instance, opponents of the promotion of traditional medicine claim that it has no effect on such infectious diseases as cholera, malaria, tuberculosis, schistosomiasis, leprosy, and others. They insist that it makes no sense to allow for or encourage ritual practices against infectious diseases. Supporters of traditional medicine as one aspect of a planned, pluralistic medical system point out that biomedicine neglects a person's psychosocial context, whereas traditional medicine is contextualized. Also, indigenous curers are more likely to know clients and their families, and this relationship facilitates therapy.

One area where progress has been made in maintaining positive aspects of traditional health care is midwifery. Many governments of developing countries have designed training programs that equip *traditional birth attendants* (TBAs) with basic

www.ablongman.com/millerwood1e   **CHAPTER 13** ■ Illness and Healing   **407** training in germ theory and provide them with, among other things, kits that include a clean razor blade for cutting the umbilical cord. Thus many thousands of TBAs working at the grassroots level around the world are not squeezed out of their work but continue to perform their important role with enhanced skills and tools.

THE BIG QUESTIONS REVISITED

▪ WHAT is ethnomedicine?

Ethnomedicine is the study of health systems of specific cultures. Health systems include categories and perceptions of illness and approaches to prevention and healing. Research in ethnomedicine shows how perceptions of the body differ cross-culturally and reveals both differences and similarities across health systems in perceptions of illness and symptoms. Culture-bound syndromes are illnesses that are locally specific in the way symptoms are clustered and causes are ascribed. Some formerly culture-bound syndromes are now undergoing globalization. Ethnomedical studies of healing, healing substances, and healers reveal a wide range of approaches. Community healing systems are more characteristic of small-scale, nonindustrial societies. They emphasize group interaction and treating the individual within the social context. In industrial societies, biomedicine emphasizes the body as a discrete unit, and treatment addresses the individual body or mind.

▪ WHAT are three major theoretical approaches in medical anthropology?

Ecological/epidemiological medical anthropology emphasizes the systemic links between environment and health. Anthropologists working in this framework have shown how certain categories of people are at risk of contracting particular diseases within various environmental contexts in historical times and the present. The interpretivist approach focuses on studying illness and healing as a set of symbols and meanings. Research in this framework shows how, cross-culturally, definitions of health problems and healing systems for these problems are embedded in meanings. Critical medical anthropologists focus on health problems and healing within their economic and political contexts and ask what power relations are involved and who benefits from particular forms of healing. Critical medical anthropologists analyze the role of inequality and poverty in health problems and have critiqued Western biomedicine as a system of social control.

▪ HOW are illness and healing changing as globalization occurs?

Health systems everywhere are facing accelerated change in the face of globalization, which includes the spread of Western capitalism as well as new diseases and new medical technologies. The "new infectious diseases" are a challenge to health care systems in terms of prevention and treatment. "Diseases of development" are new health problems caused by development projects (such as dams) that change the physical and social environments. In terms of healing systems, the spread of Western biomedicine to non-Western contexts is well under way, and as a consequence, medical pluralism exists in all countries. Clinical or applied medical anthropologists play a role in promoting change in health systems. They may inform medical care providers of more appropriate kinds of intervention and/or inform local peoples about their increasingly complex medical choices.

KEY CONCEPTS

SUGGESTED READINGS

Eric J. Bailey. *Medical Anthropology and African American Health*. New York: Greenwood Publishing Group, 2000. This book explores the relationship between cultural anthropology and African American health care. One chapter discusses how to do applied research in medical anthropology.

Nancy N. Chen. *Breathing Spaces: Qigong, Psychiatry, and Healing in China*. New York: Columbia University Press, 2003. Taking a critical medical anthropology approach, this ethnography explores *qigong,* a form of healing based on meditative breathing exercises. The author considers the impact of capitalist globalization and Western psychiatric globalization on the lives of people in China.

Paul Farmer. *AIDS and Accusation: Haiti and the Geography of Blame*. Berkeley: University of California Press, 1992. This book combines discussion of the global structures related to the spread of HIV/AIDS with in-depth study in one village in Haiti where HIV/AIDS is locally interpreted as one more phase in people's long-term exposure to affliction and suffering.

Paul Farmer. *Infections and Inequalities: The Modern Plagues*. Berkeley: University of California Press, 1999. Farmer blends interpretive medical anthropology with critical medical anthropology in this comparative study of how poverty kills through diseases such as tuberculosis and AIDS. Trained as a Western biomedical physician and as an anthropologist, Farmer takes an activist position.

Stephanie Kane. *AIDS Alibis: Sex, Drugs, and Crime in the Americas*. Philadelphia: Temple University Press, 1998. Kane provides an interpretive study of the combined forces of sex, drugs, and crime in two contexts: Chicago and Belize, Central America. An activist anthropologist, she critiques the war on drugs, the war on crime, and current public health programs in the hope that serious reconsideration of these systems can lead to useful reform.

Richard Katz. *Boiling Energy: Community Healing among the Kalahari Kung*. Cambridge. MA: Harvard University Press, 1982. This account of the healing practices of the Ju/wasi [!Kung] of the Dobe area between Namibia and Botswana focuses on several different healers, their training, and their styles.

Nancy C. Lovell. *Patterns of Injury and Illness in Great Apes: A Skeletal Analysis*. Washington, DC: Smithsonian Institution Press, 1990. The author reviews what is known from field studies and then presents results from her study of pathology in a skeletal sample in the National Museum of Natural History in Washington, DC.

Emily Martin. *The Woman in the Body: A Cultural Analysis of Reproduction*. Boston: Beacon Press, 1987. This book explores how Western medical textbooks represent women's reproductive experiences and how these descriptions compare to a sample of Baltimore women's perceptions and experiences of menstruation, childbirth, and menopause.

Carol Shepherd McClain, ed. *Women as Healers: A Cross-Cultural Perspective*. New Brunswick, NJ: Rutgers University Press, 1989. This collection of eleven studies is preceded by a general overview. Case studies include Ecuador, Sri Lanka, Mexico, Jamaica, the United States, Serbia, Korea, Southern Africa, and Benin.

Valentina Napolitano. *Migration, Mujercitas, and Medicine Men: Living in Urban Mexico*. Berkeley: University of California Press, 2002. This ethnography of Guadalajara, western Mexico focuses on how immigrants from surrounding areas adapt to urban life. The author describes their roles in the Catholic Church, the diverse health systems available, and life-cycle rituals as a focus of meaning.

Sherry Saggers and Dennis Gray. *Dealing with Alcohol: Indigenous Usage in Australia, New Zealand, and Canada*. New York: Cambridge University Press, 1998. This comparative study looks at structural issues such as European colonialism, the interests of liquor companies in creating and sustaining high rates of alcohol consumption among many indigenous groups, and the people's own understandings of their situation.

THE BIG QUESTIONS

- HOW are kinship ties created through descent, sharing, and marriage?
- WHAT is a household and what do cultural anthropologists study about household life?
- HOW are kinship systems and households changing?

CHAPTER **14**

Kinship and Domestic Life

A Minangkabau bride in Sumatra, Indonesia, wears an elaborate gold headdress. Women play a central role among the Minangkabau, whose population is around four million. (Source: © CORBIS)

Learning another culture's kinship system is as challenging as learning another language. This was true for Robin Fox during his research among the Tory Islanders of Ireland (1995 [1978]). Some of the Irish kinship terms and categories he encountered were similar to American English usage, but others were not. For example, the word *muintir* can mean "people" in its widest sense, as in English. It can also refer to people of a particular social category, as in "my people," or close relatives. Another similarity is with *gaolta*, the word for "relatives" or "those of my blood." As an adjective, gaolta refers to kindness, just as the English word *kin*, which is related to "kindness." Also, Tory Islanders have a phrase meaning "children and grandchildren," like the English term "descendants."

In contrast to American English, the word for "friend" on Tory Island is the same as the word for "kin." This usage reflects the cultural circumstances on Tory Island, with its small population, all living close together. Everyone is related by kinship. Logically, then, friends are also kin.

The closest and most intense human relationships often involve people who consider themselves linked to each other through kinship, or a sense of being related to another person or persons. All cultures have ideas about what kinship is and have rules for appropriate behavior among kin. These rules can be informal or formally defined by law. From infancy, people begin learning about their particular culture's **kinship system**—that is, the combination of ideas about who are kin and what kinds of behavior kinship relationships involve. Like one's first language, one's kinship system becomes so ingrained that it tends to be taken for granted as something "natural" rather than cultural.

This chapter first considers cross-cultural variations in kinship systems. It then examines a key unit of domestic life: the household. The last section of the chapter provides examples of change in kinship patterns and household organization.

THE STUDY OF KINSHIP

Kinship tends to be linked with economic systems. Depending on the type of economy, kinship shapes children's personality development, influences a person's marriage options, and affects the status and care of the aged. In small-scale, nonindustrial cultures, kinship is the primary, and often the only, principle that organizes people into coherent and meaningful groups. The kinship group ensures the continuity of the group by arranging marriages, maintains social order by setting moral rules and punishing offenders, and provides for the basic needs of members by regulating production, consumption, and exchange. In large-scale industrial societies, kinship ties exist, but many other forms of social affiliation draw people together into groups that have nothing to do with kinship.

Early anthropologists documented the importance of kinship in the societies they researched. Anthropologists of the nineteenth century wrote that kinship was the most important organizing principle in small-scale cultures. They also discovered that definitions of who counts as kin often differed from their own perceptions of kinship. For example, people in most Western cultures emphasize "blood" relations as relations between people linked by birth from a biological mother and father (Sault 1994). In other cultures, males in the family are thought to share "blood," whereas females are of another "blood." This latter view contrasts with the Euro-American definition that all biological children of the same parents share the same "blood."

Another variation in defining who is kin occurs among a group of Inuit living in northern Alaska among whom the word for kin literally means "addition" (Bodenhorn 2000). In their kinship system, the kin of anyone considered kin are also one's kin. These people define kin as people who act like kin. If a person ceases to act like a kinsperson, he or she is no longer considered to be kin. People in this culture may comment that someone used to be their cousin.

This section first reviews how cultural anthropologists represent and analyze information on kinship. It then considers three bases on which people cross-culturally define kinship relationships: descent, sharing, and marriage.

Kinship Analysis

Early anthropological work on kinship tended to focus on finding out who is related to whom and in what way. Typically, the anthropologist would interview one or two people, asking questions such as: What do you call your brother's daughter? Can you (as a man) marry your father's brother's daughter? What is the term you use to refer to your mother's sister?

In another approach, the anthropologist would ask an individual to name all of his or her relatives, explain how they are related to the interviewee, and provide the terms by which they refer to him or her. From this information, the anthropologist would construct a **kinship diagram,** a schematic way of presenting data on the kinship relationships of an individual, called "ego" (see Figure 14.1 for the symbols used in kinship diagrams). This diagram depicts all of ego's relatives, as remembered by ego and reported to the anthropologist, without being supplemented by having other people fill in where ego's memory failed. In cultures where kinship plays a major role in social relations, people are able to provide information on more relatives than in cultures where kinship ties are less important. When one of the authors (Barbara) took a research methods course as an undergraduate, she interviewed her Hindi language teaching assistant about his kin for a class assignment. From an upper-class family in India, he remembered over sixty relatives in his father's and mother's families, thus providing a much more extensive kinship diagram than she would have been able to provide for her middle-class Euro-American family.

In contrast to a kinship diagram, a *genealogy* begins with the earliest ancestors that can be traced and then works down to the present. The Tory Islanders were not comfortable beginning with ego when Robin Fox was attempting to gather data for kinship diagrams. They preferred to proceed genealogically, so he followed their preference. Tracing a family's complete genealogy may involve archival research in the attempt to construct as full a record as possible. In Europe and the United States, Christians often record their "family tree" in the front of the family Bible.

Decades of anthropological research have produced a great deal of information on kinship terms that people in various cultures use to refer to their kin. For example, in Euro-American kinship, children of one's father's sister and brother and children

CHARACTERS		RELATIONSHIPS		KIN ABBREVIATIONS	
◯	female	=	is married to	**Mo**	mother
△	male	≈	is cohabiting with	**Fa**	father
⊘	deceased female	≁	is divorced from	**Br**	brother
△̸	deceased male	≉	is separated from	**Z**	sister
●	female "ego" of the diagram	⊙	adopted-in female	**H**	husband
▲	male "ego" of the diagram	◬	adopted-in male	**W**	wife
		|	is descended from	**Da**	daughter
		⊓	is the sibling of	**S**	son
				Co	cousin

FIGURE 14.1
Symbols used in kinship diagrams.

(*Source:* Reprinted by permission of Allyn & Bacon.)

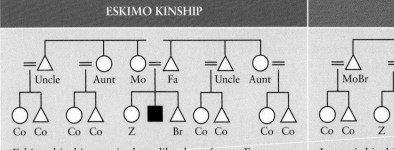

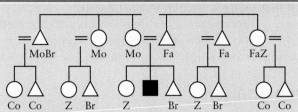

ESKIMO KINSHIP	IROQUOIS KINSHIP
Eskimo kinship terminology, like that of most Euro-Americans, has unique terms for kin within the nuclear family that are not used for any other relatives: mother, father, sister, brother. This fact is related to the importance of the nuclear family. Another feature is that the same terms are used for relatives on both the mother's side and the father's side, a feature that is related to bilineal descent.	Iroquois kinship terminology operates in unilineal systems. One result is that there are different terms for relatives on the mother's and father's sides and distinctions between cross and parallel cousins. Another feature is the "merging" of one's mother with one's mother's sister (both are referred to as "mother") and of one's father with one's father's brother (both are referred to as "father").

FIGURE 14.2

Two kinship naming systems.

(*Source:* Reprinted by permission of Allyn & Bacon.)

of one's mother's sister and brother are referred to as cousins. In many other cultures, different terms are used for cousins on the mother's and father's sides of the family. Likewise, in Euro-American kinship, the terms *grandmother* and *grandfather* refer to the parents of either one's father or one's mother. In many other cultures, however, different terms are used. For example, in North India, one's father's father is *baba* and one's mother's father is *nana*. Some kinship systems emphasize solidarity among siblings of the same gender, so one's mother and one's mother's sisters are all termed *mother*. This system is found among the Navajo, for example.

Anthropologists have classified such cross-cultural variations in kinship terminology into six basic types. Each type is named after the culture that was first discovered to have that type of system, so, for example, there is an "Iroquois" type and an "Eskimo" type (see Figure 14.2). Cultures with similar kinship terminology are placed into one of the six categories. Thus the Yanomami of the Amazon are identified as having an Iroquois naming system. These six types of kinship systems represent an earlier phase of research on kinship and are an interesting part of the history of kinship studies. However, they do not tell us much about actual kinship dynamics, a subject to which we now turn.

Toward Kinship in Action

The formalism of early kinship studies prompted many students of anthropology—and even some of their professors—to think that kinship is a boring subject. Recently, a renewed and enlivened interest in kinship has linked it to other topics, such as power relations, decision making about reproduction, women's changing work roles, and ethnic identity (Carsten 2000). Underlying all these topics are three basic ways in which kinship relations are formed: descent, sharing, and marriage.

Descent

Descent is the tracing of kinship relationships through birth and relations with a parent or parents. Descent creates a line of people from whom a person is descended, stretching through history. Cultures, however, have different ways of reckoning descent. Some have a **unilineal descent** system, which recognizes descent through only one parent, either the father or the mother. Others cultures have a **bilineal descent** system, in which a child is recognized as being related by descent to both parents. The distribution of unilineal and bilineal systems is generally related to the major modes of production (see Figure 14.3).

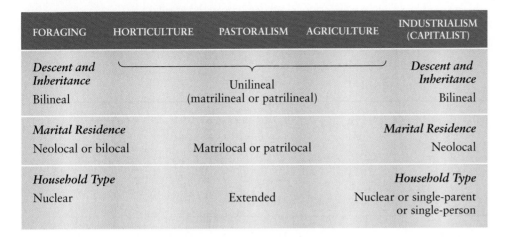

FORAGING	HORTICULTURE	PASTORALISM	AGRICULTURE	INDUSTRIALISM (CAPITALIST)
Descent and Inheritance Bilineal	Unilineal (matrilineal or patrilineal)			**Descent and Inheritance** Bilineal
Marital Residence Neolocal or bilocal	Matrilocal or patrilocal			**Marital Residence** Neolocal
Household Type Nuclear	Extended			**Household Type** Nuclear or single-parent or single-person

FIGURE 14.3
Modes of production, kinship, and household structure.

(*Source:* Reprinted by permission of Allyn & Bacon.)

Unilineal Descent. Unilineal descent systems are the most common form of descent, being the basis of kinship in about 60 percent of the world's cultures. Unilineal kinship systems are found in societies with a fixed resource base, such as farmland or herds, over which people have a sense of ownership. Inheritance rules that regulate the transmission of property through only one line help maintain cohesiveness of the resource base. Unilineal systems thus are most closely associated with pastoralism, horticulture, and agricultural modes of production.

Two patterns of unilineal descent are **patrilineal descent,** in which kinship is traced through the male line, and **matrilineal descent,** in which kinship is traced through the female line. In a patrilineal descent system, only male children are considered members of the kinship lineage. Female children "marry out" and become members of the husband's lineage. The same applies in matrilineal descent systems, in which only daughters are considered to carry on the family line.

Jack Goody (1976), a leading kinship theorist of the later twentieth century, advanced thinking in this area. He developed a comparative approach that reveals differences between the descent systems of rural sub-Saharan Africa and Eurasia. In sub-Saharan African groups that rely on horticultural production, women are prominent as producers, reproducers, marketers, and decision makers. Their matrilineal descent system recognizes and perpetuates the importance of women. In rural Eurasia, in contrast, plow agriculture has long been the mode of production. As discussed in Chapter 11, men are primarily involved with plow agricultural systems, and women play complementary roles in animal care, food processing, weeding, and harvesting. The patrilineal descent system associated with this mode of production does not give women's tasks high value. Members of the gender that controls the resources (both productive and reproductive) tend to have higher status. Thus, in general, women have higher status in matrilineal societies, and men have higher status in patrilineal societies. The question of *why* a particular culture is matrilineal or patrilineal has not been resolved.

Patrilineal descent is found among about 44 percent of all cultures. It is prevalent throughout much of India, East Asia, the Middle East, Papua New Guinea, and northern Africa. Margery Wolf's ethnography *The House of Lim* (1968) is a classic study of a patrilineal system. Wolf lived for two years with the Lims, a Taiwanese farming household (see Figure 14.4 on p. 416). She first describes the village setting and then the Lims' house, emphasizing the importance of the ancestral hall with its family altar, where the household head meets guests. Next comes a chapter on Lim Han-ci, the father and household head, followed by a chapter on Lim Hue-lieng, the eldest son. Last, Wolf introduces the females of the family: wives, sisters, and an adopted daughter. The ordering of the chapters reflects the importance of the "patriarch" (the senior, most powerful male) and his eldest son, who will, if all goes according to plan,

If you were going to write an ethnography of your family like Wolf's study of the Lims, how would you organize the chapter topics and sequence?

THINKING

OUTSIDE THE BOX

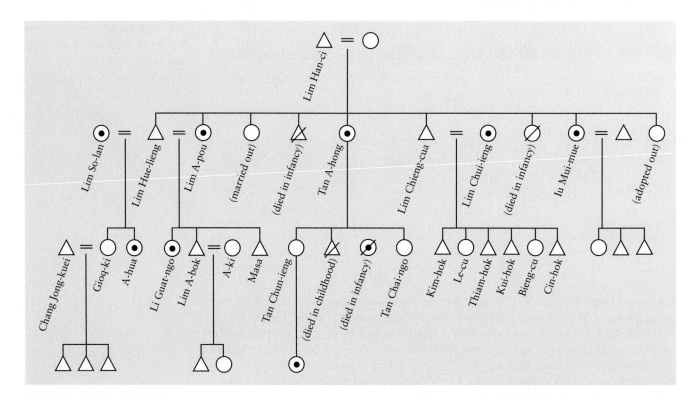

FIGURE 14.4
The Lim family of Taiwan.

(*Source:* Reprinted by permission of Allyn & Bacon.)

assume the leadership position as his father ages and dies. Daughters marry out and join other families. In-marrying females (wives, daughters-in-law) are always considered outsiders and are never fully merged into the patrilineage. The Lims' kinship system exemplifies strong patrilineality in that it allocates position, power, and property to males. In such systems, girls are raised "for other families" and are thus not fully members of their natal (birth) family; however, they never become fully merged into their marriage family either and hence are always considered somehow "outsiders." Married couples typically share a **patrilocal residence,** with or near the husband's natal family. The most strongly patrilineal systems are found in East Asia, South Asia, and the Middle East.

Matrilineal descent exists in about 15 percent of all cultures. It traces kinship through the female line exclusively, and children belong to their mother's group. It is found among many Native North American groups, across a large band of central Africa, among many groups of Southeast Asia and the Pacific and in Australia, in parts of eastern and southern India, in a small pocket of northern Bangladesh, and in localized parts of the Mediterranean coast of Spain and Portugal. Matrilineal societies vary greatly, from foragers such as the Tiwi of northern Australia to agricultural groups such as the Nayar of southern India (Lepowsky 1993:296). Most, however, are found in horticultural systems where women have primary roles in the production and distribution of food and other goods. Married couples tend to share a **matrilocal residence,** with or near the wife's natal family. Often, but not always, matrilineal kinship is associated with recognized public leadership positions for women, as among the Iroquois and Hopi.

The Minangkabau (pronounced mee-NAN-ka-bow, the last syllable rhyming with *now*) of Indonesia are the largest matrilineal group in the world (Sanday 2002). They are primarily agriculturalists, producing substantial amounts of surplus rice. Many participate in migratory labor, working for wages in Indonesian cities for a time and then returning home. In their matrilineal kinship system, women hold power through their control of land and its products, their control of agricultural employment on their land, and their dominant position in business (especially business related to rice growing and selling). Inheritance passes from mothers to daughters, making the matrilineal line the enduring controller of property. Each submatrilineage, constituting two or more generations, lives together in a lineage house or several closely located houses. The senior woman has the power in the family, and her decisions are sought in all economic and ceremonial matters. The senior male of the sublineage has the role of representing its interests to other groups, but he is only a representative, not a powerful person in his own right.

Some members of a Bedu household in Yemen. Among desert pastoralist groups throughout the Middle East, kinship tends to be strictly patrilineal. ■ Generate some hypotheses about what property Bedu women might possess. (Source: © Norbert Schiller/The Image Works)

Double Descent. A minority of cultures have double descent systems (also called *double unilineal descent*) that combine patrilineal and matrilineal descent. In these systems, offspring are believed to inherit different personal attributes and property from both their father's line and their mother's line. For example, the Bangangté of Cameroon in West Africa have a double descent system (Feldman-Savelsberg 1995). Through the maternal line, one inherits movable property (such as household goods and cattle), personality traits, and a type of witchcraft substance that resides in the intestines. Patrilineal ties determine physical resemblance and rights to land and village residence.

Bilineal Descent. Bilineal descent traces kinship from both parents equally to the child. Family groups tend to be nuclear, with strong bonds linking the father, the mother, and their children. Marital residence is predominantly **neolocal,** or involving residence for the married couple somewhere away from the residence of both the bride's and the groom's parents. Inheritance of property from the parental generation is allocated equally among all offspring regardless of their gender. Bilineal descent is found in less than one-third of the world's cultures (Murdock 1965 [1949]:57). The highest frequency of bilineal descent occurs in foraging and industrial modes of production, at the opposite ends of the production continuum (see Figure 14.3 on p. 415). For example, the Ju/wasi have bilineal descent, and bilineal descent is a

Young boys playing in Hababa, Yemen. In this patrilineal culture, public space is segregated by gender. ■ If you were a cultural anthropologist working in Yemen, how would you proceed to learn about how young Yemeni girls spend their time? (Source: © Chris Lisle/CORBIS)

How Bilineal Is American Kinship?

"AMERICAN KINSHIP" is a general model based on the bilineal system of Euro-Americans of the 1960s (Schneider 1968). According to this model, children are considered to be descended from both mother and father, and general inheritance rules suggest that property is divided equally between sons and daughters. Given the rich cultural diversity of the United States and Canada, most would now consider the label "American kinship" and its characterization as bilineal to be overgeneralized.

In reality, aspects of both patrilineality and matrilineality exist. Indicators of patrilineality include the practice of a wife dropping her surname at marriage and taking her husband's surname and the practice of using the husband's surname for offspring. Although inheritance is supposedly equal between sons and daughters, often it is not. In many business families, the business is passed from father to sons, while daughters are given a different form of inheritance such as a trust fund. On the other hand, *matrifocality* (a domestic system in which the mother is the central figure) arises from another source: high rates of divorce and the resulting trend of more young children living with the mother than with the father. A matrifocal emphasis creates mother-centered residence and child-raising patterns. It may also affect inheritance patterns.

In order to explore descent patterns in the United States, each student in the class should draw his or her own kinship diagram. Students should note their microculture or ethnicity at the top of the chart, choosing the label that they prefer. Then each student should draw a circle around the relatives who are "closest" to ego, including parents, grandparents, aunts, uncles, cousins—whoever fits in this category as defined by ego. As a group, students in the class should then consider the following questions about the kinship diagrams.

CRITICAL THINKING QUESTIONS

- How many students drew equal circles around relatives on both parents' sides?
- How many emphasized the mother's side? How many emphasized the father's side?
- Do microcultural or ethnic patterns emerge in terms of the circled kin?
- From this exercise, what can be said about "American kinship"?

common, but not universal, pattern in the United States (see the Critical Thinking box). A rare variety of bilineal descent is called *ambilineal descent*. This system recognizes that a person is descended from both parents but allows individuals to decide which descent group to be more closely affiliated with. Ambilineal descent systems are associated with *bilocal* residence, in which the married couple lives with or near either the bride's or the groom's family, with no preference involved. This system is found in parts of the South Pacific, for example, in Tahiti (Lockwood 1993).

Theorists who favor cultural materialism (review Chapter 2) attribute the numeric minority of bilineal systems to the fact that the mode of production influences the type of kinship system. They point out that bilineal kinship systems are associated mainly with two modes of production: foraging and industrialism. Both modes of production rely on a flexible gender division of labor in which males and females contribute, relatively equally, to production and exchange. Logically, then, a bilineal kinship system recognizes the strengths of both the mother's and the father's side. Bilineal kinship is adaptive for foraging and industrial populations because it fits with small family units that are spatially mobile. It offers the greatest residential flexibility, keeping open opportunities related to making a living. As the world becomes increasingly urbanized and industrialized, and if the gender division of labor and resource entitlements becomes more nearly equal, bilineal kinship is likely to increase.

Sharing

Many cultures give priority to kinship that is based on acts of sharing and support rather than on biologically defined birth and descent. These relationships may be informal or formally certified, as in legalized adoption. Ritually formalized kinship falls in this category, including *godparenthood* (kinship based on ritual ties) and blood brotherhood (kinship based on sharing of "blood" or some other substance).

Food Sharing. Sharing-based kinship is common in much of Southeast Asia, Papua New Guinea, and Australia (Carsten 1995). On an island of Malaysia, the process of developing sharing-based relatedness starts in the womb and continues throughout a person's life. The first food sharing is when the fetus is fed by the mother's blood. After birth, the infant is fed from its mother's breast. Breast milk is believed to derive from the mother's blood, and thus "blood becomes milk." This tie is crucial. After the baby is weaned, its most important food is cooked rice. Sharing cooked rice, like breast milk, becomes another way in which kinship ties are created and maintained, especially between mothers and children. Men are often away—on fishing trips, in coffee shops, or at the mosque—so they are less likely to form these rice-sharing bonds.

Adoption and Fostering. Transferring children from their birth parent to the care of others through adoption and fostering is found in all cultures. Adoption offers a cultural solution to the natural unevenness in human reproduction. Common motivations for adopting a child include infertility and the desire to obtain a particular kind of child (often a son). Motivations for the birth parent to transfer the child to someone else's care include having a premarital pregnancy in cultures that do not condone children being born outside marriage, having "too many" children as defined in that culture, and having "too many" of a particular gender of child. For example, among the Maasai, if a woman has several children, she might give one to a friend, neighbor, or aged person who has no children or no one to care for him or her.

Fostering a child is sometimes similar to a formal adoption in terms of permanence and a developed sense of a close relationship. Or it may involve a temporary placement of a child with someone else for a specific purpose, with little development of a sense of kinship. Child fostering is common throughout sub-Saharan Africa. Parents foster out children to enhance their chances of getting formal education or to help them learn a skill through apprenticeship. Most fostered children go from rural to urban areas and from poorer to better-off households.

What are the lives of these fostered children like? Insights about the lives of fostered children come from fieldwork conducted in a neighborhood in the city of Accra, Ghana (Sanjek 1990). Child fostering in the neighborhood is common: about one-fourth of the children were foster children. Twice as many of the fostered children were girls as boys. School attendance rates, however, were biased toward boys. All of the boys were attending school, but only four of the thirty-one girls were. An important factor affecting the treatment of the child involves whether the fostered child is related to his or her sponsor. As a whole, 80 percent of the children were kin of their sponsors, but among girls, only 50 percent were kin. People who sponsored non-kin fostered girls often used the girls as maids, and they made a cash payment to the girl's parents. These child maids cooked and did housecleaning. Some assisted their sponsors in market work by carrying goods or watching the trading area when the market woman was elsewhere. Fostered boys did not perform such tasks because they were attending school.

Legalized Adoption in the United States. Currently, about one of every ten couples in the United States is infertile, and many of these couples would like to have children.

An orphanage in Shanghai, China. In the 1990s, human rights activists claimed that abuse—especially of children with physical handicaps—was widespread in Chinese orphanages. After this allegation was made, foreign media were invited to visit the Shanghai Children's Welfare Institute. ■ Have you ever visited an orphanage? If so, what were your impressions? If not, find out about, and if possible, volunteer at an orphanage near you. (Source: © Reuters/Will Burgess)

A Khasi couple in their wedding clothes. The Khasi, who live in the hilly regions of northeastern India and northern Bangladesh, trace descent through women, and children take the last name of their mothers. ■ Learn about other matrilineal cultures on the Internet. (Source: © Reuters/Utpal Baruha)

Some use fertility drugs, *in vitro* fertilization, or surrogate child bearing. Many people, including those who have biologically recognized children, choose to adopt. Since the mid-1800s, adoption has been a legalized form of child transfer in the United States. It is "a procedure which establishes the relationship of parent and child between persons not so related by nature" (Leavy and Weinberg 1979, quoted in Modell 1994:2).

Judith Modell, cultural anthropologist and adoptive parent, studied people's experiences as adoptees, birth parents, and adoptive parents. According to Modell, the biological relationship of kinship is so pervasive in the United States that the legal process of adoption attempts to construct the adoptive relationship to be as much like a biological one as possible. The adopted child is given a new birth certificate, and the birth parent ceases to have any relationship to the child. This pattern is called "closed adoption." A recent trend is toward "open adoption," in which adoptees and birth parents have access to information about each other's identity and have freedom to interact with one another. Of the twenty-eight adoptees Modell talked with, most, but not all, were interested in searching for their birthparents. For many adoptees, a search for birth parents involves an attempt to discover "who I really am." For others, such a search is backward-looking and not a path toward formulating one's identity. Thus, in the United States, adoption legalizes sharing-based kinship but does not completely establish a sense of descent-based kinship for everyone involved.

Ritually Established Sharing Bonds. Ritually defined sponsorship of children who are descended from other people is common throughout the Christian—and especially the Catholic—world from Europe to South America and the Philippines. Relationships between godparents and godchildren often involve strong emotional ties and financial flows from the former to the latter. In Arembepe, a village in Bahia state in northeastern Brazil, "Children asked their godparents for a blessing the first time they saw them each day. Godparents occasionally gave cookies, candy, and money, and larger presents on special occasions" (Kottak 1992:61).

In villages in the Oaxaca Valley, southern Mexico, godparenthood is both a sign of the sponsor's status and the means to increased status for the sponsor (Sault 1985). A request to be a sponsor is public acknowledgment of one's ability to care for the child and reflects well on one's entire family. It also gives the godparent influence over the godchild. Because the godparent can call on the godchild for labor, being a godparent of many children increases one's power by bestowing the ability to amass a labor force when needed. Most sponsors are male–female couples, but a notable number of sponsors are women alone. This pattern reflects the important role and high status of women in the Maya culture of the Oaxaca region.

Marriage

The third major basis for forming kinship relationships is through marriage or other forms of "marriage-like" relationships, such as long-term cohabitation. This section discusses mainly formal marriage.

Toward a Definition. Anthropologists recognize that marriage exists in all cultures, although it takes different forms and serves different functions. What constitutes a cross-culturally valid definition of marriage, however, is open to debate. A standard definition from 1951 is now discredited: "Marriage is a union between a man and a woman such that children born to the woman are the recognized legitimate offspring of both parents" (Barnard and Good 1984:89). This definition says that the partners must be of different genders, and it implies that a child born outside a marriage is not recognized as legitimate. Exceptions exist to both these features cross-culturally. Same-gender marriages are legal in several countries, and in many cultures no distinction is made between legitimate and illegitimate children on the basis of whether or not they were born within a marriage. Many women in the Caribbean region, for example, do not marry until later in life. Before that, a woman has sequential male partners with whom she bears children. None of her children is considered more or less "legitimate" than any other.

The wedding of two gay men in the United States in 1996. Unions between people of the same sex are now legally recognized in some parts of the United States, Canada, and Europe. ■ What have you read recently about same-sex marriage? (Source: © Jim West)

Other definitions of marriage focus on rights over the spouse's sexuality. But not all forms of marriage involve sexual relations; for example, the practice of woman–woman marriage exists among the Nuer of the Sudan and some other African groups (Evans-Pritchard 1951:108–109). In this type of marriage, a woman with economic means gives gifts to obtain a "wife," goes through the marriage rituals with her, and brings her into the residential compound just as a man would who married a woman. This wife contributes her productive labor to the household. The two women do not have a sexual relationship. Instead, the in-married woman will have sexual relations with a man. Her children will belong to the compound into which she married, however. This arrangement supplies the adult woman's labor and her children's labor to the household compound.

The wide range of cross-cultural practices that are called marriage make it impossible to find a definition that will fit all cases. We suggest the following as a working definition of **marriage**: it is a more or less stable union, usually between two people who are likely to be, but are not necessarily, coresident, sexually involved with each other, and procreative with each other.

All cultures have preferences about whom one should and should not marry or with whom one should and should not have sexual intercourse. Sometimes these preferences are informal and implicit, and other times they are formal and explicit.

Selecting a Spouse: Rules of Exclusion. An **incest taboo** is a rule prohibiting marriage or sexual intercourse between certain kinship relations. All cultures have some sort of incest taboo, though there are variations in which kin types are excluded from marriage. The most basic and universal form of incest taboo is against marriage or sexual intercourse between a parent and child. In most cultures, brother–sister marriage has also been forbidden. The best known example of brother–sister marriage being allowed comes from Egypt at the time of the Roman Empire (Barnard and Good 1984:92). Between 15 and 20 percent of all marriages were between full brothers and sisters, so the practice was not limited to a few royal families. The incest taboo of many cultures excludes a large number of kin. Among the pastoralist Nuer of Sudan, the incest taboo covers the extended lineage, which may include hundreds of people.

The question of cousins is dealt with in highly contrasting ways cross-culturally. Notably, incest taboos do not universally rule out marriage or sexual intercourse with cousins. In fact, some kinship systems promote cousin marriage, as discussed next.

Selecting a Spouse: Preference Rules. In addition to incest taboos, many other rules of exclusion exist, such as prohibiting marriage to people of certain religions, races, or ethnic groups. Such exclusionary rules are often stated in the inverse—that is, as rules of preference for marriage *within* a particular religion, race, or ethnic group. For example, rules of **endogamy**, or marriage within a particular group, stipulate that the spouse must be chosen from within a defined pool of people.

Do some research on http://www.match.com to see what kinds of cultural preferences people include in their profiles.

THINKING

OUTSIDE THE BOX

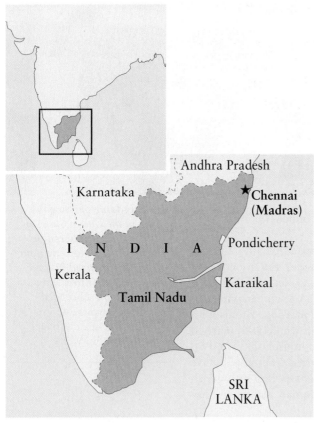

(*Source:* Reprinted by permission of Allyn & Bacon.)

Sexual dimorphism in body size and height is not marked throughout Southeast Asia, as is the case with this couple from Bali, Indonesia. ■ What are your preferences about the height of an ideal spouse or partner for you? (Source: © Rick Smolan/Stock Boston, LLC)

In kin endogamy, certain relatives are preferred, often cousins. Two major forms of cousin marriage exist. One is marriage between **parallel cousins,** children of either one's father's brother or one's mother's sister—the term *parallel* indicates that the linking siblings are of the same gender. The second is marriage between **cross cousins,** children of either one's father's sister or one's mother's brother—the term *cross* indicates the different genders of the linking siblings. Parallel-cousin marriage is favored in many Muslim cultures, especially *patrilateral parallel-cousin marriage,* a tendency for marriage to a cousin in the direction of the father's line. In contrast, Hindus of southern India favor cross-cousin marriages, especially *matrilateral cross-cousin marriage* (through the mother's line). Readers unfamiliar with cousin marriage systems may find them objectionable on the basis of genetic disabilities that might arise from close "inbreeding." A study of thousands of such marriages in the state of Tamil Nadu, South India, however, revealed only a very small difference in rates of inherited disorders compared to cultures in which cousin marriage is not practiced (Sundar Rao 1983). Marriage networks in South India offer many options for "cousins," in contrast to a closed pool such as one village. In contrast, cousin marriage that take places in a small, closed network is likely to lead to higher rates of births with genetic disorders.

Endogamy may also be based on location. Village endogamy is a common basis of marital partner selection in the eastern Mediterranean region, among both Christians and Muslims. It is also the preferred pattern among Muslims in India and among Hindus of southern India. Hindus of rural northern India forbid village endogamy and consider it a form of incest. Instead, they practice village **exogamy** (or "marriage out"). For them, a preferred spouse should live in a far-off village or town. Therefore, marriage distance is greater in the north than in the south, and brides are less likely to be able to maintain regular contact with their birth family. Songs and folktales of north Indian women convey sadness about being separated from their birth families, a theme that would make little sense in the context of village endogamy.

Status considerations often shape spouse selection. The rule of **hypergyny** requires the groom to be of higher status than the bride; in other words, the bride "marries up." Hypergyny is a strong rule in northern India, especially among upper-status groups. It is also implicitly followed among many people in the United States, where females "at the top" have the hardest time finding an appropriate partner because there are so few options "above them." Women medical students are a prime population experiencing an increased marriage squeeze because of status hypergyny. The opposite is **hypogyny,** in which the female "marries down." Status hypogyny is rare cross-culturally, as is age hypogyny, in which the groom is younger than the bride. Age hypogyny, though rare as a preferred pattern, is increasing in the United States because of the marriage squeeze on women who would otherwise prefer a husband equal in age or somewhat older. **Isogamy,** marriage between equals, is found in cultures where male and female roles and status are more equal.

The importance of romantic love as a requirement for marriage is a matter of debate between biological determinists and cultural constructionists. Biological determinists argue that feelings of romantic love are universal among all humans because they play an adaptive role in uniting males and females in care of offspring. Cultural constructionists, in contrast, argue that romantic love is far from universal—that it is an unusual, even "aberrant," factor influencing spouse selection (Little 1966, quoted in Barnard and Good 1984:94). In support of a cultural constructionist position, anthropologists point to variations in male and female economic roles to explain cross-cultural differences in an emphasis on romantic love. Romantic love is more likely to be an important factor in relationships in cultures where men contribute more to subsistence and where women are therefore economically dependent on men. Whatever the cause of romantic love, it is a common basis for marriage in many cultures (Levine et al. 1995).

Within the United States, microcultural variations exist in the degree to which women value romantic love as a basis for marriage. Dorothy Holland and Margaret Eisenhart (1990) conducted a study of young American women entering college in 1979–1981 and again in 1987 after they had graduated and begun their adult lives. The research was conducted in two southern colleges in the United States, one attended predominantly by White Euro-Americans and the other by African Americans. They found that White women were much more committed to notions of romantic love than were African American women. This pattern paral-

The Taj Mahal, located in Agra, north India, is a seventeenth-century monument to love. It was built by the Mughal emperor Shah Jahan as a tomb for his wife, Mumtaz Mahal, who died in childbirth in 1631. ■ Name some other architectural monuments to love or marriage. (Source: Jack Heaton)

leled differences in career goals and expectations of future earning ability: White women were less likely to have strong career goals and more likely to expect to be economically dependent on their spouse. The African American women expressed independence and stronger career goals. According to this study, the ideology of romantic love "derails" many young White women from competing with men in the job market. It provides a model of the heroic male provider as the ideal, the young woman's role being one of attracting him and providing the domestic context for their married life. African American women, though, are more likely to see themselves as economically autonomous, a pattern perhaps related to long-standing African traditions in which women earn money and manage their own income. Figure 14.5 (p. 424) offers three theories regarding households headed by women.

In contrast to so-called "love marriages," arranged marriages are formed on the basis of what constitutes a "good match" between the bride and groom and with the goal of linking the two families involved. Arranged marriages are common in many Middle Eastern, African, and Asian countries. Some theorists claim that arranged marriages are "traditional" and love marriages are "modern"; thus arranged marriages will disappear with modernity. Japan, however, presents a case of a highly industrialized economy with a highly educated population in which arranged marriages continue to constitute a substantial proportion of all marriages, about 25 to 30 percent (Applbaum 1995). The mechanism for arranging marriages has changed. Earlier, marriage partners were found through personal networks, perhaps with the help of an intermediary who knew both families. Now, in large cities such as Tokyo and Osaka, professional matchmakers are often used for finding marriage partners. The most common considerations in one's search for a spouse are the family's reputation and social standing, the absence of undesirable traits such as divorce or mental illness in the family, and the potential spouse's education, income, and occupation.

Marriage Gifts. Most marriages are accompanied by gift-giving, of goods or services, between the partners, members of their families, or friends (see Figure 14.6 on p. 425). There are two major forms of marital exchanges cross-culturally. The first, **dowry**, involves the transfer of goods and sometimes money from the bride's side to

What is your opinion about the relative merits of love marriages versus arranged marriages, and on what do you base your opinion?

THINKING

OUTSIDE THE BOX

FIGURE 14.5

Households headed by women: Three theories and cultural critique.

Slavery Theory	Poverty Theory	Unbalanced Sex Ratio Theory

Slavery Theory

The high frequency of woman-headed households among African Americans in the Western hemisphere is often said to be the heritage of slavery, which intentionally broke up marital ties. This theory has several problems.

If slavery were the cause of woman-headed households, one would predict that all peoples who experienced slavery would have this household form. But this is not the case. In Jamaica, which is populated mainly by descendants of African slaves, percentages of woman-headed households vary between rural and urban areas (Miller and Stone 1983). Yet both urban and rural people have the same heritage. Likewise, in the United States, no generic "Black household" exists, just as there is no generic "White household."

Homes with two coresiding parents were the norm among Black Americans following the Civil War through the mid-twentieth century. It is true that the slave system denied legal standing to adult pairings because owners did not want their slaves committed to lifetime relationships. Slaves were subject to sale, and wives and husbands, parents and children, were separated. Although such circumstances would seem to have led to a "break-up" of a conjugal [married] household tradition, it is now clear that the slaves themselves never accepted the arrangements imposed by the owners: "Once freed, blacks sought the durable unions they had been denied" (Hacker 1992:69).

In the United States, percentages of woman-headed households have increased in roughly the same proportion among Blacks and Whites. Thus similar factors may underlie the changes for both populations.

The distribution of woman-headed households throughout the world is more widespread than the distribution of slavery. Clearly, other factors must be involved in promoting the formation of this pattern.

Poverty Theory

The woman-headed household is said to be an adaptation to poverty, because in many societies, the poor have a higher frequency of woman-headed households. If so, it is only one of many possible adaptations, because not all low-income populations worldwide are characterized by high rates of woman-headed households. Within the United States, significant ethnic differences exist: low-income Chinese, Japanese, and other Asian peoples generally have low frequencies of single-parent households, and many low-income Mexican American communities have dual-parent families (Pelto, Roman, and Liriano 1982:40). As an explanatory factor, poverty needs to be considered along with male and female income-earning capabilities, other resources available, and other support systems.

In the Caribbean region and throughout Latin America, the association between poverty and woman-headed households is strong. But beneath this seemingly negative association, some positive findings appear. In the Caribbean region, about one-third of all households have been woman-headed over the past few decades (Massiah 1983, Marcoux 2000). These women have "visiting unions," involving a steady sexual relationship but separate residences. Many women who were interviewed in a study conducted in several islands (Massiah 1983) commented that they hope for financial support from their male partner or "baby father." But many others emphasized the value they place on freedom from a husband or permanent partner. One woman said, "Being single fits in with my independent thinking" (41). Another commented on her visiting union: "I like freedom, so I'm keeping it like it is."

Unbalanced Sex Ratio Theory

Woman-headed households are said to occur in contexts of high male emigration or other situations causing a shortage of males. The sheer unavailability of partners limits marriage.

In Spanish Galicia, the local economy, inheritance rules, and household formation are related (Kelley 1991). This coastal region has a high percentage of households headed by unmarried women. In the village of Ezaro, about one-fourth of all baptisms in the latter half of the nineteenth century were of "illegitimate" children. This proportion declined in the twentieth century, but the region still stands out from the rest of Spain. In Ezaro, households headed by unmarried mothers constitute about 10 percent of the total. Little or no stigma is attached to unwed motherhood in Galicia, in contrast to the generally high value that the Mediterranean kinship system places on marriage and male honor through control of the sexuality of female family members. Women household heads often hold honored positions.

What accounts for this system? The answer lies in Galicia's high rates of male emigration. The scarcity of males promotes flexible attitudes toward unwed motherhood. In Ezaro, women are in charge of agricultural work. They inherit land and gain prestige and power from owning and managing agricultural land: "Women's work is considered so critical to the prestige of the household in Ezaro that success at work is the single most important factor in the community's evaluation of a woman's character (and in her own self-evaluation). The good woman in Ezaro is the hardworking woman" (572). Thus a woman's work is more important than her marital status.

Inheritance practices reflect the importance of women's agricultural work. The goal is to ensure continuity of the *casa,* the house, which includes both the physical structure and its members. Parents usually award one of their children with a larger share of the inheritance, making that child the principal heir. Daughters are often chosen, and thus a single woman can become head of an estate. Her children ensure that the estate has continuity.

(*Source:* Reprinted by permission of Allyn & Bacon.)

FIGURE 14.6

Major types of marriage gifts and exchanges.

Dowry	Goods and money given by the bride's family to the married couple	European and Asian cultures; agriculturalists and industrialists
Groomprice	Goods and money given by the bride's family to the married couple and to the parents of the groom	South Asia, especially northern India
Brideprice	Goods and money given by the groom's family to the parents of the bride	Asian, African, and Central and South American cultures; horticulturalists and pastoralists
Brideservice	Labor given by the groom to the parents of the bride	Southeast Asian, Pacific, and Amazonian cultures; horticulturalists

the new conjugal unit for their use. This classic form of dowry includes household goods such as furniture, cooking utensils, and sometimes rights to a house. It is the predominant form of marriage transfer in a broad region of Eurasia, from Western Europe through the northern Mediterranean and into China and India, and tends to be associated with agricultural and some industrial communities (Goody 1976). In northern India, dowry is more appropriately termed *groomprice* because a substantial portion of the goods and money pass to the groom's family, not to the new couple (Billig 1992). In China during the Mao era, marriage gifts of any type were viewed as a sign of women's oppression and were made illegal. Marriage gifts are now more common with the increase in consumerism (Whyte 1993).

Brideprice, the transfer of goods or money from the groom's side to the bride's parents, is common in horticultural and pastoralist cultures. A related transfer is *brideservice,* in which the groom works for his father-in-law for a certain period of time before returning home with the bride. Less common than brideprice, brideservice is still practiced in some horticultural societies, especially in the Amazon region.

Many marriages involve transfers of gifts from both the bride's side and the groom's side, though not always gifts of equal value. For example, a common pattern in the United States is for the groom's side to pay the costs of the rehearsal dinner the night before the wedding, whereas the bride's side pays for everything else, including, mainly, the reception following the wedding ceremony.

Forms of Marriage. Cultural anthropologists distinguish two forms of marriage on the basis of the number of partners involved. **Monogamy** is marriage between two people—a male or female if the pair is heterosexual, two people of the same gender in the case of a homosexual pair. Heterosexual monogamy is the most common form of marriage cross-culturally, and in many countries, is the only legal form of marriage. **Polygamy** is marriage with multiple spouses, a pattern allowed by the majority of the world's cultures, even though the majority of people within such cultures may not practice plural marriage (Murdock 1965:24 [1949]).

Two forms of polygamous marriage exist. The predominant pattern is **polygyny,** marriage of one man with more than one woman. Within cultures that allow polygyny, the majority of unions nevertheless are monogamous. **Polyandry,** or marriage between one woman and more than one man, is rare and is found mainly in the Himalayan region of India, Nepal, and Tibet.

Anthropologists have asked why polygyny exists in some cultures and not in others (White and Burton 1988). Darwinian theory says that polygyny contributes to men's reproductive success by allowing them to maximize the spread of their genes in future generations. But this theory does not explain the cross-cultural variation in the distribution of polygyny. Economic theories have been proposed to account for

THINKING OUTSIDE THE BOX

In your microculture, what are the prevailing ideas about wedding expenses and who should pay for them?

this variation. One economic hypothesis states that polygyny is more likely where women's contribution to the economy is more important. Political and demographic factors have also been examined, especially the role of warfare in reducing the ratio of males to females, and the taking of female captives in warfare. Perhaps the most reasonable interpretation is that several interrelated factors are involved, including type of economy and warfare (White and Burton 1988).

HOUSEHOLDS AND DOMESTIC LIFE

In casual conversation, North Americans might use the words *family* and *household* interchangeably to refer to people who live together. Social scientists, however, have proposed a distinction between the two terms, both of which may refer to a *domestic group,* or people who live together. A **family** includes people who consider themselves related through kinship—descent, sharing, or marriage. In North American English, the term *family* includes both close or immediate relatives and more distant relatives. One may live with some members of one's family and see them every day but see others only once a year on a major holiday, or even less often. People who are considered close family relatives may be scattered in several different residences, including grandparents, aunts, uncles, cousins, and children of divorced parents who may live with different parents.

In contrast, the term **household** refers to a domestic group in which members may or may not be related by kinship and who share living space, including perhaps a kitchen and certain budgetary items such as food and rent. Most households around the world consist of family members who are related through kinship, but an increasing number do not. An example of a non-kin household is a group of friends who live in the same apartment. A single person living alone also constitutes a household.

This section looks at household forms and household organization cross-culturally. We also examine relationships between and among household members.

The woman at the lower right is part of a polyandrous marriage, which is common among Tibetan peoples. She is married to several brothers, two of whom stand behind her. The older man with the sash in the front row is her father-in-law. ■ For people who have grown up in monogamous cultures, the daily dynamics of polyandry are difficult to imagine. Ask yourself why this is so. (Source: © Thomas L. Kelly/ Woodfin Camp & Associates)

The Household: Variations on a Theme

In this section, we consider three major forms of households. Household organization can be categorized into several types according to how many married adults are involved. Single-person households comprise only one member, living alone. A single-parent household comprises an adult with offspring. The **nuclear household** (which many people call the nuclear family) contains one adult couple (married or partners), with or without children. **Extended households** contain more than one adult married couple. These couples may be related through the father–son line (making a patrilineal extended household such as that of the Lims of Taiwan; see Figure 14.4 on p. 416), through the mother–daughter line (a matrilineal extended household), or through sisters or brothers (a collateral extended household). Polygynous (multiple wives) and polyandrous (multiple husbands) households are complex households in which one spouse has multiple partners. They may all live together in one residence, or, as in many African polygynous households, each wife has a separate residential unit within the overall household compound. The precise cross-cultural distribution of these various types is not known.

Nuclear household units are found in all cultures (Murdock 1965:2 [1949]). The nuclear household is the exclusive household type in about one-fourth of the world's cultures. The nuclear form is most characteristic of economies at the two extremes of the continuum: in foraging groups and in industrialized societies, reflecting the need for spatial mobility and flexibility in making a living.

Extended households constitute a substantial proportion of households in horticultural, pastoral, and nonindustrial agricultural economies. Throughout Asia—(China, Japan, India), in much of Africa, and among Native North Americans, some form of complex or extended household is the ideal and frequently the reality. In India, where extended households are the preferred form, the household may contain fifty or more members. Property provides the material base to support many people, and in turn, large land holdings require a large labor force to work the land. In northern India, more households own property than in southern and eastern India, where rates of landlessness are higher. Logically, then, patrilineal extended households are more common in the northern part of the country (Kolenda 1968).

In Japan, the *ie,* or stem household, has a long history and is still important (Skinner 1993). A variant of the extended household, a **stem household** contains two (and no more) married couples related through the males. Thus only one son remains in the household, bringing in his wife, who is expected to perform the important role of caretaker for the husband's parents as they age. The patrilineal stem household is still widely preferred, yet it is increasingly difficult to achieve. The rising aspirations of children often mean that no child is willing to live with and care for the aging parents. In Japan, parents sometimes exert considerable pressure on an adult child to come and live with them (Traphagan 2000). One compromise solution is for an adult child and his or her spouse to live near the parents but not with them.

In China, the stem household system is undergoing change because many people have one daughter and no son as a result of the One Child Policy and reduced fertility. ■ Speculate about what the next generation of this household might contain. (Source: © Keren Su/ Stock Boston, LLC)

Intrahousehold Dynamics

How do household members interact with each other? What are their emotional attachments, rights, and responsibilities? What are the power relationships between and among members of various categories, such as spouses, siblings, and those of different generations? What is the status of different members?

Kinship systems provide the answers to these questions by defining ideal roles and relationships. In everyday life, people may conform more or less to the ideal. Oddly, the important dimension of how people do or do not diverge from ideal roles and relationships has been neglected for a long time by cultural anthropologists and has only recently attracted some attention. A similar gap exists in the study of everyday life and social status within households, leaving what goes on inside the household a closed book that has only recently been opened.

CROSSING
THE FIELDS

What Burials Reveal about Household Members' Status:
The Prehistoric Oneota of Wisconsin

Like the other fields of anthropology, archaeological research has recently turned its attention to the household. One study of "household archaeology" examines the details of burials in Oneota houses in southwestern Wisconsin from the late prehistoric period, around 1400–1500 (O'Gorman 2001). Burials were examined to see whether they showed signs of power or status differences among individuals within particular houses. Their condition, unfortunately, does not allow analysis of health or diet, so it is impossible to know whether various household members received preferential treatment in basic entitlements. Instead, the archaeologists consider two kinds of burial features for indications of differential power or status among different household members.

First, some context for this example. The prehistoric Oneota economic system involved diverse strategies that included gathering wild foods (especially wild rice), fishing, hunting, and horticulture. Corn, beans, and squash were major garden crops. Large-game hunting, mainly of bison, was primarily the responsibility of men. Women hunted small game and were in charge of both wild rice collecting and horticulture, as well as distributing the food products.

The Oneota's diverse economy produced surpluses, and all houses had storage areas. Ethnoarchaeological evidence suggests the possibility that women managed whether and how the surpluses, mainly grains, would be put to public use for warfare or religious ceremonies. Within the households, also, individual women may have exercised power based on their control over distributing the food they gathered and grew, as well as stored resources. As is consistent with a mixed foraging–horticultural economy, Oneota social organization was generally egalitarian with no marked differences in access to resources.

Two features of the Oneota burials were examined in an effort to learn whether burials show any evidence of status differentials among household members:

- The spatial features of the burial, including location, orientation, and position of the body.
- The number and quality of grave goods.

In terms of location, most burials within the house were of adults. Many of these were "superpositioned," or buried on top of each other. Orientation of the head toward the center of the house is more common than orientation toward the exterior walls. Both males and females were most often buried with the head toward the center of the house and the body perpendicular to the wall.

Some gender differences do emerge, however. Positioning of female heads was more varied than for males, and more female heads were oriented toward the outside walls. More of the females were buried outside the house or parallel to the side walls of the house. Body position was also more varied for females. Whereas most males were buried lying flat on their backs, females were lying on their backs, on their left side, on their right side, and semi-reclining. The interpretation offered is that the diversity of female burials reflects the greater diversity of women's economic and social roles.

A contemporary Iroquois longhouse. Like the longhouses of the Oneota people discussed in this section, those of the Iroquois provide living spaces for many household groups of the same lineage. (Source: © Nathan Benn/CORBIS)

In terms of the number and quality of grave goods, no obvious symbols of authority or differential wealth are found in the burials. Individuals are buried with a wide variety of artifacts related to everyday tasks, including stone tools and vessels. Some individuals, though, are buried with no goods, others with one or two items, and others with four to seven. Typically, infants and children are buried with none or one item, but some adult males and females also have none. Old adults always have some goods. Burials with the head pointing toward the center of the house more often have grave goods. These findings would suggest that no household member had substantially higher status than others, with the exception of slightly higher status for adults, for the aged, and for males (because more males have their heads pointing toward the center of the house, and more of these burials have goods with them).

Two complicating factors exist. First, adolescents and young adults are underrepresented in these burials. Second, some non-house burials have been found in the region. One of these included two adult females and one youth around ten years of age. The youth was buried with twenty-four projectile points and twelve copper cylinders, far more of these items than found in any of the other burials. ▪

FOOD FOR THOUGHT

▪ Generate a scenario that might explain the non-house burial of the two women and one youth.

Spouse/Partner Relationships

Anthropologists who study relationships between spouses and partners consider a range of topics: decision making, power relationships, degree of attachment and commitment, duration of commitment, and the possibility of intimate relationships outside the primary relationship. This section presents findings on levels of emotional satisfaction between spouses and how they may be related to extramarital relationships.

A landmark sociological study of marriages in Tokyo in 1959 compared marital satisfaction of husbands and wives in love marriages and arranged marriages (Blood 1967). In all marriages, marital satisfaction declined over time, but differences between the two types emerged. The decline was greatest for wives in arranged marriages and least for husbands in arranged marriages. In love-match marriages, husbands' satisfaction dropped dramatically and a bit later than their wives' satisfaction, but husbands and wives had nearly equal levels of satisfaction by the time they had been married nine years and more.

Sexual activity of couples can be both an indication of marital satisfaction and a cause of marital satisfaction. Anthropologists have not studied this topic much, but help from sociologists working with survey data is available. Analysis of reports of marital sex from a 1988 survey in the United States shows that frequency per month declines with duration of marriage, from an average of twelve times per month for people aged nineteen to twenty-four years, to less than once a month for people seventy-five years of age and older (Call, Sprecher, and Schwartz 1995). Older married people have sex less frequently, as do those who report being less happy. Within each age category, sex is more frequent among three categories of people: those who are cohabiting but not married, those who cohabited before marriage, and those who are in their second or later marriage.

Sibling Relationships

Sibling relationships are another understudied aspect of kinship dynamics. Suad Joseph (1994) provides an example of research on this topic in her study of a working-class neighborhood of Beirut, Lebanon. She got to know several families well and became especially close to Hanna, the oldest son in one of these families. Hanna was an attractive young man, considered a good marriage choice, with friends across religious and ethnic groups. He seemed peace-loving and conscientious. Therefore, the author reports, "I was shocked . . . one sunny afternoon to hear Hanna shouting at his sister Flaur and slapping her across the face" (50). Aged twelve, Flaur was the oldest daughter. "She seemed to have an opinion on most things, was never shy to speak her mind, and welcomed guests with boisterous laughter. . . . With a lively sense of humor and good-natured mischief about her, neighbors thought of her as a live wire" (50). Further consideration of the relationship between Hanna and Flaur indicated that Hanna played a fatherly role to Flaur. He would be especially irritated with her if she lingered on the street near their apartment building, gossiping with other girls: "He would forcibly escort her upstairs to their apartment, slap her, and demand that she behave with dignity" (51). Adult family members thought nothing was wrong and said that Flaur enjoyed her brother's aggressive attention. Flaur herself commented, "It doesn't even hurt when Hanna hits me," and said that she hoped to have a husband like Hanna.

An interpretation of this common brother–sister relationship in Arab culture is that it is part of the socializing process that maintains and perpetuates patriarchal family relationships: "Hanna was teaching Flaur to accept male power in the name of love . . . loving his sister meant taking charge of her and that he could discipline her if his action was understood to be in her interest. Flaur was reinforced in learning that the love of a man could include that male's violent control and that to receive his love involved submission to control" (52). This close and unequal sibling relationship persists throughout life. Even after marriage, a brother maintains a position of responsibility toward his sister and her children, as does a married sister toward her brother

Ethnography to Prevent Wife Abuse in Rural Kentucky

DOMESTIC VIOLENCE in the United States is reportedly highest in the state of Kentucky. An ethnographic study of domestic violence in Kentucky revealed several cultural factors that make it difficult to prevent wife abuse in this region (Websdale 1995). The study included interviews with fifty abused wives in eastern Kentucky, as well as with battered women in shelters, police officers, shelter employees, and social workers.

Three types of isolation make domestic violence particularly difficult to prevent in rural Kentucky:

- *Physical isolation* The women reported a feeling of physical isolation in their lives. Abusers' tactics were more effective because of geographic isolation. Batterers' strategies include removing the phone from the receiver when leaving for work, disabling motor vehicles, destroying motor vehicles, monitoring the odometer reading on motor vehicles, and discharging firearms in public (for example, at a pet).

  It is difficult to leave an abusive home located many miles from the nearest paved road, especially if the woman has children. No public transportation serves even the paved roads. Nearly one-third of households have no phones. Getting to a phone to report abuse results in delay and gives police the impression that the call is less serious.

- *Social isolation* Aspects of family life and gender roles lead to "passive policing." In rural Kentucky, men are seen as providers and women are strongly tied to domestic work and child rearing. When women do work, their wages are about 50 percent of men's wages. Residence is often in the vicinity of the husband's family, which isolates a woman from the potential support of her natal family and restricts help-seeking in the immediate vicinity because the husband's

family is likely to be nonsupportive. Police officers, especially local ones, view the family as a private unit, a man's world. They are less inclined to intervene and arrest husbands, whom they feel should be dominant in the family. In some instances, the police take the batterer's side, share the batterer's understandings of the situation, and have similar beliefs in a man's right to control his wife.

- *Institutional isolation* Battered women in rural areas face special problems in using the limited services of the state. The fact that abused women often know the people who run the services ironically inhibits the women from approaching them, given values of family privacy. In addition, social services for battered women in Kentucky are scarce. Other institutional constraints include less schooling for rural than for urban women; lack of day care centers that would give mothers the option of working outside the home; inadequate health services, with doctors appearing unfamiliar with domestic violence; and religious teaching of fundamentalist Christianity that supports patriarchal values, including the idea that it is a woman's duty to stay in a marriage, to "weather the storm."

The analysis suggests some recommendations. Women need more and better employment opportunities to reduce their economic dependency on abusive partners. Rural outreach programs should be strengthened. Increased access to telephones could decrease rural women's institutional isolation. Because of the complexity of the social situation in Kentucky, however, no single solution will be sufficient.

FOOD FOR THOUGHT

- If your job were to prevent wife battering in Kentucky, what steps would you take and why?

and his children. This loyalty can lead to conflict between husband and wife as they vie for support and resources from their spouse in competition with their siblings.

Domestic Violence

Domestic violence can occur between domestic partners, parents and children, and siblings. This section concerns the first of these. Violence between domestic partners, with males tending to be the perpetrators and women the victims, seems to be found in nearly all cultures, though in varying forms and frequencies (J. Brown 1999). A cross-cultural review revealed that wife beating is more common and more severe where men control the wealth and is less common and less severe where women's work groups are prominent (Levinson 1989). (See the Lessons Applied box.) The presence of women's work groups is related to a greater importance of women in production and to matrifocal residence. These factors provide women with the means

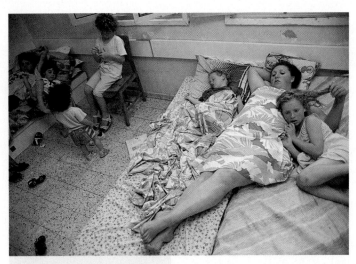

A shared bedroom in a battered women's shelter, Tel Aviv, Israel. ■ Many people wonder why abused women do not leave their abusers. Part of the answer lies in the availability and quality of shelters throughout much of the world. Think of other factors that might prevent women from leaving their abusers. (Source: © David Wells/The Image Works)

to leave an abusive relationship. For example, among the Garifuna, an African-Indian people of Belize, Central America, incidents of spouse abuse occur, but they are infrequent and not extended (Kerns 1992). Women's solidarity in this matrifocal society limits male violence against women.

Increased domestic violence worldwide brings into question the notion of the house as a refuge or place of security. In the United States, for example, there is evidence of high and increasing rates of intrahousehold abuse of children (including sexual abuse), violence between spouses or partners, and abuse of aged family members. More cross-cultural research is needed to help policy makers understand the factors affecting the safety of individuals within households in order to design more effective prevention programs.

Household Transformations

The composition of a household, and even its very existence, can change as a consequence of several factors, including divorce, death, and remarriage. This section reviews some findings on these topics.

Divorce and Kinship Patterns. Divorce and separation, like marriage and other forms of long-term union, are cultural universals, even though they may be frowned on or forbidden. Marriages may break up for several reasons: The most common reasons are voluntary separation and death of one of the partners. Globally, variations exist in the legality and propriety of divorce. Some religions, such as Roman Catholicism, prohibit divorce. In some cultures, divorce is easier for a husband to obtain than for a wife. Important questions about marital dissolution include its causes, the reasons why divorce rates appear to be rising worldwide, and the implications of divorce for the welfare of children of divorced parents.

Divorce rates vary cross-culturally. One hypothesis advanced to explain this variation suggests that divorce rates will be lower in cultures with unilineal descent, where a large descent group has control over and interests in offspring (Barnard and Good 1984:119). Royal lineages, with their strong vested interests in maintaining the family line, are examples of groups especially unlikely to favor divorce, because divorce generally means losing control of offspring. In contrast, in bilineal foraging societies, men and women quite freely form unions, dissolve them, and form others. The same is true, generally speaking, for the contemporary United States with its (more or less) bilineal system.

Another issue is whether monogamy or polygamy affects marriage durability. One case study looked at the relationship between polygyny and divorce in Nigeria and found that marriages of one husband and two wives are the most stable, whereas marriages of one husband and three or more wives have the highest rates of disruption (Gage-Brandon 1992).

Widow(er)hood. The position of a widow or widower carries altered responsibilities and rights. Women's position as widows is often marked symbolically. In Mediterranean cultures, a widow must wear modest, simple, and black clothing, sometimes for the rest of her life. Her sexuality is supposed to be virtually dead. At the same time, her new "asexual" status allows her greater spatial freedom than before. She can go to public coffeehouses and taverns, something not done by women whose husbands are living.

Extreme restrictions on widows are recorded for parts of South Asia, where social pressures on a widow enforce self-denial and self-deprivation, especially among the propertied class. A widow in India should wear a plain white sari (see the photograph on p. 47), shave her head, eat little food, and live an asexual life. Many widows are abandoned, especially if they have no son to support them. They are considered polluting and inauspicious. In a similar fashion, widows in South Africa experience symbolic and life-quality changes much more than widowers:

> A widower is encouraged to take on the challenge of picking up the pieces and to face life again. He is reminded that he must be strong and swallow his pain. His body is not marked in any significant way except to have his head shaved, as is the custom in most African communities. He also is required to wear a black button or arm band. The period of mourning for widowers is generally six months, compared to at least one year for widows. . . . The fear of the ritual danger embodied in widows is expressed in terms of "heat," "darkness," and "dirt." . . . Her body is marked in different communities by some or all of the following practices: shaving her head, smearing a mixture of herbs and ground charcoal on her body, wearing black clothes made from an inexpensive material, and covering her face with a black veil and her shoulders with a black shawl. A widow may express her liminal status in a variety of ways, [such as by] eating with her left hand, wearing clothes inside out, wearing one shoe, or eating out of a lid instead of a plate (Ramphele 1996:100).

A widow of Madeira, Portugal, wearing the typical black, modest clothing required in the Mediterranean region as a sign of widowhood. ■ What behavioral changes are required for widows and widowers in your microculture? (Source: © Andy Levin/Photo Researchers, Inc.)

Remarriage. Remarriage patterns are influenced by economic factors and gender-linked expectations that shape a person's desirability as a partner. In the United States, divorce is frequently followed by remarriage for both males and females, with a slight edge for men. In Japan, the tendency to remarry is significantly greater for men than for women (Cornell 1989). A marked age distribution in nonremarriage for women exists: "[W]hile divorced Japanese women, up to age 40, are already about 15% more likely to remain divorced than are their U.S. white female counterparts of the same age, after age 40 their situation grows rapidly more unfavorable for remarriage. In the subsequent decade it rises to 25% more divorced at age 45, 40% more at age 48, more than half again as many at age 50, and 65% more at age 51" (460). Older women's lower rates of remarriage are the result of age-hypergynous marriage and males' greater access to economic and political resources that increase their attractiveness as marriage partners in spite of their increasing age.

CHANGING KINSHIP AND HOUSEHOLD DYNAMICS

This section provides examples of how marriage and household patterns are changing. Many of these changes have roots in colonialism. Others are more the result of recent changes effected by globalization and increased population movements.

Change in Marriage

Although the institution of marriage in general remains prominent, many of its specific details are changing. Nearly everywhere, the age at first marriage is rising. This change is related to increased emphasis on completing a certain number of years of education before marriage and to rising aspirations about the potential spouse's economic status before marriage is contemplated. Arranged marriages in some contexts are being replaced by love marriages (see the Methods Close-Up box on p. 434). Marriages between people of different nations and ethnicity are increasing, partly because of increased rates of international migration. Migrants take with them many

Love Letters and Courtship in Nepal

LAURA AHERN went to a village in western Nepal to study how kinship was changing there. She used many different research methods. Her basic approach was the cornerstone method of participant observation. She attended many weddings, observed courting couples, heard stories about courtship, and participated in everyday family life. She conducted a house-to-house census of the central area of the village, visiting all forty-six households and asking about marriage and kinship patterns. This part of her study revealed that arranged marriage was declining and marriage by elopement was increasing.

Later, she conducted a survey to collect more information on marriage types and decision-making processes. She administered this survey to all 161 ever-married residents of the central ward, and two assistants administered it in two other wards. She found the quantitative data useful, but she also valued the fact that the survey brought her into contact with people she did not see everyday. From this group of respondents, she selected thirty-six for in-depth conversations about their attitudes toward marriage in general and their individual "marriage narrative."

The centerpiece of her methods, however, is quite unusual: she amassed a collection of over 200 love letters. She happened upon this form of data when, one day in casual conversation about marriage and the increase in elopements, she asked how young people courted before an elopement, given the fact that dating is not allowed. Ahern was told that the new practice of sending love letters is how young people court. One woman offered to share a love letter from her husband and gave permission for it to be copied. Eventually, many other villagers did the same. Of the 200 letters Ahern collected, 170 were written by men and 30 by women. Typically, the man starts the correspondence. For example, one man's love letter contains the following lines: "I'm helpless and I have to make friends of a notebook and pen in order to place this helplessness before you. . . . I'll let you know by a 'short cut' what I want to say: Love is the union of two souls. The 'main' meaning of love is 'life success.' I'm offering you an invitation to love" (2001:3).

Love letters became possible only in the 1990s because of increased literacy rates in the village. Literacy facilitated self-selected marriages and thus supported an increasing sense of personal agency among the younger people of the village.

FOOD FOR THOUGHT

- What means of communication are involved in courtship in your cultural world? How was it different in your parents' time?

---

of their marriage and family practices. They also adapt to rules and practices in their area of destination. Pluralistic practices evolve, such as conducting two marriage ceremonies—one based on the "original" culture and the other conforming to norms that prevail in the place of destination.

Style changes in weddings abound. Globalization of Western-style "white weddings" promotes the adoption of many features that are familiar in the West: a white wedding gown for the bride, a many-layered wedding cake, and certain kinds of floral arrangements. What the bride and groom wear is an expression of both the bride's and the groom's personal identity and may also reflect the cultural identity of their family and larger social group. Clothing choice may reflect adherence to "traditional" values or may reject those in favor of more "modern" values. Euro-American trends are prominent worldwide. Throughout much of East and Southeast Asia, advertisements and upscale stores display the Western-style white wedding gown (though less so in India, where white clothing for women signifies widowhood and is inauspicious). On the other hand, a resurgence of local "folk" styles is occurring in some contexts, such as in Morocco, where there is a trend for "modern" brides to wear a Berber costume (long robes and jewelry characteristic of the rural, mountain people) at one stage of the wedding ceremony.

Matrilineal kinship appears to be declining worldwide in the face of both colonialism and globalization. European colonial rule in Africa and Asia contributed to the decline in matrilineal kinship by registering land and other property in the names

---

of assumed male heads of household, even where females were in fact the heads (Boserup 1970). This process eroded women's previous rights and powers. Christian missionary influence also transformed matrilineal cultures into more patrilineal systems (Etienne and Leacock 1980). European influences have led to the decline of matrilineal kinship among Native North Americans (which long constituted one of the largest distributions of matrilineal descent world-wide, even though not all Native North American groups were matrilineal). A comparative study of kinship among three areas of the Navajo reservation in Arizona shows that matrilineality exists where conditions most resemble the pre-reservation era (Levy, Henderson, and Andrews 1989).

In the case of the Minangkabau of Indonesia, matrilineal kinship was undermined by Dutch colonialism, which promoted the image of male-led nuclear families as an ideal; by the Islamic faith, which currently promotes female domesticity and male household dominance; and by the modernizing Indonesian state, which insists on naming males as heads of households (Blackwood 1995).

Changing Households

Changing economic opportunities in recent times have led to rapid change in household structures and dynamics. For example, employment of daughters in electronics factories in Malaysia changed intrahousehold power structures (Ong 1987). The girls' mothers encourage them to take up factory work and urge them to contribute a proportion of their earnings to the household economy. This practice frees daughters from their father's control (traditional among Malaysian Muslims), while giving greater control to the mother.

International migration is another major cause of change in household formation. Dramatic changes in reproductive patterns can occur in one generation when members of a farming household in, for example, Taiwan or India migrate to England, France, or the United States. Having many children makes economic sense in their homeland but not in their new home. These migrants frequently decide to have only one or two children and to live in small, isolated nuclear households. International migration creates new challenges for relationships between parents and children. The children may identify strongly with the new culture and have little connection with their ancestral culture, and this pattern can be a source of anxiety for their parents. Often, values in the new culture conflict with those of the culture of origin, putting children in conflict with their parents over issues such as dating, dress, and career goals.

What about domestic life in this new millennium? Projections for the near future include the reduced economic dependence of women and the weakening of marriage in industrialized societies (Cherlin 1996: 478–480). These changes, in turn, will lead to increased movement away from nuclear household living and to increased diversity in household forms.

During the second half of the twentieth century, household size in the United States shrank from an average of 3.3 to 2.6 persons (U.S. Bureau of the Census 1999:60). The current situation contains several seemingly contradictory patterns first noted in the early 1980s by two sociologists (Cherlin and Furstenberg 1992 [1983]): (1) The number of unmarried couples living together has more than tripled since 1970, and (2) one out of four children is not living with both parents. At current rates, half of all American marriages begun in the 1980s will end in divorce.

At the start of the twenty-first century, three kinds of households are most common in the United States: households composed of couples living in their first marriage, single-parent households, and households formed through remarriage (Cherlin and Furstenberg 1992 [1983]:3). A new fourth category is the **intergenerational**

A newly married husband and wife and their relatives in front of a church in Seoul, Republic of Korea. ■ How does this wedding group resemble or differ from a wedding in your micro-culture? (Source: © Noboro Komine/Photo Researchers, Inc.)

household, in which an "adult child" returns to live with his or her parents. About one in three unmarried adults between the ages of twenty-five and fifty-five shares a home with his or her mother or father or both (*Psychology Today* 1995 [28]:16). In the United States, adult offspring spend over two hours a day doing household chores, daughters contributing about 17 hours a week and sons 14.4 hours. The daughters spend most of their time doing laundry, cooking, cleaning, and washing dishes, whereas sons are more involved in yard work and car care. Even so, the parents still do three-quarters of the housework.

Kinship and household formation are certainly not dull and static concepts. Just trying to keep up to date on their changing patterns in the United States is a daunting task, to say nothing of tracking changes in the rest of the world.

THE BIG QUESTIONS REVISITED

■ HOW are kinship ties created through descent, sharing, and marriage?

Key differences exist between unilineal and bilineal descent systems. Within unilineal systems, further important variations exist between patrilineal and matrilineal systems in terms of property inheritance, residence rules for married couples, and the relative status of males and females. Worldwide, unilineal systems are more common than bilineal systems. Within unilineal kinship systems, patrilineal kinship is more common than matrilineal kinship. A second important basis for kinship is sharing. Sharing one's child with someone else through either informal or formal processes is probably a cultural universal. Sharing-based kinship is created through food transfers, including breastfeeding (children breast-fed by the same woman are considered kin and cannot marry). Ritualized sharing creates kinship, as in the case of godparenthood. The third basis for kinship is marriage, another universal practice, although definitions of marriage differ substantially. All cultures have rules of exclusion and preference rules for spouses.

■ WHAT is a household and what do cultural anthropologists study about household life?

A household may consist of a single person living alone or may be a group comprising more than one person who may or may not be related by kinship; these individuals share a living space and, often, financial responsibilities for the household. Nuclear households consist of a mother and father and their children, but they also can be just a husband and wife without children. Nuclear households are found in all cultures but are most com-

mon in foraging and industrialized societies. Extended households include more than one nuclear household. They are most commonly found in cultures with a unilineal kinship system. Stem households, which are most common in East Asia, are a variant of an extended household in which only one child, usually the firstborn, retains residence with the parents. Household headship can be shared between two partners or can be borne by a single person, as in woman-headed households. Intrahousehold dynamics, between parents and children and among siblings, include complex power relationships as well as security, sharing, and sometimes violence. Household break-up comes about through divorce, separation of cohabiting partners, or death of a spouse or partner.

■ HOW are kinship systems and households changing?

The increasingly connected world in which we live is having marked effects on kinship formation and household patterns and dynamics. Matrilineal systems have been declining in distribution since European colonialist expansion beginning in the 1500s. Many aspects of marriage are changing. There is, for example, a trend toward later age at marriage in many developing countries. Although marriage continues to be an important basis for the formation of households, other options (such as cohabitation) are increasing in importance in many contexts, including urban areas in developed countries. What these changes in household forms and dynamics may mean for the care of dependent members (such as children, the aged, and disabled members) is a question for the future.

KEY CONCEPTS

bilineal descent, p. 414
brideprice, p. 425
cross cousin, p. 422
descent, p. 414
dowry, p. 423
endogamy, p. 421
exogamy, p. 422
extended household, p. 427
family, p. 426
household, p. 426
hypergyny, p. 422

hypogyny, p. 422
incest taboo, p. 421
intergenerational household, p. 435
isogamy, p. 422
kinship diagram, p. 413
kinship system, p. 412
marriage, p. 421
matrilocal residence, p. 416
matrilineal descent, p. 415
monogamy, p. 425
neolocal residence, p. 417

nuclear household, p. 427
parallel cousin, p. 422
patrilineal descent, p. 415
patrilocal residence, p. 416
polyandry, p. 425
polygamy, p. 425
polygyny, p. 425
stem household, p. 427
unilineal descent, p. 414

SUGGESTED READINGS

Irwin Altman and Joseph Ginat, eds. *Polygynous Families in Contemporary Society*. New York: Cambridge University Press, 1996. Based on research conducted with twenty-six Mormon families in Utah, this book provides a detailed account of polygyny as practiced in two fundamentalist communities, one rural and the other urban. Topics covered include Mormon history, how polygynous marriages are arranged, how couples manage their time and finances, and emotional relationships within the household.

Richard E. Blanton. *Houses and Households: A Comparative Study*. New York: Plenum Press, 1994. The author, an archaeologist, conducted a comparative study of the domestic architecture of several family farming communities over different periods to see whether increasing social complexity was reflected in houses, household structure, and household social relations. The sites included in the study are located in Mexico, China, Japan, Southeast Asia, and India.

John Borneman. *Belonging in the Two Berlins: Kin, State and Nation*. New York: Cambridge University Press, 1992. This book considers people's changing perceptions of the family and the government's policies related to the family.

Dorothy Ayers Counts, Judith K. Brown, and Jacquelyn C. Campbell, eds. *To Have and to Hit: Cultural Perspectives on Wife Beating*. Champaign/Urbana: University of Illinois Press, 1999. This book includes an introductory overview, case studies, and a concluding comparative essay. One chapter considers the possible evolutionary origin of wife abuse. Cases are from Australia, southern Africa, Papua New Guinea, India, Central America, the Middle East, and the Pacific.

Irene Glasser and Rae Bridgman. *Braving the Street: The Anthropology of Homelessness*. Public Issues in Anthropological Perspective, vol. 1. New York: Bergahn Books, 1999. Fieldwork with homeless people reveals complexities that have been overlooked by public officials. The authors propose solutions.

Laurel Kendall. *Getting Married in Korea: Of Gender, Morality and Modernity*. Berkeley: University of California Press, 1996. This ethnographic study examines preferences about desirable spouses, matchmaking, marriage ceremonies and their financing, and the effect of women's changing work roles on their marital aspirations.

Judith S. Modell. *A Sealed and Secret Kinship: The Culture of Policies and Practices in American Adoption*. New York, Bergahn Books, 2002. This book reviews case histories of parents, children, kin, and non-kin of adoptive families in the United States. The author discusses adoption reform, adoptees' experiences of searching for their birth parents, and changes in welfare policy.

Robert McC. Netting, Richard R. Wilk, and Eric J. Arnould, eds. *The Household: Comparative and Historical Studies of the Domestic Group*. Berkeley: University of California Press, 1984. This book includes comparative chapters on changing forms and functions of the household; case studies of contemporary Thailand, Niger, Belize, and the United States; and historical analyses of the Baltic region and Sweden.

Ellen Oxfeld. *Blood, Sweat, and Mahjong: Family and Enterprise in an Overseas Chinese Community*. Ithaca, NY: Cornell University Press, 1993. Situated in Calcutta, this ethnography provides insights into a Chinese family business and how it is organized.

Sulamith Heins Potter. *Family Life in a Northern Thai Village: A Structural Study in the Significance of Women*. Berkeley: University of California Press, 1977. This ethnography of matrifocal family life in rural Thailand focuses on work roles, rituals, and intrafamily relationships.

Nancy Tapper. *Bartered Brides: Politics, Gender and Marriage in an Afghan Tribal Society*. New York: Cambridge University Press, 1991. Based on fieldwork before the Soviet invasion, this study examines marriage among the Maduzai, a tribal society of Turkistan. The book looks at the way marriage is related to productive and reproductive aspects of society and at the role it plays in managing political conflict and competition.

Margaret Trawick. *Notes on Love in a Tamil Family*. Berkeley: University of California Press, 1992. This reflexive ethnography takes a close look at the daily dynamics of kinship in one Tamil (South Indian) family. Attention is given to sibling relationships, the role of older people, children's lives, and the way love and affection are played out.

Michael Young and Peter Willmott. *Family and Kinship in East London*. New York: Penguin Books, 1979. This classic study of kinship relationships among the working class of Bethnal Green focuses on the importance of married women's continued close relationships with their mothers, as maintained through residential proximity and visiting.

THE BIG QUESTIONS

- HOW do social groups vary cross-culturally?
- WHAT is social stratification, and what are its effects on people?
- WHAT is civil society?

CHAPTER 15

Social Groups and Social Stratification

Rock paintings at a site in Arnhemland, Australia, important to the Kunwinjku people. Arnhemland stretches across the northern part of the country and is the largest Aboriginal reserve in Australia. (Source: © Penny Tweedy/Panos Pictures)

The number of commercial sex workers worldwide is in the millions, and they are overwhelmingly at risk of contracting HIV/AIDS and of experiencing physical abuse from pimps, clients, and local police. Often trafficked and forced to work against their will, they have little power to change their situation.

A sign of hope for sex workers comes from an unlikely place: Sonagachi, one of the largest red-light districts in the world, located in India's large, eastern city of Kolkata, formerly named Calcutta (Science 2004). It is a union for sex workers, the Durbar Mahila Samanwaya Committee (DMSC), launched in 1995 through the inspiration of epidemiologist Dr. Smarajit Jana. The DMSC now includes many thousands of members in the state of West Bengal. It promotes many projects to improve the lives of sex workers, and the most famous is the Sonagachi Project.

Featured in the international media and widely recognized as a model for positive social change, the Sonagachi Project first set up a health clinic and hired local sex workers to do "peer outreach." The peer educators were given distinctive green jackets to wear and staff identity cards. They went through a training program focused on increasing confidence among the sex workers. The 65 peer educators then went from house to house, distributing free condoms and disseminating information about prevention of AIDS and other sexually transmitted infections, how to access medical care, and how to question power structures that promote violence.

DMSC negotiated with madams and pimps, convincing them of the importance of condom use to protect their investments. They opened their own bank so that sex workers could take out loans at reasonable interest rates. Condom use increased dramatically, and while HIV prevalence has skyrocketed to 50 percent among sex workers elsewhere in India, it has been held to around 11 percent in Sonagachi.

DMSC is now managing a one-million-dollar grant from the Bill & Melinda Gates Foundation to assess the replicability of the Sonagachi model and what might be involved in transferring its lessons for success to other communities of sex workers.

Several factors form the basis of social groups and organizations, including class, ethnicity and indigeneity, gender, age, and, as the DMSC story indicates, occupation. This chapter focuses on these and other ways in which people are organized into groups beyond the family and household. It first examines a variety of social groups ranging from small-scale to larger-scale, then considers the important topic of inequalities among social categories, and last looks at the emerging role of civil society.

 SOCIAL GROUPS

A **social group** is a cluster of people beyond the domestic unit who are usually related on a basis other than kinship, although kinship relationships may exist among people in the group. Two broad categories exist: the **primary group,** consisting of people who interact with each other and know each other personally, and the **secondary group,** consisting of people who identify with each other on some common ground but who may never meet with one another or interact with each other personally. Members of all social groups have rights and responsibilities in relation to the group that, if not maintained, could mean loss of membership. Membership in a primary group involves more direct accountability about rights and responsibilities than secondary group membership.

Cross-culturally, variations exist in the number and types of social groups found. One reason for such differences is the economic system (see Figure 15.1). Agricultural and industrial societies have the greatest variety of types of social groups. Mobile populations, such as foragers and pastoralists, are less likely to develop enduring social groups beyond kin relationships, simply because they move around more. But foragers and pastoralists do not completely lack social groupings. A prominent form of social group among foragers and pastoralists is an **age set,** a group

FORAGING	HORTICULTURE	PASTORALISM	AGRICULTURE	INDUSTRIALISM (CAPITALIST)
Characteristics				*Characteristics*
Informal and primary			Formal and secondary	
Egalitarian structure			Recognized leadership	
Ties based on balanced exchange		Ritual ties	Dues and fees	
Functions				*Functions*
Companionship			Special purposes	
			Work, war, lobbying government	
Types of Social Groups				*Types of Social Groups*
Friendship		Friendship		Friendship
	Age-based work groups			Urban youth gangs
	Gender-based work groups			Clubs, associations
			Status Groups:	
			Class, race, ethnicity, caste, age, gender	
			Institutional Groups:	
			Prisons, retirement homes	
			Quasi-Political Groups:	
			Human rights, environmental groups	

FIGURE 15.1
Modes of social organization.

(*Source:* Reprinted by permission of Allyn & Bacon.)

of people close in age who go through certain rituals, such as circumcision, at the same time.

A second explanation for variation, one indirectly related to economics, is that social groups emerge in settled and densely populated areas as ways of promoting cooperation, sharing knowledge, and keeping the peace. Thus social groups in this view are adaptive. This generalization is appealing and works well for many areas. Rural Africa, Latin America, and Southeast Asia have a rich diversity of social groups. For example, in northern Thailand's Chiangmai region, many social groups exist (Potter 1976). In a village, there are groups that maintain the Buddhist temple, the temple library, the school, irrigation canals, cremation grounds, and roads. Other groups are the temple festival committee, the Young People's Club, the village dancers (about a dozen young, unmarried women who manage intervillage events), and the funeral society (which provides financial aid for funeral services).

Such social groups are less common in rural areas of South Asia. In the country of Bangladesh, one of the most densely populated areas of South Asia, few indigenous social groups exist (Miller and Khan 1986). Bangladesh has gained world fame, however, for its success in forming local credit groups through an organization called the Grameen Bank, which extends loans to poor people to help them start small businesses (discussed in Chapter 21). Thus the absence of an indigenous tradition of social groups does not prevent new forms of social groups from thriving.

The following sections consider a variety of social groups, beginning with the most face-to-face, primary groups composed of two or three people and then moving to larger groups with formal membership and goals.

Friendship

Friendship is a form of primary social group. Cultural anthropologists have asked whether friendship is a cultural universal. Two factors make it difficult to answer this question. First, insufficient cross-cultural research exists to answer the question definitively. Second, defining friendship cross-culturally is problematic. It is likely,

In a low-income neighborhood in Rio de Janeiro, Brazil, men play dominoes and drink beer while others observe. ■ Discuss a comparable scene of leisure activities in your microcultural experience. (Source: © Stephanie Maze/ Woodfin Camp & Associates)

however, that something like the English-language concept of *friendship* (close ties between non-kin) is a cultural universal, although its particular shape differs from culture to culture.

Social Characteristics of Friendship

Friendship is a voluntary arrangement, in contrast to most kinship relationships. Even so, the criteria establishing who qualifies as a friend may be culturally structured. For instance, gender segregation may prevent cross-gender friendships and promote same-gender friendships, and ethnic segregation may limit cross-ethnic friendships.

Differences between men's and women's friendship patterns in southern Spain illustrate how cultural context—especially, in this case, work and gender roles—shape the kinds of friends a person has. Women's lives in this context are devoted mainly to unpaid household work within the domestic domain (Uhl 1991). Women's domestic roles sometimes draw them into the public domain—markets, town hall, taking children to school—with some time for visiting friends. Women often referred to their friends either with kin terms or as *vecina,* "neighbor," reflecting women's primary orientation to family and neighborhood.

Men's lives involve work and leisure outside the house. For men, an important category of friend is an *amigo,* a friend with whom one casually interacts. This kind of casual friendship is the friendship of bars and leisure-time male camaraderie. It grows out of work, school, common sports and hobbies, and drinking together night after night. Women do not have such friendships. Men also are more likely than women to have *amigos(as) de trabajo,* friendships based on work activities.

Differences between men and women also emerge in the category of "true friends," or *amigo(as) del verdad* or *de confianza.* True friends are those with whom one shares secrets without fear of betrayal. Most men claimed to have many more true friends than women claimed to have, a circumstance that reflects their wider social networks.

Friends are supportive of each other, psychologically and sometimes materially. Support is mutual, shared back and forth in a predictable way (as in balanced exchange, review Chapter 11). Friendship generally occurs between social equals, although there are exceptions, such as friendship between older and younger people, a supervisor and a staff worker, or a teacher and a student.

THINKING OUTSIDE THE BOX What categories of friends do you have? Are some kinds of friends "closer" or "truer" than others, and if so, why?

Friendship in a Men's Prison

Institutional cultures shape friendship in many ways. One factor that limits the formation of friendship in the particular environment of a prison is the duration of the sentence. Long-term prisoners are more likely than short-term prisoners to form enduring friendships. A study that explored friendship formation among short-term prisoners first had to deal with the difficulty of doing participant observation in the prison. The solution was to form a research team of two people, with an "insider" and an "outsider" (Schmid and Jones 1993). The "insider" was an inmate serving a short-term sentence who did participant observation, conducted interviews, and kept a journal. The "outsider" was a sociologist who met with the inmate weekly to discuss findings (he also did the analysis).

Three stages of short-term inmate adaptation are typical. First, inmates experience uncertainty and fear based on their images of what life is like in prison. They avoid contact with other prisoners and guards as much as possible. The next stage involves the creation of a survival niche. The prisoner has selective interactions with other inmates and may develop a "partnership" with another inmate. Partners hang around together and watch out for each other. In the third phase, the prisoner anticipates his eventual release, transfers to a minimum-security area, increases contact with outside visitors, and begins the transition to freedom. In this stage, partners begin to detach from each other as one of the pair moves toward the outside world.

Friendship among the Urban Poor

A study by Carol Stack of how friendship networks promote economic survival among low-income, urban African Americans is a landmark contribution to cultural anthropology (1974). Her research was conducted in the late 1960s in "The Flats," the poorest section of an African American community in a midwestern city. She learned about extensive and enduring networks of friends "supporting, reinforcing each other—devising schemes for self help, strategies for survival in a community of severe economic deprivation" (28). In this community, people use kin terms to refer to their close friends.

People in The Flats, especially women, maintain a set of friends through exchange: "swapping" goods (food, clothing) needed by someone at a particular time, sharing "child keeping," and giving or lending food stamps and money. Such exchanges are part of a clearly understood pattern—gifts and favors go back and forth over time. Friends are obligated to each another and can call on each other in time of need. Discrediting earlier theories that suggested the breakdown of social relationships among the very poor, this research documents how poor people use creativity and agency to build strong social ties that help them cope with difficult conditions.

Sharing stories is another important basis for friendship among the urban poor. In Guyana, South America, Indo-Guyanese men who have known each other since childhood reaffirm their friendship every day at the rumshop, where they eat, drink, and regale each other with stories (Sidnell 2000). Through shared storytelling about village history and other aspects of everyday life, the men affirm their equality with each other. Even the pattern of storytelling, referred to as "turn-at-talk," maintains equality; it means that everyone should have a turn at telling a story. These friendship groups are tightly knit, and the members can call on one another for economic, social, political, and ritual help.

Clubs and Fraternities

Clubs and fraternities define membership in terms of some sense of shared identity. Thus they may comprise people of the same ethnic heritage, occupation or business, religion, or gender. Although many clubs appear to exist primarily to serve functions of sociality and psychological support, these groups play economic and political roles as well.

Women's clubs in a lower-class neighborhood in Paramaribo, Suriname, have multiple functions (Brana-Shute 1976). Here, as is common throughout Latin America, clubs raise money to sponsor special events for individual celebrations, to meet personal financial needs, and to send cards and flowers for funerals. Members, as a group, attend each other's birthday parties and funerals. The clubs offer the women psychological support, entertainment, and financial help. A political aspect exists, too. Club members often belong to the same political party and attend political rallies and events together. These women constitute political interest groups that can influence political outcomes.

College fraternities and sororities are highly selective groups that serve a variety of explicit functions, such as entertainment and social service. They also forge bonds that may help members secure jobs after graduation. Unlike sociologists, few anthropologists have studied the "Greek system" (fraternities and sororities) on American campuses. One exception is Peggy Sanday, who was inspired to study college fraternities after the gang rape of a woman student by several fraternity brothers at the university where she teaches. In her book *Fraternity Gang Rape: Sex, Brotherhood, and Privilege on Campus* (1990), she explores initiation rituals; the role of pornography, ritual dances, and heavy drinking at parties; and how they are related to a pattern of male bonding solidified by victimization and ridicule of women. Gang rape, or a "train," is a prevalent practice in some—not all—fraternities. Fraternity party invitations may hint at the possibility of a "train." Typically, the brothers seek out a "party girl"—a somewhat vulnerable young woman who may be especially seeking of acceptance or especially high on alcohol or other substances (her drinks may even have been "spiked"). They take her to one of the brother's rooms, where she may or may not agree to have sex with one man—often she passes out. Then a "train" of men have sex with her. Rarely prosecuted, the male participants reinforce their sense of privilege, power, and unity with one another through this group ritual involving abuse of a female outsider.

Cross-culturally, men's clubs in which strong male–male bonds are created and reinforced by the objectification and mistreatment of women are common, but not universal. They are especially associated with cultures where male–male competitiveness is an important feature of society (Bird 1996) and in which warfare and intergroup conflict are frequent. In many indigenous Amazonian groups, the men's house is fiercely guarded from being entered by women. If a woman trespasses on male territory, she is punished by gang rape. One interpretation is that males have a high degree of anxiety about their identity as fierce warriors and as sexually potent males (Gregor 1982). Maintaining their identity as fierce toward outsiders involves taking an aggressive position in relation to women of their own group. Parallels of *gynophobic* ("women-hating" or otherwise anti-woman) men's clubs do not exist among women. College sororities are not mirror images of college fraternities. Women's groups and organizations, even if vocally anti-male, do not engage in physical abuse of males or ritualized forms of derision.

Countercultural Groups

Several kinds of groups are formed by people who seek consciously to resist conforming to the dominant cultural pattern, as in the "hippie" movement of the 1960s. This section considers examples of countercultural groups. One similarity among these groups is the importance of bonding through shared rituals.

Members of a fraternity at the University of Texas at Austin engage in public service by planting trees at an elementary school. ■ What knowledge do you have of the positive and negative social aspects of college fraternities and sororities? How could anthropological research provide a clearer picture? (Source: © Stephanie Maze/Woodfin Camp & Associates)

Youth Gangs

The term *gang* can refer to a variety of groups, such as one's friends, as in "I think I'll invite the gang over for pizza." The more specific term **youth gang** refers to a group of young people, found mainly in urban areas, who are often considered a social problem by adults and law enforcement officials (Sanders 1994).

Like clubs and fraternities, gangs often have a recognized leader, formalized rituals of initiation for new members, and symbolic markers of identity, such as tattoos or special clothing. An example of an informal youth gang with no formal leadership hierarchy or initiation rituals is the *Masta Liu* in Honiara, the capital city of the Solomon Islands, in the South Pacific (Jourdan 1995). The primary unifying feature of the male youths who become Masta Liu is the fact that they are unemployed. Most have migrated to the city from the countryside to escape what they consider an undesirable lifestyle: working in the fields under control of their elders. Some liu live with extended kin in the city; others organize liu-only households. They spend their time wandering around town (*wakabaot*) in groups of up to ten. They have developed such a distinctive lifestyle and identity, in their dress and outlook on life, that songs are written about them, and in spite of being socially marginalized, they are shaping urban youth culture in Honiara.

Street gangs are a more formal variety of youth gang. They generally have leaders and a hierarchy of membership roles and responsibilities. They are named, and their members mark their identity with tattoos or "colors." Much popular thinking associates street gangs with violence, but not all are involved in violence. A cultural anthropologist who did research among nearly forty street gangs in New York, Los Angeles, and Boston learned much about why individuals join gangs, providing insights that also contradict popular thinking (Jankowski 1991). One common perception is that young boys join gangs because they are from homes where there is no male authority figure with whom they can identify. In the gangs studied, just as many gang members were from intact nuclear households. Another common perception is that the gang replaces a missing feeling of family. This study showed that the same number of gang members reported having close family ties as those who did not.

What, then, might be the reasons behind joining a male urban gang? A particular personality type characterized many gang members, a type that could be called a *defiant individualist*. The defiant individualist type has five traits: intense competitiveness, mistrust or wariness, self-reliance, social isolation, and a strong survival instinct. A structurist (or political economy) view would say that poverty, especially urban poverty, leads to the development of this kind of personality structure. Within the

THINKING OUTSIDE THE BOX

Think of some other examples in which so-called marginal groups of people have contributed to changing styles of music, dress, and other forms of expressive culture of mainstream groups.

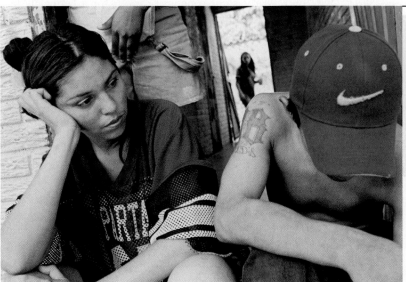

Members of the gang "18" in San Salvador, El Salvador, passing time on a street. The group's leader prohibits the use of alcohol and drugs except on Saturdays and Sundays. ■ Consider how the social life of gangs worldwide is affected by contemporary globalization. (Source: © Jerome Sessini/In Visu/CORBIS)

Left: A Tahitian chief wears tattoos that indicate his high status. Right: A woman with tattooed arms and pierced nose in the United States. ■ In your microcultural experience, what do tattoos mean? (Sources: © Charles & Josette Lenars/CORBIS, left; © Royalty-Free/CORBIS, right)

context of urban poverty, such a personality structure becomes a reasonable response to the prevailing economic obstacles and uncertainty.

In terms of explaining the global spread of urban youth gangs, structurists point to global economic changes in urban employment opportunities. In many countries, the declining urban industrial base has created persistent poverty in inner-city communities (Short 1996:326). At the same time, aspirations for a better life have been promoted through schooling and the popular media. Urban gang members, in this view, are the victims of large structural forces beyond their control. Yet research with gang members shows that they are not just passive victims of structural forces: many of these youths want to be economically successful, but social conditions channel their interests and skills into illegal pursuits rather than into legal avenues to achievement.

Body Modification Groups

One of the many countercultural movements in the United States includes people who have a sense of community strengthened through forms of body alteration. James Myers (1992) did research in California among people who feel they are a special group because of their interest in permanent body modification, especially genital piercing, branding, and cutting. Fieldwork involved participant observation and interviews. Myers was involved in six workshops organized especially for the San Francisco SM (sadomasochist) community; attended the Fifth Annual Living in Leather Convention held in Portland, Oregon, in 1990; and spent time in tattoo and piercing studios, as well as talking with students and others in his home town who were involved in these forms of body modification. The study population included males and females, heterosexuals, gays, lesbians, bisexuals, and SMers. The single largest group was made up of SM homosexuals and bisexuals. The study population was mainly Euro-American, and most had either attended or graduated from college.

Myers witnessed many modification sessions at workshops. Those seeking modification go up on stage and have their chosen procedure done by a well-known expert. Whatever the procedure, the volunteers exhibit little pain (usually a sharp intake of breath at the moment the needle passes through or the brand touches skin). After that critical moment, the audience breathes an audible sigh of relief. The volunteer stands up and adjusts clothing, and members of the audience applaud. This public event is a kind of initiation ritual that binds the expert, the volunteer, and the group together. Pain has long been recognized as an important part of rites of passage, providing an edge to the ritual drama. The audience in this case witnesses and validates the experience and also becomes joined to the initiate through witnessing.

A prominent motivation for seeking permanent body modification was a desire to identify with a specific group of people. As one person said,

> It's not that we're sheep, getting pierced or cut just because everyone else is. I like to think it's because we're a very special group and we like doing something that sets us off from others. . . . Happiness is standing in line at a cafeteria and detecting that the straight-looking babe in front of you has her nipples pierced. I don't really care what her sexual orientation is, I can relate to her. (292)

Work Groups

Work groups are organized to perform specific tasks, though they may also have other functions, including sociality and friendship among members. They are found in all modes of production, but they are more prominent in nonindustrialized horticultural and agricultural communities where land preparation, harvesting, or repair of irrigation canals requires large inputs of labor that exceed the capability of a single household unit. In her classic study of the Bemessi people of the Cameroon, West Africa, Phyllis Kaberry (1952) describes a labor group system (called a *tzo*, which is translated as "working bee"). Among the Bemessi, women were responsible mainly for carrying out horticultural work. Because of this role, women were also the ones who participated in tzos. For preparing corn beds, about ten to twelve women worked on each others' plots, whereas smaller groups of three to four women formed for weeding. At the end of the day, the women have a meal of fish provided by their husbands. A woman who fails to provide shared work is reported to the chief.

Youth work groups are common in African regions south of the Sahara, particularly in horticultural and agricultural communities. The major responsibility of the youth groups is providing field labor. The group members work one or more days in the village chief's fields for no reward or pay. They also maintain public paths and the public meeting area, construct and maintain roads between villages, build and repair canals, combat brush fires, maintain the village mosque, and prevent animals from grazing where they are not allowed (Leynaud 1961). Girls' groups exist, but in patrilocal contexts they are less durable because marriage and relocation break girls' ties with childhood companions. As adults, however, women in African cultures have many types of associations, such as mothers' groups, savings groups, and work groups.

Irrigation organizations are formal groups devoted to maintaining irrigation canals and distributing the water. These organizations are responsible for a highly valued good, and they tend to develop formal leadership and membership rules and roles. Because watershed systems cross large regions, irrigation organizations often provide links among many local groups.

The important role these organizations play is illustrated in the Chiangmai region of northern Thailand (see the map on p. 375). At the village level, care of the irrigation canals is a constant concern (Potter 1976). Each year the main dam across the Ping River is washed away by floods and must be rebuilt. This task requires two weeks of concentrated labor by all the farmers who use the system. The main canal has to be cleared at least once a year, the smaller ones more often. These tasks require much organization. The administration has three tiers. At the highest level is the overall leader of the irrigation group, who is chosen by three local political leaders. At the time of Potter's study, the head was a wealthy man of high social status who had held the position for twenty years. He had two assistants. At the next lower tier are the heads of all major canals in the system. At the most local level is the village irrigation leader, who is chosen by the village farmers. Irrigation leaders have many duties, including keeping detailed records and arbitrating disputes. They receive some benefits, such as exemption from either furnishing irrigation labor or paying a proportion of their land tax, or they can keep part of the revenues from fines levied against those who are delinquent in providing labor.

In irrigation systems worldwide, water is often allocated in proportion to land holdings (Coward 1976, 1979). Farmers who are downstream are more likely to be deprived of their fair share than the farmers who are upstream and can divert water to their fields. Another form of corruption in water allocation occurs when a farmer taps off water out of turn (Price 1995). In one area of Egypt, water theft grows more common the farther one goes from the main canal. These farmers feel justified in taking water out of turn because they feel it helps equalize their share of water, which is less than that of farmers closer to the source. Irrigation organizations everywhere face a major challenge in trying to ensure equitable distribution and prevent water theft.

Cooperatives

Cooperatives are social groups with the economic goal of enhancing production, consumption, or exchange through group action. Cooperatives have two key features: members share any surpluses, and decision making follows the democratic principle of one person, one vote (Estrin 1996). Agricultural and credit cooperatives are the most common forms of cooperatives worldwide, followed by consumer cooperatives.

This section looks at two examples of cooperatives to see how human agency, within different structures, can bring about positive results for producers. In the first, the cooperative gives its members economic strength and checks the power of the richest farmers in one region of India. In the second, craft producers in Panama join together to sell goods in the world market and also build social ties and political leadership skills.

Farmers' Cooperatives in India

In India's western state of Maharashtra, the sugar industry is largely owned and operated through cooperatives (Attwood 1992). Most shareholders are small farmers, producing just one or two acres of sugar cane. Yet the sugar industry, owned and managed cooperatively, is huge—almost as large as the state's iron and steel industry. In contrast, in the northern states where sugar cane is grown, cooperatives are not prominent.

How and why are sugar cooperatives so successful in the western state of Maharashtra but not in northern India? The answer lies in the different patterns of social stratification. The rural social stratification system in Maharashtra is simpler than in northern India. In most villages, the Marathas are the dominant group, but they constitute more of a majority and control more village land than is typical of dominant castes in northern India. They also have stronger local ties with each other because their marital arrangements are locally centralized. Thus they have a better basis for cooperating with each other in spite of class differences among themselves.

Large farmers dominate the elected board of directors of the cooperatives. These "sugar barons" use their position to gain power in state politics. However, within the cooperatives their power is held in check. They do not form cliques that exploit the cooperatives to the detriment of the less wealthy. In fact, large farmers cannot afford to alienate the small and mid-size farmers; that would mean economic ruin for the cooperative and the loss of their own profits. The technology of sugar cane processing requires wide participation of the farmers. Mechanization involves investing in expensive heavy equipment. The machinery cannot be run at a profit unless it is used at full capacity during the crushing season. If small and mid-size farmers were displeased with their treatment, they might decide to pull out of the cooperative and put their cane to other uses. Then capacity would be underused and profits would fall.

Women's Craft Cooperatives in Panama

In Panama's east coastal region, indigenous Kuna women have long sewn beautiful *molas,* or cloth with appliquéd designs. This cloth is made for their own use as clothing (Tice 1995). Since the 1960s, molas have become popular items for sale to tourists coming to Panama and on the world market. Revenue from selling molas is now an important part of the household income of the Kuna.

Some women who make molas for sale continue to operate independently, buying their own cloth and thread and selling their molas either to an intermediary who exports them or in the local tourist market. Many other women have joined cooperatives that offer them greater economic power and security. The cooperative buys cloth and thread in bulk and distributes it to the women. The women are paid almost the entire sale price for each mola, with only a small amount of that price taken out for cooperative dues and administrative costs. Their earnings are steadier than what the fluctuating tourist season offers.

Beyond these economic advantages of joining the cooperative, other benefits include its use as a consumer's cooperative (members can buy rice and sugar in bulk), as a source of mutual support, and as a place for women to develop leadership skills and become politically active.

Self-Help Groups

In recent years, there has been a proliferation of **self-help groups,** or groups formed to achieve specific personal goals (such as coping with illness or bereavement) or lifestyle change (such as trying to exercise more or lose weight). Self-help groups increasingly use the Internet to form virtual support communities. As in their examination of other social groups, anthropologists who study self-help groups focus on why members join, rituals of solidarity, and leadership and organization patterns.

Fieldwork among Alcoholic Anonymous groups in Mexico City reveals that most members are low-income, working-class males (Brandes 2002). The men migrated to Mexico City from rural areas several decades earlier to find work and improve their standard of living. Their drinking problems are related both to their poverty and to the close links between alcohol consumption and male gender identity in Mexico (a "real man" consumes a lot of alcohol). Through a dynamic of shared stories and regular meetings, AA members in Mexico City achieve a high rate of sobriety. The success of AA in Mexico is leading to a rapid proliferation of groups. Membership is growing at about 10 percent a year, a remarkably high rate of growth for a self-help organization. By the end of the twentieth century, Latin America accounted for almost one-third of the world AA membership. Thus a model of a middle-class self-help organization that originated in the United States has been culturally localized by low-income men throughout Latin America.

Stanley Brandes's research involved long-term residence in Mexico City as background but mainly focused on attending AA meetings and discussions with AA members. In contrast, an anthropologist who studied the Breast Cancer Movement in the United States participated in a diverse set of activities in order to gain a comprehensive view of the many activities of the movement's members (see the Methods Close-Up box on p. 450).

Kuna Indian woman selling molas, San Blas Islands, Panama. ■ Research molas on the Internet to find out about the people who make them, the extent to which molas are used in making different products, and how you could buy a mola if you were so inclined. (Source: © Wolfgang Kaehler)

Do research to learn about the current global distribution of Alcoholics Anonymous.

THINKING

OUTSIDE THE BOX

Multi-sited Research to Study the Breast Cancer Movement in the San Francisco Bay Area

IN 1994, Maren Klawiter began to do research about breast cancer activism in the San Francisco Bay area (2000). She started observing a breast cancer support group, and she entered a volunteer training program at the Women's Cancer Resource Center (WCRC) in Berkeley. The WCRC, the first feminist cancer community of its kind in the United States, was a hub of information and activities. Through it, she learned about and became involved in several other projects related to breast cancer activism: Race for the Cure, the Women & Cancer Walk, the Toxic Tour of the Cancer Industry, and the World Conference on Breast Cancer.

For the next several years, Klawiter conducted multi-sited participant observation in a range of settings related to breast cancer: support groups, cancer organizations, cultural events, fund-raisers, educational forums, environmental protests, public hearings, early-detection campaigns, street theater, and conferences and symposia. She supplemented the ethnographic data collected in these settings by interviewing cancer activists, experts, and women living with breast cancer. She describes her research strategy as more intuitive than deliberate—as one of "roving" ethnography, moving from site to site, with full participation and emotional engagement.

The extent of her participation in so many areas of breast cancer activism produced rich insights. For example, she learned that there is no such thing as a monolithic "breast cancer movement." Instead, she found multiple forms of mobilization. She also learned much about social movement formation in general—how movements arise, form, and change. Perhaps most important, she became keenly aware that it is impossible to draw boundaries around breast cancer activism because it is related to so many other areas of life, including her own experience as an involved and active participant researcher.

FOOD FOR THOUGHT

- Think about a social movement to which you belong, or one that you might join, and assume that you are going to conduct ethnographic research on and with the movement. What sites would be involved in the study?

SOCIAL STRATIFICATION

Social stratification, as defined in Chapter 9, refers to differences in wealth or power that separate members of society into hierarchical groups or *strata*. Stratified groups may be unequal to each other on a variety of measures, including material resources, power, human welfare, education, and symbolic attributes. People in groups in higher positions have privileges not enjoyed by those in lower groups, and they are usually interested in maintaining their privileged position. Social stratification appeared late in human history, with the emergence of farming and settled life starting around 12,000 years ago. Now, however, social stratification is widespread.

The major categories of social stratification, defined on the basis of cross-cultural analysis; differ in terms of the process by which one becomes a member of the category. The two major processes are

- **Ascription:** membership on the basis of birth.
- **Achievement:** membership through personal action.

Social groups in which membership is ascriptive include those based on "race," ethnicity, indigeneity, gender, age, and physical ability. These factors are generally beyond the control of the individual, although some flexibility exists for gender (surgery and hormonal treatments) and for certain physical conditions. Also, one can sometimes "pass" as a member of another ethnic group. Age is an unusual ascribed category because an individual, through the lifecycle, occupies different status levels associated with age.

Achievement means that a person belongs to a particular category on the basis of individual attainment. Achievement-based social systems are thus more "open" in terms of mobility within the system. Some scholars of social status believe that increasing social complexity and modernization have led to an increase in achievement-based positions and to a decline in ascription-based positions.

The Concept of Status Groups

Societies place people into categories—student, husband, child, retired person, political leader, baby, or member of Phi Beta Kappa—and these categories carry with them a particular **status**, or position in society (C. Wolf 1996). Some statuses have more prestige than others (in fact, the word *status* can be used to mean prestige, relative value, and worth). Different status groups are often distinguished by a particular lifestyle, including goods owned, leisure activities, and linguistic style. Higher-status groups often maintain power and position through exclusionary social practices in relation to lower-status groups; such practices include in-marriage, residential segregation, and socializing only within the group.

Class: Achieved Status

Ther term **class** refers to a person's or group's position in society, defined primarily in economic terms. In many cultures, class is the most important factor determining a person's status, whereas in others it is less important than other factors, such as birth into a certain family. Class and status, however, do not always match. A rich person may have become wealthy in disreputable ways and hence may never gain high status. Both status and class groups are secondary groups, because a person is unlikely to know every other member of the group, especially in large-scale societies.

In democratic capitalistic societies, the prevailing ideology is that social mobility in the system is an option available to all members. If one chooses to improve one's life, one can supposedly do so through hard work and effort. Some cultural anthropologists refer to this ideology as *meritocratic individualism*—the belief that rewards go to those who work for them and thus deserve them (Durrenberger 2001). In the United States, this popular belief is upheld and promoted in schools and universities, even in the face of substantial evidence to the contrary.

Cultural anthropologists who take a structurist perspective (review Chapter 2) point to how an individual's economic class restricts his or her ability to attain a different lifestyle, even through hard work. A person born rich is more likely to lead a lifestyle typical of that class, just as a person born poor is more likely to lead a lifestyle typical of that class. This position owes much to nineteenth-century political theorist Karl Marx. The concept of class was central to Marx's thinking, as was access of members of particular classes to the "means of production." Writing in the context of Europe's Industrial Revolution and the growth of capitalism, Marx thought that class differences, exploitation of the working class by the owners of capital (those who controlled the means of production), class consciousness among workers, and class conflict were forces of change that would eventually bring the downfall of capitalism.

Race, Ethnicity, Gender, and Caste: Ascribed Status

These major ascribed systems of social stratification are based on the division of people into unequally ranked groups on the basis of characteristics determined by birth. Like members of status and class groups, the people in these categories are in

This gold vase is one of many gold objects excavated from the dozens of elite burial sites in Ukraine, north of the Black Sea, that date from the seventh century BCE. Known mainly as horse-riding pastoralists, the Scythians gained wealth by trading grain with the Greeks. ■ What roles does gold play in your cultural world? (Source: Charles O'Rear/CORBIS)

CHAPTER 15 ■ Social Groups and Social Stratification

secondary social groups, because no one can have a personal relationship with all other members of the group. Each system takes on local characteristics depending on the context. For example, "race" and ethnicity are interrelated and overlapping in much of Latin America, although differences in what they mean in terms of identity and status occur in different contexts (de la Cadena 2001). In some places, the term *mestizaje,* which means "racial mixture," refers to people who are disenfranchised and cut off from their indigenous (Indian) roots. In others, it refers to literate and successful people who retain indigenous cultural practices. In every case, one has to know the local system of categories and meanings attached to them to understand the dynamics of inequality that go with them.

Yet systems based in difference defined in terms of "race," ethnicity, gender, and caste share with each other, and with class-based systems, some important features. First, people in lower-status groups have a lower quality life in terms of employment and income, power, security, esteem, and freedom (Berreman 1979 [1975]:213). Second, those in higher-status groups dominate others. Third, members of the dominant groups tend—consciously or unconsciously—to seek to maintain their position. They do this in two ways: through institutions that control ideology among the dominated and through institutions that physically suppress potential rebellion or subversion by the dominated (Harris 1971, quoted in Mencher 1974:469). Fourth, in spite of efforts to maintain systems of dominance, instances of subversion and rebellion do occur, indicating the potential for agency among disprivileged people and groups.

"Race" and Racism

As noted in earlier chapters of this book, the concept of "race" as referring to inborn, biological features has no scientific merit. In Western society this now discredited concept has historical roots in the meeting, on unequal footing, of formerly separate groups through colonization, slavery, and other large-group movements (Sanjek 1994). Europe's "age of discovery," beginning in the 1500s, ushered in a new era of global contact and a new stage for social stratification. In contrast, in relatively homogeneous cultures, ethnicity is usually a more important distinction than "race." Contemporary Nigeria, for example, has a relatively homogeneous population, and ethnicity is the more salient term for perceived group differences (Jinadu 1994).

A key feature of "racial thinking" is its insistence that behavioral differences among peoples are natural, inborn, or biologically caused. Throughout the history of

Boys in a small town of Brazil exhibit some of the diversity of skin color in the Brazilian population. ■ If you were a census taker and had to categorize the "race" of these boys on the basis of physical features, what categories would you use? (Source: © David G. Houser/CORBIS)

CRITICAL THINKING

What Is Missing from This Picture?

READ THE FOLLOWING summary from a news item entitled "Baseball Team Members Who Used KKK Symbol Will Receive Multi-Cultural Training" (*Jet* 1996). Then consider how anthropological research could provide a fuller understanding of racism in its social context:

A county school board in Virginia opted not to punish members of the state champion high school baseball team who used a Ku Klux Klan symbol. The team members drew the symbol in the dirt before games for good luck. Investigators believe that the symbol represents four hooded Klansmen looking down a hole, the last thing that an African American victim would see after being dropped down a well by Klansmen. The school superintendent decided to reprimand the coaches, and the school board voted to send the students for "multicultural training."

This brief news item tells us some things about the case but provides little information that would lead to deeper understanding of the cultural context. If a cultural anthropologist decided to do in-depth fieldwork in the community, what kinds of research questions would be most important? Here are some examples:

- The ethnic composition of the team.
- The ethnic composition of the school leadership (superintendent), coaches, and other local leaders.
- Patterns of social stratification in the community in which the school is located.
- Other possible forms of racist thinking and behavior in the community.
- Any generational differences that might exist in racist thinking and behavior in this community.
- The reactions of different community members to the behavior of members of the high-school baseball team; the reactions of the coaches; the reactions to the school superintendent's decision about how to treat the baseball players.
- Social programs in the schools and wider community that might reduce racism.

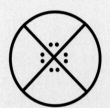

Ku Klux Klan symbol

CRITICAL THINKING QUESTIONS

- How does cultural anthropology differ from journalism in terms of research goals and methods?
- How does cultural anthropology differ from journalism in terms of research results and how they are presented?
- What are the comparative strengths and weaknesses of each approach?

racial categorizations in the West, features such as head size, head shape, and brain size have been accepted as the reasons for behavioral differences. Writing early in the twentieth century, Franz Boas contributed to de-coupling supposed racial attributes from behavior (review Chapter 1). He showed that people from different cultures who had the same head size behaved differently and that people within the same culture who had different head sizes behaved similarly. For Boas and his followers, culture, not biology, is the key explanation for differences in human behavior. In spite of some progress in reducing racism in the United States in the twentieth century, racial discrimination persists. (See the Critical Thinking box.)

Racial classifications in the Caribbean are complicated systems of status classification. This complexity results from the variety of contact over the centuries between peoples from Europe, Africa, Asia, and indigenous populations. Skin tone is a common basis of racial classification, but it is mixed with other physical features and economic status as well. In Haiti, for example, racial categories take into account physical factors such as skin texture, depth of skin tone, hair color and appearance, and facial features (Trouillot 1994). They also include a person's income, social origin, education, personality, and kinship ties. A person's "race" depends on a combination of these many variables. For example, a person with certain physical features who is poor will be considered of a different "race" than a rich person with the same physical features.

The South African policy of *apartheid*, legal segregation of Whites and Blacks, was an extreme example of racial stratification. White dominance in South Africa began in the early 1800s with European migration and settlement there. Slavery was abolished in the 1830s, but increasingly racist thinking developed among Whites at the same time (Johnson 1994). Racist images of the African population served as the rationale for colonial domination instead of outright slavery. In spite of years of African resistance to White domination, the Whites succeeded in maintaining and increasing their control for nearly two centuries.

Black South Africans constituted 90 percent of the population, but this numerical majority was dominated, through apartheid, by the White minority until 1994. Every aspect of life for the majority of Black Africans was worse than for the Whites. Every measure of life quality—infant mortality, longevity, education—showed great disparity between the Whites and the Black Africans. In addition to physical deprivation, they experienced psychological suffering through constant insecurity about raids by the police and other forms of violence.

Since the end of apartheid, many social changes have taken place. One study describes the early stages of the dismantling of apartheid in the city of Umtata, the capital of the Transkei (Johnson 1994). Before the end of apartheid, Umtata "was like other South African towns: all apartheid laws were in full force; public and private facilities were completely segregated; only whites could vote or serve in the town government; whites owned all the major economic assets" (viii). When the change came, Umtata's dominant Whites bitterly resisted at first. They did not want to lose their privileges, and they feared reprisals by the Black Africans. There were no reprisals, however. Instead, the initial stages of transition brought "neoapartheid," in which White privilege was not seriously threatened. Here, as in other colonized regions, even with independence and legal rights to their land having been restored to indigenous peoples, it has been extremely difficult to undo decades of domination.

In contrast to the explicitly racist discrimination of South African apartheid, racism also exists within contexts where no public policies or discourse about race are found—where instead there is racism with public silence (Sheriff 2000). In such contexts, the silence works to allow racial discrimination to continue in ways that may be fully as effective as a clearly stated policy such as apartheid—or perhaps more effective because it is more difficult to critique and dismantle an institution whose existence is denied. Brazil is a prime example. Brazil's public image is that of a country where race does not significantly affect people's quality of life. It is maintained that all races live together in harmony, and that Brazil is a success story in terms of racial diversity. The reality, however, is that Brazil's extreme economic inequality tends to place people who are considered "white" at the top of the class hierarchy and people who are considered "black" at the bottom.

In the United States, discrimination on the basis of race is against the law, as is discrimination on many other grounds. But even with such laws, racism and discrimination can and do occur in many areas of life—from getting jobs and pay raises to housing and educational quality. A less commonly considered aspect of racism in the United States is the neglect of the cultural heritage of minority groups. Many archaeologists are committed to changing this situation.

In 2003, the Treatment Action Campaign began a program of civil disobedience to prompt the government of South Africa to sign and implement a National Prevention and Treatment Plan for HIV/AIDS. TAC uses images of Hector Peterson, the first youth killed in the Soweto uprising against apartheid, and slogans such as "The Struggle Continues: Support HIV/AIDS Treatment Now." ■ Take a position, and be prepared to defend it, on whether the government should take responsibility for preventing and treating HIV/AIDS in any country, rich or poor. (Source: © Gideon Mendel/ CORBIS)

CROSSING
THE FIELDS

**The Role of
Archaeology
in an African
American Cultural
Heritage Project**

S ituated in western Massachusett's Berkshire Hills is a United States National Landmark site, the "Boyhood Home of William Edward Burghardt Du Bois." Anyone
passing by this site in the early 1990s would have seen a field containing scrub
bushes, poison ivy, an abandoned cellar hole, a chimney base, shards of dinner plates
and pieces of broken glass, and metal remains of tools, fences, hardware, and household appliances (Paynter et al. 1994). A small plaque attached to a fence post marked
the site but provided no further information. Michael Paynter, an archaeologist who
visited the site, comments, "A place of historical significance on the contemporary landscape should be a site for remembering . . ." (p. 285), as are Mount Vernon and Independence Hall. Instead, the Du Bois Boyhood Home was a place for forgetting an
important part of American history.

W. E. B. Du Bois was born in Great Barrington, Massachusetts, in 1868. He was one
of the foremost scholar–activists of the twentieth century. After receiving B.A. and
M.A. degrees from Fisk University, he went to Harvard University, where he wrote a dissertation on the African slave trade to the United States and received a doctorate. In
1899 he published a book entitled *The Philadelphia Negro,* the first urban ethnography created in the United States. He became a professor at Atlanta University, where
he supervised a comprehensive study of African American life, which was published in
fifteen volumes. He was a prolific writer throughout his career.

Beyond his academic work, he was a social activist and organizer. He founded the
Niagara Movement, an African American civil rights movement that shaped the subse-
quent formation of the National Association for the Advancement of Colored People
(NAACP). He died in Ghana at the age of ninety-five.

Du Bois spent many of his early years in the Great Barrington house and vacationed
there during the 1930s. It was a place that nurtured his thinking and writing, and it is
a significant landmark in African American history, American history more generally,
and international history as well.

Archaeologist Robert Paynter of the University of Massachusetts at Amherst became
involved with the site in 1983 and organized summer field schools there. As an historical archaeologist, his goal is to document the artifacts from the site, develop a description of the life of the people associated with the artifacts, and ultimately call attention
to the site and its importance. He and his team of students are aided in their work by
the vast amount of archival documentation available, including two autobiographies.
These writings provide an inside view of life at the site and help the researchers avoid
one of the common problems of African American archaeology: interpreting African
American lives through sources written by White people, which might be plagued
by distortions. As noted by Paynter, the detailed and rich reconstruction of life at the
Du Bois Boyhood Home is one way to help overcome the "cultural amnesia" in the
United States concerning African American history and to combat racism through public education. ■

FOOD FOR THOUGHT

■ Find out about more this site and other African American National Landmarks in the
United States.

Ethnicity

Ethnicity is a sense of group membership based on a sense of identity on grounds such as a shared history, language, religion, or region. *Ethnic group* is often considered a synonym for *minority group* and thus often implies lesser social standing. A rich diversity of ethnic populations, in some views, is a positive feature of a country. Many modern states, however, seek to manage ethnicity within their populations so that it does not threaten internal security.

China has one of the most formalized systems in the world for monitoring its many ethnic groups (Wu 1990). The official policy on ethnic minorities refers to non-Han groups because the Han, being the majority population, are not considered an ethnic group. The government lists a total of fifty-four ethnic groups, which together account for about 95 percent of the total population. The non-Han minorities occupy about 60 percent of China's land mass and are located in border areas. Criteria for defining an ethnic group include language, territory, economy, and "psychological disposition." The Chinese government establishes strict definitions of group membership and group characteristics. It even sets standards for ethnic costumes and dances.

The Chinese treatment of the Tibetan people has been severe and can be considered an attempt at *ethnocide* (annihilation of the culture of an ethnic group by a dominant group). In 1951, China forcibly incorporated Tibet, and the Chinese government undertook measures to bring about the social and economic transformation of what was formerly a decentralized, Buddhist feudal regime. This transformation has brought increasing ethnic conflict between Tibetans and Han Chinese, including demonstrations by Tibetans and crackdowns by the Chinese.

People of one ethnic group who move from their home area to another are often at risk of exclusionary treatment and discrimination by the local residents. Roma, or gypsies, are a **diaspora population,** a dispersed group living outside their original homeland. They are scattered throughout Europe and the United States. Their history is one of mobility and marginality since they first left India around the year 1000 (Fonseca 1995). They are universally marginalized and looked down on by the settled populations.

The traditional Roma lifestyle is one of movement, and temporary camps of their wagons often appear overnight on the outskirts of a town. For decades, European governments have tried to force the Roma to settle down. Roma migration to cities throughout continental Europe has increased in the past several years because of unemployment and the declining standard of living in rural areas. For example, in Budapest, Hungary, the Roma minority is the most disadvantaged ethnic group

THINKING
OUTSIDE
THE BOX

With which ethnic or other kind of social group do you identify? What are the bases of this identification? Is your social group relatively high or low in terms of overall social status in your home country?

A Roma encampment in Romania's Transylvania region. Not all European Roma are poor. Some urban Roma have become wealthy and have aroused the jealousy of the non-Roma population. ■ What is an example of a socially outcast group that you may have encountered in your microculture? (Source: © Bruno Barbey/Magnum Photos)

(Ladányi 1993). Although a few Roma in Budapest have gained wealth, most live in substandard housing in the slum inner areas of the city. Since the end of state socialism, discrimination against Roma people has increased. Roma houses have been torched, and their children have been harassed while going to school.

A less difficult adjustment, but still not an easy one, is being experienced by Indo-Canadians (immigrants from India to Canada). In research among a sample of nearly three hundred Indo-Canadians in Vancouver, British Columbia, nearly half of the respondents reported experiencing some form of discrimination in the recent past (Nodwell and Guppy 1992). The percentage was higher among men (54 percent) than among women (45 percent). The higher level for men was consistent across the four categories: verbal abuse, property damage, workplace discrimination, and physical harm. Verbal abuse, reported by 40 percent of both men and women, was the most frequent form of discrimination. Indo-Canadians of the Sikh faith who were born in India say that they experience the highest levels of discrimination in Canada. Apparently, however, their actual experience of discrimination is not greater than that of other Indo-Canadians.

The difference is that Sikhs who were born in India are more sensitive to discrimination than others. Sikhism, as taught and practiced in India, supports a strong sense of honor, which should be protected and, if wronged, avenged. This study helps explain differences in perception of discrimination among ethnic migrants. It does not explain why such high levels of discriminatory treatment exist in a nation committed to ethnic tolerance.

Gender and Sexism

Like other forms of social inequality, gender inequalities, based on perceived differences between people born male or female or somewhere in between, vary from one culture to another. This book has already presented many examples of gender inequality, and more will appear in later chapters. This section highlights some features of male dominance cross-culturally.

Patriarchy, or male dominance in economic, political, social, and ideological domains, is common but not universal. It also varies in severity and results. In its most severe forms, women and girls are completely under the power of men and can be killed by men with no societal response. So-called *honor killings*, for example, of girls and women who defy rules of virginity or arranged marriage and are murdered by male kin, are examples of extreme patriarchy (Kurkiala 2003). Less violent but also serious is the effect of patriarchy on girls' education. In many countries, girls are not sent to school at all, or if they are, they attend for fewer years or attend schools of lower quality than their brothers.

The logical opposite of patriarchy is **matriarchy,** or female dominance in economic, political, social, and ideological domains. Matriarchy is so rare in contemporary cultures that anthropologists are not certain that it even exists—or has ever existed. Among the Iroquois at the time the European colonialists arrived, women controlled public finances, in the form of maize, and they determined whether or not war would be waged. They also chose the leaders, although the leaders were male. It is not clear whether the Iroquois were matriarchal or might better be thought of gender egalitarian, with a mixed system of gender-based status and power. A stronger case for a matriarchal system is found in the Minangkabau people of Malaysia and Indonesia (Sanday 2002).

Immigrant farm workers from India pick strawberries on a commercial fruit farm in Kent, southern England. Immigrants from Great Britain's former colonies constitute a large and growing percentage of the population. ■ Do some research to find out about numbers of legal immigrants in your home country in the most current year for which you can find data. What are the major sending countries? (Source: © Caroline Penn/ Panos Pictures)

Caste and Casteism

The caste system is a type of social stratification found in its clearest form in India, among its Hindu population. With the migration of Hindus out of India over the past few hundred years, aspects of the caste system have spread to places such as Nepal, Sri Lanka, and Fiji. The caste system is particularly associated with Hindu peoples because ancient Hindu scriptures define the major social categories, called *varnas* (a Sanskrit word meaning "color"). The four varnas are the *brahmans*, who were priests; the *kshatriya*, or warriors; the *vaishya*, or merchants; and the *shudras*, or laborers. Of these, men of the first three varnas could go through a ritual ceremony and thereafter wear a sacred thread. These three categories are referred to as "twice-born," and their status is higher than that of the shudra varna.

Beneath the four varna groups were people considered so low that they were outside the caste system itself (hence the word *outcast*). Throughout history, people in this category have been referred to by many names in Indian languages and by the English term *untouchable*. Mahatma Gandhi, a member of an upper caste, renamed them *harijans* ("children of god") as part of his attempt to raise their status and improve their treatment. Currently, members of this category have adopted the term **dalit** (meaning "oppressed" or "ground down") as their favored name.

The four varna categories and the dalits contain within them many locally named groups called *castes*, or, more appropriately, *jatis*. The term **caste** is a Portuguese word meaning "breed" or "type" and was first used by Portuguese colonialists in the fifteenth century to refer to the closed social groups they encountered (Cohn 1971). *Jati*, which means "birth group," conveys that a Hindu is born into his or her group—membership is an ascribed status. Just as the four varnas are ranked relative to each other, so are all the jatis within them. For example, the jati of brahmans can be divided first into priestly and nonpriestly subgroups; the priestly brahmans into household priests, temple priests, and funeral priests; and the household priests into two or more endogamous (in-marrying) groups and then into lineages (Parry 1996:77). In terms of hierarchy, nonpriestly brahmans are superior to priestly ones, and household priests are superior to funeral priests.

Indian anthropologist M. N. Srinivas (1959) contributed the concept of the **dominant caste** to refer to the tendency for one caste in any particular village to control most of the land and, often, to be numerically preponderant as well. Brahmans are at the top of the social hierarchy in terms of ritual purity, and they are frequently, though not always, the dominant caste. For example, in much of northern India, the dominant caste is often from the kshatriya varna. This is the case in Pahansu village, where a group called the Gujars is dominant (Raheja 1988). The Gujars are the numerical majority, and they control most of the land (see Figure 15.2). Moreover, they dominate in the **jajmani system,** a patron–provider system in which landholding patrons (*jajmans*) are linked, through exchanges of food for services, with brahman priests, artisans (blacksmiths, potters), agricultural laborers, and other workers such as sweepers (Kolenda 1978:46–54).

Some anthropologists see the jajmani system as one of mutual interdependence that provides security for the less well-off. Others say that the system benefits those at the top to the detriment of those at the bottom and view it and the entire caste system as exploitative (Mencher 1974). The first interpretation is based on research conducted among the upper castes who present this view. From low-caste people's perspective, however, it is the patrons who have the power. Dissatisfied patrons can dismiss service providers, refuse them loans, or not pay them. Service providers

Only a special category of brahman priests can officiate at the Chidhambaram temple in south India. Here, members of an age-mixed group sit for a moment's relaxation. ■ Name some other groups in which membership cuts across age differences. (Source: Barbara Miller)

FIGURE 15.2

Caste ranking in Pahansu village, north India.

Caste Name	Traditional Occupation	Number of Households	Occupation in Pahansu
Gujar	farmer	210	owner cultivator
Brahman	priest	8	priest, postman
Baniya	merchant	3	shopkeeper
Sunar	goldsmith	2	silversmith, sugar cane press operator
Dhiman (Barhai)	carpenter	1	carpenter
Kumhar	potter	3	potter, tailor
Nai	barber	3	barber, postman
Dhobi	washerman	2	washerman
Gadariya	shepherd	4	agricultural laborer, weaver
Jhivar	water-carrier	20	agricultural laborer, basket-weaver
Luhar	ironsmith	2	blacksmith
Teli	oil-presser	2	beggar, cotton-carder, agricultural laborer
Maniharan	bangle-seller	1	bangle-seller
Chamar	leatherworker	100	agricultural laborer
Bhangi	sweeper	17	sweeper, midwife

(*Source:* From p. 19 in *The Poison in the Gift: Ritual, Prestation, and the Dominant Caste in a North Indian Village* by Gloria Goodwin Raheja. Copyright © 1988. Reprinted by permission of The University of Chicago Press.)

who are dissatisfied with the treatment they receive from their patrons have little recourse. In addition, male patrons often demand sexual relations with women of service-providing households. No matter which view one takes, it is clear that the jajmani system is being weakened by the growth of industrial manufacturing and marketing, which has reduced the need for some service providers, especially tailors, potters, and weavers. Because there is less need for their skills in the countryside, many former service providers have left the villages to work in urban areas. The ties that remain the strongest are with brahman priests, whose ritual services cannot be replaced by machines.

Several mechanisms maintain the caste system: marriage rules, spatial segregation, and ritual. Marriage rules strictly enforce jati endogamy (marriage within the jati). Marriage outside one's jati, especially in rural areas and particularly between a higher-caste female and a lower-caste male, is cause for serious, even lethal, punishment by caste elders and other local power-holders. Among urban educated elites, the trend is to allow inter-jati marriages, but such marriages are still not preferred by parents of marriage-age children.

Social mobility within the caste system has traditionally been limited, but there have been many instances of group "up-casting." Strategies include gaining wealth, merger with a next-higher jati, education, migration, and political activism (Kolenda 1978). Behavioral change is involved, too, in terms of taking on aspects of the dress and behavior of higher groups, including men wearing the sacred thread, vegetarianism, non-remarriage of widows, seclusion of women from the public, and giving of larger dowries for the marriage of a daughter.

Discrimination on the basis of caste was made illegal by the Indian constitution of 1949, but constitutional decree did not bring an end to these deeply structured inequalities. The government of India has instituted policies to promote the social and economic advancement of dalits, such as reserving places for them in medical schools, seats in the government, and public-sector jobs. This "affirmative action" plan has infuriated many of the upper castes, especially brahmans, who feel most threatened. Is the caste system on the decline? There is no question that aspects of it

A village carpenter in front of his house in a north Indian village. The status position of carpenters is mid-level, between the landholding elites or brahman priests and those who deal with polluting materials such as animal hides or refuse. ■ In your culture, what social status do carpenters, tool-makers, or other skilled manual laborers have? (Source: Barbara Miller)

are changing. Especially in large cities, people of different jatis can "pass" and participate on a more nearly equal basis in public life—if they have the economic means to do so.

CIVIL SOCIETY

Civil society consists of the social domain of diverse interest groups that function outside the government to organize economic, political, and other aspects of life. According to the German philosopher Hegel, civil society encompasses the social groups and institutions between the individual and the state (K. Kumar 1996:89). Later, Italian social theorist Gramsci wrote that there are two basic types of civic institutions: those that support the state and those that oppose state power. This section discusses recent findings from cultural anthropology on both types of institutions.

Civil Society for the State: The Chinese Women's Movement

In many instances, governments seek to build civil society to further their goals. The women's movement in China is an example of such a state-created organization. A policy goal of the Chinese government is to improve the quality of women's lives, and the Women's Federations were formed to help achieve that goal (Judd 2002). The government oversees the operation at all levels, from the national level down to the township and village. The primary objective is to mobilize women, especially rural women, to participate in literacy training and market activities.

Canadian cultural anthropologist Ellen Judd conducted a study of the women's movement in China, within the constraints that the government imposes on anthropological fieldwork by foreigners. Under Mao, foreign anthropologists were not allowed to do research of any sort in China. The situation began to change in the 1980s, when some field research became possible. But even now, the Chinese government imposes strict limitations, keeping foreigners at a distance from everyday life.

Judd has developed a long-term relationship with China over several decades, having lived there as a student from 1974 to 1977 and then undertaking long-term fieldwork there in 1986. Since 1986 she has returned almost every year for research or some other activity, such as being involved in a development project for women or attending the Beijing Fourth World Conference on Women. Through all of these activities, she gained some knowledge of Chinese women's lives, from different angles and over time.

In her latest project on the Chinese women's movement, she wanted to conduct research as a cultural anthropologist would normally do, through intensive participant observation over a long period of time. But she was not permitted to join the local women's organization. Nor could she speak privately with any of the women in the organization. Officials accompanied her on all household visits and interviews. She was allowed to attend meetings, however, and she was given access to all the public information about the goals of the Women's Federations.

Judd's fieldwork, constrained as it was by government regulations and oversight, nevertheless yielded some insights. She learned, through interviews with women members, about some women who have benefited from the programs. She discovered the important role that education plays in preparing women for market activities. The book she wrote is largely descriptive, focusing on the "public face" of the Women's Federations in one locale. Such a descriptive account is the most that can be expected from research in China at this time. Given that the women's organizations are formed by and for the government, this example stretches the concept of civil society beyond its limits.

Activist Groups

Activist groups are groups formed with the goal of changing certain conditions, such as political repression, violence, and human rights violations. In studying activist groups, cultural anthropologists are interested in learning what motivates the formation of such groups, what their goals and strategies are, and what leadership patterns they exhibit. Sometimes anthropologists join the efforts of activist groups and use their knowledge to support these groups' goals (see the Lessons Applied box on p. 462).

Many activist groups are initiated and organized by women. CO-MADRES of El Salvador is an important, women-led social movement in Latin America (Stephen 1995). CO-MADRES is a Spanish abbreviation for an organization called, in English, the Committee of Mothers and Relatives of Political Prisoners, Disappeared, and Assassinated of El Salvador. It was founded in 1977 by a group of mothers protesting the atrocities committed by the Salvadoran government and military. During the civil war that lasted from 1979 until 1992, a total of 80,000 people died and 7000 more disappeared—one in every 100 El Salvadorans.

The initial group comprised nine mothers. A year later, it had grown to nearly thirty members, including some men. In 1979 the group made its first international trip to secure wider recognition. This developed into a full-fledged and successful campaign for international solidarity in the 1980s, with support in other Latin American countries, Europe, Australia, the United States, and Canada. The group's increased visibility resulted in repression from the government. Its office was bombed in 1980 and several times since then. Forty-eight members of CO-MADRES have been detained since 1977; five were assassinated. Harassment and disappearances continued even after the signing of the Peace Accords in January 1992: "In February 1993, the son and the nephew of one of the founders of CO-MADRES were assassinated in Usulutan. This woman had already lived through the experience of her own detention, the detention and gang rape of her daughter, and the disappearance and assassination of other family members" (814).

In the 1990s, CO-MADRES focused on holding the state accountable for human rights violations during the civil war, as well as on some new areas, such as providing better protection for political prisoners, seeking assurances of human rights protection in the future, working against domestic violence, educating women about political participation, and initiating economic projects for women. The work of CO-MADRES, throughout its history, has incorporated elements of both the "personal" and the "political"—concerns of mothers and other family members for lost kin and for exposing and halting abuses of the state and military. The lesson learned from the case of CO-MADRES is that activist groups formed by women may well be based on issues related to the domestic domain (murdered children and other kin), but their activities can extend to the top of the public political hierarchy.

Another example of activist group formation under difficult conditions comes from urban Egypt (Hopkins and Mehanna 2000). The Egyptian government frowns on extra-governmental political action. Although Egyptian citizens are deeply concerned about environmental issues such as waste disposal, noise, and clean air and water, group formation for environmental causes is not easily accomplished. People interviewed in Cairo reported that they rarely discuss environmental issues with one another. One example of environmental concern, however, did result in the closing

Cultural Anthropology and Community Activism in Papua New Guinea

A CONTROVERSIAL ISSUE in applied anthropology is whether or not an anthropologist should take on the role of a community activist or act as an advocate on behalf of the people among whom he or she has conducted research (Kirsch 2002). Some say that anthropologists should maintain a neutral position in a conflict situation and simply offer information on issues—information that may be used by either side. Others say that it is appropriate and right for anthropologists to take sides and help support less powerful groups against more powerful groups. Those who endorse anthropologists' taking an activist or advocacy role argue that neutrality is never truly neutral: By seemingly taking no position, one indirectly supports the status quo, and information provided to both sides will generally serve the interests of the more powerful side in any case.

Stuart Kirsch took on an activist role after conducting field research for over fifteen years in a region of Papua New Guinea that has been negatively affected by a large copper and gold mine called the Ok Tedi mine. The mine releases 80,000 tons of mining waste into the local river system daily, causing extensive environmental damage that affects people's food and water sources. Kirsch has joined with the local community in their extended legal and political campaign to limit further pollution and to gain compensation for damages suffered. He explains his involvement with the community as a form of reciprocal exchange. The community members have provided him with information about their culture for over fifteen years. He believes that his knowledge is part of the people's cultural property and that they have a rightful claim to its use.

Kirsch's support of the community's goals took several forms. First, his scholarly research provided documentation of the problems of the people living downstream from the mine. Community activists incorporated his findings in their speeches when traveling in Australia, Europe, and the Americas to spread awareness of their case and gather international support. During the 1992 Earth Summit, one community leader presented the media with excerpts from an article by Kirsch during a press conference held aboard the Greenpeace ship *Rainbow Warrior II* in the Rio de Janeiro harbor. Second, Kirsch worked closely with local leaders, helping them decide how best to convey their views to the public and in the court. Third, he served as a cultural broker in discussions among community members, politicians, mining executives, lawyers, and representatives of non-governmental organizations (NGOs) in order to promote solutions for the problems faced by people living downstream from the mine. Fourth, in 1999 he convened an international meeting of environmental NGOs in Washington, DC, and secured funding to bring a representative from the community to the meeting.

In spite of official reports recommending that the mine be closed in 2001, its future remains uncertain. No assessment of past damages to the community has been prepared. As the case goes on, Kirsch will continue to support the community's efforts by sharing with them the results of his research, just as they have for so long shared their culture with him. Indigenous people worldwide are increasingly invoking their rights to anthropological knowledge about themselves. According to Kirsch, these claims require anthropologists to rethink their role and their relationship with the people they study. It can no longer be a relationship in which the community provides knowledge and the anthropologist keeps and controls that knowledge for his or her intellectual development alone. Although the details are still being worked out, the overall goal must be collaboration and cooperation.

FOOD FOR THOUGHT

- Consider the pros and cons of anthropological advocacy, and decide what position you would take on the Ok Tedi case. Be prepared to defend your position.

Yonggom people gather at a meeting in Atkamba village on the Ok Tedi River to discuss legal proceedings in 1996. At the end of the meeting, leaders signed an agreement to an out-of-court settlement, which was presented to the Supreme Court of Victoria in Melbourne, Australia. The current lawsuit concerns the Yonggom people's claim that the 1996 settlement agreement has been breached. (Source: Courtesy of Stuart Kirsch)

A march of the "Mothers of the Disappeared" in Argentina. This organization of women combines activism motivated by personal causes (the loss of one's child or children to political torture and death) and wider political concerns (state repressiveness in general). ■ How many activist groups in your culture can you name and what are their goals? (Source: © Peter Menzel/Stock Boston, LLC)

of a highly polluting lead smelter. In this case, the people in the affected neighborhood banded together around this particular issue and called attention to the situation in the public media, prompting high-level officials to take up their case. They were successful partly because their target was localized—one relatively small industry—and also because the industry was so clearly guilty of polluting the environment. This effort, however, did not lead to the formation of an enduring group.

New Social Movements and Cyberpower

Social scientists have begun to use the term *new social movements* to refer to the many new groups that emerged in the late 1980s and 1990s, often as the result of postsocialist transitions, but in other contexts, too (some examples are discussed in Chapter 21 in the context of international development). These groups are often constituted by disprivileged minorities—ethnic groups, women, the poor. Increasingly, they involve networks wider than the immediate social group, and most recently, they have taken advantage of cybertechnology to broaden their membership, exchange ideas, and raise funds (Escobar 2002).

Cyber-enhanced social movements are important new political forces that offer the possibility of new ways to resist, transform, and present alternatives to current political structures. The importance of cybernetworking has, of course, not been lost on formal political leaders, who are paying increased attention to their personal web sites and those of their parties.

THE BIG QUESTIONS REVISITED

■ HOW do social groups vary cross-culturally?

Groups can be classified in terms of whether all members have face-to-face interaction with one another, whether membership is based on ascription or achievement, and how formal the group's organization and leadership structure are. Thus groups extend from the most informal, face-to-face groups, such as those based on friendship, to groups that have formal membership requirements and whose members are widely dispersed and never meet each other. All groups have some criteria for membership, often based on a perceived notion of similarity. Many groups require some sort of initiation of new members, which in some cases involves dangerous or frightening activities that serve to bond members to one another through a shared experience of helplessness.

■ WHAT is social stratification, and what are its effects on people?

Social stratification consists of hierarchical relationships between and among different groups. Stratified intergroup relations are commonly based on categories such as class, "race," ethnicity, gender, age, and ability. The degree of social inequality among different status groups is highly marked in agricultural and industrial societies, whereas status inequalities are not characteristic of foraging societies and are less significant in most pastoralist and horticultural societies. India's caste-based system is an important example of a rigid structure of social inequality based on a birth group.

■ WHAT is civil society?

Civil society consists of groups and organizations that, although they are not part of the formal government, perform functions that are economic or political. Civil society groups can be roughly divided into those that support government policies and initiatives, and thus further the interests of government, and those that oppose government policies and actions, such as environmental protest groups. Some cultural anthropologists who study activist groups decide to take an advocacy role and apply their knowledge to further the goals of the group. This direction in applied anthropology is related to the view that anthropological knowledge is partly the cultural property of the groups who have shared their lives and insights with the anthropologist.

KEY CONCEPTS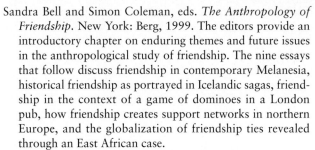

achievement, p. 450
activist group, p. 461
age set, p. 440
ascription, p. 450
caste, p. 458
civil society, p. 460
class, p. 451

cooperative, p. 448
dalit, p. 458
diaspora population, p. 456
dominant caste, p. 458
jajmani system, p. 458
matriarchy, p. 457
patriarchy, p. 457

primary group, p. 440
secondary group, p. 440
self-help group, p. 449
social group, p. 440
status, p. 451
youth gang, p. 445

SUGGESTED READINGS

Sandra Bell and Simon Coleman, eds. *The Anthropology of Friendship*. New York: Berg, 1999. The editors provide an introductory chapter on enduring themes and future issues in the anthropological study of friendship. The nine essays that follow discuss friendship in contemporary Melanesia, historical friendship as portrayed in Icelandic sagas, friendship in the context of a game of dominoes in a London pub, how friendship creates support networks in northern Europe, and the globalization of friendship ties revealed through an East African case.

Gerald Berreman. *Caste and Other Inequities: Essays on Inequality*. Delhi: Folklore Institute, 1979. These eighteen essays on caste and social inequality in India were written

over a period of twenty years. Topics include caste and economy, caste ranking, caste and social interaction, and a comparison of caste with race in the United States.

Christopher Boehm. *Hierarchy in the Forest: The Evolution of Egalitarian Behavior*. Cambridge, MA: Harvard University Press, 2001. This book, by a primatologist, asks what an egalitarian society is and how such societies evolved. Boehm traces egalitarian and despotic traits, as well as altruism, to their roots in nonhuman primate groups and early human groups.

Stanley Brandes. *Staying Sober in Mexico City*. Austin: University of Texas Press, 2002. This ethnography of Alcoholics Anonymous groups in Mexico City focuses on how AA groups help low-income men remain sober through social support. Although he emphasizes the role of human agency in these men's attempts to remain sober, the author reminds us that the high rate of alcoholism among poor Mexican men must be viewed in the context of structural conditions that make life very difficult.

Thomas A. Gregor and Donald Tuzin, eds. *Gender in Amazonia and Melanesia: An Exploration of the Comparative Method,* 2001. Two anthropologists, one a specialist on indigenous peoples of Amazonia and the other on Papua New Guinea, are the editors of this volume, which includes a theoretical overview chapter and then several chapters addressing similarities and differences between cultures of the two regions in domains such as fertility cults, rituals of masculinity, gender politics, and age-based gender roles.

Steven Gregory and Roger Sanjek, eds. *Race*. New Brunswick, NJ: Rutgers University Press, 1994. Each editor provides an introductory chapter. Seventeen other contributions cover aspects of racism in the United States and the Caribbean, how race interacts with other inequalities, and racism in higher education and anthropology.

Celeste Ray. *Highland Heritage: Scottish Americans in the American South*. Chapel Hill: University of North Carolina Press, 2001. This ethnography explores how Highland Scottish folklore and values merge with southern regional myths to produce a unique cultural identity among Scottish Americans in North Carolina. The author examines the role of people's memory of an ancestral past in creating a new community and new public rituals, such as the Tartan parade, in the present.

W. G. Runciman, ed. *The Origin of Social Institutions*. New York: Oxford University Press, 2001. This collection includes nine chapters, some by archaeologists and others by cultural anthropologists and evolutionists. They address a variety of topics, including archaeological evidence of Late Paleolithic village hierarchies in the Levant, the birth of architecture and its links to political power in early chiefdoms, the evolution of fairness norms, and social competition through cooking.

Pat Shipman. *The Evolution of Racism*. New York: Simon and Schuster, 1994. Beginning in 1857, with Darwin's publication of *On The Origin of Species*, this book traces thinking about evolution and its historic relationship with various forms of racist thinking and policies. An epilogue, entitled "Valuing Differences," considers the contemporary role of genetics in defining difference and its value in debunking the outdated notion of biological race based on phenotype.

Cris Shore and Stephen Nugent, eds. *Elite Cultures: Anthropological Perspectives*. New York: Routledge, 2002. Two introductory chapters and a concluding chapter frame twelve ethnographic cases from around the world. The major issues addressed are how elites in different societies maintain their positions, how elites represent themselves to others, how anthropologists study elites, and the implications of research on elites for the discipline of anthropology.

Miriam T. Stark, ed. *The Archaeology of Social Boundaries*. Washington, DC: Smithsonian Institution Press, 1998. Stark provides an introductory chapter describing how analysis of material culture can reveal boundaries of social groups in the past. Eight case studies address specific topics, including foragers' use of space in the Kalahari desert of southern Africa, pottery styles in West Africa, adobe architectural style in the American southwest, and Algonquian and Iroquois ceramic traditions. Two concluding chapters discuss aspects of theory and method.

Kevin A. Yelvington. *Producing Power: Ethnicity, Gender, and Class in a Caribbean Workplace*. Philadelphia, PA: Temple University Press, 1995. This ethnography examines class, race, and gender inequalities as linked processes of social stratification within the context of a factory in Trinidad and in the wider social sites of households, neighborhoods, and global interconnections.

Karin Tice. *Kuna Crafts, Gender and the Global Economy*. Austin: University of Texas Press, 1995. This ethnographic study looks at how the tourist market has affected women's production of molas in Panama and how women have organized into cooperatives to improve their situation.

THE BIG QUESTIONS

- WHAT does political anthropology cover?
- WHAT is the scope of legal anthropology?
- HOW are political and legal systems changing?

Political and Legal Systems

A political leader of the Ashanti people, Ghana. British colonialists referred to such leaders with the English term "chief" though the term "king" might have been more appropriate. (Source: © Henning Christoph/DAS FOTOARCHIV/Peter Arnold)

Recent headlines:

- Violence Continues in Iraq
- School Bus Fees Anger Parents
- Rebels in Nepal Postpone Peace Talks
- 1.7 Tons of Cocaine Seized Off Colombia
- North Korea Says It Has Nuclear Arms

These events are cultural happenings related to public power and politics. Anthropologists in all four fields address political and legal topics. Archaeologists study the evolution of centralized forms of political organization and the physical manifestations of power in monumental architecture, housing, and material possessions. Primatologists do research on dominance relationships, coalitions, and aggression among nonhuman primates. Linguistic anthropologists analyze power differences in interpersonal speech, the media, political propaganda, and more. Cultural anthropologists study cross-cultural patterns of power and politics, social control, and social conflict.

This chapter covers topics in political and legal anthropology, two subfields of cultural anthropology. *Political anthropology*, a subfield of cultural anthropology, addresses the area of human behavior and thought related to power: who has it and who doesn't, degrees of power, the bases of power, abuses of power, relationships between political and religious power, political organization and government, social conflict and social control, and morality and law. *Legal anthropology* is the subfield that addresses issues of social order and conflict resolution cross-culturally. The contemporary relevance of these two subfields is a reflection of heightened concerns worldwide about power, rights, conflict, conflict resolution and conflict prevention.

POLITICS, POLITICAL ORGANIZATION, AND LEADERSHIP

Political anthropology is the cross-cultural study of politics, political organization, and leadership. This section presents some key terms in political anthropology and then reviews four types of political organization.

Politics and Culture

When cultural anthropologists consider the concept of politics, they tend to take a broader view than a political scientist because their cross-cultural data indicate that many kinds of behavior and thought are political—not just formal party politics, voting, and government. Cultural anthropologists offer examples of political systems that are informal and only barely recognizable.

Politics: The Use of Power, Authority, and Influence

The term *politics* refers to the organized use of public power, as opposed to the more private micropolitics of family and domestic groups. **Power** is the ability to bring about results, often through the possession or use of forceful means. Closely related to power are authority and influence. **Authority** is the right to take certain forms of action. It is based on a person's achieved or ascribed status or moral reputation. Authority differs from power in that power is backed up by the potential use of force and can be wielded by individuals without their having authority in the moral sense.

Influence is the ability to achieve a desired end by exerting social or moral pressure on someone or some group. Unlike authority, influence may be exerted from a low-status and marginal position. All three terms are relational. A person's power,

Life Histories Provide Clues about Women's Political Socialization in Korea

A CULTURAL ANTHROPOLOGIST who did field research on women political leaders in the Republic of Korea asked why some women in this male-dominated society seek the role of political leadership (Soh 1993). In order to answer this question, she gathered detailed life histories of women leaders.

Korean women members of the National Assembly can be divided into two categories: elected members (active seekers) and appointed members (passive recipients). Analysis of the life history narratives of both types of female legislators for recurrent themes revealed the importance of their childhood socialization within the family. Elected women legislators, the active political seekers, had atypical family experiences related to the role of their fathers. Either the father was absent or else the father was present and was especially nurturing. Both situations facilitated a girl's development of *yŏgŏl* qualities, or an androgynous personality combining traits of both masculinity and femininity. In contrast, the presence of a "typical" father resulted in a girl's developing a more submissive and passive personality.

Korea is a strongly male-dominated society, so women political leaders represent a "notable deviance" from usual gender roles (54). This deviance is not stigmatized in Korean culture; rather, a *yŏgŏl*—a woman with "manly" accomplishments—is admired. Such a woman's personality traits include extraordinary bravery, strength, integrity, generosity, and charisma. A *yŏgŏl* is usually taller, larger, and stronger than other women and has a more resonant voice.

An intriguing question follows from these findings: What explains the different types of fathers—those who help daughters develop leadership qualities and those who socialize daughters for passivity?

Representative Kim Ok-son greets some of her constituents who are members of a local Confucian club in Seoul, Republic of Korea. She is wearing a men's style suit and has a masculine haircut. (Source: Chunghee Sarah Soh)

FOOD FOR THOUGHT

- In your microcultural experience, what socialization factors might influence boys or girls to become politicians?

---

authority, or influence exists in relation to other people. Power implies the greatest likelihood of a coercive and hierarchical relationship, and authority and influence offer the most scope for consensual, cooperative decision making. Power, authority, and influence are all related to politics, power being the strongest basis for action and decision making—and potentially the least moral.

Politics: A Cultural Universal?

Is politics a human universal? Some anthropologists would say "No." They point to instances of cultures that exhibit scarcely any institutions that can be called political, no durable ranking systems, and very little aggression. Foraging lifestyles, as a model for early human evolution, suggest that nonhierarchical social systems characterized human life for over 90 percent of our prehistory and history. Only with the emergence of private property, surpluses, and other changes did ranking systems, government, formal law, and organized aggression emerge. Also, research shows that dominance-seeking and aggression are learned behaviors, emphasized in some cultures and among some segments of the population, such as the military, and de-emphasized among others, such as religious leaders, healers, and child care providers. (See the Methods Close-Up box.)

Categories of Political Organizations

Political organization is the existence of groups for purposes such as public decision making and leadership, maintaining social cohesion and order, protecting group rights, and ensuring safety from external threats. This section describes several types of political organization, starting with the minimal forms found among foraging groups. Political organizations have several features that resemble some of the features of social groups and organizations discussed in the previous chapter, reflecting the overlap in many cases between social and political groups: criteria for membership, identity markers (clothing, card, title), internal organization (leadership hierarchy), and rules for members (Tiffany 1979).

Cultural anthropologists divide the many forms of political organization that occur cross-culturally into four major types (see Figure 16.1).

Bands

A **band** is the form of political organization found among foragers and comprises between twenty people and a few hundred people, who are related through kinship. Because foraging has been the predominant mode of production for nearly all of human history, the band has been the most long-standing form of political organization. These units come together at certain times of the year, depending on their foraging patterns and ritual schedule.

Band membership is flexible. If a person has a serious disagreement with another person, one option is to leave that band and join another. Leadership is informal,

FIGURE 16.1
Modes of political organization and social control.

FORAGING	HORTICULTURE	PASTORALISM	AGRICULTURE	INDUSTRIALISM (CAPITALIST)
Political Organization				*Political Organization*
Band	Tribe	Chiefdom	Confederacy	State
Leadership				*Leadership*
Band leader	Headman/Headwoman Big-man Big-woman	Chief	Paramount chief	King/queen/president prime minister/emperor
Social Conflict				*Social Conflict*
Face-to-face Small-scale Rarely lethal	Armed conflict Revenge killing	War		International war Technological weapons Massively lethal Ethnic conflict Standing armies
Social Control				*Social Control*
Norms Social pressure Ostracism				Laws Formal judiciary Permanent police Imprisonment

Social Control

Increased population density and residential centralization ⟶
More surpluses of resources and wealth ⟶
More social inequality/ranking ⟶
Less reliance on kinship relations as the basis of political structures ⟶
Increased internal and external social conflict ⟶
Increased power and responsibility of leaders ⟶
Increased burdens on the population to support political organization ⟶

and no one person is named as a permanent leader. Depending on events, such as organizing the group to relocate or to send people out to hunt, a particular person may come to the fore as a leader for that time. This is usually someone whose advice and knowledge about the task are especially respected.

There is no social stratification between leaders and followers. A band leader is the "first among equals." Band leaders have limited authority or influence, but no power. They cannot enforce their opinions. Social leveling mechanisms prevent anyone from accumulating much authority or influence. Political activity in bands involves mainly decision making about migration, food distribution, and resolution of interpersonal conflicts. External conflict between groups is rare because the territories of different bands are widely separated and the population density is low.

The band level of organization barely qualifies as a form of political organization because groups are flexible, leadership is ephemeral, and there are no signs or emblems of political affiliation. Some anthropologists argue that "real" politics did not exist in undisturbed band societies.

Tribes

A **tribe** is a political group that comprises several bands or lineage groups, each with similar language and lifestyle and occupying a distinct territory. Kinship is the primary basis of tribal membership, and tribal groups contain from a hundred to several thousand people. Associated with horticulture and pastoralism, tribal organization developed with the advent of these modes of production (review Chapter 8). Tribal groups may be connected to each other through a **clan** structure in which members claim descent from a common ancestor, although they may be unable to trace the exact relationship. Tribes are found in the Middle East, South Asia, Southeast Asia, the Pacific, and Africa and among Native Americans.

Tribal political organization is more formal than band-level organization. A tribal headman or headwoman (most are male) is formally recognized as a leader. Key qualifications for this position are being hardworking and generous and possessing good personal skills. A headman is a political leader on a part-time basis only, yet this role is more demanding than that of a band leader. Depending on the mode of production, a headman will be in charge of determining the times for moving herds, planting and harvesting, and setting the time for seasonal feasts and celebrations. Internal and external conflict resolution is also his responsibility. A headman relies mainly on authority and persuasion rather than on power. These strategies are effective because tribal members are all kin and have loyalty to each other.

Pastoralist tribal formations are sometimes linked in a confederacy, with local units or segments maintaining substantial autonomy. The local segments meet together rarely, usually at an annual festival. In case of an external threat, the confederacy gathers together. Once the threat is removed, local units resume their autonomy. The equality and autonomy of units, along with their ability to unite and then split, are referred to as a **segmentary model** of political organization. This form of tribal organization is found among pastoralists worldwide (Eickelman 1981).

Big-Man and Big-Woman Systems

In between tribal and chiefdom organizations is the **big-man system** or **big-woman system,** in which certain individuals develop a political following through a system of redistribution based on personal ties and grand feasts (as mentioned in Chapter 11). Research in Melanesia, a large region in the South Pacific, established the existence of the big-man type of politics, and most references to it are from this region

Chief Paul Payakan, leader of the Kayapo, a group of indigenous horticulturalists living in the rainforest of the Brazilian Amazon. Payakan was instrumental in mobilizing widespread resistance in the region to the construction of a hydroelectric dam.
■ Have you read in newspapers, or seen on television, news about the Kayapo or other Amazonian tribes recently? If so, what was the issue? If not, locate an update about the Kayapo on the Web. (Source: © Hank Wittemore/CORBIS SYGMA)

Throughout much of the South Pacific, big-man and big-woman politics has long involved the demonstration of generosity on the part of the leaders, who are expected to be able to mobilize resources for impressive feasts such as this one on Tanna Island. ■ How does this political system resemble or differ from a political system with which you are familiar? (Source: © Kal Muller/Woodfin Camp & Associates)

(Sahlins 1963, Strathern 1971). Personalistic, favor-based political groupings are found in other regions, too, however.

Unlike a tribal headman, a big-man or big-woman has a wider following that includes people in several villages. A big-man tends to have greater wealth than his followers, although people continue to expect him to be generous. Core supporters of a big-man tend to be kin, with extended networks including non-kin. A big-man has heavy responsibilities in regulating both internal affairs—cultivation—and external affairs—intergroup feasts, exchanges of goods, and war. In some instances, a big-man is assisted in carrying out his responsibilities by a group of other respected men. These councils include people from the big-man's different constituencies.

Big-man political organization is especially important in Papua New Guinea. In several tribes in the Mount Hagen area of the highlands, an aspiring big-man develops his position as a leader through making *moka* (Strathern 1971). Making moka involves exchanging gifts and favors with individuals and sponsoring large feasts where further gift-giving occurs. A crucial factor in big-manship in the Mount Hagen area is having at least one wife. An aspiring big-man urges his wife or wives to work harder than usual in order to grow more food to feed more pigs. Pigs are an important measure of a man's status and worth, and they are one of the most important items of exchange for building political support. Using his wife's (or wives') production as an exchange base, the aspiring big-man extends his political relationships, first with kin and then beyond. By giving gifts to people, he gains prestige over them. Later, the recipient will make a return gift of somewhat greater value. The exchanges go back and forth, over the years. The more he gives, and the more people in his exchange network, the greater prestige the big-man develops. Periodically, a successful big-man caps off his regular exchange efforts by staging a grand moka at which he will distribute many noteworthy and important gifts, perhaps even a jeep.

Although big-manship is an achieved position, analysis of the family patterns of big-manship in the Mt. Hagen area shows that most big-men are the sons of big-men (see Table 16.1). This is especially true of major big-men, of whom over three-quarters were sons of former big-men.

With few exceptions, the early anthropological literature about Melanesian tribal politics portrays men as dominating public exchange networks and the public political arenas. Women are mentioned in their roles as wives, in providing the material basis for men's political careers. A study of Vanatinai, however, a Pacific island that is gender-egalitarian, reveals the existence and importance of big-women as well as

TABLE 16.1

Family background of big-men in Mt. Hagen, Papua New Guinea.

	Father Was a Big-Man	Father Was Not a Big-Man	Totals
Major Big-Men	27	9	36
Minor Big-Men	31	30	61
Total	58	39	97

(*Source*: Table, p. 209, "Family background of Big-Men in Mt. Hagen, Papua New Guinea" from *The Rope of Moka: Big-Men and Ceremonial Exchange in Mount Hagen, New Guinea* by Andrew Strathern. Copyright © 1971. Reprinted by permission of Cambridge University Press.)

big-men (Lepowsky 1990). Although more Vanatinai men than women are involved in political exchange and leadership-building, some women are extremely active. These women lead sailing expeditions to neighboring islands to visit their exchange partners, who are both male and female, and they sponsor lavish feasts attended by many people.

Chiefdoms

A chiefdom, as defined in Chapter 9, is a form of political organization with a central leader encompassing several smaller political units. Compared to most tribes, chiefdoms have larger populations, often numbering in the thousands, and are more centralized and socially complex. Hereditary systems of social ranking and economic stratification are found in chiefdoms, with social divisions existing between the chiefly lineage or lineages and non-chiefly groups. Chiefs and their descendants are considered superior to commoners, and intermarriage between the two strata is forbidden. Chiefs are expected to be generous, but they may have a more luxurious lifestyle than the rest of the people. The chiefship is an "office" that must be filled at all times. When a chief dies or retires, he or she must be replaced. In contrast, the death of a band leader or big-man or big-woman does not require that someone else be chosen as a replacement. A chief has more responsibilities than a band or tribal leader. He or she regulates production and redistribution, solves internal conflicts, and plans and leads raids and warring expeditions. Criteria for becoming a chief are clearly defined. Besides ascribed criteria (birth in a chiefly lineage, or being the first son or daughter of the chief), achievement is also important. Achievement is measured in terms of personal leadership skills, charisma, and accumulated wealth. Chiefdoms have existed in most parts of the world.

Pocahontas played an important role in Native American–British relations during the early colonial period. ■ Recall the images that you have seen of her—from books, movies, stories—and ask yourself whether they might be biased in any way. (Source: North Wind Picture Archives)

Anthropologists and archaeologists are interested in how and why chiefdom systems evolved as an intermediary unit between tribes and states and in what the political implications of this evolution are (as discussed in relation to early chiefdoms in Chapter 9). Several political strategies support the expansion of power in chiefdoms: controlling more internal and external wealth and distributing feasting and gift exchanges that create debt ties; improving local production systems; applying force internally; forging stronger and wider external ties; and controlling ideological legitimacy. Depending on local conditions, different strategies are employed. For example, internal control of irrigation systems was the most important factor in the emergence of chiefdoms in prehistoric southeastern Spain, whereas control of external trade was more important in the prehistoric Aegean region (Gilman 1991).

The Iroquois of central New York offer an example of women's political power in chiefdoms (J. K. Brown 1975). Men were chiefs, but women and men councilors made up the appointing body. Most of the men were gone for extended periods, waging war as far away as Delaware and Virginia. Women controlled production and distribution of the staple crop, maize. If the women did not want the warriors to leave for a particular campaign, they would refuse to provide them with maize, thereby vetoing the plan. Men and women participated equally on the councils.

An expanded version of the chiefdom occurs when several chiefdoms are joined in a **confederacy** headed by a chief of chiefs, "big chief," or paramount chief. Many prominent confederacies have existed—for example, in Hawai'i in the late 1700s and, in North America, the Iroquois league of five nations that stretched across New York state, the Cherokee of Tennessee, and the Algonquins who dominated the Chesapeake region in present-day Virginia and Maryland. In the Algonquin confederacy, each village had a chief, and the regional council was composed of local chiefs and headed by the paramount chief. Powhatan, father of Pocahontas, was paramount chief of the Algonquins when the British arrived in the early 1600s. Confederacies were supported financially by contributions of grain from each local unit. Kept in a central storage area where the paramount chief lived, the grain was used to feed warriors during external warfare that maintained and expanded the confederacy's borders. A council building existed in the central location, where local chiefs came together to meet with the paramount chief to deliberate on questions of internal and external policy.

States

A state, as defined in Chapter 9, is a form of political organization with a bureaucracy and diversified governmental institutions with varying degrees of centralized control. The state is now the form of political organization in which all people live. Band organizations, tribes, and chiefdoms exist, but they are incorporated within state structures.

Powers of the State. Cultural anthropologists ask how states operate and relate to their citizens. In this inquiry, they focus on the enhanced power that states have over their domain compared to other forms of political organization (see Table 16.2).

Symbols of State Power. Religious beliefs and symbols are often closely tied to the power of state leadership: the ruler may be considered a deity or part deity, or may be a high priest of the state religion, or may be closely linked with the high priest, who serves as advisor. Architecture and urban planning remind the populace of the power of the state. In pre-hispanic Mexico, the central plaza of city–states, such as

---

TABLE 16.2
The powers of states.

- *States define citizenship and its rights and responsibilities.* In complex societies, since early times, not all residents were granted equal rights as citizens.

- *States monopolize the use of force and the maintenance of law and order.* Internally, the state controls the population through laws, courts, and the police. Externally, the state uses force defensively to maintain its borders and offensively to extend its territory.

- *States maintain standing armies and police* (as opposed to part-time forces).

- *States keep track of the number, age, gender, location, and wealth of their citizens through census systems that are regularly updated.* A census allows the state to maintain formal taxation systems, military recruitment, and policy planning, including population settlement, immigration quotas, and social benefits such as old-age pensions.

- *States have the power to extract resources from citizens through taxation.* All political organizations are supported by contributions of the members, but variations occur in the rate of contributions expected, the form in which they are paid, and the return that members get in terms of services. In bands, people voluntarily give time or labor for "public projects" such as a group hunt or a planned move. Public finance in states is based on formal taxation that takes many forms. **In-kind taxation** is a system of mandatory, non-cash contributions to the state. For example, the Inca state used a labor tax, to finance public works such as roads and monuments and to provide agricultural labor on state lands. Another form of in-kind taxation in early states required that farmers pay a percentage of their crop yield. Cash taxes, such as the income tax that takes a percentage of wages, emerged only in the past few hundred years.

- *States manipulate information.* Control of information to protect the state and its leaders can be done directly (through censorship, restricting access to certain information by the public, and promotion of favorable images via propaganda) and indirectly (through pressure on journalists and television networks to present information in certain ways).

Tenochtitlan (review pp. 276–277), was symbolically equivalent to the center of the cosmos and was thus the locale of greatest significance (Low 1995). The most important temples and the residence of the head of state were located around the plaza. Other houses and structures, in decreasing order of status, were located on avenues in decreasing proximity to the center. The grandness and individual character of the leader's residence indicate power, as do monuments—especially tombs to past leaders and heroes or heroines.

Gender and Leadership in States. Most states are hierarchical and patriarchal, excluding members of lower classes and women from equal participation. Some contemporary states are less male-dominated than others, but none are female-dominated. One view of gender inequality in states suggests that increasing male dominance with the evolution of the state is based on male control of the technology of production and warfare (Harris 1993). Women in most cultures have been excluded from these areas of power, and they have not been able to reverse or equalize these long-standing power relationships except in states that are relatively peaceful, such as Finland, Norway, Sweden, and Denmark.

Strongly patriarchal contemporary states preserve male dominance through ideologies that restrict women's political power, such as purdah (female seclusion and segregation from the public world), as practiced in much of the Muslim Middle East, Pakistan, and north India. In China, scientific beliefs that categorize women as less strong and dependable than men have long been used to rationalize the exclusion of women from politics (Dikötter 1998). Socialist states usually pay some attention to increasing women's political roles. The proportion of female members of legislative bodies is higher in socialist states than in capitalist democracies but is still not equal.

A few contemporary states have, or have recently had, women as prime ministers or presidents. Such powerful women include Indira Gandhi in India, Golda Meir in Israel, Margaret Thatcher in the United Kingdom, and Benazir Bhutto in Pakistan. Female heads of state are often related by kinship (as wife or daughter) to former heads of state. Indira Gandhi, for example, was the daughter of the popular first prime minister of independent India, Jawaharlal Nehru (she was not related to Mahatma Gandhi). But it is unclear whether these women's leadership positions can be explained by their inheriting the role or through the political socialization they may have received, directly or indirectly, as a result of being born into political families.

What are some of the symbols of state power in your home country?

THINKING

OUTSIDE THE BOX

The Temple of the Warriors at Chichen Itza, a Maya site on the Yucatan peninsula, Mexico. Over several hundred years, the great city of Chichen Itza went through periods of power and prominence interspersed with periods of decline. It was finally abandoned in the fourteenth century, for unknown reasons. A stone road leading north out of the site goes to the huge cenote for which the city was named. Chichen Itza means, in the Maya language, "the mouth of the well of the Itza people." ■ Go to page 16, review the map of the Yucatan peninsula, and locate Chichen Itza. (Source: © John Elk III/Elk Photography)

Women's leadership roles can also be indirect, as mothers or wives of male rulers, such as Eva Peron in Argentina and Hillary Clinton in the United States during her tenure as first lady. Women's indirect political power through their children, especially sons, is an important but understudied topic. One piece of information comes from contemporary Turkey, where most parents consider politics an undesirable career for their children. Nevertheless, in a recent survey, more women than men stated that they would say "yes" to their sons' political ambitions (Güneş-Ayara 1995). The implication is that mothers of male leaders use their position as mothers to influence politics because direct political roles are largely closed to them.

Local Power and Politics in Democratic States.   The degree to which states influence the lives of their citizens varies, as does the ability of citizens to influence the policies and actions of their governments. Some anthropologists, as citizens, use their knowledge of culture at home or abroad to influence politics in their own countries. So-called totalitarian states have the most direct control of local politics. In most other systems, local politics and local government are granted some degree of power. In highly centralized states, the central government controls public finance and legal institutions, leaving little power or autonomy in these matters to local governments. In decentralized systems, local governments are granted some forms of revenue generation (taxation) and the responsibility of providing certain services.

Local politics of various types exist within state systems, their strength and autonomy being dependent on how centralized the state apparatus is. Local politics within a democratic framework may involve another type of gift-giving and exchange in the interest of maintaining or gaining power. Here, people in elected positions of power give favors in expectation of political loyalty in return. In such contexts, various **factions** vie with each other. A faction is a politically oriented group whose members are mobilized and maintained by a leader to whom the ties of loyalty are vertical—from leader to follower (Brumfiel 1994). Factions tend to lack formal rules and formal succession in their leadership.

Two villages in Belize show a contrast in the role of factional politics (Moberg 1991). One village, Mt. Hope, is faction-free; the other, Charleston, has divisive factionalism. Economic differences between the two villages are important in explaining this difference. In Mt. Hope, the government provided residents with land and established a marketing board to purchase villagers' crops. In Charleston, most men work in small-scale fishing augmented by part-time farming. Lack of a road that would allow export of agricultural crops has inhibited the development of commercial agriculture. Intense factionalism in Charleston is sustained by outside political party patronage and favor-giving. Local faction leaders vie with one another to obtain grants and other benefits from the state. In return, state political parties look to Charleston as a base for developing political loyalties. The parties bypassed Mt. Hope because economic development created less dependence there on state favors for projects such as a cooperative or a road. Charleston, in contrast, was ripe for political manipulation.

SOCIAL ORDER AND SOCIAL CONFLICT

Socially agreed-upon ways of behaving shape people's everyday life in countless ways, inducing most people, for example, to wait in line to get on a bus and to pay for a sandwich at the deli instead of stealing it. This section discusses options for maintaining peace and order, including informal arrangements that people barely know exist and formal laws and systems of crime prevention. It moves from the study of conformity and order to the study of situations in which normal expectations and laws are not followed, and conflict and violence occur.

Anthropologists in all four fields do research on social order and social conflict. Archaeologists examine artifacts such as weapons, remains of forts, and the rise and fall of political centers. Primatologists study nonhuman primate patterns of cooperation, coalitions, conflict, and conflict resolution. Linguistic anthropologists do research on social conflict related to state language policies and on how communication patterns within the courtroom and in international mediation influence outcomes.

In anthropology, **social control** includes processes by which an orderly social life is maintained (Garland 1996:781). Social control systems include *internalized social controls* that exist through socialization for proper behavior, education, and peer pressure. In the United States and Canada, the Amish and Mennonites (Christian immigrant groups from Europe) rely on internalized social controls more than most microcultures. These groups have no police force or legal system; the way social order is maintained is through religious teaching and group pressure. If a member veers from correct behavior, punishment such as ostracism ("shunning") may be applied.

CROSSING THE FIELDS

Postconflict Reconciliation through Making Amends among Nonhuman Primates

Post-conflict contacts among former nonhuman primate opponents help to relieve the stressful effects of conflict and promote normal interaction (Silk 2002). Acts of reconciliation often appear to have short-term goals such as gaining access to desirable resources. In other instances, reconciliation appears to function as a way to repair a damaged relationship that is valuable.

Evidence of making amends, or *relationship-repair reconciliation,* appears when former opponents are seen sitting closer together than usual, or otherwise interacting peacefully, in the minutes following a conflict. Spatial proximity immediately following a conflict is often sufficient for reconciliation among some nonhuman primates.

Among baboons, however, peaceful postconflict interaction must be initiated by an attacking opponent grunting softly to the attacked opponent to signal that the conflict is over. In many postconflict situations among baboons, the grunting noise is sufficient to achieve reconciliation, though it may also be accompanied by proximity.

Conflict is stressful for primates. The heart rates of female rhesus macaques, for example, increase sharply following conflict, as do behaviors such as yawning, scratching, and body shaking. Peaceful contact among former opponents reduces stress levels by removing uncertainty about the intentions of others. ∎

Grooming, as with these baboons, is a common form of repairing relationships following a conflict among nonhuman primates. (Source: © Werner Layer/Animals Animals)

FOOD FOR THOUGHT

- In your microcultural world, what are some ways of expressing an intention for reconciliation in a postconflict situation?

Norms and Laws

Cultural anthropologists distinguish two major instruments of social control: norms and laws. A **norm** is an accepted standard for how people should behave. All societies have norms, and they are usually unwritten and learned unconsciously through socialization. Norms include, for example, the expectation that children should follow their parents' advice, that people standing in line should wait their turn, and that an individual should accept an offer of a handshake (in cultures where handshakes are the usual greeting) when meeting someone for the first time. In rural Bali, etiquette dictates certain greeting forms between people of different status: "[P]ersons of higher status and power are shown very marked respect. . . . if [they are] seated, then others moving past them crouch" (Barth 1993:114). Enforcement of norms is informal; for example, a violation may simply be considered rude and the violator avoided in the future. In others, direct action may be taken, such as asking someone who disrupts a meeting to leave.

In contrast to a norm, a **law** is a binding rule created through enactment or custom that defines right and reasonable behavior. Laws are enforceable by threat of punishment. Systems of law are more common and more elaborate in state-level societies, but many non-state societies have formalized laws. Often the legitimacy and force of law are based on religion. For example, Australian Aborigines believe that law came to humans during the "Dreamtime," a period in the mythological past when the ancestors created the world. Law and religion are synonymous in contemporary Islamic states. Secular Western states consider their laws to be neutral as regards religion, but in fact, much Western legal practice is heavily influenced by Judeo-Christian beliefs.

Systems of Social Control

This section considers forms of social control in small-scale societies as contrasted with large-scale societies, namely states. The former are more characterized by the use of norms. States rely more on legal sanctions, yet local-level groups, such as neighbors, practice social sanctions among themselves. The last part of the section takes up the question of social control systems and social inequality.

Social Control in Small-Scale Societies

Anthropologists distinguish between small-scale societies and large-scale societies in terms of prevalent forms of conflict resolution, social order, and punishment of offenses. Because bands are small, close-knit groups, disputes tend to be handled at the interpersonal level through discussion or one-on-one fights.

Group members may act together to punish an offender through shaming and ridicule. Emphasis is on maintaining social order and restoring social equilibrium, not hurtfully punishing an offender. Ostracizing an offending member (forcing the person to leave the group) is a common means of formal punishment. Capital punishment is rare but not nonexistent. For example, in some Australian Aboriginal societies, a law restricted access to religious rituals and paraphernalia to men who had gone through a ritual initiation. If an initiated man shared secrets with an uninitiated man, the elders would delegate one of their group to kill the offender. In such instances, the elders act like a court.

In non-state societies, punishment is often legitimized through belief in supernatural forces and their ability to affect people. Among highland horticulturalists of the Indonesian island of Sumba (see the map on p. 45), one of the greatest offenses is to fail to keep a promise (Kuipers 1990). Breaking a promise will bring on "supernatural assault" by the ancestors of those who have been offended by the person's misbehavior. The punishment may come in the form of damage to crops, illness or death of a relative, destruction of the offender's house, or having clothing catch on fire. When such a disaster occurs, the only recourse is to sponsor a ritual that will appease the ancestors.

THINKING OUTSIDE THE BOX

Think of various forms of conflict prevention and conflict resolution used among small-scale political groups in your cultural world. Which are more effective and why?

Legal Anthropologist Advises Resistance to "Coercive Harmony"

A CULTURAL ANTHROPOLOGIST uses cross-cultural insights to provide a critique of her own culture, with an eye to producing improved social relations (Nader 2001). Laura Nader had conducted extensive fieldwork in Latin America, as well as in the World Court in Europe. Her main interest lies in cross-cultural aspects of conflict and conflict resolution. In terms of her observations of her home country, the United States, she points out that leading politicians are currently emphasizing the need for unity, consensus, and harmony among the American people. But the United States, she points out, was founded by dissenters, and democracy depends on people speaking out. Democracy, in her view, supports the right to be indignant and the idea that "indignation can make Americans more engaged citizens" (B13).

A cultural anthropologist who teaches at the University of California at Berkeley, Nader fosters the expression of critique, opinion, and even indignation when she teaches. One of her students commented that "Dr. Nader is a pretty good professor, except she has opinions" (B13). She took that as a compliment.

Nader feels that Europeans are generally less concerned about social harmony than the United States is. Americans consider it bad manners to be contentious, whereas in Europe, debate—even bitterly contentious debate—is valued. She uses the term *coercive harmony* to refer to the informal but strong pressure in the United States to agree, to be nice, to avoid digging beneath the surface, to stifle indignation at the lack of universal health care or the low voter turnout in presidential elections. The unstated, informally enforced policy of coercive harmony labels cultural critique as bad behavior—as negative rather than positive. Nader finds it alarming that in a country that proclaims freedom as its primary feature, coercive harmony in fact suppresses contrary views and voices through the idiom of politeness, niceness, and friendliness.

How can this insight be used to improve the situation in the United States? Nader suggests one step: making sure that critique, dissent, and indignation are supported in schools. Teachers should avoid contributing to the informal enforcement of social harmony and consensus and should instead proactively encourage critique.

FOOD FOR THOUGHT

- Watch several television interview shows with politicians on BBC, and compare the style to that seen on a U.S. station. (Try especially to see Jeremy Paxman, one of Britain's most infamous interviewers.) How do the interview styles compare?

Village fission (breaking up) and ostracism are mechanisms for dealing with unresolvable conflict. The overall goal in dealing with conflict in small-scale societies is to return the group to harmony. Data on conflict resolution from nonhuman primate groups also demonstrate the importance of re-establishing peaceful interactions between former opponents as a way of promoting small-group harmony.

Social Control in States

In densely populated societies with more social stratification and more wealth, increased stress occurs in relation to the distribution of surplus, inheritance, and rights to land. In addition, not everyone knows everyone else, and face-to-face accountability exists mainly in localized groups. Three important factors of state systems of social control are the increased specialization of roles involved in social control, the formalized use of trials and courts, and the use of power-enforced forms of punishment, such as prisons and the death penalty. Yet informal mechanisms also exist. In the Lessons Applied box (above), a cultural anthropologist provides a cultural critique of informal mechanisms.

Specialization. The specialization of tasks related to law and order—police, judges, lawyers—increases with the emergence of state organization. Full-time pro-

www.ablongman.com/millerwood1e   **CHAPTER 16** ■ Political and Legal Systems   **479** fessionals, however, such as judges and lawyers, also emerged with the state. These professionals often come from powerful or elite social groups, a fact that perpetuates elite biases in the justice process itself.

Policing includes processes of surveillance and the threat of punishment related to maintaining social order (Reiner 1996). As a specialized group, police exist mainly in states.

Japan's low crime rate has attracted the attention of Western law-and-order specialists, who think that it may be the result of the police system there. They are interested in learning whether solutions to America's crime problems can be found in such Japanese policing practices as neighborhood police boxes staffed by foot patrolmen and volunteer crime prevention groups organized on a neighborhood basis. Field research among police detectives in the city of Sapporo reveals aspects of Japanese culture and policing that promote low crime rates (Miyazawa 1992). First, the police operate under high expectations that no false arrests should be made and that all arrests should lead to confession. In fact, the rate of confession is high. This may be because the police do a good job of targeting the guilty or because the police have nearly complete control of interrogation over isolated suspects for long periods of time, which may lead to wearing down resistance and potentially distorting the process of justice. In Japan, an "enabling legal environment" gives more power to the police and less to the defendant than United States law. For example, the suspect's statements are not recorded verbatim or taped. The detectives write them up and the suspect is asked to sign them.

Trials and Courts.   In societies where misdoing and punishment are defined by spirits and ancestors, a person's guilt is proved simply by the fact that misfortune has befallen him or her. If a person's crops were damaged by lightning, then that person must have done something wrong. In other instances, guilt may be determined through **trial by ordeal,** a form of trial in which the accused person is put through some kind of test that is often painful. In this case, the guilty person will be required to place a hand in boiling oil, for example, or to have a part of the body touched by a red-hot knife. Being burned is a sign of guilt, whereas not being burned means the suspect is innocent. The court system, with lawyers, judge, and jury, is used in many contemporary societies, although there is variation in how cases are presented and juries constituted. The goal of contemporary court trials is to ensure both justice and fairness. Analysis of actual courtroom dynamics and patterns of decision making in the United States and elsewhere, however, reveals serious problems in achieving these goals.

Prisons and the Death Penalty.   Administering punishment involves doing something unpleasant to someone who has committed an offense. Cultural anthropologists have examined forms of punishment cross-culturally, as well as the relationship between types of societies and forms of punishment. In small-scale societies, punishment is socially rather than judicially managed. As noted earlier, the most extreme form of punishment is usually ostracism and is only rarely death. Another common form of punishment in the case of theft or murder, especially in the Middle East, is requiring that the guilty party pay compensation to members of the harmed family.

The prison, as a place where people are forcibly detained as a form of punishment, has a long history, but it probably did not predate the state. In Europe, long-term detention of prisoners did not become common until the seventeenth century (Foucault 1977). Cross-nationally and through history, percentages of imprisoned people vary widely. The United States and Russia have high percentages compared to other contemporary Western countries: 550 and 470 prisoners per 100,000 population, respectively. The rate in the British Isles is about 100, whereas the Scandinavian countries have among the lowest rates, under 60. In the United States, nearly two million people are in prison, and the "corrections industry" is a growing commercial sector of society (Rhodes 2001).

The death penalty (capital punishment) is rare in non-state societies because condemning someone to death requires a great deal of power. A comparison of capital punishment in the contemporary United States with human sacrifice among the Aztecs of Mexico in the sixteenth century reveals striking similarities (Purdum and Paredes 1989). Both systems involve the death of mainly able-bodied males who are in one way or another socially marginal. In the United States, most people who are executed are non–Euro-Americans, have killed Euro-Americans, are poor, and have few social ties. Aztec sacrificial victims were mainly male war captives from neighboring states, but Aztec children were also sometimes sacrificed. The deaths in both contexts communicate to the general populace a political message about the state's power and strength, which is why they are highly ritualized and widely publicized events.

Social Inequality and the Law

Critical legal anthropology is the approach that examines the role of law in maintaining power relationships through discrimination against such social categories as minorities and indigenous people within various judicial systems around the world, including long-standing democracies. This section presents an example of critical legal anthropology from Australia.

At the invitation of some Aboriginal leaders, cultural anthropologist Fay Gale and colleagues conducted research comparing the treatment of Aboriginal youths and that of White youths in the judicial system (1990). The question posed by the Aboriginal leaders was: Why are our kids always in trouble? Two directions can be pursued to find the answer. First, structural factors such as Aboriginal displacement from their homeland, poverty, poor living conditions, and bleak future prospects can be investigated. These factors might make it more likely for Aboriginal youths to commit crimes than the relatively advantaged White youths. Second, the criminal justice system can be examined to see whether it treats Aboriginal and White youths equally. The researchers decided to direct their attention to the judicial system because little research had been done on that area.

Results of the study show that Aboriginal youths are overrepresented at every level of the juvenile justice system: "A far greater proportion of Aboriginal than other young people follow the harshest route. . . . [A]t each point in the system where discretion operates, young Aborigines are significantly more likely than other young persons to receive the most severe outcomes of those available to the decision-makers" (3). At the time of apprehension (being caught by the police), the suspect can be either formally arrested or informally reported. A formal arrest is made to ensure that the offender will appear in court. Officers ask the suspects for a home address and whether they have a job. Aboriginal youths are more likely than White youths to live in a poor neighborhood in an extended family, and they are more likely to be unemployed. Thus they tend to be placed in the category of "undependable," and they are formally arrested more than nonaboriginal youths for the same crime (see Table 16.3 on p. 482). The next step determines whether the suspect will be tried in Children's Court or referred to Children's Aid Panels. The Children's Aid Panels in South Australia have gained acclaim worldwide for the opportunities they give to individuals to avoid becoming repeat offenders and to take their proper place in society. But most Aboriginal youth offenders are denied access to them and instead have to appear in court, where the vast majority of youthful offenders end up pleading guilty. The clear and disturbing finding from this look at how Aboriginal youths fare is that the mode of arrest tends to determine each subsequent stage in the system.

Interior scene of the Cellular Jail in India's Andaman Islands, which was so named because all prisoners had single cells, arranged in rows, to prevent them from engaging in social interaction and possible collusion to escape or rebel. ■ Find out about how prisons in your home country are designed. (Source: Barbara Miller)

What is the current ruling on the death penalty in your home country?

THINKING

OUTSIDE THE BOX

TABLE 16.3

Comparison of outcomes for Aboriginal and White youths in the Australian judicial system.

	Aboriginal Youths (percent)	White Youths (percent)
Brought into system via arrest rather than police report	43.4	19.7
Referred to Children's Court rather than diverted to Children's Aid Panels	71.3	37.4
Proportion of Court appearances resulting in detention	10.2	4.2

Note: Most of these youths are males; data are from 1979 to 1984.

(*Source:* Table, p. 4, "Comparison of Outcomes for Aboriginal and White Youth in the Australian Judicial System" from *Aboriginal Youth and the Criminal Justice System: The Injustice of Justice?* by Faye Gale, Rebecca Bailey-Harris, and Joy Wundersitz. Copyright © 1990. Reprinted by permission of Cambridge University Press.)

Social Conflict and Violence

All systems of social control have to deal with the fact that conflict and violence may occur. Conflict can occur at any social level, from the private microlevel of the household to the public realm of international warfare. This section reviews varieties of conflict, moving from local, small-group conflict to wider, global conflict.

Banditry

Banditry is a form of aggressive conflict that involves socially patterned theft. It is usually practiced by a person or band of persons who are socially marginal and who gain a special social status from their illegal activity.

One anthropologist has humorously termed banditry "adventurist capital accumulation" (Sant Cassia 1993:793), but it is much more than that. For example, banditry, male identity and status, and the creation of social alliances are closely associated on the Greek island of Crete (Herzfeld 1985). In this sheepherding economy, manhood and male identity depend on a local form of banditry—stealing sheep. "Coming out on the branch" is a metaphor for the attainment of manhood following a young male's first theft. This phrase implies that he is now a person to be reckoned with. Not to participate in sheep raids is to be effeminate. Each theft, however, requires a counter-theft in revenge, and so the cycle goes on. For protection of his

Cultural anthropologist Michael Herzfeld (far right) observes and interacts with Glendiot men at a coffeehouse while doing fieldwork on male bonding and banditry in Crete. ■ Do you think a woman anthropologist could conduct fieldwork on the topic of male bonding in Crete? (Source: Cornelia Mayer Herzfeld)

flock from theft and to be able to avenge any theft that occurs, a shepherd relies heavily on male kin (both patrilineal kin and male kin through marriage). Sheep stealing itself is an important basis for social ties. Following a series of thefts and counter-thefts and rising hostility between the two groups, a mediator is brought in to resolve the tension. The result is that the enemies swear to be loyal friends from then on. Male identity formation through sheep stealing in highland Crete still exists, but it is declining in importance as many shepherds turn to farming. Another force of change is the government, which defines sheep stealing as a crime.

Feuding

Feuding is long-term violence between families, groups of families, or tribes. Sometimes lethal, feuding is fueled by a concept of revenge that motivates back-and-forth violence between two groups, often over many generations.

Contemporary economic change may lead to increased feuding, as happened in Thull, a Pakistani village (Keiser 1986). *Blood feuds* (which explicitly involve the death of someone in the enemy group) increased in frequency and intensity over a fifteen-year period in the 1960s and 1970s. Previously, there had been fights, expressing hostility among members of three patrilineal clans, but they rarely involved deadly weapons. According to the traditional honor code in this region, an act of avenging should equal the original act: A blow should answer a blow, a death a death. For a murder, it is best to kill the actual murderer, but a male relative is a permissible substitute. Killing women and children is unknown. Wrongs committed against a man through his wife, sister, or daughter are special, and whatever the transgression, the most appropriate response is to kill the offender. For example, one man's staring at another man's wife, daughter, or sister demands deadly retaliation. In Thull, a man killed another man for trying to catch a glimpse of his wife.

But why did blood feuds increase in Thull? The answer lies in the effects of economic change. Construction of a new road changed the economy from a blend of herding and cultivation to increased cultivation of cash crops, especially potatoes. The government started massive logging operations in the region—the reason for building the road. Logging involved local men in wage work and greatly increased the amount of cash in the area. Tension increased among men, and they grew more vigilant about defending their honor. Along with increased cash came a dramatic rise in the number of firearms owned. More guns led to more lethal feuding.

Ethnic Conflict

Ethnic conflict may result from an ethnic group's attempt to gain more autonomy or more equitable treatment (Esman 1996). It may also be caused by a dominant group's actions to subordinate, oppress, or eliminate an ethnic group by genocide or ethnocide. In the past few decades, political violence has increasingly taken place within states rather than between states. Political analysts and journalists often cite ethnicity, language, and religion as the causes of certain conflicts. It is true that ethnic identities give people an ideological sense of commitment to a cause, but it is important to look beneath the labels to see whether deeper issues exist, such as claims to land, water, ports, and other material resources.

Consider Central Asia, a vast region populated by many ethnic groups, none of which has an indigenous claim to

The Hatfield clan in West Virginia in 1899. The long-standing feud between the Hatfields and the McCoys became part of American legend. ■ What can you learn about the cultural context of this feud? (Source: © Bettmann/CORBIS)

The Yanomami: The "Fierce People"?

THE YANOMAMI are a horticultural people living in dispersed villages of between 40 and 250 people in the Venezuelan rainforest (Ross 1993). Since the 1960s, biological anthropologist Napoleon Chagnon has studied several Yanomami villages. He has written a widely read and frequently republished ethnography called *The Fierce People* (1992 [1968]) about the Yanomami and has helped to produce several classic ethnographic films about them, including "The Feast" and "The Axe Fight."

Chagnon's writings and films have promoted a long-standing view of the Yanomami as exceptionally violent and prone to lethal warfare. According to Chagnon, about one-third of adult Yanomami males die violently, about two-thirds of all adults had lost at least one close relative through violence, and over 50 percent had lost two or more close relatives (205). He reported that one village was raided twenty-five times during his first fifteen months of fieldwork. Although village alliances are sometimes formed, they are fragile, and allies may turn against each other unpredictably.

Chagnon represents the Yanomami world as one of danger, threats, and counterthreats. Enemies, human and supernatural, are everywhere. Support from one's allies is uncertain. All of this uncertainty leads to what Chagnon describes as the *waiteri* complex, a set of behaviors and attitudes that includes a fierce political and personal stance for men and forms of individual and group communication that stress aggression and independence. Fierceness is a dominant theme in socialization, as boys learn how to fight with clubs, participate in chest-pounding duels with other boys, and use a spear. Adult males are aggressive and hostile toward adult females, and young boys learn to be aggressive toward girls from an early age.

Chagnon provides a Darwinian explanation for Yanomami fierceness that is related to reproductive success. He reports that the Yanomami say that they carry out village raids and conduct warfare so that men may obtain wives. Although the Yanomami prefer to marry within their village, there is a shortage of potential brides because the Yanomami practice of female infanticide creates a scarcity of women. Taking a wife from another group is preferable to remaining a bachelor. Men in other groups, however, are unwilling to give up their women; hence the necessity for raids. Other reasons for raids include suspicion of sorcery and theft of food.

Within this system, in Chagnon's view, warfare contributes to reproductive success because successful warriors are able to gain a wife or more than one wife (polygyny is practiced). Successful warriors thus have higher reproductive rates than unsuccessful warriors. Accordingly, successful warriors have a genetic advantage for fierceness, which they pass on to their sons, leading to a higher growth rate in the population of groups with violent males through genetic selection for fierceness. Male fierceness, in this view, is biologically adaptive.

Chagnon's interpretation has created substantial controversy among anthropologists for many years. Marvin Harris, from the cultural materialist perspective, suggests that protein scarcity and population dynamics in the area are the underlying cause of warfare (1984). The Yanomami lack plentiful sources of meat, which is highly valued. Harris suggests that when game in an area became depleted, pressure would

the land. Yet every dispute in Central Asia appears on the surface to have an ethnic basis: "Russians and Ukrainians versus Kazakhs over land rights and jobs in Kazakhstan, Uzbeks versus Tajiks over the status of Samarkhand and Bukhara, conflict between Kirghiz and Uzbeks in Kyrghyzstan, and riots between Caucasian Turks and Uzbeks in the Fergana Valley of Uzbekistan" (Clay 1990:48). Attributing all these problems to ethnic differences overlooks resource competition based on regional differences. For example, Uzbekistan has most of the cities and irrigated farmland, small states such as Kyrghyzstan and Tajikistan control most of the water, and Turkmenistan has vast oil and gas riches.

Warfare

Anthropologists have contributed to war studies by offering several definitions (Reyna 1994). Is it open and declared conflict between two political units? This definition would rule out, for example, the American–Vietnam war because it was undeclared. Is it simply organized aggression? This definition is too broad because not all organized violence can be considered warfare. Perhaps the best definition is that **war** is rise to expand into the territory of neighboring groups, thus precipitating conflict. Such conflicts in turn resulted in high rates of adult male mortality. Combined with the effects of female infanticide, this meat-warfare complex kept population growth rates down to a level that the environment could support.

Another view depends on historical data. Brian Ferguson argues that the high levels of violence were caused by the intensified Western presence during the preceding one hundred years (1990). Furthermore, diseases introduced from outside, especially measles and malaria, severely depopulated the Yanomami and would have greatly increased their fears of sorcery (that is how they explain disease). The attraction to Western goods such as steel axes and guns would also boost intergroup rivalry. Thus Ferguson suggests that the "fierce people" are a creation of historical forces, especially contact and pressure from outsiders, as much as of factors internal to their society.

Following on Ferguson's position but introducing a new angle, a journalist pointed the finger of blame for Yanomami fierceness at Chagnon himself (Tierney 2000). He maintained that it was the presence of Chagnon, with his team of researchers and many boxes of trade goods, that triggered a series of lethal raids because of increased competition for those very goods. In addition, the journalist argued that

Napoleon Chagnon (center) in the field with two Yanomami men, 1995. Chagnon has been accused of using lavish distribution of goods to the Yanomami to gain their cooperation in his research, and thereby changing their culture. (Source: © Antonio Mari)

Chagnon intentionally prompted the Yanomami to act fiercely for his films and to stage raids that actually led to bad feelings where they had not existed before.

In 2001, the American Anthropological Association established the El Dorado Task Force, charging it with examining the journalist's allegations that Chagnon's and others' representations of the Yanomami may have had a negative impact on them and that the activities of anthropologists and others may have contributed to "disorganization" among the Yanomami. The report of the El Dorado Task Force appears on the AAA website (*www.aaanet.org*). Overall, the AAA position reflects the charges against Chagnon and emphasizes the harmfulness of false accusations that may jeopardize future scientific research.

CRITICAL THINKING QUESTIONS

- Do you think that Chagnon's characterization of the Yanomami as the "fierce people" is accurate? (Consider, for example, whether all Yanomami people are equally fierce.)
- Which perspective presented here seems most persuasive to you and why?
- What relevance does this case have to the theory that violence is a universal human trait?

organized group action directed against another group and involving lethal force (Ferguson 1994, quoted in Reyna 1994:30).

Archaeological evidence indicates that warfare intensified during the Neolithic era. Plant and animal domestication required more extensive land use, and they were accompanied by increased population densities. The resulting economic and demographic pressures put more and larger groups in direct and intense competition with each other. Tribal leadership patterns facilitate mobilization of warrior groups for raids. But tribal groups do not have uniform levels of warfare. At one extreme are the Yanomami of the Venezuelan and Brazilian Amazon, who have been described as "the fierce people." Some anthropologists, however, question whether this characterization of the Yanomami is correct. (See the Critical Thinking box.)

Many chiefdoms have high rates of warfare and high casualty rates. They have increased capacity for war in terms of personnel and surplus foods to support long-range expeditions. The chief could call on his or her retainers as a specialized fighting force, as well as on the general members of society. Chiefs and paramount chiefs could be organized into effective command structures (Reyna 1994:44–45). The potential for

Women near Kabul, Afghanistan, look at replicas of land mines during a mining awareness program sponsored in 2003 by the International Committee of the Red Cross. Afghanistan is still heavily mined, and rates of injury and mortality from mines are high. ■ Do Internet research to learn about international organizations involved in de-mining. (Source: © Reuters NewMedia Inc./CORBIS)

The heptamer structure of anthrax toxin protective antigen. Scientists in many disciplines, including microbiology, genetics, and anthropology, are focused on preventing, or dealing with, biochemical threats. (Source: Courtesy R. John Collier & D. Bordon Lacy)

more extensive and massive campaigns expanded as chiefdoms and confederacies evolved into state-level organizations. In states, standing armies and complex military hierarchies are supported by increased material resources through taxation and other forms of revenue generation. Greater state power allows for more powerful and effective military structures, which, in turn, increase the state's power. Thus a mutually reinforcing relationship emerges between the military and the state. States are generally highly militarized, but not all are, nor are all states equally militarized. Costa Rica does not maintain an army, whereas Turkey has one of the world's largest.

Examining the causes of war between states has occupied scholars in many fields for centuries. Some experts have pointed to common, underlying causes, such as attempts to extend boundaries, secure more resources, ensure markets, support political and economic allies, and resist aggression from other states. Others point to humanitarian concerns that prompt participation in "just wars," to defend values such as freedom or to protect human rights that are defined as such by one state but violated in another.

Causes of war in Afghanistan have changed over time (Barfield 1994). Since the seventeenth century, warfare had increasingly become a way in which kings justified their power in terms of the necessity to maintain independence from outside forces such as the British and Czarist Russia. The last Afghan king was murdered in a coup in 1978. When the Soviet Union invaded in 1979, no centralized ruling group existed to meet it. The Soviet Union deposed the ruling faction, set up one of its own, and then waged war against the Afghan population, killing over one million people, causing three million Afghans to flee the country, and displacing millions of others internally. Yet in spite of the lack of a central command, ethnic and sectarian differences, and being outmatched in equipment by Soviet forces, Afghanistan mounted a war of resistance that eventually wore down the Soviets, who withdrew in 1989.

This case suggests that war was a more effective tool of domination in the premodern period when it settled matters more definitively. In premodern times, fewer troops were needed to maintain dominance after a conquest, because continued internal revolts were less common and the main issue was defense against rivals from outside. Success in the Soviet Union's holding of Afghanistan would have required more extensive involvement and commitment, including introduction of a new economic and political system and ideology to win the population over. Current events show only too clearly that winning a war and taking over a country are the first stage in a process much more complicated than the term *regime change* implies. Afghanistan is now attempting to recover and rebuild after twenty-five years of war, although its problems of state integration and security have roots that go much deeper than the Soviet invasion (Shahrani 2002). These roots include powerful local codes of honor that value political autonomy and require vengeance for harm received, the superimposed moral system of fundamentalist Islam, the revitalized drug economy, and the effects of intervention from outside powers involving governments and corporations, including Unocal of California, Delta Oil of Saudi Arabia, and Bridas of Argentina. The difficulty of constructing a strong state with loyal citizens in the face of these conflicting internal and external factors is great.

In addition to studying the dynamics of war itself and postconflict situations, cultural anthropologists study the armed forces as social institutions, issues related to soldiers in the armed forces, and the effects of soldiers on the wider society. Cultural anthropologists are now doing more research on the armed forces. Much of their research takes the perspective of critique, viewing the armed forces as instruments of power and, often, repressive domination. Militarization in particular—that is, the intensification of labor and resources allocated to military purposes—is studied in an effort to achieve insights that might lead to its control and reduction (Lutz 2002). Parallel to critical medical anthropology (discussed in Chapter 13), this emerging area of research within political anthropology is termed **critical military anthropology,** the study of the military as a power structure.

CHANGE IN POLITICAL AND LEGAL SYSTEMS

This section considers five areas of change in political and legal systems: nationalism and transnationalism, democratization, women in politics, legal pluralism, and international organizations and world order.

Emerging Nations and Transnationalism

Many different definitions exist for the term *nation,* and some of them overlap with definitions given for the term *state* (Maybury-Lewis 1997b:125–132). One definition says that a **nation** is a group of people who share a language, culture, territorial base, political organization, and history (Clay 1990). In this sense, a nation is culturally homogeneous, and the United States would be considered not a nation but rather a unit composed of many nations. According to this definition, groups that lack a territorial base cannot be termed nations. A related term is *nation–state,* which some say refers to a state that comprises only one nation, whereas others think it refers to a state that comprises many nations.

As emerging states seek to build and maintain a sense of belonging among their plural populations, those groups are building their own solidarity and political momentum. One such group consists of the Kurds, about 20 million people who live in a region extending from Turkey into Iran, Iraq, and Syria (see map on p. 488), and most of whom speak some dialect of the Kurdish language (Major 1996). This

A political rally of indigenous people in Bolivia. ■ Do some research to discover the political concerns of indigenous peoples in Bolivia. (Source: © Roshani Kothari)

THINKING
OUTSIDE
THE BOX

How many top-level leaders in your home country are currently women?

region is mainly grasslands, interspersed with mountains, and has no coastline. Oil reserves have been found in some places, but the main resource of international interest is the headland of the Tigris and Euphrates rivers. These rivers provide life-supporting water to the surrounding region, including most of Iraq, and they provide power to Turkey, Syria, and Iraq, through hydroelectric generators built in and near the Kurd areas. In Turkey, there are 12 million Kurds who constitute 20 percent of the country's total population (J. Brown 1995). They live mainly in the southeastern portion of the country and have been battling for a separate state for many years without success. In addition, they want the right to have Kurdish-language schooling and television and radio broadcasts.

Attempts by states to force homogenization of ethnic groups prompts resistance of varying degrees from those groups that wish to retain or gain autonomy. Cultural anthropologists do research on both local and global aspects of these issues. Their findings have relevance to "peace and conflict" studies and to global policy by providing in-depth case studies and new theories based on comparative analysis.

Transnationalism, or a sense of belonging to more than one nation or country, is related to change in political organization by weakening the concept of a nation or state as clearly bounded. Puerto Rico is an illuminating example because of its continuing status as a quasi-colony of the United States and the transnationalism of much of its population (Duany 2000). Puerto Rico is neither fully a state of the United States nor an autonomous political unit. Furthermore, Puerto Rican people do not live in a bounded spatial territory. By the late 1990s, nearly as many Puerto Ricans lived on the United States mainland as on the island of Puerto Rico. Migration to Puerto Rico also occurs, creating cultural diversity there. These migrants include returning Puerto Ricans and others from the United States, such as Dominicans and Cubans. Thus, within the home country, ethnic heterogeneity is created by the diversity of people

who migrate there. The Puerto Ricans who are return migrants differ from the islanders because, amont other factors, many have adopted English as their primary language.

Democratization

Democratization is the process of transformation from an authoritarian regime to a democratic regime. This process includes several features: the end of torture, the liberation of political prisoners, the lifting of censorship, and the toleration of some opposition (Pasquino 1996). In some cases, what is achieved is more a relaxation of authoritarianism than a true transition to democracy, which would occur when the authoritarian regime is no longer in control. Political parties emerge, some representing traditional interests and others oppositional. The variety of approaches to democratization is great, and outcomes are similarly varied (Paley 2002). Of the twenty-seven states created from the former Soviet Union, nineteen are democracies, at least in name. All states in Western Europe are democracies, as are most in the Americas. The percentage is about half in Asia and the Pacific. Africa, with less than one-third of its states democracies, has the lowest percentage. The transition to democracy appears to be most difficult when the change is from highly authoritarian socialist regimes. This pattern is partly explained by the fact that democratization implies a transition from a planned economy to one based on market capitalism (Lempert 1996).

Women in Politics

Two questions arise in the area of changing patterns of women's role in contemporary politics: Is the overall participation of women at various political levels increasing? And do women in politics bring more attention to women's issues, such as the division of labor and wages, access to health care, and violence? The answer to the first question is yes, but modestly, especially at the upper levels. In recent years, only a handful of the nearly two hundred world leaders have been women. In terms of the second question, few women leaders at top levels have had a strong record of supporting women's issues. One interpretation of this pattern is that female political leaders in male-dominated contexts become "like men" or have to avoid "feminist issues" in order to maintain their position.

Women still do not have political status equal to that of men in any country (Chowdhury et al. 1994). In general, women are marginalized from formal politics and must seek to achieve their goals either indirectly (as wives or mothers of male politicians) or through channels other than formal politics, such as grassroots movements.

In some Native North American groups, however, recovery of former political power is occurring (B. G. Miller 1994). This change is taking place within the context of the greatly decreased roles of women as the result of colonialist policies. Until recently, only Native American men in the United States were allowed to vote. One explanation for the increased political participation of women is that women are obtaining many of the new managerial positions on reservations. These positions give them experience in dealing with the outside world and the authority for assuming public office. In addition, they face less resistance from Native American men than women in other, more patriarchal contexts do. Most Native Americans do not view women's roles as contradictory to public authority roles.

The resurgence in women's political participation among the Seneca of New York state and Pennsylvania echoes these themes (Bilharz 1995). From women's precontact position of at least equal political power with men, Seneca women's status then declined. Notably, when the constitution of the Seneca Nation was drawn up on a

Aung San Suu Kyi is the leader of the Burmese democracy and human rights movement. The daughter of Burma's national hero, Aung San, who was assassinated just before Burma gained its independence from the British, she has frequently been placed under house arrest since 1989. She has been awarded the Nobel Peace Prize, becoming the eighth woman to receive the award. ■ What can you learn about her and her writings from the Internet? (Source: © Daniel Simon/ Gamma Presse)

European model in 1848, men were granted the right to vote, but not women. In 1964, Seneca women finally gained the right to vote. Even before enfranchisement, women were politically active and worked on committees formed to stop the building of Kinzua Dam in Pennsylvania. For Seneca women, job creation through the Seneca Nation of Indians (SNI) brought new employment opportunities. Although no woman has run for president of the Seneca Nation as yet and only a few women have been head of a reservation, many women hold elective offices of clerk and judge, and many women head important service departments of the SNI, such as Education and Health. Women of the Seneca Nation still retain complete control over the "clearing" (the cropland), and their primacy in the home has never been challenged. Seneca women have regained a position of equality in their communities.

Electoral workers in Brasilia making preparations for electronic voting in the 2002 general elections in Brazil. ■ How are general election votes counted in your home country? (Source: © Reuters NewMedia Inc./CORBIS)

Legal Pluralism

Colonial governments, to varying degrees, attempted to learn about and rule their subject populations through what they termed "customary law" (Merry 1992). By seeking to codify customary law, colonial governments created fixed rules where flexibility and local variation had formerly existed. Often the colonialists ignored local customary law and imposed their own laws. Homicide, marriage, land rights, and indigenous religion were frequent areas of European imposition. Among the Nuer of Sudan, British legal interventions resulted in confusion about blood feuds (Hutchinson 1996). In cases of homicide, Nuer practices involved either the taking of a life in repayment or payments in cattle, depending on the relationship between the victim and the assailant, the type of weapon used, and current rates of bridewealth as an index of value. In contrast, the British determined a fixed amount of indemnity, and they imprisoned people for committing a vengeful murder. From the Nuer point of view, these practices were incomprehensible. They interpreted putting the accused in prison as a way of protecting that person from a reprisal attack.

When European administrators and missionaries encountered aspects of marriage systems different from their own, they often tried to impose their own ways. Europeans tried in most cases to stop polygamy as un-Christian and uncivilized. In South Africa, however, British and Afrikaaner Whites tolerated the traditional marriage practices of South African peoples (Chambers 2000). So-called customary law, applying to the many diverse practices of South African Black communities, permits a number of marriage forms that, despite their variety, share two basic features. First, marriage is considered a union between two families, not two individuals. Second, bridewealth is paid in nearly all groups, though formerly in cattle and now in cash. These traditions made sense in a largely rural population in which men controlled the major form of movable wealth—cattle. In the latter part of the twentieth century, many people no longer lived in rural areas within extended families, and most of these people worked in the wage economy. In the view of South African Blacks of the 1990s, much of customary marriage law appeared inequitable to women, so the 1994 Black-majority parliament that came to power adopted a new marriage law that eliminated a large part of the customary law. This change reflects a split between the views of "modernist" legislators, who favor gender equity in the law as provided for in the new constitution, and the views of especially rural elders, who feel that tradition has been forsaken.

Colonial imposition of European legal systems onto indigenous systems added another layer, and one that had pre-eminent power over others. **Legal pluralism** exists when more than one kind of legal process might be applied to identical cases (Rouland 1994:50). For example, should a case of murder in the Sudan be tried according to indigenous Sudanese principles or European ones? Post-colonial states are now attempting to reform their legal systems and develop more unified codes (Merry 1992:363).

In situations where several different cultural groups are subject to a single legal code, misunderstandings between the perspectives of both legal specialists and the affected people are likely and may result in conflict. For example, in the United States and Canada, female genital cutting (recall Chapter 12) is against the law. Yet members of some immigrant groups wish to have their daughters' genitals altered. Cultural relativists (Ahmadu 2000, Shweder 2003) support people's freedom to pursue their traditional cultural practices.

The issue of whether Muslim girls can wear head scarves in school in non-Muslim countries is another example of group rights versus state laws (Ewing 2000). For many Muslims, the head scarf is a sign of proper Muslim society, a rejection of Western secularism, and an aspect of religious freedom. Westerners typically view the head scarf as a sign of women's oppression and as a symbol of rejection of the entire ethos of schooling and modernity. In France, beginning in 1989, disputes have erupted over girls wearing head scarves in school. In 1994 the French education director stated that head scarves would not be permitted in school, yet Jewish boys, at that point, had been allowed to wear yarmulkes (head caps). Muslim leaders responded by taking the issue to court and, as of 2004, the issue has not been settled.

International Organizations and World Peace

Since the seventeenth century, the world's countries have been increasingly linked in a hierarchical structure that is largely regulated through international trade. In the seventeenth century, Holland dominated world trade. It was surpassed by England and France, which remained the two most powerful countries until around 1900. In the early part of the twentieth century, challenges for world dominance were made by the United States and, later, Germany and Japan. The outcome of World War II established the United States as world leader. Most recently, Japan, the European Union, and China have begun to play larger roles.

This scene occurred in Mantes-la-Jolie, France, in 1994. Female Muslim students who wish to wear a headscarf while attending public schools in France have been banned from doing so by the government. This ban has led to protests and court disputes for over a decade. ■ What is the current position of the French government? What is the current position of your government on clothing allowed in public schools? (Source: © Giry Daniel/CORBIS SYGMA)

Given cultural anthropology's traditional strength in the study of small-scale societies, cultural anthropologists have come late to the study of international affairs (Wilson 2000). Now, more anthropologists have expanded their focus to the international level, studying both how global changes affect local politics and how local politics affects international affairs. Worldwide communication networks facilitate global politics. Ethnic politics, although locally initiated, increasingly has international repercussions. Migrant populations promote interconnected interests across state boundaries.

A pioneering study in the anthropology of international affairs is Stacia Zabusky's (1995) research on patterns of cooperation among international scientists at the European Space Agency (ESA). The ESA involves people from different European nations seeking to cooperate in joint ventures in space and, more indirectly, to promote peaceful relations in Europe. Zabusky attended meetings and interviewed people at the European Space Research and Technology Centre, ESA's primary production site, in the Netherlands. From observing people at work roles, their styles of reaching consensus at meetings, and their informal interactions, she concluded that language plays a key part in affecting cooperation. The official languages of the ESA are English and French, but most interactions take place in English. Some nonnative English speakers felt that this gave the British an automatic advantage, especially in meetings where skill in speech can win an argument. A major divisive factor is the sheer geographic dispersal of the participants throughout Europe. This means that travel is a constant, as scientists and engineers convene for important meetings. Despite logistical problems, meetings are an important part of the "glue" that promotes cooperation above and beyond just "working together." Conversations and discussions at meetings allow people to air their differences and work toward agreement. Zabusky concludes that the ESA represents an ongoing struggle for cooperation that is motivated by more than just the urge to do science. "In working together, participants were dreaming about finding something other than space satellites, other than a unified Europe or even a functioning organization at the end of their travails. Cooperation indeed appeared to participants not only as an achievement but as an aspiration" (197).

Anthropological research on peaceful, local-level societies shows that humans are capable of living together in peace. The question is whether people living in larger groups that are globally connected can also live in peace. Numerous attempts have been made, over time, to create institutions to promote world peace. The United Nations is the most firmly established and widely respected of such institutions. One of the UN's significant accomplishments was its creation of the International Court of Justice, also known as the World Court, located in The Hague in the Netherlands (Nader 1995). In 1946, two-thirds of the Court's judges were American or Western European. Now the Court has many judges from developing countries. Despite this more balanced representation, there has been a decline in use of the World Court and an increased use of international negotiating teams for resolving disputes between countries. Laura Nader analyzed this decline and found that it follows a trend in the United States, beginning in the 1970s, to promote "alternate dispute resolution" (ADR). The goal was to move more cases out of the courts and to privatize dispute resolution. On the surface, ADR seems a more peaceful and more dignified option. Deeper analysis of actual cases and their resolution shows, however, that this bilateral process favors the stronger party. Adjudication (formal decree by a judge) would have resulted in a better deal for the weaker party than bilateral negotiation did. Thus less powerful countries are negatively affected by the United States' move away from the World Court.

What role might cultural anthropology play in international peace-keeping? Cultural anthropologist Robert Carneiro has a pessimistic response (1994). He says that during the long history of human political evolution from bands to states, warfare has been the major means by which political units enlarged their power and domain. Foreseeing no logical end to this process, he predicts that war will follow war until superstates become ever larger and one megastate is the final result. He considers the United Nations powerless in dealing with the principal obstacle to world peace: state sovereignty interests. Carneiro indicts the United Nations for its lack of coercive power and its poor record of having resolved disputes through military intervention in only a few cases. If war is inevitable, there is little hope that anthropological knowledge can be applied to peace-making efforts. Despite Carneiro's views, however, cultural anthropologists have shown that war is not a cultural universal and that different cultures have ways of solving disputes without resorting to killing.

Another positive point emerges: the United Nations does provide an arena for airing disputes. This more optimistic view suggests that international peace organizations play a major role by providing analysis of the interrelationships among world problems and by helping others see what the causes and consequences of violence are (Vickers 1993). Beyond the framework of the United Nations, many people see hope for local and global peace-making through non-governmental organizations (NGOs) and local grassroots initiatives that bridge group interests.

Representatives of ten NATO countries at the World Court in The Hague. This distinguished body of legal experts exhibits a clear pattern of age, gender, and ethnicity. ■ What might be the implications of this pattern? (Source: © Reuters/Fred Ernst)

THE BIG QUESTIONS REVISITED

■ WHAT does political anthropology cover?

Political anthropology is the study of power relationships in the public domain and how they vary and change cross-culturally. Political anthropologists study the concept of power itself and related concepts such as authority and influence. They have discovered differences and similarities between politics and political organization in small-scale and large-scale societies in looking at issues such as leadership roles and responsibilities, the distribution of power, and the emergence of the state. Patterns of political organization and leadership vary according to mode of production and global economic relationships. Foragers have a minimal form of leadership and political organization in the band. Band membership is flexible. If a band member has a serious disagreement with another person or spouse, one option is to leave that band and join another. Leadership in bands is informal. The tribe is a more formal type of political organization than the band. A tribe comprises several bands or lineage groups with a headman or headwoman as leader. Big-man and big-woman political systems are an expanded form of tribe, and leaders have influence over people in several different villages. Chiefdoms may include several thousands of people. Rank is inherited, and social divisions exist between the chiefly lineage or lineages and non-chiefly groups. The state is a centralized political unit encompassing many communities and possessing coer-

cive power. States evolved in several locations with the emergence of intensive agriculture, increased surpluses, and increased population density. Most states are hierarchical and patriarchal.

■ WHAT is the scope of legal anthropology?

Legal anthropology encompasses the study of cultural variation in social order and social conflict. Early legal anthropologists approached the subject from a functionalist viewpoint that stresses how social institutions promote social cohesion and continuity. In contrast, the more recent approach of critical legal anthropology points out how legal institutions often support and maintain social inequalities and injustice. Legal anthropologists also study the difference between norms and laws. Systems of social order and social control vary cross-culturally and over time. Legal anthropologists have examined systems of social control in small-scale societies and in large-scale societies (states). Social control in small-scale societies seeks to restore order more than to punish offenders. The presence of a wide variety of legal specialists is more associated with the state than with small-scale societies, in which social shaming and shunning are common methods of punishment. In states, imprisonment and capital punishment may exist, reflecting the greater power of the state. Cross-cultural data on levels and forms of conflict and violence indicate that high levels of lethal violence are not universal and are more often associated with the state than with earlier forms of political organization. Social conflict ranges from face-to-face conflicts, as among neighbors or domestic partners, to larger group conflicts between ethnic groups and states. Solutions that would be effective at the interpersonal level are often not applicable to large-scale, impersonalized conflict. Cultural anthropologists are turning their attention to studying global conflict and peace-keeping solutions. Key issues involve the role of cultural knowledge in dispute resolution and how international or local organizations can help achieve or maintain peace.

■ HOW are political and legal systems changing?

The anthropological study of change in political and legal systems has documented several trends, many of which are related to the powerful influences of European colonialism or contemporary capitalist globalization. Postcolonial states struggle with internal ethnic divisions

and pressures to democratize. Ethnic/national politics has emerged within and across states as groups seek to compete for increased rights within the state or autonomy from it. Women as political leaders in states are still a small minority, especially at top levels of power. In some local groups, however, women leaders are gaining ground, as among the Seneca Nation of New York State. Global colonialism and contemporary globalization have transformed indigenous systems of social control and law, often resulting in legal pluralism. Cultural anthropologists are increasingly doing research on international topics, including the internal dynamics of international organizations. Their work demonstrates the relevance of cultural anthropology in global peacekeeping and conflict resolution. Insights from archaeology about the causes of conflict in the past, and from primatologists about conflict resolution and reconciliation among non-human primates, help provide a more comprehensive view of these important issues and may lead to conflict prevention in the future.

KEY CONCEPTS

authority, p. 468
band, p. 470
banditry, p. 482
big-man or big-woman system, p. 471
clan, p. 471
confederacy, p. 473
critical legal anthropology, p. 481
critical military anthropology, p. 487
faction, p. 476

feuding, p. 483
influence, p. 468
in-kind taxation, p. 474
law, p. 478
legal pluralism, p. 490
nation, p. 487
norm, p. 478
policing, p. 480
political organization, p. 470

power, p. 468
segmentary model, p. 471
social control, p. 477
transnationalism, p. 488
trial by ordeal, p. 480
tribe, p. 471
war, p. 484

SUGGESTED READINGS

Filippo Aureli and Frans B. M. de Waal, eds. *Natural Conflict Resolution*. Berkeley: University of California Press, 2000. Eighteen chapters, as well as an introduction on "natural conflict resolution," address conflict management and post-conflict reconciliation among many animals, including hyenas, baboons, and people. Themes such as third-party roles in conflict resolution, dominance styles, and communication patterns are addressed.

Stanley R. Barrett. *Culture Meets Power*. Westport, CN: Praeger, 2002. The author examines why the concept of power has gained ascendancy in anthropology, seeming to eclipse the concept of culture. He argues that the concept of power is no less ambiguous than that of culture and that both concepts need to be considered in understanding contemporary affairs, including events such as the September 11, 2001, attacks on the United States.

John Carman, ed. *Material Harm: Archaeological Studies of War and Violence*. Glasgow, Scotland: Cruithne Press, 1997.

The editor provides an introductory chapter on archaeological approaches to violence and a concluding chapter on the need to give archaeology a moral voice. Nine case study chapters consider topics such as the identification of head injuries, Irish Bronze Age swords, West Mediterranean hill forts, and warfare and the spread of agriculture in Borneo.

Jane K. Cowan, Marie-Bénédicte Dembour, and Richard A. Wilson, eds. *Culture and Rights: Anthropological Perspectives*. New York: Cambridge University Press, 2001. This collection includes three overview/theoretical chapters, seven case studies that address issues such as child prostitution and ethnic and women's rights, and a chapter that critiques the UNESCO concept of culture.

Jack David Eller. *From Culture to Ethnicity to Conflict: An Anthropological Perspective on International Ethnic Conflict*. Ann Arbor: University of Michigan Press, 1999. Two introductory chapters discuss terminology and the relationships among culture, ethnicity, and conflict, and subsequent chapters provide case studies of Sri Lanka, the Kurds, Rwanda and Burundi, Bosnia, and Québec.

R. Brian Ferguson and Neil L. Whitehead, eds. *War in the Tribal Zone: Expanding States and Indigenous Warfare.* Santa Fe, NM: School of American Research Press, 1992. Essays on tribal and pre-state warfare include examples from pre-Columbian Mesoamerica, early Sri Lanka, West Africa, the Iroquois, the Yanomami, and highland Papua New Guinea.

Pamela Frese and Margaret Harrell, eds. *Anthropology and the United States Military: Coming of Age in the Twenty-First Century.* New York: Palgrave/Macmillan, 2003. This volume of collected essays contributes to knowledge in several core anthropological areas (such as kinship, the body, leadership, and meaning) by addressing army spouses, gender roles, weight control and physical readiness, anthrax vaccines, and the military advisor, among other topics.

Thomas Gregor, ed. *A Natural History of Peace.* Nashville: University of Tennessee Press, 1996. This book contains essays on what peace is, reconciliation among nonhuman primates, the psychological bases of violent and caring societies, community-level studies on Amazonia and Native America, and issues of peace and violence between states.

Hugh Gusterson. *Nuclear Rites: A Weapons Laboratory at the End of the Cold War.* Berkeley: University of California Press, 1996. This ethnographic study focuses on the nuclear research community of Livermore, California. It explores the scientists' motivations to develop nuclear weapons, the culture of secrecy in and around the lab, and prevalent metaphors in nuclear research, which often have to do with reproduction and birth.

Philip L. Kohl and Clare Fawcett, eds. *Nationalism, Politics, and the Practice of Archaeology.* New York: Cambridge University Press, 1995. The organizing theme of this collection is how the state uses archaeological information to support state identity and cohesion. The introduction provides a theoretical overview. Individual chapters discuss links between nationalism and archaeology in Nazi Germany, post-USSR Russia, prehistoric Korea, and postwar Japan, among others.

Roger N. Lancaster. *Life Is Hard: Machismo, Danger, and the Intimacy of Power in Nicaragua.* Berkeley: University of California Press, 1992. This ethnography of everyday life in a barrio of Managua, Nicaragua, examines interpersonal violence as well as the wider issue of how living during a revolution affected people.

David H. Lempert. *Daily Life in a Crumbling Empire.* New York: Columbia University Press, 1996. This two-volume ethnography is based on fieldwork conducted in Moscow before perestroika. It is the first comprehensive ethnography of urban Russia and its economic, political, and legal systems and reforms.

Sally Engle Merry. *Getting Justice and Getting Even: Legal Consciousness among Working-Class Americans.* Chicago: University of Chicago Press, 1990. Based on fieldwork among native-born, White, working-class Americans in a small New England town and their experiences in the court system, this book considers how the court system is perceived by the litigants as more often controlling than empowering.

Bruce Miller. *The Problem of Justice: Tradition and Law in the Coast Salish World.* Lincoln: University of Nebraska Press, 2001. The author compares several legal systems operating in the Northwest Coast region from Washington State to British Columbia. The effects of colonialism differ from group to group; some legal systems are strong and independent, and others are disintegrating.

Mark Moberg. *Citrus, Strategy, and Class: The Politics of Development in Southern Belize.* Iowa City: University of Iowa Press, 1992. The theoretical debate of structure versus agency frames this ethnography of household and village economies within the world economy and the transformation from factional politics to class formation. The author provides quantitative data as well as insights from five individual lives in a chapter entitled "Keep on Fighting It."

Dan Rabinowitz. *Overlooking Nazareth: The Politics of Exclusion in Galilee.* New York: Cambridge University Press, 1997. This ethnographic study of Palestinian citizens in an Israeli new town examines specific situations of conflict and cooperation and provides theoretical insights into nationalism and ethnicity. Biographical accounts of three Palestinians—a medical doctor, a basketball coach, and a local politician—are included.

Jennifer Schirmer. *The Guatemalan Military Project: A Violence Called Democracy.* Philadelphia: University of Pennsylvania Press, 1998. This book is an ethnography of the Guatemalan military, documenting its role in human rights violations through extensive interviews with military officers and trained torturers.

Katherine Verdery. *The Political Lives of Dead Bodies: Reburial and Postsocialist Change.* New York: Columbia University Press, 1999. Post-USSR political changes in Eastern Europe involved a rethinking and revision of the past and forward thinking about the present. An understudied aspect of post-Communist political change in Eastern Europe involved the disposition of the bodies of dead political leaders, heroes, artists, and other people. Many bodies were exhumed and relocated and have been given a new political "life."

Joan Vincent, ed. *The Anthropology of Politics: A Reader in Ethnography, Theory, and Critique.* Malden, MA: Blackwell Publishers, 2002. Over forty essays are arranged in four broad historical sections to demonstrate the dynamic interplay among theory, ethnography, and critique. First come classics of the Enlightenment (Adam Smith, Karl Marx, others). There follows a section on early ethnographies (E. E. Evans-Pritchard, others), coupled with contemporary updates (such as Sharon Hutchinson). The third section is on colonialism and imperialism (Talal Asad, June Nash, others), and the last focuses on cosmopolitanism (Aihwa Ong, James Ferguson, others).

Jack M. Weatherford. *Tribes on the Hill.* New York: Rawson, Wade Publishers, 1981. This analysis of politics within the United States Congress examines the effects of male privilege and seniority on ranking, lobbying tactics, and ritual aspects of the legislation process.

PART
IV
Communication and the Search for Meaning

SUSAN SQUIRES, a business anthropologist, is part of the brains behind the General Mills breakfast food, Go-Gurt. During its first year of production in 1991, Go-Gurt generated sales of $37 million. Squires, who earned a Ph.D. in cultural anthropology from Boston University, is one of the growing number of anthropologists who use their knowledge of anthropological theory and research methods in the business world. Some are being snapped up by companies even before they finish their dissertations.

Research into the development of Go-Gurt took Squires and an industrial designer into the homes of American families to observe their breakfast behavior and food choices. On their first day of research, they arrived at a residence at 6:30 a.m., laden with video cameras and other equipment, prepared to have breakfast with a family they had never met. General Mills had learned from focus group studies that mothers want their families to eat whole-grain breakfast foods. The fieldwork, in contrast, revealed a wider range of preferences and behavior related to individual hunger patterns and the need to leave home early for work or school.

ANTHROPOLOGY
in the Real World

■ **Susan Squires, Business Anthropologist**

Squires realized that the ideal breakfast food should be portable, healthy, fun, and come in a disposable container. The answer: yogurt packaged so that it does not require a spoon and can be frozen or refrigerated. One mother said that her daughter thinks she is eating a Popsicle when she has Go-Gurt for breakfast. Inspired by this research, Squires and another business anthropologist, Brian Byrne, co-edited a book called *Creating Breakthrough Ideas: The Collaboration of Anthropologists and Designers in the Product Development Industry* (2002).

In another research role during the 1990s, Squires was a consumer behavior analyst for Arthur Andersen, a leading accounting firm implicated in the Enron scandal. After the criminal activity at Enron was exposed, Squires and three other employees wrote a book analyzing the company's problems, *Inside Arthur Andersen: Shifting Values, Unexpected Consequences* (2003). The book discusses conflicts within the organization between a tradition of high ethical standards of accounting and the growing market demand for higher and higher profit levels.

Founding her own company takes Squires in a direction that builds on her previous ten years of experience. Tactics, LLC, provides ethnographic research for businesses, governments, and educational institutions in North America, Europe, and Asia. Squires defines her company's goal as "finding treasure" that is "buried in people's brains." So far, Tactics has created new products for telecommunication, the pharmaceutical industry, and computer software companies. It develops and evaluates business strategies, and advises on organizational management, employee training and performance, and customer satisfaction.

The work of Susan Squires demonstrates how theory and methods in cultural anthropology can benefit both the business world and the everyday lives of consumers. Two of the most valuable assets of cultural anthropology in the business world are, first, its holistic perspective, which looks at the larger context and reveals connections, and second, its attention to multiculturalism, which exposes differences in preferences, values, and behavior.

THE BIG QUESTIONS

- WHAT are the major features of human verbal language?
- HOW do language, thought, and society interact?
- WHAT is human paralanguage?

CHAPTER **17**

Communication

Tuareg men in Niger, West Africa, greeting each other. Their greetings involve lengthy handshaking and close body contact. (Source: © Charles O. Cecil)

499

Many animals have sophisticated ways of communicating about where food is available or warning others about impending danger. People are in almost constant communication with other people, with supernaturals, with pets, or with other domesticated animals.

Communication is the conveying of meaningful messages from one individual to another or others. The means of communication among humans include eye contact, body posture, position and movements of limbs, and language.

Language is a form of communication that is a systematic set of arbitrary symbols shared among a group and passed from generation to generation. It may be spoken, signed, or written.

Linguistic anthropology is devoted to the study of communication—mainly, but not exclusively, among humans. This chapter draws on work in linguistic anthropology, one of general anthropology's four fields. It first discusses the characteristics of human language that set it apart from communication in other animals and addresses the origins of languages. The role of language in our multicultural worlds is discussed in the second section: how language is related to thought and society. Last, we cover the topic of communication without the use of words.

Linguistic anthropology began in the United States, inspired by the realization that Native American languages were rapidly disappearing through population decline and assimilation into Euro-American culture. Franz Boas gained eminence for recording many of the languages, myths, and rituals of these disappearing cultures (recall Chapter 1). Another force driving the development of linguistic anthropology was the discovery, through cross-cultural fieldwork, that many existing non-Western languages had never been written down. Study of non-Western languages revealed a wide range of different sounds and exposed the inadequacy of Western alphabets to represent such varied sounds. This finding prompted the development of the International Phonetic Alphabet, which contains symbols to represent all sounds known to occur in human languages worldwide, such as the symbol "!" to indicate a click sound used in some southern African languages.

Many linguistic anthropologists are involved in applying research findings, for example, to promote improved language learning among school children, migrants, and refugee populations. The modification of standardized tests to reduce bias against children from varied cultural backgrounds is an area where applied linguistic anthropologists are increasingly active. Linguistic anthropologists also study language use in deaf communities, including research on cross-cultural differences in sign language. This work helps to promote greater public understanding of the cultures of people who are deaf and contributes to the improved teaching of sign language (see the Lessons Applied box).

HUMAN VERBAL LANGUAGE

This section begins with a discussion of some of the challenges of fieldwork in linguistic anthropology and then discusses two distinctive features of human language that separate it from other animal communication. A brief review of the formal properties of language is followed by consideration of historical linguistics and language change.

Fieldwork Challenges

Fieldwork in linguistic anthropology shares the basic method of cultural anthropology (participant observation), though some research areas require specialized data gathering and analysis. The study of language in use involves collecting data in a "natural" setting—that is, unbiased by the presence of the researcher (see the Methods

Anthropology and Public Understanding of the Language and Culture of People Who Are Deaf

ETHNOGRAPHIC STUDIES of the communication practices and culture of people who are deaf have great importance and practical application (Senghas and Monaghan 2002). First, this research demonstrates the limitations and inaccuracy of the "medical model" that construes deafness as a pathology or deficit and sees the goal as curing it. Instead, anthropologists propose the "cultural model," which views deafness simply as one possibility in the wide spectrum of cultural variation. Anthropological research shows that deafness leaves substantial room for human agency. The strongest evidence of agency among people who are deaf is sign language itself, which exhibits adaptiveness, creativity, and change. This new view helps to promote a non-victim, non-pathological identity for people who are deaf and to reduce social stigma related to deafness. Third, anthropologists working in the area of deaf culture studies examine how people who are deaf become bilingual—for example, fluent in both English and Japanese sign languages. Their findings have led to improved ways of teaching sign language.

FOOD FOR THOUGHT

■ Learn the signs for five words in English sign language and then learn the signs for the same words in another sign language. Are they the same or different, and how might one explain the similarity or difference?

Close-Up box on p. 502). It relies on tape recordings or video recordings of people and events. The tapes are then analyzed qualitatively or quantitatively. Video recordings, for example, may be subjected to a detailed "frame analysis" that pinpoints when communication breaks down or misunderstandings occur.

Linguistic anthropologists argue that the analysis of recorded data is best done when it is informed by general knowledge about the culture. This approach derives from Bronislaw Malinowski's view that communication is embedded in its social context and therefore must be studied in relation to that context. An example of such a contextualized approach is a study in Western Samoa that gathered many hours of

A Samoan kava drinking ceremony begins. Kava is made from the roots of a plant in the black pepper family. The roots are dried, pounded, and mixed with water. A social beverage, kava is a relaxant also used for healing.
■ Think of a parallel gathering in your cultural world in terms of expected forms of consumption, seating arrangements, and discourse patterns in terms of who speaks, turn-taking, and the content of the discourse itself. (Source: © Don Smetzer)

Dealing with the "Observer's Paradox"

Linguistic anthropologists who study ordinary language in use face the problem of the **observer's paradox,** the impossibility of doing research on natural communication events without affecting the very naturalness sought (McMahon 1994:234). The mere presence of the anthropologist with a tape recorder makes the speaker concentrate on speaking "correctly" and more formally. Several options exist for dealing with the observer's paradox. They include recording speakers in a group, observing and recording speech outside an interview situation, and using structured interviews in which a person is asked to perform various speech tasks at varying levels of formality. In this last technique, the research participant is first asked to read a word list and a short passage. The next stage is a question-

and-answer session. Then the interviewer encourages the participant, who may be more relaxed by now, to produce informal conversational speech by asking about childhood rhymes and sayings, encouraging digressions to get the informant to talk for longer periods, and posing questions that are likely to prompt an emotional response. Another strategy is to use "role plays" in which participants are asked to act out a particular script, such as arguing about something. Data from semistructured techniques can be compared with the more casual styles of natural speech to assess the possible bias created by being observed.

FOOD FOR THOUGHT

- Can you recall a situation in which you changed your verbal behavior because you were under observation? How did your speech change?

tape-recorded speech as well as conducting participant observation (Duranti 1994). Analysis of the transcriptions of the recorded talk revealed two major findings about how speech used in village council meetings is related to social status. First, turn-taking patterns reflected and restated people's power positions in the group. Second, people used particular grammatical forms and word choices that indirectly either praised or blamed others, thus shaping and reaffirming people's moral roles and status relations. Nonlinguistic data that helped the researchers form these interpretations included observation of seating arrangements and the order of the distribution of kava (a ritually shared intoxicating beverage). The findings about the role of language in creating and maintaining social and moral order contribute to a richer understanding of the social context of status formation in Samoa.

Most cultural and linguistic anthropologists face the challenge of translation. It involves understanding more about a language than just vocabulary in order to provide a reliable and meaningful translation. An anthropologist once translated a song that occurred at the end of a play in Zaire, central Africa (Fabian 1995). The play was presented in the Swahili language, so he assumed that the final song was, too. Thus he thought the repeated use of the word *tutubawina*, which he thought to be a Swahili word, indicated that it was a fighting song. A Swahili speaker assisting him said no, it was a soccer song. The puzzled anthropologist later learned, by writing to the theater performers, that the word *tutubawina* as used in this song was not a Swahili word but instead indicated a marching song.

Key Characteristics: Productivity and Displacement

Most anthropologists agree that nonhuman primates share with humans the ability to communicate through sounds and movements, and that some can be trained to recognize and use some of the same arbitrary symbols that humans use. Whatever progress is made in teaching nonhuman primates aspects of sign language, it is unlikely that they will ever develop the range of linguistic ability that humans possess, because human language relies heavily on two features that depend on the richness of arbitrary symbols.

Human language is said to have infinite **productivity,** or the ability to communicate many messages efficiently. In contrast, consider gibbon communication in the wild. Gibbons have nine calls that convey useful messages such as "follow me," "I am angry," "here is food," "danger," and "I am hurt." If a gibbon wants to communicate intensity in, say, the danger at hand, the only option is to repeat the "danger" call several times and at different volumes: "danger," "*danger,*" "DANGER," and so on. This variation allows some productivity, but with greater degrees of danger, the system of communication becomes increasingly inefficient. By the time twenty danger calls have been given, it may be too late. In comparison, human language's capacity for productivity makes it extremely efficient. Different levels of danger can be conveyed in these ways:

"I see a movement over there."

"I see a leopard there."

"A leopard—run!"

"Help!"

Chimpanzees have demonstrated a remarkable ability to learn aspects of human language. Here, trainer Joyce Butler signs "Nim," and Nim signs "Me." ■ Consider examples of how animals other than humans communicate with each other. (Source: © Susan Kuklin/Photo Researchers, Inc.)

Human language also uses the feature of **displacement,** which enables people to talk about displaced domains—events in the past and future—as well as about the immediate present. According to current thinking, displacement is not a prominent feature of nonhuman primate communication. A wild chimpanzee is unlikely to be able to communicate the message "Danger: there may be a leopard coming here tonight." Instead, it communicates mainly what is experienced in the present. Even if nonhuman primates do use displacement, its use among humans is far more prevalent. Among humans, the majority of language use is related to displaced domains, including reference to people and events that may never exist at all, as in fantasy and fiction.

Formal Properties of Verbal Language

Besides the general characteristics noted above, human language can be analyzed in terms of its formal properties: sounds, vocabulary, and grammar—all features that lie within the purview of formal or "structural" linguistics (Agar 1994).

Learning a new language usually involves learning different sets of sounds. The sounds that make a difference for meaning in a language are called **phonemes;** the study of phonemes is called **phonetics.** Sharon Hutchinson comments on her attraction to phonemes of the Nuer language spoken in the Sudan:

As a native English speaker, I find the seeming airy lightness and rich melodic qualities of the Nuer language to be attractive. The language contains few "hard" consonants—and those that do exist are often softened or silenced at the ends of words. A terminal "k," for instance, often slides into a breathy "gh" sound . . . or a lighter "h" sound or is suppressed entirely . . . . The apparent "airiness" of the language stems from the fact that many Nuer vowels are heavily aspirated—that is, they are released with an audible bit of breath as in the English "hi" and "hea" in "behind" and "ahead," [respectively]. Indeed, one of the earliest obstacles I faced in trying to learn the language was to hear and to control the voice's "breathiness" or "non-breathiness" in the pronunciation of various Nuer vowels. (1996:xv–xvi)

A native English-speaker trying to learn the north Indian language called Hindi is challenged to learn to produce and recognize several new sounds. For example, four different "d" sounds exist. None are the same as an English "d," which is usually

In your experience of learning a foreign language, what phonetic features have been the most difficult?

THINKING

OUTSIDE THE BOX

FIGURE 17.1

Dental and retroflex tongue positions. When making a dental sound, the speaker places the tongue against the upper front teeth (position A on the diagram). When making a retroflex sound, the speaker places the tongue up against the roof of the mouth (position B on the diagram).

(*Source:* Reprinted by permission of Allyn & Bacon.)

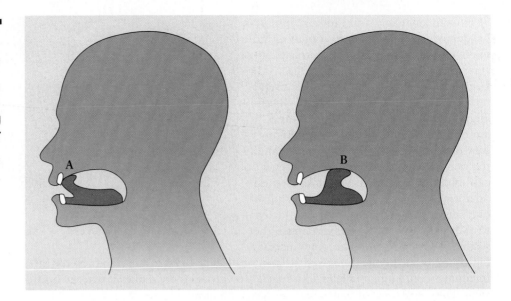

pronounced with the tongue placed on the ridge behind the upper front teeth (try it). One "d" in Hindi, which linguists refer to as a "dental" sound, is pronounced with the tongue pressed firmly behind the upper front teeth (try it). (See Figure 17.1.) Next is a dental "d" that is also aspirated (pronounced "with air"). Making this sound involves placing the tongue in the same position and expelling a puff of air during pronunciation (try it, and try the regular dental "d" again with no puff of air at all). Next is a "retroflex sound," accomplished by flipping the tongue back to the central dome of the roof of the mouth (try it, with no puff of air). Finally, there is the aspirated retroflex "d," pronounced with the tongue again in the center of the roof of the mouth and a puff of air. Once you can do this, try the whole series again with a "t," because Hindi follows the same pattern with this letter as with the "d." Several other sounds in Hindi require careful use of aspiration and placement of the tongue for communicating the right word. A puff of air at the wrong time can produce a serious error, such as saying the word for "breast" when you want to say the word for "letter."

Grammar consists of the patterns and rules by which words are organized to make sense. All languages have a grammar, although grammars vary in form. Even within the languages of contemporary Europe grammar varies. German is characterized by its placement of the verb at the end of the sentence (try to compose an English sentence with its main verb at the end). Together, phonemes, vocabulary, and grammar are the formal building blocks of language.

An Indus Valley stamp seal, carved in a fine-grained stone called steatite. Dating between 3300–1500 BCE, the seals were probably used for marking trade goods. Some have been found as far away as Mesopotamia. The seals are less than 2 inches across. This one depicts a unicorn, or a buffalo in profile, apparently eating or drinking from a raised container. The Indus Valley script, at the top, remains undeciphered. ■ How would an archaeologist of the future interpret the barcodes on contemporary products? (Source: © Borromeo/Art Resource, NY)

Origins and History

Did the first humans have language, and if so, what was it like? Did grunts and exclamations evolve into words and sentences? Did early humans attempt to imitate the sounds of nature? Did a committee meet and decide to put together a set of arbitrary symbols with meanings that everyone would accept? No one knows, nor will we ever know, how language started in the first place. The prevailing view (discussed in Chapter 8) is that humans began to develop complex verbal language around 50,000 years ago. Most paleoanthropologists think that communication before that time mainly involved grunts, facial expressions, and hand gestures. Human **paralanguage,** a category that includes all forms of nonverbal communication (such as body posture, voice tone, touch, smells, and eye and facial movements), is thus probably a continuation of the earliest phase of human language.

No contemporary human language is a "primitive" model of early human language. That would defy the principle of **linguistic relativism**— the idea that all languages have passed through thousands of years of change and that all are equally successful forms of communication. Languages differ in their structure and in the meaning they ascribe to various concepts (that is, in *semantics*), but all are capable of conveying subtle meanings and complex thoughts. Early scholars of comparative linguistics were sometimes misled by ethnocentric assumptions that the language structures of European languages were normative and that languages that did not have that same structure were deficient. Different languages exhibit complexity in different areas—sometimes in verb forms, sometimes in noun formations.

Writing Systems

Archaeological data cannot provide insights into the orgins of speech. Attempts to trace the beginnings of language are thus confined to working with records of written language. Evidence of the earliest written languages comes from Mesopotamia, Egypt, and China. The oldest writing system was in use by the fourth millennium BCE in Mesopotamia (review Chapter 9, pp. 270–273). Some scholars say that symbols found on pottery in China dated at 5000 to 4000 BCE should be counted as the earliest writing. At issue here is the definition of a writing system: Does the presence of symbolic markings on pots constitute a "writing system" or not? Most scholars say that a symbolic mark that could refer to a clan name is not necessarily evidence of a writing system that involves the use of words in relation to each other in a systematic way. All early writing systems made use of logographs, or signs that indicate a word, syllable, or sound. Over time, some logographs retained their original meaning. Others were retained but were given more abstract meaning, and nonlogographic symbols were added (see Figure 17.2).

As discussed in Chapter 9, the emergence of writing is associated with the political development of the state. Some scholars take writing as a key diagnostic feature that distinguishes the state from earlier political forms because recordkeeping was an essential task of the state. The Inca state is an exception to this generalization. It used *quipu*, or cords of knotted strings of different colors, for keeping accounts and recording events. Two interpretations of early writing systems exist. One is that the primary use of early writing was ceremonial—a view supported by the prevalence of early writing on tombs, bone inscriptions, or temple carvings. The other is that early writing was utilitarian: employed for government recordkeeping and trade. In this view, the archaeological record is biased toward durable substances and therefore ceremonial writing (because durable substances such as stone are more likely to have been used for ceremonial writing that was intended to last). Utilitarian writing is more likely to have been done on perishable materials because people would be less concerned with permanence—consider the way we treat shopping lists.

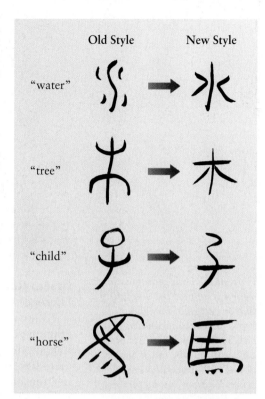

	Old Style	New Style
"water"		
"tree"		
"child"		
"horse"		

FIGURE 17.2
Logographic and current writing styles in China.

(*Source:* Courtesy of Molly Spitzer Frost.)

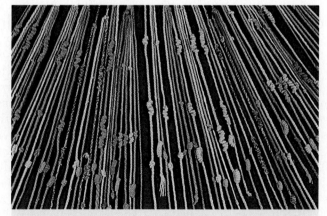

Quipu, or knotted strings, were the basis of accounting in the Incan empire. The knots convey substantial information for those who could interpret their meaning. ■
How does a quipu system compare to current technology used to keep track of government information? What do the differences suggest about contemporary states?
(Source: © M. Vautier, Anthropological & Archaeological Museum, Lima, Peru/Woodfin Camp & Associates)

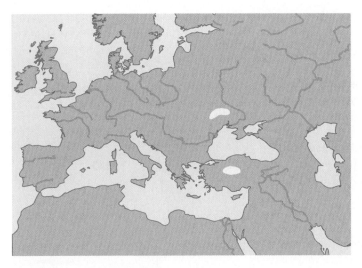

Current methods of linguistic analysis support the possibility that the original homeland of Proto-Indo-European was either among pastoralists in an area north of the Black Sea about 6000 years ago or in central Turkey among farmers over 8000 years ago.

Historical Linguistics

Historical linguistics is the study of language change through history using methods that compare shifts over time and across space in formal aspects of language such as phonetics, grammar, and semantics. This approach originated in the eighteenth century with a discovery made by Sir William Jones, a British colonial administrator working in India. During his spare time in India, he studied Sanskrit, an ancient language of India. He was the first to notice strong similarities among Sanskrit, Greek, and Latin in vocabulary and grammar. For example, the Sanskrit word for "father" is *pitr*, in Greek it is *patér*, and in Latin, *pater*. This was an astounding discovery for the time, given the prevailing European mentality that placed its cultural heritage firmly in the classical Graeco-Roman world and depicted the "Orient" as completely separate from "Europe" (Bernal 1987).

Following Jones's discovery, other scholars began comparing lists of words and grammatical forms in different languages: the French *père*, the German *Vater*, the Italian *padre*, the Old English *faeder*, the Old Norse *fadhir*, the Swedish *far*. With these lists, scholars could also determine degrees of closeness and distance in their relationships—for example, that German and English are closer to each other, and French and Spanish are closer to each other. Later scholars contributed the concept of "language families," or clusters of related languages. Attempting to reconstruct the family trees of languages was a major research interest of the nineteenth century. Comparison of contemporary and historical Eurasian languages and shifts in sound, vocabulary, and meaning yielded a model of a hypothetical early parent language called *Proto-Indo-European* (PIE). For example, the hypothetical PIE term for "father" is p#ter (the "#" symbol is pronounced like the "u" in *mutter*). Linguistic evidence suggests that PIE was located somewhere in Eurasia, either north or south of the Black Sea. From its area of origin, PIE speakers migrated to Europe, central and eastern Asia, and South Asia. The further they moved from the PIE center in terms of time and space, the more their language diverged from original PIE.

Colonialism, Globalization, and Language Change

Languages are always changing, sometimes slowly and in small ways, at other times rapidly and dramatically. We are scarcely conscious of many changes in our language.

Colonialism was a major force of change. Not only did colonial powers declare their own language as the language of government, business, and higher education, but they often took direct steps to suppress indigenous languages and literatures. A **pidgin** is a contact language, often the result of colonialism, that emerges when members of cultures with different languages come in close proximity and therefore need to communicate (McMahon 1994:253). Pidgins are generally limited to highly functional domains, such as trade. A pidgin, therefore, is no one's first language. Tok Pisin, the pidgin language of Papua New Guinea, consists of a mixture of many languages: English, Samoan, Chinese, and Malaysian. Tok Pisin has been declared one of the national languages of Papua New Guinea, where it is transforming into a **creole**—a language that is descended from a pidgin, has its own native speakers, and involves linguistic expansion and elaboration. About two hundred pidgin and creole languages exist today, mainly in West Africa, the Caribbean, and the South Pacific.

National policies of cultural assimilation of minorities have led to the extinction of many indigenous and minority languages. The Soviet attempt to build a USSR-wide

THINKING OUTSIDE THE BOX Use the Internet to access more information on Tok Pisin and choose five words or phrases in it that you would find useful in your everyday life.

commitment to communism after the 1930s included mass migration of Russian speakers into remote areas, where they eventually outnumbered indigenous peoples (Belikov 1994). In some cases, Russian officials visited areas and burned books in local languages. Children were forcibly sent away to boarding schools, where they were taught in Russian. The Komi, an indigenous group who spoke a Finno-Ugric language, traditionally formed the majority population in their area north of European Russia on the banks of the lower Pechora River. Russian immigrants eventually outnumbered the indigenous people. Russian was the language used in schools. Before long all Komi became bilingual. The Komi language may now be extinct.

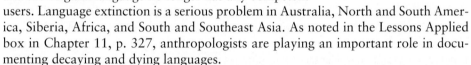

Anthropologists are concerned about the rapid loss of languages throughout the world—one result of accelerated globalization, including Western economic and media expansion (Hill 2001). **Language decay** occurs when speakers use, in some contexts, a new language in which they may be semifluent and when they have limited vocabulary in their native language. **Language extinction** occurs at the point when language speakers abandon their language in favor of another language, and the original language no longer has any competent users. Language extinction is a serious problem in Australia, North and South America, Siberia, Africa, and South and Southeast Asia. As noted in the Lessons Applied box in Chapter 11, p. 327, anthropologists are playing an important role in documenting decaying and dying languages.

Languages that are gaining currency over decaying and dying languages are called **global languages,** or world languages. They are languages that are spoken worldwide in diverse cultural contexts, notably English and Spanish. As these global languages spread to areas and cultures beyond their home area and culture, they take on new, localized identities. One scholar says that there are now many "Englishes" (Bhatt 2001). England's English was transplanted through colonial expansion to the United States, Canada, Australia, New Zealand, South Asia, Africa, Hong Kong, and the Caribbean. English became the dominant language in the colonies. It was used in government and commerce and was taught in schools. Over time, regional and subregional varieties of English have developed, often leading to a form of English that a native speaker from England cannot understand at all.

Efforts to revive or maintain local languages face a difficult challenge. Political opposition often comes from state governments that may fear local identity movements and may not wish to support, administratively or financially, bilingual or multilingual policies and programs. The English-only movement among political conservatives in the United States is an example of an attempt to control linguistic diversity (Neier 1996). Because language is such a vital part of culture, linguistic suppression can lead to cultural suppression.

LANGUAGE, THOUGHT, AND SOCIETY

This section presents material that illuminates the relationships among language, thought, and society. First, we discuss two theoretical approaches to these relationships. Then we look in greater depth at how different "levels" of language are related to thought and society.

Two Models

In the mid-twentieth century, two theoretical perspectives became influential in the study of how language, thought, and society are related. They are still important, and many anthropologists draw on both (Hill and Mannheim 1992).

Edward Sapir and Benjamin Whorf formulated a model called the **Sapir-Whorf hypothesis.** According to this model, language differences predetermine differences in thinking. For example, if a language has no word for what in English is called "snow," then a person who has been brought up in that language cannot think of "snow" as it is meant in English. Whorf first began developing this theory through study of different languages' vocabulary and grammar. He was so struck by the differences that he said that people who speak different languages inhabit different "thought worlds." This catchy phrase became the basis for what is called **linguistic determinism,** the idea that language determines consciousness of the world and behavior. Extreme linguistic determinism suggests that the frames and definitions of a person's primary language are so strong that it is impossible either to learn another language fully or to truly understand another culture (Agar 1994:67).

An alternative model to the Sapir-Whorf model was proposed by scholars working in the area of **sociolinguistics,** the study of language in relation to society. These theorists argue that a person's social position determines the content and form of language.

William Labov's research of the 1960s established this approach (1966). Labov conducted studies of the use of particular speech sounds among people of different socioeconomic classes in New York City. He hypothesized that class differences would be reflected in the use of certain sounds. For example, pronunciation of the consonant "r" in words such as *car, card, floor,* and *fourth* tends to be associated with upper-class people, whereas its absence ("caw," "cawd," "flaw," "fawth") is associated with lower-class people. In order to obtain data on discourse without the formalizing effects of taped interviews, Labov relied on the use of rapid and anonymous observations of sales clerks' speech in three Manhattan department stores. The stores were chosen to represent three class levels: Saks the highest, then R. H. Macy, then S. Klein. His assumption was that the clerks in these stores represented different class levels and statuses. Labov would approach a clerk and inquire about the location of some item that he knew was on the fourth floor. The clerk would respond, and then Labov would say, "Excuse me?" in order to prompt a more emphatic repeat of the word *fourth*. His analysis of the data confirmed the hypothesis. The higher-status "r" was pronounced both the first and second time by 44 percent of the employees in Saks, by 16 percent of the employees in R. H. Macy, and by 6 percent of the employees in S. Klein. In the rest of the cases, some of the clerks used the "r" in the emphatic, repeat response, but most uses were without the "r."

The topic of focal vocabularies illustrates the connections between the Sapir-Whorf hypothesis and sociolinguistics. **Focal vocabularies** are clusters of words that refer to important features of a particular culture. Studying focal vocabularies shows how language is both a "thought world" (according to the Sapir-Whorf hypothesis) and a cultural construction responsive to a particular context. For example, many languages of the circumpolar north recognize many different forms of snow and have many terms for these varieties. Environmental conditions that make snow such an important factor, in conjunction with economic adaptations, drive this amplification and therefore shape how circumpolar people actually think about the weather. Similarly, English speakers of the United States who are avid skiers have a

Ski enthusiasts use a more elaborate set of terms to differentiate forms of snow than most English speakers, among whom "powder" and "corn," for example, are not familiar concepts for snow.
■ What other focal vocabularies can you think of?
(Source: © Jeff Greenberg/ Photo Researchers, Inc.)

richer focal vocabulary related to forms of cold-weather precipitation than people who grow up in the Amazon region and have never seen snow or gone sledding or skiing.

Multiple Levels of Language

One characteristic of contemporary language change is the increasing numbers of people who speak more than one language. Much of this change is the result of colonialism and, now, of increased migration related to economic globalization. Another characteristic tied to multicultural diversity is the existence of variation within a single language in such matters as word choice, intonation, and even grammar.

Bilingualism

Since the era of colonial expansion beginning in the fifteenth century, people everywhere have been increasingly exposed to more than one language. One result is that more people are bilingual. Bilingualism is the capacity to speak two languages. A true bilingual has "native" speaking abilities in two languages.

French and Arabic cultural influences in Morocco result in bilingual shop signs. ■ Where have you seen bilingualism in public use? What languages were used and why? (Source: Barbara Miller)

Many world populations are bilingual because their country was colonized and a second language was introduced. As a result of their close proximity to other countries and their high exposure to many languages, most Europeans often grow up learning more than one language. The emergence of large populations speaking several languages has led to heated debates about the value of more than one "standard" language. Can **linguistic pluralism** (the presence of linguistic diversity within a particular context) be supported in view of its cost to the educational system? The effort to foster linguistic pluralism or bilingualism arises out of the belief that it will help reduce economic disparities between native speakers of the first language and non-native speakers.

Language testing of bilingual people seems to support the contention that even if people are fluent in their second language, they are still at a disadvantage in terms of majority-language competence. According to one theory, a person who has to use two languages to communicate every day does not have full capabilities in either language, because each one fills in for the other to create a unitary whole out of two partial languages (Valdés and Figueroa 1994:7). Thus, if such a person is evaluated in one of these languages, he or she will appear to have a low level of linguistic competence: "When a bilingual individual confronts a monolingual test, developed by monolingual individuals, and standardized and normed on a monolingual population, both the test taker and the test are asked to do something that they cannot. The bilingual test taker cannot perform like a monolingual. The monolingual test cannot 'measure' in the other language" (87). Given the monolingual content of existing tests, bilingual students are likely to test lower than monolingual students.

Dialects

Linguists jokingly say that a dialect is a language without an army, suggesting power differentials between speakers of a language and speakers of a dialect. A **dialect** is a way of speaking in a particular place, or, more precisely, a subordinate variety of a language arising from local circumstances (R. Williams 1983:105). Thus there is standard English, and there are dialects of English. For example, the British singing group the Beatles originated in the city of Liverpool, known for its distinct dialect called "Scouse." Cockney, spoken in London, is another prominent dialect. Speakers of these dialects are able to understand each other, but with some difficulty.

A language has the stamp of authority of the state and is taught using standardized textbooks. Dialects are used in literature and film to add "local color." Dialect speakers are often portrayed as second-class because they do not speak the standard language.

Language experts argue about whether Black English is a dialect of standard English or a language in its own right. So-called Black English has been looked down on by "linguistic conservative" champions of a standard English tradition. To them, Black English is a broken, haphazard, ungrammatical form of English that needs to be "corrected." Other educators realize that Black children in the United States learn one language at home and are then confronted with another language in school. They are expected to be bilingual because they must develop proficiency in standard English. Political scientist Andrew Hacker says that recognition of this issue is what is needed, not the teaching of Black English in schools, as the city of Oakland, California, proposed in 1997 with its promotion of teaching in "Ebonic" or Black English (1992:171).

Another thing that White teachers need to understand is that Black children may have culturally distinct styles of expression. For example, Black children should be given opportunities for expressive talking because, as Hacker notes, Black culture gives attention to both style and substance. In terms of narrative style, Black children tend to use a spiral pattern, skipping around to various topics before addressing the theme, whereas White children use a linear style. In terms of literature assignments, if more writings of Black authors were read in classrooms, Black children would thereby have a cultural anchor to their heritage, and receive respect for their traditions. At the same time White children, who might otherwise not get such exposure, would be enriched.

Language Codes

Within a single language, particular microcultures have distinctive **codes,** or ways of speaking. They may include distinctive vocabulary, grammar, and intonation depending on the age, gender, occupation, and class of the speaker and listener. Most people know more than one code and are able to *code-switch,* or move from one code to another as appropriate. For example, consider how you talk to your college friends when you are in a group, compared to how you might speak to a physician or potential employer. Code-switching can be an intentional strategy used to further the interests of the speaker. In the decolonizing nations, people may express their resistance to the colonial powers by avoiding complete switching to the colonial language but instead using code-mixing. In *code-mixing,* the speaker starts in the native language and then introduces words or phrases from the colonial language (Myers-Scotton 1993:122).

Gender codes exist in most languages. In North America, Euro-American female codes possess several features: more politeness, rising intonation at the end of sentences, and the frequent use of **tag questions,** which are questions seeking affirmation that are placed at the end of sentences: "It's a nice day, *isn't it?*" (Lakoff 1973). Male codes are less polite, maintain a flat, assertive tone in a sentence, and do not use tag questions. One conversational characteristic is that men interrupt women more than women interrupt men. In general, the female code is a subservient, complementary, "weak" form, whereas the male code is dominating, hierarchical, and "strong."

Sociolinguist Deborah Tannen's popular book *You Just Don't Understand* (1990) shows how differences in male and female communication styles in the United States may lead to miscommunication. She says that "women speak and hear a language of connection and intimacy, while men speak and hear a language of status and independence" (42). Sometimes men and women use similar linguistic styles, such as indirect response, but their differing motivations create different meanings that are embedded in their speech. For example, many husbands saw their role as one of protector in why they used an indirect response to a question:

Michele: What time is the concert?

Gary: You have to be ready by seven-thirty. (289)

Michele feels that Gary withholds information by not answering her directly, thus maintaining a power position. He feels that he is "watching out for her" by getting to the real point of her question.

Gender codes in spoken Japanese also reflect and reinforce gender differences and hierarchies (Shibamoto 1987). Certain words and sentence structures convey

THINKING OUTSIDE THE BOX Find at least one example from a recent movie in which a linguistic code was used to convey information about a character.

TABLE 17.1
Male-unmarked and female-marked nouns in Japanese.

	Male	Female
Box lunch	bentoo	obentoo
Money	kane	okane
Chopsticks	hasi	ohasi
Book	hon	ohon

(*Source:* Table, p. 28, "Male-unmarked and female-marked nouns in Japanese" from "The Womanly Woman: Manipulation of Stereotypical and Nonstereotypical Features of Japanese Female Speech" by Janet Shibamoto in *Language, Gender, and Sex in Comparative Perspective,* ed. by S. U. Philips, S. Steel, and C. Tanz. Copyright © 1987. Reprinted by permission of Cambridge University Press.)

femininity, humbleness, and politeness. A common contrast between male and female speech is the attachment, by females, of the honorific prefix "o-" to nouns (see Table 17.1). This addition gives female speech a more refined and polite tone. Polite forms of speech, cross-culturally, are more closely associated with female gender codes than with male gender codes. This gender difference carries over into related areas of speech. For example, a study of apologizing carried out on the Pacific Island of Vanuatu found that women apologize more frequently than men (Meyerhoff 1999).

Another common linguistic code is *baby talk* or *parentese,* or, even more specifically, *fatherese* or *motherese,* used when communicating with infants. Baby talk shares several features with other simplified codes, such as *foreigner talk,* talk to the elderly, talk to lovers, and talk to pets. These features include the use of short words, deletion of verbs, and high pitch. Many anthropologists agree that baby talk is widespread and may therefore have some relevance to biological theories of adaptiveness.

CROSSING
THE FIELDS

An Evolutionary Perspective
on Baby Talk

Why do mothers, fathers, and other adults use a different linguistic code when communicating with infants? Feeding hungry infants and rocking distressed infants are two behaviors that have been explained in evolutionary terms as shaped by natural selection because they contribute to survival by providing nourishment and regulating infant behavior (Fernald 1992). Baby talk could also be viewed as having evolved to serve a species-specific, biological, adaptive function. The long period of human infant dependency, compared to that of nonhuman primates, necessitates a longer and closer relationship with primary caregivers. Such attachment may be facilitated by a high-pitched code such as baby talk.

If this is the case, then the "prosodic" characteristics (mainly, pitch of the voice) of baby talk should be the same across cultures. Baby talk tends to be characterized by high pitch and exaggerated intonation compared to adult-directed speech. High tonal sounds in animals other than humans are associated with fear, appeasement, or friendliness, whereas low tonal sounds are associated with threats and punishment. Interestingly, smiling while talking forces the voice to a higher pitch. High pitch has been shown to be more effective than low pitch in gaining the attention and response of infants, which in turn contributes to infant learning and emotional connectivity. All these factors would seem to indicate that infant-directed language would be most adaptive if it involved high-pitched sounds.

Acoustic analysis of parental speech to infants in several languages—French, Italian, Japanese, German, British English, American English, and Mandarin—reveals similar prosodic modifications in speech to 12-month-old infants, with higher pitch than in adult-directed speech. Thus far, studies have been biased toward language use in industrialized countries, but one study of a nonindustrial culture, focusing on Xhosa-speaking mothers of South Africa, found raised pitch in mother–infant communication. These findings, from such diverse settings, would support an evolutionary view of species-universal raised-pitch code.

But there are complications. A few cultures (some Maya peoples) do not have high-pitched baby talk, yet their babies thrive and their cultures continue to exist. Furthermore, within the general pitch-change pattern of the several languages mentioned above, some important differences emerge. In Japanese and Mandarin Chinese, mothers employ a narrower pitch range than mothers in Europe and America. Does this difference mean that Japanese and Chinese babies have impaired chances for survival and growth? Finally, one cultural groups baby talk stands out as having the most extreme pitch modifications: middle-class Euro-American mothers. Do their babies have the best survival chances? ■

FOOD FOR THOUGHT

■ How might studies of caregiver–infant communication among the great apes shed light on this issue?

Linguistic anthropologists tend to focus their research on cultural variation in the content and meaning of baby talk in different settings. Elinor Ochs is a pioneer in studying and analyzing mother–infant talk. She recorded hundreds of hours of mother–infant "conversations" among Western Samoans and White middle-class (WMC) North Americans (1993). Her content analysis of these interactions reveals differences between the roles of mothers in the two cultures.

WMC mothers use two basic communicative strategies with their infants, both of which reflect the high level of child-centeredness of their culture. The first is their use of baby talk. Their baby talk is characterized by a restricted vocabulary, including the infant's own version of certain words, and by shorter sentences, simplified sounds (for example, choosing consonant–vowel combinations rather than consonant clusters), topical focus on the here and now, exaggerated intonation, slower pace, repetition, and providing sentence frames for the child to complete.

In the second strategy, WMC mothers interact with their infants in ways that are far beyond the infant's competence. Mothers participate in conversation-like interactions with even newborn infants, giving a speechless infant an active communicative role. WMC mothers frequently praise their babies for things they could not have done without the mother. For example, if the mother and child build a tower together, the mother will praise the child as the sole builder, thus denying her own role and creating a false sense of accomplishment of the child.

Western Samoan mothers, in contrast, do not use baby talk when talking to their infants. Western Samoan does include a prominent simplified register for foreigners who, typically in the past, were colonial government representatives or missionaries whose positions required that they be treated as honored guests. Such accommodating speech is not, however, used for babies among Western Samoans.

When Western Samoan children say something unintelligible, their mothers either ignore them or point out that they have said something unintelligible. Praising is never just one-way. When a mother praises a child, she says "Maaloo!" ("Well done!"). The child responds by saying "Maaloo!" back to the mother. Such two-directional praising patterns emphasize the contribution of both child and mother. Elinor Ochs interprets this pattern as reflecting the relatively high position of women in Western Samoan families compared to that of WMC mothers.

Discourse, Identity, and Power

Some linguistic anthropologists study discourse (or talk) in particular domains in order to learn about power dynamics, how people of different groups convey meaning, and how miscommunication occurs. They have studied thousands of conversations in varied contexts, from cursing someone to telephone conversations to chiefly speeches (the proclamations of chiefs or other leaders). Discourse styles and content provide clues about a person's social background, age, gender, and status. Consider the cultural information that can be gleaned from the following extract of a conversation:

> "So, like, you know, Ramadan?"
>
> "Yeah."
>
> "So I'm like talking to X, you know, and like she goes, 'Hey Ramadan starts next week.'"
>
> "And I'm like, 'What do you say, Happy Ramadan, Merry Ramadan?'"
> (Agar 1994:95).

If you decided the speakers were college students, you were correct. They were young women who were probably born in the United States, were native English speakers likely to be White, and were non-Muslim. The following examples illustrate how discourse is related to identity and power relationships in two quite different domains: children's arguments and teenage girls' everyday talk.

Cross-cultural research on children's disputes shows that argument style is culturally learned. For example, among Hindi-speaking Indian children of Fiji, overlapping is the norm, with little regard for strict turn-taking (Lein and Brenneis 1978). In other cultural contexts, offended feelings can arise when turn-takers try to converse with overlappers. The turn-taker feels that the overlapper is rude, and the overlapper feels that the turn-taker is distant and unengaged.

An article entitled "You Fruithead!" presents an analysis of children's arguments using data gathered among White, middle-class children of western Massachusetts (Brenneis and Lein 1977). The children were asked to do role plays, arguing about issues such as giving back a ball or who is smarter. Prominent stylistic strategies during an argument include use of volume, speed, stress, and intonation. Elevated volume was prominent, although sometimes an echo pattern of a soft statement followed by a soft response would occur. Acceleration of speed was common among older children, less so among younger children. Strict adherence to turn-taking was followed, with no overlapping. Stress and intonation were used in rhythmical patterns, sometimes with a demand for rhyming echoes, as in

> "*You're* skinny."
>
> "*You're* slimmy."
>
> "*You're* scrawny."
>
> "*You're* . . . I don't know."

The last line indicates defeat because the child was unable to come up with a meaningful term that echoed the word "scrawny." In terms of content, most arguments began with an assertion such as "I'm stronger," which calls for an identical or escalated assertion such as "*I'm* stronger," or "I'm the strongest in the world." Many of the children's arguments involved insults and counterinsults. Often the argument ended with the loser being unable to respond.

In the United States, Euro-American adolescent girls' conversations exhibit a high level of concern with their body weight and image (Nichter 2000). A study of 253 girls in the eighth and ninth grades in two urban high schools of the Southwest reveals the contexts and meanings of "fat talk." Fat talk usually starts with a girl commenting, "I'm so fat." The immediate response from her friends is "No, you're not." Girls

THINKING OUTSIDE THE BOX

Listen for examples of disputes in your cultural world(s). Pay attention to turn-taking, pitch, word choice, and other features. See if you can find any patterns in winner styles versus looser styles.

in the study say that fat talk occurs frequently throughout the day. The following representative conversation between two fourteen-year-olds was recorded during a focus group discussion:

> *Jessica:* I'm so fat.
>
> *Toni:* Shut up, Jessica. You're not fat—you know how it makes you really mad when Brenda says she's fat?
>
> *Jessica:* Yeah.
>
> *Toni:* It makes me really mad when you say that cuz it's not true.
>
> *Jessica:* Yeah, it is.
>
> *Toni:* Don't say that you're fat. (Nichter and Vuckovic 1994:112)

Yet girls who use fat talk are typically not overweight and are not dieting. The weight of the girls in the study was within "normal" range, and none suffered from a serious eating disorder. Fat talk sometimes functions as a call for positive reinforcement from friends that the initiator is an accepted group member. In other cases, it occurs at the beginning of a meal, "especially before eating a calorie-laden food or enjoying a buffet-style meal where an individual is faced with making public food choices" (115). In this context, fat talk is interpreted as functioning to absolve the girl from guilt feelings and to give her a sense that she is in control of the situation.

In many North American microcultures, teenage girls frequently discuss body weight. The girl on the scale points out the fat under her arm. ■ What are your views on female body weight? How might your views affect whom you choose for friendship or other close relationships? (Source: © Richard Lord/PhotoEdit)

Media Anthropology

Media anthropology is the cross-cultural study of public communication through electronic media such as radio, television, film, the Internet, and recorded music and print media, including newspapers, magazines, and popular literature (Spitulnik 1993). Media anthropology is an important area that links linguistic and cultural anthropology (Allen 1994). Media anthropologists study the media process and content, the audience response, and the social effects of media presentations. Media anthropology brings together the interests and goals of anthropology and the media by promoting a contextualized view. In journalism, for example, media anthropology promotes going beyond the reporting of crises and other events to presenting a more holistic, contextualized story. Another goal is to disseminate anthropology's findings to the general public via radio, television, print journalism, magazines, and the Internet.

Critical media anthropology asks to what degree access to media messages is mind-opening and liberating or propagandizing and controlling, and whose interests the media are serving.

The Media Process: Studying War Correspondents

Mark Pedelty has studied who creates news about war and how their stories are disseminated. In *War Stories* (1995), he examines the culture of war correspondents in El Salvador. He finds that their culture is highly charged with violence and terror: "War correspondents have a unique relationship to terror. . . . They need terror to realize themselves in both a professional and spiritual sense, to achieve and maintain their cultural identity as 'war correspondents'" (2). Pedelty probes the psychological ambivalence of war correspondents, who are often accused of making a living from war and violence and who become dependent on the continuation of war for their livelihood. He also addresses media censorship, direct and indirect, and how it affects what stories readers receive and the way events are described (see the Critical Thinking box on pp. 516–517).

Media Institutions and Gender: Inside a Japanese Television Station

Ethnographic research within the Japanese television station ZTV provides insights into the social organization of the workplace and how it mirrors the messages put forth through television programming (Painter 1996). Gender dynamics form the basis of his analysis, although that was not Michael Painter's original research topic. He had planned to conduct a study of power dynamics and everyday behavior at the station, not anticipating that gender is the main factor shaping those dynamics.

At ZTV, close to 90 percent of the full-time employees (*shain*) are men. Shain women rarely occupy positions of power or even minimal authority. At the time of the research, no woman had reached the level of section manager, the lowest managerial position in the company. An ideology pervasive among the male employees, especially the senior ones, depicts women as inherently inferior workers. As the president of ZTV commented one afternoon,

> [B]asically, compared to men, women are less intelligent, they have less physical strength, even their bodily structures are different—that is the philosophy I hold to—but in order to show that the company president is *not* a male chauvinist, we are also hiring women. They are people too, after all. While they may have certain limitations, there must also be "territories" where they can make use of their abilities, too. (47)

Many of the female employees at ZTV are temporary workers, pretty women who "adorned every office, tending the three pseudo-domestic zones of the Japanese workplace: the copy machine, the tea area, and the word processors" (51). These "flowers of the workplace" were occupied with answering the phone, sorting postcards from viewers, serving tea, and generally making the male employees feel important. Their behavior was consistently pleasant and subservient, their dress stylish (compare this with the discussion of Japanese hostess clubs in Chapter 12). Although these women had the lowest status in the station, they also had some freedom to joke about social hierarchies in a way that no permanent woman employee would be able to.

A parallel appears between the way female temporary workers are employed to complement and serve men and be harmonious and beautiful, and women's portrayal on Japanese television as listening to and agreeing with men. Women on television provide harmony through their roles in maintaining warm human relations, not (like men) struggling for dominance and superiority. Like the temporary workers, some women presented on television make fun of the status quo through parody and play—as long as it does not go too far. The limits are clearly defined.

The primary audience for Japanese television is the category of *shufu,* housewives. People at ZTV were preoccupied with the characteristics and preferences of shufu. They devised six categories, ranging from the strongly self-assertive "almighty housewife" to the "tranquil and prudent" housewife. A popular form of programming for housewives is the *hōmu dorama,* the "home drama" or domestic serial. These serials represent traditional values such as filial piety and the proper role of the daughter-in-law in regard to her mother-in-law. Caring for the aged is a prominent theme that supplies the central tension for many situations in which women have to negotiate relationships with each other. In contrast, television representations of men emphasize their negotiation of social hierarchies within the workplace and other public organizations.

Although most programming presents women in traditional domestic roles, many women in contemporary Japan are rejecting such shows. In response, pro-

A satellite dish dominates the scene in a village in Niger, West Africa. Throughout the world, the spread of electronic forms of communication has had many and diverse social effects. ■ Assume you are a linguistic anthropologist doing research on communication in this village. What should you study in order to assess the effects of satellite communication on the people and their culture? (Source: © Charles O. Cecil)

Watch a "soap opera" or other serial television show from a culture other than your own. What social relationships drive the plot, and how are they related to gender? **THINKING OUTSIDE THE BOX**

A Tale of Two News Stories

Mark Pedelty talked with an experienced European reporter about how she alters her story depending on which newspaper she is writing for (1995). She showed him computer printouts of two reports she had written about the same event, one for a European news institution and the other for a U.S. newspaper.

THE U.S. REPORT

Leftist rebels in El Salvador have admitted that one of their units may have executed two U.S. servicemen after their helicopter was shot down last Wednesday. An official FLMN rebel statement issued yesterday said two rebel combatants had been detained, "under the charge of suspicion of assassinating wounded prisoners of war." The U.S. helicopter was downed in the conflict[-ridden] eastern province of San Miguel as it was flying back to its base in Honduras. One pilot was killed in the crash, but a Pentagon autopsy team concluded that the other two servicemen in the helicopter were killed execution-style afterwards. Civilians confirmed that the two servicemen had survived the crash, although no one actually saw the actual execution.

"The FMLN has concluded that there are sufficient elements to presume that some of the three, in the condition of wounded prisoners, could have been assassinated by one or various members of our military unit," said the rebel statement. It also said that their investigations had determined that their initial information from units on the ground was false.

At first the guerrillas said the bodies of the Americans had been found in the helicopter. Then they said that two of the three had survived the crash but later died of wounds. Salvadoran officials have said that if the Americans were executed the guerrillas should hand over those responsible. The call was echoed by Rep. Joe Moakley (D-Mass), the Chairman of a congressional special task force on El Salvador.

"We should expect and we should demand that the FMLN turn over to the judicial authorities those responsible. If not, this lack of action will have serious consequences," he said.

But the rebel statement made no promises to do that. "If responsibility for the crime is proved, the FMLN will act with all rigor, in conformity with our normal war justice," read the statement. The rebels said that because of the nationality of the victims, the investigations would be carried out publicly. The rebels also defended shooting down the helicopter, which they said was flying in "attack position" in a conflict zone. The UH1H Huey helicopter is the same model as those used by the Salvadoran army and was flying very low to evade anti-aircraft missiles.

The rebel statement did not say whether those detained were in charge of the guerrilla unit which shot down the helicopter. Western diplomats believe it unlikely the unit would have time to radio for orders. The hilly terrain also made radio communication over any distance difficult.

A U.S. embassy spokesman in San Salvador said State Department and embassy officials are studying the rebel statement . . . .

The killings have opened up a debate in Washington as to whether another $42.5 million in military aid to El Salvador, frozen by Congress last October, should be released. The money was withheld in protest at the lack of progress in investigating the murders of six Jesuit priests by elite army soldiers a year ago. [The final four paragraphs concern the Jesuit murder case.]

THE EUROPEAN REPORT

Nestled amid the steep mountains of Northern Chalatenango province, a simple wooden cross on a hill marks the grave of a teenage guerrilla fighter. There is no name on the grave. None of the villagers from the nearby settlement of San Jose Las Flores who buried his body two years ago knew what he was called. In life the

ducers are experimenting with new sorts of dramas in which women are shown as active workers and aggressive lovers—anything but domesticated housewives. One such show is a ten-part serial aired in 1992 called *Selfish Women*. The story concerns three women: an aggressive single businesswoman who faces discrimination at work, a young mother who is raising her daughter alone while her photographer husband lives with another woman, and an ex-housewife who divorced her husband because she found home life empty and unrewarding. There are several young guerrilla had little in common with three North American servicemen who were killed last month after the rebels shot down their helicopter. They were enemies on opposite sides of a bitter war. But they shared a common death. They were all killed in cold blood after being captured.

When the young rebel was killed two years ago, I remember taking cover behind the wall of the church of San Jose Las Flores. One moment I was watching two adolescent guerrilla fighters sipping from Coke bottles and playing with a yo-yo. Then I remember seeing soldiers running, crouching, and shooting across the square. The crack of automatic rifle fire and the explosion of grenades [were] deafening in the confined space.

The whole incident lasted about twenty minutes. As soon as the soldiers left, whooping and yelling victory cries, we ran across the square to find the body of one of the teenage guerrillas still twitching. The villagers said that he had been wounded and surrendered. The soldiers had questioned him—and then finished him off at close range in the head. The bullet had blown off the top of his skull.

I remember clearly the reaction of the then U.S. ambassador when asked about the incident. "That kind of incident cannot be condoned," he said, "but I was a soldier, I can understand—it happens in a war." In a country where tens of thousands have been killed, many of them civilians murdered by the U.S.-backed military or by right-wing death squads, there was no suggestion of any investigation for the execution of a prisoner.

At the beginning of January of this year a U.S. helicopter was shot down by rebel ground fire in Eastern El Salvador. The pilot died in the crash. But two other U.S. servicemen were dragged badly wounded from the wreckage by the rebels. Before the guerrillas left they finished off the two wounded Americans execution style with a bullet in the head.

The present U.S. ambassador referred to the guerrillas in this incident as "animals." The killings made front page news internationally and provided the climate needed by President Bush to release forty-two and a half million dollars of military aid, which was frozen last October by Congress. U.S. lawmakers wanted to force the Salvadoran army to make concessions in peace talks and clean up its human rights record.

The two incidents highlight a fact of political life in El Salvador, recognized by all, that it is not worth killing Americans. Until the helicopter incident, in more than a decade of civil war the rebels have killed only six U.S. personnel. They have a deliberate policy of not targeting Americans, despite the fact that most guerrillas have a deep hatred of the U.S. government. As many have been killed by the U.S.' own allies. Extreme groups in the military, who resent U.S. interference, murdered four U.S. church workers and two government land reform advisers in the early 1980s.

In fact the rebels, because of the outcry and the policy implications in Washington, have had to admit guilt in the helicopter incident. They have arrested two of their combatants and say they will hold a trial. They have clearly got the message.

Up until the Gulf War El Salvador had easily seen the most prolonged and deepest U.S. military commitment since Vietnam. However, it is a commitment for which few Americans have felt the consequences.

(*Source:* Excerpted from pp. 9–12 in *War Stories: The Culture of Foreign Correspondents* by Mark Pedelty. Copyright © 1995. Reprinted by permission of Routledge/Taylor & Francis Books.)

CRITICAL THINKING QUESTIONS

- What are the major differences in content between the U.S. and the European news reports? (Consider the use and order of "facts" and the writer's voice and use of quotations.)
- Are these two reports giving the same message in two different ways, or are they contradictory?
- What might be the audience response to each, and how might the writing of each report lead to a different response?

male characters, but except for one, they are depicted as less interesting than the women. The show's title is ironic. In Japan, women who assert themselves are often labeled "selfish" by men. The lead women in the drama use the term in a positive way to encourage each other: "Let's become even more selfish!" Painter comments that, "though dramas like *Selfish Women* are perhaps not revolutionary, they are indicative of the fact that telerepresentations of gender in Japan are changing" (69).

BEYOND WORDS: HUMAN PARALANGUAGE

Human communication involves many nonverbal forms, including tone of voice, silence, and the full gamut of body language from posture to dress to eye movements. Referred to as *paralanguage,* these ways of communication follow patterns and rules just as verbal language does. Like verbal language, they must be learned. If not, miscommunication results. Like verbal language, paralanguage varies cross-culturally and intraculturally, and, like verbal language, it changes.

Silence

THINKING OUTSIDE THE BOX Over a day, monitor the occasions on which you use silence in a conversation. What are the contexts and what is your motivation? What if you had spoken instead of remaining silent?

Silence can be an effective form of communication. Like those of verbal language, its meanings differ cross-culturally. In Siberian households, the lowest-status person is the in-marrying daughter, and she tends to speak very little (Humphrey 1978). However, silence does not always indicate powerlessness. In American courts, comparison of speaking frequency among the judge, jury, and lawyers shows that lawyers, who have the least power, speak most, whereas the silent jury holds the most power (Lakoff 1990:97–99).

Native Americans tend to be silent more often than Euro-American speakers. Many outsiders, including social workers, have misinterpreted this either as reflecting their sense of dignity, or, more insultingly, as signaling a lack of emotion or intelligence. How wrong and ethnocentric such judgments are is revealed by a study of silence among the Western Apache of Arizona (Basso 1972 [1970]). The Western Apache use silence in four contexts. First, when meeting a stranger (someone who cannot be identified), especially at fairs, rodeos, or other public events, it is considered bad manners to speak right away. That would indicate interest in something such as money, or work, or transportation, which are possible reasons for exhibiting such bad manners. Second, silence is important in the early stages of courting. Sitting in silence and holding hands for several hours is appropriate. Speaking "too soon" would indicate sexual willingness or interest. That would be immodest. Third, when children come home after a long absence at boarding school, parents and children should meet each other with silence for about fifteen minutes rather than rushing into a flurry of greetings. It may be two or three days before sustained conversations are initiated. Last, a person should be silent when "getting cussed out," especially at drinking parties. An underlying similarity of all these contexts is the uncertainty, ambiguity, and unpredictability of the social relationships. Rather than chattering to "break the ice," the Apache response is silence. The difference between the Apache style and the Euro-American emphasis on quick and continuous verbal interactions in most contexts can cause cross-cultural misunderstandings. Outsiders, for example, have misinterpreted Apache parents' silent greeting of their returning children as a sign of child neglect.

Kinesics

Kinesics is the study of communication that occurs through body movements, positions, facial expressions, and spatial behavior. This form of nonverbal language also has rules for correct usage, possibilities for code-switching, and cross-cultural variation.

Nonverbal communication in Japanese culture is marked by frequent bowing. Two Japanese men in business meet each other, bow, and exchange business cards. ■ Describe some important forms of nonverbal communication in your cultural world(s). (Source: © Olympia/PhotoEdit)

Misunderstandings of body language can easily happen because, like verbal language and international forms of sign language, it is based on arbitrary symbols. Different cultures emphasize different "channels" more than others. Some are more touch-oriented than others, for example, or use facial expressions more. Eye contact is valued during Euro-American conversations, but in many Asian contexts, direct eye contact could be considered rude or possibly a sexual invitation. Nonverbal communication is important in communicating about social relationships, especially dominance and accommodation, or positive versus negative feelings.

Dress and Looks

Manipulation of the body is another way of sending messages. Marks on the body, clothing, and hair styles convey a range of messages about age, gender, sexual interest or availability, profession, wealth, and emotions. In the United States, gender differentiation begins in the hospital nursery with the color coding of blue for boys and pink for girls. In Japan, the kimono provides an elaborate coding system for gender, life-cycle stage, and formality of the occasion (see Figure 17.3). The more social responsibility and status one has, which depends on age and gender, the shorter the sleeve of one's kimono. An interesting contrast exists with the academic gowns worn by professors in the United States at special events such as graduation ceremonies. Professors with a doctorate (Ph.D.) wear gowns with full-length sleeves, whereas professors with a master's degree wear gowns with sleeves cut above the elbow.

Messages conveyed through dress, like other linguistic cues, have the property of arbitrariness. Consider the different meaning of the new veiling in just two cases, Egypt and Kuwait (MacLeod 1992). The "new veiling" of Kuwaiti women distinguishes them as relatively wealthy, leisured, and honorable, in contrast to poor, laboring, immigrant women workers. The new veiling in Egypt is done mainly by women from the lower and middle economic levels, where it has been adopted as a way for working-class women to accommodate to pressures from Islamic fundamentalism to veil, while preserving their right to keep working outside the home. The message of the head covering is "I am a good Muslim and a good wife/daughter." In Kuwait, the headscarf says, "I am a wealthy Kuwaiti citizen."

Human communication is a vast and exciting field. It includes verbal language and paralanguage. It varies across cultures and has rich and complex meanings. It touches every aspect of our lives from our hair styles to our jobs.

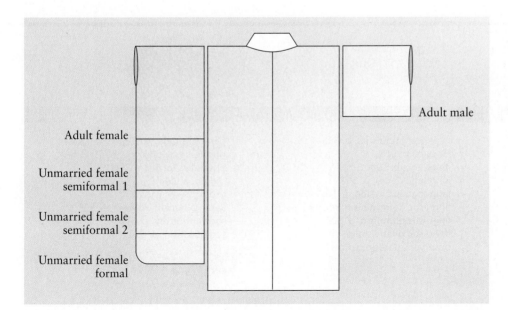

FIGURE 17.3
The social meanings of kimono sleeve length.

(*Source:* From *Kimono: Fashioning Culture* by Liza C. Dalby. Copyright © 1993 by Liza C. Dalby. Published by Unversity of Washington Press and reprinted by permission of Curtis Brown, Ltd.)

WHAT are the major features of human verbal language?

Linguistic anthropologists point to two features that distinguish human verbal language from communication that other animals use: productivity and displacement. Some study the formal, or structural, properties of verbal language, especially the basic units of meaningful sound, or phonemes. Others focus on historical linguistics, including the emergence of writing as a distinctly human form of verbal communication. Early historical linguists such as Sir William Jones discovered the relationships among languages previously thought to be unrelated, such as German and Sanskrit, and this discovery contributed to greater insights into human history and settlement patterns across Asia and Europe. Language change has been influenced by the colonialism of past decades or centuries and by the Western globalization of the current era. Many indigenous and minority languages have become extinct, and many others are in danger of doing so. National policies of cultural integration sometimes involve the repression of minority languages. Western globalization promotes the spread of English as an increasingly powerful global language with emerging localized variants that have their own distinctive character.

HOW do language, thought, and society interact?

Language, thought, and society are intimately connected in all cultural contexts. One model, the Sapir-Whorf hypothesis, emphasizes how our language structures our cultural worlds. Another model, called sociolinguistics, emphasizes how our cultural and social worlds shape our language. Many anthropologists draw on both models. Linguistic anthropologists realize how arbitrary the boundaries are between languages, dialects, and even particular linguistic codes that gain prominence. More important than hard and fast definitions of these categories is the context within which modes of communication change and the way speech is related to the social status and treatment of the speakers. Linguistic anthropologists increasingly study power relation in their attempt to understand how language is linked to dominance, agency, and identity. Media anthropology is an emerging area of anthropology. Research in media anthropology sheds light on how culture shapes media messages and on the social dynamics in media institutions.

WHAT is human paralanguage?

People use many forms of nonverbal language to communicate with each other. These include silence, body placement in relation to other people, and our physical appearance—the way we dress, hair styles, and body marking such as tattoos and other ornamentation. Like verbal language, paralanguage involves the use of arbitrary symbols, so speakers must learn it in order to communicate effectively in particular cultural contexts.

KEY CONCEPTS

SUGGESTED READINGS

William Frawley, Kenneth C. Hill, and Pamela Munro, eds. *Making Dictionaries: Preserving Indigenous Languages of the Americas.* Berkeley: University of California Press, 2002. An introductory chapter by the editors presents ten issues in the making of a dictionary. Fourteen subsequent chapters address topics such as how to standardize spelling in unwritten languages, and case studies of dictionary-making in languages such as Hopi and Nez Perce.

Faye D. Ginsburg, Lila Abu-Lughod, and Brian Larkin, eds. *Media Worlds: Anthropology on New Terrain.* Berkeley: University of California Press, 2002. The editors offer an introductory chapter on media anthropology and new directions in the field. The remaining nineteen chapters provide examples organized in five themes: cultural activism and minority claims, the cultural politics of nation–states, transnational circuits, media industry and institutions, and media technology.

Marjorie H. Goodwin. *He-Said-She-Said: Talk as Social Organization among Black Children.* Bloomington: Indiana University Press, 1990. A study of everyday talk among children of an urban African American community in the United States, this book shows how children construct social relationships among themselves through verbal interactions including disputes, pretend play, and stories.

Jack Goody. *The Power of the Written Tradition.* Washington, DC: Smithsonian Institution Press, 2000. This book focuses on how writing confers power on societies that have it, compared to those that rely on oral communication. Goody's analysis encompasses the changing power of books in the age of the Internet.

Fadwa El Guindi. *Veil: Modesty, Privacy, and Resistance.* New York: Berg, 1999. El Guindi argues that veiling in Arab-Islamic states has many functions and is more complicated than most Western stereotypical views of shame and persecution suggest. The veil may signal group identity and resistance to Western values such as materialism.

Joy Hendry. *Wrapping Culture: Politeness, Presentation and Power in Japan and Other Societies.* New York: Oxford University Press, 1993. This book explores the pervasive idiom and practice of "wrapping" in Japanese culture, including verbal language, gift-giving, and dress. In verbal language, wrapping involves the use of various forms of respect, indicating social levels of the speakers, and the use of linguistic forms of beautification, which have the effect of adornment.

Fern L. Johnson. *Speaking Culturally: Language Diversity in the United States.* Thousand Oaks, CA: Sage Publications, 2000. This book describes a variety of discourse styles in the United States, paying special attention to gender and ethnicity. Chapters address language patterns among African Americans, Latinos, and Asian Americans and within institutional contexts such as health care settings, the legal system, schools, and workplaces. The final chapter considers the issue of bilingual education.

Robin Toimach Lakoff. *Talking Power: The Politics of Language in Our Lives.* New York: Basic Books, 1990. Lakoff explores strategies of communication and language power-plays in English in the United States, providing examples from courtrooms, classrooms, summit talks, and joke-telling.

William L. Leap. *Word's Out: Gay Men's English.* Minneapolis: University of Minnesota Press, 1996. Fieldwork among gay men in the Washington, DC, area produced this ethnography. It addresses gay men's speech as a cooperative mode of discourse, bathroom graffiti, and discourse about HIV/AIDS.

Catherine A. Lutz and Jane L. Collins. *Reading National Geographic.* Chicago: University of Chicago Press, 1993. This study presents the way *National Geographic's* editors, photographers, and designers select text and images of Third World cultures and how middle-class American readers interpret the material.

Purnima Mankekar. *Screening Culture, Viewing Politics: An Ethnography of Television, Womanhood, and Nation in Postcolonial India.* Durham, NC: Duke University Press, 1999. This ethnographic study of mass media in India shows how modernity interacts with core cultural values, especially those related to the family and gender.

Daniel Miller and Don Slater. *The Internet: An Ethnographic Approach.* New York: Berg, 2000. This is the first ethnography of Internet culture. Based on fieldwork in Trinidad, it offers an account of the political and social contexts of Internet use, individual experiences of being online, and the impact of the Internet on Trinidadian people and their culture.

Susan U. Philips, Susan Steele, and Christine Tanz, ed. *Language, Gender and Sex in Comparative Perspective.* New York: Cambridge University Press, 1987. In an introductory essay followed by eleven chapters, this book explores women's and men's speech in Japan, Western Samoa, and Mexico; children's speech in American preschools and in Papua New Guinea; and sex differences in how the brain is related to speech.

Lisa Philips Valentine. *Making It Their Own: Ojibwe Communicative Practices.* Toronto: University of Toronto Press, 1995. This ethnographic study examines a variety of speech events in a small community of Ojibwe people in northern Ontario, Canada. It considers speech variations among speakers, code-switching, and multilingualism, as well as connections between spoken language and church music.

THE BIG QUESTIONS

- **WHAT** is religion and what are the basic features of religions?
- **HOW** do world religions reflect globalization and localization?
- **WHAT** are some important aspects of religious change in contemporary times?

CHAPTER **18**

Religion

Hinduism has spread from India, its place of origin, to many parts of the world, including Bali, Indonesia. A Hindu funeral procession in Bali includes symbols related to sacrifice in southern India, including a buffalo and fire. In contrast to the elaborate visual display, people in Bali do not express emotion at a funeral. (Source: © Bob Krist)

When studying the religious life of people of rural northern Greece, cultural anthropologist Loring Danforth observed rituals in which participants walk across several yards of burning coals (1989). They do not get burned, they say, because their faith and a saint protect them.

Upon his return to the United States, Danforth met an American who regularly walks on fire as part of his New Age faith and also organizes training workshops for people who want to learn how to firewalk. Danforth himself firewalked in a ceremony in rural Maine.

Not all cultural anthropologists who study religion undertake such challenges during fieldwork, but they do all share an interest in exploring humanity's understanding of the supernatural realm and relationships with it: Why do some religions have many gods and others just one? Why do some religions involve animal sacrifice? Why do some religions give greater room for women's participation? How do different religions respond to changing conditions in the political economy?

Religion has been a cornerstone topic in anthropology since the beginnings of the discipline. Over many decades, a rich collection of material has accumulated. The early focus was on religions of indigenous and tribal peoples. More recently, anthropologists have studied the major religions of state-level societies. With globalization and migration, religious traditions are changing as they adapt to new cultural contexts.

RELIGION IN COMPARATIVE PERSPECTIVE

This section sets the stage for the rest of the chapter by discussing how cultural anthropologists define religion, their theories about why religion began, and why it is so pervasive. It then covers types of religious beliefs, ritual practices, and religious specialists.

What Is Religion?

Since the earliest days of anthropology, various definitions of **religion** have been proposed. One of the simplest, offered by British anthropologist Sir Edward Tylor in the late 1800s, is that religion is the belief in spirits. A more recent definition says that religion is both beliefs and actions related to supernatural beings and forces (what Tylor referred to as spirits). Anthropologists avoid defining religion narrowly as the belief in a supreme deity. In many religions, no concept of a supreme deity exists, and others have multiple deities. Religion is related to, but is not the same as, a people's **worldview,** or their way of understanding how the world came to be, why it is the way it is, and their place in it. Worldview is a broader concept and does not include the criterion of concern with a supernatural realm. An atheist has a worldview, but not a religious one.

Magic versus Religion

In the late 1800s, Sir Edward Tylor wrote that magic, religion, and science are alike in that they are different ways in which people try to explain the physical world and events in it. Tylor thought that magical laws were false and scientific laws were true, and that religion is based on the false assumption that the world operates under the control of supernaturals. At about the same time as Tylor, Sir James Frazer defined **magic** as people's attempt to compel supernatural forces and beings to act in certain ways, in contrast to religion, which is the attempt to please supernatural forces or beings (1978 [1890]). After reviewing many cross-cultural practices he considered magical, Frazer deduced two general principles of magic. First is the "law of similarity," the basis of what he called *imitative magic*. It is founded on the assumption that if person or item X is like person or item Y, then actions done to person or item X will affect person or item Y. A familiar example is a voodoo doll. If someone sticks pins into a doll X that represents person Y, then person Y will experience pain or suffering. The second is the "law of contagion," which is the basis for *contagious magic*. The law of contagion says that persons or things that were once in contact with a person can continue to have an effect on that person. Common items for working contagious magic include a person's hair trimmings, nail clippings, teeth, spit, blood, fecal matter, and placentas. In cultures where contagious magic is practiced, people are careful about disposing of their personal wastes so that no one else can get hold of them.

Such scholars of religion as Tylor and Frazer supported an evolutionary model (review Chapter 1), with magic as the predecessor of religion. They evaluated magic as less spiritual and ethical than religion and therefore more "primitive." They assumed that in time, magic would be completely replaced by the "higher" system of religion and then, ultimately, by science as the most rational way of thinking. They would be surprised to see the widespread presence of magical religions in the modern world, as evidenced, for example, by an ethnographic study of magic and witchcraft in contemporary London (Luhrmann 1989).

Magic probably exists in all contemporary cultures. In different situations, people turn to magic, religion, or science. For example, magic is prominent in sports (Gmelch 1997 [1971]). American baseball players repeat actions or use charms (including a special shirt or hat) to help them win—on the assumption that if it worked before, it may work again. They are following Tylor's law of contagion. Such magical thinking is most common in contexts where uncertainty is greatest. In baseball, pitching and hitting involve more uncertainty than fielding, and pitchers and hitters are more likely to use magic. Magical practices are also prominent in farming, fishing, the military, and love.

Christian firewalkers in northern Greece express their faith by walking on hot coals. They reaffirm divine protection by not getting burned. ■ Speculate on why some religious rituals involve physical and mental challenges. How do these challenges compare to physical and mental challenges in secular life, such as certain sports? (Source: © Loring Danforth)

Theories of the Origin of Religion

Why did religion come into being? The existence of some form of religion in all contemporary cultures has prompted early theorists to adopt a functionalist approach. According to this view, religion provides ways of explaining and coping with universal "imponderables of life" such as birth, illness, misfortune, and death.

Tylor's theory, as proposed in his book *Primitive Culture* (1871), was based on his assumption that people needed a way to explain the difference between the living and the dead. They therefore developed the concept of a soul that exists in all living things and departs from the body after death. Tylor named this way of thinking **animism,** the belief in souls or "doubles." Eventually, Tylor speculated, the concept of the soul became personified until, later, human-like deities were conceived. For Tylor, religion evolved from animism to *polytheism* (the belief in many deities) to *monotheism* (the belief in one supreme deity). Beliefs characteristic of animism still exist. They include beliefs about angels and visitations of the dead and the New Age religious use of crystals (Stringer 1999).

In contrast to Tylor, Frazer suggested that religion developed out of the failure of magic. Neither scholar suggested a place or time period during which these developments may have occurred, and both based their theories on speculation rather than on archaeological or other empirical data.

Emile Durkheim, in his book *The Elementary Forms of the Religious Life* (1915 [1965]), offered a functional explanation for how and why religion came into being. He reviewed ethnographic data on "primitive" religions cross-culturally and was struck by their social functions. Durkheim speculated that early humans realized, through clan gatherings, that contact with one another made them feel uplifted and powerful. This positive feeling, arising from social solidarity, became attached to the clan *totem*, an emblem of the group that became the first of many objects of worship. Religion therefore originated to serve society by giving it cohesion through shared symbols and group rituals. Another functional view, that of Bronislaw Malinowski, proposed that rituals help reduce anxiety and uncertainty, thus promoting social well-being. Karl Marx took a *class conflict* perspective rather than a functional approach. He emphasized religion's role as an "opiate of the masses." By this phrase, Marx meant that religion provides a superficial form of comfort to the poor, masking the harsh realities of class inequality and thereby preventing uprisings against the rich.

Another major theoretical thread, *symbolic analysis,* informs Sigmund Freud's theory of the role of the unconscious. Many anthropologists agree with Freud that religion is a "projective system" that expresses people's unconscious thoughts, wishes, and worries. Anthropologists have also applied Freudian analysis of symbols, and of their underlying or hidden meanings in dreams, to the analysis of myths.

A last theoretical theme, which combines Durkheimian functionalism with symbolic analysis, comes from Clifford Geertz (1966), who proposed that religions are primarily *systems of meaning.* In this view, religion offers a conception of reality, "a model of life," and a pattern for how to live.

CROSSING
THE FIELDS

The Prehistoric Use
of Red Ochre
in Southern Africa
and the Origins of
Ritual

Archaeologists of religion attempt to discover and interpret evidence of behavior and beliefs related to the supernatural domain in cultures of the past. Some suggest that the first evidence of religious thinking and behavior dates from the Middle Stone Age of southern Africa and coincides with the emergence of *H. sapiens* (Watts 1999) (review Chapter 7).

The southern African evidence consists of the frequent presence of ochre, a reddish pigment, found in 74 sites dating between 100,000 and 20,000 years ago. Over this period, the frequency of appearance of ochre at the sites increases. The frequency of bright red ochres also increases relative to the frequency of lighter reds, yellows, and browns. The question, though, is what the connection between red ochre and religious beliefs and behavior might be.

To attempt to answer this question, archaeologists turned to the method of ethnoarchaeology. Fieldwork among several contemporary foraging groups of southern Africa—including the Ju/wasi, Khoisan and Xhosa—reveals the ritual importance of ochre today. Ochre is used in the important life-cycle ritual that marks a young woman's first menstruation, or menarche. The ochre may be mixed with fat and applied to women's skin or hair to create a bright and shining look. Redness in these contexts is associated with fertility, beauty, power, the coming of rain, and success of men in special hunts.

Some cultural anthropologists say that the contemporary use of ochre serves a cosmetic function, to enhance a woman's beauty, and is not related to the supernatural domain. Those supporting a ritual interpretation respond by saying that applying body coloring is both a cosmetic act for enhancing beauty and a ritual act because the domains of personal beauty and supernatural power overlap. Redness is attractive and also displays fertility and potency. In this view, the body's skin can be viewed as an early ritual implement, and body painting as the first ritual practice of our human ancestors. ■

FOOD FOR THOUGHT

■ Think of ways in which the human body is marked or symbolically transformed to demonstrate a relationship with the supernatural in a religious tradition that you know.

A stone sculpture at Mamalla-puram, south India, dating from the eighth or ninth century. It depicts the triumph of the Hindu goddess Durga (riding the lion, left of center) over the bull-headed demon Mahishasura. The story of her saving the world by killing Mahishasura has inspired countless works of art in India. ■ Think of an example from your culture in which a myth is portrayed graphically. (Source: Simon Hiltebeitel)

Varieties of Religious Beliefs

Religions comprise both beliefs and behaviors. Scholars of religion generally address belief systems first because they appear to inform patterns of religious behavior. This section considers cross-cultural variation in religious beliefs.

How Beliefs Are Expressed

Beliefs are expressed and transferred over the generations in two main forms: **myth,** narrative stories about supernatural forces or beings, and **doctrine,** direct statements about religious beliefs.

A myth is a narrative that has a plot with a beginning, middle, and end. The plot may involve recurrent motifs, the smallest units of narrative. Myths convey messages about the supernaturals indirectly, through the story itself, rather than by using logic or formal argument. Greek and Roman myths, such as the stories of Zeus, Athena, Orpheus, and Persephone, are world famous. Some people would say that the Bible is a collection of myths; others would object to that categorization because it suggests that Bible stories are not "real" or "sacred."

Myths are distinguished from folktales, which are secular stories. Borderline cases between the categories of myth and folktale exist. For example, some people would classify "Cinderella" as a folktale, whereas others would quickly point out that the fairy godmother is not an ordinary human and so "Cinderella" is a myth. Such arguments are more entertaining than enlightening.

Myths have long been part of people's oral tradition. Only with the emergence of writing were these stories recorded, and then only if they were of great importance, perhaps part of a royal or priestly tradition. Many of the world's myths are still unwritten.

Cultural anthropologists have asked why myths exist. Bronislaw Malinowski said that a myth is a "charter" for society in that it expresses core beliefs and teaches morality. Thus, for Malinowski, myths serve to maintain society by teaching people how to behave. In contrast, Claude Lévi-Strauss, probably the most famous mythologist, saw myths as functional but in a philosophical and psychological way. In his view, myths help people deal with deep conceptual contradictions, for example, between life and death and good and evil, by providing stories in which these dualities find a solution in a mediating third factor. These mythological solutions are buried within a variety of surface details in the myth. Many Pueblo Indian myths juxtapose grass-eating animals (vegetarians) with predators (carnivores). The mediating third

Celebration of Holi, a spring festival popular among Hindus worldwide. In this scene in New Delhi, India, a young woman sprays colored water on a young man as part of the joyous event. The deeper meaning of Holi is tied to a myth about a demon. ■ How is the arrival of spring marked in your microculture? (Source: © AFP/CORBIS)

character is the raven, who is a carnivore but, unlike other creatures, does not have to kill to eat meat because it is a scavenger.

A third functional view says that myths store and transmit information related to making a living and managing economic crises (Sobel and Bettles 2000). Analysis of twenty-eight myths of the Klamath and Modoc, Native Americans of Oregon and California, reveals that economic risk is a consistent theme in all of them. The myths also emphasize ways to cope with hunger, such as skill in hunting and fishing, food storage, resource diversification, resource conservation, spatial mobility, reciprocity, and the role of supernatural forces. Thus myths may promote economic survival and success of groups in the short run by imparting knowledge about crisis management, and they may contribute to long-term economic sustainability by transmitting knowledge about environmental management and conservation.

Epics are longer than myths and focus more on heroic traditions. Many epics, such as the *Odyssey* and the *Iliad* of Greece, are associated with particular ethnic groups or nations. Less well known in North America are India's two great Hindu epics, the *Mahabharata* and the *Ramayana*. Iceland's *eddas* of the thirteenth century are grouped into two categories: mythic (dealing with gods) and heroic (dealing with humans).

Doctrine, the other major form in which beliefs are expressed, explicitly defines the supernaturals—who they are, what they do, and how to relate to them through religious practice; the world and how it came to be; and people's roles in relation to the supernaturals and to other humans. Doctrine, which is written and formal, is close to law in some respects because it links incorrect beliefs and behaviors with the appropriate punishments. Many religious scriptures incorporate both myth and doctrine.

Doctrine is associated with institutionalized, large-scale religions rather than with small-scale "folk" religions. Doctrine, however, can and does change (Bowen 1998:38–40). Over the centuries, various Popes have pronounced new doctrine for the Catholic church. A papal declaration of 1854, made with the intent of reinvigorating European Catholicism, bestowed authenticity on the concept of the Immaculate Conception.

Muslim doctrine is expressed in the Qu'ran, the basic holy text of the Islamic faith, which consists of revelations made to the prophet Muhammed in the seventh century, and in collections of Muhammed's statements and deeds (Bowen 1998:38). In Kuala Lumpur, Malaysia, a small group of highly educated women called the Sisters in Islam regularly debate with members of the local *ulama*, religious authorities who are responsible for interpreting Islamic doctrine, especially that concerning families, education, and commercial affairs (Ong 1995). In recent years, these debates have addressed such issues as polygamy, divorce, women's work roles, and women's clothing.

Beliefs about Supernatural Forces and Beings

In all cultures, some concept of otherworldly beings or forces exists, even though not all members of the culture believe in their existence. Supernaturals range from impersonal forces to those that look just like humans. Supernaturals can be supreme and all-powerful creators or smaller-scale, annoying spirits that take up residence in people through "possession."

The term **animatism** refers to belief systems in which the supernatural is conceived of as an impersonal power. A well-known example is *mana,* a concept widespread throughout the Melanesian region of the South Pacific. Mana is a force outside nature that works automatically; it is neither spirit nor deity. It manifests itself in objects and people and is associated with personal status and power, because some people accumulate more of it than others. Some supernaturals are **zoomorphic**—deities that appear in the shape, or partial shape, of animals. No satisfactory theory exists to explain why some religions develop zoomorphic deities, and for what purposes, and why others do not. Religions of classical Greece and Rome and ancient and contemporary Hinduism are especially rich in zoomorphic supernaturals.

Anthropomorphic supernaturals, deities in the form of humans, are common but not universal. People's tendency to conceive of supernaturals in their own form was noted 2500 years ago by the Greek philosopher Xenophanes (who lived sometime between 570 and 470 BCE). He said, "If cattle and horses, or lions, had hands, or were able to draw with their feet and produce the worlds which men do, horses would draw the forms of gods like horses, and cattle like cattle, and they would make the gods' bodies the same shape as their own" (*Fragment* 15). Why some religions have and others do not have anthropomorphic deities is a question that is impossible to answer fully. Such deities are more common in sedentary societies than among foragers.

Anthropomorphic supernaturals, like humans, can be moved by praise, flattery, and gifts. They can be tricked. They have emotions: They get irked if neglected, they can be loving and caring, or they can be distant and nonresponsive. Most anthropomorphic supernaturals are adults. Few are very old or very young. Humans and supernaturals have similar marital and sexual patterns. Divine marriages are heterosexual. In societies where polygyny occurs, male gods may have multiple wives. Deities have sexual intercourse, within marriage and sometimes extramaritally. Gods of the Greek and Roman pantheon, the entire collection of deities, often descended to earth and kidnapped and raped human women. So far, however, legal divorce has not occurred among supernaturals. Although many supernaturals have children, grandchildren are not prominent.

In *pantheons* (collectivities of deities), a division of labor exists by which certain supernaturals are responsible for particular domains. This greater specialization among the supernaturals reflects the greater specialization in human society that emerged with agriculture. There may be deities of forests, rivers, the sky, wind and rain, agriculture, childbirth, disease, warfare, and marital happiness. Some gods are resorted to for gaining material wealth and others for academic success. The supernaturals have political roles and hierarchies. High gods, such as Jupiter and Juno of classical Roman religion, are distant from humans and hard to contact. The more approachable deities are below them in the hierarchy. Next, one finds a collection of spirits, good and bad, often unnamed and uncounted.

Deceased ancestors can also be supernaturals. In some religions, spirits of the dead can be prayed to for help, and in turn they may require respect and honor from the living (Smith 1995:46). Many African, Asian, and Native American religions have a cult of the ancestors, as did religions of ancient Mesopotamia, Greece, and Rome. In contemporary Japan, ancestor veneration is the principal religious activity of many families. Three national holidays recognize the importance of ancestors: the annual summer visit of the dead to their home and the visits by the living to graves during the two equinoxes.

Humans may also, after their death, be transformed into deities. This process, called **euhemerism**, is named after the philosopher Euhemerus of Messene (340–260 BCE), who suggested that classical Greek deities had once been earthly people.

Religion provides an important source of social cohesion and psychological support for many immigrant groups, whose places of worship attract both worshippers and cultural anthropologists interested in learning how religion fits into migrants' adaptation. This is a scene at a Lao Buddhist temple in Virginia. ■ Learn about Buddhism in North America by doing research on the Internet. (Source: Ruth Krulfeld)

Beliefs about Sacred Space

Beliefs about the sacredness of certain spaces are probably found in all religions, but such beliefs are more prominent in some religions than others. Sacred spaces may or may not be marked in a permanent way. Examples of unmarked spaces are rock formations and rapids in a river (Bradley 2000). The fact that unmarked (and therefore unidentifiable) spaces may have been religious sites in prehistory poses a major challenge to archaeologists interested in reconstructing early religion. Sometimes, though, archaeologists can find evidence of sacrifices at such sites to attest to their ritual importance.

Among the indigenous Saami people of northern Norway, Sweden, and Finland, religious beliefs were, before Christian missionary efforts, strongly associated with sacred natural sites, which were often unmarked (Mulk 1994). These sites included rock formations resembling humans, animals, or birds. The Saami sacrificed animals and fish at these sites until pressure from Christian missionaries forced them to repress their practices and beliefs. Although many Saami today still know where the sacred sites are, they will not reveal them to others.

Another important form of sacred space with no permanent physical mark occurs in an important domestic ritual conducted by Muslim women throughout the world and called the *khatam quran*, the "sealing" or reading of the holy book, the Qu'ran (Werbner 1988). A study of Pakistani migrants living in the city of Manchester, England, reveals that this ritual involves a gathering of women who read the Qu'ran and then share a ritual meal. The reason for the gathering can be to give thanks or to seek divine blessing. During the ritual, the otherwise non-sacred space of the house becomes sacred. A "portable" ritual such as this one is especially helpful in migrant adaptation, because it can be conducted without a formally consecrated ritual space. All that is required is a supportive group of kin and friends and the Qu'ran.

Many Aboriginal religions in Australia are closely tied to sacred space. During the mythological past called the Dreamtime, the ancestors walked the earth and marked out the territory belonging to a particular group. People's knowledge of where the ancestors roamed is secret. In several recent cases brought before the courts, Aboriginal peoples have claimed title to land that is being sought by business interests such as mining companies. Anthropologists have sometimes become involved in these disputes, providing expert testimony documenting the validity of the Aboriginal people's claims to their sacred space.

A gathering of modern-day Druids at Stonehenge, England. They are one of the several groups that have interests in the preservation of and access to this World Heritage Site. Debates concern possible changes in the location of nearby roads and planting or removing trees. The Druids claim that the site is a temple important to their religion. ■ As a research project, learn about the various groups and preservation issues related to Stonehenge. (Source: © Brian Seed)

Aboriginal Women's Culture, Sacred Site Protection, and the Anthropologist as Expert Witness

A GROUP of Ngarrindjeri (prounounced NAR-en-jeery) women and their lawyer hired cultural anthropologist Diane Bell to serve as a consultant to help them support their claims to a sacred site in southern Australia (Bell 1998). The area was threatened by the proposed construction of a bridge that would cross sacred waters between Goolwa and Hindmarsh Island. The women claimed protection for the area and sought to stop the bridge being built on the basis of their secret knowledge of its sacredness—knowledge that had been passed from mother to daughter over generations.

The High Commission formed by the government to investigate their claim considered it to be a hoax perpetrated to block a project important to the country. Helping the women prove their case to a White, male-dominated court system was a challenging task for Bell. A White Australian by birth, she has extensive fieldwork experience among Aboriginal women.

Bell conducted research over many months to marshal evidence related to the women's claims—including newspaper archives, early recordings of ritual songs, and oral histories of Ngarrindjeri women. She prepared reports for the courtroom about women's sacred knowledge that were general enough to avoid violating the rule of women-only knowledge but detailed enough to convince the High Court judge that the

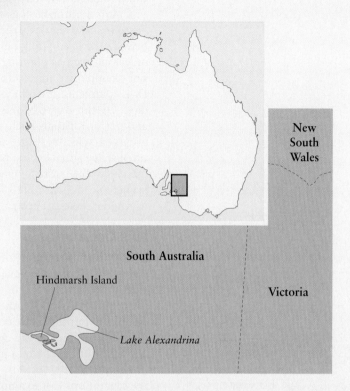

women's sacred knowledge was authentic. In the end the judge was convinced, and the bridge project was canceled in 1999.

FOOD FOR THOUGHT

- On the Internet, learn more about this case and other disputes in Australia about sacred sites.

In one such case, Aboriginal knowledge about a sacred place and its associated beliefs was gender-specific and secret: It belonged to women and could not be told to men. The anthropologist who was hired to support the women's claims was a woman and could therefore be told about the sacred places, but she would not be able to convey that knowledge in court to the male judge. These cultural rules required considerable ingenuity on the part of the anthropological consultant (see the Lessons Applied box).

Ritual Practices

Rituals are patterned forms of behavior that have to do with the supernatural realm. Many rituals are the enactment of beliefs expressed in myth and doctrine, such as the Christian ritual of communion. Rituals are distinct from *secular rituals,* such as a sorority or fraternity initiation or a common-law wedding, which are patterned forms of behavior with no connection to the supernatural realm. It is not always easy to distinguish ritual from secular ritual. Consider the holiday of Thanksgiving in the United States, which originated as a sacred meal to give thanks for the survival of the pilgrims (Siskind 1992). Its original Christian meaning is not maintained by everyone who celebrates the holiday now. It may even be rejected, for example, by Native Americans who are unlikely to consider the arrival and survival of the pilgrims a cause for celebration.

Cultural anthropologists have categorized rituals in many ways. One division is based on how regularly the ritual is performed. Regularly performed rituals are called *periodic rituals.* Many periodic rituals are performed annually to mark a seasonal milestone such as planting or harvesting or to commemorate some important event. For example, an important periodic ritual in Buddhism, Visakha Puja, or Buddha's Day, commemorates the birth, enlightenment, and death of the Buddha (all on one day). On this day, Buddhists gather at monasteries, hear sermons about the Buddha, and perform rituals such as pouring water over images of the Buddha. Calendrical events such as the shortest and longest days of the year and the new and full moons often shape ritual cycles. Nonperiodic rituals, in contrast, occur irregularly, at unpredictable times, in response to unscheduled events such as a drought or flood, or to events in a person's life such as illness, infertility, birth, marriage, or death (see the Methods Close-Up box).

Life-Cycle Rituals

Belgian cultural anthropologist Arnold van Gennep (1960 [1908]) first proposed the category of life-cycle rituals in 1909. **Life-cycle rituals,** or rites of passage, mark a change in status from one life stage to another of an individual or group. Victor Turner's (1969) fieldwork among the Ndembu, horticulturalists of Zambia, provided insights about the phases of life-cycle rituals. Turner found that among the Ndembu and cross-culturally life-cycle rituals have three phases: separation, transition, and reintegration. In the first phase, the initiate (the person undergoing the ritual) is separated physically, socially, or symbolically from normal life. Special dress may mark the separation—for example, a long white gown for a baby being baptized in a Christian church. In many cultures of the Amazon and in East and West Africa, adolescents are secluded for several years in separate huts or areas away from the village. The

THINKING Think of the stages of a life-cycle ritual you have attended, such as a baptism, wedding, or **OUTSIDE** funeral. Do Turner's **THE BOX** three stages apply to it?

An Apache teenage girl going through her coming-of-age ceremony at the Whiteriver Apache Reservation in Arizona. During the four-day ceremony, which celebrates her first menstruation, she is honored as sacred. ■ How is the beginning of menstruation marked in your microculture? (Source: © Paul Chesley/Getty Images/Stone)

Studying Birth Rituals in Indonesia

JENNIFER NOURSE went to the Indonesian island of Sulawesi to study rituals that take place around the time of giving birth (1999). She lived among Laujé people in a town on the coast. A symbolic/interpretive anthropologist by training (review Chapter 2), she was interested in learning about the symbols and meanings involved in birth rituals, and especially about the significance of "birth spirits."

The first two people she asked about birth spirits gave her an explanation that fit perfectly with Lévi-Straussian theory. The birth spirits live with the fetus, nurture it, and carry it from the womb at the time of birth. In order for the newborn baby to live, the birth spirits themselves must die. The father must perform a series of rituals to thank the spirits for bringing the baby. If they are neglected, birth spirits can bring sickness and death. Rituals include special treatment of the placenta and umbilical cord by the father—for example, wrapping the umbilical cord in a dark cloth and storing it in a special place in the house. Nourse was pleased that she had discovered a belief system that, when analyzed in a Lévi-Straussian manner, provided a clear set of binary oppositions: nature/culture, birth/ritual, and female/male.

As her research continued, however, Nourse talked with more people about birth spirits. Instead of gathering more views that substantiated the tidy binary pattern provided by the first two people, she was confronted by a diverse set of explanations about the spirits. Had she relied only on her first two findings, she would have written a highly misleading account. Upon further study of the many, seemingly chaotic interpretations of birth spirits, she began to see some coherence, but not of a binary sort. Patterns emerged that are related to the social positions of the people with whom she spoke: their class, gender, religion, and place (village, town, highland or lowland).

Nourse discovered the rich complexity of Laujé beliefs about birth spirits and how this complexity is related to the social richness of the region and its long history. She learned that the core belief in birth spirits provides a foundation upon which people can construct a wide variety of interpretations and understandings that reflect their social milieu.

FOOD FOR THOUGHT

- Consider the problem of validity in cultural anthropology fieldwork and how researchers can best address this issue.

transition phase, or *liminal phase*, is the time when the individual no longer occupies the previous status but is not yet a member of the next category. Liminality often involves the learning of specialized skills that will equip the initiate for the new status. Reintegration, the last stage, occurs when the initiate emerges and is welcomed by the community in the new status.

How can anthropologists explain variations in the occurrence, elaboration, and meaning of such rituals? Ritual marking of a baby's entry into society as a human is a common practice, but it varies according to how soon after birth the ceremony is performed. Where infant mortality rates are high, the ceremony tends to be done late, when the baby is a year old or even older. Until the ceremony has been performed, the baby is not named and is not considered "human." This timing may be a way of ensuring that the baby has survived the most dangerous period and is likely to survive before the parents make a full emotional investment. In contrast is the increasingly common practice in the United States of pregnant women purchasing an ultrasound video of their unborn fetus, a secular ritual that declares the "personhood" of the fetus before it is born. This practice is related to a context of low infant mortality.

Variations in the cross-cultural distribution of puberty rituals for boys and girls may reflect the relative economic value and status of males and females. Most societies have some form of puberty ceremony for boys, but puberty ceremonies for girls are less common. In societies where female labor is important and valued, girls have elaborate (and sometimes painful) puberty rites (J. Brown 1978). Where their labor is not important, menarche is unmarked and there is no puberty ceremony. Puberty

THINKING OUTSIDE THE BOX
What are some rituals (or secular rituals) associated with pregnancy and birth in your cultural world?

rites function to socialize the labor force, among other things (review Chapter 12 on puberty rites). For example, among the Bemba of southern Africa, during initiation, a girl learns to distinguish thirty or forty different kinds of mushrooms and to know which are edible and which are poisonous.

Pilgrimage

Pilgrimage is a round-trip to a sacred place or places for purposes of religious devotion or ritual. Prominent pilgrimage places are Varanasi in India (formerly called Banaras) for Hindus; Mecca in Saudi Arabia for Muslims; Bodh Gaya in India for Buddhists; Jerusalem in Israel for Jews, Christians, and Muslims; and Santiago de Compostela in Spain for Christians. Pilgrimage often involves hardship, with the implication that the more suffering that is involved, the more merit the pilgrim accumulates. Compared to a weekly trip to church or synagogue, pilgrimage removes a person further from everyday life, is more demanding, and therefore is potentially more transformative.

Victor Turner applied his three sequences of life-cycle rituals to pilgrimage as well: The pilgrim first separates from everyday life, then enters the liminal stage during the actual pilgrimage, and finally returns to be reintegrated into society in a transformed state. Indeed, in many pilgrimage traditions, a person who has gone on certain pilgrimages gains enhanced public status—for example, the status of *haji* (someone who has done the *haj,* or pilgrimage to Mecca) in the Islamic faith.

Connections among myth, sacred sites, and pilgrimage are strong. For example, in the Hindu goddess tradition, the story of Sati is the basis for the sanctity of four major and forty-six minor pilgrimage sites in India (Bhardwaj 1973). Because of an argument with her father over whether her husband Shiva was welcome at a big sacrifice her family was holding, the unhappy Sati committed suicide. When Shiva heard about her death, he was distraught. He picked up her body and carried it over his shoulder as he wandered across India, grieving. Along the way, parts of her body fell to the ground. The places where they dropped became holy. Some of these include her tongue at Jwala Mukhi and her throat at Vaishno Devi, both in the Himalayas, and her genitals in the eastern state of Assam.

Pilgrimage, especially among Hindus in India, may involve bathing in a sacred river, in a pond near a temple, or even in the ocean (Gold 1988). Flowing water is believed to have great powers of purification. Many of India's most famous pilgrimage sites are located on rivers, such as Varanasi (Banaras), the most prominent place of Hindu pilgrimage, which is located on the Ganges River.

Rituals of Inversion

In some rituals, normal social roles and relations are temporarily inverted. Scholars who adopt a functionalist perspective say these rituals allow for social "steam" to be let off temporarily and may also provide a reminder about the propriety of normal, everyday roles and practices to which people must inevitably return once the ritual is over.

These **rituals of inversion** are common cross-culturally, one of the best known in the West being Carnival. Carnival is celebrated throughout the northern Mediterranean region, North and South America, and the Caribbean. It is a period of riotous celebration before the Christian fast of Lent (Counihan 1985). Carnival begins at different times in different places but always ends on Mardi Gras (or Shrove Tuesday), the day before the fasting period of Lent begins. The word *Carnival* is derived from Latin and means "flesh farewell," referring to Lent.

In Bosa, a town in Sardinia, Italy, Carnival involves several aspects of social role reversal and relaxing of usual social norms: "The discotheques extend their hours, and mothers allow their daughters to attend more often and longer than at other times of the year. Men and women play sexually, fondling and flirting with each other in the discotheques and [performing] masquerades that are totally illicit at other times of the year" (14). Carnival in Bosa has three major phases. The first is impromptu street theater and masquerades that take place over several weeks, usually on Sun-

A young man dressed as an over-sexualized woman, one of the most common costumes in the Carnival street-theater masquer-ades of Sardinia. ■ Consider what might be the meaning of the object he is holding. (Source: Lorenzo Pezzatini)

days. The theatrical skits are social critiques of current events and local happenings. The masquerades mainly involve men dressing up as exaggerated women:

> Young boys thrust their padded breasts forward with their hands while brassily hiking up their skirts to reveal their thighs. . . . A youth stuffs his shirt front with melons and holds them proudly out. . . . The high school gym teacher dresses as a nun and lifts up his habit to reveal suggestive red underwear. Two men wearing nothing but bikinis, wigs, and high heels feign a stripper's dance on a table top. (15)

The second phase occurs during the morning of Mardi Gras, when hundreds of Bosans, mostly men, dress in black like widows and flood the streets. They accost passersby, shaking in their faces dolls and other objects that are maimed in some way or bloodied. They shriek at the top of their lungs as if mourning, and they say, "Give us milk, milk for our babies . . . . They are dying, they are neglected, their mothers have been gallivanting since St. Anthony's Day and have abandoned their poor children" (16). The third phase, called *Giolzi*, takes place during the evening. Men and women dress in white, wearing sheets for cloaks and pillow cases for hoods. They blacken their faces. Rushing into the street, they hold hands and chant the word "Giolzi." They storm at people, pretending to search their bodies for Giolzi and then say "Got it!" It is not clear what Giolzi is, but whatever it is, it represents something that makes everyone happy. How does a cultural anthropologist interpret these events? Carnival allows people for a short time to act out roles that are normally denied them. It is also a time when everyone has fun. In this way, rituals of inversion can be seen to function as mechanisms for maintaining social order: After the allotted days of revelry, everyone returns to his or her original place for another year.

Sacrifice

Many rituals involve **sacrifice,** or the offering of something for transfer to the supernaturals. Sacrifice has a long history throughout the world and is probably one of the oldest forms of ritual. It may involve killing and offering animals; or making human offerings (of whole people, parts of a person's body, or even bloodletting); or offering vegetables, fruits, grains, flowers, or other products. One anthropologist suggests that flowers are symbolic replacements for former animal sacrifices (Goody 1993).

Spanish documents from the sixteenth century describe Aztec state-sponsored sacrifices in which priests made offerings of humans and other animals, ostensibly to "feed" the gods on behalf of the welfare of the state. Apparently the gods were fond of human blood—as well as of quails, crocodiles, jaguars, ducks, and salamanders.

Why Did the Aztecs Practice Human Sacrifice and Cannibalism?

EVIDENCE OF state-sponsored human sacrifice and cannibalism of the victims among the Aztecs of Mexico comes from accounts written by the Spanish conquistadors (Harris 1977, 1989; Sanday 1986). The Aztec gods required human sacrifice—they "ate" human hearts and "drank" human blood. Most of the victims were prisoners of war, but many others were slaves, and sometimes young men and women, and even children.

The victims were marched up the steep steps of the pyramid, held lying on their backs over a stone altar, and slit open in the chest by a priest, who wrenched out the heart (said to be still beating), which was then burned in offering to the gods. The body was rolled down the other side of the temple, where it was retrieved by butchers and prepared for cooking. The skull was returned to the temple area to be put on display. Although no one knows for sure how many victims were sacrificed, estimates are in the hundreds of thousands. A chronicler reported that the display racks at a single site contained more than one hundred thousand skulls (Harris 1977:106). At one especially grand event, victims were arranged in four lines, each two miles long. Priests worked for four days to complete the sacrifices.

Human sacrifice and cannibalism of any scale might seem to invite the question "Why?" Certainly one must ask "why" about sacrifice and cannibalism as practiced on the grand scale of the Aztecs. Of the many attempted explanations, two perspectives are compared here: an etic view and an emic view.

Michael Harner (1977) and Marvin Harris (1977, 1989) propose a cultural materialist explanation based on references to factors in the environment and in the politics of Aztec expansionism. The region of the Aztec empire lacked sufficient animal sources of protein to satisfy its growing population. Although the ruling classes managed to maintain their supply of delicacies such as dog, turkey, duck, deer, rabbit, and fish, little was available for the poor. Yet the rulers needed to support and retain the loyalty of their army in order to protect and expand the empire's boundaries, and they needed to keep the masses happy. Providing the gods with human hearts and blood was a powerful statement of the empire's strength. It had the additional benefit of yielding huge amounts of meat for soldiers and commoners. Such "cannibal redistribution" could be manipulated by the state to reward particular groups and to compensate for periodic shortages in the agricultural cycle.

Interpretive cultural anthropologist Peggy Sanday rejects the materialist perspective and provides an interpretive one based on texts describing the Aztec people's rationale and motives (1986). Sacrifice and cannibalism, she says, followed religious logic and symbolism and were practiced to satisfy the gods' hunger, not human hunger. Aztec religion says that the gods require certain sacrifices in order for the universe to continue to operate. Human flesh was consumed not as an "ordinary meal" but as part of a religious identification with the gods, just as people would wear the skins of sacrificed victims to participate in their sacredness. Sanday says that the etic explanation, focusing on the "business" aspects of Aztec sacrifice and cannibalism, has overlooked the religious meaning for the Aztecs.

CRITICAL THINKING QUESTIONS

- How do the two explanations differ in the data they use?
- Which do you find more convincing, and why?
- Is there any other way to explain Aztec human sacrifice and cannibalism?

One of the most widely offered items for important events, such as a coronation or the naming of newborn babies, was a limited amount of ritually induced bleeding. Interpretive/symbolic anthropologists accept the religious logic involved in pleasing the gods as a sufficient explanation for blood sacrifice. Cultural materialists, on the other hand, are inclined to propose an explanation for the practice that is tied to resources, particularly sources of protein. (See the Critical Thinking box)

Religious Specialists

Not all rituals require the presence of a religious specialist, or someone with special and detailed training, but all require some level of knowledge on the part of the performer(s) about how to perform the rituals correctly. Even the daily, household veneration of an ancestor requires some knowledge gained through informal learning. At the other extreme, many rituals cannot be done without a highly trained specialist.

Shamans and Shamankas, Priests and Priestesses

General features of the categories of shaman and priest illustrate key differences between these two types of specialists (many other specialists fit somewhere in between). Shamans or shamankas (the female form with the "-ka" ending derives from the original Siberian usage) are part-time religious specialists who gain their status through direct relationships with the supernaturals, often by being "called." A potential shaman may be recognized by special signs, such as the ability to go into a trance. Anyone who demonstrates shamanic abilities can become a shaman; in other words, this is an openly available role. Shamans are more often associated with non-state societies, yet in many ways, faith healers and evangelists of the United States could be considered to fit in this category. One of the most important functions of shamanic religious specialists is healing (review Chapter 13).

Within states, the more complex occupational specialization in religion means that there is a wider variety of types of specialists, especially what anthropologists refer to as "priests" (not the same as the specific modern role of the Catholic priest) and promotes the development of religious hierarchies and power structures. The terms **priest** and **priestess** refer to a category of full-time religious specialists whose position is based mainly on abilities gained through formal training. A priest may receive a divine call, but more often the role is hereditary, passed on through priestly lineages. In terms of ritual performance, shamans are more involved with nonperiodic rituals. Priests perform a wider range of rituals, including periodic state rituals. Shamans rarely have much secular power, but priests and priestly lineages do.

Other Specialists

Certain other specialized roles are widely found. Diviners are specialists who are able to discover the will and wishes of the supernaturals through techniques such as reading animal entrails. Palm readers and tarot card readers fit into the category of diviners. Prophets are specialists who convey divine revelations usually gained through visions or dreams. They often possess charisma, have an especially attractive and powerful personality, and may be able to perform miracles. Prophets have founded new religions, some long-lasting and others short-lived. Witches use psychic powers and affect people through emotion and thought. Mainstream Western society often condemns witchcraft as negative. Some scholars of ancient and contemporary witchcraft, however, differentiate between positive forms that involve healing and negative forms that seek to harm people.

 # WORLD RELIGIONS

The term **world religions** was coined in the nineteenth century to refer to religions with many followers that crossed state borders and had other distinctive features, such as a concern with salvation (the belief that human beings require deliverance from an imperfect world). At first, the term referred only to Christianity, Islam, and Buddhism. It was later expanded to include Judaism, Hinduism, Confucianism, Taoism, and Shintoism. The category of world religions is less appropriate now, because many more religions cross country boundaries and therefore have "world" reach. Nonetheless, because college religion courses teach entire semesters of material on these "world religions," this chapter provides an anthropological perspective on five of them. In addition, because of the global importance of the African diaspora that began with the European colonial slave trade, a sixth category of world religions is included that describes key elements shared among the diversity of traditional African belief systems.

Cultural anthropologists emphasize that no world religion exists as a single monolithic entity. Rather, each has microcultural and regional variations, as well as doctrinal differences usually between reformist and fundamentalist interpretations. The world religions have long traveled outside their original borders through intentional attempts to expand and gain converts, or through migration of believers to new places. European colonialism was a major reason for the expansion of Christianity, especially (but not exclusively) through the missionary work of various Protestant sects. Now, the increased rate of population movements (Chapter 20) and the rapid expansion of television and the Internet have given even greater impetus to religious movement and change. One anthropologist says that the world religions face a "predicament" in terms of how to maintain a balance between standardization based on core beliefs and the increasingly local variants emerging everywhere (Hefner 1998). From Christian televangelism to Internet chat rooms, contemporary religion appears to be more dynamic and interactive than ever before, raising doubt about the validity of claims that modernity means the decline of religious belief and the rise of secularism.

The five world religions of long standing considered here are discussed first in terms of their history, distribution, and teachings. Then examples are given of how the same texts and teachings are localized. Often, when a world religion moves into a new cultural region, it encounters indigenous religious traditions. The two world religions that emphasize proselytizing, or seeking converts, are Christianity and Islam. Their encounters with indigenous religions have often been violent and have included physical destruction of local sacred places and objects (Corbey 2003). Common approaches include burning, overturning, dismantling, or cutting up objects, dumping them into the sea, or hiding them in caves. European Christian missionaries in the 1800s often confiscated sacred goods and shipped them to Europe for sale to private owners or museums. Both Christian and Islamic conversion efforts frequently involved the destruction of local sacred sites and the construction of their own places of worship on top of the original site.

In many cases, incoming religions and local religions coexist as separate traditions, either as complements or as competitors, in what is called **religious pluralism.** In **syncretism,** elements of two or more religions blend together. Syncretism is most likely to occur when elements of two religions form a close match with each other. For example, if a local myth involves a hero who has something to do with snakes, there may be a syncretic link with the Catholic belief in St. Patrick, who is believed to have driven snakes out of Ireland.

Many examples of non-fit can also be provided. Christian missionaries have had difficulty translating the Bible into indigenous languages because of lack of matching words or concepts, and because of differing kinship and social structures. Some Amazonian groups, for example, have no word that fits the Christian concept of "heaven" (Everett 1995). In other cases, matrilineal peoples have found it difficult to understand the significance of the Christian construct of "God the father."

Hinduism

Over 650 million people in the world are Hindus (Hiltebeitel 1995). The majority live in India, where Hinduism is practiced by 80 percent of the population. The other 20 million, the Hindu diaspora, live in the United States, Canada, the United Kingdom, Malaysia, Fiji, Trinidad, Guyana, and Hong Kong. A Hindu is typically born a Hindu, and Hinduism does not actively seek converts. The four Vedas, composed in Sanskrit in northern India between 1200 and 900 BCE, are the core texts of Hinduism. Many other scholarly texts and popular myths and epics, especially the Mahabharata (the story of a war between two lineages, the Pandavas and the Kauravas) and the Ramayana (the story of king Rama and his wife Sita), also serve as unifying scriptures. Throughout India, many local traditions exist, some of which carry forward elements from pre-Vedic times. Hinduism offers a rich polytheism and, at the same time, a philosophical tradition that reduces the multiplicity of deities into oneness. Deities range from simple stones (in Hinduism, stones can be gods) placed at the foot of a tree to elegantly carved and painted icons of gods such as Shiva and Vishnu and the goddess Durga. Everyday worship of a deity involves lighting a lamp in front of the god, chanting hymns and mantras (sacred phrases), and taking *darshan* (sight of) the deity (Eck 1985). These acts bring blessings to the worshipper.

Although certain standard features of Hinduism exist, such as acceptance of key texts and worship of important, well-known deities, many localized versions of Hinduism throughout India involve the worship of deities and practice of rituals unknown elsewhere. For example, fire-walking is an important part of goddess worship in southern and eastern India (Freeman 1981; Hiltebeitel 1988) and among some Hindu groups living outside India, notably Fiji (C. Brown 1984). Besides regional variations, caste differences in beliefs and practices are marked, even within the same area or village. Lower-caste deities prefer offerings of meat and alcohol; upper-caste deities prefer offerings of flowers, rice, and fruit. Temple structures range from magnificent buildings to a simple canopy placed over an image of the deity for shade. Yet the "unity in diversity" of Hinduism has long been recognized as real, mainly because of the shared acceptance of elements of Vedic thought.

A Nayar Fertility Ritual

The matrilineal Nayars of Kerala, South India, perform a nonperiodic ritual as a remedy for the curse of the serpent deities who cause infertility in women (Neff 1994). This ritual exemplifies the unity of Hinduism in several ritual elements, such as the use of camphor and incense, the importance of serpent deities, and offering flowers to the deity. The all-night ritual includes, first, women painting a sacred design of intertwined serpents on the floor. Several hours of worshipping the deity follow. Ritual elements include a camphor flame, incense, and flowers. Music comes from drumming, cymbals, and singing. All of these please the deity. The presence of the deity, though, is fully achieved when a Nayar woman goes into trance. Through her, matrilineal family members may speak to the deity and be blessed.

Thus, along with universal elements of Hindu ritual, the role of matrilineal kin among the Nayars provides local variation in ritual. Among the Nayars, a woman's matrilineal kin—mother, uncles, brothers—are responsible for ensuring that her desires for motherhood are fulfilled. They share her interest in her reproductive success in continuing the matrilineage. What the women say during the trance is important. They typically draw attention to family disharmonies or neglect of the deities. This message diverts blame from the infertile woman for whom the ritual is being held. It reminds family and lineage members of their responsibilities for each other.

Hindu Women and Karma in Great Britain

One of Hinduism's basic concepts is that of *karma*, translated as "destiny" or "fate." A person's karma is determined at birth on the basis of his or her previous life and how it was conducted. The karma concept has prompted many outsiders to judge Hindus as fatalistic, lacking a sense of agency. But fieldwork focused on how people actually think about karma in their everyday lives reveals much individual variation—from fatalism to a strong sense of being in charge of one's destiny. One study looked at women's perceptions of karma among Hindus living in England (Knott 1996). Some Hindu women are fatalistic in their attitudes and behavior, but others are not. One woman who had a strongly fatalistic view of karma said,

> [W]hen a baby's born . . . we have a ritual on the sixth day. That's when you name the baby, you know. And on that day, we believe the goddess comes and writes your future . . . we leave a blank white paper and a pen and we just leave it [overnight]. . . . So I believe that my future—whatever happens—is what she has written for me. That tells me [that] I have to do what I can do, and if I have a mishap in between I have to accept that. (24)

THINKING OUTSIDE THE BOX

Are there rituals (or secular rituals) related to infertility in your cultural world? If yes, what do they involve in terms of social support? If not, do you think such rituals might be helpful?

Yet another woman said that her sufferings were caused by the irresponsibility of her father and the "bad husband" to whom she had been married. She challenged her karma and left her husband: "I could not accept the karma of being with Nirmal [her husband]. If I had done so, what would have become of my children?" (25). Because Hindu women's karma dictates being married and having children, leaving one's husband is a major act of resistance. For some young women informants, questioning the role of karma was the same as questioning their parents' authority. Such intergenerational conflicts create feelings of ambiguity and confusion.

Options for women seeking support when questioning or changing their roles can be either religious (praying more and fasting) or secular (seeking the advice of a psychological counselor or social worker). Some Hindu women in England have themselves become counselors and have helped support other women's independence and self-confidence. This work involves clear subversion of the traditional rules of karma for women.

Buddhism

Buddhism originated in a founding figure, Siddhartha Gautama (ca. 566–486 BCE), revered as the Buddha, or Awakened One (Eckel 1995:135). It began in northern India, where the Buddha grew up. From there, it spread throughout the subcontinent, into Inner Asia and China, to Sri Lanka, and on to Southeast Asia. In the past two hundred years, Buddhism has spread to Europe and North America. Buddhism's popularity subsequently faded in India, and Buddhists now constitute less than 1 percent of India's population. Its global spread is matched by a great diversity of doctrine and practice, to the extent that it is difficult to point to a single essential feature (for example, no single text is accepted as authoritative for all forms of Buddhism), other than the importance of Gautama Buddha. Many Buddhists worship the Buddha as a deity, but others do not—they honor his teachings and follow the pathway he suggested for reaching nirvana, or release from worldly life.

Buddhism first arose as a protest movement against certain features of Hinduism, especially caste inequality. Yet it retained and revised several Hindu concepts, such as karma. In Buddhism, everyone has the potential for achieving nirvana (enlightenment and the overcoming of human suffering in this life), the goal of Buddhism. Good deeds are one way to achieve a better rebirth with each incarnation, until finally, release from samsara (the cycle of birth, reincarnation, death, and so on) is achieved. Compassion toward others, including animals, is a key virtue. Branches of Buddhism have different texts that they consider their canon. The major division is between the Theravada Buddhism practiced in Southeast Asia and the Mahayana Buddhism of Tibet, China, Taiwan, Korea, and Japan. Buddhism is associated with a strong tradition of monasticism through which monks and nuns renounce the everyday world and spend their lives meditating and doing good works. Buddhists have many and varied annual festivals and rituals. Some events bring pilgrims from around the world to India—to Sarnath, where the Buddha gave his first teaching, and Gaya, where he gained enlightenment.

Local Spirits and Buddhism in Southeast Asia

One theory says that wherever Buddhism exists outside India, it is never the exclusive religion of the devotees because it arrived to find established local religions already in place (Spiro 1967). In Burma, Buddhism and indigenous traditions coexist without one being dominant. Indigenous Burmese beliefs remained strong because they offer a way of dealing with everyday problems. According to Burmese Buddhism, a person's karma (as in Hinduism) is a result of

Buddhism gained a solid footing in Japan in the eighth century. The city of Nara was an important early center of Buddhism. Here an emperor sponsored the casting of a huge bronze statue of the Buddha. ■
Is there a Buddhist temple where you live? If so, have you visited it? If not, find out where the nearest one is, and visit it. (Source: Jack Heaton)

After the Chinese takeover of Tibet, many Tibetans became refugees, including the revered head of Tibetan Buddhism, the Dalai Lama. Buddhism, founded in India as a protest against Hinduism, is a minority religion in its homeland. It has millions of followers elsewhere, from Scotland to San Francisco. ■ Do some research on Buddhism as a world religion to find out where it is now established. (Source: AP/Wide World Photos)

previous births and determines his or her present condition. If something bad happens, the person can do little but suffer through it.

Burmese supernaturalism, on the other hand, says that the bad thing happened because of the actions of capricious spirits called *nats*. Ritual actions can combat the influence of nats. In other words, nats can be dealt with, but karma cannot. The continuity of belief in nats can be seen as an example of human agency and creativity. People retained what was important to them from their traditional beliefs but also adopted aspects of the new religion. Buddhism, however, became an important cultural force and the basis for social integration in Burma. Although Buddhism is held to be the supreme truth, the spirits retain control when it comes to dealing with everyday problems such as a toothache or a monetary loss.

Buddhism and Abortion in Japan

Buddhist teachings about the "fluidity" of the supernatural and human realms are important in contemporary Japan, especially in relation to the widespread practice of abortion there. In Japanese Buddhism, fetuses, like newborn infants, are not considered to be full-fledged, solid lives (LaFleur 1992). They are fluid creatures who can be "returned" through abortion (or, in previous centuries, infanticide) to the supernatural realm. People believe that a "returned" fetus may come back at a more convenient time. Women who have had an abortion commonly go to a Buddhist temple and perform a special ritual in which they pray for the good fortune of the rejected fetus. They dedicate a small statue to it that may be placed, along with hundreds of other such statues, in a cemetery-like setting (review the photo on p. 362 in Chapter 12). It is periodically adorned with clothing, cheap jewelry, and trinkets. These practices may have a positive psychological effect on the parents by diverting feelings of sadness. Thus doctrine and ritual fit with the reproductive goal of many Japanese families to have few children within the context of abortion being the predominant way of limiting the number of offspring.

Judaism

The first and basic Judaic religious system was defined around 500 BCE, following the destruction of the Temple in Jerusalem by Babylonians in 586 BCE (Neusner

1995). The early writings, called the Pentateuch, established the theme of exile and return as a paradigm for Judaism that endures today. The Pentateuch is also called the Five Books of Moses, or the Torah.

Followers of Judaism share in the belief in the Torah as the revelation of God's truth through Israel, a term for the "holy people." The Torah explains the relationship between the supernatural and human realms, and it guides people in how to carry out the Judaic worldview through appropriate actions. A key feature of all forms of Judaism is the identification of what is wrong with the present and how to escape, overcome, or survive that situation. Jewish life is symbolically interpreted as a tension between exile and return, given its foundational myth in the exile of the Jews from Israel and their period of slavery in Egypt.

Judaism is monotheistic, teaching that God is one, unique, and all-powerful. Humans have a moral duty to follow Jewish law, to protect and preserve life and health, and to follow certain duties such as observing the Sabbath. The high regard for human life is reflected in the general opposition to abortion within Jewish law and in opposition to the death penalty. Words, both spoken and written, have unique importance in Judaism: There is an emphasis on truth-telling in life and on the use of established literary formulas at precise times during worship, which are encoded in a *sidur*, or prayer book. Dietary patterns distinguish Judaism from other religions. For example, rules of kosher eating forbid the mixing of milk or milk products with meat.

Contemporary varieties of Judaism range from conservative Hasidism to Reform Judaism, which emerged in the early 1800s. One difference between these two perspectives concerns the question of who is Jewish. Jewish law traditionally defined a Jewish person as someone born of a Jewish mother. In contrast, reform Judaism also recognizes as Jewish the offspring of a Jewish father and a non-Jewish mother. Currently the Jewish population numbers about 15 million worldwide, with about half living in North America, a quarter in Israel, and another 20 percent in Europe and Russia. Other, smaller groups are scattered across the globe.

Who's Who at the Kotel

The most sacred place to all Jews is the kotel, or Western Wall in Jerusalem. Since the 1967 war, which brought Jerusalem under Israeli rule, the kotel has been the most important religious shrine and pilgrimage site of Israel. The kotel is located at one edge of the Temple Mount (or Haram Sharif), an area sacred to Jews, Muslims, and Christians. According to Jewish scriptures, God asked Abraham to sacrifice his son Isaac on this hill. Later, King Solomon built the First Temple here in the middle of the tenth century BCE. It was destroyed by Nebuchadnessar in 587 BCE, when the Jews were led into captivity in Babylon. Around 500 BCE, King Herod built the Second Temple on the same site. The kotel is a remnant of the Second Temple. Jews of all varieties and non-Jews come to the kotel in vast numbers from around the world. The kotel plaza is open to everyone. The wall is made of massive rectangular stones weighing between two and eight tons each. At its base is a synagogue area partitioned into men's and women's sections.

An ethnographic study of what goes on at the kotel reveals how this single site brings together a variety of Jewish worshippers and secular visitors. There is great diversity among the visitors, evident in the various styles of dress and gesture:

> The Hasid . . . with a fur *shtreimel* on his head may enter the synagogue area alongside a man in shorts who utilizes a cardboard skullcap available for "secular" visitors. American youngsters in jeans may ponder Israeli soldiers of their own age, dressed in uniform, and wonder what their lot might have been if they [had been] born in another country. Women from Yemen, wearing embroidered trousers under their dresses, edge close to the Wall as do women accoutred in contemporary styles whose religiosity may have been filtered through a modern education. . . . (Storper-Perez and Goldberg 1994:321)

In spite of plaques that state the prohibition against begging, there are beggars who offer to "sell a blessing" to visitors. They may remind visitors that it was the

The kotel (or Western Wall) in Jerusalem is a sacred place of pilgrimage, especially for Jews. Males pray at a section marked off on the left, women at the area on the right. Both men and women should cover their heads, and women should take care, when leaving the wall area, to keep their faces toward it and avoid turning their backs to it. ■ Think of some behavioral rules at a sacred place you know. (Source: Barbara Miller)

poor who built the wall in the first place. Another category of people is young Jewish men who, in search of prospective "born again" Jews, "hang around" looking for a "hit" (in their words). Most of the hits are young Americans who are urged to take their Jewishness more seriously and, if male, to be sure to marry a Jewish woman. Other regulars are Hebrew-speaking men who are available to organize a prayer service. One of the most frequent forms of religious expression at the kotel is the insertion of written prayers into the crevices of the wall.

The social heterogeneity of the Jewish people is thus transcended in a single space, creating what Victor Turner (1969) called *communitas,* a sense of collective unity out of individual diversity.

Passover in Kerala

The Jews of the Kochi area (formerly called Cochin) of Kerala, south India, have lived there for about 1000 years (Katz and Goldberg 1989). The Maharaja of Kochi had respect for the Jewish people, who were mainly merchants. He relied on them for external trade and contacts. In recognition of this, he allowed a synagogue, which is still standing, to be built next to his palace. Syncretism is apparent in Kochi Jewish lifestyle, social structure, and rituals. Basic aspects of Judaism are retained, along with adoption of many aspects of Hindu practices.

Three aspects of syncretism with Hinduism are apparent in passover, one of the most important annual rituals of the Jewish faith. First, the Western/European passover celebration is typically joyous and a time of feasting. In contrast, the Kochi version has adopted a tone of austerity and is called "the fasting feast." Second, Kochi passover allows no role for children, whereas at a traditional *seder* (ritual meal) children usually ask four questions as a starting-point of the narrative. The Kochi Jews chant the questions in unison. (In Hinduism, children do not have solo roles in rituals.) Third, a Kochi seder stresses purity even more than standard Jewish requirements. Standard rules about maintaining the purity of kosher wine usually mean that no gentile (non-Jew) should touch it. But Kochi Jews expand the rule to say that if the shelf or table on which the wine sits is touched by a gentile, the wine is impure. This extra level of "contagion" is influenced by Hindu concepts of pollution.

THINKING OUTSIDE THE BOX

Ask a friend to arrange for you to attend a ritual or ceremony in a religion unfamiliar to you. Take "head notes" during the event on key practices, symbols, and interactions.

Christianity

Christianity has many ties with Judaism, from which it sprang, especially in terms of the biblical teachings of a coming savior, or messiah. It began in the Middle East in the second quarter of the first century (Cunningham 1995:240–253). Most of the early believers were Jews who took up the belief in Jesus Christ as the "messiah"

A celebration of the Christian holy day of Palm Sunday in Port-au-Prince, Haiti. European colonialism brought African slaves to the New World and converted many to Christianity through missionary efforts.
■ Discover through a web site or other sources what the major Christian denominations in Haiti are. (Source: Edward Keller III)

(annointed one) who came to earth in fulfillment of prophesies contained in the Hebrew scriptures. Today, Christianity is the largest of the world's religions with about 1.5 billion adherents, or nearly one-third of the world's population. It is the majority religion of Australia, New Zealand, the Philippines, Papua New Guinea, most countries of Europe and of North and South America, and about a dozen southern African countries. Christianity is a minority religion throughout Asia, but Asian Christians constitute 16 percent of the world's total Christians and are thus a significant population.

Christians accept the Bible (Old and New Testaments) as containing the basic teachings of their faith, believe that a supreme God sent his son to earth as a sacrifice for the welfare of humanity, and look to Jesus as the model to follow for moral guidance. The three largest branches of Christianity are Roman Catholic, Protestant, and Eastern Orthodox. Within each of these branches, various denominations exist. Christianity has existed the longest in the Near East and Mediterranean regions. In contemporary times, the greatest growth in Christianity is occurring in sub-Saharan Africa, Latin America, parts of India, and Indonesia. It is currently experiencing a resurgence in Eastern Europe.

Protestantism among White Appalachians

Studies of protestantism in Appalachia describe local traditions that outsiders who are accustomed to standard, urban versions may view as "deviant." For example, some churches in rural West Virginia and North Carolina, called Old Regulars, practice three obligatory rituals: footwashing, communion (a ritual commemorating the "Last Supper" that Jesus had with his disciples), and baptism (Dorgan 1989). The footwashing ceremony occurs once a year in conjunction with communion, usually as an extension of the Sunday service. An elder is called to the front of the church, and he preaches for ten to twenty minutes. Then there is a round of handshaking and embracing. Two deaconesses come forward to "prepare the table" by uncovering the sacramental elements placed there earlier under a white tablecloth (unleavened bread, serving plates for the bread, cups for the wine, and a decanter or quart jar or two of wine). The deacons come forward and break the bread into pieces while the moderator pours the wine into the cups. Men and women form separate groups as the deacons serve the bread and wine.

After the deacons serve each other, it is time for the footwashing. The moderator may begin this part of the service by quoting from the New Testament (John 13: 4): "He riseth from supper, and laid aside his garments; and he took a towel and girded himself." He then takes a towel and basin from the communion table and puts water in the basin, selects a senior elder and removes his shoes and socks, and then washes his feet slowly and attentively. Other members come forward and take towels and basins. Soon "the church is filled with crying, shouting, and praising as these highly poignant exchanges unleash a flood of emotions . . . and literally scores of high-pathos scenes will be played out" (106). Participants take turns washing and being washed. A functional interpretation of the ritual of footwashing is that it helps maintain social cohesion.

Another feature of worship in some small, Protestant subdenominations in West Virginia involves the handling of poisonous snakes. This practice finds legitimation in the New Testament (Daugherty 1997 [1976]). According to a passage in Mark (16:15–18), "In my name shall they cast out devils; they shall speak with new tongues; they shall take up serpents; and if they drink any deadly thing, it shall not hurt them; they shall lay hands on the sick, and they shall recover." Members of "Holiness-type" churches believe that the handling of poisonous snakes is the supreme act of devotion to God. Biblical literalists, these people choose serpent-handling as their way of celebrating life, death, and resurrection and of proving that only Jesus has the power to deliver them from death.

Most serpent handlers have been bitten many times, but few have died. One interpretation of this ritual practice says that the risks of handling poisonous rattlesnakes and copperheads mirror the risks of the environment. The people are poor, with high rates of unemployment and few prospects for improvement. Outsiders might ask whether such dangerous ritual practices indicate that the people are somehow psychologically disturbed. Psychological tests indicate, however, that they are more emotionally healthy, on average, than members of mainline Protestant churches.

The Last Supper in Fiji

Among Christians in Fiji, the image of the Last Supper is a dominant motif (Toren 1988). This scene, depicted on tapestry hangings, adorns most churches and many houses. People say, "Christ is the head of this household, he eats with us and overhears us" (697). The image's popularity is the result of its fit with Fijian notions of communal eating and kava drinking. Seating rules at such events place the people of highest status, such as the chief and others close to him, at the "above" side of the room, away from the entrance. Others sit at the "lower" end, facing the highly ranked people. Intermediate positions are located on either side of the person of honor, in ranked order. Da Vinci's rendition of the Last Supper places Jesus Christ in the position of a chief, with the disciples in an ordered arrangement around him. "The image of an ordered and stratified society exemplified in people's positions relative to one another around the kava bowl is encountered virtually every day in the village" (706). The disciples and the viewers "face" the chief and eat and drink together, as is appropriate in Fijian society.

Islam

Islam is based on the teachings of the prophet Muhammed (570–632) and is the youngest of the world religions (Martin 1995:498–513). The Arabic word *Islam* means "submission" to the will of the one god, Allah, through which peace will be achieved. Islam also implies acceptance of Muhammed as the last and final messenger of god, "the seal of the prophets." Muslim-majority nations are located in northern Africa; the Middle East, including Afghanistan, Pakistan, and Bangladesh in South Asia; and several nations in Central Asia and Southeast Asia. In fact, the majority of the world's Muslims (60 percent) live in South Asia or Southeast Asia. Although Islam originally flourished among pastoralists, only 2 percent of its adherents now are in that category.

A common and inaccurate stereotype of Islam among many non-Muslims is that wherever it exists, it is the same. A comparison of Islam in highland Sumatra, Indonesia, and Morocco, North Africa, reveals culturally constructed differences (Bowen 1992). The annual Feast of Sacrifice is celebrated by Muslims around the world. It commemorates god's sparing of Abraham's son Ishmael (Isaac in Christian and Jewish traditions). It takes place everywhere on the tenth of the last month of the year, also called Pilgrimage Month. The ritual reminds Muslims of their global unity within the Islamic faith. One aspect of this event in Morocco involves the king publicly plunging a dagger into a ram's throat, a reenactment of Muhammad's performance of the sacrifice on the same day in the seventh century. Each male head of household follows the pattern and sacrifices a ram. The size and virility of the ram are a measure of the man's power and virility. Other men of the household stand to witness the sacrifice, while women and children are absent or in the background. After the ram is killed, they come forward and dab its blood on their faces. In some villages, women play a more prominent role before the sacrifice by daubing the ram with henna (red dye), thus sanctifying it, and using its blood afterward in rituals to protect the household. These state-level and household rituals symbolize male power in the public and private domains—the power of the monarchy and the power of patriarchy.

The local adaption of the ritual to Moroccan culture is clear when it is compared with its enactment in Sumatra, which has a less patriarchal culture and a political structure that does not emphasize monarchy. In Isak, a traditionalist Muslim village, people have been Muslims since the seventeenth century. They sacrifice all kinds of animals, including chickens, ducks, sheep, goats, and water buffalo. As long as the throat is cut and the meat is eaten, it satisfies the demands of god. Before cutting the victim's throat, the sacrificer dedicates it to one or more relatives. In contrast to Morocco, most sacrifices receive little notice and are done mainly in the back of the house with little fanfare. Both women and men of the household refer to it as "their" sacrifice, and there are no signs of male dominance. Women may sponsor a sacrifice, as did one wealthy woman trader who sacrificed a buffalo (the actual cutting, however, is done by a man). The Moroccan ritual emphasizes fathers and sons. The Isak ritual includes attention to a wider range of kin on both the husband's and the wife's side, daughters as well as sons, and dead relatives, too. In the Indonesian context, no centralized dynastic meanings are given to the ritual.

The differences in the way the ritual is practiced do not arise because Moroccans know the scriptures better than Sumatrans. The Isak area has many Islamic scholars who consult the scriptures and discuss issues. Rather, the cultural context, including kinship and politics, into which the same scriptural tradition is placed shapes it to local interests and needs.

African Religions

African religions have spread outside Africa through the enforced movements of people as slaves and by voluntary migration. This section attempts to summarize some key features of African religions and then offers an example of a new religion with African roots, Ras Tafari.

Features of African Religions

As of 1994, Africa's total population comprised 341 million Christians, 285 million Muslims, and about 70 million people practicing indigenous religions (Smith 1995:15–16) and the proportions are roughly the same today. With its diverse geography, cultural variation, and history, Africa encompasses a wide range of indigenous religions. Some common, but not universal, features of indigenous African religions are

- Myths about a rupture that once occurred between the creator deity and humans.
- A pantheon that includes a high god and many secondary supernaturals ranging from powerful gods to lesser spirits.

A sacred altar in Togo, West Africa. ■ Can you distinguish some of the ritual elements displayed here? How would an anthropologist begin to learn about the beliefs involved in this religion? (Source: © Gerd Ludwig/Woodfin Camp & Associates)

- Elaborate initiation rituals.
- Rituals involving animal sacrifices and other offerings, meals, and dances.
- Altars within shrines as focal places where humans and deities meet.
- Close links with healing.

Although these general features are fairly constant, African indigenous religions are rethought and reshaped with variable results (Gable 1995). Furthermore, as African religions have moved around the world to new locations with the movement of African peoples, they have been adapted in various ways to their new contexts, as discussed in the following section on the Ras Tafari religion.

Ras Tafari

Also called Rastafarianism, Ras Tafari is a relatively new religion of the Caribbean, the United States, and Europe. It is not known how many Rastafarians there are because they refuse to be counted (Smith 1995:23). Ras Tafari is an unorthodox, protest religion that shares few of the features of African religions mentioned above. Ras Tafari traces its history to several preachers of the early twentieth century who taught that Ras ("Prince") Tafari, then the Ethiopian emperor Haile Selassie, was the "Lion of Judah" who would lead Blacks to the African promised land.

Rastafarianism does not have an organized set of doctrines, and there are no written texts or enforced orthodoxy. Shared beliefs of the many diffuse groups include the belief that Ethiopia is heaven on earth, that emperor Haile Selassie is a living god, and that all Blacks will be able to return to the homeland through his help. Since the death of Haile Selassie in 1975, greater emphasis has been placed on pan-African unity and Black power, and less on Ethiopia. Rastafarianism is particularly strong in Jamaica, where it is associated with reggae music, dreadlocks, and smoking *ganja* (marijuana). Variations within the Rastafarian movement in Jamaica range from beliefs that one must fight oppression to the position that living a peaceful life brings victory against evil.

For a research project, read about the history of Rastafarianism, its contemporary distribution, and its major beliefs and rituals.

THINKING

OUTSIDE
THE BOX

DIRECTIONS OF CHANGE

All religions have established mythologies and doctrines that provide a certain degree of continuity and, often, conservativism in religious beliefs and practices. Yet nowhere are religions frozen and unchanging. Cultural anthropologists have traced the resurgence of religions that seemed to have been headed toward extinction through colonial forces, and they have documented the emergence of seemingly new religions. Likewise, they are observing the contemporary struggle of once-suppressed religions in socialist states to find a new position in the post-socialist world. Religious icons (carvings or other artistic renderings of Mary, for example), once a prominent feature in Russian Orthodox churches, had been removed and placed in museums. Now, the churches want them back. Indigenous people's beliefs about the sacredness of their land are an important part of their attempts to protect their territory from encroachment and development by outside commercial interests. The world of religious change offers these examples, and far more, as windows into wider cultural change.

Revitalization Movements

Revitalization movements are social movements that seek to bring about positive change, either through re-establishing all or parts of a religion that has been threatened by outside forces or through adopting new practices and beliefs. Such movements often arise in the context of rapid cultural change and appear to represent a way for people to try to make sense of their changing world and their place in it. One such movement that emerged as a response of Native Americans to the invasion of their land by Europeans and Euro-Americans was the Ghost Dance movement (Kehoe 1989). In the early 1870s, a shaman named Wodziwob of the Paiute tribe in California declared that the world would soon be destroyed and then renewed: Native Americans, plants, and animals would come back to life. He instructed people to perform a circle dance, known as the "Ghost Dance," at night. This movement spread to other tribes in California, Oregon, and Idaho but ended when the prophet died and his prophecy was unfulfilled.

A similar movement emerged in 1890, led by another Paiute prophet, Wovoka, who had a vision during a total eclipse. His message was the same: destruction, renewal, and the need to perform circle dances in anticipation of the impending event. The dance spread widely and had various effects. Among the Pawnee, it provided the basis for a cultural revival of old ceremonies that had fallen into disuse. The Sioux altered Wovoka's message and adopted a more overtly hostile stance toward the government and White people. Newspapers began to carry stories about the "messiah craze," referring to Wovoka. Ultimately, the U.S. government took action against the Sioux, killing Chief Sitting Bull and Chief Big Foot and about three hundred Sioux at Wounded Knee. In the 1970s, the Ghost Dance was revived again by the American Indian Movement, an activist organization that seeks to advance Native American rights.

Cargo cults are a type of revitalization movement that emerged in much of Melanesia (including Papua New Guinea and Fiji), and in New Zealand among the indigenous Maori peoples, in response to Western influences. Most prominent in the first half of the nineteenth century, cargo cults emphasize the acquisition of Western trade goods, or "cargo." Typically, a prophetic leader emerges with a vision of how the cargo will arrive. In one instance, the leader predicted that a ship would come, bringing not only cargo but also the people's dead ancestors. Followers set up tables for the expected guests, complete with flower arrangements.

Later, after World War II and the islanders' experiences of aircraft arrivals bringing cargo, the mode of anticipated arrival changed to planes. Once again, people would wait expectantly for the arrival of the plane. The cargo cults emerged as a response to the disruptive effects of new goods being suddenly introduced into indigenous settings. The outsiders imposed a new form of exchange system that emphasized the importance of Western goods and denied the importance of indigenous valuables such as shells and pigs. This transformation undermined traditional patterns

John Frum Movement supporters stand guard around one of the cult's flag poles at Sulphur Bay village on the island of Tanna, Vanuatu, in the South Pacific.
■ What does this scene remind you of from your own cultural experience? (Source: Lamont Lindstrom)

of status-gaining through the exchange of indigenous goods. Cargo cult leaders sought help, in the only way they knew, in obtaining Western goods so that they could gain social status in the new system.

Contested Sacred Sites

Religious conflict often becomes focused on sacred sites. One place of recurrent conflict is Jerusalem, where many religions and sects within religions compete for control of sacred terrain. Three major religions claim they have primary rights: Islam, Judaism, and Christianity. And even among the Christians, several different sects vie for control of the Church of the Holy Sepulchre. In India, frequent conflicts over sacred sites occur between Hindus and Muslims. Hindus claim that Muslim mosques have been built on sites sacred to Hindus. On some occasions, Hindus have destroyed mosques. Many conflicts that involve secular issues surrounding sacred sites also exist worldwide. In the United States, White racists have burned African American churches.

In Israel, some Jewish leaders object to archaeological research because the ancient Jewish burial places should remain undisturbed. The same situation exists for Native Americans, whose burial grounds have often been destroyed for the sake of development in the United States and Canada. The ongoing dispute about Kennewick man (see Chapter 9, p. 283) is an example of a dispute about the right of living people to have the skeletons of their ancestors returned to them versus scientists' claim to study them.

Around the world, large-scale development projects such as dams and mines have destroyed indigenous sacred areas. Resistance to such destruction is growing—for example, among Australian Aborigines, as discussed in this chapter's Lessons Applied Box.

Religious Freedom as a Human Right

According to a United Nations Declaration, freedom from religious persecution is a universal human right. Yet violations of this right by countries and by competing religions are common. Sometimes people who are persecuted on religious grounds can seek and obtain sanctuary in other places or nations. Thousands of Tibetan Buddhist refugees, including their leader the Dalai Lama, fled Tibet after it was taken over by the Chinese. Several Tibetan communities have been established in exile in India, the United States, and Canada, where the Tibetan people attempt to keep their religion, language, and heritage alive.

The post-9/11 policy enactments in the United States related to the "campaign against terrorism" are seen by many as dangerous steps against constitutional principles of personal liberty, and specifically, as infringements on the religious rights of practicing Muslims. The prevalent mentality in the government, and in much of the general populace, links the whole of Islam with terrorism and thereby stigmatizes all Muslims as potential terrorists. Physical attacks against people assumed to be Muslim were another aspect of such extreme thinking. Many anthropologists (for example, Mamdani 2002) have spoken out against the inaccuracy and unfairness of labeling an entire religion dangerous and putting all its members under the shadow of suspicion.

THE BIG QUESTIONS REVISITED

▪ WHAT is religion and what are the basic features of religions?

Early cultural anthropologists defined religion in contrast to magic and suggested that religion was a more evolved form of thinking about the supernatural realm. They collected information on religions of non-Western cultures and constructed theories about the origin and functions of religion. Since then, ethnographers have described the basic features of religious systems and documented a rich variety of beliefs, many forms of ritual behavior, and different types of religious specialists. Beliefs are expressed in either myth or doctrine, and they are often concerned with defining the roles and characteristics of supernatural beings and how humans should relate to them. Rituals, or the actions associated with beliefs, include life-cycle rituals, pilgrimage, rituals of inversion, and sacrifice. In some sense, all rituals are transformative for the participants. Many rituals, though not all, require the participation of a trained religious specialist such as a shaman/shamanka or priest/priestess. In states, religious specialists are often organized into hierarchies, and many specialists gain substantial secular power. In non-state societies, religious specialist roles are fewer, are less formalized, and carry less secular power and status.

▪ HOW do world religions reflect globalization and localization?

The five world religions of long standing are based on a coherent and widely agreed-upon set of teachings, but as members of these religions move around the globe, their religious beliefs and practices are contextualized into localized variants. When a religion moves into a new culture, it may be blended with indigenous systems (syncretism), may coexist with indigenous religions in a pluralistic fashion, or may take over and obliterate the original beliefs.

▪ WHAT are some important aspects of religious change in contemporary times?

Cultural anthropologists have documented religious change and sought to explain why and how it occurs. Religious movements of the past two centuries have often been prompted by colonialism and other forms of social contact. In some instances, indigenous religious leaders and cults arise in the attempt to resist unwanted outside forces of change. In other cases, they evolve as ways of incorporating selected outside elements. Issues of contemporary importance include the increasing amount of conflict surrounding sacred sites and of hostilities related to the effects of secular power interests on religious institutions and spaces. The importance of considering religion as a human right, according to United Nations policy, was brought to the fore following the 9/11 attacks on the United States, when the U.S. "campaign against terrorism" jeopardized the rights of Muslim citizens.

KEY CONCEPTS

animatism, p. 528
animism, p. 525
anthropomorphic, p. 529
cargo cult, p. 548
doctrine, p. 527
euhemerism, p. 529
life-cycle ritual, p. 532

magic, p. 524
myth, p. 527
priest/priestess, p. 537
religion, p. 524
religious pluralism, p. 538
revitalization movement, p. 547
ritual, p. 531

ritual of inversion, p. 534
sacrifice, p. 535
syncretism, p. 538
world religion, p. 537
worldview, p. 524
zoomorphic, p. 529

SUGGESTED READINGS

Nadia Abu El-Haj. *Archaeological Practice and Territorial Self-Fashioning in Israeli Society*. Chicago: University of Chicago Press, 2001. A cultural anthropologist writes about the political aspects, specifically nation-building, of archaeology in Israel. Attention is focused on contested sacred sites, how secular interests are linked to sacred site archaeology, and debates about excavation of grave sites.

Diane Bell. *Ngarrindjeri Wurruwarrin: A World That Is, Was, and Will Be*. North Melbourne, Australia: Spinifex, 1998. This is an ethnography about Australian Aboriginal women's struggles to protect their sacred land from encroachment by developers. It devotes attention to the women's own voices, the perspective of the Australian government, the media, and even disputes among anthropologists about what constitutes truth and validity.

Thomas D. Blakely, Walter E. A. van Beek, and Dennis L. Thompson. *Religion in Africa: Experience and Expression*. Portsmouth, NH: Heinemann, 1994. This book contains an introductory overview and twenty chapters on topics that include the impact of Islam and Christianity on African religious systems, women's spirit cults, myth and epic, and new religious movements.

Karen McCarthy Brown. *Mama Lola: A Vodou Priestess in Brooklyn*. Berkeley: University of California Press, 1991. The life story of Mama Lola, a Vodou practitioner, is set within an ethnographic study of a Haitian community in New York.

David L. Carmichael, Jane Hubert, Brian Reeves, and Audhold Schanche, eds. *Sacred Sites, Sacred Places*. New York: Routledge, 1994. This volume contains an introductory essay and twenty-one chapters, some by archaeologists and others by cultural anthropologists, on sacred places in California, Ireland, Cameroon, Sweden, Poland, Kenya, and New Zealand, among others. The authors discuss methods applied in studying sacred sites, as well as policy issues related to site preservation.

Susan Greenwood. *Magic, Witchcraft and the Otherworld: An Anthropology*. New York: Berg, 2000. This book examines modern magic as practiced by Pagans in Britain, focusing on the Pagan view of the essence of magic as communication with an otherworldly reality. Chapters address witchcraft, healing, Goddess worship, and the relationship between magic and morality.

Klara Bonsack Kelley and Harris Francis. *Navajo Sacred Places*. Bloomington: Indiana University Press, 1994. The authors report on the results of a research project undertaken to learn about Navajo cultural resources, especially sacred sites and the stories associated with them, in order to help protect these places.

Lorna J. Marshall. *Nyae Nyae !Kung: Beliefs and Rites*. Cambridge, MA: Peabody Museum of Archaeology and Ethnology, Harvard University, 1999. This book provides detailed descriptions of Ju/wasi [!Kung] religious beliefs, including characteristics of supernaturals and rituals for childbirth and healing. The ethnographic data are from the 1950s, when Marshall did extensive fieldwork among the Nyae Nyae area of Namibia.

Anna S. Meigs. *Food, Sex, and Pollution: A New Guinea Religion*. New Brunswick, NJ: Rutgers University Press, 1983. This book provides an analysis of taboos surrounding food, sex, and vital bodily essences among the Hua people of Papua New Guinea.

Fatima Mernissi. *Beyond the Veil: Male–Female Dynamics in Modern Muslim Society*. Bloomington: Indiana University Press, rev. ed., 1987. The author considers how Islam perceives female sexuality and seeks to regulate it on behalf of the social order. This edition contains a new chapter on Muslim women and fundamentalism.

THE BIG QUESTIONS

- HOW is culture expressed through art?
- WHAT do play and leisure activities tell us about culture?
- HOW is expressive culture changing in contemporary times?

Expressive Culture

Olmec culture flourished in the Gulf Coast region of Middle America from around 1200 to 300 BCE. At the site of San Lorenzo, archaeologists found several colossal stone sculptures of heads that weigh many tons. The sculptures probably depict individual rulers. (Source: Demetrio Carrasco © CONACULTA-INAH-MEX. Authorized reproduction by the Instituto Nacional de Antropologia e Historia/Dorling Kindersly Media Library)

In the year 2004, the Louvre, one of the world's best-known art museums, opened a huge new museum in the shadow of the Eiffel Tower that displays so-called tribal art of Africa, Asia, the South Pacific, and the Americas. This project reflects the interest of France's president, Jacques Chirac, in non-Western art. It also reflects a new appreciation for the role of anthropologists in helping museums to provide information on the cultural context for objects that are displayed, because French cultural anthropologist Maurice Godelier, a specialist on Papua New Guinea, has been involved in planning the new exhibits.

This new museum elevates "tribal" objects to the level of "art," rather than placing them in a museum of natural history, as is often done in the United States. At the same time, it places "tribal" art in a museum that is clearly separate from the Louvre. A long-standing conceptual division in European and Euro-American thinking, beginning with the Enlightenment, links the West with "civilization" and non-Western peoples with that which is uncivilized. It will be interesting to see how this new museum handles the challenge of moving beyond such a dichotomy.

This chapter considers an area of human behavior and thought called expressive culture, which, as defined in Chapter 7, consists of beliefs and behavior related to art and play (definitions of these terms are provided below). The first section discusses what the anthropology of art encompasses, theoretical perspectives about cross-cultural art, and findings from *museum anthropology*. The next section takes a cross-cultural look at another area of expressive culture: play and leisure activities. Directions of change in expressive culture, including art and play, are covered in the third section.

ART AND CULTURE

Compared to art history classes you may have taken, cultural anthropologists have a rather different view of what art is and how to study it (see the Critical Thinking box). Their approach, here as in other cultural domains, challenges Western concepts and categories and prompts us to look at art within its context. Anthropologists consider many products, practices, and processes to be art. They study the artist and the artist's place in society. In addition, they ask questions about how art, and expressive culture more generally, are related to microcultural variation, inequality, power, and change.

What Is Art?

Are ancient rock carvings art? Is subway graffiti art? An embroidered robe? A painting of a can of Campbell's soup? Philosophers, art critics, art lovers, and anthropologists all struggle with the question of what art is. The issue of how to define art involves more than mere word games. The way art is defined affects the manner in which a person values and treats artistic creations, those who create them, and their cultural context. Anthropologists propose broad definitions of art to take into account emic definitions cross-culturally. As defined in Chapter 8, art is the application of imagination, skill, and style to matter, movement, and sound that goes beyond the purely practical (Nanda 1994:383). The anthropological study of art considers both the process and the products of such human skill, the variation in art and its preferred forms cross-culturally, and the way culture constructs and changes artistic traditions. The skill involved is recognized as such in a particular culture. Such culturally judged skill can be applied to many substances and activities, and the product can be considered art—for example, a beautifully presented meal, a well-told story, or a perfectly formed basket. In this sense, art is a human universal, and no culture can be said to lack artistic activity.

Probing the Categories of Art

PROBABLY EVERY READER of this book, at one time or another, has looked at an object on display in a museum or in an art book or magazine and exclaimed, "But that's not art!" As a critical thinking research project on "what is art," visit two museums, either in person or on the Internet. One of these should be a museum of either fine art or modern art. The other should be a museum of natural history. In the former, examine at least five items on display. In the latter, examine at least five items on display that have to do with human cultures (that is, skip the bugs and rocks). Take notes on the items that you are examining. Then answer the following questions.

CRITICAL THINKING QUESTIONS

- What is the object?
- What contextual explanation does the museum provide about the object?
- Was the object intended as a work of art or as something else?
- In your opinion, is it art? Why or why not?
- Compare your notes on the objects in the two types of museums. What do your notes tell you about categories of art?

Within the general category of art, subcategories exist, denoting certain eras, such as paleolithic or modern art, or based on the medium of expression. For example, there are the graphic or plastic arts (painting, drawing, sculpture, weaving, basketry, and architecture); the decorative arts (interior design, landscaping, gardens, costume design, and body adornment such as hairstyles, tattooing, and painting); performance arts (music, dance, and theater); and verbal arts (poetry, writing, rhetoric, and telling stories and jokes). All these are Western, English-language categories that often do not correspond to emic categories.

A long-standing distinction in the Western view separates "fine art" from "folk art." This distinction is based on the Western definition of fine art as rare, expensive art produced by artists usually trained in the Western classical tradition. This is the kind of art included in college courses called Fine Arts. The implication is that all other art is less than fine and is more appropriately called folk art, ethnic art, primitive art, or crafts. The characteristics of Western fine art are as follows: It is created by a formally schooled artist, the product is made for the market (for sale or on commission), the product is associated with a particular artist, the product's uniqueness is valued, and the product is not primarily utilitarian but is rather "art for art's sake." In contrast, all the rest of the world's art that is non-Western and nonclassical is characterized by the opposite features: It is created by an artist who has not received formal training, it is not produced for the market, the artist is anonymous and does not sign or individually claim the product, and it is made primarily for use in food storage and preparation, ritual, or war. But do these two categories make sense cross-culturally?

According to anthropologists, all cultures have art, and all cultures have a sense of what makes something art. The term *esthetics* refers to agreed-upon notions of quality (Thompson 1971:374). Before anthropologists proved otherwise, however, Western art experts considered that

A South African woman painting a design on the outside of her house. ■ What kind of domestic art do you know how to do? (Source: © Roshani Kothari)

esthetics either did not exist or was poorly developed in non-Western cultures. Anthropologists know that esthetic principles, or established criteria for artistic quality, exist everywhere, whether or not they are written down and formalized. In the first half of the twentieth century, Franz Boas reviewed many forms of art in non-state societies and deduced principles that he claimed were universal: symmetry, rhythmic repetition, and naturalism. (Jonaitis 1995:37). These principles do apply in many cases, but they are not universal.

Ethno-esthetics consists of local cultural definitions of what is art. The set of standards concerning wood carving in West Africa illustrates the importance of considering cross-cultural variation in the criteria for art (Thompson 1971). Among the Yoruba of Nigeria, esthetic guidelines include the following:

- Figures should be depicted midway between complete abstraction and complete realism so that they resemble "somebody," but no one in particular (portraiture in the Western sense is considered dangerous).

- Humans should be depicted at their optimal physical peak, not in infancy or old age.

- There should be clarity of line and form.

- The sculpture should have the quality of luminosity achieved through a polished surface and the play of incisions and shadows.

- The piece should exhibit symmetry.

Some anthropological studies have documented intracultural differences in esthetic standards as well as cross-cultural variation. For example, one anthropologist showed computer-generated graphics to the Shipibo Indians of the Peruvian Amazon and learned that men liked the abstract designs, whereas women thought they were ugly (Roe in Anderson and Field 1993:257). If you are wondering why this difference would exist, consider the interpretation of the anthropologist: Shipibo men are the shamans and take hallucinogenic drugs that may give them familiarity with more "psychedelic" images.

Studying Art in Society

The anthropological study of art seeks to understand not only the products of art but also who makes it and why, the role of art in society, and its wider social meanings. Franz Boas was the first anthropologist to emphasize the importance of studying art in society. A significant thread in anthropology's theoretical history—functionalism—dominated early twentieth century research on art. Anthropologists wrote about how paintings, dance, theater, and songs serve to socialize children into the culture, provide a sense of social identity and group boundaries, and promote healing. Art may legitimize political leaders and enhance efforts in war through magical decorations on shields and weapons. Art may serve as a form of social control, as in African masks worn by dancers who represent deities visiting humans to remind them of the moral order. Or to take a more current view, art, like language, may be a catalyst for political resistance or a rallying point for ethnic solidarity in the face of the state.

The anthropology of art relies on a variety of research methods. For some projects, participant observation provides most of the necessary data. In others, participant observation is complemented by collecting and analyzing oral or written material such as video and tape recordings. Some anthropologists have become apprentices in a certain

Yoruba (West African) wood carving is done according to esthetic principles that require clarity of line and form, a polished surface that creates a play of light and shadows, symmetry, and the depiction of human figures that are neither completely abstract nor completely realistic. ■ Have you ever seen African sculptures that follow these principles? Visit an African art museum on the Web for further exploration. (Source: Courtesy of the Peabody Museum, Harvard University)

Without Participation, There Is No Meaning

READING THE INTRODUCTION to John Chernoff's book is the best way to convince yourself that fieldwork in cultural anthropology is more than simply gathering the data you think you need for the project you have in mind, especially if the project concerns processes of creativity and expression. These areas are least amenable to study through purely scientific approaches.

Chernoff makes a convincing case that only by turning standard research approaches on their heads can one get at the central concerns of creativity and expressiveness. In the words of one of his drumming teachers, "The heart sees before the eyes."

In his early months in the field, Chernoff often found himself wondering why he was there. To write a book? To tell people back in America what he learned? Why? No doubt many of the Ghanaians wondered the same thing, especially since his early drumming was laughable, although Chernoff didn't realize it because he always consumed copious quantities of gin before playing. Eventually, he became the student of a master drummer and went through a formal initiation ceremony. He had to kill two chickens and eat parts of them in a form that most North Americans would never see in a grocery store. Still, he was not playing well enough. He went through another ritual to make his wrist "smart" so it would turn faster, like a cat chasing a mouse. Before this, he had to go into the bush, ten miles outside town, and collect ingredients for the ritual. The ritual worked.

For John Chernoff, having a "cat's hand" was a good thing, but it was more important to him that along the way to getting a cat's hand, he had begun to gain an understanding of the wider social and ritual context that surrounded drumming. He could see more clearly where he fell short in terms of performance, and he learned what he needed to do to cover the gap between the Ghanaian standards for drumming and his level of achievement. He learned about Ghanaian family life and how it is connected to the individual performer and to ritual. He gained respect for the artists who taught him and admiration for their striving toward respectability. His personality, though, was also an important ingredient in the learning process: "I assumed that I did not know what to do in most situations. I accepted what people told me about myself and what I should be doing . . . I waited to see what people would make of me . . . . By staying cool I learned the meaning of character" (1979:170).

artistic tradition. For example, in one of the earliest studies of Native American potters of the Southwest, Ruth Bunzel (1972 [1929]) learned how to make pottery and gained important insights about what the potters thought were good designs. For John Chernoff, learning to play African drums was an important part of building rapport during his fieldwork in Ghana and an essential aspect of his ability to gain an understanding of the importance of the social context of music (1979). His book *African Rhythm and African Sensibility* is one of the first reflexive ethnographies (recall Chapter 4), taking into account the position and role of the ethnographer and how they shape what the ethnographer learns. (See the Methods Close-Up box.)

Focus on the Artist

In the early twentieth century, Boas urged his students to go beyond studying the products of art and study the artists. One role of the anthropologist, he said, is to add to the understanding of art by studying art from the artist's perspective. Ruth Bunzel's (1972 [1929]) research on Pueblo potters is a classic example of this tradition. She paid attention to the variety of pot shapes and motifs employed and interviewed individual potters about their personal design choices. One Zuni potter commented, "I always know the whole design before I start to paint" (49). A Laguna potter said, "I learned this design from my mother. I learned most of my designs from my mother" (52).

In Sumba, Indonesia, linguistic anthropologist Joel Kuipers interviews a ritual speaker who is adept at verbal arts performance. ■
What is a form of verbal art in a microculture you know? (Source: Joel Kuipers)

The social status of artists is another aspect of the focus on the artist. Artists may be revered and wealthy as individuals or as a group, or they may be stigmatized and economically marginal. In prehispanic Mexico, goldworkers were highly respected. In twentieth century Native American groups of the Pacific Northwest, male carvers and painters had to be initiated into a secret society, and they had higher status than other men. Often a gender division of artistic involvement exists. Among the Navajo, women weave and men do silversmithing. In the Caribbean, women of African descent are noted for their carvings of calabashes (large gourds). In the contemporary United States, most famous and successful graphic artists are male, although the profession includes a growing percentage of women.

The lifestyles of artists and performers are often outside the boundaries of mainstream society; they often challenge the social boundaries. In Morocco, a *shikha* is a female performer who sings and dances at festivities, including life-cycle ceremonies such as birth, circumcision, and marriage (Kapchan 1994). These performers appear in a group of three or four with accompanying musicians. Their performance involves suggestive songs and body movements, including reaching a state of near possession when they loosen their hair buns. With their long hair waving, they "lift the belt," a technique accomplished through an undulating movement that rolls the abdomen up to the waist. Their entertainment creates a lively atmosphere. "Through the provocative movements and loud singing of the shikhat, the audience is drawn up and into a collective state of celebration, their bodies literally pulled into the dance" (93). In their private lives, shikhat are on the social fringes, leading lives as single women who transgress limits applied to proper females. For example, they own property, drink alcohol, smoke cigarettes, and may have several lovers. Most of the shikhat have been rejected by their families. Middle- and upper-class women consider them vulgar and distance themselves from them. Yet shikhat who become successful, widening their performance spheres to larger towns and cities, manage to save money and become landowners and gain economic status. Furthermore, the modern mass media are contributing to an increased status of shikhat as performers. Recordings of shikhat music are popular in Morocco. State-produced television broadcasts carry performances of shikhat groups as a way of presenting the diverse cultures of the country.

Like those who pursue other occupations, artists are more specialized in state-level societies. Generally, among foragers, artistic activity is open to all, and artistic products are shared equally by all. Some people, however, may be singled out as especially good singers, storytellers, or carvers. With increasing social complexity and a market for art, specialized training is needed to produce certain kinds of art, and the products are sought after by those who can afford them. Class differences in artistic styles and preferences emerge along with the increasingly complex division of labor.

Microcultures, Art, and Power

Art forms and styles, like language, are often associated with microcultural groups' identity and sense of pride. For example, the Berbers of highland Morocco are associated with carpets, Maya Indians with woven and embroidered blouses, and the Inuit with stone carving. Cultural anthropologists provide many examples of links between various microcultural dimensions (especially ethnicity and gender) and power issues. In some instances, more powerful groups appropriate the art forms of less powerful groups. One study reveals how political interests in Israel take ownership of ethnic artistic expression.

Tourists who buy "arts and crafts" souvenirs rarely learn much, if anything, about the people who actually make them. Yet the tourists probably have a mental image of, for example, a village potter sitting at the wheel or a silversmith hammering at a piece of metal in a quaint workshop. Research in cultural anthropology reveals that much can be learned from close examination of what tourist shops sell and do not sell (Clifford 1988). Study of an upscale chain of stores in Israel for international tourists revealed many items for sale that are related to nationalism and national identity (Shenhav-Keller 1993). The original Maskit store in Tel Aviv, founded by the then wife of Moshe Dayan, was intended to encourage Israeli artisans to continue in their traditional crafts. The shop was envisioned as a cultural "ambassador" of Israel. Dignitaries and delegations who traveled abroad from Israel took items from Maskit to distribute, and official guests coming to Israel were given gifts from Maskit during their visit. The original shop had two floors. The top floor, where one enters, contained fashion (women's clothing, wedding gowns, and dresses with Arab embroidery), jewelry, ritual articles (prayer-books, candlesticks, goblets, incense burners), decorative items, and books. The larger lower floor had five sections: the Bar-Mitzvah Corner with prayer-books and other items, the children's corner (clothing, games, toys, T-shirts), the embroidery section (tablecloths, pillow covers, sheets, wallets, eyeglass cases), the carpet section, and a large area for ceramics, glassware, and copperware.

Over the years, however, fewer and fewer items of Jewish Israeli art have come to be sold in the Maskit stores. Many of the original artists have become famous and opened their own shops. Others have become too old to do the work. The decline is most marked in the area of Yemenite Jewish embroidery, which once dominated Maskit. Now Israeli Arab and Palestinian laborers produce most of the Maskit inventory in factories. Yet Maskit provides no information about the ethnicity of the craftspeople. The goods are presented as "Israeli" crafts.

Gender relations are also played out in expressive culture. A study of a form of popular performance art in a Florida town, male strip dancing, shows how societal power relations between men and women are reinforced in this form of leisure activity (Margolis and Arnold 1993). Advertisements in the media tell women that seeing a male strip dancer is "their chance," "their night out." Going to a male strip show is thus presumably a time of reversal of traditional gender roles in which men are dominant and women submissive. The researchers asked whether gender roles are reversed in a male stripper bar. The short answer is "no." Women customers are treated like juveniles, controlled by the manager (who tells them how to tip as they stand in line waiting for the show to open) and symbolically humbled in relation to the dancers, who take on the role of lion-tamers, for example. The "dive-bomb" is further evidence that the women are not in charge. The dive-bomb is a particular form of tipping the dancer. The woman customer gets on her hands and knees and tucks a bill held between her teeth into the dancer's g-string.

Not all forms of popular art and performance are mechanisms of social control and hierarchy maintenance, however. In the United States, for example, urban Black youths' musical performance through rap music can be seen as a form of protest through performance. Their lyrics report on their experience of economic oppression, the danger of drugs, and men's disrespect for women.

A Maya woman of Guatemala works at her hand loom. Maya identity is closely linked with weaving styles and motifs, especially evidenced in women's embroidered blouses. Three decades of warfare threatened Maya culture in Guatemala, but Maya expressive culture is being revitalized. ■ Locate a library or Internet reference on ethnic variations in styles and motifs in Maya weaving. (Source: © Douglas Mason/Woodfin Camp & Associates)

Performance Arts

The performance arts include music, dance, theater, rhetoric (public speech-making) and narrative (such as storytelling). Because so much research has been done on music,

FIGURE 19.1
Five ethnographic questions about gender and music.

If you were doing an ethnographic study of gender roles in musical performance, the following questions would be useful in starting the inquiry. But they would not exhaust the topic. Can you think of questions that should be added to the list?

1. Are men and women equally encouraged to use certain instruments and repertoires?

2. Is musical training available to all?

3. Do male and female repertoires overlap, and if so, where and for what reasons?

4. Are the performances of men and women public, private, or both? Are women and men allowed to perform together? In what circumstances?

5. Do members of the culture give equal value to the performances of men and women? On what criteria are these evaluations based, and are they the same for men and women performers?

(*Source*: Table, pp. 224–225, "Power and Gender in the Musical Experiences of Women" by Carol E. Robertson in *Women and Music in Cross-Cultural Perspective*, ed. by Ellen Koskoff. Copyright © 1987. Reprinted by permission of Greenwood Publishing Group, Inc., Westport, CT.)

this area has developed its own name: **ethnomusicology,** the cross-cultural study of music. Ethnomusicologists consider a range of topics, including the form of the music itself, the social position of musicians, how music interacts with other domains of culture, and change in musical traditions.

This section first provides a case study of the parallels between musical patterns and the gender division of labor in a foraging group in Malaysia and then an example of how theater and religion fit together in India.

Music and Gender among the Temiar of Malaysia

An important topic for ethnomusicologists is gender differences in access to performance roles in music (readers interested in approaching this topic as a research question should see Figure 19.1). A cultural materialist analysis (review Chapter 2) of this issue would predict that in cultures where gender roles and relationships in the economic system were relatively egalitarian, access to and meanings in music would tend to be more egalitarian as well. This is the case, for example, among the Temiar, a group of foragers of highland Malaysia, whose musical traditions emphasize balance and complementarity between males and females (Roseman 1987). Among the Temiar, kinship and marriage rules are relatively flexible and open. Marriages are not arranged but instead are based on the mutual desires of the partners. Descent is bilineal, and marital residence follows no particular rule after a period of bride service. Marriages often end in separation, and the usual pattern for everyone is serial monogamy.

Men, however, have a certain edge over women in political and ritual spheres. Men dominate as headmen and as spirit mediums who sing the songs that energize the spirits (although historical records indicate that women have been spirit mediums in the past). In most performances, individual male singers are the nodes through which the songs of spirit-guides enter the community. Women's performance role is significant, the male spirit-medium role is not necessarily of greater priority or higher status. The distinction

between leader and chorus establishes some priority for males, but gender distinctions are blurred through overlap between phrases and repetition. The performance is one of general community participation with integrated male and female roles—just as in Temiar society.

Theater and Myth in South India

Theater is a type of enactment that seeks to entertain through conscious forms of acting, movement, and words related to dance, music, parades, competitive games and sports, and verbal art (Beeman 1993). Cross-culturally, strong connections exist among myth, ritual, and performance.

One theatrical tradition that offers a blend of mythology, acting, and music is Kathakali ritual dance-drama of southern India (Zarrilli 1990). Stylized hand gestures, elaborate makeup, and costumes contribute to the attraction of these performances, which dramatize India's great Hindu epics, especially the Ramayana and the Mahabharata. Costumes and makeup transform the actor into one of several well-known characters from Indian mythology. The audience easily recognizes the basic character types at their first entrance through their costuming and makeup. Six makeup types exist to depict characters ranging from the most refined to the most vulgar. Characters such as kings and heroes have green facial makeup, reflecting their refinement and moral uprightness. The most vulgar characters are associated with black facial makeup and (occasionally) black beards. Female demons are in this category. Their black faces are dotted with red and white, and they are the most grotesque of Kathakali characters.

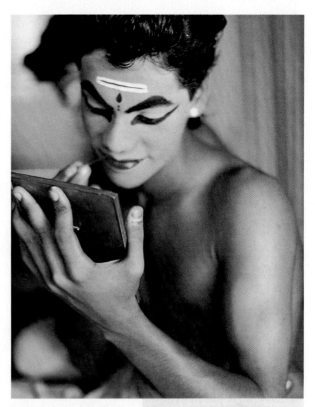

Many forms of theater combine the use of facial makeup, masks, and costumes to transform an actor into someone (or something) else. This Kathakali dancer applies makeup before a performance in Kerala, South India. ■ What forms of dance or theater in your microculture involve the use of facial makeup to depict a particular character? (Source: © Roshani Kothari)

Architecture and Decorative Arts

Like all forms of expressive culture, architecture is interwoven with other aspects of culture. Architecture may reflect and protect social rank and class differences as well as gender, age, and ethnic differences (Guidoni 1987). Decorative arts—including the interior decoration of homes and buildings and such external design features as gardens—likewise reflect people's social position and "taste." Local cultures have long defined preferred standards in these areas of expression, but global influences from the West and elsewhere, such as Japan and other non-Western cultures, have been adopted and adapted by other traditions. In turn, features of local architecture have been adopted into cosmopolitan traditions.

Architecture and Interior Design

Foragers, being mobile, build dwellings as needed and then abandon them. Because they have few possessions and no surplus goods, they need no permanent storage structures. The construction of dwellings can be done by the members of the family. Foragers' dwellings are an image of the family, not of the wider society. The dwellings' positioning in relation to each other reflects relations between families.

More elaborate shelters and greater social cohesiveness in planning occur when foraging is combined with horticulture, as in the semipermanent settlements in the Amazon rainforest. People live in the settlement part of the year but break up into smaller groups that spread out into a larger area for foraging. Important decisions concern location of the settlement site in terms of weather, availability of drinking water, and defensibility. The central plaza must be elevated for drainage, and drainage channels must be dug around the hearths. The overall plan is circular. In some groups, separate shelters are built for extended family groups; in others, they are joined into a continuous circle with connected roofs. In some cases, the headman has a separate, larger shelter.

A ring settlement design is found among many horticultural groups in the Amazon rainforest. Archaeologists have found evidence of similar settlement designs dating to several hundred years ago. ■ How might this design relate to production and social relations? (Source: © Loren McIntyre/Woodfin Camp & Associates)

Yerts in Pamir, Afghanistan. The yert form of domestic architecture is widespread across Asia among pastoralists. ■ How does a yert resemble, and how does it differ from, domestic architecture that you know? (Source: © R. & S. Michaud/Woodfin Camp & Associates)

Pastoralists have designed ingenious portable structures such as the teepee and yert. The teepee is a conical tent made with a framework of four wooden poles tied at the top with leather thongs, to which are joined other poles to complete the cone. This frame is then covered with buffalo hide. A yert is also a circular, portable dwelling, but its roof is flatter than that of a teepee. The covering is made of cloth. This lightweight structure is easy to set up, take down, and transport, and it is adaptable to all weather conditions. Encampments often arranged the teepees or yerts in several concentric circles. Social status was the structuring principle. The head chief and the council of chiefs were located in the center.

With the Neolithic and urban revolutions (Chapter 9), settlements grew larger and some showed the effects of centralized planning and power—for example, in grid-style street planning rather than haphazard street placement. The symbolic demonstration of the power, grandeur, and identity of states was—and still is—expressed architecturally through the construction of impressive monuments: temples, administrative buildings, memorials, and museums. Interior decoration of domestic dwellings also became more elaborate. Decoration was more likely to be found in settled agricultural communities and urban centers than among mobile groups. Wall paintings, sculptures, and other features distinguish the homes of wealthier individuals.

A study of interior decoration in contemporary Japan examined the contents of home decorating magazines and involved participant observation within homes (Rosenberger 1992). A recurrent theme revealed how aspects of Western decorating styles are incorporated and localized (given a particularly Japanese flavor). Home decorating magazines target middle- and upper-class housewives who seek to express their status through new consumption styles. A trend is the abandonment of three features of traditional Japanese design: *tatami, shoji,* and *fusuma.* Tatami are two-inch-thick mats, about three feet by six feet. A room's size is measured in terms of the number of tatami mats it holds. Shoji are the sliding screen doors of tatami rooms, one covered with glass and the other with translucent rice paper printed often with a design of leaves or waves. Fusuma are sliding wall panels made of thick paper; they are removable so that rooms can be enlarged for gatherings. The tatami room usually contains a low table with pillows for seating on the floor. A special alcove may contain a flower arrangement, ancestors' pictures, and a Buddhist altar. Futons are stored in closets around the edges and brought out at night for sleeping.

In distancing themselves from the old style, Japanese housewives make these changes: The kitchen is given a central rather than marginal location and is merged with a space called the DK (dining-kitchen) or LDK (living-dining-kitchen), with wood, tile, or carpeting on the floor. Western products such as carpeting and curtains (instead of the fusuma, tatami, and shoji) are used to cover surfaces and to separate rooms. Westernness is stated in the addition of a couch, dining set, VCR and stereo, and an array of small items: Western-style teapots, cuckoo clocks, and knick-knacks such as figures of the Seven Dwarfs.

These changing design choices accompany deeper social changes that involve new aspirations about marriage and family relationships. Home decorating magazines promote the idea that the new style brings happier children with better grades and closer husband–wife ties. Tensions exist, however, between these ideals and the realities of middle- and upper-class life in Japan. Women feel compelled to work either part time or full time to be able to contribute income for satisfying their new consumer needs. Yet Japanese women are discouraged from pursuing careers and are urged to devote more time to domestic pursuits, including home decorating and child care, in order to provide the kind of life portrayed in the magazines. Children are placed in the conflicting position of being indulged as new consumer targets, while the traditional value of self-discipline still holds. Husbands are put in the conflicting position of needing to be more attentive to wife and home while the corporate world calls them for a "7–11" working day. Furthermore, the Western-style, happy nuclear family image contains no plan for the aged. The wealthiest Japanese families manage to satisfy both individualistic desires and filial duties because they can afford a large house in which they dedicate a separate floor for the husband's parents, complete with tatami mats. Less wealthy people have a more difficult time dealing with these conflicting values.

Worldwide, Hilton hotels look much like each other and do not reflect local cultural architectural styles. ■ In your view, is this uniformity a good thing, or should Hiltons and other international hotels try to become more "vernacular"? (Source: © Paul Conklin/PhotoEdit)

Gardens and Flowers

Gardens for use, especially for food production, can be differentiated from gardens for decoration. Not all cultures have developed the concept of the decorative garden. Inuit peoples, for example, cannot construct gardens in the snow. Purely nomadic peoples have no gardens because they are on the move. The decorative garden seems to be a product of state-level societies, especially in the Middle East, Europe, and Asia (Goody 1993). Within these contexts, variation exists in what are considered to be the appropriate contents and design of a garden. A Japanese garden may contain no blooming flowers, focusing instead on the shape and placement of trees, shrubs, stones, and bodies of water (Moynihan 1979). Elite Muslim culture, with its core in the Middle East, has long been associated with formal decorative gardens. A garden, enclosed with four walls, is symbolically equivalent to the concept of "paradise." The Islamic garden pattern involves a square design with symmetrical layout,

Women practicing the art of flower arrangement in Japan. ■ Are there art forms in your culture that are specific to women? (Source: © Catherine Karnow/ Woodfin Camp & Associates)

fountains, waterways, and straight pathways, all enclosed within walls. Islamic gardens often surrounded the tombs of prominent people. India's Taj Mahal, built by a Muslim emperor, follows this pattern, with one modification: The tomb was placed at one edge of the garden rather than in the center. The result is a dramatic stretch of fountains and flowers leading from the main gate up to the monument (see the photograph on p. 423).

The contents of a contemporary personal garden, like a dinner menu with all its special ingredients or a collection of souvenirs from around the world with all their memories and meanings, makes a statement about its owner's identity and status. For example, in Europe during the height of colonialism, gardens contained specimens from remote corners of the globe, collected through scientific expeditions. Such gardens were created through the intentional collection and placement in one place of otherwise diverse plants, creating a **heterotopia,** or the gathering together of different "places" into one (Foucault 1970). These gardens expressed the owner's status as cosmopolitan and wealthy.

THINKING Think of several occasions in your cultural world in which flowers play a role, and what **OUTSIDE** that role is.
THE BOX

Cut flowers are now important economic products. They provide income for gardeners throughout the world. They are also exchange items. In France, women receive flowers from men more than any other kind of gift (Goody 1993:316). In much of the world, special occasions require gifts of flowers: In the West, in East Asia, funerals are times for displays of flowers. Ritual offerings to the deities in Hinduism are often flowers such as marigolds woven into a chain or necklace.

Flowers are prominent motifs in Western and Asian secular and sacred art, but less so in African art (except in Islamicized cultures of Africa, where flowers are prominent). British cultural anthropologist Jack Goody tried to understand the absence of flowers in the religion and graphic arts of Africa (1993). Some possible answers include environmental and economic factors: Eurasia possesses a greater variety of blooming plants than in many regions of Africa. Also, African horticulture, in general, is limited because less space is available for the production of luxury items. In many African kingdoms, luxury goods include fabrics, gold ornaments, or wooden carvings rather than flowers.

Museums and Culture

This section considers the concept of the museum and debates about the role of museums in exhibiting and representing culture. Museum studies, in anthropology, includes anthropologists who work in museums helping to prepare exhibits and anthropologists who study museums—what they choose to display and how they display it.

A museum is an institution that collects, preserves, interprets, and displays objects on a regular basis (Kahn 1995:324). Its purpose may be esthetic or educational. The idea of gathering and displaying objects goes back at least to the Babylonian kings of the sixth century BCE (Maybury-Lewis 1997a). The term *museum* comes from a Greek word referring to a place for the muses to congregate, and, by extension, where one would have philosophical discussions or see artistic performances. In Europe, the term came to denote a place where art objects were housed and displayed. Ethnographic and science museums came later, inspired by Europe's emerging interest in exploration in the 1500s and the accompanying effort to gather specimens from around the world and to classify them. The concept of the museum and its several forms has now diffused to most parts of the world.

The Politics of Exhibits

Within anthropology, *museum anthropology* emerged in the 1980s as a subfield concerned with studying how and why museums choose to collect and display particular objects (Ames 1992; A. Jones 1993; Stocking 1985). This subfield crosses many areas of anthropology.

Museum anthropologists are at the forefront of debates about who gets to represent whom, the ownership of particular objects, and the public-service role of museums versus their possible elitism. A major issue is whether objects from non-Western cultures should be exhibited, like Western art objects, with little or no ethnographic context (Clifford 1988, Watson 1997). Most anthropologists support the need for context, and not just for non-Western objects but for all objects on display. For example, the museum label of Andy Warhol's hyperrealistic painting of a can of Campbell's soup should include information on the social context in which such art was produced and some background on the artist. The view that all forms of expressive culture are context-bound and can be better understood and appreciated within their social context is unfortunately rare among Western art historians and critics (Best 1986).

Debate is vigorous about who should have control of objects in museums that were obtained during periods of colonial and neocolonial domination. The issue of **repatriation,** or returning objects to their cultures of origin, is a matter of international and intranational concern.

In the United States and Canada, many Native American groups have lobbied successfully for the return of ancestral bones, grave goods, and other artifacts (review earlier discussions in this book of related ethical issues). In 1990, the United States passed the Native American Graves Protection and Repatriation Act (NAGRPA) after two decades of pressure from Native American groups (Bray 1996; Rose, Green, and Green 1996). This act required universities, museums, and federal agencies in the United States to inventory their archaeological holdings in preparation for repatriating skeletons and other artifacts to their Native American descendants. One survey indicated that museums in the United States alone (not including those in Hawai'i) held over 14,000 Native American skeletons, while unofficial estimates were as high as 600,000. Unknown numbers of other items have been inventoried, a process that strains the resources of museums (Watson 1997).

The breakup of the Soviet Union prompted claims from several independent states for artistic property that had been taken to Soviet national museums in Moscow and St. Petersburg. For example, Central Asian republics lost medieval carpets to Moscow and St. Petersburg museums. There are Georgian arms in the Armory of the Moscow Kremlin. Ukrainians have sought the return of objects of historical interest,

An incised stone artifact from the Neolithic site of Skara Brae, Scotland. The significance of this small object and its designs are not known. Spirals, cups-and-rings, and rosettes are common motifs found in European rock art and on pottery during the Neolithic. ■ Assume there is an award of $500 for the best hypothesis about what this object was used for in Neolithic times: what is your entry in the contest? (Source: © Adam Woolfitt/CORBIS)

such as the ceremonial staff of their national hero, Mazepa, who fought for Ukrainian independence against Peter the Great (Akinsha 1992a). In all, Ukraine has demanded the return of about two million art objects that originated in Ukrainian territory (Akinsha 1992b). Russian museums, such as the Hermitage in St. Petersburg, face the loss of many objects.

Another area of dispute about art in post-USSR Russia concerns the state and the church. The Soviet state put many icons and other religious objects in museums and turned churches into museums. The Russian Orthodox Church has campaigned for the return of church property. Churches are demanding that "all sacred objects of the church, all church buildings, and masterpieces of church art that were confiscated by the state after 1917 must be returned without exception to the ownership of the Russian Orthodox Church" (Akinsha 1992a:102). Art historians and museum officials worry that the churches have neither the resources nor the experience to care for these treasures. On the other hand, there are threats of theft and violence to museums from those who wish to return the icons to churches and monasteries. In response, some museums have removed certain pieces from display.

PLAY, LEISURE, AND CULTURE

Leisure time and play are not limited to humans. ■ Write your own caption or "thought question" for this photograph. (Sources: © Frans Lanting/Minden Pictures)

This section turns to another area of expressive culture: what people do "for fun." It is impossible to draw a clear line between the concepts of play or leisure and art or performance, however, because they often overlap. For example, a person could paint watercolors in her leisure time yet simultaneously be creating a work of art. In most cases, though, play and leisure can be distinguished from other activities by the fact that they have no direct, utilitarian purpose for the participant. Dutch historian Johan Huizinga, in the 1930s, proposed some features of play. It is unnecessary and thus free action; it is outside of ordinary life; it is closed and limited in terms of time; it has rules for its execution; and it contains an element of tension and chance (as summarized in Hutter 1996).

Leisure activities often overlap with play, but many leisure activities, such as reading or lying on a beach, would not be considered play because they lack rules, tension, and chance. Often, depending on the context, the same activity could be considered work instead of play. For example, gardening as a hobby would be classified as a leisure activity, even though weeding, pruning, and watering are activities that could be considered work for someone else. Playing a game with a child might be considered recreational, but if one has been hired as the child's babysitter, then it is work. Professional sports are an area where the line between play and work breaks down completely because the "players" are paid to "play." Further, although play and leisure may be pursued from a nonutilitarian perspective, they are often surrounded by a wider context of commercial and political interests. For example, nonprofessional athletes competing in the Olympic games are part of a wider set of powerful interests, from advertisers to host cities to athletic equipment companies.

Within the broad category of play and leisure activities, several subcategories exist, including varieties of games, hobbies, and recreational travel. Cultural anthropologists study play and leisure within their cultural contexts. They ask, for example, why some leisure activities involve teams rather than individuals; what the social roles and status of people involved in particular activities are; what the "goals" of the games are and how they are achieved; how much danger or violence is involved; how certain activities are related to group identity; and how such activities link or separate different groups within or between societies or nations.

Games and Sports as Cultural Microcosm

Games and sports, like religious rituals and festivals, can be interpreted as reflections of social relationships and cultural ideals. In the terms of cultural anthropologist Clifford Geertz, they are both "models of" a culture, depicting basic ideals, and "models for" a culture, socializing people into adopting certain values and ideals. American football can be seen as a model for corporate culture. Leadership is vested in one person (the quarterback), and its major goal is taking territory away from the competition.

A comparison of baseball as played in the United States and baseball as played in Japan reveals core values about social relationships (Whiting 1989). These differences emerge dramatically when American players are hired by Japanese teams. The American players bring with them an intense sense of individualism, which promotes the value of "doing your own thing." This conflicts with a primary value that influences the playing style in Japan: *wa,* meaning discipline and self-sacrifice for the good of the whole. In Japanese baseball, players must seek to achieve and maintain team harmony, so extremely individualistic, egotistical plays and strategies are frowned on.

Sports and Spirituality: Men's Wrestling in India

In many non-Western settings, sports are closely tied to aspects of religion and spirituality. Asian martial arts, for example, require forms of concentration much like meditation, leading to spiritual self-control. Men's wrestling in India, a popular form of entertainment at rural fairs and other public events, involves a strong link with spiritual development and asceticism (Alter 1992). In some ways these wrestlers are just like other members of Indian society. They go to work, and they marry and have families, but their dedication to wrestling involves important differences.

A wrestler's daily routine is one of self-discipline. Every act—defecation, bathing, comportment, devotion—is integrated into a daily regimen of discipline. Wrestlers come to the *akhara* (equivalent to a gymnasium) early in the morning for practice under the supervision of a guru or other senior akhara member. They practice moves with different partners for two to three hours. In the early evening, they return for more exercise. In all, a strong young wrestler will do around 2000 push-ups and 1000 deep kneebends a day in sets of 50 to 100.

Wrestlers in the village of Sonepur, India. These wrestlers follow a rigorous regimen of dietary restrictions and exercise in order to keep their bodies and minds under control. Like Hindu holy men, they seek to build up and maintain their inner strength through such practices. ■ Think of another sport that emphasizes dietary restrictions. (Source: © CORBIS. All Rights Reserved.)

The wrestler's diet is prescribed by the wrestling way of life. Wrestlers are mainly vegetarian and avoid alcohol and tobacco, although they do consume *bhang*, a beverage made of blended milk, spices, almonds, and concentrated marijuana. In addition to regular meals, wrestlers consume large quantities of milk, *ghee* (clarified butter), and almonds. These substances are sources of strength, because according to traditional dietary principles, they help to build up the body's semen.

Several aspects of the wrestler's life are similar to those of a Hindu *sannyasi*, or holy man who renounces life in the normal world. The aspiring sannyasi studies under a guru, learns to follow a strict routine of discipline and meditation called *yoga*, and adheres to a restricted diet to achieve control of the body and its life force. Both wrestler and sannyasi roles focus on discipline to achieve a controlled self. In India, wrestling does not involve the "dumb jock" stereotype that it sometimes does in North America; rather, the image is of perfected physical and moral health.

Play, Pleasure, and Pain

THINKING OUTSIDE THE BOX

In your cultural world, what are examples of leisure activities that combine pleasure and pain? As a research project, conduct some informal interviews with participants to learn why they are attracted to such activities.

Many leisure activities combine pleasure and pain because they may involve physical discomfort. Serious injuries may result from mountain climbing, horseback riding, or playing touch football in the backyard. A more intentionally dangerous category of sports is **blood sports,** competition that explicitly seeks to bring about a flow of blood or even death. Blood sports may involve human contestants, humans contesting against animal competitors, or humans hunting animal targets (Donlon 1990). In the United States and Europe, professional boxing is an example of a highly popular blood sport that has not yet been analyzed by anthropologists. Cultural anthropologists have looked more at the use of animals in blood sports such as cockfights and bullfights. These sports have been variously interpreted as providing sadistic pleasure, as offering vicarious self-validation (usually of males) through the triumph of their representative pit bulls or fighting cocks, and as the triumph of culture over nature in the symbolism of bullfighting.

Even the seemingly pleasurable leisure experience of a Turkish bath can involve discomfort and pain. One phase involves scrubbing the skin roughly several times with a rough natural sponge, a pumice stone, or a piece of cork wood wrapped in cloth (Staats 1994). The scrubbing removes layers of dead skin and "opens the pores" so that the skin will be beautiful. In Turkey, an option for men is a massage that can be quite violent, involving deep probes of leg muscles, cracking of the back, and being walked on by the (often hefty) masseur. In Ukraine, being struck repeatedly on one's bare skin with birch branches is the final stage of the bath. However, violent scrubbing, scraping, and even beating of the skin, along with radical temperature changes in the water, are combined with valued social interaction at the bathhouse.

Leisure Travel

Anthropologists who study leisure travel, or tourism, have often commented that their work is taken less seriously than it should be because of the perspective that they are just "hanging out" at the beach or at five-star hotels. Research on tourism, however, can involve as much conflict and danger as anthropological study of any other topic. Violence does occur in tourist destinations. Even when the research site is a peaceful one, anthropological investigation of tourism involves the same amount of effort as any other fieldwork.

Tourism is now one of the major economic forces in the world, it is growing, and it has dramatic effects on people and places in tourist destination areas. Expenditure of money, time, and effort for nonessential travel is nothing new. In the past, pilgrimage to religious sites was a major preoccupation of many people (Chapter 8). Today a large percentage of worldwide tourism involves individuals from the industrialized nations of Europe, North America, and Japan traveling to the less industrialized nations. Ethnic tourism, cultural tourism, and off-the-beaten-path tourism are attracting increasing numbers of travelers.

Many international tourists increasingly prefer "cultural tourism" so that they can participate, for a while, in what is presented to them as a traditional cultural context. Safari tour groups in Africa, as in the case of this visit to Maasailand, combine exposure to wild life and to the Maasai people. ■ Consider how "cultural tourism" distorts or reflects "reality" on the basis of this photograph. (Source: © Betty Press/Woodfin Camp & Associates)

These new kinds of tourism are often marketed as providing a view of "authentic" cultures. Images of indigenous people as the "Other" figure prominently in travel brochures and advertisements (Silver 1993). Tourist promotional literature often presents a "myth" about other peoples and places and offers travel as a form of escape to a mythical land of wonder. Research on Western travel literature shows that from the time of the earliest explorers to the present, it has been full of "primitivist" images about indigenous peoples (Pratt 1992). They are portrayed as having static or "stone age" traditions, remaining largely unchanged by the forces of Western colonialism, nationalism, economic development, and tourism itself (Bruner 1991). Tourists often seek to find the culture that the tourist industry defines rather than gaining a genuine, more complicated, and perhaps less photogenic view of it (Adams 1984). For the industry, providing these desired cultural images through mass tourism involves packaging the "primitive" with the "modern" because most tourists want comfort and convenience along with their "authentic experience." Thus advertisements minimize the foreignness of the host country, noting, for example, that English is spoken and that the destination is remote yet accessible, while simultaneously promoting primitivist imagery. For example, "The Melanesian Discoverer" is a ship that cruises the Sepik River in Papua New Guinea, providing a way for affluent tourists to view the "primitive" while traveling in luxury.

The anthropology of tourism has focused most of its attention on the impact of global and local tourism on indigenous peoples and places. Such impact studies are important in exposing the degree to which tourism helps or harms local people. For example, the formation of Amboseli National Park in Kenya negatively affected the access of the Maasai to strategic water resources for their herds (Honadle 1985, as summarized in Drake 1991). The project staff promised certain benefits to the Maasai if they stayed off the reserve, but many of those benefits (including shares of the revenues from the park) never materialized. In contrast, in Costa Rica local people were included in the early planning stages of the Guanacaste National Park and have played a greater role in the park management system there.

Other studies, discussed in the following section of this chapter, document how local residents are exercising agency and playing an active role in transforming the effects of tourism to their advantage, as well as localizing outside influences to make them relevant to local conditions and frameworks of meaning.

CHANGE IN EXPRESSIVE CULTURE

Expressive culture in all its varieties changes, even in contexts where change and innovation are not valued. Anthropologists debate whether change in symbolic forms, motifs, and other features is more often the result of internal factors or more often due to the result of diffusion (defined in Chapter 9), the spread of culture from one group to another through contact. Changes in expressive culture, like changes in language (see the Crossing the Fields section in Chapter 7, pp. 217–218), can provide insight about social change more generally. For example, archaeologists have studied motifs in house-style in the South Pacific as an indicator of the route that people followed when they migrated to various islands several thousand years ago.

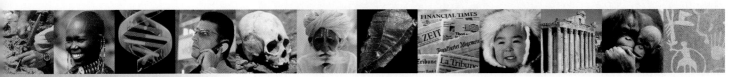

CROSSING THE FIELDS

Applying Cladistic Analysis
to Change in Oriental Carpets

Biological anthropologists look at fossil evidence for how human evolution occurred, and they ask whether changes in morphology are more determined by *cladogenesis,* in which new species are produced when the original species splits to give rise to new ones. In *anagenesis,* existing species are transformed into new ones. Through cladistic analysis (review Chapter 6, p. 175), biological anthropologists use certain morphological features to generate hypotheses about how living and fossil species are related to each other and to modern humans.

A study of change in motifs of Oriental carpets (and other woven items) applied cladistic analysis to a dataset of sixty items woven in the eighteenth and nineteenth centuries by five Turkmen groups located mainly in Turkmenistan, northern Iran, and northern Afghanistan (Tehrani and Collard 2002). The anthropologists were interested in learning if the method worked for material artifacts and if it provided insights about the dynamics of motif change as either internally generated, through cladogenesis, or if externally stimulated, through **ethnogenesis.** Specifically, they wondered whether the Russian takeover of the Turkman people in 1881 was an important ethnogenetic factor through providing an expanded market for Turkman carpets in Russia.

The results show that cladogenesis dominated ethnogenesis in explaining motif change over the entire period under study. The Russian presence, though, did have an impact. In the pre-Russian period, cladogenesis accounted for 70 percent of change and ethnogenesis 30 percent. After the Russian takeover, the effect of cladogenesis declined to 60 percent while that of ethnogenesis rose to 40 percent.

What may have happened is this: Before the Russians came, Turkmen groups were independent of each other, and their carpet-weaving practices and motifs marked their group identity. No tribal group would have been interested in adopting a motif of another group. Retention of the same motifs over generations was ensured through the prevailing gender division of labor and the kinship system. The weavers were women, and mothers passed their knowledge down to their daughters. Marriage was endogamous (within the group, see Chapter 12), so daughters—and their knowledge—stayed in the tribe.

With the Russian presence and the development of a wider market for carpets beyond the tribal group, weavers began to respond to external demand for new styles and motifs. Change and diversification in carpet styles was taken up as a way to compete in the market. ■

FOOD FOR THOUGHT

■ Think of another domain of expressive culture that might also be amenable to cladistic analysis.

Changes in expressive culture that result from outside contact often follow lines of power relations. Thus, the contemporary economic and political dominance of the United States is accompanied by the substantial spread of its forms of expressive culture to other parts of the world through globalization. Often, though, diffusion in expressive culture goes in the opposite direction, from the less powerful to the more powerful. The global influence of contemporary Caribbean music is an example of cultural spread far beyond what a simple measure of economic and political power would lead us to expect.

Some cultures appear to be more open to change than others. Depending on the context, cultures may promote change in some aspects of expressive culture yet repress it in others. Throughout history, instances of forced change in expressive culture (through European colonialism or Chinese nationalism, for example) have occurred. Local cultures may, however, adapt, localize, or ultimately reject outside factors. This section looks at how two powerful international forces—European colonialism and contemporary international tourism—have brought and are bringing changes to local systems of expressive culture.

Colonialism and Syncretism

Western colonialists had dramatic effects on the expressive culture of indigenous peoples with whom they came into contact. In some cases, colonial disapproval of particular activities resulted in the extinction of traditional art forms. For example, when colonialists banned head-hunting in various cultures, body decoration of traditional art forms, weapon decoration, and other related expressive activities were abandoned. An example follows of how colonial repression of indigenous forms succeeded in changing indigenous lifeways, but only temporarily.

In the Trobriand Islands, now part of Papua New Guinea, British administrators and missionaries sought to eradicate the frequent tribal warfare as part of a pacification process. One strategy was to replace it with intertribal competitive sports (Leach 1975). In 1903 a British missionary introduced the British game of cricket in the Trobriands as a way of promoting a new morality, separate from the former warring traditions. As played in England, cricket involves formal rules of play, and players wear white shirts and pants. In the early stages of the adoption of cricket in the Trobriands, the game followed the British pattern closely. As time passed and the game spread into more regions, it became increasingly localized. Most important, it was merged into indigenous political competition between big-men. Big-men leaders would urge their followers to increase production in anticipation of a cricket match, because the matches were followed by a redistributive feast.

The British missionaries had discouraged traditional magic in favor of Christianity, but the Trobriand Islanders transferred war-related magic to cricket. For example, spells are used to help one's team win, and bats are ritually treated in the way that war weapons were. Weather magic is also important. If things are not going well for one's team, a spell to bring rain and force cancellation of the game may be invoked.

Other changes occurred. The Trobrianders stopped wearing the crisp white clothing and instead donned paint, feathers, and shells. They announced their entry into

In the Trobriand Islands, British missionaries, starting in the late nineteenth century, tried to substitute their game of cricket for inter-tribal rivalries and warfare. It did not take long, however, for the Trobriand people to transform British rules and style to Trobriand ways. ■ If you wanted to go to a cricket match, what would be the closest place for you to go? (Source: © Wolfgang Kaehler/CORBIS)

the opposing village with songs and dances, praising their team in contrast to the opposition. Many of the teams, and their songs and dances, draw on Western elements, such as the famous entry song of the "P-K" team. (P-K is the name of a chewing gum. This team chose the name because the stickiness of gum is likened to the ability of their bat to hit the ball.) Other teams incorporated sounds and motions of airplanes, objects they had never seen until World War II. Songs and dances are explicitly sexual and are enjoyed by all, in spite of missionary attempts to suppress such "immoral" aspects of Trobriand culture.

The Trobrianders have changed some of the rules of play as well. The home team should always win, but not by too many runs. In this way, guests show respect to the hosts. Winning is not the major goal. The redistributive feast after the match is the climax for the Trobrianders.

Tourism's Complex Effects

Global tourism has had varied effects on indigenous arts. Often, tourist demand for ethnic arts and souvenirs has led to mass production of sculpture or weaving or jewelry of a lesser quality than was created before the demand. Tourists' interests in seeing an abbreviated form of traditionally long dance or theater performances has led to the presentation of "cuts" rather than an entire piece. Some scholars say, therefore, that tourism leads to the transformation of indigenous arts in a negative sense.

Tourist support for indigenous arts, however, is often the sole force maintaining them, because local people in a particular culture may be more interested in foreign music, art, or sports. Vietnamese water puppetry is an ancient performance mode, dating back at least to the Ly Dynasty of 1121 (Contreras 1995). Traditionally, water puppet shows took place in the spring during a lull in the farm work, or at special festival times. Now, water puppet shows are performed mainly for foreign tourists in large cities. Vietnamese people tend to prefer imported videos for their entertainment (Brownmiller 1994).

One positive side effect of global tourism is the growing support for preservation of **material cultural heritage,** sometimes referred to as simply "cultural heritage," which includes entire sites (for example, an ancient city), monuments (buildings as well as monumental sculpture, painting, and cave temples), and movable objects con-

A Strategy for the World Bank on Cultural Heritage

THE WORLD BANK, with headquarters in Washington, DC, and offices throughout the world, is an international organization funded by member nations that works to promote and finance economic development in poor countries. Even though most of its permanent professional staff are economists, the Bank has begun to pay more attention to noneconomic factors that affect development projects. One of the major moves in that direction occurred in 1972 when the Bank hired its first anthropologist, Michael Cernea. For three decades, Cernea has drawn attention to the cultural dimensions of development, especially in terms of the importance of local participation in development projects and people-centered approaches to project-forced resettlement (when, for example, large dams are being planned). His most recent campaign is to convince top officials at the World Bank that the Bank should become involved in supporting cultural heritage projects as potential pathways to development.

The World Bank already has in place a "do no harm" rule when it approves and financially supports construction projects. Cernea agrees that a "do no harm" rule is basic to pre-venting outright destruction, but it is a passive rule and does nothing to provide resources to preserve sites. He wants the Bank to move beyond its "do no harm" rule. He has written for the World Bank a strategy that is active, not passive. The strategy has two major objectives: (1) The World Bank should support cultural heritage projects that promote poverty reduction and cultural heritage preservation by creating employment and generating capital from tourism. (2) These projects should emphasize the educational value to both local people and international visitors on the grounds that cultural understanding has value for good will and good relations at all levels—local, national, and international.

Cernea also offers two suggestions for better management of cultural heritage projects: (1) selectivity in site selection on the basis of the impact in reducing poverty, and (2) building partnerships for project planning and implementation among local, national, and international institutions.

FOOD FOR THOUGHT

- Find, on the Internet, the UNESCO World Heritage Site that is nearest to where you live. What does the site contain, and what can you learn about its possible or potential role in generating income for the local people?

sidered of outstanding value in terms of history, art, and science (Cernea 2001). UNESCO first proposed the basic definition of material cultural heritage in 1972. Since then, many locations worldwide have been placed on its World Heritage List for preservation including Atapuerca (Chapter 7) and Cahokia (Chapter 9). In the Middle East and North Africa alone, sixty places are on UNESCO's list. Many invaluable sites and other aspects of material cultural heritage are lost to public knowledge through destructive engineering projects, war, looting, and private collecting. Many applied anthropologists, both archaeologists and cultural anthropologists, are involved in promoting stewardship of material cultural heritage. Some are motivated by a desire to preserve the record of humanity for future generations or for science. Others see that material cultural heritage, especially in poorer countries, can promote improvements in human welfare. They endorse forging a link between material cultural heritage and human development (see the Lessons Applied box).

The preservation of indigenous forms of expressive culture can also occur as a form of resistance to outside development forces. One example of this phenomenon is the resurgence of the hula, or Hawai'ian dance (Stillman 1996). Beginning in the early 1970s, the "Hawai'ian Renaissance" grew out of political protest. Hawai'ian youth began speaking out against encroaching economic development from the outside that was displacing the indigenous people from their land and their resources. They promoted a concerted effort to revive the Hawai'ian language, the hula, and canoe paddling, among other things. Since then, hula schools have proliferated, and hula competitions among the islands are widely attended. The 1990s saw the inauguration of the International Hula Festival in Honolulu, which attracts competitors from around the world. The hula competitions have helped ensure the continued

Classical dancers perform in Thailand. The intricate hand motions, with their impact augmented by metal finger extenders, have meanings that accompany the narrative being acted out. International tourism is a major support for such performance arts in Thailand. ■ Learn about UNESCO's recent declaration about "intangible" cultural heritage and speculate on what it may mean for the preservation of particular cultural forms. (Source: © Dallas and John Heaton/CORBIS)

survival of this ancient art form, although some Hawai'ians have voiced concerns. First, they feel that allowing non-Hawai'ians to compete is compromising the quality of the dancing. Second, the format of the competition violates traditional rules of style and presentation, which require more time than is allowed, so important dances have to be cut.

Post-USSR and Contemporary Chinese Transitions

Major changes have occurred in the arts in the post-communist states of the former USSR for two reasons: loss of state financial support and removal of state controls over subject matter and creativity. "A new generation of talented young artists has appeared. Many are looking for something new and different—art without ideology" (Akinsha 1992c:109). Art for art's sake—art as independent from the socialist project—is now possible. A circle of artists called the Moscow Conceptualists had been the dominant "underground" (non-official) school of art. These artists focused on political subject matter and poverty. In contrast, the new underground finds its inspiration in nostalgia for the popular culture of the 1950s and 1960s, a pack of Yugoslav chewing gum, or the cover of a Western art magazine. Commercial galleries are springing up, and a museum of modern art in Moscow may become a reality in the near future.

Theater in China is passing through a transition period with the emergence of some features of capitalism. Due to decreased state financial support, China's theater companies have experienced financial crises (Jiang 1994:72). Steep inflation means that actors can no longer live on their pay. Theater companies are urging their workers to find jobs elsewhere, such as in making movies or videos, but this is not an option for provincial troupes. Local audience preferences have changed: "People are fed up with shows that 'educate,' have too strong a political flavor, or convey 'artistic values.' They no longer seem to enjoy love stories, old Chinese legends, or Euro-American theater.

Most of the young people prefer nightclubs, discos, or karaokes. Others stay at home watching TV (73). The new materialism in China means that young people want to spend their leisure time having fun. For the theater, too, money now comes first. One outcome is a trend toward the production of Western plays. For example, Harold Pinter's *The Lover* was an immediate success when it was performed in Shanghai in 1992. Why was it so successful?

> Sex is certainly a big part of the answer. Sex has been taboo in China for a long time; it is still highly censored in theater and films. The producers warned, "no children," fueling speculation about a possible sex scene. . . . Actually, *The Lover* contains only hints of sexuality, but by Chinese standards the production was the boldest stage show in China. The actress's alluring dress, so common in the west, has seldom, if ever, been seen by Chinese theatregoers. Also, there was lots of bold language—dialog about female breasts, for example. (75–76)

Another important feature is the play's focus on private life, thoughts, and feelings. This emphasis corresponds with increasing interest in private lives in China. Change in the performing arts in China is being shaped by changes in both the global and local political economy.

THE BIG QUESTIONS REVISITED

■ HOW is culture expressed through art?

Cultural anthropologists question the narrowness of Western definitions of art. They prefer a broad definition that takes cross-cultural variations into account. In the anthropological perspective, all cultures have art and all cultures have a concept of what good art is. Ethnographers document the ways in which art is related to many aspects of culture: economics, politics, psychology, healing, social control, religion, and entertainment. Art may serve to reinforce social patterns, but it may also be a vehicle of protest and resistance. In state societies, people began collecting art objects in museums. Later, ethnographic museums were established in Europe as the result of scientific and colonialist interest in learning about other cultures. Anthropologists study museum displays as a reflection of cultural values as well as places where perceptions and values are formed and reformed.

■ WHAT do play and leisure activities tell us about culture?

Anthropological studies of play and leisure examine these activities within their cultural contexts. Games reflect and reinforce dominant social values, and these activities have thus been analyzed as cultural microcosms. Sports and leisure activities, though engaged in for nonutilitarian purposes, are often tied to economic and political interests. In some cultures, sports are also related to religion and spirituality.

■ HOW is expressive culture changing in contemporary times?

Major forces of change in expressive culture include Western colonialism and international tourism. In some cases, outside forces have led to the extinction of local forms, whereas in other cases, outside forces have promoted continuity or the recovery of practices that had been lost. The effects of change are not always on the "receiving" culture's side, however, because expressive cultures in colonial powers and in contemporary core states have also changed through exposure to other, less powerful cultures.

KEY CONCEPTS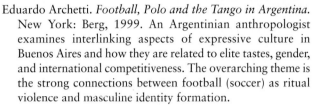

blood sports, p. 568
ethno-esthetics, p. 556
ethnogenesis, p. 570

ethnomusicology, p. 560
heterotopia, p. 564
material cultural heritage, p. 572

repatriation, p. 565
theater, p. 561

SUGGESTED READINGS

Eduardo Archetti. *Football, Polo and the Tango in Argentina.* New York: Berg, 1999. An Argentinian anthropologist examines interlinking aspects of expressive culture in Buenos Aires and how they are related to elite tastes, gender, and international competitiveness. The overarching theme is the strong connections between football (soccer) as ritual violence and masculine identity formation.

Richard Bradley. *Rock Art and the Prehistory of Atlantic Europe.* New York: Routledge, 1997. This book provides an overview of the distribution of rock carvings along the Atlantic coast from Scotland to Spain, dating between four and five thousand years ago. Prominent carvings are "ring and cup" shapes, which may have been symbolic messages that organized prehistoric ritual geography.

Shirley F. Campbell. *The Art of Kula.* New York: Berg, 2002. This ethnography of art provides insights about the contemporary importance of kula trading among men in the Trobriand Islands. Kula trading and kula art continue to be important aspects of men's culture. The author focuses on designs painted on canoes and finds that kula art and its associated male ideology linked to the sea competes with female ideology and symbolism that is linked to the earth.

Rebecca Cassidy. *The Sport of Kings: Kinship, Class, and Thoroughbred Breeding in Newmarket.* New York: Cambridge University Press, 2002. This study of the British thoroughbred racing industry is based on fieldwork conducted in Newmarket, England. Findings about how people discuss the horses, their breeding, and their capabilities reflect more widely on the British class system and the hierarchy between humans and animals.

Michael M. Cernea. *Cultural Heritage and Development: A Framework for Action in the Middle East and North Africa.* Washington, DC: The World Bank, 2001. This document provides an overview of cultural heritage projects and possibilities in the Middle East and North Africa and a proactive strategy linking efforts to reduce poverty with high-impact cultural heritage projects. The strategy was adopted for use by the Middle East and North Africa group within the World Bank.

John Miller Chernoff. *African Rhythm and African Sensibility: Aesthetics and African Musical Idioms.* Chicago: University of Chicago Press, 1979. This book describes shared features of music style and musical performance throughout Africa and also explains links to key African cultural values.

Eugene Cooper and Yinho Jiang (contributor). *The Artisans and Entrepreneurs of Dongyang County: Economic Reform and Flexible Production in China.* Armonk, NY: M. E. Sharpe, 1998. This ethnography links economic change and artistic change in China through its description of traditional and contemporary woodcarving in two villages and one town.

Ellen Dissanayake. *Home Aestheticus: Where Art Comes From and Why.* Seattle: University of Washington Press, 1992. The author presents a Darwinian argument that art was central to human evolutionary adaptation. She discusses music, poetry, and graphic art in terms of their relationship to human cognitive functioning, the human urge for control, and human emotions.

Alice C. Fletcher. *Indian Games and Dances with Native Songs: Arranged from American Indian Ceremonials and Sports.* Boston: Bison Books, 1994 [1915]. This book is a reprint of a classic study of dances, songs, and games from many tribes by the anthropologist who coined the term *Native American*. The adaptations allow readers to perform these activities themselves.

Nelson H. H. Graburn, ed. *Ethnic and Tourist Arts: Cultural Expressions from the Fourth World.* Berkeley: University of California Press, 1976. Organized regionally, twenty chapters explore the survival, revival, and reinvention of the arts of indigenous peoples in North America, Mexico and Central America, South America, Asia, Oceania, and Africa. Graburn's introduction to the book and his introductory essays preceding the sections offer theoretical and comparative insights.

James D. Keyser and Michael A. Klassen. *Plains Indian Rock Art.* Seattle: University of Washington Press, 2001. Although Native American rock carvings are found scattered throughout the vast region from the Canadian prairies to Texas, this book focuses on those in the northwestern plains. The carvings date from five thousand to one hundred years ago. Chapters provide introductory discussions of dating, interpretation, and native cultures, as well as various artistic regional traditions and motifs.

Jay R. Mandle and Joan D. Mandle. *Caribbean Hoops: The Development of West Indian Basketball.* Amsterdam: Gordon and Breach Publishers, 1994. This description and analysis of the emergence of basketball (mainly men's basketball) as a popular sport in several Caribbean nations also explores regional differences within the Caribbean.

Timothy Mitchell. *Blood Sport: A Social History of Spanish Bullfighting.* Philadelphia: University of Pennsylvania Press, 1991. Based on fieldwork and archival study, this book presents a well-rounded view of bullfighting within the context of annual Spanish village and national fiestas, consideration of the role of the matador in society, and a psychosexual interpretation of the bullfight, with comparison to blood sports in ancient Rome.

Stuart Plattner. *High Art Down Home: An Economic Ethnography of a Local Art Market*. Chicago: University of Chicago Press, 1996. Based on participant observation and interviews with artists, art dealers, and collectors in St. Louis, Missouri, this book explores concepts of value related to contemporary art and constraints that the market places on artists.

Stacy B. Schaefer. *To Think with a Good Heart: Wixárike Women, Weavers, and Shamans*. Salt Lake City: University of Utah Press, 2002. Weaving woolen textiles is a woman-centered activity among the Wixárike of western Mexico. Women generate income from weaving, and master weavers gain domestic and public status. Most previous ethnographers of the Wixárike have studied men. This book provides new insights into the world of women.

R. Anderson Sutton. *Calling Back the Spirit: Music, Dance and Cultural Politics in Lowland South Sulawesi*. New York: Oxford University Press, 2002. The author describes a wide variety of performance modes in South Sulawesi, Indonesia, from village ceremonies to studio-produced popular music. One chapter examines the role of village schools in institutionalizing local forms of music and dance. Another considers the effects of mass media. Accompanying the book is a CD with examples of music that complement points made in the book.

Roxanne Waterson. *The Living House: An Anthropology of Architecture in South-East Asia*. New York: Oxford University Press, 1990. This richly illustrated book covers a range of topics related to domestic architecture in Southeast Asia, including how house forms and decorations are related to religious symbolism, kinship, social relationships, political status, and population migration.

PART V Forces of Change and Humanity's Future

MAMPHELA RAMPHELE'S life story moves from her being subjected to racial apartheid and gender discrimination as a girl born in 1947 in rural Northern Transvaal, South Africa, to professional and personal achievement as a political activist, medical doctor, anthropologist, teacher, university administrator, mother, and (currently) one of the four managing directors of the World Bank.

As a child, Ramphele saw the injustices of apartheid inflicted on her family when the government retaliated against her relatives who worked for social equality. This experience spurred her on to political activism while she was still pursuing her education. Speaking of her school years, Ramphele says she felt confidence in her intelligence but had a difficult time overcoming the sense of inferiority that apartheid instilled in Black people.

In the early 1970s, Ramphele completed her medical studies at the University of Natal. She became a founder of South Africa's Black Consciousness movement to abolish segregation and injustice at a time when the nation's White government was engaged in some of the most brutally repressive activities in its history.

The consequence of her activism was federal censure under the Terrorism Act. Exiled for six years to Northern Transvaal, Ramphele worked with the rural poor, setting up community health programs. In the 1980s, she became a research fellow with the South African Development Research Unit at the University of Cape Town and earned a doctorate in anthropology. Her dissertation, *A Bed Called Home: Life in the Migrant Labour Hostels of Cape Town,* was later published as a book.

ANTHROPOLOGY
in the *Real World*

■ **Mamphela Ramphele, Development Anthropologist**

Ramphele also earned a BCom degree in administration and diplomas in tropical health and hygiene and public health. She served as senior research officer in the University of Cape Town's Department of Social Anthropology and, in 1996, became the first Black person and the first woman to be elected as vice-chancellor of the University of Cape Town.

Since 2000, Ramphele has been with the World Bank, the first South African to hold a position as managing director. In this position, she oversees the institution's human development activities in education; health, nutrition, and population; and social protection. She also monitors and guides the World Bank's relationships with client governments in strengthening socioeconomic support programs. In this capacity, she has worked to reduce child mortality, eradicate polio, and reduce the prevalence of HIV/AIDS, TB, and malaria.

Describing her work as "advocating with all my passion," Ramphele consults globally with several human rights initiatives. She was also an advisor to Nelson Mandela's government. She has received many awards and honors and has published books and articles on education, health, and social development.

In 2001, the South African Women for Women organization awarded Ramphele a Woman of Distinction Award that recognizes her "energetic leadership, her commitment to excellence, and her continuing dedication to transforming the lives of those around her."

THE BIG QUESTIONS

- WHAT are the major categories of migration?
- WHAT are examples of the new immigrants in North America?
- HOW do cultural anthropologists contribute to migration policies and programs?

CHAPTER 20

People on the Move

Under the rule of Saddam Hussein, the so-called Marsh Arab people of south-ern Iraq suffered from the effects of government projects that drained their region. They also endured political repression. Many who fled the country as refugees are now returning, and restoration of the marsh environment began in 2005. (Source: © Nik Wheeler/CORBIS)

The current generation of North American youths will move more times during their lives than previous generations. College graduates are likely to change jobs an average of eight times during their lives, and these changes may require relocation.

Ecological, economic, familial, and political factors are causing population movements at all-time high levels. Research in anthropology shows, however, that frequent moves during a person's life and mass movements of peoples are nothing new; they have occurred throughout human prehistory and history. Foragers, horticulturalists, and pastoralists relocate frequently as a normal part of their lives.

Migration, as defined in Chapter 12, is the movement of a person or people from one place to another. It is closely related to many aspects of life such as work, family status, and personal identity. It may also affect health and social relationships. Thus migration is of interest to many academic subjects and professions. It is one of three core areas of demography, along with fertility and mortality. Historians, economists, political scientists, sociologists, and scholars of religion, literature, art, and music have studied migration. The professions of law, medicine, education, business, architecture, urban planning, public administration, and social work have specialties that focus on the process of migration and the period of adaptation following a move. Experts working in these areas share with anthropologists an interest in the kinds of people who migrate, the causes of migration, the processes of migration, health and psychosocial adaptations to new locations, and the implications for planning and policy. Anthropologists in all four fields are often concerned with aspects of migration. This chapter, however, focuses on the work of cultural anthropologists and their findings about contemporary population movements.

Cultural anthropologists study how migration is related to economic and reproductive systems, health and human development over the life cycle, marriage and household formation, politics and social order, and religion and expressive culture. Thus, this chapter pulls together material presented earlier in this book. Given the breadth of migration studies, cultural anthropologists use the full range of research methods, from individual life histories to large-scale surveys.

Three differences distinguish migration studies from other areas of research in cultural anthropology. First, anthropologists studying migration are more likely to have conducted fieldwork in more than one location in order to understand the places of origin and estimation. Maxine Margolis (1994), for example, first did fieldwork in Brazil and then studied Brazilian immigrants in New York City. Second, studying migration challenges traditional cultural anthropology's focus on local culture and raises the need to take into wider social forces, including globalization (Basch, Glick Schiller, and Szanton Blanc 1994; Lamphere 1992). Third, anthropologists who work with migrants are more likely to be involved in applied anthropology. Anthropologists have been at the forefront of efforts to improve the situation of people forced to move by war, environmental destruction, and building projects such as dams.

This chapter first presents information on the most important categories of migrants and the opportunities and challenges they face. The second section provides descriptions of several examples of recent immigrants to the United States and Canada. The last section considers urgent applied issues related to migration, such as human rights and health care programs.

 CATEGORIES OF MIGRATION

Migration encompasses many categories, depending on the distance involved; on the purpose of the move, its duration, and the degree of voluntarism (was the move forced or more a matter of choice?); and on the migrant's status in the new destination. There are major differences between **internal migration** (movement within national boundaries) and international migration. Moving between countries is likely to create more challenges both in the process of relocation and in adjustment after arrival.

Categories Based on Spatial Boundaries

This section reviews the basic features of three categories of population movement defined in terms of the spatial and political boundaries crossed: internal migration, international migration, and transnational migration. **Transnational migrants** are migrants who regularly move back and forth between two or more countries and form a new identity that transcends a single geopolitical unit.

Internal Migration

Rural-to-urban migration was the dominant form of internal migration in most countries during the twentieth century. A major reason why people migrate to urban areas is the availability of work. According to the **push–pull theory** of labor migration, rural areas are increasingly unable to support population growth and people's rising expectations about the quality of life (the push factor). Cities (the pull factor) attract people, especially youth, for employment and lifestyle reasons. The push–pull model makes urban migration sound like a simple function of rational decision making by people who have information on the costs and benefits of rural versus urban life, weigh that information, and then opt for going or staying (recall the approach to understanding culture that emphasizes human agency discussed in Chapter 2). But many instances of urban migration are more likely to be the result of structural forces (economic need or political factors such as war) that are beyond the control of the individual.

The anonymity and rapid pace of city life and the likelihood of "psychosocial discontinuity" caused by relocation pose special challenges for migrants from rural areas. Urban life increases the risk of hypertension (elevated blood pressure through stress or tension), and hypertension is related to coronary heart disease. For example, hypertension is more prevalent in urban migrant populations than in settled rural groups in the Philippines (Hackenberg et al. 1983). The relationship between elevated health risks resulting from psychosocial adjustment problems in rural-to-urban migration exists among international immigrants as well—for example, among rural Samoans living in cities in California (Janes 1990).

The Bamiyan Valley, in Afghanistan, is located in an area long involved in trade across Asia, and linked to Europe and Africa. The use of pack animals has facilitated long-distance trade overland for thousands of years. ■ Review the discussion in Chapter 9, p. 261, of the earliest evidence of domesticated cattle being used as pack animals in the Sahara. (Source: © Ray Manley/Superstock, Inc.)

International Migration

International migration has grown in volume and significance since 1945 and especially since the mid-1980s (Castles and Miller 1993). It is estimated that nearly 2 percent of the world's population lives outside of their home countries. This is about 100 million people, including legal and undocumented immigrants. Migrants who move for work-related reasons constitute the majority of people in this category. At least 35 million people from developing countries have migrated to industrialized countries in the past three decades. The driving forces behind this trend are economic and political changes that affect labor demands and human welfare.

CROSSING THE FIELDS

Biological Anthropologists Reveal Health Effects of Immigration to the United States

Many studies have demonstrated how migration from one country to another affects health and nutritional status. Immigrants to the United States tend to adopt some of the eating patterns and lifestyle of their new country. Although one might assume that immigrants from low-income, developing countries would benefit significantly in health and nutrition by migration to the United States, a clearly positive picture does not emerge from most studies.

One case study considers the health effects of immigration, as measured by physical growth, of children in Maya families from Guatemala (Smith et al. 2002). The study is based on **anthropometric** data (measurements of the size and shape of the human body) including height for age and Body Mass Index (BMI, the ratio of weight to height). Anthropometric data for Maya children living in Guatemala are compared to similar data for Maya American children. Because the human body responds quickly to changes in food and health care, for example, anthropometry is a good indicator of quality of life. Better conditions tend to produce taller, heavier, more long-legged children. In poor conditions, in contrast, the human body conserves energy and protects internal organs by concentrating growth and development in the trunk area. Children growing up in poor conditions tend to be shorter, to be lighter, and to have shorter legs. The study also collected survey data from the Maya American children and their parents about lifestyle and socioeconomic status (SES).

Maya people of Guatemala began migrating to the United States in significant numbers, starting with the onset of civil war in Guatemala in the late 1970s. An estimated half-million Maya from Guatemala now live in the United States, where they are more likely than in their home country to have access to a clean water supply and health services. Maya immigrant children, however, are exposed to what the researchers call "unhealthy American lifestyle patterns" such as eating "junk food" and watching television a lot. Maya Americans also tend to live in poverty in the United States.

The results of the comparative anthropometric analysis show that Maya American children are on average 10 centimeters (four inches) taller than Maya children living in Guatemala, indicating better health in the immigrant children. But nearly half of the Maya American children are overweight, and most of these children fall in the obese category. Children who report watching television or playing computer games as a favorite leisure activity are more likely to be overweight. Thus immigration to the United States improves health as measured in terms of height but raises the risk of weight problems and the likelihood of health problems later in life, such as hypertension and diabetes.

FOOD FOR THOUGHT

- Explore some informational web sites on obesity to learn about the regional and class patterns of overweight and obesity among children in the United States and Canada.

The "classic" destination countries of early international immigration are the United States, Canada, Australia, New Zealand, and Argentina. The immigration policies that these nations applied in the early twentieth century are labeled "White immigration" because they explicitly limited non-White immigration (Ongley 1995). In the 1960s in Canada, changes made immigration policies less racially discriminatory and more focused on skills and experience. The "White Australia" policy formally ended in 1973. In both Canada and Australia, a combination of changing labor needs and interest in improving their international image prompted the reforms. During the 1980s and the 1990s, the United States, Canada, and Australia experienced large-scale immigration from new sources, especially from Asia, and—to the United States—from Latin America and the Caribbean.

Long-time countries of out-migration in Europe now receive many immigrants (often refugees from Asia). Italy, Spain, Hungary, Poland, and Czechoslovakia are examples of such new migrant destinations in Europe. International population flows in the Middle East are complex, and some nations (such as Turkey) are experiencing substantial movements in both directions. Millions of Turks have emigrated to Germany, while ethnic Turks in places such as Bulgaria have returned to Turkey. Turkey has also received Kurdish and Iranian refugees. Several million Palestinian refugees now live mainly in Jordan and Lebanon. Israel has attracted Jewish immigrants from Europe, northern Africa, the United States, and Russia.

Transnational Migration

Transnational migration appears to be increasing along with other aspects of globalization. We must keep in mind, however, that transnationalism is a function of the creation of nation–state boundaries. For example, pastoralist people with extensive seasonal herding routes were "transnational" migrants long before modern state boundaries cut across their pathways.

Much contemporary transnational migration is motivated by economic factors. The spread of the global capitalist economy is the basis for the growth of one category of transnational migrants nicknamed "astronauts"—businesspeople who spend most of their time flying among different cities as investment bankers or corporate executives. At the lower end of the income scale are transnational migrant laborers

Turkish people migrated to Germany in substantial numbers in the 1960s and 1970s as "guest workers" to fill jobs in German factories. German leaders expected them to work, save money, and return to Turkey. Most stayed, and their children are growing up in Germany, speaking German and having only a distant relationship with Turkey. Many incidents of violence between so-called neo-Nazis and Turkish people have occurred, including the murder of five Turkish youths in Solingen in 1993. ■ Do some Web research on the Turkish population of Germany. (Source: © David Turnley/CORBIS)

whose movements depend on the demand for their labor. An important feature of transnational migration is how it affects the migrant's identity and sense of citizenship. Constant movement weakens the sense of having a home and promotes instead a sense of belonging to a diffuse community of similar transnational migrants whose lives "in between" locations take on a new transnational cultural reality (see the Methods Close-Up box).

As a response to the increased rate of transnational migration, many of the "sending" countries (countries that are the source of emigrants) are making explicit efforts to redefine themselves as *transnational nations* (Glick Schiller and Fouron 1999). These countries, which have high proportions of emigrants, include Haiti, Colombia, Mexico, Brazil, the Dominican Republic, Portugal, Greece, and the Philippines. They confer continuing citizenship on emigrants and their descendants in order to foster a sense of belonging and willingness to continue to provide financial support in the form of **remittances,** or economic transfers of money or goods from migrants to their family back home. For example, at least 60 percent of the gross domestic product of the small Pacific island country of Tonga comes from remittances (Lee 2003:32).

Categories Based on Reason for Moving

This section considers categories of migrants that are based on the reason for relocating. Keep in mind that the spatial categories discussed above overlap with these categories based on the reason for moving: an international migrant may also be a person who moves for employment reasons, and displaced persons can be either internal or international. In other words, migrants experience different kinds of spatial change and, at the same time, have various reasons for moving.

Labor Migrants

THINKING OUTSIDE THE BOX Have you, with or separate from your family, ever moved for work-related reasons? What kinds of adjustments did you (and your family members) make in the new location?

Thousands of people migrate each year to work for a specific period of time. They do not intend to establish permanent residence and are often explicitly barred from doing so. This form of migration, when legally contracted, is called *wage labor migration*. The period of work may be brief or it may last several years, as among the many rural Egyptian men who go to Middle Eastern countries to work for an average period of four years (Brink 1991).

Asian women are the fastest-growing group among the world's 35 million migrant workers (International Labour Office 1996). About 1.5 million Asian women are working abroad. Most are in domestic service jobs, while some work as nurses and teachers. Major sending countries are Indonesia, the Philippines, Sri Lanka, and Thailand. Major receiving countries are Saudi Arabia and Kuwait, and, to a lesser degree, Hong Kong, Japan, Taiwan, Singapore, Malaysia, and Brunei. Such women are usually alone and are not allowed to marry or have a child in the country where they are temporary workers. International migrant workers are sometimes illegally recruited and have no legal protection in their working conditions.

Circular migration is a common form of labor migration involving movement in a regular pattern between two or more places. Circular migration may occur within or between countries (in the latter case, it is also referred to as transnational migration). Internal circular migrants include, for example, female domestic workers in Latin America and the Caribbean. These women have their permanent residence in the rural areas, but they work for long periods of time for better-off people in the city. They tend to leave their children at home in the care of their mother or other family members and to send regular remittances for the children's support.

Displaced Persons

Displaced persons are people who, for one reason or another, are evicted from their homes, communities, or countries and forced to move elsewhere (Guggenheim and

Studying a Virtual Community

COMPUTER-MEDIATED COMMUNICATION (CMC), such as e-mail, enables people to communicate with people they have never met. It also enables people to express opinions and share information in a participatory manner, rather than in the "top down" way typical of television and journalism. CMC creates virtual social networks and contributes to the formation of new cultural patterns. For his doctoral dissertation in cultural anthropology at Harvard University, Eriberto Lozada studied a "community in cyberspace," specifically that of the Hakka people whose homeland is in southern China (1998:148). The Hakka people have long been village-dwelling agriculturalists. Now, Hakka communities are found in many countries, including Canada, the United States, Indonesia, and Malaysia.

Hakka people worldwide are actively building web sites about Hakka culture and promoting transnational communication at levels that would not have been imagined ten years ago. Lozada had done participant observation in a Hakka village in China before he began studying the Hakka Global Network, or HGN. He conducted what he calls participant observation over the Internet for nearly two years. Using a search engine (Webcrawler), he looked for web sites that had the word "Hakka" and found five listings. He joined one and soon began receiving messages. Over the years, he collected many e-mail messages, which form his data set. His analysis was of the messages themselves, not of the people, about whom he had little data beyond knowing that they tend to be highly educated people scattered around the world.

Thus, this is a study of discourse and its possible meanings for the people engaged in it. Lozada's analysis of the messages involved the search for persistent themes. He found that the most prominent theme is preservation of Hakka culture in the face of global forces of change. Many of the messages provided announcements of television or radio programs carrying items about Hakka culture. Others included discussions of the Hakka language and of Hakka origins and customs. Many people requested information through the web site. For example, one person wrote about his grandfather, who had emigrated to Borneo and died in a certain village; he asked whether anyone knew the location of that village (158).

What can a cultural anthropologist learn about Hakka culture from studying these web sites and discussions and exchanges taking place between people who have never met each other? One conclusion of Lozada's is that through HGN,

Hakka women of rural southern China are touristically defined by their "lamp shade" hats. Here, a Hakka woman who has migrated to Hong Kong for work wears a traditional Hakka woman's hat as she pursues an urban lifestyle. (Source: © Hans Blossey/Das Fotoarchiv/Peter Arnold)

the Hakka are creating a "local global community," a new form of cultural organization that helps them deal with the present and shape the future in creative ways that no one can predict.

FOOD FOR THOUGHT

- How does a virtual community differ from a face-to-face social community? How are these kinds of communities similar?

Refugees fleeing the late-1990s violence in Rwanda on their way to neighboring Zaire. Many refugees did not survive the ordeal, although we do not have statistics adequate to assess the mortality rate. ■ Use the Internet to search for mortality rates from a recent conflict, and speculate on how accurate the data might be. (Source: © Allan Tannenbaum/The Image Works)

Cernea 1993). Colonialism, slavery, war, persecution, natural disasters, and large-scale mining and dam building are major causes of population displacement.

Refugees are a category of internationally displaced persons. Many refugees are forced to relocate because they are victims or potential victims of persecution on the basis of their race, religion, nationality, ethnicity, gender, or political views (Camino and Krulfeld 1994). Refugees constitute a large and growing category of displaced persons. An accurate count of all categories of refugees is unavailable, but it probably exceeds 10 million people globally. As of 2000, about one of every five hundred people was a refugee (Lubkemann 2002). The lack of accurate statistics about refugees is compounded by political interests, which inflate numbers in some cases and deflate them in others.

Internally displaced persons (IDPs) make up the fastest-growing category of displaced people. IDPs are people who are forced to leave their home and community but who remain within their country. Current estimates are that the number of IDPs is double that of refugees, over 20 million people (Cohen 2002). Africa is the continent with the most IDPs, and within Africa, Sudan is the country with the highest number (around 4.5 million). Because IDPs do not cross national boundaries, they do not come under the purview of the United Nations or any other international body. These institutions deal with international problems and have limited authority over problems within countries. Francis Deng, former Sudanese ambassador, has taken up the cause of IDPs and is working to raise international awareness of the immensity of the problem. His efforts led to the formal definition of IDPs and to legal recognition of their status. In his role as UN Secretary-General for Internally Displaced Persons, Deng coordinates a global coalition of institutions (including the UN, governments, and nongovernmental organizations) to provide more timely and effective assistance for IDPs. Many IDPs, like refugees, live for extended periods in camps under miserable conditions with no access to basic supports such as health care and schools.

Dr. Francis Deng, who earned a doctor of law degree from Yale University, is Representative of the United Nations Secretary-General on Internally Displaced Persons. He has been instrumental in promoting international recognition of the plight of internally displaced persons. ■ Do research on a case of IDPs and report on it to the class. (Source: AP/Wide World Photos)

Development projects are often the reason why people become IDPs. Large dam construction, mining, and other projects have displaced millions in the past several decades. Dam construction alone is estimated to have displaced 80 million people in the past fifty years (Worldwatch Institute 2003). Forced migration due to development projects is termed **development-induced displacement (DID)**. Development-induced displacement is usually internal displacement and thus has typically fallen outside international legal frameworks. Mega-dam projects are now attracting the attention of concerned people worldwide who support local resistance to massive relocation. One of the most notorious cases is India's construction of a series of high dams in the Narmada River valley, which cuts across the middle of the country. This massive project involves relocating hundreds of thousands of people—no one has a reliable estimate of the numbers. The relocation is against local residents' wishes, and government compensation to the "oustees" for the loss of their homes, land, and livelihood is completely inadequate. Thousands of people in the Narmada valley have organized protests over the many years of construction, and international environmental organizations have lent their support. A celebrated Indian novelist, Arundhati Roy, joined the cause by learning everything she could from records and interviews about the years of government planning for the Narmada dam projects and from interviews with people who have been relocated. One result of her research is a passionate essay called *The Cost of Living* (1999), which speaks out against this project. She tells about a man now living in a barren resettlement area who recalls with sadness how he used to pick fruit in the forests of the Narmada valley, forty-eight kinds in all. In the resettlement area he and his family have to purchase their food, and they cannot afford any fruit (54–55). In the other Asian giant, China, the Three Gorges Dam project will, when completed, have displaced perhaps 2 million people (McCully 2003). Mega-dam projects are promoted by governments as important to the national interest. Governments downplay the high costs for the local people who are displaced, and how the benefits are skewed toward corporate profits, energy for industrial plants, and water for urban consumers who can pay for it.

The manner in which displaced persons are relocated affects how well or poorly they adjust to their new lives. Displaced people in general have little choice about when and where they move, and refugees typically have the least choice of all. Cultural anthropologists have done substantial research with refugee populations, especially those related to war (Camino and Krulfeld 1994, Hirschon 1989, Manz 1988). They have helped discover the key factors that ease or increase relocation stresses. One major issue is the extent to which the new location resembles or differs from the home place in several features, such as climate, language, and food (Muecke 1987). Generally, the more different the places of origin and destination are, the greater the adaptational demands and stress. Other major factors are the refugee's ability to find work that is commensurate with his or her training and experience, the presence of family members, and whether people in the new location are welcoming or hostile to the refugees.

Institutional Migrants

Institutional migrants are people who move into a social institution, either voluntarily or involuntarily. They include monks and nuns, the elderly, prisoners, soldiers, and boarding school or college students. This section considers examples of students and soldiers.

Studies of student adjustment reveal similarities to many other forms of migration, especially in terms of risks for mental stress. Ethnographic research conducted among ado-

The photographs on pages 588 and 589 depict people with various face coverings. What is the purpose in each?

THINKING

OUTSIDE THE BOX

United States marines wearing gas masks as protection from oil fumes during the 1990–1991 Gulf War. Many poorly understood illnesses afflict veterans of "Desert Storm," including skin conditions, neurological disorders, chronic fatigue, and psychological-cognitive problems. ■ Do research to learn about current medical thinking on the causes of Gulf War illnesses. (Source: © David Leeson/The Image Works)

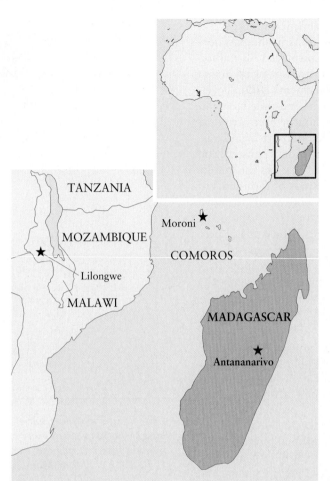

lescent boarding school children in Ambanja, a town in Madagascar, showed that girls experience more adjustment strains than boys (Sharp 1990). Boarding school children in this "boom" town constitute a vulnerable group because they have left their families and come alone to the school.

Many of the boarding school girls, who were between the ages of thirteen and seventeen, experienced spirit possession. Anthropological findings on possession patterns showed that it is correlated with a girl's being unmarried and pregnant. Many of the school girls become the mistresses of older men who shower them with expensive gifts such as perfume and gold jewelry. Such girls attract the envy of other girls and the ill will of school boys, who are being passed over in favor of adult men. Thus the girls are alienated from their schoolmates. If a girl becomes pregnant, she is expelled from the school. If the baby's father refuses to help her, she faces severe hardship because her return home will greatly disappoint her parents. Within this context, a girl's spirit possession may be understood as an expression of distress. Through the spirits, girls act out their difficult position between village and city and between girlhood and womanhood.

International students face serious challenges of spatial and cultural relocation. Like the school girls of Madagascar, they are at greater risk of adjustment stress than are local students. Many international students report mental health problems to varying degrees, depending on their age, marital status, and other factors. Spouses who accompany international students also suffer the strains of dislocation.

Soldiers are often sent on distant assignments for long periods of time. Their destination may have negative physical and mental health effects on them, in addition to the fact that they may face combat. During the British and French colonial expansion, thousands of soldiers were assigned to tropical countries (Curtin 1989). Colonial soldiers faced new diseases in their destination areas, and their death rates from disease were generally twice as high as those of soldiers who stayed home, with two exceptions—Tahiti and Hawai'i—where soldiers experienced better health than soldiers at home. Most military personnel were male, but in some colonial contexts, many wives accompanied their husbands. In India, mortality rates from disease were higher for British women than for men. This finding may be explained by the fact that the men had to pass a physical exam before enlistment, whereas the wives did not.

As noted in Chapter 16, military anthropology is an emerging specialty area within anthropology. As yet, though, little has been published by anthropologists on how military migration affects people's lives and sense of identity. It is clear, however, that U.S. military people on assignment typically lack in-depth training in how to communicate with local people and in the importance of respecting local people's cultures. A pocket-size handbook on Iraqi etiquette used by some U.S. troops in the second war in Iraq provides extremely basic guidelines (Lorch 2003). For example, one should avoid arguments and should not take more than three cups of coffee or tea when a guest. One should also avoid the "thumbs up" gesture (it is obscene in the Middle East) and should not sit with one's feet on a desk. Such basics are helpful, but they do far too little to provide the cultural understanding that is critical in conflict and post-conflict situations. Soldiers during wartime are trained primarily to seek out and destroy the enemy, not to engage in cross-cultural communication. Winning a war in contemporary times often hinges on what the conquerors do following the actual fighting. It requires even more in the way of cultural knowledge and communication skills.

THE NEW IMMIGRANTS IN THE UNITED STATES AND CANADA

The term **new immigrants** refers to international migrants who have moved since the 1960s. New immigrants worldwide include increasing proportions of refugees, many of whom are destitute and desperate for asylum. Three trends are apparent in the new international migration that began in the 1990s.

- *Globalization:* More countries are involved in international migration, leading to increased cultural diversity in both sending countries and receiving countries.
- *Acceleration:* Quantitative growth of migration has occurred in all major regions.
- *Feminization:* Women play a greater role in migration to and from all regions, and some forms of migration exhibit a majority of women.

These three trends raise new challenges for policy makers and international organizations as the cultural practices of immigrant groups and of people in the areas of destination increasingly come in contact—and sometimes in conflict—with each other.

In the United States, the category of *new immigrants* refers to people who arrived following the 1965 amendments to the Immigration and Naturalization Act. This change made it possible for far more people from developing countries to enter, especially if they were professionals or were trained in some desired skill. Later, the *family reunification* provision allowed permanent residents and naturalized citizens to bring in close family members. Most new immigrants in the United States are from Asia, Latin America, and the Caribbean, although increasing numbers are from Eastern Europe and Russia. The United States offers two kinds of visas for foreigners: immigrant visas (also called residence visas) and nonimmigrant visas for tourists and students (Pessar 1995:6). An immigrant visa is usually valid indefinitely and allows its holder to be employed and to apply for citizenship. A nonimmigrant visa is issued for a limited time and usually bars its holder from paid employment. Some immigrants are granted visas because of their special skills in relation to labor market needs, but most are admitted under the family unification provision.

The New Immigrants from Latin America and the Caribbean

Since the 1960s, substantial movements of the Latino population (people who share roots in former Spanish and Portuguese colonies in the Western hemisphere) have occurred, mainly but not entirely in the direction of the United States. Compared to numbers of legal immigrants in the 1960s, numbers doubled or tripled in the 1980s and then declined in the 1990s. For example, legal immigrants from Central America numbered about 100,000 in the 1960s, nearly 900,000 in the 1980s, and about 270,000 in the 1990s (Parrillo 1997:398). Excluding the residents of Puerto Rico, Latinos totaled about 2.4 million people, or about 9 percent of the United States population, in the 1990 census (Mahler 1995:xiii). In the United States as a whole, and in some cities (such as Los Angeles, Miami, San Antonio, and New York) Latinos are the largest minority group. Within the category of Latino new immigrants, the three largest subgroups are Mexicans, Puerto Ricans, and Cubans. Large numbers also come from the Dominican Republic, Colombia, Ecuador, El Salvador, Nicaragua, and Peru.

Mexico is by far the greatest source of foreign-born immigrants to the United States (Grieco 2003). There are currently around 10 million foreign-born Mexicans living in the United States, a number that doubled from 1990 to 2000. Most live in the main destination states of California, Texas, and Illinois, although more are now settling in states such as Georgia and North Carolina. Mexico also continues to be the leading source of unauthorized immigration to the United States.

THINKING OUTSIDE THE BOX

As a mini research project, obtain the most recent data on numbers of immigrants in the United States and Canada from Mexico.

A Dominican Day parade in New York City. ■ Learn about an ethnic festival or event that is being held in the near future. Attend it and observe what signs and symbols of ethnicity are displayed, who attends, and what messages about identity are conveyed. (Source: © Stephen Ferry/Getty Images)

Chain Migration of Dominicans

The Dominican Republic has ranked among the top ten source countries of immigrants to the United States since the 1960s (Pessar 1995). One of the fastest-growing immigrant groups in the United States, Dominicans are found in clusters in a few states, their highest concentration being in New York state. Within New York City, Washington Heights is the heart of the Dominican community. Unlike many other new immigrant streams, the Dominicans are mainly middle- and upper-class. Most have left their homeland in search of "a better life." Many hope to return to the Dominican Republic, saying that in New York, "There is work but there is no life" (xiii).

Cultural anthropologist Patricia Pessar conducted fieldwork in the Dominican Republic and in New York City. She studied the dynamics of departure (such as getting a visa), the process of arrival, and adaptation in New York. Like most anthropologists who work with immigrant groups, she became involved in helping many of her informants: "Along the way I also endeavored to repay people's help by brokering for them with institutions such as the Immigration and Naturalization Service, social service agencies, schools, and hospitals" (xv).

For Dominican immigrants, as for most other immigrant groups, the *cadena*, or chain, links one immigrant to another. **Chain migration** is the process by which a first wave of migrants attracts relatives and friends to join them in the destination place. Most Dominicans who are legal immigrants have sponsored other family members, so most legal Dominicans have entered through the family unification provision. The U.S. policy defines a family as a nuclear unit, and thus it excludes important members of Dominican extended family networks such as cousins and ritual kin (*compadres*). To overcome this barrier, some Dominicans use the technique of the "business marriage." In a business marriage, an individual pays a legal immigrant or citizen a fee of perhaps $2000 to enter into a "marriage." He or she then acquires a visa through the family unification provision. Such a "marriage" does not involve cohabitation or sexual relations; it is meant to be broken.

Dominicans have found employment in New York City's manufacturing industries, including the garment industry. Dominicans are more heavily employed in these industries than any other ethnic group. Recent declines in the numbers of New York City's manufacturing jobs and the redefining of better positions into less desirable ones through restructuring have disproportionately affected them. Dominicans also work in retail and wholesale trade, another sector that has declined since the late 1960s. Others have established their own retail businesses, or *bodegas*. A problem with this line of work is that many bodegas are located in unsafe areas, and some owners have been assaulted or killed. Declining economic opportunities for Dominicans have also been aggravated by arrivals of newer immigrants, especially from Mexico and Central America, who are willing to accept even lower wages and worse working conditions.

Although many members of middle- and upper-income families in the Dominican Republic initially secured fairly solid employment in the United States, they have declined economically since then. Dominicans now have the highest poverty rate in New York City, 37 percent, compared with an overall city average of 17 percent. Poverty is concentrated among woman-headed households with young children.

The gender gap in wages is high, and women are more likely than men to be on public assistance. On the other hand, Dominican women are more often regularly employed in the United States than they would be in the Dominican Republic. This pattern upsets a patriarchal norm in which the nuclear family depends on male earnings and female domestic responsibilities. A woman's earning power means that husband–wife decision making is more egalitarian. A working Dominican woman is likely to obtain more assistance from the man in doing household chores. These changes help explain why Dominican men are more interested in returning home than Dominican women are. As one man said, "Your country is a country for women; mine is for men" (81).

Salvadorans: Escaping War to Struggle with Poverty

Salvadorans are the fourth largest Latino population in the United States, numbering 868,000 people in 2002 (Migration Information Source 2003). The civil war in El Salvador, which began in 1979 and which continued for a decade, was the major stimulus for Salvadoran emigration (Mahler 1995). Most refugees from the war came to the United States. Many settled in New York City, and about 60,000 settled on Long Island. Suburban Washington, D.C., is a major destination for Salvadorans. Middle- and upper-class Salvadorans were able to obtain tourist or even immigration visas relatively easily, but the poor could not. Many poor Salvadorans entered the United States illegally as *mojados* ("wet-backs"), or undocumented immigrants.

Like Mexicans, they use the term *mojado* to describe their journey, but for the Salvadorans there were three rivers to cross instead of one. These three crossings are a prominent theme of their escape stories, which are full of physical and psychological hardship, including hunger, arrests, and women being beaten and raped along the way. Once they arrive, things are not easy, especially in the search for work and housing. Lack of education and marketable skills limits the job search. For those who are undocumented immigrants, getting a decent job is even harder. These factors make it more likely that Salvadorans will work in the informal sector, where they are easy targets for economic exploitation.

Cultural anthropologist Sarah Mahler conducted fieldwork among Salvadorans on Long Island (1995). She found that Salvadorans who find work on Long Island receive low wages and work in poor conditions. Jobs involve providing services to better-off Long Island households. Men do outside work such as gardening, landscaping, construction, and pool cleaning. Women work as nannies, live-in maids, house cleaners, restaurant help, and caregivers for the elderly. They often hold down a variety of jobs—for example, working at a McDonald's in the morning and cleaning houses in the afternoon. Men's pride prevents them from taking lowly ("female") jobs such as washing dishes. Women are more flexible and hence are more likely than men to find work. For the poorest Salvadoran refugees, even exploitative jobs may be an economic improvement compared to back home, where they could not support their families.

THINKING OUTSIDE THE BOX

Find a map that shows the United States, Mexico, and Central America. Trace a possible overland migration route to the United States from El Salvador and find the three rivers that would have to be crossed.

Hillary Clinton visits an orphanage in El Salvador in 1998. Many children were orphaned because their parents were killed during the civil war of the 1980s. Others were abducted by the Salvadoran military and still, two decades later, have not been reunited with their parents. ■ What do you think governments should and can do to help ensure children's safety and rights during war? (Source: © Yuri Cortez/ CORBIS)

Salvadorans were attracted to Long Island by its thriving informal economy, a sector in which few employers check for visas. Unfortunately, the cost of living on Long Island is higher than in many other places in the United States. The combination of low wages and the high cost of living has kept most Salvadorans in the category of the working poor, with few prospects for improvement. They attempt to cope with high housing costs by crowding many people into units meant for a small family. Compared to El Salvador, where most people except for the urban poor owned their own homes, only a few Salvadorans on Long Island own homes. Residential space and costs are shared among extended kin and non-kin who pay rent. This situation causes intrahousehold tension and stress.

The Catholic church has recognized that the Salvadorans are a substantial population, and it holds services in Spanish for this refugee community. Still, the refugees carry with them memories of the civil war in El Salvador and their escape from it. In spite of all these difficulties, however, most Salvadorans evaluate their experience in the United States positively.

The New Immigrants from East Asia

Koreans: Economic Achievement and Political Identity

In 1962 the South Korean government began encouraging massive emigration (Yoon 1993). This change was motivated by perceived population pressure and an interest in gaining remittances from persons working abroad. Before 1965, most Korean immigrants were wives of American servicemen or were children adopted by American parents. After 1965, most immigrants were members of nuclear families or family members being unified with earlier, "pioneer" migrants already in the United States. During the peak years of 1985 and 1987, more than 35,000 Koreans immigrated to the United States annually, making South Korea the largest immigrant source nation after Mexico and the Philippines.

Korean Americans clean up the debris from attacks on their businesses after the Los Angeles riots of May 1992. ■ Compare the situation in Los Angeles at that time to that of Baghdad in March 2003 in terms of the social cleavages involved in looting of museums and destruction of other forms of public property. (Source: © David Young-Wolff/PhotoEdit)

Latino immigrants studying English in a program in Virginia. ■ Besides learning a new language, what other kinds of learning are important for international immigrants? (Source: © David H. Wells/CORBIS)

Many of the migrants were displaced North Koreans who had fled their homeland to avoid communist rule there between 1945 and 1951. They had difficulty gaining an economic foothold in South Korea. When the opportunity arose to emigrate to South America or the United States and Canada, they were more willing to do so than many established South Koreans. In 1981 North Koreans constituted only 2 percent of the population of South Korea, but they were 22 percent of the Korean population of Los Angeles. Most of these immigrants were entrepreneurial, Christian, and middle-class. In the 1990s the number of lower-class migrants increased, and many lower-class Korean immigrants moved to Los Angeles (Sonenshein 1996).

In Los Angeles, ethnic identity is complex. Ethnic Euro-Americans constitute less than 40 percent of the population, whereas Asian Americans and Latinos account for 50 percent. The proportion of people who identify as African Americans is 14 percent. However, it is mainly African Americans and Euro-Americans who engage in electoral politics, with Latinos being involved to a lesser degree. In the area called South Central, a low-income section of the city shared by African Americans, Latinos, and Korean Americans, the African Amerians are the only politically active group. Their views are liberal, and they are mainly Democrats. A wide gap separates African American politics from interests of the Korean Americans. Although the Korean Americans are arguably exploited by larger economic interests, especially in their role as small shop owners, within South Central they are seen by other people as exploitative. One area of conflict, especially between African Americans and Korean Americans, is liquor store ownership. Over the years, many bank branches, large grocery stores, and movie theaters have left South Central. The gap was filled by stores in which the most valuable commodity sold is liquor. In South Central there are far more liquor licenses per square mile than in the rest of Los Angeles County.

Changing Patterns of Consumption among Hong Kong Chinese

Studies of how international migrants change their identity and behavior in the new destination have addressed, among other things, the question of whether consumption patterns change and, if so, how, why, and what effects such changes have on other aspects of culture.

A Canadian study focused on the topic of consumption patterns among Anglo-Canadians, new Hong Kong immigrants, long-time Hong Kong immigrants, and Hong Kong residents (Lee and Tse 1994). Since 1987, Hong Kong has been the single largest source of migrants to Canada. The new immigrant settlement pattern in

Canada is one of urban clustering. The Hong Kong Chinese have developed their own shopping centers, television and radio stations, newspapers, and country clubs. Because of generally high incomes, the Hong Kong immigrants have greatly boosted Canadian buying power.

For most migrants, however, the move brought a lowered economic situation, reflected in their consumption patterns. New immigrants tend to reduce spending on entertainment and expensive commodities. Primary needs of the new immigrants include items that only about half of all households owned: car, VCR, carpets, microwave oven, family house, and multiple TVs. Items in the secondary-needs category were a dining room set, barbecue, deep freezer, and dehumidifier. Long-time immigrants tend to own more secondary products, suggesting that, with time and increased economic standing, expanded consumption of Anglo-Canadian products occurs.

At the same time, businesses in Canada have responded to immigrant tastes by providing Hong Kong style restaurants, Chinese branch banks, and travel agencies. Supermarkets offer specialized Asian sections. Thus some consumption patterns and family ties are maintained. Two characteristics of Hong Kong immigrants distinguish them from other groups discussed in this section: their relatively secure economic status and their high level of education. Still, in Canada, they often have a difficult time finding suitable employment. Some have named Canada "Kan Lan Tai," which means "a difficult place to prosper," a fact that leads many to become "astronauts," or transnational migrants, moving back and forth between Hong Kong and Canada.

The New Immigrants from Southeast Asia

Three Patterns of Adaptation among the Vietnamese

Over one and a quarter million refugees left Vietnam during and after the wartime 1970s. Although most were relocated to the United States, many went to Canada, Australia, France, Germany, and Britain (Gold 1992). Vietnamese immigrants in the United States constitute the country's third largest Asian American group. Three subgroups are the 1970-era elite, the boat people, and the ethnic Chinese. Although they interact frequently, they experienced distinct patterns of adaptation.

The first group avoided many of the traumatic elements of flight. They were U.S. employees and members of the South Vietnamese government and military. They left before having to live under the communist regime, and they spent little time in refugee camps. Most came with intact families and received generous financial assistance. Using their education and English language skills, many found good jobs quickly and adjusted rapidly.

The boat people began to enter the United States after the outbreak of the Vietnam–China conflict of 1978. Mainly of rural origin, they lived for three years or more under communism, working in reeducation camps or "new economic zones." Their exit, either in overcrowded and leaky boats or on foot through Cambodia, was dangerous and difficult. Over 50 percent died on the way. Those who survived faced many months in refugee camps in Thailand, Malaysia, the Philippines, or Hong Kong before being admitted into the United States. Many more males than females escaped as boat people, so they are less likely to have arrived with intact families. They were less well educated than the earlier wave, half had no competence in English, and they faced the depressed American economy of the 1980s. By the time of their arrival, refugee cash assistance had been cut severely and other benefits canceled. They have had a much more difficult time adjusting to life in the United States than the 1975-era elite.

The ethnic Chinese, traditionally a distinct and socially marginalized class of entrepreneurs in Vietnam, arrived mainly as boat people. Following the 1987 outbreak of hostilities between Vietnam and China, the ethnic Chinese were allowed to leave Vietnam. Some used contacts in the overseas Chinese community and were able to reestablish their roles as entrepreneurs, but most had a difficult time in the United States

THINKING OUTSIDE THE BOX Do research to learn what is the current population of Vietnam and its age distribution. Also find the numbers of Vietnamese people living outside Vietnam and, if possible, its age distribution.

because they did not have a Western-style education. They were also sometimes subject to discrimination from other Vietnamese in the United States.

The general picture of Vietnamese adjustment in the United States shows high rates of unemployment, welfare dependency, and poverty, even after several years. Interviews with Vietnamese refugees in southern California reveal generational change and fading traditions among the younger generation. Many Vietnamese teenagers in southern California have adopted the lifestyle of other low-income American teenagers. Their American friends are of more significance than their Vietnamese heritage in defining their identities. Given social variations and regional differences in adaptation throughout the United States, however, generalizations about "Vietnamese Americans" should be made with caution.

Khmer Refugees' Interpretation of Their Suffering

Since the late 1970s, over 150,000 people from Kampuchea (formerly Cambodia) have come to the United States as refugees of the Pol Pot regime (Mortland 1994). They survived years of political repression, a difficult escape, and time in refugee camps before arriving in the United States.

Most Khmer refugees were Buddhist when they lived in Kampuchea. They have attempted to understand, within the Buddhist framework of karma, why they experienced such disasters. According to their beliefs, good actions bring good to the individual, family, and community; bad actions bring bad. Thus many Khmer Buddhists blame themselves for the suffering endured under the Pol Pot regime, thinking that they did something wrong in a previous life. Self-blame and depression characterize many Khmer refugees. Others feel that Buddhism failed, and so they turn in large numbers to Christianity, the dominant faith of the seemingly successful Americans.

Recently, a resurgence of Khmer Buddhism has occurred. Many temples have been constructed, and popular public rituals and celebrations are held in them. For these reviving Buddhists, Christianity either becomes a complementary religion or is rejected as a threat to Buddhism. Changing interpretations of religion occur over time and with new generations. It is difficult to say what the future holds for either the adults who are still trying to make sense of their suffering or for the new generation.

The New Immigrants from South Asia

Hindus of New York City Maintain Their Culture

With the 1965 change in legislation in the United States, a first wave of South Asian immigrants dominated by male professionals from India arrived (Bhardwaj and Rao 1990). Members of this first wave settled primarily in eastern and western cities. Subsequent immigrants from India have been less well educated and less wealthy, and they tend to be concentrated in New York and New Jersey. New York City has the largest population of South Asian Indians, with about one-eighth of the total number of South Asians in the United States (Mogelonsky 1995).

Members of the highly educated first wave are concentrated in professional fields such as medicine, engineering, and management (Helweg and Helweg 1990). One of the major immigrant groups in Silicon Valley, California, is South Asian Indian. Members of the less educated, later wave find work in family-run businesses or service industries. Indians dominate some trades, such as convenience stores. They have bought many budget hotels and motels and operate nearly half the establishments in this niche. More than 40 percent of New York City's licensed cab drivers are Indians, Pakistanis, or Bangladeshis (Mogelonsky 1995).

The South Asian Indian population in the United States is one of the better-off immigrant groups, and they are considered an immigrant success story. They place high value on education and urge their children to pursue careers in fields such as medicine and engineering. In the United States, they tend to have small families and to invest heavily in their children's schooling and social advancement.

THINKING OUTSIDE THE BOX

Most migrants from South Asia to the United States and Canada are Hindus, but many others are Muslims and Sikhs. Are there groups related to the major religions of South Asia on your campus? What kinds of activities and events do they sponsor?

A continuing concern of many members of the first wave, who are Hindus, is the maintenance of Hindu cultural values in the face of conflicting patterns prevalent in mainstream American culture, such as dating, premarital sex, drinking, and drugs. The Hindu population increasingly supports the construction of Hindu temples that offer Sunday school classes for young people and cultural events as a way of passing on the Hindu heritage to the next generation. They also attempt to appeal to the youth by accommodating to their preferences in terms of things like the kind of food served after rituals. Vegetarian pizza is now a common item for the young people at temple events.

Another challenge for Hinduism in the United States and Canada is to establish temples that offer ritual diversity that speaks to Hindus of many varieties. In New York City, the growth of one temple shows how its ritual flexibility helped it to expand (Lessinger 1995). The Ganesha Temple was founded in 1997 under leadership from Hindus from southern India. Temple rituals at first were the same as those conducted in south Indian temples. Over the years, though, in order to widen its reach, the temple expanded its rituals to include those that would appeal to Hindus from other regions of India. The congregation has grown, and the physical structure has expanded to provide for this growth. The daily and yearly cycle became more elaborate and varied than what one would find at a typical Hindu temple in south India. Now, the Ganesha temple is a major pilgrimage destination for Hindus who come to New York City from throughout India.

The New Immigrants from the Former Soviet Union

The breakup of the Soviet Union into fifteen separate countries spurred the movement of over 9 million people throughout Eastern Europe and Central Asia. Many are of Slavic descent, lived in Central Asia during the existence of the Soviet Union, and wanted to return to their homelands. Another large category includes people who were forcibly relocated to Siberia or Central Asia. Since 1988, people from the former Soviet Union have been the largest refugee nationality to enter the United States (Littman 1993, cited in Gold 1995).

Soviet Jews Flee Persecution

Many of the refugees from the former Soviet Union are Soviet Jews. The largest number of former Soviet Jews live in Israel, but since the mid-1960s, over 300,000 have

In January 2004, more than 50,000 Russian immigrants to Israel returned to Russia. Motivations for the move back include the difficult living conditions for many Russian immigrants in Israel, violence, and the improving economic situation in Russia. Nonetheless, people from Russia continue to migrate to Israel, and they now number over a million people, about 13 percent of the population. ■ How many people left Russia after the breakup of the Soviet Union in 1989 and where did they go? (Source: © David H. Wells/CORBIS)

settled in the United States, especially in California (Gold 1995). There are several distinguishing features of the experience of Soviet Jewish refugees. First, their origins in the Soviet Union accustomed them to the fact that the government controlled almost every aspect of life. They were used to a wide range of government services, including jobs, housing, day care, and other basic needs. They have had to find new ways of meeting these needs in a market economy. Second, as White Europeans, Soviet Jews are members of the dominant majority group in the United States. Although Soviet Jews suffered centuries of discrimination in Eastern Europe, they are much closer to the mainstream in the United States. Their education also places them in the elite of new immigrant groups. Third, they have access to established and prosperous communities of American Jews. They have well-connected sponsors when they arrive. Most other new immigrant groups do not have these advantages.

Soviet Jewish immigrants, however, face several challenges. Many have a difficult time finding a job commensurate with their education and previous work in the Soviet Union. In Pittsburgh, Pennsylvania, many Soviet Jewish immigrants are unemployed or accept menial labor far beneath their qualifications. This is especially true for women who were employed as professionals in the Soviet Union but who can find no work in the United States other than house cleaning or baby sitting. Another major challenge involves marriage options. Cultural norms promote intraethnic marriage, and few Soviet Jews are interested in marrying Americans. But, the number of Soviet Jews in the marriage pool is small. As a result, marriage brokerage businesses have developed that match women in Russia with Russian men in America.

MIGRATION POLICIES AND POLITICS IN A GLOBALIZING WORLD

Globalization and the associated increase in migration are a research focus of many anthropologists and other social scientists. Major research questions concern national and international policies of inclusion and exclusion of particular categories of people. The human rights of various categories of migrants vary dramatically. Migrants of all sorts, including long-standing migratory groups such as pastoralists and horticulturalists, seek to find ways to protect their lifestyles, maintain their health, and build a future.

The health risks to migrants are many and varied because of the wide variety of migrant types and situations. Migrants whose livelihood depends on long-standing migratory economic systems, such as foraging, horticulture, and pastoralism, constitute one area of concern. Given the frequency in recent decades of drought and food shortages in the Sahel region of Africa, anthropologists are conducting studies to see how such conditions can be prevented, monitored, and more effectively coped with through humanitarian aid (see the Lessons Applied box on p. 600).

Inclusion and Exclusion

National policies that set quotas on the number and types of immigrants who are welcome and that determine how they are treated are largely dictated by political and economic interests. Even in the cases of seemingly humanitarian quotas, governments undertake a cost–benefit analysis of how much will be gained and how much will be lost. Governments show their political support or disapproval of other governments through their immigration policies. One of the most obvious economic factors affecting policy is labor flow. Cheap—even illegal—immigrant labor is used around the world to maintain profits for businesses and services for the better-off. Flows of such labor undermine labor unions and the job security of established workers in the host country.

Studying Pastoralists' Movements for Risk Assessment and Service Delivery

PASTORALISTS ARE OFTEN vulnerable to malnutrition as a consequence of climate changes, fluctuations in food supply, and war and political upheaval. Because of their spatial mobility, they are difficult to reach with relief aid during a crisis. Cultural anthropologists are devising ways to gather and manage basic information about pastoralists' movements and nutritional needs in order to provide improved service delivery (Watkins and Fleisher 2002). The data required for such proactive planning include the following:

1. Information on the number of migrants and the size of their herds in a particular location and at a particular time. Such data can inform planners about the level of services required for public health programs, educational programs, and veterinary services. This information can be used to assess the demand on particular grazing areas and water sources and is therefore important in predicting possible future crises.

2. Information on patterns of migratory movements. This information can enable planners to move services to where the people are rather than expecting people to move to the services. Some non-governmental organizations, for example, are providing mobile banking services and mobile veterinary services. Information about pastoralist movements can be used as an early warning to prevent social conflicts that might result if several groups arrived in the same place at the same time. And conflict resolution mechanisms can be put in place more effectively if conflict does occur. The data collection involves interviews with pastoralists, often with one or two key informants, whom the anthropologists select for their specialized knowledge. Interviews cover topics such as the migratory paths followed (both typical and atypical), population levels, herd sizes, and the nutritional and water requirements of people and animals. Given the complex social systems of pastoralists, the data gathering must also include group leadership, decision-making practices, and concepts about land and water rights.

The anthropologists organize this information into a computerized database, linking the ethnographic data with geographic information systems (GIS) data on the environment and climate information from satellites. The anthropologists can then construct various scenarios and assess the relative risks that they pose to the people's health. Impending crises can be foreseen, and warning can be provided to governments and international aid agencies.

FOOD FOR THOUGHT

- The tracking system described here remains outside the control of the pastoralists themselves. How might it be managed so that they participate more meaningfully and gain greater autonomy?

In the United States, immigration law specifies who will be allowed entry and what benefits the government will provide. A court case from 1915 presents issues that still prevail today (*Gegiow v. Uhl*, 1915). The case concerned a group of Russian laborers seeking to enter the United States. All had very little money, and only one member of the group spoke some English. They wanted to settle in Portland, Oregon. The acting commissioner of immigration in the port of New York denied them entry on the grounds that they were "likely to become public charges" because employment conditions in Portland were such that they probably would be unable to obtain work. The group obtained legal counsel. The case eventually went to the Supreme Court, where the decision was handed down by Chief Justice Oliver Wendell Holmes. He focused on "whether an alien can be declared likely to become a public charge on the ground that the labor market in the city of his immediate . . . destination is overstocked." The relevant statute, Holmes declared, deals with admission to the United States, not to a particular city within it. Further, Holmes commented that a commissioner of immigration is not empowered to make decisions about possible overstocking of labor in all of the United States, for that is a matter in the hands of the president.

National immigration policies are played out in local communities. In some instances, local resentments are associated with a so-called **lifeboat mentality,** which seeks to limit enlarging a particular group because of perceived resource constraints. Influxes of immigrants who compete for jobs have led to hostility in many parts of Europe and North America. Some observers have labeled this attitude *working-class racism* because it emerges out of competition with immigrants for jobs and other benefits.

Ethnographic research in southern Italy investigated the possibility of working class racism there, given the fact that the number of immigrants has grown substantially in there since the early 1980s (Cole 1996). In the city of Palermo, with a total population of 800,000, there are between 15,000 and 30,000 immigrants from Africa, Asia, and elsewhere. Does the theory of working-class racism apply to the working class in Palermo?

Two conditions seem to predict that it would: large numbers of foreign immigrants and a high rate of unemployment. However, instead of expressing racist condemnation of the immigrants, working-class residents of Palermo accept the immigrants as fellow poor people. One critical factor may be the lack of competition for jobs, which derives from the fact that working Palmeritans and immigrants occupy different niches. Immigrant jobs are less desirable, more stigmatized, and less well-paying. African immigrant men work in bars and restaurants, as janitors, or as itinerant street vendors. African and Asian women work as domestic servants in better-off neighborhoods.

Sicilians refer to immigrants by certain racial/ethnic names, but they are used interchangeably and imprecisely. For example, a common term for all immigrants, Asian or African, is *tuichi,* which means *Turks.* The word can be applied teasingly to a Sicilian as well. In a questionnaire given to school children, a great majority agreed with the statement "a person's race is not important." The tolerance among Palermo's working class may be only temporary. Nonetheless, it suggests that the model of working-class racism against immigrants may not be universally valid.

Recent politically conservative trends in the United States have succeeded in reversing earlier, more progressive policies about immigration and minorities. Reversals of affirmative action in college admissions, initiated in California in the late 1990s, gained widespread support among "nativist" Americans. Starting at the turn of the millennium, police raids in areas thought to have many undocumented migrants have brought mass expulsion. This lifeboat mentality of exclusiveness and privilege was held mainly by the dominant White majority but has recently spread to other groups since the late twentieth century.

Migration and Human Rights

Several questions arise in the context of anthropological inquiry about migration and human rights. One important question is whether migration is forced or voluntary (see the Critical Thinking box on p. 602). Many anthropologists consider forced migration to be a violation of a person's human rights.

Another question concerns whether members of a displaced group have a guaranteed **right of return,** or repatriation, to their homeland. The right of return, which has been considered a basic human right in the West since the time of the Magna Carta, is included in the United Nations General Assembly Resolution 194 passed in 1948. It was elevated by the UN in 1974 to an "inalienable right."

The right of return is an enduring issue for Palestinian refugees, of whom hundreds of thousands fled or were driven from their homes during the 1948 war (Zureik 1994). They went mainly to Jordan, the West Bank/East Jerusalem, Gaza, Lebanon, Syria, and other Arab states. Jordan and Syria have granted Palestinian refugees rights equal to those of their citizens. In Lebanon, where estimates of the number of Palestinian refugees range between 200,000 and 600,000, the government refuses them

Haitian Cane Cutters in the Dominican Republic—A Case of Structure or Human Agency?

THE CIRCULATION of male labor from villages in Haiti to work on sugar estates in the neighboring Dominican Republic is the oldest and perhaps largest continuing population movement within the Caribbean region (Martínez 1996). Beginning in the early twentieth century, Dominican sugar cane growers began to recruit Haitian workers called *braceros*. Between 1952 and 1986, an agreement between the two countries' governments regulated and organized the labor recruitment. Since then, recruitment has become a private matter, with men crossing the border on their own or recruiters working in Haiti without official approval.

Many studies and reports have addressed this system of labor migration. Two competing perspectives exist. The exploitation position (View 1) says that the bracero system is neo-slavery and a clear violation of human rights. The human agency position (View 2) says that braceros are not slaves because they migrate voluntarily.

VIEW 1

Supporters of this position point to interviews with Haitian braceros in the Dominican Republic that indicate, they say, a consistent pattern of labor rights abuses. Haitian recruiters approach poor men, and boys as young as seven years old, and promise them easy, well-paid employment in the Dominican Republic. Those who agree to go are taken to the frontier on foot and then either transported directly to a sugar estate in the Dominican Republic or turned over to Dominican soldiers for a fee for each recruit and then passed on to the sugar estate. Once there, the workers are given only one option for survival: cutting sugar cane, for which even the most experienced workers can earn only about US$2 a day. Working and living conditions on the estates are bad. The cane cutters are coerced into working even if they are ill, and work starts before dawn and extends into the night. Many estate owners prevent Haitian laborers from leaving by having armed guards patrol the estate grounds. Many of the workers say that they cannot save enough from their meager wages to return home.

VIEW 2

According to this view, reports of coercion are greatly exaggerated and miss the point that most Haitian labor migrants cross the border of their own volition. On the basis of his fieldwork in Haiti, anthropologist Samuel Martínez comments that "Recruitment by force in Haiti seems virtually unheard of. On the contrary, if this is a system of slavery, it may be the first in history to turn away potential recruits" (20). Some recruits have even paid bribes to recruiters in order to be hired. Most

such rights (Salam 1994). The lower number is favored by Israel because it makes the problem seem less severe; the higher number is favored by the Palestinians to highlight the seriousness of their plight and by the Lebanese government to emphasize its inability to absorb so many.

Palestinians know that they are not welcome in Lebanon, but they cannot return to Israel because Israel denies them the right of return. Israel responds to the Palestinians' claims by saying that their acceptance of Jewish immigrants from Arab countries constitutes an equal exchange.

Migration is a longstanding and enduring characteristic of humanity. Our earliest human ancestors probably had extensive home ranges, offering them a variety of environments in which to find resources such as food, water, and shelter. Normally, they would have moved from one known location to another known location, unless disturbed by some outside force.

Only in the past several thousand years, as described in Chapter 9, did modern humans adopt a sedentary way of life. In our time, with globalization and increased international migration, millions of people, either voluntarily or involuntarily, have experienced a move into an unfamiliar environment and culture where they face adaptational challenges and opportunities.

people, even young people, are aware of the terrible working conditions in the Dominican Republic, so they are exercising informed choice when they decide to migrate. Repeat migration is common and is further evidence of free choice. The major means of maintaining labor discipline and productivity on the sugar estates is not force but wage incentives, especially piece-work. The life histories of braceros show that many of them move from one estate to another; this discredits the view that the estates are "concentration camps."

However, Martínez raises the question of how free the "choice" to migrate to the Dominican Republic really is, given the extreme poverty in which many Haitians live. In Haiti few work opportunities exist, and the average wage for rural workers is US$1 a day. Thus the poor are not truly free to choose to work in their home country: labor migration to the Dominican Republic becomes a necessity. What looks like a free choice to participate in the bracero system is actually "illusory," or structured, choice. It is based on the unavailability of the option to work for a decent wage in Haiti and on the forced, or structured, choice to work in the Dominican Republic.

CRITICAL THINKING QUESTIONS

- What are the comparative strengths of View 1 and View 2?
- What does each perspective support in terms of policy recommendations?
- How does the concept of structured choice change those policy recommendations?

A Haitian migrant laborer. It is a matter of debate how much choice such a laborer has in terms of whether he will migrate to the neighboring Dominican Republic for short-term work, cutting cane, given the fact that he cannot find paid work in Haiti. (Source: Edward Keller III)

THE BIG QUESTIONS REVISITED

- ## WHAT are the major categories of migration?

Migration is classified as internal, international, or transnational. Another type of categorization is based on the migrants' reason for moving: migrants are classified as labor migrants, institutional migrants, or displaced persons. People's adjustment to their new situations depends on the degree of voluntarism involved in the move, the degree of cultural difference between the place of origin and the destination, and how closely expectations about the new location are met, especially in terms of making a living and establishing social ties. Forcibly displaced persons are one of the fastest-growing categories of migrants. Refugees, fleeing from political persecution or warfare, face serious adjustment challenges because they often leave their home countries with few material resources and frequently have experienced psychological suffering. The number of internally displaced persons is growing faster than the number of refugees.

Dams and other large-scale development projects result in thousands of people becoming IDPs. Internally displaced persons do not fall under the purview of international organizations such as the United Nations, but their situation is attracting the attention of a global consortium of governments and nongovernmental organizations.

▪ WHAT are examples of the new immigrants in North America?

Worldwide, the "new immigrants" are contributing to growing transnational connections and to the formation of increasingly multicultural populations within countries. In the United States, the new immigrants from Latin America are the fastest-growing category. Immigrants from East and South Asia, who are more likely than others to have immigrated to the United States voluntarily, have achieved greater levels of economic success than most other new immigrant groups. Immigrant groups throughout the world are likely to face discrimination in their new destinations, although the degree to which discrimination occurs varies with the level of perceived resource competition from residents.

▪ HOW do cultural anthropologists contribute to migration policies and programs?

Cultural anthropologists have studied national and international migration policies and practices in terms of social inclusion and exclusion. Fieldwork in particular contexts reveals a range of patterns between local residents and immigrants. Working-class resentment among local people against immigrants is not universal and varies with the overall amount and type of employment available. Cultural anthropologists study possible infringements of the human rights of migrants, especially in terms of the degree of voluntarism in their move and the conditions they face in their destination country.

KEY CONCEPTS

anthropometrics, p. 584
chain migration, p. 592
circular migration, p. 586
development-induced displacement (DID), p. 589
displaced person, p. 586

institutional migrant, p. 589
internal migration, p. 582
internally displaced person (IDP), p. 588
lifeboat mentality, p. 601
new immigrant, p. 591
push–pull theory, p. 583

refugee, p. 588
remittance, p. 586
right of return, p. 601
transnational migrant, p. 583

SUGGESTED READINGS

Rogaia Mustafa Abusharaf. *Wanderings: Sudanese Migrants and Exiles in North America*. Ithaca, NY: Cornell University Press, 2002. This book explores the topic of Sudanese migration to the United States and Canada. The author provides historical background on the first wave, information on various Sudanese groups who have migrated, and an interpretation of Sudanese identity in North America as more unified than it is in the homeland.

Linda Basch, Nina Glick Schiller, and Christina Szanton Blanc. *Nations Unbound: Transnational Projects, Postcolonial Predicaments, and Deterritorialized Nation–States*. Langhorne, PA: Gordon and Breach Science Publishers, 1994. Eight chapters explore theoretical issues in transnational migration and present cases of migration from the Caribbean, including St. Vincent, Grenada, and Haiti.

Colin Clarke, Ceri Peach, and Steven Vertovic, eds. *South Asians Overseas: Migration and Ethnicity*. New York: Cambridge University Press, 1990. Fifteen chapters include introductory essays and several case studies. The book is divided into two sections: South Asian migrants in colonial and post-colonial contexts and South Asian migrants in contemporary Western countries and the Middle East.

Sherri Grasmuck and Patricia R. Pessar. *Between Two Islands: Dominican International Migration*. Berkeley: University of California Press, 1991. Based on fieldwork in the Dominican Republic and New York City, this volume focuses on social ties and networks facilitating migration from rural areas in the Dominican Republic to Santo Domingo and from the Dominican Republic to the United States, and on how employment opportunities shape the migration experience.

Josiah McC. Heyman. *Finding a Moral Heart for U.S. Immigration Policy: An Anthropological Perspective*. Washington, DC: American Ethnological Society, Monograph Series, Number 7, 1998. An applied anthropology perspective inspires this critique of current U.S. immigration policy, finding it to be basically anti-immigrationist. The author suggests steps toward a more inclusive policy and discusses unresolved challenges and dilemmas.

Helen Morton Lee. *Tongans Overseas: Between Two Shores.* Honolulu: University of Hawai'i Press, 2003. The author, who has done fieldwork in Tonga, turns her attention to young Tongan migrants in Australia. She combines fieldwork in Melbourne with extensive research of the messages on a Tongan Internet forum called Kava Bowl, complemented with e-mail interviews of people who participate in the forum. The book focuses on the changing and varied aspects of young Tongan migrants' identity, ties to family in Tonga, and changing aspirations.

Beatriz Manz, *Refugees of a Hidden War: The Aftermath of Counterinsurgency in Guatemala.* Albany: State University of New York Press, 1988. This study was conducted to assess whether conditions would allow the return to Guatemala of 46,000 Maya refugees living in camps in Mexico. It focuses on aspects of family and community life in the camps and in resettled villages in Guatemala where the Maya face discrimination and harassment from the military.

Jennifer Robertson. *Native and Newcomer: Making and Remaking a Japanese City.* Berkeley: University of California Press, 1991. This ethnography addresses the social and symbolic adjustments of native residents of Kodaira city and the many residents who moved to Kodaira beginning in the 1950s. Close attention is given to the role of a community festival in expressing links between natives and newcomers, while also stating and maintaining group boundaries.

Archana B. Verma. *The Making of Little Punjab in Canada: Patterns of Immigration.* Thousand Oaks, CA; Sage Publications, 2002. This book traces the historical connections between Hindu migrants from Paldi village, in India's northern state of Punjab, to Vancouver Island, British Columbia. Strong family and kinship ties continue to link the migrants to their home area. Caste group solidarity among the migrants provides support in the face of discrimination on the part of the wider Canadian society.

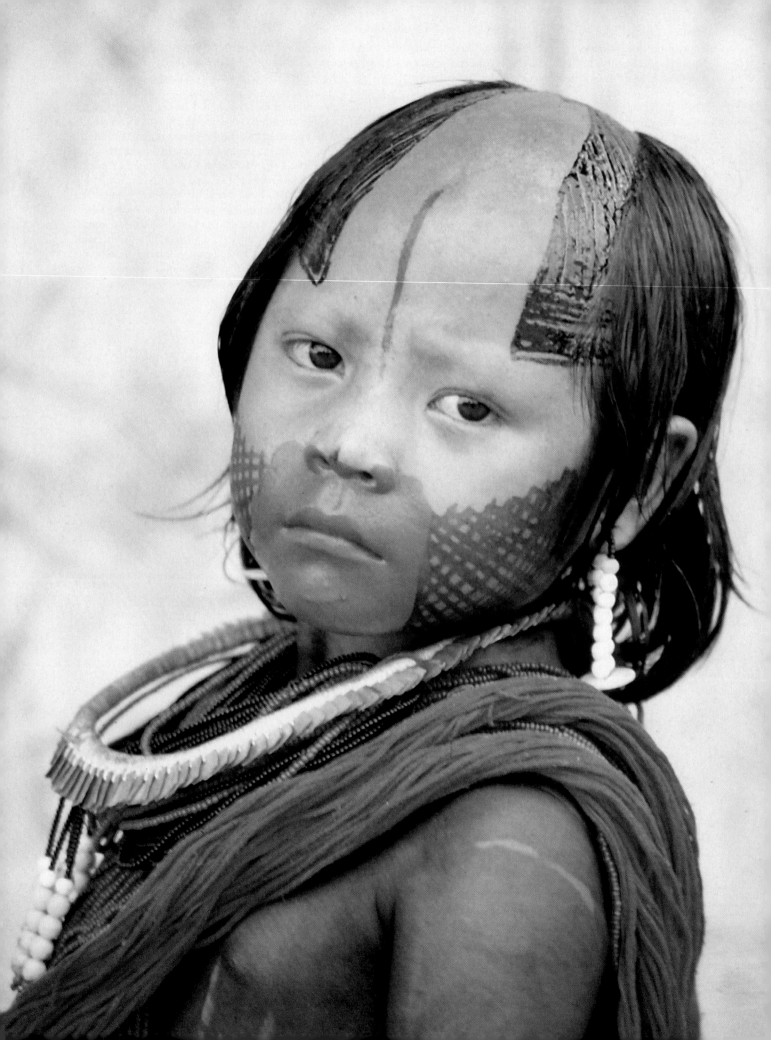

THE BIG QUESTIONS

- HOW do cultural anthropologists study change?
- WHAT are various approaches to development?
- WHAT does cultural anthropology contribute to understanding some major issues in development?

CHAPTER **21**

Development Anthropology

A Kayapo child living in Gorotire, Brazil. The Kayapo are one of many Amazonian indigenous peoples that are selectively adopting some features of Western culture and simultaneously asserting their rights to protect their land and cultural heritage. (Source © HERBERT GIRADET/Peter Arnold, Inc.)

607

We have had many visitors to Walpole Island since the French "discovered us" in the seventeenth century in our territory, Bkejwanong. In many cases, these visitors failed to recognize who we were and to appreciate our traditions. They tried to place us in their European framework of knowledge, denying that we possessed our indigenous knowledge. They attempted to steal our lands, water, and knowledge. We resisted. They left and never came back. (Dr. Dean Jacobs, Executive Director of Walpole Island First Nation, from his Foreword in VanWynsberghe 2002:ix)

The Walpole Island First Nation, located in Ontario, Canada, north of Michigan, has taken strong action in recent decades to protect its culture and environment. Its citizens have organized themselves and successfully fought to control industrial waste that was polluting its water and land. They have regained their pride and integrity.

All cultures go through change, but the causes, processes, and outcomes are varied. Cultural change can be intentional or accidental, forward-looking or backward-looking, rapid or gradual, obvious or subtle, beneficial or harmful.

Anthropologists in all four fields contribute to the understanding of how humanity has changed in the past and how it continues to change. Biological anthropologists who study human evolution and humanity's relationship to nonhuman primates take the longest view. They look back many thousands—even millions—of years to learn how human biology evolved. Archaeologists examine human cultural remains, from both prehistory and history, to learn about where and when culture and, later, social complexity developed. Linguistic anthropologists study the evolution of communication patterns and capabilities in prehistoric times, the spread and change in verbal and written languages with the emergence of settled life and of the state, and change in contemporary patterns of communication, including the effects of mass media.

In contrast to these three fields of anthropology, cultural anthropology's roots lie in the **synchronic** study of culture, or a "one-time" snapshot view of culture with minimal or no attention to the past. This early approach led to a static view of culture, perpetuating images of cultures presented in the 1960s or 1970s as if they were "timeless." Cultural anthropologists are now moving away from such time-static approaches. They are paying attention to studying cultures through time, replacing the synchronic approach with a **diachronic** (across-time) approach.

This chapter focuses on the topic of contemporary cultural change as shaped by *development,* which is directed change to achieve improved human welfare. The subject matter constitutes the subfield of **development anthropology,** or the study of how culture and development interact. The first part of the chapter discusses general processes of cultural change. Contemporary theories and models are the focus of the second part. The last section looks at three major issues in development anthropology: indigenous people, women, and human rights.

TWO PROCESSES OF CULTURAL CHANGE

Two basic processes drive all cultural change. The first is internal: the discovery of something new. The second is external: incorporation of something new from the outside. In this section, we consider some examples of cultural change brought about by each of these general processes.

Social Effects of the Green Revolution

AGRICULTURAL SCIENTISTS of the 1950s, inspired by the laudable goal of eliminating world hunger, developed genetic variations of wheat, rice, and corn. These high-yielding varieties (HYV) of seeds were promoted to farmers throughout the developing world as part of the "Green Revolution" that would feed the planet by boosting production per acre. In most places where Green Revolution agricultural practices were adopted, grain production did increase. Was world hunger conquered? The answer is no, because world hunger is not merely a problem of production; it involves distribution as well.

Analyses of the social impact of the Green Revolution in India reveal that one of its results was to increase disparities between the rich and the poor (Frankel 1971). How did this happen? Green Revolution agriculture requires several expensive inputs: purchased seeds (HYV seeds cannot be harvested from the crop and saved until the next year because they are hybridized), the heavy use of commercial fertilizers, and dependable irrigation sources. Thus farmers who could use HYV seeds successfully tended to be those who were already better off than others; they were selected for the innovation because they could afford such inputs. Small farmers who tried planting HYV seeds but could not provide these inputs experienced crop failure, went deeper into debt, and ended up having to sell the small amounts of land they had. Larger and better-off farmers took advantage of these new openings in the land market to accumulate more land and expand their holdings. With the acquisition of tractors and other mechanized equipment, large farmers became even more productive. Small farmers were unable to compete and continued to be squeezed out financially. They became hired day laborers, dependent on seasonal employment by large farmers, or they migrated to cities where they became part of the urban underclass.

Looking at the Green Revolution from a critical thinking perspective, we may see more clearly whose interests were served, whether this was the original intention or not. The big winners included the companies involved in selling chemical fertilizers (largely petroleum-based) and HYV seeds; companies that manufactured and sold mechanized farm equipment; the larger farmers whose income levels improved; and the research scientists themselves, who gained funding for their research and world fame for their discoveries. In retrospect, it is difficult to imagine that early planners in the 1950s could have been so naive as not to realize whom they would be helping and whom they might end up hurting.

CRITICAL THINKING QUESTIONS

- Is it likely that the original innovators of HYV grains considered what social transformations might occur in developing countries' agriculture as a result of their invention?
- Would they have been likely to halt their research if they had realized that it would lead to the "rich getting richer and the poor getting poorer"? Should they have done so?
- How does this example shed light on current debates about genetically modified food?

Invention

The invention of something new may prompt cultural change. Inventions usually evolve gradually, through stepwise experimentation and accumulation of knowledge, but some appear suddenly. We can all name many technological inventions that have created cultural change—for example, the printing press, gun powder, polio vaccine, and satellite communication. Concepts, such as Jeffersonian notions of democracy, are also inventions.

Not all inventions have positive social outcomes. Even innovations inspired by a socially positive goal may turn out to have mixed or even negative social effects (see the Critical Thinking box).

Be prepared to discuss in class two inventions made in your lifetime and how they affect your everyday activities, social interactions, or ways of thinking.

THINKING

OUTSIDE THE BOX

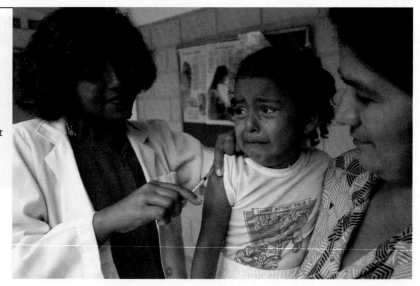

A doctor administering polio vaccine in Ecuador. The Pan American Health Organization (PAHO) established a plan in 1985 for eradicating the poliovirus from the Americas by 1990. ∎ Did the PAHO achieve its goal? If yes, when? If no, what is the current status of its effort? (Source: © Jeremy Horner/CORBIS)

Diffusion

Diffusion is the spread of culture—including technology and ways of behaving and thinking—through contact. It is logically related to invention because new discoveries are likely to spread. Diffusion can occur in several ways. First, in mutual borrowing, two societies that are roughly equal in power and level of development exchange aspects of their culture. For example, in the mid-twentieth century, the United States exported rock and roll music to England, and England in turn exported the Beatles to the United States. Second, diffusion may occur between unequal societies, involving a transfer from a dominant culture to a less powerful culture. This may occur through force or, more subtly, through education or marketing processes that promote adoption of new practices and beliefs. For example, through the Peace Corps, the United States spreads many American practices and beliefs to developing countries. Third, a more powerful culture may appropriate aspects of a less powerful culture (the latter process is called cultural imperialism). For example, the Tower of London in England is full of priceless jewels from India.

In each of these types of diffusion, the result is some degree of *acculturation,* or change in one culture as a result of contact with another culture. At one extreme, a culture may become so thoroughly acculturated that it is **assimilated,** no longer distinguishable as having a separate identity. In many cases, cultural change through diffusion has led to extreme change in the "receiving" culture, which becomes "deculturated," or extinct. Such deculturation has occurred among many indigenous peoples as the result of the introduction of new technology (see the Lessons Applied box). Other responses to acculturative influences include partial acceptance of something new with reformulation and reshaping, as in the case of cricket in the Trobriand Islands (Chapter 19, pp. 571–572), or resistance and rejection. The study of international development is concerned with the dynamics and results of a particular form of diffusion—that of Western goods, behavior, and values through international aid.

Services for photocopying and sending faxes, invented in the West, have been diffused to most parts of the world, including the formerly remote capital of India's Andaman Islands, Port Blair. A popular restaurant in Port Blair evidences diffusion of cuisine: South Indian, Chinese, and Continental. ∎ In your microcultural world, what examples of diffusion can you name? (Source: Barbara Miller)

The Saami, Snowmobiles, and the Need for Social Impact Analysis

HOW WILL ADOPTION of a new belief or practice benefit or harm a particular culture and its various members? This question is difficult to answer, but it must always be asked. A classic study of the "snowmobile disaster" among a Saami group in Finland offers a careful response to this question in a context of rapid technological diffusion (Pelto 1973). In the 1950s, the Saami of Finland (previously referred to by outsiders as Lapps, which, in the Saami language, is a derogatory term) had an economy based on fishing and reindeer herding, which provided most of their diet. Reindeer had several other important economic and social functions. They were used as draft animals, especially in the hauling of wood for fuel. Their hides were made into clothing and their sinews used for sewing. Reindeer were key items of exchange, both in external trade and internal gift-giving. A child was given a reindeer to mark the appearance of its first tooth. When a couple became engaged, they exchanged a reindeer with each other to mark the commitment. Reindeer were the most important wedding gift. Each summer the herds were let free, and then they were rounded up in the fall, a time of communal festivity.

By the 1960s, all this had changed because of the introduction of the snowmobile. Previously, the men had tended the reindeer herds on skis. The introduction of snowmobiles into herd management had several results. The herds were no longer kept closely domesticated for part of the year, during which they became tame. Instead, they were allowed to roam freely all year and thus became wilder. On snowmobiles, the men would cover larger amounts of territory at round-up time to bring in the animals, and sometimes several round-ups occurred instead of one.

Herd size declined dramatically. The reasons for the decline included the stress inflicted on the reindeer by the extra distance traveled during round-ups, the multiple round-ups replacing a single one, and the fear aroused by the noisy snowmobiles. Round-ups were held at a time when the females were near the end of their pregnancy, another factor that induced reproductive stress. As the number of snowmobiles increased, the number of reindeer decreased.

Another economic change involved dependence on the outside through links to the cash economy. Cash was needed to purchase a snowmobile, to buy gasoline, and to pay for parts and repairs. This delocalization of the economy led to social inequality, which had not existed before:

- The cash cost of effective participation in herding exceeded the resources of some families, who therefore had to drop out of serious participation in herding.
- The use of snowmobiles changed the age pattern of reindeer herding in favor of youth over age; thus older herders were squeezed out.
- The snowmobile pushed many Saami into debt.
- The dependence on cash and indebtedness forced many Saami to migrate to cities for work.

Pertti Pelto, the cultural anthropologist who documented this case, terms these transformations a disaster for Saami culture. He offers some recommendations that might be helpful for the future: The lesson of the Saami, and of some other groups, should be presented to communities that are confronting development issues before they adopt new technology so that they will better understand the potential consequences. Any group facing change should have a chance to weigh evidence on the pros and cons and make an informed judgment—something that the Saami had no opportunity to do. Pelto's work is thus one of the early warnings from anthropology about the need for **social impact assessments,** studies that gauge the potential social costs and benefits of particular innovations before the change is undertaken.

The Saami are an indigenous Nordic people currently living in Norway and Finland. Since the 1980s they have been fighting for legal rights in the countries where they live and, more broadly, in the Nordic Council, a regional association in which they have no representation. Saami activists are working on many issues, including land rights, water rights, natural resource rights, language rights, other cultural rights, and political representation. (Source: © Staffan Widstrand/ CORBIS)

FOOD FOR THOUGHT

- Speculate about what the Saami might have done if they had been able to consider, in advance, a social impact assessment of the effects of snowmobiles on their culture.

APPROACHES TO DEVELOPMENT

This section first considers several theories of and approaches to international development used by various institutions, from large-scale to small grassroots organizations. The next topic is the development project as the main mechanism that such organizations use to bring about change. Special research methods employed by applied cultural anthropologists working in international development are the last topic in this section.

Theories and Models

Five theories or models of change influence approaches to international development. They differ mainly in terms of the importance they attach to economic growth versus equitable distribution of resources, in which measures of development they assume are most meaningful (for example, income versus health or education), and in the degree to which they take into account the environmental and financial sustainability of particular development goals.

Modernization

Modernization theory focuses on change marked by industrialization, consolidation of the nation–state, bureaucratization, market economy, technological innovation, literacy, and options for social mobility. It derives from a period in Western European history, beginning in the seventeenth century, which emphasized the importance of secular, scientific thinking (Norgaard 1994). Modernization is thought to be an almost inevitable process that will, given the insights of science, spread throughout the world and lead to improvement in people's lives everywhere. The overall emphasis of modernization is on material progress and individual betterment.

Supporters and critics of modernization are found in both rich and poor countries. Supporters claim that the benefits of modernization (improved transportation; electricity; domestic comforts such as air conditioning; and technology such as washing machines, biomedical health care, and telecommunications) are worth the costs—whether those costs are calculated in terms of environmental or social costs. Other scholars regard modernization as problematic. Most cultural anthropologists are critics of modernization as a general process of social change because it leads to increased social inequality, the destruction of indigenous cultures, environmental degradation, and an overall decline in global cultural diversity. (Selected aspects of modernity, however, such as electricity and antibiotics, may be accepted as positive.) In spite of strong cautionary critiques from anthropologists and environmentalists about the negative effects of modernization, few countries have slowed their attempts to achieve it.

Growth-Oriented Development

International development emerged as a prominent theory of change after World War II, at the same time that the United States began to expand its role as a world leader. One can think of **development** as the attempt, through conscious planning and intervention, to bring the benefits of modernization to the developing world. Indeed, international development, as construed by major development institutions such as the World Bank, is similar to modernization in its ultimate goals. The process, however, emphasizes economic growth as the most crucial element in development. According to this theory, investments in economic growth in some sectors of the population will subsequently support (through the "trickle-down" effect) wider achievement of improved human welfare, such as health and education.

Since the 1950s, the United States has emphasized economic development in its foreign aid packages, especially the transfer of Western economic expertise (in the form of advisors) and technology (such as agricultural equipment) to developing countries.

THINKING OUTSIDE THE BOX

Formulate your own definition of modernization and sketch out its pros and cons for different cultures that you have learned about in this book.

Promoting growth-oriented development in poor nations, as practiced by most large-scale development organizations, includes two major economic strategies:

- Increasing economic productivity and trade through, for example, new forms of agriculture, irrigation, and markets.

- Reducing government expenditures on public services such as schools and health in order to reduce debt and reallocate resources to uses perceived to be more directly related to increased production. This strategy, called **structural adjustment,** has been promoted by the World Bank since the 1980s.

The growth-oriented development model is being spread throughout the world through economic and political globalization. As noted in Chapter 2, cultural anthropologists are now studying the effects of intensified globalization on local cultures—and the effects of those cultures on efforts at globalization.

Distributional Development

In contrast to the growth-oriented approach, a distributional approach to development views poverty as the result of global economic and political factors such as world trade imbalances between nations and unequal distribution of resources within nations and communities. This approach, which takes a structurist view, rejects the claim of other approaches that poverty is caused by some inadequacy on the part of poor people or poor countries themselves (Rahnema 1992). In terms of poverty reduction, its position is based on evidence that growth-oriented strategies applied without concern for distribution *increase* social inequality, with the "rich getting richer and the poor getting poorer."

The distributional approach is critical of structural adjustment because it further undermines the welfare of the poor by removing the few entitlements they had in the form of services. Advocates of the distributional model insist on the need to readjust access to crucial resources within countries in order to enhance the ability of the poor to produce and to provide for their own needs. Within a particular country, this perspective involves the following strategies, which differ markedly from the growth approach (Gardner and Lewis 1996). The first step—called *resource assessment*—is to do research on the social distribution of access to critical resources (see Figure 21.1). The next step, called *cultural assessment,* involves research on the positive or negative effects of development projects on the culture, with special attention to inter-

FIGURE 21.1
Key questions in assessing resources.

What are the most important resources available in the society?
How is access to these resources organized?

- Are key resources shared in the community, or do some people or groups have greater access than others?
- Are there obvious economic differences within the community? If so, what are they?
- Are key resources shared within the household, or do some members have greater access than others?

What is the distribution of decision-making power?

- Are some people or groups denied a voice?
- Do some people or groups have particular interests? If so, what are they?

Are these factors taken into consideration in the development policy or project?

(*Source:* "Key Questions in Assessing Resources," p. 86, from *Anthropology, Development and the Post-Modern Challenge* by Katy Gardner and David Lewis. Copyright © 1996. Reprinted by permission of Pluto Press.)

FIGURE 21.2
Key questions in assessing the cultural effects of a resettlement project.

How are local property relations organized in the original location?
- What access do different groups have to property or other key resources?
- What goods are highly valued?
- What are the inheritance patterns?

How is work organized?
- What are the main tasks done and during what seasons?
- What is the division of labor by gender and age?
- What is the role of kinship in allocating labor?

How is the household organized?
- Who lives where and with whom?
- How is decision making allocated within the household?
- Are there notable differences in household organization within the community? If so, what are they and how do they change over time?

What is the local political structure?
- Do some people or groups monopolize power?
- Are some groups marginalized?

How suitable is the proposed relocation site and plan, given the above economic, social, and political findings?

(*Source:* "Key Questions in Assessing Cultural Effects of a Resettlement Project," p. 86, from *Anthropology, Development and the Post-Modern Challenge* by Katy Gardner and David Lewis. Copyright © 1996. Reprinted by permission of Pluto Press.)

nal social variation (see Figure 21.2 for an example using a resettlement project). The third step is *redistribution of critical resources,* especially land, to take into account inequities discovered in the first two steps. The last step is implementation of *assistance programs,* which are another way to achieve greater social equity through the targeted provision of services such as health care and education.

Many conservative or neoliberal economists argue on economic grounds that redistribution is not a realistic or a feasible strategy. Nevertheless, cultural anthropologists report cases in which the redistribution model has worked. Research in Nadur village, in Kerala state, southern India, posed the question of whether redistribution was an effective and realistic development strategy (Franke 1993). The answer was yes. Kerala's per capita income is low compared to the rest of India and to the rest of the world. Although income remained low and stagnant, substantial material improvements occurred in many people's lives, including some of the poorest of the poor. How did this happen? Redistribution was not the result of a socialist revolution. Instead, it took place through democratic channels, prompted by protests and pressure on the government by people's groups and labor unions. These groups forced the state to reallocate land ownership, shifting some land to the landless and thereby reducing inequality (though not eradicating it completely). In other instances, people pressured government leaders to improve village conditions by improving the schools, providing school lunches for poor children, and increasing attendance by dalit children (review Chapter 15's discussion of the caste system and dalits, pp. 458–459). Throughout the 1960s and 1970s, Nadur village became a better place to live, for many people.

Human Development

Another contrast to "growth-first" strategies is called **human development**, the strategy that emphasizes investing in human welfare. The United Nations adopted the phrase *human development* to emphasize the need for improvements in human welfare in terms of health, education, and personal security and safety. According to this approach, improvements in human welfare will lead to overall development of a country and its people. The logic underlying this approach is that a growth-oriented approach, which relies on benefits "trickling down" to the less well-off, is not an effective way of raising the quality of life of the poor. It insists that resources have to be targeted directly to those in need. The motivation is both humanitarian, that is, it seeks to alleviate human suffering in the short run, and an investment in the *human capital* that will, in the longer run, contribute to strengthening the economy of the country.

Every year, the United Nations Development Program publishes its *Human Development Report*, which contains country-by-country statistics on many aspects of human welfare, such as the infant mortality rate, education levels, and health measures. Recently, it began including a measure of each country's gender gap in various measures, an important acknowledgment that measures of achievement often mask the fact that men and boys are more often the beneficiaries of gains in human development. Some regions such as the Middle East and individual countries such as India now prepare localized *Human Development Reports*.

Sustainable Development

The fifth position questions the long-term financial and environmental viability of the pursuit of economic growth. According to this view, the economic growth achieved by the wealthy nations has occurred at great cost to the environment and cannot be sustained at its present level. Since the 1980s, the term **sustainable development,** or forms of development that do not destroy nonrenewable resources and are financially supportable, has gained prominence in international development circles.

Institutional Approaches to Development

Cultural anthropologists study the institutions and organizations involved in international development, just as they would other social contexts. They have studied the management systems of large-scale institutions such as the World Bank and "local" management systems found in diverse settings. They have examined several aspects of behavior within the institutions themselves, including internal hierarchies and inequalities, social interactions, symbols of power, and institutional discourse. This section first describes some of the major development institutions and then discusses smaller, grassroots institutions.

Large-Scale Institutions

Large-scale development institutions can be separated into the *multilaterals* (those that include several nations as donors) and the *bilaterals* (those that involve a relationship between two countries, a donor and a recipient). The major multilaterals are the United Nations and the World Bank, each of which constitutes a vast and complex social system. The United Nations, established in 1945, includes over 160 member states, each contributing an amount of money assessed according to its ability and each given one vote in the General Assembly (Fasulo 2003). The United States, Germany, and Japan are major contributors. Several UN agencies exist, fulfilling a range of functions (see Figure 21.3 on p. 616). In all its units combined, the UN employs about 50,000 people.

The World Bank is supported by contributions from over 150 member countries. Founded in 1944 at a conference called by President Roosevelt in Bretton Woods, New Hampshire, "the Bank" is dedicated to promoting the concept of economic growth and expanded purchasing power throughout the world (Rich 1994). Its main strategy is to promote international investment through loans. The World Bank is guided by a Board of Governors made up of the finance ministers of member countries. Rather than following the UN's approach of one country–one vote, the World

FIGURE 21.3
Major agencies within the United Nations related to development.

Agency	Headquarters	Function
UNDP (The United Nations Development Program)	New York City, U.S.	UNDP provides many different services designed to help a country plan and manage its own development: groundwater and mineral exploration, computer and satellite technology, seed production and agricultural extension, and research. UNDP does not itself implement projects; that is done through 29 "executing agencies," some of which are listed here.
FAO (The Food and Agricultural Organization)	Rome, Italy	FAO implements agricultural field projects that receive funding from the UNDP as well as "host governments."
WHO (The World Health Organization)	Geneva, Switzerland	WHO has four goals: developing and organizing personnel and technology for disease prevention and control; eradication of major tropical diseases; immunization of all children against major childhood diseases; and establishing primary health care services.
UNICEF (The United Nations Children's Emergency Fund)	Joint headquarters: New York City and Geneva, Switzerland	UNICEF is complementary to WHO and has nearly 90 field offices in developing countries (the largest is in India). UNICEF is concerned with basic health care and social services for children. UNICEF receives about three-fourths of its funding from UN member governments and the other one-fourth from the sale of greeting cards. It is the only UN agency that receives money directly from the general public.
UNESCO (The United Nations Educational, Scientific, and Cultural Organization)	Paris, France	UNESCO is dedicated to enhancing world peace and security through education, science, and culture, as well as to promoting respect for human rights, the rule of law, and fundamental freedoms. One of UNESCO's practical concerns is to promote literacy.
UNHCR (The United Nations High Commission for Refugees)	New York City, U.S.	UNHCR is dedicated to promoting the rights and safety of refugees.
UNIFEM (The United Nations International Development Fund for Women)	New York City, U.S.	UNIFEM promotes projects directed toward raising the status of women.
UNFPA (The United Nations Fund for Population Activities)	New York City, U.S.	UNFPA supports family planning projects.

(*Source:* Table, "Major Agencies with the UN Related to Development" from *Lords of Poverty: The Power, Prestige, and Corruption of the International Aid Business* by Graham Hancock. Copyright © 1989. Reprinted by permission of Grove/Atlantis, Inc.)

Bank assigns each country a number of votes based on the size of the country's financial commitment: "There is no pretense of equality—the economic superpowers run the show" (Hancock 1989:51).

Two major units within the World Bank are the International Bank for Reconstruction and Development (IBRD) and the International Development Association (IDA). Both are administered at the World Bank headquarters in Washington, DC. They both lend for similar types of projects and often in the same country, but their conditions of lending differ. The IBRD provides loans to the poorest nations, which are generally regarded as "bad risks" on the world commercial market. Thus the IBRD is a source of interest-bearing loans to countries that otherwise would not be able to borrow. The IBRD does not allow rescheduling of debt payments. It has recorded a profit every year of its existence, so it is in the interesting position of being a profit-making aid institution. Most of its loans support large infrastructure projects and, more recently, sectoral development in health and education. The IDA is the "soft-loan" side of the World Bank because it provides interest-free loans (although there is a 0.75 percent annual "service charge") and a flexible repayment schedule averaging between 35 and 40 years (Rich 1994:77). These concessional loans are granted to the poorest countries for projects of high development priority.

Critics of the multilaterals come from many directions, including politicians, scholars, students, and people whose lives have been affected negatively by their projects. Politicians in the United States who oppose foreign aid to developing countries in any form point to the overlapping and wasteful organization of these institutions and the fact that they seem to have accomplished too little relative to the funds required of member countries to support them. Others argue that, too often, the projects supported by these institutions have failed to help the poor but, instead, provide thousands of jobs for the people in their employ and are good business investments for first-world countries. Such critics point especially to biased lending and aid policies that are shaped more by political factors than by economic need.

Prominent bilateral institutions include the Japan International Cooperation Agency (JICA), the United States Agency for International Development (USAID), the Canadian International Development Agency (CIDA), Britain's Department for International Development (DfID), the Swedish Agency for International Development (SIDA), and the Danish Organization for International Development (DANIDA). These agencies vary in terms of the total size of their aid programs, the types of programs they support, and the proportion of aid disbursed as loans that have to be repaid compared to aid disbursed as grants that do not require repayment. Another variation is whether the loans or grants are "tied" to supporting specific projects that also entail substantial donor country involvement in providing goods, services, and expertise versus being "untied," allowing the recipient country to decide how to use the funds. USAID generally offers more aid in the form of loans than grants, and more in tied than in untied aid, especially compared to aid from Sweden, the Netherlands, and Norway.

Another difference among the bilaterals is the proportion of their total aid that goes to the poorest of countries. The United Kingdom's DfID sends more than 80 percent of its aid to the poorest countries, whereas the largest chunk of U.S. foreign aid goes to Egypt and Israel. Emphasis on certain types of aid also varies from one bilateral institution to another. Cuba has long played a unique role in bilateral aid, although this fact is scarcely known in the United States. Rather than offering assistance for a wide range of development projects, Cuba has concentrated on aid for

Visit the web site of one multilateral and one bilateral aid organization to learn about their goals, programs, and internship opportunities. **THINKING OUTSIDE THE BOX**

USAID has funded many development projects worldwide, such as this improved road in rural Bangladesh. Proceeds from the tollgate will help pay for maintenance of the road. The rickshaws are parked while their drivers pay the toll. The large white vehicle belongs to USAID and was being used by American researchers. ■ What kinds of user fees have you paid in the past few months? Did you think the fees were fair? (Source: Barbara Miller)

At the Shan-Dany museum in Oaxaca, Mexico, indigenous people established a museum to house artifacts from their culture and to promote economic development for the village and the region by strengthening the local weaving industry. The museum also provides outreach to schoolchildren and encourages them to learn more about their culture. ∎ Use the Internet to learn about other museum or cultural heritage projects designed to improve the welfare of indigenous peoples. (Source: Jeffrey Cohen)

training health care providers and promoting preventive health care (Feinsilver 1993). Cuba's development assistance goes to socialist countries, including many in Africa.

Grassroots Approaches

Many countries have experimented with *grassroots approaches* to development, or locally initiated "bottom-up" projects. This alternative to the "top-down" development pursued by the large-scale agencies described in the previous section is more likely to be culturally appropriate, supported through local participation, and successful. During the 1970s, for example, Kenya sponsored a national program whereby the government committed itself to providing teachers if local communities would build schools (Winans and Haugerud 1977). This program was part of Kenya's promotion of *harambee,* or self-help, in improving health, housing, and schooling. Local people's response to the schooling program, especially, was overwhelmingly positive. They turned out in large numbers to build schools, fulfilling their part of the bargain. Given the widespread construction of schools, the government found itself hard-pressed to hold up its own end of the bargain: paying the teachers' salaries. This program shows that self-help movements can be highly successful in mobilizing local contributions, if the target—in this case, children's education—is something that is valued.

Many non-governmental, grassroots organizations have existed for several decades. Prominent international examples include Oxfam, CARE, and Feed the Children. Churches often sponsor grassroots development. In Bangladesh, for example, the Lutheran Relief Agency has played an important role in helping local people provide and maintain small-scale infrastructure projects such as village roads and canals.

Beginning with the Reagan administration's push toward privatization in the 1980s in the United States and a similar trend in the United Kingdom, an emphasis on supporting development efforts through non-governmental organizations (NGOs) emerged. This trend prompted the formation of many new NGOs in developing countries, some of which are beneficiaries of foreign aid.

The Development Project

Development institutions, whether they are large multilaterals or local NGOs, rely on the concept of the *development project* as the specific set of activities that puts policies into action. For example, suppose a government sets a policy of increased agricultural production by a certain percent within a certain period. Development projects to achieve the policy goal might include the construction of irrigation canals that would supply water to a targeted number of farmers.

Anthropologists and the Project Cycle

The details vary between organizations, but all development projects have a basic **project cycle,** or the stages of a development project from initial planning through completion and evaluation (Cernea 1985). These steps include

- *Project identification:* Selecting a project to fit a particular purpose.
- *Project design:* Preparing the details of the project.
- *Project appraisal:* Assessing the project's budgetary aspects.
- *Project implementation:* Putting the project into place.
- *Project evaluation:* Assessing whether the project goals were fulfilled.

Since the 1970s, cultural anthropologists have been hired to offer insights into the project cycle at different stages. In the early phase of their involvement in development work, they were hired primarily to do project evaluations, the last step in the project cycle, to determine whether the project had achieved its goals. Unfortunately, many anthropologists' evaluations reported the projects to be dismal failures (Cochrane 1979). Some of the most frequent findings were (1) The target group, such as the poor or women, had not been "reached," and project benefits had gone to some other group instead; (2) The project was inappropriate for the context; and (3) The intended beneficiaries were actually worse off after the project than before.

One reason for these failures was that projects were typically identified and designed by Western economists located in cities far from the project site. These experts applied a universal formula, paying little or no attention to local cultural contexts (Scott 1998). In other words, projects were designed by "people-distant" and culturally uninformed planners. But they were evaluated by "people-close" and culturally informed anthropologists. By demonstrating the weaknesses in project planning that led to failed projects, cultural anthropologists quickly gained a reputation in development circles as troublemakers and "nay-sayers"—to be avoided by those who favored a "move-ahead" approach to getting projects funded and implemented.

Cultural anthropologists are still considered a nuisance by many development economists and policy makers. On a more positive note, cultural anthropologists have lobbied for a role earlier in the project cycle, especially at the project identification and design stages. In this way, they can help prevent major blunders up front. Although they are still far less powerful than economists in defining development policy, many anthropologists have made notable strides in this direction. Their role as watchdogs and critics, furthermore, should not be discounted because it draws attention to important problems.

Sociocultural Fit

Through the years, cultural anthropologists have provided many examples of projects that were culturally inappropriate. All were a waste of time and money. One case of non-fit is a project intended to improve nutrition and health in the South Pacific by promoting increased milk consumption (Cochrane 1979). The project involved the transfer of large quantities of American powdered milk to an island community. The people, however, were lactase impersistent (unable to digest raw milk), and everyone soon had diarrhea (review Chapter 10, p. 304). Realizing what had caused the diarrhea, local people stopped making liquid milk and instead used the milk powder to whitewash their houses. Beyond wasting resources, inappropriately designed projects can result in the exclusion of the intended beneficiaries, such as when a person's signature is required among people who cannot write or when photo identification cards are requested from Muslim women, whose faces should not be shown in public.

Cultural anthropologist Conrad Kottak reviewed evaluations for sixty-eight development projects to see whether economic success of projects was related to **sociocultural fit,** or how well a project meshes with the target culture and population (1985). Results showed a strong correlation between the two factors. One role for anthropologists is to expose areas of non-fit and provide insights about how to achieve sociocultural fit in order to enhance project success. In one such case, Gerald Murray played a positive role in redesigning a costly and unsuccessful reforestation project supported by USAID in Haiti (1987). Since the colonial era in Haiti, deforestation has been dramatic; estimates are that around 50 million trees are cut annually. Some of the deforestation is driven by the market for wood for construction and for charcoal in the capital city of Port au Prince. Another aspect is that rural people are farmers and need cleared land for growing crops and grazing their

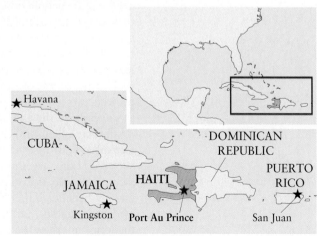

A tree nursery in Haiti established as part of a reforestation project funded by USAID. ■ Go to the USAID web site and scan the information provided there about Haiti. Is there evidence of the involvement of anthropologists? (Source: Birgit Pohl)

goats. The ecological consequences of so much clearing, however, are soil erosion and declining fertility of the land.

USAID sent millions of tree seedlings to Haiti, and the Haitian government urged rural people to plant them. But the project fell flat: farmers refused to plant the seedlings on their land and instead fed them to goats. Gerald Murray, who had done his doctoral dissertation on rural Haitian land tenure practices, was called on by USAID to suggest an alternative approach. He advised that the kind of seedling promoted be changed from fruit trees, in which the rural farmers saw little benefit because they are not to be cut, to fast-growing trees such as eucalyptus that could be cut as early as four years after planting and sold in Port au Prince. This option was quickly accepted by the farmers because it would yield profits in the foreseeable future, and they could see that losses from food production would be offset by the income. The basic incompatibility had been that USAID wanted trees planted that would stay in place for years to come, whereas the Haitian farmers viewed trees as things that were meant to be cut.

The Anthropological Critique of Development Projects

The early decades of development anthropology were dominated by **traditional development anthropology (TDA)**. In TDA, the anthropologist accepts the role of helping to make development work better, a kind of "add an anthropologist and stir" approach to development. It is an option that some economists and others involved in development realize can help make their plans more effective. For example, an anthropologist familiar with a local culture can provide information about what kinds of consumer goods the people might desire or what might induce them to relocate with less resistance. This kind of participation by anthropologists can be either positive or negative for the local people, depending on the project being undertaken.

Concern exists among many anthropologists that helping large-scale development projects work often has negative effects on local people and their environments (Bodley 1990; Horowitz and Salem-Murdock 1993; Taussig 1978). For example, a study of the welfare of local inhabitants of the middle Senegal valley (in the country of Senegal, West Africa) before and after the construction of a large dam shows that people's food insecurity increased (Horowitz and Salem-Murdock 1993). Formerly, the periodic flooding of the plain helped support a dense human population dependent on agriculture, fishing, forestry, and herding. Productivity of the wetlands had remained high for a long period of human occupation, with no signs of deterioration. The current practice of water control by the dam managers, however, does not provide periodic flooding. Instead, water is released less often and with no regard for the needs of the people downstream. In some years, they do not have enough water for their crops, and fishing has become a less secure source of food. At other times, a large flood of water is released, damaging crops. As a result, many residents have been forced to leave the area. They have become development refugees, people who must leave home because of the effects of a development project.

The awareness of the negative effects of many supposedly positive development projects has led to the emergence of **critical development anthropology (CDA)**. In this approach, the anthropologist does not simply accept a supportive role but takes on the role of cultural critique. The question is not: What can I do to make this project successful? Instead, the anthropologist asks: Is this a good project from the perspective of the target population? If the answer is yes, then that is a green light for a supportive role. If careful thinking reveals areas where revisions in the project would make it beneficial, then the anthropologist can intervene with this information. If all evidence suggests that the project will harm the target population, in the short run or the long run, then the anthropologist should assume the role of whistle-blower and try either to stop the project completely or to change the design substantially. In the case of the Senegal Valley dam project, anthropologists working with engineers and local inhabitants devised an alternative management plan of regular and controlled water release that would reduce the harm done to people downstream and restore the area's former agricultural and fishing abundance.

Methods in Development Anthropology

Many full-scale anthropological studies of cultural change and development are based on long-term fieldwork and standard research methods as described in Chapter 4. However, a development agency often needs input from an anthropologist that requires faster turnaround than long-term fieldwork allows. Specialized methods have emerged to respond to an abbreviated time frame and provide answers to the specific questions at hand. Compared to standard long-term fieldwork, the methods used in development anthropology are more focused with a less holistic research agenda, make more use of multidisciplinary research teams, and rely on specialized approaches such as rapid and participatory research methods. These three differences are related to the need to gather dependable data in a short time period.

Rapid Research Methods

Rapid research methods (RRM) are research methods designed to provide focused cultural data in a short time (Chambers 1983). They include strategies such as going to the field with a checklist of questions, conducting focus group interviews (talking to several people at the same time rather than one by one), and conducting *transect observations* (walking through a specific area with key informants and asking for explanations along the way) (Bernard 1995:139–140). When used correctly, RRMs can provide useful data for assessing the problems and opportunities related to development. Rapid research methods are most effective when several methods are used to complement each other and when researchers work in teams (see the Methods Close-Up box on p. 622).

Participatory Research Methods

Building on the RRM approach, **participatory research methods (PRM)** entail more involvement of the local people. Participatory research methods were devised in response to the growing awareness that when the target population is involved in a development project, it is more likely to be successful in the short run and sustain-

Development anthropologist Patricia Delaney (center left, wearing white shirt and trousers) facilitates a participatory research exercise with indigenous people in Guyana, South America. The woman (center) is participating in a village mapping exercise that was part of an assessment of village needs. ■ How well would you be able to draw a map of your "village"? (Source: Patricia Delaney)

The Importance of Teamwork in Development Research

AN EFFECTIVE MIX of rapid research methods was used for development project planning in rural Bali, Indonesia (Mitchell 1994). The research sought to identify environmental and social stresses that might be caused by economic development in order to make recommendations for the government to use in preparing its next five-year development plan. Cultural anthropologists and graduate students at the University of Windsor in Canada and at an Indonesian university designed an eight-village study to provide data on ecological, economic, and social factors. A four-member team studied in each village, but each team spent some time in at least two villages. Teams consisted of Indonesian and Canadian researchers, both men and women. All team members could speak Bahasa Indonesian (the national language), and at least one could also speak Bahasa Bali (the local language).

Researchers lived in the village for four weeks. The teams employed several methods for data collection: acquisition of background data from provincial documents and village records, and interviews with key informants representing the village administration, religious figures, women, youth, school teachers, health clinic personnel, and agricultural extension workers. Household interviews were conducted with fifteen men and fifteen women from different neighborhoods in the village and with a sample of primary school children. Observations were made of conditions of the village and villagers' daily activities. For each village, the research generated a profile of relevant environmental features, production and marketing, local government, health and welfare, and expressive culture. The findings offered a range of issues for the government's consideration, including the apparent environmental and social stresses being caused by external developments such as urbanization and tourism.

FOOD FOR THOUGHT

- What are the strengths that a team approach added to the research described here?

---

able over the long run. (Kabutha, Thomas-Slayter, and Ford 1993:76). Participatory research rests heavily on the anthropological assumption that local knowledge should not be bypassed but, rather, should be the foundation of development work. Participatory research proceeds by involving key community members at all stages of the research.

The best PRM work teaches local people how to collect and analyze data themselves. Local people can learn how to prepare maps and charts and other forms of descriptive data. Besides data gathering and analysis, a crucial feature of PRM is to promote participation of community members in project selection and project evaluation. Local people can then continue the data collection and analysis after the team has left. Two important effects of PRM are fostering local autonomy in planning and boosting the odds that the projects put in place will be maintained and adjusted to changing conditions.

EMERGING ISSUES IN DEVELOPMENT

This section considers three major areas in international development: indigenous people, women, and human rights. The first two are particular groups of people who have been affected by international development in various ways. They are not separate categories, because indigenous people are also women, but this section reviews findings for them separately for purposes of illustration. The issue of human rights affects all social categories, including indigenous people, ethnic minorities, women, children, and others.

Indigenous Peoples' Development

This section first raises the question of who indigenous peoples are. We next consider findings about how indigenous peoples have been victimized by many aspects of growth-oriented development (as they were by colonialism before it) and then look at how some indigenous groups are taking development into their own hands.

Who Are Indigenous Peoples?

The term *indigenous peoples* refers to groups of people who are the original inhabitants of a particular territory (recall Chapter 2). Often, indigenous peoples take the name "First Peoples" as a way of defining themselves as original claimants to a place. This naming practice highlights one of the major problems facing most indigenous peoples today: the fact that they have lost, and are still losing, claim to their ancestral lands in the face of encroachment from outsiders.

Indigenous peoples are typically a numerical minority in the states that control their territory. The United Nations distinguishes between indigenous peoples and other minority groups such as the Roma, the Tamils of Sri Lanka, and African Americans. Although this distinction is useful in some ways, it should not be taken as a hard and fast difference (Maybury-Lewis 1997b). It is better to think of all these groups as forming a continuum from more purely indigenous groups such as the Inuit to minority/ethnic groups, such as African Americans, that are not geographically original to a place but share many problems with indigenous peoples as a result of living within a more powerful majority culture.

Indigenous peoples differ from most national minorities in that they often occupy (or occupied) remote areas and were, until the era of colonial expansion, less affected by outside interests. Now governments and international businesses have recognized that their lands often contain valuable natural resources, such as natural gas in the circumpolar region and gold in Papua New Guinea and the Amazon. Different governments have paid varying degrees of attention to "integrating" indigenous peoples into "mainstream" culture in the interests of fostering nationalism at the expense of cultural pluralism.

Accurate demographic statistics on indigenous peoples are difficult to obtain (Kennedy and Perz 2000). No one agrees on whom to count as indigenous. Governments may not bother to conduct a census of indigenous people, or if they do, they may undercount indigenous people in order to downplay recognition of their existence as a group (Baer 1982:12). Some remote groups in India's Andaman Islands in the Bay of Bengal remain uncounted because Indian officials cannot gain access to them (Singh 1994). Given the difficulties involved in defining and counting indigenous people, therefore, it is possible to provide only estimates of their numbers. It is estimated that, globally, indigenous people make up about 5 percent of the total world population. (Bodley 1990:365). (See Figure 21.4 on p. 624.)

Victims of Development

Many indigenous peoples and their cultures have been exterminated as a result of contact with outsiders. Besides death and decline through contagious disease, political conflicts within indigenous people's territory often threaten their survival. In the Peruvian Andes, for example, armed conflict among the Peruvian guerrillas, the Shining Path, drug traffickers, and U.S.-backed police and army units has taken a heavy toll on Native American populations.

A Hmong woman and child, northern Thailand. The Hmong people of highland Southeast Asia have suffered decades of war in their homeland. Many have migrated to other parts of the world, including the United States and Canada, where they were classified as refugees.
■ What other cultural groups have come to your home country recently as refugees? (Source: © Roshani Kothari)

FIGURE 21.4
Population estimates of indigenous peoples.

Western Hemisphere
- less than 1 million in Canada
- 1.75 million in the United States
- less than 13 million in Mexico and Central America
- 16 million in South America

Europe
- 60,000 in Greenland
- 60,000 in Norway, Sweden, Finland, and Russia
- 28 million within the former Soviet Union

Middle East
- 5 million

Africa
- 14 million

Asia
- 52 million in India
- 31 million in China (the government terms them *national minorities*)
- 26.5 million in Southeast Asia
- 50,000 in Japan and the Pacific combined
- 550,000 in Australia and New Zealand

Total: About 5 percent of the world's total population.

(*Source:* Figure, "Population Estimates of Indigenous Peoples" from *Indigenous Peoples: Ethnic Groups and the State* by David Maybury-Lewis. Copyright © 1997 by Pearson Education. Reprinted by permission of Allyn and Bacon, Boston, MA.)

With colonialism, indigenous peoples suffered from massive efforts to take over their land by force, to prevent them from practicing their traditional lifestyle, and to integrate them into the state. Racism and other forms of oppression were the fate of many thousands of indigenous people. Many anthropologists in all four fields are involved in attempts to redress past human rights abuses.

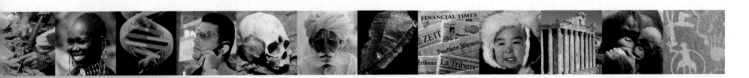

CROSSING THE FIELDS

Human Evolutionist Supports the Repatriation of Saartje Baartman's Remains to South Africa

Negotiations between the French and South African governments were completed in 2002 for the repatriation of the remains of a Khoisan woman from Paris to South Africa. Saartje Baartman (1789–1816) was a victim of colonial oppression and is now a South African symbol of that era. Phillip Tobias, a biological anthropologist who negotiated the repatriation, has summarized the facts about Saartje Baartman's life and documented the negotiations that brought about the repatriation of her remains (2002).

Saartje Baartman was born in Eastern Cape Province among people belonging to the wider San group whom European colonialists referred to by the pejorative term "Hottentots." As a young adult, she moved near Cape Town where she worked as a servant on a European's farm. The owner, Peter Cezar, was so "impressed by features of Baartman's anatomy" (107) that he convinced her to go to England with him to exhibit herself to the public. In London she became known as the "Hottentot Venus" and was shown coming out of a cage, sometimes in chains. However popular this show was among the public, the African Association in London (a scholarly society) objected to her degradation and brought the case to court. Upon questioning, she reportedly stated that her participation was voluntary and that she had no wish to return to South Africa. The case was dismissed.

In 1814, Cezar took Baartman to Paris and sold her to an animal trainer who exhibited her in the city and rented her out for parties. The French public was captivated. She also attracted the attention of French scientists. Ill health, however, soon overcame her, and she died in 1816 at the age of 26 years. No one is sure what caused her death; suggestions include smallpox, an inflammatory illness, and excess consumption of brandy.

A prominent French paleontologist, Georges Cuvier, obtained her body for dissection. He made a total body cast in wax, which resides at the Musée de l'Homme in Paris. He dissected her body, paying special attention to the buttocks and external genitalia. He characterized her buttocks as steatopygia, "great enlargement," a common feature in Khoisan peoples. He dissected her labia minora, known scientifically as macronympha, which were also enlarged compared to European standards and were crudely referred to by Westerners as the "Hottentot apron." Over half of Cuvier's 16-page report deals with her breasts, buttocks, and pelvis. Her external genitalia and brain were preserved in jars.

At that time, Cuvier and other human evolutionists were pursuing the question of where to draw the line between humans and animals, and they were asking whether the Khoisan were humans or animals. Cuvier concluded that, although some of Baartman's features resembled those of monkeys and apes, she was indeed a human being.

All that remains of Saartje Baartman's body is her skeleton, which was mounted on a stand. In addition, there is the cast of her body made by Cuvier. Her preserved brain and genitals have disappeared, amid conflicting accounts of what happened to them: lost in the museum, fallen from a shelf and destroyed, perhaps found again and on their way to South Africa as of 2002.

In 1996, the South African government began to seek the return of Saartje Baartman's remains as part of its campaign to advance the heritage of its indigenous peoples. During the colonial period, hundreds of human skulls, skeletons, and cultural objects were removed from South Africa and taken to European and North American museums. South Africa does not seek repatriation of all these remains. Unlike the many anonymous cases, that of Saartje Baartman is considered special, even unique. Her identity was known during her life, in South Africa and internationally, given the outcry of anti-slavery abolitionists in London. There are living Baartmans in South Africa who may belong to her lineage. According to Tobias, she has become "in South Africa, and internationally, a symbol of colonial and imperial excesses" (109). The government of South Africa requested the return from Paris of her skeleton, her body cast, and her bottled body parts if and when they are found.

Tobias writes, "South Africa and its people would see the return of Baartman's remains as belated recognition of her essential humanity and a gesture of reconciliation after the appalling treatment meted out to her and to the Khoisan in general" (110). In May 2002, her skeleton was returned to the land of her birth, the Gamtoos Valley, the Eastern Cape. About 10,000 people attended the burial ceremony. ▪

FOOD FOR THOUGHT

▪ European colonialism and scientific research were mutually supportive in exploiting indigenous peoples. Are there laws in place to protect indigenous peoples from similar treatment now?

The unwillingness of many states to tolerate the presence of politically sovereign tribes within their boundaries reduces the autonomy of indigenous peoples (Bodley 1988). States intervene to prevent and quell armed resistance by indigenous people, even though such resistance may be critical to the maintenance of indigenous culture and the people's welfare. Indicators that an indigenous group has lost its autonomy include inability to expel outside intruders or use force to regulate its internal affairs; introduction of formal schooling and national court systems; appointment of state-sanctioned political leaders; the institution of compulsory military service; and enforcement of the payment of taxes. These changes undermine the previous quality of life and set in motion changes that indirectly lead to the people's further impoverishment.

Anthropological analysis of government policies in Thailand for development of the highlands reveals the complex interplay between international and state government interests and the welfare of the "hill people" (Kesmanee 1994). The hill people include the Karen, Hmong, Mian, Lahu, Lisu, Akha, and others, totaling about half a million people, or 1 percent of the Thai population. International pressures are for the hill people to replace opium cultivation with other cash crops. The Thai government's concerns are with political stability and national security in this area, which borders on Burma and Laos. It therefore has promoted development projects to establish more connections between the highlands and the lowlands through transportation and marketing. Thus far, efforts to find viable substitute crops (especially among the Hmong, who have traditionally been most dependent on opium as a cash crop) have been unsuccessful. Crops that have been introduced have required extensive use of fertilizers and pesticides, which have greatly increased environmental pollution. Efforts have been made to relocate upland horticulturalists to the plains, but there they have been provided plots with poor soil, and the economic status of the people has declined.

THINKING OUTSIDE THE BOX So far, attempts in many parts of the world to suppress poppy cultivation for opium have been unsuccessful. If your job was to address this issue in Thailand, how would you proceed?

In the meantime, commercial loggers have gained access to the hills and have done more damage to the forests than the traditional patterns of shifting horticulture. Increased penetration of the hill areas by lowlanders, international tourism, and communications has also promoted the increase of HIV/AIDS rates, illegal trafficking of girls and boys for sex work, and opium addiction. The effects of thirty years of development have been disastrous for the hill people, and awareness of this fact calls for a major change in how development is pursued by international agencies and the Thai government.

The situation in Thailand is not unique. In case after case, indigenous peoples have been subjected to loss of the rights they once had, to increased impoverishment, and to widespread despair. Active resistance to their disenfranchisement has been mounted throughout history, but more effective and highly organized forms of protest and reclamation of rights have become prominent only since the 1980s. Many indigenous groups have acquired legal expertise and have confronted power-holders in world capitals, insisting on changes. One of the most basic claims of all groups is recognition of their land rights.

From Victimization to Indigenous Peoples' Development

Much evidence attests to the value of "development from within," or efforts to increase people's welfare and livelihood promoted by indigenous rather than exogenous organizations. The basic components of indigenous peoples' development include rights to resources, local initiatives in planning through local organizations, and local leadership. The following sections consider, first, resource issues (especially land) and indigenous organizations for change.

The many land and resource claims being made by indigenous peoples are a direct response to their earlier losses and a major challenge to many states. Depending on how these disputes are resolved, they can be a basis for conflicts ranging from lawsuits to attempts at secession (Plant 1994).

No Latin American country government provides protection against encroachment on the land of indigenous farm families. Throughout Latin America, increasing numbers of Indians have been forced off the land and have had to seek wage labor. Those who remain live in extreme poverty. In response, a strong resurgence of activity by indigenous people and groups that support them occurred in the 1990s (Plant 1994). Some of this activity took the form of physical resistance. Violence continues to erupt between indigenous people and state-supported power structures, especially in the southern Mexican state of Chiapas.

In Canada, the law distinguishes between two different types of Native Americans and their land claims (Plant 1994). "Specific claims" concern problems arising from previous agreements or treaties, and "comprehensive claims" are those made by Native Americans who have not been displaced and have made no treaties or agreements. Most of the former claims have led to monetary compensation. In the latter category, interest in oil and/or mineral exploration has led governments to negotiate with indigenous people in an effort to have the latter's native claims either relinquished or redefined. So far, of the over forty comprehensive claims filed, only four have been settled. In some provinces, especially British Columbia, current claims affect most of the province.

Most Asian countries have been reluctant even to recognize the concept of special land rights of indigenous people (Plant 1994). In Bangladesh, for example, the formerly protected area of the Chittagong Hill Tracts is being massively encroached upon by settlers from the crowded plains. Nonindigenous settlers now occupy the most fertile land. A large hydroelectric dam built in 1963 displaced 100,000 hill dwellers because they could no longer practice horticulture in the flooded areas. A minority received financial aid, but most did not. Tribal opposition groups began emerging, and conflict, though suppressed in the news, has been ongoing for decades. Other sites of contestation with the state over land and resources in the Asia-Pacific region include the Moros of the southern Philippines and the people of Irian Jaya. In these cases, the indigenous peoples' fight for secession from the state that controls them is costing many lives.

In Africa, political interests of state governments in establishing and enforcing territorial boundaries have created difficulties for indigenous peoples, especially pastoralists who are accustomed to moving their herds freely. Pastoralists in the Sahel region of Africa have been particularly hurt by this process. Many formerly autonomous pastoralists have been transformed into refugees living in terrible conditions. The Tuareg people, for example, have traditionally lived and herded in a territory crossing what are now five different nations: Mali, Niger, Algeria, Burkina Faso, and Libya (Childs and Chelala 1994). Because of political conflict in the region, thousands of Tuareg people now live in exile in Mauritania, and their prospects are grim. As elsewhere, resistance movements spring up, but states, international corporations, and local power interests act quickly to quell them.

The death of Ogoni leader Ken Saro-Wiwa, in 1995, is a shocking example of the personal price of resistance (Sachs 1996). Saro-Wiwa, a Nigerian writer, Nobel Peace Prize nominee, and supporter of minority people's rights, was executed by Nigerian military rulers. He spoke out against the Nigerian regime and the oil development being pursued in Ogoniland by Royal/Dutch Shell. As president and spokesperson of the Movement for the Survival of the Ogoni People (MOSOP), he had asked the government to respect the Ogoni people's right to self-determination. He asked Shell to clean up oil spills and toxic waste pits that had ruined Ogoni farming and fishing communities along the Niger River delta. His message is one that applies worldwide: states tend to impose the cost of their economic growth on the people least able to cope with it—impoverished minorities—and then apply violent means of repression if such people raise serious objections to that treatment.

Many indigenous peoples have formed their own organizations for change in order to promote "development from within." In Ethiopia, for example, many NGOs organized by local people have sprung up since the 1990s (Kassam 2002). One organization in the southern region is especially

A ritual mask from the Ogoni people of Nigeria, whose way of life is seriously threatened by oil development being pursued in their region by international companies. ■ What are some other indigenous peoples whose culture has been negatively affected by outside interests in oil? (Source: © Vanessa Vick/ Photo Researchers)

A farmer walks though an oil-soaked field. About 500,000 Ogoni people live in Ogoni, a region in Nigeria. The fertility of the Niger delta has supported farming and fishing populations at high density for many years. Since Shell discovered oil there in 1958, 100 oil wells have been constructed in Ogoniland and countless oil spills have occurred. ■ Discuss the environmental and social effects of massive oil extraction on the Ogoni people, and write a mock "briefing memo" about the consequences for the Machiguenga people of Peru, who are being pressed to open up their unspoiled lands to oil companies. (Source: © CORBIS. All Rights Reserved.)

noteworthy, because it seeks to provide a model of development based on the oral traditions of the Oromo people. This new model thus combines elements of Western-defined "development" with Oromo values and laws and provides a new approach that is culturally appropriate and goes beyond external notions of development and usual Oromo lifeways. The indigenous Oromo NGO is called Hundee, which refers to "roots," or the origins of the Oromo people—and, by extension, to all Oromo people, their land, and their culture. Hundee uses a theory of development that is based in Oromo metaphors of fertility and growth and involves gradual transformation like the spirals in the horn of a ram. Hundee relies on Oromo legal and moral principles about the communal use of natural resources and the redistribution of wealth to provide a social welfare system. These are elements of what Oromo people consider "good development," as distinguished from the "bad development" that has inflicted hunger and dependency on them.

Hundee's long-term goal is to empower Oromo communities to be self-sufficient. It takes the view the Oromo culture is a positive force for social and economic change, rather than a barrier. Hundee members use a participatory approach in all their endeavors. They consult with traditional legal assemblies to identify needs and then to shape projects to address those needs. Specific activities include the establishment of a credit association and a grain bank to help combat price fluctuations and food shortages.

In many cases, indigenous peoples' development organizations link formerly separate groups as a response to external threats (Perry 1996:245–246). In Australia, many indigenous groups have formed pan-Australian organizations and regional coalitions, such as the Pitjandjatjara Land Council, that have had success in land claim cases. In Canada, the Grand Council of the Cree has collaborated with the Inuit Tapirisat and other organizations over land issues. Many indigenous groups are taking advantage of new forms of communication in order to build and maintain links with each other over large areas.

Although it is tempting to see hope in the newly emerging forms of resistance, self-determination, and organizing among indigenous peoples, such hope cannot be generalized to all indigenous peoples. Many are making progress and their economic status is improving, while others continue to suffer from extreme political and economic repression.

Women and Development

The category of women differs from that of indigenous peoples, because women typically do not have a recognized territory associated with them as a group. The effects of development on women, however, share features with its effects on indigenous people. That is, women too have often lost economic rights and political power in their communities. For example, matrilineal kinship, which keeps property in the female line (review Chapter 12), is declining throughout the world, often as a result of Westernization and modernization.

Another factor that has had a negative effect on women's status is that Western development experts have chosen to deal with men in the context of development projects. This section first considers evidence that international development policies and programs have been biased in favor of men to the detriment of women. It next reviews examples in which women's groups are taking development into their own hands and making it work to enhance their welfare.

The Male Bias in Development

In the 1970s, researchers noticed and wrote about the fact that development projects were male-biased (Boserup 1970; Tinker 1976). Many projects completely bypassed women as beneficiaries, targeting men for such initiatives as growing cash crops and learning about new technology. This *male bias in development* contributed to increased gender inequality by giving men greater access to new sources of income and depriving women of their traditional economic roles. The development experts' image of a farmer, for example, was male, not female. Women's projects were focused on the domestic domain. Thus women's projects were typically concerned with infant feeding patterns, child care, and family planning. Over time, these emphases led to what has been labeled the *domestication of women* worldwide (Rogers 1979). For example, female horticulturalists were bypassed by agricultural projects and instead taught to spend more time in the house.

The male bias in development also increased the rate of project failure. In the West African country of Burkina Faso, for example, a reforestation project included men as the sole participants, whose tasks would include planting and caring for the trees. Cultural patterns there, however, dictate that men do not water plants; women do. Consequently, the men planted the seedlings and left them. Because women had not been included as project participants, the young trees died.

Exclusion of women from development continues to be a problem, in spite of many years of work attempting to place and keep women's issues on the development agenda. An example of an emerging development issue related to women's welfare is gender-based violence. This issue has gained attention even among the large multilaterals, where experts now realize that women cannot participate in a credit program, for example, if they fear that their husbands will beat them for leaving the house.

The United Nations Commission on the Status of Women formed a working group that drafted a declaration against violence against women; it was adopted by the General Assembly in 1993 (Heise, Pitanguy, and Germain 1994). Article 1 of the declaration states that violence against women includes "any act of gender-based violence that results in, or is likely to result in, physical, sexual or psychological harm or suffering to women, including threats of such acts, coercion or arbitrary deprivations of liberty, whether occurring in public or private life" (Economic and Social Council 1992). This definition cites "women" as the focus of concern, but it includes girls as well (see Figure 21.5 on p. 630). A weakness of programs that target issues of violence against girls and women is that they tend to deal with their effects, not the causes, often with disastrous results. For example, they may seek to increase personal security of women and girls in refugee camps by augmenting the number of guards at the camp when, in fact, the guards themselves are often guilty of abusing refugee women and girls.

Nigerian author and Nobel prize winner Ken Saro-Wiwa founded the Movement for Survival of Ogoni People (MOSOP) in 1992 to protest Shell's actions in Ogoniland and the Nigerian government's indifference. In 1995 he was arrested, tried for murder under suspicious circumstances, and executed by hanging. His execution brought about an international outcry. Shell's response was largely denial of any problem. ■ How many of your daily activities depend on the use of oil products? (Source: © CORBIS)

Women's Organizations for Change

In many countries, women have made substantial gains in improving their status and welfare through forming organizations. These organizations range from "mothers' clubs" that help provide for communal child care to lending and credit organizations that give women an opportunity to start their own businesses. Some are local and small-scale. Others are global in reach, such as Women's World Banking,

---

FIGURE 21.5

An emerging development issue: violence against girls and women throughout the life cycle.

Prebirth	Sex-selective abortion, battering during pregnancy, coerced pregnancy
Infancy	Infanticide, emotional and physical abuse, deprivation of food and medical care
Girlhood	Child marriage, genital mutilation, sexual abuse by family members and strangers, rape, deprivation of food and medical care, child prostitution
Adolescence	Dating and courtship violence, forced prostitution, rape, sexual abuse in the workplace, sexual harassment
Adulthood	Partner abuse and rape, partner homicide, sexual abuse in the workplace, sexual harassment, rape
Old Age	Abuse and neglect of widows, elder abuse

(*Source:* Figure, "An Emerging Development Issue: Violence Against Girls and Women Throughout the Life Cycle" from *Violence Against Women: The Hidden Health Burden* by Lori L. Heise, Jacqueline Pitanguay, and Adrienne Germaine. World Bank Discussion Papers # 255. Copyright © 1994. Reprinted by permission of Copyright Clearance Center, on behalf of the rightsholder.)

an international organization that grew out of credit programs for poor working women in India.

One community-based credit system in Mozambique, southern Africa, helps farm women to buy seeds, fertilizers, and supplies on loan (Clark 1992). When the loan program was started, thirty-two farm families in the village of Machel formed themselves into seven solidarity groups, each with an elected leader. The woman-headed farmer groups managed irrigation more efficiently and conferred on how to minimize the use of pesticides and chemical fertilizers. Through their efforts, the women quadrupled their harvests and were able to pay off their loans. Machel women then turned their attention to getting additional loans to improve their herds and buy a maize mill. Overall, in the midst of poverty, military conflict, the lack of government resources, and a drought, the project and the organization it fostered allowed many women farmers to increase their economic and household security.

In the southern part of Madagascar, there is pressure to grow more rice which means irrigating more land. The expansion of intensive rice cultivation will bring the death of many baobab trees and threaten the habitats of many wild animal species, including lemurs. ■ Assume you have just been appointed as Madagascar's Minister of People, Nature, and Development. What do you want your research staff to brief you about during your first months of service? (Source: © Robb Kendrick/Aurora & Quanta Productions)

Grameen Bank, a development project begun in Bangladesh to provide small loans to poor people, is one of the most successful examples of improving human welfare through "micro-credit" or small loans. Professor Mohammed Yunnus (center) founded Grameen Bank and continues to be a source of charismatic leadership for it. ■ How does the success of Grameen Bank cause you to question your previous image of Bangladesh? (Source: © Robert Nickelsberg/ Getty Images)

An informal system of social networks emerged to help support poor women vendors in San Cristobal, Mexico (Sullivan 1992). Many of the vendors around the city square are women, and most of them have been expelled from highland Chiapas because of political conflicts there. The women vendors manufacture and sell goods to tourists and thereby provide an important portion of household income. In the city, they find support in an expanded social network that compensates for the loss of support from the extensive god-parenthood system of the highlands, which has broken down because of out-migration. Instead, the vendors have established networks encompassing relatives, neighbors, and church members, as well as other vendors, regardless of religious, political, economic, or social background.

These networks originally developed in response to a series of rapes and robberies that began in 1987. The perpetrators were men of power and influence, so the women never pressed charges. Mostly single mothers and widows, they adopted a defensive strategy of self-protection: they began to group together during the slow period each afternoon. They travel in groups and carry sharpened corset bones and prongs: "If a man insults one of them, the group surrounds him and jabs him in the groin" (39–40). If a woman is robbed, the other women surround her, comfort her, and help contribute something toward compensating her for her loss. The mid-afternoon gatherings developed into support groups that provide financial assistance, child care, medical advice, and training in job skills. These groups have also publicly, and successfully, demonstrated against city officials' attempts to prevent them from continuing their vending. Through their organizational efforts, these women—poor, vulnerable refugees from highland Chiapas—forged important improvements in their lives.

Human Rights

Much of the preceding discussion of indigenous peoples and women is related to the question of human rights and development. Anthropologists' cross-cultural research and their growing sense of the importance of advocacy as part of their role place them in a key position to speak about issues of global human rights (Messer 1993). In considering what cultural anthropologists have to contribute to the issue of human rights, we must first ask some basic and difficult questions:

■ What are human rights?

■ Is there a universal set of human rights?

■ Are local cultural definitions of human rights that clash with those of other groups defensible?

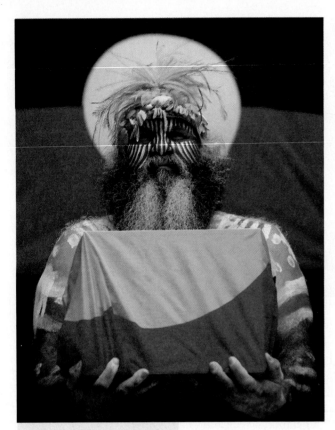

A traditional custodian from the Ngarrindjeri nation in South Australia holds a box containing four skulls of Australian Aborigines at a ceremony at Manchester University, England, 2003. The skulls returned, after 100 years in England, to a sacred keeping place. This repatriation is one result of a worldwide campaign by indigenous peoples to retrieve body parts and artifacts taken from graves during the nineteenth and twentieth centuries. (Source: © Reuters/CORBIS)

THINKING Review the discussion of nonhuman primate rights in Chapter 5, pp. 159–161. How do ques-
OUTSIDE tions of rights compare
THE BOX between nonhuman primates and humans?

Defining Human Rights

For fifty years, the United Nations has promoted human rights through its Declaration of Human Rights and other resolutions (Messer 1993). Difficulty in coming to a universal agreement on these rights is based in one sense on a split between capitalist and socialist states. The former emphasize political and civil rights such as freedom of speech as universally important. The latter emphasize socioeconomic rights such as employment and fair working conditions. Capitalist states do not acknowledge socioeconomic rights as universal human rights, and some socialist states do not recognize political rights as valid. People living in developing countries and indigenous people throughout the world have added their voices, insisting on group rights to self-determination, locally defined paths of change, and issues such as freedom from hunger. As cultural anthropologist Ellen Messer says, "[N]o state would go on record as being opposed to human rights. . . . Yet those from different states, and from different political, cultural, and religious traditions, continue to disagree on which rights have universal force and who is protected under them" (223).

Human rights are often understood to include the right of people, as members of a cultural group, to practice their cultural traditions. This provision extends the notion of human rights from including mainly the right to fulfilling basic physical needs such as health and personal security to including practices such as animal sacrifice, female genital cutting, hunting certain animals, and girls wearing headscarves in school—all issues that have received recent attention from European and North American governments and media because they differ from cultural practices in those countries. In the United States, as in many other countries, a debate about some cultural practices is carried out between human rights activists who support cultural rights and those who support animal rights.

In spring 1999, members of the Makah tribe, a Native American group living in Washington State, undertook a revival of their traditional practice of hunting gray whales (Winthrop 2000). Like that of many other native peoples of the Pacific Northwest, from Canada to the United States, the Makah traditional economy depended on fish, shellfish, and marine mammals. A treaty of 1855 acknowledged the Makah people's right to hunt whales and seals. The practice died out, however, in the twentieth century because of commercial overhunting and dwindling supplies. In 1982 the International Whaling Commission (IWC) imposed a ban on all commercial whaling but allowed continued whale hunting for subsistence purposes. In 1994 the gray whale population had recovered, and the species was taken off the endangered list. The IWC allocated the Makah a quota of twenty whales for the period from 1998 to 2002.

When, under this new plan, some Makah people killed a whale in 1999 while others watching the event cheered. The animal rights activists at the scene, in contrast, protested and said this occasion should have been one of mourning, not celebration. Although the Makah see the revival of whale hunting as a sign of cultural revival, some animal rights activists say that the way the hunt is being carried out is not culturally authentic (the Makah first harpoon the whale and then use a rifle to kill it, for example) and thus the claim of whale hunting as a traditional cultural right is not legitimate. Some of the protesters are motivated by ecological concerns for preservation of the species from extinction. Others support the concept of animal (especially mammalian) rights to life.

Human Rights and Development

This section provides two illustrations of how development and human rights are linked. In the first, ties between large-scale development institutions and military control in the Philippines result in violations of local people's human rights. The second example involves environmental destruction as a violation of human and cultural rights.

Ethnographic study of the Ifugao, an indigenous people of the Cordillera highland region of Northern Luzon, the Philippines, reveals the negative impact of militarization (Kwiatkowski 1998). The military presence is felt everywhere—in schools, in clinics, and especially at sites of large development projects such as dams. The military ensures that local people adhere to its principles and do not participate in what it considers subversive activities. Military force has been used to suppress local resistance to dam projects funded by the World Bank, including torture, killings, imprisonment, and harassment of Cordillera people for suspected subversive activities (Drucker 1988). Members of a local NGO that supports more appropriate, small-scale forms of development that would benefit people in the area have been harassed by the military. The case of the Ifugao in Northern Luzon illustrates how the powerful interests of state governments and international development institutions join together to promote their plans and projects, violating human rights in the process.

Development that leads to environmental degradation, such as pollution, deforestation, and erosion, can also be considered a form of human rights violation. Slain Ogoni leader Ken Saro-Wiwa made this point eloquently in a 1992 speech to the United Nations Working Group on Indigenous Populations:

> Environmental degradation has been a lethal weapon in the war against the indigenous Ogoni people . . . . Oil exploration has turned Ogoni into a wasteland: lands, streams, and creeks are totally and continually polluted; the atmosphere has been poisoned, charged as it is with hydrocarbon vapors, methane, carbon monoxide, carbon dioxide, and soot emitted by gas which has been flared 24 hours a day for 33 years in close proximity to human habitation . . . . All one sees and feels around is death [quoted in Sachs 1996:13–16].

Many anthropologists and other social scientists now argue, along with Saro-Wiwa, that such forms of development violate human rights because they undermine a people's way of life and threaten its continued existence (Johnston 1994).

On to the Future

During the past few decades, many anthropologists have played important roles in defining and exposing a wide range of human rights abuses around the world. Although this "whistle-blowing" can promote positive change, it is also important that anthropologists participate in advocacy work directed toward the prevention of human rights abuses. Determining exactly how anthropologists can contribute to prevention is a challenge to a discipline whose roots lie in studying what is—rather than what might be, or, in this case, what should not be.

Since its beginning, anthropology has been a product of the knowledge gained from studying "others." In the early years, this knowledge was gathered and controlled by Western centers of power. As this chapter shows, indigenous peoples, women, and other groups that have suffered from lack or loss of resources and power, often because of external forms of economic and political change, are beginning to reclaim their knowledge and identity and to rework international ideas of development and change into models of their own. Local redefinitions of development, and local approaches to achieving improved human welfare demonstrate how global forces can sometimes be transformed and remade to the advantage of marginalized and powerless people. We live in a time of war, but also a time of hope, in which insights and strength often come from those with the least in terms of material wealth but with cultural wealth beyond measure.

▪ HOW do cultural anthropologists study change?

Since the mid-twentieth century, cultural anthropologists have become more involved in the study of change. Many such cultural anthropologists have contributed to theoretical debates about how change occurs and how anthropological knowledge can contribute to culturally appropriate forms of change. Major processes of cultural change are invention and diffusion. In contemporary times, modernization has been a powerful model of change that involves diffusion of Western technologies and values to non-Western contexts. After World War II, development became increasingly important as a form of modernization that emphasizes improved human welfare.

▪ WHAT are various approaches to development?

Several theories or models of development exist, including modernization, growth-oriented development, distributional development, human development, and sustainable development. Institutional approaches to development, whether pursued by large-scale or grassroots organizations, tend to rely on the development project as a vehicle of local change. Cultural anthropologists have been hired as consultants on development projects, typically at the end of the project cycle to provide evaluations. They have advocated for involvement earlier in the project so that their cultural knowledge can be used

in project planning to avoid common errors. In order to provide relevant information in a short time frame, cultural anthropology has adapted its traditional methods of long-term participant observation. Rapid research methods are intended to maximize data gathering during a short period in spite of (and with awareness of) the greater limitations involved.

▪ WHAT does cultural anthropology contribute to understanding some major issues in development?

The status of indigenous peoples, the role of women in development, and the complex issue of defining and protecting human rights are three urgent and interrelated areas in international development that have attracted anthropological research and thinking. Research on the impact of growth-oriented, large-scale development shows that many indigenous peoples and women have suffered a decline, rather than an improvement, in their standard of living. Often, such losses are tied to violence and environmental degradation in their homelands. Such tragic occurrences lead directly to the question of what human rights are and how development affects them. Cultural anthropologists contribute insights from different cultures about perceptions of basic human and cultural rights. This knowledge, linked to advocacy, may be able to help promote socially informed and equitable development and prevent human rights abuses in the future.

KEY CONCEPTS

assimilation, p. 610
critical development anthropology (CDA), p. 620
development, p. 612
development anthropology, p. 608
diachronic, p. 608
diffusion, p. 610

human development, p. 614
modernization, p. 612
participatory research method (PRM), p. 621
project cycle, p. 618
rapid research method (RRM), p. 621
social impact assessment, p. 611

sociocultural fit, p. 619
structural adjustment, p. 613
sustainable development, p. 615
synchronic, p. 608
traditional development anthropology (TDA), p. 620

SUGGESTED READINGS

Thomas W. Collins and John D. Wingard, eds. *Communities and Capital: Local Struggles against Corporate Power and Privatization*. Athens, GA: University of Georgia Press, 2000. Nine case studies of local resistance against large capitalist forces follow an introductory chapter that sets the stage. Cases include clam farmers of North Carolina, a fishing community in Malaysia, and banana growers in Belize.

John J. Cove. *What the Bones Say: Tasmanian Aborigines, Science and Domination*. Ottawa; Canada: Carleton University Press, 1995. This book probes the links between science and global power and describes how their combination has affected indigenous peoples. The case of Tasmania, which is examined in depth, reveals how the control of indigenous people's bones is related to wider social relations and change.

Dolores Koenig, Tieman Diarra, Moussa Sow, and Ousmane Diarra. *Innovation and Individuality in African Development: Changing Production Strategies in Rural Mali*. Ann Arbor: University of Michigan Press, 1998. This ethnography of change looks at the history of Malian rural production, agricultural resources and crop production, and how lessons learned contribute to an improved anthropology of development.

David H. Lempert, Kim McCarthy, and Craig Mitchell. *A Model Development Plan: New Strategies and Perspectives*. Westport, CT: Praeger, 1995. A group of university students from different disciplines (including one anthropologist, Lempert) spent six weeks in Ecuador, visiting nearly every province and studying development issues there as the basis for their development plan for Ecuador. A preface explains the background of the project. The rest of the volume consists of a detailed presentation of the plan.

Mark Moberg. *Citrus, Strategy, and Class: The Politics of Development in Southern Belize*. Iowa City: University of Iowa Press, 1992. This ethnography of development considers the involvement of two villages in Belize, Central America, in the global citrus market. The author's "political economy" perspective sheds light on the formation of a rural class and on the increasing dependency of rural Belize through its participation in the global market. Profiles of five villagers show how people attempt to exercise some control over outside economic forces through cooperatives and labor unions.

Richard J. Perry. *From Time Immemorial: Indigenous Peoples and State Systems*. Austin: University of Texas Press, 1996. This book provides a comparative examination of the history and status of indigenous peoples of Mexico, the United States, Canada, and Australia. The conclusion offers findings about state policies, state violence, resistance of the indigenous people, and efforts at self-determination.

Richard Reed. *Forest Dwellers, Forest Protectors: Indigenous Models for International Development*. The Cultural Survival Series in Ethnicity and Change. Boston: Allyn and Bacon, 1997. This is a fieldwork-based study of the Guaraní, indigenous people of Paraguay and Brazil, now occupying one of the world's largest remaining subtropical rainforests. Chapters consider social organization, production patterns, and consumption patterns. The text focuses on Guaraní practices and their ideas about use of forest resources.

Kalima Rose. *Where Women Are Leaders: The SEWA Movement in India*. Atlantic Highlands, NJ: Zed Books, 1992. Although not written by an anthropologist, this in-depth case study of a pioneering credit scheme for poor women of India stands as a useful contribution to the "success story" literature. The book provides a history of SEWA (Self-Employed Women's Association) and describes different strategies of SEWA and its expansion throughout India and globally.

John van Willigen. *Anthropology in Action: A Source Book on Anthropological Practice*. Boulder, CO: Westview Press, 1991. This book first provides brief overviews of ethics, publications, and professional organizations in applied anthropology. There follows a series of case studies arranged alphabetically by topic, from "Agriculture" to "Women in Development."

Robert M. VanWynsberghe. *AlterNatives: Community, Identity, and Environmental Justice on Walpole Island*. Boston: Allyn and Bacon, 2002. This study documents the environmental activism of the Walpole Island First Nation, Ontario, the southernmost reserve in Canada. During the 1990s, indigenous peoples of Walpole began to organize to protect their environment from toxic pollution caused by massive discharges of industrial waste into the St. Clair River. They successfully planned for providing clean water to the community, management of the area's wetlands, and creation of a Heritage Centre.

absolute cultural relativism: the view that no one has the right to question any cultural behavior or idea anywhere because it would be ethnocentric to do so.

absolute dating method: a way of determining the age of a fossil, artifact, or site on the basis of a specific time scale, such as years before the present, or other fixed calendrical system.

Acheulian: Lower Paleolithic toolkit dominated by stone tools called handaxes (1.6 million years ago to 300,000 years ago).

achievement: the process by which an individual's membership in a social group is determined through personal action.

activist group: group formed with the goal of changing certain conditions, such as political repression, violence, and human rights violations.

adaptation: a change in response to external conditions that contributes to the survival of a species.

adaptive compromise: a change that involves trade-offs between positive and negative effects.

adaptive radiation: a form of macroevolutionary change that involves a rapid increase in the number of related species.

adolescence: a culturally defined period of maturation from the time of puberty until adulthood.

agency: the ability of an individual to make choices and exercise free will.

age set: a group of people close in age who go through certain rituals, such as circumcision, at the same time.

agriculture: a mode of production that involves growing crops with the use of plowing, irrigation, and fertilizer. Also called farming.

Allen's Rule: the generalization that members of cold-climate-adapted populations tend to have shorter arms and legs, relative to their height, than members of tropical-climate-adapted populations.

allocare: care of infants by group members.

amazon: a person who is biologically female but takes on a male gender role.

anatomically modern humans (AMH), or **modern humans:** *Homo sapiens*, the species to which modern humans belong and which differs biologically and culturally from archaic *Homo* species.

androcentrism: male-centered bias in anthropological research.

anemia: low numbers of normal red blood cells.

animatism: a belief system in which the supernatural is conceived of as an impersonal power.

animism: the belief in souls or "doubles."

anthropogenic: caused by humans, as in anthropogenic change.

anthropoids: the primate suborder that includes monkeys, apes, and humans.

anthropology: the study of humanity, including the prehistoric origins of humans and contemporary biological, cultural, and linguistic variation.

anthropometrics: measurements of the size and shape of the human body and its parts.

anthropomorphic: in the form of a human.

applied anthropology: the use of anthropological knowledge to prevent or solve problems and to shape or achieve policy goals. Also called practicing anthropology and practical anthropology.

arboreal: tree-dwelling.

archaeology: the study of past human cultures through their material remains.

Archaic: the time period in the New World, from about 8000 to 2000 BCE, when foragers began to domesticate plants.

archaic hominin: an extinct taxon that is almost certainly a hominin but which retains some ape-like characteristics.

archaic *Homo*: an extinct hominin species included in the genus *Homo* (1.9 million years ago to 18,000 years ago).

***Ardipithecus kadabba*:** a possible primitive hominin, known from fossils dated at 5.7 to 5.2 million years ago from the Middle Awash regions of Ethiopia.

***Ardipithecus ramidus*:** a probable primitive hominin, known from fossils dated at 4.5 million years ago from the Middle Awash regions of Ethiopia.

art: the application of imagination, skill, and style to matter, movement, and/or sound in a manner that goes beyond the purely utilitarian.

artifact: portable object made or modified by humans.

ascription: the process by which an individual's membership in a social group is assigned on the basis of birth.

assemblage: a cluster of similar artifacts interpreted as representing a cultural group.

assimilation: a process of culture change through which one culture becomes incorporated into another and no longer has a separate identity.

Aurignacian period: cultural phase in the European Upper Paleolithic beginning around 40,000 years ago.

Australopithecus afarensis: an archaic hominin, known from fossils dated at 4 to 3 million years ago from sites in Ethiopia and Tanzania.

Australopithecus africanus: an archaic hominin, known from fossils dated at 3 to 2.4 million years ago from sites in southern Africa.

Australopithecus anamensis: an archaic hominin, known from fossils dated at 4.5 to 4 million years ago from sites in Kenya.

Australopithecus bahrelghazali: an archaic hominin, known from fossils dated at 3.5 million years ago from a site in Chad.

Australopithecus garhi: an archaic hominin, known from fossils dated at 2.5 million years ago from Ethiopia.

australopiths: a shorthand term for species in the genus *Australopithecus.*

authority: the ability to take action based on a person's achieved or ascribed status, moral reputation, or other basis.

balanced exchange: a system of transfers involving either immediate or eventual balance in value.

band: the political organization of foraging groups.

banditry: a form of aggressive conflict that involves taking something that belongs to someone else, sometimes practiced by a person or group of persons who are socially marginal and who may gain a mythic status.

behavioral morphology: the use of fossil morphology to make inferences about behavior.

behaviorism: the view that culture consists of learned and shared patterns of behavior.

below-replacement-level fertility: a situation in which births are fewer than deaths, leading to population decline.

berdache: a blurred gender category, usually referring to a person who is biologically male but who assumes a female gender role.

Bergmann's Rule: the generalization that members of cold-climate-adapted populations tend to have wider and shorter bodies than members of tropical-climate-adapted populations.

biface: a stone tool that has been flaked on both sides.

big-man or **big-woman system:** a form of political organization midway between the tribe and the chiefdom involving reliance on the leadership of individuals who develop a political following through personal ties and redistributive feasts.

bilineal descent: a kinship system in which a child is recognized as being related by descent to both parents.

biological anthropology: the study of humans as biological organisms, including their evolution and contemporary variation. Also called physical anthropology.

biological determinism: in anthropology, an emphasis on the role of genes and hormones in shaping human culture.

bipedal: walking or running on two feet.

blade: an elongated, parallel-sided flake made from stone such as flint or obsidian, associated with modern humans.

blank: a naturally shaped stone from which stone tools are made.

blood sport: a form of competition that seeks to bring about a flow of blood, or even death, of human contestants, animal competitors, or in animal targets of human hunting.

brachiation: nonhuman primate form of arboreal travel using the forelimbs to swing from branch to branch.

breccia: a cement-like substance formed in caves when pieces of rock fall from the roof of the cave and mix with bones and sediments.

brideprice: a form of marriage exchange involving a transfer of cash and goods from the groom to the bride's father.

broad-spectrum diet: food consumption pattern in which a wide range of food items is consumed; this pattern began in the Upper Paleolithic and became prominent in the Mesolithic.

bureaucracy: a form of administration that is hierarchical, specialized, and relies on recordkeeping.

cargo cult: a form of revitalization movement that sprang up in Melanesia, the South Pacific, in response to Western and Japanese influences during World War II.

caste: a ranked group, determined by birth, often linked to a particular occupation and to South Asian cultures.

cave art: paintings or engravings on cave walls.

chain migration: the process by which first-wave migrants bring in relatives or friends, who in turn bring in others.

chiefdom: a form of political organization that has a central leader and encompasses several smaller political units.

chromosome: a structure within the nucleus of a cell that contains a pair of double-stranded DNA molecules; most genes are in chromosomes.

circular migration: a form of labor migration involving movement in a regular pattern between two or more places.

circumscription: Carneiro's model for the origin of the state, which proposes that states arise where growing populations within "circumscribed," or enclosed, environments cannot expand except through conquest warfare.

civil society: the collection of interest groups that function outside the government to organize economic and other aspects of life.

clade: a group made up of all the taxa descended from a recent common ancestor.

cladistic analysis: the use of recently evolved morphology to determine how a fossil hominin taxon is related to other fossil hominin taxa.

clan: a kinship-based group in which people claim descent from a common ancestor, although they may be unable to trace the exact relationship.

clash of civilizations: the view that the powerful advancement of Euro-American capitalism and lifeways throughout the world has created disenchantment, alienation, and resentment among people of other cultural systems, most notably in Islamic countries.

class: a social category based on people's economic position in society, usually measured in terms of income or wealth and exhibited in lifestyle.

clinical or **applied medical anthropology:** the application of anthropological knowledge to furthering the goals of health care providers.

Clovis: widespread North American prehistoric culture associated with a stone tool called the Clovis point.

code: a variant within a language that may include a distinct vocabulary, grammar, and intonation, associated with a particular microculture.

common ancestor: a primate species from which both modern humans and chimpanzees diverged between 8 and 5 million years ago.

communication: the conveying of meaningful messages from one person, animal, or insect to another through language.

community healing: way of healing that emphasizes the social context as a key component and is likely to be carried out within the public domain.

composite tool: a tool made by combining two or more separate components into a single tool.

confederacy: a form of political organization involving the joining together of several chiefdoms under the leadership of a paramount chief.

conspecific: member of the same species.

consumerism: a mode of consumption in which people's demands are many and infinite and the means of satisfying them are therefore insufficient.

consumption: the practice of using up goods or expending funds.

convergent evolution: the process by which different lineages evolve similar morphology independently.

cooperative: an economic group whose members share surpluses and who follow the democratic decision-making principle of one person, one vote.

core tool: tool made from rounded stones that have had flakes chipped off them.

corporate farm: a large agricultural enterprise that produces goods solely for sale and that is owned and operated by companies that rely entirely on hired labor.

creationism: the Bible-based belief that all species date from the Day of Creation and have always been the way they are now.

creole: a language directly descended from a pidgin but possessing its own native speakers and involving linguistic expansion and elaboration.

critical cultural relativism: the view that all cultures' practices and ideas should be examined in terms of who accepts them and why, and whom they might be harming or helping.

critical development anthropology: an approach to international development in which the anthropologist takes on a critical-thinking role and asks why and to whose benefit particular development policies and programs are pursued.

critical legal anthropology: an approach within the cross-cultural study of law that examines how law and judicial systems serve to maintain and expand dominant power interests rather than protecting marginal and less powerful people.

critical media anthropology: an approach within the cross-cultural study of mass media that examines to what degree media messages are liberating, to what degree they are propagandizing and controlling, and whose interests the media serve.

critical medical anthropology: an approach within the cross-cultural study of health and illness involving the analysis of how economic and political structures shape people's health status, their access to health care, and the prevailing medical systems that exist in relation to them.

critical military anthropology: the study of the military as a power structure in terms of its roles and internal social dynamics.

Cro-Magnon: an informal name for the earliest modern humans in Europe.

cross cousin: the offspring of either one's father's sister or one's mother's brother.

cultural anthropology: the study of living people and their cultures, including variation and change.

cultural broker: a person who is familiar with the practices and beliefs of two cultures and can promote cross-cultural understanding to prevent or mediate conflicts.

cultural constructionism: the view that human behavior and ideas are shaped by culture through learning.

cultural imperialism: a dominant group's claiming supremacy over minority cultures and changing them in its own interests and at the expense of the other cultures.

cultural materialism: an approach to studying culture that emphasizes examining the material aspects of life, such as the environmental context and how people make a living in particular environments.

cultural particularism: the idea that each culture is unique and should be studied and described within its own historical context.

cultural relativism: the idea that cultures must be understood in terms of their own values and beliefs and not judged by the standards of another culture; the assumption that no culture is better than any other.

culture: learned and shared ways of behaving and thinking.

culture-bound syndrome: a collection of signs and symptoms that is restricted to a particular culture or a limited number of cultures; also called "folk illness."

culture shock: deep feelings of uneasiness, loneliness, and anxiety that may occur when a person shifts from one culture to another.

dalit: the preferred name for the socially defined lowest groups in the Indian caste system, meaning "oppressed" or "ground down."

descent: the tracing of kinship relations through birth and relations with a parent or parents.

development: directed change to achieve improved human welfare.

developmental adaptation: gradual physiological adaptation to environmental stresses experienced during human growth.

development anthropology: the study of how culture and international development interact.

development-induced displacement (DID): forced migration due to development projects, such as dam building.

diachronic: the analysis of culture across time.

dialect: a way of speaking in a particular place or a variety of a language arising from local circumstances.

diaspora population: dispersed group of people living outside their original homeland.

differential mortality: a situation in which people of different groups, either genetic or social, experience different death rates.

differential preservation: the fact that some types of organisms and some parts of organisms are more likely than others to be preserved in the fossil record, thus creating a biased fossil record.

diffusion: the spread of culture through contact.

Diffusion Wave Model: the view that modern humans evolved recently in Africa and then spread across the Old and New Worlds, interacting and interbreeding to some extent with local populations of archaic *Homo*.

Discordance hypothesis: the hypothesis that humans are biologically adapted to Paleolithic lifestyles, not to an urban lifestyle.

discourse: language in use.

disease/illness dichotomy: the distinction between disease as an objective and universal biological pathology, and illness as the culturally specific understandings and experiences of a health problem or other form of suffering. Corresponds to the etic/emic distinction.

disease of development: a health problem caused or increased by economic development activities that affect the environment and people's relationship with it.

displaced person: someone who is forced to leave his or her home and community, or country and to settle elsewhere.

displacement: a feature of human language that allows people to talk about events in the past and future.

diurnal: active during the daytime and sleeping at night.

divination: a diagnostic procedure in which a specialist uses techniques to gain supernatural insights.

DNA: short for deoxyribose nucleic acid, a complex molecule made up of units called nucleotides that carry the genetic code.

doctrine: direct and formalized statements about religious beliefs.

domestication: the process by which human selection causes genetic changes in plants and animals.

dominance: among nonhuman primates, priority in access to valued resources and social relationships.

dominant caste: one caste in a particular locale that controls most of the land and is often numerically preponderant.

Down syndrome: a cytogenetic disorder caused by abnormal meiotic cell division that results in an additional chromosome 21. Also called DS and trisomy 21.

dowry: a form of marriage exchange involving the transfer of cash and goods from the bride's family to the bride and groom or to the groom's family.

Dynamic Model: Marcus's model for the long-term rising and falling of states, which focuses on common systemic causes of instability and change.

Early Stone Age: a time period in Africa parallel to the Lower Paleolithic.

ecological/epidemiological approach: an approach that considers how aspects of the natural environment and social environment interact to cause illness.

Edge Hypothesis: Binford's explanation for the rise of farming worldwide, which includes the idea that plant domestication first occurred outside the areas of greatest productivity.

egalitarian: characterized by an even distribution of material goods, status, and quality of life.

empire: a form of long-term political organization that involves rule over multiple states, territories, and ethnic groups.

enculturation: the process of acquiring culture through learning. Sometimes called socialization.

endogamy: marriage within a particular group or locality.

environmental determinism: the theory that environment shapes culture.

ethnicity: a sense of group affiliation based on a distinct heritage or worldview as a "people."

ethnoarchaeology: a research method that involves studying contemporary people to gain insights about past cultural patterns.

ethnobotany: an area of inquiry exploring knowledge in different cultures of plants and their uses.

ethnocentrism: judging another culture by the standards of one's own culture rather than by the standards of the other culture, usually resulting in a negative view of the other culture.

ethno-esthetics: cultural definitions of what is art.

ethnogenesis: the borrowing and blending of traits across different populations.

ethnography: a book-length description of a culture or cultures based on extended fieldwork among living people.

ethnomedicine: the medical system of a culture, including practices and ideas about the body, illness, and healing.

ethnomusicology: the cross-cultural study of music.

ethno-nosology: the cross-cultural study of classifications of health problems.

ethnopsychology: the study of how various cultures define and create personality, identity, and mental health.

euhemerism: the process by which a human who once lived is transformed into a deity; named after the philosopher Euhemerus of Messene.

evolution: inherited and cumulative change in the characteristics of species, populations, and culture.

excavation: a method for fossil or artifact recovery in which the material surrounding the evidence is removed both vertically and horizontally.

exchange: the transfer of goods or services between two or more people.

exogamy: marriage outside a particular group or locality.

expected reciprocity: an exchange of approximately equally valued goods or services, usually between people of roughly equal social status.

exposure: places where rocks of the right age for finding fossils have been revealed by water and wind erosion.

expressive culture: behavior and beliefs related to the arts and leisure.

extended household: a co-resident kinship group that comprises more than one parent–child unit.

extensive strategy: a form of production involving temporary use of large areas of land and a high degree of spatial mobility.

extinction: a form of macroevolutionary change that occurs when a living species ceases to exist or, in paleoanthropology, when one no longer finds fossil evidence of a species.

faction: a politically oriented group that has strong ties to a leader and that vies with other factions for resources and rights.

family: a group of people who consider themselves related through a form of kinship, such as descent, sharing, or marriage.

family farming: farmers that produce most of their own food using family labor.

feature: a nonportable object made or transformed by humans in the past.

female genital cutting (FGC): a term used by critics for a range of genital cutting procedures, including the excision of part or all of the clitoris, excision of part or all of the labia majora, and sometimes infibulation, the stitching together of the vaginal entry.

fertility: the rate of births in a population.

feuding: long-term, retributive violence that may be lethal between families, groups of families, or tribes.

fieldwork: research at the site where humanity lived in the past or lives in the present.

fission–fusion group: a type of nonhuman primate social pattern in which group members regularly break into subgroups of varying composition.

fitness: in genetics, the probability that an animal of a particular genotype will survive and reproduce.

flake: the sharp piece that breaks off a cobble when it is struck.

flotation: a technique by which archaeologists use water to recover the light fraction of charred or desiccated plant remains from heavier soils.

focal vocabulary: a cluster of related words referring to important features of a particular culture.

folivore: an animal whose diet consists mainly of leaves.

food production: the human management of plants and animals to increase their availability as food sources.

foraging: obtaining food available in nature through gathering, hunting, fishing, or scavenging.

fossil: the preserved remains of a plant or animal of the past, usually a bone, a tooth, or an impression such as a footprint or leaf impression.

frugivore: an animal whose diet consists mainly of fruit.

functionalism: the view, established by Malinowski, that a culture is similar to a biological organism, with various parts supporting the operation of the whole.

functional morphology: the use of morphology (form) to make inferences about the function of a particular body part.

gender: patterns of culturally constructed and learned behaviors and ideas associated with masculinity, feminity, or a "third," or blended, gender. Gender is contrasted to sex, which uses biological markers to define categories of male and female.

gene: the smallest unit of heredity; a sequence of nucleotides within a DNA molecule that determine the nature of a particular protein molecule.

generalized reciprocity: exchange involving the least conscious sense of interest in material gain or thought of what might be received in return.

genetic adaptation: a change that has been selected for over a long period of time and is part of the genetic heritage of a population.

genetic code: the information needed to make proteins, encoded as distinctive sequences of three DNA nucleotides.

genetics: the field of biology that deals with heredity.

genome: the totality of genetic information encoded in the DNA of an individual.

genome analysis: methods used to sequence parts of the genome or, increasingly, the whole genome. Also called genomic analysis.

genotype: the genetic basis, or alleles, of a trait.

globalization: a contemporary process of cultural change related to dense and rapid linkages of trade, communication, population movement, and other forms of international and transnational contact.

global language: or world language, a language spoken widely throughout the world and in diverse cultural contexts often replacing indigenous languages; notably English and Spanish.

grade: a group made up of taxa based on what an animal does.

grammar: the rules by which words are organized to make sense in a string.

grandmother hypothesis: the idea that menopause evolved because it allowed prehistoric postmenopausal females to devote their energy to caring for their grandchildren rather than producing more offspring themselves.

Gravettian period: cultural phase of the European Upper Paleolithic beginning around 28,000 years ago.

great apes: the larger apes, include orangutans, gorillas, chimpanzees, and bonobos.

gumnivore: an animal whose diet consists mainly of tree exudates.

handaxe: a bifacially flaked, pear-shaped stone tool that is the defining tool of the Acheulian tradition.

heterotopia: the creation of an internally varied place by collecting things from diverse cultures and locations.

hijira: term used in India to refer to a blurred gender role in which a person, usually biologically male, takes on female dress and behavior.

historical linguistics: the study of language change using formal methods that compare shifts over time and across space in formal aspects of language such as phonetics, grammar, and semantics.

holism: the broadest approach in anthropology, which seeks to learn about both behavior and beliefs and how they are interrelated.

hominin: a species, or an individual member of a species that is more closely related to modern humans than to chimpanzees and bonobos.

hominoids: the primate superfamily of apes, including humans.

Homo: the genus comprising modern humans and all extinct hominin species that are more closely related to modern humans than to any archaic hominin species (1.9 million years ago to the present).

Homo erectus: a species of archaic *Homo* widely distributed across the Old World (1.8 million years ago to 200,000 years ago).

Homo ergaster: the earliest archaic *Homo* species with a body size and shape more like modern humans than archaic hominins (1.9 to 1.5 million years ago).

Homo habilis: literally "handy man," a hominin that is transitional between archaic hominins and archaic *Homo*, established by Louis Leakey and his colleagues (2.4 to 1.6 million years ago).

Homo heidelbergensis: a species of archaic *Homo* that lacks the specializations seen in *H. erectus* and *H. neanderthalensis* (600,000 to 100,000 years ago).

Homo neanderthalensis: a morphologically specialized species of archaic *Homo* that lived in Europe, the Middle East, and Western Asia (400,000 to 30,000 years ago); also called Neanderthals.

homoplasy: the occurrence of similar morphologies that are not inherited from a recent common ancestor.

Homo rudolfensis: a hominin species transitional between archaic hominins and archaic *Homo* that some people include in *H. habilis* (1.8 to 1.6 million years ago).

horizon: the layer of rock or sediment. Also known as the stratigraphic layer.

horticulture: a mode of production based on growing domesticated crops in gardens using simple hand tools.

household: a group of people, who may or may not be related by kinship, who share living space and budgeting.

human development: a model of change promoted by the United Nations that emphasizes improvements in human welfare such as health, education, and personal security.

humanistic approach: the pursuit of knowledge through understanding of subjectivity and meaning.

humoral healing system: a health system that emphasizes balance among natural elements within the body.

hybridization: cultural change in which aspects of two or more cultures are mixed to form something new, a blend. Also known as syncretism, creolization, and cultural crossover.

hypergyny: marital preference rule that requires the groom to be of higher status than the bride.

hyperthermia: abnormally and destructively high body temperature.

hypogyny: marital preference rule that requires the bride to be of higher status than the groom.

hypothermia: abnormally and destructively low body temperature.

hypoxia: too little oxygen.

idealism: the view that culture consists of ideas and beliefs.

incest taboo: a strongly held prohibition against marrying or having sex with particular kin.

indigenous knowledge: local knowledge about the environment, including plants, animals, and resources.

indigenous people: a group with a long-standing connection with a home territory that predates colonial or outside societies prevailing in the territory.

industrial capital agriculture: a form of agriculture that is capital-intensive, substituting machinery and purchased inputs for human and animal labor.

industrial collective agriculture: a form of industrialized agriculture that involves estate control of land, technology, and goods produced.

industrialism: a mode of production in which goods are produced through mass employment in business and commercial operations.

infanticide: the killing of an infant or child.

infant mortality rate (IMR): the number of infant deaths per 1000 live births.

influence: the ability to achieve a desired end by exerting social or moral pressure on someone or some group.

in-kind taxation: a revenue system that involves non-cash contributions.

insectivore: an animal whose diet consists mainly of insects.

institution: an enduring group setting formed for a particular purpose.

institutional migrant: a person who moves into a social institution (such as a school or prison), voluntarily or involuntarily.

intensification: The use of inputs of increased human labor and technology such as plowing, irrigation, and fertilizer in order to increase agricultural productivity of a given plot of land.

intergenerational household: a residential group in which an "adult child" returns to live with his or her parents.

internally displaced person (IDP): people who are forced to leave their home and community but who remain within their country.

internal migration: movement within country boundaries.

interpretivist anthropology: a theoretical approach that focuses on understanding culture by studying what people think about, their explanations of their lives, and the meanings that are important to them. Also known as symbolic anthropology.

interview: the gathering of verbal information from living people through questions.

isogamy: marriage between equals.

jajmani system: an exchange system of India in which landholding patrons (jajmans) offer food grains to service providers such as brahman priests, artisans (blacksmiths, potters), and agricultural laborers.

Kenyanthropus platyops: an archaic hominin, known from fossils dated at 3.5 to 3.3 million years ago from Kenya.

kinesics: the study of communication that occurs through body movements, positions, facial expressions, and spatial behavior.

kinship diagram: a schematic way of presenting data on kinship relationships of an individual (called "ego") depicting all of ego's relatives, as remembered by ego and reported to the anthropologist.

kinship system: the predominant form of kin relationships in a culture and the kinds of behavior involved.

Kleiber's Law: the generalization that animals with larger bodies have proportionally lower metabolic rates than smaller animals.

knuckle-walking: a nonhuman primate form of terrestrial travel that involves supporting the upper body on the knuckles of the fingers.

lactase impersistence: the inability to digest lactose in adulthood.

lactase persistence: the ability to digest lactose in adulthood.

language: a form of communication that is a systematic set of arbitrary symbols shared among a group and passed on from generation to generation.

language decay: condition of a language in which speakers adopt a new language for most situations, begin to use their native language only in certain contexts, and may be only semi-fluent and have limited vocabulary in their native language.

language extinction: a situation, either gradual or sudden, in which language speakers abandon their native language in favor of a new language to the extent that the native language loses functions and no longer has competent users.

Later Stone Age (LSA): the time period in Africa defined by microlithic stone and bone technology, extending from about 45,000 to 10,000 years ago.

law: a binding rule created through enactment or custom that defines right and reasonable behavior and is enforceable by threat of punishment.

legal pluralism: the existence, within a culture, of more than one kind of legal system.

Levallois: a stone-tool-making method of preparing a core so that the tool-maker could use it to produce many standardized flakes.

lifeboat mentality: local resentment of an immigrant group because of perceived resource constraints.

life-cycle ritual: a ritual performed to mark a change in status from one life stage to another of an individual or group; also called rite of passage.

limbic system: the part of the brain that is composed of the olfactory cortex, the amygdala, and the hippocampus and is associated with emotion.

linguistic anthropology: the study of human communication, including its origins, history, and contemporary variation and change.

linguistic determinism: the theory that language determines consciousness of the world and behavior.

linguistic pluralism: the presence of linguistic diversity within a particular context.

linguistic relativism: the idea that all languages are equally valid and must be understood in their own terms.

Linnaean taxonomy: a hierarchical structure for classifying living creatures that was introduced by Linnaeus in 1758; its basic unit is the species.

localization: cultural change that occurs when global changes are received and transformed through interaction with existing cultures.

logosyllabic: a writing system wherein the sign indicates a word, a syllable, or a sound.

Lower Paleolithic (LP): the first of the three eras of the Paleolithic.

macroculture: learned and shared ways of behaving and thinking that cross local boundaries, such as a sense of national culture that some governments seek to promote to enhance unity, or the global consumer culture that pervades upper-middle-class and upper-class groups transnationally.

macroevolution: large-scale events that take place during the evolutionary history of a group of organisms, including adaptive radiations, speciation, and extinction.

Magdalenian period: cultural phase of the European Upper Paleolithic beginning around 18,000 years ago.

magic: the attempt to compel supernatural forces and beings to act in certain ways.

market exchange: the buying and selling of commodities under competitive conditions in which the forces of supply and demand determine value.

marriage: a union between two (or more) people, who are likely to be, but are not necessarily, co-resident, sexually involved with each other, and procreative.

material cultural heritage: monuments, buildings, sites, and movable objects considered to have outstanding value to humanity. Also called cultural heritage.

matriarchy: a society in which women are dominant in terms of economics, politics, and ideology.

matrifocal: characterized by females forming the core of the social group.

matrilineal descent: a kinship system that highlights the importance of women by tracing descent through the female line, favoring marital residence with or near the bride's family, and providing for property to be inherited through the female line.

matrilocality: a residence pattern in which females remain with their birth group throughout their lives.

matrilocal residence: a residence pattern in which a married couple share a residence with or near the wife's natal family.

McDonaldization: the view that world cultures are becoming homogeneous because of the powerful influence of United States–dominated corporate culture.

medicalization: labeling a particular problem as medical and requiring medical treatment when the problem is economic or political.

medical pluralism: the existence of more than one medical system in a culture, or a government policy to promote the integration of traditional medicine into biomedical practice.

meiosis: the process by which sex cells, or gametes, are produced. Also called reduction division because the number of chromosomes is reduced from 46 to 23.

melanin: the pigment largely responsible for human skin color.

Mesoamerican Triad: maize, squash, and beans: the three most important domesticated plants in the Mesoamerican Neolithic.

Mesolithic: the time period starting around 12,000 years ago and characterized by microlithic stone and bone tools, broad-spectrum diets, food management and food processing, and semi-sedentism.

microculture: distinct patterns of learned and shared behavior and ideas found in localized regions and among particular groups. Microcultures include ethnic groups, genders, and age categories. Also known as local culture.

microevolution: evolutionary changes that operate at the level of the individual and over short periods of time.

microlith: a small stone tool made from a blade, usually geometric in shape with retouched edges.

midden: a mound formed over time by deposits of human refuse.

Middle Paleolithic (MP): the second of the three eras of the Paleolithic.

Middle Stone Age (MSA): a time period in Africa parallel to the Middle Paleolithic.

minimalism: a mode of consumption that emphasizes simplicity, is characterized by few and finite (limited) consumer demands, and involves an adequate and sustainable means to achieve them.

mitosis: the process whereby one somatic cell with 46 chromosomes divides into two cells, during which time each strand of the genetic material replicates itself so that each daughter cell also has 46 chromosomes.

mode of consumption: the dominant way, in a culture, of using things up or spending resources in order to satisfy demands.

mode of exchange: the dominant pattern, in a society, of transferring goods, services, and other items between and among people and groups.

mode of production: the dominant way, in a culture, of providing for people's material and social needs.

mode of reproduction: the predominant pattern of fertility in a culture.

modernization: a model of change based on belief in the inevitable advance of science and Western secularism and processes including industrial growth, consolidation of the state, bureaucratization, market economy, technological innovation, literacy, and options for social mobility.

monogamy: marriage between two people.

monumental art: large-scale, permanent art work.

morphology: the size, shape, appearance, and/or internal structure of an organism or of part of an organism; also known as phenotype.

mortality: deaths in a population, or rate of population decline in general or from particular causes.

Mousterian: a Middle Paleolithic toolkit comprising small, specialized tools such as points, scrapers, and awls made from flakes with the Levallois technique.

multi-drug-resistant mycobacterium tuberculosis (MDRTB): one of several new strains of TB that are resistant to treatment by conventional drugs.

Multiregional Model: the view that archaic *Homo* was transformed into modern humans in several regions of the Old World—Africa, Europe, the Middle East, and various parts of Asia.

multiscalar: characterized by interpretation that moves from the micro-level to higher levels and broader implications.

mutation: an error made when DNA is copied at the time of cell division.

myth: a narrative with a plot that involves the sacred.

nation: a group of people who share a language, culture, territorial base, political organization, and history.

natural selection: the process by which organisms better adapted to the environment reproduce more effectively compared with less well adapted forms.

Neanderthal: the informal name for *Homo neanderthalensis.*

Neolithic: the "New Stone Age" characterized by stone tools related to harvesting and processing grains and, by extension, sedentary farming societies.

neolocal residence: married couple sharing a residence somewhere away from the residence of both the bride's and the groom's parents.

new immigrants: international migrants who have moved since the 1960s.

nocturnal: active during the night and sleeping during the daytime.

norm: a generally agreed-upon standard for how people should behave, usually unwritten and learned unconsciously.

nuclear household: a domestic unit containing one adult couple (married or partners), with or without children.

nucleotide: the smallest functional unit in a DNA molecule.

observer's paradox: the logical impossibility of doing research on natural communication events without affecting the naturalness sought.

obsidian: a volcanic glass that was highly prized and traded over long distances, in the Old World Neolithic, because of its excellent flaking properties and extremely sharp edges.

Oldowan: a stone toolkit dominated by cores and simple flake tools (2.6 million years ago to 300,000 years ago).

omnivore: an animal whose diet is typified not by a single food type but rather by reliance on a variety of food types. Also called multivore.

Orrorin tugenensis: a possible primitive hominin, known from fossils dated at 6 million years ago from sites in Kenya.

Paleolithic: the period during which stone tools are made and used, beginning about 2.6 million years ago. Also called the Old Stone Age.

paralanguage: nonverbal communication such as body posture, voice tone, touch, smells, and eye and facial movements.

parallel cousin: offspring of either one father's brother or one's mother's sister.

Paranthropus boisei: an archaic hominin, known from fossils dated at 2.3 to 1.3 million years ago from sites in Ethiopia, Kenya, Tanzania, and Malawi.

Paranthropus robustus: an archaic hominin, known from fossils dated at 1.9 to 1.5 million years ago from sites in southern Africa.

participant observation: a method of studying contemporary humans in which the researcher lives with and studies the people for an extended period of time.

participatory research method (PRM): a method in development anthropology that involves the local people in gathering and updating data relevant to local development projects.

pastoralism: a mode of production based on keeping domesticated animal herds and using their products, such as meat and milk, for most of the diet.

patriarchy: male dominance in economic, political, social, and ideological domains.

patrilineal descent: a kinship system that highlights the importance of men in tracing descent through the male line, determining marital residence with or near the groom's family, and providing for inheritance of property through the male line.

patrilocality: a residence pattern in which males remain with their birth group throughout their lives.

patrilocal residence: a residence pattern in which a married couple share a residence with or near the husband's natal family.

PCR: the abbreviation for polymerase chain reaction, a method used in the laboratory to make multiple accurate copies. Also called amplification of DNA.

personality: an individual's patterned and characteristic way of behaving, thinking, and feeling.

phenotype: see morphology.

phoneme: a sound that makes a difference for meaning in a language.

phonetics: the analysis of phonemes.

phytolith: microscopic fossil plant remains.

pictographic: in writing, elements in which a sign stands for a concept.

pidgin: a contact language that emerges where people with different languages need to communicate; a pidgin involves linguistic simplification and reduction.

policing: the exercise of social control through processes of surveillance and the threat of punishment related to maintaining social order.

political organization: the existence of groups for purposes of public decision making and leadership, maintaining social cohesion and order, protecting group rights, and ensuring safety from external threats.

polyandry: marriage of one wife with more than one husband.

polygamy: marriage involving multiple spouses.

polygyny: marriage of one husband with more than one wife.

population: in genetics, a group of potentially interbreeding individuals within a species.

portable art: small, movable objects that are engraved or sculpted.

postmodernist archaeology: a perspective that rejects general theories of the human past and objective interpretations of sites and artifacts in favor of rich descriptions of particular cases and intuitive interpretation of evidence. Also known as postprocessual archaeology.

potassium–argon dating: an absolute dating method based on measuring the decay rate of ^{40}K, a radioactive isotope of potassium, to argon (^{40}AR).

power: the capacity to take action in the face of resistance, through force if necessary.

prepared core: a specially selected and prepared stone cobble from which tools such as flakes are made.

priest/priestess: male or female full-time religious specialist whose position is based mainly on abilities gained through formal training.

primary group: a social group in which members meet on a face-to-face basis.

primates: the order of mammals that includes prosimians and anthropoids (monkeys, apes, and humans).

primitive hominin: a hominin taxon close to the branching point of the chimpanzee and human lineages that is still ape-like but is judged to be more closely related to modern humans than to chimpanzees.

processualism: the theory that environment and other material factors determine certain kinds of cultural changes.

production: an economic system of making goods or money.

productivity: a feature of human language that offers the ability to communicate many messages efficiently.

project cycle: the steps of a development project from initial planning to completion: project identification, project design, project appraisal, project implementation, and project evaluation.

projectile point: stone tool intended to be attached to a spear or arrow.

pronatalism: an ideology promoting high fertility.

prosimian: the primate suborder that includes the lemurs, lorises, and tarsiers.

puberty: a time in the human life cycle that occurs universally and involves a set of biological markers and sexual maturation.

pure gift: something given with no expectation or thought of a return.

push–pull theory: a theory that attributes rural-to-urban migration to the "push" of rural areas' decreasing ability to support population growth and the "pull" of cities that offer employment and a more appealing lifestyle.

quadrupedal: four-footed locomotor pattern.

qualitative: descriptive.

quantitative: numeric.

race: a group of people defined in terms of selected biological traits, usually phenotypical features; now discredited as lacking scientific validity.

radiocarbon dating: an absolute dating method based on measuring the decay rate of ^{14}C, the radioactive isotope of carbon, to stable nitrogen (^{14}N).

rapid research method (RRM): fieldwork method designed for use in development anthropology that can yield relevant data in a short period of time.

rapport: a trusting relationship between the anthropologist and the study population.

Recent African Replacement Model: the view that modern humans first emerged recently in Africa and then migrated into the Old and New Worlds with little or no interaction with local populations of archaic *Homo*.

redistribution: a form of exchange that involves one person collecting goods or money from many members of a group who then, at a later time and at a public event, "return" the pooled goods to everyone who contributed.

refugee: a person who is forced to leave their home country.

relative dating method: a way of determining the age of a fossil or artifact by placing it in a chronological sequence or matching evidence at one site with similar evidence at another site that has been dated using an absolute method.

religion: beliefs and actions related to supernatural beings and forces.

religious pluralism: when one or more religions co-exist as either complementary to each other or as competitive.

remittance: economic transfer of money or goods by a migrant to his or her family back home.

repatriation: returning bones or artifacts from museums to the people with whom they originated.

replacement-level fertility: situation when births equal deaths, leading to maintenance of current population size.

restudy: a research project in which a cultural anthropologist goes to a previously studied site.

revitalization movement: an organized movement, usually surrounding a prophetic leader, that seeks to construct a more satisfying culture, either by re-establishing all or parts of a religion that has been threatened by outside forces.

rift valley: a geological formation consisting of a sunken floor and elevated walls created by tectonic action.

right of return: United Nations guaranteed right of refugees to repatriation.

ritual: a patterned form of behavior that has to do with the supernatural realm.

ritual of inversion: a ritual in which normal social roles and order are temporarily inverted.

sacrifice: a ritual in which something is offered to the supernaturals.

Sahelanthropus tchadensis: probable primitive hominin, known from fossils dated at 7 to 6 million years ago from a site in Chad.

sample: a subset of a wider research "universe" such as a site, community, or population.

Sapir-Whorf hypothesis: a theory that claims that language determines thought.

savannah: an open plain with tall grasses and sparse patches of trees.

science: a form of knowledge-seeking based on hypothesis formation and hypothesis testing.

scientific method: a form of knowledge-seeking that entails making observations, formulating an explanatory hypothesis, testing the hypothesis, and confirming, amending, or rejecting the hypothesis.

scraper: a large flake with a sharpened edge along one side.

secondary group: people who identify with each other on some basis but may never meet with one another personally.

sedentism: the lifestyle associated with residence in permanent villages, towns, and cities, generally associated with the emergence of farming.

segmentary model: type of political organization in which smaller units unite in the face of external threats and then split when the external threat is absent.

self-help group: group formed to achieve specific personal goals.

settlement pattern research: a research approach that emphasizes the relationships of settlements with their environment and each other.

shaman or **shamanka:** male or female part-time religious specialist who gains his or her status through direct relationship with the supernaturals, often by being "called."

sickle-cell syndrome: a group of genetic disorders due to abnormal hemoglobin.

single nucleotide polymorphisms (SNPs): differences in DNA that are restricted to one nucleotide.

site: in archaeology and paleoanthropology, a location containing remains of humanity's past.

social control: processes that maintain orderly social life, including informal and formal mechanisms.

social group: a cluster of people beyond the domestic unit who are usually related on grounds other than kinship. Among non-human primates, animals that interact regularly, know each other, and spend more time with each other than with others.

social impact assessment: a study conducted to gauge the potential social costs and benefits of particular innovations before change is undertaken.

sociality: preference for living in groups.

social stratification: Inherited differences in wealth or power that separate members of society into layers (strata) or social classes.

sociocultural fit: concept that refers to how well a development project meshes with the "target" culture and population.

sociolinguistics: approach that says that culture and society and a person's social position determine the content and form of language; a field of study devoted to revealing such social effects on language.

Solutrean period: cultural phase of the European Upper Paleolithic beginning around 21,000 years ago.

speciation: a form of macroevolutionary change in which new species are produced either by the splitting of an existing species into two new species or by the transformation of an existing species into a different descendant.

species: a group of interbreeding organisms reproductively isolated from other such groups; the basic category in the Linnaean taxonomic system.

state: a form of political organization with a bureaucracy and diversified governmental institutions designed to administer large and complex societies.

status: a person's position, or standing, in society.

stem household: a coresidential group that contains only two married couples related through males, commonly found in East Asian cultures.

stratigraphy: in archaeology, the study and description of a vertical series of sediment or rock layers that have accumulated over time.

structural adjustment: an economic policy that has been pursued by the World Bank since the 1980s requiring that countries receiving World Bank loans privatize services such as health care and schools and reduce government expenditures in these areas.

structural suffering: human health problems caused by such economic and political situations as war, famine, terrorism, forced migration, and poverty. Also called structural affliction.

structurism: an approach in cultural anthropology that emphasizes the role of large, powerful structures in society (such as the economy, social and political organizations, and ideological systems) in shaping people's behavior and beliefs.

surface find: a fossil or artifact that is displaced through erosion from its horizon.

survey: a means of data collection among living people that consists of the administration of a set of written questions that are either open-ended or closed-ended.

sustainable development: a form of directed change that involves approaches to development that are not environmentally destructive, are financially supportable by the host country, and are environmentally supportable by the earth as a whole.

symbol: an object, substance, or concept that stands for something else on the basis of an arbitrary, not a logical, connection.

synchronic: a "one-time" view of a culture that devotes little or no attention to its past.

syncretism: the blending of aspects of more than one culture or aspect of culture such as religion.

tag question: a question seeking affirmation, placed at the end of a sentence.

taphonomy: scientific study of the processes by which organisms are preserved after their death and of how these processes affect the fossil and archaeological records.

taxon: any group recognized at any level in the Linnaean hierarchy (plural, *taxa*).

tell: a mound formed over time through the build-up of human settlements and the accumulation of trash.

teosinte: the wild ancestor of maize (corn).

terrestrial: ground-dwelling.

theater: a form of enactment, related to other forms such as dance, music, parades, competitive games and sports, and verbal art.

traditional development anthropology: an approach to development in which the anthropologist accepts the role of helping to make development work better by providing cultural information to planners.

transnationalism: a sense of belonging to more than one nation or country.

transnational migrant: a person who moves back and forth regularly between two or more countries and forms a new identity that transcends association of the self with a single political unit.

trial by ordeal: a way of determining innocence or guilt in which the accused person is put to a test that may be painful, stressful, or fatal.

tribe: a political group that comprises several bands or lineage groups, each with similar language and lifestyle and occupying a distinct territory.

tuberculosis (TB): a mycobacterial infection of the soft or skeletal tissues.

tuff: a rock formed from volcanic ash that is rich in potassium and argon and is useful for dating hominin fossils.

unbalanced exchange: a system of transfers in which the goal is to make a profit.

unilineal descent: a kinship system that traces descent through only one parent, either the mother or the father.

Upper Paleolithic (UP): the time period in the Old World (other than Africa) defined first by stone blade technology and later by the prominence of microlithic tools in stone and bone, extending from about 40,000 years to 10,000 years ago.

use right: a system of property relations in which a person or group has socially recognized priority in access to particular resources such as gathering, hunting, and fishing areas and water sources.

use wear: a pattern of wear on a tool caused by its use for a particular purpose.

war: organized and purposeful group action directed against another group and involving the actual or potential application of lethal force.

world economy: a global division of labor in which countries compete unequally for a share of the wealth.

world religion: a term coined in the nineteenth century to refer to religions that had many followers, that crossed state borders and that exhibited other features such as a concern with salvation.

worldview: a way of understanding how the world came to be and people's place in it with or without reference to a supernatural realm.

youth gang: a group of young people, found mainly in urban areas, who are often considered a social problem by adults and law enforcement officials.

ziggurat: a large mud-brick platform supporting public and religious structures in the early cities of Mesopotamia.

zoomorphic: in the shape, or partial shape, of an animal.

Abbate, E., A. Albianelli, A. Azzaroli, M. Benvenuti, B. Tesfamariam, P. Bruni, N. Cipriani, R. J. Clarke, G. Ficcarelli, R. Macchiarelli, G. Napoleone, M. Papini, L. Rook, M. Sagri, T. M. Tecle, D. Torre, and I. Villa. 1998
A One-million-year-old *Homo* Cranium from the Danakil (Afar) Depression of Eritrea. Nature 393:458–460.

Adams, Kathleen M. 1984
Come to Tana Toraja, "Land of the Heavenly Kings": Travel Agents as Brokers in Ethnicity. Annals of Tourism Research 11:469–485.

Adams, Robert McC. 1981
Heartland of Cities. Chicago: University of Chicago Press.

———. 1972
Patterns of Urbanization in Early Southern Mesopotamia. In Man, Settlement, and Urbanism. Peter J. Ucko, Ruth Tringham, and D. W. Dimbleby, eds. Pp. 735–749. London: Duckworth.

Adams, Vincanne. 1988
Modes of Production and Medicine: An Examination of the Theory in Light of Sherpa Traditional Medicine. Social Science and Medicine 27:505–513.

Adovasio, James M. and Jake Page. 2002
The First Americans: In Pursuit of Archaeology's Greatest Mystery. New York: Random House.

Afolayan, F. 2000
Bantu Expansion and Its Consequences. In African History before 1885. T. Falola, ed. Pp. 113–136. Durham, NC: Carolina Academic Press.

Agar, Michael. 1994
Language Shock: Understanding the Culture of Conversation. New York: William Morrow.

Agnew, N. and M. Demas. 1998
Preserving the Laetoli Footprints. Scientific American 279:26–37.

Ahern, Laura. 2001
Invitations to Love: Literacy, Love Letters, and Social Change in Nepal. Ann Arbor: University of Michigan Press.

Ahmadu, Fuambai. 2000
Rites and Wrongs: An Insider/Outside Reflects on Power and Excision. In Female "Circumcision" in Africa: Culture, Controversy, and Change. Bettina Shell-Duncan and Ylva Hernlund, eds. Pp. 283–312. Boulder, CO: Lynne Reiner Publishers.

Akinsha, Konstantin. 1992a
Russia: Whose Art Is It? ARTNews 91(5):100–105.

———. 1992b
Whose Gold? ARTNews 91(3):39–40.

———. 1992c
After the Coup: Art for Art's Sake? ARTNews 91(1):108–113.

Albarella, Umberto and Dale Serjeantson. 2002
A Passion for Pork: Meat Consumption at the British Late Neolithic Site of Durrington Walls. In Consuming Passions and Patterns of Consumption. Preston Miracle and Nicky Milner, eds. Pp. 33–49. Cambridge: University of Cambridge, McDonald Institute for Archaeological Research.

Aldenderfer, Mark. 2002
Explaining Changes in Settlement Dynamics across Transformations of Modes of Production: From Hunting to Herding in the South-Central Andes. In Beyond Foraging and Collecting: Evolutionary Change in Hunter–Gatherer Settlement Systems. Ben Fitzhugh and Junko Habu, eds. Pp. 387–412. New York: Kluwer Academic/Plenum Publishers.

Alexander, R. M. 2004
Bipedal Animals, and Their Differences from Humans. Journal of Anatomy 204:321–330.

Algaze, Guillermo. 2001
Initial Social Complexity in Southwestern Asia: The Mesopotamian Advantage. Current Anthropology 42:199–233.

Allen, Susan. 1994
What Is Media Anthropology? A Personal View and a Suggested Structure. In Media Anthropology: Informing Global Citizens. Susan L. Allen, ed. Pp. 15–32. Westport, CT: Bergin & Garvey.

Allison, Anne. 1994
Nightwork: Sexuality, Pleasure, and Corporate Masculinity in a Tokyo Hostess Club. Chicago: University of Chicago Press.

Alter, Joseph S. 1992
The Sannyasi and the Indian Wrestler: Anatomy of a Relationship. American Ethnologist 19(2):317–336.

Altmann, Jeanne. 1998
Leading Ladies. In The Primate Anthology: Essays on Primate Behavior, Ecology, and Conservation from Natural History. Russell L. Ciochon and Richard A. Nisbett, eds. Pp. 80–83. New York: Prentice-Hall.

Alvard, Michael S. 2003
The Adaptive Nature of Culture. Evolutionary Anthropology 12:136–149.

Ambrose, Stanley, Jane Buikstra, and Harold W. Krueger. 2003
Status and Gender Differences in Diet at Mound 72, Cahokia, Revealed by Isotope Analysis of Bone. Journal of Anthropological Archaeology 22:217–236.

Ames, Michael, 1992
Cannibal Tours and Glass Boxes: The Anthropology of Museums. Vancouver: University of British Columbia Press.

Anderson, Richard L. and Karen L. Field. 1993
Chapter Introduction. Art in Small-Scale Societies: Contemporary Readings. In Richard L. Anderson and Karen L. Fields, eds. P. 247. Englewood Cliffs, NJ: Prentice-Hall.

Anton, Susan. 2003
Natural History of Homo erectus. Yearbook of Physical Anthropology 46:126–170.

Applbaum, Kalman D. 1995
Marriage with the Proper Stranger: Arranged Marriage in Metropolitan Japan. Ethnology 34(1):37–51.

Archaeology. 2003
Archaeology and the Black Experience. 56(1):22.

Ariès, Philippe. 1962
Centuries of Childhood: A Social History of Family Life. Trans. Robert Baldick. New York: Vintage Books.

Árnason, E. 2003
Genetic Heterogeneity of Icelanders. Annals of Human Genetics 67:5–16.

Arsuaga, Juan-Luis, I. Martinez, J. M. Carretero, and E. Carbonell. 1993
Three New Human Skulls from the Sima de los Huesos, Middle Pleistocene Site in Sierra de Atapuerca, Spain. Nature 362:534–537.

Asfaw, Berhane, B. M. Gilbert, Y. Beyene, W. K. Hart, P. R. Renne, G. WoldeGabriel, E. S. Vrba, and T. D. White. 2002
Remains of Homo erectus from Bouri, Middle Awash, Ethiopia. Nature 416:317–320.

Attwood, Donald W. 1992
Raising Cane: The Political Economy of Sugar in Western India. Boulder, CO: Westview Press.

Aufderheide, Arthur C. 2003
The Scientific Study of Mummies. New York: Cambridge University Press.

Backwell, Lucinda R. and Francisco d'Errico. 2003
Additional Evidence on the Early Hominid Bone Tools from Swartkrans with Reference to Spatial Distribution of Lithic and Organic Artifacts. South African Journal of Science 99:259–267.

Baer, Lars-Anders. 1982
The Sami: An Indigenous People in Their Own Land. In The Sami National Minority in Sweden. Birgitta Jahreskog, ed. Pp. 11–22. Stockholm: Almqvist & Wiksell International.

Bahn, Paul G., ed. 1996
The Cambridge Illustrated History of Archaeology. New York: Cambridge University Press.

Bahn, Paul G. and Jean Vertut. 1997
Journey through the Ice Age. Berkeley: University of California Press.

Balkansky, Andrew K. 2002
The Sola Valley and the Monte Albán State: A Study of Zapotec Imperial Expansion. Ann Arbor, MI: Museum of Anthropology, University of Michigan Memoirs, Number 36.

———. 1998
Origin and Collapse of Complex Societies in Oaxaca (Mexico): Evaluating the Era from 1965 to the Present. Journal of World Prehistory 12:451–493.

Balter, Michael. 2001
Did Plaster Hold Neolithic Society Together? Science 294:2278–2281.

Barbujani, Guido and Giorgio Bertorelle. 2001
Genetics and Population History of Europe. Proceedings of the National Academy of Sciences of the United States of America 94:4516–4519.

Barfield, Thomas J. 1994
Prospects for Plural Societies in Central Asia. Cultural Survival Quarterly 18(2, 3):48–51.

Barham, Larry S. 2002
Backed Tools in Middle Pleistocene Central Africa and Their Evolutionary Significance. Journal of Human Evolution 43:585–603.

Barkey, Nanett, Benjamin C. Campbell, and Paul W. Leslie. 2001
A Comparison of Health Complaints of Settled and Nomadic Turkana Men. Medical Anthropology Quarterly 15:391–408.

Barlett, Peggy F. 1989
Industrial Agriculture. In Economic Anthropology. Stuart Plattner, ed. Pp. 253–292. Stanford: Stanford University Press.

Barnard, Alan. 2000
History and Theory in Anthropology. New York: Cambridge University Press.

Barnard, Alan and Anthony Good. 1984
Research Practices in the Study of Kinship. New York: Academic Press.

Barnosky, A. D., P. L. Koch, R. S. Feranec, S. L. Wing, and A. B. Shabel. 2004
Assessing the Causes of Late Pleistocene Extinctions on the Continents. Science 306:70–75.

Barth, Frederik. 1993
Balinese Worlds. Chicago: University of Chicago Press.

Bartlett, Thad Q., Robert W. Sussman, and James M. Cheverud. 1993
Infant Killing in Primates: A Review of Observed Cases with Specific Reference to the Sexual Selection Hypothesis. American Anthropologist 95(4):958–990.

Bar-Yosef, Ofer. 2002a
The Upper Paleolithic Revolution. Annual Review of Anthropology 31:363–393.

———. 2002b
Natufian: A Complex Society of Foragers. In Beyond Foraging and Collecting: Evolutionary Change in Hunter-Gatherer Settlement Systems. Ben Fitzhugh and Junko Habu, eds. Pp. 91–149. New York: Kluwer Academic/Plenum Publishers.

———. 1998
The Natufian Culture in the Levant: Threshold to the Origins of Agriculture. Evolutionary Anthropology 6:159–177.

Basch, Linda, Nina Glick Schiller, and Christina Szanton Blanc. 1994
Nations Unbound: Transnational Projects, Postcolonial Predicaments, and Deterritorialized Nation–States. Langhorne, PA: Gordon and Breach Science Publishers.

Basso, Keith. H. 1972 [1970]
"To Give Up on Words": Silence in Apache Culture. In Lan-

guage and Social Context. Pier Paolo Giglioni, ed. Pp. 67–86. Baltimore, MD: Penguin Books.

Bateson, Patrick, David Barker, Timothy Clutton-Brock, Debal Deb, Bruno D'Uldine, Robert A. Foley, Peter Gluckman, Keith Godfrey, Tom Kirkwood, Marta Mirazón Lahr, John McNamara, Nell B. Metcalfe, Patricia Monaghan, Hamish G. Spencer, and Sonia E. Sultan. 2004
Developmental Plasticity and Human Health. Nature 430:419–421.

Beall, Cynthia M. and A. Theodore Steegman, Jr. 2000
Human Adaptation to Climate: Temperature, Ultraviolet Radiation and Altitude. In Human Biology: An Evolutionary and Biocultural Perspective. Sara Stinson, Barry Bogin, Rebecca Huss-Ashmore, and Dennis O'Rourke, eds. Pp. 163–224. New York: Wiley-Liss.

Beals, Alan R. 1980
Gopalpur: A South Indian Village. Fieldwork edition. New York: Holt.

Beck, Benjamin. 1980
Animal Tool Behavior: The Use and Manufacture of Tools by Animals. New York: Garland Press.

Beeman, William O. 1993
The Anthropology of Theater and Spectacle. Annual Review of Anthropology 22:363–393.

Behrensmeyer, A. Kay. 1991
Terrestrial Vertebrate Accumulations. In Taphonomy: Releasing the Data Locked in the Fossil Record. P. A. Allison and D. E. G. Briggs, eds. Pp. 291–335. New York: Plenum Press.

Belikov, Vladimir. 1994
Language Death in Siberia. UNESCO Courier 1994(2): 32–36.

Bell, Diane. 1998
Ngarrindjeri Wurruwarrin: A World That Is, Was, and Will Be. North Melbourne: Spinifex.

Bellomo, R. V. 1994
Method for Determining Early Hominid Behavioural Activities Associated with the Controlled Use of Fire at FxJj 20 Main, Koobi Fora, Kenya. Journal of Human Evolution 27:173–195.

Bellwood, Peter. 2001
Early Agricultural Population Diasporas? Farming, Languages, and Genes. Annual Review of Anthropology 30: 181–207.

Benke, Paul J., Virginia Carver, and Roger Donahue. 1995
Risk and Recurrence Risk of Down Syndrome. http://www.downsyndrome.com.

Bergman, Christopher A. and John F. Doershuk. 2003
Cultural Resource Management and the Business of Archaeology. In Ethical Issues in Archaeology. Larry J. Zimmerman, Karen D. Vitelli, and Julie-Hollowell-Zimmer, eds. Pp. 85–98. Walnut Creek, CA: AltaMira Press.

Berlin, Elois Ann and Brent Berlin. 1996
Medical Ethnobiology of the Highland Maya of Chiapas, Mexico: The Gastrointestinal Diseases. Princeton, NJ: Princeton University Press.

Bermann, Marc. 1994
Lukurmata: Household Archaeology in Prehispanic Bolivia. Princeton, NJ: Princeton University Press.

Bermúdez de Castro, Jose-Maria, J. L. Arsuaga, E. Carbonell, A. Rosas, I. Martinez, and M. Mosquera. 1997
A Hominid from the Lower Pleistocene of Atapuerca, Spain: Possible Ancestor to Neandertals and Modern Humans. Science 276:1392–1395.

Bermúdez de Castro, Jose-Maria, Martinon-Torres, E. Carbonell, S. Sarmientio, A. Rosas, J. Van der Made, and M. Lozano. 2004
The Atapuerca Sites and Their Contribution to the Knowledge of Human Evolution in Europe. Evolutionary Anthropology 13:25–41.

Bernal, Martin. 1987
Black Athena: The Afroasiatic Roots of Classical Civilization. New Brunswick, NJ: Rutgers University Press.

Bernard, H. Russell. 1995
Research Methods in Anthropology: Qualitative and Quantitative Approaches. Walnut Creek, CA: AltaMira Press/Sage.

Bernardini, Wesley. 2004
Hopewell Geometric Earthworks: A Case Study in the Referential and Experiential Meaning of Monuments. Journal of Anthropological Archaeology 23:331–356.

Berreman, Gerald D. 1979 [1975]
Race, Caste, and Other Invidious Distinctions in Social Stratification. In Caste and Other Inequities: Essays on Inequality. Gerald D. Berreman, ed. Pp. 178–222. New Delhi: Manohar.

Bersaglieri, Todd, Pardis C. Sabeti, Nick Patterson, Trisha Vanderploeg, Steve F. Schaffner, Jared A. Drake, Matthew Rhodes, David E. Reich, and Joel N. Hirschhorn. 2004
Genetic Signatures of Strong Recent Positive Selection at the Lactase Gene. American Journal of Human Genetics 74: 1111–1121.

Best, David. 1986
Culture Consciousness: Understanding the Arts of Other Cultures. Journal of Art & Design Education 5(1&2): 124–135.

Beyene, Yewoubdar. 1989
From Menarche to Menopause: Reproductive Lives of Peasant Women in Two Cultures. Albany: State University of New York Press.

Bhardwaj, Surinder M. 1973
Hindu Places of Pilgrimage in India: A Study in Cultural Geography. Berkeley: University of California Press.

Bhardwaj, Surinder M. and N. Madhusudana Rao. 1990
Asian Indians in the United States: A Geographic Appraisal. In South Asians Overseas: Migration and Ethnicity. Colin Clarke, Ceri Peach, and Steven Vertovec, eds. Pp. 197–218. New York: Cambridge University Press.

Bhatt, Rakesh M. 2001
World Englishes. Annual Review of Anthropology 30: 527–550.

Bilharz, Joy. 1995
First among Equals? The Changing Status of Seneca Women. In Women and Power in Native North America. Laura F. Klein and Lillian A. Ackerman, eds. Pp. 101–112. Norman: University of Oklahoma Press.

Billig, Michael S. 1992
The Marriage Squeeze and the Rise of Groomprice in India's Kerala State. Journal of Comparative Family Studies 23:197–216.

Billman, Brian R. 2002
Irrigation and the Origins of the Southern Moche State on the North Coast of Peru. Latin American Antiquity 13:371–400.

Binford, Lewis R. 1968
Post-Pleistocene Adaptations. In New Perspectives in Archaeology. Sally R. Binford and Lewis R. Binford, eds. Pp. 313–341. Chicago: Aldine.

Bird, Sharon R. 1996
Welcome to the Men's Club: Homosociality and the Maintenance of Hegemonic Masculinity. Gender & Society 10(2):120–132.

Blackwood, Evelyn. 1995
Senior Women, Model Mothers, and Dutiful Wives: Managing Gender Contradictions in a Minangkabau Village. In Bewitching Women, Pious Men: Gender and Body Politics in Southeast Asia. Aihwa Ong and Michael Peletz, eds. Pp. 124–158. Berkeley: University of California Press.

Blaikie, Piers. 1985
The Political Economy of Soil Erosion in Developing Countries. New York: Longman.

Blanchard, Ray, Kenneth J. Zucker, Susan J. Bradley, and Caitlin S. Hume. 1995
Birth Order and Sibling Sex Ratio in Homosexual Male Adolescents and Probably Prehomosexual Feminine Boys. Developmental Psychology 31(1):22–30.

Blanton, Richard E. et al. 1999
Ancient Oaxaca: The Monte Albán State. New York: Cambridge University Press.

Bledsoe, Caroline H. 1983
Stealing Food as a Problem in Demography and Nutrition. Paper presented at the annual meeting of the American Anthropological Association.

Blim, Michael. 2000
Capitalisms in Late Modernity. Annual Review of Anthropology 29:25–38.

Blood, Robert O. 1967
Love Match and Arranged Marriage. New York: Free Press.

Blumenschine, Robert. 1987
Characteristics of an Early Hominid Scavenging Niche. Current Anthropology 38:383–407.

Blurton Jones, Nicholas G., Kristen Hawkes, and James F. O'Connell. 2002
Antiquity of Postreproductive Life: Are There Modern Impacts on Hunter–Gatherer Postreproductive Life Spans? American Journal of Human Biology 14:184–205.

Boaz, Noel T., R. L. Ciochon, Q. Xu, and J. Liu. 2004
Mapping and Taphonomic Analysis of the Homo erectus Loci at Locality 1, Zhoukoudian, China. Journal of Human Evolution 46:519–549.

Bodenhorn, Barbara. 2000
"He Used to Be My Relative." Exploring the Bases of Relatedness among the Inupiat of Northern Alaska. In Cultures of Relatedness: New Approaches to the Study of Kinship. Janet Carsten, ed. Pp. 128–148. New York: Cambridge University Press.

Bodley, John H. 1990
Victims of Progress. 3rd ed. Mountain View, CA: Mayfield.
———. 1988
Tribal Peoples and Development Issues: A Global Overview. Mountain View, CA: Mayfield.

Boëda, E. 1995
Levallois: A Volumetric Construction. In The Definition and Interpretation of Levallois Technology. H. Dibble and O. Bar-Yosef, eds. Pp. 41–68. Madison, WI: Prehistoric Press.

Boesch, Christophe and Hedwige Boesch-Achermann. 2000
The Chimpanzees of the Taï Forest. Oxford: Oxford University Press.

Bogin, Barry. 1988
Patterns of Human Growth. New York: Cambridge University Press.

Boserup, Ester. 1970
Woman's Role in Economic Development. New York: St. Martin's Press.

Bourdieu, Pierre. 1984
Distinction: A Social Critique of the Judgement of Taste. Richard Nice, trans. Cambridge, MA: Harvard University Press.

Bourgois, Philippe I. 1995
In Search of Respect: Selling Crack in El Barrio. New York: Cambridge University Press.

Bowdler, Sandra. 1988
Repainting Australian Art. Antiquity 62:517–523.

Bowen, Anne M. and Robert Trotter II. 1995
HIV Risk in Intravenous Drug Users and Crack Cocaine Smokers: Predicting Stage of Change for Condom Use. Journal of Consulting and Clinical Psychology 63:238–248.

Bowen, John R. 1998
Religions in Practice: An Approach to the Anthropology of Religion. Boston: Allyn and Bacon.
———. 1992
On Scriptural Essentialism and Ritual Variation: Muslim Sacrifice in Sumatra. American Ethnologist 19(4):656–671.

Boyd Eaton, S., Marjorie Shostak, and Melvin Konner. 1988
The Paleolithic Prescription: A Program of Diet and Exercise and a Design for Living. New York: Harper & Row.

Brace, C. Loring. 1997
Race Concept. In History of Physical Anthropology: An Encyclopedia. Volume 2. Frank Spencer, ed. Pp. 861–866. New York: Garland Publishing.

Bradley, Daniel G. 2003
Genetic Hoofprints. Natural History 112(1):36–41.

Bradley, Richard. 2000
An Archaeology of Natural Places. New York: Routledge.
———. 1997
Rock Art and the Prehistory of Atlantic Europe: Signing the Land. New York: Routledge.

Braidwood, Robert J. 1960
The Agricultural Revolution. Scientific American 203(3):130–148.

Brain, C. K. 1981
The Hunters or the Hunted? An Introduction to African Cave Taphonomy. Chicago: University of Chicago Press.

Brana-Shute, Rosemary. 1976
Women, Clubs, and Politics: The Case of a Lower-Class Neighborhood in Paramaribo, Suriname. Urban Anthropology 5(2):157–185.

Brandes, Stanley H. 2002
Staying Sober in Mexico City. Austin: University of Texas Press.
———. 1985
Forty: The Age and the Symbol. Knoxville: University of Tennessee Press.

Braswell, Geoffrey E., ed. 2003
The Maya and Teotihuacan: Reinterpreting Early Classic Interaction. Austin, TX: University of Texas Press.

Bray, Tamara L. 1996
   Repatriation, Power Relations and the Politics of the Past. Antiquity 70:440–444.

Brewer, Douglass J. and Emily Teeter. 1999
   Egypt and the Egyptians. New York: Cambridge University Press.

Brink, Judy H. 1991
   The Effect of Emigration of Husbands on the Status of Their Wives: An Egyptian Case. International Journal of Middle East Studies 23:201–211.

Brison, Karen J. and Stephen C. Leavitt. 1995
   Coping with Bereavement: Long-Term Perspectives on Grief and Mourning. Ethos 23:395–400.

Brodie, Neil and Jennifer Doole. 2001
   Illicit Antiquities. In Trade in Illicit Antiquities: The Destruction of the World's Archaeological Heritage. Neil Brodie, Jennifer Doole, and Colin Renfrew, eds. Pp. 1–6. Cambridge: University of Cambridge, McDonald Institute for Archaeological Research.

Brookes, Stuart J., C. Robinson, J. Kirkham, and W. A. Bonass. 1995
   Biochemistry and Molecular Biology of Amelogenin Proteins of Developing Dental Enamel. Archives of Oral Biology 40(1):1–14.

Brooks, Alison and P. Robertshaw. 1990
   The Glacial Maximum in Tropical Africa: 22,000 to 12,000 B.P. In The World at 18,000 B.P. Vol. 2: Low Latitudes. Olga Soffer and Clive Gamble, eds. pp. 121–169. London: Unwin Hyman.

Brooks, Alison S. and Patricia Draper. 1998 [1991]
   Anthropological Perspectives on Aging. In Anthropology Explored: The Best of AnthroNotes. Ruth Osterweis Selig and Marilyn R. London, eds. Pp. 286–297. Washington, DC: Smithsonian Institution.

Broude, Gwen J. 1988
   Rethinking the Couvade: Cross-Cultural Evidence. American Anthropologist 90(4):902–911.

Brown, Carolyn Henning. 1984
   Tourism and Ethnic Competition in a Ritual Form: The Firewalkers of Fiji. Oceania 54:223–244.

Brown, James. 1995
   The Turkish Imbroglio: Its Kurds. Annals of the American Academy of Political and Social Science 541:116–129.

Brown, Judith K. 1999
   Introduction: Definitions, Assumptions, Themes, and Issues. In To Have and To Hit: Cultural Perspectives on Wife-Beating. 2nd ed. Dorothy Ayers Counts, Judith K. Brown, and Jacquelyn C. Campbell, eds. Pp. 3–26. Urbana, IL: University of Illinois Press.

———. 1982
   Cross-Cultural Perspectives on Middle-Aged Women. Current Anthropology 23(2):143–156.

———. 1978
   The Recruitment of a Female Labor Force. Anthropos 73(1/2):41–48.

———. 1975
   Iroquois Women: An Ethnohistoric Note. In Toward an Anthropology of Women. Rayna R. Reiter, ed. Pp. 235–251. New York: Monthly Review Press.

———. 1970
   A Note on the Division of Labor by Sex. American Anthropologist 72(5):1073–1078.

Brown, Peter, T. Sutikna, M. J. Morwood, R. P. Soejono, Jatmiko, E. Wayhu Saptomo, and Rokus Awe Due. 2004
   A New Small-Bodied Hominin from the Late Pleistocene of Flores, Indonesia. Nature 431:1055–1061.

Browner, Carole H. 1986
   The Politics of Reproduction in a Mexican Village. Signs: Journal of Women in Culture and Society 11(4):710–724.

Browner, Carole H. and Nancy Ann Press. 1995
   The Normalization of Prenatal Diagnostic Screening. In Conceiving the New World Order: The Global Politics of Reproduction. Faye D. Ginsberg and Rayna Rapp, eds. Pp. 307–322. Berkeley: Universtiy of California Press.

———. 1996.
   The Production of Authoritative Knowledge in American Prenatal Care. Medical Anthropology Quarterly 10(2): 141–156.

Brownmiller, Susan. 1994
   Seeing Vietnam: Encounters of the Road and Heart. New York: HarperCollins.

Brumberg, Joan Jacobs. 1988
   Fasting Girls: The Emergence of Anorexia Nervosa as a Modern Disease. Cambridge, MA: Harvard University Press.

Brumfiel, Elizabeth M. 2003
   It's a Material World: History, Artifacts, and Anthropology. Annual Review of Anthropology 2003:205–223.

———. 1994
   Introduction. In Factional Competition and Political Development in the New World. Elizabeth M. Brumfiel and John W. Fox, eds. Pp. 3–14. New York: Cambridge University Press.

Bruner, Edward M. 1991
   The Transformation of Self in Tourism. Annals of Tourism Research 18:238–250.

Brunet, Michel, A. Beauvilain, Y. Coppens, E. Heintz, H. E. Moutaye, and D. Pilbeam. 1995
   The First Australopithecine 2500 Kilometres West of the Rift Valley. Nature 378:273–275.

Brunet, Michel, F. Guy, D. Pilbeam, H. T. Mackaye, A. Likius, D. Ahounta, A. Beauvilain, C. Blondel, H. Bocherens, J.-R. Boisserie, L. de Bonis, Y. Coppens, J. Dejax, C. Denys, P. Duringer, V. Eisenmann, D. Geraads, F. Gongdibe, P. Fronty, T. Lehmann, F. Lihoreau, A. Louchart, A. Mahamat, G. Merceron, G. Mouchelin, O. Otero, P. P. Campomanes, M. P. de Leon, J.-C. Rage, M. Sapanet, M. Schuster, J. Sudre, P. Tassy, X. Valentin, P. Vignaud, L. Viriot, A. Zazzo, and C. Zollikofer. 2002
   A New Hominid from the Upper Miocene of Chad, Central Africa. Nature 418:145–151.

Bulbeck, D. 2003
   Hunter–Gatherer Occupation of the Malay Peninsula from the Ice Age to the Iron Age. In Under the Canopy: The Archaeology of Tropical Rain Forests. Julio Mercader, ed. Pp. 119–160. New Brunswick, NJ: Rutgers University Press.

Bunn, Henry T. 1981
   Archaeological Evidence for Meat Eating by Plio-Pleistocene Hominids from Koobi Fora and Olduvai Gorge. Nature 291:574–577.

Bunzel, Ruth. 1972 [1929]
   The Pueblo Potter: A Study of Creative Imagination in Primitive Art. New York: Dover Publications.

Caldararo, Niccolo, Lee Davis, and Pete Palmer. 2002
Pesticide Contamination of Native American Objects: An Overview of a Working Conference on the Problem and Its Resolution. Museum Anthropology 25:61–66.

Call, Vaughn, Susan Sprecher, and Pepper Schwartz. 1995
The Incidence and Frequency of Marital Sex in a National Sample. Journal of Marriage and the Family 57:639–652.

Camino, Linda A. and Ruth M. Krulfeld, eds. 1994
Reconstructing Lives, Recapturing Meaning: Refugee Identity, Gender and Culture Change. Basel, Switzerland: Gordon and Breach Publishers.

Campbell, Christina, S. E. Shideler, H. E. Todd, and B. L. Lasley. 2001
Fecal Analysis of Ovarian Cycles in Female Black-Handed Spider Monkeys (Ateles geoffroyi). American Journal of Primatology 54:79–89.

Cann, Rebecca L., M. Stoneking, and A. C. Wilson. 1987
Mitochondrial DNA and Evolution. Nature 325:31–36.

Carneiro, Robert L. 1994
War and Peace: Alternating Realities in Human History. In Studying War: Anthropological Perspectives. S. P. Reyna and R. E. Downs, eds. Pp. 3–27. Langhorne, PA: Gordon and Breach Science Publishers.

———. 1970
A Theory of the Origin of the State. Science 169:733–738.

Carroll, Sean B., J. K. Grenier, and S. D. Weatherbee. 2001
From DNA to Diversity. Malden, MA: Blackwell Books.

Carstairs, G. Morris. 1967
The Twice Born. Bloomington: Indiana University Press.

Carsten, Janet. 1995
Children in Between: Fostering and the Process of Kinship on Pulau Langkawi, Malaysia. Man (n.s.) 26:425–443.

Carsten, Janet, ed. 2000
Cultures of Relatedness: New Approaches to the Study of Kinship. New York: Cambridge University Press.

Carter, William E., José V. Morales, and Mauricio P. Mamani. 1981
Medicinal Uses of Coca in Bolivia. In Health in the Andes. Joseph W. Bastien and John M. Donahue, eds. Pp. 119–149. Washington, DC: American Anthropological Association.

Cassell, Joan 1991
Expected Miracles: Surgeons at Work. Philadelphia: Temple University Press.

Cassidy, Rebecca. 2002
The Sport of Kings: Kinship, Class and Thoroughbred Breeding in Newmarket. New York: Cambridge University Press.

Castilho, L. V. and M. M. Lahr. 2001
Secular Trends in Growth among Brazilian Children of European Descent. Annals of Human Biology 28:564–574.

Castles, Stephen and Mark J. Miller. 1993
The Age of Migration: International Population Movements in the Modern World. New York: Guilford.

Cavalieri, Paola and Peter Singer. 1993
The Great Ape Project: Equality Beyond Humanity. New York: St. Martin's Press.

Cavalli-Sforza, L. Luca. 1997
Genes, Peoples, and Languages. Proceedings of the National Academy of Sciences of the United States of America 94:7719–7724.

Cernea, Michael M. 2001
Cultural Heritage and Development: A Framework for Action in the Middle East and North Africa. Washington, DC: The World Bank

———. 1985
Sociological Knowledge for Development Projects. In Putting People First: Sociological Variables and Rural Development. Michael M. Cernea, ed. Pp. 3–22. New York: Oxford University Press.

Chagnon, Napoleon. 1992 [1968]
Yanomamö. 4th ed. New York: Harcourt Brace Jovanovich.

Chakravarti, A. 2001
Single Nucleotide Polymorphisms . . . To a Future of Genetic Medicine. Nature 409:822–823.

Chambers, David L. 2000
Civilizing the Natives: Marriage in Post-Apartheid South Africa. Daedalus 129:101–124.

Chambers, Robert. 1983
Rural Development: Putting the Last First. Essex, United Kingdom: Longman.

Chambers, Robert. 1844
Vestiges of the Natural History of Creation. London: Churchill.

Chang, K. C. 1986
The Archaeology of Ancient China. New Haven, CT: Yale University Press.

Chatters, James C. 2001
Ancient Encounters: Kennewick Man and the First Americans. New York: Simon and Schuster.

Chavez, Leo R. 1992
Shadowed Lives: Undocumented Immigrants in American Society. New York: Harcourt.

Cheney, D. L., and R. M. Seyfarth. 1996
Function and Intention in the Calls of Non-human Primates. Proceedings of the British Academy 88:59–76.

Cherlin, Andrew J. 1996
Public and Private Families: An Introduction. New York: McGraw-Hill.

Cherlin, Andrew and Frank F. Furstenberg, Jr. 1992 [1983]
The American Family in the Year 2000. In One World Many Cultures. Stuart Hirschberg, ed. Pp. 2–9. New York: Macmillan.

Chernoff, John Miller. 1979
African Rhythm and African Sensibility: Aesthetics and African Musical Idioms. Chicago: University of Chicago Press.

Chikhi, Lounes, Giovanni Destro-Bisol, Giorgio Bertorell, Vincenzo Pascali, and Guido Barbujani. 1998
Clines of Nuclear DNA Markers Suggest a Largely Neolithic Ancestry of the European Gene Pool. Proceedings of the National Academy of Sciences of the United States of America 95:9053–9058.

Childe, V. Gordon. 1950
The Urban Revolution. Town Planning Review 21:3–17.

———. 1934
New Light on the Most Ancient East: The Oriental Prelude to European Prehistory. London: K. Paul, Trench, Trubner & Co.

Childs, Larry and Celina Chelala. 1994
Drought, Rebellion and Social Change in Northern Mali: The Challenges Facing Tamacheq Herders. Cultural Survival Quarterly 18(4):16–19.

Chiñas, Beverly Newbold. 1992
The Isthmus Zapotecs: A Matrifocal Culture of Mexico. New York: Harcourt.

Chowdhury, Najma and Barbara J. Nelson, with Kathryn A. Carver, Nancy J. Johnson, and Paula O'Laughlin. 1994
Redefining Politics: Patterns of Women's Political Engagement from a Global Perspective. In Women and Politics Worldwide. Barbara J. Nelson and Najma Chowdhury, eds. Pp. 3–24. New Haven: Yale University Press.

Clark, Geoff. 2002
Neanderthal Archaeology: Implications for Our Origins. American Anthropologist 104:50–67.

Clark, Gracia. 1992
Flexibility Equals Survival. Cultural Survival Quarterly 16:21–24.

Clarke, Ron J. 2002
Newly Revealed Information on the Sterkfontein Member 2 Australopithecus Skeleton. South African Journal of Science 98:523–526.

Clay, Jason W. 1990
What's a Nation? Latest Thinking. Mother Jones 15(7): 28–30.

Clifford, James. 1988
The Predicament of Culture: Twentieth Century Ethnography, Literature and Art. Cambridge: Harvard University Press.

Close, Angela E. 1996
Carry That Weight: The Use and Transportation of Stone Tools. Current Anthropology 37:545–553.

Clottes, J. 2001
Paleolithic Europe. In Handbook of Rock Art Research. D. Whitley, ed. Pp. 459–481. Walnut Creek, CA: AltaMira Press.

———. 2000
Art between 30,000 and 20,000 BP. In Hunters of the Golden Age. W. Roebroeks, M. Mussi, J. Svoboda, and K. Fennema., eds. Pp. 87–103. Leiden, The Netherlands: European Science Foundation.

Cochrane, D. Glynn. 1979
The Cultural Appraisal of Development Projects. New York: Praeger.

Cohen, Mark Nathan. 1989
Health and the Rise of Civilization. New Haven, CT: Yale University Press.

———. 1977
The Food Crisis in Prehistory. New Haven, CT: Yale University Press.

Cohen, Roberta. 2002
Nowhere to Run, No Place to Hide. Bulletin of the Atomic Scientists November/December:36–45.

Cohn, Bernard S. 1971
India: The Social Anthropology of a Civilization. New York: Prentice-Hall.

Cole, Douglas. 1991
Chiefly Feasts: The Enduring Kwakiutl Potlatch. Aldona Jonaitis, ed. Seattle: University of Washington Press/New York: American Museum of Natural History.

Cole, Jeffrey. 1996
Working-Class Reactions to the New Immigration in Palermo (Italy). Critique of Anthropology 16(2):199–220.

Cole, T. 1990
Democritus and the Sources of Greek Anthropology. Atlanta: Scholars' Press.

Collard, Mark C. and Bernard A. Wood. 2000
How Reliable Are Human Phylogenetic Hypotheses? Proceedings of the National Academy of Sciences 97:5003–5006.

Colledge, Sue, James Conolly, and Stephen Shennan. 2004
Archaeobotanical Evidence for the Spread of Farming in the Eastern Mediterranean. Current Anthropology 45:Supplement, 35–58.

Contreras, Gloria. 1995
Teaching about Vietnamese Culture: Water Puppetry as the Soul of the Rice Fields. The Social Studies 86(1):25–28.

Corbey, Raymond. 2003
Destroying the Graven Image: Religious Iconoclasm on the Christian Frontier. Anthropology Today 19:10–14.

———. 2000
Arts Premiers in the Louvre. Anthropology Today 16:3–6.

Cordain, Loren, B. A. Watkins, and N. J. Mann. 2001
Fatty Acid Composition and Energy Density of Foods Available to African Hominids. In Nutrition and Fitness: Metabolic Studies in Health and Disease, 90. A. P. Somopoulos and K. N. Pavlou, eds. Pp. 144–161. Basel, Switzerland: Karger.

Cornell, Laurel L. 1989
Gender Differences in Remarriage after Divorce in Japan and the United States. Journal of Marriage and the Family 51:45–463.

Cornia, Giovanni Andrea. 1994
Poverty, Food Consumption, and Nutrition During the Transition to the Market Economy in Eastern Europe. American Economic Review 84(2):297–302.

Counihan, Carole M. 1985
Transvestism and Gender in a Sardinian Carnival. Anthropology 9(1 & 2):11–24.

Coward, E. Walter, Jr. 1979
Principles of Social Organization in an Indigenous Irrigation System. Human Organization 38(1):28–36.

———. 1976
Indigenous Organisation, Bureaucracy and Development: The Case of Irrigation. The Journal of Development Studies 13(1):92–105.

Cowgill, George L. 1992
Toward a Political History of Teotihuacan. In Ideology and Pre-Columbian Civilizations. Arthur A. Demarest and Geoffrey W. Conrad, eds. Pp. 87–114. Santa Fe, NM: School of American Research Press.

Crapanzano, Vincent. 1980
Tuhami: Portrait of a Moroccan. Chicago: University of Chicago Press.

Creighton, Millie R. 1992
The Depáto: Merchandising the West While Selling Japanese Sameness. In Re-Made in Japan: Everyday Life and Consumer Taste in a Changing Society. Joseph J. Tobin, ed. Pp. 42–57. New Haven: Yale University Press.

Crompton, Robin H., Y. Li, S. K. Thorpe, W. J. Wang, R. Savage, and R. Payne. 2003
The Biomechanical Evolution of Erect Bipedality. Courier Forschungs-Institut Senckenberg 243:115–126.

Cunningham, Lawrence S. 1995
Christianity. In The HarperCollins Dictionary of Religion.

Jonathan Z. Smith, ed. Pp. 240–253. New York: Harper-Collins.

Curtin, Philip D. 1989
Death by Migration: Europe's Encounter with the Tropical World in the Nineteenth Century. New York: Cambridge University Press.

D'Altroy, Terence N. 2002
The Incas. Oxford, England: Blackwell Publishers.

Danforth, Loring M. 1989
Firewalking and Religious Healing: The Anestenaria of Greece and the American Firewalking Movement. Princeton, NJ: Princeton University Press.

Dannhaeuser, Norbert. 1989
Marketing in Developing Urban Areas. In Economic Anthropology. Stuart Plattner, ed. Pp. 222–252. Stanford, CA: Stanford University Press.

Darwin, Charles. 1859
On the Origin of Species by Means of Natural Selection. London: John Murray. Reprinted, Everyman edition, 1928. New York: Dutton.

Daugherty, Mary Lee. 1997 [1976]
Serpent-Handling as Sacrament. In Magic, Witchcraft, and Religion. Arthur C. Lehmann and James E. Myers, eds. Pp. 347–352. Mountain View, CA: Mayfield Publishing Company.

Davis, Lee, Niccolo Caldararo, and Peter Palmer. 2001
Recommended Actions Regarding the Pesticide Contamination of Museum Materials. Collection Forum 16:96–99.

Davis, Richard S. and Vadim A. Ranov. 1999
Recent Work on the Paleolithic of Central Asia. Evolutionary Anthropology 8:186–193.

Davis, Susan Schaefer and Douglas A. Davis. 1987
Adolescence in a Moroccan Town: Making Social Sense. New Brunswick, NJ: Rutgers University Press.

Davis-Floyd, Robbie E. 1992
Birth as an American Rite of Passage. Berkeley: University of California Press.

———. 1987
Obstetric Training as a Rite of Passage. Medical Anthropology Quarterly 1:288–318.

Day, Michael H. 1969
Omo Human Skeletal Remains. Nature 222:1135–1138.

de Beaune, S. A. 2004
The Invention of Technology. Current Anthropology 45:139–162.

Deitrick, Lynn M. 2002. Cultural Brokerage in the Newborn Nursery. Practicing Anthropology 24:53–54.

de la Cadena, Marisol. 2001
Reconstructing Race: Racism, Culture and Mestizaje in Latin America. NACLA Report on the Americas 34:16–23.

Delaney, Carol. 1988
Mortal Flow: Menstruation in Turkish Village Society. In Blood Magic: The Anthropology of Menstruation. Timothy Buckley and Alma Gottlieb, eds. Pp. 75–93. Berkeley: University of California Press.

de la Torre, Ignatio, R. Mora, M. Dominguez-Rodrigo, L. de Luque, and L. Alcala. 2003
The Oldowan industry of Peninj and Its Bearing on the Reconstruction of the Technological Skills of Lower Pleistocene Hominids. Journal of Human Evolution 44:203–224.

Demarest, Arthur A., Prudence M. Rice, and Don S. Rice, eds. 2003
The Terminal Classic in the Maya Lowlands: Collapse, Transition, and Transformation. Boulder, CO: University of Colorado Press.

Denham, T. P., Simon G. Haberle, C. J. Lentfer, Richard Fullager, J. Field, Michael Therin, Nicholas Proch, and B. Winsborough. 2003
Origins of Agriculture at Kuk Swamp in the Highlands of New Guinea. Science 301:189–193.

d'Errico, F., C. Henshilwood, G. Lawson, M. Vanhaeren, A. Tillier, M. Soressi, F. Bresson, B. Maureille, A. Nowell, J. Lakarra, L. Backwell, and M. Julien. 2003
Archaeological Evidence for the Emergence of Language, Symbolism, and Music: An Alternative Multidisciplinary Perspective. Journal of World Prehistory 17:1–70.

Devereaux, George. 1976
A Typological Study of Abortion in Primitive Societies: A Typological, Distributional, and Dynamic Analysis of the Prevention of Birth in 400 Preindustrial Societies. New York: International Universities Press.

de Waal, Frans B. M. 2000
Primates: A Natural Heritage of Conflict Resolution. Science 289(5479):586–590.

de Waal, Frans B. M. and Frans Lanting. 1997
Bonobo: The Forgotten Ape. Berkeley: University of California Press.

Di Ferdinando, George. 1999
Emerging Infectious Diseases: Biology and Behavior in the Inner City. In Urbanism, Health, and Human Biology in Industrialised Countries. Lawrence M. Schell and Stanley J. Ulijaszek, eds. Pp. 87–110. New York: Cambridge University Press.

Dikötter, Frank. 1998
Hairy Barbarians, Furry Primates and Wild Men: Medical Science and Cultural Representations of Hair in China. In Hair: Its Power and Meaning in Asian Cultures. Alf Hiltebeitel and Barbara D. Miller, eds. Pp. 51–74. Albany: State University of New York Press.

Dillehay, Thomas. 2000
The Settlement of the Americas: A New Prehistory. New York: Basic Books.

Divale, William T. and Marvin Harris. 1976
Population, Warfare and the Male Supremacist Complex. American Anthropologist 78:521–538.

DNA Sequence of the Mitochondrial Hypervariable Region II from the Neandertal Type Specimen. Proceedings of the National Academy of Sciences 96: 5581–5585.

Dolhinow, Phyllis. 1977
Normal Monkeys? American Scientist 65:266.

Dominguez-Rodrigo, M. 2002
Hunting and Scavenging by Early Humans: The State of the Debate. Journal of World Prehistory 16:1–54.

Donlon, Jon. 1990
Fighting Cocks, Feathered Warriors, and Little Heroes. Play & Culture 3:273–285.

Dorgan, Howard. 1989
The Old Regular Baptists of Central Appalachia: Brothers and Sisters in Hope. Knoxville: University of Tennessee Press.

Drake, Susan P. 1991
Local Participation in Ecotourism Projects. In Nature Tourism: Managing for the Environment. Tensie Whelan, ed. Pp. 132–155. Washington, DC: Island Press.

Drucker, Charles. 1988
Dam the Chico: Hydropower Development and Tribal Resistance. In Tribal Peoples and Development Issues: A Global Overview. John H. Bodley, ed. Pp. 151–165. Mountain View, CA: Mayfield.

Duany, Jorge. 2000
Nation on the Move: The Construction of Cultural Identities in Puerto Rico and the Diaspora. American Ethnologist 27:5–30.

Duncan, M. T. and S. M. Horvath. 1988
Physiological Adaptations to Thermal Stress in Tropical Asians. European Journal of Applied Physiology 57:440–444.

Duranti, Alessandro. 1997
Linguistic Anthropology. New York: Cambridge University Press.

———. 1994
From Grammar to Politics: Linguistic Anthropology in a Western Samoan Village. Berkeley: University of California Press.

Durkheim, Emile. 1965 [1915]
The Elementary Forms of the Religious Life. New York: The Free Press.

Durning, Alan Thein. 1993
Are We Happy Yet? How the Pursuit of Happiness Is Failing. The Futurist 27(1):20–24.

Durrenberger, E. Paul. 2001
Explorations of Class and Class Consciousness in the U.S. Journal of Anthropological Research 57:41–60.

Dyson, Tim and Mick Moore. 1983
On Kinship Structure, Female Autonomy, and Demographic Behavior in India. Population and Development Review 9:35060.

Earle, Timothy. 2004
Culture Matters in the Neolithic Transition and Emergence of Hierarchy in Thy, Denmark: Distinguished Lecture. American Anthropologist 105:111–125.

———. 1997
How Chiefs Come to Power: The Political Economy in Prehistory. Stanford, CA: Stanford University Press.

———. 1991
The Evolution of Chiefdoms. In Chiefdoms, Power, Economy, and Ideology. Timothy Earle, ed. Pp. 1–15. New York: Cambridge University Press.

Eaton, J. W. and J. I. Mucha. 1971
Increased Fertility in Males with Sickle Cell Trait? Nature 231:456–457.

Echo-Hawk, Walter R. 1997
Forging a New Ancient History for Native America. In Nina Swindler, Kurt E. Dongoske, Roger Anyon, and Alan S. Downer, eds. Native Americans and Archaeologists: Stepping Stones to Common Ground. Pp. 88–102. Walnut Creek, CA: AltaMira Press.

Eck, Diana L. 1985
Darśan: Seeing the Divine Image in India. 2nd ed. Chambersburg, PA: Anima Books.

Eckel, Malcolm David. 1995
Buddhism. In The HarperCollins Dictionary of Religion. Jonathan Z. Smith. Pp. 135–150. New York: HarperCollins.

Economic and Social Council. 1992
Report of the Working Group on Violence against Women. Vienna: United Nations. E/CN.6/WG.2/1992/L.3.

Ehret, Christopher. 1998
An African Classical Age: Eastern and Southern Africa in World History, 1000 B.C. to A.D. 400. Charlottesville: University Press of Virginia.

Eickelman, Dale F. 1981
The Middle East: An Anthropological Perspective. Englewood Cliffs, NJ: Prentice-Hall.

Eisler, Kim Isaac. 2001
Revenge of the Pequots: How a Small Native American Tribe Created the World's Most Profitable Casino. New York: Simon and Schuster.

Eldredge, Niles. 1995
Dominion. Berkeley: University of California Press.

Eller, E. 2001
Estimating Relative Population Sizes from Simulated Data Sets and the Question of Greater African Effective Size. American Journal of Physical Anthropology 116:1–12.

Elston, Robert G. and P. Jeffrey Brantingham. 2002
Microlithic Technology in Northern Asia: A Risk-Minimizing Strategy of the Late Paleolithic and Early Holocene. In Thinking Small: Perspectives on Microlithization. Robert G. Elston and S. L. Kuhn, eds. Pp. 103–116. Archaeological Papers of the American Anthropological Association, No. 12. Arlington, VA: American Anthropological Association.

Elton, Sarah, L. C. Bishop, and Bernard Wood. 2001
Comparative Context of Plio-Pleistocene Hominin Brain Evolution. Journal of Human Evolution 41:1–27.

Ember, Carol R. 1983
The Relative Decline in Women's Contribution to Agriculture with Intensification. American Anthropologist 85(2):285–304.

Enard, William, M. Przeworski, S. E. Fisher, C. S. Lai, V. Wiebe, T. Kitano, A. P. Monaco, and S. Paabo. 2002
Molecular Evolution of FOXP2, a Gene Involved in Speech and Language. Nature 418:869–872.

Endicott, Phillip, M. Thomas, P. Gilbert, Chris Stringer, Carles Lalueza-Fox, Eske Willersleve, Anders J. Hansen, and Alan Cooper. 2003
The Genetic Origins of the Andaman Islanders. American Journal of Human Genetics 72:178–184.

Escobar, Arturo. 2002
Gender, Place, and Networks: A Political Ecology of Cyberculture. In Development: A Cultural Studies Reader. Susan Schech and Jane Haggis, eds. Pp. 239–256. Malden, MA: Blackwell Publishers.

Esman, Milton. 1996
Ethnic Politics. In The Social Science Encyclopedia. Adam Kuper and Jessica Kuper, eds. Pp. 259–260. New York: Routledge.

Estrin, Saul. 1996
Co-operatives. In The Social Science Encyclopedia. Adam Kuper and Jessica Kuper, eds. Pp. 138–139. Routledge: New York.

Eswaran, V. 2002
A Diffusion Wave Out of Africa: The Mechanism of the Modern Human Revolution? Current Anthropology 43:749–774.

Etienne, Mona and Eleanor Leacock, eds. 1980
Women and Colonization: Anthropological Perspectives. New York: Praeger.

Etler, Dennis. 1996
The Fossil Evidence for Human Evolution in Asia. Annual Review of Anthropology 25:275–301.

Evans-Pritchard, E. E. 1951
Kinship and Marriage among the Nuer. Oxford: Clarendon.

Everett, Daniel. 1995
Personal communication.

Ewing, Katherine Pratt. 2000
Legislating Religious Freedom: Muslim Challenges to the Relationship between "Church" and "State" in Germany and France. Daedalus 29:31–53.

Explaining the Development of Dietary Dominance by a Single Ungulate Taxon at Grotte XVI, Dordogne, France. Journal of Archaeological Science 28:115–125.

Ezeh, Uchiechukwo O. and Onyechi Modebe. 1996
Is There Increased Fertility in Adult Males with the Sickle Cell Trait? Human Biology 68:555–562.

Fabian, Johannes. 1995
Ethnographic Misunderstanding and the Perils of Context. American Anthropologist 97(1):41–50.

Fabrega, Horacio, Jr. and Barbara D. Miller. 1995
Adolescent Psychiatry as a Product of Contemporary Anglo-American Society. Social Science and Medicine 40(7):881–894.

Fabrega, Horacio, Jr. and Daniel B. Silver. 1973
Illness and Shamanistic Curing in Zinacantan: An Ethnomedical Analysis. Stanford, CA: Stanford University Press.

Farmer, Paul, Margaret Connors, and Janie Simmons, eds. 1996
Women, Poverty, and AIDS: Sex, Drugs, and Structural Violence. Monroe, ME: Common Courage Press.

Fasulo, Linda. 2003
An Insider's Guide to the UN. New Haven, CT: Yale University Press.

Fedigan, Linda. 1992
Primate Paradigms: Sex Roles and Social Bonds. Chicago: University of Chicago Press.

Feinsilver, Julie M. 1993
Healing the Masses: Cuban Health Politics at Home and Abroad. Berkeley: University of California Press.

Feldman-Savelsberg, Pamela. 1995
Cooking Inside: Kinship and Gender in Bangangté Idioms of Marriage and Procreation. American Ethnologist 22(3):483–501.

Ferguson, James. 1994
The Anti-Politics Machine: "Development," Depoliticization, and Bureaucratic Power in Lesotho. Minneapolis: University of Minnesota Press.

Ferguson, R. Brian. 1990
Blood of the Leviathan: Western Contact and Amazonian Warfare. American Ethnologist 17(1):237–257.

Fernald, Anne. 1992
Human Maternal Vocalizations to Infants as Biologically Relevant Signals: An Evolutionary Perspective. In The Adapted Mind: Evolutionary Psychology and the Generation of Culture. Jerome H. Barlow, Leda Cosmides, and John Tooby, eds. Pp. 391–428. New York: Oxford University Press.

Fiedel, S. 2000
The Peopling of the New World. Journal of Archaeological Research 8:39–103.

Field, J., R. Fullagar, and G. Lord. 2001
A Large Area Archaeological Excavation at Cuddie Springs. Antiquity 75:696–702.

Fitzhugh, William W. and Elisabeth I. Ward, eds. 2000
Vikings: The North Atlantic Saga. Washington, DC: Smithsonian Institution Press.

Flannery, Kent V. 1999
Process and Agency in Early State Formation. Cambridge Archaeological Journal 9:3–21.

———. 1986
Guilá Naquitz: Archaic Foraging and Early Agriculture in Oaxaca, Mexico. New York: Academic Press.

Fleagle, John G. 1999
Primate Adaptation and Evolution, 2nd ed. San Diego: Academic Press.

Fonseca, Isabel. 1995
Bury Me Standing: The Gypsies and Their Journey. New York: Knopf.

Forte, Maurizio and Alberto Siliotto, eds. 1997
Virtual Archaeology: Re-creating Ancient Worlds. New York: Harry N. Abrams.

Foster, George M. and Barbara Gallatin Anderson. 1978
Medical Anthropology. New York: Knopf.

Foucault, Michel. 1977
Discipline and Punish: The Birth of the Prison. New York: Vintage.

———. 1970
The Order of Things: An Archaeology of the Human Sciences. New York: Random House.

Fowler, Brenda. 2004
African Pastoral: Archaeologists Rewrite History of Farming. New York Times July 27.

Fowler, Melvin L. 1975
A Pre-Columbian Urban Center on the Mississippi. Scientific American 232:92–101.

Fox, E. A., A. F. Sitompul, and C. P. van Schaik. 1999
Intelligent Tool Use in Wild Sumatran Orangutans. In The Mentalities of Gorillas and Orangutans: Comparative Perspectives. Sue T. Parker, R. W. Mitchell, and H. L. Miles, eds. Pp. 99–116. Cambridge, MA: Cambridge University Press.

Fox, Robin. 1995 [1978]
The Tory Islanders: A People of the Celtic Fringe. Notre Dame: University of Notre Dame Press.

Franke, Richard W. 1993
Life Is a Little Better: Redistribution as a Development Strategy in Nadur Village, Kerala. Boulder, CO: Westview Press.

Frankel, Francine R. 1971
India's Green Revolution: Economic Gains and Political Costs. Princeton, NJ: Princeton University Press.

Fratkin, Elliot. 1998
Ariaal Pastoralists of Kenya: Surviving Drought and Development in Africa's Arid Lands. Boston: Allyn and Bacon.

Frazer, Sir James. 1970 [1890]
The Golden Bough: A Study in Magic and Religion. New York: Macmillan.

———. 1978 [1890]
The Golden Bough: A Study in Magic and Religion. New York: Macmillan.

Freeman, James A. 1981
A Firewalking Ceremony That Failed. In Social and Cultural Context of Medicine in India. Giri Raj Gupta, ed. Pp.

308–336. New Delhi: Vikas Publishing House.

Frieze, Irene et al. 1978
Women and Sex Roles: A Social Psychological Perspective. New York: Norton.

Frisch, Rose. 1978
Population, Food Intake, and Fertility. Science 199:22–30.

Furst, Peter T. 1989
The Water of Life: Symbolism and Natural History on the Northwest Coast. Dialectical Anthropology 14:95–115.

Gable, Eric. 1995
The Decolonization of Consciousness: Local Skeptics and the "Will to Be Modern" in a West African Village. American Ethnologist 22(2):242–257.

Gage-Brandon, Anastasia J. 1992
The Polygyny–Divorce Relationship: A Case Study of Nigeria. Journal of Marriage and the Family 54:282–292.

Gagneux, P., C. Wills, U. Gerloff, D. Tautz, P. A. Morin, C. Boesch, B. Fruth, G. Hohmann, O. A. Ryder, and D. S. Woodruff. 1999
Mitochondrial Sequences Show Diverse Evolutionary Histories of African Hominoids. Proceedings of the National Academy of Sciences 96:5077–5082.

Gale, Faye, Rebecca Bailey-Harris, and Joy Wundersitz. 1990
Aboriginal Youth and the Criminal Justice System: The Injustice of Justice? New York: Cambridge University Press.

Galef, B. G. 1992
The Question of Animal Culture. Human Nature 3:157–178.

Galik, K., B. Senut, M. Pickford, D. Gommery, J. Treil, J. J. Kuperavage, and R. B. Eckhardt. 2004
External and Internal Morphology of the BAR 1002'00 Orrorin tugenensis Femur. Science 305:1450–1453.

Gallup, G. G. Jr., J. L. Boren, G. J. Gagliardi, and L. B. Wallnau. 1977
A Mirror for the Mind of Man, or Will the Chimpanzee Create an Identity Crisis for Homo sapiens? Journal of Human Evolution 6:303–311.

Gamble, Clive. 2001
Archaeology: The Basics. New York: Routledge.

Gannon, Patrick J., R. L. Holloway, D. C. Broadfield, and A. R. Braun. 1998
Asymmetry of Chimpanzee Planum Temporale: Human Like Pattern of Wernicke's Brain Language Area Homology. Science 279:220–222.

Gardner, Katy and David Lewis. 1996
Anthropology, Development and the Post-Modern Challenge. Chicago: Pluto Press.

Garlake, P. S. 1973
Great Zimbabwe. London: Thames & Hudson.

Garland, David. 1996
Social Control. In The Social Science Encyclopedia. Adam Kuper and Jessica Kuper, eds. pp. 780–783. Routledge: New York.

Geertz, Clifford. 1966
Religion as a Cultural System. In Anthropological Approaches to the Study of Religion. Michael Banton, ed. Pp. 1–46. London: Tavistock.

German, J. 1991
Cytogenetic Aspects of Human Disease. In Harrison's Principles of Internal Medicine. 12th ed. J. D. Wilson, E. Braunwald, K. J. Isselbacher, et al., eds. Pp. 40–55. New York: McGraw-Hill.

Gilman, Antonio. 1991
Trajectories towards Social Complexity in the Later Prehistory of the Mediterranean. In Chiefdoms: Power, Economy and Ideology. Timothy Earle, ed. Pp. 146–168. New York: Cambridge University Press.

Glick Schiller, Nina and Georges E. Fouron. 1999
Terrains of Blood and Nation: Haitian Transnational Social Fields. Ethnic and Racial Studies 22:340–365.

Gluckman, Peter D. and Mark A. Hanson. 2004
The Developmental Origins of the Metabolic Syndrome. Trends in Endocrinology and Metabolism 15:183–187.

Gmelch, George. 1997 [1971]
Baseball Magic. In Magic, Witchcraft, and Religion. Arthur C. Lehmann and James E. Myers, eds. Pp. 276–282. Mountain View, CA: Mayfield Publishing Company.

Goebel, T. 1999
Pleistocene Human Colonization of Siberia and Peopling of the Americas. Evolutionary Anthropology 8:208–227.

Gold, Ann Grodzins. 1988
Fruitful Journeys: The Ways of Rajasthani Pilgrims. Berkeley: University of California Press.

Gold, Stevan J. 1995
From the Workers' State to the Golden State: Jews from the Former Soviet Union in California. Boston: Allyn and Bacon.

———. 1992
Refugee Communities: A Comparative Field Study. Newbury Park, CA: Sage.

Goldberg, Paul, S. Weiner, O. Bar-Yosef, Q. Xu, and J. Liu. 2001
Site Formation Processes at Zhoukoudian, China. Journal of Human Evolution 41:483–530.

Goldizen, Anne Wilson. 1987
Tamarins and Marmosets: Communal Care of Offspring. In Primate Societies. Barbara Smuts, Dorothy Cheney, Robert Seyfarth, Richard Wrangham, and Thomas Struhsaker, eds. Pp. 34–43. Chicago: University of Chicago Press.

Goldsmith, Michelle. 1999
Gorilla Socioecology. In The Nonhuman Primates. Phyllis Dolhinow and Agustin Fuentes, eds. Pp. 58–63. Mountain View, CA: Mayfield Publishing Company.

Goodall, Jane. 1968
The Chimpanzees of Gombe: Patterns of Behavior. Cambridge, MA: Harvard University Press.

Goodrum, Matthew. 2002
Biblical Anthropology and the Idea of Human Prehistory in Late Antiquity. History and Anthropology 13:75–76.

Goody, Jack. 1996
The East in the West. New York: Cambridge University Press.

———. 1993
The Culture of Flowers. New York: Cambridge University Press.

———. 1976
Production and Reproduction: A Comparative Study of the Domestic Domain. New York: Cambridge University Press.

Goren-Inbar, N., N. Alperson, M. Kislev, O. Simchoni, Y. Melamed, A. Ben-Nun, and E. Werker. 2004
Evidence of Hominin Control of Fire at Gesher Benot Ya'aqov, Israel. Science 304:725–727.

Goudie, Andrew. 2000
The Human Impact on the Natural Environment, 5th ed. Cambridge, MA: MIT Press.

Gowlett, John A. J., J. W. K. Harris, D. Walton, and B. A. Wood. 1981
Early Archaeological Sites, Hominid Remains and Traces of Fire from Chesowanja, Kenya. Nature 294:125–129.

Grayson, Donald K., Françoise Delpech, Jean-Philippe Rigaud, and Jan F. Simek. 2001
Explaining the Development of Dietary Dominance by a Single Ungulate Taxon at Grotte XVI, Dordogne, France. Journal of Archaeological Science 28:115–125.

Greenhalgh, Susan. 2003
Science, Modernity, and the Making of China's One-Child Policy. Population and Development Review 29:163–196.

Gregor, Thomas. 1982
No Girls Allowed. Science 82.

Greksa, Lawrence P. 1996
Evidence for a Genetic Basis to the Enhanced Total Lung Capacity for Andean Highlanders. Human Biology 68:119–129.

———. 1991
Human Physiological Adaptation to High-Altitude Environments. In Applications of Biological Anthropology to Human Affairs. C. G. N. Mascie-Taylor and G. W. Lasker, eds. Pp. 117–142. New York: Cambridge University Press.

Gremillon, Helen. 1992
Psychiatry as Social Ordering: Anorexia Nervosa, a Paradigm. Social Science and Medicine 35(1):57–71.

Grieco, Elizabeth. 2003
The Foreign Born from Mexico to the United States. http://www.migrationinformation.

Grinker, Roy Richard. 1994
Houses in the Rainforest: Ethnicity and Inequality among Farmers and Foragers in Central Africa. Berkeley: University of California Press.

Gross, Daniel R. 1984
Time Allocation: A Tool for the Study of Cultural Behavior. Annual Review of Anthropology 13:519–558.

Gross, Daniel R. and Barbara A. Underwood. 1971
Technological Change and Caloric Costs. American Anthropologist 73:725–740.

Gross, Daniel R., George Eiten, Nancy M. Flowers, Francisca M. Leoi, Madeleine Lattman Ritter, and Dennis W. Werner. 1979
Ecology and Acculturation among Native Peoples of Central Brazil. Science 206(30):1043–1050.

Groube, L., J. Chappell, J. Muke, and D. Price. 1986
A 40,000-Year-Old Human Occupation Site at Huon Peninsula, Papua New Guinea. Nature 324:453–455.

Gruenbaum, Ellen. 2001
The Female Circumcision Controversy: An Anthropological Perspective. Philadelphia: University of Pennsylvania Press.

Guber, Rosanne. 2002
Antropología social. Anthropology Today 18(4):8–13.

Guggenheim, Scott E. and Michael M. Cernea. 1993
Anthropological Approaches to Involuntary Resettlement: Policy, Practice, and Theory. In Anthropological Approaches to Resettlement: Policy, Practice, and Theory. Michael M. Cernea and Scott E. Guggenheim, eds. Pp. 1–12. Boulder: Westview Press.

Guidoni, Enrico. 1987
Primitive Architecture. Robert Erich Wolf, trans. New York: Rizzoli.

Güneş-Ayara, Ayşe. 1995
Women's Participation in Politics in Turkey. In Women in Modern Turkish Society: A Reader. Sirin Tekeli, ed. Pp. 235–249. London: Zed Books.

Guthrie, M. 1967–1972
Comparative Bantu. 4 volumes. Farnborough, England: Gregg International.

Hackenberg, Robert A. et al. 1983
Migration, Modernization and Hypertension: Blood Pressure Levels in Four Philippine Communities. Medical Anthropology 7(1):45–71.

Hacker, Andrew. 1992
Two Nations: Black and White, Separate, Hostile, Unequal. New York: Ballantine Books.

Hahn, Robert A. 1995
Sickness and Healing: An Anthropological Perspective. New Haven: Yale University Press.

Haile-Selassie, Yohannes. 2001
Late Miocene Hominids from the Middle Awash, Ethiopia. Nature 412:178–181.

Haile-Selassie, Yohannes, Gen Suwa, and Tim D. White. 2004
Late Miocene Teeth from Middle Awash, Ethiopia, and Early Hominid Dental Evolution. Science 303:1503–1505.

Halberstein, R. A. 1997
Sickle Cell and Other Hemoglobin Variations in the Caribbean. Journal of Caribbean Studies 12:124–140.

Hallam, S. 1989
Plant Usage and Management in Southwest Australia Aboriginal Societies. In Foraging and Farming: The Evolution of Plant Exploitation. D. Harris and G. Hillman, eds. Pp. 136–151. London: WAC.

Hamblin, Dora Jane. 1987
Has the Garden of Eden Been Located at Last? Smithsonian 18(2):127–135.

Hammer, Michael F. 1995
A Recent Common Ancestry for Human Y Chromosomes. Nature 378:376–378.

Hammer, Michael F., A. B. Spurdle, T. Karafet, M. R. Bonner, and E. T. Wood. 1997
The Geographic Distribution of Human Y Chromosome Variation. Genetics 145:787–805.

Hancock, Graham. 1989
Lords of Poverty: The Power, Prestige, and Corruption of the International Aid Business. New York: Atlantic Monthly Press.

Harcourt-Smith, W. E. H. and Leslie Aiello. 2004
Fossils, Feet and the Evolution of Human Bipedal Locomotion. Journal of Anatomy 204:317–432.

Harding, R. S. O. 1981
An Order of Omnivores: Nonhuman Primate Diets in the Wild. In Omnivorous Primates: Gathering and Hunting in Human Evolution. R. S. O. Harding and Geza Teleki, eds. New York: Columbia University Press.

Hardy, B. L. and R. A. Raff. 1997
Recovery of Mammalian DNA from Middle Paleolithic Stone Tools. Journal of Archaeological Science 24:601–611.

Harlan, Jack R. 1992
Indigenous African Agriculture. In The Origins of Agricul-

ture. C. Wesley Cowan and Patty Jo Watson, eds. Pp. 59–70. Washington, DC: Smithsonian Institution Press.

Harner, Michael. 1977
The Ecological Basis of Aztec Sacrifice. American Ethnologist 4:117–135.

Harris, Jack W. K. 1978
The Karari Industry: Its Place in East African Prehistory. Berkeley: University of California Press.

Harris, Marvin. 1993
The Evolution of Human Gender Hierarchies: A Trial Formulation. In Sex and Gender Hierarchies. Barbara D. Miller, ed. Pp. 57–79. New York: Cambridge University Press.

———. 1992
Distinguished Lecture: Anthropology and the Theoretical and Paradigmatic Significance of the Collapse of Soviet and East European Communism. American Anthropologist 94:295–305.

———. 1989
Our Kind: The Evolution of Human Life and Culture. New York: Harper & Row.

———. 1984
Animal Capture and Yanomamo Warfare: Retrospect and New Evidence. Journal of Anthropological Research 40(10):183–201.

———. 1977
Cannibals and Kings: The Origins of Culture. New York: Random House.

———. 1974
Cows, Pigs, Wars and Witches: The Riddles of Culture. New York: Random House.

———. 1971
Culture, Man and Nature. New York: Thomas Y Crowell.

———. 1968
The Rise of Anthropological Theory: A History of Theories of Culture. New York: Thomas Y Crowell.

Harris, Marvin and Eric B. Ross. 1987
Death, Sex and Fertility. New York: Columbia University Press.

Harrison, Roman G. and M. Anne Katzenberg. 2003
Paleodiet Studies Using Stable Carbon Isotopes from Bone Apatite and Collagen: Examples from Southern Ontario and San Nicolas Island, California. Journal of Anthropological Archaeology 22:227–244.

Haynes, Gary. 2002
The Early Settlement of North America: The Clovis Era. New York: Cambridge University Press.

Hefner, Robert W. 1998
Multiple Modernities: Christianity, Islam, and Hinduism in a Globalizing Age. Annual Review of Anthropology 27:83–104.

Heise, Lori L., Jacqueline Pitanguy, and Adrienne Germain. 1994
Violence against Women: The Hidden Health Burden. World Bank Discussion Papers No. 255. Washington, DC: The World Bank.

Helagson, A., G. Nicholson, K. Stefánsson, and P. Donnelly. 2003
A Reassessment of Genetic Diversity in Icelanders: Strong Evidence from Multiple Loci for Relative Homogeneity Caused by Genetic Drift. Annals of Human Genetics 67:281–297.

Helweg, Arthur W. and Usha M. Helweg. 1990
An Immigrant Success Story: East Indians in America. Philadelphia: University of Pennsylvania Press.

Henshilwood, Christopher S. 1997
Identifying the Collector: Evidence for Human Processing of the Cape Dune Mole-Rate, Bathyergus suillus, from Blombos Cave, Southern Cape, South Africa. Journal of Archaeological Science 24:659–662.

Henshilwood, Christopher, Francesco d'Errico, M. Vanhaeren, K. Van Niekerk, and Z. Jacobs. 2004
Middle Stone Age Shell Beads from South Africa. Science 304:304.

Henshilwood, Christopher, Francesco d'Errico, R. Yates, Z. Jacobs, C. Tribolo, G. Duller, N. Mercier, J. Sealy, H. Valladas, I. Watts, and A. Wintle. 2002
Emergence of Modern Human Behavior: Middle Stone Age Engravings from South Africa. Science 295:1278–1280.

Herdt, Gilbert. 1987
The Sambia: Ritual and Gender in New Guinea. New York: Holt, Rinehart and Winston.

Herrnstein, Richard J. and Charles A. Murray. 1994
The Bell Curve: Intelligence and Class Structure in American Life. New York: Free Press.

Herzfeld, Michael. 1985
The Poetics of Manhood: Contest and Identity in a Cretan Mountain Village. Princeton, NJ: Princeton University Press.

Hewlett, Barry S. 1991
Intimate Fathers: The Nature and Context of Aka Pygmy Paternal Care. Ann Arbor: University of Michigan Press.

Hiatt, Betty. 1970
Woman the Gatherer. In Woman's Role in Aboriginal Society. Fay Gale, ed. Pp. 2–28. Canberra: Australia Institute of Aboriginal Studies.

Hill, Jane D. 2001
Dimensions of Attrition in Language Death. In On Biocultural Diversity: Linking Language, Knowledge, and the Environment. Luisa Maffi, ed. Pp. 175–189. Washington, DC: Smithsonian Institution.

Hill, Jane D. and Bruce Mannheim. 1992
Language and World View. Annual Review of Anthropology 21:381–406.

Hillman, G. C., and M. S. Davies. 1990
Measured Domestication Rates in Wild Wheats and Barley under Primitive Cultivation, and their Archaeological Implications. Journal of World Prehistory 4:157–222.

Hiltebeitel, Alf. 1995
Hinduism. In The HarperCollins Dictionary of Religion. Jonathan Z. Smith, ed. Pp. 424–440. New York: HarperCollins.

———. 1988
The Cult of Draupadi: Mythologies from Gingee to Kuruksetra. Chicago: University of Chicago Press.

Hinde, R. A. 1983
Primate Social Relationships: An Integrated Approach. Sunderland, MA: Sinauer Associates.

Hirschon, Renee. 1989
Heirs of the Catastrophe: The Social Life of Asia Minor Refugees in Piraeus. New York: Oxford University Press.

Hoberg, E. P., N. L. Lalkire, A. de Queroz, and A. Jones. 2001
Out of Africa: Origins of the Taenia Tapeworms. Proceedings of the Royal Society of London, Series B 268:718–787.

Hodder, Ian. 1999
  Getting to the Bottom of Things: Çatalhöyük 1999. Anatolian Archaeology 5:4–7.
———. 1996
  Archaeology. In The Social Science Encyclopedia, 2nd ed. Adam Kuper and Jessica Kuper, eds. Pp. 28–30. New York: Routledge.

Hodge, Robert W. and Naohiro Ogawa. 1991
  Fertility Change in Contemporary Japan. Chicago: University of Chicago Press.

Hoffecker, John F. 2002
  Desolate Landscapes: Ice-Age Settlements in Eastern Europe. New Brunswick, NJ: Rutgers University Press.

Holden, Clare and Ruth Mace. 1999
  Sexual Dimorphism in Stature and Women's Work: A Phylogenetic Cross-Cultural Analysis. American Journal of Physical Anthropology 110:27–45.

Holland, Dorothy C. and Margaret A. Eisenhart. 1990
  Educated in Romance: Women, Achievement, and College Culture. Chicago: University of Chicago Press.

Holliday, Trenton W. 1997
  Postcranial Evidence of Cold Adaptation in European Neandertals. American Journal of Physical Anthropology 104:245–258.

Hopkins, Nicholas S. and Sohair R. Mehanna. 2000
  Social Action against Everyday Pollution in Egypt. Human Organization 59:245–254.

Hornbein, George and Marie Hornbein. 1992
  Salamanders: A Night at the Phi Delta House. Video. College Park: Documentary Resource Center.

Horowitz, Michael M. and Muneera Salem-Murdock. 1993
  Development-Induced Food Insecurity in the Middle Senegal Valley. GeoJournal 30(2):179–184.

Hostetler, John A. and Gertrude Enders Huntington. 1992
  Amish Children: Education in the Family, School, and Community. New York: Harcourt.

Howell, Nancy. 1990
  Surviving Fieldwork: A Report of the Advisory Panel on Health and Safety in Fieldwork. Washington, DC: American Anthropological Association.
———. 1979
  Demography of the Dobe !Kung. New York: Academic Press.

Hrdy, Sarah. 1977
  The Langurs of Abu: Female and Male Strategies for Reproduction. Cambridge, MA: Harvard University Press.

Huang, Shu-Min. 1993
  A Cross-Cultural Experience: A Chinese Anthropologist in the United States. In Distant Mirrors: America as a Foreign Culture. Philip R. DeVita and James D. Armstrong, eds. Pp. 39–45. Belmont, CA: Wadsworth.

Hublin, Jean-Jacques. 2000
  Modern–Nonmodern Hominid Interactions: A Mediterranean Perspective. In The Geography of Neanderthals and Modern Humans in Europe and the Greater Mediterranean. Ofer Bar-Yosef, and David Pilbeam, eds. Pp. 157–182. Cambridge, MA: Harvard University, Peabody Museum of Archaeology and Ethnology, Peabody Museum Bulletin 8.
———. 1998
  Climatic Changes, Paleogeography, and the Evolution of the Neandertals. In Neanderthals and Modern Humans in Western Asia. T. Akazawa, K. Aoki, and O. Bar-Yosef, eds. Pp. 295–310. New York: Plenum.

Hublin, Jean-Jacques, Fred Spoor, Marc Braun, and Frans Zonneveld. 1996
  A Late Neanderthal Associated with Upper Paleolithic Artifacts. Nature 381:224–226.

Humphrey, Caroline. 1978
  Women, Taboo and the Suppression of Attention. In Defining Females: The Nature of Women in Society. Shirley Ardener, ed. Pp. 89–108. New York: Wiley.

Hunte, Pamela A. 1985
  Indigenous Methods of Fertility Regulation in Afghanistan. In Women's Medicine: A Cross-Cultural Study of Indigenous Fertility Regulation. Lucile F. Newman, ed. Pp. 44–75. New Brunswick, NJ: Rutgers University Press.

Hutchinson, Sharon E. 1996
  Nuer Dilemmas: Coping with Money, War, and the State. Berkeley: University of California Press.

Hutter, Michael. 1996
  The Value of Play. In The Value of Culture: On the Relationship between Economics and the Arts. Arjo Klamer, ed. Pp. 122–137. Amsterdam: Amsterdam University Press.

Hyslop, John. 1990
  Inka Settlement Planning. Austin, TX: University of Texas Press.

IHGSC. 2001
  Initial Sequencing and Analysis of the Human Genome. Nature 409:860–921.

Ingman, M. H., H. Kaessmann, S. Paabo, and U. Gyllensten. 2000
  Mitochondrial Genome Variation and the Origin of Modern Humans. Nature 408:708–713.

Ingstad, Anne Stine. 1977
  The Discovery of a Norse Settlement in North America. Oslo: Universitetsforlaget.

International Labour Office. 1996
  Female Asian Migrants: A Growing But Vulnerable Workforce. World of Work 15:16–17.

Isaac, Glynn L. 1978
  The Archaeological Evidence for the Activities of Early African Hominids. In Early Hominids of Africa. C. Jolly, ed. Pp. 219–254. London: Duckworth.

Jablonski, Nina G. and G. Chaplin. 2000
  The Evolution of Skin Coloration. Journal of Human Evolution 39:57–106.

Jacobsen, T. 1976
  Seventeen Thousand Years of Greek Prehistory. Scientific American 234(6):76–87.

Jahoda, Gustav. 1999
  Images of Savages: Ancient Roots of Modern Prejudices in Western Culture. New York: Routledge.

Jamison, Cheryl Sorenson, Laurel L. Cornell, Paul L. Jamison, and Hideki Nakazato. 2002.
  Are All Grandmothers Equal? A Review and a Preliminary Test of the "Grandmother Hypothesis" in Tokugawa Japan. American Journal of Physical Anthropology 119:67–76.

Janes, Craig R. 1990
  Migration, Social Change, and Health: A Samoan Community in Urban California. Stanford, CA: Stanford University Press.

Jankowski, Martín Sánchez. 1991
Islands in the Street: Gangs and American Urban Society. Berkeley: University of California Press.

Jet. 1996
Baseball Team Members Who Used KKK Symbol Will Receive Multicultural Training. Jet 88(18):39.

Jiang, David W. 1994
Shanghai Revisited: Chinese Theatre and the Forces of the Market. The Drama Review 38(2):72–80.

Jinadu, L. Adele. 1994
The Dialectics of Theory and Research on Race and Ethnicity in Nigeria. In "Race," Ethnicity and Nation: International Perspectives on Social Conflict. Peter Ratcliffe, ed. Pp. 163–178. London: University College London Press.

Jobling, Mark A. and Chris Tyler-Smith. 2000
New Uses for New Haplotypes—the Human Y Chromosome, Disease and Selection. Trends in Genetics 16:356–362.

Jobling, Mark A., M. E. Hurles, and C. Tyler-Smith. 2004
Human Evolutionary Genetics: Origins, Peoples and Disease. New York: Garland Science.

Johnson, Harriet McBryde. 2003.
Should I Have Been Killed at Birth?: The Case for My Life. New York Times Magazine, February 16:50ff.

Johnson, Walter R. 1994
Dismantling Apartheid: A South African Town in Transition. Ithaca, NY: Cornell University Press.

Johnson-Hanks, Jennifer. 2002
On the Limits of Life Stages in Ethnography: Toward a Theory of Vital Conjectures. American Anthropologist 104: 865–880.

Johnston, Barbara Rose. 1994
Environmental Degradation and Human Rights Abuse. In Who Pays the Price?: The Sociocultural Context of Environmental Crisis. Barbara Rose Johnston, ed. Pp. 7–16. Washington, DC: Island Press.

Johnston, Francis E. and P. Gordon-Larsen. 1999
Poverty, Nutrition and Obesity in the USA. In Urbanism, Health, and Human Biology in Industrialised Countries. Lawrence M. Schell and Stanley J. Ulijaszek, eds. Pp. 192–209. New York: Cambridge University Press.

Jolly, Alison. 1985
The Evolution of Primate Behavior, 2nd ed. New York: Macmillan.

Jonaitis, Aldona. 1995
A Wealth of Thought: Franz Boas on Native American Art. Seattle: University of Washington Press.

Jones, Anna Laura. 1993
Exploding Canons: The Anthropology of Museums. Annual Review of Anthropology 22:201–220.

Joralemon, Donald. 1982
New World Depopulation and the Case of Disease. Journal of Anthropological Research 38:108–127.

Jordan, Brigitte. 1983
Birth in Four Cultures. 3rd ed. Montreal: Eden Press.

Joseph, R. 2000
The Limbic Language/Language Axis Theory of Speech. Behavioral and Brain Sciences 23(3):439–440.

Joseph, Suad. 1994
Brother/Sister Relationships: Connectivity, Love, and Power in the Reproduction of Patriarchy in Lebanon. American Ethnologist 21:50–73.

Jourdan, Christine. 1995
Masta Liu. In Youth Cultures: A Cross-Cultural Perspective. Vered Amit-Talai and Helena Wulff, eds. Pp. 202–222. New York: Routledge.

Judd, Ellen. 2002
The Chinese Women's Movement: Between State and Market. Stanford, CA: Stanford University Press.

Kaberry, Phyllis. 1952
Women of the Grassfields: A Study of the Economic Position of Women in Bamenda, British Cameroons. London: Her Majesty's Stationery Office.

Kabutha, Charity, Barbara P. Thomas-Slaytor, and Richard Ford. 1993
Participatory Rural Appraisal: A Case Study from Kenya. In Rapid Appraisal Methods. Krishna Kumar, ed. Pp. 176–211. Washington, DC: The World Bank.

Kahn, Miriam. 1995
Heterotopic Dissonance in the Museum Representation of Pacific Island Cultures. American Anthropologist 97(2): 324–338.

Kano, Takayoshi. 1992
The Last Ape: Pygmy Chimpanzee Behavior and Ecology. Stanford, CA: Stanford University Press.

Kapchan, Deborah A. 1994
Moroccan Female Performers Defining the Social Body. Journal of American Folklore 107(423):82–105.

Kassam, Aneesa. 2002
Ethnodevelopment in the Oromia Regional State of Ethiopia. In Participating in Development: Approaches to Indigenous Knowledge. Paul Sillitoe, Alan Bicker, and Johan Pottier, eds. Pp. 65–81. ASA Monographs No. 39. New York: Routledge.

Katz, Nathan and Ellen S. Goldberg. 1989
Asceticism and Caste in the Passover Observances of the Cochin Jews. Journal of the American Academy of Religion 57(1):53–81.

Katz, Richard. 1982
Boiling Energy: Community Healing among the Kalahari Kung. Cambridge, MA: Harvard University Press.

Katz, Solomon H. and Fritz Maytag. 1991
Brewing an Ancient Beer. Archaeology 44(4):24–27.

Kawamura, S. 1959
The Process of Subculture Propagation among Japanese Macaques. Primates 2:43–60.

Kearney, Michael. 1986
From the Invisible Hand to Visible Feet: Anthropological Studies of Migration and Development. Annual Review of Anthropology 15:331–361.

Kehoe, Alice Beck. 1989
The Ghost Dance: History and Revitalization. Philadelphia: Holt.

Keightley, D. N. 1983
The Late Shang State: When, Where and What? In The Origins of Chinese Civilization. D. N. Keightley, ed. Pp. 523–564. Berkeley: University of California Press.

Keiser, R. Lincoln. 1986
Death Enmity in Thull: Organized Vengeance and Social Change in a Kohistani Community. American Ethnologist 13(3):489–505.

Kelley, Heidi. 1991
Unwed Mothers and Household Reputation in a Spanish Galician Community. American Ethnologist 18:565–580.

Kennedy, David P. and Stephen G. Perz. 2000
Who Are Brazil's Indígenas? Contributions of Census Data Analysis to Anthropological Demography of Indigenous Populations. Human Organization 59:311–324.

Kenoyer, Jonathan Mark. 1998
Ancient Cities of the Indus Valley Civilization. Oxford: Oxford University Press.

Kerns, Virginia. 1992
Preventing Violence against Women: A Central American Case. In Sanctions and Sanctuary: Cultural Perspectives on the Beating of Wives. Dorothy Ayers Counts, Judith K. Brown, and Jacquelyn C. Campbell, eds. Pp. 125–138. Boulder, CO: Westview Press.

Kesmanee, Chupinit. 1994
Dubious Development Concepts in the Thai Highlands: The Chao Khao in Transition. Law & Society Review 28:673–683.

Kideckel, David A. 1993
The Solitude of Collectivism: Romanian Villagers to the Revolution and Beyond. Ithaca, NY: Cornell University Press.

Kirsch, Stuart. 2002
Anthropology and Advocacy: A Case Study of the Campaign against the Ok Tedi Mine. Critique of Anthropology 22:175–200.

Klawiter, Maren. 2000
From Private Stigma to Global Assembly: Transforming the Terrain of Breast Cancer. In Global Ethnography: Forces, Connections, and Imaginations in a Postmodern World. Michael Buraway, ed. Pp. 299–334. Berkeley: University of California Press.

Kleiman, D. G., B. B. Beck, J. M. Dietz, L. A. Dietz, J. D. Ballou, and A. F. Coimbra Filho. 1986
Conservation Program for the Golden Lion Tamarin: Captive Research and Management, Ecological Studies, Educational Studies, and Reintroduction. In Primates: The Road to Self-Sustaining Populations. K. Benirschke, ed. Pp. 959–979. New York: Springer-Verlag.

Kleinman, Arthur. 1995
Writing at the Margin: Discourse between Anthropology and Medicine. Berkeley: University of California Press.

Knight, A. 2003
The Phylogenetic Relationship of Neandertal and Modern Human Mitochondrial DNAs Based on Informative Nucleotide Sites. Journal of Human Evolution 44:627–632.

Knott, Cheryl. 1999
Orangutan Behavior and Ecology. In The Nonhuman Primates. Phyllis Dolhinow and Agustin Fuentes, eds. Pp. 50–57. Mountain View, CA: Mayfield Publishing Company.

Knott, Kim. 1996
Hindu Women, Destiny and Stridharma. Religion 26:15–35.

Kolenda, Pauline M. 1978
Caste in Contemporary India: Beyond Organic Solidarity. Prospect Heights, IL: Waveland Press.

———. 1968
Region, Caste, and Family Structure: A Comparative Study of the Indian "Joint" Family. In Structure and Change in Indian Society. Milton Singer and Bernard S. Cohn, eds. Pp. 339–396. New York: Aldine.

Kondo, Dorinne. 1997
About Face: Performing "Race" in Fashion and Theater. New York: Routledge.

Konner, Melvin. 1989
Homosexuality: Who and Why? New York Times Magazine. April 2:60–61.

———. 1987
Becoming a Doctor: The Journey of Initiation in Medical School. New York: Penguin Books.

Kottak, Conrad Phillip. 1992
Assault on Paradise: Social Change in a Brazilian Village. New York: McGraw-Hill.

———. 1985
When People Don't Come First: Some Sociological Lessons from Completed Projects. In Putting People First: Sociological Variables and Rural Development. Michael M. Cernea, ed. Pp. 325–356. New York: Oxford University Press.

Krantzler, Nora J. 1987
Traditional Medicine as "Medical Neglect": Dilemmas in the Case Management of a Samoan Teenager with Diabetes. In Child Survival: Cultural Perspectives on the Treatment and Maltreatment of Children. Nancy Scheper-Hughes, ed. Pp. 325–337. Boston: D. Reidel.

Krings, M., A. Stone, R.W. Schmitz, H. Krainitzki, M. Stoneking, and S. Pääbo. 1997
Neandertal DNA Sequences and the Origin of Modern Humans. Cell 90:19–30.

Krings, M., C. Capelli, F. Tschentscher, H. Geisert, S. Meyer, A. von Haeseler, K. Grossschmidt, G. Possnert, M. Paunovic, and S. Pääbo. 2000
A View of Neandertal Genetic Diversity. Nature Genetics 26:144–146.

Krings, M., H. Geisert, R.W. Schmitz, H. Krainitzki, and S. Pääbo. 1999
DNA Sequence of the Mitochondrial Hypervariable Region II from the Neandertal Type Specimen. Proceedings of the National Academy of Sciences 96:5581–5585.

Kroeber, A. L. and Clyde Kluckhohn. 1952
Culture: A Critical Review of Concepts and Definitions. New York: Vintage Books.

Kuipers, Joel C. 1991
Matters of Taste in Weyéwa. In The Varieties of Sensory Experience: A Sourcebook in the Anthropology of the Senses. David Howes, ed. Pp. 111–127. Toronto: University of Toronto Press.

———. 1990
Power in Performance: The Creation of Textual Authority in Weyéwa Ritual Speech. Philadelphia: University of Pennsylvania Press.

Kumar, Krishna. 1996
Civil Society. In The Social Science Encyclopedia. Adam Kuper and Jessica Kuper, eds. Pp. 88–90. Routledge: New York.

Kurkiala, Mikael. 2003
Interpreting Honor Killings: The Story of Fadime Sahindal (1975–2002) in the Swedish Press. Anthropology Today 19:6–7.

Kusimba, Sibel Barut. 1999
Hunter–Gatherer Land Use Patterns in Later Stone Age East Africa. Journal of Anthropological Archaeology 18:165–200.

Kuwayama, Takami. 2003
"Natives" as Dialogic Partners. Anthropology Today 19(1):8–13.

Kwiatkowski, Lynn M. 1998
  Struggling with Development: The Politics of Hunger and Gender in the Philippines. Boulder, CO: Westview Press.
Labov, William. 1966
  The Social Stratification of English in New York City. Washington, DC: Center for Applied Linguistics.
Ladányi, János. 1993
  Patterns of Residential Segregation and the Gypsy Minority in Budapest. International Journal of Urban and Regional Research 17(1):30–41.
Laderman, Carol. 1988
  A Welcoming Soil: Islamic Humoralism on the Malay Peninsula. In Paths to Asian Medical Knowledge. Charles Leslie and Allan Young, eds. Pp. 272–288. Berkeley: University of California Press.
LaFleur, William. 1992
  Liquid Life: Abortion and Buddhism in Japan. Princeton, NJ: Princeton University Press.
Lai, C. S. L., S. E. Fisher, J. A. Hurst, F. Vargha-Khadem, and A. P. Monaco. 2001
  A Forkhead-Domain Gene Is Mutated in a Severe Speech and Language Disorder. Nature 413:519–523.
Lakoff, Robin. 1990
  Talking Power: The Politics of Language in Our Lives. New York: Basic Books.
———. 1973
  Language and Woman's Place. Language in Society 2:45–79.
Lamarck, Jean-Baptiste. 1809
  Philosophie Zoologique. Paris and London: Macmillan.
Lambert-Zazulak, Patricia I., Patricia Rutherford, and A. Rosalie David. 2003
  The International Ancient Egyptian Mummy Tissue Bank at the Manchester Museum as a Resource for the Palaeoepidemiological Study of Schistosomiasis. World Archaeology 35:223–240.
Lamphere, Louise. 1992
  Introduction: The Shaping of Diversity. In Structuring Diversity: Ethnographic Perspectives on the New Immigration. Lousie Lamphere, ed. Chicago: University of Chicago Press.
Larsen, Clark Spencer and George R. Milner. 1994
  Bioanthropological Perspectives on Postcontact Traditions. In In the Wake of Contact: Biological Responses to Conquest. Clark Spencer Larsen and George R. Milner, eds. Pp. 1–8. New York: Wiley-Liss.
Larsen, Ulla and Sharon Yan. 2000
  Does Female Circumcision Affect Infertility and Fertility? A Study of the Central African Republic, Côte d'Ivoire and Tanzania. Demography 37:313–321.
Lassiter, Luke Eric, Hurley Goodall, Elizabeth Campbell, and Michelle Natasya Johnson. 2004
  The Other Side of Middletown: Exploring Muncie's African American Community. Walnut Creek, CA: AltaMira Press.
Latinis, D. Kyle. 2000
  The Development of Subsistence System Models for Island Southeast Asia and Near Oceania: The Nature and Role of Arboriculture and Arboreal-Based Economies. World Archaeology 32:41–67.
Lawler, Andrew. 2001
  Writing Gets a Rewrite. Science 292:2418–2420.
Leach, Jerry W. 1975
  Trobriand Cricket: An Ingenious Response to Colonialism. Video. Berkeley: University of California Extension Media.

Leakey, Louis S. B., P. V. Tobias, and J. R. Napier. 1964
  A New Species of the Genus Homo from Olduvai Gorge. Nature 202:7–9.
Leakey, Mary D., and Richard L. Hay. 1979
  Pliocene Footprints in the Laetoli Beds at Laetoli, Northern Tanzania. Nature 278:317–323.
Leakey, Meave G., F. Spoor, F. H. Brown, P. N. Gathogo, C. Kiarie, L. N. Leakey, and I. McDougall. 2001
  New Hominin Genus from Eastern Africa Shows Diverse Middle Pliocene Lineages. Nature 410:433–440.
Leavy, Morton L. and R. D. Weinberg. 1979
  Law of Adoption. Dobbs Ferry, NY: Oceana.
LeBlanc, J. 1975
  Man in the Cold. Springfifeld, IL: Charles C Thomas.
Lee, Gary R. and Mindy Kezis. 1979
  Family Structure and the Status of the Elderly. Journal of Comparative Family Studies 10:429–443.
Lee, Helen Morton. 2003
  Tongans Overseas: Between Two Shores. Honolulu: University of Hawai'i Press.
Lee, Richard B. and I. DeVore, eds. 1968
  Man the Hunter. Chicago: Aldine and Atherton.
Lee, Richard Borshay. 1979
  The !Kung San: Men, Women, and Work in a Foraging Society. New York: Cambridge University Press.
Lee, Wai-Na and David K. Tse. 1994
  Becoming Canadian: Understanding How Hong Kong Immigrants Change Their Consumption. Pacific Affairs 67(1):70–95.
Lee-Thorp, Julia A., M. Sponheimer, and N. J. van der Merve. 2003
  What Do Stable Isotopes Tell Us about Hominid Dietary and Ecological Niches in the Pliocene? International Journal of Osteoarchaeology 13:104–113.
Lein, Laura and Donald Brenneis. 1978
  Children's Dispute in Three Speech Communities. Language in Society 7:299–323.
Lempert, David. 1996
  Daily Life in a Crumbling Empire. 2 volumes. New York: Columbia University Press.
Leonard, William R. 2000
  Human Nutritional Evolution. In Human Biology: An Evolutionary and Biocultural Perspective. Sara Stinson, Barry Bogin, Rebecca-Huss-Ashmore, and Dennis O'Rourke, eds. Pp. 295–344. New York: Wiley-Liss.
Lepowsky, Maria. 1993
  Fruit of the Motherland: Gender in an Egalitarian Society. New York: Columbia University Press.
———. 1990
  Big Men, Big Women, and Cultural Autonomy. Ethnology 29(10):35–50.
Levine, Robert, Suguru Sato, Tsukasa Hashimoto, and Jyoti Verma. 1995
  Love and Marriage in Eleven Cultures. Journal of Cross-Cultural Psychology 26:554–571.
Levinson, David. 1989
  Family Violence in Cross-Cultural Perspective. Newbury Park, CA: Sage Publications.
Lévi-Strauss, Claude. 1968
  Tristes Tropiques: An Anthropological Study of Primitive Societies in Brazil. New York: Atheneum.

———. 1967
Structural Anthropology. New York: Anchor Books.

Levy, Jerrold E., Eric B. Henderson, and Tracy J. Andrews. 1989
The Effects of Regional Variation and Temporal Change in Matrilineal Elements of Navajo Social Organization. Journal of Anthropological Research 45(4):351–377.

Lew, Irvina. 1994
Bathing as Science: Ancient Sea Cures Gain Support from New Research. Condé Nast Traveler 29(12):86–90.

Leynaud, Emile. 1961
Fraternités d'âge et sociétés de culture dans la Haute-Vallée du Niger. Cahiers d'Etudes Africaines 6:41–68.

Lieberman, Daniel and J. Shea. 1994
Behavioral Differences between Archaic and Modern Humans in the Levantine Mousterian. American Anthropologist 96:300–332.

Lieberman, Daniel E., Brandeis M. McBratney, and Gail Krovitz. 2002
The Evolution and Development of Cranial Form in Homo sapiens. Proceedings of the National Academy of Sciences 99:1134–1139.

Lindberg, David C. 1992
The Beginnings of Western Science: The European Scientific Tradition in Philosophical, Religious and Institutional Context, 600 B.C. to A.D. 1450. Chicago: University of Chicago Press.

Lindenbaum, Shirley. 1979
Kuru Sorcery: Disease and Danger in the New Guinea Highlands. Mountain View, CA: Mayfield.

Linduff, Katheryn M. 2003
Many Wives, One Queen in Shang China. In Ancient Queens: Archaeological Explorations. Sarah Milledge Nelson, ed. Pp. 59–76. Walnut Creek, CA: AltaMira Press.

Linnaeus, Carolus. 1758
Systema Naturae. Stockholm: Lawentii Salvii.

Little, Kenneth. 1966
The Strange Case of Romantic Love. The Listener 7 (April).

Littman, Mark. 1993
Office of Refugee Resettlement Monthly Data Report for September 1992. Washington, DC: Office of Refugee Resettlement.

Lock, Margaret. 1993
Encounters with Aging: Mythologies of Menopause in Japan and North America. Berkeley: University of California Press.

Lockwood, Victoria S. 1993
Tahitian Transformation: Gender and Capitalist Development in a Rural Society. Boulder, CO: Lynne Reiner Publishers.

Long, Austin, Bruce F. Benz, J. Donahue, A. Jull, and L. Toolin. 1989
First Direct AMS Dates on Early Maize from Tehuacán, Mexico. Radiocarbon 31:1035–1040.

Long, Jeffrey C., and Rick A. Kittles. 2003
Human Genetic Diversity and the Nonexistence of Biological Races. Human Biology 75:449–471.

Lonsdorf, Elizabeth V. and Lynn E. Eberly. 2004
Sex Differences in Learning in Chimpanzees. Nature 428:715–716.

Lorch, Donatella. 2003
Do Read This for War. Newsweek 141(11):13.

Lounsbury, Floyd G. 1972
One Hundred Years of Anthropological Linguistics. In One Hundred Years of Anthropology. J. O Brew, ed. Pp. 153–226. Cambridge, MA: Harvard University Press.

Lovejoy, C. Owen, K. G. Heiple, and R. S. Meindl. 2001
Did Our Ancestors Knuckle-walk? Nature 410:325–326.

Lovell, Nancy C. and Ira Whyte. 1999
Patterns of Dental Enamel Defects of Ancient Mendes, Egypt. American Journal of Physical Anthropology 110:69–80.

Low, Setha M. 1995
Indigenous Architecture and the Spanish American Plaza in Mesoamerica and the Caribbean. American Anthropologist 97(4):748–762.

Lozada, Eriberto P. Jr. 1998
A Hakka Community in Cyberspace: Diasporic Ethnicity and the Internet. In Sidney C. H. Cheung, ed. On the South China Track: Perspectives on Anthropological Research and Teaching. Pp. 148–182. Hong Kong: The Chinese University of Hong Kong, Hong Kong Institute of Asia-Pacific Studies.

Lubkemann, Stephen C. 2002
Refugees. In World at Risk: A Global Issues Sourcebook. Pp. 522–544. Washington, DC: CQ Press.

Luhrmann, Tanya M. 1989
Persuasions of the Witch's Craft: Ritual Magic in Contemporary England. Cambridge, MA: Harvard University Press.

Lukacs, John R. 1996
Sex Differences in Dental Caries Rates with the Origin of Agriculture in South Asia. Current Anthropology 37:147–153.

Lutz, Catherine. 2002
Making War at Home in the United States: Militarization and the Current Crisis. American Anthropologist 104:723–735.

Lyell, Charles. 1830
Principles of Geology. London: John Murray.

MacCormack, Sabine. 2001
Cuzco, Another Rome? In Empires: Perspectives from Archaeology and History. Susan E. Alcock, Terence N. D'Altroy, Kathleen D. Morrison, and Carla M. Sinopoli, eds. Pp. 419–435. New York: Cambridge University Press.

MacDonald, Kevin. 1999
Invisible Pastoralists: An Inquiry into the Origins of Nomadic Pastoralism in the West African Sahel. In The Prehistory of Food: Appetites for Change. Chris Gosden and Jon Hather, eds. Pp. 333–349. New York: Routledge.

Maclachlan, Morgan. 1983
Why They Did Not Starve: Biocultural Adaptation in a South Indian Village. Philadelphia: Institute for the Study of Human Issues.

MacLeod, Arlene Elowe. 1992
Hegemonic Relations and Gender Resistance: The New Veiling as Accommodating Protest in Cairo. Signs: The Journal of Women in Culture and Society 17(3):533–557.

MacNeish, Richard S. 1967
A Summary of the Subsistence. In The Prehistory of the Tehuacán Valley, vol. 1: Environment and Subsistence. D. Byers, ed. Pp. 290–309. Austin, TX: University of Texas Press.

Mahler, Sarah J. 1995
Salvadorans in Suburbia: Symbiosis and Conflict. Boston: Allyn and Bacon.

Major, Marc R. 1996
   No Friends But the Mountains: A Simulation on Kurdistan. Social Education 60(3):C1–C8.
Malinowski, Bronislaw. 1961 [1922]
   Argonauts of the Western Pacific. New York: E. P. Dutton.
Malthus, Thomas R. 1998 [1798]
   An Essay on the Principle of Population. Electronic New World Scholarly Publishing Project: http://www.esp.org.
Mamdani, Mahmood. 2002
   Good Muslim, Bad Muslim: A Political Perspective on Culture and Terrorism. American Anthropologist 104:766–775.
———. 1972
   The Myth of Population Control: Family, Caste, and Class in an Indian Village. New York: Monthly Review Press.
Manz, Beatriz. 1988
   Refugees of a Hidden War: The Aftermath of Counterinsurgency in Guatemala. Albany: State University of New York Press.
Manzi, Giorgio, F. Mallegni, and A. Ascenzi. 2001
   A Cranium for the Earliest Europeans: Phylogenetic Position of the Hominid from Ceprano, Italy. Proceedings of the National Academy of Sciences 98:10011–10016.
Marcoux, Alan. 2000
   The Feminization of Poverty: Facts, Hypotheses, and the Art of Advocacy. http://www.undp.org.popin.fao.womnpoor.htm. 11/6/00.
Marcus, Joyce. 1998
   The Peaks and Valleys of Ancient States: An Extension of the Dynamic Model. In Archaic States. Gary M. Feinman and Joyce Marcus, eds. Pp. 59–94. Santa Fe, NM: School of American Research Press.
———. 1992
   Mesoamerican Writing Systems: Propaganda, Myth, and History in Four Ancient Civilizations. Princeton, NJ: Princeton University Press.
———. 1974
   The Iconography of Power among the Classic Maya. World Archaeology 6:83–94.
Marcus, Joyce, and Kent V. Flannery. 1996
   Zapotec Civilization: How Urban Society Evolved in Mexico's Oaxaca Valley. New York: Thames & Hudson.
Margolis, Maxine. 1994
   Little Brazil: An Ethnography of Brazilian Immigrants in New York City. Princeton, NJ: Princeton University Press.
Margolis, Maxine L. and Marigene Arnold. 1993
   Turning the Tables? Male Strippers and the Gender Hierarchy in America. In Sex and Gender Hierarchies. Barbara D. Miller, ed. Pp. 334–350. New York: Cambridge University Press.
Marshall, Fiona, and Elisabeth Hildebrand. 2002
   Cattle before Crops: The Beginnings of Food Production in Africa. Journal of World Prehistory 16:99–143.
Martin, Richard C. 1995
   Islam. In The HarperCollins Dictionary of Religion. Jonathan Z. Smith, ed. Pp. 498–513. New York: HarperCollins.
Martínez, Samuel. 1996
   Indifference with Indignation: Anthropology, Human Rights, and the Haitian Bracero. American Anthropologist 98(1):17–25.
Massara, Emily. 1997
   Que Gordita. In Food and Culture: A Reader. Carole Counihan and Penny van Esterik, eds. Pp. 251–255. New York: Routledge.
Massiah, Joycelin. 1983
   Women as Heads of Households in the Caribbean: Family Structure and Feminine Status. Paris: UNESCO.
Maybury-Lewis, David. 1997a
   Museums and Indigenous Cultures. Cultural Survival Quarterly 21(1):3.
———. 1997b
   Indigenous Peoples, Ethnic Groups, and the State. Boston: Allyn and Bacon.
Mayor, Adrienne. 2000
   The First Fossil Hunters: Paleontology in Greek and Roman Times. Princeton: Princeton University Press.
Mayr, Ernst. 1982
   The Growth of Biological Thought: Diversity, Evolution, and Inheritance. Cambridge, MA: Harvard University Press.
McBrearty, Sally and Alison Brooks. 2000
   The Revolution That Wasn't: A New Interpretation of the Origin of Modern Human Behavior. Journal of Human Evolution 39:453–563.
McCombie, Susan C. and John K. Anarfi. 2002.
   The Influence of Sex of Interviewer on the Results of an AIDS Survey in Ghana. Human Organization 61:51–57.
McCully, Patrick. 2003
   Big Dams, Big Trouble. New Internationalist 354:14–15.
McDonald, J. Douglas, Larry J. Zimmerman, A. L. McDonald, William Tall Bull, and Ted Rising Son. 1991
   The Northern Cheyenne Outbreak of 1879: Using Oral History and Archaeology as Tools of Resistance. In The Archaeology of Inequality. Randall H. McGuire and Robert Paynter, eds. Pp. 64–78. Cambridge, MA: Basil Blackwell.
McElroy, Ann and Patricia K. Townsend. 1996
   Medical Anthropology in Ecological Perspective. 3rd ed. Boulder, CO: Westview Press.
McGovern, Thomas H. and Sophia Perdikaris. 2000
   The Vikings' Silent Saga. Natural History 109:50–57.
McGrew, William C. 1998
   Culture in Nonhuman Primates? Annual Review of Anthropology 27:301–328.
———. 1992
   Chimpanzee Material Culture: Implications for Human Evolution. Cambridge: Cambridge University Press.
McIntosh, Susan Keech, ed. 1999
   Beyond Chiefdoms: Pathways to Complexity in Africa. Cambridge: Cambridge University Press.
McKee, Jeffrey K. 2003
   Sparing Nature: The Conflict between Human Population Growth and Earth's Biodiversity. New Brunswick, NJ: Rutgers University Press.
McMahon, April M. S. 1994
   Understanding Language Change. New York: Cambridge University Press.
Mead, Margaret. 1986
   Field Work in the Pacific Islands, 1925–1967. In Women in the Field: Anthropological Experiences. Peggy Golde, ed. Pp. 293–331. Berkeley: University of California Press.
———. 1961 [1928]
   Coming of Age in Samoa: A Psychological Study of Primitive Youth for Western Civilization. New York: Dell.

Meigs, Anna S. 1984
   Food, Sex, and Pollution: A New Guinea Religion. New Brunswick, NJ: Rutgers University Press.

Mellaart, James. 1967
   Çatal Hüyük: A Neolithic Town in Anatolia. London: Thames & Hudson.

Mellars, Paul. 1996
   The Neanderthal Legacy. An Archaeological Perspective from Western Europe. Princeton, NJ: Princeton University Press.

Members of the Permanent Council of the International Association for the Study of Human Paleontology. 1999
   Resolution Regarding the Transport of Hominid Fossils beyond the Country of Origin. Journal of Human Evolution 36:459.

Mencher, Joan P. 1974
   The Caste System Upside Down, or The Not-So-Mysterious East. Current Anthropology 15(4):469–49.

Mercader, Julio and Alison Brooks. 2001
   Across Forests and Savannas: Later Stone Age Assemblages from Ituri and Semliki, Northeast Democratic Republic of Congo. Journal of Anthropological Research 57:197–217.

Mercader, Julio, Melissa Panger, and Christophe Boesch. 2002
   Excavation of a Chimpanzee Stone Tool Site in the African Rainforest. Science 296:1452–1455.

Mernissi, Fatima. 1987
   Beyond the Veil: Male–Female Dynamics in Modern Muslim Society. Rev. ed. Bloomington: Indiana University Press.

Merry, Sally Engle. 1992
   Anthropology, Law, and Transnational Processes. Annual Review of Anthropology 21:357–379.

Messer, Ellen. 2000
   Potatoes (White). In The Cambridge World History of Food. Vol. 1. Kenneth F. Kiple and Kriemhild Coneè Ornelas, eds. Pp. 187–201. New York: Cambridge University Press.

———. 1993
   Anthropology and Human Rights. Annual Review of Anthropology 22:221–249.

Meyerhoff, Miriam. 1999
   Sorry in the Pacific: Defining Communities, Defining Practice. Language in Society 28:225–238.

Michaelson, Evelyn Jacobson and Walter Goldschmidt. 1971
   Female Roles and Male Dominance among Peasants. Southwestern Journal of Anthropology 27:330–352.

Michel, Rudolph H., Patrick E. McGovern, and Virginia R. Badler. 1992
   Chemical Evidence for Ancient Beer. Nature 360:24.

Migration Information Source. 2003
   Global Data. http://www.migrationinformation.org/Global Data/countrydata.

Milanich, Jerald T. 2001
   Closing the Ignorance Gap. Archaeology 54(4):22–23.

Miller, Barbara D. 2005
   Culture, Nature and Unbalanced Juvenile Sex Ratios in India: A View from the 1871 Census to the Era of HIV/AIDS. Paper presented at the annual meeting of the Human Biology Association, Milwaukee, Wisconsin.

———. 1997 [1981]
   The Endangered Sex: Neglect of Female Children in Rural North India. New Delhi: Oxford University Press.

———. 1997
   Andaman Update: From Colonialism to "Development." Paper presented at the Annual South Asia Conference, Madison, Wisconsin.

———. 1993
   Surveying the Anthropology of Sex and Gender Hierarchies. In Sex and Gender Hierarchies. Barbara D. Miller, ed. Pp. 3–31. New York: Cambridge University Press

Miller, Barbara D. and Carl Stone. 1983
   The Low-Income Household Expenditure Survey: Description and Analysis. Jamaica Tax Structure Examination Project, Staff Paper No. 25. Syracuse, NY: Metropolitan Studies Program, Syracuse University.

Miller, Barbara D. and Showkat Hayat Khan. 1986
   Incorporating Voluntarism into Rural Development in Bangladesh. Third World Planning Review 8(2):139–152.

Miller, Bruce G. 1994
   Contemporary Native Women: Role Flexibility and Politics. Anthropologica 36:57–72.

Miller, Daniel. 2003
   Could the Internet Defetishise the Commodity? Environment and Planning D: Society and Space 21:359–372.

Millon, Rene. 1973
   Urbanization at Teotihuacan, Mexico. Austin, TX: University of Texas Press.

Mills, Mary Beth. 1995
   Attack of the Widow Ghosts: Gender, Death, and Modernity in Northeast Thailand. In Bewitching Women, Pious Men: Gender and Body Politics in Southeast Asia. Aihwa Ong and Michael G. Peletz, eds. Pp. 44–273. Berkeley: University of California Press.

Milton, Katherine. 1992
   Civilization and Its Discontents. Natural History 3/92: 37–92.

———. 1984
   The Role of Food-Processing Factors in Primate Food Choice. In Adaptations for Foraging in Nonhuman Primates: Contributions to an Organismal Biology of Prosimians, Monkeys, and Apes. P. S. Rodman and J. G. H. Cant, eds. Pp. 249–279. New York: Columbia University Press.

Mishmar, D., E. Ruiz-Pesini, P. Golik, V. Macaulay, A. G. Clark, S. Hosseini, M. Brandon, K. Easley, E. Chen, M. D. Brown, R. I. Sukernik, A. Olckers, and D. C. Wallace. 2003
   Natural Selection Shaped Regional mtDNA Variation in Humans. Proceedings of the National Academy of Sciences 100:171–176.

Mitchell, Bruce. 1994
   Sustainable Development at the Village Level in Bali, Indonesia. Human Ecology 22(2):189–211.

Mithen, Steven, Nyree Finlay, Wendy Carruthers, Stephen Carter, and Patrick Ashmore. 2001
   Plant Use in the Mesolithic: Evidence from Staosnaig, Isle of Colonsay, Scotland. Journal of Archaeological Science 28:223–234.

Mittermeier, R. A., J. F. Oates, A. E. Eudey, and J. Thornback. 1986
   Primate Conservation. In Comparative Primate Biology, Vol. 2A: Behavior, Conservation, and Ecology. G. Mitchell and J. Erwin, eds. Pp. 3–72. New York: Alan R. Liss.

Miyamoto, Michael M., B. F. Koop, J. L. Slightom, M. Goodman, and M. R. Tennant. 1988
   Molecular Systematics of Higher Primates: Genealogical Relations and Classification. Proceedings of the National Academy of Sciences 85:7627–7631.

Miyazawa, Setsuo. 1992
Policing in Japan: A Study on Making Crime. Frank G. Bennett, Jr. with John O. Haley, trans. Albany: State University of New York Press.

Moberg, Mark. 1991
Citrus and the State: Factions and Class Formation in Rural Belize. American Ethnologist 18(20):215–233.

Modell, Judith S. 1994
Kinship with Strangers: Adoption and Interpretations of Kinship in American Culture. Berkeley: University of California Press.

Moerman, Daniel E. 2002
Meaning, Medicine, and the "Placebo Effect." New York: Cambridge University Press.

Mogelonsky, Marcia. 1995
Asian-Indian Americans. American Demographics 17(8): 32–39.

Moore, A. M. T., G. C. Hillman, and A. J. Legge. 2000
Village on the Euphrates: The Excavation of Abu Hureyra. Oxford: Oxford University Press.

Morgan, William. 1977
Navaho Treatment of Sickness: Diagnosticians. In Culture, Disease, and Healing: Studies in Medical Anthropology. David Landy, ed. Pp. 163–168. New York: Macmillan.

Morkot, Robert. 2001
Egypt and Nubia: The Egyptian Empire in Nubia in the Late Bronze Age (c. 1550–1070 BCE). In Empires: Perspectives from Archaeology and History. Susan E. Alcock, Terence N. D'Altroy, Kathleen D. Morrison, and Carla M. Sinopoli, eds. Pp. 227–251. New York: Cambridge University Press.

Morris, Brian. 1998
The Power of Animals: An Ethnography. New York: Berg.

Morris, Craig. 1998
Inka Strategies of Incorporation and Governance. In Archaic States. Gary M. Feinman and Joyce Marcus, eds. Pp. 293–309. Santa Fe, NM: School of American Research Press.

Morris, Rosalind. 1994
Three Sexes and Four Sexualities: Redressing the Discourses on Gender and Sexuality in Contemporary Thailand. Positions 2:15–43.

Mortland, Carol A. 1994
Khmer Buddhism in the United States: Ultimate Questions. In Cambodian Culture Since 1975: Homeland and Exile. May M. Ebihara, Carol A. Mortland, and Judy Ledgerwood, eds. Pp. 72–90. Ithaca, NY: Cornell University Press.

Morwood, M. J., P. B. O'Sullivan, F. Aziz, and A. Raza. 1998
Fission-track Ages of Stone Tools and Fossils on the East Indonesian Island of Flores. Nature 392:173–176.

Morwood, M. J., R. P. Soejono, R. G. Roberts, T. Sutikna, C. S. M. Turney, K. E. Westaway, W. J. Rink, J.-X. Zhao, G. D. van den Bergh, Rokus Awe Due, D. R. Hobbs, M. W. Moore, M. I. Bird, and L. K. Fifield. 2004
Achaeology and Age of a New Hominin from Flores in Eastern Indonesia. Nature 431:1087–1091.

Moseley, Michael E. 1992
The Incas and Their Ancestors: The Archaeology of Peru. London: Thames & Hudson.

———. 1975
Prehistoric Principles of Labor Organization in the Moche Valley, Peru. American Antiquity 40:191–196.

Moser, Stephanie, Darren Glazier, James E. Phillips, Lamya Nasser el Nemr, Mohammed Saleh Mousa, Rascha Nasr Aiesh, Susan Richardson, Andrew Conner, and Michael Seymour. 2002
Transforming Archaeology through Practice: Strategies for Collaborative Archaeology and the Community Archaeology Project at Quesir, Egypt. World Archaeology 34:220–248.

Moynihan, Elizabeth B. 1979
Paradise as a Garden in Persia and Mughal India. New York: George Braziller.

Muecke, Marjorie A. 1987
Resettled Refugees: Reconstruction of Identity of Lao in Seattle. Urban Anthropology 16(3–4):273–289.

Mulk, Inga-Maria. 1994
Sacrificial Places and Their Meaning in Saami Society. In David L. Carmichael, Jane Hubert, Brian Reeves, and Audhild Schanche, eds. Sacred Sites, Sacred Places. Pp. 121–131. New York: Routledge.

Mull, Dorothy S. and J. Dennis Mull. 1987
Infanticide among the Tarahumara of the Mexican Sierra Madre. In Child Survival: Anthropological Perspectives on the Treatment and Maltreatment of Children. Nancy Scheper-Hughes, ed. Pp. 113–132. Boston: D. Reidel Publishing Company.

Munsiff, Sonal S., Trina Bassoff, Beth Nivin, Jiehui Li, Anu Sharma, Pablo Bifani, Barun Mathema, Jeffrey Driscoll, and Barry N. Kreiswirth. 2002
Molecular Epidemiology of Multidrug-Resistant Tuberculosis, New York City, 1995–1997. Emerging Infectious Diseases 8:1230–1238.

Murdock, George Peter. 1965 [1949]
Social Structure. New York: The Free Press.

Murphy, Yolanda and Robert F. Murphy. 1985
Women of the Forest. New York: Columbia University Press.

Murra, John V. 1985
El Archipelago Vertical Revisited. In Andean Ecology and Civilization: An Interdisciplinary Perspective on Andean Ecological Complementarity. Shozo Masuda, Izumi Shimada and Craig Morris, eds. Pp. 3–14. Tokyo: University of Tokyo Press.

Murray, Gerald F. 1987
The Domestication of Wood in Haiti: A Case Study of Applied Evolution. In Anthropological Praxis: Translating Knowledge into Action. Robert M. Wulff and Shirley J. Fiske, eds. Pp. 233–240. Boulder, CO: Westview Press.

Myers, James. 1992
Nonmainstream Body Modification: Genital Piercing, Branding, Burning, and Cutting. Journal of Contemporary Ethnography 21(3):267–306.

Myers-Scotton, Carol. 1993
Social Motivations for Code-Switching. New York: Oxford University Press.

Nader, Laura. 2001
Harmony Coerced Is Freedom Denied. The Chronicle of Higher Education, July 13:B13.

———. 1995
Civilization and Its Negotiations. In Understanding Disputes: The Politics of Argument. Pat Caplan, ed. Pp. 39–64. Providence, RI: Berg Publishers.

———. 1972
Up the Anthropologist: Perspectives Gained from Studying Up. In Reinventing Anthropology. Dell Hymes, ed. Pp. 284–311. New York: Vintage Books.

Nag, Moni. 1983
Modernization Affects Fertility. Populi 10:56–77.

———. 1972
Sex, Culture and Human Fertility: India and the United States. Current Anthropology 13:231–238.

Nag, Moni, Benjamin N. F. White, and R. Creighton Peet. 1978
An Anthropological Approach to the Study of the Economic Value of Children in Java and Nepal. Current Anthropology 19(2):293–301.

Nanda, Serena. 1994
Cultural Anthropology. Belmont, CA: Wadsworth.

———. 1990
Neither Man nor Woman: The Hijras of India. Belmont, CA: Wadsworth.

Nashida, Toshisada. 1987
Local Traditions and Cultural Transmission. In Primate Societies. Barbara Smuts, Dorothy Cheney, Robert Seyfarth, Richard Wrangham, and Thomas Struhsaker, eds. Pp. 462–474. Chicago: University of Chicago Press.

National Academy of Sciences. 2002
Rhesus Monkey Demand in Biomedical Research: A Workshop Report. Washington, DC: Research Resources Information Center.

Navarro, Arcadi and Nick H. Barton. 2003
Chromosomal Speciation and Molecular Divergence: Accelerated Evolution in Rearranged Chromosomes. Science 300:321–324.

Neff, Deborah L. 1994
The Social Construction of Infertility: The Case of the Matrilineal Nayars in South India. Social Science and Medicine 39(4):475–485.

Neier, Aryeh. 1996
Language and Minorities. Dissent 43(summer):31–35.

Nelson, Sarah M. 2003
Ancient Queens: Archaeological Explorations. Walnut Creek, CA: AltaMira Press.

———. 1997
Gender in Archaeology: Analyzing Power and Prestige. Walnut Creek, CA: AltaMira Press.

Neusner, Jacob. 1995
Judaism. In The HarperCollins Dictionary of Religion. Jonathan Z. Smith. Pp. 598–607. New York: HarperCollins.

Newman, Lucile. 1972
Birth Control: An Anthropological View. Module No. 27. Reading, MA: Addison-Wesley.

Newman Lucile, ed., 1985
Women's Medicine: A Cross-Cultural Study of Indigenous Fertility Regulation. New Brunswick, NJ: Rutgers University Press.

Ngokwey, Ndolamb. 1988
Pluralistic Etiological Systems in Their Social Context: A Brazilian Case Study. Social Science and Medicine 26:793–802.

Nichter, Mark. 1996
Vaccinations in the Third World: A Consideration of Community Demand. In Anthropology and International Health: Asian Case Studies. Mark Nichter and Mimi Nichter, eds. Pp. 329–365. Amsterdam: Gordon and Breach Publishers.

———. 1992
Of Ticks, Kings, Spirits and the Promise of Vaccines. In Paths to Asian Medical Knowledge. Charles Leslie and Allan Young, eds. pp. 224–253. Berkeley: University of California Press.

Nichter, Mimi. 2000
Fat Talk: What Girls and Their Parents Say about Dieting. Cambridge, MA: Harvard University Press.

Nichter, Mimi and Nancy Vuckovic. 1994
Fat Talk: Body Image among Adolescent Girls. In Many Mirrors: Body Image and Social Relations. Nicole Sault, ed. Pp. 109–131. New Brunswick, NJ: Rutgers University Press.

Nickens, Herbert W. 1996
The Genome Project and Health Services for Minority Populations. In The Human Genome Project and the Future of Health Care. Thomas H. Murray, Mark A. Rothstein, and Robert F. Murray, eds. Pp. 58–78. Bloomington: Indiana University Press.

Nodwell, Evelyn and Neil Guppy. 1992
The Effects of Publicly Displayed Ethnicity on Interpersonal Discrimination: Indo-Canadians in Vancouver. The Canadian Review of Sociology and Anthropology 29(1):87–99.

Norgaard, Richard B. 1994
Development Betrayed: The End of Progress and the Coevolutionary Revisioning of the Future. New York: Routledge.

Nourse, Jennifer W. 1999
Conceiving Spirits: Birth Rituals and Contested Identities among Laujé of Indonesia. Washington, DC: Smithsonian Institution Press.

Nowak, Ronald M. 1999
Walker's Primates of the World. Baltimore: Johns Hopkins University Press.

Obeyesekere, Gananath. 1981
Medusa's Hair: An Essay on Personal Symbols and Religious Experience. Chicago: University of Chicago Press.

Ochoa, Carlos M. 1991
The Potatoes of South America: Bolivia. Trans. Donald Nugent. New York: Cambridge University Press.

Ochs, Elinor. 1993
Indexing Gender. In Sex and Gender Hierarchies. Barbara D. Miller, ed. Pp. 146–169. New York: Cambridge University Press.

O'Connell, F. and H. Allen. 2004
Dating the Colonization of Sahul (Pleistocene Australia–New Guinea): A Review of Recent Research. Journal of Archaeological Science 31:835–853.

O'Connell, J. F., K. Hawkes, and N. G. Blurton Jones. 1999.
Grandmothering and the Evolution of Homo erectus. Journal of Human Evolution 36:461–485.

O'Gorman, Jodie A. 2001
Life, Death, and the Longhouse: A Gendered View of Oneota Social Organization. In Gender and the Archaeology of Death. Bettina Arnold and Nancy L. Wicker, eds. Pp. 23–49. New York: AltaMira Press.

Odegaard, Nancy and Alyce Sadongei. 2001
The Issue of Pesticides on Native American Cultural Objects: A Report on Conservation and Education Activities at the University of Arizona. Collections Forum 16:12–18.

Ohnuki-Tierney, Emiko. 1994
Brain Death and Organ Transplantation: Cultural Bases of Medical Technology. Current Anthropology 35(3):233–242.

Oinas, Felix J. 1993
Couvade in Estonia. Slavic & East European Journal 37(3): 339–345.

Olsen, Carolyn L., Philip K. Cross, and Lenore J. Gensburg. 2003
Down Syndrome: Interaction between Culture, Demography, and Biology in Determining the Prevalence of a Genetic Trait. Human Biology 75:503–520.

Ong, Aihwa. 1995
State versus Islam: Malay Families, Women's Bodies, and the Body Politic in Malaysia. In Bewitching Women, Pious Men: Gender and Body Politics in Southeast Asia. Aihwa Ong and Michael G. Peletz, eds. Pp. 159–194. Berkeley: University of California Press.

———. 1987
Spirits of Resistance and Capitalist Discipline: Factory Women in Malaysia. Albany: State University of New York Press.

Ongley, Patrick. 1995
Post-1945 International Migration: New Zealand, Australia and Canada Compared. International Migration Review 29(3):765–793.

Orser, Charles Jr. 2004
Race and Practice in Archaeological Interpretation. Philadelphia: University of Pennsylvania Press.

Ovchinnikov, I. V., A. Gotherstrom, G. P. Romanova, V. M. Khritonov, K. Liden, and W. Goodwin. 2000
Molecular Analysis of Neanderthal DNA from the Northern Caucasus. Nature 404:490–493.

Owens, K. and M.-C. King. 1999
Genomic Views of Human History. Science 286:451–453.

Pääbo, Svante. 2003
The Mosaic That Is Our Genome. Nature 421:409–412.

Painter, Andrew A. 1996
The Telerepresentation of Gender. In Re-Imaging Japanese Women. Anne E. Imamura, ed. Pp. 46–72. Berkeley: University of California Press.

Paley, Julia. 2002
Toward an Anthropology of Democracy. Annual Review of Anthropology 31:469–496.

Paley, William. 1802
Collected Works, 4: Natural Theology. London: Rilington.

Pálsson, Gísli and Kristín E. Harðardóttir. 2002
For Whom the Cell Tolls: Debates about Biomedicine. Current Anthropology 43:271–287.

Pandit, T. N. 1990
The Sentinelese. Calcutta: Seagull Books.

Panger, Melissa A. 1998
Object-Use in Free-Ranging White-Faced Capuchins (Cebus capucinus) in Costa Rica. American Journal of Physical Anthropology 106(3):311–321.

Panger, Melissa A., Alison Brooks, Brian G. Richmond, and Bernard Wood. 2002a
Older Than the Oldowan? Rethinking the Emergence of Hominin Tool Use. Evolutionary Anthropology 11(6):235–245.

Panger, Melissa A., Susan Perry, Lisa Rose, Julie Gros-Louis, Erin Vogel, Katherine C. MacKinnon, and Mary Baker. 2002b
Cross-Site Differences in Foraging Behavior of White-Faced Capuchins (Cebus capucinus). American Journal of Physical Anthropology 119:52–66.

Parrillo, Vincent N. 1997
Strangers to These Shores: Race and Ethnic Relations in the United States. Boston: Allyn and Bacon.

Parry, Jonathan P. 1966
Caste. In The Social Science Encyclopedia. Adam Kuper and Jessica Kuper, eds. Pp. 76–77. New York: Routledge.

Partridge, Tim C., D. E. Granger, M. W. Caffee, and R. J. Clarke. 2003
Lower Pliocene Hominid Remains from Sterkfontein. Science 300:607–612.

Pasquino, Gianfranco. 1996
Democratization. In The Social Science Encyclopedia. Adam Kuper and Jessica Kuper, eds. Pp. 173–174. Routledge: New York.

Patterson, Thomas C. 2001
A Social History of Anthropology in the United States. New York: Berg.

Pauketat, Timothy R. 2004
Ancient Cahokia and the Mississippians. New York: Cambridge University Press.

Pavlides, C. and C. Gosden. 1994
35,000-Year-Old Sites in the Rainforests of West New Britain, Papua New Guinea. Antiquity 68:604–610.

Pavlov, P., J. Svendsen, and S. Indrelid. 2001
Human Presence in the European Arctic Nearly 40,000 Years Ago. Nature 413:64–67.

Paynter, Robert, Susan Hautaniemi, and Nancy Muller. 1994
The Landscapes of the W. E. B. Du Bois Boyhood Homesite: An Agenda for an Archaeology of the Color Line. In Race. Steven Gregory and Roger Sanjek, eds. Pp. 285–318. New Brunswick, NJ: Rutgers University Press.

Pedelty, Mark. 1995
War Stories: The Culture of Foreign Correspondents. New York: Routledge.

Pelto, Pertti. 1973
The Snowmobile Revolution: Technology and Social Change in the Arctic. Menlo Park, CA: Cummings.

Pelto, Pertti, Maria Roman, and Nelson Liriano. 1982
Family Structures in An Urban Puerto Rican Community. Urban Anthropology 11:39–58.

Peregrine, Peter N., ed. 1992
Mississippian Evolution: A World System Perspective. Madison, WI: Prehistory Press.

Perlès, Catherine. 2001
The Early Neolithic in Greece: The First Farming Communities in Europe. New York: Cambridge University Press.

Perry, Richard J. 1996
. . . From Time Immemorial: Indigenous Peoples and State Systems. Austin: University of Texas Press.

Perry, Susan, Mary Baker, Linda Fedigan, Julie Gros-Louis, Kathy Jack, Katherine C. MacKinnon, Joe Manson, Melissa Panger, Kendra Pyle, and Lisa Rose. 2003
Social Conventions in Wild White-Faced Capuchin Monkeys: Evidence for Traditions in a Neotropical Primate. Current Anthropology 44(2):241–268.

Pessar, Patricia R. 1995
A Visa for a Dream: Dominicans in the United States. Boston: Allyn and Bacon.

Petraglia, M., P. LaPorta, and K. Paddayya. 1999
First Acheulian Quarry in India: Stone Tool Manufacture, Biface Morphology and Behaviors. Journal of Anthropological Research 55:39–70.

Pickford, Martin, B. Senut, D. Gommery, and J. Treil. 2002
Bipedalism in Orrorin tugenensis Revealed by Its Femora. Comptes Rendus Palevol 1:1–13.

Pieterse, Jan Nederveen. 2004
Globalization and Culture: Global Mélange. New York: Rowman and Littlefield.

Pilar, Luna Erreguerena. 2003
The National Institute of Anthropology and History and the Submerged Cultural Heritage in Mexico. Paper presented at the Fifth World Archaeology Congress, Washington, DC.

Pinhasi, Ron and Mark Pluciennik. 2004
A Regional Biological Approach to the Spread of Farming in Europe: Anatolia, the Levant, South-eastern Europe, and the Mediterranean. Current Anthropology 45, Supplement: S59–S82 with commentary.

Piperno, Dolores R. 2001
On Maize and the Sunflower. Science 292:2260–2261.

Piperno, Dolores R. and Karen E. Stothert. 2003
Phytolith Evidence for Early Holocene Cucurbita Domestication in Southwest Ecuador. Science 299:1054–1057.

Piperno, Dolores R., Ehud Weiss, Irene Holst, and Dani Nadel. 2004
Processing of Wild Cereal Grains in the Upper Paleolithic Revealed by Starch Grain Analysis. Nature 430:670–673.

Pitulko, V., P. Nikolsky, E. Girya, A. Basilyan, V. Tumskoy, S. Koulakov, S. Astalkhov, E. Pavlova, and M. Anisimov. 2004
The Yana RHS Site: Humans in the Arctic before the Last Glacial Maximum. Science 303:52–56.

Plant, Roger. 1994
Land Rights and Minorities. London: Minority Rights Group.

Plattner, Stuart. 1989
Markets and Marketplaces. In Economic Anthropology. Stuart Plattner, ed. Pp. 171–208. Stanford, CA: Stanford University Press.

Pollock, Susan. 1999
Ancient Mesopotamia: The Eden That Never Was. Cambridge: Cambridge University Press.

Ponce de León, Marcia S. 2002
Computerized Paleoanthropology and Neanderthals: The Case of Le Moustier 1. Evolutionary Anthropology Supplement 1:68–72.

Pope, Geoffrey G. 1989
Bamboo and Human Evolution. Natural History 98:48–57.

Posey, Darrell Addison. 1990
Intellectual Property Rights: What Is the Position of Ethnobiology? Journal of Ethnobiology 10:93–98.

Possehl, Gregory L. 2002
The Indus Civilization: A Contemporary Perspective. Walnut Creek, CA: AltaMira Press.

Potter, Jack M. 1976
Thai Peasant Social Structure. Chicago: University of Chicago Press.

Potter, Sulamith Heins. 1977
Family Life in a Northern Thai Village: A Study in the Structural Significance of Women. Berkeley: University of California Press.

Potts, Rick. 1984
Home Bases and Early Hominids. American Scientist 72: 338–334.

Pratt, Mary Louise. 1992
Imperial Eyes: Travel Writing and Transculturation. London: Routledge.

Price, David H. 1995
Water Theft in Egypt's Fayoum Oasis: Emics, Etics, and the Illegal. In Science, Materialism, and the Study of Culture. Martin F. Murphy and Maxine L. Margolis, eds. Pp. 96–110. Gainesville: University of Florida Press.

Price, T. Douglass, Anne Birgitte Gebauer, and Lawrence H. Keeley, 1995
The Spread of Farming into Europe North of the Alps. In Last Hunters–First Farmers: New Perspectives on the Transition to Agriculture. T. Douglass Price and Anne Birgitte Gebauer, eds. Pp. 95–126. Santa Fe, NM: School for American Research Press.

Prince, Raymond. 1985
The Concept of Culture-Bound Syndromes: Anorexia Nervosa and Brain-Fog. Social Science and Medicine 21(2):197–203.

Purdum, Elizabeth D. and J. Anthony Paredes. 1989
Facing the Death Penalty: Essays on Cruel and Unusual Punishment. Philadelphia: Temple University Press.

Quilter, Jeffrey. 2002
Moche Politics, Religion, and Warfare. Journal of World Prehistory 16:145–195.

Quintana-Murci, L. O., O. Semino, G. Bandelt, K. Passarino, K. McElreavey, and S. Santachiara-Benerecetti. 1999
Genetic Evidence of an Early Exit of Homo sapiens sapiens from Africa through Eastern Africa. Nature Genetics 23:437–441.

Raheja, Gloria Goodwin. 1988
The Poison in the Gift: Ritual, Prestation, and the Dominant Caste in a North Indian Village. Chicago: University of Chicago Press.

Rahnema, Majid. 1992
Poverty. In The Development Dictionary: A Guide to Knowledge and Power. Wolfgang Sachs, ed. Pp. 159–176. Atlantic Highlands, NJ: Zed Press.

Ramphele, Mamphela. 1996
Political Widowhood in South Africa: The Embodiment of Ambiguity. Daedalus 125(1):99–17.

Raphael, Dana. 1975
Matrescence: Becoming a Mother: A "New/Old" Rite de Passage. In Being Female: Reproduction, Power and Change. Dana Raphael, ed. Pp. 65–72. The Hague: Mouton Publishers.

Rappaport, Roy A. 1968
Pigs for the Ancestors: Ritual in the Ecology of a New Guinea People. New Haven, CT: Yale University Press.

Rathgeb, Elizabeth. 2002
The Creation of a "European" Identity: Anthropological Perspectives Using the Four-Field Approach. M.A. Integrating Essay, Department of Anthropology, George Washington University.

Ravaillon, Martin. 2003
The Debate on Globalization, Poverty and Inequality: Why Income Measurement Matters. International Affairs 79:739–753.

Reed, Kay E. 1997
Early Hominid Evolution and Ecological Change through the African Plio-Pleistocene. Journal of Human Evolution 32:289–322.

Reichel-Dolmatoff, G. 1971
    Amazonian Cosmos: The Sexual and Religious Symbolism of the Tukano Indians. Chicago: University of Chicago Press.

Reid, Russell M. 1992
    Cultural and Medical Perspectives on Geophagia. Medical Anthropology 13:337–351.

Reiner, R. 1996
    Police. In The Social Science Encyclopedia. Adam Kuper and Jessica Kuper, eds. Pp. 619–621. New York: Routledge.

Relethford, John H. and L. B. Jorde. 1999
    Genetic Evidence for Larger African Population Size during Human Evolution. American Journal of Physical Anthropology 108:251–260.

Renfrew, Colin. 2001
    Foreword. In Trade in Illicit Antiquities: The Destruction of the World's Archaeological Heritage. Neil Brodie, Jennifer Doole, and Colin Renfrew, eds. Pp. xi–xii. Cambridge: University of Cambridge, McDonald Institute for Archaeological Research.

Renfrew, Colin and Paul Bahn. 2004
    Archaeology: Theories, Methods and Practice. 4th ed. London: Thames and Hudson.

Reyna, Stephen P. 1994
    A Mode of Domination Approach to Organized Violence. In Studying War: Anthropological Perspectives. S. P. Reyna and R. E. Downs, eds. Pp. 29–65. Langhorne, PA: Gordon and Breach Science Publishers.

Rhode, David, David B. Madsen, P. Jeffrey Brantingham, and W. F. Goebel. 2003
    Human Occupation in the Beringian "Mammoth Steppe": Starved for Fuel, or Dung-Burner's Paradise? Current Research in the Pleistocene 20:68–70.

Rhodes, Lorna A. 2001
    Toward an Anthropology of Prisons. Annual Review of Anthropology 30:65–83.

Rich, Adrienne. 1980
    Compulsory Heterosexuality and Lesbian Existence. Signs 5:631–660.

Rich, Bruce. 1994
    Mortgaging the Earth: The World Bank, Environmental Impoverishment, and the Crisis of Development. Boston: Beacon Press.

Richard, A. F., S. J. Goldstein, and R. E. Dewar. 1989
    Weed Macaques: The Evolutionary Implications of Macaque Feeding Ecology. International Journal of Primatology 10:569–594.

Richard, Klein. 2000
    Archaeology and the Evolution of Human Behavior. Evolutionary Anthropology 9:17–36.

Richards, M. P., P. B. Pettitt, E. Trinkaus, F. H. Smith, M. Paunovic, and I. Karavanic. 2000
    Neanderthal Diet at Vindija and Neanderthal Predation: The Evidence from Stable Isotopes. Proceedings of the National Academy of Sciences 97(13):7663–7666.

Richards, Martin. 2003
    The Neolithic Invasion of Europe. Annual Review of Anthropology 32:135–162.

Richards, Michael P., Paul B. Pettitt, Mary C. Stiner, and Erik Trinkaus. 2001
    Stable Isotope Evidence for Increasing Dietary Breadth in the European Mid-Upper Paleolithic. Proceedings of the National Academy of Sciences 98:6528–6532.

Richards, Michael P., T. Douglass Price, and Eva Koch. 2003
    Mesolithic and Neolithic Subsistence in Denmark: New Stable Isotope Data. Current Anthropology 44:288–295.

Richmond, Brian and David S. Strait. 2000
    Evidence That Humans Evolved from a Knuckle-Walking Ancestor. Nature 404:382–385.

Richmond, Brian G., Leslie C. Aiello, and Bernard A. Wood. 2002
    Early Hominin Limb Proportions. Journal of Human Evolution 43:529–548.

Riding In, James. 1992
    Six Pawnee Crania: Historical and Contemporary Issues Associated with the Massacre and Decapitation of Pawnee Indians in 1869. American Indian Culture and Research Journal 16:101–120.

Rightmire, G. P. 1979
    Implications of the Border Cave Skeletal Remains for Later Pleistocene Human Evolution. Current Anthropology 20:23–35.

Rightmire, Philip. 2004
    Brain Size and Encephalization in Early to Mid-Pleistocene Homo. American Journal of Physical Anthropology 124:109–128.

Robb, John E. 1998
    The Archaeology of Symbols. Annual Review of Anthropology 27:329–346.

Roberts, Charlotte and Keith Manchester. 1997
    The Archaeology of Disease. 2nd ed. Ithaca, NY: Cornell University Press.

Roberts, R., T. Flannery, L. Ayliffe, H. Yoshida, J. Olley, G. Prideaux, G. Laslett, A. Baynes, M. Smith, R. Jones, and B. Smith. 2001
    New Ages for the Last Australian Megafauna: Continent-Wide Extinction about 46,000 Years Ago. Science 292:1888–1892.

Robins, Kevin. 1996
    Globalization. In The Social Science Encyclopedia. 2nd ed. Adam Kuper and Jessica Kuper, eds. Pp. 345–346. New York: Routledge.

Robles García, Nelly M. 2003
    The Management of Archaeological Resources in Mexico: Oaxaca as a Case Study. Jack Corbett, trans. Society for American Archaeology web site (http://www.saa.org/publications/oaxaca/cover/html).

Roche, Helen A. Delagnes, J.-P. Brigal, C. Feibel, M. Kibunjia, V. Mourre, and P.-J. Texier. 1999
    Early Hominid Stone Tool Production and Technical Skill 2.34 Myr Ago in West Turkana, Kenya. Nature 399:57–60.

Roebroeks, Wil, M. Mussi, J. Svoboda, and K. Fennema. 2000
    Hunters of the Golden Age. The Mid to Upper Paleolithic of Eurasia 30,000–20,000 BP. Leiden, The Netherlands: University of Leiden.

Rogers, Barbara. 1979
    The Domestication of Women: Discrimination in Developing Societies. New York: St. Martin's Press.

Roscoe, Will. 1991
    The Zuni Man-Woman. Albuquerque: University of New Mexico Press.

Rose, Jerome C., Thomas J. Green, and Victoria D. Green. 1996

NAGPRA Is Forever: Osteology and the Repatriation of Skeletons. Annual Review of Anthropology 25:81–103.

Roseman, Marina. 1987
Inversion and Conjuncture: Male and Female Performance among the Temiar of Peninsular Malaysia. In Women and Music in Cross-Cultural Perspective. Ellen Koskoff, ed. Pp. 131–149. New York: Greenwood Press.

Rosenberg, N. A., J. K. Pritchard, J. L. Weber, H. M. Cann, and K. K. Kidd. 2002
Genetic Structure of Human Populations. Science 298: 2381–2385.

Rosenberger, Nancy. 1992
Images of the West: Home Style in Japanese Magazines. In Re-made in Japan: Everyday Life and Consumer Taste in a Changing Society. James J. Tobin, ed. Pp. 106–125. New Haven, CT: Yale University Press.

Rosenblatt, Paul C., Patricia R. Walsh, and Douglas A. Jackson. 1976
Grief and Mourning in Cross-Cultural Perspective. New Haven: HRAF Press.

Ross, Marc Howard. 1993
The Culture of Conflict: Interpretations and Interests in Comparative Perspective. New Haven: Yale University Press.

Rouland, Norbert. 1994
Legal Anthropology. Philippe G. Planel, trans. Stanford: Stanford University Press.

Rowley-Conwy, Peter. 2004
How the West Was Lost: A Reconsideration of Agricultural Origins in Britain, Iceland, and Southern Scandinavia. Current Anthropology 45, Supplement: S83–S113, with commentary.

Roy, Arundhati. 1999
The Cost of Living. New York: The Modern Library.

Rubel, Arthur J., Carl W. O'Nell, and Rolando Collado-Ardón. 1984
Susto: A Folk Illness. Berkeley: University of California Press.

Rudwick, Martin J. S. 1997
George Cuvier, Fossil Bones, and Geological Catastrophes. Chicago: University of Chicago Press.

Ruff, Chris B. 1994
Morphological Adaptation to Climate in Modern and Fossil Hominids. Yearbook of Physical Anthropology 37: 65–107.

Ruse, M. 2003
Darwin and Design: Does Evolution Have a Purpose? Cambridge, MA: Harvard University Press.

———. 1999
The Darwinian Revolution: Science Red in Tooth and Claw. Chicago: University of Chicago Press.

Ruvolo, Maryellen. 1997
Molecular Phylogeny of the Hominoids: Inferences from Multiple Independent DNA Sequence Data Sets. Molecular Biology and Evolution 14(3):248–265.

Sabloff, Jeremy A. 1990
The New Archaeology and the Ancient Maya. New York: Scientific American Library.

Sachs, Aaron. 1996
Dying for Oil. WorldWatch, June:10–21.

Sahlins, Marshall. 1963
Poor Man, Rich Man, Big Man, Chief. Comparative Studies in Society and History 5:285–303.

Saitoti, Tepilit Ole. 1986
The Worlds of a Maasai Warrior. New York: Random House.

Salam, Nawaf A. 1994
Between Repatriation and Resettlement: Palestinian Refugees in Lebanon. Journal of Palestine Studies 24:18–27.

Samet, Jonathan M., David M. DeMarini, and Heinrich V. Malling. 2004
Do Airborne Particles Induce Heritable Mutations? Science 304:971–972.

Sanday, Peggy Reeves. 2002
Women at the Center: Life in a Modern Matriarchy. Ithaca, NY: Cornell University Press.

———. 1990
Fraternity Gang Rape: Sex, Brotherhood, and Privilege on Campus. New York: New York University Press.

———. 1986
Divine Hunger: Cannibalism as a Cultural System. New York: Cambridge University Press.

———. 1973
Toward a Theory of the Status of Women. American Anthropologist 75:1682–1700.

Sanders, Douglas E. 1999
Indigenous Peoples: Issues of Definition. International Journal of Cultural Property 8:4–13.

Sanders, William B. 1994
Gangbangs and Drive-Bys: Grounded Culture and Juvenile Gang Violence. New York: Aldine de Gruyter.

Sanders, William T. and David L. Webster. 1988
The Mesoamerican Urban Tradition. American Anthropologist 90:521–546.

Sanderson, Stephen K. 1999
Social Transformations: A General Theory of Historical Development. Lanham, MD: Rowman & Littlefield.

Sanjek, Roger. 1994
The Enduring Inequalities of Race. In Race. Steven Gregory and Roger Sanjek, eds. Pp. 1–17. New Brunswick, NJ: Rutgers University Press.

Sanjek, Roger. 1990
A Vocabulary for Fieldnotes. In Fieldnotes: The Making of Anthropology. Roger Sanjek, ed. Pp. 92–138. Ithaca, NY: Cornell University Press.

Sant Cassia, Paul. 1993
Banditry, Myth, and Terror in Cyprus and Other Mediterranean Societies. Comparative Studies in Society and History 35(4):773–795.

Sault, Nicole L. 1994
How the Body Shapes Parenthood: "Surrogate" Mothers in the United States and Godmothers in Mexico. In Many Mirrors: Body Image and Social Relations. Nicole Sault, ed. Pp. 292–318. Rutgers, NJ: Rutgers University Press.

———. 1985
Baptismal Sponsorship as a Source of Power for Zapotec Women of Oaxaca, Mexico. Journal of Latin American Lore 11(2):225–243.

Savishinsky, Joel S. 1991
The Ends of Time: Life and Work in a Nursing Home. New York: Bergin & Garvey.

———. 1974
The Trail of the Hare: Life and Stress in an Arctic Community. New York: Gordon and Breach.

Sawchuk, Lawrence A. and Stacie D. A. Burke. 2003
The Ecology of a Health Crisis: Gibraltar and the 1865 Cholera Epidemic. In Human Biologists in the Archives: Demography, Health, Nutrition and Genetics in Historical Populations. D. Ann Herring and Alan C. Swedlund, eds. Pp. 178–215. New York: Cambridge University Press.

Scheinsohn, Vivian. 2003
Hunter–Gatherer Archaeology in South America. Annual Review of Anthropology 32:339–361.

Schele, Linda and Mary Ellen Miller. 1986
The Blood of Kings: Dynasty and Ritual in Maya Art. Forth Worth, TX: Kimbell Art Museum.

Schell, Lawrence M. and D. Stark. 1999
Pollution and Child Health. In Urbanism, Health, and Human Biology in Industrialised Countries. Lawrence M. Schell and Stanley J. Ulijaszek, eds. Pp. 136–157. New York: Cambridge University Press.

Schell, Lawrence M. and Melinda Denham. 2003
Environmental Pollution in Urban Environments and Human Biology. Annual Review of Anthropology 32:111–134.

Schell, Lawrence M. and Stanley J. Ulijaszek. 1999
Urbanism, Urbanization, Health, and Human Biology: An Introduction. In Urbanism, Health, and Human Biology in Industrialised Countries. Lawrence M. Schell and Stanley J. Ulijaszek, eds. Pp. 3–20. New York: Cambridge University Press.

Scheper-Hughes, Nancy. 1992
Death without Weeping: The Violence of Everyday Life in Brazil. Berkeley: University of California Press.

———. 1990
Three Propositions for a Critically Applied Medical Anthropology. Social Science and Medicine 30:189–197.

Schick, Kathy and D. Zhuan. 1993
Early Paleolithic of China and Eastern Asia. Evolutionary Anthropology 27:2–35.

Schick, Kathy D. and Nicholas Toth. 1993
Making Silent Stones Speak. New York: Simon and Schuster.

Schlegel, Alice. 1995
A Cross-Cultural Approach to Adolescence. Ethos 23(1):15–32.

Schlegel, Alice and Herbert Barry III. 1991
Adolescence: An Anthropological Inquiry. New York: Free Press.

Schmid, Peter. 2004
Functional Intepretation of the Laetoli Footprints. In From Biped to Strider. D. J. Meldrum and C. E. Hilton, eds. Pp. 49–62. New York: Kluwer.

Schmid, Thomas J. and Richard S. Jones. 1993
Ambivalent Actions: Prison Adaptation Strategies of First-Time, Short-term Inmates. Journal of Contemporary Ethnography 21(4):439–463.

Schmitz, R. W., D. Serre, G. Bonani, S. Feine, F. Hillgruber, H. Krainitzki, S. Pääbo, and F. H. Smith. 2002
The Neandertal Type Site Revisited: Interdisciplinary Investigations of Skeletal Remains from the Neander Valley, Germany. Proceedings of the National Academy of Sciences 99(20):13342–13347.

Schneider, David M. 1968
American Kinship: A Cultural Account. Englewood Cliffs, NJ: Prentice-Hall.

Science. 2004
Sonagachi Sex Workers Stymie HIV. Science 304:506.

Scott, Eleanor. 2001
Killing the Female? Archaeological Narratives of Infanticide. In Gender and the Archaeology of Death. Bettina Arnold and Nancy L. Wicker, eds. pp. 3–21. New York: AltaMira Press.

Scott, James C. 1998
Seeing Like a State: How Certain Schemes to Improve the Human Condition Have Failed. New Haven, CT: Yale University Press.

Scrimshaw, Susan. 1984
Infanticide in Human Populations: Societal and Individual Concerns. In Infanticide: Comparative and Evolutionary Perspectives. Glenn Hausfater and Sarah Blaffer Hrdy, eds. Pp. 463–486. New York: Aldine.

Scudder, Thayer. 1973
The Human Ecology of Big Dam Projects: River Basin Development and Resettlement. Annual Review of Anthropology 2:45–55.

Semah, F., A. Semah, and T. Simanjuntak. 2003
More Than a Million Years of Human Occupation in Insular Southeast Asia. In Under the Canopy: The Archaeology of Tropical Rain Forests. Julio Mercader, ed. Pp. 161–190. New Brunswick, NJ: Rutgers University Press.

Semaw, Seleshi, M. J. Rogers, J. Quade, P. Renne, R. F. Butler, M. Dominguez-Rodrigo, D. Stout, W. S. Hart, T. Pickering, and S. W. Simpson. 2003
2.6-Million-Year-Old Stone Tools and Associated Bones from OGS-6 and OGS-7, Gona, Ethiopia. Journal of Human Evolution 45:169–177.

Senghas, Richard J. and Leila Monaghan, 2002
Signs of Their Times: Deaf Communities and the Culture of Language. Annual Review of Anthropology 31:69–97.

Senut, Brigitte, M. Pickford, D. Gommery, P. Mein, K. Cheboi, and Y. Coppens. 2001
First Hominid from the Miocene (Lukeino Formation, Kenya). Comptes rendus de l'Academie des sciences, Paris 332:137–144.

Serre, D., A. Langaney, M. Chech, M. Tescher-Nicola, and M. Paunovic. 2004
No Evidence of Neandertal mtDNA Contribution to Early Modern Humans. PloS 2:e57.

Shahrani, Nazif M. 2002
War, Factionalism, and the State in Afghanistan. American Anthropologist 104:715–722.

Sharp, Lesley. 1990
Possessed and Dispossessed Youth: Spirit Possession of School Children in Northwest Madagascar. Culture, Medicine and Psychiatry 14:339–364.

Shenhav-Keller, Shelly. 1993
The Israeli Souvenir: Its Text and Context. Annals of Tourism Research 20:182–196.

Shephard, Roy J. and Andris Rode. 1996
The Health Consequences of "Modernization": Evidence from Circumpolar Peoples. New York: Cambridge University Press.

Sheriff, Robin E. 2000
Exposing Silence as Cultural Censorship: A Brazilian Case. American Anthropologist 102:114–132.

Shibamoto, Janet. 1987
The Womanly Woman: Manipulation of Stereotypical and Nonstereotypical Features of Japanese Female Speech. In Language, Gender, and Sex in Comparative Perspective. Susan U. Philips, Susan Steel, and Christine Tanz, eds. Pp. 26–49. New York: Cambridge University Press.

Shifflett, Peggy A. and William A. McIntosh. 1986–1987
Food Habits and Future Time: An Exploratory Study of Age-Appropriate Food Habits among the Elderly. International Journal of Aging and Human Development 24(1): 2–15.

Shimada, Izumi. 1994
Pampa Grande and the Mochica Culture. Austin, TX: University of Texas Press.

Shore, Bradd. 1998
Status Reversal: The Coming of Age in Samoa. In Welcome to Middle Age! (And Other Cultural Fictions). Richard A. Shweder, ed. Pp. 101–138. Chicago: University of Chicago Press.

Shore, Cris. 1993
Inventing the "People's Europe": Critical Approaches to European Community Cultural Policy. Man 23:779–800.

Short, James F. 1966
Gangs. In The Social Science Encyclopedia. Adam Kuper and Jessica Kuper, eds. Pp. 325–326. New York: Routledge.

Shweder, Richard A. 2003
Why Do Men Barbecue? Recipes for Cultural Psychology. Cambridge: Harvard University Press.

———. 1998
Preface. In Welcome to Middle Age! (And Other Cultural Fictions). Pp. vii–viii. Chicago: University of Chicago Press.

Sidnell, Jack. 2000
Primus inter pares: Storytelling and Male Peer Groups in an Indo-Guyanese Rumshop. American Ethnologist 27:72–99.

Silk, Joan B. 2002
The Form and Function of Reconciliation among Primates. Annual Review of Anthropology 30:21–44.

Silver, Ira. 1993
Marketing Authenticity in Third World Countries. Annals of Tourism Research 20:302–318.

Simmons, Alan H. 2004
Bitter Hippos of Cyprus: The Island's First Occupants and Last Endemic Animals—Setting the Stage for Colonization. In Neolithic Revolution: New Perspectives on Southwest Asia in Light of Recent Discoveries on Cyprus. Edgar Peltenburg and Alexander Wasse, eds. Pp. 1–14. Oxford: Oxbrow Books.

Simons, Ronald C. and Charles C. Hughes, eds. 1985
The Culture-Bound Syndromes: Folk Illnesses of Psychiatric and Anthropological Interest. Boston: D. Reidel.

Sinclair, Paul J. P., Innocent Pikirayi, Gilbert Pwiti, and Robert Soper. 1993
Urban Trajectories on the Zimbabwean Plateau. In The Archaeology of Africa: Food, Metals and Towns. Thurstan Shaw, Paul Sinclair, Bassey Andah, and Alex Okpoko, eds. Pp. 705–731. New York: Routledge.

Singh, K. S. 1994
The Scheduled Tribes. Anthropological Survey of India, People of India, National Series Volume III. Delhi: Oxford University Press.

Siskind, Janet. 1992
The Invention of Thanksgiving: A Ritual of American Nationality. Critique of Anthropology 12(2):167–191.

Skinner, G. William. 1993
Conjugal Power in Tokugawa Japanese Families: A Matter of Life or Death. In Sex and Gender Hierarchies. Barbara D. Miller, ed. Pp. 236–270. New York: Cambridge University Press.

Slatkin, M. and G. Bertorelle. 2001
The Use of Intra-allelic Variability for Testing Neutrality and Estmating Population Growth Rate. Genetics 158:865–874.

Smith, Bruce D. 1998
The Emergence of Agriculture. New York: Scientific American Library.

———. 1997
The Initial Domestication of Cucurbita Pepo in the Americas 10,000 Years Ago. Science 276:932–934.

———. 1995
Seed Plant Domestication in Eastern North America. In Last Hunters–First Farmers: New Perspectives on the Transition to Agriculture. T. Douglass Price and Anne Birgitte Gebauer, eds. Pp. 193–213. Santa Fe, NM: School for American Research Press.

Smith, Bruce D., ed. 1990
Mississippian Emergence. Washington, DC: Smithsonian Institution Press.

Smith, Jonathan Z., ed. 1995
The HarperCollins Dictionary of Religion. New York: HarperCollins.

Smith, Patricia K., Barry Bogin, M. Inès Varela-Silva, Bibiana Orden, and James Loucky. 2002
Does Immigration Help or Harm Children's Health? The Mayan Case. Social Science Quarterly 83:994–1002.

Sobel, Elizabeth and Gordon Bettles. 2000
Winter Hunger, Winter Myths: Subsistence Risk and Mythology among the Klamath and Modoc. Journal of Anthropological Archaeology 19:276–316.

Soffer, Olga, James. Adovasio, D. Hyland, B. Klima, and J. Svoboda. 2001
Perishable Industries from Dolni Vestonice I: New Insights into the Nature and Origin of the Gravettian. Archaeology, Ethnology & Anthropology of Eurasia 2:48–65.

Soh, Chunghee Sarah. 1993
Women in Korean Politics. 2nd edition. Boulder: Westview Press.

Sokal, Robert R. 1991
The Continental Population Structure of Europe. Annual Review of Anthroplogy 20:119–140.

Sonenshein, Raphael J. 1996
The Battle over Liquor Stores in South Central Los Angeles: The Management of an Interminority Conflict. Urban Affairs Review 31(6):710–737.

Sparing Nature: The Conflict between Human Population Growth and Earth's Biodiversity. New Brunswick, NJ: Rutgers University Press.

Sperling, Susan. 1991
Baboons with Briefcases: Feminism, Functionalism, and Sociobiology in the Evolution of Primate Gender. Signs: Journal of Women in Culture and Society 17:1–27.

Spiro, Melford. 1967
Burmese Supernaturalism: A Study in the Explanation and Reduction of Suffering. Englewood Cliffs, NJ: Prentice-Hall.

Spitulnik, Deborah. 1993
Anthropology and Mass Media. Annual Review of Anthropology 22:293–315.

Srejović, Dragoslav. 1972
Europe's First Monumental Sculpture: New Discoveries at Lepenski Vir. New York: Stein and Day Publishers.

Srinivas, M. N. 1959
The Dominant Caste in Rampura. American Anthropologist 1:1–16.

Staats, Valerie. 1994
Ritual, Strategy or Convention: Social Meaning in Traditional Women's Baths in Morocco. Frontiers: A Journal of Women's Studies 14(3):1–18.

Stack, Carol. 1974
All Our Kin: Strategies for Survival in a Black Community. New York: Harper & Row.

Stambach, Amy. 2000
Lessons from Mount Kilimanjaro: Schooling, Community, and Gender in East Africa. New York: Routledge.

Stanford, Craig B. 1998
The Social Behavior of Chimpanzees and Bonobos: Empirical Evidence and Shifting Assumptions. Current Anthropology 39:399–407.

Stanford, D. and B. Bradley. 2002
Ocean Trails and Prairie Paths? Thoughts about Clovis Origins. Memoires of the California Academy of Sciences 27:255–271.

Stanish, Charles. 2003
Ancient Titicaca: The Evolution of Complex Society in Southern Peru and Northern Bolivia. Berkeley: University of California Press.

Stanlaw, James. 1992
"For Beautiful Human Life": The Use of English in Japan. In Re-Made in Japan: Everyday Life and Consumer Taste in a Changing Society. Joseph J. Tobin, ed. Pp. 58–76. New Haven: Yale University Press.

Stephen, Lynn. 1995
Women's Rights Are Human Rights: The Merging of Feminine and Feminist Interests among El Salvador's Mothers of the Disappeared (CO-MADRES). American Ethnologist 22(4):807–827.

Stephens, John L. 1969 [1841]
Incidents of Travel in Central America, Chiapas and Yucatan. New York: Dover Publications.

Stillman, Amy Ku'uleialoha. 1996
Hawaiian Hula Competitions: Event, Repertoire, Performance and Tradition. Journal of American Folklore 109(434):357–380.

Stiner, Mary C., Natalie D. Munro, and Todd A. Surovell. 2000
The Tortoise and the Hare: Small-Game Use, the Broad-Spectrum Revolution, and Paleolithic Demography. Current Anthropology 41:39–73.

Stivens, Maila, Cecelia Ng, and Jomo K. S., with Jahara Bee. 1994
Malay Peasant Women and the Land. Atlantic Highlands, NJ: Zed Books.

Stocking, George W. Jr., ed. 1985
Objects and Others: Essays on Museums and Material Culture. History of Anthropology Series, 3. Madison: University of Wisconsin Press.

Stoler, Ann Laura. 1989
Rethinking Colonial Categories: European Communities and the Boundaries of Rule. Comparative Studies in Society and History 31(1):134–161.

———. 1985
Capitalism and Confrontation in Sumatra's Plantation Belt, 1870–1979. New Haven: Yale University Press.

Stone, Anne C., R. C. Griffiths, S. L. Zegura, and M. F. Hammer. 2002
High Levels of Y-chromosome Nucleotide Diversity in the Genus Pan. Proceedings of the National Academy of Sciences 99:43–48.

Storper-Perez, Danielle and Harvey E. Goldberg. 1994
The Kotel: Toward an Ethnographic Portrait. Religion 24:309–332.

Stout, Dietrich, Nicholas Toth, Kathy Schick, J. C. Stout, and G. Hutchins. 2000
Stone Tool-Making and Brain Activation: Positron Emission Tomography (PET) Studies. Journal of Archaeological Science 27:1215–1223.

Strathern, Andrew. 1971
The Rope of Moka: Big-Men and Ceremonial Exchange in Mount Hagen, New Guinea. London: Cambridge University Press.

Straughan, B. and W. Schuler. 1991
The Secrets of Ancient Tiwanaku Are Benefiting Today's Bolivia. Smithsonian 12:38–47.

Strier, Karen B. 2004
Sociality among Kin and Nonkin in Nonhuman Primate Groups. In The Origins and Nature of Sociality. Robert W. Sussman and Audrey R. Chapman, eds. Pp. 191–214. New York: Aldine de Gruyter.

———. 2003
Primate Behavioral Ecology, 2nd ed. Boston: Allyn and Bacon.

Stringer, Chris B. 2003
Out of Ethiopia. Nature 423:692–695.

———. 2002
Modern Human Origins: Progress and Prospects. Philosophical Transactions of the Royal Society; Biological Sciences 357:563–579.

———. 2000
Coasting Out of Africa. Nature 405:24–26.

Stringer, Chris B. and Peter Andrews. 1988
Genetic and Fossil Evidence for the Origin of Modern Humans. Science 239:1263–1268.

Stringer, Martin D. 1999
Rethinking Animism: Thoughts from the Infancy of Our Discipline. Journal of the Royal Anthropological Institute 5:541–556.

Sullivan, Kathleen. 1992
Protagonists of Change: Indigenous Street Vendors in San Cristobal, Mexico, Are Adapting Tradition and Customs to Fit New Life Styles. Cultural Survival Quarterly 16:38–40.

Sundar Rao, P. S. S. 1983
Religion and Intensity of In-breeding in Tamil Nadu, South India. Social Biology 30(4):413–422.

Susman, Randall, ed. 1984
The Pygmy Chimpanzee: Evolutionary Biology and Behavior. New York: Plenum.

Sussman, Robert W. 1997
    Exploring Our Basic Human Nature: Are Humans Inherently Violent? AnthroNotes 19:1–10.
Sussman, Robert W. and Audrey R. Chapman, eds. 2004
    The Origins and Nature of Sociality. New York: Aldine de Gruyter.
Sussman, Robert W. and Paul A. Garber. 2004
    Rethinking Sociality: Cooperation and Aggression among Primates. In The Origins and Nature of Sociality. Robert W. Sussman and Audrey R. Chapman, eds. Pp. 161–190. New York: Aldine de Gruyter.
Suttles, Wayne. 1991
    The Traditional Kwakiutl Potlatch. In Chiefly Feasts: The Enduring Kwakiutl Potlatch. Aldona Jonaitis, ed. Pp. 71–134. Washington, DC: American Museum of Natural History.
Sutton, J. E. G. 1977
    The African Aqualithic. Antiquity 51:25–34.
Swallow, Dallas M. 2003
    Genetics of Lactase Persistence and Lactose Intolerance. Annual Review of Genetics 37:197–219.
Swallow, Dallas M. and E. J. Hollox. 2000
    The Genetic Polymorphism of Intestinal Lactase Activity in Adult Humans. In Metabolic and Molecular Bases of Inherited Disease. C. R. Scriver, A. L. Beaudet, W. S. Sly, and D. Valle, eds. Pp. 1651–1663. New York: McGraw-Hill.
Swisher, C. C. I., W. J. Rink, S. C. Anton, H. P. Schwarcz, G. H. Curtis, A. Suprijo, and Widasmoro. 1996
    Latest Homo erectus of Java: Potential Contemporaneity with Homo sapiens. Science 274:1870–1874.
Swisher, Carl C. I., G. H. Curtis, T. Jacob, A. G. Getty, A. Suprijo, and Widasmoro. 1994
    Age of the Earliest Known Hominids in Java, Indonesia. Science 263:1118–1121.
Swisher, Carl C. I., W. J. Rink, S. C. Anton, H. P. Schwarcz, G. H. Curtis, A. Suprijo, and Widasmoro. 1996
    Latest Homo erectus of Java: Potential Contemporaneity with Homo sapiens. Science 274:1870–1874.
Tainter, Joseph A. 1988
    The Collapse of Complex Societies. Cambridge: Cambridge University Press.
Tannen, Deborah. 1990
    You Just Don't Understand: Women and Men in Conversation. New York: Morrow.
Tapper, Melbourne. 1999
    In the Blood: Sickle Cell Anemia and the Politics of Race. Philadelphia: University of Pennsylvania Press.
Tattersall, Ian. 1993
    Madagascar's Lemurs. Scientific American 268:110–117.
Tauber, Henrik. 1981
    13C Evidence for Dietary Habits of Prehistoric Man in Denmark. Nature 292:332–333.
Taussig, Michael. 1978
    Nutrition, Development, and Foreign Aid: A Case Study of U.S.-Directed Health Care in a Colombian Plantation Zone. International Journal of Health Services 8(1):101–121.
Tayles, N., K. Domett, and K. Nelson. 2000
    Agriculture and Dental Caries? The Case of Rice in Prehistoric Southeast Asia. World Archaeology 32:68–83.
Taylor, Rowan. 2000
    A Step at a Time: New Zealand's Progress toward Hominid Rights. Animal Law 7:35–43.

Teaford, Mark F. and Peter S. Ungar. 2000
    Diet and the Evolution of the Earliest Human Ancestors. Proceedings of the National Academy of Sciences 97:13506–13511.
Tehrani, Jamshid and Mark Collard. 2002
    Investigating Cultural Evolution through Biological Phylogenetic Analysis of Turkmen Textiles. Journal of Anthropological Archaeology 21:443–463.
Temple, Sir Richard C. 1994 [1909]
    Andaman and Nicobar Islands. Imperial Gazetteer of India, Provincial Series. New Delhi: Asian Educational Services.
Templeton, Alan R. 2002
    Out of Africa Again and Again. Nature 416:45–51.
Theodoratus, Dorothea J. and Frank LaPena. 1994
    Wintu Sacred Geography of Northern California. In Sacred Sites, Sacred Places. David L. Carmichael, Jane Hubert, Brian Reeves and Audhild Schanche, eds. Pp. 20–31. New York: Routledge.
The Sickle Cell Information Center. 1997
    http://www.emory.edu.PEDS/SICKLE/sicklept.htm.
Thieme, H. 1997
    Lower Palaeolithic Hunting Spears from Germany. Nature 385:807–810.
Thomas, David Hurst. 2000
    Skull Wars: Kennewick Man, Archaeology, and the Battle for Native American Identity. New York: Basic Books.
Thompson, J. Eric S. 1954
    The Rise and Fall of Maya Civilization. Norman, OK: University of Oklahoma Press.
Thompson, Robert Farris. 1971
    Aesthetics in Traditional Africa. In Art and Aesthetics in Primitive Societies. Carol F. Jopling, ed. Pp. 374–381. New York: Dutton.
Thorgeirsdóttir, Sigridur. 2004
    Genes of a Nation: The Promotion of Iceland's Genetic Information. Trames 8:178–191.
Thorne, A., R. Grun, G. Mortimer, N. Spooner, J. Simpson, M. McCulloch, L. Taylor, and D. Curnoe. 1999
    Australia's Oldest Human Remains: Age of the Lake Mungo 3 Skeleton. Journal of Human Evolution 36:591–612.
Tice, Karin E. 1995
    Kuna Crafts, Gender, and the Global Economy. Austin: University of Texas Press.
Tierney, Patrick. 2000
    Darkness in El Dorado: How Scientists and Journalists Devastated the Amazon. New York: Norton.
Tiffany, Walter W. 1979
    New Directions in Political Anthropology: The Use of Corporate Models for the Analysis of Political Organizations. In Political Anthropology: The State of the Art. S. Lee Seaton and Henri J. M. Claessen, eds. Pp. 63–75. New York: Mouton.
Tinker, Irene. 1976
    The Adverse Impact of Development on Women. In Women and World Development. Irene Tinker and Michele Bo Bramsen, eds. Pp. 22–34. Washington, DC: Overseas Development Council.
Tishkoff, Sarah A. and B. C. Verrelli. 2003
    Patterns of Human Genetic Diversity. Annual Review Genomics and Human Genetics 4:293–340.
Tobias, Phillip V. 2002
    Saartje Baartman: Her Life, Her Remains, and the Negoti-

ations for Their Repatriation from France to South Africa. South African Journal of Science 98:107–110.

Toren, Christina. 1988
Making the Present, Revealing the Past: The Mutability and Continuity of Tradition as Process. Man (n.s.) 23:696–717.

Toth, Nick and K. Schick. 1993
Early Stone Industries and Inferences Regarding Language and Cognition. In Tools, Language and Cognition in Human Evolution. Kathleen Gibson and Tim Ingold, eds. Pp. 346–362. New York: Cambridge University Press.

Traphagan, John W. 2000
The Liminal Family: Return Migration and Intergenerational Conflict in Japan. Journal of Anthropological Research 56:365–385.

Trawick, Margaret. 1988
Death and Nurturance in Indian Systems of Healing. In Paths to Asian Medical Knowledge. Charles Leslie and Allan Young, eds. Pp. 129–159. Berkeley: University of California Press.

Trelease, Murray L. 1975
Dying among Alaskan Indians: A Matter of Choice. In Death: The Final Stage of Growth. Elisabeth Kübler-Ross, ed. Pp. 33–37. Englewood Cliffs, NJ: Prentice-Hall.

Trigger, Bruce G. 1989
A History of Archaeological Thought. New York: Cambridge University Press.

Trinkaus, Eric 1981
Neandertal Limb Proportions and Cold Adaptation. In Aspects of Human Evolution. Chris B. Stringer, ed. Pp. 187–224. London: Taylor and Francis.

Trotter, Robert T. II. 1987
A Case of Lead Poisoning from Folk Remedies in Mexican American Communities. In Anthropological Praxis: Translating Knowledge into Action. Robert M. Wulff and Shirley J. Fiske, eds. Pp. 146–159. Boulder, CA: Westview Press.

Trouillot, Michel-Rolph. 1994
Culture, Color, and Politics in Haiti. In Race. Steven Gregory and Roger Sanjek, eds. Pp. 146–174. New Brunswick, NJ: Rutgers University Press.

Troy, Lana. 2003
She for Whom All That Is Said Is Done: The Ancient Egyptian Queen. In Ancient Queens: Archaeological Explorations. Sarah Milledge Nelson, ed. Pp. 93–116. Walnut Creek, CA: AltaMira Press.

Tudge, Colin. 1998
Neanderthals, Bandits and Farmers: How Agriculture Really Began. New Haven, CT: Yale University Press.

Turner, Trudy R. 1999
Anthropology, Genetic Diversity and Ethics: A Workshop at the Center for Twentieth-Century Studies. Anthropology Newsletter 40(5).

Turner, Victor W. 1969
The Ritual Process: Structure and Anti-Structure. Chicago: Aldine.

Tylor, Edward Burnett. 1871
Primitive Culture: Researches into the Development of Mythology, Philosophy, Religion, Art, and Custom. 2 volumes. London: J. Murray.

Uhl, Sarah. 1991
Forbidden Friends: Cultural Veils of Female Friendship in Andalusia. American Ethnologist 18(1):90–105.

Underhill, Anne P., Gary M. Feinman, Linda M. Nicholas, Gwen Bennett, Hui Fang, Fengshi Luan, Haiguang Yu, and Fengshu Cai. 2002
Regional Survey and the Development of Complex Societies in Southeastern Shandong, China. Antiquity 76:745–755.

United Nations. 2004
Human Development Report. New York: Oxford University Press.

United Nations Development Programme. 1994
Human Development Report 1994. New York: Oxford University Press.

United States Institute of Peace. 2003
Zimbabwe and the Prospects for Nonviolent Political Change. Special Report 109. Washington, DC. August.

Valdés, Guadalupe and Richard A. Figueroa. 1994
Bilingualism and Testing: A Special Case of Bias. Norwood, NJ: Ablex Publishing Company.

van der Geest, Sjaak, Susan Reynolds Whyte, and Anita Hardon. 1996
The Anthropology of Pharmaceuticals: A Biographical Approach. Annual Review of Anthropology 25:153–178.

van der Merwe, Nikolaas J., Ronald F. Williamson, Susan Pfeiffer, Stephen Cox Thomas, and Kim Oakberg Allegretto. 2003
The Moatfield Ossuary: Isotopic Dietary Analysis of an Iroquoian Community Using Dental Tissue. Journal of Anthropological Archaeology 22:245–261.

Van Gennep, Arnold. 1960 [1908]
The Rites of Passage. Chicago: University of Chicago Press.

van Schaik, C. P., M. Ancrenaz, G. Borgen, B. Galdikas, C. D. Knott, I. Singleton, A. Suzuki, S. Utami, and M. Merrill. 2003
Orangutan Cultures and the Evolution of Material Culture. Science 299(5603):102–105.

van Schaik, Carel. 1983
Why Are Diurnal Primates Living in Groups? Behaviour 87:120–144.

VanWynsberghe, Robert M. 2002
AlterNatives: Community, Identity, and Environmental Justice on Walpole Island. Boston: Allyn and Bacon.

Vekua, A., D. Lordkipanidze, G. P. Rightmire, J. Agusti, R. Ferring, G. Maisuradze, A. Mouskhelishvili, M. Nioradze, M. Ponce De Leon, M. Tappen, M. Tvalchrelidze, and C. Zollikofer. 2002
A New Skull of Early Homo from Dmanisi, Georgia. Science 297:85–89.

Velimirovic, Boris. 1990
Is Integration of Traditional and Western Medicine Really Possible? In Anthropology and Primary Health Care. Jeannine Coreil and J. Dennis Mull, eds. Pp. 51–778. Boulder, CO: Westview Press.

Venter, J. Craig et al. 2001
The Sequence of the Human Genome. Science 291:1304–1351.

Vesilind, Priit J. 2003
Maya Water World. National Geographic 204(4):82–101.

Vesperi, Maria D. 1985
City of Green Benches: Growing Old in a New Downtown. Ithaca, NY: Cornell University Press.

Vickers, Jeanne. 1993
Women and War. Atlantic Highlands, NJ: Zed Books.

Vignaud, Patrick, P. Duringer, H. T. Mackaye, A. Likius, C. Blondel, J.-R. Boisserie, L. de Bonis, V. Eisenmann, M.-E.

Etienne, D. Geraads, F. Guy, T. Lehmann, F. Lihoreau, N. Lopez-Martinez, C. Mourer-Chauvire, O. Otero, J.-C. Rage, M. Schuster, L. Viriot, A. Zazzo, and M. Brunet. 2002
Geology and Paleontology of the Upper Miocene Toros-Menalla Hominid Locality, Chad. Nature 418:152–155.

Vilà, Carles, Peter Savolainen, Jesús E. Maldonado, Isabel R. Amorim, John E. Rice, Rodney L. Honeycutt, Keith A. Crandall, Joakim Lundeberg, and Robert K. Wayne. 1997
Multiple and Ancient Origins of the Domestic Dog. Science 276:1687–1689.

Walker, Alan, M. R. Zimmerman, and R. E. F. Leakey. 1982
A Possible Case of Hypervitaminosis A in Homo erectus. Nature 296:248–250.

Wallace, Douglas C., M. D. Brown, and M. T. Lott. 1999
Mitochondrial DNA Variation in Human Evolution and Disease. Gene 238:211–230.

Wallerstein, Immanuel. 1979
The Capitalist World-Economy. New York: Cambridge University Press.

Walsh, P., K. A. Abernathy, M. Bermejo, R. Beyers, P. de Wachter, M. E. Akou, B. Huijbregts, D. I. Mambounga, A. K. Toham, A. M. Kilbourn, S. A. Lahm, S. Latour, F. Maisels, C. Mbina, Y. Mihindou, S. N. Obiang, E. N. Effa, M. P. Starkey, P. Telfer, M. Thibault, C. E. G. Tutin, L. J. T. White, and D. S. Wilkie. 2003
Catastrophic Ape Decline in Western Equatorial Africa. Nature 422:611–614.

Walter, Robert C., Richard T. Buffler, J. Heinrich Bruggermann, Mireille M. M. Guillaune, Selfe M. Berhe, Berhanne Negassi, Yoseph Ligsekal, Hal Cheng, R. Lawrence Edwards, Rudo von Cosel, Didler Néaudeau, and Mrio Gagnon. 2000
Early Human Occupation of the Red Sea Coast of Eritrea during the Last Interglacial. Nature 405:65–69.

Wang, W.-J. and R. H. Crompton. 2004
The Role of Load-Carrying in the Evolution of Modern Body Proportions. Journal of Anatomy 204:417–430.

Ward, Martha C. 1989
Once Upon a Time. In Nest in the Wind: Adventures in Anthropology on a Tropical Island. Martha C. Ward, ed. Pp. 1–22. Prospect Heights, IL: Waveland Press.

Warren, Carol A. B. 1988
Gender Issues in Field Research. Qualitative Research Methods, Volume 9. Newbury Park, CA: Sage Publications.

Warren, D. Michael. 2001
The Role of the Global Network of Indigenous Knowledge Resource Centers in the Conservation of Cultural and Biological Diversity. In Biocultural Diversity: Linking Language, Knowledge and the Environment. Pp. 446–461. Washington, DC: Smithsonian Institution Press.

Watkins, Ben and Michael L. Fleisher. 2002
Tracking Pastoralist Migration: Lessons from the Ethiopian Somali National Regional State. Human Organization 61:328–338.

Watson, James and Francis Crick. 1953
Molecular Structure of Nucleic Acids. Nature 171:737–738.

Watson, Rubie S. 1997
Museums and Indigenous Cultures: The Power of Local Knowledge. Cultural Survival Quarterly 21(1):24–25.

Watson, William. 1966
China Before the Han Dynasty. NY: Praeger.

Watts, Ian. 1999
The Origin of Symbolic Culture. In Robin Dunbar, Chris Knight, and Camilla Power, eds. The Evolution of Culture. Pp. 113–146. New Brunswick, NJ: Rutgers University Press.

Weatherford, J. 1981
Tribes on the Hill. New York: Random House.

Websdale, Neil. 1995
An Ethnographic Assessment of the Policing of Domestic Violence in Rural Eastern Kentucky. Social Justice 22(1): 102–122.

Webster, David L. 2000
The Not So Peaceful Civilization: A Review of Maya War. Journal of World Prehistory 14:65–119.

———. 1977
Warfare and the Evolution of Maya Civilization. In The Origins of Maya Civilization. Richard E. W. Adams, ed. Pp. 335–372. Albuquerque, NM: University of New Mexico Press.

Webster, Gloria Cranmer. 1991
The Contemporary Potlatch. In Chiefly Feasts: The Enduring Kwakiutl Potlatch. Aldona Jonaitis, ed. Pp. 227–250. Washington, DC: American Museum of Natural History.

Weiner, Annette B. 1976
Women of Value, Men of Renown: New Perspectives in Trobriand Exchange. Austin: University of Texas Press.

Weiss, Kenneth M. 1995
Genetic Variation and Human Disease: Principles and Evolutionary Approaches. New York: Cambridge University Press.

Weiss, Mark L. and Alan E. Mann. 1992
Human Biology and Behavior: An Anthropological Perspective. 3rd ed. Boston: Little, Brown.

———. 1981
Human Biology and Behavior: An Anthropological Perspective. Boston: Little, Brown.

Wendorf, F., A. E. Close, and R. Schild. 1994
Africa during the Period of Homo sapiens neanderthalensis and His Contemporaries. In History of the Scientific and Cultural Development of Mankind. Vol. 1. S. J. de Laet, ed. Pp. 117–135. London: UNESCO and Routledge.

Werbner, Pnina. 1988
"Sealing the Koran": Offering and Sacrifice among Pakistani Labour Migrants. Cultural Dynamics 1:77–97.

Wheeler, Peter E. 1993
The Influence of Stature and Body Form on Hominid Energy and Water Budgets: A Comparison of Australopithecus and Early Homo Physique. Journal of Human Evolution 24: 13–28.

———. 1992
The Thermoregulatory Advantages of Large Body Size for Hominids Foraging in Savannah Environments. Journal of Human Evolution 23:351–362.

Wheeler, R. E. Mortimer. 1953
The Indus Civilization. Cambridge: Cambridge University Press.

White, Douglas R. and Michael L. Burton. 1988
Causes of Polygyny: Ecology, Economy, Kinship, and Warfare. American Anthropologist 90(4):871–887.

White, T., B. Asfaw, D. DeGusta, H. Gilbert, G. Richards, G. Suwa, and F. C. Howell. 2003
Pleistocene Homo sapiens from Middle Awash, Ethiopia. Nature:742–747.

White, Tim D., Gen Suwa, and Behane Asfaw. 1994
Australopithecus ramidus, a New Species of Early Hominid from Aramis, Ethiopia. Nature 371:306–312.

Whiten, A., J. Goodall, W. C. McGrew, T. Nishida, V. Reynolds, Y. Sugiyama, C. E. G. Tutin, R. W. Wrangham, and C. Boesch. 1999
Cultures in Chimpanzees. Nature 399:682–685.

Whiting, Beatrice B. and John W. M. Whiting. 1975
Children of Six Cultures: A Psycho-Cultural Analysis. Cambridge, MA: Harvard University Press.

Whiting, Robert. 1989
You Gotta Have Wa: When Two Baseball Cultures Collide on the Baseball Diamond. New York: Macmillan.

Whyte, Martin King. 1993
Wedding Behavior and Family Strategies in Chengdu. In Chinese Families in the Post-Mao Era. Deborah Davis and Stevan Harrell, eds. Pp. 89–218. Berkeley: University of California Press.

Wikan, Unni. 1977
Man Becomes Woman: Transsexualism in Oman as a Key to Gender Roles. Man 12(2):304–319.

Wildman, D. E., M. Uddin, L. Guozhen, L. I. Grossman, and M. Goodman. 2003
Implications of Natural Selection in Shaping 99.4% Nonsynonymous DNA Identity between Humans and Chimpanzees: Enlarging Genus Homo. Proceedings of the National Academy of Sciences 100(12):7181–7188.

Wiley, Andrea S. 2004
"Drink Milk for Fitness": The Cultural Politics of Human Biological Variation and Milk Consumption in the United States. American Anthropologist 106:506–517.

Williams, Brett. 1994
Babies and Banks: The "Reproductive Underclass" and the Raced, Gendered Masking of Debt. In Race. Steven Gregory and Roger Sanjek, eds. Pp. 348–365. Ithaca, NY: Cornell University Press.

Williams, Raymond. 1990
Key Words: A Vocabulary of Culture and Society. New York: Oxford University Press.

Williams, Walter. 1992
The Spirit and the Flesh: Sexual Diversity in American Indian Cultures. 2nd ed. Boston: Beacon Press.

Wilson, Richard. 1995
Maya Resurgence in Guatemala: Q'eqchi' Experiences. Norman, OK: University of Oklahoma Press.

Wilson, Thomas M. 2000
The Obstacles to European Union Regional Policy in the Northern Ireland Borderlands. Human Organization 59:1–10.

Winans, Edgar V. and Angelique Haugerud. 1977
Rural Self-Help in Kenya: The Harambee Movement. Human Organization 36:334–351.

Winthrop, Robert. 2000
The Real World: Cultural Rights/Animal Rights. Practicing Anthropology 22:44–45.

Winzeler, Robert L. 1974
Sex Role Equality, Wet Rice Cultivation, and the State in Southeast Asia. American Anthropologist 76(3):563–565.

Wolf, Charlotte. 1966
Status. In The Social Science Encyclopedia. Adam Kuper and Jessica Kuper, eds. Pp. 842–843. New York: Routledge.

Wolf, Margery. 1968
The House of Lim: A Study of a Chinese Farm Family. New York: Appleton-Century-Crofts.

Wolpoff, Milford H., X. Z. Wu, and A. G. Thorne. 1984
Modern Homo sapiens Origins: A General Theory of Hominid Evolution Involving the Fossil Evidence from East Asia. In The Origins of Modern Humans. F. H. Smith and F. Spencer, eds. Pp. 411–483. New York: Alan R. Liss.

Wood, Bernard A. 1992
Origin and Evolution of the Genus Homo. Nature 355:783–790.

———. 1991
Koobi Fora Research Project. Vol. 4. Hominid Cranial Remains. Oxford: Clarendon Press.

Wood, Bernard and David S. Strait. 2004
Patterns of Resource Use in Early Homo and Paranthropus. Journal of Human Evolution 46:119–162.

Wood, Bernard and Mark Collard. 1999a
The Changing Face of Genus Homo. Evolutionary Anthropology 8(6):195–207.

———. 1999b
Is Homo Defined by Culture? In World Prehistory: Studies in Memory of Grahame Clark. J. Coles, R. Bewley, and P. Mellars, eds. Pp. 11–23. Oxford: Oxford University Press.

Woolfson, Peter, Virginia Hood, Roger Secker-Walker, and Ann C. Macaulay. 1995
Mohawk English in the Medical Interview. Medical Anthropology Quarterly 9(4):503–509.

Worldwatch Institute. 2003
Vital Signs 2003: The Trends That Are Shaping Our Future. Washington, DC: Worldwatch Institute/W. W. Norton.

Wrangham, Richard and Dale Peterson. 1996
Demonic Males: Apes and the Origins of Human Violence. New York: Houghton Miffin Company.

Wrangham, Richard, J. Hollandjones, G. Laden, D. R. Pilbeam, and N.-L. Conklin-Brittain. 1999
The Raw and Stolen. Cooking and the Ecology of Human Origins. Current Anthropology 40(5):567–594.

Wright, Patricia Chapple. 1993
Variations in Male–Female Dominance and Offspring Care in Non-Human Primates. In Sex and Gender Hierarchies. Barbara D. Miller ed. Pp. 127–145. New York: Cambridge University Press.

Wright, Rita P. 1996
Technology, Gender, and Class: Worlds of Difference in Ur III Mesopotamia. In Gender and Archaeology. Pp. 79–110. Rita P. Wright, ed. Philadelphia: University of Pennsylvania Press.

Wu, David Y. H. 1990
Chinese Minority Policy and the Meaning of Minority Culture: The Example of Bai in Yunnan, China. Human Organization 49(1):1–13.

Wynn, Thomas and William C. McGrew. 1989
An Ape's View of the Oldowan. Man 24:383–398.

Yamei, H., R. Potts, Y. Baoyin, G. Zhengtang, A. Deino, W. Wei, J. Clark, X. Guangmao, and H. Weiman. 2000
Acheulean-Like Stone Technology of the Bose Basin, South China. Science 287:1622–1626.

Yellen, John, Alison Brooks, E. Cornelissen, M. Mehlman, and K. Stewart. 1995
A Middle Stone Age Worked Bone Industry from Katanda, Upper Semliki Valley, Zaire. Science 268:553–556.

Yoffee, Norman and George L. Cowgill, eds. 1988
The Collapse of Ancient States and Civilizations. Tucson, AZ: University of Arizona Press.

Yoon, In-Jin. 1993
The Social Origins of Korean Immigration to the United States from 1965 to the Present. Papers of the Program on Population, Number 121. Honolulu: East-West Center.

Young, Biloine Whiting and Melvin L. Fowler. 2000
Cahokia: The Great Native American Metropolis. Urbana: University of Illinois Press.

Zabusky, Stacia E. 1995
Launching Europe: An Ethnography of European Cooperation in Space Science. Princeton: Princeton University Press.

Zaidi, S. Akbar. 1988
Poverty and Disease: Need for Structural Change. Social Science and Medicine 27:119–127.

Zarrilli, Phillip B. 1990
Kathakali. In Indian Theatre: Traditions of Performance. Farley P. Richmond, Darius L. Swann, and Phillip B. Zarrilli, eds. Pp. 315–357. Honolulu: University of Hawaii Press.

Zeanah, David W. 2002
Central Place Foraging and Prehistoric Pinyon Utilization in the Great Basin. In Beyond Foraging and Collecting: Evolutionary Change in Hunter–Gatherer Settlement Systems. Ben Fitzhugh and Junko Habu, eds. Pp. 231–256. New York: Kluwer Academic/Plenum Publishers.

Zeder, M. and B. Hesse. 2000
The Initial Domestication of Goats (Capra hircus) in the Zagros Mountains 10,000 Years Ago. Science 287:2254–2257.

Zhu, R. X., K. A. Hoffman, R. Potts, C. L. Deng, Y. X. Pan, B. Guo, C. D. Shi, Z. T. Guo, B. Y. Yuan, Y. M. Hou, and W. W. Huang. 2001
Earliest Presence of Humans in Northeast Asia. Nature 413:413–417.

Zihlman, Adrienne and Debra R. Bolter. 2004
Mammalian and Primate Roots of Human Sociality. In The Origins and Nature of Sociality. Robert W. Sussman and Audrey R. Chapman, eds. Pp. 23–52. Hawthorne, NY: Aldine de Gruyter.

Zollikofer, Christoph. 2002
A Computational Approach to Paleoanthropology. Evolutionary Anthropology Supplement 1:64–67.

Zureik, Elia. 1994
Palestinian Refugees and Peace. Journal of Palestine Studies 24(1):5–17.

SOURCES FOR "ANTHROPOLOGY IN THE REAL WORLD"

Part I: Fredy Peccerelli

AAAS Human Rights Action Network. American Association for the Advancement of Science. 21 March 2002. Available: http://shr.aaas.org/news/050204_peccerelli.html.

Black, Richard. Guatemala Rights Scientist Honoured. BBC. 15 Feb. 2004. Available: http://news.bbc.co.uk/go/pr/fr/-/2/hi/science/nature/3489743.stm.

Digging for Truth in Guatemala. American Association for the Advancement of Science Public Release. 14 Feb. 2004. Available: http://www.eurekalert.org/pub_releases/2004-02/aaft-dft020504.php.

Elton, Catherine. Despite Threats, Guatemalan Scientists Dig for the Truth. The Christian Science Monitor. 27 March 2002. Available: http://www.csmonitor.com/2002/0327/pO8s01-woam.html.

Fredy Peccerelli, Executive Director of the Guatemalan Forensic Anthropology Foundation Speaks at AAAS. American Association for the Advancement of Science. 2004. Available: http://shr.aaas.org/news/050204_peccerelli.html.

Part II: Yohannes Haile-Selassie

Earliest Hominid Discovery; Ardipithecus ramidus kadabba. Available: http://www.priweb.org/ed/ICTHOL/ICTHOL04papers/78.html.

Perlman, David. Fossils from Ethiopia May Be Earliest Human Ancestor. San Francisco Chronicle. 12 July 2001. Available: http://news.nationalgeographic.com/news/2001/07/0712_ethiopianbones.html.

Radford, Tim. Earliest Human Ancestor Discovered. The Guardian—United Kingdom. 12 July 2001. Available: http://www.arhotaba.com/archeologie.html.

Sanders, Robert. UC Berkeley/Paleoanthropologists Find Oldest Human Ancestor in Ethiopia. University of California Berkeley Campus News Press Release. 11 July 2001. Available: http://www.berkeley.edu/news/media/releases/2001/07/11_bones.html.

Part III: Lara Tabac

Lara Tabac. Slate. 29 Sept. 2003. Available: http://slate.msn.com/id/2088748/entry/2088987/.

Part IV: Susan Squires

American Breakfast & the Mother-in-Law: How an Anthropologist Created Go-Gurt. National Association for the Practice of Anthropology. 2003–2004. Available: http://www.practicinganthropology.org/learn/index.cfm?print=1&storyid=4.

Boss, Shira J. Anthropologists on the Job. The Christian Science Monitor. 2 Jan. 2001. Available: http://csmonitor.com/cgi-bin/durableRedirect.pl?/durable/2001/01/02/fp9sl-csm.shtml.

Susan Squires, Ph.D., Research Director, Tactics LLC. Southwestern Anthropological Association. 2004. Available: http://www2.sjsu.edu/depts/anthropology/swaa/pages/PgSquires.html.

Walsh, Sharon. Corporate Anthropology: Dirt-Free Research. CNN.com/CAREER. 23 May 2001. Available: http://www.cnn.com/2001/CAREER/dayonthejob/05/23/corp.anthropologist.idg/.

Part V: Mamphela Ramphele

Across Boundaries. 21 April 1997. Online NewsHour: Zair: End of an Era. 1999, MacNeil-Lehrer Productions. Available: http://www.pbs.org/newshur/bb/africa/april97/ramph_4-21.html.

Dr. Mamphela Ramphele's Biography. Mamphela Ramphele. Available: http://www.sahistory.org.za/pages/people/ramphele-m.html.

New Vice-Chancellor Appointed. University of Capetown Department of Development and Public Affairs. 10 Dec. 1996. Available: http://web.uct.ac.za/depts/dpa/news/ramphele.html.

Ramphele, Mamphela. Higher Education in Developing Countries: Peril and Promise. 1 March 2000. Launch of the Higher Education Task Force Report. Available: http://www.tfhe.net/resources/mamphelaramphele_response.html.

Design Photo Credits

Title page, part openers and chapter openers: Chinese jar painted with a spiral decoration, © Cernuschi Museum, Paris, France/SuperStock, Inc.

The Big Questions, Key Concepts, and Suggested Readings: Kleitias and Ergotimos, the Francois vase, 570 BC, © Archeological Museum, Florence, Italy/Canali Photobank, Milan/Superstock, Inc.

Chapter introductions and Critical Thinking: Greek terra cotta vase, © Superstock, Inc.

Methods Close-Up: Bayonne vase in hammered copper, © Pyreneen Museum, Lourdes. France/Lauros-Giraudon, Paris/Superstock, Inc.

Lessons Applied: Etruscan vase, © Archeological Museum, Florence, Italy/Superstock, Inc.

Crossing the Fields, left to right: © Ray Nelson/Phototake; © Sven-Olof Lindblad/Photo Researchers, Inc.; © Kenneth Eward/BioGrafx/Photo Researchers, Inc.; © Medioimages/Alamy; © BennettPhoto/Alamy; © CORBIS Digital Stock; © Sheila Terry/Photo Researchers, Inc.; © GOODSHOOT/Alamy; © Paul Damien/National Geographic Image Collection; © Bill Lyons/Alamy; © Brand X Pictures/Alamy; © Joseph Sohm/Alamy; and closing photo: © Paul Damien/National Geographic Image Collection.

Words in boldface type indicate key terms.

Chichen Itza, 475
Chiefdoms, 473–474
  of early New World civilizations, 268, 269, 277, 281–282, 473
  origin of the state and, 268, 269
  warfare waged by, 269, 485–486
Chikhi, Lounes, 22
Childbirth. *See* Birth
Child care
  by children, 325, 329, 363, 368
  family farming and, 329
  by friends in The Flats, 443
  gender roles in, 376, 377
  grandmother hypothesis and, 377–378
  Margaret Mead's films of, 121
Childe, V. Gordon, 256, 267, 268
Children. *See also* Boys; Girls; Infants
  abuse of, 432
  adoption of, 419–420
  adult communication with, 511–512
  in agricultural societies, 329
  argument styles of, 513
  cash cropping and, 345
  "the child" as a category, 367
  conflict with parents' culture, 435
  diet of, 337, 343, 345
  and fieldwork, 117
  food stealing by, in Sierra Leone, 343
  fostering of, 419
  in global capitalist economy, 335, 336, 346
  in horticultural societies, 324–325
  "legitimacy" of, 362, 421, 424
  malnutrition in, 312, 313, 400
  Mead's fieldwork among, 364
  modes of reproduction and, 355–356
  in pastoral societies, 326
  in patrilineal system, Yemen, 417
  poverty and growth of, 584
  protection from illness, 389
  as sex workers, 626
  sleeping arrangements for, 46
  socialization of, 367–369
  value of, in fertility decision making, 359–360
Children of Six Cultures (Whiting and Whiting), 325, 329, 367–368
Childs, Larry, 627
Chimpanzee archaeology, 155–157
Chimpanzees, 150, 151, 152–154. *See also* Bonobos
  conservation programs, 160, 161
  culture in, 44, 158
  divergence from humans, 14, 133, 166, 167, 177, 188
  FOXP2 gene of, and language, 218
  genetic diversity, 293–294
  genetic relationship to humans, 14, 73, 75, 76, 87
  language capabilities, 20, 503
  learning in, 44, 135, 136

polio epidemic among, 384
sexual dimorphism, 173
social groups, 142
tool use, 135, 136, 155–157, 158, 216, 217
violence among, 145
China
  archaeology of, 39
  archaic *Homo* in, 207
  cheese and, 45
  early cities and states, 273–274
  elderly in, 353
  ethnic groups in, 456
  Hakka people of, 587
  hominin sites in, 205–206
  hookworm in, 397, 398
  human evolution as viewed in, 176–177
  humoral healing in, 393, 394
  irrigation in, 10
  local markets in, 341
  marriage gifts in, 425
  Marxist anthropology in, 42
  Neolithic period, 273, 274
  one-child-per-couple policy, 362, 427
  racial thinking in, 52, 177
  restrictions on foreign researchers, 115, 460
  sexuality in, 575
  theater in, 574–575
  Three Gorges Dam project, 589
  Tibetan culture suppressed by, 53, 456, 549
  women and power in, 475
  women's movement in, 460–461
  writing styles in, 505
Chiñas, Beverly Newbold, 329
Chinese anthropologist, 117
Chirac, Jacques, 554
Chiropractic, 394, 401
Chocolate, 46
Cholera, 387, 399, 407
  Gibraltar epidemic of 1865, 308–309
Chowdhury, Najma, 489
Christianity, 537, 538, 543–546. *See also* Biblical narrative; Catholicism; Missionaries
  abortion and, 362
  Amish people, 329, 356, 477
  Carnival and, 534
  domestic violence and, 431
  of European explorers and colonizers, 7–8, 11, 50
  European Union and, 22
  female genital cutting and, in Ethiopia, 371
  firewalking in, 524, 525
  fundamentalist, 431
  godparenthood and, 420
  Great Chain of Being and, 74, 75
  of immigrants to U.S., 594, 597
  infanticide and, 363

Jerusalem and, 549
origin of humans and, 7, 66–67, 68, 70, 77, 95
origin of language and, 40
pilgrimage in, 534
potlatch and, 347
rituals in, 531, 532
Chromosomes, 65, 81–83, 86–87
  autosomes, 293
  in Down syndrome, 306
  hot spots on, 85
  linked genes on, 88
  sex chromosomes, 293, 366–367
  speciation and, 94
Circular migration, 586
Circumcision, 371, 440, 558. *See also* Female genital cutting
Circumpolar region. *See also* Alaska; Eskimos; Inuit people; Siberia
  adaptations of humans to, 300–301
  early modern humans in, 243
  foragers of, 321–322, 363
Circumscription, 268
Cities. *See also* Urban life; Urban revolution
  defined, 267
Citizenship, 474, 586
City–states, of pre-hispanic Mexico, 474–475
Civilization
  Chinese view of, 52
  clash of, 48, 49
  culture and, 37
  Eurocentric view of, 8, 15, 38, 39, 554
  evolutionary view of, 8, 38, 40
  rise and decline of, 284–285
  state-level political systems and, 268, 269
  urban revolution and, 267–269
Civil society, 460–463
Clade, 73
Cladistic analysis, 175–176
  of Turkman carpets, 570–571
Cladogenesis, 94, 179
Cladogram, 175
Clan, 471, 525–526
Clark, Geoff, 240
Clark, Gracia, 49, 630
Clash of civilizations, 48, 49
Class, 51, 52, 451
  consumption patterns and, 334, 336
  defined, 52, 451
  of fieldworker, 116
  language and, 508
  race and, 14
  religion and, 526
  reproduction and, in industrial society, 356
Class, taxonomic, 71, 72
Classification of organisms. *See* Taxonomy
Clay, eating of, 396

Davis, Richard S., 242
Davis, Susan Schaefer, 358
Davis-Floyd, Robbie E., 365, 401
Day, Michael H., 227
Day range, 141
Dead Sea, healing properties of, 395
Deaf culture, 501
Death, 378–379. *See also* Burials
  active participation in among Alaskan
    Inuit, 379
  brain death, 385
  cremation, Upper Paleolithic, 237
  culture-bound syndromes and, 388
  forensic anthropology and, 1, 27
  Hindu funeral procession in Bali, 523
  mourning, 379
  preventive practices, 389
  spirits of the dead, 525, 529
  structural causes of, 386
  urine ritual of Native Americans, 46
  Western resistance to, 378–379
Death penalty, 478, 481, 542
de Beaune, S. A., 217
Decorative arts, 555, 561, 562–564
Deforestation, 10. *See also*
    Reforestation projects
  in Haiti, 619–620
  Kyasanur forest disease and, 403
  primate populations and, 158–159,
    160, 161
Deitrick, Lynn M., 366
de la Cadena, Marisol, 452
Delaney, Carol, 371
Delaney, Patricia, 621
de la Torre, Ignatio, 216
de Leon, Francisco, 27
Demarest, Arthur A., 279
Demas, M., 166
Democracy
  in cooperatives, 448
  expression of conflict in, 479
  meritocratic individualism and, 451
Democratization, 489
Dendrochronology, 106–107
Deng, Francis, 588
Denham, Melinda, 307, 310
Denham, T. P., 250
Denmark, Neolithic diets in, 264
Depersonalized consumption, 334, 335
Depression, 386, 401
d'Errico, Francisco, 190, 216
Desana people of Colombia, 385–386
Descent, 414–418
Descriptive linguistics, 20
Design
  argument from, 77, 95
  of products, 497
Determinism
  biological, 58–59, 422–423
  environmental, 43
  linguistic, 508
Development

anthropologists and, 608, 618–622
cultural heritage and, 573
defined, 608
as diffusion from West, 610
diseases of, 403
gender and, 615, 628–631
grassroots approaches to, 618
human rights and, 631, 633
indigenous people and, 622–628
institutional approaches to, 615–617,
  633
internally displaced persons and, 589
overview of, 634
projects in, 618–619
sociocultural fit in, 619–621
theories and models of, 612–615
women and, 628–631
Developmental adaptations, 299, 302
Development anthropology, 608,
  618–622
**Development-induced displacement
  (DID),** 589
Devereaux, George, 361
DeVore, I., 218, 284
de Waal, Frans B. M., 144, 153, 154
Diachronic approach, 608
Dialect, 509–510
Diaspora population, 456
Dichotomous trait, 80
Diet. *See also* Agriculture; Eating; Food
  adaptations involving, 303–304
  agriculture and, 284, 397
  of archaic *Homo,* 213–214
  of Arctic peoples, 301
  in Ayurvedic medicine, 399, 400
  cash cropping and, 344–345
  of children, 337, 343, 345, 584
  in countries of former Soviet Union,
    346
  cultural change and, 12, 13, 17
  of early hominins, 178, 189
  of early modern humans, 231, 232,
    236, 237, 238–239, 246–251
  fertility and, 355
  human flesh in, 337–338. *See also*
    Cannibalism
  of Indus Valley civilization, 272
  Jewish law and, 542
  lactase and, 304, 619
  maize in, health effects of, 281–282,
    284
  malnutrition in contemporary
    humans, 311, 312, 313, 400–401
  meat in. *See* Meat-eating
  Neolithic transition and, 256,
    263–264, 265, 267
  and new immigrants, 584
  nutrient requirements, 303–304
  of pastoral vs. settled Turkana, 397
  of primates, 138–140, 303–304
  of settled populations, 397
  of wrestlers in India, 568

Di Ferdinando, George, 310
Differential mortality, 309
Differential preservation, 172
Diffusion, 257–258, 610–611
Diffusion Wave Model, 226
Dikötter, Frank, 52, 176, 475
Dillehay, Thomas, 244
Dirt, eating of, 396
Disability infanticide, 354, 362
Disability rights, 354
Discordance hypothesis, 307
Discourse, 20, 41, 119, 513
Discrimination. *See also* Inequality;
    Racism; Sexism
  caste-based, 459–460
  ethnic, 53, 456–457, 509
  against homosexuals, 55, 373
  linguistic, 509
  refugees from, 588
Disease. *See also* Medical anthropology
  agriculture and, 284, 397
  in archaic *Homo,* 214
  colonialism and, 397–399
  defined, 386
  development and, 403
  doctor–patient miscommunication
    about, 391
  environment and, 396–399
  genetic factors in, 295, 296, 298,
    304–307
  in mummies, 103
  new infectious diseases, 402–403
  poverty and, 311, 312, 313
  in settled populations, 397, 398
  as threat to anthropologist, 124
  urban life and, 308–310, 311, 312,
    313, 397
  Yanomami warfare and, 485
Disease/illness dichotomy, 386
Diseases of development, 403
Displaced persons, 586–589
Displacement, in human language,
  503
Distributional development, 613–614
Diurnal nonhuman primates, 137
Diversity, 9, 10–13, 57. *See also*
    Biological variation; Pluralism
Divination, 390, 404
Diviners, 537
Division of labor
  in collectivized agriculture, 331
  in family farming, 328–329, 330
  in foraging societies, 322
  by gender. *See* Gender division of
    labor
  global, 343–344
  in horticultural societies, 323–325
  in Papua New Guinea, 47
  in pastoral societies, 325–326
Divorce, 418, 432
Dlimoumalbaye, Ahounta, 182
Dmanisi, Georgia, 204

DNA, 75. *See also* Chromosomes;
    Genome
  of Andamanese people, 92
  of chimpanzees compared to humans,
    73
  cladistic analysis and, 175
  as data type, 104
  domestication of cattle and, 261
  in forensic anthropology, 1
  heredity and, 87–88
  of hominin fossils, 175
  of Icelanders, 292
  kin relationships in primates and, 144
  mitochondrial. *See* Mitochondrial DNA
  of Neanderthal fossils, 227
  from Neanderthal stone tools, 214, 215
  PCR for amplification of, 298
  proteins coded by, 86–87
  racial thinking and, 14
  replication of, 84–85
  single-nucleotide polymorphisms in,
    294–295
  structure of, 82–84, 86–87
  taxonomic relationships and, 73, 75
Doctrine, 527, 528, 531
Dogon people of Mali, 379
Dogs
  of circumpolar foragers, 321, 322
  domestication of, 241, 263
  in Neolithic China, 273
  of pastoralists, 325
Dolhinow, Phyllis, 145
Domestication, 256. *See also*
    Agriculture; Animals; Breeding of
    animals and plants; Pastoralism
  of barley, 258, 259
  of cattle, 261, 262, 263
  defined, 256
  of dogs, 241, 263
  of horses, 66
  of maize, 258, 265–267
  in New World, 265, 267
  in Old World, 257, 258, 259,
    261–263, 264
  of potato, 280, 284
  rapidity of, 259–260
  of squash and gourds, 258, 267
  theories about origin of, 258
  warfare and, 485
  of wheat, 258, 259
Domestication of women, 629
Domestic violence, 431–432, 462, 630
Dominance. *See also* Hierarchy; Male
    dominance; Matriarchy;
    Patriarchy; Status
  in children, 367–368
  defined, 143
  discredited assumptions about, among
    nonhuman primates, 144
  in dyadic interactions among
    nonhuman primates, 144
  as learned behavior, 469

  in primates, 143–144, 154
  and sexual selection hypothesis, 145
  status and, 452
Dominant allele, 81
Dominant caste, 458
Dominguez-Rodrigo, M., 214
Dominican Republic
  Haitian cane cutters in, 602–603
  immigrants to U.S. from, 592–593
Dominion (Eldredge), 285
Donlon, Jon, 568
Doole, Jennifer, 111
Dore, 385–386
Dorgan, Howard, 544
Double descent systems, 417
Douglas, Mary, 43
Down syndrome, 306–307
Dowry, 423, 425
Drake, Susan P., 569
Draper, Patricia, 378
Dress. *See* Clothing
Drinking, 44, 45–46. *See also* Alcoholic
    beverages
  of kava, 501, 502, 545
Drucker, Charles, 633
Drugs. *See also* Healing substances
  unsafe injection practices, 289
Duany, Jorge, 488
Dubois, Eugene, 204
Du Bois, W. E. B., 455
Duncan, M. T., 299
Duranti, Alessandro, 20, 41, 502
Durkheim, Emile, 525–526
Durning, Alan Thein, 334
Durrenberger, E. Paul, 451
Dutch colonialism, in Java, 119
Dyadic interactions, 144
Dynamic Model, of civilizations, 285
Dyson, Tim, 328

Earle, Timothy, 265, 281
Early hominins, 176–191. *See also*
    Archaic hominins; Primitive
    hominins
  adaptations of, 187–191
  basic characteristics of, 178, 180
  classification of, 178–187
  diet, 178, 189
  environmental context of, 177–178, 182
  intelligence, 190
  Laetoli footprints, 111, 165, 166, 188
  language and, 190–191
  locomotion and body shape, 188–189
  overview of, 191–192
  sociality, 189–190
  tools of, 184, 185, 190, 191,
    198–199, 200, 202
Early Stone Age (ESA), 196
Earth, eating of, 396
Earth science, history of, 69, 70, 77
Eating, as cultural, 44–45. *See also*
    Diet; Food

Eating disorders, 388
Eaton, J. W., 306
Ebola fever, 161
Echo-Hawk, Walter, R., 283
Eck, Diana L., 539
Eckel, Malcolm David, 540
Ecofacts, 102, 203
Ecological/epidemiological approach,
    396–399
Ecological niche, 138
Ecology, 138
Economic anthropology, 320. *See also*
    Consumption; Exchange;
    Production
Economic change, and feuds in
    Pakistan, 483
Economic development, 612–613, 615.
    See also Development
Economic systems. *See also* Capitalism;
    Modes of production
  adaptive nature of, 44
  class and, 451
  health inequality and, 400
  kinship and, 412
  polygyny and, 425–426
Ecotourism, nonhuman primates and,
    160
Ecuador
  Neolithic plant domestication, 267
  polio vaccine in, 610
Edge Hypothesis, 258
Education
  adjustment of international students,
    590
  in bilingual populations, 509
  Black children's styles of expression
    and, 510
  development and, 613, 614, 615, 616,
    618
  gender and, 57, 419, 457, 590
  of girls in Afghanistan, 607
  incorporating anthropology into,
    29–30
  in multilingual populations, 29
  of women in China, 460, 461
Efe people of Congo, 343
"The Effectiveness of Symbols" (Lévi-
    Strauss), 399
Egalitarian behavior. *See also* Inequality
  in Aka people, 376
  male–female co-dominance among
    nonhuman primates, 144
  Middle Stone Age, 230
  of mixed foraging–horticultural
    economy, 428
  of Temiar foragers, 560–561
Ego, 413
Egypt
  brother–sister marriage in, 421
  collaborative research in, 126, 127, 128
  emergence of cities and states, 271,
    272

age categories of males and, 55
by Berber people, 12
of camels, in Rajasthan, India, 3
early African cities and, 275
lactase persistence and, 304
Neolithic, 259, 261, 262, 263
transition to, 246, 248, 251
Herdt, Gilbert, 371, 373
Heredity. *See* DNA; Genetics
Hermaphrodites, 374
Herodotus, 7
Herrnstein, Richard J., 14
Herzfeld, Michael, 482
Hesse, B., 247
Heterosexuality, as norm, 373
Heterotopia, 564
Heterozygous individual, 81
Hewlett, Barry S., 376
Hiatt, Betty, 237
Hierarchy. *See also* Inequality; Social
   stratification
   bureaucratic, 270
   in caste system, 458
   of classes, 52
   vs. difference, 51–52
   dominance, in nonhuman primates, 144
   religious, 537
   social stratification and, 450
   in states, 475
   of world's countries, 491
Hieroglyphic writing, 271
Hijira, 374
Hildebrand, Elisabeth, 261
Hill, Andrew, 166
Hill, Jane H., 507, 508
Hillman, G. C., 259
Hiltebeitel, Alf, 538, 539
Hinde, R. A., 142
Hindi, 47, 49, 503–504
Hinduism and Hindu cultures, 538–540
   abortion and, 362
   archaeology of, 39
   ascetics in Sri Lanka, 119
   caste system and, 458, 539
   conflicts with Muslims in India, 549
   cows as sacred animals in, 60, 61
   funeral procession in Bali, 523
   Jews of India and, 543
   marriage and, 422, 540
   menstruation and, 371
   myths in, 528, 538–539, 561
   in New York City, 598
   nonhuman primate survival and, 159
   pilgrimage in, 534
   ritual health protection and, 389
   rituals in, 539, 564, 598
   sexual abstinence in, 359
   zoomorphic supernaturals in, 529
Hirschon, Renee, 589
Historical archaeology, 15
   and Northern Cheyenne Outbreak of
      1879, 54

Historical archives, 119
Historical linguistics, 20, 250, 506
HIV/AIDS
   female genital cutting and, 372
   in Ghana, survey on, 358
   global epidemic of, 402–403
   mortality due to, 400
   nonhuman primate research and, 159
   sex workers in India and, 440
   in South Africa, 336, 454
   stigmatization based on, 384
   in Thailand, 626
   Treatment Action Campaign in South
      Africa, 454
   tuberculosis in, 310
Hmong people, 623, 626
Hoberg, E. P., 214
Hodder, Ian, 39, 40, 100, 261
Hodge, Robert W., 356
Hoffecker, John F., 242
Holden, Clare, 337
Holism, 37, 47, 61
Holland, Dorothy C., 423
Holliday, Trenton W., 300
Hollox, E. J., 304
Holocaust, 51
Holocene epoch, 178. *See also*
   Neolithic period
   transitions during, 246–251, 252, 256
Homeostasis, population, 355
Home range, 141
Hominin. *See also* Archaic *Homo;* Early
   hominins; *Homo;* Modern humans
   (*Homo sapiens*)
   defined, 166
   early, 111, 165, 166, 176–192,
      198–199, 200, 202
   primate taxonomy and, 148
Hominin fossils, 167–176
   in African museums, 168
   age determination, 173
   dating of, 169
   formation of, 167, 169
   gaps and biases in record, 171–173
   geographic range of, 167, 169–171
   measuring and describing, 174–175
   preservation of, 172–173, 174
   reconstructing from fragments, 174
   sex determination, 173–174
   sorting into species, 175
   species relationships, 175–176
Hominoids, 150. *See also* Apes;
   Hominin; Modern humans
Homo, 72, 73, 148, 181, 196. *See also*
   Archaic *Homo;* Modern humans
   (*Homo sapiens*)
   distinctive features of, 198–199
   jaws of, 199, 205, 207, 213
Homo antecessor, 208
Homo erectus
   in Africa and Europe, 207
   in Asia, 204–206, 235

early, 202
   island of Flores and, 207, 213, 235
   meat-eating by, 214
   origin of modern humans and,
      225–226
Homo ergaster, 202, 203, 204
   diet, 213–214
   dispersal of, 204, 207, 226
   fossilized teeth and health of, 397
   sexual dimorphism, 216
Homo floresiensis, 207, 235
Homo habilis, 200–201, 213
Homo habilis sensu stricto, 200–201
Homo heidelbergensis, 207–208, 226
Homo neanderthalensis. *See*
   Neanderthals
Homophobia, 374
Homoplasy, 175, 176
Homo rudolfensis, 187, 200–201, 202,
   213
Homo sapiens. *See* Modern humans
   (*Homo sapiens*)
Homosexuals, 373–375
   body modification by, 446–447
   discrimination against, 55, 373
   gay and lesbian anthropology, 19
   marriage of, 421, 425
Homozygous individual, 81
Hong Kong, migrants to Canada from,
   595–596
Honor killing, 457
Hookworm, 397
Hoopa (Hopi) Tribe of Arizona, 112
Hopewell culture, 281
Hopkins, Nicholas S., 461
Horizon, 102, 106
Hormones
   biological determinism and, 58, 59
   in spider monkeys, 143
Hornbein, George, 46
Hornbein, Marie, 46
Horowitz, Michael M., 120, 620
Horses
   breeding of, 66, 89–90
   as Neolithic food source, 265
Horticulture, 259, 321, 323–325
   cash cropping and, 344–345
   child personality and, 368
   consumption and, 334
   defined, 323
   descent systems and, 415, 416
   female infanticide and, 363–364
   health problems and, 385–386
   household structure and, 427
   marriage gifts and, 425
   modes of reproduction and, 354
   political organization and, 470, 471
   shelters and, 561
   social control and, 478
   social groups and, 441
   women and, 629
   work groups in, 447

Horvath, S. M., 299
Hospitals. *See also* Western biomedicine
  birth in, 365, 366
  microcultures of, 57
Hostetler, John A., 329
Hot climates, adaptations to, 299–300
Household, 426–433. *See also* Descent;
    Family; Kinship
  defined, 426
  dynamics of, 427–433
  forms of, 426–427
  headed by women, 423, 424
  recent changes in, 435–436
Household archaeology, 428
The House of Lim (Wolf), 415–416,
    427
Housing structures, 561–562. *See also*
    Architecture; Interior decoration
  of foragers, 321
  Neolithic China, 273, 274
  Upper Paleolithic, central Eurasia, 44
Howell, Nancy, 125, 355
Hrdy, Sarah, 145
Huang, Shu-Min, 117
Hua people of New Guinea, 55
Hublin, Jean-Jacques, 234, 238, 240
Huizinga, Johan, 566
Hula, 573–574
Human agency. *See* Agency
Human body. *See* Anatomy; Body
Human capital, 615
Human development, 614–615
Human Genome Diversity Project
    (HGDP), 295, 296
Humanistic approach, 5–7
Human rights
  activist groups and, 461, 462
  cultural relativism and, 51
  definitions of, 632
  development and, 631, 633
  forensic anthropology and, 1, 27
  Latin American anthropologists and,
    8
  migration and, 601–602
  religious freedom as, 549
  wars in defense of, 486
Human sacrifice. *See* Sacrifice
Human subjects, 127
Humoral healing systems, 393–394,
    399
Humphrey, Caroline, 518
Hungary, Roma minority in, 456–457
Hunte, Pamela A., 361
Hunting. *See also* Fishing; Foraging
  by archaic *Homo*, 208, 214, 218
  by Australian foragers, 237
  domesticated dogs in, 241
  by early modern people in New
    World, 244, 245
  by early Siberian–Alaska peoples, 243
  food preferences and, 45
  by foragers, 321, 322, 363

by horticulturists, 323
language and, 218
by Neolithic foragers, 259, 267
of nonhuman primates, 159, 160, 161
selective, beginning of, 247
of whales by Makah tribe, 632
Huntington, Gertrude Enders, 329
Hutchinson, Sharon E., 490, 503
Hutter, Michael, 566
Hybridization, 49, 50
Hybrids, between species, 93
Hypergyny, 422
Hypertension, 12, 583, 584
Hyperthermia, 299–300
Hypogyny, 422
Hypothermia, 300–301
Hypothesis, 5, 69, 123
Hypoxia, 301–302
Hyslop, John, 280

Ice ages, 198
  end of, 246
  land bridges during, 234–236, 243
Ice-free corridor, 243
Iceland, genome analysis, 292, 295–297
Ice Man (Ötzi), 5, 102
Idealism, 37, 43, 60
IDPs (internally displaced persons),
    588–589
IK (indigenous knowledge), 327
Illness, 386. *See also* Disease;
    Ethnomedicine
  culture-bound syndromes, 387–388,
    389, 390, 406
  healing of, 390, 391–396, 399–400
  interpretivist approach to, 399–400
  preventive practices, 389
  spirits and, 389, 390–391, 394, 395
Imitation, 44
Imitative magic, 242, 524–525
Immatures, 142
Immigration. *See* Migration
Immunostaining, 103
Imperialism, cultural, 51, 610
IMR (infant mortality rate), 308
Inca civilization, 39, 277, 280–281
  in-kind taxation in, 474
  recording system in, 505
Incest taboo, 421, 422
Inclusive fitness, 377
Independent Assortment, Law of, 81,
    82, 85
India
  air pollution in, 310
  Andaman Islands of, 90–92, 322,
    481, 623
  archaic *Homo* in, 207
  British colonialism in, 590, 610
  Buddhism's origin in, 540
  camel fair in Rajasthan, 3
  caste system in, 458–460, 539, 540,
    614

cattle in, 60–61, 403
child personality in, 368
descent systems in, 415, 416, 420
early archaeology in, 38–39
eating and drinking in, 45
elimination in, 45, 46
emigrants to Canada from, 457
emigrants to England from, 457
family planning in, 356
farmers' cooperatives in, 448–449
female farming systems in, 328
Hanuman langurs in, 140, 145
healing systems of, 393, 394, 399,
    404
herding by girls in, 326
hijiras in, 374
Hinduism, 538–540
household structure in, 427
Indus Valley civilization in, 271–273
Jews of, 543
kinship in, 414
Kyasanur forest disease in, 403
languages in, 40, 47, 49, 503–504,
    506, 538
marriage in, 422, 423, 425, 458, 459
Mesolithic rock art, 243
motherhood in, 375
Muslims in, conflicts with Hindus, 549
myths of, 527, 528, 561
Narmada dam projects, 589
new immigrants from, 597–598
nonhuman primate survival in, 159
preference for sons in, 362, 395
redistribution program in, 614
ritual health protection in, 389
Roma people's origin in, 456
sexual intercourse in, 359
sex workers in, 440
sleeping behavior in, 46
Taj Mahal, 423, 564
vaccination programs in, 407
widowhood in, 47, 432–433, 434
women's power in, 475
women's programs in, 630
wrestlers in, 567–568
Indians. *See* Native Americans
Indigenous knowledge (IK), 327
Indigenous peoples, 53, 55. *See also*
    Colonialism; Ethnicity; *specific
    peoples*
  defined, 53, 623
  development and, 622–628
  in global class structure, 52
  land rights of, 626–627
  of Latin America, "race" and, 452, 453
  population estimates of, 623, 624
  rights to knowledge about themselves,
    462
  survival of, 57
Individual agency. *See* Agency
Individualism
  meritocratic, 451

varying definitions of, 412–413
Kinship diagrams, 413–414
Kinship systems. *See also* Descent;
　　Family; Marriage; Siblings
　changing patterns of, 433–435
　descent and, 414–418
　economic systems and, 412
　intrahousehold dynamics and,
　　427–428
　marriage and, 420–426
　sharing and, 418–420
　terminology of, 413–414
　three bases of, 414
　of Tory Islanders, 412, 413
　in United States, 418, 432
Kiowa people of North America,
　127–129
Kipling, Rudyard, 50
Kirsch, Stuart, 462
Kittles, Rick A., 297
Klawiter, Maren, 450
Kleiber's Law, 303
Kleiman, D. G., 160
Klein, Richard, 231
Kleinman, Arthur, 386
Kluckhohn, Clyde, 37
Knight, A., 227
Knott, Cheryl, 152
Knott, Kim, 539
Knuckle-walking, 152, 153, 188
Kolenda, Pauline M., 427, 458, 459
Komi people of Russia, 507
Kondo, Dorinne, 116
Konner, Melvin, 57, 307, 373
Kono culture of Sierra Leone, 372
Koobi Fora, Kenya, 172, 200, 397
Korea
　immigrants to U.S. from, 594–595
　political socialization of women in,
　　469
　wedding practices in, 435
Kottak, Conrad Phillip, 420, 619
Kowalewski, Steve, 277
Krantzler, Nora J., 404, 405
Krings, M., 227
Kroeber, A. L., 37
Krulfeld, Ruth M., 588, 589
Kuipers, Joel C., 45, 478, 557
Ku Klux Klan, 453
Kula, 114, 340
Kumar, Krishna, 460
Kuna Indians of Panama, 399, 449
Kunwinjku people of Australia, 439
Kurds, 487–488
Kurin, Richard, 115–116
Kurkiala, Mikael, 457
Kuru, 337–338
Kusimba, Sibel Barut, 248
Kuwait, veiling of women in, 519
Kuwayama, Takami, 9
Kwakwaka'wakw tribe of Canada,
　332, 348

Kwiatkowski, Lynn M., 633
Kyasanur forest disease (KFD), 403

Labor migrants, 331, 586, 602–603
Labov, William, 508
Lactase impersistence, 304, 619
Lactase persistence, 304
LAD (last appearance datum), 173
Ladányi, János, 457
Laderman, Carol, 393
Laetoli, Tanzania
　Australopithecus fossils, 183
　footprints, 111, 165, 166, 188
LaFleur, William, 362, 541
Lahr, Marta M., 312
Lai, C. S. L., 218
Lake basins, 167
Lakoff, Robin, 510, 518
Lamarck, Jean Baptiste, 76
Lambert-Zazulak, Patricia I., 103
Lamphere, Louise, 582
Land. *See* Environment; Resources
Land bridges, 234–236, 243
Land mines, in Afghanistan, 486
Land rights, of indigenous peoples,
　626–627
Landscape, 9–10, 12
Language. *See also* Communication;
　　Linguistic anthropology;
　　Nonverbal communication
　Andamanese, 91
　archaic *Homo* and, 200, 218
　Bantu expansion and, 249–250
　bilingualism, 507, 509
　brain and, 146, 147, 190–191, 198,
　　200, 218
　change in, 506–507
　codes of microcultures, 510–512
　data about, 104
　defined, 19, 500
　dialects of, 509–510
　as discourse, 20, 41, 119, 513
　dying, 20, 29, 40, 507
　early hominins and, 190–191
　in Europe, 23
　extinction of, 507
　fieldworker and local language, 115,
　　117
　formal properties of, 503–504
　international cooperation and, 492
　key features of, 502–503
　in multilingual populations, 29
　vs. nonhuman primate
　　communication, 146–147
　origins and history of, 17, 68,
　　504–506
　overview of, 520
　prehistoric group behavior and, 230
　sign language, 501, 502, 503
　thought and, 507–509
　tool-making and, 217, 218, 232
　in Upper Paleolithic, 238

Language decay, 507
Language extinction, 507
Langurs, 140, 145
Lanting, Frans, 153, 154
LaPena, Frank, 36
Larsen, Clark Spencer, 398
Lascaux cave paintings, 242
Lassiter, Luke Eric, 127–129
Last appearance datum (LAD), 173
Later Stone Age (LSA), 232–233, 246,
　249
Latin, 40, 506
　in Linnean system, 72
Latin America. *See also specific*
　　countries, regions, peoples
　Alcoholics Anonymous in, 449
　Andean civilizations, 280–281, 284
　disease in colonial history of,
　　398–399
　indigenous peoples' land claims in,
　　626–627
　Neolithic, 266, 267
　new immigrants from, 591–594
　pre-Clovis, 244
　"race" and ethnicity in, 452, 453–454
　social clubs in, 444
　U.S. government and anthropologists
　　in, 24
Latinis, D. Kyle, 250
Latino peoples
　culture-bound syndromes of,
　　387–388, 406
　sickle-cell trait among, 11
　in U.S. schools, 509
Law, 478
Lawler, Andrew, 270, 272
Law of contagion in magic, 525
Law of Independent Assortment, 81,
　82, 85
Law of Segregation, 80, 81
Law of similarity in magic, 524–525
Leach, Jerry W., 571
Leacock, Eleanor, 59, 435
Leadership. *See* Political organization
Lead poisoning
　in United States, 310, 311, 406
　in urban Egypt, 463
Leakey, Louis S. B., 185, 200
Leakey, Mary, 166, 185, 188, 200
Leakey, Meave G., 184, 187
Leakey, Richard E. F., 214
Learning
　cultural constructionism and, 58–59
　as enculturation, 10, 43–44, 364–365,
　　367–369
　by nonhuman primates, 44, 135, 136,
　　157–158
Leavitt, Stephen C., 379
Leavy, Morton L., 420
Lebanon
　Palestinian refugees in, 602
　sibling relationships in, 430–431

biological markers of, 366–367
identity formation of, on Crete, 482–483
spatial skills of, 58, 59
Male strip dancing, U.S., 559
Mali, Dogon people of, 379
Malinowski, Bronislaw, 42, 114, 123, 127, 501, 526, 527
Malnutrition, 311, 312, 313, 400
Malthus, Thomas, 77
Mamani, Mauricio P., 394
Mamdani, Mahmoud, 356, 549
Mammoths, 109, 244
Mammoth steppe, 243
Man, as generic term, 37, 202
Manchester, Keith, 307
Manioc, 324
Mann, Alan E., 298, 301, 305
Mannheim, Bruce, 508
Manz, Beatriz, 589
Manzi, Giorgio, 207
Marcoux, Alan, 424
Marcus, Joyce, 277, 278, 279, 284–285
Margolis, Maxine, 559, 582
Market exchange, 341–342
development and, 612
Marmosets, 149, 151
Marriage, 420–426. *See also* Weddings
arranged, 423, 430, 433, 457
Berber engagement ceremony, 12
caste system and, 458, 459
changing patterns in, 433–435
in chiefdoms, 473
colonialism and, 490
definitions of, 420–421
divorce and, 418, 432
female genital cutting and, 371, 372, 373
gift-giving associated with, 423, 424
for immigration purposes, 592
monogamous, 425
polygamous, 425–426
relationships in, 430
remarriage, 433, 435
same-gender, 421, 425
spouse selection for, 421–423
warfare among Yanomami and, 484
widowhood and, 432–433
Marshall, Fiona, 261
Marsh Arab people of Iraq, 581
Martin, Richard C., 545
Martínez, Samuel, 602–603
Marx, Karl, 42, 52, 451, 526
Marxism, 42, 52
Massara, Emily, 336
Massiah, Joycelin, 424
Maté, 394
Material cultural heritage, 572–574. *See also* Cultural heritage
Materialism, cultural. *See* Cultural materialism
Matrescence, 375

Matriarchy, 457
Matrifocality
domestic violence and, 431–432
in United States, 418
Matrifocal species, 142
Matrilineal descent, 415, 416
decline of, worldwide, 434–435, 628
Nayar fertility ritual and, 539
in United States, 418
Matrilineal extended household, 427
Matrilocality, 142
Matrilocal residence, 416
Maya people
archaeological studies of, 16, 39, 277, 278–280, 285
arts of, 558, 559
attitudes toward pregnant woman, 389
birth among, 365
cacao drink of, 46
calendar of, 51
city of Chichen Itza, 475
civilization of, 277, 278–280, 285
funerary and religious practices of, 16
Guatemalan civil war and, 1, 27, 584
Guatemalan immigrant children's health in U.S., 584
menopause among, 377
perceptions of body among, 385
women's status, Oaxaca region, 420
Maybury-Lewis, David, 53, 487, 565, 623
Mayor, Adrienne, 15, 70
Mayr, Ernst, 72
Maytag, Fritz, 256
McBrearty, Sally, 230
McCombie, Susan C., 358
McCully, Patrick, 589
McDonald, J. Douglas, 54
McDonaldization, 48–49
McElroy, Ann, 393
McGovern, Thomas H., 275
McGrew, William C., 37, 158, 216
McIntosh, Susan Keech, 275
McIntosh, William A., 338
McKee, Jeffrey K., 245
McMahon, April M. S., 502, 506
MDRTB (multi-drug-resistant mycobacterium tuberculosis), 310
Mead, Margaret, 59, 116–117, 121, 123, 364, 371
Meadowcroft, Pennsylvania, 244
Meaning
healing systems and, 399
interpretivism and, 43, 60, 399
religion and, 526
semantics and, 505
structuralism and, 41
Meat-eating, 45
by archaic hominins, 189
by archaic *Homo,* 204, 213–214
brain enlargement and, 17

bush meat, 159
cannibalism, 7, 8, 206, 210, 536
by early modern humans, 232
by Fore people, 337–338
Neolithic transition and, 264–265
by pastoralists, 325
Yanomami warfare and, 484–485
Media anthropology, 20, 514–517
Medical anthropology. *See also* Ethnomedicine; Western biomedicine
clinical, 406–408
conflicting models of healing and, 404–406
critical, 400–402, 406
diseases of development and, 403
ecological/epidemiological approach in, 396–399
interpretivist approach in, 399–400
new infectious diseases and, 402–403
Medicalization, 400–401
Medical pluralism, 403–406
Medicine. *See* Ethnomedicine; Western biomedicine
Medicine man, 383. *See also* Healers
Medicines, 394–396
Megafauna, 109, 237, 244, 245, 246
Mehanna, Sohair R., 461
Meigs, Anna S., 55
Meiosis, 82, 85, 293
Melanesia. *See also particular subregions and groups*
animatism in, 528–529
big-man and big-woman systems in, 471–473
cargo cults in, 548–549
Melanin, 302–303
Mellaart, James, 261
Mellars, Paul, 240
Men. *See also* Gender; Male dominance; Males; Patriarchy
in patrilineal societies, 415–416
Menarche, 358, 369, 526, 532, 533
Mencher, Joan P., 452, 458
Mendel, Gregor, 78, 79–81, 82
Mendel's laws, 79–81, 82, 85
Mennonite people, social control among, 477
Menopause, 358, 377–378
Men's clubs, 444
Menstruation, 358, 371, 376. *See also* Menarche
Mental illness, 385
Mercader, Julio, 155, 156, 232
Meritocratic individualism, 451
Mernissi, Fatima, 370
Merry, Sally Engle, 490, 491
Mesoamerica
Neolithic period, 265–267
Olmec culture, stone sculptures, 553
urban tradition, 276–277
Mesoamerican Triad, 267

Native Americans *(Cont.)*
  whale hunting by, 632
  women's political power among, 489–490
Native and Newcomer (Robertson), 115
Native anthropology, 8
Natufian culture, 246–247, 258–260
Naturalist view, of language, 40
Natural resources. *See* Resources
Natural selection, 66, 76–78. *See also* Evolution; Fitness
  arguments against evolution and, 95
  in populations, 88, 92–93
  sources of variation and, 85
Natural Theology (Paley), 95
Nature
  culture and, 44–46
  Greco-Roman thought on, 67–68
  Native Americans and, 36
Navajo people of North America, 326
  arts of, 558
  ethnomedicine of, 383, 390
  kinship terms of, 414
  matrilineal descent among, 435
Navarro, Arcadi, 94
Nayar people of India, 416, 539
Ndembu people of Zambia, 532
Neanderthals, 196, 197, 208–212
  as a distinct species, 227
  expressive culture, 211
  hyperpolar body proportions of, 300
  Levant, 234
  meat-eating by, 214
  as misunderstood, 240
  modern humans and, 224–225, 226, 227, 234, 238, 240, 242
  sculpture, 212
  stone tools of, 104, 209, 211
  in Upper Paleolithic, 234, 238
  vocal tract of, 218
Neff, Deborah L., 539
Neier, Aryeh, 507
Nelson, Sarah M., 110, 242
Neolithic period
  in Africa, 261–262
  in China, 273, 274
  defined, 38, 256
  in Europe, 262–265, 565
  lactase persistence and, 304
  lessons for our world from, 284, 286
  in New World, 265–267
  in Old World, 256–265, 565
  overview of, 286
  stone circles of, 22
  warfare in, 485
Neolithic revolution, 256
Neolocal residence, 417
Nepal
  courtship in, 434
  polyandry in, 425
  Sherpa of, 404

Neusner, Jacob, 541
New immigrants, 591–599
Newman, Lucile, 361
New social movements, 463
New World archaeology, 15
  Holocene transition, 251
  Neolithic, 265–267
  Upper Paleolithic, 233, 243–246
New World Monkeys, 148, 149, 160
New York City
  crack culture in East Harlem, 124–125
  medical anthropologists in, 289
  tuberculosis in, 310
New Zealand
  animal rights in, 76
  cargo cults in, 548–549
Ngokwey, Ndolamb, 390
NGOs (non-governmental organizations), 462, 493, 618, 627–628, 633
Niche, ecological, 138
Nichter, Mark, 403, 406, 407
Nichter, Mimi, 513
Nickens, Herbert W., 306
Niger, West Africa
  millet in, 319
  satellite dish in, 519
  Tuareg men's greetings in, 499
Nigeria
  ethnic differences in, 452
  Ogoni resistance movement in, 627, 628, 629, 633
  polygyny in, 432
  Yoruba people, esthetics of, 556
Nile Valley, 248, 262, 271
Nim, 503
Nisa, 118
Nocturnal nonhuman primates, 148
Nodwell, Evelyn, 457
Non-governmental organizations (NGOs), 462, 493, 618, 627–628, 633
Nonhuman primates. *See also* Primatology; *specific primates*
  behavioral characteristics of, 137
  communication by, 20, 146–147, 502–503
  conservation of, 27, 159–161
  culture in, 10, 44, 157–158
  diet of, 138–140, 303–304
  endangered, 158–161
  environment of, 138
  ethical treatment of, 76, 160–161
  evolution of, 137
  human evolution and, 136–137, 154–158
  Kanzi, 217
  learning in, 44, 135, 136, 157–158
  morphology of, 137
  Nim, 503
  overview of, 162

reconciliation among, 477
  sign language use by, 502, 503
  social behavior of, 137, 140–146
  taxonomy of, 136, 148
  varieties of, 147–154
Nonverbal communication, 19, 20, 505, 518–519
Norgaard, Richard B., 612
Norm, 478
North America. *See also* Native Americans
  chiefdoms of, 281–282
  Neolithic period in, 266, 267
  Viking colonists, 275
Nosology, 386
Notes, 120, 122
Nourse, Jennifer W., 533
Nowak, Ronald M., 158
Nubia, 271
Nuclear DNA, 87, 292–293. *See also* DNA
Nuclear household, 427, 435
Nucleotides, 75, 82, 86
  polymorphisms of, 294–295
Nuer people of Sudan, 421, 490, 503
Num, 392
Nutrition. *See* Diet; Malnutrition; Obesity

Oaxaca, Mexico, 360, 368, 420, 618
Obesity
  increasing, in U.S. and U.K., 12, 313, 336
  in Maya American children, 584
  Western foods and, 13, 346
Obeyesekere, Gananath, 119
Observer's paradox, 502
Obsidian
  Neolithic tools made of, 259, 260
  in Teotihuacan economy, 277
Ochoa, Carlos M., 267
Ochre, 230, 231, 526
Ochs, Elinor, 511–512
O'Connell, F., 234, 236
O'Connell, J. F., 377
Odegaard, Nancy, 112
Ogawa, Naohiro, 356
Ogoni people of Nigeria, 627, 628, 629, 633
O'Gorman, Jodie A., 428
Ohnuki-Tierney, Emiko, 385, 395
Oinas, Felix J., 376
Oldowan stone tools, 201–202, 203, 204, 206, 215–216, 218
Old Stone Age. *See* Paleolithic period
Olduvai Gorge, 185–186, 200, 207
  tool-makers of, 217, 218
Old World archaeology, 15
  Neolithic, 256–265
  Upper Paleolithic, 233–243
Old World Monkeys, 148, 149–150
Olmec culture, 553

unilineal descent and, 415–416
Power grip, 188
Practical anthropology. *See* Applied anthropology
Pratt, Mary Louise, 569
Precision grip, 188, 198
Pre-Clovis, 244, 246
Pregnancy, 375. *See also* Birth
  legitimacy of, in Western societies, 362
  Maya attitudes toward woman during, 389
Prehistoric archaeology, 15
Prehistory, 38
Prepared core, 201
Price, David H., 448
Price, T. Douglass, 262
Priest, 537
Priestess, 537
Primary group, 440, 441
Primates. *See also* Archaic *Homo;* Hominin; Modern humans *(Homo sapiens);* Nonhuman primates
  taxonomy of, 136, 148
Primatology, 13–14
  applied, 27
  combined with archaeology, 155–157
  conservation programs and, 161
  language and, 20
  research questions of, 136–137
Primeval Antiquities of Denmark (Worsaac), 38
Primitive Culture (Tylor), 525
Primitive hominins, 177, 178, 180–183, 189, 190, 191. *See also* Early hominins
"Primitive" peoples, 11, 569
Prince, Raymond, 387
Principles of Geology (Lyell), 70, 77
Prisons, 480, 481
  colonialism and, 490
  friendships in, 442–443
Private property
  in agricultural societies, 327, 330
  foraging societies and, 322
  in pastoral societies, 326
Privatization, in formerly Communist countries, 346
PRMs (participatory research methods), 621–622
Processualism, 39, 43
Production. *See also* Modes of production
  defined, 320
Productivity, of human language, 503
Profit, 339, 340
Project cycle, 618–619
Projectile points, 229
Pronatalism, 355
Property relations
  in agricultural societies, 330, 331
  colonialism and, 434–435

in foraging societies, 322
in horticultural societies, 325
in pastoral societies, 326
Prophets, 537
Prosimians, 136, 147–149
Prospective medical studies, 304
Proteins
  in chromosomes, 81, 82
  dietary requirement for, 303
  genetic code and, 86, 87
Protestantism, in Appalachia, 544
Proto-Bantu, 249, 250
Proto-Indo-European (PIE), 506
Provenance, 103–104, 111
Psychiatry, 394, 401, 404
Puberty, 369, 373. *See also* Adolescence; Menarche
  rituals associated with, 526, 532, 533–534
Pueblo Indians, 527–528, 558
Puerto Rico, 488
  immigrants from, in Philadelphia, 336
Punctuated-equilibrium model, 94, 179
Punishment
  death penalty, 478, 481, 542
  prisons, 442–443, 480, 481, 490
  religious doctrine and, 528
  in small-scale societies, 478–479, 480
  in state-level societies, 479, 480–481, 482
Purdah, 475
Purdum, Elizabeth D., 481
Pure gift, 340
Push–pull theory, 583
Pyramids, Egyptian, 38, 271

Quadrupedal locomotion, 137
Qualitative data, 118, 122
Quantitative data, 118, 119, 122
Queer anthropology, 19
Quesir, Egypt, 126, 127
Quilter, Jeffrey, 280
Quintana-Murci, L. O., 227

Race
  Chinese thinking about hair and, 52, 177
  concepts of, 14
  consumption patterns and, 336
  cultural construction of, 14, 52, 298
  vs. ethnicity, 53, 452
  of fieldworker, 116
  genetics and, 297–298
  microcultures of, 37, 51, 52–53
  as scientifically discredited, 297–298
  Western classifications based on, 452–454
Racism, 52–53, 452–454
  anthropologists' recognition of, 14
  Boas on, 43
  of Nazis, 51
  W. E. B. Du Bois and, 455

working-class, 602–603
Radiocarbon dating, 107, 108
Raff, R. A., 215
Raheja, Gloria Goodwin, 458
Rahnema, Majid, 613
Ramayana, 538
Ramphele, Mamphela, 433
Random sample, 105, 118, 293
Ranov, Vadim A., 242
Rao, N. Madhusudana, 597
Rape
  gang rape, 444, 462
  in women's prisons, 57
Raphael, Dana, 375
Rapid research methods (RRMs), 621, 622
Rappaport, Roy A., 47
Rapport, 115–117
Ras Tafari, 547
Rathgeb, Elizabeth, 21
Rationalist view, of language, 40
Ravaillon, Martin, 344
Realist ethnographies, 123
Recent African Replacement Model, 226, 227
Recessive allele, 81
Reciprocity, 339–340
Recombination, genetic, 85, 92, 293
Recommended daily allowances (RDAs), 303
Recording of findings, 120, 121, 122
  in linguistic anthropology, 501–502
Recurrent levallois reduction, 234
Redistribution, 340, 471–472, 473
  development and, 613–614
Red ochre, 526
Reed, Kay E., 177
Reflexive ethnographies, 123, 557
Reforestation projects. *See also* Deforestation
  in Burkina Faso, 629
  in Haiti, 619–620
Refugees, 588, 589, 591, 596, 597, 598, 602
  African pastoralists as, 627
  development as cause of, 620
  women from Chiapas, 631
Regulatory genes, 87
Reichel-Dolmatoff, G., 385
Reid, Russell M., 396
Reindeer, 239, 325–326, 362, 611
Reiner, R., 480
Relationship-repair reconciliation, 477
Relative dating methods, 107–108
Relativism
  cultural, 43, 50–51, 491
  linguistic, 41, 505
Relethford, John H., 294
Religion, 523–550. *See also* Buddhism; Christianity; Hinduism; Islam; Judaism; Sacred spaces
  abortion and, 362, 540, 542

Religion *(Cont.)*
African, 537–538
African–Brazilian, 390–391
in Mesopotamia, 270
beliefs in, 527–531
change in, 547–549
creationism in, 77, 95
defined, 261, 524
firewalking in, 524, 525
in former Soviet Union, 566
freedom of, 549
infanticide and, 363
laws and, 478
magic and, 524–525
Maya, 279
Neolithic, 261, 264
origin of, 525–526
overview of, 549–550
revitalization movements, 547–549
ritual practices of, 526, 531–536. *See
also* Rituals
specialists in, 536–537
state leadership and, 474
in Teotihuacan, 276
world religions, 537–538. *See also
specific religions*
Religious pluralism, 538
Remarriage, 433, 435
Remittances, 586
Renaissance, European, 69
Renfrew, Colin, 108, 109, 111
Repatriation
of Australian Aborigine remains, 632
of museum exhibits, 565–566
of Native American materials,
112–113, 283, 565
of people, 601–602
of Saartje Baartman's remains,
624–625
Replacement-level fertility, 356
Reproduction. *See also* Fertility
modes of, 354–357
Reproductive success. *See also* Fitness
biological determinism and, 58
inclusive fitness and, 377
polygyny and, 425
warfare among Yanomami and, 484
Research, 100–101. *See also* Fieldwork
Research participants, 127
Research population, 127
Resources. *See also* Environment
development and, 613–614, 626–627,
628
human past and, 108–110
processualism and, 39
Restudy, 114
Retrospective medical studies, 304
Reverse culture shock, 117
Revitalization movements, 547–549
Revolution of 1989, 331
Reyna, Stephen P., 484, 485
Rhesus monkeys, 159

Rhode, David, 242, 244
Rhodes, Lorna A, 480
Rice
cultivation of, in China, 10, 397
nutrition and, 284
sharing-based kinship and, 419
wet rice agriculture, 328, 329
Rich, Adrienne, 373
Rich, Bruce, 615, 617
Richard, A. F., 159
Richards, M. P., 214
Richards, Martin, 262
Richards, Michael P., 238, 264
Richmond, Brian G., 188, 200
Riding In, James, 283
Rift valleys, 167, 169, 250
Rightmire, G. P., 227
Rightmire, Philip, 207
Right of return, 601–602
Rites of passage, 532–534
Rituals, 526, 531–536. *See also*
Initiation; Sacrifice
of African religions, 546–547
for age set, 440
of Australian Aborigines, 478, 531
at birth, 533, 558
body modification as, 447
Buddhist, 541
Christian, 544–545
defined, 531
for healing and health protection,
385, 389, 399, 407
Hindu, 539, 564
Jewish, 543
kinship based on, 419, 420
life-cycle, 526, 532–534, 558
Muslim, 545–546
ochre in, 526
sacred spaces and, 530
specialists in, 536–537
in Teotihuacan, 276
of youth gangs, 445
Rituals of inversion, 534–535
RNA, 82, 86
Robb, John E., 40
Roberts, Charlotte, 307
Roberts, R., 237
Robertshaw, P., 232
Robertson, Carol E., 560
Robertson, Jennifer, 115
Robins, Kevin, 344
Robles García, Nelly M., 279
Roche, Helen, 216
Rock paintings. *See also* Cave art
in Australia, 439
Mesolithic, 247
Neolithic, in Africa, 261, 262
Rode, Andris, 301
Roebroeks, Wil, 238
Rogers, Barbara, 629
Roma, 53, 456–457, 623
Roman, Maria, 424

Roman Catholicism. *See* Catholicism
Romania
change to market economy, 346
collectivized agriculture in, 331
Roma people in, 456
Romans, 7, 14–15, 22, 37
fossils and, 14–15, 70
human origins and, 66–68
Romantic love, 422–423, 430, 433,
434
Roosevelt, Theodore, 43
Rosaldo, Michelle Zimbalist, 124
Roscoe, Will, 374
Rose, Jerome C., 565
Roseman, Marina, 560
Rosenberg, N. A., 294
Rosenberger, Nancy, 562
Rosenblatt, Paul C., 379
Ross, Eric B., 354
Ross, Marc Howard, 484
Rouland, Norbert, 491
Rowley-Conwy, Peter, 263
Roy, Arundhati, 589
RRMs (rapid research methods), 621,
622
Rubel, Arthur J., 386, 387
Rudwick, Martin J. S., 71
Ruff, Chris B., 300
Rumbaugh, Duane, 217
Ruse, M., 68, 95
Russia. *See also* Soviet Union, former
art in, 565–566
change to market economy, 346
domestication of dogs in, 241, 263
immigrants from, 598, 599
Neanderthal fossils in, 227
prison population in, 480
religion in, 547
restrictions on foreign researchers,
115
Turkman carpets in, 570–571
Rutherford, Patricia, 103
Ruvolo, Maryellen, 166
Rwanda, refugees from, 588

Saami people of Scandinavia, 325–326,
530, 611
Sabloff, Jeremy A., 278
Sachs, Aaron, 627, 633
Sacred spaces, 530–531, 534, 538
contested, 530–531, 549
kotel in Jerusalem, 542–543
postmodernist archaeology and, 40
Sacrifice, 535–536. *See also*
Cannibalism
in African religions, 547
in Aztec civilization, 481, 535–536
in Christianity, 544
in early Chinese civilization, 273
in Islam, 545–546
in Maya civilization, 16, 279
in Moche civilization, 280

Shifting cultivation, 323, 325. *See also* Horticulture
Shimada, Izumi, 280
Shipibo Indians of Peruvian Amazon, 556
Shipwrecks, 15
Shona kingdom, 39
Shopping. *See also* Consumerism; Markets
  and credit card debt, 347
  for Western goods in Japan, 49
Shore, Bradd, 376
Shore, Cris, 23
Short, James F., 446
Shostak, Marjorie, 118, 307
Shweder, Richard A., 376, 491
Siamangs, 150, 151
Siberia
  pastoralists in, 362
  shamans in, 395, 537
  silence of daughter-in-law in, 518
  Upper Paleolithic, 242–243, 245
Siblings
  genetic differences between, 85
  incest taboo and, 421
  relationships of, 430–431
Sicily, Mead's fieldwork in, 364
Sickle-cell syndrome, 305–306
Sickle-cell trait, 11, 305
Sidnell, Jack, 443
Sierra Leone
  children's food stealing, 343
  female genital cutting in, 372
Sign language, 501, 502, 503
Sikhs, 457
Silence, 518
Silicon Valley, California, culture, 4, 5
Siliotti, Alberto, 121
Silk, Joan B., 477
Silver, Daniel B., 385
Silver, Ira, 569
Similarity, law of in magic, 524–525
Simmons, Alan H., 263
Sinclair, Paul J. P., 275
Singer, Peter, 76, 254
Singh, K. S., 623
Singing
  gender and, 560–561
  of Kuna Indians during childbirth, 399
  Moroccan female performers, 558
Single-gene effect, 78, 87
Single nucleotide polymorphisms (SNPs), 294–295
Sisal, 345
Siskind, Janet, 532
Site report, 110
Sites, 104–106
  dating of, 106–108
  preservation of, 110–111
Site-society interface, 279
Skeletons. *See also* Fossils

preservation of, 102
Skin color
  early ideas about, 7–8, 9
  in Latin America, 452, 453
  "race" and, 14, 52, 452, 453
  ultraviolet radiation and, 302–303
Skinner, G. William, 427
Slatkin, M., 307
Slavery
  African religions and, 546
  in China, 273
  control of production and, 324
  in Egypt, 271
  European colonialism and, 11, 544
  maize diet and, 282
  in Mesopotamia, 270
  pidgin languages and, 506
  in South Africa, 454
  as unbalanced exchange, 342–343
  W. E. B. Du Bois's writings on, 455
  woman-headed households and, 424
Sleeping, 44, 46
  nonhuman primate patterns, 137, 148
SM (sadomasochist) community, 446–447
Smallpox, 398
Smith, Bruce D., 267, 281, 529
Smith, Jonathan Z., 546, 547
Smith, Patricia K., 584
Snowball sampling, 118
SNPs (single nucleotide polymorphisms), 294–295
Sobel, Elizabeth, 528
Social class. *See* Class
Social conflict. *See* Conflict, social
Social control, 476–477
  coercive harmony as, 479
  defined, 477
  internalized, 477
  laws in, 478
  norms in, 478
  in small-scale societies, 478–479
  in states, 479–482
Social groups, 440–449
  in archaic *Homo*, 216
  clubs and fraternities, 443–444
  cooperatives, 448–449
  countercultural, 444–447
  defined, 440
  in early hominins, 189–190
  emergence of language and, 17
  friendship, 441–443
  Middle Stone Age, 230
  modes of production and, 440–441
  Neolithic, 264
  in nonhuman primates, 140–142, 151
  political organizations and, 470
  self-help, 449–450
  types of, 440
  variations across cultures in, 440–441
  work groups, 447–448
Social impact assessment, 611

Social inequality. *See* Inequality
Socialism, 331
  Cuban development aid and, 617
  fall of, in Soviet Union, 344
  human rights and, 632
  industrial, 356
  religion and, 547
  transition to democracy and, 489
  women's political power and, 475
Sociality
  of archaic *Homo*, 216
  of early hominins, 189–190
  infant's gender and, 367
  of primates, 137, 140, 141
Socialization. *See also* Enculturation
  norms and, 478
  sexual orientation and, 373
Social order. *See* Social control
Social stratification, 450–460. *See also* Caste; Class; Ethnicity; Gender; Hierarchy; Inequality; Power; Race; Status
  of Maya, 278
  bands of foragers and, 471
  in chiefdoms, 473
  defined, 269
  in Fiji, 545
  in states, 269, 273
Sociocultural fit, 619–621
Sociolinguistics, 20, 508–509, 510, 513
Soffer, Olga, 241
Soh, Chunghee Sarah, 469
Soil structure, 108
Sokal, Robert R., 22
Soldiers, 487, 590. *See also* Military forces; War
Solomon Islands, youth gangs in, 445
Solutrean period, 241, 245
Sonagachi Project, 440
Sonenshein, Raphael J., 595
Sororities, 444
Sound shift, 250
South Africa
  customary marriage law in, 490
  HIV/AIDS in, 336, 454
  Middle Stone Age, 227, 228, 230, 231
  racism in, 52, 336, 454
  repatriation of remains, Saartje Baartman, 624–625
  widowhood in, 433
South America. *See* Latin America
Southeast Asia. *See also specific countries, regions, and peoples*
  Buddhism in, 540–541
  early modern humans' migration to, 234–235, 236
  female farming systems in, 328
  Hmong people of, 623, 626
  new immigrants from, 596–597
  sexual dimorphism in, 422
South Pacific. *See also specific countries, regions, and peoples*

Theodoratus, Dorothea J., 36
Thieme, H., 208
Third genders, 374–375
Thissen, Jürgen, 196
Thomas, David Hurst, 283
Thomas-Slaytor, Barbara P., 622
Thompson, J. Eric S., 278
Thompson, Robert Farris, 555, 556
Thomsen, Christian Jurgen, 38
Thorgeirsdóttir, Sigridur, 292
Thorne, A., 234
Tibet, polyandry in, 425, 426
Tibetan Buddhism, 540, 549
Tibetan culture, Chinese suppression of,
    53, 456
Tibetan medicine, 386
Tice, Karin E., 449
Tierney, Patrick, 485
Tiffany, Walter W., 470
Time allocation study, 119
Tinker, Irene, 629
Tishkoff, Sarah A., 229, 294
Tiwi people of Australia, 416
Tobias, Phillip V., 170, 624, 625
Togo, religion in, 546
TOL (Tree of Life), 73–76, 87, 95, 175
Tonga, remittances to, 586
Toolkits, 104, 215–216. See also
    Acheulian stone tools; Mousterian
    tools; Oldowan stone tools
  cultural modernity and, 231–232
Tools
  archaeology and, 14, 17, 18, 38, 102,
    104
  of archaic hominins, 184, 185, 190,
    191, 198–199, 202
  bamboo, 206
  bone. See Bone tools
  as classical mark of humanity, 68
  eighteenth and nineteenth century
    discoveries, 70–71
  environment and, 12
  for excavation, 105, 106, 125
  of foragers, 321
  of horticulturists, 323
  Neolithic, 256, 259, 261
  of nonhuman primates, 135, 136,
    155–157, 158, 216–217
  obsidian, 259, 260
  plant-derived, 251
  spears, 208, 229, 232
  stone. See Stone tools
  Upper Paleolithic, 234, 236, 239–241,
    242, 244, 245, 246
Toren, Christina, 545
Torture, 489
Tory Islanders of Ireland, 412, 413
Totalitarian states, 476
Totalizing, 384
Totem, 525–526
Toth, Nicholas, 201, 203, 217
Toumai, 183

Tourism, 568–570, 572–574
  ecotourism, 160
  at Mexican archaeological sites, 279
  Panamanian women's craft
    cooperative and, 449
  Sherpas and, 404
  souvenirs and, 558–559
Townsend, Patricia K., 393
Trace fossils, 102
Trade. See also Exchange
  development and, 613
  by early African city, 275
  in Inca empire, 280
  by Indus Valley civilization, 272, 273
  as market exchange, 341–342
  in North American chiefdoms, 281
  by pastoralists, 323, 325
  pidgin languages and, 506
  in prehistoric Aegean, 473
  spread of agriculture by, 263
  urbanization and, 269, 270
  by Vikings, 275
  in world economy, 343–344
  world power and, 491
Tradition, in nonhuman primates, 157
**Traditional development anthropology
    (TDA), 620**
Transcription, of DNA, 86
Translation, of DNA into proteins, 86
Translation, of languages, 502
Transmutation of species, 76
Transnationalism, 488–489
**Transnational migrants, 583, 585, 586,
    596**
Transsexuals, 373, 374
Transvestites, 374, 375
Traphagan, John W., 427
Travel. See Tourism
Trawick, Margaret, 399
Tree of Life (TOL), 73–76, 87, 95, 175
Tree ring dating, 106–107
Trelease, Murray L., 379
Trepanation, 385
Trial by ordeal, 480
Trials, 480
Tribal art, 554
Tribe, taxonomic category of, 72
Tribes, 471, 474
  feuding by, 483
  warfare waged by, 485
Trigger, Bruce G., 37
Trinkaus, Eric, 300
Trobriand Islands
  cricket in, 571–572
  kula in, 114, 340
  Malinowski's research on, 42, 114,
    127
  Weiner's research on, 114, 127
Trotter, Robert, II, 402, 406
Trouillot, Michel-Rolph, 453
Troy, 38
Troy, Lana, 271

True fossils, 102
Tse, David K., 595
Tuareg people of North Africa, 499,
    627
Tuberculosis, 310, 312
  in developing countries, 400, 403
  traditional medicine and, 407
Tudge, Colin, 246
Tuffs, 167, 169
Tuhami (Crapanzano), 123
Turkana people of Kenya, 240, 397,
    398
Turkey
  army of, 486
  Çatalhöyük, 100, 260–261
  early modern humans in, 234, 235
  Kurds of, 487–488
  menstruation in rural areas of, 371
  population movement and, 585
  public bath and massage in, 568
  shell beads, 273
  women's political roles, 476
Turner, Trudy R., 298
Turner, Victor W., 532, 534, 543
*Two Nations: Black and White,
    Separate, Hostile, Unequal*
    (Hacker), 52
Tyler-Smith, Chris, 294
Tylor, Edward Burnett, 37, 40, 42, 524,
    525

Uhl, Sarah, 442
Ukraine
  bathhouse in, 568
  repatriation of art and, 565–566
Ulijaszek, Stanley J., 308
Uluburun shipwreck, 15
Umbanda, 390
Unbalanced exchange, 339, 340–343
Underhill, Anne P., 273
Underwater archaeology, 15–16
Underwood, Barbara A., 345
Unemployment
  among Australian Aborigine youth,
    481
  globalization and, 344
  urban youth gangs and, 446
  working-class racism and, 601
Ungar, Peter S., 189
Uniformitarianism, 70
Unilineal descent, 414, 415–416, 417
  divorce and, 432
United Nations
  development and, 614–615, 616
  displaced persons and, 588
  human rights and, 549, 602, 632
  indigenous peoples and, 623
  peace-making and, 492–493
United States. See also *specific regions
    and peoples*
  capital punishment in, 481
  coercive harmony in, 479